Cherry Hill Elementary School
32557 - 18th Avenue,
Mission, B.C. V2V 2S5
Tel: 826-9239

FRENCH-ENGLISH
ENGLISH-FRENCH
DICTIONARY

FRENCH-ENGLISH ENGLISH-FRENCH DICTIONARY

LUCEM LIBRIS

DISSEMINAMUS

GEDDES&
GROSSET

Published by Geddes & Grosset

© 1999 Geddes & Grosset,
David Dale House, New Lanark ML11 9DJ, Scotland

First published 1999
Reprinted 2000, 2001, 2002

ISBN 1 85534 358 4

Printed in Poland, OZGraf S.A.

Contents

Abbreviations

Abréviations

abrev	abbreviation	abréviation
adj	adjective	adjectif
adv	adverb	adverbe
anat	anatomy	anatomie
art	article	article
auto	automobile	automobile
aux	auxiliary	auxiliaire
bot	botany	botanique
chem, chim	chemistry	chimie
cin	cinema	cinéma
col	colloquial term	expression familière
com	commerce	commerce
compd	compound	mot composé
comput	computers	informatique
conj	conjunction	conjonction
excl	exclamation	exclamation
f	feminine noun	substantif féminin
fam	colloquial term	expression familière
fig	figurative	figuré
geol	geology	géologie
gr	grammar	grammaire
imp	impersonal	impersonnel
inform	computers	informatique
interj	interjection	interjection
invar	invariable	invariable
irr	irregular	irrégulier
jur	law term	juridique
law	law term	droit
ling	linguistics	linguistique
m	masculine noun	substantif masculin
mar	marine term	vocabulaire marin
mat, math	mathematics	mathématiques
med	medicine	médecine
mil	military term	vocabulaire militaire
mus	music	musique
n	noun	substantif
orn	ornithology	ornithologie
o.s.	oneself	
pej	pejorative	péjoratif
pl	plural	pluriel
pn	pronoun	pronom
poet	poetical term	vocabulaire poétique
p.p.	past participle	participe passé
prep	preposition	préposition
qch		quelque chose
qn		quelqu'un
rad	radio	radio
rail	railway	chemin de fer
sb	somebody, someone	
sl	slang	argot
sth	something	
thea	theatre	théâtre
tec	technology	technologie
TV	television	télévision
vi	intransitive verb	verbe intransitif
vr	reflexive verb	verbe réfléchi
vt	transitive verb	verbe transitif
zool	zoology	zoologie

French-English Dictionary

A

à *prép* (in) to; at; on; by, per; **aller ~ l'école** to go to school; **~ neuf heures** at nine o'clock; **c'est ~ toi** it's yours; it's your turn.

abaissement *m* fall, drop.

abaisser *vt* to lower; **s'~ à faire qch** to stoop to doing sth.

abandon *m* abandonment, desertion.

abandonné *adj* deserted.

abandonner *vt* to abandon, leave.

abasourdi *adj* stunned.

abasourdir *vt* to stun.

abats *mpl* giblets.

abat-jour *m* lampshade.

abattement *m* despondency; exhaustion.

abattoir *m* abattoir, slaughterhouse.

abattre *vt* to shoot; slaughter.

abattu *adj* despondent; exhausted.

abbaye *f* abbey.

abbé *m* abbot.

abbesse *f* abbess.

abcès *m* abscess.

abdiquer *vt vi* to abdicate.

abdomen *m* abdomen.

abdominal *adj* abdominal.

abeille *f* bee.

aberrant *adj* aberrant; absurd.

aberration *f* aberration.

abêtissant *adj* mindless.

abêtissement *m* mindlessness.

abîme *m* chasm.

abîmer *vt* spoil, damage; * **s'~** *vr* to get spoiled *ou* damaged.

abject *adj* abject.

abjection *f* abjectness.

abjurer *vt* to abjure.

ablatif *m* ablative.

ablation *f* (*med*) removal.

abnégation *f* abnegation.

aboiement *m* bark.

abolir *vt* to abolish.

abolition *f* abolition.

abominable *adj* abominable; **~ment** *adv* abominably.

abondamment *adv* abundantly.

abondance *f* abundance.

abondant *adj* abundant, plentiful.

abonder *vi* to be abundant *ou* plentiful.

abonné *m* **-ée** *f* subscriber.

abonnement *m* subscription.

abonner *vt* **~ qn** to subscribe, take out a subscription (*à* to); * **s'~** *vr* to subscribe, take out a subscription (*à* to).

abord *m*: **d'~** first (of all).

abordable *adj* affordable.

aborder *vt* to approach.

aborigène *mf* aborigine; * *adj* aboriginal.

aboutir *vi* to succeed.

aboutissement *m* outcome; success.

abrasif *adj* abrasive.

abrégé *m* summary; **en ~** briefly.

abréger *vt* to shorten; abridge.

abreuver *vt* to water.

abreuvoir *m* drinking trough.

abréviation *f* abbreviation.

abri *m* shelter.

abricot *m* apricot.

abriter *vt* to shelter; * **s'~** *vr* to shelter.

abroger *vt* to repeal.

abrupt *adj* abrupt; **~ement** *adv* abruptly.

abruti *m* **-e** *f* idiot; * *adj* idiotic.

abrutir *vt* to make stupid.

abrutissant *adj* stunning; mind-numbing.

abscisse *f* (*math*) abscissa.

absence *f* absence.

absent *adj* absent.

absenter (s') *vr* to leave, go out.

abside *f* apse.

absolu *adj* absolute; **~ment** *adv* absolutely; * *m* absolute.

absolution *f* absolution.

absolutisme *m* absolutism.

absorbant *adj* absorbent.

absorber *vt* to absorb.

absorption *f* absorption.

absoudre *vt* to absolve.

abstenir (s') *vr* to abstain (from).

abstention *f* abstention.

abstentionniste *mf* abstainer.

abstinence *f* abstinence.

abstraction *f* abstraction.

abstrait *adj* abstract; **~ement** *adv* in the abstract; * *m* abstract; abstract art.

absurde *adj* absurd; **~ment** *adv* absurdly.

absurdité *f* absurdity.

abus *m* abuse.

abuser *vt* **~ de** to exploit; abuse.

abusif *adj* improper.

académicien *m* **-ne** *f* academician.

académie *f* academy; learned society.

académique *adj* academic.

acajou *m* mahogany.

acariâtre *adj* cantankerous.

accablant *adj* overwhelming.

accabler *vt* to overwhelm.

accalmie *f* lull, calm.

accéder *vi*: **~ à** to reach.

accélérateur *m* accelerator.

accélération *f* acceleration.

accélérer *vi* to speed up, accelerate.

accent *m* accent.

accentuation *f* accentuation.

accentué *adj* pronounced.

accentuer *vt* to accentuate.

acceptable *adj* acceptable.

accepter *vt* to accept.

accès *m* access.

accessible *adj* accessible.

accessoire *adj* secondary; **~ment** *adv* secondarily; if need be; * *m* accessory.

accident *m* accident.

accidentel *adj* accidental; **~lement** *adv* accidentally.

acclamations *fpl* cheers; acclamation.

acclamer *vt* to acclaim, cheer.

acclimater *vt* to acclimatise; **s'~** *vr* to become acclimatised.

accolade *f* embrace.

accommodant *adj* accommodating.

accommoder *vt* to prepare; adapt.

accompagnateur *m* **-trice** *f* (*mus*) accompanist;guide.

accompagnement *m* accompaniment.

accompagner *vt* to accompany.

accomplir *vt* to achieve, accomplish.

accomplissement *m* accomplishment.

accord *m* agreement; **d'~!** okay!, all right!; **être d'~** to agree.

accordéon *m* accordion.

accorder *vt* to grant; **s'~** *vr* to agree.

accoster *vt* to accost.

accouchement *m* (*med*) delivery.

accoucher *vi* to give birth.

accoudoir *m* armrest.

accouplement *m* coupling; joining.

accourir *vi* to run up (*à, vers* to).

accoutrement *m* (*pej*) outfit, dress.

accréditer *vt* to accredit.

accroc *m* tear, breach.

accrocher *vt* to hang up (*à* on).

accroissement *m* increase.

accroître *vt* to increase.

accroupir (s') *vr* to crouch.
accueil *m* welcome, reception.
accueillant *adj* welcoming.
accueillir *vt* to welcome.
accumulateur *m* battery.
accumulation *f* accumulation.
accumuler *vt* to accumulate.
accusateur *m* **-trice** *f* accuser; * *adj* accusing.
accusatif *m* accusative (case).
accusation *f* accusation.
accusé *m* **-e** *f* (*jur*) accused, defendant.
accuser *vt* to accuse.
acerbe *adj* harsh; acrid.
acétate *m* acetate.
acétone *f* acetone.
acharné *adj* bitter, fierce; unrelenting.
acharnement *m* relentlessness; determination.
acharner (s') *vr* ~ **à faire qch** to try desperately to do sth; ~ **contre qn** to hound sb.
achat *m* purchase.
acheminer *vt* to convey.
acheter *vt* to buy.
acheteur *m* **-euse** *f* buyer, purchaser.
achèvement *m* completion.
achever *vt* to finish; complete.
acide *adj* acid, sour; * *m* acid.
acidité *f* acidity.
acidulé *adj* acid, acidulous.
acier *m* steel.
aciérie *f* steelworks.
acné *f* acne.
acompte *m* deposit, downpayment.
à-côté *m* side issue.
à-coup *m* jolt.
acoustique *adj* acoustic; * *f* acoustics.
acquéreur *m* buyer, purchaser.
acquérir *vt* to buy, purchase.
acquiescer *vi* to agree; acquiesce.
acquis *adj* acquired; * *m* experience.
acquisition *f* acquisition; purchase.
acquittement *m* payment; (*jur*) acquittal.
acquitter *vt* to acquit; pay.
acre *f* acre.
âcre *adj* acrid.
acrobate *mf* acrobat.
acrobatie *f* acrobatics.
acrobatique *adj* acrobatic.
acrylique *m*, *adj* acrylic.
acte *m* act; deed.
acteur *m*, **actrice** *f* actor.
actif *adj* active; * *m* (*ling*) active (voice).
action *f* act, action; share.

actionnaire *mf* shareholder.
actionner *vt* to activate; drive.
activement *adv* actively.
activer *vt* to speed up; **s'~** *vr* to bustle about.
activité *f* activity; hustle and bustle.
actualité *f*: **l'actualité** current events.
actuel *adj* current, present; **~lement** *adv* currently, at present.
acuité *f* acuteness; shrillness.
acuponcture *f* acupuncture.
adaptable *adj* adaptable.
adaptateur *m* adaptor.
adaptation *f* adaptation.
adapter *vt* to adapt (*à* to); **s'~** *vr* to adapt o.s. (*à* to).
additif *m* additive.
addition *f* addition; bill.
additionnel *adj* additional.
additionner *vt* to add up.
adepte *mf* follower; enthusiast.
adéquat *adj* suitable, appropriate.
adhérence *f* adhesion.
adhérent *m* **-e** *f* member, adherent; * *adj* : ~ **à** which adheres *ou* sticks to.
adhérer *vi* to adhere, stick.
adhésif *adj* adhesive.
adhésion *f* adherence; membership.
adjacent *adj* adjacent (*à* to).
adjectif *m* adjective.
adjoint *m* **-e** *f* assistant, deputy.
adjudant *m* warrant officer.
adjudication *f* sale by auction.
adjuger *vt* to auction.
admettre *vt* to admit; accept; assume.
administrateur *m* **-trice** *f* administrator.
administratif *adj* administrative.
administration *f* management; administration.
administrer *vt* to run; administer.
admirable *adj* admirable; **-ment** *adv* admirably, brilliantly.
admiratif *adj* admiring.
admiration *f* admiration.
admirativement *adv* admiringly.
admirer *vt* to admire.
admissible *adj* allowable.
admission *f* admission.
adolescence *f* adolescence.
adolescent *m* **-e** *f* adolescent.
adopter *vt* to adopt; pass.
adoption *f* adoption; passing.
adorable *adj* adorable; **~ment** *adv* delightfully.
adorer *vt* to adore, worship.
adoucir *vt* to soften.
adrénaline *f* adrenalin.

adresse *f* address; skill.
adresser *vt* to address; send; **s'~** *vr* **s'~ à** to apply to; to speak to.
adroit *adj* deft, skilful; **~ement** *adv* deftly, skilfully.
aduler *vt* to flatter.
adulte *mf* adult, grown-up; *adj* adult, full-grown.
adultère *m* adultery.
adverbe *m* adverb.
adverbial *adj*, *f* **-e** adverbial; **~ement** *adv* adverbially.
adversaire *mf* adversary, opponent.
adversité *f* adversity.
aération *f* ventilation.
aérer *vt* to air.
aérien *adj*, *f* **-ne** air, airy; aerial.
aérodrome *m* aerodrome, airfield.
aérodynamique *adj* aerodynamic; * *f* aerodynamics.
aérogare *f* (air) terminal.
aéroglisseur *m* hovercraft.
aéronautique *adj* aeronautic; * *f* aeronautics.
aéronaval *adj* air and sea.
aéroport *m* airport.
aérospatial *adj* aerospace.
affable *adj* affable.
affaiblir *vt* to weaken; **s'~** *vr* to weaken, grow weaker.
affaiblissement *m* weakening.
affaire *f* matter.
affaissement *m* subsidence.
affaisser *vt* to cause to subside *ou* cave in; **s'~** *vr* to subside; to cave in.
affamé *adj* starving.
affamer *vt* to starve.
affectation *f* allocation (*à* to); affectation.
affecté *adj* affected.
affecter *vt* to affect.
affectif *adj* emotional.
affection *f* affection.
affectueux *adj* affectionate.
affectueusement *adv* affectionately.
affermir *vt* to strengthen; to make firm.
affermissement *m* strengthening.
affichage *m* bill posting.
affiche *f* poster.
afficher *vt* to post *ou* put up.
affiner *vt* to refine.
affinité *f* affinity.
affirmatif *adj* affirmative.
affirmation *f* assertion.
affirmativement *adv* in the affirmative.
affirmer *vt* to assert.
affluent *m* tributary.
affluer *vi* to rush (*à* to).

afflux *m* influx, rush.

affolant *adj* alarming.

affolement *m* panic.

affoler *vt* to throw into a panic; **s'~** *vr* to get into a panic.

affranchir *vt* to frank, stamp; free.

affranchissement *m* stamping, franking; freeing.

affréter *vt* to charter.

affreux *adj* horrible; awful.

affreusement *adv* horribly, dreadfully.

affrontement *m* confrontation.

affronter *vt* to confront; **s'~** *vr* to confront one another.

afin *prép*: ~ **de** (in order) to; ~ **que** in order that, so that.

africain *adj*, *mf* African.

Afrique *f* Africa.

agaçant *adj* annoying.

agacer *vt* to annoy, irritate.

âge *m* age; **quel ~ as-tu?** how old are you?

âgé *adj* old; ~ **de 10 ans** 10 years old.

agence *f* agency; branch; offices.

agencement *m* organisation, arrangement; equipment.

agencer *vt* to arrange; equip.

agenda *m* diary.

agenouiller (s') *vr* to kneel (down).

agent *m* agent; policeman.

agglomération *f* town, urban area.

aggravant *adj* aggravating.

aggravation *f* worsening, aggravation; increase.

aggraver *vt* to make worse; increase; **s'~** *vr* to get worse, worsen; increase.

agile *adj* agile, nimble; **~ment** *adv* nimbly.

agilité *f* agility.

agir *vi* to act.

agitateur *m* **-trice** *f* agitator.

agitation *f* agitation.

agiter *vt* to shake; wave; **s'~** *vr* to move about; fidget.

agneau *m* lamb.

agonie *f* death throes.

agrafe *f* staple; hook.

agrafer *vt* to staple (together); fasten up.

agrafeuse *f* stapler.

agraire *adj* agrarian; land.

agrandir *vt* to make bigger; widen; expand; **s'~** *vr* to get bigger; widen; expand.

agrandissement *m* enlargement.

agréable *adj* agreeable, pleasant; **~ment** *adv* agreeably, pleasantly.

agresser *vt* to attack.

agresseur *m* attacker.

agressif *adj* aggressive.

agression *f* attack.

agressivement *adv* aggressively.

agressivité *f* aggressiveness.

agricole *adj* agricultural.

agriculteur *m* farmer.

agriculture *f* agriculture, farming.

agripper *vt* to grab (hold of); **s'~ à** *vr* to grab on to.

agronome *m* agronomist.

agronomie *f* agronomy.

agrumes *mpl* citrus fruits.

ahuri *adj* stunned; stupefied.

ahurissant *adj* staggering.

aide *f* help; aid.

aider *vt* to help.

aigle *m* eagle.

aigre *adj* sour, bitter; **~ment** *adv* sourly.

aigreur *f* sourness; acidity.

aigri *adj* bitter, embittered.

aigu *adj*, *f* **aiguè** shrill; acute; sharp.

aiguillage *m* shunting.

aiguille *f* needle.

aiguiller *vt* to direct; shunt.

aiguiser *vt* to sharpen.

ail *m* garlic.

ailé *adj* winged.

aileron *m* fin; aileron.

ailleurs *adv* elsewhere; **partout ~** everywhere else; **nulle part ~** nowhere else; **d'~** moreover; by the way.

aimable *adj* kind; **~ment** *adv* kindly.

aimant *m* magnet.

aimanter *vt* to magnetise.

aimer *vt* to love.

aîné *m*, **aînée** *f* eldest *ou* oldest child; * *adj* elder, older; eldest, oldest.

ainsi *adv* so, thus; **puisque c'est ~** since this is the way it is *ou* things are.

air *m* air; **avoir l'~ content** to look happy; **d'un ~ moqueur** in a mocking fashion.

aire *f* area.

aise *f* ease, comfort.

aisé *adj* easy; well-off; **~ment** *adv* easily.

aisselle *f* armpit.

ajournement *m* adjournment; postponement.

ajourner *vt* to adjourn; defer, postpone.

ajout *m* addition.

ajouter *vt* to add.

ajuster *vt* to adjust.

alarmant *adj* alarming.

alarme *f* alarm.

alarmer *vt* to alarm; **s'~** *vr* to get alarmed (**de** at, about).

albâtre *m* alabaster.

album *m* album.

albumine *f* albumen.

alcalin *adj* alkaline.

alcaloïde *m* alkaloid.

alchimie *f* alchemy.

alchimiste *m* alchemist.

alcool *m* alcohol.

alcoolique *adj* alcoholic; * *mf* drunkard.

alcoolisme *m* alcoholism.

aléatoire *adj* uncertain; risky.

alentours *mpl* surroundings, neighbourhood.

alerte *adj* alert; agile; * *f* alarm, alert.

alerter *vt* to alert; notify; warn.

algèbre *f* algebra.

algébrique *adj* algebraic; **~ment** *adv* algebraically.

algorithme *m* algorithm.

algue *f* seaweed.

alibi *m* alibi.

aliénation *f* alienation.

aliéner *vt* to alienate.

alignement *m* alignment; aligning.

aligner *vt* to align, line up.

aliment *m* food.

alimentaire *adj* alimentary, food.

alimentation *f* feeding; diet; food industry.

alimenter *vt* to feed; **s'~** *vr* to eat.

alinéa *m* paragraph.

allée *f* avenue; path.

alléger *vt* to make lighter; alleviate.

allégorie *f* allegory.

allégresse *f* cheerfulness.

alléguer *vt* to allege, put forward.

aller *vi* to go; **comment allez-vous?** how are you?; **allons-y** let's go; **s'en aller** to go away, leave; * *m* outward journey; single ticket.

allergie *f* allergy.

allergique *adj* allergic (**à** to).

alliage *m* alloy.

alliance *f* alliance; marriage; wedding ring.

allié *m* **-e** *f* ally; * *adj* allied.

allier *vt* to combine.

allô *excl* hello!

allocation *f* allocation; allowance.

allongé *adj* **être allongé** to be lying (down).

allonger *vt* to lengthen; **s'~** *vr* to lengthen; lie down.

allouer *vt* to allocate.

allumage *m* ignition.

allumer *vt* to light; turn *ou* switch on.

allumette *f* match.

allure *f* speed; look.
allusion *f* allusion (*à* to).
alluvions *fpl* alluvium, alluvial deposits.
alors *adv* then; ~ **que** while; whereas.
alouette *f* lark.
alourdir *vt* to make heavy; increase.
alphabet *m* alphabet.
alphabétique *adj* alphabetical; ~**ment** *adv* alphabetically.
alpinisme *m* mountaineering.
alpiniste *mf* mountaineer.
altération *f* alteration, change.
altercation *f* altercation.
altérer *vt* to change, alter.
alternance *f* alternation.
alternatif *adj* alternate.
alternative *f* alternative.
alternativement *adv* in turn, alternately.
alterner *vt vi* to alternate (*avec* with).
altitude *f* altitude, height.
altruisme *m* altruism.
aluminium *m* aluminium.
alvéole *f* cell.
amabilité *f* kindness.
amaigrir *vt* to make thin(ner).
amaigrissant *adj* slimming.
amalgame *m* mixture, amalgam.
amalgamer *vt* to combine.
amande *f* almond.
amant *m* lover.
amarrer *vt* to moor.
amas *m* pile, heap.
amasser *vt* to amass, pile up.
amateur *m* amateur; connoisseur.
ambassade *f* embassy.
ambassadeur *m* **-drice** *f* ambassador.
ambiance *f* atmosphere.
ambigu *adj,* *f* **ambigué** ambiguous.
ambiguïté *f* ambiguity.
ambitieux *adj* ambitious.
ambition *f* ambition.
ambivalence *f* ambivalence.
ambre *m* amber.
ambulance *f* ambulance.
ambulant *adj* travelling, mobile.
âme *f* soul.
amélioration *f* improvement.
améliorer *vt* to improve; **s'**~ *vr* to improve.
aménagement *m* fitting out; adjustment; development.
aménager *vt* to fit out; adjust; develop.
amende *f* fine.
amendement *m* amendment.
amener *vt* to bring.

amer *adj* bitter.
amèrement *adv* bitterly.
Américain *m* **-e** *f* American.
américain *adj* American.
Amérique *f* America.
amertume *f* bitterness.
ameublement *m* furniture.
ami *m* **-e** *f* friend.
amiante *m* asbestos.
amibe *f* amoeba.
amical *adj* friendly; ~**ement** *adv* in a friendly manner.
amincir *vt* to thin (down).
amiral *m* admiral.
amitié *f* friendship.
ammoniac *m* ammonia.
amnésie *f* amnesia.
amnistie *f* amnesty.
amnistier *vt* to grant an amnesty to.
amoindrir *vt* to weaken; reduce.
amoindrissement *m* weakening; reduction.
amoncellement *m* pile; accumulation.
amorcer *vt* to bait; begin.
amorphe *adj* apathetic.
amortir *vt* to soften; deaden.
amortissement *m* paying off.
amour *m* love.
amoureux *adj* in love (*de* with).
amovible *adj* detachable.
ampère *m* ampere, amp.
amphibie *adj* amphibious.
amphithéâtre *m* amphitheatre.
ample *adj* roomy; wide; ~**ment** *adv* amply, fully.
ampleur *f* fullness; range.
amplifier *vt* to increase; amplify.
amplitude *f* amplitude; magnitude.
ampoule *f* bulb; phial; blister.
amputation *f* amputation.
amputer *vt* to amputate.
amusant *adj* amusing.
amuser *vt* to amuse.
an *m* year; **avoir vingt** ~**s** to be 20 (years old).
anabolisant *m* anabolic steroid.
anachronisme *m* anachronism.
anagramme *m* anagram.
analgésique *adj* analgesic.
analogie *f* analogy.
analogique *adj* analogical.
analogue *adj* analogous (*à* to).
analphabète *adj* illiterate.
analyse *f* analysis; test.
analyser *vt* to analyse.
analyste *mf* analyst; psychoanalyst.
analytique *adj* analytical; ~**ment** *adv* analytically.
ananas *m* pineapple.
anarchie *f* anarchy.

anarchiste *mf* anarchist.
anathème *m* anathema.
anatomie *f* anatomy.
anatomique *adj* anatomical; ~**ment** *adv* anatomically.
ancestral *adj* ancestral.
ancêtre *m* ancestor.
anchois *m* anchovy.
ancien *adj* old; former; ~**nement** *adv* formerly.
ancienneté *f* (years of) service; seniority; age.
ancrage *m* anchorage.
ancre *f* anchor.
ancrer *vt* to anchor.
âne *m* ass, donkey.
anéantir *vt* to annihilate.
anéantissement *m* annihilation.
anecdote *f* anecdote.
anémie *f* anemia.
anémone *f* anemone.
anesthésie *f* anaesthetic; anaesthesia.
anesthésique *m* anaesthetic.
ange *m* angel.
angélique *adj* angelic; * *f* angelica.
angine *f* tonsillitis.
Anglais *m* **-e** *f* Englishman; Englishwoman.
anglais *adj* English; * *m* (*ling*) English.
angle *m* angle; corner.
Angleterre *f* England.
anglophone *adj* English-speaking; *mf* English speaker.
angoissant *adj* agonising.
angoisse *f* anguish.
angoisser *vt* to cause anguish.
animal *m* animal.
animateur *m* **-trice** *f* host, compère; leader.
animation *f* animation; hustle and bustle.
animé *adj* busy; lively.
animer *vt* to lead; host; liven up; **s'**~ *vr* to liven up.
animisme *m* animism.
animosité *f* animosity.
annales *fpl* annals.
anneau *m* ring.
année *f* year; **les** ~**s soixante** the Sixties.
annexe *f* annexe; * *adj* subsidiary.
annexer *vt* to annex; append.
annihiler *vt* to annihilate.
anniversaire *m* birthday; **joyeux** ~! happy birthday!
annonce *f* advertisement; announcement.
annoncer *vt* to announce (*à* to).
annoter *vt* to annotate.
annuaire *m* telephone directory, phone book.

annuel *adj* annual; **~lement** *adv* annually.

annulation *f* cancellation; nullification.

annuler *vt* to cancel; nullify.

anode *f* anode.

anodin *adj* insignificant.

anomalie *f* anomaly.

anonyme*adj* anonymous; impersonal; **~ment** *adv* anonymously.

anorexie *f* anorexia.

anorexique *adj, mf* anorexic.

anormal *adj* abnormal; **~ement** *adv* abnormally.

anse *f* handle.

antagonisme *m* antagonism.

antagoniste *adj* antagonistic.

antécédent *m* antecedent.

antenne *f* (*rad*, *TV*) aerial; (*zool*) feeler.

antérieur *adj* earlier, previous; **~ement** *adv* earlier, previously.

anthologie *f* anthology.

anthracite *m* anthracite.

anthropologie *f* anthropology.

anthropologue *m* anthropologist.

antiaérien *adj* antiaircraft.

anticancéreux *adj* cancer.

antichambre *f* antechamber.

anticipation *f* anticipation.

anticonceptionnel *adj* contraceptive.

anticonformiste *adj, mf* nonconformist.

anticorps *m* antibody.

anticyclone *m* anticyclone.

antidater *vt* to backdate.

antidépresseur *adj, m* antidepressant.

antidote *m* antidote.

antigel *m* antifreeze.

antimilitariste *adj, mf* antimilitarist.

antinucléaire *adj, mf* antinuclear.

antipathie *f* antipathy.

antipathique *adj* unpleasant.

antipode *m* antipodes; **aux ~s de** the polar opposite of.

antiquaire *mf* antique dealer.

antique *adj* ancient.

antiquité *f* antiquity; antique.

antirouille *adj invar* rustproof.

antisémite *mf* antisemite; *adj* antisemitic.

antiseptique *adj* antiseptic.

antisocial *adj* antisocial.

antitétanique *adj* (anti-)tetanus.

antithèse *f* antithesis.

antitoxine *f* antitoxin.

antivol *m invar* anti-theft*ou* security device; lock; * *adj invar* anti-theft.

antonyme *m* antonym.

antre *m* den.

anus *m* anus.

anxiété *f* anxiety.

anxieux *adj* anxious.

aorte *f* aorta.

août *m* August.

apaisant *adj* soothing.

apaisement *m* calm(ing down); relief.

apaiser *vt* to calm (down); relieve.

apathie *f* apathy.

apathique *adj* apathetic.

apercevoir *vt* to see; catch a glimpse of.

aperçu *m* (overall *ou* general) idea.

apéritif *m* aperitif.

apesanteur *f* weightlessness.

apeuré *adj* frightened.

aphone *adj* voiceless, hoarse.

aphrodisiaque *adj, m* aphrodisiac.

apiculteur *m* beekeeper.

apitoyer *vt* to move to pity; **s'~** *vr* to feel pity (*sur* for).

aplanir *vt* to level (out); smooth away.

aplati *adj* flat.

aplatir *vt* to flatten (out).

apocalypse *f* apocalypse.

apocalyptique *adj* apocalyptic.

apogée *m* apogee, peak.

apolitique *adj* apolitical; non-political.

apologie *f* apology.

apoplexie *f* apoplexy.

apostrophe *f* apostrophe.

apothéose *f* apotheosis.

apôtre *m* apostle.

apparaître *vi* to appear.

appareil*m* device; appliance; (tele)phone;**~-photo** camera.

appareillage *m* casting off; equipment.

appareiller *vi* (*mar*) to cast off.

apparemment *adv* apparently.

apparence *f* appearance.

apparent *adj* apparent.

apparition *f* appearance; apparition.

appartement *m* flat, apartment.

appartenance *f* membership.

appartenir *vi*: **~ à** to belong to.

appât *m* bait.

appâter *vt* to lure; bait.

appauvrir *vt* to impoverish; **s'~** *vr* to grow poorer.

appauvrissement *m* impoverishment.

appel *m* call; appeal.

appeler *vt* to call; call out; **s'~** *vr* **je m'appelle Léon** my name is Leon.

appellation *f* appellation; name.

appendicite *f* appendicitis.

appesantir *vt* to weigh down; strengthen; **s'~** *vr* to grow heavier; grow stronger.

appétissant *adj* appetizing.

appétit *m* appetite (*de* for).

applaudir *vt vi* to applaud.

applaudissements *mpl* applause.

applicable *adj* applicable (*à* to).

application *f* application; use.

appliqué *adj* thorough, industrious.

appliquer *vt* to apply (*à* to); **s'~** *vr* to apply oneself.

apport *m* supply.

apporter *vt* to bring.

apposer *vt* to append; affix.

appréciable *adj* appreciable.

appréciatif *adj* evaluative; appreciative.

appréciation *f* estimation, assessment

apprécier *vt* to appreciate; to assess

appréhender *vt* to apprehend; dread.

appréhension *f* apprehension.

apprendre *vt* to learn; **~ à lire** to learn to read; **~ à lire à un enfant** to teach a child to read.

apprenti *m* **-e** *f* apprentice.

apprentissage *m* apprenticeship.

apprêter *vt* to dress; to size; **s'~** *vr* to get ready.

apprivoiser *vt* to tame.

approbateur *adj, f* **-trice** approving.

approbation *f* approval.

approche *f* approach.

approcher *vt* to move near; approach; **s'~** *vr* to approach.

approfondir *vt* to deepen.

approfondissement *m* deepening.

approprier (s') *vr* to appropriate.

approuver *vt* to approve of.

approvisionnement *m* supplying.

approvisionner *vt* to supply; **s'~** *vr* to stock up (*de, en* with).

approximatif *adj* approximate.

approximation *f* approximation.

approximativement *adv* approximately.

appui *m* support.

appuie-tête *m invar* headrest.

appuyer *vt* to press; lean; support *vi* to press; *vr* **s'~** to lean against; *vr* **s'~ sur** to lean on; rely on.

âpre *adj* bitter, harsh; **~ment** *adv* bitterly.

après *prép* after; **après tout** after all; **d'~ elle** according to her; **collé ~ la vitre** stuck on the window; * *adv* after(wards); **tout de suite ~** immediately after *ou* afterwards.

après-demain *adv* the day after to-morrow.

après-midi *m/f invar* afternoon.

âpreté *f* bitterness.

a priori *m* apriorism; * *adv* a priori.

apte *adj* capable (*à* of).

aptitude *f* aptitude; ability.

aquarium *m* aquarium.

aquatique *adj* aquatic.

aqueduc *m* aqueduct.

aqueux *adj* aqueous, watery.

arabesque *f* arabesque.

arable *adj* arable.

arachide *f* peanut, groundnut.

araignée *f* spider.

arbalète *f* crossbow.

arbitrage *m* arbitration.

arbitraire *adj* arbitrary; **~ment** *adv* arbitrarily.

arbitre *m* arbiter; referee.

arbitrer *vt* to arbitrate; referee.

arborer *vt* to wear; bear.

arborescence *f* arborescence.

arboriculture *f* arboriculture, tree cultivation.

arbre *m* tree.

arbrisseau *m* shrub.

arbuste *m* bush.

arc *m* bow; arc; arch.

arcade *f* arcade.

arc-bouter (s') *vr* to lean.

arc-en-ciel *m*, *pl* **arcs-en-ciel** rainbow.

archaïque *adj* archaic.

archange *m* archangel.

arche *f* arch.

archéologie *f* archaeology.

archéologue *mf* archaeologist.

archétype *m* archetype.

archevêque *m* archbishop.

archipel *m* archipelago.

architecte *mf* architect.

architectonique *adj* architectonic.

architectural *adj* architectural.

architecture *f* architecture.

archiver *vt* to file, archive.

archives *fpl* archives, records.

archiviste *mf* archivist.

ardemment *adv* ardently.

ardent *adj* ardent, burning.

ardeur *f* ardour.

ardoise *f* slate.

ardu *adj* difficult.

are *f* are, a hundred square metres.

arène *f* arena.

arête *f* (fish)bone.

argent *m* silver; money.

argenté *adj* silver; silver-plated.

argenterie *f* silverware.

argile *f* clay.

argot *m* slang.

argument *m* argument.

argumentation *f* argumentation.

argumenter *vi* to argue (*sur* about).

aride *adj* arid.

aridité *f* aridity.

aristocrate *mf* aristocrat.

aristocratie *f* aristocracy.

aristocratique *adj* aristocratic.

arithmétique *f* arithmetic; * *adj* arithmetical; **~ment** *adv* arithmetically.

armature *f* (frame)work.

arme *f* arm, weapon.

armée *f* army.

armement *m* ' arms, weapons; armaments.

armer *vt* to arm; **s'~** *vr* to arm o.s.

armistice *m* armistice.

armoire *f* cupboard; wardrobe.

armure *f* armour.

aromate *m* herb; spice.

aromatique *adj* aromatic.

aromatiser *vt* to flavour.

arôme *m* aroma; flavour.

arpenteur *m* (land) surveyor.

arqué *adj* curved, arched.

arquebuse *f* arquebus.

arrachement *m* wrench; pulling *ou* tearing off.

arracher *vt* to pull (out); tear off.

arrangeant *adj* obliging.

arrangement *m* arrangement.

arranger *vt* to arrange; fix; **cela m'arrangerait** that would suit me; **s'~** *vr* to come to an arrangement; manage; get better.

arrestation *f* arrest.

arrêt *m* stopping; stop (button).

arrêté *m* order.

arrêter *vt* to stop; **s'~** *vr* to stop.

arrhes *fpl* deposit.

arrière *m invar* back; **en ~** back(wards); **à l'~** at the back; * *adj invar* back, rear.

arriéré *adj* backward.

arrière-goût *m* aftertaste.

arrière-grand-mère *f* great-grandmother.

arrière-grand-père *m* great-grandfather.

arrière-pays *m* hinterland.

arrière-pensée *f* ulterior motive.

arrière-petits-enfants *mpl* great grandchildren.

arrière-plan *m* background.

arrimer *vt* to stow.

arrivage *m* delivery.

arrivant *m* **-e** *f* newcomer.

arrivée *f* arrival, coming.

arriver *vi* to arrive, come.

arriviste *mf* careerist; social climber.

arrogance *f* arrogance.

arrogant *adj* arrogant.

arroger (s') *vr* to assume (without rights to).

arrondi *adj* round(ed).

arrondir *vt* to make round; round off.

arrondissement *m* district.

arrosage *m* watering.

arroser *vt* to water.

arsenal *m* arsenal.

arsenic *m* arsenic.

art *m* art.

artère *f* artery; road.

artériel *adj* arterial.

arthrite *f* arthritis.

artichaut *m* artichoke.

article *m* article.

articulation *f* joint; knuckle.

articuler *vt* to articulate.

artifice *m* trick.

artificiel *adj* artificial; **~lement** *adv* artificially.

artillerie *f* artillery.

artisan *m* artisan, craftsman.

artisanal *adj* craft.

artisanat *m* craft industry.

artiste *mf* artist.

artistique *adj* artistic; **~ment** *adv* artistically.

as *m* ace.

ascendance *f* ancestry.

ascendant *adj* upward, rising; * *m* (strong) influence, ascendancy (*sur* over).

ascenseur *m* lift, elevator.

ascension *f* ascent.

ascète *mf* ascetic.

ascétique *adj* ascetic.

aseptiser *vt* to sterilise; disinfect.

asexué *adj* asexual.

asiatique *adj* Asian.

asile *m* refuge; asylum.

aspect *m* appearance, look.

asperge *f* asparagus.

asperger *vt* to splash (*de* with).

aspérité *f* bump.

asphalte *m* asphalt.

asphyxie *f* asphyxiation, suffocation.

asphyxier *vt* to asphyxiate, suffocate.

aspirateur *m* vacuum cleaner.

aspiration *f* inhalation.

aspirer *vt* to inhale.

aspirine *f* aspirin.

assagir *vt* to quieten (down); **s'~** *vr* to quieten (down).

assaillant *m* assailant.

assaillir *vt* to assail.

assainir *vt* to clean up; purify.

assainissement *m* cleaning up.

assaisonnement *m* seasoning.

assaisonner *vt* to season.

assassin *m* murderer; assassin.

assassinat *m* murder; assassination.

assassiner *vt* to assassinate.

assaut *m* assault, attack (*de* on).

assécher *vt* to drain; **s'~** *vr* to dry (up *ou* out).

assemblage *m* assembly; assembling.

assemblée *f* meeting.

assembler *vt* to assemble; **s'~** *vr* to assemble.

assentiment *m* assent.

asseoir (s') *vr* to sit down.

assermenté *adj* on oath.

assertion *f* assertion.

asservissement *m* enslavement; slavery.

assez *adv* enough; quite, rather; **avoir ~ d'argent** to have enough money; **~ bien** quite well; **j'en ai ~!** I've had enough!; I'm fed up.

assidu *adj* assiduous; regular.

assiduité *f* assiduity; regularity.

assiéger *vt* to besiege.

assiette *f* plate.

assigner *vt* to assign.

assimilation *f* assimilation; comparison; classification.

assimiler *vt* to assimilate.

assis *adj* seated, sitting (down).

assistance *f* audience; assistance.

assistant *m* **-e** *f* assistant.

assister *vt* to attend; assist.

association *f* association.

associé *m* **-e** *f* associate, partner.

associer *vt* to associate (*à* with); **s'~** *vr* to join together.

assombrir *vt* to darken; **s'~** to darken.

assommer *vt* to stun.

Assomption *f* : **l'~** the Assumption.

assortiment *m* assortment.

assortir *vt* to match; **s'~** *vr* to go well together.

assoupir (s') *vr* to doze off.

assoupissement *m* doze.

assouplir *vt* to make supple; relax.

assouplissement *m* softening; relaxing.

assourdir *vt* to deafen; muffle.

assourdissant *adj* deafening.

assouvir *vt* to satisfy.

assouvissement *m* satisfying, satisfaction.

assujettir *vt* to subjugate.

assumer *vt* to assume.

assurance *f* (self-)assurance; assurance; insurance (policy).

assuré *m* **-e** *f* assured; * *adj* confident.

assurer *vt* to assure; **s'~** *vr* to insure o.s.

assureur *m* (insurance) agent; insurer(s), insurance company.

astérisque *m* asterisk.

asthmatique *adj*, *mf* asthmatic.

asthme *m* asthma.

asticot *m* maggot.

astigmate *adj* astigmatic.

astiquer *vt* to polish.

astre *m* star.

astreignant *adj* demanding.

astreindre *vt* to force, compel; **s'~** *vr* **s'~ à faire** to force *ou* compel o.s. to do.

astrologie *f* astrology.

astrologique *adj* astrological.

astrologue *m* astrologer.

astronaute *m* astronaut.

astronome *m* astronomer.

astronomie *f* astronomy.

astronomique *adj* astronomical.

astuce *f* shrewdness; (clever) trick; pun.

astucieux *adj* astute.

asymétrique *adj* asymmetric(al).

atelier *m* workshop; studio.

atermoyer *vi* to procrastinate.

athée *mf* atheist; *adj* atheistic.

athéisme *m* atheism.

athlète *mf* athlete.

athlétique *adj* athletic.

athlétisme *m* athletics.

atlas *m* atlas.

atmosphère *f* atmosphere.

atmosphérique *adj* atmospheric.

atome *m* atom.

atomique *adj* atomic.

atomiseur *m* spray; atomiser.

atout *m* trump; advantage, asset.

âtre *m* hearth.

atroce *adj* atrocious; dreadful; **~ment** *adv* atrociously; dreadfully.

atrocité *f* atrocity.

atrophié *adj* atrophied.

attachant *adj* endearing.

attache *f* fastener.

attaché *m* **-e** *f* attaché; assistant.

attachement *m* attachment (*à* to).

attacher *vt* to tie together; tie up; fasten; attach (*à* to).

attaque *f* attack.

attaquer *vt* to attack; tackle.

attarder (s') *vr* to linger.

atteindre *vt* to reach; affect; contact.

atteinte *f* attack (*à* on); **hors d'~** beyond *ou* out of reach.

attenant *adj* adjoining.

attendre *vt* to wait; **en attendant** meanwhile, in the meantime; **s'~** *vr* : **s'~ à qch** to expect sth.

attendrir *vt* to fill with pity; move; tenderise; **s'~** *vr* to be moved (*sur* by).

attendrissant *adj* touching, moving.

attendrissement *m* emotion.

attendu *adj* expected; long-awaited.

attentat *m* attack (*contre* on); murder attempt.

attente *f* wait; expectation.

attentif *adj* attentive; careful.

attention *f* attention; care.

attentionné *adj* considerate, thoughtful (*pour* towards).

attentivement *adv* attentively; carefully.

atténuation *f* alleviation; easing.

atténuer *vt* to alleviate; ease.

atterrir *vi* to land, touch down.

atterrissage *m* landing, touch down.

attester *vt* to testify to.

attirail *m* gear.

attirant *adj* attractive.

attirer *vt* to attract; **~ des ennuis à qn** to cause sb trouble.

attiser *vt* to stir up.

attitude *f* attitude; bearing.

attraction *f* attraction.

attrait *m* attraction, appeal.

attraper *vt* to catch.

attrayant *adj* attractive.

attribuer *vt* to attribute; award.

attribut *m* attribute.

attribution *f* attribution.

attrister *vt* to sadden.

attroupement *m* crowd, gathering.

au = à le.

aube *f* dawn, daybreak.

auberge *f* inn; **~ de jeunesse** youth hostel.

aubergine *f* aubergine.

aucun *adj* no; not any; any; **sans ~ doute** without (any) doubt; **~ement** *adv* in no way; not in the least; * *pn* none; not any; any (one); **~ d'entre eux** none of them.

audace *f* audacity; daring.

audacieux *adj* audacious, bold; daring.

audience *f* audience; hearing.

audiovisuel *adj* audiovisual.

auditeur *m* **-trice** *f* listener; auditor.

auditoire *m* audience.

augmentation *f* increase, rise (*de* in); increasing, raising (*de* of).

augmenter *vt* to increase, raise.

augure *f* omen; oracle.

aujourd'hui *adv* today.

aumône *f* alms; **demander/faire l'~** to beg for / give alms.

auparavant *adv* before, previously; before, first.

auprès *prép*: ~ **de** next to; (compared) with.

auquel = **à lequel**.

auréole *f* halo, aureole; ring (mark).

auriculaire *adj* auricular; * *m* little finger.

aurore *f* dawn, first light.

ausculter *vt* to auscultate.

aussi *adv* too, also; so; **nous** ~ us too; **une** ~ **belle journée** such a beautiful day; **il est** ~ **petit qu'elle** he is as small as she is.

aussitôt *adv* immediately; ~ **dit,** ~ **fait** no sooner said than done; ~ **que** as soon as.

austère *adj* austere; ~**ment** *adv* austerely.

austérité *f* austerity.

autant *adv* as much; as many; so much; such; so many; such a lot of; the same; ~ **que je sache** as far as I know; ~ **que possible** as much as possible; **elle n'est pas plus heureuse pour** ~ she's not any happier for it *ou* for all that.

autel *m* altar.

auteur *m* author.

authenticité *f* authenticity.

authentifier *vt* to authenticate.

authentique *adj* authentic; ~**ment** *adv* authentically.

autobiographie *f* autobiography.

autobiographique *adj* autobiographical.

autocar *m* coach.

autocollant *adj* self-adhesive.

autocuiseur *m* pressure cooker.

autodéfense *f* self-defence.

autodestruction *f* self-destruction.

autodidacte *adj* self-taught.

auto-école *f* driving school.

automate *m* automaton.

automatique *adj* automatic; ~**ment** *adv* automatically.

automatiser *vt* to automate.

automatisme *m* automatism.

automne *m* autumn.

automobile *f* (motor) car.

automobiliste *mf* motorist.

autonome *adj* autonomous; self-governing.

autonomie *f* autonomy; self-government.

autoportrait *m* self-portrait.

autopsie *f* autopsy, post-mortem (examination).

autoradio *m* car radio.

autorisation *f* authorisation, permission; permit.

autoriser *vt* to authorise, give permission for; allow.

autoritaire *adj* authoritarian.

autorité *f* authority.

autoroute *f* motorway.

autosatisfaction *f* self-satisfaction.

auto-stop *m* hitch-hiking; **faire de l'**~ to hitch-hike.

auto-stoppeur *m* **-euse** *f* hitch-hiker.

autour *prép* ~ **de** (a)round; * *adv* (a)round; **il y en a tout** ~ there is/are some all around.

autre *adj* other; ~ **chose** something else *ou* different; ~ **part** somewhere else; **d'**~ **part** on the other hand; moreover; * *pn* another (one); **j'en veux un** ~ I'd like another (one); **encore deux** ~**s** another two; **les cinq** ~**s** the five others; the other five.

autrefois *adv* in the past, in days gone by.

autrement *adv* differently; otherwise; **je n'ai pas pu faire** ~ I couldn't do differently *ou* otherwise.

autruche *f* ostrich.

autrui *pn* others.

aux = **à les**.

auxiliaire *adj* auxiliary; * *m* auxiliary; * *mf* assistant.

avachir (s') *vr* to become *ou* grow limp.

avalanche *f* avalanche.

avaler *vt* to swallow.

avance *f* advance; lead; **arriver en** ~ to arrive early; **payer d'**~ to pay in advance; **réserver à l'**~ to book in advance; **avoir de l'**~ **sur** to have the lead over.

avancement *m* promotion; progress; forward movement.

avancer *vt* to move forward; bring forward; put forward; **s'**~ *vr* to advance, move forward; * *vi* to move forward, advance; make progress; project, stick out.

avant *prép* before; ~ **peu** shortly; ~ **tout** above all; * *adv* before; **en** ~ in front, ahead; * *m* front; (*mar*) bow; forward.

avantage *m* advantage.

avantager *vt* to favour; flatter.

avantageux *adj* profitable, worthwhile; attractive; flattering.

avant-bras *m invar* forearm.

avant-coureur *adj* precursory.

avant-dernier *m* **-ière** *f, adj* next to last, second last, last but one.

avant-garde *f* avant-garde; vanguard.

avant-goût *m* foretaste.

avant-hier *adv* the day before yesterday.

avant-première *f* preview.

avare *mf* miser; *adj* miserly.

avarice *f* avarice, miserliness.

avarie *f* damage.

avarié *adj* rotting; damaged.

avec *prép* with; to.

avènement *m* accession (*à* to); advent.

avenir *m* future.

aventure *f* adventure; venture; experience; affair.

aventurer (s') *vr* to venture.

aventurier *m* **-ière** *f* adventurer.

avenue *f* avenue.

avérer (s') *vr* to turn out, prove to be.

averse *f* shower (of rain).

aversion *f* aversion (*pour* to); loathing (*pour* for).

avertir *vt* to warn; inform (*de* of).

avertissement *m* warning.

aveu *m* admission, confession.

aveuglant *adj* blinding.

aveugle *adj* blind; * *mf* blind person.

aveuglement *m* blindness.

aveugler *vt* to blind.

aviateur *m* **-trice** *f* pilot, aviator.

aviation *f* flying; aviation.

avide *adj* greedy; eager; ~**ment** *adv* greedily; eagerly.

avidité *f* greed; eagerness.

avilir *vt* to degrade.

avilissant *adj* degrading.

avion *m* (air)plane, aircraft.

aviron *m* oar; rowing.

avis *m* opinion.

avisé *adj* wise, sensible.

aviser *vt* to advise, inform; notice; **s'**~ *vr* **s'aviser de** to realise suddenly.

aviver *vt* to sharpen; deepen; arouse.

avocat *m* **-e** *f* lawyer, advocate; * *m* avocado (pear).

avoine *f* oats.

avoir *vt* to have; **il y a** there is/are; **il y a deux mois** two months ago; **qu'as-tu?** what's wrong (with you)?; **il n'avait qu'à le dire** he only had to say (the word); * *m* resources; credit.

avortement *m* abortion.

avorter *vi* to abort; fail.

avoué *m* solicitor.

avouer *vt* to admit (to); confess (to).

avril *m* April.

axe *m* axis; axle; main road.

axial *adj* axial.

azote *m* nitrogen.

B

babines *fpl* chops.
babiole *f* trinket, trifle.
bâbord *m* (*mar*) port.
babouin *m* baboon.
bac *m* ferry.
bâche *f* tarpaulin, cover.
bâcler *vt* to botch.
bactérie *f* bacterium.
badaud *m* idle onlooker.
badge *m* badge.
bafouer *vt* to scorn.
bafouiller *vi* to stammer; babble.
bagage *m* luggage; stock of knowledge.
bagarre *f* fight, brawl.
bagarrer (se) *vr* to fight; riot.
bagatelle *f* trinket; trifling sum.
bagne *m* penal servitude; (*fig*) grind.
bague *f* ring.
baguette *f* stick; loaf of French bread.
baie *f* (*geog*) bay.
baigner *vt vi* to bathe; * **se ~** *vr* to have a bath, swim.
baignoire *f* bath(tub).
bâiller *vi* to yawn.
bâillon *m* gag.
bâillonner *vt* to gag.
bain *m* bath; bathe; swim.
baiser *m* kiss; * *vt* to kiss.
baisse *f* fall, drop.
baisser *vi* to fall, drop; * *vt* to lower.
bal *m* dance.
balade *f* (*fam*) walk; drive.
balader (se) *vr* (*fam*) to go for a walk; to go for a drive.
balai *m* broom, brush.
balance *f* scales; balance.
balancement *m* sway; rocking.
balancer *vt* to swing; to balance.
balançoire *f* swing; seesaw.
balayer *vt* to sweep, brush.
balbutiement *m* stammering, babbling.
balbutier *vt* to stammer, babble.
balbuzard *m* osprey.
balcon *m* balcony.
baleine *f* whale.
balistique *f* ballistics.
ballast *m* ballast.
balle *f* bullet; ball.
ballet *m* ballet.
ballon *m* ball; balloon.
ballotter *vt* jolt, shake about.
balourd *adj* stupid; clumsy.

balustrade *f* balustrade; handrail.
bambou *m* bamboo.
banal *adj* banal, trite; **~ement** *adv* tritely.
banalisation *f* vulgarising; standardisation.
banalité *f* banality, triteness.
banane *f* banana.
bancaire *adj* banking, bank.
bancal, pl bancals *adj* lame; rickety.
bandage *m* bandage.
bande *f* band; tape; **~ dessinée** strip cartoon.
bandeau *m* headband; blindfold.
bander *vt* to bandage; stretch.
banderole *f* banner streamer.
bandit *m* bandit.
banlieue *f* suburbs.
bannière *f* banner.
bannir *vt* to banish; prohibit.
bannissement *m* banishment.
banque *f* bank; banking.
banqueroute *f* bankruptcy.
banquet *m* banquet.
banquette *f* seat, stool.
banquier *m* banker.
banquise *f* ice floe.
baptême *m* baptism.
baptiser *vt* to baptise.
bar *m* bar; (*zool*) bass.
barbare *adj* barbarian; barbaric.
barbarie *f* barbarism; barbarity.
barbarisme *m* (*gr*) barbarism.
barbe *f* beard.
barbelé *adj* barbed.
barbiturique *adj* barbituric; * *m* barbiturate.
barboter *vi* to dabble; splash.
barbouillage *m* scribble; daub.
barbouiller *vt* to smear; scrawl.
barbu *adj* bearded; * *m* bearded man.
barème *m* list, schedule.
baril *m* barrel, cask.
bariolé *adj* multicoloured, motley.
baromètre *m* barometer.
baron *m* baron **-ne** *f* baroness.
baroque *adj* baroque; * *m* baroque.
barque *f* small boat.
barrage *m* barrage, barrier, dam.
barre *f* bar, rod.
barré *adj* barred, blocked.
barreau *m* rung; bar (cage).
barrer *vt* to bar, block.
barrette *f* (hair) slide, brooch.
barricader *vt* to barricade; **se ~** *vr* to barricade o.s.

barrière *f* barrier; fence.
baryton *m* baritone.
bas *adj* low, base; * *n* stocking; sock; **~sement** *adv* basely, meanly.
basalte *m* basalt.
bas-côté *m* verge; aisle.
bascule *f* weighing machine, scales.
basculer *vi* to tip up, topple over.
base *f* base; basis.
baser *vt* to base; **se ~ sur** *vr* to depend on, rely on.
bas-fond *m* (*naut*) shallow, shoal.
basilic *m* (*bot*) basil.
basilique *f* basilica.
basket *m* basketball.
basketteur *m* **-euse** *f* basketball player.
bas-relief *m* bas-relief.
basse *f* (*mus*) bass.
basse-cour *f* poultry-yard.
bassesse *f* meanness; vulgarity.
bassin *m* pond, pool; dock.
bassine *f* bowl.
basson *m* bassoon.
bastion *m* bastion.
bas-ventre *m* lower abdomen.
bataille *f* battle.
batailler *vi* (*fig*) to fight, battle.
batailleur *adj* combative, aggressive.
bataillon *m* (*mil*) battalion.
bâtard *adj* bastard, illegitimate.
bateau *m* boat, ship.
batelier *m* boatman.
bâtiment *m* building; ship.
bâtir *vt* to build.
bâtisse *f* building, house.
bâton *m* stick, staff.
batracien *m* batrachian.
battant *m* clapper (bell); shutter.
batte *f* bat.
battement *m* banging; beating.
batterie *f* battery.
batteur *m* drummer; batsman.
battre *vt* to beat, defeat.
battu *adj* beaten.
baudet *m* donkey.
baume *m* balm, balsam.
bauxite *f* bauxite.
bavard *m* **-e** *f* chatterbox; * *adj* talkative, loquacious.
bavardage *m* chatting, gossiping.
bavarder *vi* to chat, gossip.
bave *f* dribble, slobber.
baver *vi* to dribble, drool.

bavure *f* smudge, blunder.

bazar *m* bazaar; general store.

B.D. *f* **(bande dessinée)** strip cartoon.

béant *adj* gaping, wide open.

béat *adj* blissful; **~ement** *adv* rapturously.

béatitude *f* beatitude; bliss.

beau, *f* belle *adj* beautiful, lovely.

beaucoup *adv* a lot, a great deal; **~ de monde** a lot of people; **~ de temps** a great deal of time.

beau-fils *m* son-in-law; stepson.

beau-frère *m* brother-in-law.

beau-père *m* father-in-law; stepfather.

beauté *f* beauty, loveliness.

beaux-arts *mpl* fine arts.

beaux-parents *mpl* parents-in-law.

bébé *m* baby.

bec *m* beak, bill.

béchamel *f* béchamel (sauce).

bée *adj* open-mouthed, flabbergasted.

bégaiement *m* stammering, faltering.

bégayer *vi* to stammer, stutter.

bégonia *m* begonia.

beige *adj* beige; * *m* beige.

beignet *m* fritter; doughnut.

bêlement *m* bleating.

bêler *vi* to bleat.

Belge *mf* Belgian.

belge *adj* Belgian.

Belgique *f* Belgium.

belle-fille *f* daughter-in-law, stepdaugher.

belle-mère *f* mother-in-law, stepmother.

belle-sœur *f* sister-in-law.

belligérant *m* **-e** *f* belligerent; * *adj* belligerent.

belliqueux *adj* aggressive; warlike.

bémol *m* (*mus*) flat.

bénédictin *m* **-e** *f* Benedictine.

bénédiction *f* benediction, blessing.

bénéfice *m* profit; benefit.

bénéficiaire *mf* beneficiary.

bénéficier *vi* to benefit; enjoy.

bénévole *adj* voluntary; unpaid; **~ment** *adv* voluntarily.

bénin, *f* bénigne *adj* benign; minor; harmless.

bénir *vt* to bless.

bénit *adj* consecrated, holy.

benne *f* skip; tipper.

benzène *m* benzene.

béquille *f* crutch; prop.

berceau *m* cradle.

bercement *m* rocking.

bercer *vt* to rock, cradle.

berceuse *f* lullaby; rocking chair.

béret *m* beret.

berge *f* riverbank.

berger *m* shepherd, **-ère** *f* shepherdess.

bergerie *f* sheepbarn.

berner *vt* to fool, hoax.

besogne *f* work; job.

besoin *m* need; want; **avoir ~ de** to need.

bestial *adj* bestial; **~ement** *adv* bestially.

bestialité *f* bestiality; brutishness.

bétail *m* livestock; cattle.

bête *adj* stupid, silly; **~ment** *adv* stupidly, foolishly; * *f* animal.

bêtifier *vt* to play the fool; prattle stupidly.

bêtise *f* stupidity, foolishness.

béton *m* concrete.

betterave *f* beetroot, beet.

beurre *m* butter.

beurrer *vt* to butter.

bévue *f* blunder.

biais *m* slant angle; bias.

biathlon *m* biathlon.

bibelot *m* curio.

biberon *m* baby's bottle.

bible *f* bible.

bibliographie *f* bibliography.

bibliothécaire *mf* librarian.

bibliothèque *f* library; bookcase.

bicarbonate *m* bicarbonate.

bicentenaire *m* bicentenary.

biceps *m* biceps.

biche *f* doe; darling, pet.

bicolore *adj* bi-coloured, two-tone.

bicyclette *f* bicycle.

bidon *m* tin, can; flask.

bidonville *m* shanty town.

bien *adv* well; properly; very; **c'est ~ cela** that's right; * *n* property, estate.

bien-être *m* well-being.

bienfaisant *adj* beneficial, kind.

bienfaiteur *m* benefactor, **-trice** *f* benefactress.

bienheureux *adj* blessed; lucky; happy.

bientôt *adv* soon.

bienveillant *adj* benevolent, kindly.

bienvenu *adj* welcome.

bienvenue *f* welcome.

bière *f* beer; coffin.

bifteck *m* steak.

bifurcation *f* bifurcation, fork.

bifurquer *vi* to fork, branch off.

bigot *adj* bigoted.

bihebdomadaire *adj* twice-weekly.

bijou *m* jewel.

bijouterie *f* jewellery.

bijoutier *m* **-ière** *f* jeweller.

bilan *m* balance sheet; assessment.

bilatéral *adj* bilateral.

bile *f* bile.

bilingue *adj* bilingual.

billard *m* billiards.

bille *f* marble; billiard ball.

billet *m* ticket; note.

billetterie *f* cash dispenser.

billion *m* billion.

bimensuel *adj* fortnightly.

bimestriel *adj* every two months.

binaire *adj* binary.

biochimie *f* biochemistry.

biochimiste *mf* biochemist.

biodégradable *adj* biodegradable.

bioéthique *f* bioethics.

biographie *f* biography.

biologie *f* biology.

biologique *adj* biological.

biologiste *mf* biologist.

biosphère *f* biosphere.

bioxyde *m* dioxide.

bipède *m* biped.

bipolaire *adj* bipolar.

bisannuel *adj* biennial.

biscornu *adj* crooked, misshapen; odd, outlandish.

biscuit *m* cake; biscuit.

bisexuel *adj* bisexual.

bissextile *adj* bissextile, leap (year).

bistouri *m* bistoury.

bitume *m* bitumen.

bitumer *vt* to asphalt, tarmac.

bizarre *adj* bizarre, strange; **~ment** *adv* strangely, oddly.

bizarrerie *f* strangeness, singularity.

blafard *adj* pale, pallid.

blague *f* joke, trick.

blaguer *vi* to joke.

blagueur *m* **-euse** *f* joker, wag; * *adj* jokey, teasing.

blaireau *m* badger.

blâme *m* blame, rebuke.

blâmer *vt* to blame, rebuke.

blanc *adj*, *f* **blanche** white; * *m* white; blank; * *mf* white person; * *f* (*mus*) minim.

blancheur *f* whiteness.

blanchir *vi* to turn white; to become lighter; * *vt* to whiten; to lighten.

blanchissage *m* laundering; refining.

blanchisserie *f* laundry.

blasé *adj* blasé.

blason *m* blazon, coat of arms.

blasphème *m* blasphemy.

blasphémer *vi* to blaspheme.

blé *m* wheat.

blême *adj* pale, wan.

blêmir *vi* to turn pale.

blessant *adj* cutting, hurtful.

blessé *adj* injured, wounded.

blesser *vt* to injure, wound.

blessure *f* injury, wound.

bleu *adj* blue; * *m* blue; bruise.

bleuet *m* cornflower.

bleuir *vt vi* to turn blue.

bleuté *adj* bluish.

blindage *m* armour plating.

blindé *adj* armoured, reinforced.

bloc *m* block, group, unit.

blocage *m* blocking, freezing.

blocus *m* blockade.

blond *adj* blond, fair.

blondir *vi* to turn blond, turn golden; * *vt* to bleach.

bloquer *vt* to block, blockade.

blottir (se) *vr* to curl up, snuggle up.

blouse *f* blouse; overall.

blouson *m* windcheater, bomber jacket.

bobine *f* reel, bobbin.

bocal *m* jar; bowl.

bœuf *m* ox, bullock.

bohémien *m* **-ne** *f* Bohemian.

boire *vt* to drink; * *vi* to drink, tipple.

bois *m* wood.

boisé *adj* wooded.

boisson *f* drink.

boîte *f* box.

boiter *vi* to limp.

boiteux *adj* lame.

boîtier *m* case, body.

boitillant *adj* limping.

boitiller *vi* to hobble slightly.

bol *m* bowl.

bolet *m* boletus.

bombardement *m* bombardment, bombing.

bombarder *vt* to bombard, bomb.

bombe *f* bomb.

bombé *adj* rounded, domed.

bon *adj*, *f* **bonne** good; * *m* slip, coupon, bond.

bonbon *m* sweet, candy.

bond *m* leap; bounce.

bonde *f* stopper, plug.

bondé *adj* packed.

bondir *vi* to jump, leap; to bounce.

bonheur *m* happiness; luck.

bonhomme *m*, *pl* **bonshommes** chap, fellow.

bonification *f* improvement; bonus.

bonifier *vt* to improve; * **se ~** *vr* to improve.

bonjour *m* hello, good morning.

bonnet *m* bonnet, hat.

bonneterie *f* hosiery.

bonsoir *m* good evening.

bonté *f* goodness, kindness.

bon vivant *m* bon vivant.

bord *m* side, edge.

bordé *adj* edged, bordered.

bordée *f* broadside, volley.

border *vt* to edge, border.

bordereau *m* note; invoice.

bordure *f* frame, border.

borgne *adj* one-eyed.

borne *f* boundary; milestone.

borné *adj* narrow-minded.

borner *vt* to restrict, limit.

bosse *f* hump, knob.

bosseler *vt* to dent, emboss.

bossu *m* **-e** *f* hunchback; * *adj* hunchbacked.

botanique *f* botany; * *adj* botanical.

botaniste *f* botanist.

botte *f* boot.

bottine *f* ankle boot, bootee.

bouche *f* mouth.

bouché *adj* cloudy, overcast.

bouchée *f* mouthful.

bouche-à-bouche *m* kiss of life.

boucher *vt* to block, clog up; * **se ~** *vr* to become cloudy; *m*, **-ère** *f* (woman) butcher.

boucherie *f* butcher's; butchery.

bouchon *m* cork.

boucle *f* curl; buckle.

boucler *vt* to buckle; to surround.

bouclier *m* shield.

bouddhisme *m* Buddhism.

boudeur *adj* sullen, sulky.

boudin *m* (black) pudding.

boue *f* mud.

bouée *f* buoy.

boueur *m* dustman.

bouffée *f* whiff, puff.

bouffi *adj* swollen, puffed up.

bouffon *m* buffoon, clown.

bougeoir *m* candlestick.

bouger *vi* to move; * *vt* to move, shift.

bougie *f* candle.

bouillant *adj* boiling.

bouillir *vi* to boil.

bouilloire *f* kettle.

bouillon *m* broth.

bouillonner *vi* to bubble, foam.

bouillotte *f* hot-water bottle.

boulanger *m* **-ère** *f* baker.

boulangerie *f* bakery.

boule *f* ball, bowl.

boulet *m* cannonball; (*fig*) millstone.

boulevard *m* boulevard.

bouleversant *adj* upsetting, confusing.

bouleversement *m* confusion, disruption.

bouleverser *vt* to confuse, disrupt.

boulimie *f* bulimia.

boulimique *adj* bulimic.

boulon *m* bolt.

bouquet *m* bouquet, posy.

bouquin *m* (*fam*) book.

bouquiniste *mf* second-hand bookseller.

bourbeux *adj* muddy.

bourbier *m* quagmire.

bourdon *m* bumblebee.

bourdonnement *m* buzz, buzzing.

bourdonner *vi* to buzz, hum.

bourg *m* market-town.

bourgeois *m* **-e** *f* bourgeois, middle-class person; * *adj* bourgeois, middle-class.

bourgeoisie *f* bourgeoisie, middle classes.

bourgeon *m* bud.

bourgeonner *vi* to bud.

bourrasque *f* squall, gust.

bourreau *m* torturer, executioner.

bourrelet *m* pad, cushion.

bourrer *vt* to stuff, cram.

bourse *f* purse; **la Bourse** stock exchange.

boursier *m* **-ière** *f* broker; speculator.

boursouflé *adj* bloated, swollen.

bousculade *f* hustle, scramble.

bousculer *vt* to jostle, hustle.

boussole *f* compass.

bout *m* end; piece, scrap.

boutade *f* whim, caprice; jest.

bouteille *f* bottle.

boutique *f* shop, store.

bouton *m* button.

boutonner *vt* to button.

boutonnière *f* buttonhole.

bouture *f* cutting.

bovin *adj* bovine.

boxe *f* boxing.

boxer *vi* to box.

boxeur *m* boxer.

boyau *m* guts, insides.

boycottage *m* boycotting.

boycotter *vt* to boycott.

bracelet *m* bracelet.

braconnier *m* poacher.

brader *vt* to sell at a discount.

braderie *f* discount sale.

braguette *f* fly (trousers).

braise *f* embers.

brancard *m* shaft, stretcher.

branche *f* branch.

branchement *m* branching; connection.

brancher *vt* to connect, link.

branchies *fpl* gills.

brandir *vt* to brandish, flourish.

branlant *adj* loose; shaky.

bras *m* arm.

brasier *m* brazier, furnace.

brasse *f* breaststroke.
brassée *f* armful.
brasser *vt* to brew; to mix.
brasserie *f* bar; brewery.
bravade *f* bravado.
brave *adj* brave, courageous; **~ment**
  adv bravely, courageously.
braver *vt* to brave, defy.
bravoure *f* bravery, courage.
brebis *f* ewe.
brèche *f* breach, gap.
bredouillant *adj* mumbling.
bredouille *adj* empty-handed.
bredouiller *vi* to mumble.
bref *adj*, *f* **brève** brief, concise; **en**
  ~ *adv* in short.
bretelle *f* strap, sling.
brevet *m* licence, patent.
breveté *adj* patented.
bribe *f* bit, scrap.
bric-à-brac *m* bric-a-brac.
bricolage *m* DIY, odd jobs.
bricole *f* small job.
bricoler *vi* to do odd jobs.
bricoleur *m* handyman, **-euse** *f*
  handywoman.
bride *f* bridle.
bridé *adj* restrained, restricted.
brider *vt* to restrain, restrict.
brièvement *adv* briefly, concisely.
brièveté *f* brevity.
brigade *f* brigade.
brigadier *m* corporal, sergeant
  (police).
brillamment *adv* brilliantly.
brillant *adj* brilliant, shining.
briller *vi* to shine.
brin *m* stalk, strand.
brindille *f* twig.
brique *f* brick, slab.
briquet *m* lighter.

brise *f* breeze.
briser *vt* to smash, shatter.
brocante *f* second-hand dealing.
brocanteur *m* **-euse** *f* second-hand
  dealer.
broche *f* brooch.
brochure *f* brochure, booklet.
broder *vt* to embroider, *vi* to embellish, elaborate.
broderie *f* embroidery.
bronche *f* bronchus.
bronchite *f* bronchitis.
bronzage *m* tan.
bronze *m* bronze.
bronzer *vi* to get a tan.
brosse *f* brush.
brosser *vt* to brush.
brouette *f* wheelbarrow.
brouillard *m* fog, mist.
brouiller *vt* to blur, confuse.
brouillon *m* rough copy, draft;
  * *adj* untidy.
broussaille *f* brushwood, undergrowth.
broussailleux *adj* bushy, overgrown.
brousse *f* undergrowth, bush.
brouter *vt* *vi* to graze.
broyer *vt* to grind, pulverise.
broyeur *adj* crushing, grinding.
bruine *f* drizzle.
bruissement *m* rustle.
bruit *m* noise, sound.
bruitage *m* sound-effects.
brûlant *adj* burning, scorching.
brûler *vt* *vi* to burn.
brûlure *f* burn.
brume *f* haze, mist.
brumeux *adj* hazy, misty.
brun *m* dark-haired man, **brune** *f*
  brunette; * *adj* brown.

brusque *adj* brusque, abrupt;
  ~ment *adv* brusquely, abruptly.
brusquer *vt* to offend; hasten.
brut *adj* crude, raw.
brutal *adj* brutal, rough; **~ement**
  adv brutally, roughly.
brutaliser *vt* to brutalise; to bully.
brutalité *f* brutality.
brute *f* brute; beast.
bruyamment *adv* noisily.
bruyant *adj* noisy.
bruyère *f* heather.
bûche *f* log.
bûcheron *m* **-ne** *f* woodcutter,
  lumberjack.
budget *m* budget.
budgétaire *adj* budgetary.
buée *f* condensation; steam.
buffet *m* sideboard, buffet.
buisson *m* bush.
bulbe *m* bulb.
bulle *f* bubble; blister.
bulletin *m* bulletin.
buraliste *mf* tobacconist.
bureau *m* office; desk.
bureaucrate *mf* bureaucrat.
bureaucratie *f* bureaucracy.
bureaucratique *adj* bureaucratic.
burin *m* chisel.
bus *m* bus.
buste *m* bust, chest.
but *m* objective, goal.
butane *m* butane.
buté *adj* stubborn.
butin *m* booty, loot.
butte *f* knoll, mound.
buvable *adj* drinkable.
buvard *m* blotting paper.
buvette *f* refreshment-room.
buveur *m* **-euse** *f* drinker.

C

ça *pn* that; it; **~ va?** How goes it?; **~ y est** that's it; **qui ~?** who (do you mean)?; **comment ~?** how (do you mean)?; **~ alors!** you don't say!

cabale *f* cabal, intrigue.

cabane *f* cabin, shed.

cabanon *m* cottage; chalet.

cabaret *m* cabaret; tavern.

cabine *f* cabin, cab; cockpit.

cabinet *m* surgery; office, study.

câble *m* cable.

câbler *vt* to cable.

cabosser *vt* to dent.

cabotage *m* coastal navigation.

cabriolet *m* convertible.

cacahuète *f* peanut.

cacao *m* cocoa.

cache *m* cache; mask; hiding place.

caché *adj* hidden, secluded.

cache-col *m invar* scarf.

cache-nez *m invar* scarf, muffler.

cacher *vt* to hide, conceal; **se ~** *vr* to hide o.s.

cacheter *vt* to seal.

cachette *f* hideout, hiding place.

cachot *m* dungeon, prison cell.

cachottier *m* **-ière** *f* secretive.

cactus *m* cactus.

cadavre *m* corpse.

cadeau *m* present.

cadenas *m* padlock.

cadenasser *vt* to padlock.

cadence *f* rhythm, time, cadence.

cadet *m* **-te** *f* youngest child.

cadrage *m* framing.

cadran *m* dial, face.

cadre *m* frame; context; scope.

cadrer *vt* to centre, fit with.

caduc *adj*, *f* **caduque** null and void; obsolete.

cafard *m* hypocrite; cockroach.

café *m* coffee.

cafétéria *f* cafeteria.

cafetière *f* coffeepot.

cage *f* cage.

cageot *m* crate.

cagoule *f* cowl; balaclava.

cahier *m* notebook.

cahot *m* jerk, jolt.

caillot *m* clot.

caillou *m* stone; pebble.

caisse *f* box; till; fund.

caissier *m* **-ière** *f* cashier.

cajoler *vt* to cajole, coax; to pet.

cajou *m* cashew.

calamité *f* calamity.

calcaire *m* calcareous, chalky.

calcination *f* calcination.

calciner *vt* to calcine; to char.

calcium *m* calcium.

calcul *m* sum, calculation.

calculateur *adj*, *f* **-trice** calculating.

calculatrice, calculette *f* calculator.

calculer *vt* to calculate, reckon; *vi* to budget carefully.

cale *f* (*mar*) wedge, hold.

caleçon *m* shorts, pants.

calembour *m* pun.

calendrier *m* calendar.

calepin *m* notebook.

caler *vi* to stall; to give up; to wedge.

calfeutrer *vt* to make airtight, draughtproof.

calibre *m* calibre, bore.

calibrer *vt* to calibrate.

calice *m* chalice.

câlin *m* cuddle; * *adj* cuddly.

câliner *vt* to cuddle.

calligraphie *f* calligraphy.

callosité *f* callosity.

calmant *m* tranquilliser, sedative; * *adj* tranquillising.

calmar *m* squid.

calme *m* calm, stillness; * *adj* calm, still; **~ment** *adv* calmly, quietly.

calmer *vt* calm, soothe, pacify.

calomnie *f* slander, calumny.

calomnier *vt* to slander; libel.

calomnieux *adj* slanderous, calumnious.

calorie *f* calorie.

calorifique *adj* calorific.

calque *m* tracing; copy.

calquer *vt* to trace; to copy.

calvaire *m* calvary; ordeal.

calvitie *f* baldness.

camarade *mf* companion, friend.

camaraderie *f* camaraderie, friendship.

cambouis *m* dirty grease.

cambré *adj* arched.

cambriolage *m* burglary.

cambrioler *vt* to burgle.

cambrioleur *m* **-euse** *f* burglar.

caméléon *m* chameleon.

camélia *m* camellia.

caméra *f* camera.

camion *m* lorry.

camionneur *m* lorry driver, trucker.

camomille *f* camomile.

camouflage *m* camouflage.

camoufler *vt* to camouflage.

camp *m* camp.

campagnard *m* countryman, **-e** *f* countrywoman; * *adj* country, rustic.

campagne *f* country, countryside.

campement *m* camp, encampment.

camper *vi* to camp.

campeur *m* **-euse** *f* camper.

canal *m* canal, channel.

canalisation *f* canalisation; mains.

canaliser *vt* to channel, funnel.

canapé *m* sofa, settee.

canard *m* duck.

cancer *m* cancer.

cancéreux *adj* cancerous.

candeur *f* ingeniousness.

candidat *m* **-e** *f* candidate.

candidature *f* candidature, candidacy.

candide *adj* guileless, ingenuous; **~ment** *adv* openly, ingenuously.

canevas *m* canvas; framework.

canicule *m* heatwave.

canif *m* penknife.

canine *f* eye tooth.

caniveau *m* gutter.

canne *f* cane, rod.

cannelle *f* cinnamon.

canoè *m* canoe.

canon *m* cannon, gun.

canot *m* boat, dinghy.

cantate *f* cantata.

cantatrice *f* opera singer.

cantine *f* canteen.

cantique *m* canticle, hymn.

canton *m* canton.

cantonner (se) *vr* to take up position in.

caoutchouc *m* rubber.

cap *f* cape; course.

capable *adj* capable, competent.

capacité *f* capacity.

cape *f* cloak.

capillaire *adj* capillary.

capitaine *m* captain.

capital *adj* capital, cardinal, major; * *m* capital, stock.

capitale *f* capital (letter, city).

capitalisme *m* capitalism.

capitaliste *mf* capitalist.

capiteux *adj* heady, strong.

capitonner *vt* to pad.

capitulation *f* capitulation.

capituler *vt* to capitulate.

caporal *m* corporal.

capot *m* bonnet, hood.

capote *f* great-coat, hood.

capoter *vt* to capsize, overturn.

câpre *m* caper.

caprice *m* caprice, whim.

capricieusement *adv* capriciously.

capricieux *adj* capricious.

capricorne *m* capricorn.

capsule *f* capsule.

capter *vt* to catch; to pick up.

capteur *m* captor; pick-up.

captif *m* **-ive** *f* captive; * *adj* captive.

captivant *adj* enthralling, captivating.

captiver *vt* to captivate, enthral.

captivité *f* captivity.

capture *f* capture.

capturer *vt* to capture.

capuche *f* hood.

car *conj* for; because; * *m* bus; van.

carabine *f* carbine, rifle.

caractère *m* character, disposition.

caractérisé *adj* marked, blatant.

caractériser *vt* to characterise.

caractéristique *f* characteristic, feature; * *adj* characteristic.

carafe *f* carafe.

carambolage *m* pile-up (car).

caramel *m* caramel.

caraméliser *vt* to caramelise.

carapace *f* carapace, shell.

carat *m* carat.

caravane *f* caravan.

caravelle *f* caravel.

carbonate *m* carbonate.

carbone *m* carbon.

carbonique *adj* carbonic.

carboniser *vt* to carbonise; to char.

carburant *m* motor-fuel.

carburateur *m* carburettor.

carburation *f* carburation.

carbure *m* carbide.

carcasse *f* carcass.

carcéral *adj* prison.

cardiaque *adj* cardiac.

cardigan *m* cardigan.

cardinal *m* cardinal; * *adj* cardinal.

cardiologie *f* cardiology.

cardiologue *m* cardiologist.

cardio-vasculaire *adj* cardiovascular.

carême *m* fast, fasting.

carence *f* deficiency; insolvency.

caressant *adj* affectionate.

caresse *f* caress.

caresser *vt* to caress, fondle.

cargaison *f* cargo, freight.

cargo *m* cargo-boat.

caricatural *adj* caricatural; grotesque.

caricature *f* caricature.

caricaturer *vt* to caricature.

caricaturiste *m* caricaturist.

carie *f* decay; caries.

carié *adj* decayed.

carillon *m* carillon, chime, peal.

caritatif *adj* charitable.

carnage *m* carnage.

carnassier *m* carnivore, **-ière** *f* gamebag; *adj* carnivorous.

carnaval *m* carnival.

carnet *m* notebook.

carnivore *mf* carnivore; *adj* carnivorous.

carotide *f* carotid.

carotte *f* carrot.

carpe *f* carp.

carpette *f* rug, doormat.

carré *m* square; * *adj* square; straightforward.

carreau *m* tile; pane.

carrefour *m* crossroads.

carrelage *m* tiling.

carrément *adv* bluntly, directly.

carrière *f* career.

carrosse *m* coach.

carrosserie *f* bodywork, coachwork.

carrossier *m* coachbuilder.

carrure *f* build, stature.

cartable *m* satchel.

carte *f* card; map.

cartel *m* cartel.

cartésien *adj* Cartesian.

cartilage *m* cartilage.

cartilagineux *adj* cartilaginous.

cartomancien *m* **-ne** *f* fortune-teller.

carton *m* cardboard.

cartonner *vt* to bind (book).

cartouche *f* cartridge.

cas *m* case; circumstance.

casanier *m* **-ière** *f* homebody.

cascade *f* waterfall; stunt.

cascadeur *m* **-euse** *f* acrobat, stuntman.

case *f* square; box.

caser *vt* (*fam*) to set up (job, marriage).

caserne *f* barracks.

casier *m* compartment; filing cabinet.

casino *m* casino.

casque *m* helmet.

casquette *f* peaked cap.

cassant *adj* brittle.

casse-croûte *m invar* snack.

casser *vt* to break; **se ~** *vr* to break.

casserole *f* saucepan.

casse-tête *m invar* puzzle, conundrum.

cassette *f* cassette; cash-box.

cassis *m* blackcurrant.

cassure *f* break, crack.

caste *f* caste.

castor *m* beaver.

castration *f* castration.

castrer *vt* to castrate.

cataclysme *m* cataclysm.

catacombe *f* catacomb.

catalogue *m* catalogue.

cataloguer *vt* to catalogue.

catalyseur *m* catalyst.

catalytique *adj* catalytic.

cataplasme *m* cataplasm.

catapulte *f* catapult.

cataracte *f* cataract.

catastrophe *f* catastrophe.

catastrophique *adj* catastrophic.

catéchisme *m* catechism.

catégorie *f* category.

catégorique *adj* categorical; **~ment** *adv* categorically.

cathédrale *f* cathedral.

cathode *f* cathode.

cathodique *adj* cathodic.

catholicisme *m* Catholicism.

catholique *adj* Catholic.

cauchemar *m* nightmare.

cause *f* cause, reason.

causer *vt* to cause; to chat; * *vi* to talk, chat.

caustique *adj* caustic.

caution *f* deposit; guarantee.

cautionner *vt* to guarantee.

cavalerie *f* cavalry.

cavalier *m* **-ière** *f* rider.

cave *f* cellar.

caveau *m* tomb; small cellar.

caverne *f* cave, cavern.

caverneux *adj* cavernous.

caviar *m* caviar.

cavité *f* cavity.

ce *adj* **cet** (*before vowel and mute* h), *f* **cette**, *pl* **ces** this, these; **cet homme-là** that man; * *pn*; **c'est le facteur** it's the postman; **~ sont mes lunettes** these are my glasses; **~ que tu veux** what you want; **c'est ~ dont je vous parle** that's what I am speaking to you about.

ceci *pn* this.

cécité *f* blindness.

céder *vi* to give in; * *vt* to give up, transfer.

ceindre *vt* to put round, encircle.

ceinture *f* belt, girdle.

ceinturer *vt* to surround.

ceinturon *m* belt.

cela *pn* that; *emphasis* **qui ~?** who? (do you mean)?; **comment ~?** how? (do you mean?).

célébration *f* celebration.

célèbre *adj* famous.

célébrer *vt* to celebrate.

célébrité *f* fame, celebrity.

célérité f celerity, speed.

céleste adj celestial.

célibat m celibacy.

célibataire mf single person; * adj single, unmarried.

cellulaire adj cellular.

cellule f cell, unit.

cellulite f cellulite.

celluloïd m celluloid.

cellulose f cellulose.

celui pn, f **celle** this one, pl **ceux** these ones.

cendre f ash.

cendrier m ashtray.

censé adj supposed; deemed.

censure f censorship.

censurer vt to censor.

cent adj a hundred; **tu as ~ fois raison** you are absolutely right; **faire les ~ pas** to walk up and down; * m a hundred; **pour ~** per cent.

centaine f about a hundred, a hundred or so.

centenaire m centenarian; * adj a hundred years old.

centésimal adj centesimal.

centième mf hundredth; * adj hundredth.

centigrade m centigrade.

centigramme m centigram.

centime m centime.

centimètre m centimetre.

central adj central.

centraliser vt to centralise.

centre m centre.

centrer vt to centre, focus.

centrifuge adj centrifugal.

centuple adj centuple, hundredfold; * mf centuple.

cependant conj however.

céramique f ceramic.

cerceau m hoop.

cercle m circle, ring.

cercueil m coffin.

céréale f cereal.

cérébral adj cerebral.

cérémonial adj ceremonial.

cérémonie f ceremony.

cérémonieux adj ceremonious.

cerf-volant m kite.

cerise f cherry.

cerisier m cherry tree.

cerne f ring.

cerner vt to circle, encompass.

certain adj certain, sure; **~ement** adv certainly, most probably; **~s** pn some, certain people.

certificat m certificate.

certifier vt to certify; to guarantee.

certitude f certainty, certitude.

cerveau m brain.

cervelle f brains.

cervical adj cervical.

césarienne f Caesarean.

cesser f to cease, stop.

cessez-le-feu m cease-fire.

cet adj, f **cette** see **ce.**

cétacé m cetacean.

ceux see **ce.**

chacun pn each one; **~e d'entre elles** each of them; **~ son tour** each in turn.

chagrin m sorrow, grief.

chahut m row, uproar.

chahuter vi to make a row.

chaîne f chain.

chaînon m link.

chair f flesh.

chaise f chair.

châle m shawl.

châlet m chalet.

chaleur f heat.

chaleureusement adv warmly.

chaleureux adj warm, cordial.

chalumeau m blowlamp.

chalutier m trawler.

chambre f room.

chameau m camel.

champ m field.

champêtre adj rural, country.

champignon m mushroom.

champion m **-ne** f champion.

championnat m championship.

chance f luck.

chancelant adj staggering, tottering.

chanceler vi to stagger, totter.

chancelier m chancellor.

chanceux adj lucky, fortunate.

chandail m sweater.

chandeleur f Candlemas.

chandelier m candlestick.

chandelle f candle.

changeant adj changeable, variable.

changement m change, changing.

changer vi to change; * vt to change.

chanson f song.

chant m song; singing.

chantage m blackmail.

chanter vt vi to sing.

chanteur m **-euse** f singer.

chantier m building site.

chantonner vt vi to hum.

chanvre m hemp.

chaos m chaos.

chaotique adj chaotic.

chapeau m hat.

chapelet m rosary; string.

chapelle f chapel.

chapiteau m capital (column).

chapitre m chapter.

chaque adj each.

char m (mil) tank; chariot.

charabia m gibberish.

charbon m coal.

charcuterie f pork meat trade.

charcutier m **-ière** f pork butcher.

chardon m thistle.

charge f load; responsibility.

chargé adj loaded.

chargement m loading; freight.

charger vt to load; **se ~ de** to take responsibility for, attend to.

chariot m waggon; freight car.

charisme m charisma.

charitable adj charitable, kind; **~ment** adv charitably.

charité f charity.

charlatan m charlatan.

charmant adj charming, delightful.

charme m charm.

charmer vt to charm, beguile.

charmeur m **-euse** f charmer; * adj winning, enchanting.

charnel adj carnal.

charnière f hinge, pivot.

charnu adj fleshy.

charogne f carrion.

charpente f structure, framework.

charpentier m carpenter.

charrette f cart.

charrier vt to cart, carry.

charrue f plough.

chasse f hunting; chase.

chasse-neige m invar snowplough.

chasser vt to hunt, chase.

chasseur m **-euse** f hunter.

châssis m chassis.

chaste adj chaste; **~ment** adv chastely.

chasteté f chastity.

chat m, **chatte** f cat.

châtaigne f chestnut.

châtain adj chestnut brown.

château m castle.

châtiment m chastisement, punishment.

chaton m kitten.

chatouiller vt to tickle.

chatoyant adj shimmering.

châtrer vt to castrate.

chaud adj warm, hot; **~ement** adv warmly, hotly.

chaudière f boiler.

chaudron m cauldron.

chauffage m heating.

chauffard m road-hog.

chauffe-eau m invar water-heater.

chauffer vi to heat; * vt to heat up.

chauffeur m driver.

chaumière f cottage.

chaussée f road, street.

chausse-pied m shoehorn.

chaussette *f* sock.
chausson *m* slipper.
chaussure *f* shoe.
chauve *adj* bald.
chauve-souris *f* bat.
chauvin *adj, f* **chauvine** chauvinistic.
chauvinisme *m* chauvinism.
chaux *f* lime.
chavirer *vi* to capsize, overturn.
chef *m* head, boss; chef.
chef-d'œuvre *m* masterpiece.
chemin *m* way, road; ~ **de fer** railway.
cheminée *f* chimney.
cheminement *m* progress; course.
chemise *f* shirt.
chemisier *m* shirtmaker.
chêne *m* oak.
chenil *m* kennel.
chenille *f* caterpillar.
chèque *m* cheque.
chéquier *m* chequebook.
cher *adj, f* **chère** dear; expensive.
chercher *vt* to look for.
chercheur *m* **-euse** *f* researcher; seeker.
chéri *m* **-ie** *f* darling, dearest; * *adj* beloved, cherished.
chétif *adj* puny, paltry.
cheval *m* horse.
chevalet *m* easel.
chevalier *m* knight.
chevelu *adj* long-haired.
chevelure *f* hair, head of hair.
chevet *m* chevet; bedside.
cheveu *m* hair.
cheville *f* ankle.
chèvre *f* goat.
chèvrefeuille *m* honeysuckle.
chevreuil *m* roe deer.
chez *prép* at home: **je rentre ~ moi** I'm going home; **~ ta tante** at your aunt's.
chic *m* style, stylishness; **avoir le ~ pour** to have the knack for.
chicorée *f* chicory.
chien *m*, **chienne** *f* dog.
chiffon *m* rag, cloth.
chiffonné *adj* crumpled, rumpled.
chiffre *m* figure.
chignon *m* chignon, bun.
chimère *f* chimera.
chimérique *adj* chimerical, fanciful.
chimie *f* chemistry.
chimique *adj* chemical; ~**ment** *adv* chemically.
chimiste *mf* chemist.
chimpanzé *m* chimpanzee.
chiot *m* puppy.
chipoteur *m* **-euse** *f* haggler.
chirurgical *adj* surgical.

chirurgie *f* surgery.
chirurgien *m* surgeon.
chlore *m* chlorine.
chloroforme *m* chloroform.
chlorophyle *f* chlorophyll.
chlorure *m* chloride.
choc *m* shock, crash.
chocolat *m* chocolate.
chœur *m* choir, chorus.
choir *vi* to fall.
choisir *vt* to choose.
choix *m* choice.
choléra *m* cholera.
chômage *m* unemployment.
chômeur *m* **-euse** *f* unemployed person.
choquant *adj* shocking, appalling.
choquer *vt* to shock.
chorale *f* choral.
chorégraphe *mf* choreographer.
choréraphie *f* choreography.
choriste *mf* chorister.
chose *f* thing, matter, object.
chou *m* cabbage.
chouette *f* owl.
chou-fleur *m* cauliflower.
choyer *vt* to cherish.
chrétien *m* **-ne** *f* Christian, *adj* christian.
christianisme *m* Christianity.
chrome *m* chromium.
chromosome *m* chromosome.
chronique *adj* chronic; * *f* chronicle, column, page.
chronologie *f* chronology.
chronologique *adj* chronological; ~**ment** *adv* chronologically.
chronomètre *m* chronometer.
chronométrer *vt* to time.
chrysanthème *m* chrysanthemum.
chuchotement *m* whisper, rustling.
chuchoter *vi* to whisper.
chuintement *m* hissing.
chuinter *vi* to hiss.
chute *f* fall, drop.
chuter *vi* to fall.
ci *adv*: **ces fleurs-ci** these flowers; **ci-joint** enclosed; **ci-dessous** below; **ci-contre** opposite; in the margin; annexed.
cible *f* target.
cibler *vt* to target.
cicatrice *f* scar.
cicatrisation *f* cicatrisation, healing.
cicatriser *vt* to heal; **se ~** *vr* to heal, form a scar.
cidre *m* cider.
ciel *m*, *pl* **cieux, ciels** sky.
cierge *m* candle.
cigale *f* cicada.
cigare *m* cigar.

cigarette *f* cigarette.
cil *m* eyelash.
ciller *vi* to blink.
cime *f* summit.
ciment *m* cement.
cimenter *vt* to cement.
cimetière *m* cemetery.
cinéaste *mf* film-maker.
cinéma *m* cinema.
cinémathèque *f* film library.
cinématographique *adj* film, cinema.
cinéphile *mf* film enthusiast.
cinétique *adj* kinetic.
cinglant *adj* bitter, lashing, cutting.
cingler *vt* to lash, sting.
cinq *m* five.
cinquantaine *f* about fifty.
cinquante *m* fifty.
cinquantenaire *m* fiftieth anniversary.
cinquantième *mf* fiftieth, *adj* fiftieth.
cinquième *mf* fifth, *adj* fifth; * ~**ment** *adv* in fifth place.
cintre *m* arch.
cirage *m* polish.
circonférence *f* circumference.
circonscription *f* division, constituency.
circonspect *adj* circumspect.
circonstance *f* circumstance.
circuit *m* circuit, tour.
circulaire *adj* circular; ~**ment** *adv* circularly.
circulation *f* circulation; traffic.
circuler *vi* to circulate, move.
cire *f* wax.
cirer *vt* to polish.
cirque *m* circus.
ciseau *m* chisel; ~**x** *pl* scissors.
citadelle *f* citadel.
citadin *m* **-e** *f* city dweller; * *adj* town, urban.
citation *f* citation, summons.
cité *f* city.
citer *vt* to quote, cite.
citerne *f* water tank.
citoyen *m* **-ne** *f* citizen.
citron *m* lemon.
citrouille *f* pumpkin.
civière *f* stretcher.
civil *adj* civil; ~**ement** *adv* civilly.
civilisation *f* civilisation.
civilisé *adj* civilised.
civiliser *vt* to civilise.
civique *adj* civic.
clair *adj* clear, bright; ~**ement** *adv* clearly.
clairière *f* clearing, glade.
clairsemé *adj* scattered.
clairvoyance *f* perspicacity; clairvoyance.

clairvoyant *adj* perceptive; clairvoyant.
clameur *f* clamour.
clan *m* clan.
clandestin *adj* clandestine; ~ement clandestinely.
clandestinité *f* secrecy.
clapoter *vi* to lap (water).
clapotis *m* lapping.
claque *f* slap, smack.
claquement *m* clapping, slamming.
claquer *vi* to bang, slam.
clarifier *vt* to clarify; **se ~** *vr* to become clear.
clarinette *f* clarinet.
clarté *f* light, brightness.
classe *f* class, standing.
classement *m* filing; grading.
classer *vt* to file, classify.
classeur *m* filing cabinet.
classification *f* classification.
classique *adj* classical, standard; ~ment *adv* classically.
clause *f* clause.
claustrer *vt* to confine.
claustrophobie *f* claustrophobia.
clavecin *m* harpsichord.
clavicule *f* collarbone.
clavier *m* keyboard.
clé, clef *f* key.
clémence *f* clemency, mildness.
clergé *m* clergy.
cliché *m* cliché; negative.
client *m* **-e** *f* client.
clientèle *f* clientele; customers.
cligner *vi* to blink.
clignotant *adj* blinking, flickering; * *m* indicator.
clignotement *m* blinking, flickering.
clignoter *vi* to blink, flicker.
climat *m* climate.
climatique *adj* climatic.
climatisation *f* air conditioning.
climatiser *vt* to air condition.
clin d'œil *m* wink.
clinique *f* clinic.
cliqueter *vi* to jingle, clink.
clitoris *m* clitoris.
clochard *m* **-e** *f* tramp.
cloche *f* bell.
clocher *m* steeple, bell tower.
clochette *f* hand-bell.
cloison *f* partition.
cloîtrer (se) *vr* to enter the monastic life.
clore *vt* to close, conclude.
clos *adj* closed, enclosed.
clôture *f* fence, hedge.
clou *m* nail.
clouer *vt* to nail.
club *m* club.

coagulation *f* coagulation.
coaguler *vi* to coagulate.
coaliser *vt vi* to form a coalition.
coalition *f* coalition.
cobalt *m* cobalt.
cobaye *m* guinea-pig.
cobra *m* cobra.
cocaïne *f* cocaine.
coccinelle *f* ladybird.
coccyx *m* coccyx.
cocher *vt* to notch, tick off.
cochon *m* **-ne** *f* pig.
code *m* code.
coder *vt* to code.
codifier *vt* to codify.
coefficient *m* coefficient.
coéquipier *m* **-ière** *f* team mate.
cœur *m* heart.
coexister *vi* to coexist.
coffre *m* chest; **~-fort** safe.
coffret *m* casket.
cogner *vi* to hammer, bang.
cohabitation *f* cohabitation.
cohabiter *vi* to cohabit.
cohérence *f* coherence.
cohérent *adj* coherent.
cohésion *f* cohesion.
cohue *f* crowd.
coiffer *vt* to arrange so's hair; **se ~** *vr* to do one's hair.
coiffeur *m* **-euse** *f* hairdresser.
coiffure *f* hairstyle.
coin *m* corner.
coincer *vt* to wedge, jam.
coïncidence *f* coincidence.
coït *m* coitus.
col *m* collar; neck.
colère *f* anger.
colérique *adj* quick-tempered, irascible.
colibri *m* hummingbird.
colique *f* diarrhoea.
colis *m* parcel.
collaborateur *m* **-trice** *f* collaborator, colleague.
collaboration *f* collaboration.
collaborer *vi* to collaborate.
collant *adj* clinging, sticky; * *m* leotard.
collecte *f* collection.
collectif *adj* collective.
collection *f* collection.
collectionner *vt* to collect.
collectionneur *m* **-euse** *f* collector.
collectivement *adv* collectively.
collectivité *f* community; collective ownership.
collège *m* secondary school.
collègue *mf* colleague.
coller *vt* to stick, glue; * *vi* to stick, be sticky.
collier *m* necklace.
colline *f* hill.

collision *f* collision.
colloque *m* colloquium.
colocataire *mf* co-tenant.
colombe *f* dove.
colon *m* colonist.
colonel *m* colonel.
colonie *f* colony.
colonisation *f* colonisation.
coloniser *vt* to colonise.
colonne *f* column.
colorant *m* colouring.
coloration *f* colouring, staining.
coloré *adj* coloured.
colorier *vt* to colour in.
coloris *m* colouring, shade.
colossal *adj* colossal.
colporter *vt* to peddle.
colza *m* rape seed.
coma *m* coma.
comateux *adj* comatose.
combat *m* combat, fight.
combatif *adj* combative.
combativité *f* combativeness.
combattant *adj* fighting, combatant.
combattre *vt* to fight, combat; * *vi* to fight.
combien *adv* how much, how many; ~ **de temps?** how much time?; ~ **sont-ils?** how many are they?
combinaison *f* combination.
combiner *vt* to combine.
comble *m* height, peak.
combler *vt* to fill; to fulfil.
combustible *m* fuel.
combustion *f* combustion.
comédie *f* comedy.
comédien *m* **-ne** *f* actor.
comestible *adj* edible.
comète *f* comet.
comique *adj* comic; ~ment *adv* comically.
comité *m* committee.
commandant *m* commander.
commande *f* command, order.
commandement *m* command, commandment.
commander *vt vi* to order, command.
commanditer *vt* to finance, sponsor.
commando *m* commando.
comme *conj* as, like; ~ **ci ~ ça** so-so; ~ **il faut** properly; *adv* how.
commémoration *f* commemoration.
commémorer *vt* to commemorate.
commencement *m* beginning, start.
commencer *vt vi* to begin, start.
comment *adv* how; ~ **dire?** how

shall we say?; ~ **cela?** what do you mean?

commentaire *m* comment; commentary.

commentateur *m* **-trice** *f* commentator.

commenter *vt* to comment.

commérage *m* piece of gossip.

commerçant *m* **-e** *f* merchant, trader.

commerce *m* business, commerce.

commercial *adj* commercial; **~ement** *adv* commercially.

commercialiser *vt* to market.

commère *f* gossip.

commettre *vt* to commit.

commissaire *m* representative; commissioner.

commissariat *m* police station; commissionership; commissariat.

commission *f* commission, committee.

commissionnaire *m* messenger; agent.

commode *adj* convenient, comfortable.

commodité *f* convenience.

commun *adj* common, joint; **~ément** *adv* commonly.

communal *adj* council; common, communal.

communautaire *adj* community.

communauté *f* community; joint estate.

commune *f* town, district.

communication *f* communication.

communier *vi* to receive communion.

communion *f* communion.

communiqué *m* communiqué.

communiquer *vt* to communicate, transmit; * *vi* to communicate.

communisme *m* communism.

communiste *mf* communist.

compact *adj* compact, dense.

compagne *f* companion.

compagnie *f* company.

compagnon *m* companion.

comparable *adj* comparable.

comparaison *f* comparison.

comparaître *vi* to appear.

comparativement *adv* comparatively.

comparer *vt* to compare.

compartiment *m* compartment.

compartimenter *vt* to compart, partition.

compas *m* compass.

compassion *f* compassion.

compatibilité *f* compatibility.

compatible *adj* compatible.

compatir *vi* to sympathise.

compatissant *adj* compassionate.

compatriote *mf* compatriot.

compensation *f* compensation.

compenser *vt* to compensate; offset; **se ~** *vr* to balance each other, make up for.

compétence *f* competence.

compétent *adj* competent, capable.

compétitif *adj* competitive.

compétition *f* competition.

compétitivité *f* competitiveness.

complaisance *f* kindness; complacency.

complaisant *adj* kind; complacent.

complément *m* complement; extension.

complémentaire *adj* complementary, supplementary.

complet *adj* complete, full.

complètement *adv* completely, fully.

compléter *vt* to complete; **se ~** *vr* to complement one another.

complexe *adj* complex, complicated.

complexé *adj* mixed up.

complication *f* complication.

complice *mf* accomplice.

complicité *f* complicity, collusion.

compliment *m* compliment.

complimenter *vt* to compliment, congratulate.

compliqué *adj* complicated, intricate.

compliquer *vt* to complicate.

complot *m* plot.

comportement *m* behaviour; performance.

comporter *vt* to consist of, comprise; **se ~** *vr* to behave.

composant *m* component, constituent.

composante *f* component.

composer *vt* to compose, make up; **se ~** *vr*: **se ~ de** to be made up of.

compositeur *m* **-trice** *f* composer; typesetter.

composition *f* composition, formation.

compréhensible *adj* comprehensible.

compréhensif *adj* comprehensive, understanding.

compréhension *f* comprehension, understanding.

comprendre *vt* to understand; consist of.

compresse *f* compress.

compresseur *m* compressor.

compression *f* compression; reduction.

comprimé *adj* compressed; restrained; * *m* tablet.

comprimer *vt* to compress; to restrain.

compromettant *adj* compromising.

compromettre *vt* to compromise.

compromis *m* compromise.

comptabilité *f* accountancy.

comptable *adj* accounting; * *mf* accountant.

compte *m* account.

compter *vt vi* to count.

compteur *m* meter.

comptoir *m* counter, bar.

comte *m* count, **comtesse** *f* countess.

concave *adj* concave.

concéder *vt* to grant, concede.

concentration *f* concentration.

concentré *adj* concentrated; reserved.

concentrer *vt* to concentrate; **se ~** *vr* to concentrate.

concept *m* concept.

conception *f* conception, design.

concerner *vt* to concern, regard.

concert *m* concert.

concertation *f* dialogue, consultation.

concession *f* concession; privilege.

concessionnaire *mf* concessionaire, grantee.

concevoir *vt* to imagine, conceive.

concierge *mf* caretaker, concierge.

conciliant *adj* conciliatory.

conciliation *f* conciliation; reconciliation.

concilier *vt* to reconcile; to attract.

concis *adj* concise.

concision *f* conciseness, brevity.

concluant *adj* conclusive, decisive.

conclure *vt* to conclude; to decide; **se ~** *vr* to conclude, come to an end.

conclusion *f* conclusion.

concombre *m* cucumber.

concordance *f* agreement, accord.

concorder *vi* to agree, coincide.

concours *m* competition; conjuncture.

concret *adj* concrete, solid.

concrètement *adv* concretely.

concrétiser *vt* to put in concrete form.

concubin *m* **-e** *f* concubine; cohabitant.

concubinage *m* concubinage; cohabitation.

concurrence *f* competition.

concurrent m **-e** f concurrent; competitor.

condamnation f condemnation; sentencing.

condamné m **-e** f convict; sentenced person; * adj sentenced.

condamner vt to condemn; to sentence.

condensation f condensation.

condensé adj condensed, evaporated.

condenser vt to condense, compress.

condescendant adj condescending.

condiment m condiment.

condition f condition, term.

conditionné adj conditioned; packaged.

conditionnement m conditioning; packaging.

conditionner vt to condition; to package.

condoléances fpl condolences.

conducteur m **-trice** f driver; operator.

conduire vt vi to lead; to drive.

conduit m conduit, pipe.

conduite f conduct; driving; behaviour.

cône m cone.

confédération f confederation.

conférence f conference.

conférencier m **-ière** f speaker; lecturer.

confesser vt to confess; **se ~** vr to go to confession.

confession f confession.

confiance f confidence, trust.

confiant adj confident; confiding.

confidence f confidence; disclosure.

confident m **-e** f confidant.

confidentiel adj confidential; ~**lement** adv confidentially.

confier vt to confide, entrust; **se ~** vr to confide in.

confiner vt to confine; **se ~** to be confined; vr: **se ~ à** to confine o.s. to.

confirmation f confirmation.

confirmer vt to confirm; **se ~** vr to be confirmed.

confiserie f confectionery.

confisquer vt to confiscate, impound.

confiture f jam.

conflictuel adj conflicting.

conflit m conflict, contention.

confondre vt to confuse, mingle.

conforme adj consistent; true.

conformément adv in accordance with.

conformer vt to model; **se ~** vr to conform.

conformiste mf conformist.

conformité f conformity; likeness.

confort m comfort.

confortable adj comfortable, cosy; ~**ment** adv comfortably.

confrère m colleague.

confrontation f confrontation; comparison.

confronter vt to confront.

confus adj confused, indistinct; ~**ément** adv confusedly, vaguely.

confusion f confusion, disorder.

congé m leave; holiday.

congédier vt to dismiss.

congélateur m freezer.

congeler vt to freeze.

congestion f congestion; stroke.

congratulation f congratulation.

congratuler vt to congratulate.

congrégation f congregation.

congrès m congress, conference.

conifère m conifer.

conjoint m **-e** f spouse; * adj joint; linked; ~**ement** adv jointly.

conjonctivite f conjunctivitis.

conjoncture f conjuncture; situation.

conjugaison f conjugation.

conjugal adj conjugal.

conjuguer vt to conjugate; to combine.

conjuration f conspiracy, plot.

conjurer vt to conspire; to implore; to ward off.

connaissance f knowledge; consciousness.

connaisseur m **-euse** f connoisseur; expert.

connaître vt to know, be acquainted with.

connecter vt to connect.

connecteur m connective.

connexion f connection, link.

connivence f connivance.

connotation f connotation.

connu adj known; famous.

conquérant m **-e** f conqueror; * adj conquering.

conquérir vt to conquer.

conquête f conquest.

conquis adj conquered, vanquished.

consacrer vt to devote, dedicate; **se ~** vr to dedicate o.s. to.

consciemment adv consciously, knowingly.

conscience f consciousness; conscience.

consciencieusement adv conscientiously.

consciencieux adv conscientious.

conscient adj conscious, aware.

consécration f consecration.

consécutif adj consecutive.

consécutivement adv consecutively.

conseil m advice, counsel.

conseiller m **-ère** f counsellor, adviser; * vt to advise, counsel.

consentant adj consenting, willing.

consentement m consent.

consentir vi to consent, acquiesce.

conséquence f consequence, result.

conséquent adj consequent; substantial.

conservateur m **-trice** f conservative; curator.

conservation f conservation.

conservatoire m conservatory; academy.

conserve f canned food.

conserver vt to keep, preserve; **se ~** vr to keep.

considérable adj considerable; notable; ~**ment** adv considerably.

considération f consideration, respect.

considérer vt to consider, regard.

consigne f orders, instructions.

consistance f consistency; strength.

consister vi: **~ en** to consist of; **cela consiste à** that consists in doing.

consolation f consolation, solace.

console f console.

consoler vt to console, comfort.

consolidation f consolidation, reinforcement.

consolider vt to consolidate, reinforce.

consommateur m **-trice** f consumer.

consommation f consumption; accomplishment.

consommé adj consummate, accomplished; * m consommé.

consommer vt to consume, use.

consonne f consonant.

conspirateur m **-trice** f conspirator.

conspiration f conspiracy, plot.

conspirer vi to conspire, plot.

constamment adv constantly, continually.

constant adj constant, continuous.

constante f constancy.

constat m report; acknowledgement.

constatation f authentication, verification.

constater vt to record; to verify.

constellation *f* constellation, galaxy.

consternation *f* consternation, dismay.

consterner *vt* to dismay.

constipation *f* constipation.

constituer *vt* to constitute, form.

constitution *f* constitution, formation.

constitutionnel *adj* constitutional; ~**lement** *adv* constitutionally.

constructeur *m* **-trice** *f* builder, maker.

constructif *adj* constructive.

construction *f* building, construction.

construire *vt* to construct, build.

consul *m* consul.

consulaire *adj* consular.

consulat *m* consulate.

consultant *m* **-e** *f* consultant; * *adj* consulting.

consultation *f* consultation, advice.

consulter *vt* to consult, take advice from.

consumer *vt* to consume, spend; **se** ~ *vr* to be burning, waste away.

contact *m* contact, touch.

contacter *vt* to contact, approach.

contagieux *adj* contagious, infectious.

contamination *f* contamination, pollution.

contaminer *vt* to contaminate, pollute.

conte *m* story, tale.

contemplation *f* contemplation, meditation.

contempler *vt* to contemplate, meditate.

contemporain *adj* contemporary.

contenance *f* capacity, volume.

contenir *vt* to contain.

contentement *m* contentment, satisfaction.

contenter *vt* to please, satisfy; **se** ~ *vr*: **se** ~ **de** to content o.s. with.

contenu *m* contents, enclosure.

contestation *f* dispute, controversy.

contester *vt* to contest, dispute.

contexte *m* context.

contigu *adj*, *f* **contiguè** contiguous, adjacent.

continent *m* continent.

continental *adj* continental.

contingent *m* quota; (*mil*) draft.

continu *adj* continuous, incessant.

continuation *f* continuation.

continuel *adj* continual, continuous; ~**lement** *adv* continuously, continually.

continuer *vt* to continue, proceed with; * *vi* to continue, go on.

contour *m* contour, outline.

contourner *vt* to bypass, skirt.

contraceptif *adj* contraceptive.

contraception *f* contraception.

contracter *vt* to contract, acquire; **se** ~ *vr* to contract, shrink.

contraction *f* contraction.

contradiction *f* contradiction, discrepancy.

contradictoire *adj* contradictory, conflicting.

contraindre *vt* to constrain, compel.

contrainte *f* constraint, compulsion.

contraire *m* opposite, contrary; * *adj* opposite, contrary; ~**ment** *adv* contrarily.

contrariant *adj* contrary; perverse.

contrarier *vt* to annoy; to oppose.

contrariété *f* annoyance, disappointment.

contraste *m* contrast.

contrat *m* contract, agreement.

contre *prép* against; **parier à 10 ~ 1** to bet at 10 to 1; ~ **toute attente** contrary to all expectations; **par** ~ on the other hand.

contre-attaque *f* counter-attack.

contre-attaquer *vi* to counter-attack.

contrebalancer *vt* to counterbalance.

contrebande *f* contraband, smuggling.

contrebandier *m* **-ière** *f* smuggler.

contrebasse *f* double bass.

contrecarrer *vt* to thwart, oppose.

contrecœur: **à** ~ reluctantly.

contrecoup *m* rebound, repercussion.

contredire *vt* to contradict, refute.

contrefaçon *f* counterfeit, forgery.

contrefaire *vt* to counterfeit, forge.

contre-indication *f* contraindication.

contremaître *m* foreman.

contre-offensive *f* counter-offensive.

contrepartie *f* compensation; consideration.

contre-plaqué *m* plywood.

contrepoison *m* antidote, counterpoison.

contresens *m* nonsense; misunderstanding; mistranslation.

contretemps *m* mishap; contretemps; (*mus*) syncopation.

contribuable *mf* taxpayer.

contribuer *vt vi* to contribute.

contribution *f* contribution; tax.

contrôle *m* control, check.

contrôler *vt* to control, check.

contrôleur *m* **-euse** *f* inspector; auditor.

controverse *f* controversy.

controversé *adj* disputed.

contusion *f* bruise, contusion.

convaincant *adj* convincing.

convaincre *vt* to convince, persuade.

convaincu *adj* convinced, persuaded.

convalescence *f* convalescence.

convenable *adj* fitting, suitable; ~**ment** *adv* suitably, fitly.

convenir *vi* to agree, accord.

convention *f* convention, agreement.

conventionnel *adj* conventional; contractual; ~**lement** *adv* conventionally.

convenu *adj* agreed; stipulated.

convergent *adj* convergent.

converger *vi* to converge.

conversation *f* conversation, talk.

conversion *f* conversion.

convertir *vt* to convert; **se** ~ *vr* to be converted.

convexe *adj* convex.

conviction *f* conviction.

convier *vt* to invite; to urge.

convivial *adj* convivial; user-friendly.

convocation *f* convocation, summoning.

convoi *m* convoy; train.

convoiter *vt* to covet.

convoquer *vt* to convoke, convene.

convulsion *f* convulsion.

coopératif *adj* cooperative.

coopération *f* cooperation.

coopérative *f* cooperative.

coopérer *vi* to cooperate, collaborate.

coordinateur *m* **-trice** *f* coordinator.

coordination *f* coordination; committee.

coordonnées *fpl* coordinates.

coordonner *vt* to coordinate.

copain *m* friend, pal.

copeau *m* shaving, chip.

copie *f* copy, reproduction.

copier *vt* to copy, reproduce.

copieusement *adv* copiously, abundantly.

copieux *adj* copious, abundant.

copilote *m* co-pilot.

copine *f* friend, mate.

coproduction *f* coproduction.

copropriété *f* co-ownership, joint ownership.

coq *m* cock, rooster.

coque *f* (*mar*) hull; shell.

coquelicot *m* poppy.

coquet *adj* stylish, smart; **~tement** *adv* stylishly, smartly.

coquetterie *f* smartness, stylishness.

coquillage *m* shellfish.

coquille *f* shell, scallop.

coquin *m* **-e** *f* naughty, mischievous.

cor *m* (*mus*) horn; corn.

corail *m* coral.

coran *m* Koran.

corbeau *m* crow.

corbeille *f* basket.

corbillard *m* hearse.

cordage *m* rope; rigging.

corde *f* rope; string.

cordée *f* roped mountaineering party.

cordial *adj* cordial, warm; **~ement** *adv* cordially, warmly.

cordialité *f* cordiality, warmth.

cordon *m* cord, string; cordon.

cordonnerie *f* shoemending.

cordonnier *m* **-ière** *f* shoemender, cobbler.

coriace *adj* tough; tight.

coriandre *m* coriander.

corne *f* horn, antler.

cornée *f* cornea.

corneille *f* crow.

cornemuse *f* bagpipes.

cornet *m* cone, cornet.

corniche *f* cornice; ledge.

cornichon *m* gherkin; greenhorn.

corporatif *adj* corporative, corporate.

corporation *f* corporation, guild.

corporatisme *m* corporatism.

corporel *adj* corporal, bodily.

corps *m* body, corpse.

corpulence *f* corpulence.

corpulent *adj* corpulent.

corpus *m* corpus.

correct *adj* correct, accurate; **~ement** *adv* correctly, accurately.

correcteur *m* **-trice** *f* examiner; proofreader.

correction *f* correction; proofreading.

corrélation *f* correlation.

correspondance *f* correspondence, communication.

correspondant *m* **-e** *f* correspondent; * *adj* corresponding.

correspondre *vi* to correspond, communicate.

corridor *m* corridor, passage.

corrigé *m* corrected version, fair copy.

corriger *vt* to correct.

corroborer *vt* to corroborate.

corroder *vt* to corrode.

corrompre *vt* to corrupt, debase.

corrompu *adj* corrupt.

corrosif *adj* corrosive.

corrosion *f* corrosion.

corruption *f* corruption, debasement.

corsage *m* blouse, bodice.

corsaire *m* corsair.

corsé *adj* rich, full-bodied.

corset *m* corset.

cortège *m* cortège, procession.

cortex *m* cortex.

cortical *adj* cortical.

cortisone *f* cortisone.

corvée *f* fatigue duty; forced labour.

cosmétique *m* cosmetic.

cosmique *adj* cosmic.

cosmonaute *mf* cosmonaut.

cosmopolite *adj* cosmopolitan.

cosmos *m* cosmos.

costume *m* costume, dress.

cotation *f* quotation, valuation.

côte *f* coast; rib; slope.

côté *m* side; point.

coteau *m* hill.

côtelé *adj* ribbed.

côtelette *f* cutlet.

coter *vt* to quote; to classify.

côtier *adj* coastal, inshore.

coton *m* cotton.

cotonneux *adj* fleecy, fluffy.

côtoyer *vt* to mix with, skirt.

cou *m* neck.

couchant *adj* setting.

couche *f* layer, coat.

coucher *vt* to put to bed; **se ~** *vr* to go to bed.

coucou *m* cuckoo.

coude *m* elbow.

coudé *adj* angled, bent.

coudoyer *vt* mix with, rub shoulders with.

coudre *vt vi* to sew.

couette *f* duvet.

coulant *adj* flowing; smooth.

couler *vi* to flow, run.

couleur *f* colour, shade.

couleuvre *f* grass snake.

coulis *m* sauce, purée.

coulissant *adj* sliding.

coulisse *f* groove; (*thea*) wings.

coulisser *vi* to slide, run.

couloir *m* corridor, passage.

coup *m* blow; shot; **~ sur ~** one after another, incessantly; **tout à ~** suddenly; **après ~** afterwards, after the event; **~ de feu** shot;

jeter un ~ d'œil to glance; **~ de coude** nudge; **~ de téléphone** phone call; **~ de soleil** sunstroke.

coupable *mf* culprit; * *adj* guilty.

coupant *adj* cutting, sharp.

coupe *f* cut; cutting.

coupe-papier *m invar* paper knife.

couper *vt* to cut, slice.

couple *m* couple, pair.

couplet *m* couplet, verse.

coupole *f* dome.

coupon *m* coupon, voucher, ticket.

coupure *f* cut; break.

cour *f* court, yard, courtyard.

courage *m* courage, daring.

courageusement *adv* courageously.

courageux *adj* courageous.

couramment *adv* fluently; commonly.

courant *adj* current; present; * *m* stream, current.

courbature *f* stiffness; ache.

courbaturé *adj* aching.

courbe *f* curve; contour.

courbé *adj* curved, stooped.

courber *vt* to curve, bend.

coureur *m* **-euse** *f* runner.

courgette *f* courgette.

courir *vi* to run, race.

couronne *f* crown, wreath.

couronnement *m* coronation.

couronner *vt* to crown.

courrier *m* mail, post.

courroie *f* strap, belt.

cours *m* course; flow; path.

course *f* running; race; flight; journey.

coursier *m* **-ière** *f* courier, messenger.

court *adj* short, brief.

court-bouillon *m* court-bouillon, wine sauce.

court-circuit *m* short-circuit.

court-circuiter *vt* to short-circuit.

courtier *m* **-ière** *f* broker, agent.

courtiser *vt* to court.

courtois *adj* courteous; **~ement** *adv* courteously.

courtoisie *f* courtesy, courteousness.

cousin *m* **-e** *f* cousin.

coussin *m* cushion, pillow.

coussinet *m* pad; bearing.

coût *m* cost, charge.

couteau *m* knife.

coûter *vt vi* to cost.

coûteusement *adv* expensively.

coûteux *adj* costly, expensive.

coutume *f* custom, habit.

coutumier *adj* customary, usual.

couture *f* sewing, needlework.

couturier *m* couturier, fashion designer.

couturière *f* dressmaker.

couvent *m* convent.

couver *vt* to hatch, incubate; * *vi* to smoulder, lurk.

couvercle *m* lid, cap.

couvert *m* shelter; cover; pretext; * *adj* covered; secret; obscure.

couverture *f* blanket; cover; roofing.

couvre-feu *m* curfew.

couvreur *m* roofer.

couvrir *vt* to cover; **se ~** *vr* to cover up; to become overcast.

crabe *m* crab.

crachement *m* spitting.

cracher *vt* to spit.

crachin *m* drizzle.

craie *f* chalk.

craindre *vt* to fear.

crainte *f* fear, dread.

craintif *adj* timid, cowardly.

crampe *f* cramp.

crampon *m* stud, spike, crampon.

cramponner *vt* to cramp, clamp; **se ~** *vr* to cling, hang on.

cran *m* notch, cog.

crâne *m* cranium, skull.

crânien *adj* cranial.

crapaud *m* toad.

crapule *f* villain.

crapuleux *adj* villainous, vicious.

craquellement *m* cracking.

craquement *m* crack, creaking, snap.

craquer *vi* to creak, squeak, crack.

crasseux *adj* grimy, filthy.

cratère *m* crater.

cravate *f* tie.

créancier *m* **-ière** *f* creditor.

créateur *m* **-trice** *f* creator, author.

créatif *adj* creative.

création *f* creation.

créativité *f* creativity.

créature *f* creature.

crèche *f* crèche; crib.

crédibilité *f* credibility.

crédible *adj* credible.

crédit *m* credit, trust.

crédit-bail *m* lease; leasing.

crédule *adj* credulous, gullible.

crédulité *f* credulity, gullibility.

créer *vt* to create, produce.

crémaillère *f* rack, chimney hook.

crème *f* cream.

crémerie *f* dairy.

crémeux *adj* creamy.

crémier *m* dairyman, **-ière** *f* dairywoman.

créneau *m* battlement.

crêpe *f* pancake; * *m* crepe, crape.

crêperie *f* pancake restaurant.

crépitement *m* crackling; rattling.

crépiter *vi* to crackle; to rattle.

crépu *adj* frizzy, woolly.

crépuscule *m* twilight, dusk.

cresson *m* watercress.

crête *f* crest, comb.

crétin *m* **-e** *f* cretin, idiot.

creuser *vi* to dig, burrow; * *vt* to dig, hollow.

creuset *m* crucible.

creux *adj* hollow, empty.

crevaison *f* puncture, flat.

crevé *adj* burst, punctured.

crever *vt* to burst; to gouge; *vi* to burst; to split.

crevette *f* prawn.

cri *m* cry, howl, yell.

criant *adj* crying; striking, glaring.

criard *adj* yelling; scolding.

crible *m* riddle, sieve; **passer au ~** to riddle; to examine closely.

cribler *vt* to sift, riddle.

cric *m* (*auto*) jack.

crier *vi* to cry, shout.

crime *m* crime, offence.

criminel *m* **-le** *f* criminal; * *adj* criminal.

crin *m* horsehair.

crinière *f* mane.

criquet *m* locust.

crise *f* crisis, attack.

crisper *vt* to shrivel; to clench.

cristal *m* crystal, glassware.

cristallin *adj* crystalline.

cristallisation *f* crystallisation.

cristalliser *vt* to crystallise.

critère *m* criterion, standard.

critiquable *adj* censurable, open to criticism.

critique *adj* critical, censorious; * *f* criticism; critique.

critiquer *vt* to criticise, censure.

croc *m* fang; hook.

croche *f* quaver.

crochet *m* hook, clasp.

crochu *adj* hooked, claw-like.

crocodile *m* crocodile.

croire *vt* to believe, think.

croisade *f* crusade.

croisement *m* crossing, junction.

croiser *vt* to cross; to fold; **se ~** *vr* to cross, intersect.

croisière *f* cruise.

croissance *f* growth, increase.

croissant *adj* growing, increasing; * *m* croissant; crescent.

croître *vi* to grow, rise.

croix *f* cross.

croque-monsieur *m* toasted cheese and ham sandwich.

croquer *vt* to crunch.

croquette *f* croquette.

croquis *m* sketch, outline.

crosse *f* (*rel*) crozier; butt, grip.

crotte *f* manure, dung.

croupir *vi* to stagnate, wallow.

croustillant *adj* crusty, crisp.

croustiller *vi* to be crusty, crispy.

croûte *f* crust.

croûton *m* crust, crouton.

croyance *f* belief.

croyant *adj* believing.

cru *adj* raw, uncooked; * *m* vineyard; wine.

cruauté *f* cruelty, inhumanity.

cruche *f* pitcher.

crucial *adj* crucial, decisive.

crucifix *m* crucifix.

crucifixion *f* crucifixion.

crudité *f* crudity, coarseness.

crue *f* flood.

cruel *adj* cruel; **~lement** *adv* cruelly.

crustacé *m* crustacean, shellfish.

crypte *m* crypt.

crypter *vt* to encode, scramble.

cube *m* cube, block.

cubique *adj* cubic.

cubisme *m* cubism.

cueillette *f* picking, gathering.

cueillir *vt* to pick, gather.

cuiller, cuillère *f* spoon, spoonful.

cuir *m* leather, hide.

cuirasse *f* (*zool*) cuirass, breastplate.

cuirassé *adj* armoured; * *m* battleship.

cuire *vi* to cook.

cuisine *f* kitchen; cookery.

cuisiner *vt vi* to cook.

cuisinier *m* **-ière** *f* cook.

cuisinière *f* cooker, stove.

cuisse *f* thigh.

cuisson *f* cooking, baking.

cuit *adj* cooked.

cuivre *m* copper.

cul *m* (*col*) bottom, ass.

culasse *f* cylinder-head; breech.

cul-de-jatte *mf* legless cripple.

cul-de-sac *m* blind alley, cul-de-sac.

culinaire *adj* culinary.

culminer *vi* to culminate, tower.

culot *m* cheek, nerve.

culotte *f* knickers; underpants; shorts.

culpabiliser *vt* to make someone feel guilty; **se ~** *vr* to feel guilty.

culpabilité *f* guilt, culpability.

culte *m* cult, veneration.

cultivable *adj* cultivable.

cultivateur *m* **-trice** *f* farmer.

cultivé *adj* cultured.

cultiver *vt* to cultivate; **se ~** *vr* to improve o.s.

culture *f* culture; cultivation.

culturel *adj* cultural.

culturisme *m* body-building.

cumin *m* cumin.

cumul *m* pluralism; accumulation.

cumuler *vt* to accumulate; to hold concurrently.

cupide *adj* greedy; **~ment** *adv* greedily.

cupidité *f* greed, cupidity.

cure *f* cure; treatment.

curé *m* parish priest, parson.

cure-dents *m* toothpick.

curieusement *adv* curiously.

curieux *m* **-euse** *f* inquisitive person; onlooker; * *adj* curious, inquisitive.

curiosité *f* curiosity, inquisitiveness.

cursus *m* degree course.

cutané *adj* skin, cutaneous.

cuve *f* vat, tank.

cuvette *f* basin, bowl.

cyanure *m* cyanide.

cybernétique *f* cybernetics.

cyclable *adj* cycle, for cycling.

cyclamen *m* cyclamen.

cycle *m* cycle; stage.

cyclique *adj* cyclical.

cyclisme *m* cycling.

cycliste *mf* cyclist; * *adj* cycle.

cyclomoteur *m* moped.

cyclone *m* cyclone.

cyclope *m* Cyclops.

cygne *m* swan.

cylindre *m* cylinder.

cylindrée *f* capacity (engine).

cylindrique *adj* cylindrical.

cymbale *f* cymbal.

cynique *adj* cynical; **~ment** *adv* cynically.

cynisme *m* cynicism.

cytologie *f* cytology.

cytoplasme *m* cytoplasm.

D

dactylographe *mf* typist.
dactylographie *f* typing, typewriting.
dactylographier *vt* to type.
dada *m* (*fam*) hobbyhorse; gee-gee.
dahlia *m* dahlia.
daigner *vt* to deign, condescend.
daim *m* deer.
dalle *f* flagstone, slab.
dalmatien *m* Dalmatian.
daltonien *adj* colour-blind.
dame *f* lady; dame.
damier *m* draughtboard.
damnation *f* damnation.
damné *adj* damned.
damner *vt* to damn.
danger *m* danger, risk.
dangereusement *adv* dangerously.
dangereux *adj* dangerous, risky.
dans *prép* in; into; **il a ~ les trente ans** he's thirty or so.
dansant *adj* dancing.
danse *f* dance; dancing.
danser *vi* to dance.
danseur *m* **-euse** *f* dancer.
dard *m* sting.
datation *f* dating.
date *f* date.
dater *vt* to date.
datif *m* dative.
datte *f* (*bot*) date.
dattier *m* date palm.
dauphin *m* dolphin.
daurade *f* sea bream.
davantage *adv* more.
de *prép* of; from; **une femme ~ quarante ans** a forty-year-old woman; **~ bonne heure** early; **deux ~ plus** two more; * *art* some, any.
dé *m* dice; thimble.
déambuler *vi* to stroll.
débâcle *f* disaster; collapse.
déballage *m* unpacking; display.
déballer *vt* to unpack; to display.
débandade *f* rout, stampede.
débarbouiller *vt* to wash; **se ~** *vr* to wash o.s.
débarcadère *m* landing; wharf.
débardeur *m* docker, stevedore.
débarquement *m* landing, disembarkment.
débarquer *vt* to land, unship; * *vi* to disembark, land.
débarrasser *vt* to clear, rid; **se ~** *vr*: **se ~ de** to rid o.s. of.
débat *m* debate; dispute, contest.

débattre *vi* to debate, discuss.
débauche *f* debauchery, dissoluteness.
débaucher *vt* to debauch, corrupt.
débile *adj* weak, feeble.
débilitant *adj* debilitating, weakening.
débit *m* debit; turnover; flow.
débiter *vt* to debit; to produce.
débiteur *m* **-trice** *f* debtor.
déblayer *vt* to clear away, remove.
déblocage *m* unblocking; freeing, releasing.
débloquer *vt* to release, unlock.
déboisement *m* deforestation.
déboiser *vt* to deforest.
déboîtement *m* dislocation.
débordant *adj* exuberant, overflowing.
débordé *adj* overwhelmed.
débordement *m* overflowing; outflanking.
déborder *vi* to overflow; to outflank.
débouché *m* outlet; issue.
déboucher *vt* to open, uncork; * *vi* to pass out, emerge.
debout *adv* upright, standing; **être ~** to stand.
déboutonner *vt* to unbutton.
débraillé *adj* untidy, disordered.
débrancher *vt* to disconnect.
débrayer *vi* to declutch; to stop work.
débris *m* debris, waste.
débrouiller *vt* to disentangle, unravel; **se ~** *vr* to cope, manage.
début *m* beginning, outset.
débutant *adj* novice.
débuter *vi* to start, begin; * *vt* to lead, start.
décadence *f* decadence, decline.
décadent *adj* decadent.
décaféiné *adj* decaffeinated.
décagone *m* decagon.
décalage *m* gap, interval; discrepancy.
décalcifier *vt* to decalcify.
décaler *vt* to shift; to stagger.
décalitre *m* decalitre.
décamètre *m* decametre.
décaper *vt* to clean, scour.
décapotable *adj* convertible; * *f* convertible.
décapsuler *vt* to take the lid off.
décapsuleur *m* bottle-opener.
décathlon *m* decathlon.

décéder *vi* to die.
décelable *adj* detectable.
déceler *vt* to detect; to disclose.
décembre *m* December.
décemment *adv* decently.
décence *f* decency.
décennal *adj* decennial.
décennie *f* decade.
décent *adj* decent, proper.
décentralisation *f* decentralisation.
décentraliser *vt* to decentralise.
déception *f* disappointment; deceit.
décerner *vt* to award, confer.
décès *m* death, decease.
décevant *adj* disappointing; deceptive.
décevoir *vt* to disappoint; to deceive.
déchaîné *adj* wild, unbridled.
déchaîner *vt* to unleash; **se ~** *vr* to break loose, run wild.
décharge *f* discharge; receipt.
déchargement *m* unloading.
décharger *vt* to unload, discharge.
décharné *adj* lean, emaciated.
déchausser *vt* to take off footwear; **se ~** *vr* to take one's shoes off.
déchéance *f* decay, decline.
déchet *m* loss, waste.
déchiffrer *vt* to decipher, decode.
déchiqueter *vt* to tear; to slash; to shred.
déchirant *adj* harrowing, excruciating.
déchirement *m* tearing, ripping.
déchirer *vt* to tear, rip.
déchirure *f* tear, rip.
déchoir *vi* to decline; to sink.
déchu *adj* fallen; declined; deposed.
décibel *m* decibel.
décidé *adj* decided; determined; **~ment** *adv* positively; resolutely; certainly.
décigramme *m* decigram.
décilitre *m* decilitre.
décimal *adj* decimal.
décimètre *m* decimetre.
décisif *adj* decisive, conclusive.
décision *f* decision.
déclamation *f* declamation.
déclamer *vt* to declaim.
déclaré *adj* professed, avowed.
déclarer *vt* to declare, announce; **se ~** *vr* to speak one's mind.

déclenchement *m* release, setting off.

déclencher *vt* to release, set off; **se ~** *vr* to release itself, go off.

déclic *m* click; trigger.

déclin *m* decline, deterioration.

déclinaison *f* declension; declination.

déclinant *adj* declining.

décliner *vi* to decline, refuse.

déclivité *f* declivity, slope.

décloisonner *vt* to decompartmentalise.

décoder *vt* to decode, decipher.

décodeur *m* decoder, decipherer.

décoiffer *vt* to disarrange so's hair.

décoincer *vt* to loose, release.

décollage *m* take-off, lift-off.

décoller *vi* to unpaste, steam off; to take off; * *vt*; **se ~** *vr* to come unstuck, become detached.

décolleté *adj* low-necked, low-cut; *m* decolletage, low neckline.

décolorant *adj* bleaching, decolorising; * *m* bleaching substance.

décolorer *vt* to decolour, bleach.

décombres *mpl* rubble, debris.

décomposer *vt* to decompose; to break up; to dissect; **se ~** *vr* to decompose, decay.

décomposition *f* decomposition, breaking up.

décompression *f* decompression.

décomprimer *vt* to decompress.

décompte *m* discount; deduction.

déconcentrer *vt* to devolve; to disperse; **se ~** *vr* to lose concentration.

déconcertant *adj* disconcerting.

déconcerter *vt* to disconcert.

décongeler *vt* to thaw, defrost.

déconnecter *vt* to disconnect.

déconnexion *f* disconnection.

décontenancé *adj* embarrassed; disconcerted.

décontracté *adj* relaxed.

décontracter *vt* to relax; **se ~** *vr* to relax.

décontraction *f* relaxation.

décor *m* scenery; setting.

décorateur *m* **-trice** *f* decorator; set designer.

décoratif *adj* decorative, ornamental.

décoration *f* decoration, embellishment.

décorer *vt* to decorate, adorn.

décortiquer *vt* to husk, shell.

découler *vi* to flow; to ensue.

découpage *m* cutting up, carving.

découper *vt* to carve, cut up.

décourageant *adj* discouraging, disheartening.

découragement *m* discouragement.

décourager *vt* to discourage, dishearten; **se ~** *vr* to become discouraged.

décousu *adj* unsewn; loose; disconnected.

découvert *adj* uncovered; open; * *m* overdraft.

découverte *f* discovery.

découvrir *vt* to discover.

décret *m* decree, enactment.

décréter *vt* to decree, enact.

décrire *vt* to describe.

décrocher *vt* to take down; to unhook.

décroissant *adj* decreasing, lessening.

décroître *vi* to decrease, diminish.

déçu *adj* disappointed.

décupler *vi* to increase tenfold.

dédaigner *vt* to disdain, scorn.

dédaigneusement *adv* disdainfully.

dédaigneux *adj* disdainful, scornful.

dédain *m* disdain, scorn.

dedans *adv* inside, indoors; * *m* inside; **au ~** inside.

dédicace *f* dedication.

dédier *vt* to consecrate, dedicate to.

dédommagement *m* compensation, damages.

dédommager *vt* to compensate, indemnify.

dédouanement *m* customs clearance.

dédoubler *vt* to divide in two; to remove lining.

déduction *f* deduction.

déduire *vt* to deduct; to deduce.

déesse *f* goddess.

défaillance *f* faintness; exhaustion; blackout.

défaillant *adj* faint; weakening.

défaillir *vi* to faint; to weaken.

défaire *vt* to undo, dismantle.

défaite *m* defeat, overthrow.

défaitiste *adj*, *mf* defeatist.

défaut *m* defect, fault.

défavorable *adj* unfavourable; **~ment** *adv* unfavourably.

défavoriser *vt* to penalise, treat unfairly.

défection *f* defection.

défectueux *adj* defective, faulty.

défendeur *m* **-eresse** *f* defendant.

défendre *vt* to defend, protect; to prohibit; **se ~** *vr* to defend o.s.

défense *f* defence; prohibition.

défenseur *m* defender.

défensif *adj* defensive.

défi *m* defiance; challenge.

défiant *adj* mistrustful, distrustful.

déficience *f* deficiency.

déficient *adj* deficient; weak.

déficit *m* deficit, shortfall.

déficitaire *adj* deficient, in deficit.

défier *vt* to challenge, defy.

défilé *m* procession, parade.

défiler *vi* to parade, march.

défini *adj* definite, precise.

définir *vt* to define, specify.

définitif *adj* definitive, final.

définition *f* definition.

définitivement *adv* definitively, finally.

déflagration *f* deflagration, explosion.

déflation *f* deflation.

défoncer *vt* to smash in; to dig deeply.

déformation *f* deformation, distortion.

déformer *vt* to deform, distort; **se ~** *vr* to bend; to lose its shape.

défoulement *m* outlet; release.

défouler *vt* to unwind, relax; **se ~** *vr* to get rid of one's inhibitions.

défricher *vt* to clear; to reclaim.

défunt *m* **-e** *f* deceased; * *adj* late, deceased.

dégagé *adj* clear; open.

dégagement *m* freeing, clearance.

dégager *vt* to free, clear; **se ~** *vr* to free o.s., extricate o.s.

dégarnir *vt* to empty; to clear.

dégât *m* havoc, damage.

dégel *m* thaw.

dégeler *vt vi* to thaw, melt.

dégénérer *vi* to degenerate, decline.

dégivrer *vt* to de-ice, defrost.

dégonfler *vt* to deflate, empty.

dégourdir *vt* to warm up, revive.

dégourdissement *m* reviving, return of circulation.

dégoût *m* disgust, distaste.

dégoûter *vt* to disgust.

dégradant *adj* degrading.

dégradation *f* degradation, debasement.

dégradé *m* shading off; gradation.

dégrader *vt* to degrade, debase; **se ~** *vr* to become degraded, debased.

dégrafer *vt* to unfasten, unhook.

dégraisser *vt* to remove grease.

degré *m* degree; grade.

dégrèvement *m* reduction; redemption.

dégripper *vt* to unblock; to unchoke.

déguisement *m* disguise.

déguiser *vt* to disguise; **se ~** *vr* to disguise o.s.

dégustation *f* tasting, sampling.

dehors *adv* outside, outdoors; **au ~** outwardly; **en ~ de** outside; apart from; * *m* outside, exterior.

déjà *adv* already.

déjeuner *vi* to lunch; * *m* lunch.

déjouer *vt* to elude; to thwart.

delà *adv*: **au ~ de** beyond; **par ~** beyond.

délabré *adj* dilapidated, ramshackle.

délacer *vt* to unlace, undo.

délai *m* delay; respite; time limit.

délaisser *vt* to abandon, quit.

délassant *adj* relaxing, refreshing.

délasser *vt* to refresh, relax; **se ~** *vr* to rest, relax.

délateur *m* **-trice** *f* informer.

délation *f* denouncement; informing.

délavé *adj* diluted; faded.

délayage *m* dragging-out, spinning-out.

délayer *vt* to thin; to drag out.

délectation *f* delectation, delight.

délecter (se) *vr* to delight, revel.

délégation *f* delegation.

délégué *m* **-e** *f* delegate, representative; * *adj* delegate, delegated.

déléguer *vt* to delegate.

délibération *f* deliberation; resolution.

délibéré *adj* deliberate; resolute; **~ment** *adv* deliberately.

délicat *adj* delicate, dainty; **~ement** *adv* delicately.

délicatesse *f* delicacy, daintiness.

délice *m* delight, pleasure.

délicieux *adj* delicious, delightful.

délier *vt* to unbind, untie.

délimitation *f* delimitation.

délimiter *vt* to delimit, demarcate.

délinquance *f* delinquency.

délinquant *m* **-e** *f* delinquent, offender; * *adj* delinquent.

délirant *adj* delirious, frenzied.

délire *m* delirium, frenzy.

délirer *vi* to be delirious.

délit *m* offence, misdemeanour.

délivrance *f* deliverance; release; delivery.

délivrer *vt* to deliver; to release; **se ~** *vr* to free o.s.

déloger *vt* to evict, dislodge.

déloyal *adj* disloyal, unfaithful; **~ement** *adv* disloyally.

déloyauté *f* disloyalty, treachery.

delta *m* delta.

deltaplane *m* hang-glider.

démagogie *f* demagogy.

démagogique *adj* demagogic.

démagogue *m* demagogue.

demain *adv* tomorrow.

demande *f* request, petition; question.

demander *vt* to ask, request; **se ~** *vr* to wonder.

démangeaison *f* itch; longing.

démaquillant *m* make-up remover; * *adj* make-up removing.

démaquiller *vt* to remove make-up; **se ~** *vr* to take one's make-up off.

démarche *f* gait, walk, step.

démarrage *m* moving off, casting off.

démarrer *vi* to start up, move off; * *vt* to start, get started.

démarreur *m* starter.

démasquer *vt* to unmask, uncover.

démêlage *m* disentangling; combing.

démêler *vt* to disentangle, unravel; comb.

déménagement *m* removal; moving (house).

déménager *vi* to move house.

déménageur *m* removal man.

démener (se) *vr* to struggle, strive.

dément *adj* mad, insane, crazy.

démenti *m* denial, refutation.

démentir *vt* to deny, refute.

démesuré *adj* excessive, inordinate; **~ment** *adv* excessively, inordinately.

démettre *vt* to dislocate; to dismiss.

demeure *f* residence, dwelling place.

demeurer *vi* to live at, reside, stay.

demi *adj* half; **à ~** halfway; * *m* half.

demi-cercle *m* semicircle.

demi-douzaine *f* half-dozen.

demi-droite *f* half-line.

demi-finale *f* semi-final.

demi-frère *m* half-brother.

demi-heure *f* half-hour.

demi-jour *m* half-light.

démilitariser *vt* to demilitarise.

demi-litre *m* half-litre.

demi-lune *f* half-moon.

demi-mesure *f* half-measure.

demi-mot *m*: **à ~** without spelling out.

demi-pension *f* half-board.

demi-sœur *f* half-sister.

démission *f* resignation.

démissionner *vi* to resign.

demi-tarif *m* half-fare.

demi-tour *m* half-turn.

démocrate *mf* democrat.

démocratie *f* democracy.

démocratique *adj* democratic; **~ment** *adv* democratically.

démocratiser *vt* to democratise.

démodé *adj* old-fashioned, out-of-date.

démographie *f* demography.

démographique *adj* demographic.

demoiselle *f* young lady; spinster; damsel.

démolir *vt* to demolish, knock down.

démolition *f* demolition.

démon *m* demon, fiend.

démoniaque *adj* demoniac, fiendish.

démonstrateur *m* **-trice** *f* demonstrator.

démonstratif *adj* demonstrative.

démonstration *f* demonstration; proof.

démontable *adj* collapsible, that can be dismantled.

démonte-pneu *m* tyre lever.

démonter *vt* to dismantle, take down, dismount; **se ~** *vr* to come apart, be nonplussed.

démontrer *vt* demonstrate; to prove.

démoralisant *adj* demoralising.

démoraliser *vt* to demoralise; **se ~** *vr* to become demoralised.

démouler *vt* to take out of a mould.

démunir *vt* to deprive; to divest.

démystifier *vt* to demystify, disabuse.

dénaturé *adj* denatured, disfigured.

dénégation *f* denial.

déneiger *vt* to clear snow from.

déni *m* denial, refusal.

dénicher *vt* to dislodge; to unearth.

dénier *vt* to deny, disclaim.

dénigrer *vt* to denigrate, disparage.

dénivellation *f* difference in level, unevenness.

dénombrer *vt* to number, enumerate.

dénomination *f* denomination, designation.

dénoncer *vt* to denounce; to inform against.

dénonciation *f* denunciation.

dénouement *m* dénouement; unravelling; outcome.

dénouer *vt* to unravel, untie, undo.

dénoyauter *vt* to stone (fruit).

denrée *f* commodity, provisions, foodstuff.

dense *adj* dense, thick.

densité *f* density, denseness.

dent *f* tooth.

dentaire *adj* dental.

dentelé *adj* jagged, perforated.

dentelle *f* lace.

dentier *m* denture, dental plate.

dentifrice *m* toothpaste.

dentiste *mf* dentist.

dentition *f* dentition, teething.

dénuder *vt* to bare, denude; **se ~** *vr* to strip off.

dénué *adj* devoid, bereft.

dénuement *m* destitution; deprivation.

déodorant *m* deodorant.

déontologie *f* deontology.

dépannage *m* repairing, fixing.

dépanner *vt* to repair, fix.

dépanneur *m* **-euse** *f* breakdown mechanic.

dépanneuse *f* breakdown lorry.

dépareillé *adj* unmatched; odd.

déparer *vt* to spoil; to disfigure.

départ *m* departure; start.

département *m* department.

dépasser *vt* to exceed; to go past.

dépaysé *adj* disoriented, out of one's element.

dépaysement *m* disorientation.

dépêcher *vt* to dispatch, send; **se ~** *vr* to hurry, rush.

dépendance *f* dependence; dependency.

dépendant *adj* dependent.

dépendre *vi* to depend on, be dependent on.

dépens *mpl*: **aux ~ de** at the expense of.

dépense *f* expenditure, outlay.

dépenser *vt* to expend, spend; **se ~** *vr* to exert o.s.

dépérir *vi* to decline, waste away.

dépeupler *vt* to depopulate; to clear.

dépistage *m* tracking; detection.

dépister *vt* to track.

dépit *m* spite; grudge; **en ~ de** in spite of.

dépité *adj* vexed; frustrated.

déplacé *adj* misplaced; ill-timed.

déplacement *m* displacement; removal.

déplacer *vt* to displace; to move; **se ~** *vr* to change residence.

déplaire *vi* to displease; to offend.

déplaisant *adj* disagreeable, unpleasant.

dépliant *m* prospectus, leaflet; * *adj* extendible; folding.

déplier *vt* to unfold; to open out.

déploiement *m* (*mil*) deployment; display.

déplorable *adj* deplorable, disgraceful.

déplorer *vt* to deplore, bewail.

déployer *vt* to deploy; to display.

dépopulation *f* depopulation.

déportation *f* deportation, transportation.

déporté *m* **-e** *f* deportee.

déporter *vt* to deport, transport.

déposer *vt* to lodge, deposit.

dépositaire *mf* depository; trustee.

déposition *f* deposition; evidence.

dépôt *m* deposit; warehouse.

dépouillement *m* scrutiny, perusal; despoiling.

dépouiller *vt* to strip; to despoil; to peruse.

dépourvu *adj* lacking, wanting; **au ~** off guard.

dépoussiérer *vt* to dust.

dépravation *f* depravity, corruption.

dépravé *adj* depraved, corrupt.

dépréciation *f* depreciation.

déprécier *vt* to depreciate; to disparage; **se ~** *vr* to depreciate, fall in value.

dépressif *adj* depressive.

dépression *f* depression, slump; dejection.

déprimant *adj* depressing.

déprimer *vt* to depress; to discourage.

depuis *prép* since, from; after.

député *m* deputy, delegate.

déracinement *m* uprooting.

déraciner *vt* to uproot.

déraillement *m* derailment.

dérailler *vi* to be derailed, run off the rails.

dérailleur *m* (*rail*) derailleur, derailer.

déraisonner *vi* to talk irrationally, rave.

dérangement *m* derangement; inconvenience.

déranger *vt* to upset, unsettle; **se ~** *vr* to move; to put o.s. out.

dérapage *m* skid.

déraper *vi* to skid, slip.

déréglé *adj* out of order; irregular; unruly.

dérèglement *m* disturbance; irregularity; dissoluteness.

dérégler *vt* to disturb; to put out of order; to upset.

dérision *f* derision, mockery.

dérisoire *adj* derisory; pathetic.

dérivation *f* derivation; diversion.

dérive *f* drift; **aller à la ~** to drift away.

dériver *vi* to drift.

dermatologie *f* dermatology.

dermatologue *mf* dermatologist.

derme *m* dermis.

dernier *adj* last; latest; back; * *m* **-ière** *f* last one; latter.

dernièrement *adv* recently; lately.

dérobade *f* sidestepping; evasion.

dérober *vt* to steal; to hide; **se ~** *vr* to steal away, escape.

dérogation *f* derogation; dispensation.

déroger *vi* to derogate; to detract.

déroulement *m* unfolding; progress, development.

dérouler *vt* to unwind, uncoil; **se ~** *vr* to develop; to unfold.

déroutant *adj* disconcerting.

déroute *f* rout, overthrow.

dérouter *vt* to rout, overthrow.

derrière *prép* behind; * *adv*; **par ~** at the back; * *m* bottom; back; **de ~** back, rear.

des *art* = **de les**; *see* **un, une**.

dès *prép* from, since; **~ que** when; as soon as.

désabusé *adj* disenchanted; disabused.

désaccord *m* disagreement, discord.

désaffecté *adj* disused.

désagréable *adj* disagreeable, unpleasant; **~ment** *adv* disagreeably, unpleasantly.

désagréger *vt* to break up, disintegrate; **se ~** *vr* to break up, disintegrate.

désagrément *m* displeasure, annoyance.

désaltérant *adj* thirst-quenching.

désaltérer *vt* to refresh; **se ~** *vi* to quench one's thirst.

désamorcer *vt* to unprime, defuse.

désapprobateur *adj* disapproving.

désapprobation *f* disapproval.

désapprouver *vt* to disapprove, object.

désarçonner *vt* to unsaddle; to nonplus, baffle.

désarmant *adj* disarming.

désarmement *m* disarmament.

désarmer *vt* to disarm; to unload.

désarroi *m* disarray, confusion.

désarticuler *vt* to dislocate; to upset.

désastre *m* disaster.

désastreux *adj* disastrous, unfortunate.

désavantage *m* disadvantage; prejudice.

désavantager *vt* to disadvantage, handicap.

désaveu *m* disavowal, retraction.

désavouer *vt* to disavow, retract.

descendance *f* descent, lineage.

descendant *m* **-e** *f* descendant; * *adj* falling, descending.

descendre *vi* to descend, go down; * *vt* to take down, bring down.

descente *f* descent, way down.

descriptif *adj* descriptive, explanatory.

description *f* description.

désemparé *adj* helpless; distraught.

désenchantement *m* disenchantment; disillusion.

désenfler *vi* to become less swollen.

désensibiliser *vt* to desensitise.

déséquilibre *m* imbalance, unbalance.

déséquilibré *adj* unbalanced, unhinged.

déséquilibrer *vt* to unbalance, throw off balance.

désert *m* desert, wilderness; * *adj* deserted.

déserter *vt* to desert.

déserteur *m* deserter.

désertification *f* desertification.

désertion *f* desertion.

désertique *adj* desert; barren.

désespérant *adj* desperate, hopeless; discouraging.

désespéré *adj* desperate, hopeless; **~ment** *adv* desperately.

désespérer *vi* to despair, give up hope.

désespoir *m* despair, despondency.

déshabiller *vt* to undress; **se ~** *vr* to undress.

désherbage *m* weeding.

désherbant *m* weed killer.

désherber *vt* to weed.

déshériter *vt* to disinherit.

déshonorant *adj* dishonourable, disgraceful.

déshonorer *vt* to dishonour, disgrace.

déshydraté *adj* dehydrated.

déshydrater *vt* to dehydrate; **se ~** *vr* to become dehydrated.

désignation *f* designation, nomination; name.

désigner *vt* to designate, indicate.

désillusion *f* disillusion; disappointment.

désillusionner *vt* to disillusion; to disappoint.

désincarné *adj* disincarnate, disembodied.

désinfectant *m* disinfectant; * *adj* disinfectant.

désinfecter *vt* to disinfect.

désinfection *f* disinfection.

désinformation *f* disinformation.

désintégration *f* disintegration.

désintégrer *vt* to split, break up; **se ~** *vr* to disintegrate.

désintéressé *adj* disinterested, unselfish.

désintéressement *m* disinterestedness, unselfishness.

désintéresser (se) *vr* to lose interest in.

désintoxiquer *vt* to detoxify; to dry out; **se faire ~** *vr* to dry out.

désinvolte *adj* easy, offhand, casual.

désinvolture *f* casualness, offhandedness.

désir *m* desire, wish, longing.

désirable *adj* desirable.

désirer *vt* to desire, wish, long.

désobéir *vi* to disobey.

désobéissance *f* disobedience.

désobéissant *adj* disobedient.

désobligeant *adj* disobliging; uncivil.

désodorisant *m* deodorant; * *adj* deodorising, deodorant.

désodoriser *vt* to deodorise.

désœuvré *adj* unoccupied, idle.

désœuvrement *m* idleness.

désolation *f* desolation; ruin; grief.

désolé *adj* desolate; disconsolate, grieved.

désordonné *adj* untidy; inordinate; reckless.

désordre *m* disorder, confusion, disturbance.

désorganisation *f* disorganisation.

désorienté *adj* disorientated.

désormais *adv* from now on, henceforth.

désossé *adj* boned.

despote *m* despot.

despotique *adj* despotic; **~ment** *adv* despotically.

dessèchement *m* dryness, drying up, withering.

dessécher *vt* to dry, parch, wither; **se ~** *vr* to dry out, become parched.

dessein *m* design, plan, scheme; **à ~** intentionally.

desserrer *vt* to loosen; to unscrew; to slacken; **se ~** *vr* to work loose, come undone.

dessert *m* dessert, sweet.

desservir *vt* to clear (table); to do a disservice to.

dessin *m* drawing, sketch; draft.

dessinateur *m* **-trice** *f* drawer, draughtsman.

dessiner *vt* to draw, sketch; to design.

dessous *adv* under, beneath; * *m* underside, bottom.

dessus *adv* over, above; * *m*; **prendre le ~** to gain the upper hand; **le ~ du panier** the upper crust, the pick of the bunch.

destabiliser *vt* to destabilise.

destin *m* destiny, fate, doom.

destinataire *mf* addressee, consignee.

destination *f* destination; purpose.

destinée *f* destiny, fate.

destiner *vt* to determine; to intend, destine, aim.

destituer *vt* to dismiss, depose.

destructeur *adj* destructive, ruinous.

destruction *f* destruction.

désuétude *f* disuse **tomber en ~** to fall into disuse.

détachable *adj* detachable.

détachant *m* cleaner, stain remover.

détaché *m* (*mus*) detached.

détachement *m* detachment, indifference.

détacher *vt* (*mus*) to detach; to unfasten; **se ~** *vr* to become detached.

détail *m* detail, particular.

détaillant *m* **-e** *f* retailer.

détailler *vt* to detail; to sell retail.

détartrage *m* descaling.

détartrant *m* descaling substance; * *adj* descaling.

détartrer *vt* to descale.

détaxe *f* reduction in tax.

détecter *vt* to detect.

détecteur *m* detector.

détection *f* detection.

détective *m* detective.

déteindre *vi* to lose colour, fade.

détendre *vt* to release, loosen; **se ~** *vr* to relax, calm down.

détendu *adj* slack; relaxed.

détenir *vt* to detain; to hold.

détente *f* relaxation, easing.

détenteur *m* **-trice** *f* holder, possessor.

détergent *m* detergent.

détérioration *f* deterioration.

détériorer *vt* to damage, impair; **se ~** *vr* to deteriorate, worsen.

déterminant *adj* determining, deciding.

détermination *f* determination; resolution.

déterminé *adj* determined, resolute.

déterminer *vt* to determine, decide.

déterrer *vt* to dig up, disinter.

détestable *adj* detestable, odious; **~ment** *adv* detestably.

détester *vt* to detest, hate.

détonateur *m* detonator.

détonation *f* detonation, explosion.

détonner *vi* to clash (colour); to go out of tune.

détour *m* detour; curve; evasion.

détourné *adj* indirect, oblique.

détournement *m* diversion, rerouting.

détourner *vt* to divert, reroute.

détracteur *m* **-trice** *f* detractor, disparager.

détraquer *vt* to upset; to disorder; **se ~** *vr* to become upset; to go wrong.

détresse *f* distress, trouble.

détriment *m*: **au ~ de** to the detriment of.

détritus *m* refuse, rubbish.

détroit *m* strait.

détrôner *vt* to dethrone, depose.

detruire *vt* to destroy, demolish.

dette *f* debt.

deuil *m* mourning, bereavement, grief.

deux *adj* two; * *m* two; **entre les ~** so-so, fair to middling; **en moins de ~** in a jiffy.

deuxième *adj* second; **~ment** *adv* secondly; * *mf* second.

deux-points *m* colon.

deux-roues *m* two-wheeled vehicle.

dévaler *vt* *vi* to hurry down, tear down.

dévaliser *vt* to burgle; to rifle.

dévalorisation *f* depreciation.

dévaloriser *vt* to depreciate, reduce the value of.

dévaluation *f* devaluation.

devancer *vt* to outstrip, outrun; to precede.

devant *prép* in front of, before; * *adv* in front; * *m* front; **prendre les ~s** to make the first move, pre-empt; **aller au-~ de** to anticipate.

devanture *f* display; shop-front.

dévaster *vt* to devastate, lay waste.

développement *m* development; growth; progress.

développer *vt* to develop, expand; **se ~** *vr* to develop, grow.

devenir *vi* to become, grow.

déverrouiller *vt* to unbolt, unlock.

déverser *vt* to pour; to dump.

dévêtir *vt* to undress; **se ~** *vr* to get undressed.

déviation *f* deviation; diversion.

dévier *vi* to deviate; to turn aside; to swerve.

devin *m* **-eresse** *f* seer, soothsayer.

deviner *vt* to guess; to solve; to foretell.

devinette *f* riddle.

devis *m* estimate, quotation.

dévisager *vt* to stare at.

devise *f* currency.

dévisser *vt* to unscrew, undo.

dévoiler *vt* to unveil, disclose.

devoir *m* duty; homework; *vt* to owe; to have to.

dévorer *vt* to devour, consume.

dévot *adj* devout, pious.

dévotion *f* devotion, piety.

dévoué *adj* devoted, dedicated.

dévouement *m* devotion, dedication.

dévouer (se) *vr* to devote o.s., sacrifice o.s.

dextérité *f* dexterity, adroitness.

diabète *m* diabetes.

diabétique *adj* diabetic.

diable *m* devil.

diablotin *m* imp; cracker (Christmas).

diabolique *adj* diabolical, devilish; **~ment** *adv* diabolically.

diagnostic *m* diagnosis.

diagnostiquer *vt* to diagnose.

diagonale *f* diagonal.

diagramme *m* diagram; graph.

dialecte *m* dialect.

dialectique *f* dialectic; * *adj* dialectic.

dialogue *m* dialogue, conversation.

dialoguer *vt* to write in dialogue form; *vi* to have talks (with).

dialyse *f* dialysis.

diamant *m* diamond.

diamètre *m* diameter.

diaphragme *m* diaphragm.

diarrhée *f* diarrhoea.

dictaphone *m* dictaphone.

dictateur *m* **-trice** *f* dictator.

dictatorial *adj* dictatorial.

dictature *f* dictatorship.

dictée *f* dictating; dictation.

dicter *vt* to dictate, impose.

dictionnaire *m* dictionary.

dicton *m* saying, dictum.

didactique *adj* didactic.

dièse *f* (*mus*) sharp.

diesel *m* diesel.

diète *f* light diet.

diététicien *m* **-ne** *f* dietician.

diététique *adj* dietary.

dieu *m* god.

diffamation *f* defamation, slandering.

diffamer *vt* to defame, slander.

différé *adj* postponed; (*rad, TV*) pre-recorded.

différemment *adv* differently.

différence *f* difference.

différenciation *f* differentiation.

différencier *vt* to differentiate.

différend *m* disagreement, difference of opinion.

différent *adj* different; various.

différer *vt* to differ; to vary.

difficile *adj* difficult; awkward, tricky; **~ment** *adv* with difficulty.

difficulté *f* difficulty; problem.

difforme *adj* deformed, misshapen.

difformité *f* deformity.

diffuser *vt* to diffuse, circulate, broadcast.

diffusion *f* diffusion, circulation, broadcasting.

digérer *vt* to digest.

digeste *adj* easily digestible.

digestif *adj* digestive.

digestion *f* digestion.

digital *adj* digital.

digne *adj* worthy; dignified; **~ment** *adv* worthily, deservedly.

dignité *f* dignity.

digression *f* digression.

digue *f* dyke; sea wall.

dilapider *vt* to squander; to embezzle.

dilatation *f* dilation, distension.

dilater *vt* to dilate, distend; **se ~** *vr* to dilate, distend.

dilemme *m* dilemma.

dilettante *mf* dilettante.

diluer *vt* to dilute.

dilution *f* dilution.

dimanche *m* Sunday.

dimension *f* dimension, size.

diminuer *vt* to diminish, reduce; * *vi* to diminish, lessen.

diminutif *m* diminutive.

diminution *f* reduction, lessening.

dinde *f* turkey hen.

dindon *m* turkey cock.

dindonneau *m* young turkey.

dîner *vi* to dine; * *m* dinner.

dinosaure *m* dinosaur.

diocèse *m* diocese.

diode *f* diode.

dioxyde *m* dioxide.

diphtérie *f* diphtheria.

diphtongue *f* diphthong.

diplomate *mf* diplomat.

diplomatie *f* diplomacy.

diplomatique *adj* diplomatic; **~ment** *adv* diplomatically.

diplôme *m* diploma, certificate.

diplômé *m* **-e** *f* graduate; * *adj* qualified.

dire *vt* to say; to tell; **se ~** to say to o.s.; to call o.s; *vr*: **se ~ que** to tell o.s. that.

direct *adj* direct; **~ement** *adv* directly; * *m* (*rail*) express.

directeur *m* **-trice** *f* director.

direction *f* direction, management.

directive *f* directive, order.

dirigeant *m* **-e** *f* leader, ruler; * *adj* ruling, executive.

diriger *vt* to run, direct; **se ~** *vr*: **se ~ vers** to head for, make for.

discernement *m* discernment, judgment.

discerner *vt* to discern, distinguish.

disciple *m* disciple.

disciplinaire *adj* disciplinary.

discipline *f* discipline.

discipliné *adj* disciplined.

discontinu *adj* discontinuous.

discordant *adj* discordant, conflicting.

discorde *f* discord, dissension.

discothèque *f* discotheque.

discours *m* speech, talking.

discourtois *adj* discourteous.

discréditer *vt* to discredit.

discret *adj* discreet.

discrétion *f* discretion, prudence.

discrétionnaire *adj* discretionary.

discrimination *f* discrimination.

discriminer *vt* to distinguish; to discriminate.

disculper *vt* to excuse, exonerate; **se ~** *vr* to justify o.s., excuse o.s.

discussion *f* discussion, debate.

discutable *adj* debatable, questionable.

discuter *vt vi* to discuss, debate.

disgrâce *f* disgrace.

disgracieux *adj* awkward, ungraceful.

disjoncter *vi* to cut off, disconnect.

disjoncteur *m* cutout, circuit breaker.

disparaître *vi* to disappear, vanish.

disparate *adj* disparate, incongruous.

disparité *f* disparity, incongruity.

disparition *f* disappearance; death; extinction.

disparu *adj* vanished; bygone; missing.

dispensaire *m* dispensary.

dispense *f* dispensation, exemption.

dispenser *vt* to dispense, exempt; **se ~** *vr*: **se ~ de** to dispense with; to avoid.

disperser *vt* to spread, scatter; **se ~** *vr* to disperse, scatter.

dispersion *f* dispersal, scattering.

disponibilité *f* availability.

disponible *adj* available; transferable.

dispos *adj* refreshed; alert; in form.

disposer *vt* to arrange, dispose; **se ~** *vr*: **se ~ à** to prepare to do; * *vi* to leave.

dispositif *m* device, mechanism.

disposition *f* arrangement, layout.

disproportionné *adj* disproportionate.

dispute *f* dispute, argument.

disputer *vt* to dispute, rival; **se ~** *vr* to quarrel, argue.

disquaire *mf* record-dealer.

disqualifier *vt* to disqualify.

disque *m* disk; record.

disquette *f* diskette.

dissection *f* dissection.

dissemblable *adj* dissimilar; different.

disséminer *vt* to disseminate, scatter.

dissentiment *m* disagreement, dissent.

disséquer *vt* to dissect.

dissertation *f* dissertation.

dissidence *f* dissidence, dissent.

dissident *adj* dissident.

dissimulation *f* dissimulation, double-dealing.

dissimulé *adj* double-faced, dissembling.

dissimuler *vt* to dissemble, conceal; **se ~** *vr* to conceal o.s.

dissipation *f* dissipation, waste.

dissipé *adj* dissipated, undisciplined.

dissiper *vt* to dispel; to dissipate; **se ~** *vr* to disperse, become undisciplined.

dissociation *f* dissociation.

dissocier *vt* to dissociate.

dissolution *f* dissolution.

dissolvant *m* solvent, dissolvent.

dissonant *adj* dissonant; discordant.

dissoudre *vt* to dissolve.

dissuader *vt* to dissuade.

dissuasif *adj* dissuasive, deterrent.

dissuasion *f* dissuasion.

distance *f* distance, interval.

distancier (se) *vr* to distance o.s. from.

distant *adj* distant.

distendre *vt* to distend, strain; **se ~** *vr* to slacken.

distillation *f* distillation.

distiller *vt* to distil.

distillerie *f* distillery.

distinct *adj* distinct, different; **~ement** *adv* distinctly.

distinctif *adj* distinctive.

distinction *f* distinction.

distingué *adj* distinguished.

distinguer *vt* to distinguish; to discern; **se ~** *vr* to distinguish o.s.

distorsion *f* distortion.

distraction *f* inattention; absent-mindedness; abstraction.

distraire *vt* to distract; to amuse; **se ~** *vr* to enjoy o.s.

distrait *adj* inattentive, absent-minded; **~ement** *adv* absent-mindedly.

distrayant *adj* entertaining, diverting.

distribuer *vt* to distribute.

distributeur *m* distributor.

distribution *f* distribution.

district *m* district.

diurétique *adj* diuretic; * *m* diuretic.

divagation *f* wandering, rambling.

divaguer *vi* to ramble, rave.

divan *m* divan.

divergence *f* divergence.

divergent *adj* divergent.

diverger *vi* to diverge, differ.

divers *adj* diverse, varied; **~ement** *adv* diversely.

diversification *f* diversification.

diversifier *vt* to vary, diversify; **se ~** *vr* to diversify.

diversion *f* diversion.

diversité *f* diversity, variety.

divertir *vt* to amuse, entertain; **se ~** *vr* to amuse o.s.

divertissant *adj* amusing, entertaining.

divertissement *m* entertainment, recreation.

dividende *m* dividend.

divin *adj* divine, exquisite; **~ement** *adv* divinely.

divination *f* divination.

divinité *f* divinity.

diviser *vt* to divide, split; **se ~** *vr* to split up, divide into.

division *f* division.

divorce *m* divorce.

divorcé *m* **-e** *f* divorcee; * *adj* divorced.

divorcer *vi* to divorce.

divulgation *f* disclosure, divulgence.

divulguer *vt* to divulge, disclose.

dix *adj, m* ten.

dix-huit *adj, m* eighteen.

dix-huitième *adj, mf* eighteenth.

dixième *adj* tenth; **~ment** *adv* tenthly; * *mf* tenth.

dix-neuf *adj, m* nineteen.

dix-neuvième *adj, mf* nineteenth.

dix-sept *adj, m* seventeen.

dix-septième *adj, mf* seventeenth.

dizaine *f* ten, ten or so.

docile *adj* docile, submissive; **~ment** *adv* docilely.

docilité *f* docility, submissiveness.

dock *m* dock, dockyard.

docteur *m* doctor.

doctorat *m* doctorate.

doctrine *f* doctrine.

document *m* document.

documentaire *adj* documentary.

documentaliste *mf* researcher.

documentation *f* documentation; information.

documenter *vt* to document; **se ~** *vr* to gather information on.

dogmatique *adj* dogmatic.

dogme *m* dogma.

doigt *m* finger; **être à deux ~s de** to come very close to doing; **obéir au ~ et à l'œil** to obey (sb) slavishly.

doigté *m* touch; fingering technique.

domaine *m* domain, estate; to sphere.

domanial *adj* state-owned.

dôme *m* dome, vault.

domestique *adj* domestic, household.

domestiquer *vt* to domesticate, tame.

domicile *m* domicile, address.

domicilié *adj* domiciled.

dominant *adj* dominant, prevailing.

dominante *f* dominant characteristic.

dominateur *adj* governing; domineering.

domination *f* domination.

dominer *vt* to dominate; to prevail; **se ~** to control o.s.

dominical *adj* Sunday.

dommage *m* damage; harm; **c'est ~** it's a pity.

dompter *vt* to tame, train.

dompteur *m* **-euse** *f* trainer, tamer.

don *m* gift; talent.

donateur *m* **-trice** *f* donor.

donation *f* donation.

donc *conj* so, therefore, thus; **pourquoi ~?** why was that?

donné *adj* given; fixed; **étant ~** seeing that, in view of.

donnée *f* datum.

donner *vt* to give; * *vi* to yield (crop).

donneur *m* **-euse** *f* giver, donor; dealer.

dont *pn* whose, of which.

dopage *m* doping.

doper *vt* to dope; **se ~** *vr* to take drugs, dope o.s.

doré *adj* gilded; tanned.

dorénavant *adv* from now on, henceforth.

dorer *vt* to gild; to tan.

dorloter *vt* to pamper, pet.

dormir *vi* to sleep, be asleep; to be still.

dortoir *m* dormitory.

dos *m* back; top; ridge.

dosage *m* mixture; balance; proportioning.

dose *f* dose; amount; quantity.

doser *vt* to measure out, proportion; to strike a balance.

dossier *m* dossier, file; case.

dot *f* dowry.

doter *vt* to provide with a dowry; to endow.

douane *f* customs.

douanier *m* customs officer.

double *adj* double, duplicate, dual; **~ment** *adv* doubly; * *m* copy, double, replica; twice as much.

doubler *vt vi* to double, duplicate.

doublure *f* lining; (*thea*) understudy.

doucement *adv* softly, gently.

doucereux *adj* sugary; mawkish; suave.

douceur *f* softness, gentleness.

douche *f* shower.

doucher *vt* to give a shower to; **se ~** *vr* to take a shower.

doué *adj* gifted, endowed with.

douille *f* case; cartridge.

douillet *adj* delicate, tender; soft.

douleur *f* pain, ache; anguish.

douloureusement *adv* painfully, grievously.

douloureux *adj* painful, grievous.

doute *m* doubt; **sans ~** without doubt.

douter *vi* to doubt, question; **se ~** *vr* **se ~ de** to suspect someone; **se ~ que** to suspect that, expect that.

douteux *adj* doubtful, dubious.

doux *adj, f* **douce** soft; sweet; mild.

douzaine *f* dozen.

douze *adj, m* twelve.

douzième *adj* twelfth; **~ment** *adv* twelfthly; * *mf* twelfth.

doyen *m* **-ne** *f* dean; doyen.

draconien *adj* draconian, drastic.

dragée *f* bonbon, sugared almond.

dragon *m* dragon.

dramatique *adj* dramatic, tragic; **~ment** *adv* dramatically.

dramatiser *vt* to dramatise.

dramaturge *mf* playwright.

drame *m* drama.

drap *m* sheet; **~-housse** fitted sheet; **être dans de beaux ~s** to be in a fine mess.

drapeau *m* flag.

draper *vt* to drape.

dressage *m* taming; pitching.

dresser *vt* to draw up; to put up; **se ~** *vr* to stand up; to rear up.

dresseur *m* **-euse** *f* trainer, tamer.

dribbler *vi* to dribble.

drogue *f* drug.

drogué *m* **-e** *f* drug addict; * *adj* drugged.

droguer *vt* to drug, administer drugs; **se ~** *vr* to dose up; to take drugs.

droguerie *f* hardware trade.

droguiste *mf* hardware storekeeper.

droit *adj* right; straight; sound; honest; **~ement** *adv* uprightly, honestly; * *adv* straight, straight ahead; * *m* right; law; tax.

droite *f* right side; right (wing); straight line.

droitier *adj* right-handed.

droiture *f* uprightness, honesty.

drôle *adj* funny, amusing; peculiar; **~ment** *adv* funnily, peculiarly.

dromadaire *m* dromedary.

dru *adj* thick, dense; sturdy.

du *art* of the.

dû *adj* owed; due; **~ment** *adv* duly.

dualité *f* duality.

dubitatif *adj* doubtful, dubious.

dubitativement *adv* doubtfully, dubiously.

duc *m* duke, **duchesse** *f* duchess.

duché *m* duchy.

duel *m* duel; dual.

duettiste *mf* duettist.

dune *f* dune.

duo *m* duo; duet.

duodénum *m* duodenum.

dupe *adj* easily duped; * *f* dupe.

duper *vt* to dupe, take in.

duplex *m* duplex, two-way.

dupliquer *vt* to duplicate.

dur *adj* hard, tough; difficult; ~**ement** *adv* harshly, severely.

durable *adj* durable, lasting; ~**ment** *adv* durably.

duralumin *m* duralumin.

durant *prép* during, for.

durcir *vt vi* to harden; **se** ~ *vr* to become hardened.

durcissement *m* hardening.

durée *f* duration, length.

durer *vi* to last.

dureté *f* hardness; austerity, harshness.

durillon *m* callus, corn.

duvet *m* down.

duveté *adj* downy.

dynamique *f* dynamic; dynamics; * *adj* dynamic; ~**ment** *adv* dynamically.

dynamiser *vt* to energise; to potentiate.

dynamisme *m* dynamism.

dynamitage *m* dynamiting.

dynamite *f* dynamite.

dynamiter *vt* to dynamite.

dynamo *f* dynamo.

dynastie *f* dynasty.

dynastique *adj* dynastic.

dysenterie *f* dysentery.

dyslexie *f* dyslexia.

dyslexique *adj* dyslexic.

E

eau *f* water; rain.

eau-de-vie *f* brandy.

ébahir *vt* to astonish, stupefy, dumbfound.

ébahissement *m* astonishment, amazement.

ébauche *f* rough draft, rough outline.

ébaucher *vt* to sketch; to roughcast.

ébène *f* ebony.

ébéniste *m* cabinetmaker.

éblouir *vt* to dazzle; to fascinate.

éblouissant *adj* dazzling; amazing.

éblouissement *m* dazzle; bedazzlement.

ébouillanter *vt* to scald; to blanch; **s'~** *vr* to scald oneself.

éboulement *m* collapse, caving in; fall.

ébouriffé *adj* tousled, ruffled.

ébranler *vt* to shake; to unsettle, disturb.

ébrécher *vt* to chip, indent; to break into (fortune).

ébriété *f* intoxication.

ébrouer (s') *vr* to shake oneself.

ébruiter *vt* to disclose, divulge; **s'~** *vr* to spread, be noised abroad.

ébullition *f* boiling; effervescence; turmoil.

écaille *f* scale; shell.

écailler *vt* to scale; to chip; **s'~** *vr* to flake off, peel off.

écarlate *adj* scarlet.

écart *m* distance; interval; discrepancy; **rester à l'~** to steer clear of.

écarteler *vt* to tear apart; to quarter.

écarter *vt* to separate; to avert; to dismiss; **s'~** *vr* to make way; to swerve.

ecchymose *f* bruise, ecchymosis.

ecclésiastique *adj* ecclesiastical; * *m* ecclesiastic, clergyman.

échafaud *m* scaffold.

échafaudage *m* scaffolding.

échange *m* exchange, barter, trade.

échanger *vt* to exchange.

échantillon *m* sample.

échappée *f* breakaway; glimpse.

échappement *m* exhaust; release.

échapper *vi* to escape, avoid, elude; **s'~** *vr* to escape from; to leak.

écharde *f* splinter, sliver.

écharpe *f* scarf; arm-sling.

échassier *m* wader.

échauffement *m* heating; warm-up; constipation.

échauffer *vt* to heat, overheat; to excite; **s'~** *vr* to warm up; to get worked up.

échéance *f* expiry; maturity date.

échec *m* failure, defeat; chess.

échelle *f* ladder; scale.

échelon *m* rung; grade.

échelonner *vt* to grade; to stagger, set at intervals; **s'~** *vr* to be graduated, staggered.

échine *f* backbone, spine; **courber l'~** to submit.

échiquier *m* chessboard.

écho *m* echo; rumour.

échographie *f* ultrasound scan.

échoir *vi* to fall due; to befall, fall to so's lot.

échouer *vi* to fail; to end up; to run aground.

éclabousser *vt* to splash, spatter.

éclair *m* flash; lightning flash; spark.

éclairage *m* lighting, light.

éclairagiste *m* electrician; lighting engineer.

éclaircie *f* clear interval, bright spot; glade.

éclaircir *vt* to lighten; to thin down; to brighten up; **s'~** *vr* to clear (up).

éclaircissement *m* clearing up, explanation, elucidation.

éclairer *vt* to light, illuminate; clarify, explain.

éclat *m* brightness, glare; splinter; splendour.

éclatant *adj* bright, blazing; resounding; blatant.

éclatement *m* explosion, bursting, rupture.

éclater *vi* to explode; to break out; to exclaim.

éclectique *adj* eclectic.

éclipse *f* eclipse.

éclipser *vt* to eclipse, overshadow; **s'~** *vr* to disappear, vanish.

éclore *vi* to hatch out; to blossom.

éclosion *f* hatching; blooming; birth.

écluse *f* lock.

écœurant *adj* disgusting, nauseating.

écœurement *m* nausea, disgust; discouragement.

écœurer *vt* to nauseate, disgust.

école *f* school, schooling; sect, doctrine.

écolier *m* schoolgirl, **-ière** *f* schoolgirl.

écologie *f* ecology.

écologique *adj* ecological.

écologiste *mf* ecologist.

économe *adj* thrifty; * *mf* steward, treasurer; (*mar*) bursar.

économie *f* economy, thrift; economics.

économique *adj* economic; **~ment** *adv* economically.

économiser *vt* to economise, save.

écorce *f* bark, peel, skin.

écorchure *f* scratch; graze.

Écossais *m* Scotsman, **-e** *f* Scotswoman.

écossais *adj* Scottish.

Écosse *f* Scotland.

écoulement *m* flow, discharge, outlet; disposal, selling.

écouler *vt* to flow, discharge; to sell; **s'~** *vr* to leak, flow out; to pass by; to sell.

écoute *f* listening, audience.

écouter *vt* to listen to.

écran *m* screen.

écrasant *adj* crushing; overwhelming.

écraser *vt* to crush; to overwhelm; to run over; **s'~** *vr* to crash; to get crushed.

écrémer *vt* to skim, cream.

écrevisse *f* crayfish.

écrin *m* box, casket.

écrire *vt* to write; to spell.

écrit *adj* written; * *m* document; piece of writing.

écriteau *m* notice, sign.

écriture *f* writing; handwriting; script.

écrivain *m* writer.

écrou *m* nut.

écroulement *m* collapse, caving in.

écrouler (s') *vr* to collapse, crumble.

écru *adj* raw; unbleached; untreated.

ectoplasme *m* ectoplasm.

écueil *m* reef, shelf; peril.

écume *f* foam, froth; scum.

écureuil *m* squirrel.

écurie f stable.

écusson m badge, shield.

eczéma m eczema.

édification f erection, construction.

édifice m edifice, building.

édifier vt to build, construct; to edify.

éditer vt to publish, produce; to edit.

éditeur m -**trice** f publisher; editor.

édition f publishing; edition; editing.

éditorial m leading article, editorial.

éducatif adj educational.

éducation f education; upbringing.

édulcorant m sweetener; * adj sweetening.

éduquer vt to educate; to bring up, raise.

effacer vt to delete, erase, wipe off; s'~ vr to wear away, become obliterated.

effaré adj alarmed, bewildered.

effaroucher vt to frighten off; to alarm.

effectif m staff; size, complement; * adj effective, positive.

effectivement adv effectively, positively.

effectuer vt to effect, execute, carry out.

effervescence f effervescence; excitement, ferment.

effervescent adj effervescent; excited.

effet m effect, impression; spin; bill, note.

efficace adj effective; efficient; ~**ment** adv effectively, efficiently.

efficacité f effectiveness, efficiency.

effleurer vt to touch lightly, skim across.

effondrement m collapse, caving in.

effondrer (s') vr to collapse, cave in.

efforcer (s') vr to endeavour, do one's best.

effort m effort, exertion; stress, strain.

effraction f breaking and entering.

effrayant adj frightening, fearsome.

effrayer vt to frighten, scare.

effriter vt to crumble; to exhaust (land); s'~ vr to crumble away, disintegrate.

effroi m terror, dismay.

effronté adj shameless, impudent, cheeky; ~**ment** adv shamelessly, impudently.

effroyable adj horrifying, appalling; ~**ment** adv horrifyingly, appallingly.

égal adj equal; even, level; equable; ~**ement** adv evenly; equally; also, as well.

égaler vt to equal, match.

égalisation f equalisation; levelling.

égaliser vt to equalise; to level out.

égalitaire adj egalitarian.

égalité f equality; equableness; evenness.

égard m consideration, respect; **à l'~ de** concerning, regarding; **à tous ~s** in all respects.

égarer vt to mislead, lead astray; s'~ vr to get lost; to wander from the point.

égayer vt to enliven, cheer up.

églantine f dog-rose, wild rose.

église f church.

égocentrique adj egocentric, self-centred.

égoïsme m selfishness, egoism.

égoïste mf egotist; * adj egotistic; ~**ment** adv egotistically.

égout m sewer.

égoutter vt to strain; to wring out.

égratignure f scratch, scrape.

éjecter vt to eject, throw out.

élaboration f elaboration, development.

élaborer vt to elaborate, develop.

élan m surge, momentum, speed; spirit, elan.

élancer (s') vr to rush, spring, hurl oneself.

élargir vt to widen, stretch; s'~ vr to get wider.

élargissement m widening, stretching, enlarging.

élastique adj elastic; flexible; * m elastic, elastic band.

électeur m -**trice** f voter, elector.

élection f election; choice.

électoral adj electoral.

électorat m electorate; constituency; franchise.

électricien m electrician.

électricité f electricity.

électrique adj electric.

électrocardiogramme m electrocardiogram.

électrode f electrode.

électrolyse f electrolysis.

électroménager m household appliance; * adj electrical (household).

électron m electron.

électronicien m electronics engineer.

électronique f electronics; * adj electronic.

élégance f elegance, stylishness.

élégant adj smart, elegant, stylish.

élément m element, component; cell; fact.

élémentaire adj elementary; basic.

éléphant m elephant.

élevage m rearing, breeding.

élève mf pupil, student.

élevé adj high; heavy; lofty, exalted.

élever vt to bring up, raise; to put up, lift up; s'~ vr to rise, go up.

éleveur m -**euse** f stockbreeder.

éligible adj eligible.

élimination f elimination.

éliminatoire adj eliminatory; * f preliminary heat.

éliminer vt to eliminate, discard.

élire vt to elect.

élite f elite.

élitisme m elitism.

elle pn she; it; her; **c'est à ~** it's up to her; it's hers; ~-**même** herself.

elliptique adj elliptic; ~**ment** adv elliptically.

élocution f elocution, diction.

éloge m praise; eulogy.

élogieux adj laudatory, eulogistic.

éloigné adj distant, remote.

éloigner vt to move away, take away; s'~ vr to go away; to grow distant.

éloquence f eloquence.

éloquent adj eloquent.

élu adj chosen, elected.

élucider vt to elucidate, clear up.

émacié adj emaciated, wasted.

émail m enamel.

émailler vt to enamel.

émancipation f emancipation, liberation.

émanciper vt to emancipate, liberate; s'~ vr to become emancipated, liberated.

émaner vi to emanate, issue.

emballage m packing paper, wrapping paper.

emballer vt to pack up, wrap up.

embarcadère m landing stage, pier.

embarcation f boat, craft.

embargo m embargo.

embarquement m loading; embarkation.

embarquer vt to embark; to load; * vi to embark, go aboard.

embarras m embarrassment, confusion; trouble.

embarrassant *adj* embarrassing, uncomfortable.

embarrassé *adj* embarrassed, self-conscious.

embarrasser *vt* to embarrass; to hinder, hamper; **s'~** *vr* to burden oneself with; to be troubled by.

embaucher *vt* to take on, hire.

embellir *vt* to beautify, make more attractive.

embellissement *m* embellishment, improvement.

embêter *vt* (*fam*) to bore; to get on one's nerves; **s'~** *vr* to be bored, fed up.

emblème *m* symbol, emblem.

emboîter *vt* to fit together; **s'~** *vr* to fit together; to fit into each other.

embonpoint *m* stoutness, plumpness.

embouchure *f* mouth (river); mouthpiece.

embouteillage *m* traffic jam; bottling.

embranchement *m* junction; side road.

embrasser *vt* to kiss, embrace.

embrayage *m* clutch.

embrayer *vi* to engage the clutch.

embrouiller *vt* to tangle up, mix up; **s'~** *vr* to become muddled, confused.

embryon *m* embryo.

embryonnaire *adj* embryonic.

embuscade *f* ambush.

émeraude *f* emerald.

émerger *vi* to emerge; to stand out.

émeri *m* emery.

émerveiller *vt* to astonish, amaze; **s'~** *vr* to marvel at.

émetteur *adj, f* **-trice** transmitting.

émettre *vt* to send out, emit, transmit.

émeute *f* riot.

émietter *vt* to crumble; to disperse, break up; **s'~** *vr* to crumble; to disperse, break up.

émigration *f* emigration.

émigré *m* **-e** *f* émigré, expatriate.

émigrer *vi* to emigrate.

éminence *f* hill, elevation; eminence, distinction.

éminent *adj* eminent, distinguished.

émir *m* emir.

émission *f* sending out; transmission; broadcast; emission.

emmêler *vt* to entangle; confuse; **s'~** *vr* to tangle.

emménager *vi* to move in.

emmener *vt* to take away; to lead.

émoi *m* agitation, emotion.

émotif *adj* emotional; emotive.

émotion *f* emotion; commotion.

émotivité *f* emotionalism.

émouvant *adj* moving, touching.

émouvoir *vt* to move, disturb, upset; **s'~** *vr* to be moved; to get worried, upset.

empailler *vt* to stuff.

empaqueter *vt* to parcel up, pack.

emparer (s') *vr* to seize, grab; to take possession of.

empêchement *m* obstacle, hitch; impediment.

empêcher *vt* to prevent, stop; **s'~** *vr*: **s'~ de** to refrain from doing something.

empereur *m* emperor.

empester *vt* to stink out; to poison, infect.

empêtrer *vt* to entangle,; **s'~** *vr* to get involved in, get mixed up in.

emphase *f* pomposity; emphasis, stress.

empiéter *vi* to encroach, overlap.

empiler *vt* to pile up, stack.

empire *m* empire; influence, ascendancy.

empirer *vi* to get worse, deteriorate.

empirique *adj* empirical; **~ment** *adv* empirically.

emplacement *m* site, location.

emploi *m* use; job, employment.

employé *m* **-e** *f* employee.

employer *vt* to use, spend; to employ.

employeur *m*, **euse** *f* employer.

empoisonner *vt* to poison; to annoy.

emporter *vt* to take; to carry off; to involve; **s'~** *vr* to lose one's temper.

empreinte *f* imprint, impression, stamp.

empresser (s') *vi* to rush to; to press around, fuss around.

emprise *f* hold, ascendancy.

emprisonner *vt* to imprison, trap.

emprunt *m* borrowing, loan.

emprunter *vt* to borrow; to assume; to derive.

ému *adj* moved, touched, excited.

émulsion *f* emulsion.

en *prép* in; to; by; on; **~ tant que** as; *pn* from there; of it, of them; **je n'~ veux plus** I don't want any more of them; **s'~ faire** to worry; **il ~ va de même pour** the same goes for.

encadré *m* box; framed text.

encadrement *m* framing; training; managerial staff.

encadrer *vt* to frame; to train; to surround.

encaissement *m* collection; receipt; cashing.

encaisser *vt* to collect, receive; to cash.

encastrer *vt* to embed, fit in, encase.

enceinte *adj* pregnant.

encens *m* incense.

encenser *vt* (*rel*) to cense; to shower praise on.

encercler *vt* to encircle, surround.

enchaînement *m* linking; link; sequence.

enchaîner *vt* to chain.

enchanté *adj* enchanted, delighted.

enchantement *m* enchantment, delight.

enchanter *vt* to enchant, delight.

enchâsser *vt* to set, imbed.

enchère *f* bid, offer.

enchevêtrement *m* entanglement, confusion.

enclave *f* enclave.

enclencher *vt* to engage; to set in motion.

enclin *adj* inclined, prone.

enclore *vt* to enclose, shut in.

enclume *f* anvil; engine block.

encoder *vt* to encode.

encolure *f* neck; collar size.

encombrant *adj* unwieldy, cumbersome.

encombrement *m* congestion; jumble; obstruction.

encombrer *vt* to clutter, obstruct; **s'~** *vr* to burden oneself.

encore *adv* still; only; again; more; **~ que** even though.

encourageant *adj* encouraging, heartening.

encouragement *m* encouragement.

encourager *vt* to encourage; to incite.

encre *f* ink.

encyclopédie *f* encyclopaedia.

endettement *m* indebtedness; debt.

endetter *vt* to get so into debt; **s'~** *vr* to get into debt.

endive *f* chicory.

endoctrinement *m* indoctrination.

endoctriner *vt* to indoctrinate.

endommager *vt* to damage.

endormir *vt* to put to sleep; **s'~** *vr* to fall asleep.

endossement *m* endorsement.

endosser *vt* to put on; to shoulder; to endorse.

endroit *m* place; side part; **à l'~** regarding.

enduire *vt* to coat, smear.

enduit *m* coating.

endurance *f* endurance, stamina.

endurci *adj* hardened; hard-hearted.

endurcir *vt* to harden; **s'~** *vr* to become hardened.

endurer *vt* to endure, bear.

énergétique *adj* energy; energising.

énergie *f* energy; spirit, vigour.

énergique *adj* energetic, vigorous; **~ment** *adv* energetically.

énervant *adj* enervating; irritating.

énervement *m* irritation; nervousness.

énerver *vt* to irritate, annoy; to get on one's nerves; **s'~** *vr* to get excited, worked up.

enfance *f* childhood; infancy.

enfant *mf* child; native.

enfanter *vt* to give birth to.

enfantillage *m* childishness.

enfantin *adj* childish, infantile.

enfer *m* hell.

enfermer *vt* to lock up; to confine; to box in.

enfiévrer *vt* to stir up, inflame.

enfiler *vt* to string, thread; to put on.

enfin *adv* at last; in short; after all.

enflammer *vt* to set on fire; to inflame, kindle; **s'~** *vr* to catch fire, ignite.

enflé *adj* swollen; bombastic, turgid.

enfler *vi* to swell up, inflate.

enfoncer *vt* to stick in, thrust; to break open; **s'~** *vr* to sink into, disappear into.

enfouir *vt* to bury.

enfuir (s') *vr* to run away, flee.

engagement *m* agreement, commitment, undertaking; engaging; opening.

engager *vt* to bind; to involve; to insert; to open; **s'~** *vr* to undertake to; to take a job.

engelure *f* chilblain.

engendrer *vt* to create, engender; to father.

engin *m* machine; instrument; contraption.

englober *vt* to include, encompass.

engloutir *vt* to wolf down; to engulf.

engorgement *m* obstruction, clogging; glut.

engouement *m* infatuation; fad, craze.

engouffrer *vt* to devour, swallow up, engulf; **s'~** *vr* to rush into, sweep, surge.

engourdi *adj* numb; dull.

engourdir *vt* to numb; to dull, blunt; **s'~** *vr* to become numb, to grow sluggish.

engourdissement *m* numbness; sleepiness.

engrais *m* fertiliser; manure.

engraisser *vi* to get fatter; * *vt* to fatten; to fertilise.

engrenage *m* gears, gearing.

énigmatique *adj* enigmatic; **~ment** *adv* enigmatically.

énigme *f* enigma, riddle.

enivrer *vt* to intoxicate, make drunk; **s'~** *vr* to get drunk.

enjeu *m* stake.

enjoliver *vt* to ornament; to embroider (truth).

enlacer *vt* to embrace, intertwine.

enlaidir *vt* to make ugly; **s'~** *vr* to become ugly.

enlèvement *m* abduction, kidnapping; removal.

enlever *vt* to remove; to take off; to deprive; to abduct.

enliser *vt* to get stuck (car); **s'~** *vr* to get bogged down, get sucked into.

enneigé *adj* snowy, snowbound.

enneigement *m* snow coverage.

ennemi *m* **-e** *f* enemy.

ennui *m* boredom, tedium, weariness.

ennuyer *vt* to bore, bother; **s'~** *vr* to get bored.

ennuyeux *adj* boring, tedious.

énorme *adj* enormous, huge.

énormément *adv* enormously.

énormité *f* enormity, hugeness; howler.

enquête *f* inquiry, investigation; survey.

enquêter *vi* to hold an inquiry; to investigate.

enraciner *vt* to implant, root; **s'~** *vr* to take root; to settle down somewhere.

enragé *adj* furious; keen.

enregistrement *m* recording; registration.

enregistrer *vt* to record; to register.

enrichi *adj* improved, enriched; nouveau riche.

enrichir *vt* to enrich, expand; **s'~** *vr* to get rich.

enrichissant *adj* enriching.

enrichissement *m* enrichment.

enrober *vt* to wrap, cover, coat.

enrôler *vt* to enlist, enrol.

enrouement *m* hoarseness.

enrouer *vt* to make hoarse.

enrouler *vt* to roll up, wind up.

enseignant *m* **-e** *f* teacher.

enseigne *f* sign; (*mil*) ensign.

enseignement *m* education, training, instruction.

enseigner *vt* to teach.

ensemble *adv* together, at the same time; * *m* unity; whole.

ensoleillé *adj* sunny.

ensorceler *vt* to bewitch, enchant.

ensuite *adv* then, next, afterwards.

entaille *f* cut, gash.

entamer *vt* to start, open, make a hole in.

entassement *m* piling up, heaping up.

entasser *vt* to pile up, heap up.

entendement *m* understanding, comprehension.

entendre *vt* to hear; to intend, mean; to understand; **s'~** *vr* to agree; to know how to.

entendu *adj* agreed; **bien ~** of course.

entente *f* harmony, understanding; accord.

enterrement *m* burial; funeral.

enterrer *vt* to bury, inter.

en-tête *m* heading, header.

entêté *adj* stubborn, obstinate.

entêtement *m* stubbornness, obstinacy.

entêter *vt* to go to the head of; **s'~** *vr* to persist in.

enthousiasme *m* enthusiasm.

enthousiasmer *vt* to fill with enthusiasm; **s'~** *vr* to be enthusiastic about.

enthousiaste *adj* enthusiastic; * *mf* enthusiast.

entier *adj* entire, whole; intact.

entièrement *adv* entirely, wholly, completely.

entité *f* entity.

entonnoir *m* funnel; swallow hole; shell-hole.

entorse *f* sprain.

entortiller *vt* to twist, twine; to hoodwink, wheedle.

entourage *m* set, circle; entourage.

entourer *vt* to surround, frame, encircle; **s'~** *vr*: **s'~ de** to surround oneself with.

entracte *m* interval, intermission.

entraide *f* mutual aid.

entraider (s') *vr* to help one another.

entrailles *fpl* entrails, guts; womb.

entrain *m* spirit, liveliness.

entraînement *m* training, coaching; force, impetus.

entraîner *vt* to drag; to lead; to train; **s'~** *vr* to train oneself.

entraîneur *m* trainer, coach.

entrave *f* hindrance, obstacle; shackle.

entraver *vt* to hold up; to shackle.

entre *prép* between, among, into.

entrebâiller *vt* to half-open; **s'~** *vr* to be half-open.

entrecôte *f* rib steak.

entrecouper *vt* to intersperse, interrupt with.

entrée *f* entry, entrance; admission; insertion; **~ en matière** introduction; **d'~ de jeu** from the outset.

entrejambes *m* crotch.

entrelacer *vt* to intertwine, interlace.

entremêler *vt* to intermingle, intermix.

entremets *m* sweet, dessert.

entreposer *vt* to store, put into storage.

entrepôt *m* warehouse, bonded warehouse.

entreprenant *adj* enterprising.

entreprendre *vt* to embark upon, undertake.

entrepreneur *m* **-euse** *f* contractor; entrepreneur.

entreprise *f* company; venture, business.

entrer *vi* to enter, go in.

entresol *m* entresol, mezzanine.

entretemps *adv* meanwhile.

entretenir *vt* to maintain, look after; to speak with.

entretien *m* upkeep, maintenance; conversation.

entrevoir *vt* to make out; to glimpse; to anticipate.

entrevue *f* meeting, interview.

entrouvert *adj* half-open.

entrouvrir *vt* to half-open; **s'~** *vr* to half-open; to gape.

énumération *f* enumeration, listing.

énumérer *vt* to enumerate, list.

envahir *vt* to invade, overrun.

envahissant *adj* invasive; intrusive; pervasive.

enveloppe *f* envelope; covering; exterior.

envelopper *vt* to envelop; to wrap up; to veil.

envergure *f* breadth, scope, scale.

envers *prép* towards, to; ***** *m*; **à l'~** inside out, upside down.

envie *f* desire, longing, inclination; envy.

envier *vt* to envy.

envieux *adj* envious.

environ *adv* about, around; **~s** *mpl* vicinity, neighbourhood.

environnant *adj* surrounding.

environnement *m* environment.

environnemental *adj* environmental.

environner *vt* to surround, encircle.

envisager *vt* to view, envisage.

envoi *m* dispatch, remittance; kick-off.

envol *m* takeoff, flight.

envoler (s') *vr* to fly away; to disappear.

envoûtant *adj* bewitching, entrancing.

envoûter *vt* to bewitch.

envoyé *m* **-e** *f* messenger, envoy.

envoyer *vt* to send, dispatch; hurl, fire.

enzyme *m* enzyme.

épais *adj* thick; deep.

épaisseur *f* thickness; depth.

épaissir *vi* to thicken; to deepen; ***** *vt*; **s'~** *vr* to thicken, get thicker.

épanoui *adj* radiant, beaming.

épanouir *vt* to brighten, light up; open out; **s'~** *vr* to bloom.

épanouissement *m* blooming; lighting up; opening out.

épargne *f* saving, savings.

épargner *vt* to save; to spare.

éparpiller *vt* to scatter, distribute; **s'~** *vr* to scatter.

épaule *f* shoulder.

épauler *vt* to support, back up.

épave *f* wreck; derelict; ruin.

épée *f* sword.

épeler *vt* to spell.

éperdu *adj* distraught, overcome; **~ment** *adv* frantically, desperately.

éperon *m* spur; (*mar*) ram.

épervier *m* sparrowhawk.

éphémère *adj* ephemeral, fleeting.

épi *m* ear; tuft.

épice *m* spice.

épicé *adj* spicy; juicy.

épicerie *f* grocery trade; grocer's shop.

épicier *m* **-ière** *f* grocer; greengrocer.

épidémie *f* epidemic.

épidémique *adj* epidemic; contagious.

épiderme *m* epidermis; skin.

épier *vt* to spy on.

épiglotte *f* epiglottis.

épilation *f* removal of hair.

épilepsie *f* epilepsy.

épileptique *adj* epileptic.

épiler *vt* to remove hair, pluck.

épilogue *m* epilogue; conclusion.

épinard *m* spinach.

épine *f* spine; thorn.

épineux *adj* thorny, prickly; tricky.

épingle *f* pin.

Épiphanie *f* Epiphany.

épique *adj* epic.

épiscopal *adj* episcopal.

épiscopat *m* episcopate.

épisode *m* episode.

épisodique *adj* occasional; transitory; **~ment** *adv* occasionally.

épitaphe *f* epitaph.

épithète *f* epithet.

éplucher *vt* to clean; to peel; to sift.

épluchure *f* peeling, paring.

éponge *f* sponge.

éponger *vt* to sponge, mop.

épopée *f* epic.

époque *f* time, epoch, age, period.

épouser *vt* to marry, wed; espouse.

épousseter *vt* to dust.

épouvantable *adj* terrible, appalling; **~ment** *adv* terribly, appallingly.

épouvantail *m* scarecrow.

épouvante *f* terror, dread.

épouvanter *vt* to terrify, appall.

époux *m* **épouse** *f* spouse.

éprendre *vr*: **s'~ de** to fall in love with.

épreuve *f* test; ordeal, trial; proof.

éprouvant *adj* trying, testing.

éprouver *vt* to feel, experience.

éprouvette *f* test tube.

épuisé *adj* exhausted; sold out.

épuisement *m* exhaustion.

épuiser *vt* to exhaust, wear out; **s'~** *vr* to run out; to exhaust oneself.

épuisette *f* landing net.

épurer *vt* to purify, refine.

équateur *m* equator.

équation *f* equation.

équatorial *adj* equatorial.

équerre *f* square; bracket.

équestre *adj* equestrian.

équilibre *m* balance, equilibrium; harmony.

équilibrer *vt* to balance; **s'~** *vr* to balance each other.

équipage *m* crew; gear, equipment.

équipe *f* team, crew, gang, staff.

équipement *m* equipment; fitting out, fittings.

équiper *vt* to equip, fit out.

équipier *m* **-ière** *f* team member.

équitable *adj* equitable, fair; **~ment** *adv* equitably, fairly.

équitation *f* equitation, riding.

équivalence *f* equivalence.

équivalent *adj* equivalent, same; * *m* equivalent.

équivoque *adj* equivocal, questionable.

érable *m* maple.

érafler *vt* to scratch, scrape.

ère *f* era.

érection *f* erection; establishment.

éreintant *adj* exhausting, backbreaking.

ergot *m* spur; *(tec)* lug.

ériger *vt* to erect; to establish.

ermite *m* hermit.

éroder *vt* to erode.

érosion *f* erosion.

érotique *adj* erotic.

érotisme *m* eroticism.

errant *adj* wandering, stray.

errer *vi* to wander, roam.

erreur *f* error, mistake, fault.

erroné *adj* erroneous.

éructation *f* eructation.

érudit *adj* erudite, learned; * *m* scholar.

érudition *f* erudition, learning.

éruptif *adj* eruptive.

éruption *f* eruption.

escabeau *m* stool; stepladder.

escadron *m* squadron, platoon.

escalade *f* climbing; escalation.

escalader *vt* to climb, scale.

escale *f* port of call, touchdown.

escalier *m* stairs, steps.

escalope *f* escalope.

escamoter *vt* to dodge, evade; to pilfer.

escapade *f* escapade; prank, jaunt.

escargot *m* snail.

escarpement *m* escarpment; steepness.

esclavage *m* slavery, bondage.

esclavagisme *m* proslavery.

esclave *mf* slave.

escompte *m* discount.

escompter *vt* to discount.

escorte *f* escort; retinue.

escorter *vt* to escort.

escrime *f* fencing.

escrimeur *m* **-euse** *f* fencer.

escroc *m* crook, con man.

escroquer *vt* to swindle, con.

ésotérique *adj* esoteric.

espace *m* space, interval.

espacement *m* spacing, interval.

espacer *vt* to space out.

espadon *m* swordfish.

espadrille *f* espadrille, rope-soled sandal.

espèce *f* sort, kind; species.

espérance *f* hope, expectation.

espérer *vt* to hope.

espion *m* **-ne** *f* spy.

espionnage *m* espionage, spying.

espionner *vt* to spy.

esplanade *f* esplanade.

espoir *m* hope.

esprit *m* mind, intellect; spirit; wit.

esquimau *m* **-de** *f* Eskimo.

esquisse *f* sketch, outline.

esquisser *vt* to sketch, outline.

esquiver *vt* to dodge; to shirk.

essai *m* test, trial; attempt; essay.

essaim *m* swarm.

essayage *m* fitting, trying on.

essayer *vt* to test, try, try on.

essence *f* petrol; essential oil.

essentiel *adj* essential, basic; **-lement** *adv* essentially, basically.

essieu *m* axle.

essorage *m* wringing, mangling.

essorer *vt* to wring, mangle.

essouffler *vt* to wind; **s'~** *vr* to get out of breath.

essuyer *vt* to wipe, mop; **s'~** *vr* to wipe oneself.

est *m* east.

esthète *mf* aesthete.

esthéticien *m* **-ne** *f* beautician.

esthétique *adj* aesthetic; **~ment** *adv* aesthetically; * *f* aesthetics.

estimation *f* valuation; estimation, reckoning.

estime *f* esteem, respect, regard.

estimer *vt* to value, assess, estimate.

estival *adj* summer; summery.

estivant *m* **-e** *f* holidaymaker, summer visitor.

estomac *m* stomach.

estomper *vt* to blur, dim; **s'~** *vr* to become blurred.

estrade *f* platform, rostrum.

estragon *m* tarragon.

et *conj* and.

étable *f* cowshed.

établi *adj* established; * *m* workbench.

établir *vt* to establish, set up; **s'~** *vr* to settle; to set oneself up as; to become established.

établissement *m* establishing, building; establishment.

étage *m* floor, storey; stage, level.

étagère *f* shelf.

étalage *m* display, display window; stall.

étalagiste *mf* window dresser.

étaler *vt* to spread, strew; to stagger; to display.

étalon *m* stallion.

étanche *adj* waterproof.

étanchéité *f* waterproofness.

étang *m* pond.

étape *f* stage, leg; staging point.

état *m* state, condition; statement.

étatique *adj* under state control.

étatiser *vt* to bring under state control, nationalise.

état-major *m* *(mil)* staff; staff headquarters.

étau *m* vice.

étayer *vt* to prop up, support.

été *m* summer.

éteindre *vt* to put out, extinguish; **s'~** *vr* to go out; to die; to evaporate.

éteint *adj* faded; extinct.

étendard *m* standard, flag.

étendre *vt* to spread, extend; to floor; **s'~** *vr* to spread; to stretch out; to increase.

étendu *adj* extensive, sprawling, wide.

étendue *f* expanse, area; duration.

éternel *adj* eternal, everlasting; **~lement** *adv* eternally.

éterniser *vt* to draw out; to immortalise; **s'~** *vr* to drag on, linger on.

éternité *f* eternity; ages.

éternuer *vi* to sneeze.

éthane *m* ethane.

éther *m* ether.

ethnie *f* ethnic unit.

ethnique *adj* ethnic.

ethnologie *f* ethnology.

ethnologue *mf* ethnologist.

étincelant *adj* sparkling; gleaming.

étinceler *vi* to sparkle, gleam.

étincelle *f* spark; gleam, glimmer.

étiqueter *vt* to label, mark.

étiquette *f* label, tag; etiquette.

étirement *m* stretching.

étirer *vt* to stretch, draw out; **s'~** *vr* to stretch out.

étoffe *f* material, fabric; stuff.

étoile *f* star.

étoilé *adj* starry.

étonnant *adj* astonishing, surprising.

étonné *adj* astonished, surprised.

étonnement *m* surprise, astonishment.

étonner *vt* to astonish, surprise; **s'~** *vr* to be astonished.

étouffant *adj* stifling.

étouffer *vt* to suffocate; to muffle; **s'~** *vr* to be suffocated, to swelter.

étourderie *f* absentmindedness.

étourdi *adj* absentminded; **~ment** *adv* absentmindedly.

étourdir *vt* to stun, daze; to deafen.

étourdissant *adj* deafening; stunning.

étourdissement *m* blackout, dizzy spell; surprise.

étourneau *m* starling.

étrange *adj* strange, funny; **~ment** *adv* strangely, oddly.

étranger *m* **-ère** *f* foreigner, stranger, alien; * *adj* foreign, strange, unknown.

étrangeté *f* strangeness, oddness.

étranglement *m* strangulation; bottleneck.

étrangler *vt* to strangle, stifle; **s'~** *vr* to strangle oneself, choke.

être *vi* to be; **c'est-à-dire** namely, that is to say; * *m* being, person, soul.

étreindre *vt* to embrace, hug; to seize.

étreinte *f* embrace; stranglehold.

étrier *m* stirrup.

étroit *adj* narrow; strict; **~ement** *adv* closely; strictly.

étude *f* study; survey; office.

étudier *vt* to study, examine.

étui *m* case; holster.

étymologie *f* etymology.

étymologique *adj* etymological.

eu = *p.p.* **avoir** had.

eucalyptus *m* eucalyptus.

eucharistie *f* eucharist.

euphémisme *m* euphemism.

euphorie *f* euphoria.

euphorique *adj* euphoric.

européen *m* **-ne** *f* European; * *adj* European.

euthanasie *f* euthanasia.

eux *pn* they, them; **c'est à ~** it's up to them; it's theirs; **~-mêmes** themselves.

évacuation *f* evacuation; emptying.

évacuer *vt* to evacuate, clear.

évader (s') *vr* to escape.

évaluation *f* evaluation, appraisal.

évaluer *vt* to evaluate, appraise.

évangélique *adj* evangelical.

évangéliser *vt* to evangelise.

évangile *m* gospel.

évanouir (s') *vr* to faint, pass out.

évanouissement *m* faint, blackout.

évaporation *f* evaporation.

évaporer (s') *vr* to evaporate.

évasif *adj* evasive.

évasion *f* escape; escapism.

évasivement *adv* evasively.

évêché *m* bishopric.

éveil *m* awakening; dawning.

éveiller *vt* to waken, arouse; **s'~** *vr* to wake up.

événement *m* event, incident.

éventail *m* fan; range.

éventaire *m* tray; stall.

éventualité *f* eventuality, possibility.

éventuel *adj* possible; **~lement** *adv* possibly.

évêque *m* bishop.

évertuer (s') *vr* to strive to.

évidemment *adv* obviously, evidently.

évidence *f* evidence, proof.

évident *adj* obvious, evident.

évier *m* sink.

évincer *vt* to oust; to evict.

éviter *vt* to avoid; to spare.

évocation *f* evocation, recall.

évolué *adj* developed, advanced; enlightened.

évoluer *vi* to evolve, develop.

évolution *f* evolution, development.

évoquer *vt* to evoke, recall.

exacerber *vt* to exacerbate, aggravate.

exact *adj* exact, accurate; **~ement** *adv* exactly.

exactitude *f* exactness, accuracy.

exagération *f* exaggeration.

exagéré *adj* exaggerated, excessive; **~ment** *adv* exaggeratedly.

exagérer *vt* to exaggerate.

exaltation *f* elation; extolling, praising.

exalter *vt* to exalt, glorify; to elate.

examen *m* examination, survey, investigation.

examinateur *m* **-trice** *f* examiner.

examiner *vt* to examine, survey.

exaspération *f* exasperation.

exaspérer *vt* to exasperate.

exaucer *vt* to fulfil, grant.

excédent *m* surplus, excess.

excédentaire *adj* surplus, excess.

excellent *adj* excellent.

exceller *vi* to excel.

excentricité *f* eccentricity.

excentrique *adj* eccentric; **~ment** *adv* eccentrically.

excepté *adj* apart, aside; * *prép* except, but for.

exception *f* exception.

exceptionnel *adj* exceptional; **~lement** *adv* exceptionally.

excès *m* excess, surplus.

excessivement *adv* excessively.

excitant *m* stimulant; * *adj* exciting, stimulating.

excitation *f* excitation, stimulation; incitement.

exciter *vt* to excite, stimulate; **s'~** *vr* to get excited.

exclamation *f* exclamation.

exclamer (s') *vr* to exclaim.

exclu *adj* excluded, outcast.

exclure *vt* to exclude, oust, expel.

exclusif *adj* exclusive.

exclusion *f* exclusion, suspension.

exclusivement *adv* exclusively.

exclusivité *f* exclusive rights.

excrément *m* excrement.

excroissance *f* (*med*) excrescence, outgrowth.

excursion *f* excursion, trip.

excursionniste *mf* tripper; walker.

excuse *f* excuse, pretext.

excuser *vt* to excuse, forgive; **s'~** *vr* to apologise for.

exécrable *adj* execrable, atrocious; **~ment** *adv* atrociously, execrably.

exécration *f* execration, loathing.

exécrer *vt* to execrate, loathe.

exécuter *vt* to execute, carry out, perform; to produce.

exécution *f* execution, carrying out, performance.

exemplaire *m* copy, archetype; * *adj* model, exemplary; **~ment** *adv* exemplarily.

exemple *m* example, model, instance.

exempt *adj* exempt, free from.

exercer *vt* to exercise, perform, fulfil; **s'~** *vr* to practise.

exercice *m* exercise, practice, use; financial year.

exhaustif *adj* exhaustive.

exhaustivement *adv* exhaustively.

exhiber *vt* to exhibit, show; to produce; **s'~** *vr* to show off; to expose oneself.

exhibition *f* exhibition, show; display.

exhibitionniste *mf* exhibitionist.

exhortation *f* exhortation.

exhorter *vt* to exhort, urge.

exigeant *adj* demanding, exacting.

exigence *f* demand, requirement; exigency.

exiger *vt* to demand, require.

exigu *adj*, *f* **exiguè** scanty, exiguous.

exiguïté *f* exiguity, scantiness.

exil *m* exile.

exilé *m* **-e** *f* exile;* *adj* exiled.

exiler *vt* to exile, banish; **s'~** *vr* to go into exile.

existant *adj* existing.

existence *f* existence, life.

exister *vi* to exist; to be.

exode *m* exodus; drift, loss.

exonération *f* exemption.

exonérer *vt* to exempt.

exorbitant *adj* exorbitant, outrageous.

exorciser *vt* to exorcise.

exotique *adj* exotic.

exotisme *m* exoticism.

expansif *adj* expansive, outgoing.

expansion *f* expansion, development.

expatrié *m* **-e** *f* expatriate; * *adj* expatriate.

expatrier *vt* to expatriate; **s'~** *vr* to expatriate oneself.

expectative *f* expectation, hope; **être dans l'~** to be waiting (to see, to hear).

expédier *vt* to send, dispatch; to dispose of.

expéditeur *m* **-trice** *f* sender; shipper, consignor.

expéditif *adj* quick, expeditious.

expédition *f* dispatch; consignment.

expérience *f* experience; experiment.

expérimental *adj* experimental; **~ement** *adv* experimentally.

expérimentateur *m* **-trice** *f* experimenter.

expérimentation *f* experimentation.

expérimenté *adj* experienced.

expérimenter *vt* to test; to experiment with.

expert *adj* expert, skilled in; * *m* expert; connoisseur; assessor.

expertise *f* expertise; expert appraisal.

expiation *f* expiation, atonement.

expier *vi* to expiate, atone for.

expiration *f* expiry; expiration, exhalation.

expirer *vi* to breathe out, expire.

explicatif *adj* explanatory.

explication *f* explanation, analysis.

explicite *adj* explicit **~ment** *adv* explicitly.

expliquer *vt* to explain, account for; to analyse.

exploitant *m* **-e** *f* farmer, smallholder.

exploitation *f* working; exploitation; operating; concern; smallholding.

exploiter *vt* to work, exploit; run, operate.

explorateur *m* **-trice** *f* explorer.

exploration *f* exploration.

explorer *vt* to explore.

exploser *vi* to explode.

explosif *adj* explosive; * *m* explosive.

explosion *f* explosion.

exportateur *m* **-trice** *f* exporter.

exportation *f* export, exportation.

exporter *vt* to export.

exposé *m* exposition, overview, statement.

exposer *vt* to display; to explain, state; to expose; **s'~** *vr* to expose oneself to, run the risk of.

exposition *f* display; exposition; exposure.

exprès *adj* express.

express *adj* fast; * *m* fast train.

expressif *adj* expressive.

expression *f* expression.

expressionnisme *m* expressionism.

expressionniste *mf* expressionist; * *adj* expressionist, expressionistic.

exprimer *vt* to express, voice; **s'~** *vr* to express oneself.

expropriation *f* expropriation.

expulser *vt* to expel; to evict.

expulsion *f* expulsion; eviction.

exquis *adj* exquisite; **~ément** *adv* exquisitely.

extase *f* ecstasy; rapture.

extasier (s') *vr* to go into ecstasies.

extensible *adj* extensible, extendable.

extension *f* extension; stretching; expansion.

exténuant *adj* exhausting.

exténuer *vt* to exhaust; **s'~** *vr* to exhaust oneself.

extérieur *m* exterior, outside; * *adj* outer, external, exterior; **~ement** *adv* externally, outwardly.

extérioriser *vt* to show, express; to exteriorise.

extermination *f* extermination.

exterminer *vt* exterminate.

externe *adj* external, outer.

extincteur *m* extinguisher.

extinction *f* extinction, extinguishing.

extraction *f* extraction; mining.

extradition *f* extradition.

extraire *vt* to extract; to mine.

extrait *m* extract; (*jur*) abstract.

extraordinaire *adj* extraordinary; **~ment** *adv* extraordinarily.

extraterrestre *mf* extraterrestrial; * *adj* extraterrestrial.

extravagant *adj* extravagant, wild.

extraverti *m* **-e** *f* extrovert; * *adj* extrovert.

extrême *adj* extreme; **~ment** *adv* extremely.

extrémiste *mf*, *adj* extremist.

extrémité *f* end, extremity, limit.

exubérance *f* exuberance.

exubérant *adj* exuberant.

exulter *vi* to exult.

F

fable *f* fable, story, tale.

fabricant *m* **-e** *f* manufacturer, maker.

fabrication *f* manufacture, production.

fabrique *f* factory.

fabriquer *vt* to manufacture; to forge; to fabricate.

fabuleux *adj* fabulous, mythical, legendary.

façade *f* façade, front.

face *f* face, side, surface, aspect; **en ~** opposite, over the road; **~ à** facing; **faire ~ à** to confront, face up to; **de ~** fullface, frontal; **~ à ~** face to face.

face à face *m* encounter, interview.

facette *f* facet.

fâché *adj* angry; sorry.

fâcher *vt* to anger, make angry; to grieve; **se ~** *vr* to get angry.

fâcheux *adj* deplorable, regrettable.

facile *adj* easy; facile; **~ment** *adv* easily.

facilité *f* easiness, ease; ability; facility.

faciliter *vt* to make easier, facilitate.

façon *f* way, fashion; make; imitation; **de toute ~** at any rate; **non merci, sans ~** no thanks, honestly; **de ~ à** so that, so as to.

façonner *vt* to shape, fashion, model; to till.

fac-similé *m* facsimile.

facteur *m* postman.

factice *adj* artificial, imitation.

faction *f* faction; sentry-duty.

facturation *f* invoicing.

facture *f* bill, invoice; construction, technique.

facturer *vt* to invoice, charge for.

facultatif *adj* optional.

faculté *f* faculty; power, ability; right.

fade *adj* insipid, bland, dull.

fagot *m* faggot, bundle of firewood.

faible *adj* weak, feeble; slight, poor; **~ment** *adv* weakly, faintly, feebly.

faiblesse *f* weakness, feebleness, faintness.

faiblir *vi* to fail, flag, weaken; to wane.

faïence *f* earthenware, crockery.

faille *f* fault; flaw; weakness.

faillir *vi*: to come close to; to fail **j'ai failli tomber** I almost fell.

faillite *f* bankruptcy; collapse.

faim *f* hunger; appetite; famine.

fainéant *m* **-e** *f* idler, loafer.

faire *vt* to do; to make; **rien à ~!** nothing doing!; **se ~ à** to get used to; **s'en ~** to worry.

faire-part *m* announcement (birth, marriage, death).

faisable *adj* feasible.

faisan *m* pheasant.

faisceau *m* bundle, stack; beam.

fait *m* event; fact; act.

faîte *m* summit; rooftop.

falaise *f* cliff.

falloir *vi*: to be necessary; **il faut, que tu partes** you must leave.

falsifier *vt* to falsify, alter.

famélique *adj* starving, scrawny.

fameux *adj* famous; excellent.

familial *adj* family, domestic.

familiariser *vt* to familiarise; **se ~** *vr* to familiarise o.s.

familiarité *f* familiarity.

familier *adj* familiar; colloquial; informal.

familièrement *adv* familiarly, informally.

famille *f* family.

famine *f* famine.

fanatique *adj* fanatic; **~ment** *adv* fanatically; * *mf* fanatic; zealot.

fanatisme *m* fanaticism.

fané *adj* faded, withered.

faner *vt* to turn (hay); to fade; **se ~** *vr* to wither, fade.

fanfare *f* fanfare, flourish; brass band.

fantaisie *f* whim, extravagance; imagination.

fantasme *m* fantasy.

fantasmer *vi* to fantasise.

fantastique *adj* fantastic; **~ment** *adv* fantastically; eerily.

fantôme *m* ghost, phantom.

faon *m* fawn.

farce *f* joke, prank; farce.

farceur *m* **-euse** *f* joker; clown.

farci *adj* stuffed, crammed, packed.

farcir *vt* to stuff, cram.

fard *m* make-up.

fardeau *m* load, burden.

farder *vt* to make up; to disguise; **se ~** *vr* to make o.s. up.

farine *f* flour.

farineux *adj* floury, powdery; * *m* starchy food.

farouche *adj* shy, timid; unsociable; fierce; **~ment** *adv* fiercely.

fascicule *m* booklet, fascicule, part, instalment.

fascinant *adj* fascinating.

fascination *f* fascination.

fasciner *vt* to fascinate, bewitch.

fascisme *m* fascism.

fasciste *mf, adj* fascist.

faste *m* pomp, ostentation.

fastidieux *adj* tedious, boring.

fastueux *adj* sumptuous, luxurious.

fatal *adj* fatal, deadly; fateful; **~ement** *adv* inevitably, unavoidably.

fataliste *mf* fatalist; * *adj* fatalistic.

fatalité *f* fatality; inevitability.

fatidique *adj* fateful; fatal.

fatigant *adj* tiring, fatiguing.

fatigue *f* fatigue, tiredness.

fatigué *adj* tired, weary; overworked, strained.

fatiguer *vt* to tire; to overwork, strain; **se ~** *vr* to get tired.

faubourg *m* suburb.

faucher *vt* to reap; to flatten, knock down.

faucille *f* sickle.

faucon *m* falcon, hawk.

faufiler *vt* to tack; to insinuate, introduce; **se ~** *vr* to worm one's way in.

faune *f* wildlife, fauna.

faussaire *mf* forger.

faussement *adv* wrongly; falsely.

fausser *vt* to distort, alter; to warp.

fausseté *f* falseness; deceitfulness.

faute *f* mistake, foul, fault; **~ de mieux** for lack of anything better.

fauteuil *m* armchair.

fautif *m* **-ive** *f* culprit, guilty party; * *adj* at fault, guilty; faulty, incorrect.

fauve *m* wild animal; fawn (colour).

faux *adj* false, forged, fake; wrong; bogus.

faux-filet *m* sirloin.

faux-fuyant *m* evasion, equivocation.

faux-semblant *m* sham, pretence.

faveur *f* favour.

favorable *adj* favourable, sympathetic; **~ment** *adv* favourably.

favori *m* **-te** *f* favourite; * *adj* favourite.

favoriser *vt* to favour, further.

fébrile *adj* feverish, febrile; **~ment** *adv* feverishly.

fébrilité *f* feverishness.

fécond *adj* fertile; prolific, fruitful; creative.

fécondation *f* impregnation, fertilisation.

féconder *vt* to impregnate; to fertilise, pollinate.

fécondité *f* fertility, fecundity.

fécule *f* starch.

féculent *adj* starchy; * *m* starchy food.

fédéral *adj* federal.

fédération *f* federation.

fée *f* fairy.

féerique *adj* magical, fairy.

feindre *vt* to feign, pretend.

feinte *f* dummy, feint.

fêlé *adj* cracked, hare-brained.

félicitation *f* congratulation.

féliciter *vt* to congratulate.

félin *adj* feline; * *m* feline.

femelle *f* female.

féminin *adj* feminine, female.

féminisme *m* feminism.

féministe *mf* feminist; * *adj* feminist.

féminité *f* femininity.

femme *f* woman; wife; **~ de ménage** cleaning woman; **~ de chambre** chambermaid.

fémur *m* femur.

fendiller *vt* to chink, crack, craze; **se ~** *vr* to be covered in small cracks.

fendre *vt* to split, cleave, crack; **se ~** *vr* to crack.

fenêtre *f* window.

fenouil *m* fennel.

fente *f* crack, fissure; slot.

féodal *adj* feudal.

fer *m* iron, point, blade; **~ à cheval** horseshoe.

férié *adj* public holiday.

ferme *adj* firm, steady; definite; **~ment** *adv* firmly; * *f* farm.

fermé *adj* closed; exclusive; inscrutable.

ferment *m* ferment, leaven.

fermentation *f* fermentation, fermenting.

fermenter *vi* to ferment, work.

fermer *vt* to close; block; turn off; **se ~** *vr* to close, shut up; to close one's mind to.

fermeté *f* firmness, steadiness.

fermeture *f* closing, shutting; latch; fastener.

fermier *m* **-ière** *f* farmer.

féroce *adj* ferocious, savage; **~ment** *adv* ferociously, savagely.

férocité *f* ferocity, fierceness.

ferraille *f* scrap iron.

ferronnerie *f* ironworks; ironwork.

ferroviaire *adj* railway.

fertile *adj* fertile, productive.

fertilisation *f* fertilisation.

fertiliser *vt* to fertilise.

fertilité *f* fertility.

fervent *adj* fervent, ardent.

ferveur *f* fervour, ardour.

fesse *f* buttock.

festin *m* feast.

festival *m* festival.

fête *f* feast, holiday.

fêter *vt* to celebrate, fête.

fétichisme *m* fetishism.

fétichiste *mf*; * *adj* fetishist.

fétide *adj* fetid.

feu *m* fire; light; hearth; **en ~** on fire.

feuillage *m* foliage, greenery.

feuille *f* leaf.

feuillet *m* leaf, page, layer.

feuilleté *adj* foliated; laminated.

feuilleter *vt* to leaf through.

feuilleton *m* serial, series.

feutre *m* felt; felt hat.

fève *f* broad bean.

fiabilité *f* accuracy; dependability.

fiable *adj* reliable; dependable.

fiançailles *fpl* engagement, betrothal.

fiancer (se) *vr* to become engaged.

fiasco *m* fiasco.

fibre *f* fibre.

fibreux *adj* fibrous, stringy.

fibrome *m* fibroid, fibroma.

ficeler *vt* to tie up.

ficelle *f* string; stick (bread).

fiche *f* card; sheet; certificate.

ficher *vt* to file, put on file.

fichier *m* catalogue; file.

fictif *adj* fictitious; imaginary.

fiction *f* imagination, fiction.

fidèle *adj* faithful, loyal; **~ment** *adv* faithfully; * *mf* believer.

fidélité *f* fidelity, loyalty.

fief *m* fief; stronghold, preserve.

fier (se) *vr* to trust, rely on.

fier *adj* proud, haughty; noble.

fièrement *adv* proudly.

fierté *f* pride; arrogance.

fièvre *f* fever, temperature; excitement.

fiévreux *adj* feverish.

figer *vt* to congeal, freeze; to clot; **se ~** *vr* to congeal, freeze; to clot.

figue *f* fig.

figuier *m* fig tree.

figurant *m* **-e** *f* extra, walk-on; stooge.

figuratif *adj* figurative, representational.

figure *f* face; figure; illustration, diagram.

figuré *adj* figurative, metaphorical, diagrammatic; * *m*: **au ~** in the figurative sense.

figurer *vt* to represent; * *vi* to appear, feature; **se ~** *vr* to imagine.

figurine *f* figurine.

fil *m* thread; wire; cord; **~ de fer** wire; **~ à plomb** plumb line; **au ~ des jours** with the passing days.

filament *m* filament, strand, thread.

filature *f* spinning; mill; tailing.

file *f* line, queue; **à la ~** in line, in succession; **stationner en double ~** to double-park.

filer *vt* to spin; to tail; to draw out; * *vi* to run, trickle; to fly by; to make off.

filet *m* dribble, trickle; fillet; net.

filiation *f* filiation; relation.

filière *f* path; procedures; network.

fille *f* daughter, girl.

fillette *f* (small) girl.

filleul *m* **-e** *f* godson, godchild.

film *m* film, picture.

filmer *vt* to film.

filon *m* vein, seam.

fils *m* son.

filtre *m* filter.

filtrer *vt* to filter; to screen.

fin *f* end, finish; **prendre ~** to terminate, come to an end; * *adj* thin, fine; delicate; **~ement** *adv* finely, delicately.

final *adj* final; **~ement** *adv* finally.

finale *f* finale.

finance *f* finance.

financement *m* financing.

financer *vt* to finance.

financier *m* **-ière** *f* financier.

financièrement *adv* financially.

finesse *f* fineness; sharpness; neatness; delicacy.

fini *adj* finished, over, complete.

finir *vt* to finish, complete; * *vi* to finish, end; to die.

finition *f* finish, finishing.

fisc *m* tax department.

fiscal *adj* fiscal, tax.

fissure *f* crack, fissure.

fixation *f* fixation; fixing, fastening.

fixe *adj* fixed, permanent, set; **~ment** *adv* fixedly, steadily.

fixer *vt* to fix, fasten; to arrange; **se ~** *vr* to settle.

flacon *m* bottle, flask.

flageolant *adj* shaky.

flageolet *m* flageolet.

flagrant *adj* flagrant, blatant.

flair *m* sense of smell, nose; intuition.

flairer *vt* to smell, sniff; to scent.

flambeau *m* torch; candlestick.

flamboyant *adj* blazing; flamboyant.

flamboyer *vi* to blaze, flash, gleam.

flamme *f* flame; fervour; ardour.

flan *m* custard tart; mould.

flanc *m* flank, side.

flanelle *f* flannel.

flâner *vi* to stroll; to lounge about.

flasque *adj* flaccid; spineless.

flatter *vt* to flatter, gratify; to pander; to delight.

flatterie *f* flattery.

flatteur *m* **-euse** *f* flatterer.

fléau *m* scourge; plague.

flèche *f* arrow.

fléchir *vi* to bend, yield, weaken; * *vt* to bend, sway.

fléchissement *m* bending; flexing; bowing.

flegmatique *adj* phlegmatic.

flegme *m* composure, phlegm.

flétrir *vt* to wither, fade; to stigmatise; **se ~** *vr* to wither, wilt.

fleur *f* flower.

fleuri *adj* in bloom; flowery.

fleurir *vi* to blossom, flower; * *vt* to decorate with flowers.

fleuriste *mf* florist.

fleuve *m* river.

flexibilité *f* flexibility.

flexible *adj* flexible, pliant.

flic *m* (*fam*) cop, policeman.

flocon *m* fleck, flake.

floraison *f* flowering, blossoming.

floral *adj* floral, flower.

flore *f* flora.

florissant *adj* flourishing, blooming.

flot *m* stream, flood; floodtide; wave.

flotte *f* fleet; (*col*) rain.

flottement *m* wavering; vagueness, imprecision.

flotter *vi* to float; to drift; to wander; to waver.

flotteur *m* float.

flou *adj* blurred, hazy.

fluctuant *adj* fluctuating.

fluctuation *f* fluctuation.

fluide *adj* fluid, flowing.

fluidité *f* fluidity.

fluor *m* fluorine.

fluorescent *adj* fluorescent.

fluorure *m* fluoride.

flûte *f* flute; French stick (bread).

flûtiste *mf* flautist.

flux *m* flood; flow; flux.

focaliser *vt* to focus; **se ~** *vr* to be focused on.

foetus *m* foetus.

foi *f* faith, trust.

foie *m* liver.

foin *m* hay.

foire *f* fair, trade fair.

fois *f* time, occasion.

folie *f* madness, insanity; extravagance.

folklore *m* folklore.

folklorique *adj* folk.

follement *adv* madly, wildly.

foncé *adj* dark, deep (colours).

foncer *vi* to hammer along, rush at; * *vt* to make darker; (*tec*) to sink, bore.

foncier *adj* land, landed, property.

foncièrement *adv* fundamentally, basically.

fonction *f* post, duty; function.

fonctionnaire *mf* civil servant.

fonctionnement *m* working, functioning, operation.

fonctionner *vi* to work, function, operate.

fond *m* bottom, back; **au ~** basically, in fact; **à ~** thoroughly, in depth; **dans le ~** in reality, basically; **~ de teint** foundation.

fondamental *adj* fundamental, basic; **~ement** *adv* fundamentally.

fondamentalisme *m* fundamentalism.

fondamentaliste *mf*; * *adj* fundamentalist.

fondant *adj* thawing, melting.

fondateur *m* **-trice** *f* founder.

fondation *f* foundation.

fondement *m* foundation; ground.

fonder *vt* to found; to base.

fondre *vi* to melt; to vanish; to slim; * *vt* to melt; to cast; to merge.

fonds *m* business; fund; money; stock.

fondu *adj* melted; molten; cast.

fontaine *f* fountain, spring.

fonte *f* melting; casting; smelting.

football *m* football, soccer.

forage *m* drilling, boring.

forain *m* **-e** *f* stallholder; fairground entertainer; * *adj* fairground.

force *f* strength, force, violence, energy; **à ~ de** by dint of.

forcé *adj* forced; emergency; **~ment** *adv* inevitably.

forcené *adj* deranged, frenzied.

forcer *vt* to force, compel; track down; * *vi* to overdo, strain; **se ~** *vr* to force o.s. to.

forestier *adj* forest; forestry.

forêt *f* forest.

forfait *m* set price, package; (*sport*) withdrawal.

forfaitaire *adj* fixed, set, inclusive.

forge *f* forge, smithy.

forger *vt* to forge, form, mould.

forgeron *m* blacksmith, smith.

formaliser (se) *vr* to take offence at.

formalité *f* formality.

format *m* format, size.

formation *f* formation; training.

forme *f* form, shape; mould, fitness; **être en ~** to be on form; **en ~ de** forming.

formel *adj* definite, positive; formal; **~lement** *adv* positively, definitely; formally.

former *vt* to form, make up; to train; **se ~** *vr* to form, gather; to train o.s.

formidable *adj* tremendous; fantastic; **~ment** *adv* tremendously, fantastically.

formulaire *m* form.

formule *f* formula; phrase; system.

formuler *vt* to formulate; express.

fort *adj* strong; high; loud; pronounced; **~ement** *adv* strongly; highly; very much; greatly; most; * *adv* loudly; greatly; most; * *m* fort; strong point; (*mus*) forte.

forteresse *f* fortress.

fortifiant *m* tonic; * *adj* fortifying; invigorating.

fortification *f* fortification.

fortifier *vt* to fortify, strengthen; **se ~** *vr* to grow stronger.

fortuit *adj* fortuitous, chance; **~ement** *adv* fortuitously.

fortune *f* fortune, luck.

fortuné *adj* wealthy; fortunate.

fosse *f* pit; grave.

fossé *m* ditch; gulf.

fossette *f* dimple.

fossile *m* fossil.

fou *adj*, *f* **folle** mad, wild; tremendous; erratic.

foudre *f* lightning, thunderbolt.

foudroyant *adj* lightning; thundering; violent.

foudroyer *vt* to strike (lightning).

fouet *m* whip; whisk.

fouetter *vt* to whip, flog.

fougère *f* fern.

fougue *f* ardour, spirit.
fougueux *adj* fiery, ardent.
fouille *f* frisking; excavations.
fouiller *vt* to search, scour.
foulard *m* scarf.
foule *f* crowd; masses, heaps.
four *m* oven; furnace; fiasco.
fourbe *adj* deceitful, two-faced.
fourbu *adj* exhausted.
fourche *f* pitchfork; crotch.
fourchette *f* fork.
fourchu *adj* forked; cloven.
fourgon *m* coach, wagon, van.
fourmi *f* ant.
fourmilière *f* anthill.
fourmillement *m* swarming, milling.
fourmiller *vi* to swarm, teem.
fourneau *m* stove.
fournir *vt* to supply, provide.
fournisseur *m* -euse *f* purveyor, supplier.
fourniture *f* supplying, provision.
fourrage *m* fodder, forage.
fourré *adj* filled; fur-lined; * *m* thicket.
fourrer *vt* to stuff; to line.
fourrière *f* pound (car).
fourrure *f* coat, fur.
foutu *adj* bloody, damned; lousy.
foyer *m* home; fireplace; club; focus.
fracas *m* crash; roar, din.
fraction *f* fraction, part.
fractionnement *m* splitting up, division.
fracture *f* fracture.
fracturer *vt* to fracture, break open.
fragile *adj* fragile, delicate.
fragilité *f* fragility, flimsiness.
fragment *m* fragment.
fragmentation *f* fragmentation; splitting up.
fragmenter *vt* to break up, fragment; **se** ~ *vr* to fragment, break up.
fraîcheur *f* freshness, coolness.
frais *mpl* expenses; * *adj*, *f* **fraîche** fresh, cool.
fraise *f* strawberry.
framboise *f* raspberry.
franc *adj*, *f* **franche** frank, open; clear; absolute.
Français *m* Frenchman, **-e** *f* Frenchwoman.
français *adj* French; * *m* French.
France *f* France.
franchement *adv* frankly, openly; boldly; clearly.
franchir *vt* to clear, get over, cross.
franchise *f* frankness, openness; exemption; franchise.

francophone *mf* French-speaker, *adj* French-speaking.
francophonie *f* French-speaking communities.
frange *f* fringe; threshold.
frappant *adj* striking.
frapper *vt* to hit; to strike down; to infringe; * *vi* to strike, knock.
fraternel *adj* fraternal; ~**lement** *adv* fraternally.
fraterniser *vi* to fraternise.
fraternité *f* fraternity.
fraude *f* fraud, cheating.
frauduleux *adj* fraudulent.
frayeur *f* fright.
frein *m* brake; check.
freinage *m* braking; slowing down.
freiner *vi* to brake, slow down; * *vt* to slow down; to curb, check.
frêle *adj* flimsy, fragile.
frémir *vi* to quiver, tremble.
frémissant *adj* quivering, trembling.
frémissement *m* shudder, quiver.
frénétique *adj* frenetic; ~**ment** *adv* frenetically.
fréquemment *adv* frequently.
fréquence *f* frequency.
fréquent *adj* frequent.
frère *m* brother.
fresque *f* fresco.
friand *adj* partial to, fond of.
friandise *f* delicacy, sweetmeat.
fric *m* (*fam*) cash, lolly.
friction *f* friction.
frigidaire *m* refrigerator.
frigide *adj* frigid.
frileux *adj* susceptible to cold; chilly.
frire *vt* to fry.
frisé *adj* curly, curly-haired.
friser *vi* to curl, be curly; * *vt* to curl; to graze, skim.
frisson *m* shiver, shudder.
frissonnant *adj* shivering, shuddering.
frissonnement *m* shuddering, shivering.
frissonner *vi* to shudder, tremble, shiver.
frite *f* chip.
friteuse *f* chip pan.
friture *f* frying; frying fat.
frivole *adj* frivolous, shallow.
frivolité *f* frivolity.
froid *adj* cold, cool; ~**ement** *adv* coldly, coolly; * *m* cold; coolness; refrigeration.
froideur *f* coldness, chilliness.
froissement *m* creasing; rustling, rustle.

froisser *vt* to crease; to offend; **se** ~ *vr* to crease; to take offence.
frôler *vt* to brush against; to verge on.
fromage *m* cheese.
front *m* forehead; face; front.
frontal *adj* frontal.
frontalier *adj* border, frontier.
frontière *f* border, frontier.
frottement *m* rubbing, scraping.
frotter *vt* to rub, scrape.
fructifier *vi* to bear fruit.
fructueux *adj* fruitful, profitable.
frugal *adj* frugal; ~**ement** *adv* frugally.
frugalité *f* frugality.
fruit *m* fruit, result.
fruité *adj* fruity.
frustration *f* frustration.
frustrer *vt* to frustrate, deprive.
fugace *adj* fleeting, transient.
fugitif *m* **-ive** *f* fugitive; * *adj* fugitive, runaway.
fugue *f* running away.
fuir *vi* to avoid; to flee; to leak.
fuite *f* flight, escape; leak.
fulgurant *adj* lightning; dazzling.
fumant *adj* smoking, fuming.
fumé *adj* smoked.
fumée *f* smoke; vapour.
fumer *vi* to smoke, steam, give off smoke; * *vt* to smoke.
fumet *m* aroma.
fumeur *m* **-euse** *f* smoker.
fumier *m* dung, manure.
funèbre *adj* funeral; funerary.
funérailles *fpl* funeral.
funéraire *adj* funeral, funerary.
funeste *adj* disastrous; harmful.
fureur *f* fury; violence.
furie *f* fury, rage.
furieusement *adv* furiously.
furieux *adj* furious, violent.
furtif *adj* furtive; stealthy.
furtivement *adv* furtively.
fusée *f* rocket, missile.
fusible *m* fuse.
fusil *m* rifle, gun.
fusillade *f* fusillade; gunfire; shoot-out.
fusiller *vt* to shoot.
fusion *f* fusion; melting; merger; blending.
fusionner *vt* to merge, combine.
fût *m* trunk; shaft; barrel.
futé *adj* crafty, cunning.
futile *adj* futile; ~**ment** *adv* futilely.
futilité *f* futility.
futur *adj* future; * *m* intended, fiancé; future.
fuyant *adj* fleeting; evasive.
fuyard *m* **-e** *f*; * *adj* runaway.

G

gabarit *m* size, build; calibre.
gâcher *vt* to mix; to waste.
gachette *f* trigger.
gâchis *m* mess.
gadget *m* gadget; gimmick.
gaffe *f* blunder; boat hook.
gage *m* security; pledge; proof.
gagnant *m* **-e** *f* winner; * *adj* winning.
gagner *vt* to earn, to win, beat; to gain; * *vi* to win; to spread.
gai *adj* cheerful, happy, gay; **~ement** *adv* cheerfully, happily.
gaieté *f* cheerfulness, gaiety.
gain *m* earnings; gain, profit, benefit; saving.
gaine *f* girdle; sheath.
gala *m* official reception; gala.
galamment *adv* courteously, gallantly.
galant *adj* gallant, courteous.
galanterie *f* gallantry.
galaxie *f* galaxy.
galère *f* galley.
galerie *f* gallery; tunnel.
galet *m* pebble.
galette *f* pancake.
Gallois *m* Welshman, **-e** *f* Welshwoman.
gallois *adj* Welsh; * *m* Welsh (language).
galon *m* braid; stripe.
galop *m* gallop; canter.
galoper *vi* to gallop; to run wild.
galvaniser *vt* to galvanise.
gamba *f* large prawn.
gamin *m* **-e** *f* kid, street urchin.
gaminerie *f* playfulness; childishness.
gamme *f* range; scale.
ganglion *m* ganglion.
gangrène *f* gangrene.
gant *m* glove.
garage *m* garage.
garagiste *mf* garage owner.
garant *m* **-e** *f* (*jur*) guarantor.
garantie *f* guarantee, surety.
garantir *vt* to guarantee, secure.
garçon *m* boy; assistant; waiter.
garde *f* custody; guard; surveillance; * *m* guard, warder.
garde-à-vous *m* standing to attention.
garde-boue *m* mudguard.
garde-chasse *m* gamekeeper.
garde-fou *m* railing, parapet; safeguard.

garder *vt* to look after; to stay in; to keep on.
garderie *f* day nursery.
garde-robe *f* wardrobe.
gardien *m* **-ne** *f* guard, guardian, warden; protector.
gare *f* rail station; (*mar*) basin; depot.
garer *vt* to park; to dock; **se ~** *vr* to avoid, steer clear of.
gargariser (se) *vr* to gargle; to crow about.
gargarisme *m* gargle.
gargouillement *m* gurgling; rumbling.
gargouiller *vi* to gurgle; to rumble.
garnir *vt* to fit with; to trim, decorate.
garnison *f* (*mil*) garrison.
garniture *f* trimming, lining; garnish.
garrot *m* garrotte; (*med*) tourniquet.
gars *m* (*fam*) lad; bloke.
gaspillage *m* waste; squandering.
gaspiller *vt* to waste, squander.
gastrique *adj* gastric.
gastronome *m* gourmet, gastronome.
gastronomie *f* gastronomy.
gâté *adj* ruined; spoiled.
gâteau *m* cake.
gâter *vt* to ruin; to spoil; **se ~** *vr* to go bad, go off.
gâteux *adj* senile; (*fam*) doddering.
gauche *adj* left; awkward, clumsy; **~ment** *adv* awkwardly; * *f* left; left wing.
gaucher *adj* left-handed.
gauchisant *m* **-e** *f* leftist; * *adj* of leftist tendencies.
gauchiste *mf*; * *adj* leftist.
gaufre *f* waffle.
gaver *vt* to force-feed, fill up; **se ~** *vr* to stuff o.s.; to devour.
gaz *m* invar gas; fizz; wind.
gaze *f* gauze.
gazelle *f* gazelle.
gazeux *adj* gaseous; fizzy.
gazon *m* lawn; turf.
gazouiller *vi* to chirp, warble.
géant *m* giant, **-e** *f* giantess.
geindre *vi* to groan; to whine.
gel *m* frost; gel.
gélatine *f* gelatine.
gelé *adj* frozen; cold, unresponsive.
gelée *f* frost; jelly.

geler *vi* to freeze, be frozen; * *vt* to freeze, turn to ice; to suspend.
gélule *f* capsule.
Gémeaux *mpl* Gemini.
gémir *vi* to groan, moan.
gémissement *m* groan, moan; groaning.
gênant *adj* annoying; awkward.
gencive *f* gum.
gendarme *m* policeman; gendarme.
gendarmerie *f* police force, constabulary.
gendre *m* son-in-law.
gêne *f* discomfort; trouble; embarrassment; **être sans ~** to be inconsiderate.
généalogie *f* genealogy.
généalogique *adj* genealogical.
gêner *vt* to bother; to hinder; to make uneasy; **se ~** *vr* to get in each other's way.
général *adj* general, broad; common; **~ement** *adv* generally; * *m* general, **-e** *f* general's wife; (*thea*) dress rehearsal.
généralisation *f* generalisation.
généraliser *vt* to generalise; **se ~** *vr* to become widespread.
généraliste *m* general practitioner; * *adj* general-interest; non-specialised.
généralité *f* majority; general points.
générateur *m* generator.
génération *f* generation.
générer *vt* to generate
généreusement *adv* generously; nobly.
généreux *adj*, *f* **-euse** generous; noble; magnanimous.
générosité *f* generosity; nobility; magnanimity.
génétique *adj* genetic; **~ment** *adv* genetically.
génial *adj* inspired, of genius.
génie *m* genius; spirit; genie.
génital *adj* genital.
génocide *m* genocide.
genou *m* knee.
genre *m* kind, type; gender; genre.
gens *mpl* people, folk.
gentil *adj*, *f* **-le** kind; good; pleasant.
gentillesse *f* kindness; favour.
gentiment *adv* kindly; nicely.
géographe *mf* geographer.

géographie *f* geography.
géographique *adj* geographic.
géologie *f* geology.
géologue *mf* geologist.
géomètre *m* land surveyor.
géométrie *f* geometry.
géométrique *adj* geometric; **~ment** *adv* geometrically.
géranium *m* geranium.
gérant *m* **-e** *f* manager.
gerbe *f* sheaf, bundle; collection.
gercer *vt* to chap, crack; **se ~** *vr* to chap, crack.
gerçure *f* (small) crack.
gérer *vt* to manage, administer.
germe *m* germ; seed.
germer *vi* to sprout, germinate.
gérondif *m* gerundive; gerund.
gésier *m* gizzard.
gestation *f* gestation.
geste *m* gesture; act, deed.
gesticuler *vi* to gesticulate.
gestion *f* management, administration.
gestionnaire *adj* administrative, management.
ghetto *m* ghetto.
gibier *m* game; prey.
gicler *vi* to spurt, squirt.
gicleur *m* jet.
gifle *f* slap, smack.
gifler *vt* to slap, smack.
gigantesque *adj* gigantic, immense.
gigot *m* leg (mutton/lamb), haunch.
gilet *m* waistcoat.
gingembre *m* ginger.
girafe *f* giraffe.
giratoire *adj* gyrating, gyratory.
girouette *f* weather vane.
gisement *m* deposit; mine; pool.
gitan *m* **-e** *f* gipsy.
gîte *m* shelter; home.
givre *m* frost, rime.
givré *adj* covered in frost.
glace *f* ice; ice cream; mirror.
glacé *adj* icy; frozen; glazed; chilly.
glacer *vt* to freeze; to chill; to glaze.
glacial *adj* icy; freezing.
glacier *m* glacier; ice cream maker.
glacière *f* icebox.
glaçon *m* icicle; ice cube.
glaïeul *m* gladiola.
glaise *f* clay.
gland *m* acorn.
glande *f* gland.
glaner *vt* to glean.
glauque *adj* murky; shabby, run-down.
glissade *f* slide, skid.
glissant *adj* slippery.

glissement *m* sliding; gliding; downturn, downswing.
glisser *vi* to slide, slip, skid.
glissière *f* slide; runner.
global *adj* global, overall; **~ement** *adv* globally.
globe *m* globe, sphere; earth.
globulaire *adj* global; (*med*) corpuscular.
globule *m* globule; corpuscle.
globuleux *adj* globular; protruding.
gloire *f* glory; distinction; celebrity.
glorieux *adj* glorious.
glorifier *vt* to glory, honour; **se ~** *vr* to glory in; to boast.
glossaire *m* glossary.
glouton *m* **-ne** *f* glutton; * *adj* gluttonous, ravenous; **~nement** *adv* gluttonously.
gluant *adj* sticky, slimy.
glucide *m* glucide.
glucose *m* glucose.
glycérine *f* glycerine.
gobelet *m* beaker, tumbler.
gober *vt* to swallow; to fall for.
goéland *m* gull.
goinfre *m* pig; * *adj* piggish.
golf *m* golf.
golfeur *m* **-euse** *f* golfer.
gomme *f* gum; rubber, eraser.
gommer *vt* to rub out; to gum.
gond *m* hinge.
gondole *f* gondola.
gondoler *vi* to crinkle, warp, buckle; **se ~** *vr* to crinkle; to split one's sides laughing.
gonflable *adj* inflatable.
gonflement *m* inflation, swelling.
gonfler *vt* to pump up, inflate; **se ~** *vr* to swell; to be puffed up.
gong *m* gong; bell.
gorge *f* throat.
gorgée *f* sip, gulp.
gorille *m* gorilla.
gosier *m* throat, gullet.
gosse *mf* (*fam*) kid.
gothique *m, adj* Gothic.
goudron *m* tar.
goudronner *vt* to tar.
gouffre *m* gulf, chasm, abyss.
goulu *adj* greedy, gluttonous.
goulûment *adv* greedily, gluttonously.
goupille *f* pin.
gourd *adj* numb (with cold).
gourde *f* gourd; flask.
gourdin *m* club, cudgel.
gourmand *adj* greedy.
gourmandise *f* greed, greediness.
gourmet *m* gourmet.
gourmette *f* chain bracelet.

gousse *f* pod.
goût *m* taste; liking; style.
goûter *vt* to taste; to appreciate; * *vi* to have a snack; to taste good; * *m* snack.
goutte *f* drop; dram; gout.
gouttière *f* gutter; drainpipe.
gouvernail *m* rudder; helm.
gouvernement *m* government.
gouvernemental *adj* government, governmental.
gouverner *vt* to govern, rule; to control; to steer.
gouverneur *m* governor.
goyave *f* guava.
grâce *f* grace; favour; mercy; pardon; **~ à** thanks to.
gracier *vt* to pardon.
gracieusement *adv* gracefully; kindly.
gracieux *adj* gracious.
grade *m* rank; grade; degree.
gradé *m* officer; * *adj* promoted.
gradin *m* tier; step; terrace.
graduel *adj* gradual; progressive; **~lement** *adv* gradually.
graduer *vt* to step up; to graduate.
graffiti *mpl* graffiti.
grain *m* grain, seed; bead.
graine *f* seed.
graissage *m* greasing, lubricating.
graisse *f* grease, fat.
graisser *vt* to grease, lubricate.
grammaire *f* grammar.
grammairien *m* **-ne** *f* grammarian.
grammatical *adj* grammatical; **~ement** *adv* grammatically.
gramme *m* gram.
grand *adj* big; tall; great; leading; **pas ~-chose** not a lot, not up to much; **~ement** *adv* greatly; a great deal; nobly.
grandeur *f* size; greatness; magnitude.
grandiose *adj* imposing, grandiose.
grandir *vi* to grow bigger, increase; * *vt* to magnify; exaggerate.
grand-mère *f* grandmother.
grand-père *m* grandfather.
grand-parents *mpl* grandparents.
granit(e) *m* granite.
granulé *m* granule; * *adj* granular.
granuleux *adj* granular; grainy.
graphique *m* graph; * *adj* graphic; **~ment** *adv* graphically.
graphite *m* graphite.
grappe *f* cluster, bunch.
gras *adj, f* **-se** fatty; fat; greasy; crude.
gratification *f* gratuity; bonus.

gratin *m* cheese dish, gratin.

gratis *adv* free, gratis.

gratitude *f* gratitude, gratefulness.

gratter *vt* to scratch, scrape.

gratuit *adj* free, gratuitous; disinterested; **~ement** *adv* free; gratuitously.

grave *adj* grave, solemn; **~ment** *adv* gravely, solemnly.

graver *vt* to engrave, imprint.

graveur *m* engraver, woodcutter.

gravier *m* gravel.

gravir *vt* to climb.

gravitation *f* gravitation.

gravité *f* gravity.

gravure *f* engraving, carving.

gré *m*: liking, taste; **au ~ de** depending on, at the mercy of; **bon ~ mal ~** like it or not, willy-nilly; **savoir ~** to be grateful.

greffe *f* transplant, graft.

greffer *vt* to transplant, graft.

grégaire *adj* gregarious.

grêle *f* hail.

grêlon *m* hailstone.

grelotter *vi* to shiver.

grenade *f* pomegranate; grenade.

grenat *m* garnet.

grenier *m* attic, garret.

grenouille *f* frog.

grès *m* sandstone; stoneware.

grésiller *vi* to sizzle; splutter.

grève *f* strike; shore.

gribouillage *m* scrawl, scribble.

gribouiller *vi* to doodle; * *vt* to scribble, scrawl.

grièvement *adv* seriously.

griffe *f* claw.

griffer *vt* to scratch.

griffonner *vt* to scribble, jot down.

grignoter *vi* to nibble at, pick at; * *vt* to nibble at; to eat away.

gril *m* grill pan; rack.

grillade *f* grilled meat.

grillage *m* toasting; grilling.

grille *f* railings; gate; grill.

grille-pain *m invar* toaster.

griller *vt* to toast, scorch; to put bars on; * *vi* to toast, grill.

grillon *m* cricket.

grimace *f* grimace; funny face.

grimper *vi* to climb up.

grincement *m* grating, creaking.

grincer *vi* to grate, creak.

grincheux *adj* grumpy.

griotte *f* Morello cherry; marble.

grippe *f* flu, influenza.

grippé *adj* suffering from flu.

gris *adj* grey.

grisant *adj* exhilarating; intoxicating.

griser *vt* to intoxicate; **se ~** *vr* to get drunk.

grisonnant *adj* greying.

grive *f* thrush.

grog *m* grog.

grognement *m* grunt, grunting.

grogner *vi* to grumble, moan.

grognon *m* grumbler, moaner, *adj* grumpy, surly.

grommeler *vi* to mutter; to grumble; * *vt* to mutter.

grondement *m* rumbling, growling.

gronder *vt* to scold; * *vi* to rumble, growl.

gros *adj*, *f* **-se** big; fat; thick; serious; heavy; coarse; **en ~** in bulk; * *m* bulk; wholesale; fat man.

groseille *f* currant.

grossesse *f* pregnancy.

grosseur *f* thickness; lump; fatness.

grossier *adj* coarse; unrefined; base.

grossièrement *adv* roughly; coarsely.

grossièreté *f* rudeness; coarseness.

grossir *vi* to get fatter; to swell, grow; * *vt* to magnify; to exaggerate.

grossiste *mf* wholesaler.

grotesque *adj* grotesque, ludicrous; **~ment** *adv* grotesquely.

grotte *f* cave; grotto.

grouiller *vi* to mill about; to swarm; **se ~** *vr* (*fam*) to get a move on.

groupe *m* group; party; cluster.

groupement *m* grouping; group.

grouper *vt* to group together; to bulk; **se ~** *vr* to gather.

grue *f* crane.

grumeau *m* lump.

gruyère *m* gruyère (cheese).

guenon *f* female monkey; hag.

guépard *m* cheetah.

guêpe *f* wasp.

guêpier *m* trap; wasp's nest.

guère *adv* hardly, scarcely.

guéri *adj* cured.

guéridon *m* pedestal table.

guérir *vi* to get better; to heal; * *vt* to cure, heal; **se ~** *vr* to get better; to recover from.

guérison *f* recovery; curing.

guérisseur *m* **-euse** *f* healer.

guerre *f* war; warfare.

guerrier *m* **-ière** *f* warrior.

guet *m* watch; **faire le ~** to be on the watch.

guetter *vt* to watch; to lie in wait for.

gueule *f* (*fam*) mouth; face; muzzle.

gueuler *vi* (*fam*) to bawl; bellow.

guichet *m* counter; ticket office, booking office.

guichetier *m* **-ière** *f* counter clerk.

guidage *m* guides; guidance.

guide *m* guide.

guider *vt* to guide; **se ~** *vr* to be guided by.

guidon *m* handlebars.

guignol *m* puppet; puppet show.

guillemet *m* inverted comma; quotation mark.

guillotine *f* guillotine.

guimauve *f* marshmallow.

guindé *adj* stiff, uptight.

guirlande *f* garland.

guise *f* manner, way; **en ~ de** by way of; **à ta ~** as you please.

guitare *f* guitar.

guitariste *mf* guitarist.

guttural *adj* guttural

gymnase *m* gymnasium.

gymnastique *f* gymnastics.

gynécologie *f* gynaecology.

gynécologue, gynécologiste *mf* gynaecologist.

gyrophare *m* revolving light.

H

habile *adj* skilful, skilled; clever; ~**ment** *adv* skilfully.

habileté *f* skill, skilfulness; clever move.

habiliter *vt* to qualify; to authorise.

habillement *m* clothing, dress, outfit.

habiller *vt* to dress, clothe; **s'~** *vr* to get dressed.

habit *m* clothes; apparel; dress-coat; outfit

habitable *adj* inhabitable.

habitant *m* -**e** *f* inhabitant; occupant; dweller.

habitat *m* habitat; housing conditions.

habitation *f* dwelling; residence; house.

habité *adj* manned.

habiter *vi* to live; * *vt* to live in; occupy.

habitude *f* habit, custom, routine.

habituel *adj* usual, customary; ~**lement** *adv* usually, generally.

habituer *vt* to accustom; to teach; **s'~** *vr* to get used to.

hache *f* axe, hatchet.

hacher *vt* to chop, mince.

hachoir *m* chopper, cleaver.

hachure *f* hatching.

hagard *adj* wild; haggard; distraught.

haie *f* hedge.

haine *f* hatred.

haineux *adj* full of hatred; malevolent.

haïr *vt* to hate, detest.

hâle *m* tan, sunburn.

hâlé *adj* tanned, sunburnt.

haleine *f* breath, breathing.

haletant *adj* panting, gasping.

haleter *vi* to pant, gasp for breath.

hall *m* hall, foyer.

halle *f* covered market; hall.

hallucination *f* hallucination.

halo *m* halo.

halte *f* stop, break; stopping place.

haltère *f* dumbbell.

hamac *m* hammock.

hameçon *m* fish-hook.

hamster *m* hamster.

hanche *f* hip; haunch.

handball *m* handball.

handballeur *m* -**euse** *f* handball player.

handicap *m* handicap.

handicaper *vt* to handicap

hangar *m* shed, barn; hangar.

hanneton *m* maybug.

hanter *vt* to haunt.

happer *vt* to snap up, snatch.

harassant *adj* exhausting, wearing.

harcèlement *m* harassment; pestering.

harceler *vt* to harass; to pester; to plague.

hardi *adj* bold, daring; brazen; ~**ment** *adv* boldly, daringly; brazenly.

hareng *m* herring.

hargne *f* spite.

hargneux *adj* aggressive, belligerent.

haricot *m* bean.

harmonica *m* harmonica.

harmonie *f* harmony; wind section.

harmonieusement *adv* harmoniously.

harmonieux *adj* harmonious; well-matched.

harmoniser *vt* to harmonise; **s'~** *vr* to be in harmony.

harnacher *m* to harness.

harnais *m* harness; equipment.

harpe *f* harp.

harpiste *mf* harpist.

harpon *m* harpoon.

hasard *m* chance; accident; hazard; risk.

hasardeux *adj* hazardous, risky.

hâte *f* haste; impatience.

hâter *vt* to hasten; to quicken; **se ~** *vr* to hurry.

hâtif *adj* precocious; early; hasty.

hâtivement *adv* hastily.

hausse *f* rise, increase.

hausser *vt* to raise; to heighten.

haut *adj* high, tall; upper; superior; ~**ement** *adv* highly.

hautain *adj* haughty, lofty.

hautbois *m* oboe.

hauteur *f* height; elevation; haughtiness; bearing.

haut-parleur *m* loudspeaker.

hebdomadaire *adj*; * *m* weekly.

hébergement *m* accommodation; lodging.

héberger *vt* to accommodate, lodge.

hectare *m* hectare.

hectogramme *m* hectogram.

hectolitre *m* hectolitre.

hectomètre *m* hectometre.

hélice *f* propeller; helix.

hélicoptère *m* helicopter.

hélium *m* helium.

hématome *m* severe bruise, haematoma.

hémicycle *m* semicircle, hemicycle; amphitheatre.

hémiplégique *mf* person paralysed on one side, hemiplegic; * *adj* hemiplegic.

hémisphère *m* hemisphere.

hémoglobine *f* haemoglobin.

hémophile *adj* haemophiliac.

hémophilie *f* haemophilia.

hémorragie *f* bleeding, haemorrhage.

hémorroïde *f* haemorrhoid, pile.

henné *m* henna.

hépatique *adj* hepatic.

hépatite *f* hepatitis.

herbe *f* grass; **en ~** in the blade.

herbivore *m* herbivore; *adj* herbivorous.

herboriste *mf* herbalist.

héréditaire *adj* hereditary.

hérédité *f* heredity; heritage; right of inheritance.

hérésie *f* heresy.

hérétique *adj* heretical.

hérissé *adj* bristling; spiked.

hérisser *vt* to bristle; to spike; * **se ~** *vr* to stand on end; to bristle.

hérisson *m* hedgehog.

héritage *m* inheritance; heritage, legacy.

hériter *vi* to inherit.

héritier *m* heir -**ière** *f* heiress.

hermaphrodite *m* hermaphrodite; * *adj* hermaphrodite.

hermétique *adj* airtight, watertight, hermetic; ~**ment** *adv* hermetically.

hermine *f* ermine; stoat.

hernie *f* hernia, rupture.

héroïne *f* heroine; heroin.

héroïque *adj* heroic; ~**ment** *adv* heroically.

héroïsme *m* heroism.

héron *m* heron.

héros *m* hero.

herpès *m* herpes; cold sore.

hésitant *adj* hesitant.
hésitation *f* hesitation.
hésiter *vi* to hesitate.
hétéroclite *adj* heterogeneous; sundry; eccentric.
hétérogène *adj* heterogeneous.
hétérosexuel *adj* heterosexual.
hêtre *m* beech.
heure *f* hour; time of day; **de bonne ~** early; **tout à l'~** a short time ago, just now.
heureusement *adv* luckily; happily.
heureux *adj* lucky; happy.
heurter *vt* to strike, hit; to jostle.
hexagone *m* hexagon.
hibernation *f* hibernation.
hibou *m* owl.
hideux *adj* hideous.
hier *adv* yesterday.
hiérarchie *f* hierarchy.
hiérarchique *adj* hierarchical; **~ment** *adv* hierarchically
hilarant *adj* hilarious, side-splitting.
hilarité *f* hilarity, laughter.
hindouisme *m* Hinduism.
hippisme *m* riding, equestrianism.
hippocampe *m* sea horse.
hippodrome *m* racecourse.
hippopotame *m* hippopotamus.
hirondelle *f* swallow.
hirsute *adj* dishevelled, tousled.
hisser *vt* to hoist, haul up.
histoire *f* history; story; business; **~ de dire** just to say.
historien *m* **-ne** *f* historian.
historique *adj* historic; historical; **~ment** *adv* historically.
hiver *m* winter.
hivernal *adj* winter; wintry.
HLM (habitation à loyer modéré) *f/m* public sector housing.
hocher *vt* to nod; to shake one's head.
hochet *m* rattle; toy.
holocauste *m* holocaust.
homard *m* lobster.
homéopathe *mf* homeopath.
homéopathie *f* homeopathy.
homicide *m* homicide.
hommage *m* homage, tribute; **rendre ~ à** to pay homage to.
homme *m* man.
homme-grenouille *m* frogman.
homogène *adj* homogeneous.
homogénéiser *vt* to homogenise.
homogénéité *f* homogeneity.
homologue *adj* homologous; equivalent.
homologuer *vt* to ratify; to approve.

homonyme *m* homonym; * *adj* homonymous.
homosexualité *f* homosexuality.
homosexuel *m* **-le** *f* homosexual.
honnête *adj* honest; decent; honourable; **~ment** *adv* honestly, decently.
honnêteté *f* honesty, decency.
honneur *m* honour; integrity; credit; **en l'~ de** in honour of.
honorable *adj* honourable; reputable; **~ment** *adv* honourably.
honoraire *adj* honorary.
honoraires *mpl* fees.
honorer *vt* to honour; to esteem; to do credit to; **s'~** *vr*: **s'~ de** to pride oneself on.
honte *f* shame, disgrace.
honteusement *adv* shamefully; disgracefully.
honteux *adj* shameful; disgraceful.
hôpital *m* hospital.
hoquet *m* hiccough, hiccup.
horaire *m* timetable; * *adj* hourly.
horizon *m* horizon.
horizontal *adj* horizontal; **~ement** *adv* horizontally.
horloge *f* clock.
horloger *m* **-ère** *f* watchmaker, clockmaker.
hormone *f* hormone.
horoscope *m* horoscope.
horreur *f* horror.
horrible *adj* horrible; dreadful; **~ment** *adv* horribly
horrifier *vt* to horrify.
hors *prép* outside; beyond; save; except; **~ série** incomparable, outstanding; special issue.
hors-bord *m invar* speedboat.
hors-d'œuvre *m invar* hors d'œuvre, starter.
hors-jeu *m invar* offside.
hors-piste *m invar* off-piste.
hortensia *m* hydrangea.
horticulteur *m* horticulturist.
horticulture *f* horticulture.
hospice *m* home, asylum; hospice.
hospitalier *adj* hospital; hospitable.
hospitalisation *f* hospitalisation.
hospitaliser *vt* to hospitalise.
hospitalité *f* hospitality.
hostie *f* host.
hostile *adj* hostile; **~ment** *adv* hostilely.
hostilité *f* hostility.
hôte *m* **hôtesse** *f* host; landlord.
hôtel *m* hotel.
hôtelier *m* **-ière** *f* hotelier; * *adj* hotel.

hôtellerie *f* inn; hotel business.
hotte *f* basket.
houblon *m* hop.
houille *f* coal.
houle *f* swell.
houleux *adj* stormy; turbulent.
houppe *f* tuft; tassel.
housse *f* cover, dust-sheet.
houx *m* holly.
hublot *m* porthole.
huer *vt* to boo.
huile *f* oil; petroleum.
huissier *m* bailiff; usher.
huit *adj, m* eight.
huitaine *f* eight or so.
huitième *adj* eighth; **~ment** *adv* eighthly; * *mf* eighth.
huître *f* oyster.
humain *adj* human; humane; **~ement** *adv* humanly; humanely; * *m* human.
humanisme *m* humanism.
humaniste *m* humanist; * *adj* humanist.
humanitaire *adj* humanitarian.
humanité *f* humanity.
humble *adj* humble; modest; **~ment** *adv* humbly.
humecter *vt* to dampen, moisten.
humeur *f* mood, humour; temper.
humide *adj* humid.
humidité *f* humidity.
humiliant *adj* humiliating.
humiliation *f* humiliation.
humilier *vt* to humiliate.
humilité *f* humility.
humoristique *adj* humorous.
humour *m* humour.
hurlement *m* roar, yell; howl.
hurler *vi*; * *vt* to roar, yell.
hutte *f* hut.
hybride *adj* hybrid; * *m* hybrid.
hydratant *adj* moisturising.
hydratation *f* hydration; moisturising.
hydrater *vt* to hydrate; to moisturise.
hydraulique *adj* hydraulic.
hydravion *m* seaplane.
hydrocarbure *m* hydrocarbon.
hydrogène *m* hydrogen.
hydrolyse *f* hydrolysis.
hydrophile *adj* absorbent.
hydroxyde *m* hydroxide.
hyène *f* hyena.
hygiène *f* hygienics; hygiene.
hygiénique *adj* hygienic; **~ment** *adv* hygienically.
hymne *m* hymn.
hyperbole *f* hyperbole; hyperbola.

hypermarché *m* hypermarket.
hypermétrope *adj* long-sighted;
* *mf* long-sighted person.
hypertension *f* hypertension.
hypertrophié *adj* (*med*) enlarged;
overdeveloped.
hypnose *f* hypnosis
hypnotique *adj* hypnotic.
hypnotiser *vt* to hypnotise.

hypocondriaque *mf* hypochondriac; * *adj* hypochondriac.
hypocrisie *f* hypocrisy.
hypocrite *mf* hypocrite; * *adj* hypocritical; ~**ment** *adv* hypocritical-
ly.
hypophyse *f* pituitary gland, hy-
pophysis.
hypothalamus *m* hypothalamus.

hypothèque *f* mortgage.
hypothéquer *vt* to mortgage.
hypothèse *f* hypothesis; assumption.
hypothétique *adj* hypothetical;
~**ment** *adv* hypothetically.
hystérie *f* hysteria.
hystérique *mf* hysterical; * *adj* hys-
teric.

I

ibis *m* ibis.
iceberg *m* iceberg.
idéal *adj*; * *m* ideal.
idéaliser *vt* to idealise.
idéaliste *adj* idealistic; * *mf* idealist.
idée *f* idea.
identifier *vt* to identify; s'~ *vr* to identify with.
identique *adj* identical; ~ment *adv* identically.
identité *f* identity; similarity.
idéologie *f* ideology.
idiot *m* -e *f* idiot, fool; * *adj* idiotic, stupid; ~ement *adv* idiotically.
idole *f* idol.
igloo *m* igloo.
ignoble *adj* ignoble, mean, base.
ignorance *f* ignorance.
ignorant *adj* ignorant; unacquainted; uninformed.
ignorer *vt* to be ignorant of; to be unaware of; to ignore.
iguane *m* iguana.
il *pn* he, it.
île *f* island, isle.
illégal *adj* illegal; unlawful; ~ement *adv* illegally.
illégalité *f* illegality.
illégitime *adj* illegitimate; unwarranted.
illettré *adj* illiterate.
illicite *adj* illicit; ~ment *adv* illicitly.
illimité *adj* unlimited; limitless.
illisible *adj* illegible, unreadable.
illogique *adj* illogical.
illumination *f* illumination, lighting.
illuminer *vt* to light up, illuminate; to enlighten.
illusion *f* illusion
illusoire *adj* illusory; illusive; ~ment *adv* illusorily.
illustration *f* illustration.
illustre *adj* illustrious, renowned.
illustrer *vt* to illustrate.
îlot *m* islet; block (flats).
image *f* image, picture; reflection.
imagé *adj* colourful; full of imagery.
imaginaire *adj* imaginary.
imagination *f* imagination.
imaginer *vt* to imagine; to suppose; to devise; s'~ *vr* to imagine o.s.; to think.
imbattable *adj* unbeatable.

imbécile *mf* idiot, imbecile; * *adj* stupid, idiotic.
imbiber *vt* to soak, moisten.
imbriquer *vt* to fit into; to overlap; s'~ *vr* to be linked.
imbuvable *adj* undrinkable; unbearable.
imitation *f* imitation; mimicry; forgery.
imiter *vt* to imitate.
immaculé *adj* spotless, immaculate.
immangeable *adj* inedible.
immatriculation *f* registration.
immatriculer *vt* to register.
immédiat *adj* immediate; instant; ~ement *adv* immediately, instantly.
immense *adj* immense, boundless.
immensément *adv* immensely; hugely.
immensité *f* immensity; immenseness.
immergé *adj* submerged.
immersion *f* immersion; submersion.
immeuble *m* building; block of flats; real estate.
immigrant *m* -e *f* immigrant.
immigration *f* immigration.
immigré *m* -e *f* immigrant.
imminent *adj* imminent, impending.
immobile *adj* motionless, still.
immobilier *adj* property; * *m* property business.
immobiliser *vt* to immobilise; to bring to a standstill; s'~ *vr* to stop, stand still.
immobilité *f* stillness; immobility; permanence.
immonde *adj* squalid; base, vile.
immoral *adj* immoral.
immoralité *f* immorality.
immortaliser *vt* to immortalise.
immortel *adj* immortal.
immuable *adj* unchanging, immutable; ~ment *adv* immutably.
immuniser *vt* to immunise.
immunité *f* immunity.
impact *m* impact.
impair *adj* odd, uneven.
impalpable *adj* impalpable.
impardonnable *adj* unforgivable, unpardonable.
imparfait *adj* imperfect; ~ement *adv* imperfectly.

impartial *adj* impartial; ~ement *adv* impartially.
impartialité *f* impartiality.
impasse *f* dead end, cul-de-sac; impasse.
impassible *adj* impassive.
impatiemment *adv* impatiently.
impatience *f* impatience.
impatient *adj* impatient.
impatienter *vt* to irritate, annoy; s'~ *vr* to grow, get impatient.
impeccable *adj* perfect; faultless, impeccable; ~ment *adv* perfectly, impeccably.
impénétrable *adj* impenetrable; inscrutable.
impensable *adj* unthinkable.
impératif *adj* imperative; mandatory; * *m* requirement; demand; constraint.
impératrice *f* empress.
imperceptible *adj* imperceptible; ~ment *adv* imperceptibly.
imperfection *f* imperfection.
impérial *adj* imperial.
impérialisme *m* imperialism.
imperméable *adj* impermeable, waterproof; ~ à impervious to.
impersonnel *adj* impersonal.
impertinence *f* impertinence.
impertinent *adj* impertinent.
imperturbable *adj* unshakeable; imperturbable; ~ment *adv* imperturbably.
impétueux *adj* impetuous.
impitoyable *adj* merciless, pitiless; ~ment *adv* mercilessly, pitilessly.
implacable *adj* implacable; ~ment *adv* implacably.
implantation *f* implantation; establishment; introduction.
implanter *vt* to introduce; to establish; to implant; s'~ *vr* to be established; to become implanted.
implication *f* implication; involvement.
implicite *adj* implicit; ~ment *adv* implicitly.
impliquer *vt* to imply; to necessitate; to implicate; s'~ *vr* to get involved in one's work.
impoli *adj* impolite, rude.
impolitesse *f* impoliteness, rudeness.
impopulaire *adj* unpopular.
importance *f* importance, significance; size.

important *adj* important, significant; sizeable.

importateur *m* **-trice** *f* importer; * *adj* importing.

importation *f* import, importation.

importer *vt* to import; * *vi* to matter; **que m'importe que** what does it matter to me that; **peu importe** whatever; **n'im-porte qui** anybody; **n'importe quoi** anything; **n'importe comment** anyhow; **n'importe quel** any.

importuner *vt* to importune, bother.

imposant *adj* imposing; stately.

imposer *vt* to impose, lay down; **s'~** *vr* to be essential; to assert o.s.

impossibilité *f* impossibility.

impossible *adj* impossible.

imposteur *m* impostor.

impôt *m* tax, duty.

impotent *adj* disabled, crippled.

imprégner *vt* impregnate; to permeate; to imbue; **s'~** *vr* to become impregnated with; to become imbued with.

impresario *m* manager, impresario.

impression *f* feeling, impression.

impressionnant *adj* impressive; upsetting.

impressionner *vt* to impress; to upset.

impressionisme *m* impressionism.

impressioniste *mf*; * *adj* impressionist.

imprévisible *adj* unforeseeable; unpredictable.

imprévoyant *adj* improvident.

imprévu *adj* unforeseen, unexpected.

imprimante *f* printer.

imprimé *adj* printed; * *m* printed form; printed material.

imprimer *vt* to print.

imprimerie *f* printing works; printing house.

imprimeur *m* printer.

improbable *adj* improbable, unlikely.

improductif *adj* unproductive.

improvisation *f* improvisation.

improviser *vt* to improvise.

improviste *adv*: **à l'~** unexpectedly.

imprudence *f* carelessness, imprudence.

imprudent *adj* careless, imprudent.

impudence *f* impudence; shamelessness.

impudique *adj* immodest, shameless.

impuissance *f* powerlessness, helplessness.

impuissant *adj* powerless, helpless.

impulsif *adj* impulsive.

impulsion *f* impulse; impetus.

impulsivement *adv* impulsively.

impunément *adv* with impunity.

impur *adj* impure; mixed.

impureté *f* impurity.

inacceptable *adj* unacceptable.

inaccessible *adj* inaccessible; obscure; incomprehensible.

inaccoutumé *adj* unusual.

inachevé *adj* unfinished, uncompleted.

inactif *adj* inactive, idle.

inaction *f* inactivity, idleness.

inactivité *f* inactivity.

inadapté *adj* unsuitable; maladjusted.

inadéquat *adj* inadequate.

inadmissible *adj* (*jur*) inadmissible.

inaltérable *adj* stable; unchanging, permanent.

inamovible *adj* irremovable; fixed.

inanimé *adj* inanimate; unconscious.

inaperçu *adj*: unnoticed **passer ~** to go unnoticed.

inappréciable *adj* invaluable, inestimable.

inapte *adj* unfit.

inattaquable *adj* unassailable; irrefutable.

inattendu *adj* unexpected, unforeseen.

inattention *f* inattention, lack of attention.

inauguration *f* inauguration, opening.

inaugurer *vt* to inaugurate, open.

inavouable *adj* shameful; undisclosable.

incapable *adj* incapable; incompetent.

incapacité *f* incompetence; disability; **être dans l'~ de** to be unable to do.

incarcérer *vt* to incarcerate.

incarnation *f* incarnation.

incarner *vt* to incarnate, embody.

incendiaire *adj* incendiary; inflammatory; * *mf* arsonist.

incendie *m* fire, blaze.

incendier *vt* to set alight; to kindle.

incertain *adj* uncertain, unsure.

incertitude *f* uncertainty; **être dans l'~** to feel uncertain.

incessant *adj* incessant, ceaseless.

inceste *m* incest.

incident *m* incident, point of law.

incinération *f* incineration; cremation.

inciser *vt* to incise; (*med*) to lance.

incisive *f* incisive; piercing.

incitation *f* incitement; incentive.

inciter *vt* to incite, urge.

inclinaison *f* incline; gradient.

incliner *vt* to bend; to slope; to bow.

inclure *vt* to include; to insert.

inclus *adj* enclosed; included; **ci-~** herein enclosed.

incohérence *f* incoherence; inconsistency.

incohérent *adj* incoherent; inconsistent.

incolore *adj* colourless; clear.

incommode *adj* inconvenient; awkward.

incommoder *vt* to disturb, bother.

incomparable *adj* incomparable; **~ment** *adv* incomparably.

incompatibilité *f* incompatibility.

incompatible *adj* incompatible.

incompétence *f* incompetence.

incompétent *adj* incompetent; inexpert.

incomplet *adj* incomplete.

incompréhensible *adj* incomprehensible.

incompréhension *f* lack of understanding.

inconcevable *adj* inconceivable.

inconciliable *adj* irreconcilable.

inconditionnel *adj* unconditional; unreserved; unquestioning.

inconfortable *adj* uncomfortable; awkward; **~ment** *adv* uncomfortably.

incongru *adj* unseemly; incongruous.

inconnu *m* **-e** *f* stranger, unknown person; * *m* unknown; * *adj* unknown.

inconsciemment *adv* unconsciously; thoughtlessly.

inconscience *f* unconsciousness; thoughtlessness.

inconscient *adj* unconscious; thoughtless, reckless; * *m* subconscious, unconscious.

inconsidéré *adj* inconsiderate; thoughtless; **~ment** *adv* inconsiderately.

inconsistant *adj* flimsy; colourless; watery.

inconsolable *adj* disconsolate; inconsolable.

inconstant *adj* fickle; variable, inconstant.

incontestable *adj* incontestable,

unquestionable; **~ment** *adv* incontestably, unquestionably.

inconvénient *m* drawback, inconvenience.

incorporation *f* incorporation; integration; blending.

incorporer *vt* to incorporate, integrate.

incorrect *adj* faulty, incorrect; **~ement** *adv* incorrectly.

incorrigible *adj* incorrigible.

incorruptible *adj* incorruptible.

incrédule *adj* incredulous; * *mf* unbeliever, non-believer.

incrédulité *f* incredulity, lack of belief.

incroyable *adj* incredible; unbelievable; **~ment** *adv* incredibly, unbelievably.

incruster *vt* to inlay; to superimpose; **s'~** *vr* to become imbedded in; to become rooted in.

inculpation *f* inculcation, instilling.

inculpé *m* **-e** *f* accused; * *adj* accused.

incurable *adj* incurable; **~ment** *adv* incurably, hopelessly.

indécent *adj* indecent, improper.

indéchiffrable *adj* indecipherable; incomprehensible.

indécis *adj* indecisive; unsettled; undefined.

indéfini *adj* undefined; indefinite; **~ment** *adv* indefinitely.

indéfinissable *adj* indefinable.

indemne *adj* unharmed, unhurt.

indemniser *vt* to indemnify; to compensate.

indemnité *f* compensation; indemnity.

indéniable *adj* undeniable, indisputable; **~ment** *adv* undeniably.

indépendance *f* independence.

indépendant *adj* independent.

indestructible *adj* indestructible.

indéterminé *adj* undetermined; unspecified; undecided.

index *m* index; index finger.

indexer *vt* to index.

indicatif *m* signature tune; dialling code; * *adj* indicative.

indication *f* indication; piece of information; instruction.

indice *m* indication; clue; sign.

indifféremment *adv* indiscriminately, equally.

indifférence *f* indifference.

indifférent *adj* indifferent; immaterial.

indigène *mf* native; local; * *adj* indigenous, native.

indigeste *adj* indigestible.

indigestion *f* indigestion.

indigne *adj* unworthy; undeserving.

indigner *vt* to annoy, make indignant; **s'~** *vr* to be indignant.

indiquer *vt* to indicate, point out; to tell.

indirect *adj* indirect; circumstantial; collateral; **~ement** *adv* indirectly.

indiscipliné *adj* undisciplined.

indiscret *adj* indiscreet; inquisitive.

indiscrétion *f* indiscretion; inquisitiveness.

indiscutable *adj* indisputable; unquestionable; **~ment** *adv* indisputably.

indispensable *adj* indispensable; essential.

indisponible *adj* unavailable.

indistinct *adj* indistinct, vague; **~ement** *adv* indistinctly.

individu *m* individual.

individuel *adj* individual; **~lement** *adv* individually.

indolore *adj* painless.

indubitable *adj* indubitable; certain; **~ment** *adv* indubitably.

indulgence *f* indulgence; leniency.

indulgent *adj* indulgent; lenient.

industrialisation *f* industrialisation.

industrie *f* industry; dexterity, ingenuity.

industriel *m* **-le** *f* industrialist, manufacturer; * *adj* industrial.

inébranlable *adj* steadfast, unwavering.

inédit *adj* unpublished; original.

inefficace *adj* ineffective; inefficient.

inefficacité *f* ineffectiveness; inefficiency.

inégal *adj* unequal; uneven; irregular; **~ement** *adv* unequally.

inégalité *f* inequality; difference, disparity.

inéluctable *adj* ineluctable, unavoidable; **~ment** *adv* ineluctably.

inépuisable *adj* inexhaustible.

inerte *adj* inert; lifeless.

inertie *f* inertia, apathy.

inespéré *adj* unexpected.

inestimable *adj* inestimable, invaluable.

inévitable *adj* inevitable, unavoidable.

inexact *adj* inexact, inaccurate.

inexactitude *f* inaccuracy.

inexistant *adj* nonexistent.

inexorable *adj* inexorable; **~ment** *adv* inexorably.

inexpérimenté *adj* inexperienced; inexpert.

inexplicable *adj* inexplicable; **~ment** *adv* inexplicably.

inexprimable *adj* inexpressible.

infaillible *adj* infallible.

infâme *adj* infamous; base, vile.

infantile *adj* infantile, childish.

infatigable *adj* indefatigable, tireless; **~ment** *adv* indefatigably.

infect *adj* vile; revolting; filthy.

infecter *vt* to infect; to contaminate; **s'~** *vr* to become infected.

infection *f* infection.

inférieur *adj* inferior; lower.

infériorité *f* inferiority.

infernal *adj* infernal, diabolical.

infester *vt* to infest, overrun.

infidèle *adj* unfaithful, disloyal.

infidélité *f* infidelity.

infiltration *f* infiltration.

infini *adj* infinite; interminable; **~ment** *adv* infinitely.

infinitif *m* infinitive.

infirme *adj* feeble; crippled, disabled.

infirmerie *f* infirmary; sick bay.

infirmier *m* **-ière** *f* nurse.

infirmité *f* disability; infirmity.

inflammation *f* inflammation.

inflation *f* inflation.

inflexible *adj* inflexible, rigid.

infliger *vt* to inflict; to impose.

influence *f* influence.

influencer *vt* to influence, sway.

informaticien *m* **-ne** *f* computer scientist.

information *f* piece of information; information; inquiry.

informatique *f* computing; data processing; * *adj* computer.

informer *vt* to inform, tell; **s'~** *vr* to find out, inquire.

infraction *f* infraction, infringement; offence.

infranchissable *adj* impassable; insuperable.

infrarouge *adj* infrared.

infrastructure *f* infrastructure; substructure.

infructueux *adj* fruitless, unsuccessful.

infusion *f* infusion, herb tea.

ingénieur *m* engineer.

ingénieux *adj* ingenious, clever.

ingénu *adj* ingenuous, naive.

ingrat *adj* ungrateful; unprofitable.

ingratitude *f* ingratitude.

ingrédient *m* ingredient; component.

inhabité *adj* uninhabited, unoccupied.

inhabituel *adj* unusual, unaccustomed.

inhumain *adj* inhuman.

inimaginable *adj* unimaginable.

inimitable *adj* inimitable.

ininterrompu *adj* uninterrupted; unbroken.

initial *adj* initial; ~**ement** *adv* initially.

initiation *f* initiation.

initiative *f* initiative; enterprise.

initier *vt* to initiate.

injecter *vt* to inject.

injection *f* injection.

injure *f* injury; insult.

injurier *vt* to abuse; insult.

injuste *adj* unjust, unfair; ~**ment** *adv* unjustly.

injustice *f* injustice.

injustifié *adj* unjustified.

inné *adj* innate, inborn.

innocence *f* innocence.

innocent *m* **-e** *f* innocent person; simpleton; * *adj* innocent.

innocenter *vt* to clear, prove innocent.

innovation *f* innovation.

innover *vi* to innovate, make innovations.

inodore *adj* odourless, scentless.

inoffensif *adj* inoffensive, harmless.

inondation *f* flood.

inonder *vt* to flood, inundate.

inopportun *adj* ill-timed, inopportune.

inoubliable *adj* unforgettable.

inouï *adj* unprecedented, unheard of.

inox *m* stainless steel.

inqualifiable *adj* unspeakable.

inquiet *adj* worried, anxious, uneasy.

inquiéter *vt* to worry, disturb; **s'~** *vr* to get worried.

inquiétude *f* restlessness, uneasiness.

insaisissable *adj* elusive; imperceptible.

insalubre *adj* insalubrious; unhealthy.

insatiable *adj* insatiable; ~**ment** *adv* insatiably.

insatisfaction *f* dissatisfaction.

inscription *f* inscription; registration; matriculation.

inscrire *vt* to inscribe; to enter; to set down; to register; **s'~** *vr* to join; to register, enrol.

insecte *m* insect.

insecticide *m* insecticide.

insémination *f* insemination.

insensé *adj* insane, demented.

insensible *adj* insensible, unfeeling, insensitive; imperceptible; ~**ment** *adv* imperceptibly; insensibly.

inséparable *adj* inseparable.

insérer *vt* to insert.

insertion *f* insertion, inserting.

insidieux *adj* insidious

insignifiant *adj* insignificant, trifling.

insinuation *f* insinuation.

insinuer *vt* to insinuate, imply; **s'~** *vr* to insinuate o.s. into; to creep into.

insipide *adj* insipid, tasteless.

insister *vi* to insist, be insistent; to stress.

insolence *f* insolence.

insolent *adj* insolent; brazen.

insolite *adj* unusual; strange.

insomnie *f* insomnia.

insouciance *f* unconcern; carelessness.

insouciant *adj* carefree; careless.

insoutenable *adj* unbearable; untenable.

inspecter *vt* to inspect, examine.

inspecteur *m* **-trice** *f* inspector

inspection *f* inspection.

inspiration *f* inspiration; suggestion.

inspirer *vt* to inspire; to breathe in; **s'~** *vr*: **s'~ de** to be inspired by.

instable *adj* unstable; unsettled.

installation *f* installation; installing.

installer *vt* to install; to fit out; **s'~** *vr* to set o.s. up; to settle down.

instant *m* moment, instant.

instantané *adj* instant, instantaneous; ~**ment** *adv* instantly.

instaurer *vt* to institute; to impose.

instinct *m* instinct.

instinctif *adj* instinctive.

instinctivement *adv* instinctively.

institut *m* institute; school.

instituteur *m* **-trice** *f* teacher.

institution *f* institution; establishment.

instructif *adj* instructive.

instruction *f* instruction; education; inquiry.

instruire *vt* to instruct; to teach; to conduct an inquiry; **s'~** *vr* to educate o.s.; to obtain information.

instrument *m* instrument, implement.

insuffisance *f* insufficiency, inadequacy.

insuffisant *adj* insufficient, inadequate.

insuline *f* insulin.

insulte *f* insult.

insulter *vt* to insult, affront.

insupportable *adj* unbearable, intolerable; ~**ment** *adv* unbearably, intolerably.

insurrection *f* insurrection, revolt.

intact *adj* intact.

intégral *adj* integral; uncut; complete; ~**ement** *adv* integrally; in full.

intégralité *f* whole; entirety.

intégrer *vt* to integrate; **s'~** *vr* to become integrated; to fit in.

intégrité *f* integrity.

intellectuel *m* **-le** *f* intellectual; * *adj* intellectual, mental.

intelligence *f* intelligence; understanding.

intelligent *adj* intelligent, shrewd, bright.

intelligible *adj* intelligible.

intempéries *fpl* bad weather.

intendant *m* **-e** *f* bursar; steward, stewardess.

intense *adj* intense; severe.

intensément *adv* intensely.

intensif *adj* intensive.

intensifier *vt* to intensify; **s'~** *vr* to intensify.

intensité *f* intensity; severity.

intention *f* intention; purpose, intent.

interaction *f* interaction.

intercaler *vt* to intercalate; to interpolate.

intercepter *vt* to intercept.

interchangeable *adj* interchangeable.

interdiction *f* interdiction, prohibition, ban.

interdire *vt* to forbid, ban, prohibit.

interdit *adj* forbidden, prohibited; dumbfounded.

intéressant *adj* interesting; attractive, worthwhile.

intéresser *vt* to interest; to concern; *vr*: **s'~ à** to be interested in.

intérêt *m* interest; significance, importance.

interférence *f* interference; conjunction.

intérieur *adj* interior, internal, inland; **à l'~** inside; within; ~**ement** *adv* inwardly.

intérimaire *adj* interim; acting; temporary.

interligne *m* line space; interlining; lead.

interlocuteur *m* **-trice** *f* interlocutor, speaker.

intermède *m* interlude.

intermédiaire *adj* intermediate; intermediary.

interminable *adj* interminable; endless; **~ment** *adv* interminably, endlessly.

intermittent *adj* intermittent, sporadic.

international *adj* international.

interne *adj* internal; * *mf* boarder; house doctor.

interpeller *vt* to call out to; (*police*) to interpellate.

interphone *m* intercom, entryphone.

interposer *vt* to interpose; **s'~** *vr* to intervene.

interprétation *f* interpretation, rendering.

interprète *mf* interpreter.

interpréter *vt* to interpret; to perform.

interrogation *f* interrogation, questioning; question.

interrogatoire *m* questioning; cross-examination.

interroger *vt* to question; to interrogate; **s'~** *vr* to wonder.

interrompre *vt* to interrupt, break; **s'~** *vr* to break off, interrupt o.s.

interrupteur *m* switch.

interruption *f* interruption, break.

intervalle *m* interval; space, distance.

intervenir *vi* to intervene; to take part in.

intervention *f* intervention; operation.

intestinal *adj* intestinal

intestin *m* intestine.

intime *adj* intimate; private; **~ment** *adv* intimately; * *mf* close friend.

intimider *vt* to intimidate.

intimité *f* intimacy; privacy.

intituler *vt* to call, entitle; **s'~** *vr* to be called; to call o.s.

intolérable *adj* intolerable.

intolérance *f* intolerance.

intolérant *adj* intolerant.

intonation *f* intonation.

intoxication *f* poisoning; indoctrination.

intransigeant *adj* intransigent, uncompromising.

intransitif *adj* intransitive.

intrépide *adj* intrepid, fearless; **~ment** *adv* intrepidly.

intrigant *adj* scheming.

introduction *f* introduction; launching; (*jur*) institution.

introduire *vt* to introduce, insert; to present; **s'~** *vr* to find one's way in; to be introduced.

introuvable *adj* undiscoverable; not to be found.

introverti *m* **-e** *f* introvert; * *adj* introverted.

intrus *m* **-e** *f* intruder; * *adj* intruding, intrusive.

intuitif *adj* intuitive.

intuition *f* intuition.

inutile *adj* useless; unavailing; pointless; **~ment** *adv* uselessly, needlessly.

inutilisable *adj* unusable.

invalide *adj* disabled; (*jur*) invalid.

invariable *adj* invariable; unvarying; **~ment** *adv* invariably.

invasion *f* invasion.

inventaire *m* inventory; stocklist.

inventer *vt* to invent; to devise; to make up.

inventeur *m* **-trice** *f* inventor.

invention *f* invention; inventiveness.

inverse *adj* opposite; * *m* opposite, reverse.

inverser *vt* to reverse, invert.

inversion *f* inversion; reversal.

investir *vt* to invest; to surround.

investissement *m* investment; investing.

invincible *adj* invincible, indomitable.

invisible *adj* invisible; unseen.

invitation *f* invitation.

invité *m* **-e** *f* guest.

inviter *vt* to invite, ask.

involontaire *adj* involuntary; unintentional; **~ment** *adv* involuntarily.

invoquer *vt* to invoke; to call up; to plead.

invraisemblable *adj* unlikely, improbable; **~ment** *adv* improbably.

invulnérable *adj* invulnerable.

iode *m* iodine.

ion *m* ion.

iris *m* iris.

Irlandais *m* Irishman, **-e** *f* Irishwoman

irlandais *adj* Irish.

Irlande *f* Ireland.

ironie *f* irony.

ironique *adj* ironic; **~ment** *adv* ironically.

irradiation *f* irradiation; radiation.

irrationnel *adj* irrational.

irrécupérable *adj* irretrievable.

irréel *adj* unreal.

irréfléchi *adj* unconsidered; hasty.

irrégularité *f* irregularity; variation; unevenness.

irrégulier *adj* irregular; varying; uneven.

irrégulièrement *adv* irregularly; unevenly.

irrémédiable *adj* irreparable; incurable; **~ment** *adv* irreparably.

irremplaçable *adj* irreplaceable.

irréparable *adj* irreparable; irretrievable; **~ment** *adv* irreparably.

irrésistible *adj* irresistible; **~ment** *adv* irresistibly.

irresponsable *adj* irresponsible

irréversible *adj* irreversible; **~ment** *adv* irreversibly.

irrigation *f* irrigation.

irriguer *vt* to irrigate.

irriter *vt* to irritate; to provoke.

irruption *f* irruption.

Islam *m* Islam.

isolement *m* loneliness; isolation; insulation.

isoler *vt* to isolate; to insulate; **s'~** *vr* to cut o.s. off.

issu *adj* descended from; stemming from.

issue *f* outlet; solution; outcome.

ivoire *m* ivory.

ivre *adj* drunk, inebriated.

ivresse *f* drunkenness.

ivrogne *mf* drunkard.

J

jachère *f* fallow; leaving land lying fallow.

jade *m* jade.

jadis *adv* formerly, long ago.

jaguar *m* jaguar.

jaillir *vi* to spout, gush; to spring.

jalon *m* staff; landmark, milestone.

jalonner *vt* to mark out.

jalousie *f* jealousy, envy.

jaloux *m* **-ouse** *f* jealous person; * *adj* jealous, envious.

jamais *adv* never, not ever; **à ~** for ever.

jambe *f* leg.

jambon *m* ham.

janvier *m* January.

jardin *m* garden.

jardinage *m* gardening.

jardiner *vi* to garden.

jardinier *m* **-ière** *f* gardener.

jargon *m* jargon, slang; gibberish.

jarret *m* hock; (*zool*) hollow of the knee.

jaser *vi* to chatter; to twitter; to babble.

jasmin *m* jasmine.

jauge *f* gauge; capacity; tonnage.

jauger *vt* to gauge the capacity of; to size up.

jaunâtre *adj* yellowish.

jaune *adj* yellow; * *m* yellow.

jaunir *vi* to yellow, turn yellow; * *vt* to make yellow.

jaunisse *f* jaundice.

jazz *m* jazz.

je, j' *pn* I.

jésuite *m* Jesuit.

jet *m* jet, spurt; throwing.

jetable *adj* disposable.

jetée *f* pier.

jeter *vt* to throw; to discard; to give out; **se ~** *vr* to throw o.s.; to rush at.

jeton *m* token; counter.

jeu *m* play; game;gambling; **~ de jambes** footwork; **~ de mots** pun, play on words; **cacher son ~** to conceal one's intentions.

jeudi *m* Thursday.

jeun *adv*: **à ~** on an empty stomach.

jeune *adj* young; junior; new; youthful; * *m* youth, young man; *f* young girl.

jeûne *m* fast.

jeûner *vi* to fast.

jeunesse *f* youth, youthfulness.

joaillerie *f* jewellery.

joaillier *m* **-ière** *f* jeweller.

joie *f* joy, happiness; pleasure.

joindre *vt* to join, link; to attach; **se ~** *vr* to join, join in.

joint *m* joint; join.

jointure *f* (*anat*) joint.

joli *adj* pretty; good, handsome; **~ment** *adv* nicely, attractively.

jonc *m* rush; cane.

joncher *vt* to strew with.

jonction *f* junction.

jongler *vi* to juggle.

jongleur *m* **-euse** *f* juggler.

jonquille *f* daffodil, jonquil.

joue *f* cheek

jouer *vi* to play; to gamble; to act.

jouet *m* toy.

joueur *m* **-euse** *f* player; gambler.

joufflu *adj* chubby; round-faced.

joug *m* yoke.

jouir *vi* to enjoy; to delight in.

jouissance *f* enjoyment; use.

jour *m* day; daylight; **tous les ~s** every day; **à ~** up to date; **vivre au ~ le ~** to live from day to day; **~ férié** public holiday; **mise à ~** updating; update; **du ~ au lendemain** overnight.

journal *m* newspaper; bulletin, journal; **~ de bord** logbook; **~ télévisé** television news.

journalisme *m* journalism.

journaliste *mf* journalist.

journée *f* day; day's work.

jovial *adj* jovial, jolly.

jovialité *f* joviality.

joyau *m* jewel, gem.

joyeusement *adv* joyfully, cheerfully.

joyeux *adj* joyful, cheerful.

jubiler *vi* to be jubilant, exult.

judaïsme *m* Judaism.

judiciaire *adj* judicial, legal.

judicieusement *adv* judiciously.

judicieux *adj* judicious.

judo *m* judo

judoka *mf* judoka.

juge *m* judge.

jugement *m* judgment; sentence; opinion.

juger *vt* to judge; to decide; to consider.

juif *m* Jew; Jewish; **juive** *f* Jewess; * *adj* Jewish.

juillet *m* July.

juin *m* June.

jumeau *m* **-elle** *f* twin; * *adj* twin; double.

jumelage *m* twinning.

jumelé *adj* twinned, twin.

jumelle(s) *f(pl)* binoculars.

jument *f* mare.

jungle *f* jungle.

jupe *f* skirt.

jurer *vt* to swear, pledge.

juridiction *f* jurisdiction; court of law.

juridique *adj* legal, juridical; **~ment** *adv* juridically, legally.

jurisprudence *f* case law, jurisprudence.

juriste *m* lawyer; jurist.

juron *m* oath, curse.

jury *m* jury; board of examiners.

jus *m* juice.

jusque, jusqu' *prép* to, as far as; until.

justaucorps *m* jerkin; leotard.

juste *adj* just, fair; exact; sound; **~ment** *adv* exactly, precisely.

justesse *f* accuracy; aptness; soundness.

justice *f* justice, fairness.

justicier *m* **-ière** *f* justiciary; dispenser of justice.

justificatif *adj* supporting, justificatory.

justification *f* justification; proof.

justifier *vt* to justify, prove; **se ~** *vr* to justify o.s.

jute *m* jute.

juteux *adj* juicy; lucrative.

juvénile *adj* young, youthful.

juxtaposer *vt* to juxtapose.

juxtaposition *f* juxtaposition.

K

kaki *adj* khaki.
kaléidoscope *m* kaleidoscope.
kangourou *m* kangaroo.
karaté *m* karate.
kayac, kayak *m* kayak.
képi *m* kepi.
kermesse *f* fair; bazaar.
kérosène *m* kerosene, aviation fuel.
kidnapper *vt* to kidnap, abduct.

kidnappeur *m* **-euse** *f* kidnapper.
kilogramme *m* kilogram.
kilohertz *m* kilohertz.
kilométrage *m* total kilometres travelled (mileage).
kilomètre *m* kilometre.
kimono *m* kimono.
kinésithérapeute *mf* physiotherapist.

kiosque *m* kiosk, stall.
kiwi *m* kiwi, Chinese gooseberry.
klaxon *m* horn.
klaxonner *vi* to sound one's horn.
kleptomane *mf* kleptomaniac.
kleptomanie *f* kleptomania.
koala *m* koala.
kyste *m* cyst.

L

la *art pn: see* **le.**

là *adv* there; over there; then; **par ~** that way; **~-dedans** inside, in there; **~-dessous** underneath, under there; **~-dessus** on that; thereupon; **~-haut** up there, up on top; **celui-~** that one.

label *m* label; seal.

labeur *m* labour, toil.

laboratoire *m* laboratory.

laborieux *adj* laborious, toilsome.

labourer *vt* to plough; to dig over; to rip open.

labyrinthe *m* labyrinth.

lac *m* lake.

lacer *vt* to lace up; to tie up.

lacérer *vt* to lacerate; to tear.

lacet *m* lace.

lâche *adj* slack; loose; lax; cowardly; **~ment** *adv* loosely; in a cowardly manner; * *mf* coward.

lâcher *vt* to loosen; to release.

lâcheté *f* cowardice; meanness.

laconique *adj* laconic; **~ment** *adv* laconically.

lacté *adj* milky, lacteal.

lactique *adj* lactic.

lacune *f* lacuna; gap.

lagon *m* lagoon.

lagune *f* lagoon.

laïc *m* layman, **laïque** *f* laywoman; * **laïque** *adj* lay, civil.

laid *adj* ugly, unsightly.

laideur *f* ugliness, unsightliness.

lainage *m* woollen article.

laine *f* wool.

laisse *f* leash, string, lead.

laisser *vt* to leave; to let; **~ tomber** to drop; **se ~ aller** to let o.s. go.

laisser-passer *m invar* pass, permit.

lait *m* milk

laitage *m* milk; milk products.

laiton *m* brass.

laitue *f* lettuce.

lama *m* (*zool*) llama; lama.

lambeau *m* shred; tatter.

lambris *m* plastering; panelling.

lame *f* blade; strip; metal plate.

lamelle *f* slide; small strip.

lamentable *adj* lamentable, distressing; **~ment** *adv* lamentably.

lamentation *f* lamentation; wailing.

lamenter (se) *vr* to lament, bewail.

laminer *vt* to laminate.

lampadaire *m* standard-lamp; street lamp.

lampe *f* lamp, light; bulb.

lance *f* lance, spear.

lance-flammes *m invar* flamethrower.

lancement *m* launching; starting up; throwing.

lance-pierres *m invar* catapult.

lancer *vt* to throw; to launch; **se ~** *vr* to leap, jump; to embark on.

lancinant *adj* nagging; haunting.

lande *f* moor.

langage *m* language, speech.

langoureux *adj* languid, languorous.

langouste *f* spiny lobster.

langoustine *f* Dublin bay prawn.

langue *f* tongue; language.

languette *f* tongue; tongue-like strip.

langueur *f* languor.

languir *vi* to languish; to linger.

lanière *f* thong; lash.

lanoline *f* lanolin.

lanterne *f* lantern; lamp.

lapin *m* **-e** *f* rabbit.

lapsus *m* slip, mistake.

laque *f* hairspray; lacquer; * *m* lacquer wax.

lard *m* fat; bacon.

lardon *m* bacon cube.

large *adj* wide; generous; lax; great; **~ment** *adv* widely; greatly.

largeur *f* width, breadth.

larguer *vt* to loose, release; cast off.

larme *f* tear.

larmoyant *adj* tearful, weeping.

larve *f* larva, grub.

laryngite *f* laryngitis.

larynx *m* larynx.

las *adj*, *f* **-se** weary, tired.

lasagne *f* lasagne.

laser *m* laser.

lasser *vt* to tire; **se ~** *vr* to grow tired.

lassitude *f* tiredness, weariness.

latent *adj* latent.

latéral *adj* lateral, side; **~ement** *adv* laterally.

latex *m* latex.

latin *adj* Latin; * *m* Latin.

latitude *f* latitude; margin.

latte *f* lath.

lauréat *m* **-e** *f* prize winner.

laurier *m* bay-tree, laurel.

lavabo *m* washbasin.

lavage *m* washing; bathing.

lavande *f* lavender.

lave *f* lava.

lavement *m* enema.

laver *vt* to wash; to cleanse; **se ~** *vr* to wash o.s.

laverie *f* laundry.

lave-vaisselle *m invar* dishwasher.

laxatif *adj* laxative; * *m* laxative.

laxisme *m* laxness.

layette *f* baby clothes.

le *art*, *f* **la**, *devant voyelle* **l'**, *pl* **les** the; * *pn* him, her, them.

lécher *vt* to lick.

leçon *f* lesson; reading; class.

lecteur *m* **-trice** *f* reader.

lecture *f* reading; perusal.

légal *adj* legal, lawful; **~ement** *adv* legally.

légaliser *vt* to legalise.

légalité *f* legality, lawfulness.

légendaire *adj* legendary.

légende *f* legend; inscription.

léger *adj* light; slight; faint; inconsiderate.

légèrement *adv* lightly; thoughtlessly.

légèreté *f* lightness; nimbleness; thoughtlessness.

légion *f* legion.

législatif *adj* legislative; * *m* legislature.

législation *f* legislation, laws.

légitime *adj* legitimate, lawful; **~ment** *adv* legitimately.

légitimité *f* legitimacy.

legs *m* legacy, bequest.

léguer *vt* to bequeath; (*jur*) to devise.

légume *m* vegetable.

lendemain *m* next day, day after.

lent *adj* slow; tardy; sluggish; **~ement** *adv* slowly.

lente *f* (*zool*) nit.

lenteur *f* slowness.

lentille *f* lentil; lens.

léopard *m* leopard.

lèpre *f* leprosy.

lépreux *m* **-euse** *f* leper; * *adj* leprous.

lequel *pn*, *f* **laquelle**, *pl* **lesquels, lesquelles** who, whom, which.

lesbienne *f* lesbian.

léser *vt* to wrong; to damage.

lésion *f* wrong; lesion, wound.

lessive *f* washing powder.

leste *adj* nimble, agile; **~ment** *adv* nimbly.

lester *vt* to fill; to ballast.

léthargie *f* lethargy.

léthargique *adj* lethargic.

lettre *f* letter, note; literature; **en toutes ~s** in black and white; **suivre à la ~** to carry out to the letter; **avant la ~** in advance, premature.

leucémie *f* leukaemia.

leucocyte *m* leucocyte.

leur *pn* them; **le ~, la ~, les ~s** theirs.

leurrer *vt* to deceive; to lure; **se ~** *vr* to delude o.s.

levain *m* leaven.

lever *vt* to lift, raise; to levy; **se ~** *vr* to get up; ***** *m* rising; getting up.

levier *m* lever.

lèvre *f* lip.

lévrier *m* greyhound.

levure *f* yeast.

lexique *m* vocabulary, lexis.

lézard *m* lizard.

lézarde *f* crack.

liaison *f* affair; connection; liaison, link.

liasse *f* bundle.

libellule *f* dragonfly.

libéral *adj* liberal; **~ement** *adv* liberally; ***** *m* liberal.

libéraliser *vt* to liberalise.

libéralisme *m* liberalism.

libéralité *f* liberality, generosity.

libération *f* release, liberation.

libérer *vt* to release; to liberate; **se ~** *vr* to free o.s.

liberté *f* liberty, freedom.

libido *f* libido.

libraire *mf* bookseller.

librairie *f* bookshop; bookselling.

libre *adj* free; independent; **~ment** *adv* freely.

licence *f* degree; permit; licentiousness.

licenciement *m* redundancy; dismissal.

licencier *vt* to make redundant; to dismiss.

lichen *m* lichen.

licorne *f* unicorn.

lie *f* dregs, sediment.

liège *m* cork.

lien *m* bond; link, connection; tie.

lier *vt* to bind; to link; **se ~** *vr*: **se ~ avec** to make friends.

lierre *m* ivy.

lieu *m* place, position; cause; occasion; **avoir ~** to take place; **en**

premier ~ in the first place; **au ~ de** instead of.

lieutenant *m* (*mil*) lieutenant.

lièvre *m* hare.

ligament *m* ligament

ligature *f* ligature; tying up.

ligne *f* line; row; range.

lignée *f* lineage; offspring.

lignite *m* lignite.

ligoter *vt* to bind hand and foot.

ligue *f* league.

lilas *m* lilac; ***** *adj* lilac.

limace *f* slug.

limande *f* dab.

lime *f* file.

limer *vt* to file down.

limitation *f* limitation, restriction.

limite *f* boundary, limit; **à la ~** ultimately.

limiter *vt* to limit, restrict; **se ~** *vr* to limit o.s. to.

limitrophe *adj* border.

limon *m* silt.

limonade *f* lemonade.

limpide *adj* limpid, clear.

limpidité *f* limpidity, clearness.

lin *m* flax; linen.

linceul *m* shroud.

linéaire *adj* linear.

linge *m* linen; washing.

lingerie *f* linen room; underwear, lingerie.

lingot *m* ingot.

linguiste *mf* linguist.

linguistique *f* linguistics; ***** *adj* linguistic.

lion *m* lion, **lionne** *f* lioness.

lionceau *m* lion cub.

lipide *m* lipid.

liquéfier *vt* to liquefy; **se ~** *vr* to liquefy.

liqueur *f* liqueur; liquid.

liquidation *f* liquidation; winding up; elimination.

liquide *m* liquid.

liquider *vt* to settle; to wind up; to eliminate

lire *vt* to read.

lis *m* lily.

lisible *adj* legible; readable; **~ment** *adv* legibly.

lisière *f* edge; border; outskirts.

lisse *adj* smooth, glossy.

lisser *vt* to smooth, gloss.

liste *f* list; (*jur*) schedule.

lit *m* bed; layer.

litanie *f* litany.

literie *f* bedding.

lithographie *f* lithography.

litière *f* litter.

litige *m* lawsuit; dispute.

litigieux *adj* litigious.

litre *m* litre.

littéraire *adj* literary.

littéral *adj* literal; **~ement** *adv* literally.

littérature *f* literature; writing.

littoral *m* coast; ***** *adj* coastal, littoral.

liturgie *f* liturgy.

livide *adj* livid, pale.

livraison *f* delivery; number, issue.

livre *m* book; ***** *f* pound (weight, currency).

livrer *vt* to deliver, hand over; to give away; **se ~** *vr* to abandon o.s.

livret *m* (*mus*) libretto; booklet.

livreur *m* delivery man, **-euse** *f* delivery woman.

lobe *m* lobe.

lobotomie *f* lobotomy.

local *adj* local; **~ement** *adv* locally.

localisation *f* localisation.

localiser *vt* to localise.

localité *f* locality; town.

locataire *mf* tenant; lodger.

location *f* renting; lease, leasing.

locomotion *f* locomotion.

locomotive *f* locomotive, engine; dynamo.

locution *f* locution, idiom.

logarithme *m* logarithm.

loge *f* lodge; dressing room; box.

logement *m* housing; accommodation.

loger *vt* to accommodate; to billet; ***** *vi* to live in.

logiciel *m* software.

logique *f* logic; ***** *adj* logical; **~ment** *adv* logically.

logistique *f* logistics.

logo *m* logo.

loi *f* law; act, statute; rule.

loin *adv* far, a long way; ***** *m*: distance; background **au ~** in the distance; **de ~** from a distance.

lointain *adj* distant, remote; ***** *m* distance; background.

loir *m* dormouse.

loisir *m* leisure, spare time.

lombaire *adj* lumbar; ***** *f* lumbar vertebra.

lombric *m* earthworm.

long *adj*, *f* **-ue** long, lengthy; **~uement** *adv* at length.

longer *vt* to border; to walk along.

longévité *f* longevity.

longitude *f* longitude.

longtemps *adv* for a long time.

longueur *f* length.

longue-vue *f* telescope.

loquace *adj* loquacious, talkative.

loque *f* rag.

loquet *m* latch; clasp.

lorgner *vt* to leer, ogle.

lors *adv* then; ~ **de** at the time of; **dès** ~ from that time.

lorsque *conj* when.

losange *m* lozenge, diamond.

lot *m* prize; lot; portion.

loterie *f* lottery; raffle.

lotion *f* lotion.

lotissement *m* allotment; site; housing development.

lotus *m* lotus.

louange *f* praise, commendation.

louche *adj* dubious; suspicious, shady.

loucher *vi* to squint; to ogle.

louer *vt* to rent, lease; to book.

loup *m* wolf.

loupe *f* magnifying glass.

louper *vt* (*fam*) to botch, bungle; to flunk.

lourd *adj* heavy; sultry; unwieldy; ~**ement** *adv* heavily.

lourdeur *f* heaviness.

loutre *f* otter.

louve *f* she-wolf.

louveteau *m* wolf-cub.

loyal *adj* loyal, faithful; ~**ement** *adv* loyally.

loyauté *f* loyalty.

loyer *m* rent.

lubrifiant *m* lubricant; * *adj* lubricating.

lubrifier *vt* to lubricate.

lubrique *adj* lustful, lecherous; ~**ment** *adv* lustfully.

lucarne *f* skylight.

lucide *adj* lucid, clear; ~**ment** *adv* lucidly.

lucidité *f* lucidity, clearness.

lucratif *adj* lucrative.

ludique *adj* play.

lueur *f* glimmer, gleam; glimpse.

luge *f* sledge, toboggan.

lugubre *adj* lugubrious, gloomy; ~**ment** *adv* lugubriously.

lui *pn* him, her, it; **c'est à** ~ it is his; ~**-même** himself, itself.

luire *vt* to shine, gleam.

luisant *adj* gleaming, shining.

lumbago *m* lumbago.

lumière *f* light; daylight; lamp; insight.

lumineux *adj* luminous; illuminated.

lunaire *adj* lunar, moon.

lunatique *adj* fantastical, whimsical, quirky.

lundi *m* Monday.

lune *f* moon.

lunette *f* telescope; ~**s** glasses.

lustré *adj* glossy; shiny.

luth *m* lute.

luthérien *adj* Lutheran.

luthiste *mf* lutanist.

lutin *m* imp;goblin.

lutte *f* struggle; contest; strife.

lutter *vi* to struggle, fight.

lutteur *m* **-euse** *f* wrestler, fighter.

luxation *f* dislocation, luxation.

luxe *m* luxury, excess.

luxueusement *adv* luxuriously.

luxueux *adj* luxurious.

luxure *f* lust.

luxuriance *f* luxuriance.

luxuriant *adj* luxuriant.

luzerne *f* lucerne, alfalfa.

lycée *m* secondary school.

lycéen *m* secondary school boy, -**ne** *f* secondary school girl.

lymphatique *adj* lymphatic.

lymphe *f* lymph.

lymphocyte *m* lymphocyte.

lyncher *vt* to lynch.

lynx *m* lynx.

lyre *f* lyre.

lyrique *adj* lyric; ~**ment** *adv* lyrically.

lyrisme *m* lyricism.

M

macabre *adj* macabre.

macadam *m* tarmac.

macaque *m* macaque.

macédoine *f* medley, hotchpotch; macedoine.

macérer *vt* to macerate; to mortify o.s.; * *vi* to macerate, steep.

mâche *f* corn-salad.

mâcher *vt* to chew.

machiavélique *adj* Machiavellian.

machin *m* (*fam*) gadget; thingamajig.

machinal *adj* mechanical, automatic; ~ement *adv* mechanically.

machination *f* machination, plot.

machine *f* machine; engine; apparatus.

machinerie *f* machinery, plant.

machiniste *m* machinist; driver; stagehand.

mâchoire *f* jaw.

maçon *m* builder, mason.

maçonnerie *f* masonry; building.

macrobiotique *adj* macrobiotic; * *f* macrobiotics

madame *f* Madam; Mrs; lady.

madeleine *f* madeleine.

mademoiselle *f* Miss; young lady.

magasin *m* shop, store; warehouse.

magazine *m* magazine.

mage *m* magus; seer.

magicien *m* **-ne** *f* magician.

magie *f* magic

magique *adj* magic; magical; ~ment *adv* magically.

magistral *adj* masterly; authoritative; ~ement *adv* in a masterly fashion.

magistrat *m* magistrate.

magistrature *f* magistracy; magistrature.

magnanime *adj* magnanimous; ~ment *adv* magnanimously.

magnanimité *f* magnanimity.

magnat *m* magnate.

magnésium *m* magnesium.

magnétique *adj* magnetic.

magnétiser *vt* to magnetise; to hypnotise.

magnétisme *m* magnetism; hypnotism.

magnétophone *m* tape recorder.

magnétoscope *m* video recorder; videotape.

magnifique *adj* magnificent; sumptuous; ~ment *adv* magnificently.

magnolia *m* magnolia.

magot *m* (*fam*) savings, hoard, nest egg.

magouille *f* (*fam*) fiddle, scam; scheming.

mai *m* May.

maigre *adj* thin; meagre, scarce; ~ment *adv* meagrely.

maigreur *f* thinness; meagreness; sparseness.

maigrir *vi* to get thinner; to waste away.

maille *f* stitch; mesh; link.

maillet *m* mallet.

maillon *m* link; shackle.

maillot *m* jersey; leotard.

main *f* hand; **avoir la ~** to have the lead; **passer la ~** to make way for so.

main-d'œuvre *f* workforce.

maintenance *f* maintenance, servicing.

maintenant *adv* now; **à partir de ~** from now on.

maintenir *vt* to keep, maintain; preserve; **se ~** *vr* to persist; to hold one's own.

maintien *m* maintenance; preservation; keeping up.

maire *m* mayor, *f* mayoress.

mairie *f* mayoralty; town hall.

mais *conj* but.

maïs *m* maize; corn.

maison *f* house; home; building; premises.

maître *m* **-esse** *f* master; ruler; lord; proprietor.

maîtresse *f* mistress; teacher.

maîtrise *f* mastery; control; expertise.

maîtriser *vt* to control; to master; **se ~** *vr* to control o.s.

majesté *f* majesty, grandeur.

majestueusement *adv* majestically.

majestueux *adj* majestic.

majeur *adj* major; main; chief; superior; * *m* major *mf* adult.

majoration *f* increased charge; overestimation.

majordome *m* majordomo, butler.

majorer *vt* to increase, raise.

majorette *f* majorette.

majoritaire *adj* majority.

majorité *f* majority.

majuscule *f* capital letter.

mal *adv* wrong, badly; * *m* evil, wrong; harm; pain.

malachite *f* malachite.

malade *adj* sick, ill; diseased; * *mf* invalid, sick person.

maladie *f* illness; malady, complaint; disorder.

maladresse *f* clumsiness; awkwardness.

maladroit *adj* clumsy, awkward; ~ement *adv* clumsily.

malaise *m* uneasiness, discomfort; indisposition.

malchance *f* ill luck; misfortune; mishap.

malchanceux *adj* unlucky, unfortunate.

mâle *m* male; * *adj* male; manly; virile.

malédiction *f* malediction, curse.

maléfique *adj* hurtful; malignant; baleful.

malencontreux *adj* unfortunate, untoward.

malentendu *m* misunderstanding.

malfaisant *adj* malevolent; harmful; wicked.

malfaiteur *m* criminal; malefactor.

malgré *prép* in spite of; despite.

malheur *m* misfortune; calamity.

malheureusement *adv* unfortunately.

malheureux *adj* unfortunate; unlucky; unhappy.

malhonnête *adj* dishonest, crooked; uncivil; ~ment *adv* dishonestly.

malhonnêteté *f* dishonesty; incivility.

malice *f* malice, spite; mischievousness.

malicieux *adj* malicious, spiteful; mischievous.

malin *adj* shrewd, cunning, crafty; malignant.

malintentionné *adj* ill-disposed, spiteful.

malle *f* trunk.

malléable *adj* malleable.

malmener *vt* to ill-treat, maltreat.

malnutrition *f* malnutrition.

malsain *adj* unhealthy, unwholesome; immoral.

malt *m* malt.

maltraiter *vt* to abuse; to handle roughly.

malveillance *f* malevolence, spite.

malveillant *adj* malevolent, spiteful.

maman *f* mother, mummy, mum.

mamelle *f* breast; udder.

mamelon *m* nipple, teat.

mammifère *m* mammal.

manche *f* sleeve; game, round; * *m* handle, shaft.

manchot *m* -e *f* one-armed person; * *adj* one-armed; * *m* penguin.

mandarin *m* mandarin; Mandarin.

mandarine *f* tangerine.

mandat *m* mandate; money order; proxy.

mandataire *mf* proxy; representative.

mandibule *f* mandible, jaw.

mandoline *f* mandolin.

manège *m* roundabout, merry-go-round.

manette *f* lever, tap.

manganèse *m* manganese.

mangeable *adj* edible.

manger *vt* to eat; to consume.

mangeur *m* -euse *f* eater.

mangouste *f* mongoose.

mangue *f* mango.

maniable *adj* handy, workable, tractable; amenable.

maniaque *adj* eccentric; fussy.; * *mf* maniac; fusspot; fanatic.

manie *f* mania.

maniement *m* handling; management, use.

manier *vt* to handle; to manipulate.

manière *f* manner, way, style.

maniéré *adj* affected.

manifestation *f* demonstration; expression, manifestation.

manifeste *adj* manifest, evident, obvious; ~**ment** *adv* manifestly, obviously; * *m* manifesto.

manifester *vt* to display, make known; to demonstrate; **se ~** *vr* to make o.s. known; to appear; to express o.s.

manigancer *vt* to contrive; to scheme.

manipulation *f* handling; manipulation.

manipuler *vt* to handle; to manipulate

manivelle *f* crank.

mannequin *m* model; dummy.

manœuvre *f* manoeuvre, operation; scheme; * *m* labourer.

manœuvrer *vt* to manoeuvre; to operate; * *vi* to manoeuvre, move.

manoir *m* manor.

manomètre *m* manometer.

manquant *adj* missing.

manque *m* lack, shortage; shortcoming, deficiency.

manquer *vt* to miss; to fail; to be absent.

mansarde *f* attic, garret.

manteau *m* coat; mantle, blanket; cloak.

manuel *m* manual, handbook; * *adj* manual; ~**lement** *adv* manually.

manufacture *f* factory; manufacture.

manufacturier *m* -ière *f* factory owner; manufacturer; * *adj* manufacturing.

manuscrit *m* manuscript; typescript; * *adj* handwritten.

manutention *f* handling.

mappemonde *f* map of the world.

maquereau *m* mackerel.

maquette *f* model; mock-up; dummy; sketch.

maquillage *m* make-up.

maquiller *vt* to make up; to fake; to fiddle; **se ~** *vr* to put make-up on.

marais *m* marsh, swamp.

marasme *m* stagnation; depression, slump.

marathon *m* marathon.

marbre *m* marble; marble statue.

marbré *adj* marbled; mottled, blotchy.

marbrier *m* marble-cutter; monumental mason.

marchand *m* -e *f* shopkeeper; dealer; merchant; * *adj* market, trade.

marchandage *m* bargaining, haggling.

marchander *vi* to bargain over, haggle.

marchandise *f* merchandise, commodity; goods.

marche *f* walk; journey; progress; movement; **mettre en ~** to start up; to turn on.

marché *m* market; transaction, contract.

marcher *vi* to walk, march; to progress; to work.

marcheur *m* -euse *f* walker, pedestrian.

mardi *m* Tuesday.

mare *f* pool, pond.

marécage *m* marsh, swamp.

maréchal *m* marshal.

marée *f* tide.

margarine *f* margarine.

marge *f* margin; latitude, freedom; mark-up.

marginal *adj* marginal.

marginaliser *vt* to marginalise.

marguerite *f* daisy.

mari *m* husband.

mariage *m* marriage.

marié *m* bridegroom; * *adj* married.

marier *vt* to marry; blend, harmonise; **se ~** *vr* to get married.

marin *m* sailor.

marine *f* navy; seascape; marine.

mariner *vi* to marinate; to hang about; * *vt* to marinate.

marionnette *f* puppet; puppet show.

maritime *adj* maritime; seaboard.

marjolaine *f* marjoram.

marmelade *f* stewed fruit; marmalade.

marmite *f* pot.

marmonner *vt* to mumble, mutter.

marmotte *f* marmot.

maroquinerie *f* tannery; fine leather craft.

maroquinier *m* leather craftsman; dealer in fine leather.

marquant *adj* outstanding, vivid.

marque *f* mark, sign; brand; make.

marquer *vt* to mark; to note down; to score.

marquis *m* marquis, -e *f* marchioness.

marraine *f* godmother; sponsor.

marron *m* chestnut; brown; * *adj* brown.

marronnier *m* chestnut tree.

mars *m* March.

marsouin *m* porpoise.

marteau *m* hammer; knocker.

marteler *vt* to hammer; to beat.

martial *adj* martial, warlike.

martin-pêcheur *m* kingfisher.

martyr *m* -e *f* martyr; * *adj* martyred.

martyre *m* martyrdom.

martyriser *vt* to torture, martyrise.

mascarade *f* farce, mascarade.

masculin *adj* masculine.

masochisme *m* masochism.

masochiste *mf* masochist; * *adj* masochistic.

masque *m* mask; facade, front.

masquer *vt* to mask, conceal; to disguise.

massacre *m* massacre; slaughter.

massacrer *vt* to massacre, slaughter.

massage *m* massage.

masse *f* mass, heap; bulk; mob.

masser *vt* to mass, assemble; to massage.

masseur *m* masseur, -euse *f* masseuse.

massif *adj* massive, solid, heavy; * *m* massif; clump.

massivement *adv* en masse, massively, heavily.

massue *f* club.

mastic *m* mastic; cement; putty.

mastiquer *vt* to chew, masticate.

masturbation *f* masturbation.

masturber *vi* se ~ *vr* to masturbate.

mat *adj* matt, dull; dead, dull-sounding.

mât *m* mast; pole.

match *m* match; game.

matelas *m* mattress.

matelassé *adj* stuffed; padded, cushioned.

matelot *m* sailor; seaman.

mater *vt* to subdue; to control, curb; to spy on; to ogle.

matérialiser *vt* to embody; se ~ *vr* to materialise.

matériaux *mpl* material, materials.

matériel *adj* material, physical; practical; ~lement *adv* materially, practically.

maternel *adj* maternal, motherly; ~lement *adv* maternally.

maternité *f* motherhood; pregnancy; maternity hospital.

mathématicien *m* -ne *f* mathematician.

mathématique *adj* mathematical; ~ment *adv* mathematically; * *f* mathematics.

matière *f* material, matter; subject; ~ première raw material.

matin *m* morning; dawn.

matinal *adj* morning.

matinée *f* morning; matinée.

matraque *f* truncheon; cosh.

matrice *f* womb; mould; matrix.

matricule *m* reference number; * *f* roll, register.

matrimonial *adj* matrimonial, marriage.

maturation *f* maturing; maturation.

maturité *f* maturity; prime.

maudire *vt* to curse.

maudit *adj* cursed; blasted, damned.

maussade *adj* sulky, sullen; ~ment *adv* sulkily, sullenly.

mauvais *adj* bad; wicked; faulty; hurtful; poor.

mauve *adj* mauve; * *f* mallow.

maximal *adj* maximal.

maxime *f* maxim.

maximum *m* maximum.

mayonnaise *f* mayonnaise.

me, m' *pn* me; myself.

mécanicien *m* -ne *f* mechanic; engineer.

mécanique *f* mechanics; mechanical engineering; * *adj* mechanical; ~ment *adv* mechanically.

mécanisme *m* mechanism, working.

mécène *m* patron.

méchamment *adv* spitefully; wickedly.

méchanceté *f* spitefulness; wickedness; mischievousness.

méchant *adj* spiteful; wicked; mischievous.

mèche *f* wick, fuse; tuft.

méconnaissable *adj* unrecognisable.

méconnu *adj* unrecognised; misunderstood.

mécontent *adj* discontent, displeased.

mécontentement *m* discontent; displeasure.

médaille *f* medal; stain, mark.

médaillon *m* medallion; locket.

médecin *m* doctor, physician.

médecine *f* medicine

médiateur *m* -trice *f* mediator; arbitrator.

médiatique *adj* media.

médical *adj* medical; ~ement *adv* medically.

médicament *m* medicine, drug.

médicinal *adj* medicinal.

médiéval *adj* medieval.

médiocre *adj* mediocre; passable; indifferent; ~ment *adv* indifferently; poorly.

médisant *adj* slanderous.

méditation *f* meditation.

méditer *vi* to meditate; * *vt* to contemplate, have in mind.

médium *m* medium.

méduse *f* jellyfish.

méfiance *f* distrust, mistrust.

méfiant *adj* distrustful, mistrustful.

méfier (se) *vr* to mistrust, distrust; to be suspicious.

mégalomane *adj* megalomaniac; * *mf* megalomaniac.

mégaphone *m* megaphone.

mégot *m* cigarette-end, stub.

meilleur *adj* better, preferable; le ~, la ~e the best.

mélancolie *f* melancholy, gloom.

mélancolique *adj* melancholy; melancholic; ~ment *adv* melancholically.

mélange *m* mixing, blending; mixture.

mélanger *vt* to mix, blend; to muddle.

mêlée *f* melée, fray; scrum.

mêler *vt* to mix; to combine; se ~ *vr* to mix, mingle; se ~ à to join; se ~ de to meddle in.

mélisse *f* lemon balm.

mélodie *f* melody, tune.

mélodieusement *adv* melodiously, tunefully.

mélodieux *adj* melodious, tuneful.

mélomane *mf* music lover.

melon *m* melon.

membrane *f* membrane.

membre *m* member; limb.

même *adv* even; tout de ~ nevertheless, all the same; * *adj* same, identical; * *pn* le ~, la ~, les ~s the same, the same ones.

mémoire *f* memory; * *m* memorandum, report.

mémorable *adj* memorable.

mémoriser *vt* to memorise.

menaçant *adj* menacing, threatening.

menace *f* threat; intimidation; danger.

menacer *vt* to threaten, menace; to impend.

ménage *m* housework, housekeeping; household.

ménager *vt* to treat with caution; to manage; to arrange.; se ~ *vr* to take care of o.s.; * *adj* household, domestic.

ménagère *f* housewife.

ménagerie *f* menagerie.

mendiant *m* -e *f* beggar.

mendier *vt* to beg; to implore.

mener *vt* to lead, guide; to steer; to manage.

meneur *m* -euse *f* leader; agitator.

menhir *m* menhir, standing stone.

méningite *f* meningitis.

ménopause *f* menopause.

menottes *fpl* handcuffs.

mensonge *m* lie, falsehood; error, illusion.

menstruation *f* menstruation.

mensuel *adj* monthly.

mental *adj* mental; ~ement *adv* mentally.

mentalité *f* mentality.

menteur *m* -euse *f* liar; * *adj* lying, deceitful.

menthe *f* mint.

menthol *m* menthol.

mention *f* mention; comment; grade.

mentionner *vt* to mention.

mentir *vi* to lie; to be deceptive.

menton *m* chin.

menu *m* menu; meal; * *adj* slender, thin; petty, minor.

menuiserie *f* joinery, carpentry.

menuisier *m* joiner, carpenter.

mépris *m* contempt, scorn.

méprisant *adj* contemptuous, scornful.

mépriser *vt* to scorn, despise.

mer *f* sea; tide.

mercenaire *m* mercenary.

mercerie *f* haberdashery.

merci *m* thank you; * *f* mercy; **sans ~** merciless; **être à la ~ de** to be at the mercy of.

mercredi *m* Wednesday.

mercure *m* mercury.

mère *f* mother.

méridien *m* meridian; midday.

méridional *adj* southern.

meringue *f* meringue.

merisier *m* wild cherry.

mérite *m* merit, worth; quality.

mériter *vt* to deserve, merit.

merlan *m* whiting.

merle *m* blackbird.

merveille *f* marvel, wonder.

merveilleusement *adv* marvellously, wonderfully.

merveilleux *adj* marvellous, wonderful.

mésange *f* (*orn*) tit.

mésentente *f* misunderstanding.

mesquin *adj* mean, niggardly; petty; **~ement** *adv* meanly, pettily.

message *m* message.

messager *m* **-ère** *f* messenger.

messagerie *f* parcels office, parcels service.

messe *f* mass.

messie *m* messiah.

mesure *f* measure; gauge; measurement; moderation; step; **au fur et à ~** as; one by one; **sans commune ~ avec** there is no possible comparison with; **dans la mesure où** insofar as; **en ~** in time.

mesurer *vt* to measure; to assess; to limit; **se ~** *vr* to try one's strength; **se ~ à** to pit o.s. against, measure one's strength against.

métabolisme *m* metabolism.

métal *m* metal.

métallique *adj* metallic.

métallisé *adj* metallic, metallised.

métallurgie *f* metallurgy.

métallurgiste *m* steelworker, metalworker.

métamorphose *f* metamorphosis.

métamorphoser *vt* to transform, metamorphose; **se ~** *vr* to be metamorphosed.

métaphore *f* metaphor.

métaphorique *adj* metaphorical; **~ment** *adv* metaphorically.

métaphysique *adj* metaphysical; * *f* metaphysics.

météore *m* meteor.

météorite *m/f* meteorite.

météorologue, météorologiste *mf* meteorologist.

méthane *m* methane.

méthode *f* method, way.

méthodique *adj* methodical; **~ment** *adv* methodically.

méthylène *m* methyl alcohol; methylene.

méticuleusement *adv* meticulously.

méticuleux *adj* meticulous

métier *m* job; occupation; **~ à tricoter** knitting machine; **~ à tisser** weaving loom.

métis *m* **-se** *f* half-caste; hybrid; mongrel; * *adj* half-caste; hybrid, mongrel.

mètre *m* metre.

métro *m* underground, metro.

métronome *m* metronome.

métropole *f* metropolis.

métropolitain *adj* metropolitan; underground.

mets *m* dish.

metteur en scène *m* (*cin*) director.

mettre *vt* to put, place; to put on; **~ en marche** to start up; **se ~** *vr* to place o.s.; to sit down; **se ~ à** to begin to; **se ~ en route** to start off.

meuble *m* piece of furniture.

meubler *vt* to furnish.

meule *f* millstone; grindstone.

meurtrier *m* murderer, **-ière** *f* murderess.

meurtrir *vt* to bruise.

meute *f* pack.

mezzanine *f* mezzanine.

mi- *adj* half; **à ~chemin** halfway; **~clos** half-closed; **à ~jambe** up to the knees; **à ~voix** in a low voice.

miauler *vi* to mew.

miche *f* round loaf.

microbe *m* germ, microbe.

microbien *adj* microbial, microbic.

microclimat *m* microclimate.

microfilm *m* microfilm.

micro-informatique *f* micro-computing.

micro-onde *f* microwave; * *m* **micro-ondes** microwave oven.

micro-ordinateur *m* microcomputer.

microphone *m* microphone.

microprocesseur *m* microprocessor.

microscope *m* microscope.

microscopique *adj* microscopic.

midi *m* midday, noon.

mie *f* crumb, soft part of a loaf.

miel *m* honey.

mien *pn*, *f* **mienne**: **le ~, la mienne, les ~s, les miennes** mine, my own.

miette *f* crumb; remnant; morsel.

mieux *m* improvement; **le ~** the best; **de ~ en ~** better and better.

mignon *adj* sweet, pretty.

migraine *f* headache; migraine.

migrateur *m* migrant.

migration *f* migration.

mijoter *vi* to simmer, be brewing; * *vt* to simmer; to scheme, plot.

milice *f* militia.

milieu *m* middle, centre; medium; environment.

militaire *m* serviceman; * *adj* military, army.

militant *m* **-e** *f* militant; * *adj* militant.

militer *vi* to militate; to be a militant.

mille *m* one thousand; * *adj* one thousand.

millénaire *m* millennium, a thousand years; thousandth anniversary; * *adj* thousand-year-old; millennial.

mille-pattes *m* millipede, centipede.

millésime *m* year, date; vintage.

millet *m* millet.

milliard *m* thousand million; billion.

milliardaire *adj* worth (many) millions; * *mf* multimillionaire.

milliardième *adj* thousand millionth; * *m* thousand millionth.

millième *adj* thousandth; * *m* thousandth.

millier *m* thousand.

milligramme *m* milligram.

millilitre *m* millilitre.

millimètre *m* millimetre.

million *m* million.

millionième *adj* millionth; * *m* millionth.

millionnaire *adj* millionaire; worth millions; * *mf* millionaire.

mime *m* mime; * *mf* mimic.

mimer *vt* to mime; to mimic, imitate.

mimétisme *m* mimicry; mimetism.

mimosa *m* mimosa.

minable *adj* seedy, shabby; **~ment** *adv* shabbily.

mince *adj* thin, slender; meagre, trivial.

mincir *vi* to get slimmer, get thinner.

mine *f* expression; appearance; mine; **avoir bonne ~** to look good.

minerai *m* ore.

minéral *adj* mineral; inorganic; * *m* mineral.

minéralogique *adj* mineralogical.

mineur *m* **-e** *f* minor; * *adj* minor; * *m* miner.

miniature *f* miniature.

mini-jupe *f* miniskirt.

minimal *adj* minimal, minimum.

minime *adj* minor, minimal.

minimum *m* minimum.

ministère *m* ministry; agency.

ministériel *adj* ministerial.

ministre *m* minister; clergyman.

minoritaire *adj* minority.

minorité *f* minority.

minuit *m* midnight.

minuscule *adj* minuscule, tiny, minute.

minute *f* minute, moment.

minuterie *f* time switch; regulator.

minutieux *adj* meticulous.

mirabelle *f* mirabelle.

miracle *m* miracle, wonder.

miraculeux *adj* miraculous.

mirage *m* mirage.

miroir *m* mirror, reflection.

misanthrope *mf* misanthrope; misanthropist; * *adj* misanthropic.

mise *f* putting, placing; stake; deposit; investment; ~ **en scène** production, staging; ~ **en liberté** release; ~ **en ordre** ordering, arrangement; ~ **en œuvre** implementation.

miser *vt* to stake, to bet.

misérable *adj* miserable; destitute; pitiable; **~ment** *adv* miserably.

misère *f* misery; poverty; destitution.

miséricorde *f* mercy, forgiveness.

misogyne *mf* misogynist; * *adj* misogynous.

missile *m* missile.

mission *f* mission, assignment.

missionnaire *m* missionary.

mi-temps *f* half-time; half.

miteux *adj* dingy, shabby, poverty-stricken.

mitigé *adj* mitigated; lukewarm.

mitoyen *adj* common; semi-detached.

mitrailler *vt* to machine-gun.

mitraillette *f* submachine gun.

mitrailleuse *f* machine gun.

mixer *vt* to mix; to blend.

mixte *adj* mixed; joint; combined.

mixture *f* mixture, concoction.

mobile *adj* moving; movable; mobile; nimble; * *m* motive; moving body.

mobilier *m* furniture; * *adj* movable; personal; transferable.

mobilisation *f* mobilisation, calling up.

mobilité *f* mobility.

mobylette *f* moped.

moche *adj* (*fam*) ugly, lousy.

mode *f* fashion; custom; * *m* form, mode; way.

modèle *m* model; pattern; design; example.

modeler *vt* to model; to shape; **se ~** *vr*: **se ~ sur** to model o.s. on.

modem *m* modem.

modération *f* moderation; diminution.

modéré *adj* moderate; **~ment** *adv* in moderation.

modérer *vt* moderate, restrained; **se ~** *vr* to control o.s., keep one's temper.

moderne *adj* modern, up-to-date.

moderniser *vt* to modernise.

modeste *adj* modest, simple; unassuming; **~ment** *adv* modestly.

modestie *f* modesty.

modification *f* modification.

modifier *vt* to modify, alter; **se ~** *vr* to be modified.

modulation *f* modulation; adjustment.

moelle *f* marrow; core.

moelleux *adj* mellow; soft; smooth.

mœurs *fpl* morals; customs.

moi *pn* me, I; **c'est à ~** it is mine, it is my turn; **~-même** myself.

mois *m* month.

moisi *adj* mouldy, mildewed; * *m* mould.

moisir *vi* to go mouldy.

moisissure *f* mould, mildew.

moisson *f* harvest.

moissonner *vt* to reap, harvest.

moite *adj* moist, damp.

moitié *f* half.

molaire *f* molar.

molécule *f* molecule.

mollement *adv* softly; gently.

mollusque *m* mollusc.

moment *m* moment, instant, while; time; opportunity.

momentané *adj* momentary; brief; **~ment** *adv* momentarily.

momie *f* mummy.

mon *pn*, *f* **ma**, *pl* **mes** my, my own.

monarchie *f* monarchy.

monastère *m* monastery.

mondain *adj* worldly, mundane; society, fashionable.

monde *m* world, earth; society, company; **il y a du ~** there are some people there.

mondial *adj* world, world-wide; **~ement** *adv* the world over.

monétaire *adj* monetary.

moniteur *m* **-trice** *f* instructor, coach; supervisor.

monnaie *f* currency; coin; change.

monoculture *f* single-crop farming, monoculture.

monologue *m* monologue.

monopole *f* monopoly.

monopoliser *vt* to monopolise.

monotone *adj* monotonous.

monotonie *f* monotony, sameness.

monseigneur *m* my lord, your grace.

monsieur *m* sir, gentleman, Mr, *pl* **messieurs** gentlemen, Messrs.

monstre *m* monster.

monstrueux *adj* monstrous.

mont *m* mountain; mount.

montage *m* assembly; setting up; editing.

montagnard *m* **-e** *f* mountain dweller.

montagne *f* mountain.

montagneux *adj* mountainous.

montant *m* upright; total, total sum; * *adj* upward, rising; upstream.

montée *f* climb, climbing; ascent; rise.

monter *vi* to go up, ascend; get into (vehicle); * *vt* to go up; to carry/bring up.

monteur *m* **-euse** *f* fitter; editor.

montre *f* watch.

montrer *vt* to show, point to; to prove; **se ~** *vr* to appear; to prove o.s.

monture *f* mount; setting; frame.

monument *m* monument, memorial.

monumental *adj* monumental, colossal.

moquer (se) *vr* to make fun, jeer, laugh at.

moqueur *m* **-euse** *f* mocker, scoffer; * *adj* mocking.

moral *adj* moral, ethical; intellectual; **~ement** *adv* morally.

moralité *f* morals, morality.

morbide *adj* morbid, unhealthy.

morceau *m* piece, morsel, fragment; extract.

mordant *adj* cutting, mordant; * *m* mordant.

mordre *vt* to bite, gnaw; to grip.

morgue *f* morgue; mortuary.

morille *f* morel.

morne *adj* gloomy, dismal.

morose *adj* sullen, morose.

morphine *f* morphine.

morphologie *f* morphology.

morse *m* Morse; walrus.

morsure *f* bite.

mort *m* dead man, **-e** *f* dead woman; * *adj* dead; * *f* death.

mortalité *f* mortality; death rate.

mortel *adj* mortal; fatal; **~lement** *adv* mortally.

mortier *m* mortar.

mortuaire *adj* mortuary; funeral.

morue *f* cod.

mosaïque *f* mosaic.

mosquée *f* mosque.

mot *m* word; saying; **~s croisés** crossword.

moteur *m* engine, motor; * *adj* motor, driving.

motif *m* motive, grounds; motif, design.

motion *f* motion; **~ de censure** censure motion.

motivation *f* motivation.

motiver *vt* to justify; to motivate.

moto *f* motorbike.

moto-cross *m* motocross, scrambling.

motte *f* clod, lump; slab.

mou *adj*, *f* **molle** soft; gentle; muffled.

mouche *f* fly.

moucher *vt* to wipe sb's nose; **se ~** *vr* to blow one's nose.

moucheron *m* midge, gnat.

moucheté *adj* speckled; flecked.

mouchoir *m* handkerchief.

moudre *vt* to mill, grind.

moue *f* pout; **faire la ~** to pout.

mouette *f* gull.

moufle *f* mitten.

mouillé *adj* wet, soaked.

mouiller *vt* to wet; to water down; **se ~** *vr* to get wet.

moulage *m* moulding, casting.

moule *m* mould; * *f* mussel.

mouler *vt* to mould; to model.

moulin *m* mill.

moulu *adj* ground; bruised.

mourant *m* dying man, **-e** *f* dying woman; * *adj* dying.

mourir *vi* to die.

mousse *f* moss; foam, froth.

mousser *vi* to froth, foam.

mousseux *adj* sparkling; frothy; * *m* sparkling wine.

moustache *f* moustache; whiskers.

moustachu *adj* moustached; * *m* moustached man.

moustiquaire *f* mosquito net.

moustique *m* mosquito.

moutarde *f* mustard.

mouton *m* sheep; mutton.

mouvement *m* movement, motion; animation.

mouvementé *adj* eventful; turbulent.

mouvoir *vt* to drive, power; **se ~** *vr* to move.

moyen *m* means; way; * *adj* average, medium, moderate; **~nement** *adv* fairly, moderately; **~ âge** Middle Ages.

moyenne *f* average.

moyeu *m* hub; boss.

mue *f* moulting; shedding.

muer *vi* to moult; to slough.

muet *m* mute (man), **muette** *f* mute (woman); * *adj* dumb; silent, mute.

mufle *m* muffle; muzzle.

muguet *m* lily-of-the-valley; (*med*) thrush.

mule *f* she-mule.

mulet *m* mule.

multicolore *adj* multicoloured.

multinationale *f* multinational.

multiple *adj* numerous, multiple; * *m* multiple.

multiplication *f* multiplication.

multiplier *vt* **se ~** *vr* to multiply, increase.

multitude *f* multitude, crowd.

municipal *adj* municipal; local.

municipalité *f* town, municipality.

munir *vt* to provide, equip with; **se ~** *vr* to equip o.s.

munition *f* munition, ammunition.

mur *m* wall.

mûr *adj* ripe, mature; worn out.

muraille *f* city wall, rampart.

mûre *f* blackberry.

mûrir *vi* to ripen, mature.

murmure *m* murmur; muttering; grumbling.

murmurer *vi* to murmur; to whisper; grumble; to babble * *vt* to murmur.

muscle *m* muscle.

musclé *adj* muscular, brawny.

musculaire *adj* muscular.

muse *f* muse.

museau *m* muzzle, snout.

musée *m* art gallery, museum.

musicien *m* **-ne** *f* musician; * *adj* musical.

musique *f* music.

musulman *m* **-e** *f* Moslem; * *adj* Moslem.

mutant *m* **-e** *f* mutant; * *adj* mutant.

mutation *f* transfer; transformation; mutation.

muter *vt* to transfer, move.

mutilation *f* mutilation, maiming.

mutiler *vt* to mutilate; **se ~** *vr* to injure o.s.

mutisme *m* silence; dumbness, muteness.

mutuel *adj* mutual; **~lement** *adv* mutually.

mutuelle *f* mutual insurance company.

mycose *f* mycosis.

mygale *f* tarantula.

myope *mf* short-sighted person; * *adj* short-sighted.

myopie *f* short-sightedness, myopia.

myosotis *m* forget-me-not.

myrtille *f* bilberry, blueberry.

mystère *m* mystery.

mystérieusement *adv* mysteriously.

mystérieux *adj* mysterious.

mystifier *vt* to mystify; to hoax.

mystique *adj* mystical; * *mf* mystic.

mythe *m* myth.

mythique *adj* mythical.

mythologie *f* mythology.

N

nacre *f* mother-of-pearl.
nacré *adj* nacreous, pearly, iridescent.
nageoire *f* fin, flipper.
nager *vi* to swim.
nageur *m* **-euse** *f* swimmer; rower.
naïf *adj* naïve, artless, ingenuous.
nain *m* **-e** *f* dwarf; * *adj* dwarfish, dwarf.
naissance *f* birth, extraction; dawn, beginning.
naître *vi* to be born; to arise, spring up.
naïvement *adv* naïvely.
naïveté *f* naïvety, artlessness, gullibility.
nanti *m* rich man, *adj* rich, well-to-do.
nappe *f* tablecloth; layer; sheet, expanse.
napper *vt* to top with.
napperon *m* tablemat.
narcisse *m* narcissus.
narcotique *m* drug, narcotic; * *adj* narcotic.
narguer *vt* to flout, defy; to cheek.
narine *f* nostril.
narrateur *m* **-trice** *f* narrator.
narration *f* narration, narrative.
nasal *adj* nasal.
naseau *m* nostril.
natalité *f* birth rate.
natation *f* swimming.
nation *f* nation.
national *adj* national; domestic.
nationaliser *vt* to nationalise.
nationaliste *mf* nationalist; * *adj* nationalist.
nationalité *f* nationality.
natte *f* plait, braid.
naturalisation *f* naturalisation.
naturaliste *mf* naturalist; taxidermist; * *adj* naturalistic.
nature *f* nature; kind, sort; temperament.
naturel *adj* natural; native; unsophisticated; **~lement** *adv* naturally; of course.
naufrage *m* shipwreck; ruin, foundering.
nausée *f* nausea.
nautique *adj* nautical, water.
naval *adj* naval, shipbuilding.
navet *m* turnip.
navette *f* shuttle; **faire la ~** to shuttle between.
navigateur *m* navigator, sailor.

navigation *f* sailing, navigation.
navire *m* ship, vessel.
navrant *adj* distressing, upsetting.
ne *adv* no, not.
né *adj* born.
néanmoins *adv* nevertheless.
néant *m* nothing, nothingness, emptiness.
nécessaire *adj* necessary; requisite; indispensable; **~ment** *adv* necessarily.
nécessité *f* necessity; need; inevitability.
nécessiter *vt* to require, necessitate.
nécropole *f* necropolis.
nectar *m* nectar.
nectarine *f* nectarine.
néfaste *adj* harmful; unlucky; ill-fated.
négatif *adj* negative.
négation *f* negation; negative.
négativement *adv* negatively.
négligemment *adv* negligently; carelessly; nonchalantly.
négligence *f* negligence, carelessness.
négligent *adj* negligent, careless; nonchalant.
négliger *vt* to neglect; to be negligent about.
négociant *m* **-e** *f* merchant.
négociation *f* negotiation.
négocier *vi* to negotiate; to trade; * *vt* to negotiate.
neige *f* snow.
neiger *vi* to snow, be snowing.
nénuphar *m* water-lily.
néophyte *mf* neophyte; novice * *adj* newly converted.
nerf *m* nerve.
nerveusement *adv* nervously; irritably.
nerveux *adj* nervous; vigorous; excitable.
nervosité *f* nervousness; excitability.
nervure *f* nervure, vein; rib.
net *adj*, *f* **-te** clean; clear; plain; sharp; net; **~tement** *adv* cleanly; clearly; plainly.
netteté *f* neatness; clearness; sharpness.
nettoyage *m* cleaning; clearing up.
nettoyer *vt* to clean; to ruin, clean out.
neuf *adj* nine; * *m* nine.

neurologie *f* neurology.
neurone *m* neurone.
neutraliser *vt* to neutralise.
neutralité *f* neutrality.
neutre *adj* neutral; neuter.
neutron *m* neutron.
neuvième *adj* ninth; **~ment** *adv* ninthly; * *f* ninth.
neveu *m* nephew.
névralgie *f* neuralgia.
névrose *f* neurosis.
nez *m* nose; flair; **avoir du ~** to have flair.
niais *adj* silly, simple, inane; **~ement** *adv* inanely.
niche *f* niche, nook; kennel; trick.
nickel *m* nickel.
nicotine *f* nicotine.
nid *m* nest; den; berth.
nièce *f* niece.
nier *vt* to deny; to repudiate.
nigaud *m* **-e** *f* simpleton.
nitrate *m* nitrate.
nitroglycérine *f* nitroglycerine.
niveau *m* level; standard; par; gauge.
niveler *vt* to level; to even out, equalise.
noble *adj* noble, dignified; **~ment** *adv* nobly.
noblesse *f* nobleness, nobility.
noce *f* wedding, wedding feast; marriage ceremony.
nocif *adj* noxious, harmful.
noctambule *mf* night reveller, night owl; sleepwalker; * *adj* enjoying night life; noctambulant.
nocturne *adj* nocturnal, night; * *f* evening fixture; late night opening.
nodule *m* nodule.
Noël *m* Christmas.
nœud *m* knot, bow; crux.
noir *adj* black; dark; * *m* black; darkness; black man.
noircir *vt* to blacken; to dirty; **se ~** *vr* to darken, grow black.
noire *f* black woman.
noisetier *m* hazel tree.
noisette *f* hazel.
noix *f* walnut.
nom *m* name; fame; noun.
nomade *mf* nomad.
nombre *m* number, quantity.
nombreux *adj* numerous, frequent.
nombril *m* navel.

nomenclature *f* list, catalogue; nomenclature.

nominal *adj* nominal; noun; **~ement** *adv* nominally.

nominatif *m* nominative.

nomination *f* appointment; nomination.

nommer *vt* to appoint; nominate.

non *adv* no; not.

nonchalance *f* nonchalance.

nonchalant *adj* nonchalant.

non-conformiste *mf* nonconformist; * *adj* nonconformist.

non-lieu *m* (*jur*) no ground for prosecution.

non-sens *m* nonsense.

non-violence *f* non-violence.

nord *m* north, northerly (wind).

nordique *adj* Nordic; Scandinavian.

normal *adj* normal, usual; standard-sized; **~ement** *adv* normally, usually.

norme *f* norm; standard.

nostalgie *f* nostalgia.

nostalgique *adj* nostalgic.

notable *adj* notable; noteworthy; **~ment** *adv* notably.

notaire *m* notary; solicitor.

notamment *adv* notably; in particular.

note *f* note; minute; mark; bill.

noter *vt* to note down; to notice; to mark.

notice *f* note; directions; instructions.

notion *f* notion, idea.

notoire *adj* notorious; well-known, acknowledged; **~ment** *adv* notoriously.

notoriété *f* notoriety; fame.

notre *adj*, *pl* **nos** ours, our own.

nôtre *pn*: **le ~, la ~, les ~s** ours, our own.

nouer *vt* to tie, knot; **se ~** *vr* to join together.

nouille *f* (piece of) pasta.

nourrice *f* child-minder, nanny.

nourrir *vt* to feed, provide for; to stoke; **se ~** *vr* to feed o.s.

nourrissant *adj* nourishing, nutritious.

nourrisson *m* infant, nursling.

nourriture *f* food; sustenance.

nous *pn* we; us; **c'est à ~** it's ours; it's our turn; **~-mêmes** ourselves.

nouveau *adj* new; recent; additional.

nouveau-né *m* **-e** *f* new-born child.

nouveauté *f* novelty; newness.

nouvelle *f* piece of news; short story.

novembre *m* November.

novice *mf* novice, beginner; * *adj* novice, unpractised, inexperienced.

noyade *f* drowning, drowning incident.

noyau *m* stone, pit; core; nucleus.

noyer *vt* to drown; to flood; **se ~** *vr* to drown, drown o.s.; * *m* walnut (tree).

nu *adj* naked, nude; plain, unadorned.

nuage *m* cloud.

nuageux *adj* cloudy, overcast.

nuance *f* shade, hue; faint difference, nuance.

nucléaire *adj* nuclear; * *m* nuclear energy.

nudiste *mf* nudist; * *adj* nudist.

nudité *f* nakedness, nudity.

nuée *f* dense cloud; horde, swarm.

nuire *vi* to harm, injure; to prejudice.

nuisible *adj* harmful; noxious; **~ment** *adv* harmfully.

nuit *f* night, darkness.

nul *adj* no; nil; null and void; non-existent; **~lement** *adv* not at all, not in the least.

nullité *f* nullity; uselessness.

numéral *adj* numeral; * *m* numeral.

numérique *adj* numerical; digital.

numéro *m* number; issue.

numérotation *f* numbering, numeration.

numéroter *vt* to number.

nuptial *adj* nuptial, wedding.

nuque *f* nape (of the neck).

nutritif *adj* nutritious, nourishing.

nutrition *f* nutrition.

nylon *m* nylon.

nymphe *f* nymph.

O

oasis *m* oasis.

obéir *vt* to obey, be obedient; to comply.

obéissance *f* obedience; compliance.

obéissant *adj* obedient.

obèse *adj* obese.

obésité *f* obesity.

objecter *vt* to object.

objectif *adj* objective, unbiased; * *m* objective, target.

objection *f* objection.

objectivement *adv* objectively.

objet *m* object, thing; purpose; matter.

obligation *f* obligation, duty; bond.

obligatoire *adj* obligatory, compulsory; ~ment *adv* obligatorily.

obligé *adj* obliged, compelled; inevitable; necessary.

obliger *vt* to oblige, require; (*jur*) to bind.

oblique *adj* oblique, sidelong.

oblitérer *vt* to obliterate; to cancel (stamp).

obscène *adj* obscene.

obscénité *f* obscenity.

obscur *adj* obscure, dark, gloomy; ~ément *adv* obscurely.

obscurcir *vt* to darken; to obscure; s'~ *vr* to get dark.

obscurité *f* obscurity; darkness.

obséder *vt* to obsess, haunt.

obsèques *fpl* funeral.

observateur *m* -trice *f* observer; * *adj* observant.

observation *f* observation; remark.

observatoire *m* observatory.

observer *vt* to observe, watch; to notice; to comply with.

obsession *f* obsession.

obstacle *m* obstacle, hindrance.

obstétrique *f* obstetrics.

obstination *f* obstinacy, stubbornness.

obstiné *adj* obstinate, stubborn; ~ment *adv* obstinately.

obstiner (s') *vr* to insist, persist.

obtenir *vt* to obtain, procure, get; to achieve.

obturation *f* stopping, closing up, obturation.

obus *m* shell.

occasion *f* occasion, opportunity; cause; bargain; d'~ second-hand.

occident *m* west.

occidental *adj* western; Occidental.

occulte *adj* occult.

occupant *m* -e *f* occupant, occupier.

occupation *f* occupation, pursuit; work; occupancy.

occuper *vt* to occupy; to employ; to inhabit; s'~ *vr* to keep busy.

océan *m* ocean.

ocre *m* ochre; * *adj* ochre.

octane *m* octane.

octave *f* octave.

octet *m* byte.

octobre *m* October.

octroyer *vt* to grant, bestow; s'~ *vr* to allow oneself.

oculaire *adj* ocular.

odeur *f* smell, odour.

odieux *adj* hateful, obnoxious.

odorat *m* smell (sense).

oedème *m* oedema.

œil *m, pl* yeux eye; look; bud.

œillet *m* carnation.

oesophage *m* oesophagus.

œuf *m* egg.

œuvre *f* work; action, deed; production.

offense *f* offence; injury, wrong.

offenser *vt* to offend; to injure, shock; s'~ *vr* to take offence.

offensif *adj* offensive; forceful, aggressive.

offensive *f* offensive, attack.

office *m* office, bureau; duty; function.

officiel *adj* official; ~lement *adv* officially.

officier *m* officer.

officieusement *adv* officiously; unofficially.

officieux *adj* officious, over-obliging; unofficial.

offrande *f* offering.

offre *f* offer, tender, bid.

offrir *vt* to offer.

offusquer *vt* to offend; s'~ *vr* to take offence; to be offended.

ogive *f* ogive, pointed arch.

ogre *m* ogre, -sse *f* ogress.

ohm *m* ohm.

oie *f* goose.

oignon *m* onion; bulb.

oiseau *m* bird.

oisif *adj* idle.

oisiveté *f* idleness.

oléagineux *adj* oleaginous, oily.

oléoduc *m* oil pipeline.

olfactif *adj* olfactory.

oligarchie *f* oligarchy.

oligo-élément *m* trace element.

olive *f* olive.

olivier *m* olive tree.

olympique *adj* Olympic.

ombilical *adj* umbilical.

ombragé *adj* shaded, shady.

ombre *f* shade, shadow.

omelette *f* omelette.

omettre *vt* to leave out, miss out.

omission *f* omission.

omnibus *m* local train; omnibus.

omnipotent *adj* omnipotent.

omniprésent *adj* omnipresent.

omoplate *f* shoulder blade.

on *pn* one; someone, anyone.

once *f* ounce.

oncle *m* uncle.

onctueux *adj* smooth, creamy.

onde *f* wave.

ondoyant *adj* undulating, flowing; changeable.

ondulation *f* undulation; wave.

onduler *vi* to undulate; to ripple.

onéreux *adj* onerous; expensive, costly.

ongle *m* nail; claw, talon; hoof.

onomatopée *f* onomatopoeia.

onyx *m* onyx.

onze *adj* eleven; * *m* eleven.

onzième *adj* eleventh; ~ment *adv* in eleventh place; * *mf* eleventh.

opale *f* opal.

opaque *adj* opaque; impenetrable.

opéra *m* opera.

opération *f* operation, performance; transaction, deal.

opérationnel *adj* operational.

opératoire *adj* operating; operative, surgical.

opérer *vt* to operate; to carry out, implement.

opérette *f* operetta, light opera.

ophtalmie *f* ophthalmia.

opiniâtre *adj* stubborn; persistent; ~ment *adv* stubbornly; persistently.

opinion *f* opinion, view.

opium *m* opium.

opportun *adj* timely, opportune; ~ément *adv* opportunely.

opportuniste *mf* opportunist; * *adj* opportunist.

opportunité *f* opportuneness, expediency, timeliness.

opposant *m* -e *f* opponent; * *adj* opposing.

opposé *adj* opposite, contrary; facing; * *m* opposite; **à l'~** contrary to.

opposer *vt* to oppose; to contrast; to object; **s'~** *vr* to be opposed to; to clash, conflict.

opposition *f* opposition; conflict.

oppresser *vt* to oppress, weigh down.

oppressif *adj* oppressive.

oppression *f* oppression.

opprimer *vt* to oppress, crush.

opticien *m* **-ne** *f* optician.

optimisme *m* optimism.

optimiste *mf* optimist; * *adj* optimistic.

option *f* option, choice.

optionnel *adj* optional.

optique *adj* optical; * *f* optics.

opulence *f* opulence, wealth.

opulent *adj* opulent, wealthy.

or *m* gold; * *conj* now.

oracle *m* oracle.

orage *m* storm, tempest, thunderstorm.

orageux *adj* stormy.

oral *adj* oral, verbal; **~ement** *adv* orally.

orange *f* orange; * *adj invar* orange.

oranger *m* orange tree.

orang-outan(g) *m* orang-utang.

orateur *m* **-trice** *f* orator.

orbite *f* orbit; socket; sphere.

orchestral *adj* orchestral.

orchestre *m* orchestra.

orchestrer *vt* to orchestrate, score.

orchidée *f* orchid.

ordinaire *adj* ordinary, common, usual; **~ment** *adv* ordinarily, usually; * *m* custom, usual routine; **d'~, à l'~** ordinarily, usually.

ordinateur *m* computer.

ordonnance *f* prescription, order, edict.

ordonner *vt* to arrange; to order; to prescribe.

ordre *m* order, command; class.

ordure *f* filth, dirt; excrement; rubbish.

oreille *f* ear; hearing; wing; handle.

oreiller *m* pillow.

oreillons *mpl* mumps.

orfèvre *m* silversmith, goldsmith.

orfèvrerie *f* silversmith's (goldsmith's) craft.

organe *m* organ; instrument; medium.

organigramme *m* organisational chart.

organique *adj* organic.

organisateur *m* **-trice** *f* organiser.

organisation *f* organisation.

organiser *vt* to organise, arrange; **s'~** *vr* to organise o.s.

organisme *m* organism.

organiste *mf* organist.

orgasme *m* orgasm.

orge *f* barley.

orgie *f* orgy.

orgue *m* (*mus*) organ.

orgueil *m* pride, arrogance.

orgueilleux *adj* proud, arrogant.

orient *m* orient, east.

oriental *adj* eastern, oriental.

orientation *f* orientation; positioning; directing; trend.

orienter *vt* to orientate; to position; to direct; **s'~** *vr* to ascertain one's position; to turn towards.

orifice *m* orifice; aperture, opening.

originaire *adj* originating from, native to; **~ment** *adv* originally, primitively.

original *adj* original, novel; peculiar, bizarre; * *m* original; top copy.

originalité *f* originality; oddness.

origine *f* origin, source, derivation; **à l'~** originally.

originel *adj* original, primitive.

orme *m* elm.

ornement *m* ornament, embellishment.

ornemental *adj* ornamental.

orner *vt* to adorn, decorate.

ornière *f* rut.

ornithologie *f* ornithology.

ornithologiste, ornithologue *mf* ornithologist.

orphelin *m* **-e** *f* orphan.

orphelinat *m* orphanage.

orteil *m* toe.

orthodoxe *adj* orthodox; * *mf* orthodox.

orthogonal *adj* orthogonal.

orthographe *f* spelling.

orthopédie *f* orthopaedics.

orthopédique *adj* orthopaedic.

ortie *f* nettle.

orvet *m* slow-worm.

os *m* bone.

oscillation *f* oscillation, swinging.

osciller *vi* to oscillate, swing.

oseille *f* sorrel.

oser *vt* to dare.

osier *m* osier, willow, wicker.

osmose *f* osmosis.

ossature *f* skeleton; framework.

ossements *mpl* bones.

ostensible *adj* open, conspicuous; **~ment** *adv* openly; conspicuously.

ostentation *f* ostentation.

ostéopathe *mf* osteopath.

ostracisme *m* ostracism.

otage *m* hostage.

otarie *f* sea-lion.

ôter *vt* to take away, remove; to deprive, deduct.

otite *f* ear infection.

oto-rhino-laryngologie *f* oto-rhinolaryngology.

oto-rhino(-laryngologiste) *mf* ear, nose and throat specialist.

ou *conj* or.

où *adv* where, in which; *pn* where.

ouate *f* cotton wool.

oubli *m* forgetfulness; oblivion; oversight, omission.

oublier *vt* to forget; to omit, neglect.

oubliette *f* oubliette.

ouest *m* west; *adj* west.

oui *adv* yes.

ouïe *f* hearing (sense).

ouragan *m* hurricane, whirlwind.

ourlet *m* hem.

ours *m* **-e** *f* bear.

oursin *m* sea urchin.

ourson *m* bear cub.

outil *m* tool, implement.

outillage *m* (set of) tools; equipment.

outiller *vt* to equip; to provide with tools.

outrage *m* outrage, insult, wrong.

outrageant *adj* outrageous, insulting.

outre *prép* as well as, besides; **en ~** moreover; **~ mesure** to excess, inordinately; **passer ~** to go on, to take no notice; * *f* goatskin, leather bottle.

outré *adj* excessive, exaggerated.

outremer *m* ultramarine.

outrepasser *vt* to exceed; to transgress.

ouvert *adj* open; exposed; frank; **~ement** *adv* openly, overtly.

ouverture *f* opening; mouth; overture; means, way.

ouvrable *adj* working, business.

ouvrage *m* work; piece of work.

ouvre-boîte *m* tin-opener.

ouvre-bouteille *m* bottle-opener.

ouvrier *m* **-ière** *f* worker; * *adj* working-class; industrial; labour.

ouvrir *vt* to open; to unlock; to broach; **s'~** *vr* to open; to open one's mind; to cut o.s.

ovaire *m* ovary.

ovale *adj* oval; * *m* oval.

ovation *f* ovation.

ovni *m* UFO.

ovulation *f* ovulation.

ovule *m* ovum; ovule.

oxydation *f* oxidation.

oxyde *m* oxide.

oxyder *vt* to oxidise; **s'~** *vr* to become oxidised.

oxygène *m* oxygen.

ozone *f* ozone.

P

pacifier *vt* to pacify.

pacifique *adj* peaceful, pacific; **~ment** *adv* peacefully, pacifically.

pacifiste *mf* pacifist; * *adj* pacifist.

pacte *m* pact, treaty.

pactiser *vt* to treat with sb; to come to terms with.

pagaie *f* paddle.

pagayer *vi* to paddle.

page *f* page; passage.

pagne *m* loincloth.

paiement *m* payment.

païen *m* **-ne** *f* pagan; * *adj* pagan.

paillasse *f* straw mattress.

paillasson *m* doormat.

paille *f* straw.

paillette *f* sequin; spangle.

pain *m* bread; loaf; bar.

pair *adj* even; * *m* peer; par; **hors ~** outstanding, matchless.

paire *f* pair; yoke; brace.

paisible *adj* peaceful; calm; **~ment** *adv* peacefully; calmly.

paître *vi* to graze.

paix *f* peace; quiet; stillness; tranquillity.

palais *m* palace; law courts; palate.

palan *m* hoist.

pâle *adj* pale, pallid.

palette *f* palette; pallet; paddle.

pâleur *f* paleness, pallor.

palier *m* landing; level; degree.

pâlir *vi* to turn pale; to dim; to fade.

palissade *f* fence; boarding; stockade.

palliatif *m* palliative; * *adj* palliative.

pallier *vt* to palliate; to offset.

palmarès *m* prize list; medal record.

palme *f* palm leaf; palm.

palmé *adj* palmate; webbed.

palmeraie *f* palm grove.

palmier *m* palm tree.

palmipède *m* palmiped.

palpable *adj* palpable.

palper *vt* to feel, touch; to palpate.

palpitation *f* palpitation; throbbing; quivering.

palpiter *vi* to palpitate; to beat; to race.

paludisme *m* malaria.

pamplemousse *m* grapefruit.

panache *m* panache; gallantry.

panaché *adj* variegated; motley.

pancarte *f* sign, notice; placard.

pancréas *m* pancreas.

panda *m* panda.

pané *adj* covered in breadcrumbs.

panier *m* basket; pannier (mode).

panique *f* panic.

paniquer *vi* to panic, get panicky.

panne *f* breakdown; fault, problem.

panneau *m* panel; sign, notice.

panoplie *f* outfit; display.

panorama *m* panorama.

panoramique *adj* panoramic.

pansement *m* dressing, bandage.

panser *vt* to dress, bandage.

pantalon *m* trousers; pants; knickers.

panthéon *m* pantheon.

panthère *f* panther.

pantin *m* jumping-jack; puppet.

pantomime *f* pantomime; mime.

pantoufle *f* slipper.

paon *m* peacock.

papa *m* dad; daddy.

papauté *f* papacy.

papaye *f* papaya.

pape *m* pope.

papeterie *f* stationery; stationer's shop; paper mill.

papetier *m* **-ière** *f* stationer; paper-maker.

papier *m* paper; article; wrapper.

papillon *m* butterfly.

papillote *f* sweet wrapper.

papoter *vi* to chatter.

Pâques *fpl* Easter.

paquebot *m* liner, steamer.

pâquerette *f* daisy.

paquet *m* packet, pack; bag; parcel.

par *prép* by, with, through;from; along; **~-ci**, **~-là** here and there, now and then; **~-derrière** round the back; **~-dessous** underneath; **~-dessus** over, above.

parabole *f* (*math*) parabola; parable.

parachever *vt* to perfect; to complete.

parachute *m* parachute.

parachuter *vt* to parachute.

parachutiste *mf* parachutist.

parade *f* parade, show; parry.

paradis *m* paradise; (*thea*) gallery.

paradoxal *adj* paradoxical; **~ement** *adv* paradoxically.

paradoxe *m* paradox.

paraffine *f* paraffin.

parages *mpl* vicinity; **dans les ~** in the area.

paragraphe *m* paragraph; section.

paraître *vi* to appear; to be published; to look, seem; **il paraît que** apparently.

parallèle *adj* parallel; **~ment** *adv* parallel; at the same time.

paralyser *vt* to paralyse.

paralysie *f* paralysis.

paralytique *mf* paralytic; * *adj* paralytic.

paramètre *m* parameter.

paranoïa *f* paranoia.

paranoïaque *adj* paranoiac, paranoid; * *mf* paranoiac, paranoid.

paraphraser *vt* to paraphrase.

parapluie *m* umbrella.

parasite *m* parasite, sponger.

parasol *m* parasol; sunshade.

paratonnerre *m* lightning conductor.

paravent *m* folding screen, partition.

parc *m* park; grounds; depot.

parcelle *f* fragment, particle; parcel.

parce que *conj* because.

parchemin *m* parchment.

parcimonie *f* parsimony.

parcmètre *m* meter (parking).

parcourir *vt* to travel through; to scour; to traverse.

pardon *m* pardon, forgiveness.

pardonner *vt* to pardon; to excuse, overlook.

pare-brise *m invar* windscreen.

pare-chocs *m invar* bumper.

pareil *m* **-le** *f* equal; match; **sans ~** unparalleled, unequalled; * *adj* like, equal, similar; identical; **~lement** *adv* likewise, equally.

parent *m* **-e** *f* relative, relation; **~s** (*pl*) parents.

parental *adj* parental.

parenté *f* relationship, kinship.

parenthèse *f* parenthesis, digression.

parer *vt* to adorn, deck out; to ward off; to parry; **~ à** to deal with, overcome.

paresse *f* laziness; sluggishness.

paresseux *m* **-euse** *f* lazy person, loafer; * *adj* lazy.

parfaire *vt* to perfect, bring to perfection.

parfait *adj* perfect, flawless; ~**ement** *adv* perfectly; completely, absolutely.

parfois *adv* sometimes, occasionally.

parfumer *vt* to perfume, scent; **se** ~ *vr* to put perfume on.

parfumerie *f* perfumery.

parfumeur *m* **-euse** *f* perfumer.

pari *m* bet, wager.

parier *vt* to bet, wager.

parking *m* car park; parking.

parlement *m* Parliament.

parlementaire *adj* parliamentary; * *mf* member of parliament.

parler *vi* to talk, speak; * *vt* to speak.

parmesan *m* parmesan.

parmi *prép* among.

parodie *f* parody.

paroi *f* wall; surface.

paroisse *f* parish.

parole *f* word; speech; voice; lyrics.

paroxysme *m* paroxysm; crisis.

parquer *vt* to park; to enclose, pen.

parquet *m* floor, floorboards.

parrain *m* godfather; patron; promoter.

parrainage *m* sponsorship; promoting; patronage.

parrainer *vt* to sponsor; propose.

parsemer *vt* to sprinkle, strew.

part *f* part; share; portion; **prendre** ~ **à** to participate in; **faire** ~ **de** to announce; **de sa part** for his part; **autre** ~ elsewhere; **nulle** ~ nowhere; **d'autre** ~ moreover.

partage *m* sharing, distribution; portion.

partager *vt* to divide up, share out.

partenaire *mf* partner.

parti *m* party; option; match.

partial *adj* partial, biased; ~**ement** *adv* in a biased way.

participant *m* **-e** *f* participant, member; * *adj* participant, participating.

participation *f* participation; involvement.

participe *m* participle.

participer *vi* to take part in, participate.

particularité *f* particularity, characteristic.

particule *f* particle.

particulier *adj* particular, specific; peculiar, characteristic; * *m* person, private individual; character.

particulièrement *adv* particularly, especially.

partie *f* part; subject; game; party; **faire** ~ **de** to be a part of.

partiel *adj* part, partial; ~**lement** *adv* partially, in part.

partir *vi* to leave, set off; to start up; **à** ~ **de** from.

partisan *m* **-e** *f* partisan, supporter, proponent.

partition *f* partition; score.

partout *adv* everywhere.

parvenir *vi*: ~ **à** to reach; to achieve.

pas *m* step; pace; footprint; gait; * *adv* no, not.

passable *adj* passable, tolerable; ~**ment** *adv* tolerably; reasonably.

passage *m* passage, passing by; transit.

passager *m* **-ère** *f* passenger; * *adj* passing, transitory.

passant *m* **-e** *f* passer-by, wayfarer; * *adj* much-frequented, busy.

passe *f* pass; permit; channel.

passé *m* past.

passeport *m* passport.

passer *vi* to pass; to elapse; to disappear, fade; **se** ~ *vr* to pass; to take place; **se** ~ **de** to do without.

passerelle *f* footbridge; bridge; gangway.

passe-temps *m invar* pastime.

passif *adj* passive; * *m* passive.

passion *f* passion; fondness.

passionnant *adj* fascinating; exciting.

passionné *adj* passionate, impassioned; ~**ment** *adv* passionately.

passionner *vt* to fascinate; to interest deeply, impassion; **se** ~ *vr* to be fascinated by, have a passion for.

passivement *adv* passively.

passivité *f* passivity, passiveness.

pastel *m* pastel.

pastèque *f* watermelon.

pasteur *m* minister, pastor.

pasteuriser *vt* to pasteurise.

pastiche *m* pastiche.

pastille *f* pastille, lozenge.

patate *f* (*fam*) spud; sweet potato.

patauger *vi* to wade about, splash about.

pâte *f* pastry, pasta, dough, batter.

pâté *m* pâté.

paternel *adj* paternal, fatherly; ~**lement** *adv* paternally.

paternité *f* paternity; fatherhood.

pathétique *adj* pathetic.

patiemment *adv* patiently.

patience *f* patience, endurance.

patient *adj* patient, enduring.

patienter *vi* to wait.

patin *m* skate; ~ **à glace** iceskate; ~ **à roulettes** roller skate.

patinage *m* skating; slipping; spinning.

patiner *vi* to skate; to slip; to spin.

patineur *m* **-euse** *f* skater.

patinoire *f* ice rink.

pâtisserie *f* cake shop, confectioner's.

pâtissier *m* **-ière** *f* pastry cook, confectioner.

patois *m* patois, provincial dialect.

patrie *f* homeland, country.

patrimoine *m* inheritance, patrimony.

patriote *mf* patriot; * *adj* patriotic.

patriotisme *m* patriotism.

patron *m* **-ne** *f* owner, boss, proprietor.

patronat *m* employers.

patronner *vt* to patronise, sponsor.

patrouille *f* patrol.

patte *f* leg, paw, foot.

pâturage *m* pasture, pasturage, grazing.

pâture *f* pasture; food.

paume *f* palm.

paumer *vt* (*fam*) to lose; **se** ~ *vr* to get lost.

paupière *f* eyelid.

paupiette *f* stuffed slice of meat.

pause *f* pause; half-time.

pauvre *adj* poor; indigent; scanty; weak; ~**ment** *adv* poorly; * *mf* poor person, pauper.

pavé *m* cobblestone, paving stone.

pavillon *m* house; pavilion; flag.

pavot *m* poppy.

paye *f* pay, wages.

payer *vt* to pay, settle; to reward.

pays *m* country; region; village; land.

paysage *m* landscape; scenery.

paysan *m* countryman, farmer; **-ne** *f* countrywoman.

PDG (président-directeur général) *m* chairman and managing director.

péage *m* toll; tollgate.

peau *f* skin; hide, pelt.

pêche *f* peach; fishing.

pécher *vi* to sin.

pêcher *vt* to fish; to catch; * *m* peach tree.

pécheur *m* **-eresse** *f* sinner.

pêcheur *m* fisherman, **-euse** *f* fisherwoman.

pectoral *adj* pectoral; cough.

pectoraux *mpl* pectorals.

pédagogie *f* education; educational methods.

pédagogue *mf* teacher; educationalist; * *adj* pedagogic.

pédale *f* pedal; treadle.

pédaler *vi* to pedal.
pédalier *m* pedal-board, crank-gear.
pédestre *adj* pedestrian.
pédiatre *mf* paediatrician.
pédicure *mf* chiropodist.
peigne *m* comb.
peigner *vt* to comb; to card; **se ~** *vr* to comb one's hair.
peignoir *m* dressing gown.
peindre *vt* to paint; to depict, portray.
peine *f* effort; sadness; pain; punishment; difficulty.
peiner *vi* to toil; to struggle.
peintre *m* painter; portrayer.
peinture *f* painting, picture; paintwork.
péjoratif *adj* pejorative.
pelage *m* coat, fur.
peler *vi* to peel.
pèlerin *m* pilgrim; peregrine falcon.
pèlerinage *m* pilgrimage.
pélican *m* pelican.
pelle *f* shovel; spade.
pellicule *f* film; thin layer.
pelote *f* ball; pelota ball.
peloton *m* pack; squad; platoon.
pelouse *f* lawn, field; ground.
pelure *f* peeling, piece of peel.
pénal *adj* penal; criminal.
pénaliser *vt* to penalise.
pénalité *f* penalty.
penalty *m* penalty (kick).
pencher *vi* to lean; to tilt; (*mar*) to list; * *vt* to tip up; tilt; **se ~** *vr* to bend down; to study, look at.
pendant *prép* during; for; **~ que** while, whilst; * *adj* hanging, drooping; pending.
pendentif *m* pendant; pendentive.
pendre *vi* to hang, dangle; * *vt* to hang; **se ~** *vr* to hang o.s.
pendule *f* clock; * *m* pendulum.
pénétrant *adj* penetrating, piercing; searching; acute.
pénétration *f* penetration; perception.
pénétrer *vi* to enter, penetrate; * *vt* to penetrate, pierce; to pervade.
pénible *adj* hard, tiresome; difficult; laborious; **~ment** *adv* painfully; with difficulty.
péniche *f* barge.
péniciline *f* penicillin.
péninsule *f* peninsula.
pénis *m* penis.
pénitence *f* penitence, penance; punishment.
pénitencier *m* prison, penitentiary.
pénitent *m* **-e** *f* penitent; * *adj* penitent.

pénombre *f* half-light; penumbra (astronomy).
pensée *f* thought; thinking; mind.
penser *vt* to think, suppose, believe; * *vi* to think.
pensif *adj* pensive, thoughtful.
pension *f* pension; boarding house.
pensionnaire *mf* boarder; lodger.
pensionnat *m* boarding school.
pensivement *adv* pensively, thoughtfully.
pentagone *m* pentagon.
pentathlon *m* pentathlon.
pente *f* slope; gradient.
Pentecôte *f* Pentecost, Whitsun.
pénurie *f* shortage, scarcity; penury.
pépère *m* granddad, grandpa.
pépin *m* pip; snag, hitch.
pépinière *f* tree nursery; breeding-ground.
pépite *f* nugget.
perçant *adj* piercing, shrill.
percée *f* opening, clearing; breach; breakthrough.
perce-oreille *m* earwig.
perception *f* perception; collection.
percer *vt* to pierce; to drill; to see through.
percevoir *vt* to perceive, detect; to collect.
percher *vt* to stick; to place on; **se ~** *vr* to perch.
percussion *f* percussion.
percussionniste *mf* percussionist.
percuter *vt* to strike; to crash into.
perdant *m* **-e** *f* loser; * *adj* losing.
perdre *vt* to lose; to waste; to miss; * *vi* to lose; **se ~** *vr* to lose one's way.
perdrix *f* partridge.
perdu *adj* lost; wasted; missed.
père *m* father; sire.
péremptoire *adj* peremptory.
perfection *f* perfection.
perfectionnement *m* perfection, perfecting; improvement.
perfectionner *vt* to improve, perfect; **se ~** *vr* to improve, improve o.s.
perfectionniste *mf* perfectionist; * *adj* perfectionist.
perfide *adj* perfidious, treacherous; **~ment** *adv* perfidiously.
perforation *f* perforation.
perforer *vt* to perforate; to pierce.
performance *f* result, performance.
performant *adj* outstanding; high-performance, high-return.

péricliter *vi* to collapse; to be in jeopardy.
péril *m* peril, danger.
périlleux *adj* perilous.
périmé *adj* out-of-date; expired.
périmètre *m* perimeter.
période *f* period; epoch, era; wave, spell.
périodique *adj* periodic; **~ment** *adv* periodically.
péripétie *f* event, episode.
périphérie *f* periphery.
périphérique *adj* peripheral, outlying; * *m* ring road; peripheral.
périple *m* voyage; journey.
périr *vi* to perish, die.
périscope *m* periscope.
périssable *adj* perishable.
perle *f* pearl; bead; gem.
permanence *f* permanence; permanency.
permanent *adj* permanent, continuous.
permanente *f* perm.
permanenter *vt* to perm.
perméable *adj* permeable; pervious.
permettre *vt* to allow, permit; **se ~** *vr* to allow o.s.
permis *adj* permitted; * *m* permit, licence.
permission *f* permission; leave.
permutation *f* permutation.
permuter *vt* to change, switch round; to permutate.
pernicieux *adj* pernicious.
perpendiculaire *adj* perpendicular; **~ment** *adv* perpendicularly.
perpétuel *adj* perpetual; permanent; **~lement** *adv* perpetually.
perpétuer *vt* to perpetuate, carry on; **se ~** *vr* to be perpetuated; to survive.
perpétuité *f* perpetuity.
perplexe *adj* perplexed, confused.
perplexité *f* perplexity, confusion.
perquisition *f* search.
perquisitionner *vt* to make a search.
perron *m* flight of steps.
perroquet *m* parrot.
perruche *f* budgerigar; chatterbox.
perruque *f* wig.
persécuter *vt* to persecute; to harass.
persécution *f* persecution.
persévérance *f* perseverance.
persévérant *adj* persevering.
persévérer *vi* to persevere; to persist in.
persil *m* parsley.
persistance *f* persistence.

persistant *adj* persistent; ever-green.

persister *vi* to persist, keep up.

personnage *m* character, individual.

personnaliser *vt* to personalise.

personnalité *f* personality.

personne *f* person; self; appearance; **en ~** in person; * *pn* anyone, anybody; nobody.

personnel *adj* personal; selfish; **~lement** *adv* personally.

personnifier *vt* to personify.

perspective *f* perspective; view; angle.

perspicace *adj* shrewd, perspicacious.

perspicacité *f* insight, perspicacity.

persuader *vt* to persuade; to convince.

persuasif *adj* persuasive; convincing.

persuasion *f* persuasion; conviction.

perte *f* loss, losing; ruin.

pertinent *adj* pertinent.

perturbation *f* disruption; perturbation.

perturber *vt* to disrupt, disturb.

pervenche *f* periwinkle.

pervers *adj* perverse; perverted.

perversité *f* perversity.

pesant *adj* heavy, weighty.

pesanteur *f* gravity; heaviness.

pèse-personne *m* scales.

peser *vt* to weigh; to press; to evaluate; * *vi* to weigh, weigh down; to hang over; **se ~** to weigh o.s.

pessimisme *m* pessimism.

pessimiste *mf* pessimist; * *adj* pessimistic.

peste *f* pest, nuisance; plague.

pesticide *m* pesticide.

pétale *f* petal.

pétanque *f* petanque.

pétard *m* firecracker; detonator; charge; racket, row.

pétillant *adj* bubbly, fizzy.

pétiller *vi* to crackle; to bubble; to sparkle.

petit *adj* small, tiny; slim; young.

petitesse *f* smallness, modesty; meanness.

petit-fils *m* grandson.

petite-fille *f* granddaughter.

pétition *f* petition.

petits-enfants *mpl* grandchildren.

pétrifié *adj* petrified; transfixed; fossilised.

pétrin *m* kneading trough; scrape, mess, tight spot.

pétrir *vt* to knead; to mould, shape.

pétrole *m* oil, petroleum.

pétrolier *m* oil tanker; * *adj* petroleum, oil, oil-producing.

pétrolifère *adj* oil-bearing.

pétunia *m* petunia.

peu *adv* little, not much; few; **un petit ~** a little bit; **quelque ~** a little; **pour ~ que** however little; **~ de** little, few.

peuplade *f* tribe, people.

peuple *m* people, nation; crowd.

peuplement *m* populating; stocking.

peupler *vt* to populate, stock; to plant.

peuplier *m* poplar.

peur *f* fear, terror, apprehension; **avoir ~** to be afraid.

peureux *adj* fearful, timorous.

peut-être *adv* perhaps.

phalange *f* phalanx.

phallocrate *m* male chauvinist.

pharaon *m* pharaoh.

phare *m* lighthouse; headlight.

pharmaceutique *adj* pharmaceutical.

pharmacie *f* pharmacy; pharmacology.

pharmacien *m* **-ne** *f* pharmacist; chemist.

pharynx *m* pharynx.

phase *f* phase, stage.

phénoménal *adj* phenomenal.

phénomène *m* phenomenon; freak; character.

philanthrope *mf* philanthropist.

philatélie *f* philately, stamp collecting.

philologie *f* philology.

philosophe *mf* philosopher; * *adj* philosophical.

philosopher *vi* to philosophise.

philosophie *f* philosophy.

philosophique *adj* philosophical; **~ment** *adv* philosophically.

phobie *f* phobia.

phonétique *f* phonetics; * *adj* phonetic; **~ment** *adv* phonetically.

phoque *m* seal; sealskin.

phosphate *m* phosphate.

phosphore *m* phosphorus.

phosphorescent *adj* luminous, phosphorescent.

photo *f* photo.

photocopie *f* photocopy.

photocopier *vt* to photocopy.

photocopieur *m*, **-euse** *f* photocopier.

photogénique *adj* photogenic.

photographe *mf* photograph.

photographie *f* photography.

photographier *vt* to photograph.

photographique *adj* photographic.

phrase *f* sentence; phrase.

physicien *m* **-ne** *f* physicist.

physiologie *f* physiology.

physiologique *adj* physiological.

physionomie *f* countenance, physiognomy.

physionomiste *adj* good at remembering faces.

physiothérapie *f* physiotherapy.

physique *f* physics; * *adj* physical; **~ment** *adv* physically.

pianiste *mf* pianist.

piano *m* piano.

pic *m* peak; **à ~** vertically, sheer.

pichet *m* pitcher, jug.

picorer *vt* to peck; to nibble.

picot *m* picot; (*bot*) burr; (*tec*) tooth.

picotement *m* tickle; prickling.

picoter *vt* to tickle; to prickle; to smart, sting.

pictural *adj* pictorial.

pie *f* magpie; chatterbox.

pièce *f* piece; object; component; room; paper, document.

pied *m* foot; track; hoof; bottom; **à ~** on foot; **être sur ~** to be underway.

pied-à-terre *m invar* pied-à-terre.

piédestal *m* pedestal.

piège *m* trap; pit; snare.

piéger *vt* to trap, set a trap.

pierre *f* stone.

piété *f* piety.

piétiner *vi* to stamp (one's foot); * *vt* to trample on.

piéton *m* pedestrian; * *adj* pedestrian.

pieu *m* post, stake, pile.

pieusement *adv* piously, devoutly.

pieux *adj* pious, devout.

pigeon *m* pigeon; dupe, mug.

pigment *m* pigment.

pigmentation *f* pigmentation.

pignon *m* gable; cogwheel.

pile *f* pile; pier; battery; * *adv* dead; just, right, exactly.

piler *vt* to crush, pound.

pilier *m* pillar.

pillage *m* pillaging, looting.

piller *vt* to pillage, loot.

pilon *m* pestle; wooden leg.

pilote *m* pilot; driver.

piloter *vt* to pilot, fly; to drive.

pilotis *m* stilts; pilotis.

pilule *f* pill.

piment *m* hot pepper, capsicum.

pimenter *vt* to add spice.

pin *m* pine.

pince *f* pliers, crowbar; pincer; dart.

pinceau *m* brush, paintbrush.

pincée *f* pinch.

pincer *vt* to pinch, nip; to grip.

pinède *f* pine forest.

pingouin *m* penguin.

ping-pong *m* table tennis.

pintade *f* guinea-fowl.

pinte *f* pint.

pioche *f* pick, pickaxe.

piocher *vt* to use a pick; to swot.

piolet *m* ice axe.

pion *m* pawn; draught.

pionnier *m* pioneer.

pipe *f* pipe.

pipette *f* pipette.

piquant *adj* prickly; pungent; piquant; * *m* quill, spine; prickle.

pique *f* pike, lance.

pique-nique *m* picnic.

pique-niquer *vi* to picnic.

piquer *vt* to sting, bite; to goad; to puncture.

piquet *m* post, picket.

piqûre *f* prick; sting; bite.

pirate *m* pirate.

pire *adj* worse; **le ~, la ~, les ~s** the worst.

pirogue *f* pirogue, dugout canoe.

pirouette *f* pirouette; about-turn.

pis *m* udder.

pis-aller *m invar* last resort, stop-gap.

piscine *f* swimming pool.

pissenlit *m* dandelion.

pistache *f* pistachio.

piste *f* track, trail; course; runway; lead, clue.

pistolet *m* pistol, gun.

piston *m* piston.

pistonner *vt* to pull strings for, recommend.

piteux *adj* pitiful, pathetic.

pitié *f* pity, mercy.

pitoyable *adj* pitiful, pitiable.

pittoresque *adj* picturesque.

pivoine *f* peony.

pivot *m* pivot; mainspring.

pivoter *vi* to revolve, pivot.

placard *m* cupboard; poster, notice.

place *f* place; square; seat; space; position; **à la ~ de** instead of.

placebo *m* placebo.

placement *m* placing; investment.

placenta *m* placenta; afterbirth.

placer *vt* to place, put; to fit; to seat; to sell; to invest; **se ~** *vr* to take up position; to stand; to find a job.

placide *adj* placid, calm.

placidité *f* placidity, calmness.

plafond *m* ceiling; roof.

plafonner *vi* to reach a ceiling/maximum.

plage *f* beach.

plagiat *m* plagiarism, plagiary.

plagier *vt* to plagiarise.

plaider *vt* to plead; to defend; * *vi* to plead for, go to court.

plaidoirie *f* defence speech; plea.

plaidoyer *m* defence speech; plea.

plaie *f* wound, cut; scourge.

plaignant *m* **-e** *f* plaintiff.

plaindre *vt* to pity; to begrudge; **se ~** *vr* to complain.

plaine *f* plain.

plainte *f* complaint; moan, groan.

plaintif *adj* plaintive, complaining.

plaire *vi* to please, be pleasant; **se ~** *vr* to enjoy, take pleasure in.

plaisant *adj* pleasant, agreeable.

plaisanter *vi* to joke, jest.

plaisanterie *f* joking; pleasantry; humour.

plaisir *m* pleasure; delight; entertainment; **faire ~** to please.

plan *m* plan, scheme, project; plane, level.

planche *f* plank, board; plate; shelf.

plancher *m* floor.

planchette *f* small board, small shelf.

plancton *m* plankton.

planer *vi* to glide, soar; to hover over.

planétaire *adj* planetary.

planète *f* planet.

planeur *m* glider.

planifier *vt* to plan.

planisphère *m* planisphere.

planning *m* programme, schedule.

plantation *f* plantation; planting.

plante *f* plant.

planter *vt* to plant; to hammer in; to stick, dump.

plantureux *adj* copious, ample.

plaque *f* sheet, plate; plaque; slab.

plaqué *adj* plated.

plaquer *vt* to plate, veneer; to jilt; to tackle.

plaquette *f* plaque; tablet; slab.

plasma *m* plasma.

plastifier *vt* to coat with plastic.

plastique *m* plastic; * *adj* plastic.

plat *adj* flat; straight; dull, insipid; **~ement** *adv* dully, insipidly; * *m* plate, dish; course.

platane *m* plane tree.

plateau *m* tray; turntable; plateau; stage.

plate-bande *f* border, flower-bed.

plate-forme *f* platform.

platine *m* platinum; * *f* deck; turntable; stage.

platitude *f* platitude; flatness, dullness.

platonique *adj* platonic.

plâtre *m* plaster.

plâtrer *vt* to plaster; to set in plaster.

plâtrier *m* plasterer.

plausible *adj* plausible.

plébiscite *m* plebiscite.

plébisciter *vt* to elect by plebiscite.

plein *adj* full; entire, whole; busy; **~ement** *adv* fully, in full; wholly; * *m* filling up; full house; height, middle.

plénitude *f* plenitude, fullness.

pléonasme *m* pleonasm.

pleur *m* tear, sob; **en ~s** in tears.

pleurer *vi* to cry, weep; * *vt* to mourn for, lament.

pleurésie *f* pleurisy.

pleuvoir *vi* to rain; to shower down, rain down.

plexus *m* plexus.

pli *m* fold; crease; wrinkle; envelope.

pliant *adj* collapsible, folding.

plier *vt* to fold; to bend; * *vi* to bend; to yield; **se ~** *vr* to fold up; to submit.

plinthe *f* plinth; skirting board.

plissement *m* creasing, folding; puckering.

plisser *vt* to pleat, fold; to pucker; * *vi* to become creased.

pliure *f* fold; bend.

plomb *m* lead; sinker; fuse.

plombage *m* weighting; leading; filling.

plomber *vt* to weight; to fill.

plomberie *f* plumbing.

plombier *m* plumber.

plongée *f* diving, dive.

plongeoir *m* diving board.

plongeon *m* dive.

plonger *vi* to dive; to plunge, dip sharply.

plongeur *m* **-euse** *f* diver; washer-up.

ployer *vi* to bend, to sag.

pluie *f* rain; shower.

plumage *m* plumage, feathers.

plume *f* feather.

plumeau *m* feather duster.

plumer *vt* to pluck.

plupart *f* most, most part, majority; **la ~ de** most of.

pluriel *m* plural; * *adj* plural.

plus *adv* more, most; **~ grand que** bigger than; **de ~ en ~** more and more; **de ~** besides, moreover; **non ~** neither, not either.

plusieurs *adj* several.

plus-que-parfait *m* pluperfect.

plus-value *f* appreciation; increase in value.

plutonium *m* plutonium.

plutôt *adv* rather, quite, fairly; sooner.

pluvieux *adj* rainy, wet.

pneu *m* tyre.

pneumatique *adj* pneumatic; * *m* tyre.

pneumonie *f* pneumonia.

poche *f* pocket; pouch; bag.

pocher *vt* to poach.

pochette *f* pocket handkerchief; wallet; envelope.

pochoir *m* stencil.

podium *m* podium.

poêle *m* stove; * *f* frying pan.

poème *m* poem.

poésie *f* poetry.

poète *m* poet.

poétique *adj* poetic; **~ment** *adv* poetically.

poids *m* weight, influence; **~ lourd** heavyweight; **~ plume** featherweight.

poignant *adj* poignant.

poignard *m* dagger.

poignarder *vt* to stab.

poigne *f* grip; hand.

poignée *f* handful; **~ de mains** handshake.

poignet *m* wrist; cuff.

poil *m* hair; coat; bristle.

poilu *adj* hairy.

poinçon *m* hallmark, style; awl.

poinçonner *vt* to stamp; to hallmark.

poindre *vi* to break, dawn.

poing *m* fist; **coup de ~** punch.

point *m* point, spot; stage; full stop; **mettre au ~** to finalise; to perfect; **faire le ~** (*mar*) to take bearings; **être sur le ~ de** to be about to; **à~** medium, just right, when due; **~-virgule** semicolon; **~ de vue** point of view.

pointage *m* checking off; sighting; scrutiny.

pointe *f* point, head; spike, tack; **tailler en ~** to cut to a point; **sur la ~ des pieds** on tiptoe.

pointer *vi* to clock in; to soar up; to peep out; * *vt* to check off; to clock in; to stick into.

pointillé *m* stipple engraving; dotted line.

pointilleux *adj* particular, fastidious.

pointu *adj* pointed, sharp; subtle.

pointure *f* size, number.

poire *f* pear.

poireau *m* leek.

poirier *m* pear tree.

pois *m* pea; **~ chiche** chickpea; **petits ~** garden peas.

poison *m* poison.

poisseux *adj* sticky.

poisson *m* fish.

poissonnerie *f* fishmonger's, fish shop.

poissonnier *m* **-ière** *f* fishmonger.

poitrail *m* breast, chest.

poitrine *f* chest, breast; bosom.

poivre *m* pepper.

poivrer *vt* to pepper, put pepper in.

poivrière *f* pepperpot.

poivron *m* green pepper, capsicum.

polaire *adj* polar.

polariser *vt* to polarise; to attract.

polarité *f* polarity.

polaroïd *m* polaroid; * *adj* polaroid.

pôle *m* pole; centre.

polémique *f* controversy, polemic; * *adj* controversial, polemic.

poli *adj* polite; polished, smooth; **~ment** *adv* politely.

police *f* police; policing; regulations.

polichinelle *m* buffoon.

policier *m* policeman, **-ière** *f* policewoman.

poliomyélite *f* poliomyelitis.

polir *vt* to polish; to refine.

politesse *f* politeness, courtesy.

politicien *m* **-ne** *f* politician; * *adj* (*pej*) politicking.

politique *f* politics; policy; * *adj* political; **~ment** *adv* politically.

politiser *vt* to politicise; to make a political issue of.

pollen *m* pollen.

polluant *adj* polluting; * *m* pollutant.

polluer *vt* to pollute.

pollution *f* pollution.

polo *m* polo.

poltron *m* **-ne** *f* coward; * *adj* cowardly, craven.

polyamide *m* polyamide.

polycopier *vt* to duplicate, stencil.

polyester *m* polyester.

polygame *m* polygamist.

polygamie *f* polygamy.

polyglotte *adj* polyglot; * *mf* polyglot.

polygone *m* polygon.

polymère *m* polymer; * *adj* polymeric.

polyvalent *adj* polyvalent; varied; versatile.

pommade *f* ointment.

pomme *f* apple.

pomme de terre *f* potato.

pommette *f* cheekbone.

pommier *m* apple tree.

pompe *f* pump.

pomper *vt* to pump.

pompeux *adj* pompous; pretentious.

pompier *m* fireman.

pompiste *mf* pump attendant.

poncer *vt* to sand down, rub down.

ponction *f* (*med*) puncture.

ponctualité *f* punctuality.

ponctuation *f* punctuation.

ponctuel *adj* punctual; **~lement** *adv* punctually.

ponctuer *vt* to punctuate; to phrase.

pondéré *adj* weighted; levelheaded.

pondre *vt* to lay; to produce.

poney *m* pony.

pont *m* bridge; deck; axle.

ponte *f* laying; clutch.

pontifical *adj* pontifical.

ponton *m* pontoon; landing stage.

populaire *adj* popular; working-class; vernacular.

populariser *vt* to popularise.

popularité *f* popularity.

population *f* population.

porc *m* pig; pork.

porcelaine *f* porcelain, china.

porc-épic *m* porcupine.

porche *m* porch.

porcherie *f* pigsty.

pore *m* pore.

poreux *adj* porous.

pornographique *adj* pornographic.

port *m* port, harbour; carrying, wearing.

portail *m* portal, gate.

portatif *adj* portable.

porte *f* door; gate; threshold.

porte-avions *m invar* aircraft carrier.

porte-bagages *m invar* luggage rack.

porte-bonheur *m invar* lucky charm.

porte-clefs, porte-clés *m invar* key ring.

porte-documents *m invar* briefcase.

portée *f* reach, range; capacity; impact, significance; **à la ~ de** within reach; **hors de ~** out of reach.

portefeuille *m* wallet; portfolio.

porte-jarretelles *m invar* suspender belt.

portemanteau *m* coat hanger; hat stand.

porte-parole *m invar* spokesperson.

porte-plume *m invar* penholder.

porter *vt* to carry; to take; to wear; to hold, keep; **se ~** *vr* to put o.s. forward; to go.

porteur *m* **-euse** *f* porter; carrier; * *adj* booster; strong, buoyant.

portier *m* commissionaire.

portière *f* door.

portillon *m* gate, barrier.

portion *f* portion, share.

portique *m* portico.

portrait *m* portrait.

portraitiste *mf* portraitist.

pose *f* pose, posture; laying, fitting, setting.

poser *vt* to put; to install; to set out; to ask; **se ~** *vr* to land, settle; to come up, arise.

positif *adj* positive, definite.

position *f* position; situation; state; stance.

positionner *vt* to position, locate.

positivement *adv* positively.

posologie *f* posology.

posséder *vt* to possess, have; to know inside out.

possesseur *m* possessor, owner.

possessif *adj* possessive.

possession *f* possession, ownership.

possibilité *f* possibility; potential.

possible *adj* possible, feasible; potential; * *m*; **faire son ~** to do one's best.

postal *adj* postal, mail.

poste *f* post office, post; * *m* post, position; station; job.

poster *vt* to post, mail; to station; **se ~** *vr* to take up a position.

postérieur *adj* later, subsequent; back, posterior.

postérité *f* posterity; descendants.

posthume *adj* posthumous.

postiche *adj* false; postiche; pretended; * *m* hairpiece; toupee.

postier *m* **-ière** *f* post office worker.

postillon *m* postilion.

postulant *m* **-e** *f* applicant.

postuler *vt* to apply for; to postulate.

posture *f* posture, position.

pot *m* jar; pot; can.

potable *adj* drinkable; passable.

potage *m* soup.

potager *m* kitchen garden; * *adj* vegetable, edible.

potassium *m* potassium.

pot-au-feu *m invar* stew.

pot-de-vin *m* bribe.

poteau *m* post, stake.

potée *f* hotpot.

potelé *adj* plump, chubby.

potence *f* gallows; bracket.

potentiel *adj* potential; * *m* potential.

poterie *f* pottery, piece of pottery.

potiche *f* vase, mere, puppet.

potier *m* potter.

potion *f* potion.

potiron *m* pumpkin.

pou *m* louse.

poubelle *f* dustbin.

pouce *m* thumb; big toe; inch.

poudre *f* powder, dust.

poudrer *vt* to powder.

poudrière *f* powder magazine.

poulailler *m* henhouse.

poulain *m* foal; protégé.

poule *f* hen, fowl.

poulet *m* chicken.

poulie *f* pulley.

poulpe *m* octopus.

pouls *m* pulse.

poumon *m* lung.

poupe *f* stern.

poupée *f* doll.

poupon *m* baby.

pouponnière *f* day nursery, crèche.

pour *prép* for; to; in favour of; on account of; in order to; **~ que** so that, in order that; **être ~** to be in favour of.

pourboire *m* tip.

pourceau *m* pig, swine.

pourcentage *m* percentage.

pourchasser *vt* to pursue; to harry.

pourparlers *mpl* talks, negotiations.

pourpre *adj* crimson; * *m* crimson.

pourquoi *adv* why; **~ pas?** why not?; * *m* reason, question.

pourri *adj* rotten, decayed; corrupt; * *m* rotten part, rottenness.

pourrir *vi* to rot, go rotten; to deteriorate.

pourriture *f* rot, rottenness.

poursuite *f* pursuit; prosecution.

poursuivant *m* **-e** *f* pursuer; plaintiff.

poursuivre *vt* to pursue; to seek; to prosecute.

pourtant *adv* however, yet, nevertheless.

pourtour *m* circumference, perimeter.

pourvoir *vt* to provide, equip.

pourvu *conj* **~ que** provided that.

pousse *f* shoot; sprouting.

poussée *f* pressure, pushing; thrust; upsurge.

pousser *vt* to push; to drive; to incite; * *vi* to push; to grow, expand; **se ~** *vr* to move, shift.

poussette *f* pushchair.

poussière *f* dust.

poussiéreux *adj* dusty.

poussin *m* chick; junior.

poutre *f* beam.

pouvoir *vi* can, be able; may, be allowed; * *m* power, ability; authority; proxy.

pragmatique *adj* pragmatic.

prairie *f* meadow, prairie.

pralin *m* praline.

praline *f* sugared almond.

praticable *adj* practicable; passable.

pratiquant *m* **-e** *f* churchgoer; * *adj* practising.

pratique *f* practice; exercise; observance; * *adj* practical; **~ment** *adv* practically.

pratiquer *vt* to practise, exercise; to carry out.

pré *m* meadow.

préalable *adj* preliminary; previous; **~ment** *adv* previously, first.

préambule *m* preamble, prelude.

préau *m* covered playground; inner yard.

préavis *m* notice, advance warning.

précaire *adj* precarious.

précarité *f* precariousness.

précaution *f* precaution; care.

précautionneux *adj* cautious, careful.

précédent *adj* previous, preceding; * *m* precedent.

précéder *vt* to precede, go before.

précepte *m* precept.

prêcher *vt* to preach; * *vi* to preach, sermonise.

prêcheur *m* **-euse** *f* preacher.

précieux *adj* precious; invaluable.

précipice *m* precipice; abyss.

précipitamment *adv* hurriedly, hastily.

précipitation *f* haste, violent hurry.

précipiter *vt* to throw, push down; to hasten, precipitate; **se ~** *vr* to rush forward; to speed up.

précis *adj* precise, exact; **~ément** *adv* precisely.

préciser *vt* to specify; to clarify; **se ~** *vr* to become clear.

précision *f* precision, preciseness.

précoce *adj* precocious, premature.

préconçu *adj* preconceived.

préconiser *vt* to recommend; to advocate.

précurseur *m* forerunner, precursor; * *adj* precursory, preceding.

prédateur *m* predator.

prédécesseur *m* predecessor.

prédestiné *adj* predestined, fated.

prédiction *f* prediction.

prédire *vt* to predict, foretell.

prédisposition *f* predisposition.

prédominance *f* predominance.

prédominant *adj* predominant.

prédominer *vi* to predominate.

préfabriqué *adj* prefabricated.

préface *f* preface, prelude.

préfecture *f* prefecture.

préférable *adj* preferable; better; ~**ment** *adv* preferably.

préféré *m* **-e** *f* favourite; *adj* favourite, preferred.

préférence *f* preference.

préférer *vt* to prefer.

préfet *m* prefect.

préfigurer *vt* to prefigure.

préhistoire *f* prehistory.

préhistorique *adj* prehistoric.

préjudice *m* loss; harm; wrong; damage.

préjudiciable *adj* prejudicial, detrimental.

préjudicier *vt* to be prejudicial.

préjugé *m* prejudice.

prélasser (se) *vr* to sprawl, lounge.

prélèvement *m* taking; levying; imposition.

prélever *vt* to take; to levy; to deduct.

préliminaire *m* preliminary; * *adj* preliminary.

prélude *m* prelude; warm-up.

prématuré *adj* premature; untimely; ~**ment** *adv* prematurely.

préméditation *f* premeditation.

prémédité *adj* premeditated.

premier *m* first, first floor, **-ière** *f* first, first gear; * *adj* first; former; chief; early; primary.

première *f* première.

premièrement *adv* firstly, in first place.

prémonition *f* premonition.

prémonitoire *adj* premonitory.

prénatal *adj* prenatal.

prendre *vt* to take; to pick up; to catch; * *vi* to take root; to harden; to start; **se** ~ *vr* to consider o.s.; **s'y** ~ **mal** to set about the wrong way; **s'en** ~ **à** to set upon, take it out on.

prénom *m* first name, forename.

préoccuper *vt* to worry; to preoccupy; **se** ~ *vr* to concern o.s.

préparatif *m* preparation.

préparation *f* preparation; making up; training.

préparatoire *adj* preparatory.

préparer *vt* to prepare, get ready; to train; **se** ~ *vr* to prepare o.s.

prépondérant *adj* preponderant, dominating.

préposition *f* preposition.

prérogative *f* prerogative.

près *adv* near, close; nearly, almost; **de** ~ closely; **à peu** ~ just about, near enough; **à peu de choses** ~ more or less.

présage *m* omen; harbinger.

presbytère *m* presbytery.

presbytie *f* long-sightedness, presbyopia.

prescrire *vt* to prescribe; to stipulate.

présélection *f* preselection.

présence *f* presence.

présent *m* present, gift; **-e** *f* this letter, the present letter; * *adj* present; * *m* present; **à** ~ just now.

présentable *adj* presentable.

présentateur *m* **-trice** *f* host, compère; presenter.

présentation *f* presentation; introduction; **faire les** ~**s** to make the introductions.

présenter *vt* to introduce; to present; to explain; **se** ~ *vr* to appear; to come forward; to introduce o.s.

présentoir *m* display shelf.

préservatif *m* condom.

préserver *vt* to preserve; to protect; **se** ~ *vr* to protect o.s.

présidence *f* presidency; chairmanship.

président *m* **-e** *f* president.

présidentiel *adj* presidential.

présider *vt* to preside, chair; to direct.

présomption *f* presumption, assumption.

présomptueux *adj* presumptuous.

presque *adv* almost, nearly; hardly, scarcely.

presqu'île *f* peninsula.

pressant *adj* urgent, pressing.

presse *f* press, newspapers; throng.

pressé *adj* hurried, urgent.

presse-citron *m invar* lemon squeezer.

pressentiment *m* presentiment, foreboding, premonition.

pressentir *vt* to have a presentiment of.

presse-papiers *m invar* paperweight.

presser *vt* to press; to squeeze; to hurry up; **se** ~ *vr* to hurry; to crowd around.

pression *f* pressure.

pressoir *m* press (wine, cider).

prestation *f* benefit; service; payment; allowance.

prestidigitateur *m* **-trice** *f* conjurer; magician.

prestige *m* prestige.

prestigieux *adj* prestigious.

présumer *vt* to presume, assume.

prêt *adj* ready; prepared, willing; * *m* loan, lending.

prêt-à-porter *m* ready-to-wear.

prétendant *m* **-e** *f* candidate.

prétendre *vt* to claim, maintain; to want; to intend, mean.

prétendu *adj* so-called, supposed; ~**ment** *adv* supposedly, allegedly.

prétentieux *adj* pretentious.

prétention *f* pretension, claim; pretentiousness.

prêter *vt* to lend; to attribute; to give.

prétérit *m* preterite tense.

prétexte *m* pretext, excuse.

prêtre *m* priest.

preuve *f* proof, evidence.

prévaloir *vi* to prevail.

prévenant *adj* considerate, thoughtful.

prévenir *vt* to prevent; to warn, inform; to anticipate.

préventif *adj* preventive.

prévention *f* prevention.

prévisible *adj* foreseeable.

prévision *f* prediction; forecast.

prévoir *vt* to anticipate; to plan; to provide for.

prévoyance *f* foresight, forethought.

prévoyant *adj* provident.

prévu *adj* provided for.

prier *vi* to pray; * *vt* to pray to; to beg; to invite.

prière *f* prayer; entreaty.

primaire *adj* primary; elementary.

primate *m* primate.

primauté *f* primacy.

prime *f* premium, subsidy; free gift.

primer *vi* to dominate; to take first place; * *vt* to outdo, prevail.

primeurs *fpl* early fruit and vegetable.

primevère *f* primrose.

primitif *adj* primitive.

primordial *adj* primordial, essential.

prince *m* prince.

princesse *f* princess.

principal *m* principal; headmaster; * *adj* main, principal; ~**ement** *adv* principally.

principe *m* principle; origin; element; **en ~** in principle.

printanier *adj* spring.

printemps *m* spring.

prioritaire *adj* having priority, priority.

priorité *f* priority.

pris *adj* taken; busy, engaged.

prise *f* hold, grip; catch; plug; dose; **lâcher ~** to let go one's hold; **~ de sang** blood sample; **~ de courant** plug, power point; **~ de conscience** awareness, realisation.

prisme *m* prism.

prison *f* prison; jail.

prisonnier *m* **-ière** *f* prisoner; * *adj* captive.

privation *f* deprivation; forfeiture.

privatiser *vt* to privatise.

privé *adj* private; unofficial; independent.

priver *vt* to deprive; **se ~** *vr* to go without.

privilège *m* privilege.

privilégié *m* **-e** *f* privileged person; * *adj* privileged, favoured.

privilégier *vt* to favour.

prix *m* price, cost; prize.

probabilité *f* probability, likelihood.

probable *adj* probable, likely; **~ment** *adv* probably.

problématique *adj* problematical; * *f* problem; problematics.

problème *m* problem, issue.

procédé *m* process; behaviour.

procéder *vi* to proceed.

procédure *f* procedure; proceedings.

procès *m* proceedings; lawsuit, trial.

procession *f* procession.

processus *m* process; progress.

procès-verbal *m* minutes; report.

prochain *adj* next; imminent; **~ement** *adv* soon, shortly; * *m* neighbour.

proche *adj* nearby; close, imminent.

proclamation *f* proclamation.

proclamer *vt* to proclaim, declare.

procuration *f* proxy, power of attorney.

procurer *vt* to procure, provide; **se ~** *vr* to procure, obtain for o.s.

procureur *m* prosecutor.

prodige *m* marvel, wonder.

prodigieusement *adv* prodigiously, incredibly.

prodigieux *adj* prodigious.

prodiguer *vt* to be lavish, be unsparing; to squander.

producteur *m* **-trice** *f* producer; * *adj* producing, growing.

productif *adj* productive.

production *f* production; generation; output.

productivité *f* productivity.

produire *vt* to produce; to grow; to generate; **se ~** *vr* to happen, take place.

produit *m* product; goods; yield, profit.

proéminent *adj* prominent.

profane *adj* secular, profane; * *mf* layman, lay person.

profaner *vt* to profane; to defile.

proférer *vt* to utter, pronounce.

professeur *m* teacher, professor.

profession *f* profession; occupation, trade.

professionnel *m* **-le** *f* professional; skilled worker; * *adj* professional; occupational; technical; **~lement** *adv* professionally.

profil *m* profile, outline.

profiler *vt* to profile; to streamline; **se ~** *vr* to stand out, be profiled.

profit *m* profit; advantage, benefit.

profitable *adj* profitable; **~ment** *adv* profitably.

profiter *vi* to profit; to thrive.

profiteur *m* **-euse** *f* profiteer.

profond *adj* deep, profound; heavy; **~ément** *adv* deeply, profoundly.

profondeur *f* depth; profundity.

profusion *f* profusion, wealth; **à ~** plenty, in profusion.

programme *m* program; syllabus; schedule.

programmer *vt* to program; to schedule.

progrès *m* progress; improvement; advance.

progresser *vi* to progress; to advance.

progression *f* progress; progression, spread.

progressivement *adv* progressively.

prohiber *vt* to prohibit, ban.

proie *f* prey, victim.

projecteur *m* projector; spotlight, floodlight.

projectile *m* projectile; missile.

projection *f* projection, casting; showing.

projet *m* plan; draft.

projeter *vt* to plan; to throw out; to cast, project.

prolétaire *mf* proletarian.

prolétariat *m* proletariat.

prolifération *f* proliferation.

proliférer *vi* to proliferate.

prologue *m* prologue.

prolongation *f* prolongation, extension.

prolongement *m* continuation, extension.

prolonger *vt* to prolong, extend; **se ~** *vr* to go on, persist.

promenade *f* walk, stroll; drive, spin.

promener *vt* to take out for a walk; **se ~** *vr* to go for a walk.

promeneur *m* **-euse** *f* walker.

promesse *f* promise.

prometteur *adj* promising.

promettre *vt* to promise.

promontoire *m* promontory, headland.

promoteur *m* **-trice** *f* promoter, instigator.

promotion *f* promotion; advancement.

promouvoir *vt* to promote, upgrade.

prompt *adj* prompt; swift; ready; **~ement** *adv* promptly; swiftly.

promptitude *f* promptness; swiftness.

promulgation *f* promulgation.

promulguer *vt* to promulgate.

prôner *vt* to advocate.

pronom *m* pronoun.

prononcer *vt* to pronounce, utter; **se ~** *vr* to reach a verdict.

prononciation *f* pronunciation.

pronostic *m* forecast; prognosis; tip.

pronostiquer *vt* to forecast, prognosticate.

propagande *f* propaganda.

propagation *f* propagation; spreading.

propager *vt* to propagate, spread; **se ~** *vr* to spread, be propagated.

propane *m* propane.

prophète *m* prophet.

prophétie *f* prophecy.

prophétique *adj* prophetic.

prophétiser *vt* to prophesy.

propice *adj* propitious, favourable.

proportion *f* proportion, ratio.

proportionné *adj* proportional; proportionate.

proportionnel *adj* proportional; **~lement** *adv* proportionally.

propos *m* talk, remarks; intention; **à ~ de** about, on the subject of; **hors de ~** irrelevant.

proposer *vt* to propose, suggest; **se ~** *vr* to offer one's services; to intend to.

proposition *f* proposition, suggestion.

propre *adj* clean, neat; honest; own; peculiar; suitable; ~**ment** *adv* cleanly; exactly; specifically.

propreté *f* cleanliness; tidiness.

propriétaire *mf* owner; landlord.

propriété *f* ownership, property; appropriateness, suitability.

propulser *vt* to propel, power.

propulsion *f* propulsion.

prorogation *f* prorogation; deferment; extension.

proroger *vt* to prorogue; to defer; to extend.

prosaïque *adj* mundane, prosaic.

proscrire *vt* to proscribe; to prohibit.

prose *f* prose.

prospecter *vt* to prospect; to canvass.

prospecteur *m* -**trice** *f* prospector.

prospection *f* prospecting; canvassing.

prospectus *m* leaflet; prospectus.

prospère *adj* prosperous, flourishing.

prospérer *vi* to prosper, flourish.

prospérité *f* prosperity.

prostate *f* prostate.

prosterner (se) *vr* to prostrate o.s.

prostituée *f* prostitute.

prostitution *f* prostitution.

prostré *adj* prostrate, prostrated.

protagoniste *m* protagonist.

protecteur *m* -**trice** *f* protector; patron; * *adj* protective; patronising.

protection *f* protection; patronage.

protectionnisme *m* protectionism.

protégé *m* -**e** *f* favourite, protegé; * *adj* protected, sheltered.

protéger *vt* to protect; to patronise; **se ~** *vr* to protect o.s.

protéine *f* protein.

protestant *m* -**e** *f* Protestant; * *adj* Protestant.

protestantisme *m* Protestantism.

protestation *f* protest, protestation.

protester *vi* to protest; to affirm.

prothèse *f* prosthesis; prosthetics.

protocole *m* protocol; etiquette.

prototype *m* prototype.

protubérance *f* protuberance, bulge.

proue *f* prow; bows.

prouesse *f* prowess.

prouver *vt* to prove; to demonstrate.

provenir *vi* to come from; to be due to.

proverbe *m* proverb.

proverbial *adj* proverbial.

providence *f* providence.

providentiel *adj* providential.

province *f* province.

provincial *m* -**e** *f* provincial; * *adj* provincial.

provision *f* provision; supply, stock.

provisoire *adj* provisional, temporary; ~**ment** *adv* provisionally.

provocant *adj* provocative.

provocation *f* provocation.

provoquer *vt* to provoke; to cause.

proximité *f* proximity, closeness; imminence.

prudemment *adv* prudently, carefully.

prudence *f* prudence, care.

prudent *adj* prudent, careful.

prune *f* plum.

pruneau *m* prune.

prunelle *f* sloe; pupil, eye.

prunier *m* plum tree.

psaume *m* psalm.

pseudonyme *m* pseudonym; pen name; alias.

psoriasis *m* psoriasis.

psychanalyse *f* psychoanalysis.

psychanalyser *vt* to psychoanalyse.

psychanalyste *mf* psychoanalyst.

psychédélique *adj* psychedelic.

psychiatre *mf* psychiatrist.

psychiatrie *f* psychiatry.

psychiatrique *adj* psychiatric.

psychique *adj* psychic, mental.

psychisme *m* psyche, mind.

psychologie *f* psychology.

psychologique *adj* psychological; ~**ment** *adv* psychologically.

psychologue *mf* psychologist; * *adj* psychological.

psychopathe *mf* psychopath; mentally ill person.

psychose *f* psychosis; obsessive fear.

psychosomatique *adj* psychosomatic.

psychothérapie *f* psychotherapy.

puberté *f* puberty.

pubis *m* pubis.

public *adj, f* **publique** public, state; * *m* public, audience; public sector.

publication *f* publication, publishing.

publicité *f* publicity.

publier *vt* to publish; to make public.

publiquement *adv* publicly.

puce *f* flea.

puceron *m* aphid, greenfly.

pudeur *f* modesty, decency.

pudique *adj* modest; chaste; ~**ment** *adv* modestly.

puer *vi* to stink; * *vt* to stink.

puéricultrice *f* paediatric nurse.

puéril *adj* puerile, childish; ~**ement** *adv* puerilely, childishly.

puérilité *f* puerility, childishness.

puis *adv* then, next.

puiser *vt* to draw from, extract.

puisque *conj* since; as, seeing that.

puissance *f* power, strength; output; force.

puissant *adj* powerful; potent.

puits *m* well; shaft.

pull-over *m* pullover, sweater.

pulluler *vi* to swarm, pullulate.

pulmonaire *adj* pulmonary, lung.

pulpe *f* pulp.

pulsation *f* beat; beating; pulsation.

pulsion *f* drive, urge.

pulvériser *vt* to pulverise; to powder.

puma *m* puma.

punaise *f* bug; drawing pin.

punir *vt* to punish.

punition *f* punishment.

pupille *f* pupil; ward.

pupitre *m* desk; console; lectern.

pur *adj* pure; neat; clear; ~**ement** *adv* purely.

purée *f* mashed potatoes; purée.

pureté *f* purity, pureness.

purge *f* purge; purgative; draining.

purger *vt* to purge; to drain.

purifier *vt* to purify, cleanse.

purin *m* liquid manure, slurry.

puritain *m* -**e** *f* puritan; * *adj* puritan.

puritanisme *m* puritanism.

pur-sang *m invar* thoroughbred.

purulent *adj* purulent.

pus *m* pus.

putois *m* polecat; skunk.

putréfaction *f* putrefaction.

putréfier *vt* to putrefy, rot.

pyjama *m* pyjamas.

pylône *m* pylon.

pyramide *f* pyramid.

pyrex *m* Pyrex.

pyromane *mf* pyromaniac; arsonist.

python *m* python.

Q

quadragénaire *adj mf* forty-year-old.

quadrangle *m* quadrangle.

quadrature *f* quadrature.

quadriceps *m* quadriceps.

quadrilatère *m* quadrilateral.

quadrillage *m* covering, control; check pattern.

quadriller *vt* to mark out in squares; to cover, control.

quadrupède *adj m* quadruped.

quadruple *adj m* quadruple.

quai *m* quay, wharf; platform.

qualificatif *adj* qualifying.

qualification *f* qualification.

qualifier *vt* to describe; to qualify; **se ~** *vr* to qualify for; to call o.s.

qualitatif *adj* qualitative.

qualitativement *adv* qualitatively.

qualité *f* quality; skill; position.

quand *conj* when, whenever, while.

quant *prép*: **~ à lui** as for him/it.

quantifier *vt* to quantify.

quantitatif *adj* quantitative.

quantitativement *adv* quantitatively.

quantité *f* quantity, amount.

quarantaine *f* about forty; **avoir la ~** to be in one's forties.

quarante *adj, m inv* forty.

quarantième *adj, mf* fortieth.

quart *m* quarter; beaker; watch.

quartette *m* quartet.

quartier *m* district, neighbourhood; quarters; quarter.

quartz *m* quartz.

quasi *adv* almost, nearly.

quasiment *adv* almost, nearly.

quaternaire *adj* quaternary. * *m* Quaternary.

quatorze *adj, m* fourteen.

quatorzième *adj, mf* fourteenth; **~ment** *adv* in fourteenth place.

quatre *adj, m* four.

quatre-vingt(s) *adj, m* eighty.

quatre-vingt-dix *adj, m* ninety.

quatre-vingtième *adj, mf* eightieth.

quatrième *adj, mf* fourth; **~ment** *adv* in fourth place.

quatuor *m* quartet.

que *conj* that; than; * *pn* that; whom; what; which.

quel, f quelle *adj* who, what, which.

quelconque *adj* some, any; least, slight; poor, indifferent.

quelque *adj* some; **~ part** somewhere.

quelque chose *pn* something.

quelquefois *adv* sometimes

quelqu'un, f -une someone, somebody, *pl* **quelques-uns, -unes** *pn* some, a few; **il y a ~?** is there someone there?

quémander *vt* to beg for.

querelle *f* quarrel; row; debate.

quereller (se) *vr* to quarrel, squabble.

question *f* question; matter, issue.

questionnaire *m* questionnaire.

questionner *vt* to question.

quête *m* quest, search; collection; **en ~ de** in search of.

quêter *vi* to seek; to collect money.

queue *f* tail; stalk; queue; **faire la ~** to queue.

qui *pn* who, whom; which.

quiche *f* quiche.

quiconque *pn* whoever, whosoever.

quiétude *f* quiet; peace; tranquillity.

quille *f* skittle; (*mar*) keel.

quincaillerie *f* hardware, ironmongery.

quinine *f* quinine.

quinquagénaire *adj mf* fifty-year-old.

quinquennal *adj* five-year, quinquennial.

quinquina *m* cinchona.

quinte *f* (*mus*) fifth; coughing fit.

quintette *m* quintet.

quintuple *adj* quintuple; * *m* quintuple.

quintupler *vt* to multiply by five; * *vi* to quintuple, increase fivefold.

quintuplés *mpl* **-ées** *fpl* quintuplets.

quinzaine *f* about fifteen; fortnight.

quinze *adj, m* fifteen.

quinzième *adj, mf* fifteenth; **~ment** *adv* in fifteenth place.

quiproquo *m* mistake; misunderstanding.

quittance *f* receipt; bill.

quitte *adj* even, quits; **être ~ envers** to be quits, all square with; **~ à** even if it means, although it may mean; **~ ou double** double or quits.

quitter *vt* to leave; to give up; **se ~** *vr* to part company, separate.

quoi *pn* what; **~ que** whatever.

quoique *conj* although, though.

quolibet *m* gibe, jeer.

quote-part *f* share.

quotidien *adj* daily, everyday; **~nement** *adv* daily, every day; * *m* everyday life.

quotient *m* quotient; quota.

R

rabâcher *vi* to harp on, keep on; * *vt* to rehearse, harp on.

rabais *m* reduction, discount; **au ~** at a reduced price.

rabaisser *vt* to humble, disparage; to reduce; **se ~** *vr* to belittle o.s.

rabattre *vt* to close; to pull down; to reduce; **se ~** *vr* to cut across, pull in front of; **se ~ sur** to fall back on.

rabbin *m* rabbi.

rabot *m* plane.

raboter *vt* to plane; to scrape.

rabougri *adj* stunted, puny.

racaille *f* rabble, scum.

raccommodage *m* mending, repairing.

raccommoder *vt* to mend, repair.

raccompagner *vt* to see back to; to accompany home.

raccord *m* join; link; pointing.

raccordement *m* linking; joining; connecting.

raccorder *vt* to link up, join up; **se ~** *vr* to link, join up.

raccourci *m* shortcut; **en ~** in short.

raccourcir *vt* to shorten, curtail; * *vi* to shrink; to grow shorter.

raccrocher *vt* to ring off; to hang up; to grab; **se ~** *vr* to catch; to cling to.

race *f* race; stock; breed.

rachat *m* repurchase, purchase.

racheter *vt* to repurchase; to redeem; to ransom.

rachitique *adj* rachitic; scrawny.

racial *adj* racial.

racine *f* root; **~ carrée** square root.

racisme *m* racism.

raciste *mf* racist; * *adj* racist.

racler *vt* to scrape; to rake.

racoler *vt* to accost; to solicit.

raconter *vt* to tell, recount.

radar *m* radar.

rade *f* (*mar*) harbour, roads.

radeau *m* raft.

radiateur *m* radiator; heater.

radiation *f* radiation.

radical *adj* radical; **~ement** *adv* radically.

radieux *adj* radiant, dazzling.

radin *m* **-e** *f* skinflint; * *adj* mean, stingy.

radio *f* radio; X-ray.

radioactif *adj* radioactive.

radioactivité *f* radioactivity.

radiodiffuser *vt* to broadcast (radio).

radiodiffusion *f* broadcasting (radio).

radiographie *f* radiography; X-ray photography.

radiologie *f* radiology.

radiologue *mf* radiologist.

radiophonique *adj* radio.

radioscopie *f* radioscopy.

radio-taxi *m* radio taxi.

radis *m* radish.

radium *m* radium.

radoter *vi* to ramble; to dote.

radoucir *vt* to soften; **se ~** *vr* to calm down; to mellow.

rafale *f* gust, blast; flurry.

raffermir *vt* to harden; to strengthen; **se ~** *vr* to become strengthened.

raffinage *m* refining.

raffiné *adj* refined, sophisticated.

raffinement *m* refinement, sophistication.

raffiner *vt* to refine.

raffoler *vi*: **~ de** to be crazy about.

rafle *f* raid, round-up.

rafraîchir *vt* to cool, freshen, chill; **se ~** *vr* to freshen up; to get colder.

rafraîchissant *adj* refreshing, cooling.

rafraîchissement *m* cooling; cold drink.

rage *f* rage, fury; mania; rabies.

rageur *adj* quick-tempered; bad-tempered.

ragot *m* (*fam*) malicious gossip.

ragoût *m* ragout; stew.

raid *m* raid; trek.

raide *adj* stiff; steep; rough; (*col*) broke.

raideur *f* stiffness; steepness; roughness.

raidir *vt* to stiffen; to tighten; to harden.

raie *f* line; furrow; scratch.

raifort *m* horseradish.

rail *m* rail; railway.

railler *vt* to scoff at, mock.

raillerie *f* mockery, scoffing.

railleur *adj* mocking, scoffing.

rainette *f* tree frog.

raisin *m* grape.

raison *f* reason; motive; sense; ground; ratio; **avoir ~** to be right; **en ~ de** because of.

raisonnable *adj* reasonable, sensible; **~ment** *adv* reasonably.

raisonnement *m* reasoning; argument.

raisonner *vi* to reason; to argue.

rajeunir *vi* to feel younger; to be modernised; * *vt* to rejuvenate.

rajouter *vt* to put in; to add; **en ~** to exaggerate.

rajuster *vt* to readjust, rearrange; to tidy up.

râle *m* groan; death rattle.

ralenti *adj* slow; slackened; * *m* slow motion; **au ~** ticking over, idling.

ralentir *vi* to slow down, let up; * *vt* to slow down, check.

ralentissement *m* slowing down; slowing up.

râler *vi* to groan, moan.

ralliement *m* rallying, winning over; uniting.

rallier *vt* to rally; to win over; **se ~** *vr* to join; to side with.

rallonge *f* extension, lengthening; extension lead.

rallumer *vt* to relight; to switch on again; to revive.

ramadan *m* Ramadan.

ramage *m* song; foliage.

ramassage *m* collection; gathering.

ramasser *vt* to pick up; to collect, gather.

rambarde *f* guardrail.

rame *f* oar; underground train; stake.

rameau *m* branch; ramification.

ramener *vt* to bring back, restore.

ramer *vi* to row.

rameur *m* **-euse** *f* rower.

ramification *f* ramification.

ramifier (se) *vr* to ramify; to branch out.

ramollir *vt* to soften; to weaken; **se ~** *vr* to go soft.

ramoner *vt* to sweep.

ramoneur *m* chimney sweep.

rampant *adj* crawling, creeping.

rampe *f* ramp, slope; gradient.

ramper *vi* to crawl, slither.

rance *adj* rancid, rank.

rancœur *f* rancour, resentment.

rançon *f* ransom.

rancune *f* grudge, resentment.

rancunier *adj* rancorous, spiteful.

randonnée *f* drive; ride; ramble.

randonneur *m* **-euse** *f* hiker, rambler.

rang *m* row, line; rank; class.

rangée *f* row, range, tier.

rangement *m* arranging, putting in order.

ranger *vt* to arrange, array; to put in order; **se ~** *vr* to line up; to make room; to park.

ranimer *vt* to reanimate, revive; to rekindle.

rapace *m* bird of prey.

rapatrié *m* **-e** *f* repatriate; * *adj* repatriated.

rapatriement *m* repatriation.

rapatrier *vt* to repatriate.

râpe *f* rasp, rough file.

râper *vt* to grate; to rasp.

râpeux *adj* rough.

rapide *adj* rapid, quick; steep; **~ment** *adv* rapidly, quickly.

rapidité *f* rapidity, quickness.

rapiécer *vt* to patch up.

rappel *m* recall; reminder.

rappeler *vt* to recall; to remind; **se ~** *vr* to remember.

rapport *m* report; relation; reference; profit; **en ~ avec** in touch with.

rapporter *vt* to report; to bring back; to yield; **se ~** *vr*: **se ~ à** to relate to.

rapporteur *m* **-euse** *f* reporter; telltale; * *adj* tell-tale; * *m* (*math*) protractor.

rapprochement *m* drawing closer; reconciliation.

rapprocher *vt* to bring nearer; to reconcile; **se ~** *vr* to approach; to come together, be reconciled.

rapt *m* abduction.

raquette *f* racket.

rare *adj* rare; few, odd; exceptional; **~ment** *adv* rarely, seldom.

raréfier (se) *vr* to rarefy; become scarce.

rareté *f* rarity; scarcity; infrequency.

rarissime *adj* extremely rare.

ras *adj* close-shaven, shorn; **à ~** short; level with; **à ~ bords** to the brim; **en avoir ~ le bol** (*fam*) to be fed up.

rasage *m* shaving; shearing.

raser *vt* to shave off; to scrape; to raze; **se ~** *vr* to have a shave.

rasoir *m* razor.

rassasier *vt* to fill sb up.

rassemblement *m* assembling, mustering; crowd; political group.

rassembler *vt* to rally, gather together; **se ~** *vr* to gather, assemble.

rasseoir (se) *vr* to sit down again.

rasséréner *vt* to clear up, restore serenity to.

rassis *adj* settled; calm; stale.

rassurant *adj* reassuring, comforting.

rassurer *vt* to reassure; to comfort; **se ~** *vr* to be reassured.

rat *m* rat.

ratatiner *vt* to shrivel; to wrinkle; **se ~** *vr* to become wrinkled.

ratatouille *f* ratatouille.

rate *f* spleen.

raté *m* **-e** *f* failure; * *m* misfire.

râteau *m* rake.

râtelier *m* rack; denture.

rater *vt* to miss; to spoil; to fail; * *vi* to misfire; to miss.

ratification *f* ratification.

ratifier *vt* to ratify, confirm.

ration *f* ration, allowance.

rationnel *adj* rational.

rationnement *m* rationing.

rationner *vt* to ration, put on rations; **se ~** *vr* to ration o.s.

ratisser *vt* to rake; to comb.

rattacher *vt* to refasten; to attach; to link.

rattraper *vt* to catch again, retake; to recover; **se ~** *vr* to catch hold of; to make up for.

rature *f* crossing-out.

raturer *vt* to cross out.

rauque *adj* hoarse, raucous.

ravage *m* havoc; ravaging, laying waste.

ravager *vt* to ravage; devastate.

ravaler *vt* to swallow again; to restore.

ravi *adj* delighted.

ravin *m* ravine, gully.

ravir *vt* to delight.

raviser (se) *vr* to think better of it, change one's mind.

ravissant *adj* ravishing, delightful.

ravitaillement *m* supplies; refuelling.

ravitailler *vt* to resupply; **se ~** *vr* to be resupplied; to refuel.

raviver *vt* to revive, reanimate; **se ~** *vr* to be revived.

rayer *vt* to scratch; to cross out.

rayon *m* ray, beam; spoke; shelf.

rayonnant *adj* radiant, beaming.

rayonnement *m* radiance, effulgence; influence.

rayonner *vi* to radiate, shine; to be influential.

rayure *f* stripe; streak; groove.

réaccoutumer *vt* to reaccustom; **se ~** *vr* to become reaccustomed.

réacteur *m* reactor; jet-engine.

réaction *f* reaction.

réactionnaire *adj* reactionary; * *mf* reactionary.

réactiver *vt* to reactivate.

réadaptation *f* rehabilitation; readjustment.

réadapter *vt* to readjust; to rehabilitate.

réagir *vi* to react.

réalisateur *m* **-trice** *f* director, filmmaker.

réalisation *f* realisation; carrying out; achievement.

réaliser *vt* to realise; to carry out; to achieve; **se ~** *vr* to be realised, come true.

réalisme *m* realism.

réaliste *adj* realistic; * *mf* realist.

réalité *f* reality; **en ~** in fact, in reality.

réanimation *f* resuscitation.

réanimer *vt* to reanimate; to resuscitate.

réapparaître *vi* to reappear.

rébarbatif *adj* stern, grim, forbidding.

rebattu *adj* hackneyed.

rebelle *mf* rebel; * *adj* rebel, rebellious.

rebeller (se) *vr* to rebel.

rébellion *f* rebellion.

reboisement *m* reafforestation.

reboiser *vt* to reafforest.

rebondir *vi* to bounce; to rebound.

rebondissement *m* rebound; bouncing.

rebord *m* rim, edge; hem.

rebrousser *vt* to brush back; **~ chemin** to turn back.

rébus *m* rebus, puzzle.

rebut *m* scrap; repulse, rebuff.

récalcitrant *adj* recalcitrant, stubborn.

récapituler *vt* to recapitulate, sum up.

receler *vt* to receive; to harbour.

récemment *adv* recently.

recensement *m* census, inventory.

recenser *vt* to make a census of; to record.

récent *adj* recent; new.

récépissé *m* receipt.

récepteur *m* receiver.

réceptif *adj* receptive.

réception *f* reception, welcome; receipt.

réceptionniste *mf* receptionist.

récession *f* recession.

recette *f* recipe; formula; receipt.

receveur *m* **-euse** *f* recipient; collector.

recevoir *vt* to receive, welcome; to take, collect.

rechange *m*: change; spare; **de ~** spare.

recharge *f* recharging; reloading.

rechargeable *adj* rechargeable; reloadable; refillable.

recharger *vt* to recharge; to reload; to refill.

réchaud *m* stove; dish-warmer.

réchauffer *vt* to reheat; to warm up; **se ~** *vr* to get warmer.

rêche *adj* rough, harsh.

recherche *f* search; inquiry; investigation; research; **être à la ~ de** to be in search of.

recherché *adj* sought after, in demand; choice, exquisite.

rechercher *vt* to seek; to investigate.

rechigner *vt* to balk; to grumble.

rechute *f* relapse; lapse.

récidive *f* second offence, relapse into crime; (*med*) recurrence.

récidiver *vi* to reoffend; to recur.

récidiviste *mf* recidivist, habitual criminal.

récif *m* reef.

récipient *m* container, receptacle.

réciproque *adj* reciprocal, mutual; **~ment** *adv* reciprocally.

récit *m* account, story.

récital *m, pl* **-als** recital.

récitation *f* recitation; recital.

réciter *vt* to recite.

réclamation *f* complaint; demand; claim.

réclame *f* advertisement; publicity; **en ~** on offer.

réclamer *vt* to claim, demand, ask for; * *vi* to complain.

reclus *adj* shut up, secluded.

réclusion *f* reclusion; confinement.

recoiffer *vt* to do sb's hair; **se ~** *vr* to do one's hair.

recoin *m* corner, nook.

recoller *vt* to restick.

récolte *f* harvest; collection; result.

récolter *vt* to harvest; to collect.

recommandation *f* recommendation, reference.

recommander *vt* to recommend; to commend; to register (letter).

recommencement *m* renewal; fresh beginning.

recommencer *vi* to begin again; * *vt* to begin again, resume.

récompense *f* reward; award.

réconciliation *f* reconciliation.

réconcilier *vt* to reconcile; **se ~** *vr* to become reconciled.

reconduire *vt* to bring back; to see home, escort.

réconfort *m* comfort.

réconfortant *adj* comforting; tonic.

réconforter *vt* to comfort; to fortify; **se ~** *vr* to take some refreshment.

reconnaissance *f* recognition; acknowledgement; gratitude.

reconnaissant *adj* grateful.

reconnaître *vt* to recognise; to acknowledge; to be grateful.

reconnu *adj* recognised, accepted.

reconquérir *vt* to reconquer; to recover.

reconsidérer *vt* to reconsider.

reconstituer *vt* to reconstitute; rebuild, restore.

reconstitution *f* reconstitution; rebuilding, restoration.

reconstruire *vt* to reconstruct, rebuild.

reconversion *f* reconversion, redeployment.

recopier *vt* to copy out.

record *m* record.

recoudre *vt* to sew up.

recoupement *m* crosscheck.

recourbé *adj* curved, hooked.

recourir *vi* to run again; **~ à** to resort to.

recours *m* recourse; redress; (*jur*) appeal.

recouvrir *vt* to cover again; to cover up.

récréatif *adj* recreative; entertaining.

récréation *f* recreation; break.

récrimination *f* recrimination, remonstration.

récriminer *vi* to recriminate, remonstrate.

recroqueviller (se) *vr* to shrivel up.

recrudescence *f* recrudescence; upsurge; further outbreak.

recrue *f* recruit.

recrutement *m* recruiting, recruitment.

recruter *vt* to recruit.

rectal *adj* rectal.

rectangle *m* rectangle.

rectangulaire *adj* rectangular.

recteur *m* priest, rector.

rectificatif *m* correction; * *adj* corrected, rectified.

rectification *f* rectification; correction.

rectifier *vt* to rectify, correct; to adjust.

rectiligne *adj* straight; rectilinear.

recto *m* recto, first side; front.

rectum *m* rectum.

reçu *p.p.* **recevoir** accepted, successful; * *m* receipt.

recueil *m* collection, miscellany.

recueillement *m* meditation.

recueillir *vt* to gather, collect; to record; **se ~** *vr* to collect one's thoughts.

recul *m* retreat; recession; decline.

reculer *vi* to fall back, retreat; * *vt* to move back; to defer.

récupération *f* recovery; retrieval.

récupérer *vt* to recover, retrieve; to recuperate; * *vi* to recover.

récurer *vt* to scour.

recycler *vt* to recycle.

rédacteur *m* **-trice** *f* editor, compiler; drafter; writer; sub-editor.

rédaction *f* drafting, drawing up.

rédemption *f* redemption.

redescendre *vi* to go down again; * *vt* to bring down again.

redevable *adj* indebted, owing; liable.

redevance *f* rent; tax; fees.

rediffusion *f* repeat, reshowing.

rédiger *vt* to write; to compile; to draft.

redire *vt* to repeat, say again; **trouver à ~ à** to find fault with.

redoubler *vt* to increase, intensify; * *vi* to increase, intensify; **~ de** redouble.

redoutable *adj* redoubtable, formidable.

redouter *vt* to dread, fear.

redresser *vt* to rectify; to true; to set up again; **se ~** *vr* to stand up; to right oneself.

réduction *f* reduction; discount; mitigation.

réduire *vt* to reduce, diminish; **se ~** *vr*: **se ~ à** to boil down to.

réduit *adj* reduced, limited; miniature; * *m* retreat; recess; small room.

rééducation *f* re-education; rehabilitation.

rééduquer *vt* to re-educate; to rehabilitate.

réel *adj* real, genuine; **~lement** *adv* really.

réélire *vt* to re-elect.

rééquilibrer *vt* to restabilise.

réévaluer *vt* to revalue.

refaire *vt* to redo; to remake; to renew.

réfectoire *m* canteen, refectory.

référence *f* reference.

référendum *m* referendum.

refermer *vt* to close again.

réfléchi *adj* well-considered; reflective, thoughtful.

réfléchir *vi* to think, reflect; * *vt* to realise; to mirror.

reflet *m* reflection; reflex.

refléter *vt* to reflect, mirror.

réflexe *m* reflex.

réflexion *f* thought, reflection; remark; **à la** ~ on reflection; ~ **faite** all things considered.

reflux *m* reflux, ebb.

réforme *f* reform, amendment; discharge.

réformer *vt* to reform, correct; to invalid out; to scrap.

refouler *vt* to drive back, repel.

réfraction *f* refraction.

refrain *m* refrain, chorus.

réfréner *vt* to curb, hold in check.

réfrigérateur *m* refrigerator.

réfrigérer *vt* to refrigerate.

refroidir *vt* to cool; * *vi* to cool down, get cold.

refroidissement *m* cooling; chill.

refuge *m* refuge, shelter; lay-by.

réfugié *m* **-e** *f* refugee; * *adj* refugee.

réfugier (se) *vr* to take refuge.

refus *m* refusal.

refuser *vt* to refuse; to reject; to deny; **se** ~ *vr* to deny o.s.; **se** ~ **à** to reject.

réfuter *vt* to refute.

regagner *vt* to regain, win back.

regain *m* renewal; revival.

régal *m* delight, treat.

régaler *vt* to regale; to treat; **se** ~ *vr* to treat o.s.

regard *m* look; glance; expression; peephole.

regardant *adj* particular, meticulous; stingy.

regarder *vt* to look at; to glance; to be opposite; to concern; ~ **à** to think about.

régates *fpl* regattas.

régénération *f* regeneration.

régénérer *vt* to regenerate, revive.

régent *m* **-e** *f* regent.

régenter *vt* to rule over, domineer.

régie *f* administration; state control.

régime *m* system, régime; scheme; diet; rate, speed.

régiment *m* regiment.

région *f* region, area.

régional *adj* regional.

régir *vt* to govern, rule.

régisseur *m* manager; steward; bailiff.

registre *m* register, record; style; compass.

réglable *adj* adjustable.

réglage *m* regulation, adjustment; tuning.

règle *f* rule; order; regularity; period.

règlement *m* regulation, rules; settlement.

réglementaire *adj* regulation; statutory.

réglementation *f* regulations; control.

réglementer *vt* to regulate, control.

régler *vt* to settle, pay; to regulate.

réglisse *f* liquorice.

règne *m* reign.

régner *vi* to reign; to prevail.

regorger *vi*: ~ **de** to overflow with, abound in.

régresser *vi* to regress; to recede.

régression *f* regression.

regret *m* regret, yearning; **à** ~ regretfully.

regrettable *adj* regrettable.

regretter *vt* to regret, be sorry; to miss.

regroupement *m* gathering together; merger.

regrouper *vt* to group together; to reassemble; **se** ~ *vr* to gather together.

régulariser *vt* to regularise; straighten out.

régularité *f* regularity; consistency.

régulier *adj* regular; consistent; steady; even; legitimate.

régulièrement *adv* regularly; consistently; lawfully.

réhabilitation *f* rehabilitation; discharge; reinstatement.

réhabiliter *vt* to rehabilitate; to discharge; to reinstate.

réhabituer *vt* to reaccustom sb to; **se** ~ *vr* to reaccustom o.s. to.

rehausser *vt* to heighten, raise.

rein *m* kidney.

réincarnation *f* reincarnation.

reine *f* queen.

reine-claude *f* greengage.

réinsertion *f* reinsertion, reintegration.

réintégrer *vt* to reinstate; to return to.

réitérer *vt* to reiterate, repeat.

rejaillir *vi* to gush out; to rebound on.

rejet *m* rejection, dismissal; throwing up.

rejeter *vt* to reject, dismiss; throw up.

rejoindre *vt* to rejoin; to catch up with.

rejouer *vt* to replay; to perform again; * *vi* to play again.

réjouir *vt* to delight; to entertain; **se** ~ *vr* to rejoice, be delighted.

réjouissance *f* rejoicing, merry-making.

relâche *f* intermission, respite; **faire** ~ to be closed; **sans** ~ relentlessly.

relâchement *m* relaxation, loosening; laxity.

relâcher *vt* to relax, slacken; **se** ~ *vr* to relax; to become lax.

relais *m* relay; shift; staging post.

relatif *adj* relative; relating to.

relation *f* relation, relationship; reference; acquaintance; account; **être en** ~ **avec** to be in contact with.

relativement *adv* relatively.

relativisme *m* relativism.

relativité *f* relativity.

relaxant *adj* relaxing.

relaxation *f* relaxation.

relaxer *vt* to relax; to acquit; to release; **se** ~ *vr* to relax.

relayer *vt* to relieve, take the place of; to relay; **se** ~ *vr* to take turns.

relecture *f* rereading.

reléguer *vt* to relegate; to banish.

relève *f* relief; relief party.

relevé *m* statement; list; bill; * *adj* turned up, rolled up; elevated.

relever *vt* to set up again, raise again; to rebuild; to relieve; **se** ~ *vr* to stand up again; to get up.

relief *m* relief; contours; depth.

relier *vt* to link up, connect; to bind.

religieux *m* monk, **-euse** *f* nun; * *adj* religious.

religion *f* religion.

relique *f* relic.

relire *vt* to reread.

reliure *f* binding; bookbinding.

reluire *vi* to gleam, shine.

remaniement *m* recasting; altering; revision; amendment.

remanier *vt* to recast, revise; to amend.

remarquable *adj* remarkable, notable; **~ment** *adv* remarkably.

remarque *f* remark, comment.

remarquer *vt* to remark; to notice.

rembourrer *vt* to stuff; to pad.

remboursement *m* reimbursement, repayment.

rembourser *vt* to reimburse, pay back.

remède *m* remedy, cure.

remédier *vi*: ~ **à** to remedy, cure.

remerciement *m* thanks; thanking.

remercier *vt* to thank.

remettre *vt* to put back; to replace; to restart; to revive; **se** ~ *vr* to recover, get better; **se** ~ **à** to start doing sth again; **se** ~ **de** to get over sth.

réminiscence *f* reminiscence.

remise *f* delivery; remittance; discount; deferment; ~ **en état** repairing; ~ **à neuf** restoration; ~ **en jeu** throw-in; ~ **en question** calling into question; ~ **en cause** calling into question; ~ **de peine** remission.

remmener *vt* to take back.

remontant *m* tonic; * *adj* invigorating, fortifying.

remonte-pente *m* ski tow.

remonter *vi* to go up again; to rise, increase; to return; * *vt* to go up; to take up.

remontrance *f* remonstrance.

remords *m* remorse.

remorque *f* trailer; towrope.

remorquer *vt* to tow.

remorqueur *m* tug.

rémouleur *m* knife-grinder.

remous *m* back-wash; eddy, swirl.

rempailler *vt* to reseat (chair).

rempart *m* rampart; defence.

remplaçant *m* -**e** *f* substitute.

remplacement *m* replacing; substitution.

remplacer *vt* to replace, stand in for.

remplir *vt* to fill; to fill in; to fulfil; **se** ~ *vr* to fill up.

remplissage *m* filling up; padding.

remporter *vt* to take away.

remuant *adj* restless, fidgety.

remue-ménage *m invar* commotion; hullabaloo.

remuer *vi* to move; to fidget; * *vt* to move, shift; to stir; **se** ~ *vr* to move; to shift o.s.

rémunération *f* remuneration, payment.

rémunérer *vt* to remunerate, pay.

renaissance *f* rebirth, Renaissance.

renaître *vi* to be reborn; to be revived; to reappear.

renard *m* fox.

renchérir *vi* to go further, go one better; to bid higher.

renchérissement *m* increase in price.

rencontre *f* meeting, encounter; conjuncture; collision.

rencontrer *vt* to meet; to find; to strike; **se** ~ *vr* to meet each other.

rendement *m* yield; output.

rendez-vous *m* appointment; date; meeting place.

rendormir *vt* to put to sleep again; **se** ~ *vr* to go back to sleep.

rendre *vt* to render; to give back, return; to yield; **se** ~ *vr* to surrender; to give way.

rêne *f* rein.

renfermé *adj* withdrawn, close; * *m* fusty/close smell.

renfermer *vt* to contain, hold.

renflement *m* bulge.

renflouer *vt* to refloat; to bail out.

renfoncement *m* recess.

renfoncer *vt* to drive further in; to recess.

renforcer *vt* to strengthen, reinforce.

renfort *m* reinforcement; help.

renfrogné *adj* frowning, glum.

renier *vt* to repudiate, disown.

renifler *vt* to sniff, snuffle.

renne *m* reindeer.

renom *m* renown, fame.

renommée *f* renowned, famed.

renoncement *m* renouncement; renunciation.

renoncer *vi* to renounce, give up.

renonciation *f* renunciation; waiver.

renouer *vt* to retie; to renew.

renouveau *m* spring; renewal.

renouveler *vt* to renew; to revive; **se** ~ *vr* to be renewed.

renouvellement *m* renewal; revival.

rénovation *f* renovation; renewal.

rénover *vt* to renovate.

renseignement *m* information; intelligence.

renseigner *vt* to inform, give information to; **se** ~ *vr* to ask for information.

rentabiliser *vt* to make profitable.

rentable *adj* profitable.

rente *f* rent; profit; annuity.

rentier *m* -**ière** *f* stockholder, fundholder; rentier.

rentrée *f* reopening; reassembly; reappearance.

rentrer *vi* to re-enter; to return home; to begin again; * *vt* to bring in.

renversement *m* inversion; reversal; overturning.

renverser *vt* to turn upside down; to reverse; to overturn.

renvoi *m* sending back; returning; dismissal.

renvoyer *vt* to send back; to return; to dismiss.

réorganisation *f* reorganisation.

réorganiser *vt* to reorganise.

réouverture *f* reopening.

repaire *m* den, lair.

répandre *vt* to pour out; to scatter, spread; **se** ~ *vr* to spread; to be spilled.

répandu *adj* widespread.

réparateur *m* -**trice** *f* repairer.

réparation *f* repairing; restoration.

réparer *vt* to repair; to restore; to make up for.

repartie *f* retort; **avoir de la** ~ to have a quick wit.

repartir *vi* to set off again; to start up again.

répartir *vt* to share out; to distribute; **se** ~ *vr* to share out.

répartition *f* sharing out; allocation.

repas *m* meal.

repassage *m* ironing; grinding, sharpening.

repasser *vt* to iron; to cross again; to resit; * *vi* to go past again.

repêcher *vt* to fish out, retrieve.

repeindre *vt* to repaint.

repenti *adj* repentant.

repentir *m* repentance, contrition.

repentir (se) *vr* to repent, rue.

répercussion *f* repercussion.

répercuter *vt* to reverberate; to echo; **se** ~ *vr* to reverberate; to echo.

repère *m* line, mark; **point de** ~ indication, reference mark.

repérer *vt* to spot, pick out; to mark out.

répertoire *m* index, catalogue; repertory.

répertorier *vt* to itemise; to index.

répéter *vt* to repeat; to rehearse; **se** ~ *vr* to repeat o.s.; to reoccur.

répétitif *adj* repetitive.

répétition *f* repetition; rehearsal.

repiquer *vt* to plant out, transplant.

répit *m* respite, rest.

repli *m* fold, coil, meander; withdrawal; downturn.

replier *vt* to fold up; to withdraw; **se** ~ *vr* to coil up, curl up.

réplique *f* reply, retort; counterattack.

répliquer *vt* to reply; to retaliate.

répondant *m* -**e** *f* guarantor; bail; surety.

répondeur *m* answering machine.

répondre *vt* to answer, reply.

réponse *f* response, reply.

report *m* postponement, deferment; carrying forward.

reportage *m* report; commentary; reporting.

reporter *vt* to postpone; to carry forward; to transfer; * *m* reporter.

repos *m* rest; tranquillity; landing.

reposant *adj* restful, refreshing.

reposer *vt* to put back; to rest; to ask again; **se ~** *vr* to rest.

repoussant *adj* repulsive; repellent.

repousser *vt* to push back; to repel.

reprendre *vt* to retake, recapture; to resume; **se ~** *vr* to correct o.s.; to pull o.s. together.

représailles *fpl* reprisals; retaliation.

représentant *m* representative.

représentatif *adj* representative.

représentation *f* representation; performance.

représenter *vt* to represent, depict; to perform; to symbolise.

répressif *adj* repressive.

répression *f* repression.

réprimande *f* reprimand, rebuke.

réprimander *vt* to reprimand, rebuke.

réprimer *vt* to repress; to quell.

reprise *f* resumption; recapture, taking back; **à plusieurs ~s** several times.

repriser *vt* to darn.

réprobation *f* reprobation.

reproche *m* reproach; objection.

reprocher *vt* to reproach, blame.

reproduction *f* reproduction; copy; duplicate.

reproduire *vt* to reproduce, copy; to repeat; **se ~** *vr* to reproduce, breed.

reptile *m* reptile.

repu *adj* full, satiated.

républicain *m* **-e** *f* republican; * *adj* republican.

république *f* republic.

répudier *vt* to repudiate; to renounce.

répugnance *f* repugnance, disgust.

répugnant *adj* repugnant, disgusting, revolting.

répulsion *f* repulsion, repugnance.

réputation *f* reputation; character; fame.

réputé *adj* reputable, renowned; supposed, reputed.

requérir *vt* to call for, request.

requête *f* petition, request.

requin *m* shark.

requis *adj* required, requisite.

réquisition *f* requisition; conscription.

réquisitionner *vt* to requisition; to conscript.

rescapé *m* **-e** *f* survivor.

réseau *m* network, net.

réservation *f* reservation, booking.

réserve *f* reserve; reservation, caution.

réservé *f* reserved.

réserver *vt* to reserve, save; to book; to lay by.

réservoir *m* tank; reservoir.

résidence *f* residence; apartment block.

résidentiel *adj* residential.

résider *vi* to reside, dwell.

résidu *m* residue.

résignation *f* resignation.

résigner (se) *vr* to resign o.s.

résilier *vt* to terminate; to annul.

résine *f* resin.

résistance *f* resistance.

résistant *adj* resistant; tough, unyielding.

résister *vi* to resist, withstand.

résolu *adj* resolved, determined; **~ment** *adv* resolutely.

résolution *f* resolution, determination.

résonner *vi* to resound, resonate.

résorber *vt* to reduce; to absorb; **se ~** *vr* to be reduced.

résoudre *vt* to solve; to resolve; to annul; **se ~** *vr*: **se ~ à** to decide to do.

respect *m* respect, regard, deference.

respectable *adj* respectable; sizeable.

respecter *vt* to respect; to comply with.

respectif *adj* respective.

respectivement *adv* respectively.

respectueusement *adv* respectfully.

respectueux *adj* respectful.

respirable *adj* breathable.

respiration *f* breathing, respiration.

respiratoire *adj* respiratory.

respirer *vi* to breathe, respire; to rest; * *vt* to breathe in.

resplendissant *adj* shining, radiant.

responsabilité *f* responsibility; liability.

responsable *adj* responsible; liable; * *mf* official, manager.

resquiller *vi* to sneak in; to take a free ride.

ressaisir (se) *vr* to regain one's self-control.

ressemblance *f* resemblance, likeness; similarity.

ressemblant *adj* lifelike.

ressembler *vi* to resemble, be like; **se ~** *vr* to be alike.

ressemelage *m* soling, resoling.

ressentiment *m* resentment.

ressentir *vt* to feel, experience; **se ~** *vr*: **se ~ de** to feel the effects of.

resserrement *m* contraction, tightening; narrowing.

resserrer *vt* to tighten; to strengthen; **se ~** *vr* to grow tighter.

ressort *m* spring; motivation.

ressortir *vi* to go out again; to stand out.

ressortissant *m* **-e** *f* national.

ressource *f* resource, resort, expedient.

ressusciter *vi* to revive, reawaken; to come back to life; * *vt* to resuscitate; to revive.

restant *adj* remaining; * *m* rest, remainder.

restaurant *m* restaurant.

restaurateur *m* **-trice** *f* restaurateur; restorer.

restauration *f* restoration, rehabilitation; catering.

restaurer *vt* to restore; to feed; **se ~** *vr* to eat.

reste *m* rest, left-over, remainder; **du ~** besides; **être en ~** to be outdone.

rester *vi* to remain, stay; to be left; to continue; to pause.

restituer *vt* to return, restore; to refund.

restitution *f* restoration; restitution.

restreindre *vt* to restrict, curtail; **se ~** *vr* to restrain o.s.

restreint *adj* restricted, limited.

restrictif *adj* restrictive.

restriction *f* restriction, limitation; reserve.

restructurer *vt* to restructure.

résultat *m* result, outcome; profit.

résulter *vi*: **~ de** to result, follow from, ensue.

résumé *m* summary, recapitulation; **en ~** in brief.

résumer *vt* to sum up; **se ~** *vr*: **se ~ à** to amount to.

résurrection *f* resurrection.

rétablir *vt* to re-establish, restore; **se ~** *vr* to recover, get well again.

rétablissement *m* re-establishment, restoring.

retard *m* lateness; delay; **être en ~** to be late; to be behind; to be backward.

retardataire *mf* latecomer; * *adj* obsolete.

retardé *adj* backward, slow.

retarder *vt* to delay; to hinder; to put back; * *vi* to be out of touch.

retenir *vt* to hold back, retain; to remember; **se ~** *vr* to control o.s.

rétention *f* retention; withholding.

retentir *vi* to resound; to ring.

retentissant *adj* resounding; ringing.

retenue *f* discretion; deduction, stoppage; reservoir.

réticence *f* reticence.

réticent *adj* reticent.

rétine *f* retina.

retiré *adj* remote, isolated.

retirer *vt* to take off; to take out, withdraw; to redeem; **se ~** *vr* to retire, withdraw; to stand down.

retombée *f* fallout; repercussions.

retomber *vi* to fall again; to have a relapse; **~ sur** to come across again.

rétorquer *vt* to retort.

retouche *f* touching up; alteration.

retoucher *vt* to touch up; to alter.

retour *m* return; recurrence; vicissitude, reversal; **être de ~** to be back.

retournement *m* reversal; turnaround.

retourner *vt* to reverse, turn over; to return; * *vi* to return, go back; **se ~** *vr* to turn over; to overturn.

rétracter *vt* to retract, take back; **se ~** *vr* to retract, withdraw one's evidence.

retrait *m* ebb; retreat; withdrawal; **être en ~** to be set back.

retraite *f* retreat; retirement; refuge; **à la ~** retired.

retraité *m* **-e** *f* pensioner; * *adj* retired.

retranchement *m* curtailment; entrenchment.

retrancher *vt* to curtail; to entrench.

retransmettre *vt* to retransmit.

retransmission *f* retransmission.

rétrécir *vi* to narrow; to shrink; * *vt* to take in, make narrower; **se ~** *vr* to narrow; to shrink.

rétrécissement *m* narrowing; shrinking.

rétribuer *vt* to remunerate.

rétribution *f* retribution.

rétroactif *adj* retrospective; retroactive.

rétroaction *f* retroaction; retrospective action.

rétrograde *adj* reactionary, backward.

rétrograder *vi* to go backward, regress.

rétroprojecteur *m* overhead projector.

rétrospectif *adj* retrospective.

rétrospective *f* retrospective.

rétrospectivement *adv* retrospectively.

retrousser *vt* to roll up, hitch up.

retrouvailles *fpl* reunion.

retrouver *vt* to find again, to regain; to recover; to recognise; **se ~** *vr* to meet up; to end up in.

rétroviseur *m* rear-view mirror.

réunifier *vt* to reunify.

réunion *f* reunion, gathering.

réunir *vt* to unite; to collect, gather; to combine; **se ~** *vr* to meet; to assemble.

réussir *vi* to succeed, be a success; * *vt* to make a success of.

réussite *f* success, successful outcome.

revanche *f* revenge; **en ~** on the other hand.

rêvasser *vi* to daydream.

rêve *m* dream, dreaming; illusion.

réveil *m* waking, awaking; alarm clock.

réveiller *vt* to wake; **se ~** *vr* to awaken.

réveillon *m* midnight feast.

révélation *f* revelation, disclosure; developing.

révéler *vt* to reveal, disclose; **se ~** *vr* to be revealed; to prove to be.

revenant *m* **-e** *f* ghost.

revendeur *m* **-euse** *f* retailer; dealer.

revendication *f* claiming; claim; demand.

revendiquer *vt* to claim; to demand.

revendre *vt* to resell.

revenir *vi* to come back, reappear; to happen again; **ne pas en ~** to not recover from, not pull through; **~ à soi** to come round.

revenu *m* income, revenue.

rêver *vi* to dream; to muse; * *vt* to dream of.

réverbération *f* reverberation.

réverbère *m* street lamp.

révérence *f* bow, curtsey.

révérend *adj* reverend.

révérer *vt* to revere.

rêverie *f* reverie, musing.

revers *m* back, reverse; counterpart.

réversible *adj* reversible.

revêtement *m* coating, surface.

revêtir *vt* to don; to assume.

rêveur *m* **-euse** *f* dreamer; * *adj* dreamy.

revigorer *vt* to invigorate; to revive.

revirement *m* change of mind; reversal; turnaround.

réviser *vt* to review; to revise.

révision *f* review; auditing; revision.

revivre *vt* to relive; * *vi* to live again, come alive again.

révocation *f* removal; dismissal; revocation.

revoir *vt* to see again; **se ~** *vr* to meet each other again.

révoltant *adj* revolting, appalling.

révolte *f* revolt, rebellion.

révolter *vt* to revolt, outrage; **se ~** *vr* to rebel, revolt.

révolu *adj* past, bygone.

révolution *f* revolution.

révolutionnaire *mf* revolutionary; * *adj* revolutionary.

révolutionner *vt* to revolutionise; to upset.

revolver *m* revolver.

révoquer *vt* to revoke; to dismiss.

revue *f* review; inspection.

rez-de-chaussée *m invar* ground floor.

rhabiller *vt* to dress (sb) again; to fit (sb) out again; **se ~** *vr* to get dressed again.

rhésus *m* rhesus.

rhétorique *f* rhetoric; * *adj* rhetorical.

rhinocéros *m* rhinoceros.

rhododendron *m* rhododendron.

rhubarbe *f* rhubarb.

rhum *m* rum.

rhumatisme *m* rheumatism.

rhume *m* cold.

riant *adj* smiling; cheerful.

ribambelle *f* swarm, herd.

ricanement *m* snigger, sniggering.

ricaner *vi* to snigger, giggle.

riche *adj* rich, wealthy; abundant; **~ment** *adv* richly; * *mf* rich person.

richesse *f* richness; wealth; abundance.

ricochet *m* ricochet; rebound.

rictus *m* grin; grimace.

ride *f* wrinkle; ripple; ridge.

ridé *adj* wrinkled.

rideau *m* curtain.

ridicule *adj* ridiculous; * *m* ridiculousness; absurdity; ridicule.

ridiculiser *vt* to ridicule.

rien *pn* nothing; **de ~** don't mention it; **il n'en est ~** it's nothing of the sort; * *m* nothingness; mere nothing; pinch, shade; **en un ~ de temps** in no time; **pour un ~** at the slightest little thing.

rieur *adj* cheerful; laughing.

rigide *adj* rigid; **~ment** *adv* rigidly.

rigidité *f* rigidity, stiffness.

rigole *f* channel; rivulet.

rigoler *vi* (*fam*) to have a good laugh.

rigoureusement *adv* harshly, rigorously.

rigoureux *adj* rigorous, harsh.

rigueur *f* rigour; harshness, severity.

rime *f* rhyme.

rimer *vi* to rhyme (with).

rince-doigts *m invar* finger-bowl.

rincer *vt* to rinse out; to rinse.

ring *m* boxing ring.

riposte *f* riposte, retort.

riposter *vi* to answer back, retaliate.

rire *vi* to laugh; to smile; to joke; * *m* laughter, laugh.

risée *f* laugh; ridicule; mockery, derision.

risible *adj* laughable, ridiculous.

risque *m* risk, hazard.

risqué *adj* risky, hazardous; risqué.

risquer *vt* to risk; to venture; **se ~** *vr* to venture, dare.

ristourne *f* discount, rebate.

rite *m* rite.

rituel *adj* ritual.

rivage *m* shore.

rival *m* **-e** *f* rival; **sans ~** unrivalled; * *adj* rival.

rivaliser *vi* to rival, compete with; **~ de** to vie with.

rivalité *f* rivalry.

rive *f* shore, bank.

river *vt* to clinch; to rivet.

riverain *m* **-e** *f* lakeside resident; riverside resident; * *adj* lakeside, riverside.

rivière *f* river.

riz *m* rice.

robe *f* dress; gown; **~ de chambre** dressing gown.

robinet *m* tap.

robot *m* robot.

robotique *f* robotics.

robuste *adj* robust.

robustesse *f* robustness.

roc *m* rock.

rocaille *f* loose stones; rocky ground.

rocailleux *adj* rocky.

roche *f* rock.

rocher *m* rock, boulder.

rodage *m* grinding; running in, breaking in.

roder *vt* to grind; to run in.

rôder *vi* to roam; to prowl about.

rôdeur *m* **-euse** *f* prowler.

rogner *vt* to pare, prune, clip.

rognon *m* kidney.

roi *m* king.

rôle *m* role, character; roll, catalogue.

roman *m* novel; romance.

romancier *m* **-ière** *f* novelist.

romanesque *adj* fabulous; storybook; fictional.

romantique *adj* romantic.

romantisme *m* romanticism.

rompre *vt* to break; to snap; to dissolve; * *vi* to break; to burst.

ronce *f* bramble.

rond *m* circle, ring; slice, round; * *adj* round; chubby, plump; frank, **~ement** *adv* briskly, frankly.

ronde *f* patrol; round; beat.

rondelle *f* slice, round; disc.

rondeur *f* plumpness; roundness.

rondin *m* log.

rond-point *m* roundabout.

ronflement *m* snore, snoring; humming; roaring.

ronfler *vi* to snore; to hum; to roar.

ronger *vt* to gnaw.

ronronner *vi* to purr; to hum.

rosbif *m* roast beef.

rose *f* rose; * *adj* pink; * *m* pink.

roseau *m* reed.

rosée *f* dew.

rosier *m* rosebush.

rossignol *m* nightingale.

rot *m* belch, burp.

roter *vi* to belch, burp.

rotation *f* rotation; turnover.

rôti *m* joint, roast.

rotin *m* rattan.

rôtir *vt* to roast.

rôtisserie *f* rotisserie, steak-house.

rotonde *f* rotunda; roundhouse.

rotule *f* kneecap, patella.

rouage *m* cog; gearwheel.

roucouler *vi* to coo; to bill.

roue *f* wheel.

rouge *adj* red; * *m* red; **~ à lèvres** lipstick.

rouge-gorge *m* robin.

rougeole *f* measles.

rougeur *f* redness, blushing.

rougir *vi* to blush, go red; * *vt* to make red, redden.

rouille *f* rust.

rouiller *vi* to rust; * *vt* to make rusty.

roulant *adj* on wheels; moving.

rouleau *m* roll; roller.

roulement *m* rotation; movement; rumble, rumbling.

rouler *vt* to wheel, roll along; * *vi* to go, run (train); to drive.

roulette *f* castor; trundle; roulette.

roulis *m* rolling.

roulotte *f* caravan.

rouquin *m* **-e** *f* redhead; * *adj* redhaired.

route *f* road; way; course, direction.

routier *adj* road; * *m* lorry driver; transport café.

routine *f* routine.

routinier *adj* humdrum, routine.

roux *m*, **rousse** *f* redhead; * *adj* red, auburn.

royal *adj* royal, regal; **~ement** *adv* royally.

royaliste *mf* royalist; * *adj* royalist.

royaume *m* kingdom.

royauté *f* monarchy.

ruade *f* kick (horse).

ruban *m* ribbon; tape, band.

rubéole *f* rubella.

rubis *m* ruby.

rubrique *f* column; heading, rubric.

ruche *f* hive.

rude *adj* rough; hard; unrefined; **~ment** *adv* roughly, harshly.

rudesse *f* roughness; harshness.

rudiment *m* rudiment; principle.

rudimentaire *adj* rudimentary.

rudoyer *vt* to treat harshly.

rue *f* street.

ruée *f* rush, stampede.

ruelle *f* alley.

ruer *vi* to kick (horse); **se ~** *vr* to pounce on.

rugby *m* rugby.

rugbyman *m* rugby player.

rugir *vi* to roar.

rugissement *m* roar, roaring.

rugueux *adj* rough; coarse.

ruine *f* ruin; wreck.

ruiner *vt* to ruin.

ruineux *adj* ruinous; extravagant.

ruisseau *m* stream, brook.

ruisseler *vi* to stream, flow.

ruissellement *m* streaming; cascading.

rumeur *f* rumour; murmur; hum.

ruminer *vt* to ruminate; to brood over.

rupture *f* break, rupture; breach; split.

rural *adj* rural, country.

ruse *f* cunning, slyness.

rusé *adj* cunning, crafty.

rustine ® *f* rubber repair patch.

rustique *adj* rustic.

rutilant *adj* gleaming, rutilant.

rythme *m* rhythm; rate, speed.

rythmique *adj* rhythmic.

S

sabbatique *adj* sabbatical.

sable *m* sand.

sablé *m* shortbread biscuit; * *adj* sandy, sanded.

sablier *m* hourglass, sandglass.

sabot *m* clog; hoof.

sabotage *m* sabotage.

saboter *vt* to sabotage; to mess up.

saboteur *m* **-euse** *f* saboteur; bungler.

sabre *m* sabre

sac *m* bag, sack; ~ **à main** handbag; ~ **de voyage** travelling bag.

saccade *f* jerk, jolt.

saccadé *adj* jerky, broken, staccato.

saccager *vt* to sack; to wreck, devastate.

saccharine *f* saccharin.

sacerdoce *m* priesthood.

sacerdotal *adj* priestly, sacerdotal.

sachet *m* bag; sachet; packet.

sacoche *f* saddlebag, satchel.

sacre *m* coronation; consecration.

sacré *adj* sacred, holy; damned, confounded.

Sacré-Cœur *m* Sacred Heart.

sacrer *vt* to crown; to consecrate.

sacrifice *m* sacrifice.

sacrifier *vt* to sacrifice; to give up; **se** ~ *vr* to sacrifice o.s.

sacrilège *m* sacrilege.

sacristie *f* sacristy.

sacrum *m* sacrum.

sadique *adj* sadistic; * *mf* sadist.

sadisme *m* sadism.

sadomasochiste *adj* sadomasochistic; * *mf* sadomasochist.

safari *m* safari.

safran *m* saffron.

saga *f* saga.

sagace *adj* sagacious, shrewd.

sagacité *f* sagacity, shrewdness.

sage *adj* wise, sensible; well-behaved; **~ment** *adv* wisely, sensibly; * *m* sage, wise man.

sage-femme *f* midwife.

sagesse *f* wisdom, sense; good behaviour.

sagittaire *m* archer; Sagittarius.

saignant *adj* bleeding; underdone.

saignement *m* bleeding.

saigner *vi* to bleed; * *vt* to bleed; to stick.

saillant *adj* prominent, protruding.

saillie *f* projection; sally; flash of wit.

saillir *vi* to gush out; to project, jut.

sain *adj* healthy; sound; sane; **~ement** *adv* healthily; soundly.

saindoux *m* lard.

saint *m* **-e** *f* saint; * *adj* holy, saintly; **Saint-Sylvestre** New Year's Eve; **Saint-Esprit** Holy Spirit.

saint-bernard *m* St Bernard.

sainteté *f* saintliness; holiness.

saisie *f* (*jur*) seizure, distraint; capture.

saisir *vt* to take hold of; (jur) to seize, distrain; to capture.

saisissant *adj* gripping, startling, striking.

saison *f* season.

saisonnier *adj* seasonal.

salade *f* salad; jumble, miscellany.

saladier *m* salad bowl.

salaire *m* salary, pay; reward.

salamandre *f* salamander.

salarié *m* **-e** *f* salaried employee; * *adj* salaried.

sale *adj* dirty, filthy; obscene; nasty; **~ment** *adv* dirtily.

salé *adj* salty, salted; savoury.

saler *vt* to salt, add salt.

saleté *f* dirtiness, dirt; rubbish; obscenity.

salière *f* saltcellar.

salin *adj* saline.

salir *vt* to make dirty, soil; **se** ~ *vr* to get dirty.

salissant *adj* dirty; that gets dirty easily.

salive *f* saliva.

saliver *vi* to salivate; to drool.

salle *f* room; hall; theatre; audience; ~ **de séjour** living room; ~ **à manger** dining room; ~ **de bain** bathroom; ~ **de cinéma** cinema.

salon *m* lounge, sitting room; exhibition.

salopette *f* overalls.

salpêtre *m* saltpetre.

salsifis *m* salsify.

salubre *adj* healthy, salubrious.

saluer *vt* to greet; to salute.

salut *m* safety, salvation; welfare; wave (hand); salute.

salutaire *adj* salutary; profitable; healthy.

salutation *f* salutation, greeting.

samedi *m* Saturday.

sanatorium *m* sanatorium.

sanctifier *vt* to sanctify, bless.

sanction *f* sanction, penalty; approval.

sanctionner *vt* to punish; to sanction, approve.

sanctuaire *m* sanctuary.

sandale *f* sandal.

sandwich *m* sandwich.

sang *m* blood; race; kindred.

sang-froid *m* sangfroid, cool, calm.

sanglant *adj* bloody, gory; bloodshot; blood-red.

sangle *f* strap; girth.

sanglier *m* wild boar.

sanglot *m* sob.

sangloter *vi* to sob.

sangsue *f* leech.

sanguinaire *adj* sanguinary, bloodthirsty.

sanitaire *adj* health, sanitary.

sans-abris *mf invar* homeless person.

sans-gêne *adj* inconsiderate; * *m invar* inconsiderate type.

santal *m* sandalwood.

santé *f* health, healthiness.

saper *vt* to undermine, sap.

sapeur-pompier *m* fireman.

saphir *m* sapphire.

sapin *m* fir tree, fir.

sarcasme *m* sarcasm.

sarcastique *adj* sarcastic.

sarcler *vt* to weed; to hoe.

sarcophage *m* sarcophagus.

sardine *f* sardine.

sardonique *adj* sardonic

SARL (société à responsabilité limitée) *f* limited liability company.

sarrasin *m* buckwheat.

sas *m* airlock; sieve.

satanique *adj* satanic, diabolical.

satellite *m* satellite.

satiété *f* satiety, satiation; **à** ~ ad nauseam.

satin *m* satin.

satiné *adj* satiny, satin-smooth; glazed.

satire *f* satire, lampoon.

satirique *adj* satirical.

satisfaction *f* satisfaction; gratification; appeasement.

satisfaire *vt* to satisfy; to gratify; to appease.

satisfaisant *adj* satisfactory; satisfying.

satisfait *adj* satisfied.

saturation *f* saturation.
saturé *adj* saturated; overloaded, jammed.
saturer *vt* to saturate; to surfeit; to congest.
satyre *m* satyr.
sauce *f* sauce, dressing.
saucière *f* sauceboat.
saucisse *f* sausage.
saucisson *m* large sausage; salami.
sauf *prép* save, except; unless; * *adj* safe, unhurt.
sauge *f* sage.
saugrenu *adj* preposterous, absurd.
saule *m* willow.
saumon *m* salmon.
sauna *m* sauna.
saupoudrer *vt* to sprinkle; to dust.
saut *m* jump, bound; waterfall.
sauté *adj* sauté.
sauter *vi* to jump, leap; to blow up; to get sacked.
sauterelle *f* grasshopper.
sautiller *vi* to hop, skip.
sauvage *adj* savage, wild; unsociable; ~**ment** *adv* savagely.
sauvegarde *f* safeguard; backup.
sauvegarder *vt* to safeguard.
sauver *vt* to save, rescue; to preserve; **se** ~ *vr* to save o.s.; to escape.
sauvetage *m* rescue; salvage.
sauveteur *m* rescuer.
savant *adj* learned; expert; skilled; * *m* scientist, scholar.
savate *f* old shoe.
saveur *f* flavour; savour.
savoir *vt* to know; to be aware; to understand; to be able; * *m* learning, knowledge.
savoir-faire *m* know-how.
savoir-vivre *m* good manners, good breeding.
savon *m* soap.
savonner *vt* to soap, lather.
savonnette *f* bar of soap.
savoureux *adj* tasty, savoury.
saxophone *m* saxophone.
saxophoniste *mf* saxophonist.
scabreux *adj* scabrous; dangerous; improper.
scalpel *m* scalpel.
scandale *m* scandal.
scandaleux *adj* scandalous.
scandaliser *vt* to scandalise, shock deeply; **se** ~ *vr* to be scandalised.
scanner *m* scanner.
scaphandre *m* diving suit.
scarabée *m* beetle, scarab.
scarlatine *f* scarlet fever.

sceau *m* seal.
scélérat *m* **-e** *f* villain, rascal; * *adj* villainous, wicked.
sceller *vt* to seal.
scénario *m* scenario; screenplay.
scénariste *mf* scriptwriter.
scène *f* stage; scenery, scene.
scepticisme *m* scepticism.
sceptique *adj* sceptical; * *mf* sceptic.
sceptre *m* sceptre.
schéma *m* diagram, sketch; outline.
schématique *adj* diagrammatic, schematic; ~**ment** *adv* diagrammatically.
schématiser *vt* to schematise.
schisme *m* schism; split.
schiste *m* schist, shale.
schizophrène *mf* schizophrenic; * *adj* schizophrenic.
schizophrénie *f* schizophrenia.
sciatique *f* sciatica.
scie *f* saw; bore.
sciemment *adv* knowingly, on purpose.
science *f* science; skill; knowledge.
science-fiction *f* science fiction.
scientifique *adj* scientific; ~**ment** *adv* scientifically.
scierie *f* sawmill.
scinder *vt* to split, divide up.
scintillant *adj* sparkling, glistening.
scintillement *m* sparkling, glistening.
scintiller *vi* to sparkle, glisten.
scission *f* split, scission.
sciure *f* sawdust.
sclérose *f* sclerosis.
scléroser (se) *vr* to become sclerotic.
scolaire *adj* school; academic.
scolariser *vt* to send to school; to provide schools.
scolarité *f* schooling.
scoliose *f* scoliosis, curvature of the spine.
scooter *m* scooter.
score *m* score.
scorie *f* slag, scoria.
scorpion *m* scorpion.
scout *m* scout, boy scout.
script *m* printing; script.
scrupule *m* scruple, qualm, doubt.
scrupuleusement *adv* scrupulously.
scrupuleux *adj* scrupulous.
scruter *vt* to scrutinise, scan.
scrutin *m* ballot, poll.
sculpter *vt* to sculpt; to carve.
sculpteur *m* sculptor.
sculpture *f* sculpture.

se *pn* oneself, himself, herself, itself, themselves.
séance *f* meeting, sitting, session; seat.
seau *m* bucket, pail.
sec *adj*, *f* **sèche** dry, arid; barren; unfeeling; curt; neat.
sécateur *m* secateurs.
séchage *m* drying; seasoning.
sèche-cheveux *m invar* hair-drier
sèchement *adv* dryly; curtly.
sécher *vi* to dry, dry out; * *vt* to dry, wipe.
sécheresse *f* drought; dryness.
séchoir *m* drying room; ~ **à linge** clothes horse.
second *adj* second, in second place; * *m* second; second floor; second in command; * *f* second.
secondaire *adj* secondary.
seconder *vt* to assist, help.
secouer *vt* to shake, toss; **se** ~ *vr* to shake o.s.
secourir *vt* to help, assist.
secouriste *mf* first-aid worker.
secours *m* help, assistance; relief; rescue.
secousse *f* jolt, bump.
secret *m* secret; privacy; mystery; * *adj* secret; private; discreet.
secrétaire *mf* secretary; * *m* writing desk.
secrétariat *m* office of secretary; secretariat.
secrètement *adv* secretly.
secréter *vt* to secrete, exude.
sécrétion *f* secretion.
secte *f* sect.
secteur *m* sector, section, district.
section *f* section, division; branch.
sectionner *vt* to sever; to divide into sections.
séculaire *adj* secular, century-old, once a century.
sécurisant *adj* reassuring, lending security.
sécuriser *vt* to make sb feel secure.
sécuritaire *adj* security.
sécurité *f* security; safety.
sédatif *m* sedative; * *adj* sedative.
sédentaire *adj* sedentary; * *m* sedentary.
sédiment *m* sediment.
sédimentation *f* sedimentation.
séducteur *m* seducer **-trice** *f* seductress.
séduction *f* seduction; captivation.
séduire *vt* to seduce; to charm, captivate.
séduisant *adj* seductive; enticing, attractive.
segment *m* segment.
segmenter *vt* to segment.

ségrégation *f* segregation.
seigle *m* rye.
seigneur *m* lord, nobleman; master.
sein *m* breast, bosom; womb; **au ~ de** within.
séisme *m* earthquake, seism.
seize *adj, m* sixteen.
seizième *adj, mf* sixteenth; **~ment** *adv* in sixteenth place.
séjour *m* stay, sojourn; abode; **salle de ~** living room.
séjourner *vi* to stay, sojourn.
sel *m* salt; wit.
sélecteur *m* selector; gear lever.
sélectif *adj* selective.
sélection *f* choosing, selection.
sélectionner *vt* to select, pick.
sélectivement *adv* selectively.
self-service *m* self-service restaurant.
selle *f* saddle.
selon *prép* according to; pursuant to.
semaine *f* week.
semblable *adj* like, similar, alike; such.
semblant *m* appearance, look; pretence; **faire ~ (de)** to pretend to.
sembler *vi* to seem, appear.
semelle *f* sole.
semence *f* seed; semen.
semer *vt* to sow; to scatter, strew.
semestre *m* half-year; semester.
semestriel *adj* half-yearly; semestral.
semi-conducteur *m* semiconductor.
séminaire *m* seminary; seminar.
semi-remorque *f* trailer, semitrailer.
semis *m* seedling; sowing; seedbed.
semoule *f* semolina.
sénat *m* senate.
sénateur *m* senator.
sénile *adj* senile.
sénilité *f* senility.
sens *m* sense; judgement; consciousness; meaning; direction; **bon ~** good sense.
sensation *f* sensation, feeling.
sensationnel *adj* fantastic, sensational.
sensé *adj* sensible.
sensibiliser *vt* to make sensitive to, heighten awareness of.
sensibilité *f* sensitivity, sensitiveness.
sensible *adj* sensitive; perceptive; appreciable; **~ment** *adv* approximately; noticeably.
sensoriel *adj* sensory.

sensualité *f* sensuality.
sensuel *adj* sensual.
sentence *f* sentence; maxim.
sentencieux *adj* sententious.
sentier *m* path, track.
sentiment *m* feeling, sentiment; emotion.
sentimental *adj* sentimental.
sentimentalisme *m* sentimentalism.
sentinelle *f* sentry, sentinel.
sentir *vt* to feel; to perceive, guess; to smell.
séparation *f* separation; division; pulling apart.
séparatiste *mf* separatist.
séparément *adv* separately.
séparer *vt* to separate, divide; to pull off; to split; **se ~** *vr* to separate, divide; to part with.
sept *adj, m* seven.
septembre *m* September
septième *adj, mf* seventh; **~ment** *adv* in seventh place.
sépulture *f* sepulture, burial.
séquelle *f* after-effect.
séquence *f* sequence.
séquestre *m* sequestration, confiscation.
séquestrer *vt* to sequester, impound.
serein *adj* serene, calm; **~ement** *adv* serenely.
sérénade *f* serenade.
sérénité *f* serenity, calmness.
sergent *m* sergeant; **~ de ville** police constable.
série *f* series, string; class; rank.
sérieusement *adv* seriously, responsibly.
sérieux *adj* serious; responsible; * *m* seriousness, reliability.
seringue *f* syringe.
serment *m* oath; pledge.
sermon *m* sermon.
sermonner *vt* to lecture, reprimand.
séropositif *adj* HIV positive, seropositive.
serpe *f* billhook, bill.
serpent *m* serpent, snake.
serpenter *vi* to meander, wind.
serpentin *m* coil; streamer.
serre *f* greenhouse; claw.
serré *adj* tight; close, compact.
serrer *vt* to tighten, fasten; to clench; **se ~** *vr* to crowd, huddle.
serrure *f* lock.
serrurerie *f* locksmithing.
serrurier *m* locksmith.
sérum *m* serum.
servante *f* servant, maidservant.
serveur *m* waiter, **-euse** *f* waitress.
serviable *adj* obliging, helpful.

service *m* service; function; department; operation; **rendre ~** to do a favour; **~ militaire** national service.
serviette *f* towel; serviette, napkin.
servile *adj* servile, slavish; **~ment** *adv* servilely, slavishly.
servilité *f* servility.
servir *vi* to be of use, be useful; * *vt* to serve, attend to; **se ~** *vr* to help o.s.; **se ~ de** to use, make use of.
servitude *f* servitude; *(jur)* easement.
sésame *m* sesame.
session *f* session, sitting.
seuil *m* threshold.
seul *adj* alone; single; sole; **~ement** *adv* only; but; solely.
sève *f* sap; pith, vigour.
sévère *adj* severe, austere; **~ment** *adv* severely; strictly.
sévérité *f* severity; strictness.
sévir *vi* to deal severely; to rage, hold sway.
sevrer *vt* to wean; to deprive.
sexe *m* sex; genitals.
sexiste *mf* sexist; * *adj* sexist.
sexualité *f* sexuality.
sexuel *adj* sexual, sex; **~lement** *adv* sexually.
sexy *adj* sexy.
seyant *adj* becoming.
shampooing *m* shampoo.
shooter *vt* to shoot, make a shot.
shopping *m* shopping.
short *m* shorts.
si *adv* so, so much, however much; yes; * *conj* if; whether.
siamois *adj* Siamese.
sida *m* Aids.
sidéral *adj* sidereal.
sidérer *vt* to flabbergast, stagger.
sidérurgie *f* steel metallurgy
sidérurgique *adj* steel-making.
sidérurgiste *mf* steel maker.
siècle *m* century; period.
siège *m* seat, bench; head office.
siéger *vi* to sit; to be located.
sien *pn, f* **sienne: le ~** his, its, his own, its own, **la sienne** her, its, her own, its own, **les ~s, les siennes** their, their own.
sieste *f* nap, snooze; siesta.
sifflement *m* whistling; hissing.
siffler *vi* to whistle; to hiss; * *vt* to whistle for; to hiss, boo.
sifflet *m* whistle; catcall.
sigle *m* abbreviation; acronym.
signal *m* signal, sign.
signalement *m* description, particulars.

signaler *vt* to signal, indicate; to point out.

signalisation *f* signalling system; installing signs.

signature *f* signature; signing.

signe *m* sign; mark; indication; symptom.

signer *vt* to sign; to hallmark.

signet *m* bookmark.

significatif *adj* significant, revealing.

signification *f* significance; meaning.

signifier *vt* to mean, signify; to make known; to serve notice.

silence *m* silence; stillness.

silencieusement *adv* silently.

silencieux *adj* silent; still.

silhouette *f* silhouette, outline.

silice *f* silica.

silicone *f* silicone.

sillage *m* wake; slipstream; trail.

sillon *m* furrow; fissure.

sillonner *vt* to plough, furrow; to criss-cross.

silo *m* silo.

similaire *adj* similar.

similarité *f* similarity.

similitude *f* similitude.

simple *adj* simple; mere; single; common; ~**ment** *adv* simply, merely.

simplicité *f* simplicity; simpleness.

simplification *f* simplification.

simplifier *vt* to simplify.

simpliste *adj* simplistic.

simulation *f* simulation.

simuler *vt* to simulate, feign.

simultané *adj* simultaneous; ~**ment** *adv* simultaneously.

sincère *adj* sincere, honest; ~**ment** *adv* sincerely.

sincérité *f* sincerity, honesty.

singe *m* monkey.

singulariser *vt* to singularise; make conspicuous; **se** ~ *vr* to make o.s. conspicuous.

singularité *f* singularity; peculiarity.

singulier *adj* singular; peculiar; remarkable.

singulièrement *adv* singularly; remarkably.

sinistre *m* disaster; accident; * *adj* sinister; ~**ment** *adv* in a sinister way.

sinistré *m* -**e** *f* disaster victim; * *adj* disaster-stricken.

sinon *conj* otherwise, if not; except.

sinueux *adj* sinuous, winding.

sinus *m* sinus; (*math*) sine.

sinusite *f* sinusitis.

siphon *m* siphon.

sirène *f* mermaid; siren, hooter.

sirop *m* syrup.

sirupeux *adj* syrupy.

sismique *adj* seismic.

site *m* setting, beauty spot.

sitôt *adv* so soon, as soon; **pas de** ~ not for a while; ~ **que** as soon as.

situation *f* situation, position; state of affairs.

situer *vt* to site, situate; **se** ~ *vr* to place o.s.; to be situated.

six *adj*, *m* six.

sixième *adj*, *mf* sixth; ~**ment** *adv* in sixth place.

sketch *m* sketch.

ski *m* ski, skiing.

skier *vi* to ski.

skieur *m* -**euse** *f* skier.

slalom *m* slalom.

slip *m* briefs, panties, swimming trunks.

slogan *m* slogan.

snack(-bar) *m* snack bar.

snob *adj* snobbish.

snobisme *m* snobbery, snobbishness.

sobre *adj* sober, temperate; ~**ment** *adv* soberly, temperately.

sobriété *f* sobriety, temperance.

sobriquet *m* nickname.

sociable *adj* sociable; social.

social *adj* social; ~**ement** *adv* socially.

social-démocrate *mf* social democrat; * *adj* social democrat.

socialisme *m* socialism.

socialiste *mf* socialist; * *adj* socialist.

sociétaire *mf* member.

société *f* society; company; partnership.

socio-économique *adj* socio-economic.

sociologie *f* sociology.

sociologique *adj* sociological; ~**ment** *adv* sociologically.

sociologue *mf* sociologist.

socle *m* pedestal, plinth; base.

socquette *f* ankle sock.

sodium *m* sodium.

sodomie *f* sodomy.

sœur *f* sister; nun.

sofa *m* sofa.

soi *pn* one(self); self; ~-**même** oneself, himself, herself, itself; ~-**disant** so called.

soie *f* silk.

soif *f* thirst.

soigné *adj* neat, well-kept.

soigner *vt* to look after, care for; **se** ~ *vr* to take care of o.s.

soigneusement *adv* neatly; carefully.

soigneux *adj* neat; careful.

soin *m* care; attention; trouble.

soir *m* evening; night.

soirée *f* evening; evening party.

soit *conj* either; or; whether; * *adv* granted; that is to say.

soixantaine *f* about sixty.

soixante *adj*, *m* sixty.

soixantième *adj*, *mf* sixtieth.

soja *m* soya.

sol *m* ground; floor; soil.

solaire *adj* solar.

soldat *m* soldier.

solde *f* pay; * *m* balance; clearance sale.

solder *vt* to pay; to settle, discharge; **se** ~ *vr*: **se** ~ **par** to show (profit, loss).

sole *f* sole; hearth.

soleil *m* sun, sunshine; sunflower.

solennel *adj* solemn; ~**lement** *adv* solemnly.

solfège *m* musical theory; sol-fa.

solidaire *adj* jointly liable; interdependent; ~**ment** *adv* jointly.

solidarité *f* solidarity.

solide *adj* solid; stable; sound; ~**ment** *adv* solidly; soundly.

solidifier *vt* **se** ~ *vr* to solidify.

solidité *f* solidity; soundness.

soliste *mf* soloist.

solitaire *mf* recluse, hermit; * *adj* solitary, lone; ~**ment** *adv* alone.

solitude *f* solitude; loneliness.

sollicitation *f* entreaty, appeal.

solliciter *vt* to seek, solicit; to appeal to.

sollicitude *f* solicitude, concern.

solo *m* solo.

solstice *m* solstice.

soluble *adj* soluble, solvable.

solution *f* solution; solving; answer.

solvable *adj* solvent; creditworthy.

solvant *m* solvent.

somatique *adj* somatic.

sombre *f* dark; gloomy, dismal.

sombrer *vi* to sink, founder.

sommaire *m* summary, argument; * *adj* basic, brief, summary; ~**ment** *adv* basically, summarily.

sommation *f* summons; demand.

somme *m* nap, snooze.

sommeil *m* sleep; sleepiness, drowsiness.

sommeiller *vi* to slumber, doze.

sommelier *m* wine waiter.

sommet *m* summit; top; crest; apex.

sommier *m* springs, divan base; ledger (construction).

sommité *f* leading light, eminent person.

somnambule *mf* sleepwalker; * *adj* sleepwalking.

somnifère *m* sleeping pill; * *adj* soporific.

somnolent *adj* sleepy, drowsy.

somnoler *vi* to doze, drowse.

somptueux *adj* sumptuous, lavish.

son *m* sound; * *adj*, *f* **sa**; *pl* **ses** his, her, its.

sonate *f* sonata.

sondage *m* drilling; probing; sounding.

sonde *f* sounding line; probe; drill.

sonder *vt* to sound; to probe; to drill.

songe *m* dream.

songer *vt* to dream; to imagine; to consider.

songeur *adj* pensive.

sonner *vi* to ring; to go off; * *vt* to ring, sound.

sonnerie *f* ringing, bells; chimes.

sonnette *f* small bell; house-bell.

sonore *adj* resonant, deep-toned.

sonorisation *f* sound recording; sound system.

sonorité *f* sonority, tone; resonance.

sophistiqué *adj* sophisticated.

soporiphique *m* sleeping drug; soporific; * *adj* soporific.

soprano *mf* soprano.

sorbet *m* sorbet, water ice.

sorcellerie *f* witchcraft, sorcery.

sorcier *m* sorcerer.

sorcière *f* witch, sorceress.

sordide *adj* sordid, squalid; **~ment** *adv* sordidly, squalidly.

sort *m* fate, destiny, lot.

sortant *adj* outgoing, retiring.

sorte *f* sort, kind, manner.

sortie *f* exit, way out; trip; sortie; outburst; export.

sortilège *m* spell (magical).

sortir *vi* to go out, emerge; to result; to escape; **se ~** *vr* to get out of; to extricate o.s.; **s'en ~** to get over, pull through.

sosie *m* double, second self.

sot *adj*, *f* **-te** silly, foolish; **~tement** *adv* foolishly, stupidly.

sottise *f* stupidity; stupid remark, action.

sou *m* five centimes; cent.

soubresaut *m* jolt; start.

souche *f* stump; stock.

souci *m* worry; concern.

soucier (se) *vr*: **se ~ de** to care about.

soucieux *adj* concerned, worried.

soucoupe *f* saucer.

soudain *adj* sudden, unexpected; **~ement** *adv* suddenly.

soude *f* soda.

souder *vt* to solder; to weld.

soudeur *m* **-euse** *f* solderer; welder.

soudoyer *vt* to bribe, buy over.

soudure *f* soldering, welding.

souffle *m* blow, puff; breath.

soufflé *m* soufflé; * *adj* flabbergasted.

souffler *vi* to blow; to breathe; to puff.

soufflerie *f* bellows.

soufflet *m* slap in the face; affront; bellows.

souffrance *f* suffering; pain.

souffrant *adj* suffering; in pain.

souffrir *vi* to suffer, be in pain.

souhait *m* wish.

souhaitable *adj* desirable.

souhaiter *vt* to wish for, desire.

souiller *vt* to soil, dirty; to tarnish.

soulagement *m* relief.

soulager *vt* to relieve, soothe.

soulèvement *m* uprising.

soulever *vt* to lift, raise; to excite, stir up; **se ~** *vr* to rise; to revolt.

soulier *m* shoe.

souligner *vt* to underline.

soumettre *vt* to subdue, subjugate; to submit, deliver; **se ~** *vr* to subject o.s. to.

soumis *adj* submissive.

soumission *f* submission.

soupape *f* valve; safety valve.

soupçon *m* suspicion, conjecture; hint.

soupçonner *vt* to suspect, surmise.

soupçonneux *adj* suspicious.

soupe *f* soup.

soupeser *vt* to feel the weight of; to weigh up.

soupière *f* soup tureen.

soupir *m* sigh; gasp.

soupirail *m* basement window.

soupirer *vi* to sigh; to gasp.

souple *adj* supple; pliable; **~ment** *adv* supply, flexibly.

souplesse *f* suppleness; flexibility.

source *f* source; origin; spring.

sourcil *m* eyebrow.

sourd *m* **-e** *f* deaf person; * *adj* deaf; muted; veiled; **~ement** *adv* dully; silently.

sourdine *f* mute.

sourd(e)-muet(te) *m(f)* deaf-mute; * *adj* deaf and dumb.

souriant *adj* smiling, cheerful.

sourire *m* smile, grin.

souris *f* mouse.

sournois *adj* deceitful; sly; **~ement** *adv* deceitfully.

sous *prép* under, beneath, below.

sous-alimenté *adj* undernourished.

sous-bois *m* undergrowth.

sous-chef *m* second-in-command.

souscrire *vi* to subscribe.

sous-développé *adj* underdeveloped.

sous-directeur *m* **-trice** *f* sub-manager.

sous-entendre *vt* to imply, infer.

sous-entendu *m* innuendo, understood.

sous-estimer *vt* to underestimate.

sous-jacent *adj* subjacent, underlying.

sous-louer *vt* to sublet.

sous-marin *m* submarine; * *adj* underwater.

sous-multiple *m* submultiple.

sous-officier *m* non-commissioned officer.

sous-préfecture *f* sub-prefecture.

sous-préfet *m* sub-prefect.

soussigné *adj* undersigned.

sous-sol *m* subsoil; basement.

sous-titre *m* subtitle.

sous-titrer *vt* to subtitle.

soustraction *f* subtraction.

soustraire *vt* to subtract; to remove; **se ~** *vr*: **se ~ à** to escape, elude.

sous-traitance *f* subcontracting.

sous-traitant *m* subcontractor.

sous-traiter *vi* to subcontract.

sous-vêtement *m* undergarment.

soutane *f* cassock, soutane.

soute *f* hold; baggage hold.

soutenir *vt* to hold up; to sustain; to endure.

souterrain *m* underground passage; * *adj* underground.

soutien *m* support.

soutien-gorge *m* bra.

soutirer *vt* to extract from.

souvenir *m* memory; recollection; reminder.

souvenir (se) *vr* to remember, recollect.

souvent *adv* often, frequently.

souverain *m* **-e** *f* sovereign; * *adj* sovereign; supreme; **~ement** *adv* supremely.

soyeux *adj* silky.

spacieux *adj* spacious, roomy.

spaghetti *mpl* spaghetti.

sparadrap *m* sticking plaster.

spasme *m* spasm.

spasmophilie *f* spasmophilia.

spatial *adj* spatial; space.

spatule *f* spatula.

spécial *adj* special, particular; **~ement** *adv* specially.

spécialisation *f* specialisation.

spécialiser *vt* to specialise; **se ~** *vr* to be a specialist in sth.

spécialiste *mf* specialist.

spécialité *f* speciality; specialism.

spécieux *adj* specious.

spécification *f* specification.

spécifier *vt* to specify, determine.

spécifique *adj* specific; **~ment** *adv* specifically.

spécimen *m* specimen; sample.

spectacle *m* spectacle, scene.

spectaculaire *adj* spectacular.

spectateur *m* **-trice** *f* spectator.

spectre *m* ghost.

spéculateur *m* **-trice** *f* speculator.

spéculation *f* speculation.

spéculer *vi* to speculate.

spéléologie *f* speleology; caving.

spermatozoïde *m* sperm; spermatozoon.

sperme *m* sperm, semen.

sphère *f* sphere.

sphérique *adj* spherical.

sphinx *m* sphinx.

spirale *f* spiral.

spiritisme *m* spiritualism.

spiritualité *f* spirituality.

spirituel *adj* witty; spiritual; **~lement** *adv* wittily; spiritually.

splendeur *f* splendour, brilliance.

splendide *adj* splendid, magnificent; **~ment** *adv* splendidly.

spongieux *adj* spongy.

sponsoriser *vt* to sponsor.

spontané *adj* spontaneous; **~ment** *adv* spontaneously.

sporadique *adj* sporadic.

sport *m* sport.

sportif *m* sportsman, **-ive** *f* sportswoman; * *adj* sports; competitive; athletic.

square *m* (public) square.

squatter *vi* to squat in.

squelette *m* skeleton.

squelettique *adj* skeleton-like, scrawny.

stabiliser *vt* to stabilise, consolidate; **se ~** *vr* to stabilise, become stabilised.

stabilité *f* stability.

stable *adj* stable, steady.

stade *m* stadium; stage.

stage *m* training course; probation.

stagiaire *mf* trainee.

stagnation *f* stagnation.

stagner *vi* to stagnate.

standard *m* standard; switchboard; * *adj* standard.

standardiser *vt* to standardise.

standardiste *mf* switchboard operator.

starter *m* choke.

station *f* station; stage, stop; resort; posture.

stationnaire *adj* stationary.

stationnement *m* parking.

stationner *vi* to park.

station-service *f* service station.

statique *adj* static.

statistique *f* statistics; * *adj* statistical.

statue *f* statue.

statuer *vt* to rule, give a verdict.

statu quo *m* status quo.

statut *m* statute, ordinance; status.

statutaire *adj* statutory; **~ment** *adv* statutorily.

stencil *m* stencil.

sténodactylo *mf* shorthand typist.

sténographie *f* shorthand.

stentor *m*: **une voix de ~** stentorian voice.

steppe *f* steppe.

stère *m* stere.

stéréo(phonique) *adj* stereophonic.

stéréotype *m* stereotype.

stérile *adj* sterile, infertile.

stérilet *m* coil, IUD.

stériliser *vt* to sterilise.

stérilité *f* sterility.

sternum *m* breastbone, sternum.

stéroïde *adj* steroidal; * *m* steroid.

stigmate *m* mark, scar; stigmata.

stimulant *adj* stimulating; * *m* stimulant, stimulus.

stimulation *f* stimulation.

stimuler *vt* to stimulate, spur on.

stipuler *vt* to stipulate, specify.

stock *m* stock, supply.

stockage *m* stocking; stockpiling.

stocker *vt* to stock, stockpile.

stoïcisme *m* stoicism.

stoïque *adj* stoical; **~ment** *adv* stoically; * *mf* stoic.

stop *m* stop; stop sign; brake-light.

stopper *vt* to stop, halt; * *vi* to stop, halt.

store *m* blind, shade.

strabisme *m* squinting; strabismus.

strapontin *m* foldaway seat; minor role.

stratégie *f* strategy.

stratégique *adj* strategic; **~ment** *adv* strategically.

stratifié *adj* stratified.

stress *m* stress.

stressant *adj* stressful.

stresser *vt* to cause stress to.

strict *adj* strict, severe; **~ement** *adv* strictly.

strident *adj* strident, shrill.

strié *adj* streaked, striped, ridged.

stroboscope *m* stroboscope.

strophe *f* verse, stanza.

structural *adj* structural.

structure *f* structure.

structurel *adj* structural.

structurer *vt* to structure; **se ~** *vr* to develop a structure.

stuc *m* stucco.

studieux *adj* studious.

studio *m* studio; film theatre.

stupéfaction *f* stupefaction, amazement.

stupéfait *adj* astounded, dumbfounded.

stupéfiant *adj* astounding, amazing; drug, narcotic.

stupéfier *vt* to stupefy; to astound.

stupeur *f* amazement; stupor.

stupide *adj* stupid, foolish; **~ment** *adv* stupidly.

stupidité *f* stupidity.

style *m* style; stylus.

stylet *m* stiletto.

styliste *mf* designer; stylist.

stylo *m* pen.

su *m* knowledge.

suave *adj* suave, smooth.

subalterne *mf* subordinate; * *adj* subordinate.

subconscient *m* subconscious; * *adj* subconscious.

subdiviser *vt* to subdivide.

subdivision *f* subdivision.

subir *vt* to sustain, support; to undergo, suffer.

subit *adj* sudden; **~ement** *adv* suddenly.

subjectif *adj* subjective.

subjectivement *adv* subjectively.

subjectivité *f* subjectivity.

subjonctif *m* subjunctive; * *adj* subjunctive.

subjuguer *vt* to subjugate; to captivate.

sublime *adj* sublime; * *m* sublime.

sublimer *vt* to sublimate.

subliminal *adj* subliminal.

submerger *vt* to submerge, flood; to engulf.

submersible *m* submersible; * *adj* submersible.

subordination *f* subordination.

subordonné *m* **-e** *f* subordinate; * *adj* subordinate.

subordonner *vt* to subordinate.

subreptice *adj* surreptitious; **~ment** *adv* surreptitiously.

subséquent *adj* subsequent.

subside *m* grant.

subsidiaire *adj* subsidiary.

subsistance *f* subsistence, maintenance, sustenance.

subsister *vi* to subsist; to live on.

substance *f* substance.

substantiel *adj* substantial; **~lement** *adv* substantially.

substantif *m* noun, substantive; * *adj* substantival, nominal.

substituer *vt* to substitute, replace.

substitut *m* substitute.

substitution *f* substitution.

subterfuge *m* subterfuge.

subtil *adj* subtle; **~ement** *adv* subtly.

subtiliser *vt* to steal, spirit away.

subtilité *f* subtlety.

subvenir *vi*: **~ à** to provide for.

subvention *f* grant, subsidy.

subventionner *vt* to subsidise.

subversif *adj* subversive.

suc *m* sap; juice.

succéder *vi*: **~ à** to succeed, follow; * **se ~** *vr* to succeed one another.

succès *m* success; hit.

successeur *m* successor.

successif *adj* successive.

succession *f* succession; inheritance, estate.

successivement *adv* successively.

succinct *adj* succinct; **~ement** *adv* succinctly.

succomber *vi* to succumb, give way.

succulent *adj* succulent, delicious.

succursale *f* branch.

sucer *vt* to suck.

sucette *f* lollipop; dummy.

suçon *m* love bite.

sucre *m* sugar.

sucrer *vt* to sugar, sweeten.

sucrerie *f* sugar refinery.

sucrier *m* sugar bowl; * *adj* sugar; sugar-producing.

sud *m* south.

suer *vi* to sweat, perspire.

sueur *f* sweat.

suffire *vi* to suffice, be sufficient; **il suffit de** it is enough to, it only takes.

suffisamment *adv* sufficiently, enough.

suffisant *adj* sufficient, adequate.

suffoquer *vi* to choke, suffocate; * *vt* to choke, stifle.

suffrage *m* suffrage; vote; commendation, approval.

suggérer *vt* to suggest, put forward.

suggestion *f* suggestion.

suicidaire *adj* suicidal; * *mf* person with suicidal tendencies.

suicide *m* suicide.

suicider (se) *vr* to commit suicide.

suie *f* soot.

suif *m* tallow.

suintement *m* oozing; sweating.

suinter *vi* to ooze; to sweat.

suite *f* rest; sequel; continuation; series; connection; progress; **tout de ~** at once; **deux fois de ~** two times in a row; **et ainsi de ~** and so on; **à la suite de** after, behind; **par la ~** afterwards; **donner ~ à** to follow up.

suivant *m* **-e** *f* next one; attendant; * *adj* following, next; * *prép* according to; **~ que** according to whether.

suivi *adj* steady, regular; widely adopted; * *m* follow-up.

suivre *vt* to follow; to attend, accompany; to exercise; **~ son cours** to take its course; **à suivre** to be continued; **se ~** *vr* to follow each other; to be continuous.

sujet *m* subject, topic; ground; reason; * *adj*: **être ~ à** to be subject to, liable to.

sujétion *f* subjection; constraint.

sulfate *m* sulphate.

sulfater *vt* to apply copper sulphate.

sulfure *m* sulphur.

sulfureux *adj* sulphurous.

sulfurique *adj* sulphuric.

sultan *m* sultan, **-e** *f* sultana.

summum *m* climax, height.

super *m* super, four-star petrol; * *adj* (*fam*) ultra, super.

superbe *adj* superb, splendid; **~ment** *adv* superbly.

supercarburant *m* high-octane petrol.

supercherie *f* trick, trickery.

superficie *f* area, surface.

superficiel *adj* superficial; **~lement** *adv* superficially.

superflu *adj* superfluous.

supérieur *adj* upper; superior; higher, greater; **~ement** *adv* exceptionally well.

supériorité *f* superiority.

superlatif *m* superlative; * *adj* superlative.

superposer *vt* to superpose, stack; to superimpose; **se ~** *vr* to be superimposed.

superposition *f* superposing; superimposition.

supersonique *adj* supersonic.

superstitieux *adj* superstitious.

superstition *f* superstition.

superviser *vt* to supervise.

supplanter *vt* to supplant, oust.

suppléant *m* **-e** *f* substitute, understudy; * *adj* substitute.

supplément *m* supplement; extra charge.

supplémentaire *adj* supplementary, additional.

suppliant *adj* beseeching, entreating.

supplication *f* supplication; entreaty.

supplice *m* corporal punishment; torture.

supplier *vt* to beseech, entreat.

support *m* support, prop; stand.

supporter *vt* to support; to endure, bear.

supporter *m* supporter.

supposer *vt* to suppose; to assume; to imply.

supposition *f* supposition, surmise.

suppositoire *m* suppository.

suppression *f* suppression; deletion; cancellation.

supprimer *vt* to suppress; to cancel.

suppurer *vi* to suppurate.

suprématie *f* supremacy.

suprême *adj* supreme.

sur *prép* on; over, above; into; out of, from.

sûr *adj* sure, certain; secure; **~ de soi** self-assured; **bien ~** of course; **à coup ~** for sure; **~ement** *adv* surely, certainly.

surabondance *f* overabundance.

suranné *adj* outmoded, outdated.

surcharge *f* overloading; excess; surcharge.

surcharger *vt* to overload.

surchauffe *f* overheating.

surcroît *m*: surplus, excess; **de ~** in addition.

surdité *f* deafness.

sureau *m* elder (tree).

surélever *vt* to raise, heighten.

surenchérir *vi* to outbid.

surestimer *vt* to overestimate; to overvalue.

sûreté *f* safety; guarantee, surety; **être en ~** to be safe.

surexcité *adj* overexcited.

surface *f* surface.

surgeler *vt* to deep-freeze.

surgir *vi* to rise, appear; to arise, crop up.

surhomme *m* superman.

surintendant *m* superintendent.

surlendemain *m* day after tomorrow.

surmenage *m* overwork; overtaxing.

surmener *vt* to overwork; **se ~** *vr* to overwork.

surmonter *vt* to surmount, overcome.

surnager *vi* to float.

surnaturel *adj* supernatural.

surnom *m* nickname.

surnommer *vt* to nickname.

surpasser *vt* to surpass, outdo.

surplomb *m* overhang; **en ~** overhanging.

surplomber *vt* to overhang.

surplus *m* surplus, remainder, excess.

surpopulation *f* overpopulation.

surprenant *adj* surprising, amazing.

surprendre *vt* to surprise, amaze.

surprise *f* surprise.

surproduction *f* overproduction.

surréalisme *m* surrealism.

surréaliste *mf* surrealist; * *adj* surrealistic.

sursaut *m* start, jump.

sursauter *vi* to start, jump.

sursis *m* reprieve; deferment.

sursitaire *adj* deferred; suspended.

surtaxe *f* surcharge.

surtout *adv* especially; above all.

surveillance *f* surveillance; supervision; inspection.

surveillant *m* **-e** *f* warder, guard.

surveiller *vt* to watch; to supervise; to inspect.

survenir *vi* to take place, occur.

survêtement *m* tracksuit.

survie *f* survival.

survivant *m* **-e** *f* survivor; * *adj* surviving.

survivre *vi* to survive.

survoler *vt* to fly over.

susceptible *adj* sensitive; susceptible; capable; likely; **être ~ de** to be liable to.

susciter *vt* to arouse, incite.

suspect *m* **-e** *f* suspect; * *adj* suspicious, suspect.

suspecter *vt* to suspect.

suspendre *vt* to hang up; to suspend, defer.

suspendu *adj* hanging; suspended.

suspens *m*: **en ~** in abeyance; shelved.

suspense *m* suspense.

suspension *f* suspension; deferment; adjournment.

suspicieux *adj* suspicious.

suspicion *f* suspicion.

susurrer *vt* to whisper.

suture *f* suture; **points de ~** stitches.

svelte *adj* svelte, slim.

SVP *abrév de* **s'il vous plaît** please.

syllabe *f* syllable.

sylvestre *adj* forest.

symbole *m* symbol.

symbolique *adj* symbolic; token; nominal; **~ment** *adv* symbolically.

symboliser *vt* to symbolise.

symbolisme *m* symbolism.

symétrie *f* symmetry.

symétrique *adj* symmetrical; **~ment** *adv* symmetrically.

sympa *adj invar* (*fam*) nice, friendly.

sympathie *f* liking; fellow feeling; sympathy.

sympathique *adj* likeable, nice; friendly.

sympathisant *m* **-e** *f* sympathiser; * *adj* sympathising.

sympathiser *vi* to get on well with.

symphonie *f* symphony.

symphonique *adj* symphonic.

symptomatique *adj* symptomatic.

symptôme *m* symptom.

synagogue *f* synagogue.

synchronisation *f* synchronisation.

synchroniser *vt* to synchronise.

syncope *f* blackout, syncope.

syncopé *adj* syncopated.

syndical *adj* trade-union.

syndicalisme *m* trade unionism.

syndicaliste *mf* trade unionist; * *adj* trade union.

syndicat *m* trade union; association.

syndiquer *vt* to unionise; **se ~** *vr* to form a trade union.

syndrome *m* syndrome.

synonyme *m* synonym; * *adj* synonymous.

syntaxe *f* syntax.

synthèse *f* synthesis.

synthétique *adj* synthetic.

synthétiser *vt* to synthesise.

synthétiseur *m* synthesiser.

syphilis *f* syphilis.

systématique *adj* systematic; **~ment** *adv* systematically.

système *m* system.

T

tabac *m* tobacco.
tabagisme *m* nicotine addiction.
tabatière *f* snuffbox; skylight.
table *f* table; ~ **de nuit** bedside table; ~ **ronde** round-table conference.
tableau *m* table; chart; timetable; scene; ~ **de bord** dashboard.
tablette *f* bar; tablet; block.
tablier *m* apron; pinafore; overall.
tabou *m* taboo.
tabouret *m* stool.
tache *f* mark; stain; spot.
tâche *f* task, assignment; work.
taché *adj* stained, blemished.
tâcher *vi* to endeavour.
tacheté *adj* spotted; freckled.
tachycardie *f* tachycardia.
tacite *adj* tacit; **~ment** *adv* tacitly.
taciturne *adj* taciturn, silent.
tact *m* tact; **avoir du** ~ to have tact, be tactful.
tactile *adj* tactile.
tactique *f* tactics; * *adj* tactical.
taffetas *m* taffeta.
tagliatelles *fpl* tagliatelli.
taillader *vt* to slash, gash.
taille *f* waist; height, stature, size; **de** ~ considerable, sizeable; **être de** ~ **à** to be up to it.
taille-crayons *m* pencil sharpener.
tailler *vt* to cut; to carve; to sharpen; **se** ~ *vr* (*fam*) to clear off, split.
tailleur *m* tailor; cutter, hewer.
taillis *m* copse, coppice.
taire *vt* to hush up; to conceal; **se** ~ *vr* to be quiet; to fall silent.
talc *m* talc, talcum powder.
talent *m* talent, ability.
talentueux *adj* talented.
talisman *m* talisman.
talon *m* heel; end; pile.
talonner *vt* to follow closely; to hound.
talquer *vt* to put talcum powder on.
talus *m* embankment.
tambour *m* drum; barrel.
tambourin *m* tambourine.
tambouriner *vi* to drum; to beat, hammer.
tamis *m* sieve; riddle.
tamiser *vt* to sieve; to sift.
tampon *m* stopper, plug; tampon; buffer.
tamponner *vt* to mop up; to stamp.

tam-tam *m* tom-tom; row.
tandem *m* tandem; duo.
tandis *conj*: ~ **que** while; whereas.
tangent *adj* tangent, tangential.
tangible *adj* tangible.
tango *m* tango.
tanguer *vi* to pitch (ship).
tanière *f* den, lair.
tank *m* tank.
tanné *adj* tanned; weathered.
tanner *vt* to tan, weather.
tanneur *m* tanner.
tant *adv* so much; ~ **que** as long as; ~ **soit peu** ever so slightly; ~ **mieux** so much the better; that's a good job; ~ **pis** too bad; ~ **bien que mal** as well as can be expected.
tante *f* aunt.
tantôt *adv* sometimes; this afternoon; shortly.
taon *m* horsefly, gadfly.
tapage *m* din, uproar, racket.
tapageur *adj* noisy, rowdy; showy.
tape *f* slap.
taper *vi* to hit, tap, stamp; to beat down; * *vt* to beat; to slap; to type.
tapioca *m* tapioca.
tapir (se) *vr* to crouch; to hide away.
tapir *m* tapir.
tapis *m* carpet; rug; cloth.
tapisser *vt* to wallpaper; to cover; to carpet.
tapisserie *f* tapestry; tapestry-making; **faire** ~ to be a wallflower.
tapoter *vt* to pat; to tap; to strum.
taquin *adj* teasing.
taquiner *vt* to tease; to plague.
tarauder *vt* to tap; to torment.
tard *adv* late.
tarder *vi* to delay, put off; to dally.
tardif *adj* late; tardy; slow; backward.
tardivement *adv* late; tardily.
tare *f* tare; defect, flaw.
taré *adj* tainted, corrupt; sickly.
tari *adj* dried up.
tarif *m* tariff; price-list.
tarir *vt* to dry up; to exhaust; **se** ~ *vr* to dry up.
tarot *m* tarot.
tartare *adj* Tartar.
tarte *f* tart, flan.
tartelette *f* tartlet, tart.

tartine *f* slice of buttered bread.
tartiner *vt* to spread with butter, jam, etc.
tartre *m* tartar; fur, scale.
tas *m* heap, pile; lot, set.
tasse *f* cup.
tassement *m* settling, sinking.
tasser *vt* to heap up; **se** ~ *vr* to sink; subside.
tata *f* auntie.
tâter *vt* to feel, try; **se** ~ *vr* to feel o.s.
tâtonnement *m* trial and error; experimentation.
tâtonner *vi* to feel one's way, grope along.
tatouage *m* tattooing; tattoo.
tatouer *vt* to tattoo.
taudis *m* hovel, slum.
taupe *f* mole.
taureau *m* bull.
tauromachie *f* bullfighting.
taux *m* rate; ratio; ~ **de change** exchange rate.
taverne *f* tavern.
taxation *f* taxation, taxing.
taxe *f* tax; duty; rate.
taxer *vt* to tax; to fix the price of.
taxi *m* taxi.
tchin-tchin! *interj* cheers!
te *pn* you, yourself.
technicien *m* **-ne** *f* technician.
technique *f* technique; * *adj* technical; **~ment** *adv* technically.
technocrate *m* technocrat.
technocratie *f* technocracy.
technologie *f* technology.
technologique *adj* technological.
téflon *m* teflon.
teigne *f* moth; ringworm.
teindre *vt* to dye.
teint *m* complexion, colouring.
teinte *f* tint, colour, shade.
teinter *vt* to tint; to stain.
teinture *f* dye; dyeing.
teinturerie *f* dyeing; dye-works; dry cleaner's.
teinturier *m* **-ère** *f* dyer; dry cleaner.
tel *adj* such; like, similar; ~ **quel** such as it is; **en tant que** ~ as such, in such a capacity; **il n'y a rien de** ~ there's nothing like…
télé *f* TV, telly.
télécarte *f* phonecard.
télécommande *f* remote control.
télécommunication *f* telecommunication.

télécopie *f* facsimile transmission; fax.

télécopieur *m* fax machine.

télédiffusion *f* television broadcasting.

téléphérique *m* cableway; cable-car.

télégramme *m* telegram; cable.

télégraphier *vt* to telegraph, cable.

téléguider *vt* to radio-control.

télématique *f* telematics.

téléobjectif *m* telephoto lens.

télépathie *f* telepathy.

téléphone *m* telephone.

téléphoner *vi* to telephone.

téléphonique *adj* telephone; telephonic.

télescope *m* telescope.

télescopique *adj* telescopic.

télésiège *m* chairlift.

téléski *m* lift, ski tow.

téléspectateur *m* **-trice** *f* television viewer.

téléviseur *m* television set.

télévision *f* television.

télex *m* telex.

tellement *adv* so, so much; ~ **de** so many, so much.

téméraire *adj* rash, reckless; ~**ment** *adv* rashly; recklessly.

témérité *f* rashness; recklessness.

témoignage *m* testimony; evidence; certificate.

témoigner *vi* to testify.

témoin *m* witness; evidence; proof.

tempérament *m* constitution; temperament; character.

tempérance *f* temperance.

température *f* temperature.

tempéré *adj* temperate; tempered.

tempérer *vt* to temper; to assuage, soothe.

tempête *f* tempest.

temple *m* temple.

tempo *m* tempo, pace.

temporaire *adj* temporary; ~**ment** *adv* temporarily.

temporel *adj* worldly, temporal.

temporiser *vi* to temporise, delay.

temps *m* time; while; tense; beat; weather; **de** ~ **en** ~ from time to time; **entre** ~ meanwhile.

tenace *adj* tenacious, stubborn, persistent.

ténacité *f* tenacity; stubbornness.

tenaille *f* pincers; tongs.

tenailler *vt* to torture; to rack.

tendance *f* tendency; leaning; trend.

tendancieux *adj* tendentious.

tendinite *f* tendinitis.

tendon *m* tendon, sinew.

tendre *adj* tender, soft; delicate;

~**ment** *adv* tenderly, affectionately.

tendresse *f* tenderness; fondness.

tendu *adj* tight; stretched; concentrated; delicate, fraught.

ténèbres *fpl* darkness, gloom.

ténébreux *adj* dark, gloomy.

teneur *f* terms; content; grade.

tenir *vt* to hold, keep; to stock; to run; * *vi* to hold, stay in place; ~ **à** to value, care about; ~ **de** to take after; **se** ~ *vr* to hold on to; to behave; **s'en** ~ **à** to limit o.s. to, stick to.

tennis *m* tennis; ~ **de table** table tennis.

ténor *m* tenor; leading light.

tentacule *m* tentacle.

tentant *adj* tempting, inviting.

tentation *f* temptation.

tentative *f* attempt, bid.

tente *f* tent.

tenter *vt* to tempt.

tenture *f* hanging; curtain.

tenue *f* holding; session; deportment, good behaviour; dress, appearance.

tergal *m* terylene.

tergiverser *vi* to procrastinate, beat about the bush.

terme *m* term; termination, end; word, expression; **au** ~ **de** at the end of.

terminaison *f* ending.

terminal *adj* terminal; * *m* terminal.

terminer *vt* to terminate; to finish off; **se** ~ *vr* to terminate; to come to an end.

terminologie *f* terminology.

termite *m* termite.

terne *adj* colourless; lustreless, drab; spiritless.

ternir *vt* to tarnish, dull.

terrain *m* ground, soil, earth; plot; position; site; field.

terrasse *f* terrace.

terrasser *vt* to floor, knock down; to strike down, overcome.

terre *f* earth; world; ground, land; **mettre pied à** ~ to land, alight.

terre à terre *adj* down to earth, commonplace.

terreau *m* compost.

terre-plein *m* (*mil*) terreplein; platform; central reservation.

terrer (se) *vr* to crouch down; to lie low, go to ground.

terrestre *adj* land; terrestrial.

terreur *f* terror, dread.

terreux *adj* earthy; dirty; ashen.

terrible *adj* terrible, dreadful; terrific, great; ~**ment** *adv* terribly.

terrien *m* countryman; earthling; -**ne** *f* countrywoman; earthling.

terrier *m* burrow; earth; terrier.

terrifiant *adj* terrifying, fearsome.

terrifier *vt* to terrify.

terrine *f* earthenware dish, terrine.

territoire *m* territory, area.

territorial *adj* land, territorial.

terroir *m* land.

terroriser *vt* to terrorise.

terrorisme *m* terrorism.

terroriste *mf* terrorist; * *adj* terrorist.

tertiaire *adj* tertiary.

test *m* test.

testament *m* will, testament.

tester *vt* to test; to make out one's will.

testicule *m* testicle, testis.

tétanos *m* tetanus; lockjaw.

têtard *m* tadpole.

tête *f* head; face; front; top; sense, judgment; **tenir** ~ to stand up to sb; **faire la** ~ to pout, sulk; ~ **de turc** whipping boy; ~ **de mort** skull and crossbones; **être en** ~ to head.

tête à tête *m* private conversation; **en** ~ in the lead.

tétée *f* feeding; nursing.

téter *vt* to suck.

tétine *f* teat; udder; dummy.

téton *m* breast.

têtu *adj* headstrong, stubborn.

texte *m* text.

textile *adj* textile.

textuel *adj* textual, literal, exact; ~**lement** *adv* literally; word for word.

texture *f* texture.

thé *m* tea.

théâtral *adj* theatrical, dramatic.

théâtre *m* theatre; drama.

théière *f* teapot.

thématique *adj* thematic.

thème *m* theme.

théologie *f* theology.

théorème *m* theorem.

théoricien *m* **-ne** *f* theoretician, theorist.

théorie *f* theory.

théorique *adj* theoretical; ~**ment** *adv* theoretically.

thérapeute *mf* therapist.

thérapie *f* therapy.

thermal *adj* thermal; hydropathic.

thermique *adj* thermal; thermic.

thermomètre *m* thermometer.

thermos *f/m* thermos.

thermostat *m* thermostat.

thésaurus *m* thesaurus.

thèse *f* thesis.

thon *m* tuna.

thoracique *adj* thoracic; **cage ~** rib-cage.

thorax *m* thorax.

thrombose *f* thrombosis.

thym *m* thyme.

thyroïde *f* thyroid.

tibia *m* tibia.

tic *m* twitch, tic; mannerism.

ticket *m* ticket.

tiède *adj* lukewarm, tepid.

tien *pn, f* **tienne: le ~, la tienne, les ~s, les tiennes** yours, your own.

tiers *adj* third; **~-monde** Third World; * *m* third; third party.

tige *f* stem, stalk.

tigre *m* tiger.

tigresse *f* tigress.

tilleul *m* lime, linden.

timbale *f* kettledrum.

timbre *m* stamp; postmark; bell; tone, timbre.

timbré *adj* stamped; resonant.

timbrer *vt* to stamp; to postmark.

timide *adj* timid, shy; **~ment** *adv* timidly.

timidité *f* timidity, shyness.

timonier *m* (*mar*) helmsman.

tintamarre *m* hubbub, uproar.

tintement *m* ringing; chiming; toll.

tinter *vi* to ring, toll; to chime.

tique *f* tick.

tiquer *vi* to wince.

tir *m* shooting, firing, fire; shot; **~ à l'arc** archery.

tirade *f* tirade; monologue.

tirage *m* drawing, drawing off; printing; circulation; friction.

tiraillement *m* tugging; pulling.

tirailler *vt* to tug; to plague; to pester.

tire-bouchon *m* corkscrew.

tire-fesses *m* ski tow.

tirelire *f* moneybox.

tirer *vt* to pull; to draw; to extract; **se ~** *vr* (*fam*) to clear off; **bien s'en ~** to make a good job of sth.

tiret *m* dash; hyphen.

tireur *m* **-euse** *f* gunner, sharp-shooter; printer; drawer (cheque).

tiroir *m* drawer.

tison *m* brand.

tisonnier *m* poker.

tissage *m* weaving.

tisser *vt* to weave.

tissu *m* texture, fabric; tissue.

titan *m* titan.

titane *m* titanium.

titanesque *adj* titanic.

titre *m* title; heading; denomination; claim, right; deed; **à ~ de**

by right of; **à juste ~** deservedly, justly; **en ~** titular, acknowledged.

tituber *vi* to stagger.

titulaire *mf* incumbent, holder; * *adj* titular; entitled.

toast *m* slice of toast; toast; **porter un ~** to drink a toast.

toboggan *m* toboggan.

toc *m* tap, knock; sham jewellery etc.; **en ~** imitation, fake.

toi *pn* you; **~-même** yourself; **c'est à ~** it's your's; it's your turn.

toile *f* cloth; canvas; sheet

toilette *f* cleaning, grooming; washstand; **faire sa ~** to wash oneself; **cabinet de ~** bathroom.

toiser *vt* to survey; to evaluate.

toison *f* fleece.

toit *m* roof; home.

toiture *f* roof, roofing.

tôle *f* sheet metal.

tolérable *adj* tolerable, bearable.

tolérance *f* tolerance.

tolérant *adj* tolerant.

tolérer *vt* to tolerate; to put up with.

tomate *f* tomato.

tombe *f* tomb; grave.

tombeau *m* tomb.

tomber *vi* to fall; to sink; to decay; **laisser ~** to drop; **~ malade** to fall sick; **~ amoureux** to fall in love; **~ sur** to come across; **bien/mal ~** to be lucky/unlucky.

tombola *f* tombola.

tome *m* book; volume.

ton *adj, f* **ta**, *pl* **tes** your; * *m* tone; pitch; shade.

tonalité *f* tonality; key.

tondeuse *f* clippers, shears; mower.

tondre *vt* to shear, clip; mow.

tonifiant *m* tonic; * *adj* bracing; invigorating.

tonifier *vt* to tone up; to invigorate.

tonique *adj* tonic; fortifying; invigorating *m* tonic.

tonitruant *adj* thundering.

tonnage *m* tonnage; displacement.

tonne *f* ton.

tonneau *m* barrel, cask.

tonnelle *f* bower, arbour.

tonnerre *m* thunder.

tonton *m* (*fam*) uncle.

tonus *m* tone; energy.

top *m* pip, stroke.

topaze *f* topaz.

topographie *f* topography.

toquade *f* infatuation; fad, craze.

toque *f* fur hat; cap.

toquer *vi* to tap, rap.

torche *f* torch.

torcher *vt* to wipe, mop up; **se ~** *vr* to wipe oneself.

torchon *m* cloth; duster.

tordre *vt* to twist, contort; **se ~** *vr* to bend, twist; to sprain.

tordu *adj* twisted, crooked, bent.

tornade *f* tornado.

torpeur *f* torpor.

torpille *f* torpedo.

torpiller *vt* to torpedo.

torréfaction *f* roasting; toasting.

torrent *m* torrent.

torrentiel *adj* torrential.

torride *adj* torrid; scorching.

torsade *f* twist; cable moulding.

torse *m* chest; torso.

torsion *f* twisting; torsion.

tort *m* fault; wrong; prejudice; **avoir ~** to be wrong; **en ~** in the wrong; **à ~ ou à raison** wrongly or rightly; **faire du ~** to harm; **à ~ et à travers** wildly; here, there and everywhere.

torticolis *m* stiff neck; torticollis.

tortiller *vt* to twist; **se ~** *vr* to wriggle; to squirm.

tortionnaire *mf* torturer; * *adj* pertaining to torture.

tortue *f* tortoise.

tortueux *adj* tortuous, winding, meandering.

torture *f* torture.

torturer *vt* to torture.

tôt *adv* early; soon, quickly; **au plus ~** as soon as possible; **plus ~** sooner.

total *adj* total; absolute; **~ement** *adv* totally.

totaliser *vt* to totalise, add up.

totalitaire *adj* totalitarian.

totalitarisme *m* totalitarianism.

totalité *f* totality; whole.

totem *m* totem.

touchant *adj* touching, moving.

touche *f* touch; trial; stroke; key.

toucher *vt* to touch; to feel; * *m* touch, feeling.

touffe *f* tuft, clump.

touffu *adj* bushy, thick.

toujours *adv* always; still; all the same; **pour ~** for ever; **~ est-il que** the fact remains that.

toupet *m* quiff, tuft; cheek.

toupie *f* spinning top.

tour *f* tower; * *m* turn, round; circuit; tour; trick; **faire un ~** to take a stroll; **faire le tour de** to go around; **fermer à double ~** to double-lock; **jouer un ~** to play a trick; **~ à ~** by turns.

tourbe *f* peat.

tourbillon *m* whirlwind, whirlpool.

tourbillonner *vi* to whirl, eddy.

tourisme *m* tourism.

touriste *mf* tourist.

touristique *adj* tourist.

tourment *m* torment, agony.

tourmente *f* storm, tempest.

tourmenter *vt* to rack, torment; **se ~** *vr* to fret; to worry.

tournage *m* turning; (*cin*) shooting.

tournant *m* bend; turning point; * *adj* revolving, swivel; winding.

tournedos *m* fillet steak.

tournée *f* tour; round.

tourner *vt* to turn; to round; * *vi* to turn; to work; to change; **se ~** *vr* to turn round; to change.

tournesol *m* sunflower.

tourneur *m* turner.

tournevis *m* screwdriver.

tourniquet *m* tourniquet; turnstile.

tournis *m* (*vet*) sturdy, staggers; **avoir le ~** to feel giddy.

tournoi *m* tournament.

tournoyer *vi* to whirl, swirl.

tournure *f* turn; turn of phrase.

tourte *f* pie.

tourerelle *f* turtledove.

tourtière *f* pie tin.

Toussaint *f* All Saints' Day.

tousser *vi* to cough.

tout *adj*, *pl* **tous**, **toutes** all; whole; every; **~ le monde** everybody; * *pn* everything; all; **c'est ~** that is all; * *m* whole, only thing; **pas du ~** not at all; **du ~ au ~** completely; * *adv* entirely, quite; **~ droit** straight on; **~ à fait** completely, quite; **~ de suite** immediately.

toutefois *adv* however.

tout-puissant *adj* all-powerful.

toux *f* cough.

toxicomane *mf* drug addict; * *adj* drug addicted.

toxicomanie *f* drug addiction.

toxine *f* toxin.

toxique *adj* toxic.

trac *m* nerves, stage fright.

tracas *m* bustle, turmoil; worry.

tracasser *vt* to worry; to harass.

trace *f* track, impression; outline, sketch; vestige, trace.

tracé *m* layout, plan.

tracer *vt* to draw, trace; to open up.

trachée *f* trachea, windpipe.

tract *m* leaflet, tract.

tractation *f* transaction; bargaining.

tracteur *m* tractor.

traction *f* traction; pulling.

tradition *f* tradition.

traditionaliste *mf* traditionalist; * *adj* traditionalist.

traditionnel *adj* traditional; usual; **~lement** *adv* traditionally.

traducteur *m* **-trice** *f* translator.

traduction *f* translation.

traduire *vt* to translate.

trafic *m* traffic; trading; dealings.

trafiquant *m* **-e** *f* trafficker.

trafiquer *vi* to fiddle, tamper with.

tragédie *f* tragedy.

tragédien *m* **-ne** *f* tragedian, tragic actor.

tragique *adj* tragic; **~ment** *adv* tragically.

trahir *vt* to betray.

trahison *f* betrayal, treason.

train *m* train; pace, rate; **être en ~ de** to be in the act of doing sth.

traînasser *vi* to dawdle; to loiter.

traîne *f* dragging; train; **être à la ~** to be in tow.

traîneau *m* sleigh, sledge.

traînée *f* trail, track; drag.

traîner *vi* to lag, dawdle; to drag on; * *vt* to drag, pull; to protract; **se ~** *vr* to drag o.s.; to crawl along.

train-train *m* humdrum routine.

traire *vt* to milk.

trait *m* trait, feature; deed; relation; **avoir ~ à** to have reference; **~ d'union** hyphen, connecting link.

traite *f* trade; draft, bill; milking.

traité *m* treaty; treatise, tract.

traitement *m* treatment; salary; processing.

traiter *vt* to treat; to process; * *vi* to treat, negotiate.

traiteur *m* caterer; trader.

traître *m* traitor **-sse** *f* traitress.

traîtrise *f* treachery, treacherousness.

trajectoire *f* trajectory.

trajet *m* distance; journey; course, path.

trame *f* framework; web.

tramer *vt* to plot; to weave.

trampoline *m* trampoline.

tramway *m* tram, tramway.

tranchant *adj* sharp, cutting.

tranche *f* slice; edge; section.

tranchée *f* trench; cutting.

trancher *vt* to cut, sever; to conclude; to settle; * *vi* to cut; to resolve; to stand out.

tranquille *adj* quiet, tranquil; **~ment** *adv* quietly, tranquilly.

tranquillisant *m* tranquilliser; * *adj* soothing, tranquillising.

tranquilliser *vt* to reassure.

tranquillité *f* tranquillity.

transaction *f* transaction, arrangement.

transatlantique *m* transatlantic liner; * *adj* transatlantic.

transcendant *adj* transcendent; transcendental.

transcender *vt* to transcend.

transcription *f* transcription; copy.

transcrire *vt* to transcribe; copy out.

transe *f* trance.

transept *m* transept.

tranférer *vt* to transfer.

transfert *m* transfer; conveyance.

transfiguration *f* transfiguration.

transfigurer *vt* to transfigure.

transformateur *m* transformer.

transformation *f* transformation.

transformer *vt* to transform, change; **se ~** *vr* to be transformed; to change.

transfuge *mf* defector.

transfuser *vt* to transfuse.

transfusion *f* transfusion.

transgresser *vt* to transgress, infringe.

transgression *f* transgression, infringement.

transi *adj* numb, paralysed.

transiger *vi* to compromise, come to terms.

transistor *m* transistor.

transit *m* transit.

transiter *vi* to pass in transit.

transitif *adj* transitive.

transition *f* transition.

transitoire *adj* transitory.

translucide *adj* translucent.

transmettre *vt* to transmit; to pass on, hand down.

transmissible *adj* transmissible.

transmission *f* transmission; passing on; handing down.

transmuter *vt* to transmute.

transparaître *vi* to show through.

transparence *f* transparency.

transparent *adj* transparent.

transpercer *vt* to pierce; to penetrate.

transpiration *f* transpiration; perspiration.

transpirer *vi* to perspire; to come to light.

transplanter *vt* to transplant.

transport *m* carrying; transport; conveyance; transfer.

transportable *adj* transportable.

transporter *vt* to carry; to transport.

transporteur *m* haulier; carrier.

transposer *vt* to transpose.

transposition *f* transposition.

transsexuel *adj* transsexual.

transvaser *vt* to decant.

transversal *adj* transverse; **~ement** *adv* crosswise; transversely.

transvider *vt* to pour into another container.

trapèze *m* trapeze.

trapéziste *mf* trapeze artist.

trappe *f* trap door.

trappeur *m* trapper.

trapu *adj* squat; thickset.

traquer *vt* to track; to hunt down.

traumatisant *adj* traumatising.

traumatiser *vt* to traumatise.

traumatisme *m* traumatism.

travail *m* work; job, occupation; labour; *pl* **travaux** work, labour.

travailler *vi* to work; to endeavour; * *vt* to work, shape; to cultivate; to fatigue.

travailleur *m* **-euse** *f* worker; * *adj* diligent; hard-working.

travers *m* breadth; irregularity; fault; **à ~** through, across; **de ~** obliquely, askew; **en ~** across, crosswise.

traversée *f* crossing, going through; traverse.

traverser *vt* to cross, traverse.

traversin *m* bolster.

travesti *m* drag artist; transvestite; * *adj* disguised.

trébucher *vi* to stumble, trip up.

trèfle *m* clover.

tréfonds *m* subsoil, bottom.

treille *f* climbing vine.

treillis *m* trellis; wire mesh.

treize *adj, m* thirteen.

treizième *adj, mf* thirteenth; **~ment** *adv* in thirteenth place.

tréma *m* dieresis.

tremblant *adj* trembling, shaking.

tremblement *m* trembling; shiver; vibration; **~ de terre** earthquake.

trembler *vi* to tremble, shake.

trembloter *vi* to tremble slightly, flicker.

trémousser (se) *vr* to wriggle.

tremper *vt* to soak; to dip; * *vi* to soak; to take part in.

tremplin *m* springboard; ski-jump.

trentaine *f* about thirty.

trente *adj, m* thirty.

trentième *adj, mf* thirtieth.

trépasser *vi* to pass away.

trépidant *adj* pulsating, quivering.

trépied *m* tripod.

trépigner *vi* to stamp one's feet.

très *adv* very; most; very much.

trésor *m* treasure.

trésorerie *f* treasury.

trésorier *m* **-ière** *f* treasurer.

tressaillir *vi* to thrill; to shudder.

tressauter *vi* to start, jump.

tresse *f* plait, braid.

tresser *vt* to plait, braid.

tréteau *m* trestle.

treuil *m* winch.

trêve *f* truce; respite, rest.

tri *m* sorting out; selection; grading.

triage *m* sorting out.

triangle *m* triangle.

triangulaire *adj* triangular.

triathlon *m* triathlon.

tribal *adj* tribal.

tribord *m* starboard.

tribu *f* tribe.

tribunal *m* court, tribunal.

tribune *f* gallery, stand; rostrum.

tribut *m* tribute.

tributaire *adj* dependent, tributary.

tricher *vi* to cheat.

tricheur *m* **-euse** *f* cheater.

trichloréthylène *m* trichlorethylene.

tricolore *adj* three-coloured, tricolour.

tricot *m* jumper; knitting.

tricoter *vt* to knit.

tridimensionnel *adj* three-dimensional.

triennal *adj* triennial; three-yearly.

trier *vt* to sort out; to pick over.

trifouiller *vi* (*fam*) to rummage about; * *vt* to rummage about in.

trigonométrie *f* trigonometry.

trilingue *adj* trilingual.

trilogie *f* trilogy.

trimer *vi* to slave away.

trimestre *m* quarter; term.

trimestriel *adj* quarterly; three-monthly.

tringle *f* rod.

trinité *f* trinity.

trinquer *vi* to toast; to booze.

trio *m* trio.

triomphal *adj* triumphal; **~ement** *adv* triumphantly.

triomphant *adj* triumphant.

triomphe *m* triumph, victory.

triompher *vi* to triumph.

triparti, tripartite *adj* tripartite.

tripe *f* tripe; guts.

triple *adj* triple, treble.

tripler *vi* to triple, increase threefold; * *vt* to triple, treble.

tripoter *vt* to play with, speculate with.

trique *f* cudgel.

triste *adj* sad, melancholy; **~ment** *adv* sadly.

tristesse *f* sadness; melancholy.

triton *m* triton; tritone.

triturer *vt* to grind up, triturate.

trivial *adj* mundane, trivial; coarse, crude.

trivialité *f* triviality; crudeness.

troc *m* exchange; barter.

troglodyte *m* cave dweller, troglodyte.

trognon *m* core; stalk.

trois *adj, m* three.

troisième *adj, mf* third; **~ment** *adv* thirdly.

trombe *f*: **~ d'eau** cloudburst, downpour; **entrer/sortir en ~** to dash in/out.

trombone *m* trombone.

trompe *f* trumpet; trunk, snout.

trompe-l'œil *m invar* trompe-l'oeil.

tromper *vt* to deceive, trick; **se ~** *vr* to be mistaken.

tromperie *f* deception, deceit.

trompette *f* trumpet.

trompettiste *mf* trumpet player.

trompeur *adj* deceitful; deceptive.

tronc *m* trunk, shaft.

tronçon *m* section, part.

tronçonner *vt* to cut up, cut into sections.

tronçonneuse *f* chain saw.

trône *m* throne.

trôner *vi* to sit on the throne.

tronquer *vt* to truncate, curtail.

trop *adv* too; too much, unduly; *m* **~** too much, too many.

trophée *m* trophy.

tropical *adj* tropical.

tropique *m* tropic.

trop-plein *m* overflow; excess.

troquer *vt* to barter, swap.

trot *m* trot.

trotter *vi* to trot; to run about; to toddle.

trottiner *vi* to jog along; to trot along.

trottinette *f* scooter.

trottoir *m* pavement.

trou *m* hole; gap; cavity.

troublant *adj* disturbing, disquieting.

trouble *adj* unclear; murky, suspicious; * *m* disturbance, confusion; disorder.

trouble-fête *mf* spoilsport, killjoy.

troubler *vt* to disturb, disconcert; to cloud, darken; **se ~** *vr* to become cloudy; to become flustered.

trouer *vt* to make a hole in; to pierce.

trouille *f*: **avoir la ~** to have the wind up.

troupe *f* troupe; troop, band.

troupeau *m* herd, drove.

trousse *f* case, kit; wallet.

trousseau *m* trousseau; outfit.

trouvaille *f* windfall; inspired idea.

trouver *vt* to find, detect; to think; **se ~** *vr* to find o.s.; to be located; **il se trouve que** it happens that.

truand *m* (*fam*) gangster; tramp.

truc *m* (*fam*) trick; gadget, thingummy.

truculent *adj* truculent; colourful, vivid.

truelle *f* trowel.

truffe *f* truffle.

truie *f* sow.

truite *f* trout.

truquage *m* rigging, fixing; fiddling.

truquer *vt* to rig, fix; to fiddle.

tsar *m* tsar.

tu *pn* you.

tuant *adj* exhausting; exasperating.

tuba *m* tuba, snorkel.

tube *m* tube, pipe; duct.

tuberculose *f* tuberculosis.

tuer *vt* to kill; **se ~** *vr* to be killed; to kill o.s.

tuerie *f* slaughter.

tueur *m* **-euse** *f* killer.

tuile *f* tile.

tulipe *f* tulip.

tulle *m* tulle.

tuméfié *adj* puffed-up, swollen.

tumeur *f* tumour.

tumulte *m* tumult, commotion.

tumultueux *adj* tumultuous, stormy.

tungstène *m* tungsten.

tunique *f* tunic; smock.

tunnel *m* tunnel.

turban *m* turban.

turbine *f* turbine.

turbo *m* turbo.

turbulence *f* turbulence; excitement.

turbulent *adj* turbulent.

turpitude *f* turpitude, baseness.

tutelle *f* guardianship, supervision.

tuteur *m* **-trice** *f* guardian; * *m* stake, prop.

tutoyer *vt* to address sb as '*tu*'.

tuyau *m* pipe.

tuyauterie *f* piping.

TVA (taxe à la valeur ajoutée) *f* VAT.

tympan *m* eardrum, tympanum.

type *m* type; model; sample; bloke, chap.

typé *adj* typical.

typhoïde *f* typhoid; * *adj* typhoid.

typhon *m* typhoon.

typhus *m* typhus.

typique *adj* typical; **~ment** *adv* typically.

tyran *m* tyrant.

tyrannie *f* tyranny.

tyrannique *adj* tyrannical.

tyranniser *vt* to tyrannise.

U

ulcère *m* ulcer.

ulcérer *vt* to sicken; to embitter.

ultérieur *adj* later, subsequent; ~**ement** *adv* later, subsequently.

ultimatum *m* ultimatum.

ultime *adj* ultimate, final.

ultra-violet *m* ultraviolet ray; * *adj* ultraviolet.

un, une *art* a, an; (number) one; **l'~ l'autre, les ~s les autres** one another.

unanime *adj* unanimous; ~**ment** *adv* unanimously.

uni *adj* plain, self-coloured; close; smooth; ~**ment** *adv* plainly, smoothly.

unification *f* unification; standardisation.

unifier *vt* to unify; to standardise.

uniforme *adj* uniform, regular; * *m* uniform.

uniformément *adv* uniformly, regularly.

uniformité *f* uniformity; regularity.

unilatéral *adj* unilateral.

union *f* union; combination, blending.

unique *adj* only, single; unique; ~**ment** *adv* only, solely, exclusively; merely.

unir *vt* to unite; to join; to combine; **s'~** *vr* to unite; to be joined in marriage.

unisson *m* unison; **à l'~** in unison.

unitaire *adj* unitary, unit.

unité *f* unity; unit.

univers *m* universe; world.

universalité *f* universality.

universel *adj* universal; all-purpose; ~**lement** *adv* universally.

universitaire *adj* university; * *mf* academic.

université *f* university.

uranium *m* uranium.

urbain *adj* urban, city.

urbanisation *f* urbanisation.

urbaniser *vt* to urbanise.

urbanisme *m* town planning.

urbaniste *mf* town planner.

urée *f* urea.

urgence *f* urgency; emergency.

urgent *adj* urgent.

urinaire *adj* urinary.

urine *f* urine.

uriner *vi* to urinate.

urne *f* ballot box; urn.

urticaire *f* hives, urticaria.

usage *m* use; custom; usage; practice; wear; **faire ~ de** to exercise; to make use of.

usagé *adj* worn, old.

usager *m* **-ère** *f* user.

usé *adj* worn; threadbare; banal, trite.

user *vt* to make use of, enjoy; to wear out; **~ de** to exercise; to employ; **s'~** *vr* to wear out.

usine *f* factory.

usiner *vt* to machine; to manufacture.

usité *adj* in common use, common.

ustensile *m* implement; utensil.

usuel *adj* ordinary; everyday; ~**lement** *adv* ordinarily.

usufruit *m* (*jur*) usufruct.

usure *f* usury.

usurier *m* **-ière** *f* usurer.

usurper *vt* to usurp.

utérus *m* womb, uterus.

utile *adj* useful; ~**ment** *adv* usefully.

utilisateur *m*, **-trice** *f* user.

utilisation *f* use, utilisation.

utiliser *vt* to use, utilise; to make use of.

utilitaire *adj* utilitarian.

utilité *f* usefulness; use; profit.

utopie *f* utopia.

utopique *adj* utopian.

V

vacance *f* vacancy; **~s** holiday, vacation.
vacancier *m* **-ière** *f* holidaymaker.
vacant *adj* vacant, unoccupied.
vacarme *m* racket, row.
vaccin *m* vaccine.
vaccination *f* vaccination.
vacciner *vt* to vaccinate.
vache *f* cow; cowhide.
vachement *adv* (*fam*) damned, bloody.
vacher *m* **-ère** *f* cowherd.
vacherie *f* (*fam*) rottenness, meanness; nasty remark/trick.
vaciller *vi* to sway, totter; to falter.
va-et-vient *m invar* comings and goings; to and fro.
vagabond *m* **-e** *f* tramp, vagabond.
vagabondage *m* wandering, roaming; (*jur*) vagrancy.
vagabonder *vi* to wander, roam.
vagin *f* vagina.
vaginal *adj* vaginal.
vague *adj* vague, hazy, indistinct; **~ment** *adv* vaguely; * *m* vagueness; * *f* wave.
vaguer *vi* to wander, roam.
vaillamment *adv* bravely, courageously.
vaillant *adj* brave, courageous.
vain *adj* vain; empty, hollow; shallow; **en ~** in vain; **~ement** *adv* vainly.
vaincre *vt* to defeat, overcome.
vaincu *adj* defeated, beaten.
vainqueur *m* conqueror, victor.
vaisseau *m* vessel; ship.
vaisselle *f* crockery; dishes; **faire la ~** to do the washing up.
valable *adj* valid, legitimate; worthwhile.
valet *m* valet; servant.
valeur *f* value, worth; security; share; meaning.
valide *adj* able, able-bodied; **~ment** *adv* validly.
valider *vt* to validate.
validité *f* validity.
valise *f* suitcase.
vallée *f* valley.
vallon *m* vale, dale.
vallonné *adj* undulating, hilly.
valoir *vt* to be worth; to be valid; **il vaut mieux** it is better to; **~ la peine** to be worth the trouble.
valoriser *vt* to valorise.
valse *f* waltz.

valser *vi* to waltz.
valve *f* valve.
vampire *m* vampire.
vandale *mf* vandal.
vandalisme *m* vandalism.
vanille *f* vanilla.
vanité *f* vanity, conceit.
vaniteux *adj* vain, conceited.
vanne *f* gate, sluice.
vannerie *f* basketry; wickerwork.
vantard *adj* boastful, bragging.
vantardise *f* boastfulness; boast.
vanter *vt* to praise, vaunt; **se ~** *vr* to boast, brag.
vapeur *f* haze, vapour.
vaporeux *adj* filmy, vaporous.
vaporisateur *m* spray, atomiser.
vaporiser *vt* to spray; to vaporise.
varappe *f* rock-climbing.
variable *adj* variable, changeable.
variante *f* variant; variation.
variation *f* variation, change.
varice *f* varicose vein.
varicelle *f* chickenpox.
varié *adj* varied; variegated; various.
varier *vi* to vary, change; * *vt* to vary.
variété *f* variety, diversity.
variole *f* smallpox.
vasculaire *adj* vascular.
vase *m* vase, bowl; * *f* silt, mud.
vaseline *f* vaseline.
vaseux *adj* woolly, muddled; muddy, silty.
vasistas *m* fanlight.
vaste *adj* vast, huge.
vaudeville *m* vaudeville.
vaudou *m* voodoo.
vaurien *m* **-ne** *f* good-for-nothing.
vautour *m* vulture.
vautrer (se) *vr* to wallow in.
veau *m* calf; veal.
vecteur *m* vector.
vécu *adj* real, true-life; lived; * *m* real-life.
vedette *f* star; (*mar*) launch.
végétal *adj* vegetable.
végétarien *m* **-ne** *f* vegetarian; * *adj* vegetarian.
végétatif *adj* vegetative.
végétation *f* vegetation.
végéter *vi* to vegetate; to stagnate.
véhémence *f* vehemence.
véhément *adj* vehement.
véhicule *m* vehicle.
veille *f* wakefulness; watch; eve.

veillée *f* evening; evening meeting.
veiller *vi* to stay up, sit up.
veilleur *m* watchman.
veilleuse *f* night light; sidelight.
veinard *m* **-e** *f* lucky person; * *adj* lucky, jammy.
veine *f* vein, seam; inspiration; luck.
vêler *vi* to calve.
velléité *f* vague desire, vague impulse.
vélo *m* bike.
vélodrome *m* velodrome.
vélomoteur *m* moped.
velours *m* velvet.
velouté *adj* velvety, downy.
velu *adj* hairy.
vénal *adj* venal, mercenary.
vendange *f* wine harvest.
vendanger *vt* to harvest grapes from; * *vi* to harvest the grapes.
vendangeur *m* **-euse** *f* grape-picker.
vendetta *f* vendetta.
vendeur *m* **-euse** *f* seller, salesperson.
vendre *vt* to sell.
vendredi *m* Friday.
vénéneux *adj* poisonous.
vénérable *adj* venerable.
vénération *f* veneration.
vénérer *vt* to venerate.
vénérien *adj* venereal.
vengeance *f* vengeance, revenge.
venger *vt* to avenge; **se ~** *vr* to avenge o.s.
venimeux *adj* venomous, poisonous; vicious.
venin *m* venom; poison.
venir *vi* to come; to happen; to grow; **~ de** to come from; to derive from; **~ au monde** to be born.
vent *m* wind; breath; emptiness.
vente *f* sale; selling; auction; **en ~** for sale.
ventilateur *m* ventilator, fan.
ventiler *vt* to ventilate; to divide up.
ventouse *f* sucker; suction disc.
ventre *m* stomach, belly; womb.
ventricule *m* ventricle.
ventriloque *mf* ventriloquist; * *adj* ventriloquous.
venue *f* coming.

ver *m* worm; grub; ~ **de terre** earthworm.

véracité *f* veracity; truthfulness.

véranda *f* veranda.

verbal *adj* verbal; **~ement** *adv* verbally.

verbe *m* verb; language, word.

verbiage *m* verbiage.

verdeur *f* vigour, vitality.

verdict *m* verdict.

verdir *vi* to go green; * *vt* to turn green.

verdure *f* greenery, verdure.

verge *f* stick, cane.

verger *m* orchard.

verglas *m* black ice.

véridique *adj* truthful, veracious; **~ment** *adv* truthfully.

vérification *f* check; verification.

vérifier *vt* to verify, check; to audit.

véritable *adj* real, genuine; **~ment** *adv* really, genuinely.

vérité *f* truth; truthfulness, sincerity; **en ~** really, actually.

vermeil *adj* vermilion, ruby, cherry; * *m* vermeil.

vermicelle *m* vermicelli.

vermillon *m* vermilion; scarlet.

vermine *f* vermin.

vermisseau *m* small worm.

vermoulu *adj* worm-eaten.

verni *adj* varnished.

vernis *m* varnish; glaze; shine.

vernissage *m* varnishing; glazing.

verre *m* glass; lens; drink.

verrerie *f* glassworks; glass-making.

verrière *f* window; glass roof.

verrou *m* bolt.

verrouillage *m* bolting; locking.

verrouiller *vt* to bolt; to lock.

verrue *f* wart, verruca.

vers *prép* towards; around; about; * *m* line, verse.

versatile *adj* versatile.

verse *f*: **pleuvoir à ~** to pour down.

Verseau *m* Aquarius.

verser *vt* to pour, shed; to pay; (*mil*) to assign.

verset *m* verse.

version *f* version.

verso *m* back.

vert *m* green; * *adj* green; **langue ~e** slang; **~ement** *adv* sharply, brusquely.

vertébral *adj* vertebral.

vertèbre *f* vertebra.

vertical *adj* vertical; **~ement** *adv* vertically.

vertige *m* vertigo; dizziness.

vertigineux *adj* vertiginous, breathtaking.

vertu *f* virtue; courage; **en ~ de** in accordance with.

vertueux *adj* virtuous.

verve *f* verve, vigour.

verveine *f* verbena.

vésicule *f* vesicle; gall bladder.

vessie *f* bladder.

veste *f* jacket.

vestiaire *m* cloakroom; changing-room.

vestibule *m* hall, vestibule.

vestige *m* relic; trace, vestige.

veston *m* jacket.

vêtement *m* garment.

vétéran *m* veteran.

vétérinaire *mf* veterinary surgeon; * *adj* veterinary.

vêtir *vt* to clothe, dress; **se ~** *vr* to dress o.s.

veto *m* veto.

vêtu *adj* dressed; clad, wearing.

vétuste *adj* dilapidated, ancient.

veuf *m* widower; * *adj* widowed.

veule *adj* spineless.

veuve *f* widow; * *adj* widowed.

vexant *adj* annoying, vexing.

vexer *vt* to annoy; to hurt.

viable *adj* viable.

viaduc *m* viaduct.

viande *f* meat.

vibration *f* vibration.

vibrer *vi* to vibrate; to quiver.

vibromasseur *m* vibrator.

vicaire *m* curate, vicar.

vice *m* vice; fault, defect.

vice-président *m* vice-president; deputy chairman.

vice-versa *adv* vice versa.

vicieux *adj* licentious; dissolute; incorrect.

vicissitude *f* vicissitude, change; trial.

vicomte *m* viscount, **-esse** *f* viscountess.

victime *f* victim, casualty; **être ~ de** to be the victim of.

victoire *f* victory.

victorieusement *adv* victoriously.

victorieux *adj* victorious.

vidange *f* emptying; waste outlet.

vidanger *vt* to empty; to drain off.

vide *adj* empty, vacant, devoid; * *m* vacuum; gap; void.

vidéo *f* video; * *adj invar* video.

vidéocassette *f* videocassette.

vide-ordures *m invar* rubbish chute.

vider *vt* to empty; to drain; to vacate; to gut.

videur *m* bouncer.

vie *f* life; living; **être en ~** to be alive.

vieillard *m* old man.

vieillesse *f* old age; the elderly; oldness.

vieillir *vi* to get old; * *vt* to age; to put years on.

vieillissement *m* ageing; obsolescence.

vierge *f* virgin; * *adj* virgin; blank; unexposed.

vieux *adj*, *f* **vieille** old; ancient; obsolete.

vif *adj* alive, lively; quick; eager, passionate.

vigilance *f* vigilance.

vigilant *adj* vigilant.

vigile *m* vigil.

vigne *f* vine; vineyard.

vigneron *m* **-ne** *f* wine grower.

vignette *f* vignette; illustration; seal.

vignoble *m* vineyard.

vigoureusement *adv* vigorously, energetically.

vigoureux *adj* vigorous.

vigueur *f* vigour, strength, energy.

vil *adj* vile; lowly.

vilain *m* naughty boy, **-e** *f* naughty girl.

villa *f* villa, detached house.

village *m* village.

villageois *adj* village, rustic.

ville *f* town, city.

villégiature *f* holiday; vacation.

vin *m* wine.

vinaigre *m* vinegar.

vinaigrette *f* vinaigrette, oil and vinegar dressing, French dressing.

vindicatif *adj* vindictive.

vingt *adj*, *m* twenty.

vingtaine *f* about twenty; score.

vingtième *adj*, *mf* twentieth; **~ment** *adv* in twentieth place.

vinicole *adj* wine, wine-growing.

vinyl *m* vinyl.

viol *m* rape.

violation *f* violation; transgression.

violemment *adv* violently.

violence *f* violence; force, duress.

violent *adj* violent; considerable, excessive.

violer *vt* to violate, desecrate; to rape.

violet *adj* purple, violet; * *m* purple, violet.

violette *f* (*bot*) violet.

violeur *m* rapist.

violon *m* violin.

violoncelle *m* cello, violoncello.

violoncelliste *mf* cello player.

violoniste *mf* violinist.

vipère *f* viper, adder.

virage *m* turn, bend; tacking.

viral *adj* viral.

virement *m* turning, tacking; transfer, clearance.

virer *vt* to transfer; * *vi* to turn, tack.

virevolter *vi* to spin round, pirouette.

virginité *f* virginity; purity.

virgule *f* comma; (*math*) point.

viril *adj* virile; male, masculine; **~ement** *adv* in a virile way.

virilité *f* virility; masculinity.

virtuel *adj* virtual; potential; **~lement** *adv* virtually.

virtuose *mf* virtuoso, master.

virulence *f* virulence, viciousness.

virulent *adj* virulent, vicious.

virus *m* virus.

vis *f* screw.

visa *m* stamp, visa.

visage *m* face; expression.

vis-à-vis *prép*: opposite; **~ de** towards; as regards; * *m* encounter; person opposite; **en ~** opposite each other.

viscéral *adj* visceral; deep-rooted.

viscère *f* viscera; intestines.

viser *vt* to aim, target; to visa.

viseur *m* sight; viewfinder.

visibilité *f* visibility.

visible *adj* visible; evident, obvious; **~ment** *adv* visibly; obviously.

visière *f* peak; eyeshade; visor.

vision *f* eyesight; vision.

visionnaire *mf* visionary; * *adj* visionary.

visite *f* visit; visiting, inspection; visitor.

visiter *vt* to visit; to examine, inspect.

visiteur *m* **-euse** *f* visitor; representative.

vison *m* mink.

visqueux *adj* viscous, thick.

visser *vt* to screw on.

visuel *adj* visual.

vital *adj* vital.

vitalité *f* energy, vitality.

vitamine *f* vitamin.

vite *adv* quickly, fast; soon; * *adj* swift; quick.

vitesse *f* speed, swiftness; gear.

viticole *adj* wine, wine-growing.

viticulteur *m* wine grower.

vitrage *m* glazing; windows.

vitrail *m* stained-glass window.

vitre *f* pane, window.

vitreux *adj* glassy, glazed, vitreous.

vitrier *m* glazier.

vitrine *f* shop window; display cabinet.

vitriol *m* vitriol.

vitupérer *vi* to vituperate, reprimand.

vivace *adj* hardy, perennial; enduring.

vivacité *f* vivacity, liveliness; vividness; acuteness.

vivant *adj* alive, living; lively.

vivement *adv* quickly, briskly; keenly, acutely.

vivier *m* fishpond.

vivifiant *adj* refreshing, invigorating.

vivifier *vt* to enliven, invigorate, refresh.

vivre *vi* to live, be alive; to last, endure; **vive la mariée!** three cheers for the bride; * *vt* to live, spend; to live through.

vivres *mpl* victuals, supplies.

VO (version originale) *f* original version.

vocabulaire *m* vocabulary.

vocal *adj* vocal; **~ement** *adv* vocally.

vocalise *f* singing exercise.

vocation *f* vocation, calling.

vociférer *vi* to vociferate, bawl.

vœu *m* vow; wish.

vogue *f* fashion, vogue; **en ~** in fashion.

voici *prép* here is, here are; ago, past.

voie *f* way, road; means; process; **~ ferrée** railway; **~ d'eau** leak; **en ~ de** in the process of.

voilà *prép* there is, there are; ago; **et ~!** so there!

voile *f* sail; * *m* veil.

voilé *adj* veiled; hazy, blurred.

voiler *vt* to veil, shroud; **se ~** *vr* to wear a veil; to mist over.

voilier *m* sailing boat, yacht.

voir *vt* to see; to deal with; to understand; **avoir à ~ avec** to have to do with; **se ~** *vr* to find o.s.; to show.

voisin *m* **-e** *f* neighbour; fellow; * *adj* neighbouring, next.

voisinage *m* neighbourhood, vicinity.

voiture *f* car; carriage; cart.

voix *f* voice; vote; **parler à ~ basse/haute** to speak in a low/high voice.

vol *m* flight; flock; **à ~ d'oiseau** as the crow flies.

volaille *f* fowl, poultry.

volant *m* steering wheel; * *adj* flying.

volatile *adj* volatile.

volatiliser *vt* to volatilise; to extinguish; **se ~** *vr* to volatilise; to vanish.

volcan *m* volcano.

volcanique *adj* volcanic.

volée *f* flight; volley; **à la ~** in midair; rashly, at random; **demi-~** half-volley.

voler *vi* to fly; **~ en éclats** to smash into pieces; * *vt* to steal; to rob.

volet *m* shutter; flap, paddle.

voleur *m* **-euse** *f* thief; * *adj* dishonest, thieving.

volley-ball *m* volleyball.

volleyeur *m* **-euse** *f* volleyball player.

volontaire *adj* voluntary; intentional; **~ment** *adv* voluntarily; intentionally.

volonté *f* will, wish; willingness; willpower.

volontiers *adv* willingly; gladly.

volt *m* volt.

volte-face *f invar* volte-face, about-turn; **faire ~** to turn round.

voltige *f* acrobatics; trick riding.

voltiger *vi* to flutter about.

volubile *adj* voluble.

volume *m* volume.

volumineux *adj* voluminous, bulky.

volupté *f* voluptuousness, sensual pleasure.

voluptueux *adj* voluptuous.

volute *f* volute, scroll; wreath.

vomir *vi* to vomit, be sick; * *vt* to vomit, bring up.

vomissement *m* vomiting.

vorace *adj* voracious; **~ment** *adv* voraciously.

voracité *f* voracity, voraciousness.

vos = *pl* **votre**.

votant *m* **-e** *f* voter.

vote *m* vote; voting.

voter *vi* to vote.

votre *adj*, *pl* **vos** your, your own.

vôtre *pn*: **le ~, la ~, les ~s** yours, your own.

vouer *vt* to vow; to devote, dedicate.

vouloir *vt* to want, wish; to require; to try; **~ du mal à** to wish sb harm; **en ~ à** to bear a grudge against sb; **bien ~** to be happy that.

voulu *adj* required; deliberate.

vous *pn* you, yourself.

voûte *f* vault.

voûté *adj* vaulted.

vouvoyer *vt* to use the '*vous*' form.

voyage *m* journey, trip; travelling.

voyager *vi* to travel, journey.

voyageur *m* **-euse** *f* traveller, passenger.

voyant *m* **-e** *f* visionary, seer; * *m* signal light; * *adj* gaudy, showy.

voyelle *f* vowel.

voyeur *m* **-euse** *f* voyeur.

voyou *m* lout, loafer, hoodlum.

vrac *adv*: **en ~** in bulk.

vrai *adj* true, genuine; **~ment** *adv* truly, really.

vraisemblable *adj* likely, probable; **~ment** *adv* probably.

vrille *f* tendril; spiral; **descendre en ~** to come down in a spin.

vrombir *vi* to roar, hum.

vu *adj* seen; considered, regarded; **être bien/mal ~** to be well/poorly thought of; **ni ~ ni connu** you won't discover anything; * *prép* in view of.

vue *f* sight, eyesight; **en ~ de** with a view to; **avoir des ~s sur** to have designs on.

vulgaire *adj* vulgar, crude; **~ment** *adv* vulgarly.

vulgariser *vt* to popularise; to coarsen.

vulgarité *f* vulgarity, coarseness.

vulnérable *adj* vulnerable.

vulve *f* vulva.

W, X, Y, Z

wagon *m* wagon, truck, freight car; wagonload.
wagon-citerne *m* tanker.
wagon-lit *m* sleeper.
wagon-restaurant *m* restaurant car.
water-polo *m* water polo.
watt *m* watt.
W-C (water-closet) *mpl* lavatory.
week-end *m* weekend.
western *m* western.
whisky *m* whisky.
xénophobe *mf* xenophobe; * *adj* xenophobic.
xénophobie *f* xenophobia.
xylophone *m* xylophone.
yacht *m* yacht.
yang *m* yang.

yaourt *m* yoghurt.
yard *m* yard.
yeux *pl* = **œil**.
yin *m* yin.
yoga *m* yoga.
yogi *m* yogi.
yogourt *m* = **yaourt**.
yo-yo *m* yo-yo.
yucca *m* yucca.
yuppie *mf* yuppy.
zèbre *m* zebra.
zébu *m* zebu.
zèle *m* zeal.
zélé *adj* zealous.
zen *m* Zen.
zénith *m* zenith.
zéro *m* zero, nought, nothing.
zézayer *vi* to lisp.

zigzag *m* zigzag.
zigzaguer *vi* to zigzag.
zinc *m* zinc.
zizanie *f* ill-feeling.
zizi *m* (*fam*) willy.
zodiaque *m* zodiac.
zona *m* shingles.
zone *f* zone, area.
zoo *m* zoo.
zoologie *f* zoology.
zoologiste *mf* zoologist.
zoom *m* zoom; zoom lens.
zoophile *adj* zoophilic, zoophilous.
zozoter *vi* (*fam*) to lisp.
ZUP (zone à urbaniser en priorité) *f* urban development zone.
zut *interj* damn! rubbish! shut up!

English-French Dictionary

A

a *art* un, une.

aback *adv* **to be taken ~** *vi* être décontenancé.

abacus *n* abaque, boulier *m*.

abandon *vt* abandonner, laisser.

abandonment *n* abandon *m*.

abase *vt* avilir; humilier.

abasement *n* avilissement *m*; humiliation *f*.

abash *vt* couvrir de honte.

abate *vt* baisser; * *vi* baisser; se calmer.

abatement *n* baisse, réduction *f*.

abbess *n* abbesse *f*.

abbey *n* abbaye *f*.

abbot *n* abbé *m*.

abbreviate *vt* abréger, raccourcir.

abbreviation *n* abréviation *f*.

abdicate *vt* abdiquer; renoncer à.

abdication *n* abdication *f*; renonciation *f*.

abdomen *n* abdomen *m*.

abdominal *adj* abdominal.

abduct *vt* kidnapper, enlever.

abductor *n* abducteur *m*.

abed *adv* au lit.

aberrant *adj* aberrant.

aberration *n* aberration *f*.

abet *vt*: **to aid and ~** être complice
de.

abeyance *n* suspension *f*.

abhor *vt* abhorrer, exécrer.

abhorrence *n* exécration, horreur
f.

abhorrent *adj* exécrable.

abide *vt* supporter, souffrir.

ability *n* capacité, aptitude *f*; **abi-
lities** *pl* talents *mpl*.

abject *adj* misérable; abject, méprisable; **~ly** *adv* misérable-
ment.

abjure *vt* abjurer; renoncer à.

ablative *n* (*gr*) ablatif *m*.

ablaze *adj* enflammé.

able *adj* capable; **to be ~** pouvoir.

able-bodied *adj* robuste.

ablution *n* ablution *f*.

ably *adv* habilement.

abnegation *n* renoncement *m*.

abnormal *adj* anormal.

abnormality *n* anomalie *f*.

aboard *adv* à bord.

abode *n* domicile *m*.

abolish *vt* abolir, supprimer.

abolition *n* abolition, suppression
f.

abominable *adj* abominable; **~bly**
adv abominablement.

abomination *n* abomination *f*.

aboriginal *adj* aborigène.

aborigines *npl* aborigènes *mpl*.

abort *vi* avorter.

abortion *n* avortement *m*.

abortive *adj* raté.

abound *vi* abonder; **~ with** abonder en.

about *prep* au sujet de; vers; **I
carry no money ~ me** je n'ai pas
d'argent sur moi; * *adv* çà et là;
to be ~ to être sur le point de; **to
go ~** aller de- ci de- là; **to go ~ a
thing** entreprendre quelque
chose; **all ~** partout.

above *prep* au-dessus de; * *adv* au-
dessus; **~ all** surtout, principalement; **~ mentioned** mention-
né ci-dessus.

aboveboard *adj* franc.

abrasion *n* écorchure *f*.

abrasive *adj* abrasif.

abreast *adv* de front.

abridge *vt* abréger, raccourcir.

abridgment *n* abrégement *m*; version abrégée *f*.

abroad *adv* à l'étranger; **to go ~** se
rendre à l'étranger.

abrogate *vt* abroger.

abrogation *n* abrogation *f*.

abrupt *adj* abrupt; brusque; **~ly**
adv brusquement; rudement.

abscess *n* abcès *m*.

abscond *vi* s'enfuir.

absence *n* absence *f*.

absent *adj* absent; * *vi* s'absenter.

absentee *n* absent *m* -e *f*.

absenteeism *n* absentéisme *m*.

absent-minded *adj* distrait.

absolute *adj* absolu; **~ly** *adv* absolument.

absolution *n* absolution *f*.

absolutism *n* absolutisme *m*.

absolve *vt* absoudre.

absorb *vt* absorber.

absorbent *adj* absorbant.

absorbent cotton *n* coton hydrophile *m*.

absorption *n* absorption *f*.

abstain *vi* s'abstenir.

abstemious *adj* sobre; **~ly** *adv* sobrement.

abstemiousness *n* sobriété *f*.

abstinence *n* abstinence *f*.

abstinent *adj* abstinent.

abstract *adj* abstrait; * *n* abrégé *m*;
in the ~ dans l'abstrait.

abstraction *n* abstraction *f*; extraction *f*.

abstractly *adv* abstraitement.

abstruse *adj* abstrus, obscur; **~ly**
adv obscurément.

absurd *adj* absurde; **~ly** *adv* absur-
dement.

absurdity *n* absurdité *f*.

abundance *n* abondance *f*.

abundant *adj* abondant; **~ly** *adv*
abondamment.

abuse *vt* abuser de; insulter; maltraiter; * *n* abus *m*; injures *fpl*;
mauvais traitements *mpl*.

abusive *adj* injurieux; **~ly** *adv* injurieusement.

abut *vi* être contigu.

abysmal *adj* abominable.

abyss *n* abîme *m*.

acacia *n* acacia *m*.

academic *adj* universitaire; scolaire; théorique.

academician *n* académicien *m* -ne
f.

academy *n* académie *f*.

accede *vi* accéder.

accelerate *vt* accélérer.

accelerator *n* accélérateur *m*.

acceleration *n* accélération *f*.

accent *n* accent *m*; * *vt* accentuer.

accentuate *vt* accentuer.

accentuation *n* accentuation *f*.

accept *vt* accepter.

acceptable *adj* acceptable.

acceptability *n* acceptabilité *f*.

acceptance *n* acceptation *f*.

access *n* accès *m*.

accessible *adj* accessible.

accession *n* augmentation *f*; accession *f*.

accessory *n* accessoire *m*; (*law*)
complice *m*.

accident *n* accident *m*; hasard *m*.

accidental *adj* accidentel; **~ly** *adv*
par hasard.

acclaim *vt* acclamer.

acclamation *n* acclamation *f*.

acclimate *vt* (US) acclimater.

accommodate *vt* loger; accommoder.

accommodating *adj* obligeant.

accommodations *npl* logement
m.

accompaniment *n* (*mus*) accompagnement *m*.

accompanist *n* (*mus*) accompagnateur *m* -trice *f*.

accompany *vt* accompagner.

accomplice *n* complice *mf*.

accomplish *vt* accomplir.

accomplished *adj* accompli.

accomplishment *n* accomplissement *m*; ~s *pl* talents *mpl*.

accord *n* accord *m*; **with one ~** d'un commun accord; **of one's own ~** de son propre chef.

accordance *n*: **in ~ with** conformément à.

according *prep* selon; **~ as** selon que; **~ly** *adv* en conséquence.

accordion *n* (*mus*) accordéon *m*.

accost *vt* accoster.

account *n* compte *m*; **on no ~** en aucun cas; **on ~ of** en raison de; **to call to ~** demander des comptes; **to turn to ~** mettre à profit; * *vt* ~ **for** expliquer; représenter.

accountability *n* responsabilité *f*.

accountable *adj* responsable.

accountancy *n* comptabilité *f*.

accountant *n* comptable *mf*.

account book *n* livre *m* de comptes.

account number *n* numéro de compte *m*.

accrue *vi* s'accumuler; revenir.

accumulate *vt* accumuler; * *vi* s'accumuler.

accumulation *n* accumulation *f*.

accuracy *n* exactitude *f*.

accurate *adj* exact; **~ly** *adv* exactement.

accursed *adj* maudit.

accusation *n* accusation *f*.

accusative *n* (*gr*) accusatif *m*.

accusatory *adj* accusateur.

accuse *vt* accuser.

accused *n* accusé *m* -e *f*.

accuser *n* accusateur *m* -trice *f*.

accustom *vt* accoutumer.

accustomed *adj* accoutumé.

ace *n* as *m*; **within an ~ of** à deux doigts de.

acerbic *adj* acerbe.

acetate *n* (*chem*) acétate *m*.

ache *n* douleur *f*; * *vi* faire mal.

achieve *vt* réaliser; obtenir.

achievement *n* réalisation *f*; exploit *m*.

acid *adj* acide; aigre; * *n* acide *m*.

acidity *n* acidité *f*.

acknowledge *vt* reconnaître, admettre.

acknowledgment *n* reconnaissance *f*.

acme *n* apogée *m*.

acne *n* acné *f*.

acorn *n* gland *m*.

acoustics *n* acoustique *f*.

acquaint *vt* informer, aviser.

acquaintance *n* connaissance *f*.

acquiesce *vi* acquiescer, consentir.

acquiescence *n* consentement *m*.

acquiescent *adj* consentant.

acquire *vt* acquérir.

acquisition *n* acquisition *f*.

acquit *vt* acquitter.

acquittal *n* acquittement *m*.

acre *n* acre *f*.

acrid *adj* âcre; acerbe.

acrimonious *adj* acrimonieux.

acrimony *n* acrimonie *f*.

across *adv* en travers, d'un côté à l'autre; * *prep* à travers; **to come ~** tomber sur.

act *vt* jouer; * *vi* agir; jouer la comédie; * *n* acte *m*; **~s of the apostles** Actes des Apôtres *mpl*.

acting *adj* intérimaire.

action *n* action *f*; combat *m*.

action replay *n* répétition *f*.

activate *vt* activer.

active *adj* actif; **~ly** *adv* activement.

activity *n* activité *f*.

actor *n* acteur *m*.

actress *n* actrice *f*.

actual *adj* réel; concret; **~ly** *adv* en fait; réellement.

actuary *n* actuaire *mf*.

acumen *n* perspicacité *f*.

acute *adj* aigu; perspicace; **~ accent** *n* accent aigu *m*; **~ angle** *n* angle aigu *m*; **~ly** *adv* vivement; avec perspicacité.

acuteness *n* finesse *f*, intensité *f*.

ad *n* annonce *f*.

adage *n* adage *m*.

adamant *adj* inflexible.

adapt *vt* adapter, ajuster.

adaptability *n* adaptabilité *f*.

adaptable *adj* adaptable.

adaptation *n* adaptation *f*.

adaptor *n* adaptateur *m*.

add *vt* ajouter; **~ up** additionner.

addendum *n* addendum *m*.

adder *n* vipère *f*.

addict *n* intoxiqué *m* -e *f*.

addiction *n* dépendance *f*.

addictive *adj* qui crée une dépendance.

addition *n* addition *f*.

additional *adj* additionnel; **~ly** *adv* de plus.

additive *n* additif *m*.

address *vt* adresser; s'adresser à; * *n* adresse *f*; discours *m*.

adduce *vt* mentionner, citer.

adenoids *npl* végétations *fpl*.

adept *adj* expert.

adequacy *n* suffisance *f*; capacité *f*.

adequate *adj* adéquat; suffisant; **~ly** *adv* convenablement; suffisamment.

adhere *vi* adhérer.

adherence *n* adhérence *f*.

adherent *n* adhérent, partisan *m*.

adhesion *n* adhérence *f*; adhésion *f*.

adhesive *adj* adhésif.

adhesive tape *n* (*med*) sparadrap *m*; papier *m* collant.

adhesiveness *n* adhérence *f*.

adieu *adv* adieu; * *n* adieux *mpl*.

adipose *adj* adipeux.

adjacent *adj* adjacent, contigu.

adjectival *adj* adjectival; **~ly** *adv* adjectivalement.

adjective *n* adjectif *m*.

adjoin *vi* être contigu.

adjoining *adj* contigu.

adjourn *vt* reporter, remettre.

adjournment *n* ajournement *m*.

adjudicate *vt* décider; juger.

adjunct *n* subalterne *mf*; annexe *f*.

adjust *vt* ajuster, adapter.

adjustable *adj* ajustable, adaptable.

adjustment *n* ajustement *m*; réglage *m*.

adjutant *n* (*mil*) adjudant *m*.

ad lib *vt* improviser.

administer *vt* administrer; distribuer; **~ an oath** faire prêter serment.

administration *n* administration *f*; gouvernement *m*.

administrative *adj* administratif.

administrator *n* administrateur *m* -trice *f*.

admirable *adj* admirable; **~bly** *adv* admirablement.

admiral *n* amiral *m*.

admiralship *n* amirauté *f*.

admiralty *n* ministère de la Marine *m*.

admiration *n* admiration *f*.

admire *vt* admirer.

admirer *n* admirateur *m* -trice *f*.

admiringly *adv* avec admiration.

admissible *adj* admissible.

admission *n* admission, entrée *f*.

admit *vt* admettre; **~ to** reconnaître, avouer.

admittance *n* admission *f*.

admittedly *adv* il est vrai (que).

admixture *n* mélange *m*.

admonish *vt* admonester, réprimander.

admonition *n* admonestation *f*; conseil *m*.

admonitory *adj* d'admonestation.

ad nauseam *adv* à saturation.

ado *n* agitation *f*.
adolescence *n* adolescence *f*.
adopt *vt* adopter.
adopted *adj* adoptif.
adoption *n* adoption *f*.
adoptive *adj* adoptif.
adorable *adj* adorable.
adorably *adv* adorablement.
adoration *n* adoration *f*.
adore *vt* adorer.
adorn *vt* orner.
adornment *n* ornement *m*.
adrift *adv* à la dérive.
adroit *adj* adroit, habile.
adroitness *n* adresse *f*.
adulation *n* adulation *f*.
adulatory *adj* adulateur.
adult *adj* adulte; * *n* adulte *mf*.
adulterate *vt* falsifier; * *adj* falsifié.
adulteration *n* falsification *f*.
adulterer *n* adultère *m*.
adulteress *n* adultère *f*.
adulterous *adj* adultère.
adultery *n* adultère *m*.
advance *vt* avancer; * *vi* avancer; faire des progrès; * *n* avance *f*.
advanced *adj* avancé.
advancement *n* avancement *m*.
advantage *n* avantage *m*; **to take ~ of** profiter de.
advantageous *adj* avantageux; **~ly** *adv* avantageusement.
advantageousness *n* avantage *m*.
advent *n* venue *f*; **Advent** *n* Avent *m*.
adventitious *adj* accidentel.
adventure *n* aventure *f*.
adventurer *n* aventurier *m* -ière *f*.
adventurous *adj* aventureux; **~ly** *adv* aventureusement.
adverb *n* adverbe *m*.
adverbial *adj* adverbial; **~ly** *adv* adverbialement.
adversary *n* adversaire *mf*.
adverse *adj* défavorable, contraire.
adversity *n* adversité *f*; malheur *m*.
advertise *vt* faire de la publicité pour; mettre une annonce pour.
advertisement *n* publicité *f*; annonce *f*.
advertising *n* publicité *f*.
advice *n* conseil *m*; avis *m*.
advisability *n* opportunité *f*.
advisable *adj* prudent, conseillé.
advise *vt* conseiller; aviser.
advisedly *adv* de manière avisée.
advisory *adj* consultatif.
advocacy *n* défense *f*.
advocate *n* avocat *m*; * *vt* plaider pour.
aerial *n* antenne *f*.
aerobics *npl* aérobic *m*.

aerometer *n* aéromètre *m*.
aeroplane *n* avion *m*.
aerosol *n* aérosol *m*.
aerostat *n* aérostat *m*.
aesthetic *adj* esthétique; **~s** *npl* esthétique *f*.
afar *adv* au loin; **from ~** de loin.
affability *n* affabilité *f*.
affable *adj* affable; **~bly** *adv* affablement.
affair *n* affaire *f*.
affect *vt* toucher; affecter.
affectation *n* affectation *f*.
affected *adj* affecté; **~ly** *adv* avec affectation.
affectingly *adv* avec émotion.
affection *n* affection *f*.
affectionate *adj* affectueux; **~ly** *adv* affectueusement.
affidavit *n* déclaration sous serment *f*.
affiliate *vt* affilier.
affiliation *n* affiliation *f*.
affinity *n* affinité *f*.
affirm *vt* affirmer, déclarer.
affirmation *n* affirmation *f*.
affirmative *adj* affirmatif; **~ly** *adv* affirmativement.
affix *vt* coller; apposer; * *n* (*gr*) affixe *m*.
afflict *vt* affliger.
affliction *n* affliction *f*.
affluence *n* abondance *f*.
affluent *adj* riche; abondant.
afflux *n* afflux *m*, affluence *f*.
afford *vt* fournir; **to be able to ~** avoir les moyens d'acheter.
affray *n* (*law*) rixe *f*.
affront *n* affront *m*, injure *f*; * *vt* affronter; insulter.
aflame *adv* en flammes.
afloat *adv* à flot.
afore *prep* avant; * *adv* d'abord.
afraid *adj* apeuré; **I am ~** j'ai peur.
afresh *adv* à nouveau.
aft *adv* (*mar*) en poupe.
after *prep* après; * *adv* après; **~ all** après tout.
afterbirth *n* placenta *m*.
after-crop *n* deuxième récolte *f*.
after-effects *npl* répercussions *fpl*.
afterlife *n* vie après la mort *f*.
aftermath *n* conséquences *fpl*.
afternoon *n* après-midi *mf*.
afterpains *npl* tranchées utérines *fpl*.
aftershave *n* après-rasage *m*.
aftertaste *n* arrière-goût *m*.
afterward(s) *adv* ensuite.
again *adv* à nouveau; **~ and ~** de nombreuses fois; **as much ~** encore autant.

against *prep* contre; **~ the grain** à contre fil; de mauvaise volonté.
agate *n* agate *f*.
age *n* âge *m*; vieillesse *f*; **under ~** mineur; * *vt* vieillir.
aged *adj* âgé.
agency *n* agence *f*.
agenda *n* ordre du jour *m*.
agent *n* agent *m*.
agglomerate *vt* agglomérer.
agglomeration *n* agglomération *f*.
aggrandisement *n* avancement *m*.
aggravate *vt* aggraver; énerver.
aggravation *n* aggravation *f*; énervement *m*.
aggregate *n* agrégat *m*.
aggregation *n* agrégation *f*.
aggression *n* agression *f*.
aggressive *adj* agressif.
aggressor *n* agresseur *m*.
aggrieved *adj* offensé.
aghast *adj* horrifié.
agile *adj* agile; adroit.
agility *n* agilité *f*; adresse *f*.
agitate *vt* agiter.
agitation *n* agitation *f*.
agitator *n* agitateur *m* -trice *f*.
ago *adv*: **how long ~?** il y a combien de temps?
agog *adj* en émoi; impatient.
agonising *adj* atroce, angoissant.
agony *n* douleur *f* atroce; angoisse *f*.
agrarian *adj* agraire.
agree *vt* convenir; * *vi* être d'accord.
agreeable *adj* agréable; **~bly** *adv* agréablement; **~ with** conforme à.
agreeableness *n* caractère agréable *m*.
agreed *adj* convenu; **~!** *adv* d'accord!
agreement *n* accord *m*.
agricultural *adj* agricole.
agriculture *n* agriculture *f*.
agriculturist *n* agriculteur *m*.
aground *adv* (*mar*) échoué.
ah! *excl* ah!
ahead *adv* en avant; à l'avance; (*mar*) sur l'avant.
ahoy! *excl* (*mar*) ohé!
aid *vt* aider, secourir; **~ and abet** être complice de; * *n* aide *f*, secours *m*; aide *mf*.
aide-de-camp *n* (*mil*) aide de camp *m*.
AIDS *n* SIDA *m*.
ail *vt* affliger.
ailing *adj* souffrant.
ailment *n* maladie *f*.
aim *vt* pointer; viser; aspirer à; * *n* but *m*; cible *f*.
aimless *adj* sans but; **~ly** à la dérive, sans but.

air *n* air *m*; * *vt* aérer.

air balloon *n* ballon *m*.

airborne *adj* aéroporté.

air-conditioned *adj* climatisé.

air-conditioning *n* climatisation *f*.

aircraft *n* avion *m*.

air cushion *n* coussin d'air *m*.

air force *n* armée de l'air *f*.

air freshener *n* appareil de conditionnement d'air *m*.

air gun *n* carabine à air comprimé *f*.

air hole *n* trou d'aération *m*.

airiness *n* aération, ventilation *f*.

airless *adj* mal aéré, mal ventilé.

airlift *n* pont aérien *m*.

airline *n* ligne aérienne *f*.

airmail *n*: **by ~** par avion.

airport *n* aéroport *m*.

air pump *n* compresseur *m*.

airsick *adj*: **to be ~** avoir le mal de l'air.

airstrip *n* piste d'atterrissage *f*.

air terminal *n* aérogare *f*.

airtight *adj* hermétique.

airy *adj* aéré; léger.

aisle *n* nef d'église *f*.

ajar *adj* entrouvert.

akimbo *adj* les poings sur les hanches.

akin *adj* ressemblant.

alabaster *n* albâtre *m*; * *adj* d'albâtre.

alacrity *n* vivacité *f*.

alarm *n* alarme *f*; * *vt* alarmer; inquiéter.

alarm bell *n* sonnette d'alarme *f*.

alarmist *n* alarmiste *mf*.

alas *adv* hélas.

albeit *conj* bien que.

album *n* album *m*.

alchemist *n* alchimiste *m*.

alchemy *n* alchimie *f*.

alcohol *n* alcool *m*.

alcoholic *adj* alcoolisé; * *n* alcoolique *mf*.

alcove *n* alcôve *f*.

alder *n* aulne *m*.

ale *n* bière *f*.

alehouse *n* taverne, brasserie *f*.

alert *adj* vigilant; vif; * *n* alerte *f*.

alertness *n* vigilance *f*; vivacité *f*.

algae *npl* algues *fpl*.

algebra *n* algèbre *f*.

algebraic *adj* algébrique.

alias *adj* alias.

alibi *n* (*law*) alibi *m*.

alien *adj* étranger; * *n* étranger *m* -ère *f*; extra-terrestre *mf*.

alienate *vt* aliéner.

alienation *n* aliénation *f*.

alight *vi* mettre pied à terre; * *adj* en feu.

align *vt* aligner.

alike *adj* semblable, égal; * *adv* de la même façon.

alimentary *n* (*med*) digestif *m*.

alimony *n* (*law*) pension *f* alimentaire.

alive *adj* en vie, vivant; actif.

alkali *n* alcali *m*.

alkaline *adj* alcalin.

all *adj* tout; * *adv* totalement; **~ at once, ~ of a sudden** soudain; **~ the same** cependant; **~ the better** tant mieux; **not at ~!** pas du tout!; il n'y a pas de quoi!; **once and for ~** une fois pour toutes; * *n* tout *m*.

allay *vt* apaiser.

all clear *n* feu vert *m*.

allegation *n* allégation *f*.

allege *vt* alléguer.

allegiance *n* loyauté, fidélité *f*.

allegorical *adj* allégorique; **~ly** *adv* allégoriquement.

allegory *n* allégorie *f*.

allegro *n* (*mus*) allegro *m*.

allergy *n* allergie *f*.

alleviate *vt* alléger.

alleviation *n* allègement *m*.

alley *n* ruelle *f*.

alliance *n* alliance *f*.

allied *adj* allié.

alligator *n* alligator *m*.

alliteration *n* allitération *f*.

all-night *adj* ouvert toute la nuit.

allocate *vt* allouer.

allocation *n* allocation *f*.

allot *vt* assigner.

allow *vt* permettre; accorder; **~ for** tenir compte de.

allowable *adj* admissible, permis.

allowance *n* allocation *f*; concession *f*.

alloy *n* alliage *m*.

all right *adv* bien.

all-round *adj* complet.

allspice *n* piment *m* de la Jamaïque.

allude *vi* faire allusion à.

allure *n* charme, attrait *m*.

alluring *adj* attrayant; **~ly** *adv* avec charme.

allurement *n* attrait *m*.

allusion *n* allusion *f*.

allusive *adj* allusif; **~ly** *adv* par allusion.

alluvial *adj* alluvial.

ally *n* allié *m* -e *f*; * *vt* allier.

almanac *n* almanach *m*.

almighty *adj* omnipotent, tout-puissant.

almond *n* amande *f*.

almond-milk *n* lait d'amandes *m*.

almond tree *n* amandier *m*.

almost *adv* presque.

alms *n* aumône *f*.

aloft *prep* en l'air; en haut.

alone *adj* seul; * *adv* seul; **to leave ~** laisser tranquille.

along *adv* le long (de); **~ side** à côté.

aloof *adj* distant.

aloud *adj* à voix haute.

alphabet *n* alphabet *m*.

alphabetical *adj* alphabétique; **~ly** *adv* par ordre alphabétique, alphabétiquement.

alpine *adj* alpin.

already *adv* déjà.

also *adv* aussi.

altar *n* autel *m*.

altarpiece *n* retable *m*.

alter *vt* modifier.

alteration *n* modification *f*.

altercation *n* altercation *f*.

alternate *adj* alterné; * *vt* alterner; **~ly** *adv* alternativement.

alternating *adj* alterné.

alternation *n* alternance *f*.

alternator *n* alternateur *m*.

alternative *n* alternative *f*; * *adj* alternatif; **~ly** *adv* sinon.

although *conj* bien que, malgré.

altitude *n* altitude *f*.

altogether *adv* complètement.

alum *n* alun *m*.

aluminium *n* aluminium *m*.

aluminous *adj* alumineux.

always *adv* toujours.

a.m. *adv* du matin.

amalgam *n* amalgame *m*.

amalgamate *vt* amalgamer; *vi* s'amalgamer.

amalgamation *n* amalgamation *f*.

amanuensis *n* copiste *mf*.

amaryllis *n* (*bot*) amaryllis *f*.

amass *vt* accumuler, amasser.

amateur *n* amateur *m*.

amateurish *adj* d'amateur.

amatory *adj* amoureux; galant.

amaze *vt* stupéfier.

amazement *n* stupéfaction *f*.

amazing *adj* stupéfiant; **~ly** *adv* incroyablement.

amazon *n* amazone *f*.

ambassador *n* ambassadeur *m*.

ambassadress *n* ambassadrice *f*.

amber *n* ambre *m*; * *adj* ambré.

ambidextrous *adj* ambidextre.

ambient *adj* ambiant.

ambiguity *n* ambiguïté *f*.

ambiguous *adj* ambigu; **~ly** *adv* de manière ambiguè.

ambition *n* ambition *f*.

ambitious *adj* ambitieux; **~ly** *adv* ambitieusement.

amble *vi* marcher tranquillement.

ambulance *n* ambulance *f*.

ambush *n* embuscade *f*; **to lie in ~** être embusqué; * *vt* tendre une embuscade à.

ameliorate *vt* améliorer.

amelioration *n* amélioration *f*.

amenable *adj* responsable.

amend *vt* modifier; amender.

amendable *adj* réparable, corrigible.

amendment *n* modification *f*; amendement *m*.

amends *npl* compensation *f*.

amenities *npl* commodités *fpl*.

America *n* Amérique *f*.

American *adj* américain.

amethyst *n* améthyste *f*.

amiability *n* amabilité *f*.

amiable *adj* aimable.

amiableness *n* amabilité *f*.

amiably *adv* aimablement.

amicable *adj* amical; **~bly** *adv* amicalement.

amid(st) *prep* entre, parmi.

amiss *adv*: **something's ~** quelque chose ne va pas.

ammonia *n* ammoniaque *m*.

ammunition *n* munitions *fpl*.

amnesia *n* amnésie *f*.

amnesty *n* amnistie *f*.

among(st) *prep* entre, parmi.

amoral *adj* amoral.

amorous *adj* amoureux; **~ly** *adv* amoureusement.

amorphous *adj* informe.

amount *n* montant *m*; quantité *f*; * *vi* s'élever (à).

amp(ere) *n* ampère *m*.

amphibian *n* amphibie *m*.

amphibious *adj* amphibie.

amphitheatre *n* amphithéâtre *m*.

ample *adj* spacieux; abondant, gros.

ampleness *n* abondance *f*.

amplification *n* amplification *f*.

amplifier *n* amplificateur *m*.

amplify *vt* amplifier.

amplitude *n* amplitude *f*.

amply *adv* amplement.

amputate *vt* amputer.

amputation *n* amputation *f*.

amulet *n* amulette *f*.

amuse *vt* distraire, divertir.

amusement *n* distraction *f*, divertissement *m*.

amusing *adj* divertissant; **~ly** *adv* de manière divertissante.

an *art* un, une.

anachronism *n* anachronisme *m*.

anaemia *n* anémie *f*.

anaemic *adj* (*med*) anémique.

anaesthetic *n* anesthésique *m*.

analog *adj* (*comput*) analogique.

analogous *adj* analogue.

analogy *n* analogie *f*.

analyse *vt* analyser.

analysis *n* analyse *f*.

analyst *n* analyste *mf*.

analytical *adj* analytique; **~ly** *adv* analytiquement.

anarchic *adj* anarchique.

anarchist *n* anarchiste *mf*.

anarchy *n* anarchie *f*.

anatomical *adj* anatomique; **~ly** *adv* anatomiquement.

anatomise *vt* disséquer.

anatomy *n* anatomie *f*.

ancestor *n* ancêtre *mf*.

ancestral *adj* ancestral.

ancestry *n* ascendance *f*.

anchor *n* ancre *f*; * *vi* jeter l'ancre.

anchorage *n* ancrage *m*.

anchovy *n* anchois *m*.

ancient *adj* ancien, antique; **~ly** *adv* anciennement.

ancillary *adj* auxiliaire.

and *conj* et.

anecdotal *adj* anecdotique.

anecdote *n* anecdote *f*.

anemone *n* (*bot*) anémone *f*.

anew *adv* de nouveau.

angel *n* ange *m*.

angelic *adj* angélique.

anger *n* colère *f*; * *vt* mettre en colère, irriter.

angle *n* angle *m*; * *vi* pêcher à la ligne.

angled *adj* anguleux.

angler *n* pêcheur à la ligne *m*.

anglicism *n* anglicisme *m*.

angling *n* pêche à la ligne *f*.

angrily *adv* avec colère.

angry *adj* en colère, irrité.

anguish *n* angoisse *f*.

angular *adj* angulaire.

angularity *n* caractère anguleux *m*.

animal *n adj* animal *m*.

animate *vt* animer; * *adj* vivant.

animated *adj* animé.

animation *n* animation *f*.

animosity *n* animosité *f*.

animus *n* haine *f*.

anise *n* anis *m*.

aniseed *n* graine d'anis *f*.

ankle *n* cheville *f*; **~bone** astragale *m*.

annals *n* annales *fpl*.

annex *vt* annexer; * *n* annexe *f*.

annexation *n* annexion *f*.

annihilate *vt* annihiler, anéantir.

annihilation *n* anéantissement *m*.

anniversary *n* anniversaire (de) *m*.

annotate *vt* annoter.

annotation *n* annotation *f*.

announce *vt* annoncer.

announcement *n* annonce *f*.

announcer *n* présentateur *m* -trice *f*.

annoy *vt* ennuyer.

annoyance *n* ennui *m*.

annoying *adj* ennuyeux.

annual *adj* annuel; **~ly** *adv* annuellement.

annuity *n* rente viagère *f*.

annul *vt* annuler, abroger.

annulment *n* annulation *f*.

annunciation *n* annonciation *f*.

anodyne *adj* calmant.

anoint *vt* oindre.

anomalous *adj* anormal.

anomaly *n* anomalie, irrégularité *f*.

anon *adv* = **anonymous**.

anonymity *n* anonymat *m*.

anonymous *adj* anonyme; **~ly** *adv* anonymement.

anorexia *n* anorexie *f*.

another *adj* un autre; **one ~** l'un l'autre.

answer *vt* répondre à; **~ for** répondre de; **~ to** répondre à; * *n* réponse *f*.

answerable *adj* responsable.

answering machine *n* répondeur téléphonique *m*.

ant *n* fourmi *f*.

antagonise *vt* provoquer.

antagonism *n* antagonisme *m*; rivalité *f*.

antagonist *n* antagoniste *mf*.

antarctic *adj* antarctique.

anteater *n* fourmilier *m*.

antecedent *n*: **~s** *pl* antécédents *mpl*.

antechamber *n* antichambre *f*.

antedate *vt* antidater.

antelope *n* antilope *f*.

antenna *n* antenne *f*.

anterior *adj* antérieur, précédent.

anthem *n* hymne *m*.

anthill *n* fourmilière *f*.

anthology *n* anthologie *f*.

anthracite *n* anthracite *m*.

anthropology *n* anthropologie *f*.

antiaircraft *adj* antiaérien.

antibiotic *n* antibiotique *m*.

antibody *n* anticorps *m*.

Antichrist *n* Antéchrist *m*.

anticipate *vt* prévoir.

anticipation *n* attente *f*; prévision *f*.

anticlockwise *adv* dans le sens contraire des aiguilles d'une montre.

antidote *n* antidote *m*.

antifreeze *n* antigel *m*.

antimony *n* antimoine *m*.

antipathy *n* antipathie *f*.

antipodes *npl* antipodes *fpl*

antiquarian *n* antiquaire *mf*.
antiquated *adj* vieux; suranné.
antique *n* meuble *m* ancien.
antiquity *n* antiquité *f*.
antiseptic *adj* antiseptique.
antisocial *adj* antisocial.
antithesis *n* antithèse *f*.
antler *n* corne *f*.
anvil *n* enclume *f*.
anxiety *n* anxiété *f*; désir *m*.
anxious *adj* anxieux; **~ly** *adv* anxieusement.
any *adj pn* n'importe quel, n'importe quelle; un, une; tout; **~body** quelqu'un; n'importe qui; personne; **~how** de toute façon; de n'importe quelle manière; **~more** plus; **~place** n'importe où; nulle part; **~thing** quelque chose; n'importe quoi; rien.
apace *adv* rapidement.
apart *adv* séparément.
apartment *n* appartement *m*.
apartment house *n* immeuble *m*.
apathetic *adj* apathique.
apathy *n* apathie *f*.
ape *n* singe *m*; * *vt* singer.
aperture *n* ouverture *f*.
apex *n* sommet *m*; apex *m*.
aphorism *n* aphorisme *m*.
apiary *n* rucher *m*.
apiece *adv* chacun, chacune.
aplomb *n* aplomb *m*.
Apocalypse *n* Apocalypse *f*.
apocrypha *npl* apocryphes *mpl*.
apocryphal *adj* apocryphe.
apologetic *adj* d'excuse.
apologise *vt* excuser.
apologist *n* apologiste *mf*.
apology *n* apologie, défense *f*.
apoplexy *n* apoplexie *f*.
apostle *n* apôtre *m*.
apostolic *adj* apostolique.
apostrophe *n* apostrophe *f*.
apotheosis *n* apothéose *f*.
appall *vt* horrifier, atterrer.
appalling *adj* horrible.
apparatus *n* appareil *m*.
apparel *n* vêtements *mpl*.
apparent *adj* évident, apparent; **~ly** *adv* apparemment.
apparition *n* apparition, vision *f*.
appeal *vi* faire appel; * *n* (*law*) appel *m*.
appealing *adj* attrayant.
appear *vi* paraître.
appearance *n* apparence *f*.
appease *vt* apaiser.
appellant *n* (*law*) appelant *m*.
append *vt* annexer.
appendage *n* appendice *m*.
appendicitis *n* appendicite *f*.

appendix *n* appendice *m*.
appertain *vi* appartenir (à).
appetising *adj* appétissant.
appetite *n* appétit *m*.
applaud *vt vi* applaudir.
applause *n* applaudissements *mpl*.
apple *n* pomme *f*.
apple pie *n* tourte aux pommes *f*; **in ~ order** parfaitement en ordre.
apple tree *n* pommier *m*.
appliance *n* appareil *m*.
applicability *n* applicabilité *f*.
applicable *adj* applicable.
applicant *n* candidat *m* -e *f*.
application *n* application *f*; candidature *f*.
applied *adj* appliqué.
apply *vt* appliquer; * *vi* s'adresser.
appoint *vt* nommer.
appointee *n* personne nommée *f*.
appointment *n* rendez-vous *m*; nomination *f*.
apportion *vt* répartir.
apportionment *n* répartition *f*.
apposite *adj* approprié, juste.
apposition *n* apposition *f*.
appraisal *n* estimation *f*.
appraise *vt* évaluer.
appreciable *adj* appréciable, sensible.
appreciably *adv* sensiblement.
appreciate *vt* apprécier; être conscient de.
appreciation *n* appréciation *f*.
appreciative *adj* reconnaissant.
apprehend *vt* appréhender.
apprehension *n* appréhension *f*; arrestation *f*.
apprehensive *adj* appréhensif.
apprentice *n* apprenti *m*; * *vt* mettre en apprentissage.
apprenticeship *n* apprentissage *m*.
apprise *vt* informer.
approach *vi* (s')approcher; * *vt* (s')approcher de; * *n* approche *f*.
approachable *adj* accessible, approchable.
approbation *n* approbation *f*.
appropriate *vt* s'approprier; * *adj* approprié, adéquat.
approval *n* approbation *f*.
approve (of) *vt* approuver.
approximate *vi* s'approcher; * *adj* approximatif; **~ly** *adv* approximativement.
approximation *n* approximation *f*.
apricot *n* abricot *m*.
April *n* avril *m*.
apron *n* tablier *m*.
apse *n* abside *f*.
apt *adj* idéal; susceptible; **~ly** *adv* opportunément.
aptitude *n* aptitude *f*.

aqualung *n* scaphandre autonome *m*.
aquarium *n* aquarium *m*.
Aquarius *n* Verseau *m* (signe du zodiaque).
aquatic *adj* aquatique.
aqueduct *n* aqueduc *m*.
aquiline *adj* aquilin.
arabesque *n* arabesque *f*.
arable *adj* arable.
arbiter *n* arbitre *m* (de la mode).
arbitrariness *n* caractère arbitraire *m*.
arbitrary *adj* arbitraire.
arbitrate *vt* arbitrer.
arbitration *n* arbitrage *m*.
arbitrator *n* arbitre *m*.
arbour *n* tonnelle *f*.
arcade *n* galerie *f*.
arch *n* arc *m*; * *adj* malicieux.
archaic *adj* archaïque.
archangel *n* archange *m*.
archbishop *n* archevêque *m*.
archbishopric *n* archevêché *m*.
archeological *adj* archéologique.
archeology *n* archéologie *f*.
archer *n* archer *m*.
archery *n* tir à l'arc *m*.
architect *n* architecte *mf*.
architectural *adj* architectural.
architecture *n* architecture *f*.
archives *npl* archives *fpl*.
archivist *n* archiviste *mf*.
archly *adv* malicieusement.
archway *n* arcade, voûte *f*.
arctic *adj* arctique.
ardent *adj* ardent; **~ly** *adv* ardemment.
ardour *n* ardeur *f*.
arduous *adj* ardu, difficile.
area *n* région *f*; domaine *m*.
arena *n* arène *f*.
arguably *adv* peut-être, sans doute.
argue *vi* se disputer; * *vt* soutenir.
argument *n* argument *m*; dispute *f*.
argumentation *n* argumentation *f*.
argumentative *adj* raisonneur.
aria *n* (*mus*) aria *f*.
arid *adj* aride.
aridity *n* aridité *f*.
Aries *n* Bélier *m* (signe du zodiaque).
aright *adv* correctement; **to set ~** rectifier.
arise *vi* se lever; survenir.
aristocracy *n* aristocratie *f*.
aristocrat *n* aristocrate *mf*.
aristocratic *adj* aristocratique; **~ally** *adv* aristocratiquement.
arithmetic *n* arithmétique *f*.
arithmetical *adj* arithmétique; **~ly** *adv* arithmétiquement.

ark *n* arche *f*.

arm *n* bras *m*; arme *f*; * *vt* armer; * *vi* (s')armer.

armament *n* armement *m*.

armchair *n* fauteuil *m*.

armed *adj* armé.

armful *n* brassée *f*.

armhole *n* emmanchure *f*.

armistice *n* armistice *m*.

armour *n* armure *f*.

armoured car *n* voiture blindée *f*.

armoury *n* arsenal *m*.

armpit *n* aisselle *f*.

armrest *n* accoudoir *m*.

army *n* armée *f*.

aroma *n* arôme *m*.

aromatic *adj* aromatique.

around *prep* autour de; * *adv* autour.

arouse *vt* éveiller; exciter.

arraign *vt* traduire en justice.

arraignment *n* accusation *f*; procès criminel *m*.

arrange *vt* arranger, organiser.

arrangement *n* arrangement *m*.

arrant *adj* fieffé.

array *n* série *f*.

arrears *npl* arriéré *m*; retard *m*.

arrest *n* arrestation *f*; * *vt* arrêter.

arrival *n* arrivée *f*.

arrive *vi* arriver.

arrogance *n* arrogance *f*.

arrogant *adj* arrogant; ~**ly** *adv* avec arrogance.

arrogate *vt* s'arroger.

arrogation *n* usurpation *f*.

arrow *n* flèche *f*.

arsenal *n* (*mil*) arsenal *m*.

arsenic *n* arsenic *m*.

arson *n* incendie criminel *m*.

art *n* art *m*.

arterial *adj* artériel.

artery *n* artère *f*.

artesian well *n* puits artésien *m*.

artful *adj* malin, astucieux.

artfulness *n* astuce *f*; habileté *f*.

art gallery *n* musée d'art *m*.

arthritis *n* arthrite *f*.

artichoke *n* artichaut *m*.

article *n* article *m*.

articulate *vt* articuler.

articulated *adj* articulé.

articulation *n* articulation *f*.

artifice *n* artifice *m*.

artificial *adj* artificiel; ~**ly** *adv* artificiellement.

artificiality *n* caractère artificiel *m*.

artillery *n* artillerie *f*.

artisan *n* artisan *m*.

artist *n* artiste *mf*.

artistic *adj* artistique.

artistry *n* habileté *f*.

artless *adj* naturel, simple; ~**ly** *adv* naturellement, simplement.

artlessness *n* simplicité *f*, naturel *m*.

art school *n* école des beaux-arts *f*.

as *conj* comme; pendant que; aussi; ~ **for**, ~ **to** quant à.

asbestos *n* asbeste *m*, amiante *f*.

ascend *vi* monter.

ascendancy *n* ascendant *m*.

ascension *n* ascension *f*.

ascent *n* montée *f*.

ascertain *vt* établir.

ascetic *adj* ascétique; * *n* ascète *mf*.

ascribe *vt* attribuer.

ash *n* (*bot*) frêne *m*; cendre *f*.

ashamed *adj* honteux.

ashbin *n* poubelle *f*.

ashore *adv* à terre; **to go** ~ débarquer.

ashtray *n* cendrier *m*.

Ash Wednesday *n* mercredi des Cendres *m*.

aside *adv* de côté.

ask *vt* demander; ~ **after** demander des nouvelles de; ~ **for** demander; ~ **out** inviter à sortir.

askance *adv* avec méfiance.

askew *adv* de côté.

asleep *adj* endormi; **to fall** ~ s'endormir.

asparagus *n* asperge *f*.

aspect *n* aspect *m*.

aspen *n* (*bot*) tremble *m*.

aspersion *n* calomnie *f*.

asphalt *n* asphalte *m*.

asphyxia *n* (*med*) asphyxie *f*.

asphyxiate *vt* asphyxier.

asphyxiation *n* asphyxie *f*.

aspirant *n* aspirant *m* -e *f*.

aspirate *vt* aspirer; * *n* aspirée *f*.

aspiration *n* aspiration *f*.

aspire *vi* aspirer, désirer.

aspirin *n* aspirine *f*.

ass *n* âne *m*; **she** ~ ânesse *f*.

assail *vt* assaillir, attaquer.

assailant *n* assaillant, agresseur *m*.

assassin *n* assassin *m*.

assassinate *vt* assassiner.

assassination *n* assassinat *m*.

assault *n* assaut *m*; agression *f*; * *vt* agresser.

assemblage *n* assemblage *m*.

assemble *vt* assembler; * *vi* s'assembler.

assembly *n* assemblée *f*.

assembly line *n* chaîne de montage *f*.

assent *n* assentiment *m*; * *vi* donner son assentiment.

assert *vt* soutenir; affirmer.

assertion *n* assertion *f*.

assertive *adj* péremptoire.

assess *vt* évaluer.

assessment *n* évaluation *f*.

assessor *n* assesseur *m*.

assets *npl* biens *mpl*.

assiduous *adj* assidu; ~**ly** *adv* assidûment.

assign *vt* assigner.

assignation *n* rendez-vous *m*; (*law*) cession *f*.

assignment *n* (*law*) cession *f*; mission *f*.

assimilate *vt* assimiler.

assimilation *n* assimilation *f*.

assist *vt* assister, aider; secourir.

assistance *n* assistance, aide *f*; secours *m*.

assistant *n* aide *mf*, assistant *m* -e *f*.

associate *vt* associer; * *adj* associé; * *n* associé *m* -e *f*.

association *n* association *f*.

assonance *n* assonance *f*.

assorted *adj* assorti.

assortment *n* assortiment *m*.

assuage *vt* calmer, adoucir.

assume *vt* assumer; supposer.

assumption *n* supposition *f*; **Assumption** *n* Assomption *f*.

assurance *n* assurance *f*.

assure *vt* assurer.

assuredly *adv* assurément.

asterisk *n* astérisque *m*.

astern *adv* (*mar*) en poupe.

asthma *n* asthme *m*.

asthmatic *adj* asthmatique.

astonish *vt* surprendre, stupéfier.

astonishing *adj* stupéfiant; ~**ly** *adv* incroyablement.

astonishment *n* surprise, stupéfaction *f*.

astound *vt* ébahir.

astray *adv*: **to go** ~ s'égarer; **to lead** ~ détourner du droit chemin.

astride *adv* à califourchon.

astringent *adj* astringent.

astrologer *n* astrologue *mf*.

astrological *adj* astrologique.

astrology *n* astrologie *f*.

astronaut *n* astronaute *mf*.

astronomer *n* astronome *mf*.

astronomical *adj* astronomique.

astronomy *n* astronomie *f*.

astute *adj* malin.

asylum *n* asile, refuge *m*.

at *prep* à; en; ~ **once** tout de suite; ~ **all** du tout; ~ **all events** en tout cas; ~ **first** au début, d'abord; ~ **last** enfin.

atheism *n* athéisme *m*.

atheist *n* athée *mf*.

athlete *n* athlète *mf*.

athletic *adj* athlétique.

atlas *n* atlas *m*.

atmosphere *n* atmosphère *f*.

atmospheric *adj* atmosphérique.
atom *n* atome *m.*
atom bomb *n* bombe atomique *f.*
atomic *adj* atomique.
atone *vt* expier.
atonement *n* expiation *f.*
atop *adv* en haut.
atrocious *adj* atroce; ~**ly** *adv* atrocement.
atrocity *n* atrocité, énormité *f.*
atrophy *n* (*med*) atrophie *f.*
attach *vt* joindre.
attaché *n* attaché *m* -e *f.*
attachment *n* attachement *m.*
attack *vt* attaquer; * *n* attaque *f.*
attacker *n* attaquant *m* -e *f.*
attain *vt* atteindre, obtenir.
attainable *adj* accessible.
attempt *vt* essayer; * *n* essai *m*, tentative *f.*
attend *vt* servir; assister à; ~ **to** s'occuper de; * *vi* faire attention.
attendance *n* service *m*; assistance *f*; présence *f.*
attendant *n* serviteur *m.*
attention *n* attention *f*; soin *m.*
attentive *adj* attentif; ~**ly** *adv* attentivement.
attenuate *vt* atténuer.
attest *vt* attester.
attic *n* grenier *m.*
attire *n* atours *mpl.*
attitude *n* attitude *f.*
attorney *n* avocat *m.*
attract *vt* attirer.
attraction *n* attraction *f*; attrait *m.*
attractive *adj* attrayant.
attribute *vt* attribuer; * *n* attribut *m.*
attrition *n* usure *f.*
auburn *adj* auburn.
auction *n* vente aux enchères *f.*
auctioneer *n* commissaire-priseur *m.*
audacious *adj* audacieux, téméraire; ~**ly** *adv* audacieusement.
audacity *n* audace, témérité *f.*
audible *adj* audible; ~**ly** *adv* audiblement.

audience *n* audience *f*; auditoire *m.*
audit *n* audit *m*; * *vt* vérifier.
auditor *n* vérificateur(-trice) de comptes *m(f)*; auditeur *m* -trice *f.*
auditory *adj* auditif.
augment *vt vi* augmenter.
augmentation *n* augmentation *f.*
August *n* août *m.*
august *adj* auguste, majestueux.
aunt *n* tante *f.*
au pair *n* (jeune fille) au pair *f.*
aura *n* aura *f.*
auspices *npl* auspices *mpl.*
auspicious *adj* favorable, propice; ~**ly** *adv* favorablement.
austere *adj* austère, sévère; ~**ly** *adv* austèrement.
austerity *n* austérité *f.*
authentic *adj* authentique; ~**ally** *adv* authentiquement.
authenticate *vt* légaliser.
authenticity *n* authenticité *f.*
author *n* auteur *m.*
authoress *n* femme auteur *f.*
authorisation *n* autorisation *f.*
authorise *vt* autoriser.
authoritarian *adj* autoritaire.
authoritative *adj* autoritaire; ~**ly** *adv* autoritairement.
authority *n* autorité *f.*
authorship *n* paternité *f* (d'un livre).
auto *n* voiture *f.*
autocrat *n* autocrate *mf.*
autocratic *adj* autocratique.
autograph *n* autographe *m.*
automated *adj* automatisé.
automatic *adj* automatique.
automaton *n* automate *m.*
autonomy *n* autonomie *f.*
autopsy *n* autopsie *f.*
autumn *n* automne *m.*
autumnal *adj* automnal.
auxiliary *adj* auxiliaire.
avail *vt*: **to ~ oneself of** profiter de; * *n*: **to no ~** en vain.
available *adj* disponible.

avalanche *n* avalanche *f.*
avarice *n* avarice *f.*
avaricious *adj* avare.
avenge *vt* venger.
avenue *n* avenue *f.*
aver *vt* affirmer, déclarer.
average *vt* atteindre la moyenne de; * *n* moyenne *f*, moyen terme *m.*
aversion *n* aversion *f*, dégoût *m.*
avert *vt* détourner, écarter.
aviary *n* volière *f.*
avoid *vt* éviter; échapper à.
avoidable *adj* évitable.
await *vt* attendre.
awake *vt* réveiller; * *vi* se réveiller; * *adj* éveillé.
awakening *n* réveil *m.*
award *vt* attribuer; * *n* prix *m*; décision *f.*
aware *adj* conscient; au courant.
awareness *n* conscience *f.*
away *adv* absent; loin; ~! va-t-en!; allez-vous-en! **far and ~** de loin.
away game *n* match à l'extérieur *m.*
awe *n* peur, crainte *f.*
awe-inspiring, awesome *adj* terrifiant; imposant.
awful *adj* horrible, terrible; ~**ly** *adv* horriblement, terriblement.
awhile *adv* un moment.
awkward *adj* gauche, maladroit; délicat; ~**ly** *adv* maladroitement.
awkwardness *n* maladroitesse *f*; difficulté *f.*
awl *n* alêne *f.*
awning *n* (*mar*) taud *m.*
awry *adv* de travers.
axe *n* hache *f*; * *vt* licencier; supprimer.
axiom *n* axiome *m.*
axis *n* axe *m.*
axle *n* axe *m.*
ay(e) *excl* oui.

B

baa *n* bêlement *m*; * *vi* bêler.

babble *vi* bavarder, babiller; ~, babbling *n* bavardage, babillage *m*.

babbler *n* bavard *m*.

babe, baby *n* bébé, enfant en bas-âge *m*; nourrisson *m*.

baboon *n* babouin *m*.

baby carriage *n* voiture d'enfant *f*.

babyhood *n* petite enfance *f*.

babyish *adj* enfantin; puéril.

baby linen *n* layette *f*.

bachelor *n* célibataire *m*; (diplôme) licencié *m* -e *f*.

bachelorship *n* célibat *m*.

back *n* dos *m*; * *adv* en arrière, à l'arrière; a few years ~ il y a quelques années, quelques années en arrière; * *vt* soutenir, appuyer, renforcer.

backbite *vt* médire de, sur.

backbiter *n* détracteur *m* -trice *f*.

backbone *n* colonne vertébrale, épine dorsale *f*.

backdate *vt* antidater.

backdoor *n* porte de derrière *f*.

backer *n* partisan *m* -e *f*.

backgammon *n* (jeu de) jacquet *m*.

background *n* fond *m*.

backlash *n* réaction violente *f*.

backlog *n* accumulation de travail en retard *f*.

back number *n* vieux numéro (magazine, journal) *m*.

backpack *n* sac à dos *m*.

back payment *n* rappel de salaire *m*.

backside *n* derrière *m*.

back-up lights *npl* (*auto*) feux de marche arrière *mpl*.

backward *adj* rétrograde; retardé; lent; * *adv* en arrière.

bacon *n* lard *m*.

bad *adj* mauvais, de mauvaise qualité; méchant; malade; ~ly *adv* mal.

badge *n* plaque *f*, insigne *m*, badge *m*; symbole *m*; signe *m*.

badger *n* blaireau *m*; * *vt* harceler.

badminton *n* badminton *m*.

badness *n* mauvaise qualité *f*; méchanceté *f*.

baffle *vt* déconcerter, confondre.

bag *n* sac *m*; valise *f*.

baggage *n* bagages *mpl*; équipement *m*.

bagpipe *n* cornemuse *f*.

bail *n* mise en liberté sous caution, caution *f*; * *vt* mettre en liberté sous caution; mettre en dépôt.

bailiff *n* huissier *m*; régisseur *m*.

bait *vt* tourmenter; appâter; * *n* appât *m*; amorce *f*.

baize *n* serge *f*.

bake *vt* faire cuire au four.

baker *n* boulanger *m* -ère *f*; ~'s dozen treize à la douzaine.

bakery *n* boulangerie *f*.

baking *n* cuisson *f*; fournée *f*.

baking powder *n* levure *f*.

balance *n* balance *f*; équilibre *m*; solde d'un compte *m*; to lose one's ~ perdre l'équilibre; * *vt* peser; peser le pour et le contre; solder; équilibrer.

balance sheet *n* bilan *m*.

balcony *n* balcon *m*.

bald *adj* chauve.

baldness *n* calvitie *f*.

bale *n* balle *f*; * *vt* emballer; écoper.

baleful *adj* sinistre, funeste, maléfique; ~ly *adv* sinistrement.

ball *n* balle *f*; boule *f*; ballon *m*.

ballad *n* ballade *f*.

ballast *n* lest *m*; * *vt* lester.

ballerina *n* ballerine *f*.

ballet *n* ballet *m*.

ballistic *adj* balistique.

balloon *n* montgolfière *f*, aérostat *m*.

ballot *n* scrutin *m*; vote *m*; * *vi* voter au scrutin.

ballpoint (pen) *n* stylo à bille *m*.

ballroom *n* salle de bal *f*.

balm, balsam *n* baume *m*.

balmy *adj* balsamique, parfumé; doux.

balustrade *n* balustrade *f*.

bamboo *n* bambou *m*.

bamboozle *vt* (*fam*) embobiner.

ban *n* interdiction *f*; * *vt* interdire.

banal *adj* banal.

banana *n* banane *f*.

band *n* bande *f*; reliure *f*; courroie de transmission *f*; orchestre *m*.

bandage *n* bande *f*, bandage *m*; * *vt* bander.

bandaid *n* pansement *m* adhésif.

bandit *n* bandit *m*.

bandstand *n* kiosque à musique *m*.

bandy *vt* avoir des mots.

bandy-legged *adj* aux jambes arquées.

bang *n* coup violent, claquement *m*, détonation *f*; * *vt* frapper violemment; claquer.

bangle *n* bracelet *m*.

bangs *npl* (US) frange (courte et droite) *f*.

banish *vt* bannir, exiler, chasser, expatrier.

banishment *n* exil, bannissement *m*.

banister(s) *n(pl)* rampe d'escalier *f*.

banjo *n* banjo *m*.

bank *n* rive *f*; remblai *m*; banque *f*; banc *m*; digue *f*; * *vt* déposer de l'argent à la banque; ~ on compter sur.

bank account *n* compte en banque *m*.

bank card *n* carte bancaire *f*.

banker *n* banquier *m* -ière *f*.

banking *n* opérations bancaires *fpl*.

banknote *n* billet de banque *m*.

bankrupt *adj* failli; * *n* failli *m*.

bankruptcy *n* banqueroute, faillite *f*.

bank statement *n* relevé de compte *m*.

banner *n* bannière *f*; étendard *m*.

banquet *n* banquet *m*.

baptise *vt* baptiser.

baptism *n* baptême *m*.

baptismal *adj* de baptême, baptismal.

baptistery *n* baptistère *m*.

bar *n* bar *m*; barre *f*; obstacle *m*; (law) barreau *m*; * *vt* empêcher; interdire; exclure.

barbarian *n* barbare *mf*; * *adj* barbare, cruel.

barbaric *adj* barbare.

barbarism *n* (*gr*) barbarisme *m*; barbarie *f*.

barbarity *n* barbarie, atrocité *f*.

barbarous *adj* barbare, cruel.

barbecue *n* barbecue *m*.

barber *n* coiffeur (pour hommes) *m*.

bar code *n* code barres *m*.

bard *n* barde *m*; poète *m*.

bare *adj* nu, dépouillé; simple; pur; * *vt* dénuder, découvrir.

barefaced *adj* éhonté, impudent.

barefoot(ed) *adj* aux pieds nus.

bareheaded *adj* nu-tête.

barelegged *adj* aux jambes nues.

barely *adv* à peine, tout juste.

bareness *n* nudité *f*.

bargain *n* affaire *f*; contrat, marché *m*; occasion *f*; * *vi* conclure un marché; négocier; ~ **for** s'attendre à.

barge *n* péniche *f*.

baritone *n* (*mus*) baryton *m*.

bark *n* écorce *f*; aboiement *m*; * *vi* aboyer.

barley *n* orge *m*.

barmaid *n* serveuse *f*.

barman *n* barman *m*.

barn *n* grange *f*; étable *f*.

barnacle *n* anatife *m*, bernacle *f*.

barometer *n* baromètre *m*.

baron *n* baron *m*.

baroness *n* baronne *f*.

baronial *adj* de baron.

barracks *npl* caserne *f*.

barrage *n* barrage *m*; (*fig*) torrent *m*.

barrel *n* tonneau, fût *m*; canon de fusil *m*.

barrelled *adj* (firearms) à canons.

barrel organ *n* orgue de Barbarie *m*.

barren *adj* stérile, infertile, improductif.

barricade *n* barricade *f*; barrière *f*; * *vt* barricader, barrer.

barrier *n* barrière *f*; obstacle *m*.

barring *adv* excepté, sauf.

barrow *n* brouette *f*.

bartender *n* barman *m*.

barter *vi* faire du troc; * *vt* troquer, échanger.

base *n* base *f*; partie inférieure *f*; pied *m*; point de départ *m*; * *vt* fonder sur; * *adj* vil, abject.

baseball *n* baseball *m*.

baseless *adj* sans fondement, injustifié.

basement *n* sous-sol *m*.

baseness *n* bassesse, vilenie *f*.

bash *vt* frapper.

bashful *adj* timide, modeste; ~ly *adv* timidement.

basic *adj* fondamental, de base; ~ally *adv* fondamentalement.

basilisk *n* (*zool*) basilic *m*.

basin *n* cuvette *f*; lavabo *m*.

basis *n* base *f*; fondement *m*.

bask *vi* se prélasser.

basket *n* panier *m*, corbeille *f*.

basketball *n* basket-ball *m*.

bass *n* (*mus*) contrebasse *f*.

bassoon *n* basson *m*.

bass viol *n* viole de gambe *f*.

bass voice *n* voix de basse *f*.

bastard *n*, *adj* bâtard *m*.

bastardy *n* bâtardise *f*.

baste *vt* arroser la viande de son jus; bâtir.

basting *n* bâti *m*; jus (de viande) *m*; rossée *f*.

bastion *n* (*mil*) bastion *m*.

bat *n* chauve-souris *f*.

batch *n* fournée *f*.

bath *n* bain *m*.

bathe *vt* (*vi*) (se) baigner.

bathing suit *n* maillot de bain *m*.

bathos *n* platitudes (dans un texte littéraire) *fpl*.

bathroom *n* salle de bain *f*.

baths *npl* piscine *f*.

bathtub *n* baignoire *f*.

baton *n* matraque *f*.

battalion *n* (*mil*) bataillon *m*.

batter *vt* battre; frapper, martyriser; * *n* pâte à frire *f*.

battering ram *n* (*mil*) bélier *m*.

battery *n* pile, batterie *f*.

battle *n* bataille *f*; combat *m*; * *vi* se battre, combattre.

battle array *n* ordre de bataille *m*.

battlefield *n* champ de bataille *m*.

battlement *n* remparts *mpl*.

battleship *n* cuirassé *m*.

bawdy *adj* paillard.

bawl *vi* brailler, (*fam*) gueuler.

bay *n* baie *f*; laurier *m*; * *vi* aboyer, hurler; * *adj* bai.

bayonet *n* baïonnette *f*.

bay window *n* fenêtre en saillie *f*.

bazaar *n* bazar *m*.

be *vi* être.

beach *n* plage *f*.

beacon *n* phare, signal lumineux *m*.

bead *n* perle *f*; ~**s** *npl* chapelet *m*.

beagle *n* beagle *m*.

beak *n* bec *m*.

beaker *n* gobelet *m*.

beam *n* rayon *m*; poutre *f*; * *vi* rayonner, resplendir.

bean *n* haricot *m*; **French ~** haricot *m* vert.

beansprouts *npl* germes de soja *mpl*.

bear *vt* porter, supporter, produire; * *vi* se diriger.

bear *n* ours *m*; **she ~** ourse *f*.

bearable *adj* supportable.

beard *n* barbe *f*.

bearded *adj* barbu.

bearer *n* porteur *m* -euse *f*; arbre fructifère *m*.

bearing *n* relation *f*; maintien, port *m*.

beast *n* bête *f*; brute *f*; ~ **of burden** bête de somme *f*.

beastliness *n* bestialité, brutalité *f*.

beastly *adj* bestial, brutal; abominable; * *adv* terriblement.

beat *vt* battre; * *vi* battre, palpiter; * *n* battement *m*; pulsation *f*.

beatific *adj* béatifique; béat.

beatify *vt* béatifier, sanctifier.

beating *n* correction, raclée *f*; battement *m*.

beatitude *n* béatitude *f*.

beautiful *adj* beau, belle, magnifique; ~ly *adv* à la perfection, merveilleusement.

beautify *vt* embellir; décorer.

beauty *n* beauté *f*; ~ **salon** *n* institut de beauté *m*; ~ **spot** *n* site touristique *m*.

beaver *n* castor *m*.

because *conj* parce que; * *prép*: ~ **of** en raison de.

beckon *vi* faire signe.

become *vt* convenir, aller à; * *vi* devenir, se faire.

becoming *adj* convenable, seyant.

bed *n* lit *m*.

bedclothes *npl* couvertures et draps *mpl*.

bedding *n* literie *f*.

bedecked *adj* orné.

bedlam *n* maison *f* de fous; chahut *m*.

bed-post *n* colonne de lit *f*.

bedridden *adj* cloué au lit; grabataire.

bedroom *n* chambre *f*.

bedspread *n* dessus-de-lit *m invar*.

bedtime *n* heure d'aller au lit *f*.

bee *n* abeille *f*.

beech *n* hêtre *m*.

beef *n* bœuf (viande) *m*.

beefburger *n* hamburger *m*.

beefsteak *n* bifteck *m*.

beehive *n* ruche *f*.

beeline *n* ligne droite *f*.

beer *n* bière *f*.

beeswax *n* cire *f*.

beet *n* betterave *f*.

beetle *n* scarabée *m*.

befall *vi* arriver, survenir; * *vt* arriver à.

befit *vt* convenir à.

before *adv*, *prep* avant; devant; * *conj* avant de, avant que.

beforehand *adv* à l'avance, au préalable.

befriend *vt* traiter en ami; aider.

beg *vt* mendier; solliciter; supplier; * *vi* demander la charité.

beget *vt* engendrer.

beggar *n* mendiant *m* -e *f*.

begin *vt vi* commencer.

beginner *n* débutant *m* -e *f*; novice *mf*.

beginning *n* commencement, début *m*, origine *f*.

begrudge *vt* donner à contrecœur; envier.

behalf *n* faveur *f*, intérêt *m*; nom *m*, part *f*.

behave *vi* se comporter, se conduire.

behaviour *n* conduite *f*; comportement *m*.

behead *vt* décapiter.

behind *prep* derrière; * *adv* derrière, par-derrière, en arrière.

behold *vt* voir; contempler; observer.

behove *vi* (*impers*) incomber à.

beige *adj* beige.

being *n* existence *f*; être *m*.

belated *adj* tardif.

belch *vi* éructer; * *vt* vomir; * *n* éructation *f*, rot *m*.

belfry *n* beffroi, clocher *m*.

belie *vt* démentir, tromper.

belief *n* foi, croyance *f*; conviction, opinion *f*, credo *m*.

believable *adj* croyable.

believe *vt* croire; * *vi* penser, croire.

believer *n* croyant *m* -e *f*; adepte *mf*, partisan *m* -e *f*.

belittle *vt* rabaisser.

bell *n* cloche *f*.

bellicose *adj* belliqueux.

belligerent *adj* belligérant.

bellow *vi* beugler, mugir; hurler; * *n* beuglement, mugissement *m*.

bellows *npl* soufflet *m*.

belly *n* ventre *m*.

bellyful *n* ventrée *f*; ras-le-bol *m*.

belong *vi* appartenir à.

belongings *npl* affaires *fpl*.

beloved *adj* chéri, bien-aimé.

below *adv* en dessous, en bas; * *prep* sous, au-dessous de, en dessous.

belt *n* ceinture *f*.

beltway *n* (US) périphérique *m*.

bemoan *vt* déplorer; pleurer.

bemused *adj* déconcerté.

bench *n* banc *m*.

bend *vt* courber, plier; incliner; * *vi* se courber, s'incliner; * *n* courbe *f*.

beneath *adv* au-dessous; * *prep* sous, au-dessous de.

benediction *n* bénédiction *f*.

benefactor *n* bienfaiteur *m* -trice *f*.

benefice *n* bénéfice *m*; bénéfice ecclésiastique *m*.

beneficent *adj* bienfaisant.

beneficial *adj* profitable, salutaire, utile.

beneficiary *n* bénéficiaire *mf*.

benefit *n* intérêt, avantage *m*; profit *m*; bienfait *m*; * *vt* profiter à; * *vi* bénéficier.

benefit night *n* soirée de bienfaisance *f*.

benevolence *n* bienveillance *f*; générosité *f*.

benevolent *adj* bienveillant; de bienfaisance.

benign *adj* bienveillant, doux, affable; bénin.

bent *n* penchant *m*.

benzine *n* (*chem*) benzine *f*.

bequeath *vt* léguer à.

bequest *n* legs *m*.

bereave *vt* priver.

bereavement *n* perte *f*; deuil *m*.

beret *n* béret *m*.

berry *n* baie *f*.

berserk *adj* fou furieux.

berth *n* (*mar*) couchette *f*.

beseech *vt* supplier, implorer, conjurer.

beset *vt* assaillir.

beside(s) *prep* à côté de; excepté; * *adv* de plus, en outre.

besiege *vt* assiéger, assaillir.

best *adj* le meilleur, la meilleure; * *adv* le mieux; * *n* le meilleur, le mieux *m*.

bestial *adj* bestial, brutal; ~**ly** *adv* bestialement.

bestiality *n* bestialité, brutalité *f*.

bestow *vt* accorder, conférer; consacrer.

bestseller *n* best-seller *m*.

bet *n* pari *m*; * *vt* parier.

betray *vt* trahir.

betrayal *n* trahison *f*.

betroth *vt* promettre en mariage.

betrothal *n* fiançailles *fpl*.

better *adj adv* meilleur, mieux; **so much the** ~ tant mieux; * *vt* améliorer.

betting *n* pari *m*.

between *prep* entre;* *adv* au milieu.

bevel *n* biseau *m*.

beverage *n* boisson *f*.

bevy *n* bande *f*, groupe *m*.

beware *vi* prendre garde.

bewilder *vt* déconcerter, dérouter.

bewilderment *n* perplexité *f*.

bewitch *vt* ensorceler, enchanter.

beyond *prep* au-delà de; au-dessus de; plus de; sauf; * *adv* au-delà, plus loin.

bias *n* préjugé *m*; tendance, inclination *f*.

bib *n* bavoir *m*.

Bible *n* Bible *f*.

biblical *adj* biblique.

bibliography *n* bibliographie *f*.

bicarbonate of soda *n* bicarbonate de soude *m*.

bicker *vi* se chamailler.

bicycle *n* bicyclette *f*.

bid *vt* ordonner, commander; offrir; * *n* offre, tentative *f*.

bidding *n* ordre *m*; enchère, offre *f*.

benevolent *adj* bienveillant; de bienfaisance.

biennial *adj* biennal, bisannuel.

bifocals *npl* verres à double foyer *mpl*.

bifurcated *adj* divisé en deux branches.

big *adj* grand, gros; important.

bigamist *n* bigame *mf*.

bigamy *n* bigamie *f*.

Big Dipper *n* Grande Ourse *f*.

bigheaded *adj* frimeur.

bigness *n* grandeur, grosseur *f*.

bigot *n* fanatique *mf*.

bigoted *adj* fanatique.

bike *n* vélo *m*.

bikini *n* bikini *m*.

bilberry *n* airelle *f*.

bile *n* bile *f*.

bilingual *adj* bilingue.

bilious *adj* bilieux.

bill *n* bec (d'oiseau) *m*; addition *f*; billet *m*.

billboard *n* panneau d'affichage *m*.

billet *n* logement *m*.

billfold *n* (US) portefeuille *m*.

billiards *npl* billard *m*.

billiard table *n* table de billard *f*.

billion *n* milliard *m*.

billy *n* (US) matraque *f*.

bin *n* coffre *m*.

bind *vt* attacher; lier; entourer; relier.

binder *n* relieur *m* -euse *f*.

binding *n* reliure *f*, extra-fort *m*.

binge *n* beuverie, bringue *f*.

bingo *n* loto *m*.

binoculars *npl* jumelles *fpl*.

biochemistry *n* biochimie *f*.

biographer *n* biographe *mf*.

biographical *adj* biographique.

biography *n* biographie *f*.

biological *adj* biologique.

biology *n* biologie *f*.

biped *n* bipède *m*.

birch *n* bouleau *m*.

bird *n* oiseau *m*.

bird's-eye view *n* vue d'ensemble *f*.

bird-watcher *n* ornithologue *mf*.

birth *n* naissance *f*.

birth certificate *n* extrait de naissance *m*.

birth control *n* limitation des naissances *f*.

birthday *n* anniversaire *m*.

birthplace *n* lieu de naissance *m*.

birthright *n* droit de naissance *m*.

biscuit *n* biscuit *m*.

bisect *vt* couper en deux.

bishop *n* évêque *m*.

bison *n* bison *m*.

bit *n* morceau *m*; peu *m*.

bitch *n* chienne *f*; (*fig*) plainte *f*.

bite *vt* mordre; ~ **the dust** (*fam*) mordre la poussière; * *n* morsure *f*.

bitter *adj* amer, âpre; cuisant, acerbe; glacial; ~**ly** *adv* amèrement; avec amertume; âprement.

bitterness *n* amertume *f*; rancœur *f*.

bitumen *n* bitume *m*.

bizarre *adj* étrange, bizarre.

blab *vi* jacasser; lâcher le morceau.

black *adj* noir, obscur; * *n* noir *m*.

blackberry *n* mûre *f*.

blackbird *n* merle *m*.

blackboard *n* tableau (noir) *m*.

blacken *vt* noircir, ternir.

black ice *n* verglas *m*.

blackjack *n* vingt-et-un *m*.

blackleg *n* jaune *m* (pendant une grève).

blacklist *n* liste noire *f*.

blackmail *n* chantage *m*; * *vt* faire chanter.

black market *n* marché noir *m*.

blackness *n* couleur noire *f*; obscurité *f*; noirceur *f*.

black pudding *n* boudin *m*.

black sheep *n* brebis galeuse *f*.

blacksmith *n* forgeron *m*.

blackthorn *n* épine noire *f*.

bladder *n* vessie *f*.

blade *n* lame *f*.

blame *vt* blâmer; * *n* faute *f*.

blameless *adj* irréprochable; ~**ly** *adv* irréprochablement.

blanch *vt* blanchir.

bland *adj* affable, suave; doux; apaisant.

blank *adj* blanc; vide, déconcerté; * *n* blanc *m*.

blank cheque *n* chèque en blanc *m*.

blanket *n* couverture *f*.

blare *vi* retentir.

blase *adj* blasé.

blaspheme *vt* blasphémer.

blasphemous *adj* blasphématoire.

blasphemy *n* blasphème *m*.

blast *n* souffle d'air *m*; explosion *f*; * *vt* faire sauter.

blast-off *n* lancement *m*, mise à feu *f*.

blatant *adj* flagrant.

blaze *n* flamme *f*; * *vi* flamber; resplendir.

bleach *vt* blanchir; décolorer; * *vi* blanchir; * *n* eau de Javel *f*.

bleached *adj* blanchi; décoloré.

bleachers *npl* gradins *mpl*.

bleak *adj* morne, lugubre, glacial, désolé.

bleakness *n* froid *m*; austérité *f*.

bleary(-eyed) *adj* larmoyant.

bleat *n* bêlement *m*; * *vi* bêler.

bleed *vt vi* saigner.

bleeding *n* saignement *m*.

bleeper *n* bip *m*.

blemish *n* gâter; ternir; * *n* tache *f*; infamie *f*.

blend *vt* mélanger.

bless *vt* bénir.

blessing *n* bénédiction *f*; bienfait *m*.

blight *vt* détruire.

blind *adj* aveugle; ~ **alley** *n* impasse *f*; * *vt* aveugler; éblouir; * *n* aveugle *mf*; **(Venetian)** ~ store vénitien *m*.

blinders *npl* (US) œillères *fpl*.

blindfold *vt* bander les yeux de; ~ed *adj* les yeux bandés.

blindly *adv* à l'aveuglette, aveuglément.

blindness *n* cécité *f*.

blind side *n* côté faible de quelqu'un *m*.

blind spot *n* angle mort *m*.

blink *vi* clignoter.

blinkers *npl* clignotants *mpl*.

bliss *n* bonheur extrême *m*; félicité *f*.

blissful *adj* heureux; béat, bienheureux; ~**ly** *adv* heureusement.

blissfulness *n* bonheur extrême *m*, félicité *f*.

blister *n* ampoule *f*, cloque *f*; * *vi* se couvrir de cloques.

blitz *n* bombardement aérien *m*.

blizzard *n* tempête de neige *f*.

bloated *adj* gonflé, boursouflé, bouffi.

blob *n* goutte, tache *f*.

bloc *n* bloc *m*.

block *n* bloc *m*; encombrement, blocage *m*; pâté de maisons *m*; ~ **(up)** *vt* bloquer.

blockade *n* blocus *m*; * *vt* faire le blocus, bloquer.

blockage *n* obstruction *f*.

blockbuster *n* grand succès *m*.

blockhead *n* lourdaud, sot, crétin *m*.

blond *adj* blond; * *n* blond *m* -e *f*.

blood *n* sang *m*.

blood donor *n* donneur(-euse) de sang *m(f)*.

blood group *n* groupe sanguin *m*.

bloodhound *n* limier *m*.

bloodily *adv* cruellement.

bloodiness *n* (*fig*) cruauté *f*.

bloodless *adj* exangue, anémié; sans effusion de sang.

blood poisoning *n* empoisonnement du sang *m*.

blood pressure *n* pression artérielle *f*.

bloodshed *n* effusion de sang *f*; carnage *m*.

bloodshot *adj* injecté de sang.

bloodstream *n* système sanguin *m*.

bloodsucker *n* sangsue *f*; (*fig*) vampire *m*.

blood test *n* analyse de sang *f*.

bloodthirsty *adj* sanguinaire.

blood transfusion *n* transfusion sanguine *f*.

blood vessel *n* veine *f*; vaisseau sanguin *m*.

bloody *adj* sanglant, ensanglanté; cruel; ~ **minded** *adj* pas commode, buté.

bloom *n* fleur *f*; (also *fig*); * *vi* éclore, fleurir.

blossom *n* fleur *f*.

blot *vt* tacher; sécher; effacer; * *n* tache *f*.

blotchy *adj* marbré; couvert de taches.

blotting pad *n* buvard *m*.

blotting paper *n* papier buvard *m*.

blouse *n* chemisier *m*.

blow *vi* souffler; sonner; * *vt* souffler; faire voler; jouer de; ~ **up** exploser; * *n* coup *m*.

blowout *n* éclatement *m*.

blowpipe *n* sarbacane *f*.

blubber *n* blanc de baleine *m*; * *vi* pleurnicher.

bludgeon *n* gourdin *m*; matraque *f*.

blue *adj* bleu.

bluebell *n* campanule *f*.

bluebottle *n* (*bot*) bleuet *m*; mouche bleue *f*.

blueness *n* bleu *m*.

blueprint *n* (*fig*) projet *m*.

bluff *n* esbrouffe *f*; * *vt* faire de l'esbrouffe.

bluish *adj* bleuâtre.

blunder *n* gaffe *f*; * *vi* faire une gaffe.

blunt *adj* émoussé, obtus; direct; * *vt* émousser.

bluntly *adv* carrément; sans ménagements.

bluntness *n* brusquerie, rudesse *f*.

blur *n* image *f* floue; * *vt* brouiller.

blurt out *vt* laisser échapper.

blush *n* rougeur *f*; fard à joues *m*; * *vi* rougir.

blustery *adj* de tempête, violent.

boa *n* boa *m* (serpent).

boar *n* verrat *m*; **wild** ~ sanglier *m*.

board *n* planche *f*; table *f*; conseil *m*; * *vt* monter à bord de.

boarder *n* pensionnaire *mf*.

boarding card *n* carte d'embarquement *f.*

boarding house *n* internat *m;* pension (de famille) *f.*

boarding school *n* pensionnat *m.*

boast *vi* se vanter; * *n* vantardise *f;* rodomontade *f.*

boastful *adj* vantard.

boat *n* bateau *m;* canot *m;* barque *f.*

boating *n* canotage *m;* promenade en bateau *f.*

bobsleigh *n* bobsleigh *m.*

bode *vt* présager, augurer.

bodice *n* corsage *m.*

bodily *adj adv* physique(ment).

body *n* corps *m;* cadavre *m;* **any ~** n'importe qui; **every ~** tout le monde.

body-building *n* culturisme *m.*

bodyguard *n* garde du corps *m.*

bodywork *n* (*auto*) carrosserie *f.*

bog *n* marécage *m.*

boggy *adj* marécageux.

bogus *adj* faux.

boil *vi* bouillir; * *vt* faire bouillir; * *n* furoncle *m;* ébullition *f.*

boiled egg *n* œuf à la coque *m.*

boiled potatoes *npl* pommes de terre à l'eau *fpl.*

boiler *n* casserole *f;* chaudière *f.*

boiling point *n* point d'ébullition *m.*

boisterous *adj* bruyant; turbulent; tumultueux; **~ly** *adv* bruyamment, tumultueusement.

bold *adj* audacieux, téméraire, osé, hardi; **~ly** *adv* audacieusement, hardiment.

boldness *n* intrépidité *f;* audace *f;* effronterie *f.*

bolster *n* traversin *m;* * *vt* soutenir.

bolt *n* verrou *m;* * *vt* verrouiller, fermer au verrou.

bomb *n* bombe *f;* **~ disposal** déminage *m.*

bombard *vt* (*phys*) bombarder.

bombardier *n* bombardier *m.*

bombardment *n* bombardement *m.*

bombshell *n* (*fig*) bombe *f.*

bond *n* lien *m;* attache *f;* engagement *m;* obligation *f.*

bondage *n* esclavage, asservissement *m.*

bond holder *n* obligataire *mf.*

bone *n* os *m;* * *vt* désosser.

boneless *adj* désossé, sans os.

bonfire *n* feu (de joie) *m.*

bonnet *n* bonnet *m.*

bonny *adj* joli.

bonus *n* prime *f.*

bony *adj* osseux.

boo *vt* huer.

booby trap *n* mine *f.*

book *n* livre *m;* **to bring to ~** *vt* obliger à rendre des comptes.

bookbinder *n* relieur(-euse) de livres *m(f).*

bookcase *n* bibliothèque *f.*

bookkeeper *n* comptable *mf.*

bookkeeping *n* comptabilité *f.*

bookmaking *n* prise des paris *f.*

bookmarker *n* signet *m.*

bookseller *n* libraire *mf.*

bookstore *n* librairie *f.*

bookworm *n* rat de bibliothèque *m.*

boom *n* grondement *m;* essor *m;* * *vi* gronder.

boon *n* bienfait *m,* aubaine *f;* faveur *f.*

boor *n* rustre *m;* brute *f.*

boorish *adj* rustre, rustique.

boost *n* stimulation *f;* * *vt* stimuler.

booster *n* propulseur *m.*

boot *n* botte *f;* coffre *m;* **to ~** *adv* de plus, de surcroît.

booth *n* cabine *f;* baraque *f.*

booty *n* butin *m.*

booze *vi* se saôuler; * *n* alcool *m.*

border *n* bord *m;* bordure *f;* lisière *f;* frontière *f;* * *vt* border, avoisiner.

borderline *n* limite *f.*

bore *vt* forer, percer; ennuyer; * *n* perceuse *f;* calibre *m;* raseur *m.*

boredom *n* ennui *m.*

boring *adj* ennuyeux.

born *adj* né; originaire.

borrow *vt* emprunter.

borrower *n* emprunteur *m* -euse *f.*

bosom *n* sein *m,* poitrine *f.*

bosom friend *n* ami(e) intime *m(f).*

boss *n* chef *m;* patron(ne) *m(f).*

botanic(al) *adj* botanique.

botanist *n* botaniste *mf.*

botany *n* botanique *f.*

botch *vt* cochonner.

both *pn* tou(te)s les deux, l'un(e) et l'autre; * *adj* les deux; * *conj* à la fois; autant que.

bother *vt* ennuyer, déranger; * *n* ennui, problème *m.*

bottle *n* bouteille *f;* * *vt* mettre en bouteille.

bottleneck *n* embouteillage *m;* goulot *m.*

bottle-opener *n* ouvre-bouteille *m invar.*

bottom *n* fond *m;* fondement *m;* * *adj* du bas; dernier.

bottomless *adj* sans fond, insondable; inépuisable.

bough *n* branche *f;* rameau *m.*

boulder *n* gros galet *m.*

bounce *vi* rebondir; bondir, faire des bonds; * *n* bond, rebond *m.*

bound *n* limite *f;* saut *m;* répercussion *f;* * *vi* bondir, sauter; * *adj* à destination de.

boundary *n* limite *f;* frontière *f.*

boundless *adj* illimité, infini.

bounteous, bountiful *adj* abondant; prodigue, généreux; bienfaisant.

bounty *n* libéralité, générosité *f.*

bouquet *n* bouquet *m.*

bourgeois *adj* bourgeois.

bout *n* attaque *f;* accès *m;* combat *m.*

bovine *adj* bovin.

bow *vt* incliner, baisser; * *vi* se courber; faire une révérence; * *n* salut *m,* révérence *f.*

bow *n* arc *m;* archet *m;* nœud *m.*

bowels *npl* intestins *mpl;* entrailles *fpl.*

bowl *n* bol, saladier *m;* boule *f;* * *vi* jouer aux boules.

bowling *n* boules *fpl.*

bowling alley *n* bowling *m.*

bowling green *n* terrain de boules *m.*

bowstring *n* corde (d'arc) *f.*

bow tie *n* nœud papillon *m.*

box *n* boîte, caisse *f;* loge *f;* **~ on the ear** gifle *f;* * *vt* mettre en boîte; * *vi* boxer.

boxer *n* boxeur *m.*

boxing *n* boxe *f.*

boxing gloves *npl* gants de boxe *mpl.*

boxing ring *n* ring *m.*

box office *n* guichet *m.*

box-seat *n* place à côté du siège du cocher *f.*

boy *n* garçon *m.*

boycott *vt* boycotter; * *n* boycottage *m.*

boyfriend *n* petit ami *m.*

boyish *adj* d'enfant, puéril; de garçon.

bra *n* soutien-gorge *m.*

brace *n* attache *f;* bretelle *f;* appareil dentaire *m.*

bracelet *n* bracelet *m*

bracken *n* (*bot*) fougère *f.*

bracket *n* tranche *f;* parenthèse *f;* crochet *m;* * **~ with** *vt* réunir par une accolade; mettre ensemble.

bracing *adj* vivifiant, tonifiant.

brag *n* fanfaronnade *f;* * *vi* se vanter, fanfaronner.

braid *n* tresse *f;* * *vt* tresser.

brain *n* cerveau *m;* tête *f;* * *vt* assommer, défoncer le crâne à.

brainchild *n* invention personnelle *f.*

brainless *adj* stupide.

brainwash *vt* faire un lavage de cerveau à.

brainwave *n* idée lumineuse *f*.

brainy *adj* intelligent.

brake *n* frein *m*; * *vi* freiner.

brake fluid *n* liquide de frein *m*.

brake light *n* feu de stop *m*.

bramble *n* ronce *f*.

bran *n* son *m*.

branch *n* branche *f*; ramification *f*; * *vi* se ramifier.

branch line *n* (*rail*) ligne d'embranchement *f*.

brand *n* marque *f*; marque au fer *f*; * *vt* marquer au fer.

brandish *vt* brandir.

brand-new *adj* flambant-neuf.

brandy *n* cognac *m*.

brash *adj* grossier; impertinent.

brass *n* cuivre *m*.

brassiere *n* soutien-gorge *m*.

brat *n* môme, gosse *mf*.

bravado *n* bravade *f*.

brave *adj* courageux, brave, vaillant; * *vt* braver; * *n* brave *m*; ~**ly** *adv* bravement, courageusement.

bravery *n* bravoure *f*; courage *m*; magnificence *f*.

brawl *n* bagarre, rixe *f*; * *vi* se bagarrer.

brawn *n* muscle *m*; fromage de tête *m*.

bray *vi* braire; * *n* braiment *m*.

braze *vt* souder au laiton.

brazen *adj* de cuivre; impudent, effronté; * *vi* crâner.

brazier *n* brasero *m*.

breach *n* rupture *f*; brèche *f*; violation *f*.

bread *n* pain *m*; (*also fig*); **brown ~** pain bis *m*.

breadbox *n* panière *f*.

breadcrumbs *npl* chapelure *f*.

breadth *n* largeur *f*.

breadwinner *n* soutien de famille *m*.

break *vt* casser; briser; violer; interrompre; * *vi* se casser; ~ **into** entrer par effraction; ~ **out** s'échapper; * *n* cassure, rupture *f*; interruption *f*; ~ **of day** point du jour *m*, aube *f*.

breakage *n* casse *f*.

breakdown *n* panne *f*; dépression nerveuse *f*.

breakfast *n* petit déjeuner *m*; * *vi* déjeuner.

breaking *n* bris *m*; violation *f*; fracture *f*.

breakthrough *n* percée, innovation *f*.

breakwater *n* digue *f*.

breast *n* poitrine *f*, sein *m*; cœur *m*.

breastbone *n* sternum *m*.

breastplate *n* pectoral *m*; plastron *m*.

breaststroke *n* brasse *f*.

breath *n* haleine *f*; respiration *f*; souffle *m*.

breathe *vt vi* respirer; exhaler.

breathing *n* respiration *f*; souffle *m*.

breathing space *n* moment de répit *m*.

breathless *adj* hors d'haleine.

breathtaking *adj* stupéfiant.

breed *n* race, espèce *f*; * *vt* élever, engendrer; produire; éduquer; * *vi* se reproduire.

breeder *n* éleveur *m* -euse *f*.

breeding *n* élevage *m*; éducation *f*.

breeze *n* brise *f*.

breezy *adj* frais.

brethren *npl* frères *mpl*.

breviary *n* bréviaire *m*.

brevity *n* brièveté *f*; concision *f*.

brew *vt* faire infuser; brasser; comploter * *vi* infuser; se tramer; * *n* infusion *f*.

brewer *n* brasseur *m*.

brewery *n* brasserie *f*.

briar, brier *n* ronce *f*; églantier *m*.

bribe *n* pot-de-vin *m*; * *vt* acheter, soudoyer.

bribery *n* corruption *f*.

bric-a-brac *n* bric-à-brac *m*.

brick *n* brique *f*; * *vt* bâtir en briques.

bricklayer *n* maçon *m*.

bridal *adj* de noces, nuptial.

bride *n* mariée *f*.

bridegroom *n* marié *m*.

bridesmaid *n* demoiselle d'honneur *f*.

bridge *n* pont *m*; arête du nez *f*; chevalet *m*; ~ **(over)** *vt* relier par un pont.

bridle *n* bride *f*; frein *m*; * *vt* brider; réfréner.

brief *adj* bref, concis, succinct; * *n* affaire *f*; résumé *m*.

briefcase *n* serviette *f*.

briefly *adv* brièvement, en peu de mots.

brigade *n* (*mil*) brigade *f*.

brigadier *n* (*mil*) général de brigade *m*.

brigand *n* bandit, brigand *m*.

bright *adj* clair, brillant, éclatant; ~**ly** *adv* avec éclat.

brighten *vt* faire briller; * *vi* s'éclairer.

brightness *n* éclat, brillant *m*.

brilliance *n* éclat *m*.

brilliant *adj* éclatant; génial; ~**ly** *adv* avec éclat.

brim *n* bord *m*.

brimful *adj* plein jusqu'au bord.

bring *vt* apporter; amener; persuader; ~ **about** entraîner, provoquer; ~ **forth** produire; provoquer; ~ **up** élever.

brink *n* bord *m*.

brisk *adj* vif, rapide, frais.

brisket *n* poitrine *f* (de bœuf).

briskly *adv* vivement; rapidement.

bristle *n* poil *m*; soie *f*; * *vi* se hérisser.

bristly *adj* hérissé.

brittle *adj* cassant, fragile.

broach *vt* aborder.

broad *adj* large.

broadbeans *npl* fèves *fpl*.

broadcast *n* émission *f*; * *vt vi* diffuser, émettre.

broadcasting *n* radiodiffusion *f*; émission de télévision *f*.

broaden *vt* élargir; * *vi* s'élargir.

broadly *adv* généralement.

broad-minded *adj* tolérant, aux idées larges.

broadness *n* largeur *f*.

broadside *n* flanc (d'un navire) *m*; attaque *f* cinglante.

broadways *adv* en large, dans le sens de la largeur.

brocade *n* brocart *m*.

broccoli *n* brocoli *m*.

brochure *n* brochure *f*, dépliant *m*.

brogue *n* accent *m* du terroir.

broil *vt* griller.

broken *adj* cassé; interrompu; ~ **English** mauvais anglais *m*.

broker *n* courtier *m*.

brokerage *n* courtage *m*.

bronchial *adj* des bronches.

bronchitis *n* bronchite *f*.

bronze *n* bronze *m*; * *vt* bronzer, brunir.

brooch *n* broche *f*.

brood *vi* couver; ruminer; * *n* couvée *f*; nichée *f*.

brood-hen *n* couveuse *f*.

brook *n* ruisseau *m*.

broom *n* genêt *m*; balai *m*.

broomstick *n* manche à balai *m*.

broth *n* bouillon de viande et de légumes *m*.

brothel *n* bordel *m*.

brother *n* frère *m*.

brotherhood *n* fraternité *f*.

brother-in-law *n* beau-frère *m*.

brotherly *adj* fraternel; *adv* fraternellement.

brow *n* sourcil *m*; front *m*; sommet *m*.

browbeat *vt* intimider.

brown *adj* marron; brun; ~ **paper** *n*

papier d'emballage m; ~ **sugar** n cassonade f; * n marron m; * vt brunir.

browse vt parcourir; * vi paître.

bruise vt faire un bleu à; * n bleu m, ecchymose f.

brunette n brune f.

brunt n choc m.

brush n brosse f; pinceau m; accrochage m; * vt brosser.

brushwood n broussailles fpl; brindilles fpl.

brusque adj brusque.

Brussels sprout n chou de Bruxelles m.

brutal adj brutal; ~**ly** adv brutalement.

brutalise vt brutaliser.

brutality n brutalité f.

brute n brute f; * adj bestial, féroce.

brutish adj brutal, bestial; féroce; ~**ly** adv brutalement.

bubble n bulle f; * vi faire des bulles, bouillonner; pétiller.

bubblegum n bubble-gum m.

bucket n seau m.

buckle n boucle f; * vt attacher, boucler; * vi se déformer.

bucolic adj bucolique.

bud n bourgeon, bouton m; * vi bourgeonner.

Buddhism n bouddhisme m.

budding adj en bouton.

buddy n copain m.

budge vi bouger, remuer; céder.

budgerigar n perruche f.

budget n budget m.

buff n mordu m.

buffalo n bison m.

buffers npl (rail) pare-chocs m invar.

buffet n buffet m; * vt gifler; frapper.

buffoon n bouffon m.

bug n punaise f.

bugbear n épouvantail, croquemitaine m.

bugle(horn) n clairon m.

build vt construire, bâtir.

builder n constructeur m; entrepreneur m.

building n bâtiment m; immeuble, édifice m.

building society n organisme de crédit immobilier m.

bulb n bulbe m; oignon m.

bulbous adj bulbeux.

bulge vi se renfler; * n gonflement, renflement m.

bulk n masse f; volume m; grosseur f; majeure partie f; **in** ~ en gros.

bulky adj volumineux; encombrant.

bull n taureau m.

bulldog n bouledogue m.

bulldozer n bulldozer m.

bullet n balle f.

bulletin board n panneau d'affichage m.

bulletproof adj pare-balles, blindé.

bullfight n corrida f.

bullfighter n torero m.

bullfighting n tauromachie f.

bullion n or en barre m.

bullock n bouvillon m.

bullring n arène f.

bull's-eye n centre de la cible m.

bully n tyran m; * vt tyraniser.

bulwark n rempart m.

bum n clochard m.

bumblebee n bourdon m.

bump n heurt m; secousse f; bosse f; * vt heurter.

bumpkin n rustre m; plouc m.

bumpy adj cahoteux, bosselé.

bun n petit pain m; chignon m.

bunch n botte f; groupe m.

bundle n paquet m, liasse f; ballot m; fagot m; * vt empaqueter, mettre en liasse.

bung n bonde f; * vt boucher.

bungalow n bungalow m.

bungle vt bousiller; * vi faire mal les choses.

bunion n (med) oignon m.

bunk n couchette f.

bunker n abri m; bunker m.

buoy n (mar) bouée f.

buoyancy n flottabilité f; optimisme m.

buoyant adj flottable; gai, enjoué.

burden n charge f; fardeau m; * vt charger.

bureau n commode f; bureau m.

bureaucracy n bureaucratie f.

bureaucrat n bureaucrate mf.

burglar n cambrioleur m -euse f.

burglar alarm n signal d'alarme, signal antivol m.

burglary n cambriolage m.

burial n enterrement m; obsèques fpl.

burial place n lieu de sépulture m.

burlesque n caricature, parodie f; * adj burlesque, caricatural.

burly adj robuste, de forte carrure.

burn vt brûler; incendier, mettre le feu à; * vi brûler; * n brûlure f.

burner n brûleur m.

burning adj brûlant.

burrow n terrier m; * vi se terrer.

bursar n intendant(e) m(f).

burst vi éclater; ~ **into tears** éclater en sanglots; ~ **out laughing** éclater de rire; * vt ~ **into** faire

irruption dans; * n éclatement m; explosion f.

bury vt enterrer, inhumer.

bus n (auto)bus m.

bush n buisson, taillis m.

bushy adj touffu, plein de buissons.

busily adv activement, avec empressement.

business n entreprise f; commerce m; affaires fpl; activité f.

businesslike adj sérieux.

businessman n homme d'affaires m.

business trip n voyage d'affaires m.

businesswoman n femme d'affaires f.

bust n buste m.

bus-stop n arrêt d'autobus m.

bustle vi s'affairer; s'activer; * n remue-ménage m; animation f.

bustling adj animé.

busy adj occupé; actif.

busybody n mouche du coche f.

but conj mais; sauf, excepté, seulement.

butcher n boucher m -ère f; * vt abattre, massacrer.

butcher's (shop) n boucherie f.

butchery n boucherie f, carnage m.

butler n majordome m.

butt n butte f; mégot m; * vt donner un coup de tête à.

butter n beurre m; * vt beurrer.

buttercup n (bot) bouton d'or m.

butterfly n papillon m.

buttermilk n babeurre m.

buttocks npl fesses fpl.

button n bouton m; * vt boutonner.

buttonhole n boutonnière f.

buttress n contre-fort m; soutien m; * vt soutenir.

buxom adj bien en chair.

buy vt acheter.

buyer n acheteur m -euse f.

buzz n bourdonnement, murmure m; * vi bourdonner.

buzzard n buse f.

buzzer n interphone m.

by prep à côté de, près de; par; de; ~ **and** ~ bientôt; ~ **the** ~ à propos; ~ **much** de loin; ~ **all means** certainement; * adv près.

bygone adj passé.

by-law n arrêté municipal m.

bypass n route de contournement f.

by-product n sous-produit m.

by-road n chemin de traverse m.

bystander n spectateur m -trice f, badaud m -e f.

byte n (comput) octet m.

byword n proverbe, dicton m.

C

cab *n* taxi *m*.

cabbage *n* chou *m*.

cabin *n* cabine *f*; cabane *f*.

cabinet *n* conseil des ministres *m*; meuble de rangement *m*; console *f*.

cabinet-maker *n* ébéniste *m*.

cable *n* (*mar*) câble *m*.

cable car *n* téléphérique *m*.

cable television *n* télévision par câble *f*.

caboose *n* (*mar*) coquerie *f*.

cabstand *n* station de taxis *f*.

cache *n* cachette *f*.

cackle *vi* caqueter, jacasser; * *n* caquetage *m*; jacasserie *f*.

cactus *n* cactus *m*.

cadence *n* (*mus*) cadence *f*.

cadet *n* cadet *m*.

cadge *vt* taper (*fam*).

cafe *n* café *m*.

cafeteria *n* cafétéria *f*.

caffein(e) *n* caféine *f*.

cage *n* cage *f*; prison *f*; * *vt* mettre en cage; emprisonner.

cagey *adj* circonspect.

cajole *vt* cajoler pour amadouer.

cake *n* gâteau *m*.

calamitous *adj* calamiteux, catastrophique.

calamity *n* calamité *f*, désastre *m*.

calculable *adj* calculable.

calculate *vt* calculer, compter.

calculation *n* calcul *m*.

calculator *n* calculatrice *f*.

calculus *n* calcul *m*.

calendar *n* calendrier *m*.

calf *n* veau *m*; vachette *f*; mollet *m*.

calibre *n* calibre *m*.

calisthenics *npl* gymnastique rythmique *f*.

call *vt* appeler; appeler au téléphone; convoquer; **to ~ for** demander, nécessiter ; aller chercher quelqu'un; **to ~ on** rendre visite à; **to ~ attention** demander l'attention; **to ~ names** insulter; * *n* appel *m*; cri *m*; visite *f*; nomination *f*; vocation *f*; profession *f*.

caller *n* visiteur *m*, -euse *f*.

calligraphy *n* calligraphie *f*.

calling *n* profession, vocation *f*.

callous *adj* dur ; insensible.

calm *n* calme *m*, tranquillité *f*; * *adj* calme, tranquille; * *vt* calmer; apaiser ; **~ly** *adv* calmement.

calmness *n* calme *m*, tranquillité *f*.

calorie *n* calorie *f*.

calumny *n* calomnie *f*.

Calvary *n* Calvaire *m*.

calve *vi* vêler, mettre bas.

Calvinist *n* calviniste *mf*.

camel *n* chameau *m*.

cameo *n* camée *m*.

camera *n* appareil photographique *m*; caméra *f*.

cameraman *n* cameraman, cadreur *m*.

camomile *n* camomille *f*.

camouflage *n* camouflage *m*.

camp *n* camp *m*; * *vi* camper.

campaign *n* campagne *f*; * *vi* faire campagne.

campaigner *n* militant, candidat en campagne électorale *m*.

camper *n* campeur *m* -euse *f*.

camphor *n* camphre *m*.

campsite *n* camping *m*.

can *v aux* pouvoir; * *n* boîte de conserve *f*.

canal *n* conduit *m*; canal *m*.

cancel *vt* annuler.

cancellation *n* annulation *f*.

cancer *n* cancer *m*.

Cancer *n* Cancer *m* (signe du zodiaque).

cancerous *adj* cancéreux.

candid *adj* candide, simple, sincère; **~ly** *adv* candidement, franchement.

candidate *n* candidat(e) *m(f)*.

candied *adj* confit.

candle *n* bougie *f*; cierge *m*.

candlelight *n* lueur d'une bougie *f*.

candlestick *n* bougeoir *m*.

candour *n* candeur *f*; sincérité *f*.

candy *n* bonbon *m*.

cane *n* canne *f*; bâton *m*.

canine *adj* canin.

canister *n* boîte *f* métallique.

cannabis *n* cannabis *m*.

cannibal *n* cannibale *mf*; anthropophage *mf*.

cannibalism *n* cannibalisme *m*.

cannon *n* canon *m*.

cannonball *n* boulet de canon *m*.

canny *adj* rusé; prudent.

canoe *n* canoë *m*.

canon *n* canon *m*; règle *f*; **~law** droit canon *m*.

canonisation *n* canonisation *f*.

canonise *vt* canoniser.

can opener *n* ouvre-boîte *m*.

canopy *n* baldaquin *m*, marquise *f*.

cantankerous *adj* acariâtre, atrabilaire.

canteen *n* cantine *f*.

canter *n* petit galop *m*.

canvas *n* toile *f*.

canvass *vt* sonder, examiner; débattre; * *vi* solliciter des voix; faire du démarchage.

canvasser *n* prospecteur *m* -trice *f*, démarcheur *m* -euse *f*.

canyon *n* canyon *m*.

cap *n* casquette *f*.

capability *n* capacité, aptitude, faculté *f*; potentiel *m*.

capable *adj* capable.

capacitate *vt* rendre capable.

capacity *n* capacité, aptitude *f*; potentiel *m*.

cape *n* cap, promontoire *m*.

caper *n* cabriole *f*; gambade *f*; * *vi* cabrioler; gambader.

capillary *adj* capillaire.

capital *adj* capital; principal; * *n* capital *m*; capitale *f*; majuscule *f*.

capitalise *vt* capitaliser; **~ on** profiter de.

capitalism *n* capitalisme *m*.

capitalist *n* capitaliste *mf*.

capital punishment *n* peine de mort, peine capitale *f*.

Capitol *n* Capitole *m*.

capitulate *vi* capituler.

capitulation *n* capitulation *f*.

caprice *n* caprice *m*.

capricious *adj* capricieux, **~ly** *adv* capricieusement.

Capricorn *n* Capricorne *m* (signe du zodiaque).

capsize *vt* (*mar*) chavirer.

capsule *n* capsule *f*.

captain *n* capitaine *m*.

captaincy, captainship *n* grade de capitaine *m*; statut de capitaine *m*.

captivate *vt* captiver.

captivation *n* fascination *f*.

captive *n* captif *m* -ive *f*, prisonnier *m* -ière *f*.

captivity *n* captivité *f*.

capture *n* capture *f*; * *vt* prendre, capturer.

car *n* voiture *f*, automobile *f*; wagon *m*.

carafe *n* carafe *f*.

caramel *n* caramel *m*.

carat *n* carat *m*.

caravan *n* caravane *f*.

caraway *n* (*bot*) cumin *m*.

carbohydrates *npl* hydrates de carbone *mpl*.

carbon *n* carbone *m*.

carbon copy *n* copie carbone *f*, double carbone *m*.

carbonise *vt* carboniser.

carbon paper *n* papier carbone *m*.

carbuncle *n* escarboucle *f*; furoncle *m*, tumeur maligne *f*.

carburettor *n* carburateur *m*.

carcass *n* cadavre *m*.

card *n* carte *f*.

cardboard *n* carton *m*.

card game *n* jeu de cartes *m*.

cardiac *adj* cardiaque.

cardinal *adj* cardinal, principal; * *n* cardinal *m*.

card table *n* table de jeu *f*.

care *n* soin *m*; souci *m*; * *vi* se soucier de, être concerné par; **what do I ~?** qu'est-ce que cela peut me faire?; **~ for** *vt* soigner; aimer.

career *n* carrière *f*; cours *m*; * *vi* aller à toute vitesse.

carefree *n* insouciant.

careful *adj* soigneux, consciencieux, prudent; **~ly** *adv* soigneusement.

careless *adj* insouciant, négligent; indolent; **~ly** *adv* négligemment.

carelessness *n* négligence, indifférence *f*.

caress *n* caresse *f*; * *vt* caresser.

caretaker *n* gardien *m* -ne *f*, concierge *mf*.

car-ferry *n* ferry *m*.

cargo *n* cargaison de navire *f*.

car hire *n* location de voiture *f*.

caricature *n* caricature *f*; * *vt* caricaturer.

caries *n* carie *f*.

caring *adj* aimant; humanitaire.

Carmelite *n* carmélite *f*.

carnage *n* carnage *m*.

carnal *adj* charnel; sensuel; **~ly** *adv* charnellement.

carnation *n* œillet *m*.

carnival *n* carnaval *m*.

carnivorous *adj* carnivore.

carol *n* chant *m* (de Noël).

carpenter *n* charpentier *m*; **~'s bench** banc de menuisier *m*.

carpentry *n* charpenterie *f*.

carpet *n* tapis *m*; * *vt* recouvrir d'un tapis; moquetter.

carpeting *n* moquette *f*.

carriage *n* port *m*; voiture *f*; wagon *m*.

carriage-free *adj* franco de port.

carrier *n* porteur, transporteur *m*.

carrier pigeon *n* pigeon voyageur *m*.

carrion *n* charogne *f*.

carrot *n* carotte *f*.

carry *vt* porter; transporter; conduire; * *vi* porter; **~ the day** être victorieux; **~ on** continuer.

cart *n* charrette *f*; chariot *m*; * *vt* charrier.

cartel *n* cartel *m*.

carthorse *n* cheval de trait *m*.

Carthusian *n* chartreux *m*.

cartilage *n* cartilage *m*.

cartload *n* charretée *f*.

carton *n* pot *m*; boîte *f*.

cartoon *n* dessin animé *m*.

cartridge *n* cartouche *f*.

carve *vt* tailler, sculpter, ciseler.

carving *n* sculpture *f*.

carving knife *n* couteau à découper *m*.

car wash *n* station de nettoyage pour voitures *f*.

case *n* boîte *f*; valise *f*; cas *m*; étui *m*; enveloppe *f*; **in ~** au cas où.

cash *n* espèces *fpl*; * *vt* encaisser.

cash card *n* carte bancaire *f*.

cash dispenser *n* distributeur automatique de billets *m*.

cashier *n* caissier *m* -ière *f*.

cashmere *n* cachemire *m*.

casing *n* chambranle *m*; enveloppe *f*.

casino *n* casino *m*.

cask *n* tonneau, fût *m*.

casket *n* cercueil *m*.

casserole *n* cocotte *f*.

cassette *n* cassette *f*.

cassette player, recorder *n* lecteur de cassettes, magnétophone *m*.

cassock *n* soutane *f*.

cast *vt* jeter, lancer; couler; * *n* coup *m*; moule *m*.

castanets *npl* castagnettes *fpl*.

castaway *n* réprouvé, paria *m*.

caste *n* caste *f*.

castigate *vt* punir sévèrement.

casting vote *n* voix prépondérante *f*.

cast iron *n* fonte *f*.

castle *n* château *m*.

castor oil *n* huile de ricin *f*.

castrate *vt* castrer.

castration *n* castration *f*.

cast steel *n* acier fondu *m*.

casual *adj* accidentel, fortuit; **~ly** *adv* par hasard, fortuitement.

casualty *n* victime *f*, mort *m* -e *f*.

cat *n* chat *m*, chatte *f*.

catalogue *n* catalogue *m*.

catalyst *n* catalyseur *m*.

cataplasm *n* cataplasme *m*.

catapult *n* catapulte *f*.

cataract *n* cataracte *f*.

catarrh *n* rhume *m*; catarrhe *m*.

catastrophe *n* catastrophe *f*.

catcall *n* sifflet *m*.

catch *vt* attraper, saisir; prendre; surprendre; **~ cold** attraper froid; **~ fire** prendre feu; * *n* prise *f*; capture *f*; (*mus*) canon *m*; attrape *f*.

catching *adj* contagieux, communicatif.

catchphrase *n* rengaine *f*.

catchword *n* slogan *m*.

catchy *adj* qui attire l'attention; accrocheur.

catechise *vt* cathéchiser; interroger.

catechism *n* catéchisme *m*.

categorical *adj* catégorique; **~ly** *adv* catégoriquement.

categorise *vt* classer par catégories.

category *n* catégorie *f*.

cater *vi* approvisionner en nourriture.

caterer *n* fournisseur, traiteur *m*.

catering *n* restauration *f*.

caterpillar *n* chenille *f*.

catgut *n* boyau de chat *m*.

cathedral *n* cathédrale *f*.

catholic *adj n* catholique *mf*.

Catholicism *n* catholicisme *m*.

cattle *n* bétail *m*.

cattle show *n* exposition bovine *f*.

caucus *n* réunion d'un comité électoral *f*.

cauliflower *n* chou-fleur *m*.

cause *n* cause *f*; raison *f*; motif *m*; procès *m*; * *vt* causer.

causeway *n* chaussée *f*.

caustic *adj n* caustique *m/f*.

cauterise *vt* cautériser.

caution *n* prudence, précaution *f*; avertissement *m*; * *vt* avertir.

cautionary *adj* d'avertissement.

cautious *adj* prudent, circonspect.

cavalier *adj* cavalier.

cavalry *n* cavalerie *f*.

cave *n* grotte *f*; caverne *f*.

caveat *n* avertissement *m*; mise en garde *f*; (*law*) notification *f*.

cavern *n* caverne *f*.

cavernous *adj* caverneux.

cavity *n* cavité *f*.

cease *vt* cesser, arrêter; * *vi* cesser.

ceasefire *n* cessez-le-feu *m*.

ceaseless *adj* incessant, continuel; **~ly** *adv* continuellement.

cedar *n* cèdre *m*.

cede *vt* (*law*) céder.

ceiling *n* plafond *m*.

celebrate *vt* célébrer, fêter.

celebration *n* fête *f*.

celebrity *n* célébrité *f*.

celery *n* céleri *m*.

celestial *adj* céleste, divin.

celibacy *n* célibat *m*.

celibate *adj* célibataire.

cell *n* cellule *f*.

cellar *n* cave *f*; cellier *m*.

cello *n* violoncelle *m*.

cellophane *n* cellophane *f*.

cellular *adj* cellulaire.

cellulose *n* (*chem*) cellulose *f*.

cement n ciment m; (also fig); * vt cimenter.

cemetery n cimetière m.

cenotaph n cénotaphe m.

censor n censeur m, critique mf.

censorious adj sévère, critique.

censorship n censure f.

censure n censure, critique f; * vt censurer, condamner; critiquer.

census n recensement m.

cent n centime m.

centenarian n centenaire mf.

centenary n centenaire m; * adj centenaire.

centennial adj centenaire.

centigrade n centigrade m.

centilitre n centilitre m.

centimetre n centimètre m.

centipede n mille-pattes m invar.

central adj central; ~ly adv de façon centralisée; dans le centre.

centralise vt centraliser.

centre n centre m; * vt centrer; concentrer; * vi se concentrer.

centrifugal adj centrifuge.

century n siècle m.

ceramic adj en céramique.

cereals npl céréales fpl.

cerebral adj cérébral.

ceremonial adj n cérémonial m; rituel m.

ceremonious adj cérémonieux; ~ly adv solennellement.

ceremony n cérémonie f; cérémonies fpl.

certain adj certain, sûr; ~ly adv certainement, sans aucun doute.

certainty, certitude n certitude, conviction f.

certificate n certificat, acte m.

certification n authentification f.

certified mail n envoi avec accusé de réception m.

certify vt certifier, assurer.

cervical adj cervical.

cessation n cessation f.

cesspool n cloaque m; fosse d'aisances f.

chafe vt irriter; frotter.

chaff n menue paille f.

chaffinch n pinson m.

chagrin n dépit m.

chain n chaîne f; série, suite f; * vt enchaîner; attacher avec une chaîne.

chain reaction n réaction en chaîne f.

chainstore n grand magasin à succursales m.

chair n chaise f; * vt présider.

chairman n président m.

chalice n calice m.

chalk n craie f.

challenge n défi m; * vt défier.

challenger n provocateur m -trice f.

challenging adj provocateur.

chamber n pièce f; chambre f.

chambermaid n femme de chambre f.

chameleon n caméléon m.

chamois leather n peau de chamois f.

champagne n champagne m.

champion n champion m -ne f; * vt défendre.

championship n championnat m.

chance n hasard m; chance f; occasion f; **by ~** par hasard; * vt faire par hasard.

chancellor n chancelier m.

chancery n chancellerie f.

chandelier n lustre m.

change vt changer; * vi changer, se transformer; * n changement m, modification f; variété f; change m.

changeable adj changeant, variable; inconstant.

changeless adj constant, immuable.

changing adj variable, changeant.

channel n canal m; chaîne f; * vt canaliser.

chant n chant m scandé; * vt scander.

chaos n chaos m.

chaotic adj chaotique.

chapel n chapelle f.

chaplain n chapelain m.

chapter n chapitre m.

char vt carboniser.

character n caractère m; personnage m.

characterise vt caractériser.

characteristic adj caractéristique; ~ally adv typiquement.

characterless adj sans caractère.

charade n charade f.

charcoal n charbon de bois m.

charge vt charger; accuser; * n fardeau m; accusation f; (mil) attaque f; prix m.

chargeable adj passible.

charge card n carte de crédit f.

charitable adj caritatif; charitable; ~bly adv charitablement.

charity n charité, bienfaisance f; aumône f.

charlatan n charlatan m.

charm n charme m; attrait m; * vt charmer, enchanter.

charming adj charmant.

chart n carte de navigation f; diagramme m.

charter n charte f; privilège m; * vt affréter.

charter flight n vol charter m.

chase vt donner la chasse à; poursuivre; * n chasse f.

chasm n abîme m.

chaste adj chaste; pur; sobre.

chasten vt châtier, corriger.

chastise vt châtier, punir, corriger.

chastisement n châtiment m.

chastity n chasteté, pureté f.

chat vi causer; * n petite conversation f, bavardage m.

chatter vi bavarder; jacasser; * n bavardage m; jacasserie f.

chatterbox n moulin à paroles m, pipelette f.

chatty adj bavard.

chauffeur n chauffeur m.

chauvinist n chauvin m -e f.

cheap adj bon marché, peu cher; ~ly adv bon marché.

cheapen vt baisser le prix de.

cheaper adj moins cher.

cheat vt tromper, frauder; * n fraude, tricherie f; tricheur m -euse f.

check vt vérifier; contrôler; réprimer, enrayer; stopper; enregistrer; * n contrôle m.

checkmate n échec et mat m.

checkout n caisse f.

checkpoint n poste de contrôle m.

checkroom n (US) consigne f.

checkup n bilan de santé m.

cheek n joue f; culot m (fam) m.

cheekbone n pommette f.

cheer n gaieté f; joie f; applaudissement m; * vt réconforter, égayer.

cheerful adj gai, enjoué, joyeux; ~ly adv gaiement.

cheerfulness, cheeriness n gaieté f; bonne humeur f.

cheese n fromage m.

chef n chef (de cuisine) m.

chemical adj chimique.

chemist n chimiste mf; pharmacien m -ne f.

chemistry n chimie f.

cheque n chèque m.

cheque account n compte courant m.

chequerboard n échiquier m.

chequered adj à carreaux.

cherish vt chérir, aimer.

cheroot n petit cigare m.

cherry n cerise f; * adj vermeil.

cherrytree n cerisier m.

cherub n chérubin m.

chess n échecs mpl.

chessboard n échiquier m.

chessman n pièce de jeu d'échecs f.

chest n poitrine f; cage thoracique f; **~ of drawers** commode f.

chestnut n châtaigne f.

chestnut tree n châtaigner m.

chew vt mâcher, mastiquer.

chewing gum n chewing-gum m.

chic adj chic.

chicanery n chicane, chicanerie f.

chick n poussin m; (fig) poulette (fam) f, nana (fam) f.

chicken n poulet m.
chickenpox n varicelle f.
chickpea n pois chiche m.
chicory n chicorée f.
chide vt gronder, réprimander.
chief adj principal, en chef; ~**ly** adv principalement; * n chef m.
chief executive n directeur général m.
chieftain n chef m (de tribu).
chiffon n mousseline de soie f.
chilblain n engelure f.
child n enfant m; **from a** ~ tout enfant; **with** ~ enceinte.
childbirth n accouchement m.
childhood n enfance f.
childish adj enfantin, puéril; ~**ly** adv puérilement.
childishness n enfantillage m, puérilité f.
childless adj sans enfants.
childlike adj d'enfant.
children npl de **child**: enfants mpl.
chill adj froid, frais, f fraîche; * n froid m; * vt refroidir; glacer.
chilly adj froid, très frais.
chime n carillon m; harmonie f; * vi sonner; s'accorder.
chimney n cheminée f.
chimpanzee n chimpanzé m.
chin n menton m.
china(ware) n porcelaine f.
chink n fente f; tintement m; * vi tinter.
chip vt ébrécher; * vi s'ébrécher; * n fragment, éclat m; puce f; frite f.
chiropodist n pédicure mf.
chirp vi pépier, gazouiller; * n pépiement, gazouillis m.
chirping n chant des oiseaux m.
chisel n ciseau m; * vt ciseler.
chitchat n bavardage, papotage m.
chivalrous adj chevaleresque.
chivalry n chevalerie f.
chives npl ciboulette f.
chlorine n chlore m.
chloroform n chloroforme m.
chock-full adj plein à craquer, comble.
chocolate n chocolat m.
choice n choix m, préférence f; assortiment m; sélection f; * adj de choix, de qualité.
choir n chœur m.
choke vt étrangler; étouffer.
cholera n choléra m.
choose vt choisir, élire.
chop vt trancher, couper, hacher; * n côtelette f; ~**s** pl (sl) babines fpl.
chopper n hélicoptère m.
chopping block n billot m.
chopsticks npl baguettes fpl.
choral adj choral.

chord n corde f, (mus) accord m.
chore n corvée f; travail routinier m.
chorist, chorister n choriste mf.
chorus n chœur m.
Christ n Jésus-Christ.
christen vt baptiser.
Christendom n christianisme m; chrétienté f.
christening n baptême m.
Christian adj n chrétien m -ne f; ~ **name** prénom m.
Christianity n christianisme m; chrétienté f.
Christmas n Noël f.
Christmas card n carte de Noël f.
Christmas Eve n veille de Noël f.
chrome n chrome m.
chronic adj chronique.
chronicle n chronique f.
chronicler n chroniqueur m.
chronological adj chronologique; ~**ly** adv chronologiquement.
chronology n chronologie f.
chronometer n chronomètre m.
chubby adj potelé.
chuck vt lancer, jeter.
chuckle vi rire, glousser.
chug vi souffler, haleter.
chum n copain m, copine f.
chunk n gros morceau m.
church n église f.
churchyard n cimetière m.
churlish adj fruste, grossier; hargneux.
churn n baratte f; * vt baratter.
cider n cidre m.
cigar n cigare m.
cigarette n cigarette f.
cigarette case n étui à cigarettes m.
cigarette end n mégot m.
cigarette holder n fume-cigarette m invar.
cinder n braise f.
cinema n cinéma m.
cinnamon n cannelle f.
cipher n chiffre m (code).
circle n cercle m; groupe m; * vt encercler; tourner autour de * vi décrire des cercles.
circuit n circuit m; tour m; tournée f.
circuitous adj détourné, indirect.
circular adj circulaire; * n circulaire f.
circulate vi circuler.
circulation n circulation f.
circumcise vt circoncire.
circumcision n circoncision f.
circumference n circonférence f.
circumflex n accent circonflexe m.
circumlocution n circonlocution f.
circumnavigate vt contourner.
circumnavigation n circumnavigation f.
circumscribe vt circonscrire.

circumspect adj circonspect.
circumspection n circonspection f.
circumstance n circonstance, situation f.
circumstantial adj circonstancié; accessoire.
circumstantiate vt détailler.
circumvent vt circonvenir.
circumvention n évitement m; tricherie f.
circus n cirque m.
cistern n citerne f.
citadel n citadelle f.
citation n citation f.
cite vt citer.
citizen n citoyen m -ne f.
citizenship n citoyenneté f.
city n ville f.
civic adj civique.
civil adj civil, courtois; ~**ly** adv poliment.
civil defence n défense passive f.
civil engineer n ingénieur des travaux publics m.
civilian n civil m -e f.
civilisation n civilisation f.
civilise vt civiliser.
civility n civilité, courtoisie f.
civil law n droit civil m.
civil war n guerre civile f.
clad adj vêtu, habillé.
claim vt revendiquer, réclamer; * n demande f; réclamation f.
claimant n demandeur m.
clairvoyant n voyant m -e f.
clam n palourde f.
clamber vi grimper (avec difficulté).
clammy adj moite.
clamour n clameur f, cris mpl; * vi vociférer, crier.
clamp n attache f; * vt serrer; imposer; ~ **down on** resserrer le contrôle.
clan n clan, groupe m.
clandestine adj clandestin.
clang n bruit métallique m; * vi faire un bruit métallique.
clap vt vi applaudir.
clapping n applaudissements mpl.
claret n vin rouge de Bordeaux m.
clarification n clarification f, éclaircissement m.
clarify vt clarifier, éclaircir.
clarinet n clarinette f.
clarity n clarté f.
clash vi se heurter; s'entrechoquer; * n choc m; affrontement m.
clasp n fermoir m; boucle f; étreinte f; * vt agrafer; étreindre.
class n classe f; catégorie f; * vt classer, classifier.
classic(al) adj classique; * n auteur classique m.

classification *n* classification *f.*

classified advertisement *n* petite annonce *f.*

classify *vt* classifier, classer.

classmate *n* camarade de classe *mf.*

classroom *n* salle de classe *f.*

clatter *vi* résonner; cliqueter; * *n* cliquetis *m.*

clause *n* (*gr*) proposition *f;* clause *f.*

claw *n* griffe *f;* serre *f;* pince *f;* * *vt* griffer; agripper.

clay *n* argile *m.*

clean *adj* propre; net; * *vt* nettoyer.

cleaning *n* nettoyage *m.*

cleanliness *n* propreté, pureté *f.*

cleanly *adj* propre; * *adv* proprement, nettement.

cleanness *n* propreté *f.*

cleanse *vt* nettoyer.

clear *adj* clair; net; transparent; évident; * *adv* distinctement; * *vt* clarifier, éclaircir; dégager; disculper; * *vi* s'éclaircir.

clearance *n* déblaiement *m;* autorisation *f.*

clear-cut *adj* net.

clearly *adv* clairement; manifestement.

cleaver *n* couperet *m.*

clef *n* (*mus*) clé *f.*

cleft *n* fissure, crevasse *f.*

clemency *n* clémence *f.*

clement *adj* clément.

clenched *adj* serré.

clergy *n* clergé *m.*

clergyman *n* ecclésiastique *m.*

clerical *adj* clérical, ecclésiastique.

clerk *n* ecclésiastique *m;* employé *m.*

clever *adj* intelligent; habile; astucieux; **~ly** *adv* intelligemment, habilement.

click *vt* claquer; * *vi* faire un bruit sec.

client *n* client *m* -e *f.*

cliff *n* falaise *f.*

climate *n* climat *m.*

climatic *adj* climatique.

climax *n* point culminant *m,* apogée *m.*

climb *vt* grimper, escalader; * *vi* grimper, escalader.

climber *n* alpiniste *mf.*

climbing *n* alpinisme *m.*

clinch *vt* serrer fort.

cling *vi* s'accrocher (à); se cramponner (à); adhérer, (se) coller.

clinic *n* clinique *f.*

clink *vt* faire tinter; * *vi* tinter, résonner; * *n* tintement *m.*

clip *vt* couper; * *n* clip *m;* pince *f.*

clipping *n* coupure *f.*

clique *n* clique *f.*

cloak *n* cape *f;* prétexte *m;* * *vt* masquer.

cloakroom *n* vestiaire *m.*

clock *n* horloge *f.*

clockwork *n* mécanisme d'horloge *m;* * *adj* précis.

clod *n* motte (de terre) *f.*

clog *n* sabot *m;* * *vi* se boucher.

cloister *n* cloître *m.*

close *vt* fermer; clore, conclure; terminer; * *vi* se fermer; * *n* fin *f;* conclusion *f;* * *adj* proche; étroit; ajusté; dense; réservé; * *adv* de près; **~ by** tout près.

closed *adj* fermé.

closely *adv* étroitement; de près.

closeness *n* proximité *f;* fidélité, exactitude *f;* intimité *f;* minutie *f.*

closet *n* placard *m.*

close-up *n* gros plan *m.*

closure *n* fermeture *f;* clôture *f.*

clot *n* caillot *m;* grumeau *m.*

cloth *n* tissu *m;* chiffon *m;* toile *f;* clergé *m.*

clothe *vt* habiller, vêtir.

clothes *npl* vêtements *mpl;* linge *m;* **bed ~** draps et couvertures *mpl.*

clothes basket *n* panière à linge *f.*

clotheshorse *n* séchoir à linge *m.*

clothesline *n* corde à linge *f.*

clothespin *n* pince à linge *f.*

clothing *n* vêtements *mpl.*

cloud *n* nuage *m;* nuée *f;* * *vt* rendre trouble; assombrir; * *vi* se couvrir; s'obscurcir.

cloudiness *n* nébulosité *f;* obscurité *f.*

cloudy *adj* nuageux, nébuleux; obscur; sombre, trouble.

clout *n* coup de poing *m.*

clove *n* clou de girofle *m.*

clover *n* trèfle *m.*

clown *n* clown *m.*

club *n* matraque *f;* club *m.*

club car *n* wagon-bar *m* (1ère classe).

clue *n* indice *m,* indication *f;* idée *f.*

clump *n* massif *m.*

clumsily *adv* gauchement.

clumsiness *n* gaucherie *f.*

clumsy *adj* gauche, maladroit; lourd.

cluster *n* bouquet *m;* grappe *f;* groupe *m;* * *vt* grouper; * *vi* se rassembler.

clutch *n* prise *f;* embrayage *m;* * *vt* empoigner, agripper.

clutter *vt* encombrer.

coach *n* autocar *m;* wagon *m;* entraîneur *m;* * *vt* entraîner, donner des cours particuliers à.

coach trip *n* excursion en car *f.*

coagulate *vt* coaguler; agglutiner; * *vi* se coaguler; s'agglutiner.

coal *n* charbon *m.*

coalesce *vi* s'unir, se fondre.

coalfield *n* gisement charbonnier *m.*

coalition *n* coalition *f.*

coalman *n* charbonnier *m.*

coalmine *n* mine de charbon, houillère *f.*

coarse *adj* rude; grossier; **~ly** *adv* grossièrement.

coast *n* côte *f.*

coastal *adj* côtier.

coastguard *n* gendarmerie maritime *f,* garde-côte *m.*

coastline *n* littoral *m.*

coat *n* manteau *m;* pelage *m;* couche *f;* * *vt* enduire, revêtir.

coat hanger *n* cintre *m.*

coating *n* revêtement *m.*

coax *vt* cajôler.

cob *n* épi de maïs *m.*

cobbler *n* cordonnier *m.*

cobbles, cobblestones *npl* pavés ronds *mpl.*

cobweb *n* toile d'araignée *f.*

cocaine *n* cocaïne *f.*

cock *n* coq *m;* (*zool*) mâle *m;* * *vt* armer; dresser.

cock-a-doodle-doo *n* cocorico *m.*

cockcrow *n* chant du coq *m.*

cockerel *n* jeune coq *m.*

cockfight(ing) *n* combat de coqs *m.*

cockle *n* (*zool*) coque *f.*

cockpit *n* cabine de pilotage *f.*

cockroach *n* cafard *m.*

cocktail *n* cocktail *m.*

cocoa *n* cacao *m.*

coconut *n* noix de coco *f.*

cocoon *n* cocon *m.*

cod *n* morue *f.*

code *n* code *m;* indicatif *m.*

cod-liver oil *n* huile de foie de morue *f.*

coefficient *n* coefficient *m.*

coercion *n* coercition, contrainte *f.*

coexistence *n* coexistence *f.*

coffee *n* café *m.*

coffee break *n* pause-café *f.*

coffee house *n* café *m.*

coffeepot *n* cafetière *f.*

coffee table *n* table basse *f.*

coffer *n* coffre *m;* caisse *f.*

coffin *n* cercueil *m.*

cog *n* dent d'engrenage *f.*

cogency *n* puissance, force *f.*

cogent *adj* convaincant, puissant; **~ly** *adv* d'une manière convaincante.

cognac *n* cognac *m.*

cognate *adj* apparenté.

cognisance *n* connaissance *f;* compétence *f.*

cognisant *adj* instruit; (*law*) compétent.

cognition *n* connaissance *f;* cognition *f.*

cogwheel *n* roue dentée *f.*

cohabit *vi* cohabiter.
cohabitation *n* cohabitation *f*.
cohere *vi* se tenir; être cohérent.
coherence *n* cohérence *f*.
coherent *adj* cohérent; logique.
cohesion *n* cohésion *f*.
cohesive *adj* cohésif.
coil *n* rouleau *m*; bobine *f*; * *vt* enrouler.
coin *n* pièce de monnaie *f*; * *vt* frapper.
coincide *vi* coïncider.
coincidence *n* coïncidence *f*.
coincident *adj* coïncident.
coke *n* coke *m*.
colander *n* passoire *f*.
cold *adj* froid; indifférent; ~**ly** *adv* froidement; avec froideur; * *n* froid *m*; rhume *m*.
cold-blooded *adj* insensible.
coldness *n* froideur *f*.
cold sore *n* bouton de fièvre *m*.
coleslaw *n* salade de chou cru *f*.
colic *n* coliques *fpl*.
collaborate *vi* collaborer.
collaboration *n* collaboration *f*.
collapse *vi* s'écrouler; * *n* écroulement; (*med*) évanouissement *m*.
collapsible *adj* pliant.
collar *n* col *m*.
collarbone *n* clavicule *f*.
collate *vt* collationner, confronter.
collateral *adj* concomitant; parallèle; * *n* nantisse ment *m*.
collation *n* collation *f*.
colleague *n* collègue *mf*, confrère *m*, consœur *f*.
collect *vt* rassembler; collectionner.
collection *n* collection *f*.
collective *adj* collectif; ~**ly** collectivement.
collector *n* collectionneur *m* -euse *f*.
college *n* faculté *f*.
collide *vi* entrer en collision, se heurter.
collision *n* collision *f*, heurt *m*.
colloquial *adj* familier; parlé; ~**ly** *adv* familièrement.
colloquialism *n* expression familière *f*.
collusion *n* collusion *f*.
colon *n* deux-points *m invar*; (*med*) colon *m*.
colonel *n* (*mil*) colonel *m*.
colonial *adj* colonial.
colonise *vt* coloniser.
colonist *n* colon *m*.
colony *n* colonie *f*.
colossal *adj* colossal.
colossus *n* colosse *m*.
colour *n* couleur *f*; prétexte *m*; ~**s** *pl* drapeau *m*; * *vt* colorer; * *vi* se colorer.

colour-blind *adj* daltonien.
colourful *adj* coloré.
colouring *n* teint *m*; coloris *m*.
colourless *adj* sans couleur, incolore.
colour television *n* télévision en couleur *f*.
colt *n* poulain *m*.
column *n* colonne *f*.
columnist *n* chroniqueur *m*.
coma *n* coma *m*.
comatose *adj* comateux.
comb *n* peigne *m*; * *vt* peigner.
combat *n* combat *m*; **single** ~ duel *m*; * *vt* combattre.
combatant *n* combattant *m* -e *f*.
combative *adj* combatif.
combination *n* combinaison, association *f*.
combine *vt* combiner; * *vi* s'unir.
combustion *n* combustion *f*.
come *vi* venir; ~ **across**, ~ **upon** *vt* rencontrer par hasard, tomber sur; ~ **by** *vt* obtenir; ~ **down** *vi* descendre; se résumer à, baisser (prices); ~ **from** *vt* provenir de; être originaire de; ~ **in for** *vt* être l'objet de; ~ **into** *vt* hériter de; ~ **round**, ~ **to** *vi* revenir à soi; ~ **up with** *vt* suggérer.
comedian *n* comédien *m*; comique *m*.
comedienne *n* comédienne *f*; comique *f*.
comedy *n* comédie *f*.
comet *n* comète *f*.
comfort *n* confort *m*; aises *fpl*; commodités *fpl*; consolation *f*; * *vt* réconforter; soulager; consoler.
comfortable *adj* confortable; réconfortant.
comfortably *adv* confortablement; agréablement.
comforter *n* personne qui réconforte *f*; édredon *m*.
comic(al) *adj* comique; ~**ly** *adv* comiquement.
coming *n* venue, arrivée *f*; * *adj* à venir.
comma *n* (*gr*) virgule *f*.
command *vt* ordonner, commander; * *n* ordre *m*.
commander *n* commandant *m*.
commandment *n* commandement *m*.
commando *n* commando *m*.
commemorate *vt* commémorer.
commemoration *n* commémoration *f*.
commence *vt vi* commencer.
commencement *n* commencement *m*.
commend *vt* recommander, confier à; louer.
commendable *adj* louable.
commendably *adv* élogieusement.

commendation *n* louange *f*; recommandation *f*.
commensurate *adj* proportionné.
comment *n* commentaire *m*; * *vt* commenter.
commentary *n* commentaire *m*; observation *f*.
commentator *n* commentateur *m* -trice *f*.
commerce *n* commerce *m*, affaires *fpl*; relations *fpl*.
commercial *adj* commercial.
commiserate *vt* compatir.
commiseration *n* commisération, pitié *f*.
commissariat *n* (*mil*) intendance *f*, ravitaillement *m*.
commission *n* commission *f*; * *vt* commissionner; commander.
commissioner *n* commissionnaire, coursier *m*.
commit *vt* commettre; confier à; engager.
commitment *n* engagement *m*.
committee *n* comité *m*.
commodity *n* produit *m*, denrée *f*.
common *adj* commun; ordinaire; **in** ~ en commun; * *n* terrain communal *m*.
commoner *n* roturier *m* -ière *f*.
common law *n* droit coutumier *m*.
commonly *adv* communément, généralement.
commonplace *n* lieux communs *mpl*; * *adj* banal.
common sense *n* bon sens *m*.
Commonwealth *n* Commonwealth *m*.
commotion *n* vacarme *m*; perturbation *f*.
commune *vi* discuter avec sincérité.
communicable *adj* communicable, transmissible.
communicate *vt* communiquer, transmettre; * *vi* communiquer.
communication *n* communication *f*.
communicative *adj* communicatif.
communion *n* communion *f*.
communiqué *n* communiqué *m*.
communism *n* communisme *m*.
communist *n* communiste *mf*.
community *n* communauté *f*.
community centre *n* centre social *m*.
community chest *n* fonds commun *m*.
commutable *adj* interchangeable, permutable.
commutation ticket *n* carte d'abonnement *f*.
commute *vt* échanger.
compact *adj* compact, serré, dense; * *n* accord, contrat *m*; ~**ly** *adv* de façon compacte; en peu de mots.

compact disc *n* disque compact *m*.

companion *n* compagnon *m*, compagne *f*.

companionship *n* camaraderie *f*; compagnie *f*.

company *n* compagnie, fréquentation *f*; société *f*.

comparable *adj* comparable.

comparative *adj* comparatif; ~**ly** *adv* comparativement.

compare *vt* comparer.

comparison *n* comparaison *f*.

compartment *n* compartiment *m*.

compass *n* boussole *f*.

compassion *n* compassion *f*.

compassionate *adj* compatissant.

compatibility *n* compatibilité *f*.

compatible *adj* compatible.

compatriot *n* compatriote *mf*.

compel *vt* contraindre, obliger, forcer.

compelling *adj* irrésistible.

compensate *vt* compenser.

compensation *n* compensation *f*; dédommagement *m*.

compère *n* animateur *m* -trice *f*.

compete *vi* rivaliser (avec), faire concurrence (à).

competence *n* compétence *f*; aptitude *f*.

competent *adj* compétent; suffisant; ~**ly** *adv* avec compétence.

competition *n* compétition *f*; concurrence *f*.

competitive *adj* concurrentiel, compétitif.

competitor *n* concurrent *m* -e *f*.

compilation *n* compilation *f*.

compile *vt* compiler.

complacency *n* suffisance *f*.

complacent *adj* suffisant.

complain *vi* se plaindre; déposer une plainte.

complaint *n* plainte *f*; réclamation *f*.

complement *n* complément *m*.

complementary *adj* complémentaire.

complete *adj* complet; achevé; ~**ly** *adv* complètement; * *vt* achever, mener à bien, compléter.

completion *n* achèvement *m*.

complex *adj* complexe.

complexion *n* teint *m*; aspect *m*.

complexity *n* complexité *f*.

compliance *n* conformité *f*; soumission *f*.

compliant *adj* docile, soumis.

complicate *vt* compliquer.

complication *n* complication *f*.

complicity *n* complicité *f*.

compliment *n* compliment *m*; * *vt* complimenter.

complimentary *adj* flatteur; à titre gracieux.

comply *vi* se soumettre, se plier, se conformer.

component *adj* composant.

compose *vt* composer; constituer.

composed *adj* calme, posé.

composer *n* auteur *m*; compositeur *m* -trice *f*.

composite *adj* composite, composé.

composition *n* composition *f*.

compositor *n* compositeur *m* -trice *f*.

compost *n* compost *m*.

composure *n* maîtrise de soi *f*, calme *m*, sang-froid *m*.

compound *vt* composer, combiner; * *adj* *n* composé *m*.

comprehend *vt* comprendre; englober.

comprehensible *adj* compréhensible; ~**ly** *adv* intelligiblement.

comprehension *n* compréhension *f*; inclusion *f*.

comprehensive *adj* global; complet; compréhensif; ~**ly** *adv* globalement.

compress *vt* comprimer, concentrer; * *n* compresse *f*.

comprise *vt* comprendre, embrasser.

compromise *n* compromis *m*; * *vt* compromettre; * *vi* adopter un compromis.

compulsion *n* contrainte *f*; compulsion *f*.

compulsive *adj* compulsif; ~**ly** *adv* compulsivement.

compulsory *adj* obligatoire.

compunction *n* remords, scrupule *m*.

computable *adj* computable, calculable.

computation *n* computation *f*, calcul *m*.

compute *vt* calculer.

computer *n* ordinateur *m*.

computerise *vt* traiter par ordinateur, informatiser.

computer programming *n* programmation *f*.

computer science *n* informatique *f*.

comrade *n* camarade *mf*, compagnon *m*, compagne *f*.

comradeship *n* camaraderie *f*.

con *vt* duper; * *n* duperie *f*.

concave *adj* concave.

concavity *n* concavité *f*.

conceal *vt* cacher, dissimuler.

concealment *n* dissimulation *f*; recel *m*.

concede *vt* concéder, accorder.

conceit *n* vanité *f*; trait d'esprit *m*.

conceited *adj* vaniteux, prétentieux.

conceivable *adj* concevable.

conceive *vt* concevoir; * *vi* concevoir.

concentrate *vt* concentrer.

concentration *n* concentration *f*.

concentration camp *n* camp de concentration *m*.

concentric *adj* concentrique.

concept *n* concept *m*.

conception *n* conception *f*.

concern *vt* concerner, toucher; * *n* affaire *f*; souci *m*.

concerning *prep* en ce qui concerne, concernant.

concerto *n* concerto *m*.

concession *n* concession *f*.

conciliate *vt* concilier.

conciliation *n* conciliation *f*.

conciliatory *adj* conciliateur, conciliant.

concise *adj* concis, succinct; ~**ly** *adv* avec concision.

conclude *vt* conclure; décider; déduire.

conclusion *n* conclusion, déduction *f*; fin *f*.

conclusive *adj* décisif, concluant; ~**ly** *adv* de façon concluante.

concoct *vt* confectionner, fabriquer.

concoction *n* préparation *f*; élaboration *f*.

concomitant *adj* concomitant.

concord *n* entente, harmonie *f*.

concordance *n* accord *m*.

concordant *adj* concordant.

concourse *n* rassemblement *m*; carrefour *m*; foule *f*.

concrete *n* béton *m*; * *vt* bétonner.

concubine *n* concubine *f*.

concur *vi* coïncider; s'entendre.

concurrence *n* consentement *m*, coïncidence *f*; union *f*.

concurrently *adv* simultanément.

concussion *n* commotion *f*.

condemn *vt* condamner; désapprouver.

condemnation *n* condamnation *f*.

condensation *n* condensation *f*.

condense *vt* condenser.

condescend *vi* condescendre; daigner.

condescending *adj* condescendant.

condescension *n* condescendance *f*.

condiment *n* condiment *m*.

condition *vt* conditionner; * *n* condition, situation *f*; état *m*.

conditional *adj* conditionnel, hypothétique; ~**ly** *adv* conditionnellement.

conditioned *adj* conditionné.

conditioner *n* après-shampoing *m*.

condolences *npl* condoléances *fpl*.

condom *n* préservatif *m*.

condominium *n* condominium *m*, copropriété *f*.

condone *vt* pardonner, fermer les yeux sur.

conducive *adj* propice, opportun.

conduct *n* conduite *f*; comportement *m*; * *vt* conduire, mener.

conductor *n* receveur *m*; chef d'orchestre *m*; conducteur *m*.

conduit *n* conduit *m*; tuyau *m*.

cone *n* cône *m*.

confection *n* sucrerie, confiserie *f*; confection *f*.

confectioner *n* confiseur *m* -euse *f*.

confectioner's (shop) *n* confiserie *f*; pâtisserie *f*.

confederacy *n* confédération *f*.

confederate *vi* se confédérer; * *adj* *n* confédéré *m*.

confer *vt* *vi* conférer.

conference *n* conférence *f*.

confess *vt* confesser; * *vi* se confesser.

confession *n* confession *f*.

confessional *n* confessionnal *m*.

confessor *n* confesseur *m*.

confidant *n* confident *m* -e *f*.

confide *vt* confier; ~ **in** se confier à.

confidence *n* confiance *f*; assurance *f*.

confidence trick *n* abus de confiance *m*, escroquerie *f*.

confident *adj* confiant, assuré, sûr (de soi).

confidential *adj* confidentiel.

configuration *n* configuration *f*.

confine *vt* limiter; emprisonner.

confinement *n* détention *f*; alitement *m*.

confirm *vt* confirmer; ratifier.

confirmation *n* confirmation *f*; ratification *f*; corroboration *f*.

confirmed *adj* invétéré, endurci.

confiscate *vt* confisquer.

confiscation *n* confiscation *f*.

conflagration *n* incendie *m*; conflagration *f*.

conflict *n* conflit *m*; lutte *f*; dispute *f*.

conflicting *adj* contradictoire.

confluence *n* confluence *f*; rencontre *f*.

conform *vt* conformer, adapter; * *vi* se conformer (à), s'adapter (à).

conformity *n* conformité *f*, accord *m*.

confound *vt* confondre.

confront *vt* confronter; affronter.

confrontation *n* affrontement *m*, confrontation *f*.

confuse *vt* confondre; embarrasser; embrouiller.

confusing *adj* déroutant.

confusion *n* confusion *f*; désordre *m*.

congeal *vt* solidifier, congeler; * *vi* se solidifier, se congeler.

congenial *adj* sympathique; similaire.

congenital *adj* congénital.

congested *adj* encombré, congestionné.

congestion *n* encombrement *m*, congestion *f*.

conglomerate *vt* conglomérer, agglomérer; * *adj* aggloméré; * *n* (com) conglomérat *m*.

conglomeration *n* conglomération *f*.

congratulate *vt* complimenter, féliciter.

congratulations *npl* félicitations *fpl*.

congratulatory *adj* de félicitations.

congregate *vt* rassembler, réunir.

congregation *n* assemblée *f*, rassemblement *m*.

congress *n* congrès *m*; conférence *f*.

congressman *n* membre du Congrès *m*.

congruity *n* congruence *f*.

congruous *adj* congru, approprié.

conic(al) *adj* conique.

conifer *n* conifère *m*.

coniferous *adj* (bot) conifère.

conjecture *n* conjecture, supposition *f*; * *vt* conjecturer, supposer.

conjugal *adj* conjugal.

conjugate *vt* (gr) conjuguer.

conjugation *n* conjugaison *f*.

conjunction *n* conjonction *f*; union *f*.

conjuncture *n* conjoncture *f*; occasion *f*.

conjure *vt* conjurer; exorciser.

conjurer *n* magicien *m* -ne *f*, illusionniste *mf*.

con man *n* escroc *m*.

connect *vt* relier, joindre, rattacher.

connection *n* liaison, connexion *f*.

connivance *n* connivence *f*.

connive *vi* fermer les yeux (sur); être de connivence.

connoisseur *n* connaisseur *m* -euse *f*.

conquer *vt* conquérir; vaincre.

conqueror *n* vainqueur *m*; conquérant *m*.

conquest *n* conquête *f*.

conscience *n* conscience *f*.

conscientious *adj* consciencieux; de conscience; ~**ly** *adv* consciencieusement.

conscious *adj* conscient; intentionnel; ~**ly** *adv* consciemment, sciemment.

consciousness *n* conscience *f*.

conscript *n* conscrit *m*.

conscription *n* conscription *f*.

consecrate *vt* consacrer.

consecration *n* consécration *f*.

consecutive *adj* consécutif; ~**ly** *adv* consécutivement.

consensus *n* consensus *m*.

consent *n* consentement *m*; assentiment *m*; * *vi* consentir.

consequence *n* conséquence *f*; importance *f*.

consequent *adj* consécutif; ~**ly** *adv* par conséquent.

conservation *n* conservation *f*.

conservative *adj* conservateur.

conservatory *n* conservatoire *m*.

conserve *vt* conserver; * *n* conserve *f*.

consider *vt* considérer, examiner; * *vi* penser, délibérer.

considerable *adj* considérable; important; ~**bly** *adv* considérablement.

considerate *adj* prévenant, attentionné; prudent; ~**ly** *adv* avec prévenance; prudemment.

consideration *n* considération *f*; réflexion *f*; estime *f*; rémunération *f*.

considering *conj* étant donné que; ~ **that** vu que; étant donné que.

consign *vt* confier, remettre, expédier.

consignment *n* expédition *f*, envoi *m*.

consist *vi* consister (en).

consistency *n* consistance *f*; cohérence *f*; constance *f*.

consistent *adj* constant; cohérent; compatible; ~**ly** *adv* régulièrement.

consolable *adj* consolable.

consolation *n* consolation *f*; réconfort *m*.

consolatory *adj* consolateur.

console *vt* consoler.

consolidate *vt* consolider, grouper; * *vi* se consolider.

consolidation *n* consolidation *f*.

consonant *adj* en accord; * *n* (gr) consonne *f*.

consort *n* consort *m*; associé *m* -e *f*.

conspicuous *adj* voyant, manifeste; notable; ~**ly** *adv* manifestement.

conspiracy *n* conspiration *f*.

conspirator *n* conspirateur *m* -trice *f*.

conspire *vi* conspirer.

constancy *n* constance, fermeté d'âme *f*; persévérance *f*.

constant *adj* constant; persévérant; ~**ly** *adv* constamment.

constellation *n* constellation *f*.

consternation *n* consternation *f*.

constipated *adj* constipé.

constituency *n* électorat *m*; circonscription *f*.

constituent *n* composant *m*; * *adj* constituant.

constitute *vt* constituer; établir.

constitution *n* constitution *f*.

constitutional *adj* constitutionnel.

constrain *vt* contraindre, forcer, obliger.

constraint *n* contrainte *f*.

constrict *vt* serrer; gêner.

construct *vt* construire, bâtir.

construction *n* construction *f*.

construe *vt* interpréter, analyser.

consul *n* consul *m*.

consular *adj* consulaire.

consulate, consulship *n* consulat *m*.

consult *vt* consulter; * *vi* (se) consulter.

consultation *n* consultation, délibération *f*.

consume *vt* consommer; dissiper; consumer, brûler; * *vi* se consommer.

consumer *n* consommateur *m* -trice *f*.

consumer goods *npl* biens de consommation *mpl*.

consumerism *n* consumérisme *m*.

consumer society *n* société de consommation *f*.

consummate *vt* consommer, accomplir; perfectionner; * *adj* accompli, consommé.

consummation *n* consommation *f*; perfection *f*.

consumption *n* consommation *f*.

contact *n* contact *m*.

contact lenses *npl* lentilles de contact *fpl*.

contagious *adj* contagieux.

contain *vt* contenir, renfermer; refréner.

container *n* récipient *m*.

contaminate *vt* contaminer; ~d *adj* contaminé.

contamination *n* contamination *f*.

contemplate *vt* contempler.

contemplation *n* contemplation *f*.

contemplative *adj* contemplatif.

contemporaneous,contemporary *adj* contemporain.

contempt *n* mépris, dédain *m*.

contemptible *adj* méprisable, vil; ~bly *adv* vilement.

contemptuous *adj* méprisant, dédaigneux; ~ly *adv* dédaigneusement.

contend *vi* combattre, lutter; * *vt* affirmer.

content *adj* content, satisfait; * *vt* contenter, satisfaire; * *n* contentement *m*; ~s *pl* contenu *m*; table des matières *f*.

contentedly *adv* avec contentement.

contention *n* querelle, altercation *f*.

contentious *adj* litigieux; querelleur; ~ly *adv* en chicanant.

contentment *n* contentement *m*, satisfaction *f*.

contest *vt* contester, discuter, disputer; * *n* concours *m*; altercation *f*.

contestant *n* concurrent *m* -e *f*.

context *n* contexte *m*.

contiguous *adj* contigu, voisin.

continent *adj* continent, chaste; * *n* continent *m*.

continental *adj* continental.

contingency *n* contingence *f*; événement imprévu *m*; éventualité *f*.

contingent *n* contingent *m*; * *adj* contingent, éventuel; ~ly fortuitement.

continual *adj* continuel; ~ly *adv* continuellement.

continuation *n* continuation, reprise, suite *f*.

continue *vt vi* continuer.

continuity *n* continuité *f*.

continuous *adj* continu; ~ly *adv* sans interruption.

contort *vt* tordre, déformer.

contortion *n* contorsion *f*.

contour *n* contour *m*.

contraband *n* contrebande *f*; * *adj* de contrebande.

contraception *n* contraception *f*.

contraceptive *n* contraceptif *m*; * *adj* contraceptif.

contract *vt* contracter; * *vi* se contracter; * *n* contrat *m*.

contraction *n* contraction *f*.

contractor *n* entrepreneur *m*.

contradict *vt* contredire.

contradiction *n* contradiction *f*.

contradictory *adj* contradictoire.

contraption *n* gadget, bidule (*fam*) *m*.

contrariness *n* esprit de contradiction *m*.

contrary *adj* contraire, opposé; * *n* contraire *m*; **on the ~** au contraire.

contrast *n* contraste *m*; * *vt* contraster, mettre en contraste.

contrasting *adj* contrasté, opposé.

contravention *n* infraction *f*.

contributary *adj* contributif.

contribute *vt* contribuer.

contribution *n* contribution *f*; cotisation *f*.

contributor *n* souscripteur(-trice), collaborateur(-trice) *m(f)*.

contributory *adj* contribuant.

contrite *adj* contrit, repentant.

contrition *n* contrition *f*, repentir *m*.

contrivance *n* dispositif *m*; invention *f*.

contrive *vt* inventer, combiner; trouver le moyen de.

control *n* contrôle *m*; maîtrise *f*; autorité *f*; * *vt* maîtriser; réguler; contrôler; gouverner.

control room *n* salle des commandes *f*.

control tower *n* tour de contrôle *f*.

controversial *adj* polémique.

controversy *n* polémique *f*.

contusion *n* contusion *f*.

conundrum *n* énigme *f*.

conurbation *n* conurbation *f*.

convalesce *vi* être en convalescence.

convalescence *n* convalescence *f*.

convalescent *adj* convalescent.

convene *vt* convoquer; réunir; * *vi* se réunir.

convenience *n* commodité, convenance *f*.

convenient *adj* commode, pratique; qui convient; ~ly *adv* commodément.

convent *n* couvent *m*.

convention *n* convention *f*; contrat *m*; assemblée *f*.

conventional *adj* conventionnel.

converge *vi* converger.

convergence *n* convergence *f*.

convergent *adj* convergent.

conversant *adj* au courant; compétent.

conversation *n* conversation *f*.

converse *vi* converser.

conversely *adv* inversement, réciproquement.

conversion *n* conversion; transformation *f*.

convert *vt* convertir; * *n* converti *m* -e *f*.

convertible *adj* convertible; * *n* décapotable *f*.

convex *adj* convexe.

convexity *n* convexité *f*.

convey *vt* transporter; transmettre, communiquer.

conveyance *n* transport *m*; transfert *m*; cession *f*.

conveyancer *n* notaire *m*.

convict *vt* déclarer coupable; * *n* détenu *m* -e *f*.

conviction *n* condamnation *f*; conviction *f*.

convince *vt* convaincre, persuader.

convincing *adj* convaincant.

convincingly *adv* de façon convaincante.

convivial *adj* jovial.

conviviality *n* jovialité *f*.

convoke *vt* convoquer.

convoy *n* convoi *m*.

convulse *vt* ébranler, convulser.

convulsion *n* convulsion *f*; bouleversement *m*; forte agitation *f*.

convulsive *adj* convulsif; ~**ly** *adv* convulsivement.

coo *vt vi* roucouler.

cook *n* cuisinier *m* -ière *f*; * *vt* cuire; falsifier; * *vi* faire la cuisine, cuisiner.

cookbook *n* livre de cuisine *m*.

cooker *n* cuisinière *f*.

cookery *n* cuisine *f*.

cookie *n* gâteau *m* sec.

cool *adj* frais; calme; * *n* fraîcheur *f*; * *vt* rafraîchir, refroidir.

coolly *adv* fraîchement; de sang-froid.

coolness *n* fraîcheur *f*; froideur *f*; sang-froid *m*.

cooperate *vi* coopérer.

cooperation *n* coopération *f*.

cooperative *adj* coopératif.

coordinate *vt* coordonner.

coordination *n* coordination *f*.

cop *n* (*fam*) flic *m*.

copartner *n* coassocié *m* -e *f*.

cope *vi* se débrouiller.

copier *n* photocopieuse *f*.

copious *adj* copieux, abondant; ~**ly** *adv* abondamment.

copper *n* cuivre *m*.

coppice, copse *n* taillis *m*.

copulate *vi* copuler.

copy *n* copie *f*; reproduction *f*; exemplaire *m*; * *vt* copier; imiter.

copybook *n* cahier *m*.

copying machine *n* photocopieuse *f*.

copyist *n* copiste *mf*.

copyright *n* droit d'auteur *m*.

coral *n* corail *m*.

coral reef *n* récif de corail *m*.

cord *n* cordon *m*, corde *f*.

cordial *adj* cordial, chaleureux; ~**ly** *adv* cordialement.

corduroy *n* velours côtelé *m*.

core *n* trognon *m*; noyau, centre, cœur *m*.

cork *n* liège *m*; bouchon *m*; * *vt* boucher.

corkscrew *n* tire-bouchon *m*.

corn *n* maïs *m*; grain *m*; blé *m*.

corncob *n* épi de maïs *m*.

cornea *n* cornée *f*.

corned beef *n* corned-beef *m*.

corner *n* coin *m*; angle *m*.

cornerstone *n* pierre angulaire *f*.

cornet *n* cornet *m*.

cornfield *n* champ de maïs *m*.

cornflakes *npl* flocons de maïs, cornflakes *mpl*.

cornice *n* corniche *f*.

cornstarch *n* (US) farine de maïs *f*.

corollary *n* corollaire *m*.

coronary *n* infarctus *m*.

coronation *n* couronnement *m*.

coroner *n* coroner *m*.

coronet *n* couronne *f*.

corporal *n* caporal *m*.

corporate *adj* en commun; d'entreprise.

corporation *n* corporation *f*; société par actions *f*.

corporeal *adj* corporel.

corps *n* (*mil*) corps *m*.

corpse *n* cadavre *m*.

corpulent *adj* corpulent.

corpuscle *n* corpuscule *m*; électron *m*.

corral *n* corral *m*.

correct *vt* corriger; rectifier; * *adj* correct, juste; ~**ly** *adv* correctement.

correction *n* correction *f*; rectification *f*.

corrective *adj* correcteur, correctif; * *n* rectificatif *m*.

correctness *n* correction *f*.

correlation *n* corrélation *f*.

correlative *adj* corrélatif.

correspond *vi* correspondre.

correspondence *n* correspondance *f*.

correspondent *adj* correspondant; * *n* correspondant *m* -e *f*.

corridor *n* couloir, corridor *m*.

corroborate *vt* corroborer.

corroboration *n* corroboration *f*.

corroborative *adj* qui corrobore.

corrode *vt* corroder.

corrosion *n* corrosion *f*.

corrosive *adj* n corrosif *m*.

corrugated iron *n* tôle ondulée *f*.

corrupt *vt* corrompre; * *vi* se corrompre, se pourrir; * *adj* corrompu; dépravé.

corruptible *adj* corruptible.

corruption *n* corruption *f*; dépravation *f*.

corruptive *adj* qui corrompt.

corset *n* corset *m*, gaine *f*.

cortege *n* cortège *m*.

cosily *adv* confortablement, douillettement.

cosmetic *adj* n cosmétique *m*.

cosmic *adj* cosmique.

cosmonaut *n* cosmonaute *mf*.

cosmopolitan *adj* cosmopolite.

cosset *vt* dorloter.

cost *n* prix, coût *m*; * *vi* coûter.

costly *adj* coûteux, cher.

costume *n* costume *m*.

cosy *adj* douillet.

cottage *n* cottage *m*.

cotton *n* coton *m*.

cotton candy *n* barbe à papa *f*.

cotton mill *n* filature de coton *f*.

cotton wool *n* coton hydrophile *m*.

couch *n* canapé, divan *m*.

couchette *n* couchette *f*.

cough *n* toux *f*; * *vi* tousser.

council *n* conseil *m*.

councillor *n* membre du conseil *m*; conseiller *m* -ère *f*.

counsel *n* conseil *m*; avocat *m*.

counsellor *n* conseiller *m* -ère *f*; avocat *m*.

count *vt* compter, dénombrer; calculer; ~ **on** compter sur; * *n* compte *m*; calcul *m*; chef d'accusation *m*; comte *m*.

countdown *n* compte à rebours *m*.

countenance *n* visage *m*; aspect *m*; mine *f*.

counter *n* comptoir *m*; pion *m*.

counteract *vt* contrecarrer; neutraliser; contrebalancer.

counterbalance *vt* contrebalancer; compenser; * *n* contrepoids *m*.

counterfeit *vt* contrefaire; * *adj* faux.

countermand *vt* annuler.

counterpart *n* contrepartie *f*; homologue *mf*.

counterproductive *adj* qui va à l'encontre du but visé.

countersign *vt* contresigner.

countess *n* comtesse *f*.

countless *adj* innombrable.

countrified *adj* rustique; campagnard.

country *n* pays *m*; patrie *f*; campagne *f*; région *f*; * *adj* rustique; campagnard.

country house *n* maison de campagne *f*.

countryman *n* campagnard *m*; compatriote *m*.

county *n* comté *m*.

coup *n* coup *m* d'État.

coupé *n* coupé *m*.

couple *n* couple *m*; **a** ~ **of** deux; * *vt* unir, associer.

couplet *n* distique *m*; couplet *m*.

coupon *n* coupon *m*, bon *m*.

courage *n* courage *m*.

courageous *adj* courageux; ~**ly** *adv* courageusement.

courier *n* messager *m*; guide *m*.

course *n* cours *m*; route *f*; chemin *m*; plat *m*; marche à suivre *f*; **of** ~ bien sûr, naturellement.

court *n* cour *f*; tribunal *m*; * *vt* courtiser; solliciter.

courteous *adj* courtois; poli; **~ly** *adv* courtoisement.

courtesan *n* courtisane *f*.

courtesy *n* courtoisie *f*.

courthouse *n* palais de justice *m*.

courtly *adj* élégant, raffiné.

court-martial *n* conseil de guerre *m*.

courtroom *n* salle de tribunal *f*.

courtyard *n* cour *f*.

cousin *n* cousin *m* -e *f*; **first ~** cousin(e) germain(e) *m(f)*.

cove *n* (*mar*) crique, anse *f*.

covenant *n* contrat *m*; convention *f*; * *vi* convenir, stipuler par contrat.

cover *n* couverture *f*; abri *m*; prétexte *m*; * *vt* (re)couvrir; dissimuler; protéger.

coverage *n* reportage *m*, couverture *f*.

coveralls *npl* bleu de travail *m*.

covering *n* couverture *f*; couche *f*.

cover letter *n* lettre explicative *f*.

covert *adj* voilé; caché, secret; **~ly** *adv* secrètement.

cover-up *n* dissimulation *f*.

covet *vt* convoiter.

covetous *adj* avide, cupide.

cow *n* vache *f*.

coward *n* lâche *mf*.

cowardice *n* lâcheté *f*.

cowardly *adj* lâche; *adv* lâchement.

cowboy *n* cowboy *m*.

cower *vi* se tapir.

cowherd *n* vacher *m*.

coy *adj* timide; coquet; évasif; **~ly** *adv* évasivement.

coyness *n* timidité *f*; modestie *f*.

crab *n* crabe *m*.

crab-apple *n* pomme sauvage *f*; **crab-apple tree** *n* pommier sauvage *m*.

crack *n* craquement *m*; fente, fissure *f*; * *vt* fêler, craquer; **~ down on** sévir; * *vi* se fêler; craquer.

cracker *n* pétard *m*; biscuit salé *m*.

crackle *vi* crépiter, pétiller.

crackling *n* crépitement *m*; friture *f*.

cradle *n* berceau *m*; * *vt* bercer.

craft *n* habileté *f*; métier manuel *m*; barque *f*.

craftily *adv* astucieusement.

craftiness *n* astuce, ruse *f*.

craftsman *n* artisan *m*.

craftsmanship *n* artisanat *m*.

crafty *adj* astucieux, rusé.

crag *n* rocher escarpé *m*.

cram *vt* bourrer; fourrer; * *vi* s'entasser.

crammed *adj* bourré.

cramp *n* crampe *f*; * *vt* entraver.

cramped *adj* à l'étroit.

crampon *n* crampon *m*.

cranberry *n* canneberge *f*.

crane *n* grue *f*.

crash *vi* s'écraser; * *n* fracas *m*; collision *f*.

crash helmet *n* casque *m*.

crash landing *n* atterrissage en catastrophe *m*.

crass *adj* grossier, crasse.

crate *n* caisse *f*; cageot *m*.

crater *n* cratère *m*.

cravat *n* foulard *m*, cravate *f*.

crave *vt* avoir extrêmement besoin de.

craving *n* désir extrême *m*, soif *f*.

crawfish *n* écrevisse *f*.

crawl *vi* ramper; **~ with** grouiller de.

crayfish *n* écrevisse *f*.

crayon *n* crayon de couleur *m*.

craze *n* manie *f*, engouement *m*.

craziness *n* folie *f*.

crazy *adj* fou.

creak *vi* grincer, craquer.

cream *n* crème *f*; * *adj* crème.

creamy *adj* crémeux.

crease *n* pli *m*; * *vt* froisser.

create *vt* créer; causer.

creation *n* création *f*.

creative *adj* créatif.

creator *n* créateur *m* -trice *f*.

creature *n* créature *f*.

credence *n* créance *f*; crédit *m*.

credentials *npl* lettres de créance *fpl*; preuves d'identité *fpl*.

credibility *n* crédibilité *f*.

credible *adj* crédible.

credit *n* crédit *m*; honneur *m*; reconnaissance *f*; * *vt* croire, reconnaître; créditer.

creditable *adj* estimable, honorable; **~bly** *adv* honorablement.

credit card *n* carte de crédit *f*.

creditor *n* créancier *m* -ière *f*.

credulity *n* crédulité *f*.

credulous *adj* crédule; **~ly** *adv* avec crédulité.

creed *n* credo *m*.

creek *n* ruisseau *m*.

creep *vi* ramper; avancer lentement.

creeper *n* (*bot*) plante grimpante *f*.

creepy *adj* terrifiant, qui donne la chair de poule.

cremate *vt* incinérer.

cremation *n* incinération, crémation *f*.

crematorium *n* crématoire *m*.

crescent *adj* croissant; * *n* croissant de lune *m*.

cress *n* cresson *m*.

crest *n* crête *f*.

crested *adj* à crête.

crestfallen *adj* découragé, abattu.

crevasse *n* crevasse *f*.

crevice *n* fissure, lézarde *f*.

crew *n* bande, équipe *f*; équipage *m*.

crib *n* berceau *m*; mangeoire *f*.

cricket *n* grillon *m*.

crime *n* crime *m*; délit *m*.

criminal *adj* criminel; **~ly** *adv* criminellement; * *n* criminel *m* -le *f*.

criminality *n* criminalité *f*.

crimson *adj* cramoisi *m*.

cripple *n*, *adj* invalide *mf*; * *vt* estropier; (*fig*) paralyser.

crisis *n* crise *f*.

crisp *adj* frais; croquant.

crispness *n* croquant *m*.

criss-cross *adj* entrecroisé.

criterion *n* critère *m*.

critic *n* critique *m*.

critical *adj* critique; exigeant, sévère; **~ly** *adv* d'un œil critique; sévèrement.

criticise *vt* critiquer.

criticism *n* critique *f*.

croak *vi* coasser, croasser.

crochet *n* crochet *m*; * *vt* faire au crochet; *vi* faire du crochet.

crockery *n* poterie *f*.

crocodile *n* crocodile *m*.

crony *n* copain *m* (copine *f*) de longue date.

crook *n* escroc *m*; filou *m*.

crooked *adj* tordu; malhonnête.

crop *n* culture *f*; récolte *f*; * *vt* récolter.

cross *n* croix *f*; croisement *m*; * *adj* de mauvaise humeur, fâché; * *vt* traverser, croiser; **~ over** traverser.

crossbar *n* barre transversale *f*.

crossbreed *n* hybride *m*.

cross-country *n* cross-country *m*.

cross-examine *vt* soumettre à un contre-interrogatoire.

crossfire *n* feux croisés *mpl*.

crossing *n* traversée *f*; passage pour piétons *m*.

cross-purpose *n* malentendu *m*; quiproquo *m*; **to be at ~s** comprendre (quelqu'un) de travers.

cross-reference *n* renvoi *m*, référence *f*.

crossroad *n* carrefour *m*.

crosswalk *n* (US) passage clouté *m*.

crotch *n* entre-jambes *m*.

crouch *vi* s'accroupir, se tapir.

crow *n* corbeau *m*; chant du coq *m*; * *vi* chanter victoire.

crowd *n* foule *f*; monde *m*; * *vt* entasser; * *vi* s'entasser.

crown *n* couronne *f*; sommet *m*; * *vt* couronner.

crown prince *n* prince héritier *m*.

crucial *adj* crucial.

crucible *n* creuset *m*.

crucifix *n* crucifix *m*.

crucifixion *n* crucifixion *f*.

crucify *vt* crucifier.

crude *adj* brut, grossier; **~ly** *adv* crûment.

cruel *adj* cruel; **~ly** *adv* cruellement.

cruelty *n* cruauté *f*.

cruet *n* huilier-vinaigrier *m*.

cruise *n* croisière *f*; * *vi* croiser.

cruiser *n* croiseur *m*.

crumb *n* miette *f*.

crumble *vt* émietter; effriter; * *vi* s'émietter; se désintégrer.

crumple *vt* froisser.

crunch *vt* croquer; * *n* (*fig*) crise *f*.

crunchy *adj* croquant.

crusade *n* croisade *f*.

crush *vt* écraser; opprimer; * *n* cohue *f*.

crust *n* croûte *f*.

crusty *adj* croustillant; hargneux, bourru.

crutch *n* béquille *f*.

crux *n* cœur *m* (d'une question).

cry *vt vi* crier; pleurer; * *n* cri *m*; sanglot *m*.

crypt *n* crypte *f*.

cryptic *adj* énigmatique.

crystal *n* cristal *m*.

crystal-clear *adj* clair comme de l'eau de roche.

crystalline *adj* cristallin; pur.

crystallise *vi* se cristalliser; * *vt* cristalliser.

cub *n* petit *m* (animal).

cube *n* cube *m*.

cubic *adj* cubique.

cuckoo *n* coucou *m*.

cucumber *n* concombre *m*.

cud *n*: **to chew the ~** ruminer (*also fig*).

cuddle *vt* embrasser; * *vi* s'enlacer; * *n* étreinte *f*, câlin *m*.

cudgel *n* gourdin *m*, trique *f*.

cue *n* queue de billard *f*.

cuff *n* manchette *f*; revers de pantalon *m*.

culinary *adj* culinaire.

cull *vt* sélectionner; éliminer.

culminate *vi* culminer.

culmination *n* point culminant *m*.

culpability *n* culpabilité *f*.

culpable *adj* coupable; blâmable; **~bly** *adv* coupablement.

culprit *n* coupable *mf*.

cult *n* culte *m*.

cultivate *vt* cultiver; améliorer, perfectionner.

cultivation *n* culture *f*.

cultural *adj* culturel.

culture *n* culture *f*.

cumbersome *adj* encombrant; lourd, pesant.

cumulative *adj* cumulatif.

cunning *adj* astucieux, rusé; **~ly** *adv* astucieusement; habilement; * *n* astuce, finesse *f*.

cup *n* tasse, coupe *f*; (*bot*) corolle *f*.

cupboard *n* placard *m*.

curable *adj* guérissable.

curate *n* vicaire *m*.

curator *n* conservateur *m*; curateur *m*.

curb *n* frein *m*; bord du trottoir *m*; * *vt* freiner, juguler, modérer.

curd *n* lait caillé *m*.

curdle *vt* cailler, figer; *vi* se cailler, se figer.

cure *n* remède *m*; cure *f*; * *vt* guérir.

curfew *n* couvre-feu *m*.

curing *n* salaison *f*.

curiosity *n* curiosité *f*.

curious *adj* curieux; **~ly** *adv* avec curiosité; curieusement.

curl *n* boucle de cheveux *f*; * *vt* boucler; friser; * *vi* friser.

curling iron *n*, **curling tongs** *npl* fer à friser *m*.

curly *adj* frisé, bouclé.

currant *n* raisin *m* sec.

currency *n* monnaie *f*; circulation *f*; cours *m*.

current *adj* courant; actuel; * *n* cours *m*; tendance *f*; courant *m*.

current affairs *npl* actualité *f*; problèmes actuels *mpl*.

currently *adv* actuellement.

curriculum vitae *n* curriculum vitae *m*.

curry *n* curry *m*.

curse *vt* maudire; * *vi* jurer; * *n* malédiction *f*.

cursor *n* curseur *m*.

cursory *adj* superficiel; hâtif.

curt *adj* succinct; sec.

curtail *vt* réduire; écourter.

curtain *n* rideau *m*.

curtain rod *n* tringle à rideaux *f*.

curtsy *n* révérence *f*; * *vi* faire une révérence.

curvature *n* courbure *f*.

curve *vt* courber; * *n* courbe *f*.

cushion *n* coussin *m*.

custard *n* crème anglaise *f*.

custodian *n* gardien *m* -ne *f*.

custody *n* garde *f*; emprisonnement *m*.

custom *n* coutume *f*, usage *m*.

customary *adj* habituel, coutumier, ordinaire.

customer *n* client *m* -e *f*.

customs *npl* douane *f*.

customs duty *n* droits de douane *mpl*.

customs officer *n* douanier *m*.

cut *vt* découper; couper; tailler; réduire; blesser; **~ short** écourter; interrompre; **~ a tooth** percer une dent; * *vi* couper; se couper; * *n* coupe *f*; coupure *f*; réduction *f*; **~ and dried** *adj* arrangé.

cutback *n* réduction *f*.

cute *adj* mignon.

cutlery *n* couverts *mpl*.

cutlet *n* côtelette *f*.

cut-rate *adj* à prix réduit.

cut-throat *n* assassin *m*; * *adj* acharné.

cutting *n* coupure *f*; * *adj* coupant; tranchant.

cyanide *n* cyanure *m*.

cycle *n* cycle *m*; bicyclette *f*; * *vi* aller à bicyclette.

cycling *n* cyclisme *m*.

cyclist *n* cycliste *mf*.

cyclone *n* cyclone *m*.

cygnet *n* jeune cygne *m*.

cylinder *n* cylindre *m*; rouleau *m*.

cylindric(al) *adj* cylindrique.

cymbals *n* cymbale *f*.

cynic(al) *adj* cynique; sceptique; * *n* cynique *mf*.

cynicism *n* cynisme *m*.

cypress *n* cyprès *m*.

cyst *n* kyste *m*.

czar *n* tsar *m*.

D

dab *n* petit peu *m*; touche *f*.
dabble *vi* barboter.
Dacron *n* dacron *m*.
dad(dy) *n* papa *m*.
daddy-long-legs *n* (*zool*) cousin *m*.
daffodil *n* narcisse *m*, jonquille *f*.
dagger *n* poignard *m*.
daily *adj* quotidien; * *adv* quotidiennement, tous les jours; * *n* quotidien *m*.
daintily *adv* délicatement.
daintiness *n* élégance *f*; délicatesse *f*.
dainty *adj* délicat; élégant.
dairy *n* laiterie *f*.
dairy farm *n* laiterie *f*.
dairy produce *n* produits laitiers *mpl*.
daisy *n* marguerite *f*.
daisy wheel *n* marguerite *f*.
dale *n* vallée *f*.
dally *vi* traîner.
dam *n* barrage *m*; * *vt* endiguer.
damage *n* dommage *m*; tort *m*; * *vt* endommager; faire du tort à.
damask *n* damas *m*; * *adj* damassé.
dame *n* dame *f*; fille *f*.
damn *vt* condamner; * *adj* maudit.
damnable *adj* maudit; ~**bly** *adv* terriblement.
damnation *n* damnation *f*.
damning *adj* accablant.
damp *adj* humide; * *n* humidité *f*; * *vt* humidifier.
dampen *vt* humidifier.
dampness *n* humidité *f*.
damson *n* prune de Damas *f*.
dance *n* danse *f*; soirée dansante *f*; * *vt vi* danser.
dance hall *n* dancing *m*.
dancer *n* danseur *m* -euse *f*.
dandelion *n* pissenlit *m*.
dandruff *n* pellicules *fpl*.
dandy *adj* génial.
danger *n* danger *m*.
dangerous *adj* dangereux; ~**ly** *adv* dangereusement.
dangle *vi* pendre.
dank *adj* humide.
dapper *adj* soigné.
dappled *adj* tacheté.
dare *vi* oser; * *vt* défier.
daredevil *n* casse-cou *m invar*.
daring *n* audace *f*; * *adj* audacieux; ~**ly** *adv* audacieusement.

dark *adj* sombre, obscur; * *n* obscurité *f*; ignorance *f*.
darken *vt* assombrir, obscurcir; * *vi* s'assombrir, s'obscurcir.
dark glasses *npl* lunettes de soleil *fpl*.
darkness *n* obscurité *f*.
darkroom *n* chambre noire *f*.
darling *n*, *adj* chéri *m* -e *f*.
darn *vt* repriser.
dart *n* dard *m*.
darts *n* jeu de fléchettes *m*.
dash *vi* se dépêcher; * *n* goutte *f*; tiret, trait *m*; **at one** ~ tout d'un coup.
dashboard *n* tableau de bord *m*.
dashing *adj* impétueux; élégant.
dastardly *adj* infâme.
data *n* données *fpl*.
database *n* base de données *f*.
data processing *n* traitement de données *m*.
date *n* date *f*; rendez-vous *m*; (*bot*) datte *f*; * *vt* dater; sortir avec.
dated *adj* démodé.
dative *n* (*gr*) datif *m*.
daub *vt* barbouiller.
daughter *n* fille *f*; ~ **in-law** belle-fille *f*.
daunting *adj* décourageant.
dawdle *vi* traîner.
dawn *n* aube *f*; * *vi* se lever.
day *n* jour *m*, journée *f*; **by** ~ de jour; ~ **by** ~ de jour en jour.
daybreak *n* aube *f*.
day laborer *n* (US) journalier *m*.
daylight *n* lumière du jour, lumière naturelle *f*; ~ **saving time** *n* heure d'été *f*.
daytime *n* journée *f*, jour *m*.
daze *vt* étourdir.
dazed *adj* étourdi.
dazzle *vt* éblouir.
dazzling *adj* éblouissant.
deacon *n* diacre *m*.
dead *adj* mort; ~**wood** *n* bois mort *m*; ~ **silence** *n* silence de mort *m*; **the** ~ *npl* les morts *mpl*.
dead-drunk *adj* ivre-mort.
deaden *vt* amortir.
dead heat *n* arrivée ex-aequo *f*.
deadline *n* date limite *f*.
deadlock *n* impasse *f*.
deadly *adj* mortel; * *adv* terriblement.
dead march *n* marche funèbre *f*.
deadness *n* inertie *f*.

deaf *adj* sourd.
deafen *vt* assourdir.
deaf-mute *n* sourd(e)-muet(te) *mf*.
deafness *n* surdité *f*.
deal *n* accord *m*; marché *m*; **a great** ~ beaucoup; **a good** ~ pas mal; * *vt* distribuer, donner; * *vi* ~ **in** être dans le commerce de; ~ **with** avoir affaire à.
dealer *n* commerçant *m*; trafiquant *m*; donneur *m*.
dealings *npl* rapports *mpl*; transactions *fpl*.
dean *n* doyen *m*.
dear *adj* ~**ly** *adv* cher.
dearness *n* cherté *f*.
dearth *n* pénurie *f*.
death *n* mort *f*.
deathbed *n* lit de mort *m*.
deathblow *n* coup mortel *m*.
death certificate *n* acte de décès *m*.
death penalty *n* peine de mort *f*.
death throes *npl* agonie *f*.
death warrant *n* condamnation à mort *f*.
debacle *n* débâcle *f*.
debar *vt* exclure.
debase *vt* dégrader.
debasement *n* dégradation *f*.
debatable *adj* discutable.
debate *n* débat *m*; * *vt* discuter; examiner.
debauched *adj* débauché.
debauchery *n* débauche *f*.
debilitate *vt* débiliter.
debit *n* débit *m*; * *vt* (*com*) débiter.
debt *n* dette *f*; **to get into** ~ s'endetter.
debtor *n* débiteur *m* -trice *f*.
debunk *vt* démystifier.
decade *n* décennie *f*.
decadence *n* décadence *f*.
decaffeinated *adj* décaféiné.
decanter *n* carafe *f*.
decapitate *vt* décapiter.
decapitation *n* décapitation *f*.
decay *vi* décliner; pourrir; * *n* déclin *m*; pourrissement *m*; carie *f*.
deceased *adj* décédé.
deceit *n* tromperie *f*.
deceitful *adj* trompeur; ~**ly** *adv* faussement.
deceive *vt* tromper.
December *n* décembre *m*.
decency *n* décence *f*; pudeur *f*.

decent *adj* décent; bien, bon; **~ly** *adv* décemment.

deception *n* tromperie *f*.

deceptive *adj* trompeur.

decibel *n* décibel *m*.

decide *vt* decider; * *vi* se décider.

decided *adj* décidé.

decidedly *adv* décidément.

deciduous *adj* (*bot*) à feuilles caduques.

decimal *adj* décimal.

decimate *vt* décimer.

decipher *vt* déchiffrer.

decision *n* décision, détermination *f*.

decisive *adj* décisif; **~ly** *adv* avec décision.

deck *n* pont *m*; * *vt* orner.

deckchair *n* chaise longue *f*.

declaim *vt vi* déclamer.

declamation *n* déclamation *f*.

declaration *n* déclaration *f*.

declare *vt* déclarer.

declension *n* déclinaison *f*.

decline *vt* (*gr*) décliner; refuser; * *vi* décliner; * *n* déclin *m*; décadence *f*.

declutch *vi* débrayer.

decode *vt* décoder.

decompose *vt* décomposer.

decomposition *n* décomposition *f*.

decor *n* décor *m*; décoration *f*.

decorate *vt* décorer, orner.

decoration *n* décoration *f*.

decorative *adj* décoratif.

decorator *n* décorateur *m* -trice *f*.

decorous *adj* bienséant, convenable; **~ly** *adv* convenablement.

decorum *n* décorum *m*.

decoy *n* leurre *m*.

decrease *vt* diminuer; * *n* diminution *f*.

decree *n* décret *m*; * *vt* décréter; ordonner.

decrepit *adj* décrépit.

decry *vt* décrier.

dedicate *vt* dédier; consacrer.

dedication *n* dédicace *f*; consacration *f*.

deduce *vt* déduire, conclure.

deduct *vt* déduire, soustraire.

deduction *n* déduction *f*.

deed *n* action *f*; exploit *m*.

deem *vt* juger, considérer.

deep *adj* profond.

deepen *vt* approfondir.

deep-freeze *n* congélateur *m*.

deeply *adv* profondément.

deepness *n* profondeur *f*.

deer *n* cerf *m*.

deface *vt* défigurer.

defacement *n* défiguration *f*.

defamation *n* diffamation *f*.

default *n* défaut *m*; manque *m*; * *vi* manquer à ses engagements.

defaulter *n* (*law*) défaillant *m* -e *f*.

defeat *n* défaite *f*; * *vt* vaincre; frustrer.

defect *n* défaut *m*.

defection *n* désertion *f*.

defective *adj* défectueux.

defend *vt* défendre; protéger.

defendant *n* accusé *m* -e *f*.

defense *n* défense *f*; protection *f*.

defenseless *adj* sans défense.

defensive *adj* défensif; **~ly** *adv* défensivement.

defer *vt* déférer.

deference *n* déférence *f*.

deferential *adj* respectueux.

defiance *n* défi *m*.

defiant *adj* provocant.

deficiency *n* défaut *m*; manque *m*.

deficient *adj* insuffisant.

deficit *n* déficit *m*.

defile *vt* souiller.

definable *adj* définissable.

define *vt* définir.

definite *adj* sûr; précis; **~ly** *adv* sans aucun doute.

definition *n* définition *f*.

definitive *adj* définitif; **~ly** *adv* définitivement.

deflate *vt* dégonfler.

deflect *vt* dévier.

deflower *vt* déflorer.

deform *vt* déformer.

deformity *n* déformité *f*.

defraud *vt* escroquer.

defray *vt* payer.

defrost *vt* dégivrer; décongeler.

defroster *n* dégivreur *m*.

deft *adj* habile; **~ly** *adv* habilement.

defunct *adj* défunt.

defuse *vt* désamorcer.

degenerate *vi* dégénérer; * *adj* dégénéré.

degeneration *n* dégénération *f*.

degradation *n* dégradation *f*.

degrade *vt* dégrader.

degree *n* degré *m*; diplôme *m*.

dehydrated *adj* déshydraté.

de-ice *vt* dégivrer.

deign *vi* daigner.

deity *n* divinité *f*.

dejected *adj* découragé.

dejection *n* découragement *m*.

delay *vt* retarder; * *n* retard *m*.

delectable *adj* délectable.

delegate *vt* déléguer; * *n* délégué *m* -e *f*.

delegation *n* délégation *f*.

delete *vt* effacer.

deliberate *vt* examiner; * *adj* délibéré; **~ly** *adv* délibérément, exprès.

deliberation *n* délibération *f*.

deliberative *adj* délibérant.

delicacy *n* délicatesse *f*.

delicate *adj* délicat; **~ly** *adv* délicatement.

delicious *adj* délicieux, exquis; **~ly** *adv* délicieusement.

delight *n* délice *m*; enchantement *m*; * *vt* enchanter; * *vi* adorer.

delighted *adj* enchanté.

delightful *adj* charmant; **~ly** *adv* merveilleusement.

delineate *vt* décrire; délimiter.

delineation *n* tracé *m*.

delinquency *n* délinquance *f*.

delinquent *n* délinquant *m* -e *f*.

delirious *adj* délirant.

delirium *n* délire *m*.

deliver *vt* livrer; délivrer; prononcer.

deliverance *n* libération *f*.

delivery *n* livraison *f*; accouchement *m*.

delude *vt* tromper.

deluge *n* déluge *m*.

delusion *n* tromperie *f*; illusion *f*.

delve *vi* creuser; chercher.

demagogue *n* démagogue *m*.

demand *n* demande *f*; * *vt* exiger; réclamer.

demanding *adj* exigeant.

demarcation *n* démarcation *f*.

demean *vi* s'abaisser.

demeanour *n* conduite *f*, comportement *m*.

demented *adj* dément.

demise *n* disparition *f*.

democracy *n* démocratie *f*.

democrat *n* démocrate *mf*.

democratic *adj* démocratique.

demolish *vt* démolir.

demolition *n* démolition *f*.

demon *n* démon, diable *m*.

demonstrable *adj* démontrable; **~bly** *adv* manifestement.

demonstrate *vt* démontrer, prouver; * *vi* manifester.

demonstration *n* démonstration *f*; manifestation *f*.

demonstrative *adj* démonstratif.

demonstrator *n* manifestant *m* -e *f*.

demoralisation *n* démoralisation *f*.

demoralise *vt* démoraliser.

demote *vt* rétrograder.

demur *vi* émettre une objection; rechigner.

demure *adj* réservé; **~ly** *adv* avec réserve.

den *n* antre *m*.

denatured alcohol *n* alcool dénaturé *m*.

denial *n* dénégation *f*.

denims *npl* jean *m.*

denomination *n* valeur *f;* dénomination *f.*

denominator *n* (*math*) dénominateur *m.*

denote *vt* dénoter, indiquer.

denounce *vt* dénoncer.

dense *adj* dense, épais.

density *n* densité *f.*

dent *n* bosse *f;* * *vt* cabosser.

dental *adj* dentaire.

dentifrice *n* dentifrice *m.*

dentist *n* dentiste *mf.*

dentistry *n* dentisterie *f.*

denture *n* dentier *m.*

denude *vt* dénuder, dépouiller.

denunciation *n* dénonciation *f.*

deny *vt* nier.

deodorant *n* déodorant *m.*

deodorise *vt* déodoriser.

depart *vi* partir.

department *n* département *m;* service *m.*

department store *n* grand magasin *m.*

departure *n* départ *m.*

departure lounge *n* salle d'embarquement *f.*

depend *vi* dépendre; ~ **on/upon** compter sur.

dependable *adj* fiable; sûr.

dependant *n* personne à charge *f.*

dependency *n* dépendance *f.*

dependent *adj* dépendant.

depict *vt* dépeindre, décrire.

depleted *adj* réduit.

deplorable *adj* déplorable, lamentable; **~bly** *adv* déplorablement.

deplore *vt* déplorer, lamenter.

deploy *vt* (*mil*) déployer.

depopulated *adj* dépeuplé.

depopulation *n* dépopulation *f.*

deport *vt* déporter; expulser.

deportation *n* déportation *f;* expulsion *f.*

deportment *n* comportement *m.*

deposit *vt* déposer; * *n* dépôt *m;* caution *f.*

deposition *n* déposition *f.*

depositor *n* déposant *m* -e *f.*

depot *n* dépôt *m.*

deprave *vt* dépraver, corrompre.

depraved *adj* dépravé.

depravity *n* dépravation *f.*

deprecate *vt* désapprouver.

depreciate *vi* se déprécier.

depreciation *n* dépréciation *f.*

depredation *n* déprédation *f.*

depress *vt* déprimer.

depressed *adj* déprimé.

depression *n* dépression *f.*

deprivation *n* privation *f.*

deprive *vt* priver.

deprived *adj* défavorisé.

depth *n* profondeur *f.*

deputation *n* députation *f.*

depute *vt* députer, déléguer.

deputise *vi* remplacer.

deputy *n* remplaçant *m* -e *f;* député *m;* délégué *m* -e *f.*

derail *vt* faire dérailler.

deranged *adj* dérangé.

derby *n* chapeau melon *m.*

derelict *adj* abandonné, en ruines.

deride *vt* se moquer de.

derision *n* dérision *f.*

derisive *adj* ridicule; moqueur.

derivable *adj* déductible.

derivation *n* dérivation *f.*

derivative *n* dérivé *m.*

derive *vt vi* dériver.

derogatory *adj* désobligeant.

derrick *n* derrick *m.*

descant *n* (*mus*) déchant *m.*

descend *vi* descendre.

descendant *n* descendant *m* -e *f.*

descent *n* descente *f.*

describe *vt* décrire.

description *n* description *f.*

descriptive *adj* descriptif.

descry *vt* distinguer.

desecrate *vt* profaner.

desecration *n* profanation *f.*

desert *n* désert *m;* * *adj* désert; * *vt* abandonner; déserter.

deserter *n* déserteur *m.*

desertion *n* désertion *f.*

deserve *vt* mériter.

deservedly *adv* à juste titre.

deserving *adj* méritant.

déshabillé *n* déshabillé *m.*

desideratum *n* desideratum *m.*

design *vt* concevoir; dessiner; * *n* dessein *m;* design *m;* dessin *m.*

designate *vt* désigner.

designation *n* désignation *f.*

designedly *adv* exprès, délibérément.

designer *n* créateur *m* -trice *f;* styliste *mf.*

desirability *n* avantage *m;* attrait *m.*

desirable *adj* désirable.

desire *n* désir *m;* * *vt* désirer.

desirous *adj* désireux.

desist *vi* abandonner.

desk *n* bureau *m.*

desolate *adj* désert, désolé.

desolation *n* désolation *f.*

despair *n* désespoir *m;* * *vi* se désespérer.

despairingly *adv* désespérément.

despatch = dispatch.

desperado *n* bandit *m.*

desperate *adj* désespéré; **~ly** *adv* désespérément; extrêmement.

desperation *n* désespoir *m.*

despicable *adj* méprisable.

despise *vt* mépriser.

despite *prep* malgré.

despoil *vt* dépouiller.

despondency *n* abattement *m.*

despondent *adj* abattu.

despot *n* despote *m.*

despotic *adj* despotique; **~ally** *adv* despotiquement.

despotism *n* despotisme *m.*

dessert *n* dessert *m.*

destination *n* destination *f.*

destine *vt* destiner.

destiny *n* destin, sort *m.*

destitute *adj* indigent.

destitution *n* indigence *f.*

destroy *vt* détruire.

destruction *n* destruction *f.*

destructive *adj* destructeur.

desultory *adj* irrégulier; sans méthode.

detach *vt* séparer, détacher.

detachable *adj* détachable.

detachment *n* (*mil*) détachement *m.*

detail *n* détail *m;* **in ~** en détail; * *vt* détailler.

detain *vt* retenir; détenir.

detect *vt* détecter.

detection *n* détection *f;* découverte *f.*

detective *n* détective *m.*

detector *n* détecteur *m.*

detention *n* détention *f.*

deter *vt* dissuader.

detergent *n* détergent *m.*

deteriorate *vt* détériorer.

deterioration *n* détérioration *f.*

determination *n* détermination *f.*

determine *vt* déterminer, décider.

determined *adj* déterminé.

deterrent *n* force de dissuasion *f.*

detest *vt* détester.

detestable *adj* détestable.

dethrone *vt* détrôner.

dethronement *n* détrônement *m.*

detonate *vi* détoner.

detonation *n* détonation *f.*

detour *n* déviation *f.*

detract *vi* nuire à.

detriment *n* détriment *m.*

detrimental *adj* préjudiciable.

deuce *n* deux *m;* égalité *f.*

devaluation *n* dévaluation *f.*

devalue = devaluate.

devastate *vt* dévaster.

devastating *adj* dévastateur.

devastation *n* dévastation *f.*

develop *vt* développer.

development *n* développement *m.*

deviate *vi* dévier.

deviation *n* déviation *f.*

device *n* mécanisme *m.*

devil *n* diable, démon *m*.

devilish *adj* diabolique; **~ly** *adv* diaboliquement.

devious *adj* tortueux.

devise *vt* inventer; concevoir.

devoid *adj* dépourvu.

devolve *vt* déléguer.

devote *vt* consacrer.

devoted *adj* dévoué.

devotee *n* partisan *m* -e *f*.

devotion *n* dévotion *f*.

devotional *adj* dévot.

devour *vt* dévorer.

devout *adj* dévot, pieux; **~ly** *adv* pieusement.

dew *n* rosée *f*.

dewy *adj* couvert de rosée; ingénu.

dexterity *n* dextérité *f*.

dexterous *adj* adroit, habile.

diabetes *n* diabète *m*.

diabetic *n* diabétique *mf*.

diabolic *adj* diabolique; **~ally** *adv* diaboliquement.

diadem *n* diadème *m*.

diagnosis *n* (*med*) diagnostic *m*.

diagnostic *adj* diagnostique; * *npl* **~s** diagnostic *m*.

diagonal *adj* diagonal; **~ly** *adv* diagonalement; * *n* diagonale *f*.

diagram *n* diagramme *m*.

dial *n* cadrant *m*.

dial code *n* code *m*.

dialect *n* dialecte *m*.

dialogue *n* dialogue *m*.

dial tone *n* tonalité *f*.

diameter *n* diamètre *m*.

diametrical *adj* diamétral; **~ly** *adv* diamétralement.

diamond *n* diamant *m*.

diamond-cutter *n* tailleur de diamant *m*.

diamonds *npl* (cards) carreaux *mpl*.

diaper *n* couche *f*.

diaphragm *n* diaphragme *m*.

diarrhoea *n* diarrhée *f*.

diary *n* journal *m*.

dice *npl* dés *mpl*.

dictate *vt* dicter; * *n* ordre *m*.

dictation *n* dictée *f*.

dictatorial *adj* dictatorial.

dictatorship *n* dictature *f*.

diction *n* diction *f*

dictionary *n* dictionnaire *m*.

didactic *adj* didactique.

die *vi* mourir; **~ away** s'affaiblir; **~ down** s'éteindre.

die *n* (*sing de* **dice**) dé *m*.

diehard *n* réactionnaire *mf*.

diesel *n* diesel *m*.

diet *n* diète *f*; régime *m*; * *vi* être au régime.

dietary *adj* diététique.

differ *vi* différer.

difference *n* différence *f*.

different *adj* différent; **~ly** *adv* différemment.

differentiate *vt* différencier.

difficult *adj* difficile.

difficulty *n* difficulté *f*.

diffidence *n* timidité *f*; manque d'assurance *m*.

diffident *adj* timide; mal assuré; **~ly** *adv* avec timidité.

diffraction *n* diffraction *f*.

diffuse *vt* diffuser, répandre; * *adj* diffus.

diffusion *n* diffusion *f*.

dig *vt* creuser; * *n* coup *m*.

digest *vt* digérer.

digestible *adj* digestible.

digestion *n* digestion *f*.

digestive *adj* digestif.

digger *n* excavatrice *f*.

digit *n* chiffre *m*.

digital *adj* digital; numérique.

dignified *adj* digne.

dignitary *n* dignitaire *m*.

dignity *n* dignité *f*.

digress *vi* faire une digression.

digression *n* digression *f*.

dike *n* digue *f*.

dilapidated *adj* délabré.

dilapidation *n* délabrement *m*.

dilate *vt* dilater; * *vi* se dilater.

dilemma *n* dilemme *m*.

diligence *n* assiduité *f*.

diligent *adj* assidu; **~ly** *adv* avec assiduité.

dilute *vt* diluer.

dim *adj* indistinct; faible; sombre; * *vt* affaiblir; troubler.

dime *n* pièce de dix cents *f*.

dimension *n* dimension *f*.

diminish *vt vi* diminuer.

diminution *n* diminution *f*.

diminutive *n* diminutif *m*.

dimly *adv* indistinctement; faiblement.

dimmer *n* interrupteur d'intensité *m*.

dimple *n* fossette *f*.

din *n* vacarme *m*.

dine *vi* dîner.

diner *n* restaurant (économique) *m*; dîneur *m* -euse *f*.

dinghy *n* canot pneumatique *f*.

dingy *adj* sale; miteux.

dinner *n* dîner *m*.

dinner time *n* heure du dîner *f*.

dinosaur *n* dinosaure *m*.

dint *n*: **by ~ of** à force de.

diocese *n* diocèse *m*.

dip *vt* tremper.

diphtheria *n* diphtérie *f*.

diphthong *n* diphtongue *f*.

diploma *n* diplôme *m*.

diplomacy *n* diplomatie *f*.

diplomat *n* diplomate *m*.

diplomatic *adj* diplomatique.

dipsomania *n* dipsomanie *f*.

dipstick *n* (*auto*) jauge *f*.

dire *adj* atroce, affreux.

direct *adj* direct; * *vt* diriger.

direction *n* direction *f*; instruction *f*.

directly *adv* directement; immédiatement.

director *n* directeur *m* -trice *f*.

directory *n* annuaire *m*.

dirt *n* saleté *f*.

dirtiness *n* saleté *f*.

dirty *adj* sale.

disability *n* incapacité *f*; infirmité *f*.

disabled *adj* infirme.

disabuse *vt* détromper.

disadvantage *n* désavantage *m*; * *vt* désavantager.

disadvantageous *adj* désavantageux.

disaffected *adj* mécontent.

disagree *vi* ne pas être d'accord.

disagreeable *adj* désagréable; **~bly** *adv* désagréablement.

disagreement *n* désaccord *m*.

disallow *vt* rejeter.

disappear *vi* disparaître.

disappearance *n* disparition *f*.

disappoint *vt* décevoir.

disappointed *adj* déçu.

disappointing *adj* décevant.

disappointment *n* déception *f*.

disapproval *n* désapprobation *f*.

disapprove *vt* désapprouver.

disarm *vt* désarmer.

disarmament *n* désarmement *m*.

disarray *n* désordre *m*.

disaster *n* désastre *m*.

disastrous *adj* désastreux.

disband *vt* disperser.

disbelief *n* incrédulité *f*.

disbelieve *vt* ne pas croire.

disburse *vt* débourser.

discard *vt* jeter.

discern *vt* discerner, percevoir.

discernible *adj* perceptible.

discerning *adj* perspicace.

discernment *n* perspicacité *f*.

discharge *vt* décharger; régler (une dette); remplir; * *n* décharge *f*; règlement *m*.

disciple *n* disciple *m*.

discipline *n* discipline *f*; * *vt* discipliner.

disclaim *vt* nier.

disclaimer *n* dénégation *f*.

disclose *vt* révéler.

disclosure *n* révélation *f*.

disco *n* discothèque *f*.

discoloration *n* décoloration *f*.

discolour *vt* décolorer.

discomfort *n* incommodité *f.*

disconcert *vt* déconcerter.

disconnect *vt* débrancher.

disconsolate *adj* inconsolable; ~**ly** *adv* inconsolablement.

discontent *n* mécontentement *m;* * *adj* mécontent.

discontented *adj* mécontent.

discontinue *vt* interrompre.

discord *n* discorde *f.*

discordant *adj* discordant.

discount *n* escompte *m;* remise *f;* * *vt* escompter.

discourage *vt* décourager.

discouraged *adj* découragé.

discouragement *n* découragement *m.*

discouraging *adj* décourageant.

discourse *n* discours *m.*

discourteous *adj* discourtois; ~**ly** *adv* de manière discourtoise.

discourtesy *n* manque de courtoisie *m.*

discover *vt* découvrir.

discovery *n* découverte *f.*

discredit *vt* discréditer.

discreditable *adj* peu honorable.

discreet *adj* discret; ~**ly** *adv* discrètement.

discrepancy *n* contradiction *f.*

discretion *n* discrétion *f.*

discretionary *adj* discrétionnaire.

discriminate *vt* distinguer; discriminer.

discrimination *n* discrimination *f.*

discursive *adj* discursif.

discuss *vt* discuter.

discussion *n* discussion *f.*

disdain *vt* dédaigner; * *n* dédain, mépris *m.*

disdainful *adj* dédaigneux, méprisant; ~**ly** *adv* dédaigneusement, avec mépris.

disease *n* maladie *f.*

diseased *adj* malade.

disembark *vt vi* débarquer.

disembarkation *n* (*mil*) débarquement *m.*

disenchant *vt* désenchanter.

disenchanted *adj* désenchanté.

disenchantment *n* désenchantement *m.*

disengage *vt* dégager.

disentangle *vt* démêler.

disfigure *vt* défigurer.

disgrace *n* honte *f;* scandale *m;* * *vt* déshonorer.

disgraceful *adj* honteux; scandaleux; ~**ly** *adv* honteusement.

disgruntled *adj* mécontent.

disguise *vt* déguiser; * *n* déguisement *m.*

disgust *n* dégoût *m;* * *vt* dégoûter.

disgusting *adj* dégoûtant.

dish *n* plat *m;* assiette *f;* * *vt* servir dans un plat; ~ **up** servir.

dishcloth *n* torchon à vaisselle *m.*

dishearten *vt* démoraliser.

dishevelled *adj* ébouriffé.

dishonest *adj* malhonnête; ~**ly** *adv* malhonnêtement.

dishonesty *n* malhonnêteté *f.*

dishonour *n* déshonneur *m;* * *vt* déshonorer.

dishonourable *adj* déshonorable; ~**bly** *adv* de manière déshonorante.

dishtowel *n* torchon à vaisselle *m.*

dishwarmer *n* chauffe-plats *m.*

dishwasher *n* lave-vaisselle *m;* plongeur *m* -euse *f.*

disillusion *vt* désillusionner.

disillusioned *adj* désillusionné.

disincentive *n* élément dissuasif *m.*

disinclination *n* aversion *f.*

disinclined *adj* peu enclin.

disinfect *vt* désinfecter.

disinfectant *n* désinfectant *m.*

disinherit *vt* déshériter.

disintegrate *vi* se désintégrer.

disinterested *adj* désintéressé; ~**ly** *adv* de manière désintéressée.

disjointed *adj* déréglé; décousu.

disk *n* disque *m;* disquette *f.*

diskette *n* disque *m,* disquette *f.*

dislike *n* aversion *f;* * *vt* ne pas aimer.

dislocate *vt* disloquer.

dislocation *n* dislocation *f.*

dislodge *vt* déloger.

disloyal *adj* déloyal; ~**ly** *adv* déloyalement.

disloyalty *n* déloyauté *f.*

dismal *adj* triste, lugubre.

dismantle *vt* démonter.

dismay *n* consternation *f.*

dismember *vt* démembrer.

dismiss *vt* renvoyer; écarter.

dismissal *n* renvoi *m;* rejet *m.*

dismount *vt* désarçonner; * *vi* descendre.

disobedience *n* désobéissance *f.*

disobedient *adj* désobéissant.

disobey *vt* désobéir.

disorder *n* désordre *m.*

disorderly *adj* en désordre, confus.

disorganisation *n* désorganisation *f.*

disorganised *adj* désorganisé.

disorientated *adj* désorienté.

disown *vt* renier.

disparage *vt* dénigrer.

disparaging *adj* désobligeant.

disparity *n* disparité *f.*

dispassionate *adj* impartial; calme.

dispatch *vt* envoyer; * *n* envoi *m;* dépêche *f.*

dispel *vt* dissiper.

dispensary *n* dispensaire *m.*

dispense *vt* dispenser; distribuer.

disperse *vt* disperser.

dispirited *adj* démoralisé.

displace *vt* déplacer.

display *vt* exposer; faire preuve de; * *n* exposition *f;* déploiement *m.*

displeased *adj* mécontent.

displeasure *n* mécontentement *m.*

disposable *adj* à jeter.

disposal *n* disposition *f.*

dispose *vt* disposer.

disposed *adj* disposé.

disposition *n* disposition *f.*

dispossess *vt* déposséder.

disproportionate *adj* disproportionné.

disprove *vt* réfuter.

dispute *n* dispute *f;* controverse *f;* * *vt* mettre en cause.

disqualify *vt* exclure; disqualifier.

disquiet *n* inquiétude *f.*

disquieting *adj* inquiétant.

disquisition *n* dissertation *f.*

disregard *vt* ne pas tenir compte de; mépriser; * *n* dédain *m.*

disreputable *adj* de mauvaise réputation.

disrespect *n* irrévérence *f.*

disrespectful *adj* irrespectueux; ~**ly** *adv* irrespectueusement.

disrobe *vt* dévêtir.

disrupt *vt* interrompre.

disruption *n* interruption *f.*

dissatisfaction *n* mécontentement *m.*

dissatisfied *adj* mécontent.

dissect *vt* disséquer.

dissection *n* dissection *f.*

disseminate *vt* disséminer.

dissension *n* dissension *f.*

dissent *vi* être en dissension; * *n* dissension *f.*

dissenter *n* dissident *m* -e *f.*

dissertation *n* thèse *f.*

dissident *n* dissident *m* -e *f.*

dissimilar *adj* dissemblable.

dissimilarity *n* dissemblance *f.*

dissimulation *n* dissimulation *f.*

dissipate *vt* dissiper.

dissipation *n* dissipation *f.*

dissociate *vt* dissocier.

dissolute *adj* dissolu.

dissolution *n* dissolution *f.*

dissolve *vt* dissoudre; * *vi* se dissoudre.

dissonance *n* dissonance *f.*

dissuade *vt* dissuader.

distance *n* distance *f;* **at a ~** de loin; * *vt* distancer.

distant *adj* distant.

distaste *n* dégoût *m*.

distasteful *adj* désagréable.

distend *vt* distendre.

distil *vt* distiller.

distillation *n* distillation *f*.

distillery *n* distillerie *f*.

distinct *adj* distinct; **~ly** *adv* distinctement.

distinction *n* distinction *f*.

distinctive *adj* distinctif.

distinctness *n* clarté *f*.

distinguish *vt* distinguer; discerner.

distort *vt* déformer.

distorted *adj* déformé.

distortion *n* distortion *f*.

distract *vt* distraire.

distracted *adj* distrait; **~ly** *adv* distraitement.

distraction *n* distraction *f*; confusion *f*.

distraught *adj* éperdu.

distress *n* souffrance *f*; détresse *f*; * *vt* désoler; affliger.

distressing *adj* affligeant.

distribute *vt* distribuer, répartir.

distribution *n* distribution *f*.

distributor *n* distributeur *m*.

district *n* district *m*.

district attorney *n* procureur de la République *m*.

distrustful *adj* méfiant.

disturb *vt* déranger.

disturbance *n* dérangement *m*; trouble *m*.

disturbed *adj* troublé.

disturbing *adj* troublant.

disuse *n* désuétude *f*.

disused *adj* abandonné.

ditch *n* fossé *m*.

dither *vi* hésiter.

ditto *adv* idem.

ditty *n* chansonnette *f*.

diuretic *adj* (*med*) diurétique.

dive *vi* plonger.

diver *n* plongeur *m* -euse *f*.

diverge *vi* diverger.

divergence *n* divergence *f*.

divergent *adj* divergent.

diverse *adj* divers, différent; **~ly** *adv* différemment.

diversion *n* diversion *f*.

diversity *n* diversité *f*.

divert *vt* dévier; divertir.

divest *vt* dénuder; dépouiller.

divide *vt* diviser; * *vi* se diviser.

dividend *n* dividende *m*.

dividers *npl* (*math*) compas à pointes sèches *m*.

divine *adj* divin.

divinity *n* divinité *f*.

diving *n* plongeon *m*.

diving board *n* plongeoir *m*.

divisible *adj* divisible.

division *n* (*math*) division *f*.

divisor *n* (*math*) diviseur *m*.

divorce *n* divorce *m*; * *vi* divorcer.

divorced *adj* divorcé.

divulge *vt* divulguer.

dizziness *n* vertige *m*.

dizzy *adj* pris de vertige.

DJ *n* disc-jockey, DJ *m*.

do *vt* faire.

docile *adj* docile.

dock *n* dock *m*; * *vi* entrer aux docks.

docker *n* docker *m*.

dockyard *n* chantier *m* naval.

doctor *n* docteur *m*.

doctrinal *adj* doctrinal.

doctrine *n* doctrine *f*.

document *n* document *m*.

documentary *adj* documentaire.

dodge *vt* esquiver.

doe *n* biche *f*; **~ rabbit** lapine *f*.

dog *n* chien *m*.

dogged *adj* tenace; **~ly** *adv* tenacement.

dog kennel *n* refuge pour chiens *m*.

dogmatic *adj* dogmatique; **~ly** *adv* dogmatiquement.

doings *npl* faits *mpl*.

do-it-yourself *n* bricolage *m*.

doleful *adj* lugubre, triste.

doll *n* poupée *f*.

dollar *n* dollar *m*.

dolphin *n* dauphin *m*.

domain *n* domaine *m*.

dome *n* dôme *m*.

domestic *adj* domestique.

domesticate *vt* domestiquer.

domestication *n* domestication *f*.

domesticity *n* domesticité *f*.

domicile *n* domicile *m*.

dominant *adj* dominant.

dominate *vi* dominer.

domination *n* domination *f*.

domineer *vi* dominer.

domineering *adj* autoritaire.

dominion *n* domination *f*.

dominoes *npl* domino *m*.

donate *vt* donner, faire don de.

donation *n* donation *f*.

done *p*, *adj* fait; cuit.

donkey *n* âne *m*.

donor *n* donneur *m*; donateur *m*.

doodle *vi* gribouiller.

doom *n* sort *m*.

door *n* porte *f*.

doorbell *n* sonnette *f*.

door handle *n* poignée de porte *f*.

doorman *n* portier *m*.

doormat *n* paillasson *m*.

doorplate *n* plaque *f*.

doorstep *n* pas de porte *m*.

doorway *n* entrée *f*.

dormant *adj* latent; dormant.

dormer window *n* lucarne *f*.

dormitory *n* dortoir *m*.

dormouse *n* loir *m*.

dosage *n* dose *f*; dosage *m*.

dose *n* dose *f*; * *vt* doser; donner une dose à.

dossier *n* dossier *m*.

dot *n* point *m*.

dote *vi* adorer.

dotingly *adv* avec adoration.

double *adj* double; * *vt* doubler; * *n* double *m*.

double bed *n* lit *m* à deux places.

double-breasted *adj* croisé.

double chin *n* double menton *m*.

double-dealing *n* duplicité *f*.

double-edged *adj* à double tranchant.

double entry *n* (*com*) comptabilité en partie double *f*.

double-lock *vt* fermer à double tour.

double room *n* chambre pour deux *f*.

doubly *adv* doublement.

doubt *n* doute *m*; * *vt* douter de.

doubtful *adj* douteux.

doubtless *adv* indubitablement.

dough *n* pâte *f*.

douse *vt* éteindre.

dove *n* colombe *f*.

dovecot *n* colombier *m*.

dowdy *adj* mal habillé.

down *n* duvet *m*; * *prep* en bas; **to sit ~** s'asseoir; **upside ~** à l'envers.

downcast *adj* démoralisé; baissé.

downfall *n* ruine *f*.

downhearted *adj* découragé.

downhill *adv* en descendant, dans la descente.

down payment *n* acompte *m*.

downpour *n* grosse averse *f*.

downright *adj* manifeste.

downstairs *adv* en bas.

down-to-earth *adj* pratique; terre à terre.

downtown *adv* dans le centre, en ville.

downward(s) *adv* vers le bas.

dowry *n* dot *f*.

doze *vi* somnoler.

dozen *n* douzaine *f*.

dozy *adj* somnolent.

drab *adj* gris; morne.

draft *n* brouillon *m*; traite *f*.

drag *vt* tirer; * *n* drague *f*; ennui *m*.

dragnet *n* seine *f*; filet *m*.

dragon *n* dragon *m*.

dragonfly *n* libellule *f*.

drain *vt* drainer; vider; * *n* tuyau d'écoulement *m*.

drainage *n* drainage *m*.

drainboard *n* égouttoir *m*.

drainpipe *n* tuyau d'écoulement *m*.

drake *n* canard mâle *m*.

dram *n* petit verre *m*.

drama *n* drame *m*.

dramatic *adj* dramatique; **~ally** *adv* dramatiquement.

dramatise *vt* dramatiser.

dramatist *n* dramaturge *mf*.

drape *vt* draper.

drapes *npl* tentures *fpl*.

drastic *adj* radical.

draught *n* courant d'air *m*.

draughts *npl* jeu de dames *m*.

draughty *adj* exposé aux courants d'air.

draw *vt* tirer; dessiner; ~ **nigh** s'approcher.

drawback *n* désavantage, inconvénient *m*.

drawer *n* tiroir *m*.

drawing *n* dessin *m*.

drawing board *n* planche à dessin *f*.

drawing room *n* salon *m*.

drawl *vi* parler d'une voix traînante.

dread *n* terreur *f*; * *vt* redouter, craindre.

dreadful *adj* horrible; **~ly** *adv* horriblement.

dream *n* rêve *m*; * *vt vi* rêver.

dreary *adj* triste, morne.

dredge *vt* draguer.

dregs *npl* lie *f*.

drench *vt* tremper.

dress *vt* habiller; panser; * *vi* s'habiller; * *n* robe *f*.

dresser *n* buffet *m*.

dressing *n* pansement *m*; sauce *f*.

dressing gown *n* peignoir *m*.

dressing room *n* loge *f*; garde-robe *f*.

dressing table *n* coiffeuse *f*.

dressmaker *n* couturier *m* -ière *f*.

dressy *adj* élégant.

dribble *vi* tomber goutte à goutte.

dried *adj* séché.

drift *n* amoncellement *m*; courant *m*; sens *m*; * *vi* aller à la dérive.

driftwood *n* bois flottant *m*.

drill *n* perceuse *f*; (*mil*) exercice *m*; * *vt* percer.

drink *vt vi* boire; * *n* boisson *f*.

drinkable *adj* potable; buvable.

drinker *n* buveur *m* -euse *f*.

drinking bout *n* beuverie *f*.

drinking water *n* eau potable *f*.

drip *vi* goutter; * *n* goutte *f*; goutte-à-goutte *m*.

dripping *n* graisse *f*.

drive *vt* conduire; pousser; * *vi* conduire; * *n* promenade en voiture *f*; allée, entrée *f*.

drivel *n* imbécilités *fpl*; * *vi* baver; dire des imbécilités.

driver *n* conducteur *m* -trice *f*; chauffeur *m*.

driveway *n* allée, entrée *f*.

driving *n* conduite *f*.

driving instructor *n* moniteur (-trice) d'auto-école *m(f)*.

driving licence *n* permis *m* de conduire.

driving school *n* auto-école *f*.

driving test *n* examen *m* du permis de conduire.

drizzle *vi* bruiner.

droll *adj* drôle.

drone *n* bourdonnement *m*.

droop *vi* tomber.

drop *n* goutte *f*; * *vt* laisser tomber; * *vi* tomber; ~ **out** se retirer; abandonner.

drop-out *n* marginal *m*.

dropper *n* compte-gouttes *m invar*.

dross *n* scories *fpl*.

drought *n* sécheresse *f*.

drove *n*: in ~s en troupe.

drown *vt* noyer; * *vi* se noyer.

drowsiness *n* somnolence *f*.

drowsy *adj* somnolent.

drudgery *n* corvée *f*.

drug *n* drogue *f*; * *vt* droguer.

drug addict *n* drogué *m* -e *f*.

druggist *n* pharmacien *m* -ne *f*.

drugstore *n* pharmacie *f*.

drum *n* tambour *m*; * *vi* jouer du tambour.

drum majorette *n* majorette *f*.

drummer *n* batteur *m*.

drumstick *n* baguette de tambour *f*.

drunk *adj* ivre.

drunkard *n* ivrogne *mf*.

drunken *adj* ivre.

drunkenness *n* ivresse *f*.

dry *adj* sec; * *vt* faire sécher; * *vi* sécher.

dry-cleaning *n* nettoyage à sec *m*.

dry-goods store *n* (US) mercerie *f*.

dryness *n* sécheresse *f*.

dry rot *n* pourriture *f*.

dual *adj* double.

dual-purpose *adj* à double emploi.

dubbed *adj* doublé.

dubious *adj* douteux.

duck *n* canard *m*; * *vt vi* plonger.

duckling *n* caneton *m*.

dud *adj* nul; faux.

due *adj* dû, *f* due; * *adv* exactement; * *n* droit *m*; chose due *f*.

duel *n* duel *m*.

duet *n* (*mus*) duo *m*.

dull *adj* terne; insipide; gris; * *vt* ternir; atténuer.

duly *adv* dûment; en temps voulu.

dumb *adj* muet; **~ly** *adv* sans dire un mot.

dumbbell *n* haltère *m*; (US) abruti *m*.

dumbfounded *adj* interloqué.

dummy *n* mannequin *m*; prête-nom *m*.

dump *n* tas *m*; * *vt* jeter; laisser tomber.

dumping *n* (*com*) dumping *m*.

dumpling *n* boulette de pâte *f*.

dumpy *adj* boulot, -te *f*.

dunce *n* cancre *m*.

dune *n* dune *f*.

dung *n* fumier *m*.

dungarees *npl* salopette *f*.

dungeon *n* donjon *m*; cachot *m*.

dupe *n* dupe *f*; * *vt* duper.

duplex *n* duplex *m*.

duplicate *n* duplicata *m*; copie *f*; * *vt* dupliquer.

duplicity *n* duplicité *f*.

durability *n* durabilité *f*.

durable *adj* durable.

duration *n* durée *f*.

during *prep* pendant.

dusk *n* crépuscule *m*.

dust *n* poussière *f*; * *vt* épousseter.

duster *n* chiffon *m*.

dusty *adj* poussiéreux.

Dutch courage *n* courage puisé dans la boisson *m*.

duteous *adj* fidèle, loyal.

dutiful *adj* obéissant, soumis; **~ly** *adv* avec obéissance.

duty *n* devoir *m*; obligation *f*.

duty-free *adj* hors taxe.

dwarf *n* nain *m*, naine *f*; * *vt* rapetisser.

dwell *vi* habiter, vivre.

dwelling *n* habitation *f*; domicile *m*.

dwindle *vi* diminuer.

dye *vt* teindre; * *n* teinture *f*.

dyer *n* teinturier *m*.

dyeing *n* teinturerie *f*; teinture *f*.

dye-works *npl* teinturerie *f*.

dying *adj* mourant, agonisant; * *n* mort *f*.

dynamic *adj* dynamique.

dynamics *n* dynamique *f*.

dynamite *n* dynamite *f*.

dynamiter *n* dynamiteur *m* -euse *f*.

dynamo *n* dynamo *f*.

dynasty *n* dynastie *f*.

dysentery *n* dysenterie *f*.

dyspepsia *n* (*med*) dyspepsie *f*.

dyspeptic *adj* dyspeptique.

E

each *pn* chacun(e); ~ **other** les un(e)s les autres.

eager *adj* enthousiaste; ardent; **~ly** *adv* avec enthousiasme; ardemment.

eagerness *n* enthousiasme *m*; ardeur *f*; désir *m*.

eagle *n* aigle *m*.

eagle-eyed *adj* aux yeux d'aigle.

eaglet *n* aiglon *m*.

ear *n* oreille *f*; ouïe *f*; **by ~** en improvisant.

earache *n* mal d'oreille *m*.

eardrum *n* tympan *m*.

early *adj* premier; *adv* tôt, de bonne heure.

earmark *vt* (*fig*) désigner.

earn *vt* gagner.

earnest *adj* sérieux; **~ly** *adv* sérieusement.

earnestness *n* sérieux *m*.

earnings *npl* revenus *mpl*.

earphones *npl* écouteurs *mpl*.

earring *n* boucle d'oreille *f*.

earth *n* terre *f*; * *vt* brancher à la terre.

earthen *adj* de terre.

earthenware *n* poterie *f*.

earthquake *n* tremblement de terre *m*.

earthworm *n* ver de terre *m*.

earthy *adj* terreux; truculent.

earwig *n* perce-oreille *m*.

ease *n* aise *f*; facilité *f*; **at ~** à l'aise; * *vt* apaiser; soulager.

easel *n* chevalet *m*.

easily *adv* facilement.

easiness *n* facilité *f*.

east *n* est *m*; orient *m*.

Easter *n* Pâques *fpl*.

Easter egg *n* œuf de Pâques *m*.

easterly *adj* d'est.

eastern *adj* de l'est, oriental.

eastward(s) *adv* vers l'est.

easy *adj* facile; commode; **~ going** décontracté.

easy chair *n* fauteuil *m*.

eat *vt vi* manger.

eatable *adj* comestible; mangeable; * **~s** *npl* vivres *mpl*.

eau de Cologne *n* eau *f* de Cologne.

eaves *npl* avant-toit *m*.

eavesdrop *vt* espionner; écouter discrètement.

ebb *n* reflux *m*; * *vi* refluer; décliner.

ebony *n* ébène *f*.

eccentric *adj* excentrique.

eccentricity *n* excentricité *f*.

ecclesiastic *adj* ecclésiastique.

echo *n* écho *m*; * *vi* résonner.

eclectic *adj* éclectique.

eclipse *n* éclipse *f*; * *vt* éclipser.

ecology *n* écologie *f*.

economic(al) *adj* économique; économe.

economics *npl* économie *f*.

economise *vt* économiser.

economist *n* économiste *mf*.

economy *n* économie *f*.

ecstasy *n* extase *f*.

ecstatic *adj* extatique; **~ally** *adv* avec extase.

eczema *n* eczéma *m*.

eddy *n* tourbillon *m*; * *vi* tourbillonner.

edge *n* fil *m*; pointe *f*; bord *m*; acrimonie *f*; * *vt* border; affiler.

edgeways, edgewise *adv* de côté.

edging *n* bordure *f*.

edgy *adj* nerveux.

edible *adj* mangeable; comestible.

edict *n* édit *m*; décret *m*.

edification *n* édification *f*.

edifice *n* édifice *m*.

edify *vt* édifier.

edit *vt* diriger; rédiger; couper.

edition *n* édition *f*.

editor *n* directeur *m* -trice *f*; rédacteur *m* -trice *f*.

editorial *adj* rédactionnel; * *n* éditorial *m*.

educate *vt* éduquer; instruire.

education *n* éducation *f*; instruction *f*.

eel *n* anguille *f*.

eerie *adj* inquiétant; surnaturel.

efface *vt* effacer.

effect *n* effet *m*; réalité *f*; **~s** *npl* biens *mpl*; * *vt* effectuer.

effective *adj* efficace; effectif; **~ly** *adv* effectivement, en effet.

effectiveness *n* efficacité *f*.

effectual *adj* efficace; **~ly** *adv* efficacement.

effeminacy *n* caractère efféminé *m*.

effeminate *adj* efféminé.

effervescence *n* effervescence *f*.

effete *adj* (*bot*) stérile; faible.

efficacy *n* efficacité *f*.

efficiency *n* efficacité *f*.

efficient *adj* efficace.

effigy *n* effigie *f*.

effort *n* effort *m*.

effortless *adj* sans effort.

effrontery *n* effronterie *f*.

effusive *adj* chaleureux; expansif.

egg *n* œuf *m*; * **~ on** *vt* encourager.

eggcup *n* coquetier *m*.

eggplant *n* (US) aubergine *f*.

eggshell *n* coquille d'œuf *f*.

ego(t)ism *n* égoïsme *m*.

ego(t)ist *n* égoïste *mf*.

ego(t)istical *adj* égoïste.

eiderdown *n* édredon *m*.

eight *adj n* huit *m*.

eighteen *adj n* dix-huit *m*.

eighteenth *adj n* dix-huitième *mf*.

eighth *adj n* huitième *mf*.

eightieth *adj n* quatre-vingtième *mf*.

eighty *adj n* quatre-vingt.

either *pn* n'importe lequel, n'importe laquelle; * *conj* ou, soit.

ejaculate *vi* s'exclamer; éjaculer.

ejaculation *n* exclamation *f*; éjaculation *f*.

eject *vt* éjecter, expulser.

ejection *n* éjection, expulsion *f*.

ejector seat *n* siège éjectable *m*.

eke *vt* augmenter; prolonger.

elaborate *vt* élaborer; * *adj* élaboré; compliqué; **~ly** *adv* avec soin.

elapse *vi* s'écouler.

elastic *adj* élastique.

elasticity *n* élasticité *f*.

elated *adj* exultant.

elation *n* exultation *f*.

elbow *n* coude *m*; * *vt* pousser du coude.

elbow-room *n* espace *m*; (*fig*) liberté, latitude *f*.

elder *n* sureau *m*; * *adj* aîné.

elderly *adj* d'un âge avancé.

elders *npl* anciens *mpl*.

eldest *adj* aîné.

elect *vt* élire; choisir; * *adj* élu; choisi.

election *n* élection *f*; choix *m*.

electioneering *n* propagande électorale *f*.

elective *adj* facultatif; électif.

elector *n* électeur *m* -trice *f*.

electoral *adj* électoral.

electorate *n* électorat *m*.

electric(al) *adj* électrique.

electric blanket *n* couverture électrique *f*.

electric cooker *n* cuisinière électrique *f*.

electric fire *n* radiateur électrique *m*.

electrician *n* électricien *m*.

electricity *n* électricité *f*.

electrify *vt* électriser.

electron *n* électron *m*.

electronic *adj* électronique; **~s** *npl* électronique *f*.

elegance *n* élégance *f*.

elegant *adj* élégant; **~ly** *adv* élégamment.

elegy *n* élégie *f*.

element *n* élément *m*.

elemental, elementary *adj* élémentaire.

elephant *n* éléphant *m*.

elephantine *adj* lourd.

elevate *vt* élever, hausser.

elevation *n* élévation *f*; hauteur *f*.

elevator *n* ascenseur *m*.

eleven *adj n* onze *m*.

eleventh *adj n* onzième *mf*.

elf *n* elfe *m*.

elicit *vt* tirer, obtenir.

eligibility *n* éligibilité *f*.

eligible *adj* éligible.

eliminate *vt* éliminer, écarter.

elk *n* élan *m*.

elliptic(al) *adj* elliptique.

elm *n* orme *m*.

elocution *n* élocution *f*.

elocutionist *n* professeur d'élocution *m*.

elongate *vt* allonger.

elope *vi* s'échapper, s'enfuir.

elopement *n* fugue, évasion *f*.

eloquence *n* éloquence *f*.

eloquent *adj* éloquent; **~ly** *adv* éloquemment.

else *pn* autre.

elsewhere *adv* ailleurs.

elucidate *vt* élucider, expliquer.

elucidation *n* élucidation, explication *f*.

elude *vt* éluder; éviter.

elusive, elusory *adj* insaisissable.

emaciated *adj* émacié.

emanate (from) *vi* émaner (de).

emancipate *vt* émanciper; affranchir.

emancipation *n* émancipation *f*; affranchissement *m*.

embalm *vt* embaumer.

embankment *n* talus *m*; quai *m*.

embargo *n* embargo *m*.

embark *vt* embarquer.

embarkation *n* embarcation *f*.

embarrass *vt* embarrasser.

embarrassed *adj* embarrassé.

embarrassing *adj* embarrassant.

embarrassment *n* embarras *m*.

embassy *n* ambassade *f*.

embed *vt* enchâsser; intégrer.

embellish *vt* embellir, orner.

embellishment *n* ornement *m*.

ember *n* braise *f*.

embezzle *vt* détourner.

embezzlement *n* détournement de fonds *m*.

embitter *vt* rendre amer.

emblem *n* emblème *m*.

emblematic(al) *adj* emblématique, symbolique.

embodiment *n* (*law*) incorporation *f*; incarnation *f*.

embody *vt* (*law*) incorporer; incarner.

embrace *vt* étreindre; comprendre; * *n* étreinte *f*.

embroider *vt* broder.

embroidery *n* broderie *f*.

embroil *vt* impliquer.

embryo *n* embryon *m*.

emendation *n* correction *f*.

emerald *n* émeraude *f*.

emerge *vi* émerger; apparaître.

emergency *n* urgence *f*.

emergency cord *n* sonnette d'alarme *f*.

emergency exit *n* sortie de secours *f*.

emergency landing *n* atterrissage forcé *m*.

emergency meeting *n* réunion extraordinaire *f*.

emery *n* émeri *m*.

emigrant *n* émigré *m* -e *f*.

emigrate *vi* émigrer.

emigration *n* émigration *f*.

eminence *n* hauteur *f*; éminence, excellence *f*.

eminent *adj* élevé; éminent, distingué; **~ly** *adv* éminemment.

emission *n* émission *f*.

emit *vt* émettre.

emoluments *npl* émoluments *mpl*.

emotion *n* émotion *f*.

emotional *adj* émotionnel; ému.

emotive *adj* émotif.

emperor *n* empereur *m*.

emphasis *n* emphase *f*.

emphasise *vt* souligner, accentuer.

emphatic *adj* emphatique; **~ally** *adv* avec emphase.

empire *n* empire *m*.

employ *vt* employer.

employee *n* employé *m* -e *f*.

employer *n* employeur *m*.

employment *n* emploi, travail *m*.

emporium *n* grand magasin *m*.

empress *n* impératrice *f*.

emptiness *n* vide *m*; futilité *f*.

empty *adj* vide; vain; * *vt* vider.

empty-handed *adj* les mains vides.

emulate *vt* imiter.

emulsion *n* émulsion *f*.

enable *vt* permettre.

enact *vt* promulguer; représenter.

enamel *n* émail *m*; * *vt* émailler.

enamour *vt* s'éprendre de.

encamp *vi* camper.

encampment *n* campement *m*.

encase *vt* entourer.

enchant *vt* enchanter.

enchanting *adj* enchanteur.

enchantment *n* enchantement *m*.

encircle *vt* encercler.

enclose *vt* entourer; inclure, joindre.

enclosure *n* clôture *f*; enceinte *f*.

encompass *vt* comprendre.

encore *adv* encore.

encounter *n* rencontre *f*; combat *m*; * *vt* rencontrer.

encourage *vt* encourager.

encouragement *n* encouragement *m*.

encroach *vi* empiéter (sur).

encroachment *n* empiètement *m*.

encrusted *adj* incrusté.

encumber *vt* embarrasser.

encumbrance *n* embarras *m*.

encyclical *adj* encyclique.

encyclopedia *n* encyclopédie *f*.

end *n* fin *f*; extrémité *f*; bout *m*; dessein *m*; **to that ~** afin que; **to no ~** en vain; **on ~** debout; * *vt* terminer, conclure; * *vi* terminer.

endanger *vt* mettre en danger.

endear *vt* faire aimer.

endearing *adj* attachant.

endearment *n* expression de tendresse *f*.

endeavour *vi* s'efforcer, tenter; * *n* effort *m*.

endemic *adj* endémique.

ending *n* fin, conclusion *f*; dénouement *m*; terminaison *f*.

endive *n* (*bot*) endive *f*.

endless *adj* infini, perpétuel; **~ly** *adv* sans fin, perpétuellement.

endorse *vt* endosser; approuver.

endorsement *n* endos *m*; approbation *f*.

endow *vt* doter.

endowment *n* dotation *f*.

endurable *adj* supportable.

endurance *n* endurance *f*; patience *f*.

endure *vt* supporter; * *vi* durer.

endways, endwise *adv* debout.

enemy *n* ennemi *mf*.

energetic *adj* énergique, vigoureux.

energy *n* énergie, force *f*.

enervate *vt* débiliter.

enfeeble *vt* affaiblir.

enfold *vt* envelopper.

enforce *vt* mettre en vigueur.

enforced *adj* forcé.

enfranchise *vt* émanciper.

engage *vt* aborder; engager.

engaged *adj* fiancé; occupé.

engagement *n* engagement *m*; combat *m*; fiançailles *fpl*; ~ **ring** *n* bague de fiançailles *f*.

engaging *adj* attrayant.

engender *vt* engendrer; produire.

engine *n* moteur *m*; locomotive *f*.

engine driver *n* conducteur *m*.

engineer *n* ingénieur *m*; mécanicien *m*.

engineering *n* ingénierie *f*.

engrave *vt* graver.

engraving *n* gravure *f*.

engrossed *adj* absorbé.

engulf *vt* submerger.

enhance *vt* améliorer; réhausser.

enigma *n* énigme *f*.

enjoy *vt* aimer; jouir de; ~ **o.s.** s'amuser.

enjoyable *adj* agréable; amusant.

enjoyment *n* plaisir *m*; jouissance *f*.

enlarge *vt* agrandir; étendre; dilater.

enlargement *n* agrandissement *m*; extension *f*; dilatation *f*.

enlighten *vt* éclairer.

enlightened *adj* éclairé.

Enlightenment *n*: **the** ~ le Siècle des lumières *m*.

enlist *vt* recruter.

enlistment *n* recrutement *m*.

enliven *vt* animer; égayer.

enmity *n* inimitié *f*; haine *f*.

enormity *n* énormité *f*; atrocité *f*.

enormous *adj* énorme; ~**ly** *adv* énormément.

enough *adv* suffisamment; assez; * *n* assez *m*.

enounce *vt* déclarer.

enquire *vt* = inquire.

enrage *vt* rendre furieux.

enrapture *vt* enchanter, enthousiasmer.

enrich *vt* enrichir; orner.

enrichment *n* enrichissement *m*.

enrol *vt* enrôler; inscrire.

enrolment *n* inscription *f*.

en route *adv* en route.

ensign *n* (*mil*) drapeau *m*; porte-étendard *m*; (*mar*) pavillon *m*.

enslave *vt* asservir.

ensue *vi* s'ensuivre.

ensure *vt* assurer.

entail *vt* impliquer, entraîner.

entangle *vt* emmêler, embrouiller.

entanglement *n* emmêlement *m*.

enter *vt* entrer dans; inscrire; ~ **for**

se présenter à; ~ **into** commencer; faire partie de.

enterprise *n* entreprise *f*.

enterprising *adj* entreprenant.

entertain *vt* divertir; recevoir; avoir.

entertainer *n* artiste *mf*.

entertaining *adj* divertissant, amusant.

entertainment *n* divertissement, passe-temps *m*.

enthralled *adj* captivé.

enthralling *adj* captivant.

enthrone *vt* introniser.

enthusiasm *n* enthousiasme *m*.

enthusiast *n* enthousiaste *mf*.

enthusiastic *adj* enthousiaste.

entice *vt* tenter; séduire.

entire *adj* entier, complet; parfait; ~**ly** *adv* entièrement.

entirety *n* intégralité *f*.

entitle *vt* intituler; conférer un droit à.

entitled *adj* intitulé; **to be** ~ **to** avoir le droit de.

entity *n* entité *f*.

entourage *n* entourage *m*.

entrails *npl* entrailles *fpl*.

entrance *n* entrée *f*; admission *f*.

entrance examination *n* examen d'entrée *m*.

entrance fee *n* droit d'inscription *m*.

entrance hall *n* vestibule *m*.

entrance ramp *n* bretelle d'accès *f*.

entrant *n* participant *m* -e *f*; candidat *m* -e *f*.

entrap *vt* piéger.

entreat *vt* implorer, supplier.

entreaty *n* supplication, prière *f*.

entrepreneur *n* entrepreneur *m*.

entrust *vt* confier.

entry *n* entrée *f*.

entry phone *n* interphone *m*.

entwine *vt* entrelacer.

enumerate *vt* énumérer.

enunciate *vt* énoncer.

enunciation *n* énonciation *f*.

envelop *vt* envelopper.

envelope *n* enveloppe *f*.

enviable *adj* enviable.

envious *adj* envieux; ~**ly** *adv* avec envie.

environment *n* environnement *m*.

environmental *adj* relatif à l'environnement.

environs *npl* environs *mpl*.

envisage *vt* envisager.

envoy *n* envoyé *m* -e *f*.

envy *n* envie *f*; * *vt* envier.

ephemeral *adj* éphémère.

epic *adj* épique; * *n* récit épique *m*.

epidemic *adj* épidémique; * *n* épidémie *f*.

epilepsy *n* épilepsie *f*.

epileptic *adj* épileptique.

epilogue *n* épilogue *m*.

Epiphany *n* Epiphanie *f*.

episcopacy *n* épiscopat *m*.

episcopal *adj* épiscopal.

episcopalian *n* épiscopalien *m* -ne *f*.

episode *n* épisode *m*.

epistle *n* épître *f*.

epistolary *adj* épistolaire.

epithet *n* épithète *f*.

epitome *n* modèle *m*; résumé *m*.

epitomise *vt* incarner; résumer.

epoch *n* époque *f*.

equable *adj* uniforme; ~**bly** *adv* uniformément.

equal *adj* égal; semblable; * *n* égal *m* -e *f*; * *vt* égaler.

equalise *vt* égaliser.

equaliser *n* point égalisateur *m*.

equality *n* égalité *f*.

equally *adv* également.

equanimity *n* équanimité *f*.

equate *vt* comparer; assimiler.

equation *n* équation *f*.

equator *n* équateur *m*.

equatorial *adj* équatorial.

equestrian *adj* équestre.

equilateral *adj* équilatéral.

equilibrium *n* équilibre *m*.

equinox *n* équinoxe *m*.

equip *vt* équiper.

equipment *n* équipement *m*.

equitable *adj* équitable, impartial; ~**bly** *adv* équitablement.

equity *n* équité, justice, impartialité *f*.

equivalent *adj n* équivalent *m*.

equivocal *adj* équivoque, ambigu; ~**ly** *adv* d'une manière équivoque.

equivocate *vt* équivoquer, user d'équivoques.

equivocation *n* faux-fuyants *mpl*.

era *n* ère *f*.

eradicate *vt* supprimer; extirper.

eradication *n* suppression *f*; extirpation *f*.

erase *vt* effacer; gommer.

eraser *n* gomme *f*.

erect *vt* ériger; élever; * *adj* droit, debout.

erection *n* érection *f*; structure *f*.

ermine *n* hermine *f*.

erode *vt* éroder; ronger.

erotic *adj* érotique.

err *vi* se tromper.

errand *n* message *m*; commission *f*.

errand boy *n* garçon de courses, messager *m*.

errata *npl* errata *m*.

erratic *adj* changeant; irrégulier.

erroneous *adj* erroné, faux; **~ly** *adv* erronément, faussement.

error *n* erreur *f*.

erudite *adj* érudit.

erudition *n* érudition *f*.

erupt *vi* entrer en éruption; faire éruption.

eruption *n* éruption *f*.

escalate *vi* monter en flèche; s'intensifier.

escalation *n* montée en flèche *f*; intensification *f*.

escalator *n* escalier roulant *m*.

escapade *n* fredaine *f*.

escape *vt* éviter; échapper à; * *vi* s'évader, s'échapper; * *n* évasion, fuite *f*; **to make one's ~** prendre la fuite.

escapism *n* évasion de la réalité *f*.

eschew *vt* fuir; éviter.

escort *n* escorte *f*; * *vt* escorter.

esoteric *adj* ésotérique.

especial *adj* spécial; **~ly** *adv* spécialement.

espionage *n* espionnage *m*.

esplanade *n* (*mil*) esplanade *f*.

espouse *vt* épouser.

essay *n* essai *m*.

essence *n* essence *f*.

essential *n* essentiel *m*; * *adj* essentiel, principal; **~ly** *adv* essentiellement.

establish *vt* établir; fonder; démontrer.

establishment *n* établissement *m*; fondation *f*; institution *f*.

estate *n* état *m*; domaine *m*; biens *mpl*.

esteem *vt* estimer; apprécier; * *n* estime *f*; considération *f*.

esthetic *adj* (US) esthétique; **~s** *npl* esthétique *f*.

estimate *vt* estimer; évaluer.

estimation *n* estimation, évaluation *f*; opinion *f*.

estrange *vt* éloigner, séparer.

estranged *adj* séparé.

estrangement *n* séparation *f*; distance *f*.

estuary *n* estuaire *m*.

etch *vt* graver à l'eau forte.

etching *n* gravure à l'eau forte *f*.

eternal *adj* éternel, perpétuel; **~ly** *adv* éternellement.

eternity *n* éternité *f*.

ether *n* éther *m*.

ethical *adj* éthique, moral; **~ly** *adv* éthiquement.

ethics *npl* éthique *f*.

ethnic *adj* ethnique.

ethos *n* génie *m*, esprit *m*.

etiquette *n* étiquette *f*.

etymological *adj* étymologique.

etymologist *n* étymologiste *mf*.

etymology *n* étymologie *f*.

Eucharist *n* Eucharistie *f*.

eulogy *n* éloge *m*.

eunuch *n* eunuque *m*.

euphemism *n* euphémisme *m*.

evacuate *vt* évacuer.

evacuation *n* évacuation *f*.

evade *vt* éviter; échapper à.

evaluate *vt* évaluer.

evangelic(al) *adj* évangélique.

evangelist *n* évangéliste *m*.

evaporate *vt* faire évaporer; * *vi* s'évaporer; se volatiliser.

evaporated milk *n* lait condensé *m*.

evaporation *n* évaporation *f*.

evasion *n* dérobade *f*.

evasive *adj* évasif; **~ly** *adv* évasivement.

eve *n* veille *f*.

even *adj* égal; uni; pair; * *adv* même; encore; * *vt* égaliser; unir; * *vi*: **~ out** s'égaliser.

even-handed *adj* impartial, équitable.

evening *n* soir *m*, soirée *f*.

evening class *n* cours du soir *m*.

evening dress *n* robe du soir *f*; tenue de soirée *f*.

evenly *adv* également; uniment.

evenness *n* égalité *f*; uniformité *f*; régularité *f*; impartialité *f*.

event *n* événement *m*; épreuve *f*.

eventful *adj* mouvementé.

eventual *adj* final; **~ly** *adv* finalement, en fin de comptes.

eventuality *n* éventualité *f*.

ever *adv* toujours; jamais; déjà; **for ~ and ~** pour toujours; **~ since** depuis.

evergreen *adj* à feuilles persistantes; * *n* arbre à feuilles persistantes *m*.

everlasting *adj* éternel.

evermore *adv* toujours.

every *adj* chacun, chacune; **~ where** partout; **~ thing** tout; **~ one, ~ body** tout le monde.

evict *vt* expulser.

eviction *n* expulsion *f*.

evidence *n* évidence *f*; témoignage *m*; preuve *f*; * *vt* témoigner de.

evident *adj* évident; manifeste; **~ly** *adv* manifestement, de toute évidence.

evil *adj* mauvais; malveillant; * *n* mal *m*.

evil-minded *adj* malintentionné.

evocative *adj* évocateur.

evoke *vt* évoquer.

evolution *n* évolution *f*.

evolve *vt* développer; * *vi* se développer, évoluer.

ewe *n* brebis *f*.

exacerbate *vt* exacerber.

exact *adj* exact; * *vt* exiger.

exacting *adj* exigeant.

exaction *n* exaction *f*; extorsion *f*.

exactly *adv* exactement.

exactness, exactitude *n* exactitude *f*.

exaggerate *vt* exagérer.

exaggeration *n* exagération *f*.

exalt *vt* exalter; élever.

exaltation *n* exaltation *f*; élévation *f*.

exalted *adj* exalté; élevé.

examination *n* examen *m*.

examine *vt* examiner.

examiner *n* examinateur *m* -trice *f*.

example *n* exemple *m*.

exasperate *vt* exaspérer, irriter.

exasperation *n* exaspération, irritation *f*.

excavate *vt* exhumer, creuser.

excavation *n* excavation *f*.

exceed *vt* excéder, dépasser.

exceedingly *adv* trop; extrêmement.

excel *vt* surpasser; *vi* exceller.

excellence *n* excellence *f*; supériorité *f*.

Excellency *n* Excellence (titre) *f*.

excellent *adj* excellent; **~ly** *adv* excellemment, admirablement.

except *vt* excepter, exclure; **~(ing)** *prep* excepté, à l'exception de.

exception *n* exception *f*.

exceptional *adj* exceptionnel.

excerpt *n* extrait *m*.

excess *n* excès *m*.

excessive *adj* excessif; **~ly** *adv* excessivement.

exchange *vt* échanger; permuter; * *n* échange *m*; change *m*.

exchange rate *n* taux de change *m*.

excise *n* taxe *f*.

excitability *n* excitabilité *f*.

excitable *adj* excitable.

excite *vt* exciter; animer; enthousiasmer; stimuler.

excited *adj* animé, enthousiaste; excité.

excitement *n* animation *f*, enthousiasme *m*.

exciting *adj* passionnant; stimulant.

exclaim *vi* s'exclamer.

exclamation *n* exclamation *f*.

exclamation mark *n* point d'exclamation *m*.

exclamatory *adj* exclamatif.

exclude *vt* exclure.

exclusion *n* exclusion *f*; exception *f*.

exclusive *adj* exclusif; **~ly** *adv* exclusivement.

excommunicate *vt* excommunier.

excommunication *n* excommunion *f*.

excrement *n* excrément *m*.

excruciating *adj* atroce, horrible.

exculpate *vt* disculper; justifier.

excursion *n* excursion *f*; digression *f*.

excusable *adj* excusable.

excuse *vt* excuser; pardonner; * *n* excuse *f*.

execute *vt* exécuter.

execution *n* exécution *f*.

executioner *n* bourreau *m*.

executive *adj* exécutif.

executor *n* exécuteur testamentaire *m*.

exemplary *adj* exemplaire.

exemplify *vt* exemplifier.

exempt *adj* exempt.

exemption *n* exemption *f*.

exercise *n* exercice *m*; * *vi* prendre de l'exercice; * *vt* exercer; montrer.

exercise book *n* cahier *m*.

exert *vt* employer, exercer; **~ o.s.** s'efforcer.

exertion *n* effort *m*.

exhale *vt* exhaler; expirer.

exhaust *n* échappement *m*; * *vt* épuiser.

exhausted *adj* épuisé.

exhaustion *n* épuisement *m*.

exhaustive *adj* exhaustif, complet.

exhibit *vt* exhiber; montrer; * *n* (*law*) pièce à conviction *f*.

exhibition *n* exposition, présentation *f*.

exhilarating *adj* stimulant, grisant.

exhilaration *n* joie *f* intense.

exhort *vt* exhorter.

exhortation *n* exhortation *f*.

exhume *vt* exhumer, déterrer.

exile *n* exil *m*; * *vt* exiler, déporter.

exist *vi* exister.

existence *n* existence *f*.

existent *adj* existant.

existing *adj* actuel, présent.

exit *n* sortie *f*; * *vi* sortir.

exit ramp *n* bretelle d'accès *f*.

exodus *n* exode *m*.

exonerate *vt* disculper; décharger.

exoneration *n* disculpation *f*; décharge *f*.

exorbitant *adj* exorbitant, excessif.

exorcise *vt* exorciser.

exorcism *n* exorcisme *m*.

exotic *adj* exotique.

expand *vt* étendre; dilater.

expanse *n* étendue *f*.

expansion *n* expansion *f*.

expansive *adj* expansif.

expatriate *vt* expatrier.

expect *vt* attendre; espérer; penser.

expectance, expectancy *n* attente *f*; espoir *m*.

expectant *adj* d'attente.

expectant mother *n* femme enceinte *f*.

expectation *n* expectative *f*; attente *f*.

expediency *n* convenance *f*; opportunité *f*.

expedient *adj* opportun; * *n* expédient *m*; **~ly** *adv* de manière opportune.

expedite *vt* accélérer; expédier.

expedition *n* expédition *f*.

expeditious *adj* expéditif; **~ly** *adv* de manière expéditive.

expel *vt* expulser.

expend *vt* dépenser; utiliser.

expendable *adj* jetable; consommable.

expenditure *n* dépense *f*.

expense *n* dépense *f*; coût *m*.

expense account *n* frais *mpl* de représentation.

expensive *adj* cher; coûteux; **~ly** *adv* de manière coûteuse.

experience *n* expérience *f*; pratique *f*; * *vt* ressentir, éprouver; connaître.

experienced *adj* expérimenté.

experiment *n* expérience *f*; * *vi* expérimenter.

experimental *adj* expérimental; **~ly** *adv* expérimentalement.

expert *adj* expert.

expertise *n* compétences *fpl*.

expiration *n* expiration *f*.

expire *vi* expirer.

explain *vt* expliquer.

explanation *n* explication *f*.

explanatory *adj* explicatif.

expletive *adj* explétif.

explicable *adj* explicable.

explicit *adj* explicite; **~ly** *adv* explicitement.

explode *vt* faire exploser; *vi* exploser.

exploit *vt* exploiter; * *n* exploit *m*.

exploitation *n* exploitation *f*.

exploration *n* exploration *f*.

exploratory *adj* exploratoire.

explore *vt* explorer, examiner; sonder.

explorer *n* explorateur *m* -trice *f*.

explosion *n* explosion *f*.

explosive *adj n* explosif *m*.

exponent *n* (*math*) exposant *m*.

export *vt* exporter.

export, exportation *n* exportation *f*.

exporter *n* exportateur *m* -trice *f*.

expose *vt* exposer; dévoiler.

exposed *adj* exposé.

exposition *n* exposition *f*; interprétation *f*.

expostulate *vi* faire des remonstrances.

exposure *n* exposition *f*; temps de pose *m*; cliché *m*.

exposure meter *n* photomètre *m*.

expound *vt* exposer; interpréter.

express *vt* exprimer; * *adj* exprès; * *n* exprès *m*; (*rail*) rapide *m*.

expression *n* expression *f*; locution *f*.

expressionless *adj* inexpressif.

expressive *adj* expressif; **~ly** *adv* d'une manière expressive.

expressly *adv* expressément.

expressway *n* autoroute *f*.

expropriate *vt* exproprier.

expropriation *n* (*law*) expropriation *f*.

expulsion *n* expulsion *f*.

expurgate *vt* expurger.

exquisite *adj* exquis; **~ly** *adv* exquisément.

extant *adj* existant.

extempore *adv* à l'improviste.

extemporise *vi* improviser.

extend *vt* étendre; élargir; * *vi* s'étendre.

extension *n* extension *f*.

extensive *adj* étendu; important; **~ly** *adv* considérablement.

extent *n* extension *f*.

extenuate *vt* atténuer.

extenuating *adj* atténuant.

exterior *adj n* extérieur *m*.

exterminate *vt* exterminer; supprimer.

extermination *n* extermination *f*; suppression *f*.

external *adj* externe; **~ly** *adv* extérieurement; **~s** *npl* apparence *f*.

extinct *adj* disparu; éteint.

extinction *n* extinction *f*.

extinguish *vt* éteindre; supprimer.

extinguisher *n* extincteur *m*.

extirpate *vt* extirper.

extol *vt* louer, exalter.

extort *vt* extorquer; arracher.

extortion *n* extorsion *f*.

extortionate *adj* exorbitant.

extra *adv* particulièrement; *n* supplément *m*.

extract *vt* extraire; * *n* extrait *m*.

extraction *n* extraction *f*; origine *f*.

extracurricular *adj* périscolaire.

extradite *vt* extrader.

extradition *n* (*law*) extradition *f*.

extramarital *adj* extérieur au mariage.

extramural *adj* extra-muros.

extraneous *adj* superflu; sans rapport.

extraordinarily *adv* extraordinai-
rement.

extraordinary *adj* extraordinaire.

extravagance *n* extravagance *f*;
gaspillage *m*.

extravagant *adj* extravagant; exorbitant; gaspilleur; ~**ly** *adv* de manière extravagante; en gaspillant.

extreme *adj* extrême; suprême; ultime; * *n* extrême *m*; ~**ly** *adv* extrêmement.

extremist *adj n* extrémiste *mf*.

extremity *n* extrémité *f*.

extricate *vt* extirper, démêler.

extrinsic(al) *adj* extrinsèque.

extrovert *adj n* extraverti *m* -e *f*.

exuberance *n* exubérance *f*.

exuberant *adj* exubérant; ~**ly** *adv*
avec exubérance.

exude *vi* exsuder.

exult *vi* exulter, triompher.

exultation *n* exultation *f*.

eye *n* œil *m*; * *vt* regarder, observer; lorgner.

eyeball *n* globe oculaire *m*.

eyebrow *n* sourcil *m*.

eyelash *n* cil *m*.

eyelid *n* paupière *f*.

eyesight *n* vue *f*.

eyesore *n* monstruosité *f*.

eyetooth *n* canine *f*.

eyewitness *n* témoin oculaire *m*.

eyrie *n* aire *f*, nid *m* d'aigle.

F

fable *n* fable *f*; légende *f*.

fabric *n* tissu *m*.

fabricate *vt* fabriquer; inventer.

fabrication *n* fabrication *f*; invention *f*.

fabulous *adj* fabuleux; ~**ly** *adv* fabuleusement.

facade *n* façade *f*.

face *n* visage *m*, figure *f*; surface *f*; façade *f*; mine *f*; apparence *f*; * *vt* faire face à; affronter; ~ **up to** faire face à.

face cream *n* crème pour le visage *f*.

face-lift *n* lifting *m*.

face powder *n* poudre de riz *f*.

facet *n* facette *f*.

facetious *adj* facétieux, plaisant, spirituel; ~**ly** *adv* facétieusement.

face value *n* valeur nominale *f*.

facial *adj* facial.

facile *adj* facile; superficiel.

facilitate *vt* faciliter.

facility *n* facilité *f*; équipement *m*, infrastructure *f*.

facing *n* revers *m*; * *prep* en face de.

facsimile *n* fac-similé *m*.

fact *n* fait *m*; réalité *f*; **in** ~ en fait.

faction *n* faction *f*; dissension *f*.

factor *n* facteur *m*.

factory *n* usine *f*.

factual *adj* factuel, basé sur les faits.

faculty *n* faculté *f*; le corps enseignant *m*.

fad *n* engouement *m*.

fade *vi* se faner; perdre son éclat.

fail *vt* échouer à; omettre; manquer à ses engagements envers; * *vi* échouer; faiblir; manquer.

failing *n* défaut *m*.

failure *n* échec *m*; panne *f*; raté *m*; faillite *f*; manquement *m*.

faint *vi* s'évanouir, défaillir; * *n* évanouissement *m*; * *adj* faible; ~**ly** *adv* faiblement.

fainthearted *adj* timide, timoré, pusillanime.

faintness *n* faiblesse *f*; légèreté *f*.

fair *adj* beau; blond; clair; favorable; juste, équitable; considérable; passable; * *adv* loyalement; * *n* foire *f*.

fairly *adv* équitablement; absolument.

fairness *n* beauté *f*; justice *f*.

fair play *n* fair-play, franc-jeu *m*.

fairy *n* fée *f*.

fairy tale *n* conte de fées *m*.

faith *n* foi *f*; croyance *f*; fidélité *f*.

faithful *adj* fidèle, loyal; ~**ly** *adv* fidèlement.

faithfulness *n* fidélité, loyauté *f*.

fake *n* falsification *f*; imposteur *m*; * *adj* faux; * *vt* feindre; falsifier.

falcon *n* faucon *m*.

falconry *n* fauconnerie *f*.

fall *vi* tomber; s'effondrer; diminuer, baisser; ~ **asleep** s'endormir; ~ **back** reculer; ~ **back on** avoir recours à; ~ **behind** être à la traîne; ~ **down** tomber; ~ **for** se faire avoir; tomber amoureux de; ~ **in** s'effondrer; ~ **short** échouer; ~ **sick** tomber malade; ~ **in love** tomber amoureux; ~ **off** tomber; diminuer; ~ **out** se produire; se quereller; * *n* chute *f*; automne *m*.

fallacious *adj* fallacieux, trompeur; ~**ly** *adv* d'une manière fallacieuse.

fallacy *n* erreur *f*; sophisme *m*; tromperie *f*.

fallibility *n* faillibilité *f*.

fallible *adj* faillible.

fallout *n* retombées *fpl*.

fallout shelter *n* abri antiatomique *m*.

fallow *adj* en jachère; ~ **deer** *n* daim *m*.

false *adj* faux; ~**ly** *adv* faussement.

false alarm *n* fausse alerte *f*.

falsehood, falseness *n* mensonge *m*; fausseté *f*.

falsify *vt* falsifier.

falsity *n* fausseté *f*.

falter *vi* vaciller; faiblir.

faltering *adj* chancelant.

fame *n* réputation *f*; renommée, notoriété *f*.

famed *adj* célèbre.

familiar *adj* familier; domestique; ~**ly** *adv* familièrement.

familiarise *vt* familiariser.

familiarity *n* familiarité *f*.

family *n* famille *f*.

family business *n* affaire de famille *f*.

family doctor *n* médecin de famille *m*.

famine *n* famine *f*; disette *f*.

famished *adj* affamé.

famous *adj* célèbre, fameux; ~**ly** *adv* fameusement.

fan *n* éventail *m*; ventilateur *m*; jeune admirateur *m* -trice *f*; * *vt* éventer; attiser.

fanatic *adj n* fanatique *mf*.

fanaticism *n* fanatisme *m*.

fan belt *n* courroie de ventilateur *f*.

fanciful *adj* fantasque, capricieux; ~**ly** *adv* capricieusement.

fancy *n* fantaisie, imagination *f*; caprice *m*; * *vt* avoir envie de; s'imaginer.

fancydress ball *n* bal masqué *m*.

fancy goods *npl* nouveautés *fpl*.

fanfare *n* (*mus*) fanfare *f*.

fang *n* croc *m*.

fantastic *adj* fantastique; excentrique; ~**ally** *adv* fantastiquement.

fantasy *n* imagination *f*.

far *adv* loin; * *adj* lointain, éloigné; ~ **and away** de très loin; ~ **off** lointain.

faraway *adj* lointain.

farce *n* farce *f*.

farcical *adj* grotesque.

fare *n* prix (du voyage) *m*; tarif *m*; nourriture *f*; voyageur *m* -euse *f*; client *m* -e *f*.

farewell *n* adieu *m*; ~! *excl* adieu!

farm *n* ferme *f*, exploitation agricole *f*; * *vt* cultiver.

farmer *n* fermier *m*; agriculteur *m*.

farmhand *n* ouvrier agricole *m*.

farmhouse *n* ferme *f*.

farming *n* agriculture *f*.

farmland *n* terres arables *fpl*.

farmyard *n* cour de ferme *f*.

far-reaching *adj* d'une grande portée, considérable.

fart *n* (*sl*) pet *m*; * *vi* péter.

farther *adv* plus loin; * *adj* plus éloigné.

farthest *adv* le plus lointain; le plus loin; au plus.

fascinate *vt* fasciner, captiver.

fascinating *adj* fascinant.

fascination *n* fascination *f*; charme *m*.

fascism *n* fascisme.

fashion *n* manière, façon *f*; forme *f*; coutume *f*; mode *f*; style *m*; **people of** ~ personnes élégantes *fpl*; * *vt* façonner, confectionner.

fashionable adj à la mode; chic; **the ~ world** le beau monde; **~bly** adv à la mode.

fashion show n défilé de mode m.

fast vi jeûner; * n jeûne m; * adj rapide; ferme, stable; * adv rapidement; fermement; solidement.

fasten vt attacher; fixer; attribuer; * vi se fixer, s'attacher.

fastener, fastening n attache f; fermoir m.

fast food n restauration rapide f.

fastidious adj minutieux, méticuleux; **~ly** adv minutieusement.

fat adj gros, gras; * n graisse f.

fatal adj mortel; néfaste; **~ly** adv mortellement.

fatalism n fatalisme m.

fatalist n fataliste mf.

fatality n accident mortel m, fatalité f.

fate n destin, sort m.

fateful adj fatidique.

father n père m.

fatherhood n paternité f.

father-in-law n beau-père m.

fatherland n patrie f.

fatherly adj (adv) paternel(lement).

fathom n brasse (mesure) f; * vt sonder; pénétrer.

fatigue n fatigue f; * vt fatiguer, lasser.

fatten vt vi engraisser.

fatty adj gras, graisseux.

fatuous adj imbécile, stupide, niais.

faucet n (US) robinet m.

fault n défaut m, faute f; délit m; faille f.

faultfinder n chicaneur m -euse f.

faultless adj irréprochable.

faulty adj défectueux.

fauna n faune f.

faux pas n impair m.

favour n faveur f; approbation f; avantage m; * vt favoriser, préférer.

favourable adj favorable, propice; **~bly** adv favorablement.

favoured adj favorisé.

favourite n favori m; * adj favori.

favouritism n favoritisme m.

fawn n faon m; * vi flatter servilement.

fawningly adv d'une flatterie servile.

fax n télécopieur, fax m; télécopie f, fax m; * vt envoyer par fax, télécopier.

fear vt craindre; * n crainte f.

fearful adj effrayant; craintif, peureux; **~ly** adv terriblement; craintivement.

fearless adj intrépide, courageux; **~ly** adv courageusement.

fearlessness n intrépidité f.

feasibility n faisabilité f.

feasible adj faisable, réalisable.

feast n festin, banquet m; fête f; * vi banqueter.

feat n exploit m; prouesse f.

feather n plume f;.

feather bed n lit de plumes m.

feature n caractéristique f; trait m; * vi figurer.

feature film n long métrage m.

February n février m.

federal adj fédéral.

federalist n fédéraliste mf.

federate vt fédérer; * vi se fédérer.

federation n fédération f.

fed-up adj: **to be ~** en avoir marre.

fee n honoraires mpl; frais mpl.

feeble adj faible, frêle.

feebleness n faiblesse f.

feebly adv faiblement.

feed vt nourrir; alimenter; **~ on** se nourrir de; * vi manger; se nourrir; * n nourriture f; alimentation f.

feedback n réaction f, répercussion f.

feel vt sentir; toucher; croire; **~ around** tâtonner, fouiller; * n sensation f; toucher m.

feeler n antenne f; (fig) tentative f.

feeling n sensation f; sentiment m.

feelingly adv avec émotion.

feign vt inventer; feindre, simuler.

feline adj félin.

fellow n homme, type m; membre m.

fellow citizen n concitoyen m -enne f.

fellow countryman n compatriote m.

fellow feeling n sympathie f.

fellow men npl semblables mpl.

fellowship n camaraderie f; association f.

fellow student n copain (copine) de fac m(f).

fellow traveller n compagnon (compagne) de voyage m(f).

felon n criminel m -le f.

felony n crime m.

felt n feutre m.

felt-tip pen n feutre m.

female n femelle f; * adj de sexe féminin, femelle.

feminine adj féminin.

feminist n féministe mf.

fen n marais m.

fence n barrière f; clôture f; * vt clôturer; * vi faire de l'escrime.

fencing n escrime f.

fender n pare-chocs m invar.

fennel n (bot) fenouil m.

ferment n agitation f; * vi fermenter.

fern n (bot) fougère f.

ferocious adj féroce; **~ly** adv férocement.

ferocity n férocité f.

ferret n furet m; * vt fureter; **~ out** découvrir, dénicher.

ferry n bac m; ferry m; * vt transporter.

fertile adj fertile, fécond.

fertilise vt fertiliser.

fertiliser n engrais m.

fertility n fertilité, fécondité f.

fervent adj fervent; ardent; **~ly** adv avec ferveur.

fervid adj ardent, véhément.

fervour n ferveur, ardeur f.

fester vi suppurer; s'envenimer.

festival n fête f; festival m.

festive adj de fête.

festivity n fête f, réjouissances fpl.

fetch vt aller chercher.

fetching adj charmant, séduisant.

fête n fête f.

fetid adj fétide, nauséabond.

fetus n fœtus m.

feud n rivalité f, dissension f.

feudal adj féodal.

feudalism n féodalité f.

fever n fièvre f.

feverish adj fiévreux.

few adj peu; **a ~** quelques; **~ and far between** rares.

fewer adj moins (de); * adv moins.

fewest adj le moins (de).

fiancé n fiancé m.

fiancée n fiancée f.

fib n bobard m; * vi raconter des bobards.

fibre n fibre f.

fibreglass n fibre de verre f.

fickle adj volage, inconstant.

fiction n fiction f; invention f.

fictional adj fictif.

fictitious adj fictif, imaginaire; feint; **~ly** adv fictivement.

fiddle n violon m; combine f; * vi jouer du violon.

fiddler n violoneux m.

fidelity n fidélité, loyauté f.

fidget vi s'agiter, s'impatienter.

fidgety adj agité, remuant.

field n champ m; étendue f; domaine m.

field day n (mil) jour de grandes manœuvres m.

fieldmouse n mulot m.

fieldwork n recherches sur le terrain fpl.

fiend *n* démon *m*; mordu *m*.
fiendish *adj* diabolique.
fierce *adj* féroce, violent; acharné, furieux; **~ly** *adv* férocement.
fierceness *n* férocité, fureur *f*.
fiery *adj* ardent; fougueux.
fifteen *adj n* quinze *m*.
fifteenth *adj n* quinzième *mf*.
fifth *adj n* cinquième *mf*; **~ly** *adv* cinquièmement.
fiftieth *adj n* cinquantième *mf*.
fifty *adj n* cinquante *m*.
fig *n* figue *f*.
fight *vt vi* se battre (contre); combattre; lutter; * *n* bataille *f*; combat *m*; lutte *f*.
fighter *n* combattant *m*; lutteur *m*; chasseur *m*.
fighting *n* combat *m*.
fig-leaf *n* feuille de figuier *f*.
fig tree *n* figuier *m*.
figurative *adj* figuratif; **~ly** *adv* figurativement.
figure *n* figure *f*; forme, silhouette *f*; image *f*; chiffre *m*; * *vi* figurer; avoir du sens; **~ out** comprendre.
figurehead *n* figure de proue *f*.
filament *n* filament *m*; fibre *f*.
filch *vt* chiper.
filcher *n* voleur *m* -euse *f*.
file *n* file *f*; liste *f*; (*mil*) colonne, rangée *f*; lime *f*; dossier *m*; fichier *m*; * *vt* enregistrer; limer; classer; déposer; * *vi* **~ in/out** entrer/sortir en file; **~ past** défiler devant.
filing cabinet *n* classeur (meuble) *m*.
fill *vt* remplir; **~ in** remplir; **~ up** remplir (jusqu'au bord).
fillet *n* filet *m*.
fillet steak *n* filet de bœuf *m*.
filling station *n* station-service *f*.
fillip *n* (*fig*) coup de fouet *m*.
filly *n* pouliche *f*.
film *n* pellicule *f*; film *f*; cellophane *m*; * *vt* filmer; * *vi* s'embuer.
film star *n* vedette de cinéma *f*.
filmstrip *n* film *m*.
filter *n* filtre *m*; * *vt* filtrer.
filter-tipped *adj* à bout filtre.
filth(iness) *n* immondice, ordure *f*; saleté, crasse *f*.
filthy *adj* crasseux, dégoûtant.
fin *n* nageoire *f*.
final *adj* dernier; définitif; **~ly** *adv* finalement.
finale *n* finale *m*.
finalise *vt* parachever, rendre définitif.
finalist *n* finaliste *mf*.
finance *n* finance *f*.

financial *adj* financier.
financier *n* financier *m*.
find *vt* trouver, découvrir; **~ out** découvrir; démasquer; **~ o.s.** se retrouver; * *n* trouvaille *f*.
findings *npl* résultats *mpl*, conclusions *fpl*; verdict *m*.
fine *adj* fin; pur; aigu; raffiné; beau, *f* belle; délicat; subtil; élégant; * *n* amende *f*; * *vt* infliger une amende à.
fine arts *npl* beaux arts *mpl*.
finely *adv* magnifiquement.
finery *n* parure *f*.
finesse *n* finesse, subtilité *f*.
finger *n* doigt *m*; * *vt* toucher, manier.
fingernail *n* ongle *m*.
fingerprint *n* empreinte digitale *f*.
fingertip *n* bout du doigt *m*.
finicky *adj* pointilleux, difficile.
finish *vt* finir, terminer, achever; **~ off** finir; **~ up** terminer; * *vi*: **~ up** se retrouver.
finishing line *n* ligne d'arrivée *f*.
finishing school *n* école privée (pour jeunes filles) *f*.
finite *adj* fini.
fir *n* sapin *m*
fire *n* feu *m*; incendie *m*; * *vt* mettre le feu à; incendier; tirer; * *vi* s'enflammer, faire feu.
fire alarm *n* alarme d'incendie *f*.
firearm *n* arme à feu *f*.
fireball *n* boule de feu *f*.
fire department *n* pompiers *mpl*.
fire engine *n* voiture de pompiers *f*.
fire escape *n* escalier de secours *m*.
fire extinguisher *n* extincteur *m*.
firefly *n* luciole *f*.
fireman *n* pompier *m*.
fireplace *n* cheminée *f*, foyer *m*.
fireproof *adj* ignifugé.
fireside *n* coin du feu *m*.
fire station *n* caserne de pompiers *f*.
firewater *n* eau de vie *f*.
firewood *n* bois de chauffage *m*.
fireworks *npl* feu d'artifice *m*.
firing *n* fusillade *f*.
firing squad *n* peloton d'exécution *m*.
firm *adj* ferme, solide; constant; * *n* (*com*) compagnie *f*; **~ly** *adv* fermement.
firmament *n* firmament *m*.
firmness *n* fermeté *f*; résolution *f*.
first *adj* premier; * *adv* premièrement; **at ~** d'abord; **~ly** *adv* en premier lieu.

first aid *n* premiers secours *mpl*.
first-aid kit *n* trousse de premiers secours *f*.
first-class *adj* de première classe, de première catégorie.
first-hand *adj* de première main.
First Lady *n* (US) première dame, femme du président d'un pays *f*.
first name *n* prénom *m*.
first-rate *adj* de première qualité.
fiscal *adj* fiscal.
fish *n* poisson *m*; * *vi* pêcher.
fishbone *n* arête *f*.
fisherman *n* pêcheur *m*.
fish farm *n* entreprise de pisciculture *f*.
fishing *n* pêche *f*.
fishing line *n* ligne de pêche *f*.
fishing rod *n* canne à pêche *f*.
fishing tackle *n* attirail de pêche *m*.
fish market *n* marché au poisson *m*.
fishseller *n* poissonnier *m* -ière *f*.
fishstore *n* poissonnerie *f*.
fishy *adj* (*fig*) suspect.
fissure *n* fissure, crevasse *f*.
fist *n* poing *m*.
fit *n* accès *m*, attaque *f*; crise *f*; * *adj* en forme; capable; adapté à, qui convient; * *vt* aller à; ajuster, adapter; **~ out** équiper; * *vi* (bien) aller; **~ in** s'accorder avec; être en harmonie avec.
fitment *n* meuble encastré *m*.
fitness *n* forme physique *f*; aptitude *f*.
fitted carpet *n* moquette *f*.
fitted kitchen *n* cuisine encastrée *f*.
fitter *n* monteur *m*.
fitting *adj* qui convient, approprié, juste; * *n* accessoire *m*; **~s** *pl* installations *fpl*.
five *adj n* cinq *m*.
five spot *n* (*sl*) (US) billet *m* de cinq dollars.
fix *vt* fixer, établir; **~ up** arranger.
fixation *n* obsession *f*.
fixed *adj* fixe.
fixings *npl* garniture *f*; accessoires *mpl*.
fixture *n* (sport) rencontre *f*.
fizz *vi* pétiller.
fizzy *adj* gazeux.
flabbergasted *adj* abasourdi.
flabby *adj* mou, *f* molle, flasque.
flaccid *adj* flasque, mou, *f* molle.
flag *n* drapeau *m*; (*bot*) iris *m*; * *vi* s'affaiblir.
flagpole *n* mât *m* de drapeau.
flagrant *adj* flagrant.
flagship *n* vaisseau amiral *m*.

flagstop n (US) arrêt m facultatif.
flair n flair m; talent m.
flak n tir antiaérien m; critiques fpl.
flake n flocon m; paillette f; * vi s'effriter, s'écailler.
flaky adj floconneux; friable.
flamboyant adj flamboyant; ostentatoire.
flame n flamme f; ardeur f.
flamingo n flamant m.
flammable adj inflammable.
flank n flanc m; (also mil); * vt flanquer.
flannel n flanelle f.
flap n battement m; rabat m; * vt vi battre.
flare vi luire, briller; ~ **up** s'embraser; se mettre en colère; éclater; * n flamme f.
flash n éclat m; éclair m; * vt faire briller; allumer.
flashbulb n ampoule de flash f.
flash cube n cube de flash m.
flashlight n lampe f de poche.
flashy adj tape-à-l'œil, voyant.
flask n flasque f; flacon m.
flat adj plat; uniforme; insipide; * n plaine f; plat m; (mus) bémol m; ~**ly** adv horizontalement; platement; également; caté-goriquement.
flatness n égalité f; monotonie f.
flatten vt aplanir; aplatir.
flatter vt flatter.
flattering adj flatteur.
flattery n flatterie f.
flatulence n (med) flatulence f.
flaunt vt étaler, afficher.
flavour n saveur m; * vt parfumer; assaisonner.
flavoured adj savoureux; parfumé.
flavourless adj insipide.
flaw n défaut m; imperfection f.
flawless adj parfait.
flax n lin m.
flea n puce f.
flea bite n piqûre de puce f.
fleck n petite tache f; particule f.
flee vt fuir de; * vi s'enfuir; fuir.
fleece n toison f; * vt (sl) tondre.
fleet n flotte f; (autos) parc m.
fleeting adj fugace, fugitif.
flesh n chair f.
flesh wound n blessure superficielle f.
fleshy adj charnu.
flex n cordon m; * vt fléchir.
flexibility n flexibilité f.
flexible adj flexible, souple.
flick n petit coup m; * vt donner un petit coup à.

flicker vt vaciller; trembloter.
flier n aviateur m -trice f.
flight n vol m; fuite f; volée f; (fig) envolée f.
flight attendant n steward m, hôtesse de l'air f.
flight deck n cabine de pilotage f.
flimsy adj léger; fragile.
flinch vi sourciller.
fling vt lancer, jeter.
flint n silex m.
flip vt lancer.
flippant adj désinvolte, cavalier.
flipper n nageoire f.
flirt vi flirter; * n charmeur m -euse f.
flirtation n flirt f.
flit vi voler, voleter.
float vt faire flotter; lancer; * vi flotter; * n flotteur m; char (de carnaval) m; provision f.
flock n troupeau m; volée f; foule f; * vi affluer.
flog vt fustiger.
flogging n fustigation, flagellation f.
flood n inondation f; marée haute f; déluge m; * vt inonder.
flooding n inondation f.
floodlight n projecteur m.
floor n sol m; plancher m; étage m; * vt parqueter; déconcerter.
floorboard n planche f.
floor lamp n lampadaire m.
floor show n spectacle de cabaret m.
flop n four, fiasco m.
floppy adj lâche; * n disquette f.
flora n flore f.
floral adj floral.
florescence n floraison f.
florid adj fleuri.
florist n fleuriste mf.
florist's (shop) n boutique de fleuriste f.
flotilla n (mar) flotille f.
flounder n flet m; * vi patauger.
flour n farine f.
flourish vi fleurir; prospérer; * n fioriture f; (mus) fioriture f.
flourishing adj florissant.
flout vt mépriser, se moquer de.
flow vi couler; circuler; monter (marée); ondoyer; * n flux m; écoulement m; flot m.
flow chart n organigramme m.
flower n fleur f; * vi fleurir.
flowerbed n parterre de fleurs m.
flowerpot n pot de fleurs m.
flowery adj fleuri.
flower show n exposition de fleurs f.
fluctuate vi fluctuer.

fluctuation n fluctuation f.
fluency n aisance f.
fluent adj coulant; facile; ~**ly** adv couramment.
fluff n peluche f; ~**y** adj duveteux.
fluid adj n fluide m.
fluidity n fluidité f.
fluke n (sl) veine f.
fluoride n fluorure m.
flurry n rafale f; agitation f.
flush vt: **to ~ out** nettoyer à grande eau; * vi rougir; * n rougeur f; éclat m.
flushed adj rouge.
fluster vt énerver.
flustered adj énervé.
flute n flûte f.
flutter vi voleter; s'agiter; * n agitation f; émoi m.
flux n flux m.
fly vt piloter; transporter par avion; * vi voler; fuir; ~ **away/off** s'envoler; * n mouche f; braguette f.
flying n aviation f.
flying saucer n soucoupe volante f.
flypast n défilé aérien m.
flysheet n feuille volante f.
foal n poulain m.
foam n écume f; * vi écumer.
foam rubber n caoutchouc mousse m.
foamy adj écumeux.
focus n foyer m; centre m.
fodder n fourrage m.
foe n ennemi m -e f, adversaire mf.
fog n brouillard m.
foggy adj brumeux.
fog light n feu de brouillard m.
foible n point faible m.
foil vt déjouer; * n papier d'aluminium m; fleuret m.
fold n pli m; parc à moutons m; * vt plier; ~ **up** faire faillite; * vi: ~ **up** plier, replier.
folder n chemise f; dépliant m.
folding adj pliant.
folding chair n chaise pliante f.
foliage n feuillage m.
folio n folio m.
folk n gens mpl.
folklore n folklore m.
folk song n chant folklorique m.
follow vt suivre; ~ **up** suivre; exploiter; * vi suivre, s'ensuivre, résulter.
follower n serviteur m; disciple mf, partisan m -e f; adhérent m -e f; admirateur m -trice f.
following adj suivant; * n partisans mpl.
folly n folie, extravagance f.

foment *vt* fomenter.

fond *adj* affectueux; **to be ~ of** aimer; **~ly** *adv* affectueusement.

fondle *vt* caresser.

fondness *n* prédilection *f*; affection *f*.

font *n* fonts baptismaux *mpl*.

food *n* nourriture *f*.

food mixer *n* mixer *m*.

food poisoning *n* intoxication alimentaire *f*.

food processor *n* robot *m* ménager.

foodstuffs *npl* denrées alimentaires *fpl*.

fool *n* imbécile *mf*, idiot *m* -e *f*; * *vt* duper.

foolhardy *adj* téméraire.

foolish *adj* idiot, insensé; **~ly** *adv* bêtement.

foolproof *adj* infaillible.

foolscap *n* papier ministre *m*.

foot *n* pied *m*; patte *f*; **on** or **by ~** à pied.

footage *n* métrage *m*.

football *n* football *m*; ballon de football *m*.

footballer *n* footballeur *m* -euse *f*.

footbrake *n* frein à pied *m*.

footbridge *n* passerelle *f*.

foothills *npl* contreforts *mpl*.

foothold *n* prise (pour le pied) *f*.

footing *n* prise (pour le pied) *f*; statut *m*; situation *f*; plan *m*.

footlights *npl* feux de la rampe *mpl*.

footman *n* valet de pied *m*; soldat d'infanterie *m*.

footnote *n* note (de bas de page) *f*.

footpath *n* sentier *m*.

footprint *n* empreinte (de pas) *f*.

footsore *adj* aux pieds endoloris.

footstep *n* pas *m*.

footwear *n* chaussures *fpl*.

for *prep* pour; en raison de; pendant; * *conj* car; **as ~ me** quant à moi; **what ~?** pourquoi?; pourquoi faire?

forage *n* fourrage *m*; * *vt* fourrager; fouiller.

foray *n* incursion *f*.

forbid *vt* interdire, défendre; empêcher; **God ~!** pourvu que non!

forbidding *adj* menaçant; sévère.

force *n* force *f*; puissance, vigueur *f*; violence *f*; **~s** *pl* forces armées *fpl*; * *vt* forcer, obliger, contraindre; imposer.

forced *adj* forcé.

forced march *n* (*mil*) marche forcée *f*.

forceful *adj* énergique.

forceps *n* forceps *m*.

forcible *adj* énergique, vigoureux, puissant; **~bly** *adv* énergiquement, avec véhémence.

ford *n* gué *m*; * *vt* passer à gué.

fore *n*: **to the ~** en évidence.

forearm *n* avant-bras *m*.

foreboding *n* pressentiment *m*.

forecast *vt* prévoir; * *n* prévision *f*.

forecourt *n* avant-cour *f*.

forefather *n* aïeul, ancêtre *m*.

forefinger *n* index *m*.

forefront *n*: **in the ~ of** au premier plan de.

forego *vt* renoncer à, s'abstenir de.

foregone *adj* passé; anticipé.

foreground *n* premier plan *m*.

forehead *n* front *m*.

foreign *adj* étranger.

foreigner *n* étranger *m* -ère *f*.

foreign exchange *n* devises *fpl*.

foreleg *n* patte de devant *f*.

foreman *n* contremaître *m*; (*law*) premier juré *m*.

foremost *adj* principal.

forenoon *n* matinée *f*.

forensic *adj* médico-légal.

forerunner *n* précurseur *m*; signe avant-coureur *m*.

foresee *vt* prévoir.

foreshadow *vt* présager.

foresight *n* prévoyance *f*; prescience *f*.

forest *n* forêt *f*.

forestall *vt* anticiper; prévenir.

forester *n* garde forestier *m*.

forestry *n* sylviculture *f*.

foretaste *n* avant-goût *m*.

foretell *vt* prédire.

forethought *n* prévoyance *f*; préméditation *f*.

forever *adv* toujours; un temps infini.

forewarn *vt* avertir, prévenir.

foreword *n* préface *f*.

forfeit *n* amende *f*; confiscation *f*; * *vt* perdre.

forge *n* forge *f*; usine métallurgique *f*; * *vt* forger; contrefaire * *vi*: **~ ahead** aller de l'avant.

forger *n* faussaire *mf*.

forgery *n* contrefaçon *f*.

forget *vt vi* oublier.

forgetful *adj* étourdi; négligent.

forgetfulness *n* étourderie *f*; négligence *f*.

forget-me-not *n* (*bot*) myosotis *m*.

forgive *vt* pardonner.

forgiveness *n* pardon *m*; indulgence *f*.

fork *n* fourchette *f*; fourche *f*; * *vi* bifurquer; **~ out** (*sl*) casquer.

forked *adj* fourchu.

fork-lift truck *n* chariot élévateur *m*.

forlorn *adj* malheureux, abandonné.

form *n* forme *f*; formule *f*; formulaire *m*; formalité *f*; moule *m*; * *vt* former.

formal *adj* formel; méthodique; cérémonieux; **~ly** *adv* formellement.

formality *n* formalité *f*; cérémonie *f*.

format *n* format *m*; * *vt* formater.

formation *n* formation *f*.

formative *adj* formateur *m* -trice *f*.

former *adj* précédent, ancien; **~ly** *adv* autrefois, jadis.

formidable *adj* effrayant, terrible.

formula *n* formule *f*.

formulate *vt* formuler.

forsake *vt* abandonner, renoncer à.

fort *n* fort *m*.

forte *n* fort *m*.

forthcoming *adj* prochain; sociable.

forthright *adj* franc.

forthwith *adv* immédiatement, tout de suite.

fortieth *adj n* quarantième *mf*.

fortification *n* fortification *f*.

fortify *vt* fortifier, renforcer.

fortitude *n* stoïcisme *m*; courage *m*.

fortnight *n* quinze jours *mpl*; deux semaines *fpl*; * *adj* **~ly** bimensuel; * *adv* **~ly** tous les quinze jours.

fortress *n* (*mil*) forteresse *f*.

fortuitous *adj* fortuit; imprévu; **~ly** *adv* fortuitement.

fortunate *adj* chanceux; **~ly** *adv* heureusement.

fortune *n* chance *f*, sort *m*; fortune *f*.

fortune-teller *n* diseuse de bonne aventure *f*.

forty *adj n* quarante *m*.

forum *n* forum *m*, tribune *f*.

forward *adj* avancé; précoce; présomptueux; **~(s)** *adv* en avant, vers l'avant; * *vt* transmettre; promouvoir; expédier.

forwardness *n* précocité *f*; effronterie *f*.

fossil *adj* fossilisé; * *n* fossile *m*.

foster *vt* encourager.

foster child *n* enfant adoptif *m*.

foster father *n* père adoptif *m*.

foster mother *n* mère adoptive *f*.

foul *adj* infect, ignoble; vil, dé-

loyal; ~ **copy** *n* copie illisible *f*;
~**ly** *adv* salement; ignoblement;
* *vt* polluer.

foul play *n* jeu déloyal *m*; meurtre
m.

found *vt* fonder, créer; établir, édifier; fondre.

foundation *n* foundation *f*; fondement *m*.

founder *n* fondateur *m* -trice *f*;
fondeur *m*; * *vi* (*mar*) couler.

foundling *n* enfant trouvé(e) *mf*.

foundry *n* fonderie *f*.

fount, fountain *n* fontaine *f*.

fountainhead *n* source, origine *f*.

four *adj n* quatre *m*.

fourfold *adj* quadruple.

four-poster (bed) *n* lit à baldaquin
m.

foursome *n* groupe de quatre personnes *m*.

fourteen *adj n* quatorze *m*.

fourteenth *adj n* quatorzième *mf*.

fourth *adj n* quatrième *mf*; * *n* quart
m; ~**ly** *adv* quatrièmement.

fowl *n* volaille *f*.

fox *n* renard *f*; (*fig*) rusé *m*.

foyer *n* vestibule *m*.

fracas *n* rixe *f*.

fraction *n* fraction *f*.

fracture *n* fracture *f*; * *vt* fracturer.

fragile *adj* fragile; frêle.

fragility *n* fragilité *f*; faiblesse, délicatesse *f*.

fragment *n* fragment *m*.

fragmentary *adj* fragmentaire.

fragrance *n* parfum *m*.

fragrant *adj* parfumé, odorant; ~**ly**
adv en exhalant un parfum.

frail *adj* frêle, fragile.

frailty *n* fragilité *f*; faiblesse *f*.

frame *n* charpente *f*; châssis *m*, armature *f*; cadre *m*; structure *f*;
monture *f*; * *vt* encadrer; concevoir; construire; former.

frame of mind *n* état d'esprit *m*.

framework *n* charpente *f*; structure *f*, cadre *m*.

franchise *n* droit de vote *m*; franchise *f*.

frank *adj* franc, direct.

frankly *adv* franchement.

frankness *n* franchise *f*.

frantic *adj* frénétique, effréné.

fraternal *adj* ~**ly** *adv* fraternel(lement).

fraternise *vi* fraterniser.

fraternity *n* fraternité *f*.

fratricide *n* fratricide *mf*.

fraud *n* fraude, tromperie *f*.

fraudulence *n* caractère frauduleux *m*.

fraudulent *adj* frauduleux; ~**ly** *adv*
frauduleusement.

fraught *adj* accablé, tendu.

fray *n* rixe, bagarre, querelle *f*.

freak *n* caprice *m*; phénomène *m*.

freckle *n* tache de rousseur *f*.

freckled *adj* couvert de taches de
rousseur.

free *adj* libre; autonome; gratuit;
dégagé; * *vt* affranchir; libérer;
débarrasser.

freedom *n* liberté *f*.

free-for-all *n* mêlée générale *f*.

free gift *n* prime *f*.

freehold *n* propriété libre *f*.

free kick *n* coup franc *m*.

freelance *adj* indépendant; * *adv*
en indépendant.

freely *adv* librement; franchement;
libéralement.

freemason *n* franc-maçon *m*.

freemasonry *n* franc-maçonnerie *f*.

freepost *n* port payé *m*.

free-range *adj* de plein air.

freethinker *n* libre-penseur *m* -
euse *f*.

freethinking *n* libre pensée *f*.

free trade *n* libre échange *m*.

freeway *n* (US) autoroute *f*.

freewheel *vi* rouler en roue libre.

free will *n* libre arbitre *m*.

freeze *vi* geler; * *vt* congeler; geler.

freeze-dried *adj* lyophilisé.

freezer *n* congélateur *m*.

freezing *adj* gelé.

freezing point *n* point de congéla-
tion *m*.

freight *n* cargaison *f*; fret *m*.

freighter *n* affréteur *m*.

freight train *n* train de marchandises *m*.

French bean *n* haricot vert *m*.

French fries *npl* frites *fpl*.

French window *n* porte-fenêtre *f*.

frenzied *adj* fou, frénétique.

frenzy *n* frénésie *f*; folie *f*.

frequency *n* fréquence *f*.

frequent *adj* fréquent; ~**ly** *adv* fréquemment; * *vt* fréquenter.

fresco *n* fresque *f*.

fresh *adj* frais; nouveau, récent; ~
water *n* eau douce *f*.

freshen *vt* rafraîchir; * *vi* se rafraîchir.

freshly *adv* nouvellement; récemment.

freshman *n* nouveau *m*, nouvelle *f*.

freshness *n* fraîcheur *f*.

freshwater *adj* d'eau douce.

fret *vi* s'agiter, se tracasser.

friar *n* moine *m*.

friction *n* friction *f*.

Friday *n* vendredi *m*; **Good** ~ Vendredi Saint *m*.

friend *n* ami *m* -e *f*.

friendless *adj* sans amis.

friendliness *n* amitié, bienveillance *f*.

friendly *adj* amical.

friendship *n* amitié *f*.

frieze *n* frise *f*.

frigate *n* (*mar*) frégate *f*.

fright *n* peur, frayeur *f*.

frighten *vt* effrayer.

frightened *adj* effrayé, apeuré.

frightening *adj* effrayant.

frightful *adj* épouvantable, effroyable; ~**ly** *adv* affreusement, ef-
froyablement.

frigid *adj* froid, glacé; frigide; ~**ly**
adv froidement.

fringe *n* frange *f*.

fringe benefits *npl* avantages *mpl*
en nature.

frisk *vt* fouiller.

frisky *adj* vif, fringant.

fritter *vt*: **to ~ away** gaspiller.

frivolity *n* frivolité *f*.

frivolous *adj* frivole, léger.

frizz *vt* friser.

frizzle *vt vi* grésiller.

frizzy *adj* frisé.

fro *adv*: **to go to and ~** aller et venir.

frock *n* robe *f*.

frog *n* grenouille *f*.

frolic *vi* folâtrer, gambader.

frolicsome *adj* folâtre, gai.

from *prep* de; depuis; à partir de.

front *n* avant, devant *m*; façade *f*;
front *m*; * *adj* de devant; premier.

frontal *adj* de front.

front door *n* porte d'entrée *f*.

frontier *n* frontière *f*.

front page *n* première page *f*.

front-wheel drive *n* (*auto*) traction
avant *f*.

frost *n* gel *m*; gelée *f*; * *vt* geler.

frostbite *n* engelure *f*.

frostbitten *adj* gelé.

frosted *adj* gelé, givré.

frosty *adj* glacial; givré.

froth *n* écume *f*; * *vi* écumer.

frothy *adj* mousseux, écumeux.

frown *vt* froncer les sourcils; * *n*
froncement de sourcils *m*.

frozen *adj* gelé.

frugal *adj* frugal; économique;
simple; ~**ly** *adv* frugalement.

fruit *n* fruit *m*.

fruiterer *n* fruitier *m* -ière *f*.

fruiterer's (shop) *n* fruiterie *f*.

fruitful *adj* fécond, fertile; fructueux, utile; ~**ly** *adv* fructueuse-
ment.

fruitfulness *n* fertilité *f*; caractère
fructueux *m*.

fruition *n* réalisation *f*.

fruit juice *n* jus de fruit *m*.

fruitless *adj* stérile; infécond; **~ly** *adv* vainement, inutilement.

fruit salad *n* salade de fruits *f*.

fruit tree *n* arbre fruitier *m*.

frustrate *vt* contrecarrer; frustrer; énerver.

frustrated *adj* frustré.

frustration *n* frustration *f*.

fry *vt* frire.

frying pan *n* poêle *f*.

fuchsia *n* (*bot*) fuchsia *m*.

fudge *n* caramel *m* mou.

fuel *n* combustible, carburant *m*.

fuel tank *n* réservoir à carburant *m*.

fugitive *adj n* fugitif *m* -ive *f*.

fugue *n* (*mus*) fugue *f*.

fulcrum *n* pivot *m*.

fulfil *vt* accomplir; réaliser.

fulfilment *n* accomplissement *m*.

full *adj* plein, rempli; complet; * *adv* pleinement, entièrement.

full-blown *adj* complet.

full-length *adj* en pied; de long métrage.

full moon *n* pleine lune *f*.

fullness *n* plénitude *f*; abondance *f*.

full-scale *adj* grandeur nature; total, complet.

full-time *adj* à plein temps.

fully *adv* pleinement, entièrement.

fully fledged *adj* diplômé, qualifié.

fulsome *adj* exagéré.

fumble *vi* manier gauchement; farfouiller.

fume *vi* exhaler des vapeurs; rager, fumer; * **~s** *npl* exhalaisons *fpl*.

fumigate *vt* fumiger.

fun *n* amusement *m*; plaisir *m*; **to have ~** (bien) s'amuser.

function *n* fonction *f*.

functional *adj* fonctionnel.

fund *n* fonds *m*; * *vt* financer.

fundamental *adj* fondamental; **~ly** *adv* fondamentalement.

funeral *n* enterrement *m*.

funeral service *n* service *m* funèbre.

funereal *adj* funèbre, lugubre.

fungus *n* champignon *m*; moisissure *f*.

funnel *n* entonnoir *m*; cheminée *f*.

funny *adj* amusant; curieux.

fur *n* fourrure *f*.

fur coat *n* manteau de fourrure *m*.

furious *adj* furieux; déchaîné; **~ly** *adv* furieusement.

furlong *n* mesure de longueur (220 yards = 201 mètres), furlong *m*.

furnace *n* fourneau *m*; chaudière *f*.

furnish *vt* meubler; fournir; pourvoir.

furnishings *npl* ameublement *m*.

furniture *n* meubles *mpl*.

furrow *n* sillon *m*; * *vt* sillonner; rider.

furry *adj* à poil.

further *adj* supplémentaire; plus lointain; * *adv* plus loin, plus avant; en outre; de plus; * *vt* faire avancer; favoriser; promouvoir.

further education *n* formation *f* postscolaire.

furthermore *adv* de plus.

furthest *adv* le plus loin, le plus éloigné.

furtive *adj* furtif; secret; **~ly** *adv* furtivement.

fury *n* fureur *f*; furie *f*; colère *f*.

fuse *vt* fondre; faire sauter; * *vi* fondre, sauter; * *n* fusible *m*; amorce *f*.

fuse box *n* boîte à fusibles *f*.

fusion *n* fusion *f*.

fuss *n* tapage *m*; histoires *fpl*.

fussy *adj* tatillon, chipoteur.

futile *adj* futile, vain.

futility *n* futilité *f*.

future *adj* futur; * *n* futur *m*; avenir *m*.

fuzzy *adj* flou, confus; crépu.

G

gab *n* (*fam*) bavardage *m*.

gabble *vi* baragouiner; * *n* charabia *m*.

gable *n* pignon *m*.

gadget *n* gadget *m*.

gaffe *n* gaffe *f*, bévue *f*.

gag *n* bâillon *m*; blague *f*; * *vt* bâillonner.

gaiety *n* gaieté *f*.

gaily *adv* gaiement.

gain *n* gain *m*; bénéfice *m*; * *vt* gagner; atteindre.

gait *n* démarche *f*; maintien *m*.

gala *n* gala *m*.

galaxy *n* galaxie *f*.

gale *n* grand vent *m*.

gall *n* bile *f*; fiel *m*.

gallant *adj* galant.

gall bladder *n* vésicule biliaire *f*.

gallery *n* galerie *f*.

galley *n* galère *f*; (*mar*) cuisine *f*.

gallon *n* gallon *m* (mesure).

gallop *n* galop *m*; * *vi* galoper.

gallows *n* potence *f*.

gallstone *n* calcul biliaire *m*.

galore *adv* en abondance.

galvanise *vt* galvaniser.

gambit *n* stratagème *m*.

gamble *vi* jouer; spéculer; * *n* risque *m*; pari *m*.

gambler *n* joueur *m* -euse *f*.

gambling *n* jeu *m* (d'argent).

game *n* jeu *m*; divertissement *m*; partie *f*; gibier *m*; * *vi* jouer.

gamekeeper *n* garde-chasse *m*.

gaming *n* jeu *m* (d'argent).

gammon *n* jambon *m*.

gamut *n* (*mus*) gamme *f*.

gander *n* jars *m*.

gang *n* gang *m*, bande *f*.

gangrene *n* gangrène *f*.

gangster *n* gangster *m*.

gangway *n* passerelle *f*.

gap *n* trou *m*; vide *m*; intervalle, écart *m*.

gape *vi* être bouche bée; bâiller.

gaping *adj* béant.

garage *n* garage *m*.

garbage *n* ordures *fpl*.

garbage can *n* poubelle *f*.

garbage man *n* éboueur *m*.

garbled *adj* confus.

garden *n* jardin *m*.

garden hose *n* tuyau d'arrosage *m*.

gardener *n* jardinier *m* -ière *f*.

gardening *n* jardinage *m*.

gargle *vi* se gargariser.

gargoyle *n* gargouille *f*.

garish *adj* tapageur.

garland *n* guirlande *f*.

garlic *n* ail *m*.

garment *n* vêtement *m*.

garnish *vt* garnir, décorer; * *n* garniture *f*.

garret *n* mansarde *f*.

garrison *n* (*mil*) garnison *f*; * *vt* (*mil*) mettre en garnison; protéger d'une garnison.

garrote *vt* étrangler, garrotter.

garrulous *adj* locace, bavard.

garter *n* jarretelle *f*.

gas *n* gaz *m*; essence *f*.

gas burner *n* brûleur à gaz *m*.

gas cylinder *n* bouteille de gaz *f*.

gaseous *adj* gazeux.

gas fire *n* radiateur à gaz *m*.

gash *n* entaille *f*; fente *f*; * *vt* entailler.

gasket *n* joint d'étanchéité *m*.

gasp *vi* haleter; * *n* halètements *mpl*.

gas mask *n* masque à gaz *m*.

gas meter *n* compteur à gaz *m*.

gasoline *n* (US) essence *f*.

gas pedal *n* (US) accélérateur *m*.

gas ring *n* brûleur à gaz *m*.

gas station *n* (US) poste d'essence *m*.

gassy *adj* gazeux.

gas tap *n* robinet de gaz *m*.

gastric *adj* gastrique.

gastronomic *adj* gastronomique.

gasworks *npl* usine à gaz *f*.

gate *n* porte *f*; portail *m*.

gateway *n* porte *f*.

gather *vt* rassembler; ramasser; comprendre; * *vi* se rassembler.

gathering *n* réunion *f*; récolte *f*.

gauche *adj* gauche, maladroit.

gaudy *adj* criard.

gauge *n* calibre *m*; écartement *m*; * *vt* mesurer; calibrer.

gaunt *adj* décharné.

gauze *n* gaze *f*.

gay *adj* gai; vif; homosexuel.

gaze *vi* contempler, considérer; * *n* regard *m*.

gazelle *n* gazelle *f*.

gazette *n* gazette *f*.

gazetteer *n* répertoire géographique *m*.

gear *n* équipement *m*, matériel *m*; appareil *m*; affaires *fpl*; vitesse *f*.

gearbox *n* boîte de vitesses *f*.

gear shift *n* levier de vitesse *m*.

gear wheel *n* roue d'engrenage *f*.

gel *n* gel *m*.

gelatin(e) *n* gélatine *f*.

gelignite *n* gélignite *f*.

gem *n* pierre précieuse *f*; perle *f*.

Gemini *n* Gémeaux *mpl* (signe du zodiaque).

gender *n* genre *m*.

gene *n* gène *m*.

genealogical *adj* généalogique.

genealogy *n* généalogie *f*.

general *adj* général; commun, usuel; **in ~** en général; **~ly** *adv* généralement; * *n* général *m*; générale *f*.

general delivery *n* (US) poste restante *f*.

general election *n* élections générales *fpl*.

generalisation *n* généralisation *f*.

generalise *vt* généraliser.

generality *n* généralité; majeure partie *f*.

generate *vt* engendrer; produire; causer.

generation *n* génération *f*.

generator *n* générateur *m*.

generic *adj* générique.

generosity *n* générosité, libéralité *f*.

generous *adj* généreux.

genetics *npl* génétique *f*.

genial *adj* cordial; doux.

genitals *npl* organes génitaux *mpl*.

genitive *n* (*gr*) génitif *m*.

genius *n* génie *m*.

genteel *adj* distingué.

gentle *adj* doux, *f* douce, modéré.

gentleman *n* gentleman *m*.

gentleness *n* douceur *f*.

gently *adv* doucement.

gentry *n* aristocratie *f*.

gents *n* toilettes pour hommes *fpl*.

genuflexion *n* génuflexion *f*.

genuine *adj* authentique; sincère; **~ly** *adv* authentiquement; sincèrement.

genus *n* genre *m*.

geographer *n* géographe *mf*.

geographical *adj* géographique.

geography *n* géographie *f*.

geological *adj* géologique.

geologist *n* géologue *mf*.

geology *n* géologie *f*.

geometric(al) *adj* géométrique.

geometry *n* géométrie *f*.
geranium *n* (*bot*) géranium *m*.
geriatric *n* malade gériatrique *mf*;
　* *adj* gériatrique.
germ *n* (*bot*) germe *m*.
germinate *vi* germer.
gesticulate *vi* gesticuler.
gesture *n* geste *m*.
get *vt* avoir; obtenir; atteindre; ga-
　gner; attraper; * *vi* devenir; aller;
　~ **the better** avoir l'avantage,
　surpasser.
geyser *n* geyser *m*; chauffe-eau *m*
　invar.
ghastly *adj* affreux; sinistre.
gherkin *n* cornichon *m*.
ghost *n* fantôme, spectre *m*.
ghostly *adj* spectral.
giant *n* géant *m* -e *f*.
gibberish *n* charabia *m*; sornettes
　fpl.
gibe *vi* se moquer; * *n* moquerie *f*.
giblets *npl* abattis (de volaille)
　mpl.
giddiness *n* vertige *m*.
giddy *adj* vertigineux.
gift *n* cadeau *m*; don *m*; talent *m*.
gifted *adj* talentueux; doué.
gift voucher *n* bon-cadeau *m*.
gigantic *adj* gigantesque.
giggle *vi* rire bêtement.
gild *vt* dorer.
gilding, gilt *n* dorure *f*.
gill *n* quart de pinte *m*; ~**s** *pl* bran-
　chies *fpl*.
gilt-edged *adj* de premier ordre.
gimmick *n* truc *m*.
gin *n* gin *m*.
ginger *n* gingembre *m*.
gingerbread *n* pain d'épice *m*.
ginger-haired *adj* roux, *f* rousse.
giraffe *n* girafe *f*.
girder *n* poutre *f*.
girdle *n* gaine *f*; ceinture *f*.
girl *n* fille *f*.
girlfriend *n* amie *f*; petite amie *f*.
girlish *adj* de fille.
giro *n* virement *m*.
girth *n* sangle *f*; circonférence *f*.
gist *n* essence *f*.
give *vt* donner; offrir; prononcer,
　faire; consacrer; ~ **away** offrir;
　trahir; révéler; ~ **back** rendre; ~
　in *vi* céder; *vt* remettre; ~ **off** dé-
　gager; ~ **out** distribuer; ~ **up** *vi*
　abandonner; *vt* renoncer à.
gizzard *n* gésier *m*.
glacial *adj* glacial.
glacier *n* glacier *m*.
glad *adj* joyeux, content; **I am ~ to**
　see that je me réjouis de voir
　que; ~**ly** *adv* avec joie, avec plai-
　sir.

gladden *vt* réjouir.
gladiator *n* gladiateur *m*.
glamorous *adj* attrayant, sédui-
　sant.
glamour *n* attrait *m*, séduction *f*.
glance *n* regard *m*; * *vi* regarder; je-
　ter un coup d'œil.
glancing *adj* oblique.
gland *n* glande *f*.
glare *n* éclat *m*; regard féroce *m*;
　* *vi* éblouir, briller; lancer des re-
　gards indignés.
glaring *adj* éclatant; évident; fu-
　rieux.
glass *n* verre *m*; longue-vue *f*; mi-
　roir *m*; ~**es** *pl* lunettes *fpl*; * *adj* en
　verre.
glassware *n* verrerie *f*.
glassy *adj* vitreux, cristallin.
glaze *vt* vitrer; vernisser.
glazier *n* vitrier *m*.
gleam *n* rayon *m*; * *vi* rayonner,
　briller.
gleaming *adj* brillant.
glean *vt* glaner.
glee *n* joie *f*; exultation *f*.
glen *n* vallée *f*.
glib *adj* facile; volubile; ~**ly** *adv* fa-
　cilement; volubilement.
glide *vi* glisser; planer.
gliding *n* vol plané *m*.
glimmer *n* lueur *f*; * *vi* luire.
glimpse *n* aperçu *m*; vision *f*; * *vt*
　entrevoir.
glint *vi* briller, scintiller.
glisten, glitter *vi* luire, briller.
gloat *vi* exulter.
global *adj* global; mondial.
globe *n* globe *m*; sphère *f*.
gloom, gloominess *n* obscurité *f*;
　mélancolie, tristesse *f*; ~**ily** *adv*
　sombrement; tristement.
gloomy *adj* sombre, obscur; triste,
　mélancolique.
glorification *n* glorification *f*.
glorify *vt* glorifier, célébrer.
glorious *adj* glorieux, illustre; ~**ly**
　adv glorieusement.
glory *n* gloire, célébrité *f*.
gloss *n* glose *f*; lustre *m*; * *vt* gloser,
　interpréter; lustrer; ~ **over** pas-
　ser sur.
glossary *n* glossaire *m*.
glossy *adj* lustré, brillant.
glove *n* gant *m*.
glove compartment *n* boîte à
　gants *f*.
glow *vi* rougeoyer; rayonner; * *n*
　rougeoiement *m*; éclat *m*; feu *m*.
glower *vi* lancer des regards noirs.
glue *n* colle *f*; * *vt* coller.
gluey *adj* gluant, visqueux.
glum *adj* abattu, triste.

glut *n* surabondance *f*.
glutinous *adj* glutineux.
glutton *n* glouton *m* -ne *f*.
gluttony *n* gloutonnerie *f*.
glycerine *n* glycérine *f*.
gnarled *adj* noueux.
gnash *vt*: **to ~ one's teeth** grincer
　des dents.
gnat *n* moucheron *m*.
gnaw *vt* ronger.
gnome *n* gnome *m*.
go *vi* aller; s'en aller, partir; dispa-
　raître; se perdre; ~ **ahead** conti-
　nuer; ~ **away** s'en aller; ~ **back**
　repartir; ~ **by** passer; *vt* se
　lancer sur; aimer; ~ **in** entrer; ~
　off s'en aller, partir; se passer; se
　gâter; ~ **on** continuer; se passer;
　~ **out** sortir; s'éteindre; ~ **up**
　monter.
goad *n* aiguillon *m*; * *vt* aiguillon-
　ner; stimuler.
go-ahead *adj* entreprenant; * *n* feu
　vert *m*.
goal *n* but, objectif *m*.
goalkeeper *n* gardien de but *m*.
goalpost *n* poteau de but *m*.
goatherd *n* chevrier *m* -ière *f*.
gobble *vt* engloutir, avaler.
go-between *n* intermédiaire *mf*.
goblet *n* coupe *f*.
goblin *n* lutin *m*.
God *n* Dieu *m*.
godchild *n* filleul *m* -e *f*.
goddaughter *n* filleule *f*.
goddess *n* déesse *f*.
godfather *n* parrain *m*.
godforsaken *adj* perdu.
godhead *n* divinité *f*.
godless *adj* impie, athée.
godlike *adj* divin.
godliness *n* piété, dévotion, sain-
　teté *f*.
godly *adj* pieux, dévot, religieux;
　droit.
godmother *n* marraine *f*.
godsend *n* don du ciel *m*.
godson *n* filleul *m*.
goggle-eyed *adj* aux yeux exorbi-
　tés de surprise.
goggles *npl* lunettes *fpl*; lunettes
　de plongée *fpl*.
going *n* départ *m*; sortie *f*; progrès
　m.
gold *n* or *m*.
golden *adj* doré; d'or; excellent; ~
　rule règle d'or *f*.
goldfish *n* poisson rouge *m*.
gold-plated *adj* plaqué or.
goldsmith *n* orfèvre *m*.
golf *n* golf *m*.
golf ball *n* balle de golf *f*.
golf club *n* club de golf *m*.

golf course *n* terrain de golf *m*.

golfer *n* golfeur *m* -euse *f*.

gondolier *n* gondolier *m*.

gone *adj* parti; perdu; passé; fini; mort, disparu.

gong *n* gong *m*.

good *adj* bon; bienveillant; favorable; valable; * *adv* bien; * *n* bien *m*; avantage *m*; ~s *pl* biens *mpl*; marchandises *fpl*.

goodbye ! *excl* au revoir!

Good Friday *n* Vendredi Saint *m*.

goodies *npl* gourmandises *fpl*.

good-looking *adj* beau.

good nature *n* bon caractère *m*.

good-natured *adj* qui a bon caractère.

goodness *n* bonté *f*; qualité *f*.

goodwill *n* bienveillance *f*.

goose *n* oie *f*.

gooseberry *n* groseille à maquereau *f*.

goosebumps *npl* chair de poule *f*.

goose-step *n* pas de l'oie *m*.

gore *n* sang *m*; * *vt* blesser d'un coup de corne.

gorge *n* (*geogr*) gorge *f*; * *vt* engloutir, avaler.

gorgeous *adj* merveilleux.

gorilla *n* gorille *m*.

gorse *n* ajonc *m*.

gory *adj* sanglant.

goshawk *n* autour *m*.

gospel *n* évangile *m*.

gossamer *n* gaze *f*; toile d'araignée *f*.

gossip *n* commérages, cancans *mpl*; * *vi* cancaner, faire des commérages.

gothic *adj* gothique.

gout *n* goutte *f* (maladie).

govern *vt* gouverner, diriger.

governess *n* gouvernante *f*.

government *n* gouvernement *m*; administration publique *f*.

governor *n* gouverneur *m*.

gown *n* toge *f*; robe *f*; robe de chambre *f*.

grab *vt* saisir.

grace *n* grâce *f*; faveur *f*; pardon *m*; grâces *fpl*; **to say ~** dire le bénédicité; * *vt* orner; honorer.

graceful *adj* gracieux; ~ly *adv* gracieusement.

gracious *adj* gracieux; favorable; ~ly *adv* gracieusement.

gradation *n* gradation *f*.

grade *n* grade *m*; degré *m*; classe *f*.

grade crossing *n* (US) passage à niveau *m*.

grade school *n* (US) école primaire *f*.

gradient *n* (*rail*) rampe *f*.

gradual *adj* graduel; ~ly *adv* graduellement.

graduate *vi* obtenir son diplôme.

graduation *n* remise des diplômes *f*.

graffiti *n* graffiti *mpl*.

graft *n* greffe *f*; * *vt* greffer.

grain *n* grain *m*; graine *f*; céréales *fpl*.

gram *n* gramme *m*.

grammar *n* grammaire *f*.

grammatical *adj* ~ly *adv* grammatical(lement).

granary *n* grenier *m*.

grand *adj* grandiose; magnifique.

grandchild *n* petit-fils *m*; petite-fille *f*; **grandchildren** *pl* petits-enfants *mpl*.

grandad *n* pépé *m*.

granddaughter *n* petite-fille *f*; **great~** arrière-petite-fille *f*.

grandeur *n* grandeur *f*; pompe *f*.

grandfather *n* grand-père *m*; **great~** arrière-grand-père *m*.

grandiose *adj* grandiose.

grandma *n* mémé *f*.

grandmother *n* grand-mère *f*; **great~** arrière-grand-mère *f*.

grandparents *npl* grands-parents *mpl*.

grand piano *n* piano à queue *m*.

grandson *n* petit-fils *m*; **great~** arrière-petit-fils *m*.

grandstand *n* tribune *f*.

granite *n* granit *m*.

granny *n* mamie *f*.

grant *vt* accorder; **to take for ~ed** considérer comme acquis; * *n* bourse *f*; allocation *f*.

granulate *vt* granuler.

granule *n* granule *m*.

grape *n* grain *m* de raisin; **bunch of ~s** grappe *f* de raisin.

grapefruit *n* pamplemousse *m*.

graph *n* graphe, graphique *m*.

graphic(al) *adj* graphique; pittoresque; ~ally *adv* graphiquement.

graphics *n* art graphique *m*; graphiques *mpl*.

grapnel *n* (*mar*) grappin *m*.

grasp *vt* saisir, empoigner; comprendre; * *n* poigne *f*; compréhension *f*; prise *f*.

grasping *adj* avide.

grass *n* herbe *f*.

grasshopper *n* sauterelle *f*.

grassland *n* prés *mpl*.

grass-roots *adj* populaire; de base.

grass snake *n* couleuvre *f*.

grassy *adj* herbeux.

grate *n* grille *f*; * *vt* râper; grincer (des dents); * *vi* grincer.

grateful *adj* reconnaissant; ~ly *adv* avec reconnaissance.

gratefulness *n* gratitude, reconnaissance *f*.

gratification *n* satisfaction *f*.

gratify *vt* satisfaire; faire plaisir à.

gratifying *adj* réjouissant.

grating *n* grillage *m*; grincement *m*; * *adj* grinçant; énervant.

gratis *adv* gratis, gratuitement.

gratitude *n* gratitude, reconnaissance *f*.

gratuitous *adj* gratuit; volontaire; ~ly *adv* gratuitement.

gratuity *n* gratification *f*.

grave *n* tombe *f*; * *adj* grave, sérieux; ~ly *adv* gravement, sérieusement.

grave digger *n* fossoyeur *m*.

gravel *n* gravier *m*.

gravestone *n* pierre tombale *f*.

graveyard *n* cimetière *m*.

gravitate *vi* graviter.

gravitation *n* gravitation *f*.

gravity *n* gravité *f*.

gravy *n* jus de viande *m*; sauce *f*.

graze *vt* paître; effleurer; * *vi* paître.

grease *n* graisse *f*; * *vt* graisser.

greaseproof *adj* (papier) sulfurisé.

greasy *adj* gras.

great *adj* grand; important; fort; ~ly *adv* énormément.

greatcoat *n* pardessus *m*.

greatness *n* grandeur *f*; importance *f*; pouvoir *m*; noblesse *f*.

greedily *adv* avidement.

greediness, greed *n* avidité *f*; gloutonnerie *f*.

greedy *adj* avide; glouton.

Greek *n* grec *m*; Grec *m* Grecque *f*.

green *adj* vert; inexpérimenté; * *n* vert *m*; verdure *f*; ~s *npl* légumes verts *mpl*.

greenback *n* (US) billet *m*.

green belt *n* zone verte *f*.

green card *n* carte verte *f*; (US) permis de travail *m*.

greenery *n* verdure *f*.

greengrocer *n* marchand(e) de fruits et légumes *m(f)*.

greenhouse *n* serre *f*.

greenish *adj* verdâtre.

greenness *n* verdure *f*; manque d'expérience *m*.

green room *n* foyer des artistes *m*.

greet *vt* saluer; accueillir.

greeting *n* salutation *f*; accueil *m*.

greeting(s) card *n* carte de vœux *f*.

grenade *n* (*mil*) grenade *f*.

grenadier *n* grenadier *m*.

grey *adj* gris; * *n* gris *m*.

grey-haired *adj* aux cheveux gris.

greyhound *n* lévrier *m*.

greyish *adj* grisâtre; grisonnant.

greyness *n* couleur grise *f*; grisaille *f*.

grid *n* grille *f*; réseau *m*.

gridiron *n* gril *m*; terrain de football américain *m*.

grief *n* chagrin *m*, douleur, peine *f*.

grievance *n* grief *m*; doléance *f*; différend *m*; injustice *f*; tort *m*.

grieve *vt* peiner, affliger; * *vi* se chagriner, s'affliger.

grievous *adj* douloureux; grave, atroce; ~**ly** *adv* douloureusement; cruellement.

griffin *n* griffon *m*.

grill *n* gril *m*; grillade *f*; * *vt* faire griller; interroger, cuisiner.

grille *n* grille *f*.

grim *adj* peu engageant; sinistre.

grimace *n* grimace *f*; moue *f*.

grime *n* saleté *f*.

grimy *adj* crasseux.

grin *n* grimace *f*; sourire *m*; * *vi* grimacer; sourire.

grind *vt* moudre; piler, broyer; affûter, aiguiser; * *vi* grincer.

grinder *n* moulin *m*; rémouleur *m*; molaire *f*.

grip *n* prise *f*; poignée *f*; sac *m* de voyage; * *vt* saisir, agripper.

gripping *adj* passionnant.

grisly *adj* horrible; sinistre.

gristle *n* cartilage *m*.

gristly *adj* cartilagineux.

grit *n* gravillon *m*; cran *m*.

groan *vi* gémir; grogner; * *n* gémissement *m*; grognement *m*.

grocer *n* épicier *m* -ière *f*.

groceries *npl* épicerie *f*, provisions *fpl*.

grocer's (shop) *n* épicerie *f*.

groggy *adj* sonné, étourdi.

groin *n* aine *f*.

groom *n* palefrenier *m*; valet *m*; marié *m*; * *vt* panser; préparer.

groove *n* rainure *f*.

grope *vt* chercher à tâtons; * *vi* tâtonner.

gross *adj* gros, corpulent; épais; grossier; brut; ~**ly** *adv* énormément.

grotesque *adj* grotesque.

grotto *n* grotte *f*.

ground *n* terre *f*, sol *m*; terrain, territoire *m*; fondement *m*; raison fondamentale *f*; fond *m*; * *vt* retenir au sol; fonder; mettre une prise de terre à.

ground floor *n* rez-de-chaussée *m*.

grounding *n* connaissances de base *fpl*.

groundless *adj* sans fondement; ~**ly** *adv* sans fondement.

ground staff *n* personnel au sol *m*.

groundwork *n* travaux de préparation *mpl*.

group *n* groupe *m*; * *vt* regrouper.

grouse *n* grouse *f*, coq de bruyère *m*; * *vi* grogner.

grove *n* bosquet *m*.

grovel *vi* se traîner; ramper.

grow *vt* cultiver; faire pousser; * *vi* pousser; grandir; augmenter; ~ **up** grandir.

grower *n* cultivateur *m* -trice *f*; producteur *m* -trice *f*.

growing *adj* croissant; grandissant.

growl *vi* grogner; * *n* grognement *m*.

grown-up *n* adulte *mf*.

growth *n* croissance *f*; augmentation *f*; poussée *f*.

grub *n* asticot *m*.

grubby *adj* sale.

grudge *n* rancune *f*; * *vt* accorder à contrecœur; *vi* avoir de la rancune.

grudgingly *adv* à contrecœur.

gruelling *adj* difficile, pénible.

gruesome *adj* horrible.

gruff *adj* brusque; ~**ly** *adv* brusquement.

gruffness *n* brusquerie *f*.

grumble *vi* grogner; grommeler.

grumpy *adj* ronchon, grincheux.

grunt *vi* grogner; * *n* grognement *m*.

G-string *n* cache-sexe *m*.

guarantee *n* garantie *f*; * *vt* garantir.

guard *n* garde *f*; garde *m*; * *vt* garder; défendre.

guarded *adj* prudent; surveillé.

guardroom *n* (*mil*) corps de garde *m*.

guardian *n* tuteur *m* -trice *f*; gardien *m* -ne *f*.

guardianship *n* tutelle *f*.

guerrilla *n* guérillero *m*.

guerrilla warfare *n* guérilla *f*.

guess *vt* deviner; supposer; * *vi* deviner; * *n* conjecture *f*.

guesswork *n* conjectures *fpl*.

guest *n* invité *m* -ée *f*; client *m* -e *f*.

guest room *n* chambre d'amis *f*.

guffaw *n* éclat de rire *m*.

guidance *n* guidage *m*; direction *f*.

guide *vt* guider, diriger; * *n* guide *m*.

guidebook *n* guide *m*.

guide dog *n* chien d'aveugle *m*.

guidelines *npl* directives *fpl*.

guild *n* association *f*; corporation *f*.

guile *n* astuce *f*.

guillotine *n* guillotine *f*; * *vt* guillotiner.

guilt *n* culpabilité *f*.

guiltless *adj* innocent.

guilty *adj* coupable.

guinea pig *n* cochon d'Inde, cobaye *m*.

guise *n* apparence *f*.

guitar *n* guitare *f*.

gulf *n* golfe *m*; abîme *m*.

gull *n* mouette *f*.

gullet *n* œsophage *m*.

gullibility *n* crédulité *f*.

gullible *adj* crédule.

gully *n* ravine *f*.

gulp *n* gorgée *f*; * *vt* *vi* avaler.

gum *n* gomme *f*; gencive *f*; chewing-gum *m*; * *vt* coller.

gum tree *n* gommier *m*.

gun *n* pistolet *m*; fusil *m*.

gunboat *n* canonnière *f*.

gun carriage *n* affût de canon *m*.

gunfire *n* coups de feu *mpl*.

gunman *n* homme armé *m*.

gunmetal *n* bronze à canon *m*.

gunner *n* artilleur *m*.

gunnery *n* artillerie *f*.

gunpoint *n*: at ~ sous la menace d'une arme à feu.

gunpowder *n* poudre à canon *f*.

gunshot *n* coup de feu *m*.

gunsmith *n* armurier *m*.

gurgle *vi* gargouiller.

guru *n* gourou *m*.

gush *vi* jaillir; bouillonner; * *n* jaillissement *m*.

gushing *adj* jaillissant; très exubérant.

gusset *n* soufflet *m*.

gust *n* rafale *f*; bouffée *f*.

gusto *n* plaisir *m*, délectation *f*.

gusty *adj* venteux.

gut *n* intestin *m*; ~**s** *npl* cœur au ventre *m*; * *vt* vider.

gutter *n* gouttière *f*; caniveau *m*.

guttural *adj* guttural.

guy *n* mec, type *m*.

guzzle *vt* bouffer, engloutir; avaler.

gym(nasium) *n* gymnase *m*.

gymnast *n* gymnaste *mf*.

gymnastic *adj* gymnastique; ~**s** *npl* gymnastique *f*.

gynaecologist *n* gynécologue *mf*.

gypsy *n* gitan *m* -e *f*.

gyrate *vi* tourner.

H

haberdasher *n* mercier *m* -ière *f*.

haberdashery *n* mercerie *f*.

habit *n* habitude *f*.

habitable *adj* habitable.

habitat *n* habitat *m*.

habitual *adj* habituel; ~ly *adv* d'habitude, habituellement.

hack *n* coupure, entaille *f*; * *vt* entailler, couper.

hackneyed *adj* rebattu.

haddock *n* aiglefin *m*.

haemorrhage *n* hémorragie *f*.

haemorrhoids *npl* hémorroïdes *fpl*.

hag *n* sorcière *f*.

haggard *adj* exténué; défait.

haggle *vi* marchander.

hail *n* grêle *f*; * *vt* saluer; * *vi* grêler.

hailstone *n* grêlon *m*.

hair *n* cheveux *mpl*; poil *m*.

hairbrush *n* brosse à cheveux *f*.

haircut *n* coupe de cheveux *f*.

hairdresser *n* coiffeur *m* -euse *f*.

hairdryer *n* séchoir à cheveux *m*.

hairless *adj* chauve; sans poils.

hairnet *n* filet à cheveux *m*.

hairpin *n* épingle à cheveux *f*.

hairpin bend *n* virage en épingle à cheveux *m*.

hair remover *n* crème dépilatoire *f*.

hairspray *n* laque à cheveux *f*.

hairstyle *n* coiffure *f*.

hairy *adj* chevelu; poilu.

hale *adj* vigoureux.

half *n* moitié *f*; * *adj* demi; * *adv* à moitié.

half-caste *adj* métis.

half-hearted *adj* peu enthousiaste.

half-hour *n* demi-heure *f*.

half-moon *n* demi-lune *f*.

half-price *adj* à moitié prix.

half-time *n* mi-temps *f*.

halfway *adv* à mi-chemin.

hall *n* vestibule *m*.

hallmark *n* marque *f*.

hallow *vt* consacrer, sanctifier.

hallucination *n* hallucination *f*.

halo *n* halo *m*.

halt *vi* s'arrêter; * *n* arrêt *m*; halte *f*.

halve *vt* couper en deux.

ham *n* jambon *m*.

hamlet *n* hameau *m*.

hammer *n* marteau *m*; * *vt* marteler.

hammock *n* hamac *m*.

hamper *n* panier *m*; * *vt* embarrasser, entraver.

hamstring *vt* couper les jarrets à.

hand *n* main *f*; ouvrier *m* -ière *f*; aiguille *f*; **at ~** à portée de main; * *vt* donner, passer.

handbag *n* sac à main *m*.

handbell *n* sonnette *f*.

handbook *n* manuel *m*.

handbrake *n* frein à main *m*.

handcuff *n* menotte *f*.

handful *n* poignée *f*.

handicap *n* handicap *m*.

handicapped *adj* handicapé.

handicraft *n* artisanat *m*.

handiwork *n* travail manuel *m*.

handkerchief *n* mouchoir *m*.

handle *n* manche *m*, queue *f*; anse *f*; poignée *f*; * *vt* manier; traiter; prendre.

handlebars *npl* guidon *m*.

handling *n* maniement *m*; traitement *m*.

handrail *n* garde-fou *m*.

handshake *n* poignée de mains *f*.

handsome *adj* beau; ~ly *adv* élégamment.

handwriting *n* écriture *f*.

handy *adj* pratique; adroit.

hang *vt* accrocher; pendre; * *vi* pendre, être accroché; être pendu.

hanger *n* cintre *m*.

hanger-on *n* parasite *m*.

hangings *npl* tapisserie *f*.

hangman *n* bourreau *m*.

hangover *n* gueule de bois *f*.

hang-up *n* complexe *m*.

hanker *vi* avoir envie.

haphazard *adj* fortuit.

hapless *adj* malheureux.

happen *vi* se passer; **I ~ to have one** il se trouve que j'en ai un.

happening *n* événement *m*.

happily *adv* heureusement; gaiement.

happiness *n* bonheur *m*.

happy *adj* heureux.

harangue *n* harangue *f*; * *vt* haranguer.

harass *vt* harceler; tourmenter.

harbinger *n* précurseur *m*.

harbour *n* port *m*; * *vt* héberger; entretenir, nourrir.

hard *adj* dur; pénible; sévère, rigide; **~ of hearing** dur d'oreille; **~ by** tout près.

harden *vt* *vi* durcir.

hard-headed *adj* réaliste.

hard-hearted *adj* au cœur dur, insensible.

hardiness *n* robustesse *f*.

hardly *adv* à peine; **~ ever** presque jamais.

hardness *n* dureté *f*; difficulté *f*; sévérité *f*.

hardship *n* épreuve(s) *f(pl)*.

hard-up *adj* fauché, sans le sou.

hardware *n* matériel *m*; quincaillerie *f*.

hardwearing *adj* résistant.

hardy *adj* fort, robuste; résistant.

hare *n* lièvre *m*.

hare-brained *adj* écervelé.

hare-lipped *adj* qui a un bec de lièvre.

haricot *n* haricot blanc *m*.

harlequin *n* arlequin *m*.

harm *n* mal *m*; tort *m*; * *vt* faire du mal à; nuire à.

harmful *adj* nuisible.

harmless *adj* inoffensif.

harmonic *adj* harmonique.

harmonious *adj* harmonieux; ~ly *adv* harmonieusement.

harmonise *vt* harmoniser.

harmony *n* harmonie *f*.

harness *n* harnais *m*; * *vt* harnacher.

harp *n* harpe *f*.

harpist *n* harpiste *mf*.

harpoon *n* harpon *m*.

harpsichord *n* clavecin *m*.

harrow *n* herse *f*.

harry *vt* harceler; dévaster.

harsh *adj* dur; austère; rude; ~ly *adv* sévèrement; durement.

harshness *n* aspérité, dureté *f*; austérité *f*.

harvest *n* récolte *f*; moisson *f*; * *vt* récolter; moissonner.

harvester *n* moissonneur *m* -euse *f*; moissonneuse *f* (machine).

hash *n* hachis *m*; gâchis *m*.

hassock *n* agenouilloir *m*.

haste *n* hâte *f*; **to be in ~** être pressé.

hasten *vt* accélérer, hâter; * *vi* se dépêcher.

hastily *adv* à la hâte, précipitamment.

hastiness *n* précipitation *f*.

hasty *adj* hâtif; irréfléchi.

hat *n* chapeau *m*.

hatbox *n* carton à chapeau *m*.

hatch *vt* couver; faire éclore; tramer; * *n* écoutille *f.*

hatchback *n* (*auto*) voiture à hayon arrière *f.*

hatchet *n* hachette *f.*

hatchway *n* (*mar*) écoutille *f.*

hate *n* haine *f;* * *vt* haïr, détester.

hateful *adj* odieux, détestable.

hatred *n* haine *f.*

hatter *n* chapelier *m* -ière *f.*

haughtily *adv* hautainement.

haughtiness *n* orgueil *m;* hauteur *f.*

haughty *adj* hautain, orgueilleux.

haul *vt* tirer; * *n* prise *f;* butin *m.*

haulier *n* camionneur *m.*

haunch *n* hanche *f.*

haunt *vt* hanter; fréquenter; * *n* repaire *m.*

have *vt* avoir; posséder.

haven *n* refuge *m.*

haversack *n* sac à dos *m.*

havoc *n* ravages *mpl.*

hawk *n* faucon *m;* * *vi* chasser au faucon.

hawthorn *n* aubépine *f.*

hay *n* foin *m.*

hay fever *n* rhume des foins *m.*

hayloft *n* fenil *m.*

hayrick, haystack *n* meule de foin *f.*

hazard *n* risque, danger *m;* * *vt* risquer.

hazardous *adj* risqué, dangereux.

haze *n* brume *f.*

hazel *n* noisetier *m;* * *adj* noisette.

hazelnut *n* noisette *f.*

hazy *adj* brumeux.

he *pn* il.

head *n* tête *f;* chef *m;* esprit *m;* * *vt* conduire; ~ **for** se diriger vers.

headache *n* mal de tête *m.*

headdress *n* coiffe *f.*

headland *n* promontoire *m.*

headlight *n* phare *m.*

headline *n* titre *m.*

headlong *adv* à toute allure.

headmaster *n* directeur *m.*

head office *n* siège social *m.*

headphones *npl* écouteurs *mpl.*

headquarters *npl* (*mil*) quartier général *m;* siège social *m.*

headroom *n* hauteur *f.*

headstrong *adj* têtu.

headwaiter *n* maître d'hôtel *m.*

headway *n* progrès *m(pl).*

heady *adj* capiteux.

heal *vt vi* guérir.

health *n* santé *f.*

healthiness *n* bonne santé *f.*

healthy *adj* en bonne santé; sain.

heap *n* tas *m;* * *vt* entasser.

hear *vt* entendre; écouter; * *vi* entendre; avoir des nouvelles.

hearing *n* ouïe *f.*

hearing aid *n* audiophone *m.*

hearsay *n* rumeur *f.*

hearse *n* corbillard *m.*

heart *n* cœur *m;* **by** ~ par cœur; **with all my** ~ de tout cœur.

heart attack *n* crise cardiaque *f.*

heartbreaking *adj* à fendre le cœur.

heartburn *n* acidité *f* gastrique.

heart failure *n* arrêt cardiaque *m.*

heartfelt *adj* sincère.

hearth *n* foyer *m.*

heartily *adv* sincèrement, cordialement.

heartiness *n* cordialité, sincérité *f.*

heartless *adj* cruel; ~**ly** *adv* cruellement.

hearty *adj* cordial.

heat *n* chaleur *f;* * *vt* chauffer.

heater *n* radiateur *m.*

heather *n* (*bot*) bruyère *f.*

heathen *n* païen *m*, païenne *f;* ~**ish** *adj* sauvage, barbare.

heating *n* chauffage *m.*

heatwave *n* onde de chaleur *f.*

heave *vt* lever; tirer; * *n* effort *m.*

heaven *n* ciel *m.*

heavenly *adj* divin.

heavily *adv* lourdement.

heaviness *n* lourdeur *f.*

heavy *adj* lourd, pesant; considérable.

Hebrew *n* hébreu *m* (langue).

heckle *vt* interrompre.

hectic *adj* agité.

hedge *n* haie *f;* * *vt* entourer d'une haie.

hedgehog *n* hérisson *m.*

heed *vt* tenir compte de; * *n* soin *m;* attention *f.*

heedless *adj* inattentif, étourdi; ~**ly** *adv* étourdiment.

heel *n* talon *m;* **to take to one's** ~**s** prendre ses jambes à son cou.

hefty *adj* costaud, puissant.

heifer *n* génisse *f.*

height *n* hauteur *f;* altitude *f.*

heighten *vt* rehausser; augmenter; intensifier.

heinous *adj* atroce.

heir *n* héritier *m;* ~ **apparent** héritier présomptif *m.*

heiress *n* héritière *f.*

heirloom *n* héritage *m.*

helicopter *n* hélicoptère *m.*

hell *n* enfer *m.*

hellish *adj* infernal.

helm *n* (*mar*) barre *f.*

helmet *n* casque *m.*

help *vt* aider, secourir; **I cannot** ~ **it** je n'y peux rien; je ne peux pas m'en empêcher; * *n* aide *f;* secours *m.*

helper *n* aide *mf.*

helpful *adj* utile; qui rend service.

helping *n* portion *f.*

helpless *adj* impuissant; ~**ly** *adv* désespérément; sans pouvoir rien faire.

helter-skelter *adv* n'importe comment, en désordre.

hem *n* ourlet *m;* * *vt* ourler.

he-man *n* dur, mâle *m.*

hemisphere *n* hémisphère *m.*

hemp *n* chanvre *m.*

hen *n* poule *f.*

henchman *n* acolyte *m.*

henceforth, henceforward *adv* dorénavant.

hen-house *n* poulailler *m.*

hepatitis *n* hépatite *f.*

her *pn* son, sa, ses; elle; la; lui.

herald *n* héraut *m.*

heraldry *n* héraldique *f.*

herb *n* herbe *f;* ~**s** *pl* fines herbes *fpl.*

herbaceous *adj* herbacé.

herbalist *n* herboriste *mf.*

herbivorous *adj* herbivore.

herd *n* troupeau *m.*

here *adv* ici.

hereabout(s) *adv* dans les environs.

hereafter *adv* plus tard; ci-après.

hereby *adv* par la présente.

hereditary *adj* héréditaire.

heredity *n* hérédité *f.*

heresy *n* hérésie *f.*

heretic *n, adj* hérétique *mf.*

herewith *adv* avec ceci.

heritage *n* patrimoine, héritage *m.*

hermetic *adj* hermétique; ~**ly** *adv* hermétiquement.

hermit *n* ermite *m.*

hermitage *n* ermitage *m.*

hernia *n* hernie *f.*

hero *n* héros *m.*

heroic *adj* héroïque; ~**ally** *adv* héroïquement.

heroine *n* héroïne *f.*

heroism *n* héroïsme *m.*

heron *n* héron *m.*

herring *n* hareng *m.*

hers *pn* le sien, la sienne, le(s) sien(ne)s, à elle.

herself *pn* elle-même.

hesitant *adj* hésitant.

hesitate *vi* hésiter.

hesitation *n* hésitation *f.*

heterogeneous *adj* hétérogène.

heterosexual *adj n* hétérosexuel *m* -le *f.*

hew *vt* tailler; couper.

heyday *n* apogée *m.*

hi *excl* salut!

hiatus *n* (*gr*) hiatus *m.*

hibernate *vi* hiberner.

hiccup *n* hoquet *m*; * *vi* avoir le hoquet.

hickory *n* noyer d'Amérique *m*.

hide *vt* cacher; * *n* cuir *m*; peau *f*.

hideaway *n* cachette *f*.

hideous *adj* hideux; horrible; ~ly *adv* horriblement.

hiding-place *n* cachette *f*.

hierarchy *n* hiérarchie *f*.

hieroglyphic *adj* hiéroglyphique; * *n* hiéroglyphe *m*.

hi-fi *n* hi-fi *f invar*.

higgledy-piggledy *adv* pêle-mêle.

high *adj* haut; élevé.

high altar *n* maître-autel *m*.

high chair *n* chaise haute *f*.

high-handed *adj* tyrannique.

highlands *npl* terres montagneuses *fpl*.

highlight *n* point fort *m*.

highly *adv* extrêmement, hautement.

highness *n* hauteur *f*; altesse *f*.

high school *n* lycée *m*.

high-strung *adj* nerveux, tendu.

high water *n* marée haute *f*.

highway *n* grande route *f*.

hike *vi* faire une randonnée.

hijack *vt* détourner.

hijacker *n* pirate de l'air *m*.

hilarious *adj* hilarant; hilare.

hill *n* colline *f*.

hillock *n* petite colline *f*.

hillside *n* coteau *m*.

hilly *adj* montagneux.

hilt *n* poignée *f*.

him *pn* lui; le.

himself *pn* lui-même; soi.

hind *adj* derrière; * *n* biche *f*.

hinder *vt* gêner, entraver.

hindrance *n* gêne *f*, obstacle *m*.

hindmost *adj* dernier.

hindquarter *n* arrière-train *m*.

hindsight *n*: with ~ rétrospectivement.

hinge *n* charnière *f*; gond *m*.

hint *n* allusion *f*; insinuation *f*; * *vt* insinuer; suggérer.

hip *n* hanche *f*.

hippopotamus *n* hippopotame *m*.

hire *vt* louer; * *n* location *f*.

his *pn* son, sa, ses; le sien, la sienne, les sien(ne)s; à lui.

Hispanic *adj* hispanique.

hiss *vt vi* siffler.

historian *n* historien *m* -ne *f*.

historic(al) *adj* historique; ~ally *adv* historiquement.

history *n* histoire *f*.

histrionic *adj* théâtral.

hit *vt* frapper; atteindre; heurter; * *n* coup *m*; succès *m*.

hitch *vt* accrocher; * *n* nœud *m*; anicroche *f*.

hitchhike *vi* faire du stop.

hitherto *adv* jusqu'à présent, jusqu'ici.

hive *n* ruche *f*.

hoard *n* stock *m*; trésor caché *m*; * *vt* accumuler, amasser.

hoarfrost *n* givre *m*.

hoarse *adj* rauque; ~ly *adv* d'une voix rauque.

hoarseness *n* voix rauque *f*.

hoax *n* canular *m*; * *vt* faire un canular à.

hobble *vi* boitiller.

hobby *n* passe-temps *m invar*.

hobbyhorse *n* cheval de bataille *m*.

hobo *n* vagabond *m*.

hockey *n* hockey *m*.

hodge-podge *n* confusion *f*.

hoe *n* binette *f*; * *vt* biner.

hog *n* porc *m*.

hoist *vt* hisser; * *n* grue *f*.

hold *vt* tenir; détenir; contenir; ~ on to se tenir à; * *vi* valoir; * *n* prise *f*; pouvoir *m*.

holder *n* détenteur *m* -trice *f*; titulaire *mf*.

holding *n* possession *f*.

holdup *n* hold-up *m*; retard *m*.

hole *n* trou *m*.

holiday *n* jour de congé *m*; jour férié *m*; ~s *pl* vacances *fpl*.

holiness *n* sainteté *f*.

hollow *adj* creux; * *n* creux *m*; * *vt* creuser, vider.

holly *n* (*bot*) houx *m*.

hollyhock *n* rose trémière *f*.

holocaust *n* holocauste *m*.

holster *n* étui de révolver *m*.

holy *adj* saint; bénit; sacré.

holy water *n* eau bénite *f*.

holy week *n* semaine sainte *f*.

homage *n* hommage *m*.

home *n* maison *f*; patrie *f*; domicile *m*; ~ly *adj* simple.

home address *n* domicile *m*.

homeless *adj* sans abri.

homeliness *n* simplicité *f*.

home-made *adj* fait maison.

homesick *adj* nostalgique, qui a le mal du pays.

homesickness *n* nostalgie *f*, mal du pays *m*.

hometown *n* ville natale *f*.

homeward *adj* vers chez soi; vers son pays.

homework *n* devoirs *mpl*.

homicidal *adj* homicide.

homicide *n* homicide *m*; homicide *mf*.

homoeopathist *n* homéopathe *mf*.

homoeopathy *n* homéopathie *f*.

homogeneous *adj* homogène.

homosexual *adj n* homosexuel *m* -le *f*.

honest *adj* honnête; ~ly *adv* honnêtement.

honesty *n* honnêteté *f*.

honey *n* miel *m*.

honeycomb *n* rayon de miel *m*.

honeymoon *n* lune de miel *f*.

honeysuckle *n* (*bot*) chèvrefeuille *m*.

honorary *adj* honoraire.

honour *n* honneur *m*; * *vt* honorer.

honourable *adj* honorable.

honourably *adv* honorablement.

hood *n* capot *m*; capuche *f*.

hoodlum *n* truand *m*.

hoof *n* sabot *m*.

hook *n* crochet *m*; hameçon *m*; by ~ or by crook coûte que coûte; * *vt* accrocher.

hooked *adj* crochu.

hooligan *n* vandale *m*.

hoop *n* cerceau *m*.

hooter *n* sirène *f*.

hop *n* (*bot*) houblon *m*; saut *m*; * *vi* sauter.

hope *n* espoir *m*, espérance *f*; * *vi* espérer.

hopeful *adj* plein d'espoir; prometteur; ~ly *adv* avec espoir.

hopefulness *n* bon espoir *m*.

hopeless *adj* désespéré; ~ly *adv* désespérément.

horde *n* horde *f*.

horizon *n* horizon *m*.

horizontal *adj* horizontal; ~ly *adv* horizontalement.

hormone *n* hormone *f*.

horn *n* corne *f*.

horned *adj* à cornes.

hornet *n* frelon *m*.

horny *adj* calleux.

horoscope *n* horoscope *m*.

horrendous *adj* horrible.

horrible *adj* horrible.

horribly *adv* horriblement; énormément.

horrid *adj* horrible.

horrific *adj* horrible, affreux.

horrify *vt* horrifier.

horror *n* horreur *f*.

horror film *n* film d'horreur *m*.

hors d'oeuvre *n* hors-d'œuvre *m invar*.

horse *n* cheval *m*.

horseback *adv*: on ~ à cheval.

horse-breaker *n* dresseur(-euse) de chevaux *m(f)*.

horse chestnut *n* marron d'Inde *m*.

horsefly *n* taon *m*.

horseman *n* cavalier *m*.

horsemanship *n* équitation *f*.

horsepower *n* cheval-vapeur *m*; puissance en chevaux *f*.

horse race *n* course de chevaux *f*.

horseradish *n* raifort *m*.

horseshoe *n* fer à cheval *m*.

horsewoman *n* cavalière *f*.

horticulture *n* horticulture *f*.

horticulturist *n* horticulteur *m* -trice *f*.

hose-pipe *n* tuyau *m*.

hosiery *n* bonneterie *f*.

hospitable *adj* hospitalier.

hospitably *adv* avec hospitalité.

hospital *n* hôpital *m*.

hospitality *n* hospitalité *f*.

host *n* hôte *m*; hostie *f*.

hostage *n* otage *m*.

hostess *n* hôtesse *f*.

hostile *adj* hostile.

hostility *n* hostilité *f*.

hot *adj* chaud; épicé.

hotbed *n* foyer *m*.

hotdog *n* hot-dog *m*.

hotel *n* hôtel *m*.

hotelier *n* hôtelier *m* -ière *f*.

hotheaded *adj* exalté.

hothouse *n* serre *f*.

hotline *n* téléphone rouge *m*.

hotplate *n* plaque chauffante *f*.

hotly *adv* violemment.

hound *n* chien de chasse *m*.

hour *n* heure *f*.

hourglass *n* sablier *m*.

hourly *adv* toutes les heures.

house *n* maison *f*; maisonnée *f*; * *vt* loger.

houseboat *n* péniche *f*.

housebreaker *n* cambrioleur *m*.

housebreaking *n* cambriolage *m*.

household *n* famille *f*, ménage *m*.

householder *n* propriétaire *mf*; chef de famille *m*.

housekeeper *n* gouvernante *f*.

housekeeping *n* travaux ménagers *mpl*.

houseless *adv* sans abri.

house-warming party *n* pendaison de crémaillère *f*.

housewife *n* ménagère *f*.

housework *n* travaux ménagers *mpl*.

housing *n* logement *m*.

housing development *n* urbanisation *f*.

hovel *n* taudis *m*.

hover *vi* planer.

how *adv* comme; comment; ~ **do you do!** enchanté.

however *adv* de quelque manière que; cependant, néanmoins.

howl *vi* hurler; * *n* hurlement *m*.

hub *n* centre *m*; moyeu *m*.

hubbub *n* vacarme *m*.

hubcap *n* enjoliveur *m*.

hue *n* teinte *f*; nuance *f*.

huff *n*: **in a ~** fâché.

hug *vt* étreindre; * *n* étreinte *f*.

huge *adj* énorme; ~**ly** *adv* énormément.

hulk *n* (*mar*) carcasse *f*; ponton *m*.

hull *n* (*mar*) coque *f*.

hum *vi* chantonner.

human *adj* humain.

humane *adj* humain; ~**ly** *adv* humainement.

humanise *vt* humaniser.

humanist *n* humaniste *mf*.

humanitarian *adj* humanitaire.

humanity *n* humanité *f*.

humanly *adv* humainement.

humble *adj* humble, modeste; * *vt* humilier.

humbleness *n* humilité *f*.

humbly *adv* humblement.

humbug *n* blagues *fpl*.

humdrum *adj* monotone.

humid *adj* humide.

humidity *n* humidité *f*.

humiliate *vt* humilier.

humiliation *n* humiliation *f*.

humility *n* humilité *f*.

hummingbird *n* colibri *m*.

humorist *n* humoriste *mf*.

humorous *adj* humoristique; ~**ly** *adv* avec humour.

humour *n* sens de l'humour *m*, humour *m*; * *vt* complaire à.

hump *n* bosse *f*.

hunch *n* intuition *f*; ~**backed** *adj* bossu.

hundred *adj* cent; * *n* centaine *f*.

hundredth *adj* centième.

hundredweight *n* quintal *m*.

hunger *n* faim *f*; * *vi* avoir faim.

hunger strike *n* grève de la faim *f*.

hungrily *adv* avidement.

hungry *adj* qui a faim, affamé.

hunt *vt* chasser; poursuivre; chercher; * *vi* chasser; * *n* chasse *f*.

hunter *n* chasseur *m*.

hunting *n* chasse *f*.

huntsman *n* chasseur *m*.

hurdle *n* haie *f*.

hurl *vt* lancer avec violence, jeter.

hurricane *n* ouragan *m*.

hurried *adj* fait à la hâte; précipité; ~**ly** *adv* hâtivement; précipitamment.

hurry *vt* presser; * *vi* se presser, se dépêcher; * *n* hâte *f*.

hurt *vt* faire mal à; blesser; * *n* mal *m*.

hurtful *adj* blessant; ~**ly** *adv* de manière blessante.

husband *n* mari *m*.

husbandry *n* agriculture *f*.

hush! chut!, silence!; * *vt* faire taire; * *vi* se taire.

husk *n* coque *f* (graine).

huskiness *n* voix rauque *f*.

husky *adj* rauque.

hustings *n* plate-forme électorale *f*.

hustle *vt* pousser avec force, bousculer.

hut *n* cabane, hutte *f*.

hutch *n* clapier *m*.

hyacinth *n* jacinthe *f*.

hydrant *n* bouche d'incendie *f*.

hydraulic *adj* hydraulique; ~**s** *npl* hydraulique *f*.

hydroelectric *adj* hydroélectrique.

hydrofoil *n* hydroptère *m*.

hydrogen *n* hydrogène *m*.

hydrophobia *n* hydrophobie *f*.

hyena *n* hyène *f*.

hygiene *n* hygiène *f*.

hygienic *adj* hygiénique.

hymn *n* hymne *m*.

hyperbole *n* hyperbole *f*.

hypermarket *n* hypermarché *m*.

hyphen *n* (*gr*) trait d'union *m*.

hypochondria *n* hypocondrie *f*.

hypochondriac *adj* *n* hypocondriaque *mf*.

hypocrisy *n* hypocrisie *f*.

hypocrite *n* hypocrite *mf*.

hypocritical *adj* hypocrite.

hypothesis *n* hypothèse *f*.

hypothetical *adj* ~**ly** *adv* hypothétique(ment).

hysterical *adj* hystérique.

hysterics *npl* hystérie *f*; crise de nerfs *f*.

I

I *pn* je, j'; moi
ice *n* glace *f*; * *vt* glacer; geler.
ice-axe *n* piolet *m*.
iceberg *n* iceberg *m*.
ice-bound *adj* fermé par les glaces.
icebox *n* glacière *f*.
ice cream *n* glace *f*.
ice rink *n* patinoire *f*.
ice skating *n* patinage sur glace *m*.
icicle *n* stalactite *f*, glaçon *m*.
iconoclast *n* iconoclaste *mf*.
icy *adj* glacé.
idea *n* idée *f*.
ideal *adj* idéal; **~ly** *adv* idéalement.
idealist *n* idéaliste *mf*.
identical *adj* identique.
identification *n* identification *f*.
identify *vt* identifier.
identity *n* identité *f*.
ideology *n* idéologie *f*.
idiom *n* expression idiomatique *f*.
idiomatic *adj* idiomatique.
idiosyncrasy *n* idiosyncrasie *f*.
idiot *n* imbécile *mf*.
idiotic *adj* idiot, bête.
idle *adj* désœuvré; au repos; inutile.
idleness *n* paresse *f*; oisiveté *f*.
idler *n* paresseux *m* -euse *f*.
idly *adv* oisivement; paresseusement; vainement.
idol *n* idole *f*.
idolatry *n* idôlatrie *f*.
idolise *vt* idôlatrer.
idyllic *adj* idyllique.
i.e. *adv* c.-à-d., c'est-à-dire.
if *conj* si; ~ **not** sinon.
ignite *vt* allumer, enflammer.
ignition *n* (*chem*) ignition *f*; allumage *m*.
ignition key *n* clé de contact *f*.
ignoble *adj* infâme; bas.
ignominious *adj* ignominieux; **~ly** *adv* ignominieusement.
ignominy *n* ignominie, infamie *f*.
ignoramus *n* ignorant *m* -e *f*.
ignorance *n* ignorance *f*.
ignorant *adj* ignorant; **~ly** *adv* par ignorance.
ignore *vt* ne pas tenir compte de.
ill *adj* malade; * *n* mal *m*; dommage *m*; * *adv* mal.
ill-advised *adj* malavisé.
illegal *adj* **~ly** *adv* illégal(ement).
illegality *n* illégalité *f*.
illegible *adj* illisible.
illegibly *adv* illisiblement.

illegitimacy *n* illégitimité *f*.
illegitimate *adj* illégitime; **~ly** *adv* illégitimement.
ill feeling *n* rancœur *f*.
illicit *adj* illicite.
illiterate *adj* analphabète, illettré.
illness *n* maladie *f*.
illogical *adj* illogique.
ill-timed *adj* inopportun.
ill-treat *vt* maltraiter.
illuminate *vt* illuminer.
illumination *n* illumination *f*.
illusion *n* illusion *f*.
illusory *adj* illusoire.
illustrate *vt* illustrer.
illustration *n* illustration *f*.
illustrative *adj* qui illustre.
illustrious *adj* illustre.
ill-will *n* malveillance *f*.
image *n* image *f*.
imagery *n* images *fpl*.
imaginable *adj* imaginable.
imaginary *adj* imaginaire.
imagination *n* imagination *f*.
imaginative *adj* imaginatif.
imagine *vt* imaginer.
imbalance *n* déséquilibre *m*.
imbecile *adj* imbécile, idiot.
imbibe *vt* boire; imbiber; absorber.
imbue *vt* imprégner.
imitate *vt* imiter.
imitation *n* imitation *f*.
imitative *adj* imitatif.
immaculate *adj* immaculé.
immaterial *adj* insignifiant.
immature *adj* pas mûr.
immeasurable *adj* incommensurable.
immeasurably *adv* immensément.
immediate *adj* immédiat; **~ly** *adv* immédiatement.
immense *adj* immense; énorme; **~ly** *adv* immensément.
immensity *n* immensité *f*.
immerse *vt* immerger.
immersion *n* immersion *f*.
immigrant *n* immigrant *m* -e *f*.
immigration *n* immigration *f*.
imminent *adj* imminent.
immobile *adj* immobile.
immobility *n* immobilité *f*.
immoderate *adj* immodéré, excessif; **~ly** *adv* immodérément.
immodest *adj* immodeste.
immoral *adj* immoral.
immorality *n* immoralité *f*.
immortal *adj* immortel.

immortalise *vt* immortaliser.
immortality *n* immortalité *f*.
immune *adj* immunisé.
immunise *vt* immuniser.
immunity *n* immunité *f*.
immutable *adj* immuable.
imp *n* lutin *m*.
impact *n* impact *m*.
impair *vt* diminuer; affaiblir.
impale *vt* empaler.
impalpable *adj* impalpable.
impart *vt* communiquer.
impartial *adj* **~ly** *adv* impartial-(ement).
impartiality *n* impartialité *f*.
impassable *adj* impraticable; infranchissable.
impasse *n* impasse *f*.
impassive *adj* impassible.
impatience *n* impatience *f*.
impatient *adj* impatient; **~ly** *adv* impatiemment.
impeach *vt* (*law*) mettre en accusation.
impeccable *adj* impeccable.
impecunious *adj* impécunieux.
impede *vt* empêcher; entraver.
impediment *n* obstacle *m*.
impel *vt* pousser.
impending *adj* imminent.
impenetrable *adj* impénétrable.
imperative *adj* impératif.
imperceptible *adj* imperceptible.
imperceptibly *adv* imperceptiblement.
imperfect *adj* **~ly** imparfait(ement); * *n* (*gr*) imparfait *m*.
imperfection *n* imperfection *f*; défaut *m*.
imperial *adj* impérial.
imperialism *n* impérialisme *m*.
imperious *adj* impérieux; **~ly** *adv* impérieusement.
impermeable *adj* imperméable.
impersonal *adj* **~ly** *adv* impersonel-(lement).
impersonate *vt* se faire passer pour; imiter.
impertinence *n* impertinence *f*.
impertinent *adj* impertinent; **~ly** *adv* impertinemment.
imperturbable *adj* imperturbable.
impervious *adj* imperméable; indifférent.
impetuosity *n* impétuosité *f*.
impetuous *adj* impétueux; **~ly** *adv* impétueusement.

impetus *n* élan *m*.
impiety *n* impiété *f*.
impinge (on) *vi* affecter; empiéter (sur).
impious *adj* impie.
implacable *adj* implacable.
implacably *adv* implacablement.
implant *vt* implanter.
implement *n* outil *m*; ustensile *m*.
implicate *vt* impliquer.
implication *n* implication *f*.
implicit *adj* implicite; ~ly *adv* implicitement.
implore *vt* supplier.
imply *vt* supposer.
impolite *adj* impoli.
impoliteness *n* impolitesse *f*.
impolitic *adj* maladroit; impolitique.
import *vt* importer; * *n* importation *f*.
importance *n* importance *f*.
important *adj* important.
importation *n* importation *f*.
importer *n* importateur *m* -trice *f*.
importunate *adj* importun.
importune *vt* importuner.
importunity *n* importunité *f*.
impose *vt* imposer.
imposing *adj* imposant.
imposition *n* imposition *f*.
impossibility *n* impossibilité *f*.
impossible *adj* impossible.
impostor *n* imposteur *m*.
impotence *n* impotence *f*.
impotent *adj* impotent; ~ly *adv* faiblement.
impound *vt* confisquer.
impoverish *vt* appauvrir.
impoverished *adj* appauvri.
impoverishment *n* appauvrissement *m*.
impracticability *n* impraticabilité *f*.
impracticable *adj* impraticable.
impractical *adj* peu pratique.
imprecation *n* imprécation, malédiction *f*.
imprecise *adj* imprécis.
impregnable *adj* inexpugnable.
impregnate *vt* imprégner; féconder.
impregnation *n* fécondation *f*; imprégnation *f*.
impress *vt* impressionner.
impression *n* impression *f*; édition *f*.
impressionable *adj* impressionnable.
impressive *adj* impressionnant.
imprint *n* empreinte *f*; * *vt* imprimer; marquer.
imprison *vt* emprisonner.

imprisonment *n* emprisonnement *m*.
improbability *n* improbabilité *f*.
improbable *adj* improbable.
impromptu *adj* impromptu.
improper *adj* indécent; déplacé; impropre; ~ly *adv* indécemment; de manière déplacée; improprement.
impropriety *n* impropriété *f*; inconvenance *f*.
improve *vt* améliorer; * *vi* s'améliorer.
improvement *n* amélioration *f*.
improvident *adj* imprévoyant.
improvise *vt* improviser.
imprudence *n* imprudence *f*.
imprudent *adj* imprudent.
impudence *n* impudence *f*.
impudent *adj* impudent; ~ly *adv* impudemment.
impugn *vt* attaquer, contester.
impulse *n* impulsion *f*.
impulsive *adj* impulsif.
impunity *n* impunité *f*.
impure *adj* impur; ~ly *adv* impurement.
impurity *n* impureté *f*.
in *prep* dans; en.
inability *n* incapacité *f*.
inaccessible *adj* inaccessible.
inaccuracy *n* inexactitude *f*.
inaccurate *adj* inexact.
inaction *n* inaction *f*.
inactive *adj* inactif.
inactivity *n* inactivité *f*.
inadequate *adj* inadéquat.
inadmissible *adj* inadmissible.
inadvertently *adv* par inadvertance.
inalienable *adj* inaliénable.
inane *adj* inepte.
inanimate *adj* inanimé.
inapplicable *adj* inapplicable.
inappropriate *adj* impropre.
inasmuch *adv* attendu que.
inattentive *adj* inattentif.
inaudible *adj* inaudible.
inaugural *adj* inaugural.
inaugurate *vt* inaugurer.
inauguration *n* inauguration *f*.
inauspicious *adj* peu propice.
in-between *adj* intermédiaire.
inborn, inbred *adj* inné.
incalculable *adj* incalculable.
incandescent *adj* incandescent.
incantation *n* incantation *f*.
incapable *adj* incapable.
incapacitate *vt* mettre dans l'incapacité.
incapacity *n* incapacité *f*.
incarcerate *vt* incarcérer.
incarnate *adj* incarné.

incarnation *n* incarnation *f*.
incautious *adj* imprudent; ~ly *adv* imprudemment.
incendiary *n* bombe incendiaire *f*; incendiaire *mf*.
incense *n* encens *m*; * *vt* exaspérer.
incentive *n* stimulant *m*; prime, aide *f*.
inception *n* commencement *m*.
incessant *adj* incessant, continuel; ~ly *adv* continuellement.
incest *n* inceste *m*.
incestuous *adj* incestueux.
inch *n* pouce *m*; ~ by ~ petit à petit.
incidence *n* fréquence *f*.
incident *n* incident *m*.
incidental *adj* fortuit; ~ly *adv* incidemment.
incinerator *n* incinérateur *m*.
incipient *adj* naissant.
incise *vt* inciser.
incision *n* incision *f*.
incisive *adj* incisif.
incisor *n* incisive *f*.
incite *vt* inciter, encourager.
inclement *adj* inclément.
inclination *n* inclination, propension *f*.
incline *vt* incliner; * *vi* s'incliner.
include *vt* inclure, comprendre.
including *prep* inclus, y compris.
inclusion *n* inclusion *f*.
inclusive *adj* inclus; tout compris.
incognito *adv* incognito.
incoherence *n* incohérence *f*.
incoherent *adj* incohérent; ~ly *adv* d'une manière incohérente.
income *n* revenu *m*; recettes *fpl*.
income tax *n* impôt sur le revenu *m*.
incoming *adj* entrant; nouveau.
incomparable *adj* incomparable.
incomparably *adv* incomparablement.
incompatibility *n* incompatibilité *f*.
incompatible *adj* incompatible.
incompetence *n* incompétence *f*.
incompetent *adj* incompétent; ~ly *adv* de manière incompétente.
incomplete *adj* incomplet.
incomprehensibility *n* incompréhensibilité *f*.
incomprehensible *adj* incompréhensible.
inconceivable *adj* inconcevable.
inconclusive *adj* peu concluant; * *adv* d'une manière peu concluante.
incongruity *n* incongruité *f*.
incongruous *adj* incongru; ~ly *adv* incongrûment.

inconsequential *adj* inconséquent.
inconsiderate *adj* sans considération; inconsidéré; ~**ly** *adv* sans considération.
inconsistency *n* inconsistance *f*.
inconsistent *adj* inconsistant.
inconsolable *adj* inconsolable.
inconspicuous *adj* discret.
incontinence *n* incontinence *f*.
incontinent *adj* incontinent.
incontrovertible *adj* indéniable.
inconvenience *n* inconvénient, désagrément *m*; * *vt* incommoder.
inconvenient *adj* incommode; ~**ly** *adv* incommodément.
incorporate *vt* incorporer; * *vi* s'incorporer.
incorporated company *n* société constituée *f*.
incorporation *n* incorporation *f*.
incorrect *adj* incorrect, inexact; ~**ly** *adv* incorrectement.
incorrigible *adj* incorrigible.
incorruptibility *n* incorruptibilité *f*.
incorruptible *adj* incorruptible.
increase *vt vi* augmenter; * *n* augmentation *f*.
increasing *adj* croissant; *adv* ~**ly** de plus en plus.
incredible *adj* incroyable.
incredulity *n* incrédulité *f*.
incredulous *adj* incrédule.
increment *n* augmentation *f*.
incriminate *vt* incriminer.
incrust *vt* incruster.
incubate *vi* couver.
incubator *n* couveuse *f*.
inculcate *vt* inculquer.
incumbent *adj* en exercice; * *n* titulaire *mf*.
incur *vt* encourir.
incurability *n* incurabilité *f*.
incurable *adj* incurable.
incursion *n* incursion *f*.
indebted *adj* endetté; redevable.
indecency *n* indécence *f*.
indecent *adj* indécent; ~**ly** *adv* indécemment.
indecision *n* indécision, irrésolution *f*.
indecisive *adj* indécis, irrésolu.
indecorous *adj* inconvenant.
indeed *adv* vraiment.
indefatigable *adj* infatigable.
indefinite *adj* ~**ly** *adv* indéfini(ment).
indelible *adj* indélébile.
indelicacy *n* indélicatesse *f*.
indelicate *adj* peu délicat.
indemnify *vt* indemniser.
indemnity *n* indemnité *f*.

indent *vt* bosseler; renfoncer.
independence *n* indépendance *f*.
independent *adj* indépendant; ~**ly** *adv* indépendamment.
indescribable *adj* indescriptible.
indestructible *adj* indestructible.
indeterminate *adj* indéterminé.
index *n* (*math*) indice *m*; index *m*.
index card *n* fiche *f*.
indexed *adj* indexé.
index finger *n* index *m*.
indicate *vt* indiquer.
indication *n* indication *f*; indice *m*.
indicative *adj n* (*gr*) indicatif *m*.
indicator *n* indicateur *m*.
indict *vt* accuser.
indictment *n* accusation *f*.
indifference *n* indifférence *f*.
indifferent *adj* indifférent; ~**ly** *adv* indifféremment.
indigenous *adj* indigène.
indigent *adj* indigent.
indigestible *adj* indigeste.
indigestion *n* indigestion *f*.
indignant *adj* indigné.
indignation *n* indignation *f*.
indignity *n* indignité *f*.
indigo *n* indigo *m*.
indirect *adj* indirect; ~**ly** *adv* indirectement.
indiscreet *adj* indiscret; ~**ly** *adv* indiscrètement.
indiscretion *n* indiscrétion *f*.
indiscriminate *adj* ~**ly** *adv* sans discernement.
indispensable *adj* indispensable.
indisposed *adj* indisposé.
indisposition *n* indisposition *f*.
indisputable *adj* indiscutable.
indisputably *adv* indiscutablement.
indistinct *adj* indistinct, confus; ~**ly** *adv* indistinctement.
indistinguishable *adj* indiscernable.
individual *adj* ~**ly** *adv* individuel(lement); * *n* individu *m*.
individuality *n* individualité *f*.
indivisible *adj* ~**bly** *adv* indivisible(ment).
indoctrinate *vt* endoctriner.
indoctrination *n* endoctrinement *m*.
indolence *n* indolence *f*.
indolent *adj* indolent; ~**ly** *adv* indolemment.
indomitable *adj* indomptable.
indoors *adv* à l'intérieur.
indubitably *adv* indubitablement.
induce *vt* persuader; causer, provoquer.

inducement *n* encouragement *m*; incitation *f*.
induction *n* induction *f*.
indulge *vt* céder à; *vi* se permettre, se laisser aller.
indulgence *n* indulgence *f*.
indulgent *adj* indulgent; ~**ly** *adv* avec indulgence.
industrial *adj* industriel.
industrialise *vt* industrialiser.
industrialist *n* industriel *m*.
industrial park *n* zone industrielle *f*.
industrious *adj* travailleur.
industry *n* industrie *f*.
inebriated *vt* ivre.
inebriation *n* ivresse *f*.
inedible *adj* non comestible.
ineffable *adj* ineffable.
ineffective, ineffectual *adj* inefficace; ~**ly** *adv* inefficacement.
inefficiency *n* inefficacité *f*.
inefficient *adj* inefficace.
ineligible *adj* inéligible.
inept *adj* inepte; déplacé.
ineptitude *n* ineptie *f*; manque d'à-propos *m*.
inequality *n* inégalité *f*.
inert *adj* inerte.
inertia *n* inertie *f*.
inescapable *adj* inévitable.
inestimable *adj* inestimable.
inevitable *adj* inévitable.
inevitably *adv* inévitablement.
inexcusable *adj* inexcusable.
inexhaustible *adj* inépuisable.
inexorable *adj* inexorable.
inexpedient *adj* imprudent, inopportun.
inexpensive *adj* bon marché.
inexperience *n* inexpérience *f*.
inexperienced *adj* inexpérimenté.
inexpert *adj* néophyte.
inexplicable *adj* inexplicable.
inexpressible *adj* indicible; inexprimable.
inextricably *adv* inextricablement.
infallibility *n* infaillibilité *f*.
infallible *adj* infaillible.
infamous *adj* vil, infâme; ~**ly** *adv* vilement.
infamy *n* infamie *f*.
infancy *n* enfance *f*.
infant *n* bébé *m*; enfant *mf*.
infanticide *n* infanticide *mf*.
infantile *adj* infantile.
infantry *n* infanterie *f*.
infatuated *adj* fou.
infatuation *n* folie *f*; obsession *f*.
infect *vt* infecter.
infection *n* infection *f*.
infectious *adj* contagieux; infectieux.

infer *vt* inférer.

inference *n* inférence *f*.

inferior *adj* inférieur; * *n* subordonné *m* -e *f*.

inferiority *n* infériorité *f*.

infernal *adj* infernal.

inferno *n* enfer *m*.

infest *vt* infester.

infidel *n* infidèle *mf*.

infidelity *n* infidélité *f*.

infiltrate *vi* s'infiltrer.

infinite *adj* ~**ly** *adv* infini(ment).

infinitive *n* (*gr*) infinitif *m*.

infinity *n* infini *m*; infinité *f*.

infirm *adj* infirme.

infirmary *n* infirmerie *f*.

infirmity *n* infirmité *f*.

inflame *vt* enflammer; * *vi* s'enflammer.

inflammation *n* inflammation *f*.

inflammatory *adj* inflammatoire.

inflatable *adj* gonflable.

inflate *vt* gonfler.

inflation *n* inflation *f*.

inflection *n* inflexion *f*.

inflexibility *n* inflexibilité *f*.

inflexible *adj* inflexible.

inflexibly *adv* inflexiblement.

inflict *vt* infliger.

influence *n* influence *f*; * *vt* influencer.

influential *adj* influent.

influenza *n* grippe *f*.

influx *n* afflux *m*.

inform *vt* informer.

informal *adj* informel; simple; familier.

informality *n* simplicité *f*.

informant *n* informateur *m* -trice *f*

information *n* information *f*.

infraction *n* infraction *f*.

infrared *adj* infrarouge.

infrastructure *n* infrastructure *f*.

infrequent *adj* ~**ly** *adv* rare(ment).

infringe *vt* enfreindre.

infringement *n* infraction *f*.

infuriate *vt* rendre furieux.

infuse *vt* infuser.

infusion *n* infusion *f*.

ingenious *adj* ingénieux; ~**ly** *adv* ingénieusement.

ingenuity *n* ingéniosité *f*.

ingenuous *adj* ~**ly** *adv* ingénu(ment); sincère(ment).

inglorious *adj* infamant; ~**ly** *adv* honteusement.

ingot *n* lingot *m*.

ingrained *adj* invétéré.

ingratiate *vi*: ~ **with sb** chercher à entrer dans les bonnes grâces de qn.

ingratitude *n* ingratitude *f*.

ingredient *n* ingrédient *m*.

inhabit *vt vi* habiter.

inhabitable *adj* habitable.

inhabitant *n* habitant *m* -e *f*.

inhale *vt* inhaler.

inherent *adj* inhérent.

inherit *vt* hériter.

inheritance *n* héritage *m*.

inheritor *n* héritier *m* -ière *f*.

inhibit *vt* inhiber.

inhibited *adj* inhibé.

inhibition *n* inhibition *f*.

inhospitable *adj* inhospitalier.

inhospitality *n* inhospitalité *f*.

inhuman *adj* inhumain; ~**ly** *adv* inhumainement.

inhumanity *n* inhumanité, cruauté *f*.

inimical *adj* hostile, ennemi.

inimitable *adj* inimitable.

iniquitous *adj* inique, injuste.

iniquity *n* iniquité, injustice *f*.

initial *adj* initial; * *n* initiale *f*.

initially *adv* au début.

initiate *vt* commencer; initier.

initiation *n* début, commencement *m*; initiation *f*.

initiative *n* initiative *f*.

inject *vt* injecter.

injection *n* injection *f*.

injudicious *adj* peu judicieux.

injunction *n* injonction *f*; ordre *m*.

injure *vt* blesser.

injury *n* blessure *f*; tort *m*.

injury time *n* arrêts de jeu *mpl*.

injustice *n* injustice *f*.

ink *n* encre *f*.

inkling *n* soupçon *m*.

inkstand *n* encrier *m*.

inlaid *adj* incrusté.

inland *adj* intérieur; * *adv* vers l'intérieur, dans les terres.

in-laws *npl* belle-famille *f*.

inlay *vt* incruster.

inlet *n* entrée *f*; bras de mer *m*.

inmate *n* détenu *m* -e *f*.

inmost *adj* le plus profond.

inn *n* auberge *f*; hôtel *m*.

innate *adj* inné.

inner *adj* intérieur.

innermost *adj* le plus profond.

inner tube *n* chambre à air *f*.

innkeeper *n* aubergiste *mf*, hôtelier *m* -ière *f*.

innocence *n* innocence *f*.

innocent *adj* innocent; ~**ly** *adv* innocemment.

innocuous *adj* inoffensif; ~**ly** *adv* de manière inoffensive.

innovate *vt* innover.

innovation *n* innovation *f*.

innuendo *n* allusion *f*; insinuation *f*.

innumerable *adj* innombrable.

inoculate *vt* inoculer.

inoculation *n* inoculation *f*.

inoffensive *adj* inoffensif.

inopportune *adj* inopportun.

inordinately *adv* démesurément.

inorganic *adj* inorganique.

in-patient *n* patient(e) hospitalisé(e) *m(f)*.

input *n* entrée *f*; consommation *f*.

inquest *n* enquête *f*.

inquire *vt vi* demander; ~ **about** s'informer de; ~ **after** *vt* demander des nouvelles de; ~ **into** *vt* faire des recherches sur; enquêter sur.

inquiry *n* demande de renseignements *f*; enquête *f*.

inquisition *n* investigation *f*.

inquisitive *adj* curieux.

inroad *n* incursion *f*.

insane *adj* fou, *f* folle.

insanity *n* folie *f*.

insatiable *adj* insatiable.

inscribe *vt* inscrire; dédier.

inscription *n* inscription *f*; dédicace *f*.

inscrutable *adj* impénétrable.

insect *n* insecte *m*.

insecticide *n* insecticide *m*.

insecure *adj* peu assuré.

insecurity *n* insécurité *f*.

insemination *n* insémination *f*.

insensible *adj* inconscient; insensible.

insensitive *adj* insensible.

inseparable *adj* inséparable.

insert *vt* introduire, insérer.

insertion *n* insertion *f*.

inshore *adj* côtier.

inside *n* intérieur *m*; * *adv* à l'intérieur.

inside out *adv* à l'envers; à fond.

insidious *adj* insidieux; ~**ly** insidieusement.

insight *n* perspicacité *f*.

insignia *npl* insignes *mpl*.

insignificant *adj* insignifiant.

insincere *adj* peu sincère.

insincerity *n* manque de sincérité *m*.

insinuate *vt* insinuer.

insinuation *n* insinuation *f*.

insipid *adj* insipide.

insist *vi* insister.

insistence *n* insistance *f*.

insistent *adj* insistant.

insole *n* semelle intérieure *f*.

insolence *n* insolence *f*.

insolent *adj* insolent; ~**ly** *adv* insolemment.

insoluble *adj* insoluble.

insolvency *n* insolvabilité *f*.

insolvent *adj* insolvable.

insomnia *n* insomnie *f*.
insomuch *conj* à tel point.
inspect *vt* examiner, inspecter.
inspection *n* inspection *f*.
inspector *n* inspecteur *m* -trice *f*.
inspiration *n* inspiration *f*.
inspire *vt* inspirer.
instability *n* instabilité *f*.
instal *vt* installer.
installation *n* installation *f*.
instalment *n* installation *f*; verse-ment *m*.
instalment plan *n* plan de vente à tempérament *m*.
instance *n* exemple *m*; **for ~** par exemple.
instant *adj* instantané; **~ly** *adv* im-médiatement; * *n* instant, mo-ment *m*.
instantaneous *adj* **~ly** *adv* instan-tané(ment).
instead (of) *pr* au lieu, à la place (de).
instep *n* cou-de-pied *m*.
instigate *vt* inciter; susciter.
instigation *n* incitation *f*.
instil *vt* instiller; inspirer.
instinct *n* instinct *m*.
instinctive *adj* instinctif; **~ly** *adv* instinctivement, d'instinct.
institute *vt* instituer; * *n* institut *m*.
institution *n* institution *f*.
instruct *vt* instruire.
instruction *n* instruction *f*.
instructive *adj* instructif.
instructor *n* professeur *m*; moni-teur *m* -trice *f*.
instrument *n* instrument *m*.
instrumental *adj* instrumental.
insubordinate *adj* insubordonné.
insubordination *n* insubordina-tion *f*.
insufferable *adj* insupportable.
insufferably *adv* insupportable-ment.
insufficiency *n* insuffisance *f*.
insufficient *adj* insuffisant; **~ly** *adv* insuffisamment.
insular *adj* insulaire; borné.
insulate *vt* isoler; insonoriser.
insulating tape *n* ruban isolant *m*.
insulation *n* isolation *f*; insonori-sation *f*.
insulin *n* insuline *f*.
insult *vt* insulter; * *n* insulte *f*.
insulting *adj* insultant.
insuperable *adj* insurmontable.
insurance *n* (*com*) assurance *f*.
insurance policy *n* police d'assu-rance *f*.
insure *vt* assurer.
insurgent *n* insurgé, rebelle *m*.
insurmountable *adj* insurmontable.

insurrection *n* insurrection *f*.
intact *adj* intact.
intake *n* admission *f*; consomma-tion *f*.
integral *adj* intégrant; (*chem*) inté-gral; * *n* intégrale *f*.
integrate *vt* intégrer.
integration *n* intégration *f*.
integrity *n* intégrité *f*.
intellect *n* intellect *m*.
intellectual *adj* intellectuel.
intelligence *n* intelligence *f*.
intelligent *adj* intelligent.
intelligentsia *n* intelligentsia *f*.
intelligible *adj* intelligible.
intelligibly *adv* intelligiblement.
intemperate *adj* **~ly** *adv* im-modéré(ment).
intend *vt* avoir l'intention de.
intendant *n* intendant *m* -e *f*.
intended *adj* voulu.
intense *adj* intense; **~ly** *adv* inten-sément.
intensify *vt* intensifier.
intensity *n* intensité *f*.
intensive *adj* intensif.
intensive care unit *n* service de soins intensifs *m*.
intent *adj* résolu; attentif; **~ly** *adv* attentivement; * *n* intention *f*, dessein *m*.
intention *n* intention *f*, dessein *m*.
intentional *adj* intentionnel; **~ly** *adv* à dessein, intentionnelle-ment.
inter *vt* enterrer.
interaction *n* interaction *f*.
intercede *vi* intercéder.
intercept *vt* intercepter.
intercession *n* intercession *f*.
interchange *n* échange *m*.
intercom *n* interphone *m*.
intercourse *n* relations sexuelles *fpl*.
interest *vt* intéresser; * *n* intérêt *m*.
interesting *adj* intéressant.
interest rate *n* taux d'intérêt *m*.
interfere *vi* s'ingérer.
interference *n* ingérence *f*; interfé-rence *f*.
interim *adj* intérimaire.
interior *adj* intérieur.
interior designer *n* décorateur (-trice) d'intérieur *m(f)*.
interjection *n* (*gr*) interjection *f*.
interlock *vi* s'entremêler.
interlocutor *n* interlocuteur *m* -tri-ce *f*.
interloper *n* intrus *m* -e *f*.
interlude *n* intermède *m*.
intermarriage *n* intermariage *m*.
intermediary *n* intermédiaire *mf*.
intermediate *adj* intermédiaire.

interment *n* enterrement *m*.
interminable *adj* interminable.
intermingle *vt* entremêler; * *vi* s'entremêler.
intermission *n* entracte *m*; inter-ruption *f*.
intermittent *adj* intermittent.
intern *n* interne *mf*.
internal *adj* intérieur; interne; **~ly** *adv* intérieurement.
international *adj* international.
interplay *n* interaction *f*.
interpose *vt* interposer.
interpret *vt* interpréter.
interpretation *n* interprétation *f*.
interpreter *n* interprète *mf*.
interregnum *n* interrègne *m*.
interrelated *adj* en corrélation.
interrogate *vt* interroger.
interrogation *n* interrogatoire *m*.
interrogative *adj* interrogatif.
interrupt *vt* interrompre.
interruption *n* interruption *f*.
intersect *vi* se croiser.
intersection *n* croisement *m*.
intersperse *vt* parsemer.
intertwine *vt* entrelacer.
interval *n* intervalle *m*; mi-temps *f*.
intervene *vi* intervenir.
intervention *n* intervention *f*.
interview *n* entrevue *f*; interview *f*; * *vt* faire passer une entrevue à; interviewer.
interviewer *n* interviewer *m*.
interweave *vt* entrelacer.
intestate *adj* intestat.
intestinal *adj* intestinal.
intestine *n* intestin *m*.
intimacy *n* intimité *f*.
intimate *n* intime *mf*; * *adj* **~ly** *adv* intime(ment); * *vt* insinuer, lais-ser entendre.
intimidate *vt* intimider.
into *prep* dans, en.
intolerable *adj* intolérable.
intolerably *adv* intolérablement.
intolerance *n* intolérance *f*.
intolerant *adj* intolérant.
intonation *n* intonation *f*.
intoxicate *vt* enivrer.
intoxication *n* ivresse *f*.
intractable *adj* intraitable.
intransitive *adj* (*gr*) intransitif.
intravenous *adj* intraveineux.
in-tray *n* courrier à l'arrivée *m*.
intrepid *adj* intrépide; **~ly** *adv* in-trépidement.
intrepidity *n* intrépidité *f*.
intricacy *n* complexité *f*.
intricate *adj* complexe, compliqué; **~ly** *adv* de manière compliquée.
intrigue *n* intrigue *f*; * *vi* intriguer.
intriguing *adj* intrigant.

intrinsic *adj* **~ally** *adv* intrinsèque-(ment).

introduce *vt* introduire.

introduction *n* introduction *f*.

introductory *adj* d'introduction.

introspection *n* introspection *f*.

introvert *n* introverti *m* -ie *f*.

intrude *vi* s'ingérer, s'immiscer.

intruder *n* intrus *m* -e *f*.

intrusion *n* intrusion *f*.

intuition *n* intuition *f*.

intuitive *adj* intuitif.

inundate *vt* inonder.

inundation *n* inondation *f*.

inure *vt* endurcir.

invade *vt* envahir.

invader *n* envahisseur *m* -euse *f*.

invalid *adj* invalide; * *n* invalide *mf*.

invalidate *vt* invalider, annuler.

invaluable *adj* inappréciable.

invariable *adj* invariable.

invariably *adv* invariablement.

invasion *n* invasion *f*.

invective *n* invective *f*.

inveigle *vt* persuader, entraîner.

invent *vt* inventer.

invention *n* invention *f*.

inventive *adj* inventif.

inventor *n* inventeur *m* -trice *f*.

inventory *n* inventaire *m*.

inverse *adj* inverse.

inversion *n* inversion *f*.

invert *vt* inverser.

invest *vt* investir.

investigate *vt* faire des recherches sur; examiner.

investigation *n* investigation *f*; recherches *fpl*.

investigator *n* investigateur *m* -trice *f*; chercheur *m* -euse *f*.

investment *n* investissement *m*.

inveterate *adj* invétéré.

invidious *adj* odieux; désobligeant.

invigilate *vt* surveiller.

invigorating *adj* vivifiant.

invincible *adj* invincible.

invincibly *adv* invinciblement.

inviolable *adj* inviolable.

invisible *adj* invisible.

invisibly *adv* invisiblement.

invitation *n* invitation *f*.

invite *vt* inviter.

inviting *adj* attrayant, tentant.

invoice *n* (*com*) facture *f*.

invoke *vt* invoquer.

involuntarily *adv* involontairement.

involuntary *adj* involontaire.

involve *vt* impliquer, entraîner.

involved *adj* compliqué; impliqué.

involvement *n* implication *f*; confusion *f*.

invulnerable *adj* invulnérable.

inward *adj* intérieur; intime; ~, ~s *adv* vers l'intérieur.

iodine *n* (*chem*) iode *m*.

IOU (I owe you) *n* reçu *m*.

irascible *adj* irascible.

irate, ireful *adj* irrité.

iris *n* iris *m*.

irksome *adj* fastidieux, ennuyeux.

iron *n* fer *m*; * *adj* de fer; * *vt* repasser.

ironic *adj* **~ally** *adv* ironique-(ment).

ironing *n* repassage *m*.

ironing board *n* table *f* à repasser.

iron ore *n* minerai de fer *m*.

ironwork *n* ferronnerie *f*; ~s *pl* ferronneries *fpl*.

irony *n* ironie *f*.

irradiate *vt* irradier.

irrational *adj* irrationnel.

irreconcilable *adj* irréconciliable; inconciliable.

irregular *adj* irrégulier; **~ly** *adv* irrégulièrement.

irregularity *n* irrégularité *f*.

irrelevant *adj* hors de propos.

irreligious *adj* irréligieux.

irreparable *adj* irréparable.

irreplaceable *adj* irremplaçable.

irrepressible *adj* irrépressible.

irreproachable *adj* irréprochable.

irresistible *adj* irrésistible.

irresolute *adj* **~ly** *adv* irrésolu-(ment).

irresponsible *adj* irresponsable.

irretrievably *adv* irréparablement.

irreverence *n* irrévérence *f*.

irreverent *adj* irrévérencieux; **~ly** *adv* irrévérencieusement.

irrigate *vt* irriguer.

irrigation *n* irrigation *f*.

irritability *n* irritabilité *f*.

irritable *adj* irritable.

irritant *n* (*med*) irritant *m*.

irritate *vt* irriter.

irritating *adj* irritant.

irritation *n* irritation *f*.

Islam *n* Islam *m*.

island *n* île *f*.

islander *n* insulaire *mf*.

isle *n* île *f*.

isolate *vt* isoler.

isolation *n* isolement *m*.

issue *n* sujet *m*, question *f*; * *vt* publier; distribuer; fournir.

isthmus *n* isthme *m*.

it *pn* il, elle; le, la; cela, ça, ce, c'.

italic *n* italique *m*.

itch *n* démangeaison *f*; * *vi* avoir des démangeaisons.

item *n* article *m*.

itemise *vt* détailler.

itinerant *adj* ambulant, itinérant.

itinerary *n* itinéraire *m*.

its *pn* son, sa, ses.

itself *pn* lui-même, elle-même.

ivory *n* ivoire *m*.

ivy *n* lierre *m*.

J

jab *vt* planter, enfoncer.
jabber *vi* baragouiner.
jack *n* cric *m*; valet *m*.
jackal *n* chacal *m*.
jackboots *npl* bottes de militaire *fpl*.
jackdaw *n* choucas *m*.
jacket *n* veste *f*; couverture *f*.
jackknife *vi* se mettre en travers.
jack plug *n* prise à fiche *f*.
jackpot *n* gros lot *m*.
jade *n* jade *m*.
jagged *adj* dentelé.
jaguar *n* jaguar *m*.
jail *n* prison *f*.
jailbird *n* prisonnier *m* -ière *f*.
jailer *n* geôlier *m* -ière *f*.
jam *n* confiture *f*; embouteillage *m*.
jangle *vi* cliqueter.
janitor *n* portier *m*.
January *n* janvier *m*.
jar *vi* se heurter; (*mus*) détonner; grincer; * *vt* pot *m*.
jargon *n* jargon *m*.
jasmine *n* jasmin *m*.
jaundice *n* jaunisse *f*.
jaunt *n* promenade *f*.
jaunty *adj* enjoué.
javelin *n* javelot *m*.
jaw *n* mâchoire *f*.
jay *n* geai *m*.
jealous *adj* jaloux.
jealousy *n* jalousie *f*.
jeans *npl* jean *m*.
jeer *vi* se moquer, railler; * *n* raillerie, moquerie *f*.
jelly *n* gelée *f*.
jellyfish *n* méduse *f*.
jeopardise *vt* risquer, mettre en péril.
jerk *n* secousse *f*; * *vt* donner une secousse à.
jerky *adj* saccadé.
jersey *n* jersey *m*, tricot *m*.
jest *n* blague, plaisanterie *f*.
jester *n* bouffon *m*.
jestingly *adv* en plaisantant.
Jesuit *n* jésuite *m*.
Jesus *n* Jésus *m*.

jet *n* avion à réaction *m*; jet *m*; gicleur *m*.
jet engine *n* moteur à réaction *m*.
jettison *vt* se défaire de.
jetty *n* jetée *f*.
Jew *n* Juif *m*.
jewel *n* bijou *m*.
jeweller *n* bijoutier *m* -ière *f*.
jewellery *n* bijoux *mpl*.
jewellery store *n* bijouterie *f*.
Jewess *n* Juive *f*.
Jewish *adj* juif.
jib *n* (*mar*) foc *m*.
jibe *n* raillerie, moquerie *f*.
jig *n* gigue *f*.
jigsaw *n* puzzle *m*.
jilt *vt* laisser tomber.
jinx *n* porte-malheur *m invar*.
job *n* travail *m*.
jockey *n* jockey *m*.
jocular *adj* joyeux; facétieux.
jog *vi* faire du jogging.
join *vt* joindre, unir; ~ **in** participer à; * *vi* se réunir; se joindre.
joiner *n* menuisier *m*.
joinery *n* menuiserie *f*.
joint *n* articulation *f*; * *adj* commun.
jointly *adv* conjointement.
joint-stock company *n* (*com*) société par actions *f*.
joke *n* blague, plaisanterie *f*; * *vi* blaguer, plaisanter.
joker *n* blagueur *m* -euse *f*.
jollity *n* gaieté *f*.
jolly *adj* gai, joyeux.
jolt *vt* secouer; * *n* secousse *f*.
jostle *vt* bousculer.
journal *n* revue *f*.
journalism *n* journalisme *m*.
journalist *n* journaliste *mf*.
journey *n* voyage *m*; * *vi* voyager.
jovial *adj* jovial, gai; ~**ly** *adv* jovialement.
joy *n* joie *f*.
joyful, joyous *adj* joyeux, gai; ~**ly** *adv* joyeusement.
joystick *n* manche à balai *m*.
jubilant *adj* réjoui.
jubilation *n* jubilation *f*.

jubilee *n* jubilé *m*.
Judaism *n* judaïsme *m*.
judge *n* juge *m*; * *vt* juger.
judgment *n* jugement *m*.
judicial *adj* ~**ly** *adv* judiciaire(ment).
judiciary *n* pouvoir judiciaire *m*.
judicious *adj* judicieux.
judo *n* judo *m*.
jug *n* cruche *f*.
juggle *vi* jongler.
juggler *n* jongleur *m* -euse *f*.
juice *n* jus *m*; suc *m*.
juicy *adj* juteux.
jukebox *n* juke-box *m*.
July *n* juillet *m*.
jumble *vt* mélanger; * *n* mélange *m*; fouillis *m*.
jump *vi* sauter; * *n* saut *m*.
jumper *n* pull *m*; sauteur *m* -euse *f*.
jumpy *adj* nerveux.
juncture *n* joncture *f*.
June *n* juin *m*.
jungle *n* jungle *f*.
junior *adj* plus jeune.
juniper *n* (*bot*) genièvre *m*.
junk *n* cochonnerie *f*; bric-à-brac *m invar*.
junta *n* junte *f*.
jurisdiction *n* juridiction *f*.
jurisprudence *n* jurisprudence *f*.
jurist *n* juriste *mf*.
juror, juryman *n* juré *m*.
jury *n* jury *m*.
just *adj* juste; * *adv* justement, exactement; ~ **as** juste quand; ~ **now** tout de suite.
justice *n* justice *f*.
justifiably *adv* légitimement.
justification *n* justification *f*.
justify *vt* justifier.
justly *adv* justement.
justness *n* justesse *f*.
jut *vi*: **to** ~ **out** faire saillie, dépasser.
jute *n* jute *m*.
juvenile *adj* juvénile; pour enfants.
juxtaposition *n* juxtaposition *f*.

K

kaleidoscope *n* kaléidoscope *m*.
kangaroo *n* kangourou *m*.
karate *n* karaté *m*.
kebab *n* brochette *f*.
keel *n* (*mar*) quille *f*.
keen *adj* aiguisé; vif; enthousiaste.
keenness *n* enthousiasme *m*.
keep *vt* garder, conserver; tenir.
keeper *n* gardien *m* -ne *f*.
keepsake *n* souvenir *m*.
keg *n* baril *m*.
kennel *n* niche *f*.
kernel *n* amande *f*; noyau *m*.
kerosene *n* kérosène *m*.
kettle *n* bouilloire *f*.
kettle-drum *n* timbale *f*.
key *n* clé, clef *f*; (*mus*) ton *m*; touche *f*.
keyboard *n* clavier *m*.
keyhole *n* trou de la serrure *m*.
keynote *n* (*mus*) tonique *f*.
key ring *n* porte-clefs *m invar*.
keystone *n* clef de voûte *f*.
khaki *n* kaki *m*.
kick *vi* (*vt*) donner un coup de pied (à); * *n* coup de pied *m*; plaisir *m*.
kid *n* gamin *m* -e *f*.
kidnap *vt* kidnapper.
kidnapper *n* kidnappeur *m* -euse *f*.
kidnapping *n* kidnapping *m*.

kidney *n* rein *m*; rognon *m*.
killer *n* assassin *m*.
killing *n* assassinat *m*.
kiln *n* four *m*.
kilo *n* kilo *m*.
kilobyte *n* kilo-octet *m*.
kilogram *n* kilogramme *m*.
kilometre *n* kilomètre *m*.
kin *n* parents *mpl*; next of ~ parent proche *m*.
kind *adj* gentil; * *n* genre *m*, sorte *f*.
kindergarten *n* jardin d'enfants *m*.
kind-hearted *adj* bon.
kindle *vt* allumer; * *vi* s'allumer.
kindliness *n* gentillesse, bonté *f*.
kindly *adj* bon, bienveillant.
kindness *n* bonté *f*.
kindred *adj* apparenté.
kinetic *adj* cinétique.
king *n* roi *m*.
kingdom *n* royaume *m*.
kingfisher *n* martin-pêcheur *m*.
kiosk *n* kiosque *m*.
kiss *n* baiser *m*; * *vt* embrasser.
kissing *n* baisers *mpl*.
kit *n* équipement *m*.
kitchen *n* cuisine *f*.
kitchen garden *n* potager *m*.
kite *n* cerf-volant *m*.
kitten *n* chaton *m*.
knack *n* don, chic *m*.
knapsack *n* sac à dos *m*.

knave *n* fripouille *f*; (*cards*) valet *m*.
knead *vt* pétrir.
knee *n* genou *m*.
knee-deep *adj* jusqu'aux genoux.
kneel *vi* s'agenouiller.
knell *n* glas *m*.
knife *n* couteau *m*.
knight *n* chevalier *m*.
knit *vt vi* tricoter; ~ the brows froncer les sourcils.
knitter *n* tricoteur *m* -euse *f*.
knitting pin *n* aiguille à tricoter *f*.
knitwear *n* tricots *mpl*.
knob *n* bouton *m*; nœud *m* (du bois).
knock *vt vi* cogner, frapper; ~ down abattre; * *n* coup *m*.
knocker *n* heurtoir *m*.
knock-kneed *adj* aux genoux cagneux.
knock-out *n* knock-out *m*.
knoll *n* butte *f*.
knot *n* nœud *m*; * *vt* nouer.
knotty *adj* emmêlé; épineux.
know *vt vi* savoir; connaître.
know-all *n* je-sais-tout *m*.
know-how *n* savoir-faire *m*.
knowing *adj* entendu; ~ly *adv* en connaissance de cause.
knowledge *n* connaissances *fpl*.
knowledgeable *adj* bien informé.
knuckle *n* articulation *f*.

L

label *n* étiquette *f*.

laboratory *n* laboratoire *m*.

laborious *adj* laborieux; pénible; ~**ly** *adv* laborieusement.

labour *n* travail *m*; **to be in** ~ être en train d'accoucher; * *vi* travailler.

labourer *n* ouvrier *m*.

labour union *n* syndicat *m*.

labyrinth *n* labyrinthe *m*.

lace *n* lacet *m*; dentelle *f*; * *vt* lacer.

lacerate *vt* lacérer.

lack *vt* manquer de; * *vi* manquer; * *n* manque *m*.

lackadaisical *adj* nonchalant.

lackey *n* laquais *m*.

laconic *adj* laconique.

lacquer *n* laque *f*.

lad *n* garçon *m*.

ladder *n* échelle *f*.

ladle *n* louche *f*.

ladleful *n* louchée *f*.

lady *n* dame *f*.

ladybird *n* coccinelle *f*.

ladykiller *n* bourreau des cœurs *m*.

ladylike *adj* distingué.

ladyship *n* madame *f*.

lag *vi* se laisser distancer.

lager *n* bière blonde *f*.

lagoon *n* lagune *f*.

laidback *adj* décontracté.

lair *n* repaire *m*.

laity *n* laïcat *m*.

lake *n* lac *m*.

lamb *n* agneau *m*; * *vi* agneler.

lambswool *n* laine d'agneau *f*.

lame *adj* boiteux.

lament *vt* se lamenter sur; * *vi* se lamenter; * *n* lamentation *f*.

lamentable *adj* lamentable, déplorable.

lamentation *n* lamentation *f*.

laminated *adj* laminé.

lamp *n* lampe *f*.

lampoon *n* satire *f*.

lampshade *n* abat-jour *m invar*.

lance *n* lance *f*; bistouri *m*; * *vt* inciser.

lancet *n* bistouri *m*.

land *n* pays *m*; terre *f*; * *vt* débarquer; * *vi* atterrir, débarquer.

land forces *npl* armée de terre *f*.

landholder *n* propriétaire terrien *m*.

landing *n* atterrissage *m*.

landing strip *n* piste d'atterrissage *f*.

landlady *n* propriétaire *f*.

landlord *n* propriétaire *m*.

landlubber *n* marin d'eau douce *m*.

landmark *n* point de repère *m*.

landowner *n* propriétaire terrien *m*.

landscape *n* paysage *m*.

landslide *n* glissement de terrain *m*.

lane *n* allée, ruelle *f*; file *f*.

language *n* langue *f*; langage *m*.

languid *adj* languissant; ~**ly** *adv* languissamment.

languish *vi* languir.

lank *adj* raide, plat.

lanky *adj* grand et maigre.

lantern *n* lanterne *f*.

lap *n* genoux *mpl*; * *vt* laper.

lapdog *n* chien *m* de salon.

lapel *n* revers *m*.

lapse *n* laps *m*; défaillance *f*; * *vi* expirer, se périmer; se relâcher.

larceny *n* vol *m*.

larch *n* mélèze *m*.

lard *n* saindoux *m*.

larder *n* garde-manger *m invar*.

large *adj* grand; **at** ~ en liberté; ~**ly** *adv* en grande partie.

large-scale *adj* à grande échelle.

largesse *n* largesse *f*.

lark *n* alouette *f*.

larva *n* larve *f*.

laryngitis *n* laryngite *f*.

larynx *n* larynx *m*.

lascivious *adj* lascif; ~**ly** *adv* lascivement.

laser *n* laser *m*.

lash *n* coup de fouet *m*; * *vt* fouetter; attacher.

lasso *n* lasso *m*.

last *adj* dernier; **at** ~ enfin; ~**ly** *adv* finalement; * *n* dernier *m*, dernière *f*; forme *f* (de cordonnier); * *vi* durer.

last-ditch *adj* ultime.

lasting *adj* ~**ly** *adv* durable(ment).

last-minute *adj* de dernière minute.

latch *n* loquet *m*.

latchkey *n* clef de porte d'entrée *f*.

late *adj* en retard; défunt; (*rail*) **the train is ten minutes** ~ le train a dix minutes de retard; * *adv* tard; ~**ly** *adv* récemment.

latecomer *n* retardataire *mf*.

latent *adj* latent.

lateral *adj* ~**ly** *adv* latérale(ment).

lathe *n* tour *m*.

lather *n* mousse *f*.

latitude *n* latitude *f*.

latrine *n* latrine *f*.

latter *adj* dernier; ~**ly** *adv* récemment.

lattice *n* treillis *m*.

laudable *adj* louable.

laudably *adv* louablement.

laugh *vi* rire; ~ **at** *vt* rire de, se moquer de; * *n* rire *m*.

laughable *adj* risible; dérisoire.

laughing stock *n* risée *f*.

laughter *n* rires *mpl*.

launch *vt* lancer; * *vi* se lancer; * *n* (*mar*) vedette *f*.

launching *n* lancement *m*.

launching pad *n* rampe de lancement *f*.

launder *vt* laver.

laundrette, laundromat *n* laverie automatique *f*.

laundry *n* lessive *f*.

laurel *n* laurier *m*.

lava *n* lave *f*.

lavatory *n* toilettes *fpl*.

lavender *n* (*bot*) lavande *f*.

lavish *adj* prodigue; ~**ly** *adv* avec prodigalité; * *vt* prodiguer.

law *n* loi *f*; droit *m*.

law-abiding *adj* respectueux de la loi.

law and order *n* ordre public *m*.

law court *n* tribunal *m*.

lawful *adj* légal; légitime; ~**ly** *adv* légalement.

lawless *adj* anarchique.

lawlessness *n* anarchie *f*.

lawmaker *n* législateur *m* -trice *f*.

lawn *n* pelouse *f*, gazon *m*.

lawnmower *n* tondeuse à gazon *f*.

law school *n* faculté de droit *f*.

law suit *n* procès *m*.

lawyer *n* avocat *m*; juriste *m*.

lax *adj* relâché.

laxative *n* laxatif *m*.

laxity *n* relâchement *m*; flou *m*.

lay *vt* coucher; mettre; pondre; ~ **claim** réclamer; prétendre (à); * *vi* pondre.

layabout *n* paresseux *m* -euse *f*.

layer *n* couche *f*.

layette *n* layette *f*.

layman *n* laïc *m*.

layout n disposition f; présentation f.

laze vi paresser.

lazily adv paresseusement.

laziness n paresse f.

lazy adj paresseux.

lead n plomb m; * vt vi conduire, mener.

leader n chef m.

leadership n direction f.

leading adj principal; premier; ~ **article** n article de fond m.

leaf n feuille f.

leaflet n feuillet m; prospectus m.

leafy adj feuillu.

league n ligue f; lieue f.

leak n fuite f; * vi (mar) faire eau.

leaky adj qui fuit.

lean vt appuyer; * vi s'appuyer; * adj maigre.

leap vi sauter; * n saut m.

leapfrog n saute-mouton m.

leap year n année bisextile f.

learn vt vi apprendre.

learned adj instruit.

learner n élève mf; débutant m -e f.

learning n érudition f.

lease n bail m; * vt louer.

leasehold n bail m.

leash n laisse f.

least adj moindre; **at ~** au moins; **not in the ~** pas du tout.

leather n cuir m.

leathery adj qui a l'aspect du cuir.

leave n permission f; congé m; **to take ~** prendre congé; * vt laisser.

leaven n levain m; * vt faire lever.

leavings npl restes mpl.

lecherous adj lascif, lubrique.

lecture n conférence f; * vi faire une conférence.

lecturer n conférencier m -ière f.

ledge n rebord m.

ledger n (com) registre m.

lee n (mar) côté sous le vent m.

leech n sangsue f.

leek n (bot) poireau m.

leer vt regarder d'un œil lascif.

lees npl lie f.

leeward adj (mar) sous le vent.

leeway n liberté d'action f.

left adj gauche; **on the ~** à gauche.

left-handed adj gaucher.

left-luggage office n consigne f.

leftovers npl restes mpl.

leg n jambe f; patte f.

legacy n héritage, legs m.

legal adj légal, légitime; **~ly** adv légalement.

legal holiday n jour férié m.

legalise vt légaliser.

legality n légalité, légitimité f.

legal tender n monnaie légale f.

legate n légat m.

legatee n légataire mf.

legation n légation f.

legend n légende f.

legendary adj légendaire.

legible adj lisible.

legibly adv lisiblement.

legion n légion f.

legislate vt vi légiférer.

legislation n législation f.

legislative adj législatif.

legislator n législateur m -trice f.

legislature n corps législatif m.

legitimacy n légitimité f.

legitimate adj légitime; **~ly** adv légitimement; * vt légitimer.

leisure n loisir m; **~ly** adj tranquille; **at ~** au calme.

lemon n citron m.

lemonade n limonade f.

lemon tea n thé au citron m.

lemon tree n citronnier m.

lend vt prêter.

length n longueur f; durée f; **at ~** longuement; enfin.

lengthen vt allonger; * vi s'allonger.

lengthways, lengthwise adv dans le sens de la longueur.

lengthy adj long.

lenient adj indulgent.

lens n lentille f (optique).

Lent n Carême m.

lentil n lentille f.

Leo n Lion m (signe du zodiaque).

leopard n léopard m.

leotard n justaucorps m.

leper n lépreux m -euse f.

leprosy n lèpre f.

lesbian n lesbienne f.

less adj moins; * adv moins.

lessen vt vi diminuer.

lesser adj moindre.

lesson n leçon f.

lest conj de crainte que.

let vt laisser, permettre; louer.

lethal adj mortel.

lethargic adj léthargique.

lethargy n léthargie f.

letter n lettre f.

letter bomb n lettre piégée f.

letter box boite aux lettres f.

lettering n inscription f.

letter of credit n lettre de crédit f.

lettuce n salade f.

leukaemia n leucémie f.

level adj plat, égal; à niveau; * n niveau m; * vt niveler.

level-headed adj sensé.

lever n levier m.

leverage n effet de levier m; prise f.

levity n légèreté f.

levy n levée f; prélèvement m; * vt prélever.

lewd adj obscène.

lexicon n lexique m.

liability n responsabilité f.

liable adj sujet (à); responsable.

liaise vi effectuer une liaison.

liaison n liaison f.

liar n menteur m -euse f.

libel n diffamation f; * vt diffamer.

libellous adj diffamatoire.

liberal adj libéral; généreux; **~ly** adv libéralement.

liberality n libéralité, générosité f.

liberate vt libérer.

liberation n libération f.

libertine n libertin m -e f.

liberty n liberté f.

Libra n Balance f (signe du zodiaque).

librarian n bibliothécaire mf.

library n bibliothèque f.

libretto n livret m.

licence n licence f; permis m; permission f.

licentious adj licencieux.

lichen n (bot) lichen m.

lick vt lécher.

lid n couvercle m.

lie n mensonge m; * vi mentir; être allongé.

lieu n: **in ~ of** au lieu de.

lieutenant n lieutenant m.

life n vie f; **for ~** pour toute la vie.

life belt n gilet de sauvetage m.

lifeboat n canot de sauvetage m.

lifeguard n maître nageur m; garde du corps m.

life jacket n gilet de sauvetage m.

lifeless adj mort; sans vie.

lifelike adj naturel.

lifeline n bouée de sauvetage f.

life sentence n condamnation à perpétuité f.

life-sized adj grandeur nature.

lifespan n durée de vie f.

lifestyle n style de vie m.

life-support system n système de respiration artificielle m.

lifetime n vie f.

lift vt lever.

ligament n ligament m.

light n lumière f; * adj léger; clair; * vt allumer; éclairer.

light bulb n ampoule f.

lighten vi s'éclaircir; * vt éclairer; éclaircir; alléger.

lighter n briquet m.

light-headed adj étourdi.

lighthearted adj joyeux.

lighthouse n (mar) phare m.

lighting n éclairage m.

lightly adv légèrement.

lightning *n* éclair *m*.

lightning rod *n* paratonnerre *m*.

light pen *n* crayon optique *m*.

lightweight *adj* léger.

light year *n* année-lumière *f*.

ligneous *adj* ligneux.

like *adj* pareil; * *adv* comme; * *vt vi* aimer.

likeable *adj* sympathique.

likelihood *n* probabilité *f*.

likely *adj* probable, vraisemblable.

liken *vt* comparer.

likeness *n* ressemblance *f*.

likewise *adv* pareillement.

liking *n* goût *m*.

lilac *n* lilas *m*.

lily *n* lis *m*; ~ **of the valley** muguet *m*.

limb *n* membre *m*.

limber *adj* flexible, souple.

lime *n* chaux *f*; lime *f*; ~ **tree** tilleul *m*.

limestone *n* pierre à chaux *f*.

limit *n* limite *f*; * *vt* limiter.

limitation *n* limitation *f*; restriction *f*.

limitless *adj* illimité.

limo(usine) *n* limousine *f*.

limp *vi* boiter; * *n* boitement *m*; * *adj* mou.

limpet *n* patelle *f*.

limpid *adj* limpide.

line *n* ligne *f*; ride *f*; * *vt* rayer; rider.

lineage *n* lignage *m*.

linear *adj* linéaire.

lined *adj* rayé; ridé.

linen *n* lin *m*; linge *m* de maison.

liner *n* transatlantique *m*.

linesman *n* juge de ligne *m*.

linger *vi* traîner.

lingerie *n* lingerie *f*.

lingering *adj* long.

linguist *n* linguiste *mf*.

linguistic *adj* linguistique.

linguistics *n* linguistique *f*.

liniment *n* liniment *m*.

lining *n* doublure *f*.

link *n* chaînon *m*; * *vt* relier.

linnet *n* linotte *f*.

linoleum *n* linoléum *m*.

linseed *n* graine de lin *f*.

lint *n* peluche *f*.

lintel *n* linteau *m*.

lion *n* lion *m*.

lioness *n* lionne *f*.

lip *n* lèvre *f*; bord *m*.

lip-read *vi* lire sur les lèvres.

lip salve *n* pommade pour les lèvres *f*.

lipstick *n* rouge à lèvres *m*.

liqueur *n* liqueur *f*.

liquid *adj* liquide; * *n* liquide *m*.

liquidate *vt* liquider.

liquidation *n* liquidation *f*.

liquidise *vt* liquéfier.

liquor *n* spiritueux *m*.

liquorice *n* réglisse *m/f*.

liquor store *n* magasin de vins et spiritueux *m*.

lisp *vi* zézayer; * *n* zézaiement *m*.

list *n* liste *f*; * *vt* faire une liste de.

listen *vi* écouter.

listless *adj* indifférent.

litany *n* litanie *f*.

literal *adj* ~**ly** *adv* littéral(ement).

literary *adj* littéraire.

literate *adj* cultivé.

literature *n* littérature *f*.

lithe *adj* agile.

lithograph *n* lithographie *f*.

lithography *n* lithographie *f*.

litigation *n* litige *m*.

litigious *adj* litigieux.

litre *n* litre *m*.

litter *n* litière *f*; ordures *fpl*; * *vt* recouvrir, joncher.

little *adj* petit; ~ **by** ~ petit à petit; * *n* peu *m*.

liturgy *n* liturgie *f*.

live *vi* vivre; habiter; ~ **on** *vt* se nourrir de; ~ **up to** *vt* faire honneur à; * *adj* vivant.

livelihood *n* moyens de subsistance *mpl*.

liveliness *n* vivacité *f*.

lively *adj* vif.

liven up *vt* animer.

liver *n* foie *m*.

livery *n* livrée *f*.

livestock *n* bétail *m*.

livid *adj* livide; furieux.

living *n* vie *f*; * *adj* vivant.

living room *n* salle de séjour *f*.

lizard *n* lézard *m*.

load *vt* charger; * *n* charge *f*.

loaded *adj* chargé.

loaf *n* pain *m*.

loafer *n* paresseux *m* -euse *f*.

loam *n* terreau *m*.

loan *n* prêt *m*.

loathe *vt* détester.

loathing *n* aversion *f*.

loathsome *adj* répugnant.

lobby *n* vestibule *m*.

lobe *n* lobe *m*.

lobster *n* langouste *f*.

local *adj* local.

local anaesthetic *n* anesthésique local *m*.

local government *n* administration *f* municipale, administration *f* locale.

localise *vt* localiser.

locality *n* localité *f*.

locally *adv* localement.

locate *vt* localiser.

location *n* situation *f*.

lock *n* serrure *f*; * *vt* fermer à clé.

locker *n* casier *m*.

locket *n* médaillon *m*.

lockout *n* grève patronale *f*.

locksmith *n* serrurier *m*.

lock-up *n* cellule *f*.

locomotive *n* locomotive *f*.

locust *n* sauterelle *f*.

lodge *n* loge du gardien *f*; * *vi* se loger.

lodger *n* locataire *mf*.

loft *n* grenier *m*.

lofty *adj* haut.

log *n* bûche *f*.

logbook *n* (*mar*) journal de bord *m*.

logic *n* logique *f*.

logical *adj* logique.

logo *n* logo *m*.

loins *npl* reins *mpl*.

loiter *vi* s'attarder.

loll *vi* se prélasser.

lollipop *n* sucette *f*.

lonely, lonesome *adj* seul, solitaire.

loneliness *n* solitude *f*.

long *adj* long, *f* longue; * *vi* désirer.

long-distance *n*: ~ **call** appel interurbain *m*.

longevity *n* longévité *f*.

long-haired *adj* aux cheveux longs.

longing *n* désir *m*.

longitude *n* longitude *f*.

longitudinal *adj* longitudinal.

long jump *n* saut en longueur *m*.

long-playing record *n* trente-trois tours *m*.

long-range *adj* à longue portée.

long-term *adj* à long terme.

long wave *n* grandes ondes *fpl*.

long-winded *adj* prolixe.

look *vi* regarder; sembler; ~ **after** *vt* s'occuper de; garder; ~ **for** *vt* chercher; ~ **forward to** *vt* attendre avec impatience; ~ **out for** *vt* guetter; * *n* aspect *m*; regard *m*.

looking glass *n* miroir *m*.

look-out *n* (*mil*) sentinelle *f*; vigie *f*.

loom *n* métier à tisser *m*; * *vi* menacer.

loop *n* boucle *f*.

loophole *n* échappatoire *f*.

loose *adj* lâché; desserré; ~**ly** *adv* approximativement; ~, **loosen** *vt* lâcher; desserrer.

loot *vt* piller; * *n* butin *m*.

lop *vt* élaguer.

lopsided *adj* de travers; déséquilibré.

loquacious *adj* loquace.
loquacity *n* loquacité *f*.
lord *n* seigneur *m*.
lore *n* savoir *m* (traditionnel).
lose *vt vi* perdre.
loss *n* perte *f*; **to be at a ~** ne pas savoir que faire.
lost and found *n* objets trouvés *mpl*.
lot *n* sort *f*; lot *m*; **a ~** beaucoup.
lotion *n* lotion *f*.
lottery *n* loterie *f*.
loud *adj* fort, bruyant; **~ly** *adv* bruyamment; haut.
loudspeaker *n* haut-parleur *m*.
lounge *n* salon *m*.
louse *n* (*pl* **lice**) pou *m*.
lousy *adj* minable.
lout *n* vaurien *m*.
lovable *adj* sympathique.
love *n* amour *m*; **to fall in ~** tomber amoureux; ** vt* aimer.
love letter *n* lettre d'amour *f*.
love life *n* vie sentimentale *f*.
loveliness *n* beauté *f*.
lovely *adj* beau.
lover *n* amant *m*.
love-sick *adj* fou amoureux.
loving *adj* affectueux.
low *adj* bas; ** vi* meugler.
low-cut *adj* décolleté.
lower *adj* plus bas; ** vt* baisser.
lowest *adj* le plus bas.
lowland *n* plaine *f*.

lowliness *n* humilité *f*.
lowly *adj* humble.
low-water *n* basse mer *f*.
loyal *adj* loyal, fidèle; **~ly** *adv* loyalement.
loyalty *n* loyauté *f*; fidélité *f*.
lozenge *n* pastille *f*.
lubricant *n* lubrifiant *m*.
lubricate *vt* lubrifier.
lucid *adj* lucide.
luck *n* chance *f*.
luckily *adv* heureusement, par chance.
luckless *adj* malchanceux.
lucky *adj* chanceux, qui a de la chance.
lucrative *adj* lucratif.
ludicrous *adj* absurde.
lug *vt* traîner.
luggage *n* bagages *mpl*.
lugubrious *adj* lugubre, triste.
lukewarm *adj* tiède.
lull *vt* bercer; ** n* répit *m*.
lullaby *n* berceuce *f*.
lumbago *n* lumbago *m*.
lumberjack *n* bûcheron *m*.
lumber room *n* débarras *m*.
luminous *adj* lumineux.
lump *n* bosse *f*; grosseur *f*; morceau *m*; ** vt* réunir.
lump sum *n* somme globale *f*.
lunacy *n* folie *f*.
lunar *adj* lunaire.
lunatic *adj* fou, *f* folle.

lunch, luncheon *n* déjeuner *m*.
lungs *npl* poumons *mpl*.
lurch *n* embardée *f*.
lure *n* leurre *m*; attrait *m*; ** vt* séduire, attirer.
lurid *adj* criard (couleur); horrible.
lurk *vi* être tapi.
luscious *adj* délicieux.
lush *adj* luxuriant.
lust *n* luxure *f*; sensualité *f*; désir *m*; ** vi* désirer; **~ after** *vt* convoiter.
lustful *adj* luxurieux, voluptueux; **~ly** *adv* luxurieusement.
lustily *adv* vigoureusement.
lustre *n* lustre *m*.
lusty *adj* fort, vigoureux.
lute *n* luth *m*.
Lutheran *n* luthérien *m* -ne *f*.
luxuriance *n* exubérance, luxuriance *f*.
luxuriant *adj* exubérant, luxuriant.
luxuriate *vi* pousser de manière exubérante.
luxurious *adj* luxueux; **~ly** *adv* luxueusement.
luxury *n* luxe *m*.
lying *n* mensonges *mpl*.
lymph *n* lymphe *f*.
lynch *vt* lyncher.
lynx *n* linx *m*.
lyrical *adj* lyrique.
lyrics *npl* paroles *fpl*.

M

macaroni *n* macaronis *mpl.*

macaroon *n* macaron *m.*

mace *n* massue *f*; macis *m.*

macerate *vt* macérer.

machination *n* machination *f.*

machine *n* machine *f.*

machine gun *n* mitrailleuse *f.*

machinery *n* machinerie *f*; mécanisme *m.*

mackerel *n* maquereau *m.*

mad *adj* fou, *f* folle; furieux; insensé.

Madam *n* madame *f.*

madden *vt* rendre fou; rendre furieux.

madder *n* (*bot*) garance *f.*

madhouse *n* asile de fous *m.*

madly *adv* à la folie; comme un fou.

madman *n* fou *m.*

madness *n* folie *f.*

magazine *n* magazine *m*, revue *f*; (*mil*) magasin *m.*

maggot *n* asticot *m.*

magic *n* magie *f*; * *adj* ~**ally** *adv* magique(ment).

magician *n* magicien *m* -ne *f.*

magisterial *adj* ~**ly** *adv* magistral(ement).

magistracy *n* magistrature *f.*

magistrate *n* magistrat *m.*

magnanimity *n* magnanimité *f.*

magnanimous *adj* ~**ly** *adv* magnanime(ment).

magnet *n* aimant *m.*

magnetic *adj* magnétique.

magnetism *n* magnétisme *m.*

magnificence *n* magnificence *f.*

magnificent *adj* ~**ly** *adv* magnifique(ment).

magnify *vt* grossir; exagérer.

magnifying glass *n* loupe *f.*

magnitude *n* magnitude *f.*

magpie *n* pie *f.*

mahogany *n* acajou *m.*

maid *n* bonne *f.*

maiden *n* jeune fille *f.*

maiden name *n* nom de jeune fille *m.*

mail *n* courrier *m.*

mailbox *n* boîte aux lettres *f.*

mail coach *n* malle-poste *f.*

mailing list *n* fichier-clientèle *m.*

mail-order *n* vente par correspondance *f.*

mail train *n* (*rail*) train-poste *m.*

maim *vt* mutiler.

main *adj* principal; essentiel; **in the ~** en général.

mainland *n* continent *m.*

main line *n* (*rail*) grande ligne *f.*

mainly *adv* principalement, essentiellement.

main street *n* rue principale *f.*

maintain *vt* maintenir; soutenir.

maintenance *n* entretien *m.*

maize *n* maïs *m.*

majestic *adj* majestueux; ~**ally** *adv* majestueusement.

majesty *n* majesté *f.*

major *adj* majeur; * *n* (*mil*) commandant *m.*

majority *n* majorité *f.*

make *vt* faire; ~ **for** se diriger vers; ~ **up** inventer; ~ **up for** compenser; * *n* marque *f.*

make-believe *n* invention *f.*

makeshift *adj* improvisé, de fortune.

make-up *n* maquillage *m.*

make-up remover *n* démaquillant *m.*

malady *n* maladie *f.*

malaise *n* malaise *m.*

malaria *n* malaria *f.*

malcontent *adj n* mécontent *m* -e *f.*

male *adj* mâle; masculin; * *n* mâle *m.*

malevolence *n* malveillance *f.*

malevolent *adj* malveillant; ~**ly** *adv* avec malveillance.

malfunction *n* mauvais fonctionnement *m.*

malice *n* méchanceté *f.*

malicious *adj* méchant; ~**ly** *adv* méchamment.

malign *adj* nocif; * *vt* calomnier.

malignant *adj* malfaisant; ~**ly** *adv* méchamment.

mall *n* centre commercial *m.*

malleable *adj* malléable.

mallet *n* maillet *m.*

mallow *n* (*bot*) mauve *f.*

malnutrition *n* malnutrition *f.*

malpractice *n* malversations *fpl.*

malt *n* malt *m.*

maltreat *vt* maltraiter.

mammal *n* mammifère *m.*

mammoth *adj* gigantesque.

man *n* homme *m*; * *vt* (*mar*) équiper en personnel.

manacle *n* entrave *f*; ~**s** *pl* menottes *fpl.*

manage *vt* diriger; réussir; * *vi* réussir.

manageable *adj* maniable.

management *n* direction *f.*

manager *n* directeur *m.*

manageress *n* directrice *f.*

managerial *adj* directorial.

managing director *n* directeur *m* général.

mandarin *n* mandarine *f*; mandarin *m.*

mandate *n* mandat *m.*

mandatory *n* obligatoire.

mane *n* crinière *f.*

manfully *adv* vaillamment.

manger *n* mangeoire *f.*

mangle *n* essoreuse *f*; * *vt* mutiler.

mangy *adj* miteux.

manhandle *vt* maltraiter; manutentionner.

manhood *n* âge d'homme *m*; virilité *f.*

man-hour *n* heure *f* de main d'œuvre.

mania *n* manie *f.*

maniac *n* maniaque *mf.*

manic *adj* obsessionnel.

manicure *n* manucure *f.*

manifest *adj* manifeste; * *vt* manifester.

manifestation *n* manifestation *f.*

manifesto *n* manifeste *m.*

manipulate *vt* manipuler.

manipulation *n* manipulation *f.*

mankind *n* humanité *f.*

manlike *adj* viril; d'homme.

manliness *n* virilité *f*; courage *m.*

manly *adj* viril.

man-made *adj* artificiel.

manner *n* manière *f*; attitude *f*; ~**s** *pl* manières *fpl.*

manoeuvre *n* manœuvre *f.*

manpower *n* main-d'œuvre *f.*

mansion *n* château *m.*

manslaughter *n* homicide involontaire *m.*

mantelpiece *n* manteau de cheminée *m.*

manual *adj n* manuel *m.*

manufacture *n* fabrication *f*; * *vt* fabriquer.

manufacturer *n* fabricant *m.*

manure *n* fumier *m*; engrais *m*; purin *m*; * *vt* fumer.

manuscript *n* manuscrit *m.*

many *adj* beaucoup de; ~ **a time** de

nombreuses fois; **how ~?** combien?; **as ~ as** autant que.

map *n* carte *f*; plan *m*; * *vt* dessiner un plan de; **~ out** programmer.

maple *n* érable *m*.

mar *vt* gâter, gâcher.

marathon *n* marathon *m*.

marauder *n* maraudeur *m* -euse *f*.

marble *n* marbre *m*; * *adj* marbré.

March *n* mars *m*.

march *n* marche *f*; * *vi* marcher.

marchpast *n* défilé *m*.

mare *n* jument *f*.

margarine *n* margarine *f*.

margin *n* marge *f*; bord *m*.

marginal *adj* marginal.

marigold *n* (*bot*) calendula *f*, souci *m*.

marijuana *n* marijuana *f*.

marinate *vt* mariner.

marine *adj* marin; * *n* fusilier *m* marin.

mariner *n* marin *m*.

marital *adj* matrimonial.

maritime *adj* maritime.

marjoram *n* marjolaine *f*.

mark *n* marque *f*; signe *m*; * *vt* marquer.

marker *n* marque *f*; marqueur *m*.

market *n* marché *m*.

marketable *adj* vendable.

marketing *n* marketing *m*.

marketplace *n* marché *m*.

market research *n* étude de marché *f*.

market value *n* valeur sur le marché *f*.

marksman *n* tireur d'élite *m*.

marmalade *n* confiture d'oranges *f*.

maroon *adj* marron rouge.

marquee *n* tente *f*.

marriage *n* mariage *m*.

marriageable *adj* mariable.

marriage certificate *n* acte de mariage *m*.

married *adj* marié; conjugal.

marrow *n* moelle *f*.

marry *vi* se marier.

marsh *n* marécage *m*.

marshal *n* maréchal *m*.

marshy *adj* marécageux.

marten *n* martre *f*.

martial *adj* martial; **~ law** *n* loi martiale *f*.

martyr *n* martyr *m* -e *f*.

martyrdom *n* martyre *m*.

marvel *n* merveille *f*; * *vi* s'émerveiller.

marvellous *adj* merveilleux; **~ly** *adv* merveilleusement.

marzipan *n* massepain *m*, pâte d'amandes *f*.

mascara *n* mascara *m*.

masculine *adj* masculin, viril.

mash *n* bouillie, purée *f*.

mask *n* masque *m*; * *vt* masquer.

masochist *n* masochiste *mf*.

mason *n* maçon *m*.

masonry *n* maçonnerie *f*.

masquerade *n* mascarade *f*.

mass *n* masse *f*; messe *f*; multitude *f*.

massacre *n* massacre *m*; * *vt* massacrer.

massage *n* massage *m*.

masseur *n* masseur *m*.

masseuse *n* masseuse *f*.

massive *adj* énorme.

mass media *npl* média *mpl*.

mast *n* mât *m*.

master *n* maître *m*; * *vt* maîtriser.

masterly *adj* magistral.

mastermind *vt* diriger.

masterpiece *n* chef-d'œuvre *m*.

mastery *n* maîtrise *f*.

masticate *vt* mastiquer.

mastiff *n* mastiff *m*.

mat *n* tapis *m*.

match *n* allumette *f*; match *m*; * *vt* égaler; * *vi* bien aller ensemble.

matchbox *n* boîte d'allumettes *f*.

matchless *adj* incomparable, sans pareil.

matchmaker *n* marieur *m* -euse *f*.

mate *n* camarade *mf*; * *vt* accoupler.

material *adj* **~ly** *adv* matériel(lement).

materialism *n* matérialisme *m*.

maternal *adj* maternel.

maternity dress *n* robe de grossesse *f*.

maternity hospital *n* maternité *f*.

mathematical *adj* **~ly** *adv* mathématique(ment).

mathematician *n* mathématicien *m* -ne *f*.

mathematics *npl* mathématiques *fpl*.

maths *n* maths *fpl*.

matinee *n* matinée *f*.

mating *n* accouplement *m*.

matins *npl* matines *fpl*.

matriculate *vt* immatriculer.

matriculation *n* immatriculation *f*.

matrimonial *adj* matrimonial.

mat(t) *adj* mat.

matted *adj* emmêlé.

matter *n* matière, substance *f*; sujet *m*; affaire *f*; **what is the ~?** que se passe-t-il?; **a ~ of fact** un fait; * *vi* importer.

mattress *n* matelas *m*.

mature *adj* mûr; * *vi* mûrir.

maturity *n* maturité *f*.

maul *vt* meurtrir.

mausoleum *n* mausolée *m*.

mauve *adj* mauve.

maxim *n* maxime *f*.

maximum *n* maximum *m*.

may *v aux* pouvoir; **~be** peut-être.

May *n* mai *m*.

Mayday *n* le Premier Mai *m*.

mayor *n* maire *m*.

mayoress *n* mairesse *f*.

maze *n* labyrinthe *m*.

me *pn* moi; me.

meadow *n* prairie *f*, pré *m*.

meagre *adj* pauvre.

meagreness *n* pauvreté *f*.

meal *n* repas *m*; farine *f*.

mealtime *n* heure du repas *f*.

mean *adj* avare, mesquin; moyen; **in the ~time, ~while** pendant ce temps-là; **~s** *npl* moyens *mpl*; * *vt vi* signifier.

meander *vi* serpenter.

meaning *n* sens *m*, signification *f*.

meaningful *adj* significatif.

meaningless *adj* vide de sens.

meanness *n* avarice, mesquinerie *f*.

meantime, meanwhile *adv* pendant ce temps-là.

measles *npl* rougeole *f*.

measure *n* mesure *f*; * *vt* mesurer.

measurement *n* mesure *f*.

meat *n* viande *f*.

meatball *n* boulette de viande *f*.

meaty *adj* riche en viande.

mechanic *n* mécanicien *m*.

mechanical *adj* **~ly** *adv* mécanique(ment).

mechanics *npl* mécanique *f*.

mechanism *n* mécanisme *m*.

medal *n* médaille *f*.

medallion *n* médaillon *m*.

medallist *n* médaillé *m* -e *f*.

meddle *vi* se mêler des affaires des autres.

meddler *n* fouineur *m* -euse *f*, indiscret *m* -ète *f*.

media *npl* média *mpl*.

median *n* médiane *f*.

mediate *vi* agir en tant que médiateur.

mediation *n* médiation *f*.

mediator *n* médiateur *m* -trice *f*.

medical *adj* médical.

medicate *vt* traiter.

medicated *adj* médical.

medicinal *adj* médicinal.

medicine *n* médecine *f*; médicament *m*.

medieval *adj* médiéval.

mediocre *adj* médiocre.

mediocrity *n* médiocrité *f*.

meditate *vi* méditer.

meditation n méditation f.
meditative adj méditatif.
Mediterranean adj méditerra-néen.
medium n milieu m; médium m; * adj moyen.
medium wave n ondes moyennes fpl.
medley n mélange m.
meek adj docile; ~**ly** adv docile-ment.
meekness n docilité f.
meet vt rencontrer; ~ **with** retrou-ver; * vi se rencontrer; se retrou-ver.
meeting n réunion f; congrès m.
megaphone n mégaphone m.
melancholy n mélancolie f; * adj mélancolique.
mellow adj moelleux; doux; * vi mûrir.
mellowness n moelleux m.
melodious adj mélodieux; ~**ly** adv mélodieusement.
melody n mélodie f.
melon n melon m.
melt vt faire fondre; * vi fondre.
melting point n point de fusion m.
member n membre m.
membership n adhésion f.
membrane n membrane f.
memento n mémento m.
memo n note de service f.
memoir n mémoire m.
memorable adj mémorable.
memorandum n mémorandum m; note de service f.
memorial n monument commé-moratif, mémorial m.
memorise vt mémoriser.
memory n mémoire f; souvenir m.
menace n menace f; * vt menacer.
menacing adj menaçant.
menagerie n ménagerie f.
mend vt réparer; raccommoder.
mending n réparation f; raccom-modage m.
menial adj vil.
meningitis n méningite f.
menopause n ménopause f.
menstruation n menstruation f.
mental adj mental.
mentality n mentalité f.
mentally adv mentalement.
mention n mention f; * vt mention-ner.
menu n menu m.
mercantile adj commercial.
mercenary adj n mercenaire m.
merchandise n marchandise f.
merchant n négociant m -e f.
merchantman n navire marchand m.

merchant marine n marine mar-chande f.
merciful adj miséricordieux.
merciless adj ~**ly** adv impitoyable-(ment).
mercury n mercure m.
mercy n pitié f.
mere adj ~**ly** adv simple(ment).
merge vt vi fusionner.
merger n fusion f.
meridian n méridien m.
merit n mérite m; * vt mériter.
meritorious adj méritoire.
mermaid n sirène f.
merrily adv joyeusement.
merriment n divertissement m; ré-jouissance f.
merry adj joyeux.
merry-go-round n manège m.
mesh n maille f.
mesmerise vt hypnotiser.
mess n désordre m; confusion f; (mil) mess m; ~ **up** vt mettre en désordre.
message n message m.
messenger n messager m -ère f.
metabolism n métabolisme m.
metal n métal m.
metallic adj métallique.
metallurgy n métallurgie f.
metamorphosis n métamorphose f.
metaphor n métaphore f.
metaphoric(al) adj métaphorique.
metaphysical adj métaphysique.
metaphysics npl métaphysique f.
mete (out) vt distribuer.
meteor n météore m.
meteorological adj météorolo-gi-que.
meteorology n météorologie f.
meter n compteur m.
method n méthode f.
methodical adj ~**ly** adv méthodique(ment).
Methodist n méthodiste mf.
metre n mètre m.
metric adj métrique.
metropolis n métropole f.
metropolitan adj métropolitain.
mettle n courage m.
mettlesome adj courageux.
mew vi miauler.
mezzanine n mezzanine f.
microbe n microbe m.
microphone n microphone m.
microchip n microprocesseur m, puce f.
microscope n microscope m.
microscopic adj microscopique.
microwave n four à micro-ondes m.
mid adj demi; mi-.

midday n midi m.
middle adj moyen; du milieu; * n milieu m.
middle name n deuxième prénom m.
middleweight n poids moyen m.
middling adj moyen, passable.
midge n moucheron m.
midget n nain m -e f.
midnight n minuit m.
midriff n diaphragme m; estomac m.
midst n milieu m.
midsummer n milieu de l'été m.
midway adv à mi-chemin.
midwife n sage-femme f.
midwifery n obstétrique f.
might n force f.
mighty adj fort, puissant.
migraine n migraine f.
migrate vi émigrer.
migration n émigration f.
migratory adj migratoire.
mike n micro m.
mild adj doux; modéré; ~**ly** adv doucement.
mildew n moisissure f; mildiou m.
mildness n douceur f.
mile n mile m.
mileage n kilométrage m.
milieu n milieu m.
militant adj militant.
military adj militaire.
militate vi militer.
militia n milice f.
milk n lait m; * vt traire; exploiter.
milkshake n milk-shake m.
milky adj laiteux; **M~ Way** n Voie lactée f.
mill n moulin m; * vt moudre.
millennium n millénaire m.
miller n meunier m.
millet n (bot) millet m.
milligram n milligramme m.
millilitre n millilitre m.
millimetre n millimètre m.
milliner n chapelier m -ière f.
millinery n chapellerie f.
million n million m.
millionaire n millionaire mf.
millionth adj n millionième mf.
millstone n meule f.
mime n mime m.
mimic vt mimer.
mimicry n mimique f.
mince vt hacher.
mind n esprit m; * vt prendre soin de; * vi: **do you ~?** est-ce que cela vous dérange?
minded adj disposé.
mindful adj soucieux; attentif.
mindless adj insouciant.
mine pn le mien, la mienne, les

miens, les miennes; à moi; * *n* mine *f*; * *vi* exploiter la mine.

minefield *n* champ de mines *m*.

miner *n* mineur *m*.

mineral *adj* in minéral *m*.

mineralogy *n* minéralogie *f*.

mineral water *n* eau minérale *f*.

minesweeper *n* dragueur de mines *m*.

mingle *vt* mêler.

miniature *n* miniature *f*.

minimal *adj* minime.

minimise *vt* minimiser.

minimum *n* minimum *m*.

mining *n* exploitation minière *f*.

minion *n* larbin *m*; favorit(te) *m(f)*.

minister *n* ministre *m*; * *vt* servir.

ministerial *adj* ministériel.

ministry *n* ministère *m*.

mink *n* vison *m*.

minnow *n* vairon *m*.

minor *adj* mineur; * *n* mineur *m* -e *f*.

minority *n* minorité *f*.

minstrel *n* ménestrel *m*.

mint *n* (*bot*) menthe *f*; hôtel de la Monnaie *m*; * *vt* frapper la monnaie.

minus *adv* moins.

minute *adj* minuscule; ~ly *adv* minutieusement.

minute *n* minute *f*.

miracle *n* miracle *m*.

miraculous *adj* miraculeux.

mirage *n* mirage *m*.

mire *n* bourbe *f*.

mirky *adj* trouble; ténébreux.

mirror *n* miroir *m*.

mirth *n* allégresse *f*.

mirthful *adj* joyeux.

misadventure *n* mésaventure *f*.

misanthropist *n* misanthrope *mf*.

misapply *vt* mal appliquer.

misapprehension *n* méprise *f*.

misbehave *vi* se conduire mal.

misbehaviour *n* mauvaise conduite *f*.

miscalculate *vt* mal calculer.

miscarriage *n* fausse couche *f*.

miscarry *vi* faire une fausse couche; échouer.

miscellaneous *adj* divers, varié.

miscellany *n* mélange, assortiment *m*.

mischief *n* mal, tort *m*.

mischievous *adj* mauvais; espiègle.

misconception *n* méprise *f*.

misconduct *n* mauvaise conduite *f*.

misconstrue *vt* mal interpréter.

miscount *vt* mal compter.

miscreant *n* scélérat *m*.

misdeed *n* méfait *m*.

misdemeanour *n* délit *m*.

misdirect *vt* mal diriger.

miser *n* avare *mf*.

miserable *adj* malheureux.

miserly *adj* mesquin, avare.

misery *n* malheur *m*; misère *f*.

misfit *n* inadapté *m* -e *f*.

misfortune *n* infortune *f*.

misgiving *n* doute *m*.

misgovern *vt* mal gouverner.

misguided *adj* malencontreux; malavisé.

mishandle *vt* maltraiter; mal s'y prendre avec.

mishap *n* mésaventure *f*.

misinform *vt* mal renseigner.

misinterpret *vt* mal interpréter.

misjudge *vt* méjuger.

mislay *vt* égarer.

mislead *vt* induire en erreur.

mismanage *vt* mal administrer.

mismanagement *n* mauvaise administration *f*.

misnomer *n* (*law*) nom inapproprié *m*.

misogynist *n* misogyne *mf*.

misplace *vt* égarer.

misprint *vt* mal imprimer; * *n* coquille *f*.

misrepresent *vt* mal représenter.

Miss *n* Mlle, Mademoiselle *f*.

miss *vt* rater; s'ennuyer de.

missal *n* missel *m*.

misshapen *adj* déformé.

missile *n* missile *m*.

missing *adj* perdu; absent.

mission *n* mission *f*.

missionary *n* missionnaire *mf*.

misspent *adj* gaspillé.

mist *n* brouillard *m*.

mistake *vt* confondre; * *vi* se tromper; **to be mistaken** se tromper; * *n* méprise *f*; erreur *f*.

Mister *n* monsieur *m*.

mistletoe *n* (*bot*) gui *m*.

mistress *n* maîtresse *f*.

mistrust *vt* se méfier de; * *n* méfiance *f*.

mistrustful *adj* méfiant.

misty *adj* brumeux.

misunderstand *vt* mal comprendre.

misunderstanding *n* malentendu *m*.

misuse *vt* faire un mauvais usage de; abuser de.

mitigate *vt* atténuer.

mitigation *n* atténuation *f*.

mitre *n* mitre *f*.

mittens *npl* moufles *fpl*.

mix *vt* mélanger.

mixed *adj* mélangé; mixte.

mixed-up *adj* confus.

mixer *n* mixeur *m*.

mixture *n* mélange *m*.

mix-up *n* confusion *f*.

moan *n* gémissement *m*; * *vi* gémir; se plaindre.

moat *n* fossé *m*.

mob *n* foule *f*; masse *f*.

mobile *adj* mobile.

mobile home *n* caravane *f*.

mobilise *vt* (*mil*) mobiliser.

mobility *n* mobilité *f*.

moccasin *n* mocassin *m*.

mock *vt* se moquer de.

mockery *n* moquerie *f*.

mode *n* mode *m*.

model *n* modèle *m*; * *vt* modeler.

moderate *adj* ~ly *adv* modéré(ment); * *vt* modérer.

moderation *n* modération *f*.

modern *adj* moderne.

modernise *vt* moderniser.

modest *adj* ~ly *adv* modeste(ment).

modesty *n* modestie *f*.

modicum *n* minimum *m*.

modification *n* modification *f*.

modify *vt* modifier.

modulate *vt* moduler.

modulation *n* (*mus*) modulation *f*.

module *n* module *m*.

mogul *n* magnat *m*.

mohair *n* mohair *m*.

moist *adj* humide.

moisten *vt* humidifier.

moisture *n* humidité *f*.

molar *n* molaire *f*.

molasses *npl* mélasse *f*.

mole *n* taupe *f*.

molecule *n* molécule *f*.

molehill *n* taupinière *f*.

molest *vt* importuner.

mollify *vt* apaiser.

mollusc *n* mollusque *m*.

mollycoddle *vt* dorloter.

molten *adj* fondu.

mom, mommy *n* maman *f*.

moment *n* moment *m*.

momentarily *adv* momentanément.

momentary *adj* momentané.

momentous *adj* capital.

momentum *n* vitesse *f*; élan *m*.

monarch *n* monarque *m*.

monarchy *n* monarchie *f*.

monastery *n* monastère *m*.

monastic *adj* monastique.

Monday *n* lundi *m*.

monetary *adj* monétaire.

money *n* argent *m*; pièce de monnaie *f*.

money order *n* mandat *m*.

mongol *n* (*med*) mongolien *m* -ne *f*.
mongrel *adj n* bâtard *m* -e *f*.
monitor *n* moniteur *m* -trice *f*.
monk *n* moine *m*.
monkey *n* singe *m*.
monochrome *adj* monochrome.
monocle *n* monocle *m*.
monologue *n* monologue *m*.
monopolise *vt* monopoliser.
monopoly *n* monopole *m*.
monosyllable *n* monosyllabe *m*.
monotonous *adj* monotone.
monotony *n* monotonie *f*.
monsoon *n* mousson *f*.
monster *n* monstre *m*.
monstrosity *n* monstruosité *f*.
monstrous *adj* monstrueux; ~**ly** *adv* monstrueusement.
montage *n* montage *m*.
month *n* mois *m*.
monthly *adj* mensuel; *adv* mensuellement.
monument *n* monument *m*.
monumental *adj* monumental.
moo *vi* meugler.
mood *n* humeur *f*.
moodiness *n* mauvaise humeur *f*.
moody *adj* de mauvaise humeur; lunatique.
moon *n* lune *f*.
moonbeams *npl* rayons de lune *mpl*.
moonlight *n* clair de lune *m*.
moor *n* lande *f*; * *vt* (*mar*) amarrer.
moorland *n* lande *f*.
moose *n* élan *m*, orignal *m*.
mop *n* lavette *f*; * *vt* éponger.
mope *vi* se morfondre.
moped *n* vélomoteur *m*.
moral *adj* ~**ly** *adv* moral(ement); ~**s** *npl* moralité *f*.
morale *n* moral *m*.
moralise *vt vi* moraliser.
moralist *n* moraliste *mf*.
morality *n* moralité *f*.
morass *n* marais *m*.
morbid *adj* morbide.
more *adj adv* plus; **never** ~ plus jamais; **once** ~ encore une fois; ~ **and** ~ de plus en plus; **so much the** ~ d'autant plus.
moreover *adv* de plus, en outre.
morgue *n* morgue *f*.
morning *n* matin *m*; **good** ~ bonjour.
moron *n* imbécile *mf*.
morose *adj* morose.
morphine *n* morphine *f*.
morse *n* morse *m*.
morsel *n* bouchée *f*; morceau *m*.
mortal *adj* ~**ly** *adv* mortel(lement); * *n* mortel *m* -le *f*.
mortality *n* mortalité *f*.

mortar *n* mortier *m*.
mortgage *n* hypothèque *f*; * *vt* hypothéquer.
mortgage company *n* banque de prêts hypothécaires *f*.
mortgager *n* débiteur(-trice) hypothécaire *m*(*f*).
mortification *n* mortification *f*.
mortify *vt* mortifier.
mortuary *n* morgue *f*.
mosaic *n* mosaïque *f*.
mosque *n* mosquée *f*.
mosquito *n* moustique *m*.
moss *n* (*bot*) mousse *f*.
mossy *adj* moussu.
most *adj pn* la plupart de; * *adv* extrêmement; **at** ~ au maximum; ~**ly** *adv* surtout, essentiellement.
moth *n* papillon de nuit *m*; mite *f*.
mothball *n* boule de naphtaline *f*.
mother *n* mère *f*.
motherhood *n* maternité *f*.
mother-in-law *n* belle-mère *f*.
motherless *adj* sans mère.
motherly *adj* maternel.
mother-of-pearl *n* nacre *f*.
mother-to-be *n* future maman *f*.
mother tongue *n* langue maternelle *f*.
motif *n* (*art, mus*) motif *m*.
motion *n* mouvement *m*.
motionless *adj* immobile.
motion picture *n* film *m*.
motivated *adj* motivé.
motive *n* motif *m*.
motley *adj* bigarré.
motor *n* moteur *m*.
motorbike *n* moto *f*.
motorboat *n* canot à moteur *m*.
motorcycle *n* motocyclette *f*.
motor vehicle *n* automobile *f*.
mottled *adj* marbré, tacheté.
motto *n* devise *f*.
mould *n* moule *m*; * *vt* mouler.
moulder *vi* s'effriter.
mouldy *adj* moisi.
moult *vi* muer.
mound *n* monticule *m*.
mount *n* mont *m*; * *vt* gravir.
mountain *n* montagne *f*.
mountaineer *n* alpiniste *mf*.
mountaineering *n* alpinisme *m*.
mountainous *adj* montagneux.
mourn *vt* pleurer.
mourner *n* personne en deuil *f*.
mournful *adj* ~**ly** *adv* triste(ment).
mourning *n* deuil *m*.
mouse *n* (*pl* **mice**) souris *f*.
mouth *n* bouche *f*; embouchure *f*.
mouthful *n* bouchée *f*.
mouth organ *n* harmonica *m*.
mouthpiece *n* bec *m*; microphone *m*.

mouthwash *n* eau dentifrice *f*.
mouthwatering *adj* appétissant.
movable *adj* mobile.
move *vt* déplacer; toucher, émouvoir; * *vi* bouger; * *n* mouvement *m*.
movement *n* mouvement *m*.
movie *n* film *m*.
movie camera *n* caméra *f*.
moving *adj* touchant, émouvant.
mow *vt* tondre.
mower *n* tondeuse *f*.
Mrs *n* Mme, Madame *f*.
much *adj pn* beaucoup; *adv* beaucoup, très.
muck *n* saleté *f*.
mucous *adj* muqueux.
mucus *n* mucus *m*.
mud *n* boue *f*.
muddle *vt* confondre; embrouiller; * *n* confusion *f*; désordre *m*.
muddy *adj* boueux.
mudguard *n* garde-boue *m invar*.
muffle *vt* assourdir.
mug *n* tasse *f*.
muggy *adj* lourd, étouffant.
mulberry *n* mûre *f*; ~ **tree** mûrier *m*.
mule *n* mulet *m*; mule *f*.
mull *vt* méditer.
multifarious *adj* divers.
multiple *adj* multiple.
multiplication *n* multiplication *f*; ~ **table** table de multiplication *f*.
multiply *vt* multiplier.
multitude *n* multitude *f*.
mumble *vt vi* grommeler.
mummy *n* momie *f*.
mumps *npl* oreillons *mpl*.
munch *vt* mâcher.
mundane *adj* banal.
municipal *adj* municipal.
municipality *n* municipalité *f*.
munificence *n* munificence *f*.
munitions *npl* munitions *fpl*.
mural *n* mural *m*.
murder *n* assassinat, meurtre *m*; homicide volontaire *m*; * *vt* assassiner.
murderer *n* assassin, meurtrier *m*.
murderess *n* meurtrière *f*.
murderous *adj* meurtrier.
murky *adj* obscur, glauque.
murmur *n* murmure *m*; * *vt vi* murmurer.
muscle *n* muscle *m*.
muscular *adj* musculaire.
muse *vi* méditer, rêver.
museum *n* musée *m*.
mushroom *n* (*bot*) champignon *m*.

music *n* musique *f.*
musical *adj* musical; mélodieux.
musician *n* musicien *m* -ne *f.*
musk *n* musc *m.*
muslin *n* mousseline *f.*
mussel *n* moule *f.*
must *v aux* devoir.
mustard *n* moutarde *f.*
muster *vt* rassembler.
musty *adj* moisi.
mute *adj* muet, silencieux.
muted *adj* assourdi.
mutilate *vt* mutiler.

mutilation *n* mutilation *f.*
mutiny *n* mutinerie *f; vi* se mutiner, se révolter.
mutter *vt vi* grommeler, marmonner; * *n* grommellement *m.*
mutton *n* mouton *m* (viande).
mutual *adj* ~**ly** *adv* mutuel(lement), réciproque(ment).
muzzle *n* muselière *f;* museau *m;* * *vt* museler.
my *pn* mon, ma, mes.
myriad *n* myriade *f.*

myrrh *n* myrrhe *f.*
myrtle *n* myrte *m.*
myself *pn* moi-même.
mysterious *adj* mystérieux; ~**ly** *adv* mystérieusement.
mystery *n* mystère *m.*
mystic(al) *adj* mystique.
mystify *vt* mystifier; laisser perplexe.
mystique *n* mystique *f.*
myth *n* mythe *m.*
mythology *n* mythologie *f.*

N

nab *vt* coincer, pincer.

nag *n* bourrin *m*; * *vt* harceler.

nagging *adj* persistant; * *npl* harcèlement *m*.

nail *n* ongle *m*; clou *m*; * *vt* clouer.

nailbrush *n* brosse à ongles *f*.

nailfile *n* lime à ongles *f*.

nail polish *n* vernis à ongles *m*.

nail scissors *npl* ciseaux à ongles *mpl*.

naive *adj* naïf.

naked *adj* nu; dénudé; pur, simple.

name *n* nom *m*; réputation *f*; * *vt* nommer; mentionner.

nameless *adj* anonyme.

namely *adv* à savoir.

namesake *n* homonyme *m*.

nanny *n* nourrice *f*.

nap *n* sieste *f*, somme *m*.

napalm *n* napalm *m*.

nape *n* nuque *f*.

napkin *n* serviette *f*.

narcissus *n* (*bot*) narcisse *m*.

narcotic *adj n* narcotique *m*.

narrate *vt* narrer, raconter.

narrative *adj* narratif; * *n* narration *f*.

narrow *adj* ~**ly** *adv* étroit(ement); * *vt* resserrer; limiter.

narrow-minded *adj* à l'esprit étroit.

nasal *adj* nasal.

nasty *adj* méchant; mauvais; sale.

natal *adj* natal.

nation *n* nation *f*.

national *adj* ~**ly** *adv* national-(ement).

nationalise *vt* nationaliser.

nationalism *n* nationalisme *m*.

nationalist *adj n* nationaliste *mf*.

nationality *n* nationalité *f*.

nationwide *adj* au niveau national.

native *adj* natal; * *n* autochtone *mf*.

native language *n* langue maternelle *f*.

Nativity *n* Nativité *f*.

natural *adj* ~**ly** *adv* naturel(lement).

natural gas *n* gaz naturel *m*.

naturalise *vt* naturaliser.

naturalist *n* naturaliste *mf*.

nature *n* nature *f*; sorte *f*.

naught *n* zéro *m*.

naughty *adj* méchant.

nausea *n* nausée, envie de vomir *f*.

nauseate *vt* donner des nausées à.

nauseous *adj* écœurant.

nautic(al), naval *adj* nautique.

nave *n* nef (d'église) *f*.

navel *n* nombril *m*.

navigate *vi* naviguer.

navigation *n* navigation *f*.

navy *n* marine *f*.

Nazi *n* nazi *m* -e *f*.

near *prep* près de; * *adv* près; à côté; * *adj* proche.

nearby *adj* proche.

nearly *adv* presque.

near-sighted *adj* myope.

neat *adj* soigné; net, propre; ~**ly** *adv* proprement; élégamment.

nebulous *adj* nébuleux.

necessarily *adv* nécessairement.

necessary *adj* nécessaire.

necessitate *vt* nécessiter.

necessity *n* nécessité *f*.

neck *n* cou *m*; * *vi* se bécoter.

necklace *n* collier *m*.

necktie *n* cravate *f*.

nectar *n* nectar *m*.

née *adj*: ~ **Brown** née Brown.

need *n* besoin *m*; pauvreté *f*; * *vt* avoir besoin de, nécessiter.

needle *n* aiguille *f*.

needless *adj* superflu, inutile.

needlework *n* couture *f*.

needy *adj* nécessiteux, pauvre.

negation *n* négation *f*.

negative *adj* négatif; ~**ly** *adv* négativement; * *n* négative *f*; négation *f*; négatif *m*.

neglect *vt* négliger; * *n* négligence *f*.

negligee *n* négligé, déshabillé *m*.

negligence *n* négligence *f*; manque de soin *m*.

negligent *adj* négligent; ~**ly** *adv* négligemment.

negligible *adj* négligeable.

negotiate *vt vi* négocier.

negotiation *n* négociation *f*.

Negress *n* Noire *f*.

Negro *adj* noir; * *n* Noir *m*.

neigh *vi* hennir; * *n* hennissement *m*.

neighbour *n* voisin *m* -e *f*; * *vt* être voisin de.

neighbourhood *n* voisinage *m*.

neighbouring *adj* voisin.

neighbourly *adj* sociable.

neither *conj* ni; * *pn* aucun(e), ni l'un(e) ni l'autre.

neon *n* néon *m*.

neon light *n* lumière au néon *f*.

nephew *n* neveu *m*.

nepotism *n* népotisme *m*.

nerve *n* nerf *m*; courage *m*; toupet *m*.

nerve-racking *adj* exaspérant.

nervous *adj* nerveux.

nervous breakdown *n* dépression nerveuse *f*.

nest *n* nid *m*; nichée *f*.

nest egg *n* (*fig*) économies *fpl*.

nestle *vt vi* se blottir.

net *n* filet *m*.

net curtain *n* voile *m*.

netting *n* filet *m*.

nettle *n* ortie *f*.

network *n* réseau *f*.

neurosis *n* névrose *f*.

neurotic *adj n* névrosé *m* -e *f*.

neuter *adj* (*gr*) neutre.

neutral *adj* neutre.

neutralise *vt* neutraliser.

neutrality *n* neutralité *f*.

neutron *n* neutron *m*.

neutron bomb *n* bombe à neutrons *f*.

never *adv* jamais; ~ **mind** ça ne fait rien.

never-ending *adj* interminable.

nevertheless *adv* cependant, néanmoins.

new *adj* neuf; nouveau; dernier; ~**ly** *adv* nouvellement.

newborn *adj* nouveau-né, *f* nouvelle-née.

newcomer *n* nouveau venu *m*, nouvelle venue *f*.

new-fangled *adj* moderne.

news *npl* nouvelles, informations *fpl*.

news agency *n* agence de presse *f*.

newscaster *n* présentateur *m* -trice *f*.

newsdealer *n* (US) marchand(e) de journaux *m(f)*.

news flash *n* flash d'information *m*.

newsletter *n* bulletin *m*.

newspaper *n* journal *m*.

newsreel *n* actualités *fpl*.

New Year *n* Nouvel An *m*; ~**'s Day** *n* Jour du Nouvel An *m*; ~**'s Eve** Saint-Sylvestre *f*.

next *adj* prochain; **the ~ day** le jour suivant; * *adv* ensuite, après.

nib *n* pointe *f*; plume *f*.

nibble *vt* mordiller.

nice *adj* gentil(le) *m(f)*; agréable; joli; **~ly** *adv* gentiment; bien.

nice-looking *adj* beau, *f* belle.

niche *n* niche *f*.

nick *n* entaille *f*; * *vt* (*sl*) faucher.

nickel *n* nickel *m*; (US) pièce *f* de cinq cents.

nickname *n* surnom *m*; * *vt* surnommer.

niece *n* nièce *f*.

niggling *adj* insignifiant.

night *n* nuit *f*; **by ~** de nuit; **good ~** bonne nuit.

nightclub *n* boîte de nuit *f*.

nightfall *n* tombée de la nuit *f*.

nightingale *n* rossignol *m*.

nightly *adv* tous les soirs; toutes les nuits; * *adj* nocturne.

nightmare *n* cauchemar *m*.

night school *n* cours du soir *mpl*.

night shift *n* équipe de nuit *f*.

night-time *n* nuit *f*.

nihilist *n* nihiliste *mf*.

nimble *adj* léger; agile, souple.

nine *adj n* neuf *m*.

nineteen *adj n* dix-neuf *m*.

nineteenth *adj n* dix-neuvième *mf*.

ninetieth *adj n* quatre-vingt-dixième *mf*.

ninety *adj n* quatre-vingt-dix *m*.

ninth *adj n* neuvième *mf*.

nip *vt* pincer; mordre.

nipple *n* mamelon *m*; tétine *f*.

nit *n* lente *f*.

nitrogen *n* nitrogène *m*.

no *adv* non; * *adj* aucun; pas de.

nobility *n* noblesse *f*.

noble *adj* noble; * *n* noble *mf*.

nobleman *n* noble *m*.

nobody *pn* personne.

nocturnal *adj* nocturne.

nod *n* signe de tête *m*; * *vi* faire un signe de la tête; somnoler.

noise *n* bruit *m*.

noisily *adv* bruyamment.

noisiness *n* bruit, tapage *m*.

noisy *adj* bruyant.

nominal *adj* **~ly** *adv* nominal(ement).

nominate *vt* nommer.

nomination *n* nomination *f*.

nominative *n* (*gr*) nominatif *m*.

nominee *n* candidat *m* -e *f*.

nonalcoholic *adj* non alcoolisé.

non-aligned *adj* non-aligné.

nonchalant *adj* nonchalant.

noncommittal *adj* réservé.

nonconformist *n* non-conformiste *mf*.

nondescript *adj* quelconque.

none *pn* aucun; personne.

nonentity *n* nullité *f*.

nonetheless *adv* cependant.

nonexistent *adj* inexistant.

nonfiction *n* ouvrages non romanesques *mpl*.

nonplussed *adj* perplexe.

nonsense *n* absurdité *f*.

nonsensical *adj* absurde.

nonsmoker *n* non-fumeur *m*.

nonstick *adj* anti-adhérent.

nonstop *adj* direct; * *adv* sans s'arrêter.

noodles *npl* nouilles *fpl*.

noon *n* midi *m*.

noose *n* nœud coulant *m*.

nor *conj* ni.

normal *adj* normal.

north *n* nord *m*; * *adj* du nord.

North America *n* Amérique du Nord *f*.

northeast *n* nord-est *m*.

northerly, northern *adj* du nord.

North Pole *n* pôle Nord *m*.

northward(s) *adv* vers le nord.

northwest *n* nord-ouest *m*.

nose *n* nez *m*.

nosebleed *n* saignement de nez *m*.

nosedive *n* piqué *m*.

nostalgia *n* nostalgie *f*.

nostril *n* narine *f*.

not *adv* pas; non.

notable *adj* notable.

notably *adv* notamment.

notary *n* notaire *m*.

notch *n* cran *m*, dent *f*; * *vt* denteler.

note *n* note *f*; billet *m*; mot *m*; marque *f*; * *vt* noter, marquer; remarquer.

notebook *n* carnet *m*.

noted *adj* célèbre, connu.

notepad *n* bloc-notes *m*.

notepaper *n* papier à lettres *m*.

nothing *n* rien *m*; **good for ~** bon à rien.

notice *n* notice *f*; avis *m*; * *vt* remarquer.

noticeable *adj* visible.

notification *n* notification *f*.

notify *vt* notifier.

notion *n* notion *f*; opinion *f*; idée *f*.

notoriety *n* notoriété *f*.

notorious *adj* notoire; **~ly** *adv* notoirement.

notwithstanding *conj* quoique.

nougat *n* nougat *m*.

nought *n* zéro *m*.

noun *n* (*gr*) nom, substantif *m*.

nourish *vt* nourrir, alimenter.

nourishing *adj* nourrissant.

nourishment *n* nourriture *f*, aliments *mpl*.

novel *n* roman *m*.

novelist *n* romancier *m* -ière *f*.

novelty *n* nouveauté *f*.

November *n* novembre *m*.

novice *n* novice *mf*, débutant(e) *m(f)*.

now *adv* maintenant; **~ and then** de temps en temps.

nowadays *adv* de nos jours, à l'heure actuelle.

nowhere *adv* nulle part.

noxious *adj* nocif.

nozzle *n* douille *f*.

nuance *n* nuance *f*.

nuclear *adj* nucléaire.

nucleus *n* noyau *m*.

nude *adj* nu.

nudge *vt* donner un coup de coude à.

nudist *n* nudiste *mf*.

nudity *n* nudité *f*.

nuisance *n* ennui *m*; gêne *f*.

nuke *n* (*col*) bombe atomique *f*; * *vt* atomiser.

null *adj* nul.

nullify *vt* annuler; invalider.

numb *adj* engourdi; * *vt* engourdir.

number *n* numéro, nombre *m*; quantité *f*; * *vt* numéroter; compter.

numberplate *n* plaque d'immatriculation *f*.

numbness *n* engourdissement *m*.

numeral *n* chiffre *m*.

numerical *adj* numérique.

numerous *adj* nombreux.

nun *n* religieuse *f*.

nunnery *n* couvent *m*.

nuptial *adj* nuptial; **~s** *npl* noces *fpl*.

nurse *n* infirmière *f*; * *vt* soigner; ménager.

nursery *n* crèche *f*; chambre d'enfant *f*.

nursery rhyme *n* comptine *f*.

nursery school *n* (école) maternelle *f*.

nursing home *n* maison de repos *f*.

nurture *vt* élever, soigner.

nut *n* noix *f*.

nutcrackers *npl* casse-noix *m invar*, casse-noisettes.

nutmeg *n* noix de muscade *f*.

nutritious *adj* nutritif.

nut shell *n* coquille de noix *f*.

nylon *n* nylon *m*; * *adj* en nylon.

O

oak *n* chêne *m*.

oar *n* rame *f*.

oasis *n* oasis *f*.

oat *n* avoine *f*.

oath *n* serment *m*.

oatmeal *n* flocons d'avoine *mpl*.

oats *npl* avoine *f*.

obedience *n* obéissance *f*.

obedient *adj* obéissant; ~ly *adv* avec obéissance.

obese *adj* obèse.

obesity *n* obésité *f*.

obey *vt* obéir à.

obituary *n* nécrologie *f*.

object *n* objet *m*; * *vt* objecter.

objection *n* objection *f*.

objectionable *adj* désagréable.

objective *adj n* objectif *m*.

obligation *n* obligation *f*.

obligatory *adj* obligatoire.

oblige *vt* obliger; rendre service à.

obliging *adj* obligeant.

oblique *adj* oblique; indirect; ~ly *adv* obliquement.

obliterate *vt* effacer.

oblivion *n* oubli *m*.

oblivious *adj* oublieux.

obnoxious *adj* odieux.

oboe *n* hautbois *m*.

obscene *adj* obscène.

obscenity *n* obscénité *f*.

obscure *adj* obscur; ~ly *adv* obscurément; * *vt* obscurcir.

obscurity *n* obscurité *f*.

observance *n* observation *f*; observance *f*.

observant *adj* observateur; respectueux.

observation *n* observation *f*.

observatory *n* observatoire *m*.

observe *vt* observer.

observer *n* observateur *m* -trice *f*.

observingly *adv* attentivement.

obsess *vt* obséder.

obsessive *adj* obsédant.

obsolete *adj* désuet.

obstacle *n* obstacle *m*.

obstinate *adj* obstiné; ~ly *adv* obstinément.

obstruct *vt* obstruer; entraver.

obstruction *n* obstruction *f*; encombrement *m*.

obtain *vt* obtenir.

obtainable *adj* disponible.

obtrusive *adj* importun.

obtuse *adj* obtus.

obvious *adj* évident; ~ly *adv* évidemment.

occasion *n* occasion *f*; * *vt* occasionner, causer.

occasional *adj* occasionnel; ~ly *adv* occasionnellement.

occupant, occupier *n* occupant *m* -e *f*; locataire *mf*.

occupation *n* occupation *f*; emploi *m*.

occupy *vt* occuper.

occur *vi* se produire, arriver.

occurrence *n* incident *m*.

ocean *n* océan *m*.

ocean-going *adj* de haute mer.

oceanic *adj* océanique.

ochre *n* ocre *m*.

octave *n* octave *f*.

October *n* octobre *m*.

octopus *n* poulpe *m*.

odd *adj* impair; étrange; quelconque; ~ly *adv* étrangement.

oddity *n* singularité, particularité *f*.

odd jobs *npl* petits travaux *mpl*.

oddness *n* étrangeté *f*; singularité *f*.

odds *npl* chances *fpl*.

odious *adj* odieux.

odometer *n* (US) odomètre *m*.

odorous *adj* odorant.

odour *n* odeur *f*; parfum *m*.

of *prep* de; à.

off *adj* éteint; fermé; annulé; en congé; ~! *excl* du vent!

offence *n* offense *f*; injure *f*.

offend *vt* offenser, blesser; choquer; * *vi* pécher.

offender *n* délinquant *m* -e *f*.

offensive *adj* offensant; injurieux; ~ly *adv* d'une manière offensante.

offer *vt* offrir; * *n* offre *f*.

offering *n* offrande *f*; offre *f*.

offhand *adj* désinvolte; * *adv* soudainement.

office *n* bureau *m*; poste *m*, fonctions *fpl*; service *m*.

office automation *n* bureautique *f*.

office building *n* immeuble de bureaux *m*.

office hours *npl* heures de bureau *fpl*.

officer *n* officier *m*; fonctionnaire *mf*.

office worker *n* employé(e) de bureau *m(f)*.

official *adj* ~ly *adv* officiel(lement); * *n* employé *m* -e *f*.

officiate *vi* officier.

officious *adj* officieux; ~ly *adv* officieusement.

off-line *adj adv* hors ligne.

off-peak *adj* aux heures creuses.

off-season *adj adv* hors-saison.

offset *vt* compenser; décaler.

offshoot *n* ramification *f*.

offshore *adj* côtier.

offside *adj* hors jeu.

offspring *n* progéniture *f*; descendance *f*.

offstage *adv* en coulisses.

off-the-rack *adj* prêt-à-porter.

ogle *vt* lorgner.

oil *n* huile *f*; * *vt* huiler.

oilcan *n* burette d'huile *f*; bidon d'huile *m*.

oilfield *n* gisement pétrolifère *m*.

oil filter *n* filtre à huile *m*.

oil painting *n* peinture à l'huile *f*.

oil rig *n* derrick *m*.

oil tanker *n* pétrolier *m*.

oil well *n* puits pétrolifère *m*.

oily *adj* huileux; gras.

ointment *n* onguent *m*.

OK, okay *excl* O.K., d'accord; * *adj* bien; * *vt* approuver.

old *adj* vieux, *f* vieille.

old age *n* vieillesse *f*.

old-fashioned *adj* démodé.

olive *n* olivier *m*; olive *f*.

olive oil *n* huile d'olive *f*.

omelet(te) *n* omelette *f*.

omen *n* augure, présage *m*.

ominous *adj* menaçant.

omission *n* omission *f*; négligence *f*.

omit *vt* omettre.

omnipotence *n* omnipotence *f*.

omnipotent *adj* omnipotent, tout-puissant.

on *prep* sur, dessus; en; pour; * *adj* allumé; branché; ouvert; de service.

once *adv* une fois; at ~ tout de suite; all at ~ tout d'un coup; ~ more encore une fois.

oncoming *adj* qui arrive.

one *adj* un, une; ~ by ~ un par un.

one-day excursion *n* billet d'aller-retour valable une journée *m*.

one-man *adj* individuel.

onerous *adj* lourd; (*law*) dur.

oneself *pn* soi-même.

one-sided *adj* partial.

one-to-one *adj* face à face.

ongoing *adj* continu; en cours.

onion *n* oignon *m*.

on-line *adj adv* en ligne.

onlooker *n* spectateur *m* -trice *f*.

only *adj* seul, unique; * *adv* seulement.

onset, onslaught *n* début *m*; attaque *f*.

onus *n* obligation *f*.

onward(s) *adv* en avant.

ooze *vi* suinter.

opaque *adj* opaque.

open *adj* ouvert; public; déclaré; sincère, franc; **~ly** *adv* ouvertement; * *vt* ouvrir; * *vi* s'ouvrir; commencer; **~ on to** donner sur; **~ up** *vt* ouvrir; *vi* s'ouvrir.

opening *n* ouverture *f*; *(com)* débouché *m*; inauguration *f*; commencement *m*.

open-minded *adj* aux idées larges.

openness *n* clareté *f*; franchise, sincérité *f*.

opera *n* opéra *m*.

opera house *n* théâtre de l'opéra *m*.

operate *vi* fonctionner; opérer.

operation *n* fonctionnement *m*; opération *f*.

operational *adj* opérationnel.

operative *adj* actif; en vigueur.

operator *n* opérateur *m* -trice *f*; téléphoniste *mf*.

ophthalmic *adj* ophtalmique.

opine *vt* être d'avis (que).

opinion *n* opinion *f*; jugement *m*.

opinionated *adj* entêté.

opinion poll *n* sondage *m*.

opponent *n* opposant *m* -e *f*; adversaire *mf*.

opportune *adj* opportun.

opportunist *n* opportuniste *mf*.

opportunity *n* occasion *f*.

oppose *vt* s'opposer à.

opposing *adj* opposé.

opposite *adj* opposé; contraire; * *adv* en face; *prep* en face de; * *n* contraire *m*.

opposition *n* opposition *f*; résistance *f*.

oppress *vt* opprimer.

oppression *n* oppression *f*.

oppressive *adj* oppressif.

oppressor *n* oppresseur *m*.

optic(al) *adj* optique; **~s** *npl* optique *f*.

optician *n* opticien *m* -ne *f*.

optimist *n* optimiste *mf*.

optimistic *adj* optimiste.

option *n* option *f*.

optional *adj* optionnel; facultatif.

opulent *adj* opulent.

or *conj* ou.

oracle *n* oracle *m*.

oral *adj* oral, verbal; **~ly** *adv* oralement.

orange *n* orange *f*.

orator *n* orateur *m* -trice *f*.

orbit *n* orbite *f*.

orchard *n* verger *m*.

orchestra *n* orchestre *m*.

orchestral *adj* orchestral.

orchid *n* orchidée *f*.

ordain *vt* ordonner.

ordeal *n* épreuve *f*.

order *n* ordre *m*; commande *f*; mandat *m*; classe *f*; * *vt* ordonner; commander; mettre en ordre.

order form *n* bon de commande *m*.

orderly *adj* ordonné; réglé.

ordinarily *adv* ordinairement.

ordinary *adj* ordinaire.

ordination *n* ordination *f*.

ordnance *n* artillerie *f*.

ore *n* minerai *m*.

organ *n* organe *m*; orgue *m*.

organic *adj* organique.

organisation *n* organisation *f*.

organise *vt* organiser.

organism *n* organisme *m*.

organist *n* organiste *mf*.

orgasm *n* orgasme *m*.

orgy *n* orgie *f*.

oriental *adj* oriental.

orifice *n* orifice *m*.

origin *n* origine *f*.

original *adj* original; originel; **~ly** *adv* à l'origine; originalement.

originality *n* originalité *f*.

originate *vi* provenir (de); être originaire (de).

ornament *n* ornement *m*; * *vt* ornementer, décorer.

ornamental *adj* ornemental.

ornate *adj* ornementé.

orphan *adj n* orphelin *m* -e *f*.

orphanage *n* orphelinat *m*.

orthodox *adj* orthodoxe.

orthodoxy *n* orthodoxie *f*.

orthography *n* orthographe *f*.

orthopaedic *adj* orthopédique.

oscillate *vi* osciller.

osprey *n* balbuzard pêcheur *m*.

ostensibly *adv* selon les apparences.

ostentatious *adj* ostentatoire.

osteopath *n* ostéopathe *mf*.

ostracise *vt* frapper d'ostracisme.

ostrich *n* autruche *f*.

other *pn* autre.

otherwise *adv* autrement.

otter *n* loutre *f*.

ouch *excl* aïe!

ought *v aux* devoir; falloir.

ounce *n* once *f*.

our *pn* notre, *pl* nos.

ours *pn* le nôtre, la nôtre, les nôtres; à nous.

ourselves *pn pl* nous-mêmes.

oust *vt* évincer; déposséder.

out *adv* dehors; éteint.

outback *n* intérieur *m*.

outboard *adj*: **~ motor** (moteur) hors-bord *m*.

outbreak *n* éruption *f*; explosion *f*.

outburst *n* explosion *f*.

outcast *n* paria *m*.

outcome *n* résultat *m*.

outcry *n* protestations *fpl*.

outdated *adj* démodé; périmé.

outdo *vt* surpasser.

outdoor *adj* de plein air, **~s** *adv* à l'extérieur.

outer *adj* extérieur.

outermost *adj* extrême; le plus à l'extérieur.

outer space *n* espace *m*.

outfit *n* tenue *f*; équipement *m*.

outfitter *n* confectionneur *m* -euse *f*.

outgoing *adj* extroverti; sortant.

outgrow *vt* devenir plus grand que.

outhouse *n* dépendances *fpl*.

outing *n* excursion *f*.

outlandish *adj* bizarre.

outlaw *n* hors-la-loi *m*; * *vt* proscrire.

outlay *n* dépenses *fpl*, frais *mpl*.

outlet *n* sortie *f*; débouché *m*.

outline *n* contour *m*; grandes lignes *fpl*.

outlive *vt* survivre à.

outlook *n* perspective *f*.

outlying *adj* distant, éloigné.

outmoded *adj* démodé.

outnumber *vt* être plus nombreux que.

out-of-date *adj* périmé; démodé.

out-patient *n* patient(e) en consultation externe *m(f)*.

outpost *n* avant-poste *m*.

output *n* rendement *m*; sortie *f*.

outrage *n* outrage *m*; * *vt* outrager.

outrageous *adj* outrageant; atroce; **~ly** *adv* outrageusement; atrocement.

outright *adv* absolument, complètement; * *adj* absolu, complet.

outrun *vt* gagner de vitesse, distancer.

outset *n* commencement *m*.

outshine *vt* éclipser.

outside *n* surface *f*; extérieur *m*; apparence *f*; * *adv* dehors; * *prep* en dehors de.

outsider *n* étranger *m* -ère *f*.

outsize *adj* grande taille.

outskirts *npl* périphérie *f*, alentours *mpl*.

outspoken *adj* franc.

outstanding *adj* exceptionnel; en suspens.

outstretch *vi* s'étendre.

outstrip *vt* devancer; surpasser.

out-tray *n* courrier au départ *m*.

outward *adj* extérieur; vers l'extérieur; d'aller; ~**ly** *adv* à l'extérieur, extérieurement.

outweigh *vt* peser plus lourd que; l'emporter sur.

outwit *vt* être plus spirituel que.

oval *n, adj* ovale *m*.

ovary *n* ovaire *m*.

oven *n* four *m*.

ovenproof *adj* allant au four.

over *prep* sur, dessus; plus de; pendant; **all** ~ de tous côtés; * *adj* fini; en trop, en plus; ~ **again** à nouveau; ~ **and** ~ de nombreuses fois.

overall *adj* total; * *adv* dans l'ensemble; ~**s** *npl* salopette *f*.

overawe *vt* impressionner.

overbalance *vi* perdre l'équilibre.

overbearing *adj* despotique.

overboard *adv* (*mar*) par-dessus bord.

overbook *vt* surréserver.

overcast *adj* couvert.

overcharge *vt* surcharger; faire payer un prix excessif à.

overcoat *n* pardessus *m*.

overcome *vt* vaincre; surmonter.

overconfident *adj* trop confiant.

overcrowded *adj* bondé; surpeuplé.

overdo *vi* exagérer.

overdraft *n* découvert *m*.

overdrawn *adj* à découvert.

overdress *vi* s'habiller trop élégamment.

overdue *adj* en retard; arriéré.

overeat *vi* trop manger.

overestimate *vt* surestimer.

overflow *vt* déborder de; * *vi* déborder; * *n* inondation *f*; surplus *m*.

overgrown *adj* envahi.

overgrowth *n* végétation envahissante *f*.

overhang *vt* surplomber.

overhaul *vt* réviser; * *n* révision *f*.

overhead *adv* en l'air, au-dessus.

overhear *vt* entendre par hasard.

overjoyed *adj* fou de joie.

overkill *n* (*fig*) matraquage *m*.

overland *adj adv* par voie de terre.

overlap *vi* se chevaucher.

overleaf *adv* au dos.

overload *vt* surcharger.

overlook *vt* dominer; donner sur; oublier; laisser passer, tolérer; négliger.

overnight *adv* pendant la nuit; * *adj* de nuit.

overpass *n* pont surélevé *m*.

overpower *vt* dominer, écraser.

overpowering *adj* écrasant.

overrate *vt* surévaluer.

override *vt* outrepasser.

overriding *adj* prédominant.

overrule *vt* rejeter; annuler.

overrun *vt* envahir; infester; dépasser.

overseas *adv* à l'étranger; outremer; * *adj* étranger.

oversee *vt* inspecter, surveiller.

overseer *n* contremaître *m*.

overshadow *vt* éclipser.

overshoot *vt* dépasser.

oversight *n* oubli *m*; erreur *f*.

oversleep *vi* se réveiller en retard.

overspill *n* excédent de population *m*.

overstate *vi* exagérer.

overstep *vt* dépasser.

overt *adj* ouvert; public; ~**ly** *adv* ouvertement.

overtake *vt* doubler.

overthrow *vt* renverser; détruire; * *n* renversement *m*; ruine, déroute *f*.

overtime *n* heures supplémentaires *fpl*.

overtone *n* harmonique *mf*; connotation *f*.

overture *n* ouverture *f*.

overturn *vt* renverser.

overweight *adj* trop lourd.

overwhelm *vt* écraser; submerger.

overwhelming *adj* écrasant; irrésistible.

overwork *vi* se surmener, trop travailler.

owe *vt* devoir; être redevable de.

owing *adj* dû; ~ **to** en raison de.

owl *n* chouette *f*.

own *adj* propre; **my** ~ mon, ma, mes propre(s); * *vt* posséder; ~ **up** *vi* confesser.

owner *n* propriétaire *mf*.

ownership *n* possession *f*.

ox *n* bœuf *m*; ~**en** *pl* bœufs *mpl*.

oxidise *vt* oxyder.

oxygen *n* oxygène *m*.

oxygen mask *n* masque à oxygène *m*.

oxygen tent *n* tente à oxygène *f*.

oyster *n* huître *f*.

ozone *n* ozone *m*.

P

pa *n* papa *m*.

pace *n* pas *m*; allure *f*; * *vt* arpenter; * *vi* marcher.

pacemaker *n* meneur *m* -euse *f* de train; (*med*) pacemaker *m*.

pacific(al) *adj* pacifique.

pacification *n* pacification *f*.

pacify *vt* pacifier.

pack *n* paquet *m*; jeu de cartes *m*; bande *f*; * *vt* empaqueter; remplier; * *vi* faire ses valises.

package *n* paquet *m*; accord *m*.

package tour *n* voyage organisé *m*.

packet *n* paquet *m*.

packing *n* emballage *m*.

pact *n* pacte *m*.

pad *n* bloc *m*; coussinet, tampon *m*; plateforme *f*; (*sl*) piaule *f*; * *vt* rembourrer.

padding *n* rembourrage *m*.

paddle *vi* ramer; * *n* pagaie *f*.

paddle steamer *n* vapeur à roues *m*.

paddock *n* paddock *m*.

paddy *n* rizière *f*.

paediatrics *n* pédiatrie *f*.

pagan *adj n* païen *m*, païenne *f*.

page *n* page *f*; page *m*.

pageant *n* grand spectacle *m*.

pageantry *n* pompe *f*.

pail *n* seau *m*.

pain *n* douleur *f*; mal *m*; peine *f*; * *vt* peiner.

pained *adj* peiné.

painful *adj* douloureux; pénible; ~**ly** *adv* douloureusement; péniblement; à grand-peine.

painkiller *n* analgésique *m*.

painless *adj* indolore; sans peine.

painstaking *adj* soigneux.

paint *vt* peindre.

paintbrush *n* pinceau *m*.

painter *n* peintre *m*.

painting *n* peinture *f*; tableau *m*.

paintwork *n* peinture *f*.

pair *n* pair *m*.

pajamas *npl* = **pyjamas**.

pal *n* copain *m*, copine *f*, pote *m*.

palatable *adj* savoureux.

palate *n* palais *m*.

palatial *adj* grandiose.

palaver *n* discussions *fpl*; situation embrouillée *f*.

pale *adj* pâle; clair.

palette *n* palette *f*.

paling *n* palissade *f*.

pall *n* nuage *m* (de fumée); * *vi* perdre sa saveur.

pallet *n* palette *f*.

palliative *adj n* palliatif *m*.

pallid *adj* pâle.

pallor *n* pâleur *f*.

palm *n* (*bot*) palme *f*, palmier *m*.

palmistry *n* chiromancie *f*.

Palm Sunday *n* Dimanche des Rameaux *m*.

palpable *adj* palpable; évident.

palpitation *n* palpitation *f*.

paltry *adj* dérisoire; mesquin.

pamper *vt* gâter, dorloter.

pamphlet *n* pamphlet *m*; brochure *f*.

pan *n* casserole *f*; poêle *f*.

panacea *n* panacée *f*.

panache *n* panache *m*.

pancake *n* crêpe *f*.

pandemonium *n* pandémonium *m*.

pane *n* vitre *f*.

panel *n* panneau *m*; comité *m*.

panelling *n* lambrissage *m*.

pang *n* angoisse *f*; tourment *m*.

panic *adj n* (de) panique *f*.

panicky *adj* paniqué, affolé.

panic-stricken *adj* pris de panique.

pansy *n* (*bot*) pensée *f*.

pant *vi* haleter.

panther *n* panthère *f*.

panties *npl* (petite) culotte *f*.

pantihose *n* collant *m*.

pantry *n* placard *m*.

pants *npl* slip *m*; pantalon *m*.

papacy *n* papauté *f*.

papal *adj* papal.

paper *n* papier *m*; journal *m*; épreuve *f* d'examen; exposé *m*, étude *f*; ~**s** *pl* documents *mpl*; (*com*) fonds *mpl*; * *adj* en papier; * *vt* garnir de papier; tapisser.

paperback *n* livre de poche *m*.

paper bag *n* sac en papier *m*.

paper clip *n* trombone *m*.

paperweight *n* presse-papiers *m*.

paperwork *n* paperasserie *f*.

paprika *n* paprika *m*.

par *n* équivalence *f*; égalité *f*; pair *m*; **at ~** (*com*) au pair.

parable *n* parabole *f*.

parachute *n* parachute *m*; * *vi* sauter en parachute.

parade *n* parade *f*; (*mil*) défilé *m*; * *vt* faire défiler, faire parader; * *vi* défiler, parader; se pavaner.

paradise *n* paradis *m*.

paradox *n* paradoxe *m*.

paradoxical *adj* paradoxal.

paragon *n* modèle absolu *m*.

paragraph *n* paragraphe *m*.

parallel *adj* parallèle; * *n* parallèle *f*; * *vt* mettre en parallèle; comparer.

paralyse *vt* paralyser.

paralysis *n* paralysie *f*.

paralytic(al) *adj* paralytique.

paramedic *n* auxiliaire médical(e) *m(f)*.

paramount *adj* suprême, supérieur.

paranoid *adj* paranoïaque.

paraphernalia *n* affaires *fpl*; attirail *m*.

parasite *n* parasite *m*.

parasol *n* parasol *m*.

paratrooper *n* parachutiste *m*.

parcel *n* paquet *m*; parcelle *f*; * *vt* empaqueter, emballer.

parch *vt* dessécher.

parched *adj* desséché.

parchment *n* parchemin *m*.

pardon *n* pardon *m*; * *vt* pardonner.

parent *n* parent *m* -e *f*; ~**s** parents *mpl*.

parentage *n* parenté *f*; origine *f*.

parental *adj* parental.

parenthesis *n* parenthèse *f*.

parish *n* paroisse *f*; * *adj* paroissial.

parishioner *n* paroissien *m* -ne *f*.

parity *n* parité *f*.

park *n* parc *m*; * *vt* garer; *vi* se garer.

parking *n* stationnement *m*.

parking lot *n* parking *m*.

parking meter *n* parcomètre *m*.

parking ticket *n* amende pour stationnement interdit *f*.

parlance *n* langage *m*.

parliament *n* parlement *m*.

parliamentary *adj* parlementaire.

parlour *n* parloir *m*; salon *m*.

parody *n* parodie *f*; * *vt* parodier.

parole *n*: **on ~** sur parole.

parricide *n* parricide *m*; parricide *mf*.

parrot *n* perroquet *m*.

parry *vt* parer.

parsley *n* (*bot*) persil *m*.

parsnip *n* (*bot*) navet *m*.

part *n* partie *f*; part *f*; rôle (d'acteur) *m*; raie *f*; ~**s** *pl* parties *fpl*; parages *mpl*; * *vt* séparer; diviser; * *vi* se séparer; se diviser; ~ **with** céder; se défaire de; donner; ~**ly** *adv* en partie.

partial *adj* partial; ~**ly** *adv* avec partialité; partiellement.

participant *n* participant *m* -e *f*.

participate *vi* participer (à).

participation *n* participation *f*.

participle *n* (*gr*) participe *m*.

particle *n* particule *f*.

particular *adj* particulier, singulier; ~**ly** *adv* particulièrement; * *n* particulier *m*; particularité *f*.

parting *n* séparation *f*; raie (dans les cheveux) *f*.

partisan *n* partisan *m* -e *f*.

partition *n* partition, séparation *f*; * *vt* diviser en plusieurs parties, partager,

partner *n* associé *m* -e *f*.

partnership *n* association *f*; société *f*.

partridge *n* perdrix *f*.

party *n* parti *m*; fête *f*.

pass *vt* passer; dépasser; adopter; être admis à; * *vi* passer; * *n* permis *m*; passage *m*; ~ **away** *vi* mourir; ~ **by** *vi* passer; *vt* négliger, oublier; ~ **on** *vt* transmettre; passer.

passable *adj* passable; praticable.

passage *n* passage *m*; traversée *f*; couloir *m*.

passbook *n* livret *m* (bancaire).

passenger *n* passager *m* -ère *f*.

passer-by *n* passant *m* -e *f*.

passing *adj* passager.

passion *n* passion *f*; amour *m*; emportement *m*.

passionate *adj* passionné; ~**ly** *adv* passionnément; ardemment.

passive *adj* passif; ~**ly** *adv* passivement.

passkey *n* passe-partout *m invar*.

Passover *n* Pâque *f* juive.

passport *n* passeport *m*.

passport control *n* contrôle des passeports *m*.

password *n* mot de passe *m*.

past *adj* passé; * *n* (*gr*) prétérit *m*; passé *m*; * *prep* au-delà de; après.

pasta *n* pâtes *fpl*.

paste *n* pâte *f*; colle *f*; * *vt* coller.

pasteurised *adj* pasteurisé.

pastime *n* passe-temps *m invar*; divertissement *m*.

pastor *n* pasteur *m*.

pastoral *adj* pastoral.

pastry *n* pâtisserie *f*.

pasture *n* pâture *f*.

pasty *adj* pâteux; pâle.

pat *vt* tapoter.

patch *n* pièce *f*; tache *f*; terrain *m*; * *vt* rapiécer; ~ **up** réparer; se réconcilier.

pâté *n* pâté *m*.

patent *adj* breveté; évident; * *n* brevet *m*; * *vt* faire breveter.

patentee *n* détenteur d'un brevet *m*.

patent leather *n* cuir verni *m*.

paternal *adj* paternel.

paternity *n* paternité *f*.

path *n* chemin, sentier *m*.

pathetic *adj* ~**ally** *adv* pathétique(ment); lamentable(ment).

pathological *adj* pathologique.

pathology *n* pathologie *f*.

pathos *n* pathétique *m*.

pathway *n* sentier *m*.

patience *n* patience *f*.

patient *adj* patient; ~**ly** *adv* patiemment; * *n* patient *m* -e *f*.

patio *n* patio *m*.

patriarch *m* patriarche *m*.

patriot *n* patriote *mf*.

patriotic *adj* patriotique.

patriotism *n* patriotisme *m*.

patrol *n* patrouille *f*; * *vi* patrouiller.

patrol car *n* voiture de patrouille *f*.

patrolman *n* agent de police *m*.

patron *n* protecteur *m*; client *m* -e *f*.

patronage *n* patronage *m*; clientèle *f*.

patronise *vt* patronner, protéger.

patter *n* trottinement *m*; bavardage *m*; * *vi* trottiner.

pattern *n* motif *m*; modèle *m*.

paunch *n* panse *f*; ventre *m*.

pauper *n* pauvre *mf*.

pause *n* pause *f*; * *vi* faire une pause; hésiter.

pave *vt* paver; carreler.

pavement *n* trottoir *m*.

pavilion *n* pavillon *m*.

paving stone *n* pavé *m*.

paw *n* patte *f*; * *vt* tripoter.

pawn *n* pion *m*; gage *m*; * *vt* engager.

pawn broker *n* prêteur(-euse) sur gages *m(f)*.

pawnshop *n* mont-de-piété *m*.

pay *vt* payer; ~ **back** *vt* rembourser; ~ **for** payer; ~ **off** *vt* liquider; *vi* payer; rapporter; * *n* paie *f*; salaire *m*.

payable *adj* payable.

pay day *n* jour de paie *m*.

payee *n* bénéficiaire *mf*.

pay envelope *n* enveloppe de paie *f*.

paymaster *n* caissier *m*.

payment *n* paiement *m*.

pay-phone *n* téléphone public *m*.

payroll *n* liste des employés *f*.

pea *n* pois *m*.

peace *n* paix *f*.

peaceful *adj* paisible; pacifique.

peach *n* pêche *f*.

peacock *n* paon *m*.

peak *n* pic *m*; maximum *m*.

peak hours, peak period *n* heures de pointe *fpl*.

peal *n* carillon *m*; grondement *m*.

peanut *n* cacahuète *f*.

pear *n* poire *f*.

pearl *n* perle *f*.

peasant *n* paysan *m* -ne *f*.

peat *n* tourbe *f*.

pebble *n* caillou *m*; galet *m*.

peck *n* coup de bec *m*; * *vt* picoter.

pecking order *n* hiérarchie *f*.

peculiar *adj* étrange, singulier; ~**ly** *adv* étrangement.

peculiarity *n* particularité, singularité *f*.

pedal *n* pédale *f*; * *vi* pédaler.

pedant *n* pédant *m* -e *f*.

pedantic *adj* pédant.

peddler *n* colporteur *m*.

pedestal *n* piédestal *m*.

pedestrian *n* piéton *m* -ne *f*; * *adj* pédestre.

pediatrics *n* (US) pédiatrie *f*.

pedigree *n* généalogie *f*; pedigree *m*; * *adj* de race.

peek *vi* regarder à la dérobée.

peel *vt* peler; éplucher; * *vi* peler; * *n* peau *f*; pelure *f*.

peer *n* pair *m*.

peerless *adj* incomparable.

peeved *adj* fâché.

peevish *adj* maussade, ronchon (*fam*).

peg *n* cheville *f*; piquet *m*; * *vt* cheviller.

pelican *n* pélican *m*.

pellet *n* boulette *f*.

pelt *n* fourrure *f*; * *vt* arroser; * *vi* pleuvoir à verse.

pen *n* stylo *m*; plume *f*; enclos *m*.

penal *adj* pénal.

penalty *n* peine *f*; sanction *f*; amende *f*.

penance *n* pénitence *f*.

pence *n* = *pl* of **penny**.

pencil *n* crayon *m*.

pencil case *n* trousse *f*.

pendant *n* pendentif *m*.

pending *adj* pendant.

pendulum *n* pendule *m*.

penetrate *vt* pénétrer (dans).

penguin *n* pingouin *m*.

penicillin *n* pénicilline *f*.

peninsula *n* péninsule *f*.

penis *n* pénis *m*.

penitence n pénitence f.

penitent adj n pénitent m -e f.

penitentiary n pénitencier m.

penknife n canif m.

pennant n fanion m.

penniless adj sans le sou.

penny n penny m.

penpal n correspondant m -e f.

pension n pension f; * vt pensionner.

pensive adj pensif; ~ly adv pensivement.

pentagon n: the P~ le Pentagone.

Pentecost n la Pentecôte f.

penthouse n appartement situé sur le toit d'un immeuble m.

pent-up adj réprimé, refoulé.

penultimate adj pénultième, avant-dernier.

penury n pénurie f.

people n peuple m; nation f; gens mpl; * vt peupler.

pep n énergie f; ~ up vt animer.

pepper n poivre m; * vt poivrer.

peppermint n menthe poivrée f.

per prep par.

per annum adv par an.

per capita adj adv par habitant.

perceive vt percevoir.

percentage n pourcentage m.

perception n perception f; notion f.

perch n perche f.

perchance adv par hasard.

percolate vt filtrer.

percolator n percolateur m.

percussion n percussion f.

perdition n perte, ruine f.

peremptory adj péremptoire; décisif.

perennial adj perpétuel.

perfect adj parfait; idéal; ~ly adv parfaitement; * vt parfaire, perfectionner.

perfection n perfection f.

perforate vt perforer.

perforation n perforation f.

perform vt exécuter; effectuer; * vi donner une représentation, tenir un rôle.

performance n exécution f; accomplissement m; rendement m; représentation f.

performer n exécutant m -e f; acteur m -trice f.

perfume n parfum m; * vt parfumer.

perhaps adv peut-être.

peril n péril, danger m.

perilous adj dangereux; ~ly adv dangereusement.

perimeter n périmètre m.

period n période f; époque f; règles fpl.

periodic(al) adj périodique; ~ally adv périodiquement.

periodical n journal m.

peripheral adj périphérique; * n unité périphérique f.

perish vi périr.

perishable adj périssable.

perjure vt parjurer.

perjury n parjure m.

perk n extra, à-côté m.

perky adj animé, plein d'entrain.

perm n permanente f.

permanent adj permanent; ~ly adv en permanence.

permeate vt pénétrer, traverser.

permissible adj permis.

permission n permission f.

permissive adj permissif.

permit vt permettre; * n permis m.

permutation n permutation f.

perpendicular adj ~ly adv perpendiculaire(ment); * n perpendiculaire f.

perpetrate vt perpétrer, commettre.

perpetual adj perpétuel; ~ly adv perpétuellement.

perpetuate vt perpétuer, éterniser.

perplex vt confondre, laisser perrplexe.

persecute vt persécuter; importuner.

persecution n persécution f.

perseverance n persévérance f.

persevere vi persévérer.

persist vi persister.

persistence n persistance f.

persistent adj persistant.

person n personne f.

personable adj attrayant.

personage n personnage m.

personal adj ~ly adv personnel(lement).

personal assistant n secrétaire mf de direction.

personal column n annonces personnelles fpl.

personal computer n ordinateur individuel m.

personality n personnalité f.

personification n personnification f.

personify vt personnifier.

personnel n personnel m.

perspective n perspective f.

perspiration n transpiration f.

perspire vi transpirer.

persuade vt persuader.

persuasion n persuasion f.

persuasive adj persuasif; ~ly adv de manière persuasive.

pert adj plein d'entrain.

pertaining: ~ to prep relatif à.

pertinent adj pertinent; ~ly adv de manière pertinente.

pertness n impertinence f; entrain m.

perturb vt perturber.

perusal n lecture f.

peruse vt lire; examiner attentivement.

pervade vt pénétrer, traverser.

perverse adj pervers, dépravé; ~ly adv perversement.

pervert vt pervertir, corrompre.

pessimist n pessimiste mf.

pest n insecte nuisible m; (fam) casse-pieds mf invar.

pester vt importuner, fatiguer.

pestilence n peste f.

pet n animal domestique m; préféré m -e f; * vt gâter; * vi (fam) se peloter.

petal n (bot) pétale m.

petite adj menue.

petition n pétition f; * vt présenter une pétition à; supplier.

petrified adj pétrifié.

petroleum n pétrole m.

petticoat n jupon m.

pettiness n insignifiance f.

petty adj mesquin; insignifiant.

petty cash n argent destiné aux dépenses courantes m.

petty officer n second maître m.

petulant adj pétulant.

pew n banc m.

pewter n étain m.

phantom n fantôme m.

Pharisee n Pharisien m.

pharmaceutic(al) adj pharmaceutique.

pharmacist n pharmacien m -ienne f.

pharmacy n pharmacie f.

phase n phase f.

pheasant n faisan m.

phenomenal adj phénoménal.

phenomenon n phénomène m.

phial n fiole f.

philanthropic adj philanthropique.

philanthropist n philanthrope mf.

philanthropy n philanthropie f.

philologist n philologue mf.

philology n philologie f.

philosopher n philosophe mf.

philosophical(ly) adj (adv) philosophique(ment).

philosophise vi philosopher.

philosophy n philosophie f; natural ~ physique f.

phlegm n flegme m.

phlegmatic(al) adj flegmatique.

phobia n phobie f.

phone n téléphone m; * vt téléphoner à; ~ **back** *vt vi* rappeler; ~ **up** *vt* appeler au téléphone.

phone book *n* annuaire *m*.

phone box, phone booth *n* cabine téléphonique *f*.

phone call *n* coup de téléphone *m*.

phosphorus *n* phosphore *m*.

photocopier *n* photocopieuse *f*.

photocopy *n* photocopie *f*.

photograph *n* photo(graphie) *f*; * *vt* photographier.

photographer *n* photographe *mf*.

photographic *adj* photographique.

photography *n* photo(graphie) *f*.

phrase *n* phrase *f*; locution *f*; * *vt* exprimer.

phrase book *n* guide de conversation *m*.

physical *adj* ~**ly** *adv* physique(ment).

physical education *n* éducation physique *f*.

physician *n* médecin *m*.

physicist *n* physicien *m* -ne *f*.

physiological *adj* physiologique.

physiologist *n* physiologiste, physiologue *mf*.

physiology *n* physiologie *f*.

physiotherapy *n* physiothérapie *f*.

physique *n* physique *m*.

pianist *n* pianiste *mf*.

pick *vt* choisir; cueillir; gratter; ~ **on** *vt* s'en prendre à; ~ **out** *vt* choisir; ~ **up** *vi* s'améliorer; se remettre; * *vt* ramasser; décrocher; arrêter; acheter; * *n* pic *m*; choix *m*.

pickaxe *n* pic *m*.

picket *n* piquet *m*.

pickle *n* saumure *f*; * *vt* saumurer.

pickpocket *n* pickpocket *m*.

pickup *n* (*auto*) fourgonnette *f*.

picnic *n* pique-nique *m*.

pictorial *adj* pictural; illustré.

picture *n* image *f*; peinture *f*; photo *f*; * *vt* dépeindre; se figurer.

picture book *n* livre d'images *m*.

picturesque *adj* pittoresque.

pie *n* gâteau *m*; tarte *f*; pâté en croûte *m*.

piece *n* morceau *m*; pièce *f*; tranche *f*; * *vt* raccommoder.

piecemeal *adv* petit à petit; * *adj* partiel.

piecework *n* travail à la pièce *m*.

pier *n* jetée *f*.

pierce *vt* percer, transpercer.

piercing *adj* perçant.

piety *n* piété, dévotion *f*.

pig *n* cochon *m*.

pigeon *n* pigeon *m*.

pigeonhole *n* casier *m*.

piggy bank *n* tirelire *f*.

pigheaded *adj* têtu.

pigsty *n* porcherie *f*.

pigtail *n* natte *f*.

pike *n* brochet *m*; pique *f*.

pile *n* tas *m*; pile *f*; amas *m*; poil *m*; ~**s** *pl* hémorroïdes *fpl*; * *vt* entasser, empiler.

pile-up *n* carambolage *m*.

pilfer *vt* chaparder.

pilgrim *n* pèlerin *m*.

pilgrimage *n* pèlerinage *m*.

pill *n* pilule *f*.

pillage *vt* piller, mettre à sac.

pillar *n* pilier *m*.

pillion *n* siège arrière *m*.

pillow *n* oreiller *m*.

pillow case *n* taie d'oreiller *f*.

pilot *n* pilote *m*; * *vt* piloter; (*fig*) mener.

pilot light *n* témoin *m*.

pimp *n* proxénète, maquereau (*fam*) *m*.

pimple *n* bouton *m*.

pin *n* épingle *f*; goupille *f*; ~**s and needles** *npl* fourmis *fpl*; * *vt* épingler; goupiller.

pinafore *n* tablier *m*.

pinball *n* flipper *m*.

pincers *n* tenailles *fpl*.

pinch *vt* pincer; (*sl*) piquer, faucher; * *vi* serrer; * *n* pincement *m*; pincée *f*.

pincushion *n* pelote à épingles *f*.

pine *n* (*bot*) pin *m*; * *vi* languir.

pineapple *n* ananas *m*.

ping *n* tintement *m*.

pink *adj n* rose *m*.

pinnacle *n* sommet *m*.

pinpoint *vt* préciser; souligner.

pint *n* pinte *f*.

pioneer *n* pionnier *m*.

pious *adj* pieux, dévot, ~**ly** *adv* pieusement.

pip *n* pépin *m*.

pipe *n* tube, tuyau *m*; pipe *f*; ~**s** tuyauterie *f*.

pipe cleaner *n* cure-pipe *m*.

pipe dream *n* rêve impossible *m*.

pipeline *n* canalisation *f*; oléoduc *m*; gazoduc *m*.

piper *n* joueur de cornemuse *m*.

piping *adj* bouillant; aigu, *f* aiguë.

pique *n* pique *f*; dépit *m*.

piracy *n* piraterie *f*.

pirate *n* pirate *m*.

pirouette *n* pirouette *f*; *vi* pirouetter.

Pisces *n* Poissons *mpl* (signe du zodiaque).

piss *n* (*sl*) pisse *f*; * *vi* pisser.

pistol *n* pistolet *m*.

piston *n* piston *m*.

pit *n* noyau *m*; mine *f*; fosse *f*.

pitch *n* lancement *m*; ton *m*; * *vt* lancer, jeter; * *vi* tomber; piquer du nez.

pitchblack *adj* noir comme dans un four.

pitcher *n* cruche *f*.

pitchfork *n* fourche *f*.

pithy *adj* moelleux; vigoureux.

pitiable *adj* pitoyable; déplorable.

pitiful *adj* pitoyable; lamentable; ~**ly** *adv* pitoyablement.

pittance *n* salaire de misère *m*; pitance *f*.

pity *n* pitié *f*; * *vt* avoir pitié de.

pivot *n* pivot, axe *m*.

pizza *n* pizza *f*.

placard *n* affiche *f*.

placate *vt* apaiser.

place *n* endroit, lieu *m*; place *f*; * *vt* placer; mettre.

placid *adj* placide, calme; ~**ly** *adv* placidement.

plagiarism *n* plagiat *m*.

plague *n* peste *f*; * *vt* tourmenter; infester.

plaice *n* carrelet *m*.

plaid *n* tartan *m*; plaid *m*.

plain *adj* uni; simple; clair, sincère; commun; évident; ~**ly** *adv* simplement; clairement; * *n* plaine *f*.

plaintiff *n* (*law*) plaignant *m* -e *f*.

plait *n* tresse *f*; * *vt* tresser.

plan *n* plan *m*; projet *m*; * *vt* projeter.

plane *n* avion *m*; plan *m*; rabot *m*; * *vt* aplanir; raboter.

planet *n* planète *f*.

planetary *adj* planétaire.

plank *n* planche *f*.

planner *n* planificateur *m* -trice *f*.

planning *n* planification *f*.

plant *n* plante *f*; usine *f*; machinerie *f*; * *vt* planter.

plantation *n* plantation *f*.

plaque *n* plaque *f*.

plaster *n* plâtre *m*; emplâtre *m*; * *vt* plâtrer; emplâtrer.

plastered *adj* (*sl*) bourré, soûl.

plasterer *n* plâtrier *m*.

plastic *adj* plastique.

plastic surgery *n* chirurgie esthétique *f*.

plate *n* assiette *f*; plaque *f*; lame *f*.

plateau *n* (*geol*) plateau *m*.

plate glass *n* vitre *f*.

platform *n* plateforme *f*.

platinum *n* platine *m*.

platitude *n* platitude *f*.

platoon *n* (*mil*) peloton *m*.

platter *n* écuelle *f*; plat *m*.

plaudit *n* applaudissement *m*.

plausible *adj* plausible.

play *n* jeu *m*; pièce de théâtre *f*; * *vt vi* jouer; (*also mus*) ~ **down** *vt* rabaisser; minimiser.

playboy *n* playboy *m*.

player *n* joueur *m* -euse *f*; acteur *m* -trice *f*.

playful *adj* enjoué, amusé; ~**ly** *adv* d'une manière enjouée; pour s'amuser.

playmate *n* camarade de jeu *mf*.

playground *n* cour de récréation *f*; jardin d'enfants *m*.

playgroup *n* halte-garderie *f*.

play-off *n* prolongation *f* (match).

playpen *n* parc pour enfant *m*.

plaything *n* jouet *m*.

playwright *n* dramaturge *mf*.

plea *n* appel *m*; excuse *f*, prétexte *m*.

plead *vt* plaider; prétexter.

pleasant *adj* agréable; plaisant; aimable; ~**ly** *adv* agréablement.

please *vt* faire plaisir à.

pleased *adj* content.

pleasing *adj* agréable, plaisant.

pleasure *n* plaisir *m*; gré *m*, volonté *f*.

pleat *n* pli *m*.

pledge *n* promesse *f*; gage *m*; * *vt* engager; promettre.

plentiful *adj* copieux; abondant.

plenty *n* abondance *f*; ~ **of** beaucoup de.

plethora *n* pléthore *f*.

pleurisy *n* pleurésie *f*.

pliable, pliant *adj* pliable, pliant; souple.

pliers *npl* pinces *fpl*.

plight *n* épreuve *f*; situation difficile *f*.

plinth *n* plinthe *f*.

plod *vi* se traîner, avancer péniblement.

plot *n* petit morceau de terrain *m*; complot *m*; intrigue *f*; * *vt* tracer; comploter; conspirer.

plough *n* charrue *f*; * *vt* labourer; ~ **back** *vt* réinvestir; ~ **through** *vi* se faire un chemin; avancer péniblement.

ploy *n* truc *m*.

pluck *vt* tirer; arracher; déplumer; * *n* courage *m*.

plucky *adj* courageux.

plug *n* tampon *m*; bouchon *m*; bougie *f*; prise *f*; * *vt* boucher.

plum *n* prune *f*.

plumage *n* plumage *m*.

plumb *n* aplomb *m*; * *adv* d'aplomb; * *vt* plomber; sonder.

plumber *n* plombier *m*.

plume *n* plume *f*, panache *m*.

plump *adj* rondouillet, dodu.

plum tree *n* prunier *m*.

plunder *vt* mettre à sac, piller; * *n* pillage *m*; butin *m*.

plunge *vi* plonger; s'élancer.

plunger *n* piston *m*.

pluperfect *n* (*gr*) plus-que-parfait *m*.

plural *adj n* pluriel *m*.

plurality *n* pluralité *f*.

plus *n* signe plus *m*; * *prep* plus.

plush *adj* en peluche.

plutonium *n* plutonium *m*.

ply *vt* manier avec vigueur; * *vi* s'appliquer; (*mar*) faire la navette.

plywood *n* contreplaqué *m*.

pneumatic *adj* pneumatique.

pneumatic drill *n* marteau pneumatique *m*.

pneumonia *n* pneumonie *f*.

poach *vt* pocher; braconner; *vi* braconner.

poached *adj* poché.

poacher *n* braconnier *m*.

poaching *n* braconnage *m*.

pocket *n* poche *f*; * *vt* empocher.

pocketbook *n* portefeuille *m*.

pocket money *n* argent de poche *m*.

pod *n* cosse *f*.

podgy *adj* boudiné.

poem *n* poème *m*.

poet *n* poète *m*.

poetess *n* poétesse *f*.

poetic *adj* poétique.

poetry *n* poésie *f*.

poignant *adj* poignant.

point *n* pointe *f*; point *m*; promontoire *m*; ~ **of view** *n* point de vue *m*; * *vt* pointer; tailler en pointe; indiquer.

point-blank *adv* à bout portant; directement.

pointed *adj* pointu; acéré; ~**ly** *adv* subtilement.

pointer *n* auguille *f*; pointer *m*.

pointless *adj* inutile.

poise *n* attitude *f*; équilibre *m*.

poison *n* poison *m*; * *vt* empoisonner.

poisoning *n* empoisonnement *m*.

poisonous *adj* vénéneux.

poke *vt* attiser; donner un coup de coude à; pousser du doigt.

poker *n* tison *m*; poker *m*.

poker-faced *adj* au visage impassible.

poky *adj* exigu, *f* exiguè.

polar *adj* polaire.

pole *n* pôle *m*; mât *m*; perche *f*.

pole bean *n* haricot en rames *m*.

pole vault *n* saut à la perche *m*.

police *n* police *f*.

police car *n* voiture de police *f*.

policeman *n* agent de police *m*.

police state *n* état policier *m*.

police station *n* commissariat *m*.

policewoman *n* femme agent de police *f*.

policy *n* politique *f*; police d'assurance *f*.

polio *n* polio *f*.

polish *vt* polir; cirer; ~ **off** *vt* parachever; expédier; * *n* poli *m*.

polished *adj* poli; ciré; élégant.

polite *adj* ~**ly** *adv* poli(ment), courtois(ement).

politeness *n* politesse, courtoisie *f*.

politic *adj* politique; rusé.

political *adj* politique.

politician *n* homme (femme) politique *m(f)*.

politics *npl* politique *f*.

polka *n* polka *f*; ~ **dot** *n* pois *m*.

poll *n* liste électorale *f*; vote *m*; sondage *m*.

pollen *n* (*bot*) pollen *m*.

pollute *vt* polluer; corrompre.

pollution *n* pollution, contamination *f*.

polyester *n* polyester *m*.

polyethylene *n* polyéthylène *m*.

polygamy *n* polygamie *f*.

polystyrene *n* polystyrène *m*.

polytechnic *n* école d'enseignement technique *f*.

pomegranate *n* grenade *f*.

pomp *n* pompe *f*; splendeur *f*.

pompom *n* pompon *m*.

pompous *adj* pompeux.

pond *n* mare *f*; étang *m*.

ponder *vt* considérer; réfléchir à.

ponderous *adj* lourd, pesant.

pontiff *n* pontife *m*.

pontoon *n* ponton *m*.

pony *n* poney *m*.

ponytail *n* queue de cheval *f*.

pool *n* flaque d'eau *f*; piscine *f*; * *vt* grouper.

poor *adj* pauvre; mauvais; ~**ly** *adv* pauvrement; **the** ~ *n* les pauvres *mpl*.

pop *n* pop *m*; papa *m*; boisson gazeuse *f*; éclatement *m*; * ~ **in/out** *vi* entrer/sortir un instant.

pop concert *n* concert de musique pop *m*.

popcorn *n* popcorn *m*.

Pope *n* pape *m*.

poplar *n* peuplier *m*.

poppy *n* (*bot*) pavot *m*.

popsicle *n* (US) sucette *f* glacée.

populace *n* populace *f*.

popular *adj* ~**ly** *adv* populaire(ment).

popularise *vt* populariser.
popularity *n* popularité *f*.
populate *vi* peupler.
population *n* population *f*.
populous *adj* populeux.
porcelain *n* porcelaine *f*.
porch *n* porche *m*.
porcupine *n* porc-épic *m*.
pore *n* pore *m*.
pork *n* porc *m* (viande).
pornography *n* pornographie *f*.
porous *adj* poreux.
porpoise *n* marsouin *m*.
porridge *n* porridge *m*, flocons d'avoine *mpl*.
port *n* port *m*; (*mar*) sabord *m*; babord *m*; porto (vin) *m*.
portable *adj* portable, portatif.
portal *n* portail *m*.
porter *n* portier *m*; garçon *m*.
portfolio *n* serviette *f*; carton *m*; portefeuille *m*.
porthole *n* hublot *m*.
portico *n* portique *m*.
portion *n* portion, part *f*.
portly *adj* corpulent.
portrait *n* portrait *m*.
portray *vt* faire le portrait de; dépeindre.
pose *n* posture *f*; pose *f*; * *vt vi* poser.
posh *adj* chic; bourgeois.
position *n* position *f*; situation *f*; * *vt* mettre en position.
positive *adj* positif; réel; favorable; ~**ly** *adv* positivement; assurément.
posse *n* peloton *m*, détachement *m*.
possess *vt* posséder.
possession *n* possession *f*.
possessive *adj* possessif.
possibility *n* possibilité *f*.
possible *adj* possible; ~**ly** *adv* peut-être.
post *n* courrier *m*; poste *f*; emploi *m*; poste *m*; pieu *m*; * *vt* poster; fixer.
postage *n* affranchissement *m*.
postage stamp *n* timbre *m*.
postcard *n* carte postale *f*.
postdate *vt* postdater.
posterior *n* postérieur *m*.
posterity *n* postérité *f*.
postgraduate *n* licencié *m* -e *f*.
posthumous *adj* posthume.
postman *n* facteur *m*.
postmark *n* cachet de la poste *m*.
postmaster *n* receveur des postes *m*.
post office *n* poste *f*, bureau de poste *m*.
postpone *vt* remettre; différer.

postscript *n* post-scriptum *m*.
posture *n* posture *f*.
postwar *adj* d'après-guerre.
posy *n* petit bouquet de fleurs *m*.
pot *n* pot *m*; marmite *f*; (*sl*) marijuana *f*; * *vt* empoter; mettre en pot.
potato *n* pomme de terre, patate (*fam*) *f*.
potato peeler *n* couteau éplucheur *m*.
potbellied *adj* ventru.
potent *adj* puissant.
potential *adj* potentiel.
pothole *n* trou *m*.
potion *n* potion *f*.
potted *adj* en pot.
potter *n* potier *m*.
pottery *n* poterie *f*.
potty *adj* insignifiant; (*sl*) fou, maboul.
pouch *n* sac *m*.
poultice *n* cataplasme *m*.
poultry *n* volaille *f*.
pound *n* livre *f*; livre sterling *f*; fourrière *f*; * *vt* concasser; * *vi* taper fort.
pour *vt* verser; servir; * *vi* couler; pleuvoir à verse.
pout *vi* faire la moue.
poverty *n* pauvreté *f*.
powder *n* poudre *f*; * *vt* saupoudrer.
powder compact *n* poudrier *m*.
powdered milk *n* lait en poudre *m*.
powder puff *n* houppette *f*.
powder room *n* toilettes *fpl*.
powdery *adj* poudreux.
power *n* pouvoir *m*; puissance *f*; empire *m*; autorité *f*; force *f*; * *vt* propulser.
powerful *adj* puissant; ~**ly** *adv* puissamment; avec force.
powerless *adj* impuissant.
power station *n* centrale électrique *f*.
practicable *adj* praticable; faisable.
practical *adj* ~**ly** *adv* pratique(ment).
practicality *n* faisabilité *f*.
practical joke *n* farce *f*.
practice *n* pratique *f*; usage *m*; entraînement *m*; ~**s** *pl* agissements *mpl*.
practise *vt* pratiquer, exercer; * *vi* s'exercer, s'entraîner.
practitioner *n* médecin *m*.
pragmatic *adj* pragmatique.
prairie *n* prairie *f*.
praise *n* éloge *m*; louange *f*; * *vt* louer.
praiseworthy *adj* digne d'éloges.

prance *vi* cabrioler.
prank *n* folie, extravagance *f*.
prattle *vi* jacasser; * *n* jacasserie *f*.
prawn *n* crevette *f*.
pray *vi* prier.
prayer *n* prière *f*.
prayer book *n* livre de messe *m*.
preach *vt* prêcher.
preacher *n* prédicateur *m*.
preamble *n* préambule *m*.
precarious *adj* précaire, incertain; ~**ly** *adv* précairement.
precaution *n* précaution *f*.
precautionary *adj* préventif.
precede *vt* précéder.
precedence *n* précédence *f*.
precedent *adj n* précédent *m*.
precinct *n* limite *f*; enceinte *f*; circonscription *f*.
precious *adj* précieux.
precipice *n* (*fig*) précipice *m*.
precipitate *vt* précipiter; * *adj* précipité.
precise *n* précis, exact; ~**ly** *adv* précisément, exactement.
precision *n* précision, exactitude *f*.
preclude *vt* exclure, empêcher.
precocious *adj* précoce, prématuré.
preconceive *vt* préconcevoir.
preconception *n* préjugé *m*; idée préconçue *f*.
precondition *n* condition préalable *f*.
precursor *n* précurseur *m*.
predator *n* prédateur *m*.
predecessor *n* prédécesseur *m*.
predestination *n* prédestination *f*.
predicament *n* situation difficile *f*.
predict *vt* prédire.
predictable *adj* prévisible.
prediction *n* prédiction *f*.
predilection *n* prédilection *f*.
predominant *adj* prédominant.
predominate *vt* prédominer.
preen *vt* nettoyer (ses plumes).
prefab *n* maison préfabriquée *f*.
preface *n* préface *f*.
prefer *vt* préférer.
preferable *adj* préférable.
preferably *adv* de préférence.
preference *n* préférence *f*.
preferential *adj* préférentiel.
preferment *n* promotion *f*; préférence *f*.
prefix *vt* préfixer; * *n* (*gr*) préfixe *m*.
pregnancy *n* grossesse *f*.
pregnant *adj* enceinte.
prehistoric *adj* préhistorique.
prejudice *n* (*law*) préjudice, tort *m*; préjugé *m*; * *vt* préjudicier à, faire du tort à.

prejudiced *adj* qui a des préjugés; partial.

prejudicial *adj* préjudiciable.

preliminary *adj* préliminaire.

prelude *n* prélude *m*.

premarital *adj* préconjugal.

premature *adj* ~ly *adv* prématuré(ment).

premeditation *n* préméditation *f*.

premier *n* premier ministre *m*.

première *n* (*thea*) première *f*.

premise *n* prémisse *f*.

premises *npl* locaux *mpl*.

premium *n* prix *m*; indemnité *f*; prime *f*.

premonition *n* pressentiment *m*, prémonition *f*.

preoccupied *adj* préoccupé; absorbé.

prepaid *adj* port payé.

preparation *n* préparation *f*.

preparatory *adj* préparatoire.

prepare *vt* préparer; * *vi* se préparer.

preponderance *n* prépondérance *f*.

preposition *n* préposition *f*.

preposterous *adj* ridicule, absurde.

prerequisite *n* condition requise *f*.

prerogative *n* prérogative *f*.

prescribe *vt* prescrire.

prescription *n* prescription *f*; ordonnance *f*.

presence *n* présence *f*.

present *n* cadeau *m*; * *adj* présent; actuel; ~ly *adv* actuellement; * *vt* offrir, donner; présenter.

presentable *adj* présentable.

presentation *n* présentation *f*.

present-day *adj* actuel.

presenter *n* présentateur *m* -trice *f*.

presentiment *n* pressentiment *m*, prémonition *f*.

preservation *n* préservation *f*.

preservative *n* préservatif *m*.

preserve *vt* préserver; conserver; faire des conserves de; * *n* conserve *f*; confiture *f*.

preside *vi* présider; diriger.

presidency *n* présidence *f*.

president *n* président *m*.

presidential *adj* présidentiel.

press *vt* appuyer sur; serrer; pressurer; * *vi* se presser; * *n* presse *f*; pressoir *m*; pression *f*.

press agency *n* agence de presse *f*.

press conference *n* conférence de presse *f*.

pressing *adj* pressant; urgent; ~ly *adv* de manière pressante; d'urgence.

pressure *n* pression *f*.

pressure cooker *n* autocuiseur *m*.

pressure group *n* groupe de pression *m*.

pressurised *adj* pressurisé.

prestige *n* prestige *m*.

presumable *adj* vraisemblable.

presumably *adv* vraisemblablement.

presume *vt* présumer, supposer.

presumption *n* présomption *f*.

presumptuous *adj* présomptueux.

presuppose *vt* présupposer.

pretence *n* prétexte *m*; simulation *f*; prétention *f*.

pretend *vi* prétendre; faire semblant.

pretender *n* prétendant *m*.

pretension *n* prétention *f*.

pretentious *adj* prétentieux.

preterite *n* prétérit *m*.

pretext *n* prétexte *m*.

pretty *adj* joli, mignon; * *adv* assez; plutôt.

prevail *vi* prévaloir; prédominer.

prevailing *adj* dominant.

prevalent *adj* prédominant.

prevent *vt* prévenir; empêcher; éviter.

prevention *n* prévention *f*.

preventive *adj* préventif.

preview *n* avant-première *f*.

previous *adj* précédent; antérieur; ~ly *adv* auparavant.

prewar *adj* d'avant-guerre.

prey *n* proie *f*.

price *n* prix *m*.

priceless *adj* inappréciable.

price list *n* tarif *m*.

prick *vt* piquer; exciter; * *n* piqûre *f*; pointe *f*.

prickle *n* picotement *m*; épine *f*.

prickly *adj* épineux.

pride *n* orgueil *m*; vanité *f*; fierté *f*.

priest *n* prêtre *m*.

priestess *n* prêtresse *f*.

priesthood *n* sacerdoce *m*, prêtrise *f*.

priestly *adj* sacerdotal.

priggish *adj* affecté, bégueule.

prim *adj* prude, affecté.

primacy *n* primauté *f*.

primarily *adv* principalement, surtout.

primary *adj* primaire; principal, premier.

primate *n* primate *m*.

prime *n* (*fig*) fleur *f*; commencement *m*; * *adj* premier; principal; excellent; * *vt* amorcer.

prime minister *n* premier ministre *m*.

primeval *adj* primitif.

priming *n* amorçage *m*.

primitive *adj* primitif; ~ly *adv* primitivement.

primrose *n* (*bot*) primevère *f*.

prince *n* prince *m*.

princess *n* princesse *f*.

principal *adj* ~ly *adv* principal(ement); * *n* principal *m*.

principality *n* principauté *f*.

principle *n* principe *m*.

print *vt* imprimer; * *n* impression *f*; estampe *f*; caractères imprimés *mpl*; **out of** ~ épuisé (livres).

printed matter *n* imprimés *mpl*.

printer *n* imprimeur *m*; imprimante *f*.

printing *n* impression *f*.

prior *adj* antérieur, précédent; * *n* prieur *m*.

priority *n* priorité *f*.

priory *n* prieuré *m*.

prise *vt*: **to** ~ **open** ouvrir par la force, forcer.

prism *n* prisme *m*.

prison *n* prison *f*.

prisoner *n* prisonnier *m* -ière *f*.

pristine *adj* d'origine; intact.

privacy *n* intimité *f*.

private *adj* privé; secret; particulier; ~ **soldier** *n* simple soldat *m*; ~ly *adv* en privé.

private eye *n* détective privé *m*.

privet *n* troène *m*.

privilege *n* privilège *m*.

prize *n* prix *m*; * *vt* apprécier, évaluer.

prize-giving *n* distribution des prix *f*.

prizewinner *n* gagnant *m* -e *f*.

pro *prep* pour.

probability *n* probabilité *f*; vraisemblance *f*.

probable *adj* probable, vraisemblable; ~bly *adv* probablement.

probation *n* essai *m*; probation *f*.

probationary *adj* d'essai.

probe *n* sonde *f*; enquête *f*; * *vt* sonder; * *vi* faire des recherches.

problem *n* problème *m*.

problematical *adj* ~ly *adv* problématique(ment).

procedure *n* procédure *f*.

proceed *vi* procéder; provenir; poursuivre; ~**s** *npl* produit *m*; montant *m*; **gross** ~**s** bénéfices bruts *mpl*; **net** ~**s** bénéfices nets *mpl*.

proceedings *n* procédure *f*; procédé *m*; procès *m*.

process *n* processus *m*; procédé *m*.

procession *n* procession *f*.

proclaim *vt* proclamer; promulguer.

proclamation *n* proclamation *f*; décret *m*.

procrastinate *vt* différer, retarder.

proctor *n* censeur *m*.

procure *vt* procurer.

procurement *n* obtention *f*.

prod *vt* pousser.

prodigal *adj* prodigue.

prodigious *adj* prodigieux; ~ly *adv* prodigieusement.

prodigy *n* prodige *m*.

produce *vt* produire; créer; fabriquer; * *n* produit *m*.

produce dealer *n* revendeur *m* -euse *f*.

producer *n* producteur *m* -trice *f*.

product *n* produit *m*; œuvre *f*; fruit *m*.

production *n* production *f*; produit *m*.

production line *n* chaîne *f* de fabrication.

productive *adj* productif.

productivity *n* productivité *f*.

profane *adj* profane.

profess *vt* professer; exercer; déclarer.

profession *n* profession *f*.

professional *adj* professionnel.

professor *n* professeur *m*.

proficiency *n* capacité *f*.

proficient *adj* compétent.

profile *n* profil *m*.

profit *n* bénéfice, profit *m*; avantage *m*; * *vi* profiter (de).

profitability *n* rentabilité *f*.

profitable *adj* profitable, avantageux.

profiteering *n* exploitation *f*, mercantilisme *m*.

profound *adj* ~ly *adv* profond-(ément).

profuse *adj* profus; prodigue; ~ly *adv* à profusion.

program(me) *n* programme *m*.

programming *n* programmation *f*.

programmer *n* programmeur *m* -euse *f*.

progress *n* progrès *m*; cours *m*; * *vi* progresser.

progression *n* progression *f*; avance *f*.

progressive *adj* progressif; ~ly *adv* progressivement.

prohibit *vt* prohiber; défendre.

prohibition *n* prohibition *f*.

project *vt* projeter; * *n* projet *m*.

projectile *n* projectile *m*.

projection *n* projection *f*.

projector *n* projecteur *m*.

proletarian *adj* prolétaire.

proletariat *n* prolétariat *m*.

prolific *adj* prolifique, fécond.

prolix *adj* prolixe.

prologue *n* prologue *m*.

prolong *vt* prolonger.

prom *n* bal *m*; concert-promenade *m*.

promenade *n* promenade *f*.

prominence *n* proéminence *f*; éminence *f*.

prominent *adj* proéminent.

promiscuous *adj* immoral, débauché.

promise *n* promesse *f*; * *vt* promettre.

promising *adj* prometteur.

promontory *n* promontoire *m*.

promote *vt* promouvoir.

promoter *n* promoteur *m*.

promotion *n* promotion *f*.

prompt *adj* ~ly *adv* prompt-(ement); * *vt* suggérer; inciter; souffler (au théâtre).

prompter *n* souffleur *m* -euse *f*.

prone *adj* enclin (à).

prong *n* dent *f* (fourchette).

pronoun *n* pronom *m*.

pronounce *vt* prononcer; déclarer.

pronounced *adj* marqué, prononcé.

pronouncement *n* déclaration *f*.

pronunciation *n* prononciation *f*.

proof *n* preuve *f*; * *adj* imperméable; résistant.

prop *vt* soutenir; * *n* appui, soutien *m*; tuteur *m*.

propaganda *n* propagande *f*.

propel *vt* propulser.

propeller *n* hélice *f*.

propensity *n* propension, tendance *f*.

proper *adj* propre; convenable; exact; approprié; ~ly *adv* convenablement; correctement.

property *n* propriété *f*.

prophecy *n* prophétie *f*.

prophesy *vt* prophétiser, prédire.

prophet *n* prophète *m*.

prophetic *adj* prophétique.

proportion *n* proportion *f*; symétrie *f*.

proportional *adj* proportionnel.

proportionate *adj* proportionné.

proposal *n* proposition *f*; offre *f*.

propose *vt* proposer.

proposition *n* proposition *f*.

proprietor *n* propriétaire *mf*.

propriety *n* propriété *f*.

pro rata *adv* au prorata.

prosaic *adj* prosaïque.

prose *n* prose *f*.

prosecute *vt* poursuivre en justice.

prosecution *n* poursuites *fpl*; accusation *f*.

prosecutor *n* (*law*) procureur *m*.

prospect *n* perspective *f*; espoir *m*; * *vt vi* prospecter.

prospecting *n* prospection *f*.

prospective *adj* probable; futur.

prospector *n* prospecteur *m* -trice *f*.

prospectus *n* prospectus *m*.

prosper *vi* prospérer.

prosperity *n* prospérité *f*.

prosperous *adj* prospère.

prostitute *n* prostituée *f*.

prostitution *n* prostitution *f*.

prostrate *adj* prostré.

protagonist *n* protagoniste *mf*.

protect *vt* protéger; abriter.

protection *n* protection *f*.

protective *adj* protecteur.

protector *n* protecteur *m* -trice *f*.

protégé *n* protégé *m* -e *f*.

protein *n* protéine *f*.

protest *vi* protester; * *n* protestation *f*.

Protestant *n* protestant *m* -e *f*.

protester *n* manifestant *m* -e *f*; protestataire *mf*.

protocol *n* protocole *m*.

prototype *n* prototype *m*.

protracted *adj* prolongé.

protrude *vi* déborder, ressortir.

proud *adj* fier, orgueilleux; ~ly *adv* fièrement.

prove *vt* prouver; justifier; * *vi* s'avérer; se révéler.

proverb *n* proverbe *m*.

proverbial *adj* ~ly *adv* proverbial-(ement).

provide *vt* fournir; ~ for pourvoir aux besoins de; prévoir.

provided *conj*: ~ that pourvu que.

providence *n* providence *f*.

province *n* province *f*; compétence *f*.

provincial *adj n* provincial *m* -e *f*.

provision *n* provision *f*; disposition *f*.

provisional *adj* ~ly *adv* provisoire-(ment).

proviso *n* stipulation *f*.

provocation *n* provocation *f*.

provocative *adj* provocateur.

provoke *vt* provoquer.

prow *n* (*mar*) proue *f*.

prowess *n* prouesse *f*.

prowl *vi* rôder.

prowler *n* rôdeur *m* -euse *f*.

proximity *n* proximité *f*.

proxy *n* procuration *f*; délégué *m* -e *f*.

prudence *n* prudence *f*.

prudent *adj* prudent, circonspect; ~ly *adv* prudemment.

prudish *adj* prude.

prune *vt* tailler; * *n* pruneau *m*.

prussic acid *n* acide prussique *m*.

pry *vi* espionner; ~ **open** *vt* (US) forcer.

psalm *n* psaume *m*.

pseudonym *n* pseudonyme *m*.

psyche *n* psyché *f*.

psychiatric *adj* psychiatrique.

psychiatrist *n* psychiatre *mf*.

psychiatry *n* psychiatrie *f*.

psychic *adj* psychique.

psychoanalysis *n* psychanalyse *f*.

psychoanalyst *n* psychanaliste *mf*.

psychological *adj* psychologique.

psychologist *n* psychologue *mf*.

psychology *n* psychologie *f*.

puberty *n* puberté *f*.

public *adj* public; commun; ~**ly** *adv* publiquement; * *n* public *m*.

public address system *n* sonorisation *f*.

publican *n* patron(ne) de pub *m(f)*.

publication *n* publication *f*; édition *f*.

publicise *vt* faire de la publicité pour.

publicity *n* publicité *f*.

public opinion *n* opinion publique *f*.

public school *n* école privée *f*.

publish *vt* publier.

publisher *n* éditeur *m* -trice *f*.

publishing *n* édition *f*.

pucker *vt* plisser.

pudding *n* pudding *m*; dessert *m*.

puddle *n* flaque d'eau *f*.

puerile *adj* puéril.

puff *n* souffle *m*; bouffée *f*; * *vt* souffler; dégager; * *vi* souffler; bouffer.

puff pastry *n* pâte feuilletée *f*.

puffy *adj* bouffi, gonflé.

pull *vt* tirer; arracher; ~ **down** faire descendre; abattre; ~ **in** *vi* s'arrêter; entrer en gare; ~ **off** enlever; ~ **out** *vi* partir; * *vt* arra-

cher; ~ **through** *vi* s'en sortir; se remettre; ~ **up** *vi* s'arrêter; * *vt* arracher; arrêter; * *n* tirage *m*; secousse *f*.

pulley *n* poulie *f*.

pulp *n* pulpe *f*.

pulpit *n* chaire *f*.

pulsate *vi* palpiter.

pulse *n* pouls *m*; légumes *mpl* secs.

pulverise *vt* pulvériser.

pumice *n* pierre ponce *f*.

pummel *vt* marteler.

pump *n* pompe *f*; * *vt* pomper; puiser.

pumpkin *n* citrouille *f*.

pun *n* jeu de mots *m*; * *vi* faire des jeux de mots.

punch *n* coup de poing *m*; poinçon *m*; punch *m*; * *vt* cogner; perforer; poinçonner.

punctual *adj* ponctuel, exact; ~**ly** *adv* ponctuellement.

punctuate *vt* ponctuer.

punctuation *n* ponctuation *f*.

pundit *n* expert *m*.

pungent *adj* piquant, âcre; mordant.

punish *vt* punir.

punishment *n* châtiment *m*, punition *f*; peine *f*.

punk *n* punk *mf*; minable *mf*; ~ **(music)** punk *m*.

punt *n* bateau plat *m*.

puny *adj* chétif, maigrelet.

pup, puppy *n* chiot *m*; * *vi* avoir des chiots, mettre bas.

pupil *n* élève *mf*; pupille *mf*.

puppet *n* marionnette *f*.

purchase *vt* acheter; * *n* achat *m*; acquisition *f*.

purchaser *n* acheteur *m* -euse *f*.

pure *adj* pur; ~**ly** *adv* purement.

purée *n* purée *f*.

purge *vt* purger.

purification *n* purification *f*.

purify *vt* purifier.

purist *n* puriste *mf*.

puritan *n* puritain *m* -e *f*.

purity *n* pureté *f*.

purl *n* maille à l'envers *f*.

purple *adj n* pourpre, violet *m*.

purport *vt*: **to ~ to** prétendre.

purpose *n* intention *f*; but, dessein *m*; **to the ~** à propos; **to no ~** en vain; **on ~** exprès, à dessein.

purposeful *adj* résolu.

purr *vi* ronronner.

purse *n* sac à main *m*; porte-monnaie *m invar*.

purser *n* commissaire *m* de bord.

pursue *vi* poursuivre; suivre.

pursuit *n* poursuite *f*; occupation *f*.

purveyor *n* fournisseur *m* -euse *f*.

push *vt* pousser; presser; ~ **aside** écarter; ~ **off** *vi* (sl) se casser; ~ **on** *vi* continuer; * *n* poussée *f*; impulsion *f*; effort *m*; énergie *f*.

pusher *n* trafiquant de drogues *m*.

push-up *n* (gymn) pompe *f*.

put *vt* mettre, poser; proposer; obliger; ~ **away** ranger; ~ **down** poser par terre; rabaisser; attribuer; ~ **forward** avancer; ~ **off** remettre; décourager; ~ **on** mettre; allumer; prendre; affecter; ~ **out** éteindre; faire sortir; déranger; ~ **up** lever; augmenter; loger.

putrid *adj* putride.

putt *n* putt *m*;* *vt vi* putter.

putty *n* mastic *m*.

puzzle *n* énigme *f*; casse-tête *m invar*.

puzzling *adj* étrange, mystérieux.

pyjamas *npl* pyjama *m*.

pylon *n* pylône *m*.

pyramid *n* pyramide *f*.

python *n* python *m*.

Q

quack *vi* cancaner; * *n* canard *m*; (*sl*) charlatan *m*.

quadrangle *n* quadrilatère *m*.

quadrant *n* quadrant *m*.

quadrilateral *adj* quadrilatéral.

quadruped *n* quadrupède *m*.

quadruple *adj* quadruple.

quadruplet *n* quadruplé *m* -e *f*.

quagmire *n* marécage *m*.

quail *n* caille *f*.

quaint *adj* désuet; bizarre.

quake *vi* trembler.

Quaker *n* quaker *m*.

qualification *n* qualification *f*; diplôme *m*.

qualified *adj* qualifié; diplômé.

qualify *vt* qualifier; modérer; * *vi* se qualifier.

quality *n* qualité *f*.

qualm *n* scrupule *m*.

quandary *n* incertitude *f*, doute *m*.

quantitative *adj* quantitatif.

quantity *n* quantité *f*.

quarantine *n* quarantaine *f*.

quarrel *n* dispute, querelle *f*; * *vi* se disputer, se quereller.

quarrelsome *adj* querelleur.

quarry *n* carrière *f*.

quarter *n* quart *m*; **a ~ of an hour** un quart d'heure; * *vt* diviser en quatre.

quarterly *adj* trimestriel; * *adv* tous les trimestres.

quartermaster *n* (*mil*) intendant *m*.

quartet *n* (*mus*) quartette *m*; quatuor *m*.

quartz *n* (*min*) quartz *m*.

quash *vt* écraser; annuler.

quay *n* quai *m*.

queasy *adj* qui a des nausées; écœurant.

queen *n* reine *f*; dame *f* (cartes).

queer *adj* extrange; (*sl*) pédale *f*.

quell *vt* étouffer; apaiser.

quench *vt* assouvir; éteindre.

query *n* question *f*; * *vt* demander.

quest *n* recherche *f*.

question *n* question *f*; sujet *m*; doute *m*; * *vt* douter de; mettre en question; questionner.

questionable *adj* discutable; douteux.

questioner *n* interrogateur *m*.

question mark *n* point d'interrogation *m*.

questionnaire *n* questionnaire *m*.

quibble *vi* chicaner.

quick *adj* rapide; vif; prompt; **~ly** *adv* rapidement, vite.

quicken *vt* presser; accélérer; * *vi* s'accélérer.

quicksand *n* sables mouvants *mpl*.

quicksilver *n* mercure *m*.

quick-witted *adj* à l'esprit vif.

quiet *adj* calme; silencieux; **~ly** *adv* calmement.

quietness *n* calme *m*, tranquillité *f*; silence *m*.

quinine *n* quinine *f*.

quintet *n* (*mus*) quintette *m*.

quintuple *adj* quintuple.

quintuplet *n* quintuplé *m* -e *f*.

quip *n* sarcasme *m*; * *vt* railler.

quirk *n* particularité *f*.

quit *vt* arrêter de; quitter; * *vi* abandonner; démissionner; * *adj* quitte.

quite *adv* assez; complètement, absolument.

quits *adj* quitte.

quiver *vi* trembler.

quixotic *adj* donquichottesque.

quiz *n* concours *m*; examen *m*; * *vt* interroger.

quizzical *adj* railleur.

quota *n* quota *m*.

quotation *n* citation *f*.

quotation marks *npl* guillemets *mpl*.

quote *vt* citer.

quotient *n* quotient *m*.

R

rabbi *n* rabbi, rabbin *m*.

rabbit *n* lapin *m*.

rabbit hutch *n* clapier *m*.

rabble *n* cohue *f*.

rabid *adj* forcené, enragé.

rabies *n* rage *f*.

race *n* course *f*; race *f*; * *vt* faire une course avec; * *vi* courir; faire une course; aller très vite; foncer.

racer *n* cheval de course *m*.

racial *adj* racial; ~**ist** *adj n* raciste *mf*.

raciness *n* vivacité *f*.

racing *n* courses *fpl*.

rack *n* casier *m*; étagère *f*; * *vt* soumettre au supplice du chevalet; tourmenter.

racket *n* vacarme *m*; raquette *f*.

rack-rent *n* loyer démesuré *m*.

racy *adj* piquant, plein de verve.

radiance *n* rayonnement *m*, éclat *m*.

radiant *adj* rayonnant, radieux.

radiate *vt vi* rayonner, irradier.

radiation *n* irradiation *f*.

radiator *n* radiateur *m*.

radical(ly) *adj* (*adv*) radical(ement).

radicalism *n* radicalisme *m*.

radio *n* radio *f*.

radioactive *adj* radioactif.

radish *n* radis *m*.

radius *n* radius *m*.

raffle *n* tombola *f*; * *vt* mettre en tombola.

raft *n* radeau, train de flottage *m*.

rafter *n* chevron *m*.

rag *n* lambeau *m*, loque *f*.

ragamuffin *n* va-nu-pieds *m invar*; galopin *m*.

rage *n* rage *f*; fureur *f*; * *vi* être furieux; faire rage.

ragged *adj* déguenillé.

raging *adj* furieux, déchaîné, enragé.

ragman, ~ picker *n* chiffonnier *m*.

raid *n* raid *m*; * *vt* faire un raid sur.

raider *n* raider *m*, pillard *m*.

rail *n* rambarde *f*, garde-fou *m*; (*rail*) rail, chemin de fer *m*; * *vt* entourer d'une barrière.

raillery *n* taquinerie *f*.

railroad, railway *n* chemin de fer *m*.

raiment *n* vêtements *mpl*.

rain *n* pluie *f*; * *vi* pleuvoir.

rainbow *n* arc-en-ciel *m*.

rainwater *n* eau de pluie *f*.

rainy *adj* pluvieux.

raise *vt* lever, soulever; ériger, édifier; élever.

raisin *n* raisin sec *m*.

rake *n* râteau *m*; libertin *m*; * *vt* ratisser.

rakish *adj* libertin, débauché.

rally *vt* (*mil*) rallier; * *vi* se rallier.

ram *n* bélier *m*; navire bélier *m*; * *vt* enfoncer.

ramble *vi* errer; faire une randonnée; * *n* excursion à pied, randonnée *f*.

rambler *n* excursionniste *mf*.

ramification *n* ramification *f*.

ramify *vi* se ramifier.

ramp *n* rampe *f*.

rampant *adj* exubérant.

rampart *n* terre-plein *m*; (*mil*) rempart *m*.

ramrod *n* baguette *f*; refouloir *m*.

ramshackle *adj* délabré.

ranch *n* ranch *m*.

rancid *adj* rance.

rancour *n* rancœur *f*.

random *adj* fortuit, fait au hasard; **at ~** au hasard.

range *vt* ranger, classer; * *vi* s'étendre; * *n* rangée *f*; ordre *m*; portée *f*; chaîne *f*; champ de tir *m*; fourneau de cuisine *m*.

ranger *n* garde forestier *m*.

rank *adj* exubérant; fétide; flagrant; * *n* rang *m*, classe *f*, grade *m*.

rankle *vi* rester sur le cœur.

rankness *n* exubérance *f*; odeur rance *f*.

ransack *vt* saccager, piller.

ransom *n* rançon *f*.

rant *vi* déclamer.

rap *vi* donner un coup sec; * *n* petit coup sec *m*.

rapacious *adj* rapace; ~**ly** *adv* avec rapacité.

rapacity *n* rapacité *f*.

rape *n* viol *m*; rapt *m*; (*bot*) colza *m*; * *vt* violer.

rapid *adj* ~**ly** *adv* rapide(ment).

rapidity *n* rapidité *f*.

rapier *n* rapière *f*.

rapist *n* violeur *m*.

rapt *adj* extasié; absorbé.

rapture *n* ravissement *m*; extase *f*.

rapturous *adj* de ravissement.

rare *adj* ~**ly** *adv* rare(ment).

rarity *n* rareté *f*.

rascal *n* vaurien *m*.

rash *adj* imprudent, téméraire; ~**ly** *adv* sans réfléchir; * *n* vague *f*; éruption (cutanée) *f*.

rashness *n* imprudence *f*.

rasp *n* râpe *f*; * *vt* râper.

raspberry *n* framboise *f*; ~ **bush** framboisier *m*.

rat *n* rat *m*.

rate *n* taux, prix, cours *m*; classe *f*; vitesse *f*; * *vt* estimer, évaluer.

rather *adv* plutôt; quelque peu.

ratification *n* ratification *f*.

ratify *vt* ratifier.

rating *n* estimation *f*; classement *m*; indice *m*.

ratio *n* rapport *m*.

ration *n* ration *f*; (*mil*) vivres *mpl*.

rational *adj* rationnel; raisonnable; ~**ly** *adv* rationnellement.

rationality *n* rationalité *f*.

rattan *n* (*bot*) rotin *m*.

rattle *vi* s'entrechoquer; cliqueter * *vt* faire s'entrechoquer; * *n* fracas *m*; cliquetis *m*.

rattlesnake *n* serpent à sonnettes *m*.

ravage *vt* ravager, piller; dévaster; * *n* ravage *m*.

rave *vi* délirer.

raven *n* corbeau *m*.

ravenous *adj* ~**ly** *adv* vorace(ment).

ravine *n* ravin *m*.

ravish *vt* enchanter; ravir.

ravishing *adj* enchanteur.

raw *adj* cru; brut; novice.

rawboned *adj* décharné; maigre.

rawness *n* crudité *f*; inexpérience *f*.

ray *n* rayon *m*; (*fish*) raie *f*.

raze *vt* raser.

razor *n* rasoir *m*.

reach *vt* atteindre; arriver à; * *vi* s'étendre, porter; * *n* portée *f*.

react *vi* réagir.

reaction *n* réaction *f*.

read *vt vi* lire.

readable *adj* lisible.

reader *n* lecteur *m* -trice *f*.

readily *adv* volontiers; facilement.

readiness *n* bonne volonté *f*; empressement *m*.

reading *n* lecture *f*.

reading room *n* salle de lecture *f*.

readjust *vt* réajuster, réadapter.

ready *adj* prêt; enclin; disposé.

real *adj* réel, vrai; **~ly** *adv* vraiment.

realisation *n* réalisation *f*.

realise *vt* se rendre compte de; réaliser.

reality *n* réalité *f*.

realm *n* royaume *m*.

ream *n* rame *f* de papier.

reap *vt* moissonner.

reaper *n* moissonneuse *f* (machine).

reappear *vi* réapparaître.

rear *n* arrière *m*; derrière *m*; * *vt* élever, dresser.

rearmament *n* réarmement *m*.

reason *n* raison *f*; cause *f*; * *vt vi* raisonner.

reasonable *adj* raisonnable.

reasonableness *n* bon sens *m*, sagesse *f*.

reasonably *adv* raisonnablement.

reasoning *n* raisonnement *m*.

reassure *vt* rassurer; (*com*) réassurer.

rebel *n* rebelle *mf*; * *vi* se rebeller.

rebellion *n* rébellion *f*.

rebellious *adj* rebelle.

rebound *vi* rebondir.

rebuff *n* rebuffade *f*; * *vt* repousser.

rebuild *vt* reconstruire.

rebuke *vt* réprimander; * *n* réprimande *f*.

rebut *vt* réfuter.

recalcitrant *adj* récalcitrant.

recall *vt* (se) rappeler; retirer; * *n* retrait *m*.

recant *vt* rétracter, désavouer.

recantation *n* rétractation *f*.

recapitulate *vt vi* récapituler.

recapitulation *n* récapitulation *f*.

recapture *n* reprise *f*.

recede *vi* reculer.

receipt *n* reçu *m*; réception *f*; **~s** *npl* recettes *fpl*.

receivable *adj* recevable.

receive *vt* recevoir; accueillir.

recent *adj* récent, neuf; **~ly** *adv* récemment.

receptacle *n* récipient *m*.

reception *n* réception *f*.

recess *n* (*law*) vacance *f*; renfoncement *m*; recoin *m*.

recession *n* recul *m*; (*com*) récession *f*.

recipe *n* recette *f*.

recipient *n* destinataire *mf*.

reciprocal *adj* **~ly** *adv* réciproque(ment).

reciprocate *vi* rendre la pareille.

reciprocity *n* réciprocité *f*.

recital *n* récit *m*; récital *m*.

recite *vt* réciter; exposer, énumérer.

reckless *adj* téméraire; **~ly** *adv* imprudemment.

reckon *vt* compter, calculer; * *vi* calculer.

reckoning *n* compte *m*; calcul *m*.

reclaim *vt* assainir; récupérer.

reclaimable *adj* remboursable; récupérable.

recline *vt* reposer; * *vi* être allongé.

recluse *n* reclus *m* -e *f*.

recognise *vt* reconnaître.

recognition *n* reconnaissance *f*.

recoil *vi* reculer.

recollect *vt* se rappeler, se souvenir de.

recollection *n* souvenir *m*.

recommence *vt* recommencer.

recommend *vt* recommander.

recommendation *n* recommandation *f*.

recompense *n* récompense *f*; * *vt* récompenser.

reconcilable *adj* conciliable.

reconcile *vt* réconcilier.

reconciliation *n* réconciliation *f*.

recondite *adj* abstrus, obscur.

reconnoitre *vt* (*mil*) reconnaître.

reconsider *vt* reconsidérer.

reconstruct *vt* reconstruire.

record *vt* enregistrer; consigner par écrit; * *n* rapport *m*, registre *m*; disque *m*; record *m*; **~s** *pl* archives *fpl*.

recorder *n* magnétophone *m*, archiviste *mf*; (*mus*) flûte à bec *f*.

recount *vt* raconter.

recourse *n* recours *m*.

recover *vt* retrouver; reprendre; récupérer; * *vi* se remettre, se rétablir.

recoverable *adj* récupérable.

recovery *n* guérison *f*; reprise *f*.

recreation *n* détente *f*; récréation *f*.

recriminate *vi* récriminer.

recrimination *n* récrimination *f*.

recruit *vt* recruter; * *n* (*mil*) recrue *f*.

recruiting *n* recrutement *m*.

rectangle *n* rectangle *m*.

rectangular *adj* rectangulaire.

rectification *n* rectification *f*.

rectify *vt* rectifier.

rectilinear *adj* rectiligne.

rectitude *n* rectitude *f*.

rector *n* pasteur *m*.

recumbent *adj* couché, étendu.

recur *vi* se reproduire.

recurrence *n* répétition *f*.

recurrent *adj* répétitif.

red *adj* rouge; * *n* rouge *m*.

redden *vt vi* rougir.

reddish *adj* rougeâtre.

redeem *vt* racheter, rembourser.

redeemable *adj* rachetable.

Redeemer *n* Rédempteur *m*.

redemption *n* rachat *m*.

redeploy *vt* réaffecter.

redhanded *adj*: **to catch sb ~** prendre quelqu'un la main dans le sac.

redhot *adj* brûlant, ardent.

red-letter day *n* jour à marquer d'une pierre blanche *m*.

redness *n* rougeur, rousseur *f*.

redolent *adj* parfumé, odorant.

redouble *vt vi* redoubler.

redress *vt* réparer; corriger; redresser; * *n* réparation *f*, redressement *m*.

redskin *n* Peau-Rouge *mf*.

red tape *n* (*fig*) paperasserie *f*.

reduce *vt* réduire; diminuer; abaisser.

reducible *adj* réductible.

reduction *n* réduction *f*; baisse *f*.

redundancy *n* licenciement *m*.

redundant *adj* superflu; licencié.

reed *n* roseau *m*.

reedy *adj* couvert de roseaux.

reef *n* (*mar*) ris *m*; récif *m*.

reek *n* puanteur *f*; * *vi* empester; puer.

reel *n* bobine *f*; bande *f*; dévidoir *m*; * *vi* chanceler.

re-election *n* réélection *f*.

re-engage *vt* rengager.

re-enter *vt* rentrer.

re-establish *vt* rétablir; réhabiliter.

re-establishment *n* rétablissement *m*; restauration *f*.

refectory *n* réfectoire *m*.

refer *vt* soumettre, renvoyer; se référer à; * *vi* se référer.

referee *n* arbitre *m*.

reference *n* référence, allusion *f*.

refine *vt* raffiner, affiner.

refinement *n* raffinement *m*; raffinerie *f*; culture *f*.

refinery *n* raffinerie *f*.

refit *vt* réparer (*also mar*).

reflect *vt* réfléchir, refléter; * *vi* réfléchir.

reflection *n* réflexion, pensée *f*.

reflector *n* réflecteur *m*; cataphote *m*.

reflex *adj* réflexe.

reform *vt* réformer; * *vi* se réformer.

reform, reformation *n* réforme *f*.

reformer *n* réformateur *m* -trice *f*.

reformist *n* réformiste *mf*.

refract *vt* réfracter.

refraction *n* réfraction *f*.

refrain *vi*: **to ~ from sth** s'abstenir de qch.

refresh *vt* rafraîchir.

refreshment *n* rafraîchissement *m*.

refrigerator *n* glacière *f*; réfrigérateur *m*.

refuel *vi* se ravitailler (en carburant).

refuge *n* refuge, asile *m*.

refugee *n* réfugié *m* -e *f*.

refund *vt* rembourser; * *n* remboursement *m*.

refurbish *vt* rénover.

refusal *n* refus *m*.

refuse *vt* refuser; * *n* déchets *mpl*.

refute *vt* réfuter.

regain *vt* recouvrer, reprendre.

regal *adj* royal.

regale *vt* régaler.

regalia *n* insignes *mpl*.

regard *vt* considérer; * *n* considération *f*; respect *m*.

regarding *pr* en ce qui concerne.

regardless *adv* quand même, malgré tout.

regatta *n* régate *f*.

regency *n* régence *f*.

regenerate *vt* régénérer; * *adj* régénéré.

regeneration *n* régénération *f*.

regent *n* régent *m*.

regime *n* régime *m*.

regiment *n* régiment *m*.

region *n* région *f*.

register *n* registre *m*; * *vt* enregistrer; **~ed letter** *n* lettre recommandée *f*.

registrar *n* officier d'état civil *m*.

registration *n* enregistrement *m*.

registry *n* enregistrement *m*.

regressive *adj* régressif.

regret *n* regret *m* * *vt* regretter.

regretful *adj* plein de regrets.

regular *adj* régulier; ordinaire; **~ly** *adv* régulièrement; * *n* habitué *m* -e *f*.

regularity *n* régularité *f*.

regulate *vt* régler, réglementer.

regulation *n* règlement *m*; réglementation *f*.

regulator *n* régulateur *m*.

rehabilitate *vt* réhabiliter.

rehabilitation *n* réhabilitation *f*.

rehearsal *n* répétition *f*.

rehearse *vt* répéter; raconter.

reign *n* règne *m*; * *vi* régner.

reimburse *vt* rembourser.

reimbursement *n* remboursement *m*.

rein *n* rêne *f*; * *vt* **~ in** (*fig*) contenir.

reindeer *n* renne *m*.

reinforce *vt* renforcer.

reinstate *vt* réintégrer.

reinsure *vt* (*com*) réassurer.

reissue *n* réédition *f*.

reiterate *vt* réitérer.

reiteration *n* réitération, répétition *f*.

reject *vt* rejeter.

rejection *n* refus, rejet *m*.

rejoice *vt* réjouir; * *vi* se réjouir.

rejoicing *n* réjouissance *f*.

relapse *vi* retomber; * *n* rechute *f*.

relate *vt* relater; rapprocher; * *vi* se rapporter.

related *adj* apparenté.

relation *n* rapport *m*; parent *m*.

relationship *n* lien de parenté *m*; relation *f*; rapport *m*.

relative *adj* relatif; **~ly** *adv* relativement; * *n* parent *m* -e *f*.

relax *vt* relâcher; détendre; * *vi* se relâcher; se détendre.

relaxation *n* relâchement *m*; détente *f*.

relay *n* relais *m*; * *vt* retransmettre.

release *vt* libérer, relâcher; * *n* libération *f*; décharge *f*.

relegate *vt* reléguer.

relegation *n* relégation *f*.

relent *vi* s'adoucir.

relentless *adj* implacable.

relevant *adj* pertinent.

reliable *adj* fiable, digne de confiance.

reliance *n* confiance *f*.

relic *n* relique *f*.

relief *n* soulagement *m*; secours *m*.

relieve *vt* soulager, alléger; secourir.

religion *n* religion *f*.

religious *adj* religieux; **~ly** *adv* religieusement.

relinquish *vt* abandonner, renoncer à.

relish *n* saveur *f*; goût *m*; attrait *m*; * *vt* savourer, se délecter de.

reluctance *n* répugnance *f*.

reluctant *adj* peu disposé.

rely *vi* compter sur, avoir confiance en.

remain *vi* rester, demeurer.

remainder *n* reste, restant *m*.

remains *npl* restes, vestiges *mpl*; dépouille *f*.

remand *vt*: **to ~ in custody** mettre en détention préventive.

remark *n* remarque, observation *f*; * *vt* (faire) remarquer, (faire) observer.

remarkable *adj* remarquable, notable.

remarkably *adv* remarquablement.

remarry *vi* se remarier.

remedial *adj* de rattrapage.

remedy *n* remède, recours *m*; * *vt* remédier à.

remember *vt* se souvenir de; se rappeler.

remembrance *n* mémoire *f*; souvenir *m*.

remind *vt* rappeler.

reminiscence *n* réminiscence *f*.

remiss *adj* négligent.

remission *n* rémission *f*.

remit *vt* remettre, pardonner; * *vi* diminuer.

remittance *n* remise *f*.

remnant *n* reste, restant *m*.

remodel *vt* remodeler.

remonstrate *vi* protester.

remorse *n* remords *m*.

remorseless *adj* implacable.

remote *adj* lointain, éloigné; **~ly** *adv* au loin, de loin.

remoteness *n* éloignement *m*; isolement *m*.

removable *adj* amovible.

removal *n* suppression *f*; déménagement *m*.

remove *vt* enlever; * *vi* déménager.

remunerate *vt* rémunérer.

remuneration *n* rémunération *f*.

render *vt* rendre, remettre; traduire; (*law*) rendre.

rendezvous *n* rendez-vous *m*; point de ralliement *m*.

renegade *n* renégat *m* -e *f*.

renew *vt* renouveler.

renewal *n* renouvellement *m*.

rennet *n* présure *f*.

renounce *vt* renoncer à.

renovate *vt* rénover.

renovation *n* rénovation *f*.

renown *n* renommée *f*; célébrité *f*.

renowned *adj* célèbre, renommé.

rent *n* loyer *m*; location *f*; * *vt* louer.

rental *n* loyer *m*.

renunciation *n* renonciation *f*.

reopen *vt* rouvrir.

reorganisation *n* réorganisation *f*.

reorganise *vt* réorganiser.

repair *vt* réparer; * *n* réparation *f*.

repairable *adj* réparable.

reparation *n* réparation *f*.

repartee *n* repartie, réplique *f*.

repatriate *vt* rapatrier.

repay *vt* rembourser; rendre, récompenser.

repayment *n* remboursement *m*.

repeal *vt* abroger, annuler; * *n* abrogation, annulation *f*.

repeat *vt* répéter.

repeatedly *adv* à plusieurs reprises.

repeater *n* montre à répétition *f*.

repel *vt* repousser, rebuter.

repent *vi* se repentir.

repentance *n* repentir *m*.

repentant *adj* repentant.

repertory *n* répertoire *m*.
repetition *n* répétition, réitération *f*.
replace *vt* replacer; remplacer.
replant *vt* replanter.
replenish *vt* remplir de nouveau.
replete *adj* rempli, rassasié.
reply *n* réponse *f*; * *vi* répondre.
report *vt* rapporter, relater; rendre compte de; * *n* rapport *m*; compte rendu *m*; rumeur *f*.
reporter *n* journaliste *mf*.
repose *vi* (se) reposer; * *n* repos *m*.
repository *n* dépôt *m*.
repossess *vt* reprendre possession de.
reprehend *vt* condamner.
reprehensible *adj* répréhensible.
represent *vt* représenter.
representation *n* représentation *f*.
representative *adj* représentatif; * *n* représentant(e) *m(f)*.
repress *vt* réprimer, contenir.
repression *n* répression *f*.
repressive *adj* répressif.
reprieve *vt* accorder un sursis *ou* un répit à; * *n* sursis *m*.
reprimand *vt* réprimander, blâmer; * *n* blâme *m*; réprimande *f*.
reprint *vt* réimprimer.
reprisal *n* représailles *fpl*.
reproach *n* reproche, opprobre *m*; * *vt* reprocher.
reproachful *adj* réprobateur; ~**ly** *adv* d'un air de reproche.
reproduce *vt* reproduire.
reproduction *n* reproduction *f*.
reptile *n* reptile *m*.
republic *n* république *f*.
republican *adj n* républicain *m* -e *f*.
republicanism *n* républicanisme *m*.
repudiate *vt* renier.
repugnance *n* répugnance f, dégoût *m*.
repugnant *adj* répugnant; ~**ly** *adv* avec répugnance.
repulse *vt* repousser, rejeter; * *n* rebuffade *f*; refus *m*.
repulsion *n* répulsion *f*.
repulsive *adj* répulsif.
reputable *adj* honorable.
reputation *n* réputation *f*.
repute *n* renom *m*.
request *n* demande, requête *f*; * *vt* demander.
require *vt* demander, nécessiter.
requirement *n* besoin *m*; exigence *f*.
requisite *adj* nécessaire, indispensable; * *n* objet(s) nécessaire(s) *m(pl)*.
requisition *n* demande; (*mil*) réquisition *f*.
requite *vt* rembourser.

rescind *vt* annuler, abroger.
rescue *vt* sauver, secourir; * *n* secours *m*, délivrance *f*.
research *vt* faire des/de la recherche(s); * *n* recherche(s) *f(pl)*.
resemblance *n* ressemblance *f*.
resemble *vt* ressembler à.
resent *vt* être contrarié/irrité par.
resentful *adj* plein de ressentiment; amer; ~**ly** *adv* avec ressentiment.
resentment *n* ressentiment *m*.
reservation *n* réserve *f*; réservation *f*.
reserve *vt* réserver; * *n* réserve *f*.
reservedly *adv* avec réserve.
reservoir *n* réservoir *m*.
reside *vi* résider.
residence *n* résidence *f*; séjour *m*.
resident *adj* résidant; * *n* résident *m* -e *f*.
residuary *adj* restant; ~ **legatee** *n* (*law*) légataire universel *m*.
residue *n* reste, résidu *m*.
residuum *n* (*chem*) résidu *m*.
resign *vt* démissionner de, renoncer à, céder; se résigner à; * *vi* démissionner.
resignation *n* démission *f*.
resin *n* résine *f*.
resinous *adj* résineux.
resist *vt* résister, s'opposer.
resistance *n* résistance *f*.
resolute *adj* ~**ly** *adv* résolu(ment).
resolution *n* résolution *f*.
resolve *vt* résoudre; * *vi* (se) résoudre, (se) décider.
resonance *n* résonance *f*.
resonant *adj* résonant.
resort *vi* recourir; * *n* lieu de vacances *m*; recours *m*.
resound *vi* résonner.
resource *n* ressource(s) *f(pl)*; expédient *m*.
respect *n* respect *m*; égard *m*; rapport *m*; ~**s** *pl* respects *mpl*; * *vt* respecter.
respectability *n* respectabilité *f*.
respectable *adj* respectable; considérable; ~**bly** *adv* convenablement.
respectful *adj* respectueux; ~**ly** *adv* respectueusement.
respecting *prep* en ce qui concerne.
respective *adj* respectif; ~**ly** *adv* respectivement.
respirator *n* respirateur *m*.
respiratory *adj* respiratoire.
respite *n* répit *m*; (*law*) sursis *m*; * *vt* repousser, différer.
resplendence *n* resplendissement *m*, splendeur *f*.

resplendent *adj* resplendissant.
respond *vi* répondre; réagir.
respondent *n* (*law*) défendeur *m* -deresse *f*.
response *n* réponse, réaction *f*.
responsibility *n* responsabilité *f*.
responsible *adj* responsable.
responsive *adj* sensible à, réceptif.
rest *n* repos *m*; (*mus*) pause *f*; reste, restant *m*; * *vt* faire/*or* laisser reposer; appuyer; * *vi* se reposer, reposer.
resting place *n* lieu de repos *m*.
restitution *n* restitution *f*.
restive *adj* rétif, récalcitrant; agité.
restless *adj* agité; instable.
restoration *n* restauration *f*.
restorative *adj* fortifiant.
restore *vt* restituer, restaurer.
restrain *vt* retenir, contenir.
restraint *n* contrainte, entrave *f*.
restrict *vt* restreindre, limiter.
restriction *n* restriction *f*.
restrictive *adj* restrictif.
rest room *n* (*US*) toilettes *fpl*.
result *vi* résulter; * *n* résultat *m*.
resume *vt* reprendre.
resurrection *n* résurrection *f*.
resuscitate *vt* réanimer.
retail *vt* vendre au détail, détailler; * *n* vente au détail *f*.
retain *vt* retenir, conserver.
retainer *n* serviteur *m*; ~**s** *pl* arrhes *fpl*; suite *f*.
retake *vt* reprendre.
retaliate *vi* se venger.
retaliation *n* représailles *fpl*.
retardation *n* retard *m*.
retarded *adj* retardé.
retch *vi* avoir des haut-le-cœur.
retention *n* rétention *f*.
retentive *adj* qui retient bien.
reticence *n* réticence *f*.
reticule *n* réticule *m*.
retina *n* rétine *f*.
retire *vt* mettre à la retraite; * *vi* se retirer; prendre sa retraite.
retired *adj* retraité, à la retraite.
retirement *n* isolement *m*; retraite *f*.
retort *vt* rétorquer; * *n* réplique *f*.
retouch *vt* retoucher.
retrace *vt* retracer.
retract *vt* rétracter; retirer.
retrain *vt* recycler.
retraining *n* recyclage *m*.
retreat *n* repli *m*; * *vi* se retirer.
retribution *n* châtiment *m*; récompense *f*.
retrievable *adj* récupérable; réparable.
retrieve *vt* récupérer, recouvrer.
retriever *n* chien d'arrêt *m*.

retrograde *adj* rétrograde.

retrospect, retrospection *n* regard rétrospectif *m*.

retrospective *adj* rétrospectif.

return *vt* rendre; restituer; renvoyer; * *n* retour *m*; renvoi *m*; récompense *f*; revenu *m*; remboursement *m*.

reunion *n* réunion *f*.

reunite *vt* réunir; * *vi* se réunir.

reveal *vt* révéler.

revel *vi* faire la fête.

revelation *n* révélation *f*.

reveller *n* fêtard *m*.

revelry *n* fête *f*.

revenge *vt* venger; * *n* vengeance *f*.

revengeful *adj* vindicatif.

revenue *n* revenu *m*; rente *f*.

reverberate *vt* réverbérer; * *vi* résonner, retentir; se réverbérer.

reverberation *n* répercussion *f*; réverbération *f*.

revere *vt* révérer, vénérer.

reverence *n* vénération *f*; * *vt* révérer.

reverend *adj* révérend; vénérable; * *n* curé *m*.

reverent, reverential *adj* révérenciel, respectueux.

reversal *n* renversement *m*; annulation *f*.

reverse *vt* renverser; annuler; * *vi* faire marche arrière; * *n* inverse *m*; contraire *m*; revers *m*.

reversible *adj* révocable; réversible.

reversion *n* retour *m*; réversion *f*.

revert *vi* revenir; retourner.

review *vt* revoir; (*mil*) passer en revue; * *n* revue *f*; examen *m*.

reviewer *n* critique *m*.

revile *vt* vilipender.

revise *vt* réviser; mettre à jour.

reviser *n* réviseur *m*.

revision *n* révision *f*.

revisit *vt* retourner voir.

revival *n* reprise *f*; renouveau *m*.

revive *vt* ranimer; raviver; * *vi* reprendre connaissance; reprendre.

revocation *n* révocation *f*.

revoke *vt* révoquer, annuler.

revolt *vi* se révolter; * *n* révolte *f*.

revolting *adj* exécrable.

revolution *n* révolution *f*.

revolutionary *adj n* révolutionnaire *mf*.

revolve *vt* (re)tourner; * *vi* tourner.

revolving *adj* tournant.

revue *n* revue *f*.

revulsion *n* écœurement *m*.

reward *n* récompense *f*; * *vt* récompenser.

rhapsody *n* r(h)apsodie *f*.

rhetoric *n* rhétorique *f*.

rhetorical *adj* rhétorique.

rheumatic *adj* rhumatisant.

rheumatism *n* rhumatisme *m*.

rhinoceros *n* rhinocéros *m*.

rhombus *n* rhombe *m*.

rhomboid *n* rhomboïd *m*.

rhubarb *n* rhubarbe *f*.

rhyme *n* rime *f*; vers *mpl*; * *vi* rimer.

rhythm *n* rythme *m*.

rhythmical *adj* rythmique.

rib *n* côte *f*.

ribald *adj* paillard.

ribbon *n* ruban *m*; lambeaux *mpl*.

rice *n* riz *m*.

rich *adj* riche; somptueux; abondant; ~**ly** *adv* richement.

riches *npl* richesse *f*.

richness *n* richesse *f*; abondance *f*.

rickets *n* rachitisme *m*.

rickety *adj* rachitique.

rid *vt* débarrasser; se débarrasser de.

riddance *n*: good ~! bon débarras!

riddle *n* énigme *f*; crible *m*; * *vt* cribler.

ride *vi* monter à cheval; aller en voiture; * *n* promenade à cheval *ou* en voiture *f*.

rider *n* cavalier *m* -ière *f*.

ridge *n* arête, crête *f*; chaîne *f*; * *vt* rider, strier.

ridicule *n* ridicule *m*; raillerie *f*; * *vt* ridiculiser.

ridiculous *adj* ~**ly** *adv* ridicule(ment).

riding *n* équitation *f*; monte *f*.

riding habit *n* tenue d'amazone *f*.

riding school *n* manège *m*.

rife *adj* répandu, abondant.

riffraff *n* racaille *f*.

rifle *vt* dévaliser, piller; strier, rayer; * *n* fusil *m*.

rifleman *n* fusilier *m*.

rig *vt* équiper; truquer; (*mar*) gréer; * *n* gréement *m*; plateforme de forage *f*.

rigging *n* (*mar*) gréement *m*.

right *adj* droit, bien; juste; équitable; ~! bien!, bon!; ~**ly** *adv* bien; correctement; à juste titre; * *n* justice *f*; raison *f*; droit *m*; droite *f*; * *vt* redresser.

righteous *adj* droit, vertueux; ~**ly** *adv* vertueusement.

righteousness *n* droiture *f*; vertu *f*.

rigid *adj* rigide; sévère, strict; ~**ly** *adv* rigidement.

rigidity *n* rigidité *f*; sévérité *f*.

rigmarole *n* galimatias *m*.

rigorous *adj* rigoureux; ~**ly** *adv* rigoureusement.

rigour *n* rigueur *f*; sévérité *f*.

rim *n* bord *m*, monture *f*.

rind *n* peau, écorce *f*.

ring *n* anneau, cercle, rond *m*; bague *f*; tintement *m* de cloche; * *vt* sonner; * *vi* sonner, retentir; ~ **the bell** sonner.

ringer *n* carillonneur *m*.

ringleader *n* meneur *m*.

ringlet *n* anglaise *f*.

ringworm *n* (*med*) teigne *f*.

rink *n* (*also* **ice ~**) patinoire *f*.

rinse *vt* rincer.

riot *n* émeute *f*; * *vi* se livrer à une émeute.

rioter *n* émeutier *m*, -ière *f*.

riotous *adj* séditieux; dissolu; ~**ly** *adv* de façon tapageuse.

rip *vt* déchirer, fendre.

ripe *adj* mûr.

ripen *vt vi* mûrir.

ripeness *n* maturité *f*.

rip-off *n* (*sl*): it's a ~! c'est du vol!

ripple *vt* rider; * *vi* se rider; * *n* ondulation *f*, ride *f*.

rise *vi* se lever; naître; se soulever; monter; provenir de; s'élever; croître; ressusciter; * *n* hausse *f*; augmentation *f*; montée *f*; lever *m*; source *f*.

rising *n* insurrection *f*; levée, clôture *f*.

risk *n* risque, danger *m*; * *vt* risquer.

risky *adj* risqué.

rissole *n* rissole *f*.

rite *n* rite *m*.

ritual *adj n* rituel *m*.

rival *adj* rival; * *n* rival *m* -e *f*; * *vt* rivaliser avec, concurrencer.

rivalry *n* rivalité *f*.

river *n* rivière *f*.

rivet *n* rivet *m*; * *vt* riveter, river.

rivulet *n* petit ruisseau *m*.

roach *n* blatte *f*.

road *n* route *f*.

roadsign *n* panneau de signalisation *m*.

roadstead *n* (*mar*) rade *f*.

roadworks *npl* travaux routiers *mpl*.

roam *vt* parcourir; errer dans; * *vi* errer.

roan *adj* rouan.

roar *vi* hurler, rugir; mugir; * *n* hurlement *m*; rugissement, mugissement *m*; grondement *m*.

roast *vt* rôtir; griller.

roast beef *n* rôti de bœuf *m*.

rob *vt* voler.

robber *n* voleur *m* -euse *f*.

robbery *n* vol *m*.

robe *n* robe (de cérémonie) *f*; peignoir de bain *m*; * *vt* revêtir d'une robe de cérémonie.

robin (redbreast) *n* rouge-gorge *m*.

robust *adj* robuste.

robustness *n* robustesse *f*.

rock *n* roche *f*; rocher *m*; roc *m*; * *vt* bercer; balancer; ébranler; * *vi* (se) balancer.

rock and roll *n* rock (and roll) *m*.

rock crystal *n* cristal de roche *m*.

rocket *n* fusée *f*.

rocking chair *n* fauteuil à bascule *m*.

rock salt *n* sel gemme *m*.

rocky *adj* rocheux.

rod *n* baguette, tringle, canne *f*.

rodent *n* rongeur *m*.

roe *n* chevreuil *m*; œufs *mpl* de poisson.

roebuck *n* chevreuil (mâle) *m*.

rogation *n* rogations *fpl*.

rogue *n* coquin, polisson *m*; gredin *m*.

roguish *adj* coquin.

roll *vt* rouler; étendre; enrouler; * *vi* (se) rouler; * *n* roulement *m*; rouleau *m*; liste *f*; catalogue *m*; liasse *f*; petit pain *m*.

roller *n* rouleau, cylindre *m*.

roller skates *npl* patins à roulettes *mpl*.

rolling pin *n* rouleau à pâtisserie *m*.

Roman Catholic *adj n* catholique *mf*.

romance *n* romance *f*; roman *m*; conte *m*; fable *f*.

romantic *adj* romantique.

romp *vi* jouer bruyamment.

roof *n* toit *m*; voûte *f*; * *vt* couvrir.

roofing *n* toiture *f*.

rook *n* freux *m*; tour *f* (*aux échecs*).

room *n* pièce, salle *f*; place *f*, espace *m*; chambre *f*.

roominess *n* grande envergure *f*.

rooming house *n* pension *f*.

roomy *adj* spacieux.

roost *n* perchoir *m*; * *vi* se percher.

root *n* racine *f*; origine *f*; * *vt vi* ~ out extirper; dénicher.

rooted *adj* enraciné; ancré.

rope *n* corde *f*; cordage *m*; * *vi* attacher.

ropemaker *n* cordier *m*.

rosary *n* rosaire *m*.

rose *n* rose *f*.

rosebed *n* massif de roses *m*.

rosebud *n* bouton de rose *m*.

rosebush *n* rosier *m*.

rosemary *n* (*bot*) romarin *m*.

rosette *n* rosette *f*.

rosé wine *n* (vin) rosé *m*.

rosewood *n* bois de rose *m*.

rosiness *n* couleur rosée *f*.

rosy *adj* rosé.

rot *vi* pourrir; * *n* pourriture *f*.

rotate *vt* faire tourner; * *vi* tourner.

rotation *n* rotation *f*.

rote *n*: by ~ par cœur.

rotten *adj* pourri; corrompu.

rottenness *n* pourriture *f*.

rotund *adj* rond, replet, arrondi.

rouble *n* rouble *m*.

rouge *n* rouge (à joues) *m*.

rough *adj* accidenté, inégal, rugueux; rude, brutal, brusque; houleux; ~ly *adv* rudement.

roughcast *n* crépi *m*.

roughen *vt* rendre rugueux.

roughness *n* rugosité *f*; rudesse, brusquerie *f*; agitation *f*.

round *adj* rond, circulaire; rondelet; franc; * *n* cercle *m*; rond *m*; tour *m*; tournée *f*; partie *f*; ronde *f*; canon *m*; série *f*; * *adv* autour de; environ; ~ly *adv* rondement; franchement; * *vt* contourner; arrondir.

roundabout *adj* détourné, indirect; * *n* rond-point *m*.

roundness *n* rondeur *f*.

rouse *vt* réveiller; exciter.

rout *n* déroute, débâcle *f*; * *vt* mettre en déroute.

route *n* itinéraire *m*; route *f*.

routine *adj* habituel; * *n* routine *f*; numéro *m*.

rove *vi* vagabonder, errer.

rover *n* vagabond *m* -e *f*; pirate *m*.

row *n* querelle *f*; vacarme *m*.

row *n* rangée, file *f*; * *vt* (*mar*) ramer.

rowdy *n* hooligan, voyou *m*.

rower *n* rameur *m* -euse *f*.

royal *adj* royal; princier; ~ly *adv* royalement.

royalist *n* royaliste *mf*.

royalty *n* royauté *f*; droits d'auteur *mpl*; royalties *fpl*; redevance *f*; membres de la famille royale *mpl*.

rub *vt* frotter; irriter; * *n* frottement *m*; (*fig*) ennui *m*; difficulté *f*.

rubber *n* caoutchouc *m*, gomme *f*; préservatif *m*.

rubber band *n* élastique *m*.

rubbish *n* détritus *mpl*; ordures *fpl*; bêtises *fpl*; décombres *mpl*.

rubric *n* rubrique *f*.

ruby *n* rubis *m*.

rucksack *n* sac à dos *m*.

rudder *n* gouvernail *m*.

ruddiness *n* teint vif *m*, rougeur *f*.

ruddy *adj* coloré, rouge.

rude *adj* impoli, rude, brusque; grossier, primitif; ~ly *adv* impoliment, grossièrement.

rudeness *n* impolitesse *f*; rudesse, insolence *f*.

rudiment *n* rudiments *mpl*.

rue *vt* regretter amèrement; * *n* (*bot*) rue *f*.

rueful *adj* triste.

ruffian *n* voyou *m*, brute *f*; * *adj* brutal.

ruffle *vt* ébouriffer, déranger; rider.

rug *n* tapis *m*, carpette *f*.

rugged *adj* accidenté, déchiqueté; rude; robuste.

ruin *n* ruine *f*; perte *f*; ruines *fpl*; * *vt* ruiner; détruire.

ruinous *adj* ruineux.

rule *n* règle *f*; règlement *m*; pouvoir *m*; domination *f*; * *vt* gouverner, dominer; décider, régler, diriger.

ruler *n* dirigeant *m* -e *f*; règle *f*.

rum *n* rhum *m*.

rumble *vi* gronder, tonner.

ruminate *vt* ruminer.

rummage *vi* fouiller.

rumour *n* rumeur *f*; * *vt* faire courir le bruit.

rump *n* croupe *f*.

run *vt* diriger; organiser; faire couler; passer; ~ the risk courir le risque; * *vi* courir; fuir, se sauver; filer; fonctionner; aller; couler; concourir; * *n* course, compétition *f*; parcours *m*; cours *m*; série *f*; mode *f*; ruée *f*.

runaway *n* fugitif *m* -ive *f*, fuyard *m*.

rung *n* barreau, échelon *m*.

runner *n* coureur *m*; concurrent *m* -e *f*; messager *m*.

running *n* course *f*; direction *f*.

runway *n* piste de décollage *f*.

rupture *n* rupture *f*; hernie *f*; * *vt* rompre; * *vi* se rompre.

rural *adj* rural, champêtre.

ruse *n* ruse *f*, stratagème m.

rush *n* jonc *m*; ruée *f*; hâte *f*; * *vt* pousser vivement; * *vi* se précipiter, s'élancer.

rusk *n* biscotte *f*.

russet *adj* roux.

rust *n* rouille *f*; * *vi* se rouiller.

rustic *adj* rustique; * *n* paysan, rustaud *m*.

rustiness *n* rouille *f*.

rustle *vi* bruire; * *vt* faire bruire; froisser.

rustling *n* vol de bétail *m*; bruissement *m*.

rusty *adj* rouillé; roux.

rut *n* (*zool*) rut *m*; ornière *f*.

ruthless *adj* cruel, impitoyable; ~ly *adv* sans pitié.

rye *n* (*bot*) seigle *m*.

S

Sabbath *n* sabbat *m*; dimanche *m*.
sable *n* zibeline *f*.
sabotage *n* sabotage *m*.
sabre *n* sabre *m*.
saccharin *n* saccharine *f*.
sack *n* sac *m*; * *vt* mettre à sac; renvoyer.
sacrament *n* sacrement *m*; Eucharistie *f*.
sacramental *adj* sacramentel.
sacred *adj* saint, sacré; inviolable.
sacredness *n* (caractère) sacré *m*.
sacrifice *n* sacrifice *m*; * *vt* sacrifier.
sacrificial *adj* sacrificiel.
sacrilege *n* sacrilège *m*.
sacrilegious *adj* sacrilège.
sad *adj* triste, déprimé; attristant; regrettable; **~ly** *adv* tristement.
sadden *vt* attrister.
saddle *n* selle *f*; col *m*; * *vt* seller.
saddlebag *n* sacoche de selle *f*.
saddler *n* sellier *m*.
sadness *n* tristesse *f*.
safe *adj* sûr; en sécurité; hors de danger; sans danger; **~ly** *adv* sans accident; **~ and sound** sain et sauf; * *n* coffre-fort *m*.
safe-conduct *n* sauf-conduit *m*.
safeguard *n* sauvegarde *f*; * *vt* sauvegarder, protéger.
safety *n* sécurité *f*; sûreté *f*.
safety belt *n* ceinture de sécurité *f*.
safety pin *n* épingle de nourrice *f*.
saffron *n* safran *m*.
sage *n* (*bot*) sauge *f*; sage *m*; * *adj* sage; **~ly** *adv* avec sagesse.
Sagittarius *n* Sagittaire *m* (signe du zodiaque).
sago *n* (*bot*) sagou *m*.
sail *n* voile *f*; * *vt* piloter; * *vi* aller à la voile, naviguer.
sailing *n* navigation *f*.
sailor *n* marin *m*.
saint *n* saint *m* -e *f*.
sainted, saintly *adj* saint.
sake *n* bien *m*, égard *m*; **for God's ~** pour l'amour de Dieu.
salad *n* salade *f*.
salad bowl *n* saladier *m*.
salad dressing *n* vinaigrette *f*.
salad oil *n* huile de table *f*.
salamander *n* salamandre *f*.
salary *n* salaire *m*.
sale *n* vente *f*; solde *m*.
saleable *adj* vendable.
salesman *n* vendeur *m*.

saleswoman *n* vendeuse *f*.
salient *adj* saillant.
saline *adj* salin.
saliva *n* salive *f*.
sallow *adj* jaunâtre, cireux.
sally *n* (*mil*) sortie, saillie *f*; * *vi* saillir.
salmon *n* saumon *m*.
salmon trout *n* truite saumonée *f*.
saloon *n* bar *m*.
salt *n* sel *m*; * *vt* saler.
salt cellar *n* salière *f*.
saltness *n* salinité *f*.
saltpetre *n* salpêtre *m*.
saltworks *npl* salines *fpl*.
salubrious *adj* salubre, sain.
salubrity *n* salubrité *f*.
salutary *adj* salutaire.
salutation *n* salutation(s) *f(pl)*.
salute *vt* saluer; * *n* salut *m*.
salvage *n* (*mar*) droit de sauvetage *m*.
salvation *n* salut *m*.
salve *n* baume, onguent *m*.
salver *n* plateau *m*.
salvo *n* salve *f*.
same *adj* même, identique.
sameness *n* monotonie *f*.
sample *n* échantillon *m*; prélèvement *m*; * *vt* goûter.
sampler *n* échantillonneur *m* -euse *f*; modèle *m*.
sanatorium *n* sanatorium *m*.
sanctify *vt* sanctifier.
sanctimonious *adj* cagot.
sanction *n* sanction *f*; * *vt* sanctionner.
sanctity *n* sainteté *f*.
sanctuary *n* sanctuaire *m*; asile *m*.
sand *n* sable *m*; * *vt* sabler.
sandal *n* sandale *f*.
sandbag *n* (*mil*) sac *m* de sable.
sandpit *n* carrière de sable *f*.
sandstone *n* grès *m*.
sandy *adj* sablonneux, sableux.
sane *adj* sain.
sanguinary *adj* sanguinaire, sanglant.
sanguine *adj* sanguin.
sanitary towel *n* serviette *f* hygiénique.
sanity *n* santé mentale, raison *f*.
sap *n* sève *f*; * *vt* miner.
sapient *adj* sage, prudent.
sapling *n* jeune arbre *m*.
sapphire *n* saphir *m*.
sarcasm *n* sarcasme *m*.

sarcastic *adj* sarcastique, caustique; **~ally** *adv* d'une manière sarcastique.
sarcophagus *n* sarcophage *m*.
sardine *n* sardine *f*.
sash *n* écharpe *f*; ceinture *f*.
sash window *n* fenêtre à guillotine *f*.
sassy *adj* (US) insolent.
Satan *n* Satan *m*.
satanic(al) *adj* satanique.
satchel *n* cartable *m*.
satellite *n* satellite *m*.
satiate, sate *vt* rassasier, assouvir.
satin *n* satin *m*; * *adj* en *ou* de satin.
satire *n* satire *f*.
satirical *adj* satirique; **~ly** *adv* d'une manière satirique.
satirise *vt* faire la satire de.
satirist *n* écrivain satirique *m*.
satisfaction *n* satisfaction *f*.
satisfactorily *adv* d'une manière satisfaisante.
satisfactory *adj* satisfaisant.
satisfy *vt* satisfaire; convaincre.
saturate *vt* saturer.
Saturday *n* samedi *m*.
saturnine *adj* saturnien, sombre.
satyr *n* satyre *m*.
sauce *n* sauce *f*; assaisonnement *m*; * *vt* assaisonner.
saucepan *n* casserole *f*.
saucer *n* soucoupe *f*.
saucily *adv* avec impertinence.
sauciness *n* impertinence, insolence *f*.
saucy *adj* impertinent.
saunter *vi* flâner, se balader.
sausage *n* saucisse *f*.
savage *adj* sauvage, barbare; **~ly** *adv* sauvagement; * *n* sauvage *mf*.
savageness *n* sauvagerie *f*; barbarie *f*.
savagery *n* sauvagerie, barbarie *f*.
savannah *n* savane *f*.
save *vt* sauver; économiser; épargner; éviter; conserver; * *adv* sauf, à l'exception de; * *n* (*sport*) arrêt *m*.
saveloy *n* cervelas *m*.
saver *n* libérateur *m* -trice *f*; épargnant *m* -e *f*.
saving *adj* économique, économe; * *prep* sauf, à l'exception de; * *n*

sauvetage *m*; ~s *pl* économies *fpl*, épargne *f.*

savings account *n* compte d'épargne *m.*

savings and loan association *n* (US) organisme *m* de crédit immobilier.

savings bank *n* caisse d'épargne *f.*

Saviour *n* Sauveur *m.*

savour *n* saveur *f*; goût *m*; * *vt* déguster, savourer.

savouriness *n* goût *m*; saveur *f.*

savoury *adj* savoureux.

saw *n* scie *f*; * *vt* scier.

sawdust *n* sciure *f.*

sawfish *n* poisson scie *m.*

sawmill *n* scierie *f.*

sawyer *n* scieur *m.*

saxophone *n* saxophone *m.*

say *vt* dire.

saying *n* dicton, proverbe *m.*

scab *n* gale *f*; croûte *f.*

scabbard *n* gaine *f*; fourreau *m.*

scabby *adj* galeux.

scaffold *n* échafaud *m*; échafaudage *m.*

scaffolding *n* échafaudage *m.*

scald *vt* échauder; * *n* brûlure *f.*

scale *n* balance *f*; échelle *f*; gamme *f*; écaille *f*; * *vt* escalader; écailler.

scallion *n* échalote *f.*

scallop *n* feston *m*; coquille *f* St Jacques; * *vt* festonner.

scalp *n* cuir chevelu *m*; * *vt* scalper.

scamp *n* coquin *m.*

scamper *vi* galoper.

scampi *npl* langoustines *fpl.*

scan *vt* scruter; explorer; scander.

scandal *n* scandale *m*; infamie *f.*

scandalise *vt* scandaliser.

scandalous *adj* scandaleux; ~ly *adv* scandaleusement.

scant, scanty *adj* rare, insuffisant.

scantily *adv* pauvrement, insuffisamment.

scantiness *n* insuffisance, pauvreté *f.*

scapegoat *n* bouc émissaire *m.*

scar *n* cicatrice *f*; * *vt* marquer d'une cicatrice.

scarce *adj* rare; ~ly *adv* à peine.

scarcity *n* rareté *f*; pénurie *f.*

scare *vt* effrayer; * *n* peur; panique *f.*

scarecrow *n* épouvantail *m.*

scarf *n* écharpe *f.*

scarlatina *n* scarlatine *f.*

scarlet *n* écarlate *f*; * *adj* écarlate.

scarp *n* escarpement *m.*

scat *interj* (*sl*) ouste!

scatter *vt* éparpiller; disperser.

scavenger *n* charognard *m*; éboueur *m.*

scenario *n* scénario *m*; (*also fig*).

scene *n* scène *f*; lieu *m*; spectacle *m*, vue *f.*

scenery *n* vue *f*; décor (de théâtre) *m.*

scenic *adj* scénique.

scent *n* parfum *m*, odeur *f*; odorat *m*; piste *f*; * *vt* parfumer.

scent bottle *n* flacon à parfum *m.*

scentless *adj* sans odeur, inodore.

sceptic *n* sceptique *mf.*

sceptic(al) *adj* sceptique.

scepticism *n* scepticisme *m.*

sceptre *n* sceptre *m.*

schedule *n* horaire *m*; programme *m*; liste *f.*

scheme *n* projet, plan *m*; schéma *m*; système *m*; machination *f*; * *vt* machiner; * *vi* intriguer.

schemer *n* conspirateur *m* -trice *f*, intrigant *m* -e *f.*

schism *n* schisme *m.*

schismatic *n* schismatique *mf.*

scholar *n* élève *mf*; érudit *m* -e *f.*

scholarship *n* savoir *m*, science *f*; bourse (d'études) *f.*

scholastic *adj* scolaire.

school *n* école *f*; * *vt* instruire.

schoolboy *n* écolier, élève *m.*

schoolgirl *n* écolière, élève *f.*

schooling *n* instruction, éducation *f.*

schoolmaster *n* instituteur, maître (d'école) *m.*

schoolmistress *n* institutrice, maîtresse (d'école) *f.*

schoolteacher *n* instituteur/trice *mf*; professeur *mf.*

schooner *n* (*mar*) goélette *f.*

sciatica *n* sciatique *f.*

science *n* science *f.*

scientific *adj* ~ally *adv* scientifique(ment).

scientist *n* scientifique *mf.*

scimitar *n* cimeterre *m.*

scintillate *vi* scintiller, étinceler.

scintillating *adj* brillant, scintillant.

scission *n* scission, division *f.*

scissors *npl* ciseaux *mpl.*

scoff *vi* se moquer.

scold *vt* réprimander; * *vi* grogner.

scoop *n* louche *f*; pelle *f*; exclusivité *f*; * *vt* évider; écoper.

scooter *n* scooter *m*; trottinette *f.*

scope *n* portée, envergure, étendue *f*; zone de compétence *f*; liberté d'action *f.*

scorch *vt* brûler; roussir, griller; * *vi* se brûler, roussir.

score *n* score *m*; marque *f*; entaille, rayure *f*; titre, égard *m*; compte *m*; (*mus*) partition *f*; vingtaine *f*;

* *vt* marquer; souligner; * *vi* marquer un/des point(s).

scoreboard *n* tableau (d'affichage) *m.*

scorn *vt* mépriser; dédaigner; * *n* dédain, mépris *m.*

scornful *adj* dédaigneux; ~ly *adv* avec mépris.

Scorpio *n* Scorpion *m* (signe du zodiaque).

scorpion *n* scorpion *m.*

scotch *vt* contrecarrer.

Scotch *n* whisky *m.*

Scotch tape *n* scotch *m.*

scoundrel *n* vaurien *m.*

scour *vt* récurer, frotter; nettoyer; * *vi* battre la campagne.

scourge *n* fouet *m*; châtiment *m*; * *vt* fouetter; châtier.

scout *n* (*mil*) éclaireur *m* -euse *f*; guetteur *m*; reconnaissance *f*; * *vi* aller en reconnaissance.

scowl *vi* se renfrogner; * *n* mine renfrognée *f.*

scragginess *n* décharnement *m*, maigreur extrême *f*; rugosité *f.*

scraggy *adj* rugueux; famélique.

scramble *vi* avancer à quatre pattes; grimper; se battre, se disputer; * *n* bousculade, ruée *f*; ascension *f.*

scrap *n* bout *m*; restes *mpl*; petit morceau *m*; bagarre *f*; ferraille *f.*

scrape *vt* *vi* racler, gratter; * *vt* érafler; * *n* embarras *m*, ennui *m.*

scraper *n* racloir *m.*

scratch *vt* griffer, égratigner; gratter, griffonner; * *n* égratignure *f.*

scrawl *vt* *vi* gribouiller; * *n* griffonnage *m.*

scream, screech *vi* hurler, pousser des cris; * *n* cri perçant, hurlement *m.*

screen *n* écran *m*; paravent *m*; rideau *m*; écran de cheminée *m*; * *vt* abriter, cacher; projeter; passer au crible, sélectionner.

screenplay *n* scénario *m.*

screw *n* vis *f*; * *vt* visser; extorquer, soutirer.

screwdriver *n* tournevis *m.*

scribble *vt* gribouiller; * *n* gribouillage *m.*

scribe *n* scribe *m.*

scrimmage *n* mêlée *f.*

script *n* scénario *m*; script *m.*

scriptural *adj* biblique.

Scripture *n* Écriture *f* sainte.

scroll *n* rouleau (de papier *ou* parchemin) *m.*

scrub *vt* nettoyer à la brosse, récurer; annuler; * *n* broussailles *fpl.*

scruffy *adj* mal soigné.

scruple *n* scrupule *m*.

scrupulous *adj* scrupuleux; **~ly** *adv* scrupuleusement.

scrutinise *vt* étudier minutieusement, examiner.

scrutiny *n* examen minutieux *m*.

scuffle *n* échauffourée, rixe *f*; * *vi* se bagarrer.

scull *n* aviron *m*.

scullery *n* arrière-cuisine *f*.

sculptor *n* sculpteur *m* -trice *f*.

sculpture *n* sculpture *f*; * *vt* sculpter.

scum *n* écume *f*; crasse *f*; rebut *m*.

scurrilous *adj* injurieux; vil, ignoble; **~ly** *adv* injurieusement.

scurvy *n* scorbut *m*; * *adj* vil, mesquin.

scuttle *n* corbeille *f*; * *vi* courir précipitamment.

scythe *n* faux *f*.

sea *n* mer *f*; * *adj* marin; **heavy ~** mer houleuse *f*.

sea breeze *n* brise de mer *f*.

seacoast *n* côte *f*.

sea fight *n* combat naval *m*.

seafood *n* fruits de mer *mpl*.

sea front *n* bord de mer *m*.

seagreen *adj* vert glauque.

seagull *n* mouette *f*.

sea horse *n* hippocampe *m*.

seal *n* sceau *m*; phoque *m*; * *vt* sceller.

sealing wax *n* cire à cacheter *f*.

seam *n* couture *f*; * *vt* faire une couture.

seaman *n* marin *m*.

seamanship *n* habileté à naviguer *f*.

seamstress *n* couturière *f*.

seamy *adj* sordide.

sea plane *n* hydravion *m*.

seaport *n* port de mer *m*.

sear *vt* cautériser.

search *vt* fouiller; inspecter; examiner; scruter, sonder; * *n* fouille *f*; recherche *f*; perquisition *f*.

searchlight *n* projecteur *m*.

seashore *n* rivage *m*, bord de mer *m*.

seasick *adj* sujet au mal de mer.

seasickness *n* mal de mer *m*.

seaside *n* bord de mer *m*.

season *n* saison *f*; moment opportun *m*; assaisonnement *m*; * *vt* assaisonner; dessécher.

seasonable *adj* opportun, à propos.

seasonably *adv* de façon opportune, à propos.

seasoning *n* assaisonnement *m*.

season ticket *n* carte d'abonnement *f*.

seat *n* siège *m*; place *f*; derrière *m*; fond *m*; * *vt* (faire) asseoir; placer.

seat belt *n* ceinture de sécurité *f*.

seaward *adj* du large; **~s** *adv* vers le large.

seaweed *n* algue *f*.

seaworthy *adj* en état de naviguer.

secede *vi* faire sécession, se séparer.

secession *n* sécession *f*; séparation *f*.

seclude *vt* éloigner, isoler.

seclusion *n* solitude *f*; isolement *m*.

second *adj* **~(ly)** *adv* deuxième(ment); * *n* second *m*; seconde *f*; (*mus*) seconde *f*; * *vt* aider; seconder.

secondary *adj* secondaire.

secondary school *n* collège d'enseignement secondaire *m*.

secondhand *n* article d'occasion *m*.

secrecy *n* secret *m*; discrétion *f*.

secret *adj* *n* secret *m*; **~ly** *adv* secrètement.

secretary *n* secrétaire *mf*.

secrete *vt* cacher; (*med*) sécréter.

secretion *n* sécrétion *f*.

secretive *adj* secret, dissimulé.

sect *n* secte *f*.

sectarian *n* sectaire *mf*.

section *n* section *f*.

sector *n* secteur *m*.

secular *adj* séculaire.

secularise *vt* séculariser.

secure *adj* sûr; en sûreté; **~ly** *adv* en sécurité; * *vt* mettre en sûreté; assurer.

security *n* sécurité *f*; sûreté *f*; protection *f*; caution *f*.

sedan *n* (US) berline *f*.

sedan chair *n* chaise à porteurs *f*.

sedate *adj* **~ly** *adv* calme(ment), posé(ment).

sedateness *n* calme *m*.

sedative *n* sédatif *m*.

sedentary *adj* sédentaire.

sedge *n* (*bot*) carex *m*.

sediment *n* sédiment *m*; lie *f*; dépôt *m*.

sedition *n* sédition *f*.

seditious *adj* séditieux.

seduce *vt* séduire; corrompre.

seducer *n* séducteur *m* -trice *f*.

seduction *n* séduction *f*.

seductive *adj* séduisant.

sedulous *adj* assidu; **~ly** *adv* assidûment.

see *vt* voir, remarquer, découvrir; connaître; juger; comprendre; * *vi* voir; comprendre; **~!** regarde!; tu vois!

seed *n* graine, semence *f*; * *vi* monter en graine.

seedling *n* semis *m*.

seedsman *n* grainetier *m*.

seed time *n* (époque des) semailles *f(pl)*.

seedy *adj* minable.

seeing *conj*: **~ that** vu que.

seek *vt* chercher; demander.

seem *vi* paraître, sembler.

seeming *n* apparence *f*; **~ly** *adv* apparemment.

seemliness *n* bienséance *f*.

seemly *adj* convenable, bienséant.

seer *n* prophète *m*.

seesaw *n* bascule *f*; * *vi* osciller.

seethe *vi* bouillir, bouillonner.

segment *n* segment *m*.

seize *vt* saisir, attraper; opérer la saisie de.

seizure *n* capture *f*; saisie *f*.

seldom *adv* rarement, peu souvent.

select *vt* sélectionner, choisir; * *adj* choisi, sélectionné.

selection *n* sélection *f*.

self *n* soi-même; **the ~** le moi; * *pref* auto-.

self-command *n* maîtrise de soi *f*.

self-conceit *n* vanité *f*.

self-confident *adj* sûr de soi.

self-defence *n* autodéfense *f*.

self-denial *n* abnégation de soi *f*.

self-employed *adj* indépendant.

self-evident *adj* évident, qui va de soi.

self-governing *adj* autonome.

self-interest *n* intérêt personnel *m*.

selfish *adj* **~ly** *adv* égoïste(ment).

selfishness *n* égoïsme *m*.

self-pity *n* apitoiement sur soi-même *m*.

self-portrait *n* autoportrait *m*.

self-possession *n* sang-froid *m*, assurance *f*.

self-reliant *adj* indépendant.

self-respect *n* respect de soi *m*.

selfsame *adj* exactement le même, identique.

self-satisfied *adj* suffisant.

self-seeking *adj* égoïste.

self-service *adj* libre-service.

self-styled *adj* autoproclamé.

self-sufficient *adj* autosuffisant.

self-taught *adj* autodidacte.

self-willed *adj* obstiné, volontaire.

sell *vt* vendre; attraper; * *vi* se vendre.

seller *n* vendeur *m* -euse *f*.

selling-off *n* liquidation *f*.

semblance *n* semblant *m*, apparence *f*.

semen *n* sperme *m*.

semester *n* semestre *m*.

semicircle *n* demi-cercle *m*.

semicircular *adj* semi-circulaire.

semicolon *n* point-virgule *m*.

semiconductor *n* semi-conducteur *m*.

seminary *n* séminaire *m*.

semitone *n* (*mus*) demi-ton *m*.

senate *n* sénat *m*.

senator *n* sénateur *m* -trice *f*.

senatorial *adj* sénatorial.

send *vt* envoyer, expédier, adresser; émettre; pousser.

sender *n* expéditeur *m* -trice *f*.

senile *adj* sénile.

senility *n* sénilité *f*.

senior *n* aîné *m* -e *f*; * *adj* aîné; supérieur.

seniority *n* ancienneté *f*.

senna *n* (*bot*) séné *m*.

sensation *n* sensation *f*.

sense *n* sens *m*; sensation *f*; raison *f*; bon sens *m*; sentiment *m*.

senseless *adj* insensé; sans connaissance; ~**ly** *adv* stupidement.

senselessness *n* manque de bon sens *m*; absurdité *f*.

sensibility *n* sensibilité *f*.

sensible *adj* sensé, raisonnable; sensible.

sensibly *adv* raisonnablement.

sensitive *adj* sensible.

sensual, sensuous *adj* ~**ly** *adv* sensuel(lement).

sensuality *n* sensualité *f*.

sentence *n* phrase *f*; condamnation *f*; * *vt* condamner, prononcer une sentence contre.

sententious *adj* sentencieux; ~**ly** *adv* sentencieusement.

sentient *adj* sensible.

sentiment *n* sentiment *m*; opinion *f*.

sentimental *adj* sentimental.

sentinel, sentry *n* sentinelle *f*.

sentry box *n* guérite *f*.

separable *adj* séparable.

separate *vt* séparer; * *vi* se séparer; * *adj* séparé; distinct; ~**ly** *adv* séparément.

separation *n* séparation *f*.

September *n* septembre *m*.

septennial *adj* septennal.

septuagenarian *n* septuagénaire *m*.

sepulchre *n* sépulcre *m*.

sequel *n* conséquence *f*; suite *f*.

sequence *n* ordre *m*, série *f*.

sequester, sequestrate *vt* séquestrer.

sequestration *n* séquestration *f*.

seraglio *n* sérail *m*.

seraph *n* séraphin *m*.

serenade *n* sérénade *f*; * *vt* jouer une sérénade pour.

serene *adj* serein; ~**ly** *adv* sereinement.

serenity *n* sérénité *f*.

serf *n* serf *m*, serve *f*.

serge *n* serge *f*.

sergeant *n* sergent *m*; (US) caporal-chef *m*; brigadier *m*.

serial *adj* de/en série; * *n* feuilleton *m*; téléroman *m*.

series *n* série *f*.

serious *adj* sérieux, grave; ~**ly** *adv* sérieusement.

sermon *n* sermon *m*.

serous *adj* séreux.

serpent *n* serpent *m*.

serpentine *adj* sinueux; * *n* (*chem*) serpentine *f*.

serrated *adj* en dents de scie.

serum *n* sérum *m*.

servant *n* domestique *mf*.

servant-girl *n* servante, bonne *f*.

serve *vt* servir; desservir; faire; accomplir; * *vi* servir; être utile; ~ **a warrant** remettre un mandat.

service *n* service *m*; office *m*; entretien *m*; * *vt* entretenir; réviser.

serviceable *adj* utilisable; pratique.

service station *n* station-service *f*.

servile *adj* servile.

servitude *n* servitude *f*, esclavage *m*.

session *n* séance, session *f*; réunion *f*.

set *vt* mettre, poser, placer; fixer, déterminer; * *vi* se coucher (soleil); se figer; se mettre; * *n* jeu *m*; service *m*; ensemble *m*; (*cine*) plateau *m*; set *m*; groupe *m*, bande *f*; * *adj* fixe, figé; prêt; déterminé.

settee *n* canapé *m*.

setting *n* disposition *f*; cadre *m*; monture *f*; ~ **of the sun** coucher du soleil *m*.

settle *vt* poser, installer, arranger; régler; calmer; * *vi* se poser; s'installer; se calmer.

settlement *n* règlement *m*; établissement *m*; accord *m*; résolution *f*; colonie *f*; colonisation *f*.

settler *n* colon *m*, colonisateur *m* -trice *f*.

set-to *n* lutte *f*; combat *m*.

seven *adj n* sept *m*.

seventeen *adj n* dix-sept *m*.

seventeenth *adj n* dix-septième *mf*.

seventh *adj n* septième *mf*.

seventieth *adj n* soixante-dixième *mf*.

seventy *adj n* soixante-dix *m*.

sever *vt* séparer.

several *adj pn* plusieurs.

severance *n* séparation *f*.

severe *adj* sévère, rigoureux, austère, dur; ~**ly** *adv* sévèrement.

severity *n* sévérité *f*.

sew *vt vi* coudre.

sewer *n* égout *m*.

sewerage *n* (système d') égouts *mpl*; eaux d'égout *fpl*.

sewing machine *n* machine à coudre *f*.

sex *n* sexe *m*.

sexist *adj n* sexiste *mf*.

sextant *n* sextant *m*.

sexton *n* sacristain *m*.

sexual *adj* sexuel.

sexy *adj* sexy.

shabbily *adv* petitement, mesquinement.

shabbiness *n* aspect décrépit *ou* miteux *m*.

shabby *adj* miteux.

shackle *vt* enchaîner; ~**s** *npl* chaînes *fpl*.

shade *n* ombre, obscurité *f*; nuance *f*; abat-jour *m*; * *vt* ombrager; abriter; atténuer.

shadiness *n* ombre *f*; ombrage *m*.

shadow *n* ombre *f*.

shadowy *adj* ombragé; sombre; indistinct.

shady *adj* ombreux, ombragé; sombre.

shaft *n* flèche *f*; fût *m*; puits *m*; (*tech*) arbre *m*; rayon *m*.

shag *n* tabac *m*; cormoran huppé *m*.

shaggy *adj* hirsute.

shake *vt* secouer; agiter; * *vi* trembler; chanceler; ~ **hands** se serrer la main; * *n* secousse *f*; tremblement *m*.

shaking *adj* tremblant.

shaky *adj* tremblant.

shallow *adj* peu profond, superficiel; futile.

shallowness *n* manque de profondeur *m*; futilité *f*.

sham *vt* feindre; * *n* imitation *f*; imposture *f*; * *adj* feint, simulé.

shambles *npl* désordre *m*.

shame *n* honte *f*; * *vt* faire honte à, déshonorer.

shamefaced *adj* honteux, confus.

shameful *adj* honteux; scandaleux; ~**ly** *adv* honteusement.

shameless *adj* ~**ly** *adv* effronté(ment).

shamelessness *n* effronterie, impudeur *f*.

shammy *n* (peau de) chamois *m*.

shampoo *vt* faire un shampooing à; * *n* shampooing *m*.

shamrock *n* trèfle *m*.

shank *n* jambe *f*; hampe *f*; tuyau (de pipe) *m*; canon *m*.

shanty *n* baraque *f*.

shanty town *n* bidonville *m*.

shape *vt* former; façonner; modeler; * *vi* prendre forme; * *n* forme, figure *f*; modèle *m*.

shapeless *adj* informe.

shapely *adj* bien proportionné.

share *n* part, portion *f*; (*com*) action *f*; soc (de charrue) *m*; * *vt* partager; répartir; * *vi* partager.

sharer *n* participant *m*.

shark *n* requin *m*.

sharp *adj* aigu, acéré; malin; fin; pénétrant; âpre, mordant, cinglant; perçant; vif, violent; * *n* (*mus*) dièse *m*; * *adv* pile.

sharpen *vt* aiguiser, affûter.

sharply *adv* brusquement; sévèrement; vivement; nettement.

sharpness *n* tranchant *m*; finesse, acuité *f*; aigreur *f*.

shatter *vt* fracasser, détruire; * *vi* se fracasser.

shave *vt* raser, raboter; * *vi* se raser; *n* rasage *m*.

shaver *n* rasoir électrique *m*.

shaving *n* rasage *m*.

shaving brush *n* blaireau *m*.

shaving cream *n* crème à raser *f*.

shawl *n* châle *m*.

she *pn* elle.

sheaf *n* gerbe *f*; liasse *f*.

shear *vt* tondre; ~s *npl* cisailles *fpl*.

sheath *n* fourreau *m*.

shed *vt* verser, répandre; perdre; * *n* hangar *m*; cabane *f*.

sheen *n* lustre *m*.

sheep *n* mouton *m*.

sheepfold *n* parc à moutons *m*.

sheepish *adj* penaud; timide.

sheepishness *n* timidité *f*, air penaud *m*.

sheep-run *n* pâturage pour moutons *m*.

sheepskin *n* peau de mouton *f*.

sheer *adj* pur, absolu, véritable; abrupt; * *adv* abruptement.

sheet *n* drap *m*; plaque *f*; feuille (de papier) *f*; (*mar*) écoute *f*.

sheet anchor *n* ancre de veille *f*.

sheeting *n* toile pour draps *f*.

sheet iron *n* tôle *f*.

sheet lightning *n* éclairs en nappes *mpl*.

shelf *n* étagère *f*; (*mar*) écueil *m*; saillie *f*; **on the ~** au rancart.

shell *n* coquille *f*; carcasse *f*; écorce *f*; obus *m*; * *vt* écosser, décortiquer; bombarder; * *vi* se décortiquer.

shellfish *npl invar* crustacé *m*; fruits de mer *mpl*.

shelter *n* abri *m*; asile, refuge *m*; * *vt* abriter; protéger; * *vi* s'abriter.

shelve *vt* mettre au rancart.

shelving *n* rayonnage *m*.

shepherd *n* berger *m*.

shepherdess *n* bergère *f*.

sherbet *n* sorbet *m*.

sheriff *n* shérif *m*.

sherry *n* xérès *m*.

shield *n* bouclier *m*; écran protecteur *m*; * *vt* protéger.

shift *vi* changer; se déplacer; * *vt* changer, bouger; transférer; * *n* changement *m*; roulement *m*.

shinbone *n* tibia *m*.

shine *vi* briller, reluire, illuminer; * *vt* cirer; * *n* éclat *m*.

shingle *n* galets *mpl*; ~s *pl* (*med*) zona *m*.

shining *adj* resplendissant; * *n* éclat *m*.

shiny *adj* brillant, reluisant.

ship *n* bateau *m*; navire *m*; bâtiment *m*; * *vt* embarquer; transporter.

shipbuilding *n* construction navale *f*.

shipmate *n* (*mar*) camarade de bord *m*.

shipment *n* cargaison *f*.

shipowner *n* armateur *m*.

shipwreck *n* naufrage *m*.

shirt *n* chemise *f*.

shit *excl* (*sl*) merde!

shiver *vi* frissonner.

shoal *n* banc *m* (de poissons).

shock *n* choc *m*; décharge *f*; coup *m*; * *vt* bouleverser; choquer.

shock absorber *n* amortisseur *m*.

shoddy *adj* de mauvaise qualité.

shoe *n* chaussure *f*; fer (à cheval) *m*; * *vt* chausser; ferrer (un cheval).

shoeblack *n* cireur de chaussures *m*.

shoehorn *n* chausse-pied *m*.

shoelace *n* lacet de chaussure *m*.

shoemaker *n* cordonnier *m*.

shoestring *n* lacet de chaussure *m*.

shoot *vt* tirer, lancer, décocher; * *vi* pousser, bourgeonner; passer en flèche; s'élancer; * *n* pousse *f*.

shooter *n* tireur *m* -euse *f*.

shooting *n* fusillade *f*; tir *m*.

shop *n* magasin *m*; atelier *m*.

shopfront *n* devanture *f*.

shoplifter *n* voleur(-euse) à l'étalage *m(f)*.

shopper *n* acheteur *m* -euse *f*.

shopping *n* courses *fpl*.

shopping centre *n* centre commercial *m*.

shore *n* rivage, bord *m*, côte *f*.

short *adj* court, bref, succinct, con-cis; ~ly *adv* brièvement; rapidement.

shortcoming *n* insuffisance *f*; défaut *m*.

shorten *vt* raccourcir; abréger.

shortness *n* petitesse *f*; brièveté *f*.

short-sighted *adj* myope.

short-sightedness *n* myopie *f*.

shortwave *n* ondes courtes *fpl*.

shot *n* coup *m*; décharge *f*; plomb *m*; tentative *f*; prise *f*.

shotgun *n* fusil de chasse *m*.

shoulder *n* épaule *f*; accotement *m*; * *vt* charger sur son épaule.

shout *vi* crier; * *vt* crier; * *n* cri *m*, acclamation *f*.

shouting *n* cris *mpl*.

shove *vt vi* pousser; * *n* poussée *f*.

shovel *n* pelle *f*; * *vt* pelleter.

show *vt* montrer; faire voir, présenter; prouver; expliquer; * *vi* se voir; * *n* exposition *f*; spectacle *m*; manifestation *f*; salon *m*.

show business *n* monde du spectacle *m*.

shower *n* averse *f*; douche *f*; (*fig*) torrent *m*; * *vi* pleuvoir.

showery *adj* pluvieux.

showroom *n* salle d'exposition *f*.

showy *adj* voyant, ostentatoire.

shred *n* lambeau *m*, parcelle *f*; * *vt* mettre en lambeaux.

shrew *n* mégère *f*; musaraigne *f*.

shrewd *adj* astucieux; perspicace; ~ly *adv* astucieusement.

shrewdness *n* astuce *f*.

shriek *vt vi* hurler; * *n* hurlement *m*.

shrill *adj* aigu, strident.

shrillness *n* ton aigu *m*.

shrimp *n* crevette *f*; nabot *m* -e *f*, avorton *m*.

shrine *n* lieu saint *m*.

shrink *vi* rétrécir; se réduire, rapetisser.

shrivel *vi* se ratatiner, se flétrir; * *vt* ratatiner.

shroud *n* voile *m*; linceul *m*; * *vt* envelopper, voiler; ensevelir.

Shrove Tuesday *n* Mardi gras *m*.

shrub *n* arbuste *m*.

shrubbery *n* massif d'arbustes *m*.

shrug *vt* hausser les épaules; * *n* haussement d'épaules *m*.

shudder *vi* frissonner; * *n* frisson *m*.

shuffle *vt* mélanger; battre.

shun *vt* fuir, éviter.

shunt *vt* (*rail*) aiguiller.

shut *vt* fermer; *vi* (se) fermer.

shutter *n* volet *m*.

shuttle *n* navette *f*.

shuttlecock *n* volant *m*.

shy *adj* timide; réservé; embarrassé, gauche; **~ly** *adv* timidement.

shyness *n* timidité *f*.

sibling *n*: **~s** enfants de mêmes parents *mpl*.

sibyl *n* sibylle *f*.

sick *adj* malade; écœuré.

sicken *vt* rendre malade; * *vi* tomber malade.

sickle *n* faucille *f*.

sick leave *n* congé de maladie *m*.

sickliness *n* état maladif *m*.

sickly *adj* maladif.

sickness *n* maladie *f*.

sick pay *n* indemnité de maladie *f*.

side *n* côté *m*; flanc *m*; camp *m*; parti *m*; * *adj* latéral; secondaire; * *vi* se ranger du côté de.

sideboard *n* buffet *m*.

sidelight *n* veilleuse *f*.

sidelong *adj* oblique.

sideways *adv* de côté, obliquement.

siding *n* (*rail*) voie de garage *f*.

sidle *vi* avancer de côté; avancer furtivement.

siege *n* (*mil*) siège *m*.

sieve *n* tamis *m*; crible *m*; passoire *f*; * *vt* tamiser.

sift *vt* tamiser; passer au crible; dégager.

sigh *vi* soupirer, gémir; * *n* soupir *m*.

sight *n* vue *f*; mire *f*; spectacle *m*.

sightless *adj* aveugle.

sightly *adj* agréable à regarder; séduisant.

sightseeing *n* tourisme *m*.

sign *n* signe *m*, indication *f*; panneau *m*; geste *m*; trace *f*; * *vt* signer.

signal *n* signal *m*; * *adj* insigne, remarquable.

signalise *vt* signaler.

signal lamp *n* (*rail*) lampe de signalisation *f*.

signalman *n* (*rail*) aiguilleur *m*.

signature *n* signature *f*.

signet *n* sceau *m*.

significance *n* importance *f*.

significant *adj* considérable.

signify *vt* signifier.

signpost *n* poteau indicateur *m*.

silence *n* silence *m*; * *vt* imposer le silence à.

silent *adj* silencieux; **~ly** *adv* silencieusement.

silex *n* silex *m*.

silicon chip *n* puce *f* électronique.

silk *n* soie *f*.

silken *adj* soyeux; satiné.

silkiness *n* soyeux *m*.

silkworm *n* ver à soie *m*.

silky *adj* soyeux; satiné.

sill *n* rebord *m*; seuil *m*.

silliness *n* stupidité, bêtise, niaiserie *f*.

silly *adj* bête, stupide.

silver *n* argent *m*; * *adj* en argent.

silversmith *n* orfèvre *m*.

silvery *adj* argenté.

similar *adj* semblable; similaire; **~ly** *adv* de la même façon.

similarity *n* ressemblance *f*.

simile *n* comparaison *f*.

simmer *vi* cuire à feu doux, mijoter.

simony *n* simonie *f*.

simper *vi* minauder; * *n* sourire affecté *m*.

simple *adj* simple; naïf.

simpleton *n* nigaud *m* -e *f*.

simplicity *n* simplicité *f*; naïveté *f*.

simplification *n* simplification *f*.

simplify *vt* simplifier.

simply *adv* simplement; seulement.

simulate *vt* simuler, feindre.

simulation *n* simulation *f*.

simultaneous *adj* simultané.

sin *n* péché *m*; * *vi* pécher.

since *adv* depuis; * *prep* depuis; * *conj* depuis que; puisque.

sincere *adj* **~ly** *adv* sincère(ment); **yours ~ly** veuillez agréer, Monsieur/Madame, l'expression de mes salutations distinguées.

sincerity *n* sincérité *f*.

sinecure *n* sinécure *f*.

sinew *n* tendon *m*.

sinewy *adj* musclé; tendineux.

sinful *adj* coupable, honteux; **~ly** *adv* honteusement.

sinfulness *n* corruption *f*, péché *m*.

sing *vt* *vi* chanter; (*poet*) *vt* célébrer.

singe *vt* roussir.

singer *n* chanteur *m* -euse *f*.

singing *n* chant *m*.

single *adj* seul, unique, simple; célibataire; * *n* aller simple *m*; 45 tours *m*; * *vt* distinguer; séparer.

singly *adv* séparément.

singular *adj* singulier, rare; * *n* singulier *m*; **~ly** *adv* singulièrement.

singularity *n* singularité *f*.

sinister *adj* sinistre; de mauvais augure, funeste.

sink *vi* couler; sombrer; s'affaisser; tomber très bas, baisser; * *vt* couler, faire sombrer; ruiner; * *n* évier *m*.

sinking fund *n* fonds d'amortissement *m*.

sinner *n* pécheur *m*; pécheresse *f*.

sinuosity *n* sinuosité *f*.

sinuous *adj* sinueux.

sinus *n* sinus *m*.

sip *vt* boire à petites gorgées; * *n* petite gorgée *f*.

siphon *n* siphon *m*.

sir *n* monsieur *m*.

sire *n* étalon *m*.

siren *n* sirène *f*.

sirloin *n* aloyau (de bœuf) *m*.

sister *n* sœur *f*.

sisterhood *n* solidarité féminine *f*.

sister-in-law *n* belle-sœur *f*.

sisterly *adj* de sœur.

sit *vi* s'asseoir; se trouver; * *vt* se présenter à.

site *n* emplacement *m*; site *m*.

sit-in *n* sit-in *m*, manifestation avec occupation de lieux publics *f*.

sitting *n* séance, réunion *f*; position assise *f*.

sitting room *n* salle de séjour *f*.

situated *adj* situé.

situation *n* situation *f*.

six *adj* *n* six *m*.

sixteen *adj* *n* seize *m*.

sixteenth *adj* *n* seizième *mf*.

sixth *adj* *n* sixième *mf*.

sixtieth *adj* *n* soixantième *mf*.

sixty *adj* *n* soixante *m*.

size *n* taille, grandeur *f*; volume *m*; dimension *f*; ampleur *f*; étendue *f*.

sizeable *adj* assez grand.

skate *n* patin *m*; * *vi* patiner.

skateboard *n* planche à roulettes *f*, skateboard *m*.

skating *n* patinage *m*.

skating rink *n* patinoire *f*.

skein *n* écheveau *m*.

skeleton *n* squelette *m*.

skeleton key *n* passe(-partout) *m*.

sketch *n* croquis *m*; esquisse *f*; * *vt* equisser, faire un croquis de.

skewer *n* broche *f*; brochette *f*; * *vt* embrocher.

ski *n* ski *m*; * *vi* skier.

ski boot *n* chaussure de ski *f*.

skid *n* dérapage *m*; * *vi* déraper.

skier *n* skieur *m* -euse *f*.

skiing *n* ski *m*.

skilful *adj* **~ly** *adv* adroit(ement), habile(ment).

skilfulness *n* habileté *f*.

skill *n* habileté, adresse, dextérité *f*.

skilled *adj* adroit; qualifié.

skim *vt* écrémer; effleurer.

skimmed milk *n* lait écrémé *m*.

skimmer *n* écumoire *f*.

skin *n* peau *f*; * *vt* écorcher.

skin diving *n* plongée sous-marine *f*.

skinned *adj* dépouillé.

skinny *adj* maigre, efflanqué.

skip *vi* sautiller, gambader; * *vt* sauter, passer; * *n* saut, bond *m*; benne *f*.

ski pants *npl* fuseau (de ski) *m*.

skipper *n* capitaine *m*.

skirmish *n* escarmouche *f*; * *vi* s'engager dans une escarmouche.

skirt *n* jupe *f*; bordure *f*; * *vt* contourner.

skit *n* parodie, satire *f*.

skittish *adj* espiègle, fantasque; coquet; inconstant; **~ly** *adv* d'une manière espiègle.

skittle *n* quille *f*.

skulk *vi* se cacher, rôder furtivement.

skull *n* crâne *m*.

skullcap *n* calotte *f*.

sky *n* ciel *m*.

skylight *n* lucarne *f*.

skyrocket *n* fusée *f*.

skyscraper *n* gratte-ciel *m invar*.

slab *n* dalle *f*.

slack *adj* lâche, mou, indolent, négligent.

slack(en) *vt* relâcher; ralentir; diminuer; * *vi* se relâcher; ralentir.

slackness *n* manque d'énergie, ralentissement *m*; laisser-aller *m*.

slag *n* scories *fpl*.

slam *vt* claquer violemment; * *vi* se refermer en claquant.

slander *vt* calomnier, dire du mal de; * *n* calomnie *f*.

slanderer *n* calomniateur *m* -trice *f*.

slanderous *adj* calomnieux; **~ly** *adv* calomnieusement.

slang *n* argot *m*.

slant *vi* pencher; être incliné; * *n* inclinaison *f*; point de vue *m*.

slanting *adj* en pente, incliné.

slap *n* claque *f*; (*on the face*) gifle *f*; * *adv* en plein; * *vt* donner une claque à, gifler.

slash *vt* entailler; * *n* entaille *f*.

slate *n* ardoise *f*.

slater *n* ardoisier *m*.

slating *n* recouvrement en ardoises *m*.

slaughter *n* carnage, massacre *m*; * *vt* abattre; massacrer.

slaughterer *n* tueur, meurtrier *m*.

slaughterhouse *n* abattoir *m*.

slave *n* esclave *mf*; * *vi* travailler comme un nègre.

slaver *n* bave *f*; * *vi* baver.

slavery *n* esclavage *m*.

slavish *adj* servile, d'esclave; **~ly** *adv* servilement.

slavishness *n* servilité *f*.

slay *vt* tuer.

slayer *n* tueur *m* -euse *f*.

sleazy *adj* louche, sordide.

sledge, sleigh *n* traîneau *m*.

sledgehammer *n* marteau de forgeron *m*.

sleek *adj* lisse et brillant, luisant.

sleep *vi* dormir; * *n* sommeil *m*.

sleeper *n* dormeur *m* -euse *f*.

sleepily *adv* d'un air endormi.

sleepiness *n* envie de dormir *f*.

sleeping bag *n* sac de couchage *m*.

sleeping pill *n* somnifère *m*.

sleepless *adj* sans sommeil.

sleepwalking *n* somnambulisme *m*.

sleepy *adj* qui a envie de dormir; endormi.

sleet *n* neige fondue *f*.

sleeve *n* manche *f*.

sleight *n*: **~ of hand** tour de passe-passe *m*.

slender *adj* svelte, mince, élancé; faible; **~ly** *adv* faiblement.

slenderness *n* sveltesse *f*, minceur *f*; faiblesse *f*.

slice *n* tranche *f*; spatule *f*; * *vt* couper (en tranches).

slide *vi* glisser; faire des glissades; * *n* glissade *f*; coulisse *f*; diapositive *f*; toboggan *m*.

sliding *adj* glissant; coulissant.

slight *adj* léger, mince, petit; * *n* affront *m*; * *vt* manquer d'égards pour.

slightly *adv* légèrement.

slightness *n* fragilité *f*; insignifiance *f*.

slim *adj* mince; * *vi* maigrir.

slime *n* vase *f*; dépôt visqueux *m*.

sliminess *n* viscosité *f*.

slimming *n* amaigrissement *m*.

slimy *adj* visqueux, gluant.

sling *n* fronde *f*; écharpe *f*; * *vt* lancer.

slink *vi* s'en aller furtivement; s'éclipser.

slip *vi* (se) glisser, se faufiler; * *vt* glisser; * *n* glissade *f*; faux pas *m*; oubli *m*; fiche *f*.

slipper *n* pantoufle *f*.

slippery *adj* glissant.

slipshod *adj* négligé.

slipway *n* (*mar*) cale *f*.

slit *vt* fendre, inciser; * *n* fente, incision *f*.

slobber *n* bave *f*.

sloe *n* (*bot*) prunelle *f*.

slogan *n* slogan *m*.

sloop *n* (*mar*) sloop *m*.

slop *n* fange *f*; bouillon *m*; **~s** *pl* eaux sales *fpl*.

slope *n* inclinaison *f*; pente *f*; déclivité *f*; versant *m*; * *vt* incliner.

sloping *adj* en pente; incliné.

sloppy *adj* négligé; peu soigné.

sloth *n* paresse *f*.

slouch *vi* manquer de tenue; se tenir d'une façon négligée.

slovenliness *n* négligence *f*; manque de soin *m*.

slovenly *adj* négligé, sale, débraillé.

slow *adj* lent; lourd; ennuyeux; **~ly** *adv* lentement.

slowness *n* lenteur, lourdeur *f*, manque d'intérêt *m*.

slow worm *n* orvet *m*.

slug *n* lingot *m*; limace *f*; jeton *m*; coup *m*.

sluggish *adj* paresseux; léthargique; **~ly** *adv* paresseusement.

sluggishness *n* paresse, mollesse *f*.

sluice *n* écluse *f*; * *vt* lâcher les vannes.

slum *n* taudis *m*; quartier pauvre *m*.

slumber *vi* dormir paisiblement; * *n* sommeil paisible *m*.

slump *n* effondrement *m*.

slur *vt* dénigrer; calomnier; mal articuler; * *n* calomnie *f*.

slush *n* neige fondante *f*.

slut *n* traînée *f*.

sly *adj* rusé; **~ly** *adv* de façon rusée.

slyness *n* ruse, finesse *f*.

smack *n* léger goût *m*; claque *f*; gros baiser retentissant *m*; * *vi* sentir; embrasser bruyamment; * *vt* donner une claque à.

small *adj* petit, menu.

smallish *adj* assez petit.

smallness *n* petitesse *f*.

smallpox *n* variole *f*.

smalltalk *n* conversation *f* banale.

smart *adj* élégant; rapide; astucieux; vif; * *vi* brûler.

smartly *adv* astucieusement, vivement; avec élégance; habilement.

smartness *n* astuce, vivacité, finesse *f*.

smash *vt* casser, briser; détruire; * *vi* se briser (en mille morceaux), se fracasser; * *n* fracas *m*; coup violent *m*.

smattering *n* connaissances superficielles *fpl*.

smear *n* (*med*) frottis *m*; * *vt* enduire; salir.

smell *vt vi* sentir; * *n* odorat *m*; odeur *f*; mauvaise odeur *f*.

smelly *adj* malodorant.

smelt *n* éperlan *m*; * *vt* fondre.

smelter *n* fondeur *m*.

smile *vi* sourire; * *n* sourire *m*.

smirk *vi* sourire d'un air affecté.

smite *vt* frapper.

smith *n* forgeron *m*.

smithy *n* forge *f*.

smock *n* blouse *f*.

smoke *n* fumée *f*; vapeur *f*; * *vt vi* fumer.

smokeless *adj* sans fumée.

smoker *n* fumeur *m* -euse *f*.

smoke shop *n* (US) bureau de tabac *m*.

smoking: 'no ~' 'interdiction de fumer'.

smoky *adj* enfumé; qui fume.

smooth *adj* lisse, uni, égal; doucereux, mielleux; * *vt* lisser; aplanir; adoucir.

smoothly *adv* facilement; doucement.

smoothness *n* douceur *f*; aspect lisse *m*; air doucereux *m*.

smother *vt* étouffer; réprimer.

smoulder *vi* couver, se consumer.

smudge *vt* étaler; * *n* tache *f*.

smug *adj* suffisant.

smuggle *vt* passer en contrebande.

smuggler *n* contrebandier *m* -ière *f*.

smuggling *n* contrebande *f*.

smut *n* saleté *f*; trace de suie *f*.

smuttiness *n* suie *f*; obscénité *f*.

smutty *adj* noirci; obscène.

snack *n* collation *f*.

snack bar *n* snack-bar *m*.

snag *n* obstacle *m*.

snail *n* escargot *m*.

snake *n* serpent *m*.

snaky *adj* sinueux.

snap *vt* casser net; * *vi* se casser net; claquer; mordre; parler sèchement; **~ one's fingers** faire claquer ses doigts; * *n* claquement *m*; photographie *f*.

snapdragon *n* (*bot*) gueule-de-loup *f*.

snap fastener *n* bouton-pression *m*.

snare *n* piège *m*; collet *m*.

snarl *vi* gronder férocement.

snatch *vt* saisir; s'emparer de; * *n* geste vif *m*; vol *m*; fragment *m*.

sneak *vi* se glisser furtivement; * *n* faux-jeton *m*.

sneakers *npl* chaussures de basket *fpl*.

sneer *vi* parler d'un ton méprisant; ricaner.

sneeringly *adv* d'un ton méprisant.

sneeze *vi* éternuer.

sniff *vt* renifler; * *vi* renifler.

snigger *vi* ricaner.

snip *vt* donner de petits coups de ciseaux dans; * *n* petit coup de ciseaux *m*; petit bout *m*.

snipe *n* bécassine *f*.

sniper *n* franc-tireur *m*.

snivel *n* pleurnicherie *f*; * *vi* pleurnicher.

sniveller *n* pleurnicheur *m* -euse *f*.

snobbish *adj* snob.

snooze *n* petit somme *m*; * *vi* faire un somme.

snore *vi* ronfler.

snorkel *n* tube respiratoire *m*.

snort *vi* renifler fortement.

snout *n* museau *m*; groin *m*.

snow *n* neige *f*; * *vi* neiger.

snowball *n* boule de neige *f*.

snowdrop *n* (*bot*) perce-neige *m invar*.

snowman *n* bonhomme de neige *m*.

snowplough *n* chasse-neige *m invar*.

snowy *adj* neigeux; enneigé.

snub *vt* repousser, rejeter.

snub-nosed *adj* au nez retroussé.

snuff *n* tabac à priser *m*.

snuffbox *n* tabatière *f*.

snuffle *vi* parler d'une voix nasillarde, nasiller; renifler.

snug *adj* confortable, douillet; bien abrité.

so *adv* si, tellement, aussi; ainsi.

soak *vi* tremper; * *vt* faire tremper.

soap *n* savon *m*; * *vt* savonner.

soap bubble *n* bulle de savon *f*.

soap opera *n* feuilleton à l'eau de rose *m*.

soap powder *n* lessive *f*.

soapsuds *n* mousse de savon *f*.

soapy *adj* savonneux.

soar *vi* monter en flèche.

sob *n* sanglot *m*; * *vi* sangloter.

sober *adj* sobre; sérieux; **~ly** *adv* sobrement; sérieusement.

sobriety *n* sobriété *f*; sérieux, calme *m*.

soccer *n* football *m*.

sociability *n* sociabilité *f*.

sociable *adj* sociable, liant.

sociably *adv* sociablement.

social *adj* social, sociable; **~ly** *adv* socialement.

socialism *n* socialisme *m*.

socialist *n* socialiste *mf*.

social work *n* assistance sociale *f*.

social worker *n* assistant(e) social(e) *m(f)*.

society *n* société *f*; compagnie *f*.

sociologist *n* sociologue *mf*.

sociology *n* sociologie *f*.

sock *n* chaussette *f*.

socket *n* prise de courant *f*.

sod *n* gazon *m*.

soda *n* soude *f*; eau *f* de Seltz, soda *m*.

soft *adj* doux, moelleux; aimable, gentil; **~ly** *adv* doucement; tendrement.

soften *vt* (r)amollir, adoucir; atténuer.

soft-hearted *adj* compatissant.

softness *n* douceur, mollesse *f*.

soft-spoken *adj* à la voix douce.

software *n* logiciel *m*.

soil *vt* salir, souiller; * *n* salissure, souillure *f*; sol *m*; terre *f*.

sojourn *vi* séjourner; * *n* séjour *m*.

solace *vt* consoler, soulager; * *n* consolation *f*.

solar *adj* solaire.

solder *vt* souder; * *n* soudure *f*.

soldier *n* soldat *m*.

soldierly *adj* militaire.

sole *n* plante du pied *f*; semelle (de chaussure) *f*; sole *f*; * *adj* seul, unique.

solecism *n* (*gr*) solécisme *m*.

solemn *adj* **~ly** *adv* solennel(lement).

solemnise *vt* solenniser.

solemnity *n* solennité *f*.

solicit *vt* solliciter; quémander.

solicitation *n* sollicitation *f*.

solicitor *n* notaire *m*.

solicitous *adj* plein de sollicitude; **~ly** *adv* avec sollicitude.

solicitude *n* sollicitude *f*.

solid *adj* solide, compact; * *n* solide *m*; **~ly** *adv* solidement.

solidify *vt* solidifier.

solidity *n* solidité *f*.

soliloquy *n* soliloque *m*.

solitaire *n* solitaire *m* (jeu).

solitary *adj* solitaire, retiré; * *n* anachorète *m*.

solitude *n* solitude *f*.

solo *n* (*mus*) solo *m*.

solstice *n* solstice *m*.

soluble *adj* soluble.

solution *n* solution *f*.

solve *vt* résoudre.

solvency *n* solvabilité *f*.

solvent *adj* solvable; *n* (*chem*) solvant *m*.

some *adj* du, de la, de l', des; quelques; quelconque; certain(e)s; quelque.

somebody *pn* quelqu'un.

somehow *adv* d'une façon ou d'une autre.

someplace *adv* quelque part.

something *pn* quelque chose.

sometime *adv* au cours de, un jour ou l'autre.

sometimes *adv* quelquefois, parfois.

somewhat *adv* quelque peu.

somewhere *adv* quelque part.

somnambulism *n* somnambulisme *m*.

somnambulist *n* somnambule *mf*.

somnolence *n* somnolence *f*.

somnolent *adj* somnolent.

son *n* fils *m*.

sonata *n* (*mus*) sonate *f*.

song *n* chanson *f*.

son-in-law *n* gendre *m*.

sonnet *n* sonnet *m*.

sonorous *adj* sonore.

soon *adv* bientôt; **as ~ as** dès que.

sooner *adv* plus tôt; plutôt.

soot *n* suie *f*.

soothe *vt* calmer, apaiser; flatter.

soothsayer *n* devin *m*.

sop *n* pain trempé *m*.

sophism *n* sophisme *m*.

sophist *n* sophiste *mf*.

sophistical *adj* sophistiqué.

sophisticate *vt* falsifier; sophistiquer.

sophisticated *adj* sophistiqué.

sophistry *n* sophistique *f*.

sophomore *n* (US) étudiant(e) *m(f)* de seconde année.

soporific *adj* soporifique.

sorcerer *n* sorcier *m*.

sorceress *n* sorcière *f*.

sorcery *n* sorcellerie *f*.

sordid *adj* sordide, sale.

sordidness *n* bassesse *f*, saleté *f*.

sore *n* plaie, blessure *f*; * *adj* douloureux, sensible; contrarié; **~ly** *adv* fortement.

sorrel *n* (*bot*) oseille *f*; * *adj* alezan, roux.

sorrow *n* peine *f*; chagrin *m*; * *vi* se lamenter.

sorrowful *adj* triste, affligé; **~ly** *adv* tristement.

sorry *adj* désolé, navré; déplorable; **I am ~** je suis désolé.

sort *n* sorte *f*; genre *m*; espèce *f*; race *f*; manière *f*; * *vt* classer; trier.

soul *n* âme *f*; essence *f*; personne *f*.

sound *adj* sain; solide; valide; **~ly** *adv* sainement, solidement; * *n* son *m*; bruit *m*; * *vt* sonner (de); * *vi* sonner, retentir; ressembler; sembler.

sound effects *npl* bruitage *m*.

sounding board *n* table d'harmonie *f*; abat-voix *m*.

soundings *npl* (*mar*) sondages *mpl*; (*mar*) fonds *mpl*.

soundness *n* santé *f*; solidité *f*.

soundtrack *n* bande sonore *f*.

soup *n* soupe *f*.

sour *adj* aigre, acide; acerbe; revêche; **~ly** *adv* aigrement; * *vt* aigrir, faire tourner; * *vi* s'aigrir; tourner.

source *n* source *f*; origine *f*.

sourness *n* acidité, aigreur *f*; acrimonie *f*.

souse *n* (*sl*) soûlard *m* -e *f*; * *vt* mariner; faire tremper.

south *n* sud *m*; * *adj* sud, du sud, au sud; * *adv* au sud; vers le sud.

southerly, southern *adj* du sud, sud, méridional.

southward(s) *adv* vers le sud.

southwester *n* (*mar*) vent du sud-ouest *m*; suroît *m*.

sovereign *adj* *n* souverain *m* -e *f*.

sovereignty *n* souveraineté *f*.

sow *n* truie *f*.

sow *vt* semer; disperser.

sowing time *n* époque des semailles *f*.

soy *n* soja *m*.

space *n* espace *m*; intervalle *m*; * *vt* espacer.

spacecraft *n* vaisseau spatial *m*.

spaceman/woman *n* astronaute *mf*.

spacious *adj* spacieux, ample; **~ly** *adv* spacieusement.

spaciousness *n* dimensions spacieuses *fpl*, espace *m*.

spade *n* bêche *f*; pique *m* (carte).

span *n* envergure *f*; * *vt* enjamber; embrasser.

spangle *n* paillette *f*; * *vt* orner de paillettes.

spaniel *n* épagneul *m*.

Spanish *adj* espagnol; * *n* espagnol *m*; Espagnol *m* -e *f*.

spar *n* (*mar*) espar *m*; * *vi* s'entraîner.

spare *vt* *vi* épargner; ménager; éviter; se passer de; * *adj* de trop; de réserve.

sparing *adj* limité, modéré, économe; **~ly** *adv* frugalement, avec modération.

spark *n* étincelle *f*.

sparkle *n* scintillement *m*, étincelle *f*; * *vi* étinceler; briller.

spark plug *n* bougie *f*.

sparrow *n* moineau *m*.

sparrowhawk *n* épervier *m*.

sparse *adj* clairsemé; épars; **~ly** *adv* faiblement.

spasm *n* spasme *m*.

spasmodic *adj* spasmodique.

spatter *vt* éclabousser; * *vi* gicler.

spatula *n* spatule *f*.

spawn *n* frai *m*; * *vt* pondre; engendrer.

spawning *n* frai *m*.

speak *vt* parler; dire; * *vi* parler, s'entretenir; prendre la parole.

speaker *n* haut-parleur *m*; interlocuteur *m* -trice *f*; orateur *m*.

spear *n* lance *f*; harpon *m*; * *vt* transpercer d'un coup de lance.

special *adj* spécial, particulier; **~ly** *adv* spécialement.

speciality *n* spécialité *f*.

species *n* espèce *f*.

specific *adj* spécifique; * *n* remède spécifique *m*.

specifically *adv* spécifiquement; explicitement.

specification *n* spécification *f*.

specify *vt* spécifier.

specimen *n* spécimen *m*; exemple *m*.

specious *adj* spécieux.

speck(le) *n* grain, tache *f*; * *vt* tacheter, moucheter.

spectacle *n* spectacle *m*.

spectator *n* spectateur *m* -trice *f*.

spectral *adj* spectral; **~ analysis** *n* analyse spectrale *f*.

spectre *n* spectre *m*.

speculate *vi* spéculer; méditer.

speculation *n* spéculation *f*; conjecture *f*; méditation *f*.

speculative *adj* spéculatif, méditatif.

speculum *n* spéculum *m*.

speech *n* parole *f*; discours *m*; langage *m*; élocution *f*.

speechify *vi* discourir, pérorer.

speechless *adj* muet.

speed *n* vitesse *f*; rapidité *f*; * *vt* presser; accélérer; * *vi* se presser.

speedboat *n* vedette *f*.

speedily *adv* rapidement, vite.

speediness *n* rapidité, promptitude, célérité *f*.

speed limit *n* limitation de vitesse *f*.

speedometer *n* compteur de vitesse *m*.

speedway *n* piste de course *f*.

speedy *adj* rapide, prompt.

spell *n* charme, sortilège *m*; période *f*; * *vt* écrire; épeler; ensorceler, envoûter; * s'écrire; s'épeler.

spelling *n* orthographe *f*.

spend *vt* dépenser; passer; épuiser; gaspiller.

spendthrift *n* dépensier *m* -ière *f*.

spent *adj* épuisé.

sperm *n* sperme *m*.

spermaceti *n* spermaceti *m*.

spew *vi* (*sl*) vomir.

sphere n sphère f.

spherical adj sphérique; **~ly** adv de forme sphérique.

spice n épice f; * vt épicer.

spick-and-span adj impeccable; tiré à quatre épingles.

spicy adj épicé.

spider n araignée f.

spigot n clef de robinet f.

spike n pointe f; clou m; * vt clouter.

spill vt renverser, répandre; * vi se répandre.

spin vt filer; inventer, fabriquer; faire tourner; * vi tourner; * n tournoiement m; tour (en voiture) m.

spinach n épinard m.

spinal adj spinal.

spindle n fuseau m; broche f.

spine n colonne vertébrale, épine dorsale f.

spinet n (mus) épinette f.

spinner n fileur m; fileuse f.

spinning wheel n rouet m.

spin-off n sous-produit m.

spinster n célibataire f.

spiral adj **~ly** adv en spirale.

spire n flèche f; aiguille f; tige f.

spirit n esprit m; âme f; caractère m, disposition f; courage m; humeur f; * vt encourager; animer; **~ away** faire disparaître comme par enchantement.

spirited adj vif, fougueux; **~ly** adv fougueusement.

spirit lamp n lampe à alcool f.

spiritless adj sans entrain, abattu.

spiritual adj **~ly** adv spirituel(lement).

spiritualist n spiritualiste mf.

spirituality n spiritualité f.

spit n crachat m; salive f; * vt vi cracher; crépiter.

spite n dépit m, rancune f; **in ~ of** en dépit de, malgré; * vt vexer.

spiteful adj rancunier, malveillant; **~ly** adv par méchanceté, par rancune.

spitefulness n méchanceté f; rancune f.

spittle n salive f; crachat m.

splash vt éclabousser, faire gicler; * vi barboter; * n éclaboussure f; tache f.

spleen n rate f; spleen m.

splendid adj splendide, magnifique; **~ly** adv splendidement.

splendour n splendeur f; magnificence f.

splice vt (mar) épisser, abouter.

splint n éclisse f.

splinter n éclat m; esquille f; échar-

de f; * vt (vi) (se) fendre en éclats.

split n fente f; rupture f; * vt fendre, diviser; * vi se fendre.

spoil vt abîmer; gâter; gâcher.

spoiled adj abîmé; gâté.

spoke n rayon (de roue) m.

spokesman/woman n porte-parole mf.

sponge n éponge f; * vt éponger; * vi être un parasite.

sponger n parasite m.

sponginess n spongiosité f.

spongy adj spongieux.

sponsor n caution m; parrain m; marraine f.

sponsorship n parrainage m.

spontaneity n spontanéité f.

spontaneous adj **~ly** adv spontané(ment).

spool n bobine f; rouleau m.

spoon n cuiller f.

spoonful n cuillerée f.

sporadic(al) adj sporadique.

sport n sport m; jeu m; divertissement, amusement m.

sports car n voiture de sport f.

sports jacket n veste sport f.

sportsman/woman n sportif m -ive f.

sportswear n vêtements de sport mpl.

spot n tache f; point m; endroit m; pois m; * vt apercevoir; tacher.

spotless adj impeccable, immaculé.

spotlight n feu de projecteur m.

spotted, spotty adj tacheté; à pois.

spouse n époux m, épouse f.

spout vi jaillir; gicler; déblatérer; * vt faire jaillir; * n bec m; gargouille f; jet m.

sprain vt fouler; * n entorse f.

sprawl vi s'étaler.

spray n spray m; pulvérisation f; embruns mpl.

spread vt étendre, étaler; répandre, propager; * vi s'étendre, se répandre; * n propagation, diffusion f.

spree n fête f.

sprig n brin m.

sprightliness n vivacité f, entrain m.

sprightly adj alerte, vif, fringant.

spring vi bondir, sauter; provenir, découler; émaner, naître; * n printemps m; élasticité f; ressort m; saut m; source f.

springiness n élasticité f.

springtime n printemps m.

springwater n eau de source f.

springy adj élastique.

sprinkle vt arroser.

sprinkling n arrosage m.

sprout n pousse f, germe m; **~s** npl choux de Bruxelles mpl; * vi germer.

spruce adj net, impeccable; **~ly** adv tiré à quatre épingles; * vi se mettre sur son trente-et-un.

spruceness n élégance f.

spur n éperon m; ergot (coq) m; stimulant m; * vt éperonner; stimuler.

spurious adj faux, feint; falsifié, de contrefaçon.

spurn vt repousser avec mépris.

sputter vi postillonner; bredouiller; bafouiller.

spy n espion m -ne f; * vt apercevoir; espionner; vi espionner.

squabble vi se disputer, se quereller; * n querelle, dispute f.

squad n escouade f; brigade f; équipe f.

squadron n (mil) escadron m.

squalid adj misérable, sordide.

squall n rafale f; bourrasque f; * vi brailler.

squally adj qui souffle en rafales.

squalor n saleté f; misère f.

squander vt gaspiller, dilapider.

square adj carré; catégorique; honnête; * n carré m; place f; équerre f; * vt cadrer; mettre en ordre, régler; * vi cadrer.

squareness n forme carrée f.

squash vt écraser; * n squash m.

squat vi s'accroupir; * adj accroupi; trapu, courtaud.

squaw n squaw, femme peau-rouge f.

squeak vi grincer, crier; * n cri, couinement m.

squeal vi pousser un cri aigu, couiner.

squeamish adj impressionable; délicat.

squeeze vt presser, tordre; comprimer; * n pression f; serrement de main m; cohue f.

squid n calmar m.

squint adj atteint de strabisme; * vi loucher; * n strabisme.

squirrel n écureuil m.

squirt vt faire gicler; * n giclée f; jet m.

stab vt poignarder; * n coup de couteau m.

stability n stabilité, solidité f.

stable n écurie f; * vt mettre à l'écurie; * adj stable.

stack n pile f; * vt empiler.

staff n personnel m; bâton m; soutien m.

stag n cerf m.

stage n étape f; scène f; échafaudage *m*; théâtre *m*; stade *m*; estrade *f*.

stagger *vi* vaciller, tituber; hésiter; * *vt* stupéfier; échelonner.

stagnation *n* stagnation *f*.

stagnant *adj* stagnant.

stagnate *vi* stagner.

staid *adj* posé, sérieux, guindé.

stain *vt* tacher; ternir; * *n* tache *f*.

stainless *adj* sans tache; immaculé.

stair *n* marche *f*; ~s *pl* escalier *m*.

staircase *n* escalier *m*.

stake *n* pieu *m*; enjeu *m*; * *vt* marquer; délimiter.

stale *adj* rassis, rance.

staleness *n* manque de fraîcheur *m*; rance *m*.

stalk *vi* avancer d'un air majestueux; * *n* tige, queue *f*, trognon *m*.

stall *n* stalle *f*; stand, étalage *m*; (fauteuil d') orchestre *m*; emplacement *m*; * *vt* caler; * *vi* caler; atermoyer.

stallion *n* étalon *m*.

stalwart *n* partisan fidèle *m*.

stamen *n* étamine *f*.

stamina *n* résistance *f*.

stammer *vi* bégayer; * *n* bégaiement *m*.

stamp *vt* trépigner; timbrer; affranchir; tamponner; * *vi* trépigner; * *n* timbre *m*; cachet *m*; tampon *m*; empreinte *f*; estampille *f*.

stampede *n* débandade *f*.

stand *vi* être debout, se tenir; se maintenir; résister; être situé, se trouver; rester, durer; s'arrêter, faire halte; * *vt* poser; résister; soutenir, supporter; * *n* position, prise de position *f*; pied, support *m*; étalage *m*; état *m*; tribune *f*; stand *m*.

standard *n* étendard *m*; modèle *m*; étalon *m*; norme *f*; * *adj* normal.

standing *adj* permanent, fixe, établi; en pied; * *n* durée *f*; importance *f*; rang *m*.

standstill *n* arrêt *m*; immobilisation *f*.

staple *n* agrafe *f*; * *adj* principal, de base; * *vt* agrafer.

star *n* étoile *f*; astérisque *m*.

starboard *n* tribord *m*.

starch *n* amidon *m*; * *vt* amidonner.

stare *vi*: **to ~ at** regarder fixement; * *n* regard fixe *m*.

stark *adj* raide, rigide; cru; * *adv* complètement.

starling *n* étourneau *m*.

starry *adj* étoilé.

start *vi* commencer, débuter; sursauter, tressaillir; démarrer, se mettre en route; * *vt* commencer; amorcer; lancer; mettre en marche; * *n* début *m*; ouverture *f*; sursaut *m*; départ *m*; avance *f*.

starter *n* starter, démarreur *m*.

starting point *n* point de départ *m*.

startle *vt* faire sursauter.

startling *adj* surprenant, alarmant.

starvation *n* inanition, faim *f*.

starve *vi* mourir de faim.

state *n* état *m*; condition *f*; pompe *f*, apparat *m*; **the S~s** les Etats-Unis *mpl*; * *vt* déclarer; exposer.

stateliness *n* majesté, grandeur *f*.

stately *adj* majestueux, imposant.

statement *n* déclaration, affirmation *f*.

statesman *n* homme d'État *m*.

statesmanship *n* qualité d'homme politique *f*.

static *adj* statique; * *n* parasites *mpl*.

station *n* station *f*; place, position *f*; condition *f*, rang *m*; situation *f*; condition *f*; (*rail*) gare *f*; * *vt* placer.

stationary *adj* stationnaire, immobile.

stationer *n* papetier *m* -ière *f*.

stationery *n* papeterie *f*.

station wagon *n* (US) break *m*.

statistical *adj* statistique.

statistics *npl* statistiques *fpl*.

statuary *n* statuaire *f*.

statue *n* statue *f*.

stature *n* stature, taille *f*.

statute *n* statut *m*; loi *f*.

stay *n* séjour *m*; ~s *npl* corset *m*; * *vi* rester, demeurer; tenir; loger; ~ **in** rester à la maison; ~ **on** rester encore quelque temps; ~ **up** ne pas se coucher.

stead *n* place *f*, lieu *m*.

steadfast *adj* ferme, résolu, inébranlable; ~**ly** *adv* fermement, résolument.

steadily *adv* fermement; régulièrement.

steadiness *n* fermeté, stabilité *f*.

steady *adj* stable, solide; * *vt* affermir.

steak *n* bifteck *m*; steak *m*.

steal *vt vi* voler.

stealth *n* discrétion *f*; **by ~** à la dérobée.

stealthily *adv* furtivement.

stealthy *adj* furtif.

steam *n* vapeur *f*; buée *f*; * *vt* cuire à la vapeur; * *vi* fumer.

steam engine *n* locomotive à vapeur *f*.

steamer, steamboat *n* (bateau à) vapeur, paquebot *m*.

steel *n* acier *m*; * *adj* d'acier.

steelyard *n* balance romaine *f*.

steep *adj* abrupt; excessif; * *vt* tremper.

steeple *n* clocher *m*; flèche *f*.

steeplechase *n* steeple (course) *m*.

steepness *n* raideur *f*; escarpement *m*.

steer *n* bouvillon *m*; * *vt* conduire; diriger; gouverner; * *vi* tenir le gouvernail.

steering *n* direction *f*.

steering wheel *n* volant *m*.

stellar *adj* stellaire.

stem *n* tige *f*, tronc *m*; souche *f*; pied *m*; tuyau *m*; * *vt* endiguer.

stench *n* odeur fétide *f*.

stencil *n* stencil *m*, pochoir *m*.

stenographer *n* sténographe *mf*.

stenography *n* sténographie *f*.

step *n* pas *m*, marche *f*; trace *f*; * *vi* faire un pas; marcher.

stepbrother *n* demi-frère *m*.

stepdaughter *n* belle-fille *f*.

stepfather *n* beau-père *m*.

stepmother *n* belle-mère *f*.

stepping stone *n* pierre de gué *f*.

stepsister *n* demi-sœur *f*.

stepson *n* beau-fils *m*.

stereo *n* stéréo *f*.

stereotype *n* stéréotype *m*; * *vt* stéréotyper.

sterile *adj* stérile.

sterility *n* stérilité *f*.

sterling *adj* de bon aloi, vrai, véritable; * *n* livres sterling *fpl*.

stern *adj* sévère, rigide, strict; * *n* (*mar*) poupe *f*; ~**ly** *adv* sévèrement.

stethoscope *n* (*med*) stéthoscope *m*.

stevedore *n* (*mar*) docker *m*.

stew *vt* faire cuire à l'étouffée; * *n* ragoût *m*.

steward *n* intendant *m*; (*mar*) steward *m*.

stewardess *n* hôtesse de l'air *f*.

stewardship *n* intendance *f*.

stick *n* bâton *m*; canne *f*; baguette *f*; * *vt* coller; piquer, planter; supporter; * *vi* tenir; se planter; rester fidèle.

stickiness *n* viscosité *f*.

stick-up *n* braquage *m*, hold-up *m*.

sticky *adj* collant, poisseux.

stiff *adj* raide, rigide; inflexible; dur; entêté; ~**ly** *adv* raidement; obstinément.

stiffen *vt* raidir, renforcer; * *vi* se raidir.

stiff neck *n* torticolis *m*.

stiffness n raideur, rigidité f; opiniâtreté f.

stifle vt étouffer.

stifling adj suffocant.

stigma n stigmate m.

stigmatise vt stigmatiser.

stile n tourniquet m.

stiletto n stylet m; talon aiguille m.

still vt calmer, apaiser; faire taire; * adj silencieux, calme; * n alambic m; * adv encore; toujours; quand même, tout de même.

stillborn adj mort-né.

stillness n calme m, tranquillité f.

stilts npl échasses fpl.

stimulant n stimulant m.

stimulate vt stimuler.

stimulation n stimulant m; stimulation f.

stimulus n stimulant m.

sting vt piquer; * vi brûler; * n dard m; piqûre f; aiguillon m.

stingily adv avec avarice.

stinginess n mesquinerie, avarice f.

stingy adj mesquin, avare, pingre.

stink vi puer; * n puanteur f.

stint n tâche assignée f.

stipulate vt stipuler.

stipulation n stipulation f.

stir vt remuer; agiter; exciter; * vi remuer, bouger; * n agitation f; émoi m.

stirrup n étrier m.

stitch vt coudre; * n point m; point de suture m.

stoat n hermine f.

stock n réserve f; provision f; bouillon m; souche f; lignée f; capital m; fonds mpl; ~s pl valeurs mobilières fpl; * vt approvisionner, stocker.

stockade n prison militaire f.

stockbroker n agent de change m.

stock exchange n Bourse f.

stockholder n actionnaire mf.

stocking n bas m.

stock market n Bourse f.

stoic n stoïque mf.

stoical adj ~ly adv stoïque(ment).

stoicism n stoïcisme m.

stole n étole f.

stomach n estomac m; ventre m; * vt digérer; endurer.

stone n pierre f; caillou m; noyau m; * adj de pierre; * vt lancer des pierres sur; dénoyauter; empierrer.

stone deaf adj sourd comme un pot.

stoning n empierrement m.

stony adj pierreux, rocailleux; dur.

stool n tabouret m; rebord, appui m.

stoop vi se baisser, se pencher; * n inclination en avant f.

stop vt arrêter, interrompre; boucher; * vi s'arrêter, cesser; * n arrêt m; halte f; pause f; point m.

stopover n escale; étape f.

stoppage, stopping n obstruction f; engorgement m; (rail) suppression f.

stopwatch n chronomètre m.

storage n emmagasinage m; entreposage m.

store n provision f; réserve f; entrepôt m, magasin m; * vt mettre en réserve, accumuler, emmagasiner.

storekeeper n marchand m -e f.

storey n (UK) étage m.

stork n cigogne f.

storm n tempête f, orage m; assaut m; * vt prendre d'assaut; * vi faire rage.

stormily adv violemment.

stormy adj orageux; houleux.

story n histoire f; récit m; (US) étage m.

stout adj corpulent, robuste, vigoureux; solide; ~ly adv solidement; vaillamment; résolument.

stoutness n vigueur f; puissance f; corpulence f.

stove n poêle m; cuisinière f.

stow vt ranger, mettre en place; (mar) arrimer.

straggle vi être disséminé.

straggler n traînard m -e f.

straight adj droit; direct; franc; * adv droit; directement.

straightaway adv immédiatement, tout de suite.

straighten vt redresser.

straightforward adj honnête; franc; direct.

straightforwardness n honnêteté f.

strain vt tendre; fouler; forcer; mettre à l'épreuve; * vi peiner; * n tension f; effort m; entorse f; contrainte f; lignée f; accent m; ton m.

strainer n passoire f.

strait n détroit m; embarras m; situation critique f.

strait-jacket n camisole de force f.

strand n brin m; rivage m, rive f.

strange adj inconnu; étrange; ~ly adv étrangement, curieusement.

strangeness n étrangeté f; nouveauté f.

stranger n inconnu(e) m(f), étranger m -ère f.

strangle vt étrangler.

strangulation n strangulation f.

strap n lanière, sangle f; courroie f; * vt attacher avec une courroie.

strapping adj robuste, charpenté.

stratagem n stratagème m.

strategic adj stratégique m.

strategy n stratégie f.

stratum n strate f.

straw n paille f.

strawberry n fraise f.

stray vi s'égarer; vagabonder; * adj perdu; errant.

streak n raie, bande f; filet m; * vt strier.

stream n ruisseau m, rivière f; torrent m; * vi ruisseler.

streamer n serpentin m.

street n rue f.

streetcar n tramway m.

strength n force, puissance f; vigueur f; robustesse f.

strengthen vt fortifier; confirmer, renforcer.

strenuous adj ardu; vigoureux.

stress n pression f; stress m; tension f; contrainte f; importance f; accent m; * vt souligner; accentuer.

stretch vt étendre, étirer; élargir; forcer; * vi s'étendre, s'étirer; * n extension f; étendue f; période f.

stretcher n brancard m.

strew vt éparpiller; semer.

strict adj strict, sévère; exact, rigoureux, précis; ~ly adv strictement, sévèrement.

strictness n sévérité f; rigueur f.

stride n grand pas m; * vi marcher à grandes enjambées.

strife n conflit m, lutte f.

strike vt frapper; heurter; attaquer; rayer; * vi frapper; se mettre en grève; sonner; * n coup m; grève f; découverte f.

striker n gréviste mf.

striking adj frappant; saisissant; ~ly adv remarquablement.

string n ficelle f; corde f; cordon m; rang m; fibre f; * vt munir d'une corde; enfiler; suspendre.

stringent adj rigoureux.

stringy adj filandreux.

strip vt déshabiller, dévêtir; * vi se déshabiller; * n bande f; langue f; bandelette f.

stripe n raie, rayure f; coup de fouet m; * vt rayer.

strive vi s'efforcer; s'évertuer; lutter, se battre.

stroke n coup m; trait m; course f; caresse f; apoplexie f; * vt caresser.

stroll n petit tour; * vi flâner.

strong adj fort, vigoureux, robuste; puissant; intense; **~ly** *adv* fortement, énergiquement.

strongbox *n* coffre-fort *m*.

stronghold *n* forteresse *f*.

strophe *n* strophe *f*.

structure *n* structure *f*; construction *f*.

struggle *vi* lutter; se battre; se démener; * *n* lutte *f*.

strum *vt* (*mus*) tapoter de.

strut *vi* se pavaner; * *n* démarche affectée *f*.

stub *n* souche *f*; bout *m*; talon *m*.

stubble *n* chaume *m*; barbe de plusieurs jours *f*.

stubborn *adj* entêté, obstiné; **~ly** *adv* obstinément.

stubbornness *n* entêtement *m*, obstination *f*.

stucco *n* stuc *m*.

stud *n* clou *m*; crampon *m*; écurie *f*.

student *n*, *adj* étudiant *m* -e *f*.

stud horse *n* étalon *m*.

studio *n* studio, atelier *m*.

studio apartment *n* studio *m*.

studious *adj* studieux; sérieux; **~ly** *adv* studieusement, sérieusement.

study *n* étude *f*; études *fpl*; méditation *f*; * *vt* étudier; observer; * *vi* étudier; faire des études.

stuff *n* matière *f*; matériaux *mpl*; étoffe *f*; * *vt* (rem)bourrer, remplir; empailler.

stuffing *n* rembourrage *m*.

stuffy *adj* mal aéré; collet monté.

stumble *vi* trébucher; * *n* faux pas, trébuchement *m*.

stumbling block *n* hésitation *f*; pierre d'achoppement *f*.

stump *n* souche *f*; moignon *m*; bout *m*.

stun *vt* étourdir; stupéfier.

stunner *n* personne *ou* chose extraordinaire *f*.

stunt *n* cascade *f*; coup de publicité *m*; * *vt* empêcher de croître.

stuntman *n* cascadeur *m*.

stupefy *vt* hébéter; stupéfier.

stupendous *adj* prodigieux, remarquable.

stupid *adj* **~ly** *adv* stupide(ment).

stupidity *n* stupidité *f*.

stupor *n* stupeur *f*.

sturdily *adv* fortement.

sturdiness *n* force, robustesse *f*; résolution *f*.

sturdy *adj* vigoureux, robuste, fort; hardi, résolu.

sturgeon *n* esturgeon *m*.

stutter *vi* bégayer.

sty *n* porcherie *f*; taudis *m*.

stye *n* orgelet *m*.

style *n* style *m*; mode *f*; * *vt* appeler, dénommer; créer, dessiner.

stylish *adj* élégant, qui a du chic.

suave *adj* suave.

subdivide *vt* subdiviser.

subdivision *n* subdivision *f*.

subdue *vt* subjuguer, assujettir; contenir, réfréner; adoucir.

subject *adj* soumis; sujet à; * *n* sujet *m*; thème *m*; * *vt* soumettre; exposer.

subjection *n* sujétion *f*.

subjugate *vt* subjuguer, assujettir.

subjugation *n* subjugation *f*.

subjunctive *n* subjonctif *m*.

sublet *vt* sous-louer.

sublimate *vt* sublimer.

sublime *adj* sublime, suprême; **~ly** *adv* sublimement; * *n* sublime *m*.

sublimity *n* sublimité *f*.

submachine gun *n* mitraillette *f*.

submarine *adj n* sous-marin *m*.

submerge *vt* submerger.

submersion *n* submersion *f*.

submission *n* soumission *f*.

submissive *adj* soumis, docile; **~ly** *adv* avec soumission.

submissiveness *n* docilité *f*; soumission *f*.

submit *vt* soumettre; * *vi* se soumettre.

subordinate *adj* subalterne, inférieur; * *vt* subordonner.

subordination *n* subordination *f*.

subpoena *n* assignation *f* à comparaître; * *vt* assigner.

subscribe *vi* souscrire; * *vt* apposer; signer.

subscriber *n* souscripteur *m* -trice *f*.

subscription *n* souscription *f*.

subsequent *adj* **~ly** *adv* ultérieur(ement).

subservient *adj* subordonné; utile.

subside *vi* s'affaisser, baisser.

subsidence *n* affaissement *m*.

subsidiary *adj* subsidiaire.

subsidise *vt* subventionner, fournir des subsides à.

subsidy *n* subvention *f*; subside *m*.

subsist *vi* subsister; exister.

subsistence *n* existence *f*; subsistance *f*.

substance *n* substance *f*; fond *m*; essentiel *m*.

substantial *adj* considérable; réel, substantiel; solide; **~ly** *adv* considérablement.

substantiate *vt* justifier.

substantive *n* substantif *m*.

substitute *vt* substituer; * *n* remplaçant *m* -e *f*.

substitution *n* substitution *f*.

substratum *n* substrat *m*.

subterfuge *n* subterfuge *m*; fauxfuyant *m*.

subterranean *adj* souterrain.

subtitle *n* sous-titre *m*.

subtle *adj* subtile.

subtlety *n* subtilité *f*.

subtly *adv* subtilement.

subtract *vt* (*math*) soustraire.

suburb *n* banlieue *f*.

suburban *adj* de banlieue.

subversion *n* subversion *f*.

subversive *adj* subversif.

subvert *vt* subvertir, renverser.

subway *n* (US) métro *m*.

succeed *vi* réussir; succéder; avoir du succès; * *vt* succéder à, suivre.

success *n* succès *m*.

successful *adj* couronné de succès, qui réussit; **~ly** *adv* avec succès.

succession *n* succession *f*.

successive *adj* successif; **~ly** *adv* successivement.

successor *n* successeur *m*.

succinct *adj* succinct, concis; **~ly** *adv* succinctement.

succulent *adj* succulent.

succumb *vi* succomber.

such *adj* tel, pareil; **~ as** tel que.

suck *vt vi* sucer; *vi* téter.

suckle *vt* allaiter.

suckling *n* nourrisson *m*.

suction *n* succion *f*.

sudden *adj* **~ly** *adv* soudain(ement), subit(ement).

suddenness *n* soudaineté *f*.

suds *npl* mousse de savon *f*.

sue *vt* poursuivre en justice; supplier.

suede *n* daim *m*.

suet *n* graisse de rognon *f* de bœuf.

suffer *vt* souffrir, subir; tolérer, endurer; * *vi* souffrir.

suffering *n* souffrance *f*; douleur *f*.

suffice *vi* suffire, être suffisant.

sufficiency *n* quantité suffisante *f*; aisance *f*.

sufficient *adj* suffisant; **~ly** *adv* suffisamment.

suffocate *vt vi* étouffer.

suffocation *n* suffocation *f*.

suffrage *n* suffrage, vote *m*.

suffuse *vt* baigner, se répandre sur.

sugar *n* sucre *m*; * *vt* sucrer.

sugar beet *n* betterave à sucre *f*.

sugar cane *n* canne à sucre *f*.

sugar loaf *n* pain de sucre *m*.

sugar plum *n* bonbon *m*.

sugary *adj* sucré.

suggest *vt* suggérer.

suggestion *n* suggestion *f*.

suicidal *adj* suicidaire.

suicide *n* suicide *m*; suicidé *m* -e *f*.

suit *n* procès *m*; pétition *f*; costume *m*; tailleur *m*; requête *f*; * *vt* convenir à; aller à; arranger, adapter.

suitable *adj* qui convient, approprié.

suitably *adv* convenablement.

suitcase *n* valise *f*.

suite *n* suite *f*; escorte *f*; mobilier *m*; cortège *m*.

suitor *n* plaideur *m*; prétendant *m*.

sulkiness *n* bouderie *f*.

sulky *adj* boudeur, maussade.

sullen *adj* maussade; sombre; **~ly** *adv* d'un air maussade; de mauvaise grâce.

sullenness *n* maussaderie *f*; silence *m*.

sulphur *n* soufre *m*.

sulphurous *adj* sulfureux.

sultan *n* sultan *m*.

sultana *n* sultane *f*; raisin sec *m*.

sultry *adj* étouffant; chaud.

sum *n* somme *f*; total *m*; **~ up** *vt* résumer; récapituler; * *vi* résumer.

summarily *adv* sommairement.

summary *adj n* résumé *m*.

summer *n* été *m*.

summerhouse *n* gloriette *f*, pavillon de jardin *m*.

summit *n* sommet *m*; cime *f*.

summon *vt* convoquer, citer à comparaître; sommer; (*mil*) sommer de se rendre.

summons *n* convocation *f*; sommation *f*.

sumptuous *adj* somptueux; **~ly** *adv* somptueusement.

sun *n* soleil *m*.

sunbathe *vi* prendre un bain de soleil, se faire bronzer.

sunburnt *adj* bronzé, hâlé.

Sunday *n* dimanche *m*.

sundial *n* cadran solaire *m*.

sundry *adj* divers, différent.

sunflower *n* tournesol *m*.

sunglasses *npl* lunettes de soleil *fpl*.

sunless *adj* sans soleil.

sunlight *n* lumière du soleil *f*.

sunny *adj* ensoleillé; radieux.

sunrise *n* lever de soleil *m*.

sun roof *n* toit ouvrant *m*.

sunset *n* coucher de soleil *m*.

sunshade *n* parasol *m*.

sunshine *n* (lumière du) soleil *m*; ensoleillement *m*.

sunstroke *n* insolation *f*.

suntan *n* bronzage *m*.

suntan oil *n* huile solaire *f*.

super *adj* (*fam*) sensationnel.

superannuated *adj* en retraite.

superannuation *n* retraite, pension de retraite *f*.

superb *adj* **~ly** *adv* superbe(ment).

supercargo *n* (*mar*) subrécargue *m*.

supercilious *adj* hautain, dédaigneux; **~ly** *adv* avec dédain.

superficial *adj* **~ly** *adv* superficiel(lement).

superfluity *n* surabondance, superfluité *f*.

superfluous *adj* superflu.

superhuman *adj* surhumain.

superintendent *n* directeur *m* -trice *f*.

superior *adj n* supérieur *m* -e *f*.

superiority *n* supériorité *f*.

superlative *adj* superlatif *m*; **~ly** *adv* extrêmement, au suprême degré.

supermarket *n* supermarché *m*.

supernatural *n* surnaturel.

supernumerary *adj* surnuméraire.

superpower *n* superpuissance *f*.

supersede *vt* remplacer; supplanter.

supersonic *adj* supersonique.

superstition *n* superstition *f*.

superstitious *adj* superstitieux; **~ly** *adv* superstitieusement.

superstructure *n* superstructure *f*.

supertanker *n* gros pétrolier, supertanker *m*.

supervene *vi* survenir.

supervise *vt* surveiller, superviser.

supervision *n* surveillance *f*.

supervisor *n* surveillant *m* -e *f*.

supine *adj* couché, étendu sur le dos; indolent.

supper *n* dîner *m*.

supplant *vt* supplanter.

supple *adj* souple, flexible; obséquieux.

supplement *n* supplément *m*.

supplementary *adj* supplémentaire.

suppleness *n* souplesse *f*.

suppli(c)ant *n* suppliant *m* -e *f*.

supplicate *vt* supplier.

supplication *n* supplique, supplication *f*.

supplier *n* fournisseur *m*.

supply *vt* fournir, approvisionner; suppléer à, remédier à; * *n* approvisionnement *m*; provision *f*.

support *vt* soutenir; supporter, appuyer; * *n* appui *m*.

supportable *adj* supportable.

supporter *n* partisan *m*; supporter *m*, adepte *mf*.

suppose *vt vi* supposer.

supposition *n* supposition *f*.

suppress *vt* supprimer.

suppression *n* suppression *f*.

supremacy *n* suprématie *f*.

supreme *adj* **~ly** *adv* suprême(ment).

surcharge *vt* surcharger; * *n* surtaxe *f*.

sure *adj* sûr, certain; infaillible; **to be ~** certainement; **~ly** *adv* sûrement, certainement, sans doute.

sureness *n* certitude, sûreté *f*.

surety *n* certitude *f*; caution *f*.

surf *n* (*mar*) ressac *m*.

surface *n* surface *f*; * *vt* revêtir; * *vi* remonter à la surface.

surfboard *n* planche (de surf) *f*.

surfeit *n* excès *m*.

surge *n* vague, montée *f*; * *vi* déferler.

surgeon *n* chirurgien *m*.

surgery *n* chirurgie *m*.

surgical *adj* chirurgical.

surliness *n* air revêche, bourru *m*.

surly *adj* revêche, bourru.

surmise *vt* conjecturer; * *n* conjecture *f*.

surmount *vt* surmonter.

surmountable *adj* surmontable.

surname *n* nom de famille *m*.

surpass *vt* surpasser, dépasser.

surpassing *adj* sans pareil, incomparable.

surplice *n* surplis *m*.

surplus *n* excédent *m*; surplus *m*; * *adj* en surplus.

surprise *vt* surprendre; * *n* surprise *f*.

surprising *adj* surprenant.

surrender *vt* rendre; céder; * *vi* se rendre; * *n* reddition *f*.

surreptitious *adj* **~ly** *adv* subreptice(ment).

surrogate *vt* remplacer; * *n* substitut *m*.

surrogate mother *n* mère porteuse *f*.

surround *vt* entourer, cerner, encercler.

survey *vt* examiner, inspecter; faire le relevé de; * *n* enquête *f*; relevé (des plans) *m*.

survive *vi* survivre; * *vt* survivre à.

survivor *n* survivant *m* -e *f*.

susceptibility *n* sensibilité *f*.

susceptible *adj* sensible.

suspect *vt* soupçonner; * *n* suspect *m* -e *f*.

suspend *vt* suspendre.

suspense *n* incertitude *f*; suspense *m*.

suspension *n* suspension *f*.

suspension bridge n pont suspendu m.

suspicion n soupçon m.

suspicious adj soupçonneux; **~ly** adv soupçonneusement.

suspiciousness n caractère soupçonneux m.

sustain vt soutenir, supporter, maintenir; subir.

sustenance n (moyens de) subsistance f.

suture n suture f.

swab n tampon m; prélèvement m.

swaddle vt emmailloter.

swaddling clothes npl langes mpl.

swagger vi plastronner.

swallow n hirondelle f; * vt avaler.

swamp n marais m.

swampy adj marécageux.

swan n cygne m.

swap vt échanger; * n échange m.

swarm n essaim m; grouillement m; nuée f; * vi fourmiller; grouiller de monde; pulluler.

swarthy adj basané.

swarthiness n teint basané m.

swashbuckling adj fanfaron.

swath n andain m.

swathe vt emmailloter; * n bande f.

sway vt balancer; * vi se balancer, osciller; * n balancement m; emprise, domination, puissance f.

swear vt jurer; faire prêter serment; * vi jurer.

sweat n sueur f; * vi suer, transpirer.

sweater, sweatshirt n pullover m.

sweep vt balayer; ramoner; * vi s'étendre; avancer rapidement, majestueusement; * n coup de balai m; grand geste m; champ m.

sweeping adj rapide; **~s** pl balayures fpl.

sweepstake n sweepstake m.

sweet adj sucré, doux, agréable; suave; gentil; mélodieux; adorable; * adv doux; sucré; * n bonbon m.

sweetbread n ris de veau m.

sweeten vt sucrer; adoucir; assainir; purifier.

sweetener n édulcorant m.

sweetheart n petit(e) ami(e) m(f); chéri m -e f.

sweetmeats npl sucreries fpl.

sweetness n goût sucré m, douceur f.

swell vi gonfler; enfler; augmenter; * vt gonfler, enfler, grossir; * n houle f; * adj (fam) génial, épatant.

swelling n gonflement m; boursouflure, tuméfaction f.

swelter vi étouffer de chaleur.

swerve vi faire un écart; * vt dévier.

swift adj rapide, prompt, vif; * n martinet m.

swiftly adv rapidement.

swiftness n rapidité, promptitude f.

swill vt boire avidement; * n pâtée f.

swim vi nager; * vt traverser à la nage; * n baignade f.

swimming n natation f, nage f; vertige m.

swimming pool n piscine f.

swimsuit n maillot de bain m.

swindle vt escroquer.

swindler n escroc m.

swine n pourceau, porc m.

swing vi se balancer, osciller; virer; * vt balancer; faire tourner; influencer; * n balancement m; rythme m.

swinging adj (fam) rythmé.

swinging door n porte battante f.

swirl n tourbillon.

switch n baguette f; interrupteur m; (rail) aiguille f; * vt changer de; **~ off** éteindre; **~ on** allumer.

switchboard n standard (téléphonique) m.

swivel vt faire pivoter.

swoon vi s'évanouir; * n évanouissement m, défaillance f.

swoop vi fondre sur; * n descente en piqué f; descente, rafle f; **in one ~** d'un seul coup.

sword n épée f.

swordfish n espadon m.

swordsman n tireur d'épée m.

sycamore n sycomore m.

sycophant n sycophante mf.

syllabic adj syllabique.

syllable n syllabe f.

syllabus n programme m (d'un cours).

syllogism n syllogisme m.

sylph n sylphe m; sylphide f.

symbol n symbole m.

symbolic(al) adj symbolique.

symbolise vt symboliser.

symmetrical adj **~ly** adv symétrique(ment).

symmetry n symétrie f.

sympathetic adj compatissant; **~ally** adv avec compassion.

sympathise vi compatir.

sympathy n compassion f.

symphony n symphonie f.

symptom n symptôme m.

synagogue n synagogue f.

synchronism n synchronisme m.

syndicate n syndicat m.

syndrome n syndrome m.

synod n synode m.

synonym n synonyme m.

synonymous adj synonyme; **~ly** adv de façon synonyme.

synopsis n synopsis f; résumé m.

synoptical adj synoptique.

syntax n syntaxe f.

synthesis n synthèse f.

syringe n seringue f; * vt seringuer.

system n système m.

systematic adj **~ally** adv systématique(ment).

systems analyst n analyste de systèmes mf.

T

tab *n* patte *f*; étiquette *f*.
tabernacle *n* tabernacle *m*.
table *n* table *f*; * *vt* mettre en forme de tableau; ajourner; ~ **d'hôte** repas à prix fixe *m*.
tablecloth *n* nappe *f*.
tablespoon *n* grande cuiller *f*.
tablet *n* tablette *f*; comprimé *m*.
table tennis *n* ping-pong *m*.
taboo *adj n* tabou *m*; * *vt* proscrire.
tabular *adj* tabulaire.
tacit *adj* ~**ly** *adv* tacite(ment).
taciturn *adj* taciturne.
tack *n* broquette *f*; bordée *f*; * *vt* clouer; * *vi* tirer des bordées.
tackle *n* attirail, équipement, matériel *m*; plaquage *m*; (*mar*) appareil de levage *m*, apparaux *mpl*.
tactician *n* tacticien *m*.
tactics *npl* tactique *f*.
tadpole *n* têtard *m*.
taffeta *n* taffetas *m*.
tag *n* ferret *m*; étiquette *f*; * *vt* ferrer.
tail *n* queue *f*; basque *f*; * *vt* suivre, filer.
tailgate *n* hayon arrière *m*.
tailor *n* tailleur *m*.
tailoring *n* métier de tailleur *m*.
tailor-made *adj* fait sur mesure.
tailwind *n* vent arrière *m*.
taint *vt* infecter, polluer; vicier; * *n* tache, souillure *f*.
tainted *adj* infecté; souillé.
take *vt* prendre, saisir; apporter, emporter; conduire; enlever, retirer; passer; * *vi* prendre; ~ **away** *vt* enlever; emporter; ~ **back** *vt* reprendre; raccompagner; ~ **down** *vt* descendre; prendre (notes); ~ **in** *vt* saisir, comprendre; recevoir; ~ **off** *vi* décoller; *vt* enlever; imiter; ~ **on** *vt* accepter; engager; s'attaquer à; ~ **out** *vt* sortir; enlever; ~ **to** *vt* se prendre d'amitié pour; ~ **up** *vt* monter; occuper; se mettre à; * *n* prise *f*.
takeoff *n* décollage *m*.
takeover *n* prise *f* de contrôle.
takings *npl* recette *f*.
talent *n* talent *m*; don *m*.
talented *adj* talentueux.
talisman *n* talisman *m*.
talk *vi* parler, bavarder; causer; * *n* conversation *f*; discussion *f*; entretien *m*.
talkative *adj* loquace.

talk show *n* débat télévisé *m*.
tall *adj* grand, élevé; incroyable.
tally *vi* correspondre.
talon *n* serre *f*.
tambourine *n* tambourin *m*.
tame *adj* apprivoisé, domestiqué; ~**ly** *adv* docilement; fadement; * *vt* apprivoiser, domestiquer.
tameness *n* nature apprivoisée *f*; soumission *f*.
tamper *vi* tripoter.
tampon *n* tampon *m*.
tan *vt vi* bronzer; * *n* bronzage *m*.
tang *n* saveur forte *f*.
tangent *n* tangente *f*.
tangerine *n* mandarine *f*.
tangible *adj* tangible.
tangle *vt* enchevêtrer, embrouiller.
tank *n* réservoir *m*; citerne *f*.
tanker *n* pétrolier *m*; camion-citerne *m*.
tanned *adj* bronzé.
tantalising *adj* tentant.
tantamount *adj* équivalent (à).
tantrum *n* accès de colère *m*.
tap *vt* taper doucement; exploiter; inciser; * *n* petite tape *f*; robinet *m*.
tape *n* ruban *m*; * *vt* enregistrer.
tape measure *n* mètre à ruban *m*.
taper *n* cierge *m*.
tape recorder *n* magnétophone *m*.
tapestry *n* tapisserie *f*.
tar *n* goudron *m*.
target *n* cible *f*.
tariff *n* tarif *m*.
tarmac *n* piste *f* (d'aéroport).
tarnish *vt* ternir.
tarpaulin *n* bâche (goudronnée) *f*.
tarragon *n* (*bot*) estragon *m*.
tart *adj* acidulé; * *n* tarte, tartelette *f*.
tartar *n* tartre *m*.
task *n* tâche *f*.
tassel *n* gland *m* (décoration).
taste *n* goût *m*; saveur *f*; pincée *f*; penchant *m*; * *vt* sentir le goût de; goûter à; déguster; savourer; * *vi* avoir du goût.
tasteful *adj* de bon goût; ~**ly** *adv* avec goût.
tasteless *adj* insipide, sans goût.
tasty *adj* savoureux.
tattoo *n* tatouage *m*; * *vt* tatouer.
taunt *vt* railler; accabler de sarcasmes; * *n* raillerie *f*, sarcasme *m*.
Taurus *n* Taureau *m* (signe du zodiaque).

taut *adj* tendu.
tautological *adj* tautologique.
tautology *n* tautologie *f*.
tawdry *adj* tapageur, voyant, clinquant.
tax *n* impôt *m*; contribution *f*; * *vt* imposer; mettre à l'épreuve.
taxable *adj* imposable.
taxation *n* imposition *f*.
tax collector *n* percepteur *m*.
tax-free *adj* exonéré d'impôts.
taxi *n* taxi *m*; * *vi* rouler sur la piste.
taxi driver *n* chauffeur de taxi *m*.
taxi stand *n* station de taxis *f*.
tax payer *n* contribuable *mf*.
tax relief *n* dégrèvement fiscal *m*.
tax return *n* déclaration d'impôts *f*.
tea *n* thé *m*.
teach *vt* enseigner, apprendre; * *vi* enseigner.
teacher *n* professeur *m*; instituteur *m* -trice *f*.
teaching *n* enseignement *m*.
teacup *n* tasse à thé *f*.
teak *n* teck *m*.
team *n* équipe *f*.
teamster *n* (US) routier *m*.
teamwork *n* travail d'équipe *m*.
teapot *n* théière *f*.
tear *vt* déchirer; ~ **up** mettre en morceaux.
tear *n* larme *f*.
tearful *adj* larmoyant; ~**ly** *adv* en pleurant.
tear gas *n* gaz lacrymogène *m*.
tease *vt* taquiner.
tea-service, tea-set *n* service à thé *m*.
teaspoon *n* petite cuiller *f*.
teat *n* tétine *f*, mamelon *m*.
technical *adj* technique.
technicality *n* technicité *f*.
technician *n* technicien *m* -ne *f*.
technique *n* technique *f*.
technological *adj* technologique.
technology *n* technologie *f*.
teddy (bear) *n* ours en peluche *m*.
tedious *adj* ennuyeux, fastidieux; ~**ly** *adv* fastidieusement.
tedium *n* ennui, manque d'intérêt *m*.
teem *vi* grouiller (de).
teenage *adj* adolescent; ~**r** *n* adolescent(e) *m(f)*.
teens *npl* adolescence (de 13 à 20 ans) *f*.
tee-shirt *n* T-shirt *m*.

teeth *npl* de **tooth**.

teethe *vi* faire ses premières dents.

teetotal *adj* antialcoolique, qui ne boit jamais d'alcool.

teetotaller *n* personne qui ne boit jamais d'alcool *f*.

telegram *n* télégramme *m*.

telegraph *n* télégraphe *m*.

telegraphic *adj* télégraphique.

telegraphy *n* télégraphie *f*.

telepathy *n* télépathie *f*.

telephone *n* téléphone *m*.

telephone booth *n* cabine téléphonique *f*.

telephone call *n* appel téléphonique *m*.

telephone directory *n* annuaire *m*.

telephone number *n* numéro de téléphone *m*.

telescope *n* télescope *m*.

telescopic *adj* télescopique.

televise *vt* téléviser.

television *n* télévision *f*.

television set *n* téléviseur, poste de télévision *m*.

telex *n* télex *m*; *vt* envoyer par télex.

tell *vt* dire; raconter.

teller *n* (banque) caissier *m* -ière *f*.

telling *adj* révélateur.

telltale *adj* dénonciateur.

temper *vt* tempérer, modérer; * *n* colère *f*.

temperament *n* tempérament *m*.

temperance *n* tempérance, modération *f*.

temperate *adj* tempéré, modéré, mesuré.

temperature *n* température *f*.

tempest *n* tempête *f*.

tempestuous *adj* de tempête.

template *n* gabarit *m*.

temple *n* temple *m*; tempe *f*.

temporarily *adv* temporairement.

temporary *adj* temporaire.

tempt *vt* tenter.

temptation *n* tentation *f*.

tempting *adj* tentant.

ten *adj n* dix *m*.

tenable *adj* défendable.

tenacious *adj* tenace, ~**ly** *adv* avec ténacité.

tenacity *n* ténacité *f*.

tenancy *n* location *f*.

tenant *n* locataire *mf*.

tend *vt* garder, surveiller; * *vi* avoir tendance (à).

tendency *n* tendance *f*.

tender *adj* tendre, délicat; sensible; ~**ly** *adv* tendrement; * *n* offre *f*; * *vt* offrir.

tenderness *n* tendresse *f*.

tendon *n* tendon *m*.

tenement *n* appartement *m*.

tenet *n* doctrine *f*; principe *m*.

tennis court *n* court *ou* terrain de tennis *m*.

tennis player *n* joueur(-euse) de tennis *m(f)*.

tennis racket *n* raquette de tennis *f*.

tennis shoes *npl* chaussures de tennis *fpl*.

tenor *n* (*mus*) ténor *m*; sens *m*; substance *f*.

tense *adj* tendu; * *n* (*gr*) temps *m*.

tension *n* tension *f*.

tent *n* tente *f*.

tentacle *n* tentacule *m*.

tentative *adj* timide, hésitant; ~**ly** *adv* à titre d'essai.

tenth *adj n* dixième *mf*.

tenuous *adj* ténu.

tenure *n* titularisation *f*.

tepid *adj* tiède.

term *n* terme *m*; trimestre *m*; mot *m*; condition, clause *f*; * *vt* appeler, nommer.

terminal *adj* terminal; * *n* aérogare *f*; terminal *m*.

terminate *vt* terminer.

termination *n* fin, conclusion *f*.

terrace *n* terrace *f*.

terrain *n* (*mil*) terrain *m*.

terrestrial *adj* terrestre.

terrible *adj* terrible.

terribly *adv* terriblement.

terrier *n* terrier *m* (chien).

terrific *adj* terrifiant; fantastique.

terrify *vt* terrifier, épouvanter.

territorial *adj* territorial.

territory *n* territoire *m*.

terror *n* terreur *f*.

terrorise *vt* terroriser.

terrorism *n* terrorisme *m*.

terrorist *n* terroriste *mf*.

terse *adj* concis, net.

test *n* essai *m*; épreuve *f*; * *vt* essayer; examiner.

testament *n* testament *m*.

tester *n* contrôleur *m* -euse *f*.

testicles *npl* testicules *mpl*.

testify *vt* témoigner, déclarer sous serment.

testimonial *n* certificat *m*.

testimony *n* témoignage *m*.

test pilot *n* pilote d'essai *m*.

test tube *n* éprouvette *f*.

testy *adj* irritable.

tetanus *n* tétanos *m*.

tether *vt* attacher.

text *n* texte *m*.

textbook *n* manuel *m*.

textiles *npl* textile *m*.

textual *adj* textuel.

texture *n* texture *f*; (*med*) tissu *m*.

than *adv* que; de.

thank *vt* remercier, dire merci à.

thankful *adj* reconnaissant; ~**ly** *adv* avec reconnaissance.

thankfulness *n* reconnaissance *f*.

thankless *adj* ingrat.

thanks *npl* remerciement(s) *m(pl)*.

thanksgiving *n* action de grâce *f*.

that *pn* cela, ça, ce; qui, que; celui-là; * *conj* que; afin que; **so** ~ pour que.

thatch *n* chaume *m*; * *vt* couvrir de chaume.

thaw *n* dégel *m*; * *vi* fondre, dégeler.

the *art* le, la, l', les.

theatre *n* théâtre *m*.

theatre-goer *n* habitué(e) du théâtre *m(f)*.

theatrical *adj* théâtral.

theft *n* vol *m*.

their *pn* leur(s); ~**s** le leur; la leur; les leurs; à elles; à eux.

them *pn* les; leur.

theme *n* thème *m*.

themselves *pn pl* eux-mêmes *mpl*, elles-mêmes *fpl*; se.

then *adv* alors, à cette époque-là; ensuite; en ce cas; * *conj* donc; en ce cas; * *adj* d'alors; **now and** ~ de temps en temps.

theological *adj* théologique.

theologian *n* théologien *m* -ne *f*.

theology *n* théologie *f*.

theorem *n* théorème *m*.

theoretical *adj* ~**ly** *adv* théorique(ment).

theorise *vt* théoriser.

theorist *n* théoricien *m* -ne *f*.

theory *n* théorie *f*.

therapeutics *n* thérapeutique *f*.

therapist *n* thérapeute *mf*.

therapy *n* thérapie *f*.

there *adv* y, là.

thereabout(s) *adv* par là, près de là.

thereafter *adv* par la suite; après.

thereby *adv* de cette façon.

therefore *adv* donc, par conséquent.

thermal *adj* thermal.

thermal printer *n* imprimante thermique *f*.

thermometer *n* thermomètre *m*.

thermostat *n* thermostat *m*.

thesaurus *n* trésor *m*; dictionnaire de synonymes *m*.

these *pn pl* ceux-ci, celles-ci.

thesis *n* thèse *f*.

they *pn pl* ils, elles.

thick *adj* épais, gros; dense; obtus.

thicken *vi* (s')épaissir, grossir.

thicket *n* fourré *m*.

thickness n épaisseur f.

thickset adj trapu; râblé.

thick-skinned adj endurci, blindé.

thief n voleur m -euse f.

thigh n cuisse f.

thimble n dé (à coudre) m.

thin adj mince, fin, maigre; clair; * vt amincir; délayer; éclaircir.

thing n chose f; objet m; truc m.

think vi penser, réfléchir, imaginer; * vt penser, croire, juger; ~ **over** vt réfléchir à; ~ **up** vt imaginer.

thinker n penseur m -euse f.

thinking n pensée f; réflexion f; opinion f.

third adj troisième; * n troisième mf; tiers m; ~**ly** adv troisièmement.

third rate adj médiocre, de mauvaise qualité.

thirst n soif f.

thirsty adj assoiffé.

thirteen adj n treize m.

thirteenth adj n treizième mf.

thirtieth adj n trentième mf.

thirty adj n trente m.

this adj ce, cet, cette, ces; * pn ceci, ce.

thistle n chardon m.

thorn n épine f; aubépine f.

thorny adj épineux.

thorough adj consciencieux, approfondi; ~**ly** adv minutieusement, à fond.

thoroughbred adj pur-sang, de race.

thoroughfare n rue, artère f.

those pn pl ceux-là, celles-la; * adj ces, ces… là.

though conj bien que, malgré le fait que; * adv pourtant.

thought n pensée, réflexion f; opinion f; intention f.

thoughtful adj pensif.

thoughtless adj étourdi; irréfléchi; ~**ly** adv étourdiment, à la légère.

thousand adj n mille m.

thousandth adj n millième mf.

thrash vt battre; rouer de coups.

thread n fil m; filetage m; * vt enfiler.

threadbare adj râpé, élimé.

threat n menace f.

threaten vt menacer.

three adj n trois m.

three-dimensional adj à trois dimensions, tridimensionnel.

three-ply adj à trois fils ou épaisseurs.

threshold n seuil m.

thrifty adj économe.

thrill vt faire frissonner; * n frisson m.

thriller n film ou roman à suspense m.

thrive vi prospérer; bien se développer.

throat n gorge f.

throb vi palpiter; vibrer; lanciner.

throne n trône m.

throng n foule f; * vi affluer.

throttle n accélérateur m; * vt étrangler.

through prep à travers; pendant; par, grâce à; * adj direct; * adv complètement.

throughout prep partout dans; * adv partout.

throw vt jeter, lancer, projeter; * n jet m; lancement m; ~ **away** vt jeter; ~ **off** vt rejeter; ~ **out** vt jeter dehors; ~ **up** vt vi vomir.

throwaway adj jetable.

thru (US) = **through.**

thrush n grive f.

thrust vt pousser violemment; enfoncer; * n poussée f.

thud n bruit sourd m.

thug n voyou m.

thumb n pouce m.

thumbtack n punaise f.

thump n coup de poing m; * vi frapper, cogner; * vt cogner à.

thunder n tonnerre m; * vi tonner.

thunderbolt n foudre f.

thunderclap n coup de tonnerre m.

thunderstorm n orage m.

thundery adj orageux.

Thursday n jeudi m.

thus adv ainsi, de cette manière.

thwart vt contrecarrer.

thyme n (bot) thym m.

thyroid n thyroïde f.

tiara n tiare f.

tic n tic m.

tick n tic-tac m; instant m; * vt cocher; ~ **over** vi tourner au ralenti; aller doucement.

ticket n billet, ticket m; étiquette f; carte f.

ticket collector n (rail) contrôleur m -euse f.

ticket office n guichet m.

tickle vt chatouiller.

ticklish adj chatouilleux.

tidal adj (mar) de la marée.

tidal wave n raz-de-marée m.

tide n marée f; (fig) afflux m, cours m.

tidy adj rangé, en ordre; ordonné; soigné.

tie vt attacher, nouer; * vi se nouer; ~ **up** vt ficeler; attacher; amarrer; conclure; * n attache f; lacet m; égalité f.

tier n gradin m; étage m.

tiger n tigre m.

tight adj raide, tendu; serré; hermétique; * adv très fort.

tighten vt (re)serrer, tendre.

tightfisted adj avare.

tightly adv très fort.

tightrope n corde raide f.

tigress n tigresse f.

tile n tuile f; carreau m; * vt couvrir de tuiles.

tiled adj en tuiles, carrelé.

till n caisse f; * vt labourer, cultiver.

tiller n barre du gouvernail f.

tilt vt pencher; * vi s'incliner.

timber n bois de construction m; arbres mpl.

time n temps m; période f; heure f; moment m; (mus) mesure f; **in** ~ à temps; **from** ~ **to** ~ de temps en temps; * vt fixer; chronométrer.

time bomb n bombe à retardement f.

time lag n décalage m.

timeless adj éternel.

timely adj opportun.

time off n temps libre m.

timer n sablier m; minuteur m.

time scale n durée f.

time zone n fuseau horaire m.

timid adj timide, timoré; ~**ly** adv timidement.

timidity n timidité f.

timing n chronométrage m.

tin n étain m; boîte (de conserve) f.

tinfoil n papier d'aluminium m.

tinge n teinte f.

tingle vi picoter; vibrer, frissonner.

tingling n picotement m; frisson m.

tinker n rétameur m.

tinkle vi tinter.

tinplate n fer-blanc m.

tinsel n guirlande f.

tint n teinte f; * vt teinter.

tinted adj teinté; fumé.

tiny adj minuscule, tout petit.

tip n pointe f, bout m; pourboire m; conseil, tuyau m; * vt donner un pourboire à; pencher; effleurer.

tip-off n avertissement m.

tipsy adj gai, éméché.

tiptop adj excellent, de premier ordre.

tirade n diatribe f.

tire n (US) pneu m; * vt fatiguer; * vi se fatiguer; se lasser.

tireless adj infatigable.

tire pressure n (US) pression f des pneus.

tiresome adj ennuyeux, fatigant.

tiring *adj* fatigant.

tissue *n* (US) tissu *m(bot)*; mouchoir *m* en papier.

tissue paper *n* papier *m* de soie.

titbit *n* friandise *f*; bon morceau *m*.

titillate *vt* titiller.

title *n* titre *m*.

title deed *n* titre de propriété *m*.

title page *n* page de titre *f*.

titter *vi* rire sottement; * *n* petit rire sot *m*.

titular *adj* titulaire.

to *prep* à; vers; en; chez; moins; de.

toad *n* crapaud *m*.

toadstool *n* (*bot*) champignon vénéneux *m*.

toast *vt* (faire) griller; porter un toast à la santé de; * *n* toast *m*.

toaster *n* grille-pain *m invar*.

tobacco *n* tabac *m*.

tobacconist *n* marchand(e) de tabac *m(f)*.

tobacco pouch *n* blague à tabac *f*.

tobacco shop *n* bureau de tabac *m*.

toboggan *n* toboggan *m*, luge *f*.

today *adv* aujourd'hui.

toddler *n* enfant qui commence à marcher *m*.

toddy *n* grog *m*.

toe *n* orteil *m*; pointe *f*.

together *adv* ensemble; en même temps.

toil *vi* travailler dur, peiner; se donner du mal; * *n* dur travail *m*; labeur *m*; peine *f*.

toilet *n* toilette *f*; toilettes *fpl*; * *adj* de toilette.

toilet bag *n* trousse de toilette *f*.

toilet bowl *n* cuvette des toilettes *f*.

toilet paper *n* papier hygiénique *m*.

toiletries *npl* articles de toilette *mpl*.

token *n* signe *m*; marque *f*; souvenir *m*; bon *m*; jeton *m*.

tolerable *adj* tolérable; passable.

tolerance *n* tolérance *f*.

tolerant *adj* tolérant.

tolerate *vt* tolérer.

toll *n* péage *m*; nombre de victimes *m*; * *vi* sonner le glas.

tomato *n* tomate *f*.

tomb *n* tombeau *m*; tombe *f*.

tomboy *n* garçon manqué *m*.

tombstone *n* pierre tombale *f*.

tomcat *n* matou *m*.

tomorrow *adv*, *n* demain *m*.

ton *n* tonne *f*.

tone *n* ton *m*; tonalité *f*; * *vi* s'harmoniser; ~ **down** *vt* adoucir.

tone-deaf *adj* qui n'a pas l'oreille musicale.

tongs *npl* pinces *fpl*.

tongue *n* langue *f*.

tongue-tied *adj* muet.

tongue-twister *n* phrase difficile à prononcer *f*.

tonic *n* (*med*) tonique *m*.

tonight *adv*, *n* ce soir (*m*).

tonnage *n* tonnage *m*.

tonsil *n* amygdale *f*.

tonsure *n* tonsure *f*.

too *adv* aussi; trop.

tool *n* outil *m*; ustensile *m*.

tool box *n* caisse à outils *f*.

toot *vi* klaxonner.

tooth *n* dent *f*.

toothache *n* rage de dents *f*.

toothbrush *n* brosse à dents *f*.

toothless *adj* édenté.

toothpaste *n* dentifrice *m*.

toothpick *n* cure-dent *m*.

top *n* sommet *m*, cime *f*; haut *m*; tête *f*; dessus *m*; couvercle *m*; étage supérieur *m*; * *adj* du haut; premier; * *vt* dépasser; être au sommet de; ~ **off** couronner.

topaz *n* topaze *f*.

top floor *n* dernier étage *m*.

top-heavy *adj* instable, déséquilibré.

topic *n* sujet *m*; ~**al** *adj* d'actualité.

topless *adj* torse nu, aux seins nus.

top-level *adj* au plus haut niveau.

topmost *adj* le plus haut.

topographic(al) *adj* topographique.

topography *n* topographie *f*.

topple *vt* renverser; * *vi* basculer.

top-secret *adj* ultra-secret.

topsy-turvy *adv* sens dessus dessous.

torch *n* torche *f*.

torment *vt* tourmenter; * *n* tourment *m*.

tornado *n* tornade *f*.

torrent *n* torrent *m*.

torrid *adj* torride.

tortoise *n* tortue *f*.

tortoiseshell *adj* en écaille de tortue.

tortuous *adj* tortueux, sinueux.

torture *n* torture *f*; * *vt* torturer.

toss *vt* lancer, jeter; agiter, secouer.

total *adj* total, global; ~**ly** *adv* totalement.

totalitarian *adj* totalitaire.

totality *n* totalité *f*.

totter *vi* chanceler.

touch *vt* toucher; ~ **on** effleurer; ~ **up** retoucher; * *n* toucher *m*; contact *m*; touche *f*.

touch-and-go *adj* incertain, précaire.

touchdown *n* atterrissage *m*; but *m*.

touched *adj* touché; timbré.

touching *adj* touchant, attendrissant.

touchstone *n* pierre de touche *f*.

touchwood *n* amadou *m*.

touchy *adj* susceptible.

tough *adj* dur; pénible; résistant; fort; * *n* dur *m*.

toughen *vt* durcir.

toupee *n* postiche *m*.

tour *n* voyage *m*; visite *f*; * *vt* visiter.

touring *n* tourisme *m*.

tourism *n* tourisme *m*.

tourist *n* touriste *mf*.

tourist office *n* office de tourisme *m*.

tournament *n* tournoi *m*.

tow *n* remorquage *m*; * *vt* remorquer.

toward(s) *prep* vers, dans la direction de; envers, à l'égard de.

towel *n* serviette *f*.

towelling *n* tissu éponge *m*.

towel rack *n* porte-serviette *m invar*.

tower *n* tour *f*.

towering *adj* imposant.

town *n* ville *f*.

town clerk *n* secrétaire de mairie *mf*.

town hall *n* mairie *f*.

towrope *n* câble de remorquage *m*.

toy *n* jouet *m*.

toyshop *n* magasin de jouets *m*.

trace *n* trace, piste *f*; * *vt* tracer, esquisser; retrouver.

track *n* trace *f*; empreinte *f*; chemin *m*; voie *f*; piste *f*; * *vt* suivre à la trace.

tracksuit *n* survêtement *m*.

tract *n* étendue *f*, région *f*; brochure *f*.

traction *n* traction *f*.

trade *n* commerce *m*, affaires *fpl*; échange *m*; métier *m*; * *vi* faire le commerce (de), commercer.

trade fair *n* foire commerciale *f*.

trademark *n* marque de fabrique *f*.

trade name *n* raison commerciale *f*.

trader *n* négociant *m* -e *f*.

tradesman *n* fournisseur, commerçant *m*.

trade(s) union *n* syndicat *m*.

trade unionist *n* syndicaliste *mf*.

trading *n* commerce *m*; * *adj* commercial.

tradition *n* tradition *f*

traditional *adj* traditionnel.

traffic *n* circulation *f*; négoce *m*; * *vi* faire le commerce (de).

traffic circle *n* (US) rond-point *m*.

traffic jam *n* embouteillage *m*.

trafficker *n* trafiquant *m* -e *f*.

traffic lights *npl* feux de signalisation *mpl*.

tragedy *n* tragédie *f*.

tragic *adj* ~**ally** *adv* tragique(ment).

tragicomedy *n* tragi-comédie *f*.

trail *vt* suivre la piste de; traîner; *vi* traîner; * *n* traînée *f*; trace *f*; queue *f*.

trailer *n* remorque *f*; caravane *f*; bande-annonce *f*.

train *vt* entraîner; former; * *n* train *m*; traîne *f*; file *f*.

trained *adj* qualifié; diplômé.

trainee *n* stagiaire *mf*.

trainer *n* entraîneur *m*.

training *n* formation *f*; entraînement *m*.

trait *n* trait *m*.

traitor *n* traître *m*.

tramp *n* clochard *m* -e *f*; (*sl*) putain *f*; * *vi* marcher d'un pas lourd; * *vt* piétiner.

trample *vt* piétiner.

trampoline *n* trampoline *m*.

trance *n* transe *f*; extase *f*.

tranquil *adj* tranquille.

tranquillise *vt* tranquilliser.

tranquilliser *n* tranquillisant *m*.

transact *vt* traiter.

transaction *n* transaction *f*; opération *f*.

transatlantic *adj* transatlantique.

transcend *vt* transcender, dépasser; surpasser.

transcription *n* transcription *f*; copie *f*.

transfer *vt* transférer, déplacer; * *n* transfert *m*; mutation *f*; décalcomanie *f*.

transform *vt* transformer.

transformation *n* transformation *f*.

transfusion *n* transfusion *f*.

transient *adj* transitoire, passager.

transit *n* transit *m*.

transition *n* transition *f*; passage *m*.

transitional *adj* de transition.

transitive *adj* transitif.

translate *vt* traduire.

translation *n* traduction *f*.

translator *n* traducteur *m* -trice *f*.

transmission *n* transmision *f*.

transmit *vt* transmettre.

transmitter *n* transmetteur *m*; émetteur *m*.

transparency *n* transparence *f*; diapositive *f*.

transparent *adj* transparent.

transpire *vi* transpirer; arriver.

transplant *vt* transplanter; * *n* transplantation *f*.

transport *vt* transporter; * *n* transport *m*.

transportation *n* moyen de transport *m*.

trap *n* piège *m*; * *vt* prendre au piège; bloquer.

trap door *n* trappe *f*.

trapeze *n* trapèze *m*.

trappings *npl* ornements *mpl*.

trash *n* camelote *f*; inepties *fpl*.

trash can *n* poubelle *f*.

trashy *adj* sans valeur, de mauvaise qualité.

travel *vi* voyager; * *vt* parcourir; * *n* voyage *m*.

travel agency *n* agence de voyages *f*.

travel agent *n* agent de voyages *m*.

traveller *n* voyageur *m* -euse *f*.

traveller's cheque *n* chèque de voyage *m*.

travelling *n* voyages *mpl*.

travel sickness *n* mal de mer/de l'air *m*.

travesty *n* parodie *f*.

trawler *n* chalutier *m*.

tray *n* plateau *m*; tiroir *m*.

treacherous *adj* traître, perfide.

treachery *n* traîtrise *f*.

tread *vi* marcher; écraser; * *n* pas *m*; bruit de pas *m*; bande de roulement *f*.

treason *n* trahison *f*; **high** ~ haute trahison *f*.

treasure *n* trésor *m*; * *vt* conserver précieusement.

treasurer *n* trésorier *m* -ière *f*.

treat *vt* traiter; offrir; * *n* cadeau *m*; plaisir *m*.

treatise *n* traité *m*.

treatment *n* traitement *m*.

treaty *n* traité *m*.

treble *adj* triple; * *vt vi* tripler; * *n* (*mus*) soprano *m*.

treble clef *n* clef de sol *f*.

tree *n* arbre *m*.

trek *n* randonnée *f*.

trellis *n* treillis *m*.

tremble *vi* trembler.

trembling *n* tremblement *m*; frisson *m*.

tremendous *adj* terrible; énorme; formidable.

tremor *n* tremblement *m*.

trench *n* fossé *m*; (*mil*) tranchée *f*.

trend *n* tendance *f*; direction *f*; mode *f*.

trendy *adj* dernier cri.

trepidation *n* vive inquiétude *f*.

trespass *vt* transgresser, violer.

tress *n* boucle de cheveu *f*; ~**es** chevelure *f*.

trestle *n* tréteau, chevalet *m*.

trial *n* procès *m*; épreuve *f*; essai *m*; peine *f*.

triangle *n* triangle *m*.

triangular *adj* triangulaire.

tribal *adj* tribal.

tribe *n* tribu *f*.

tribulation *n* tribulation *f*.

tribunal *n* tribunal *m*.

tributary *adj n* tributaire *m*.

tribute *n* tribut *m*.

trice *n* instant *m*.

trick *n* ruse, astuce *f*, tour *m*; blague *f*; pli *m*; * *vt* attraper.

trickery *n* supercherie *f*.

trickle *vi* couler goutte à goutte; * *n* filet *m*.

tricky *adj* délicat; difficile.

tricycle *n* tricycle *m*.

trifle *n* bagatelle, vétille *f*; * *vi* jouer; badiner.

trifling *adj* futile, insignifiant.

trigger *n* gâchette *f*; ~ **off** *vt* déclencher.

trigonometry *n* trigonométrie *f*.

trill *n* trille *f*; * *vi* triller.

trim *adj* net, soigné; bien tenu; en parfait état; * *vt* arranger; tailler; orner.

trimmings *npl* ornements *mpl*.

Trinity *n* Trinité *f*.

trinket *n* bibelot *m*, babiole *f*; colifichet *m*.

trio *n* (*mus*) trio *m*.

trip *vt* faire trébucher; * *vi* trébucher; faire un faux pas; ~ **up** *vi* trébucher; *vt* faire trébucher; * *n* faux pas *m*; voyage *m*.

tripe *n* tripes *fpl*; bêtises *fpl*.

triple *adj* triple; * *vt vi* tripler.

triplets *npl* triplés *mpl*.

triplicate *n* copie en trois exemplaires *f*.

tripod *n* trépied *m*.

trite *adj* banal; usé.

triumph *n* triomphe *m*; * *vi* triompher.

triumphal *adj* triomphal.

triumphant *adj* triomphant; victorieux; ~**ly** *adv* triomphalement.

trivia *npl* futilités *fpl*.

trivial *adj* insignifiant, sans importance; ~**ly** *adv* banalement.

triviality *n* banalité *f*.

trolley *n* chariot *m*.

trombone *n* trombone *m*.

troop *n* bande *f*; ~**s** *npl* troupes *fpl*.

trooper *n* soldat de cavalerie *m*.

trophy *n* trophée *m*.

tropical *adj* tropical.

trot *n* trot *m*; * *vi* trotter.

trouble *vt* affliger; tourmenter; * *n* problème *m*; ennui *m*; difficulté *f*; affliction, peine *f*.

troubled *adj* inquiet; agité.

troublemaker *n* agitateur *m* -trice *f*.

troubleshooter *n* médiateur *m*.

troublesome *adj* pénible.

trough *n* abreuvoir *m*; auge *f*.

troupe *n* troupe *f*.

trousers *npl* pantalon *m*.

trout *n* truite *f*.

trowel *n* truelle *f*.

truce *n* trêve *f*.

truck *n* camion *m*; wagon *m*.

truck driver *n* routier *m*.

truck farm *n* jardin maraîcher *m*.

truculent *adj* brutal, agressif.

trudge *vi* marcher lourdement.

true *adj* vrai, véritable; sincère; exact.

truelove *n* bien-aimé *m* -e *f*.

truffle *n* truffe *f*.

truly *adv* vraiment; sincèrement.

trump *n* atout *m*.

trumpet *n* trompette *f*.

trunk *n* malle *f*, coffre *m*; trompe *f*.

truss *n* botte *f*; * *vt* botteler; trousser.

trust *n* confiance *f*; trust *m*; fidéicommis *m*; * *vt* avoir confiance en; confier à.

trusted *adj* de confiance.

trustee *n* fidéicommissaire *m*, curateur *m* -trice *f*.

trustful *adj* confiant.

trustily *adv* fidèlement.

trusting *adj* confiant.

trustworthy *adj* digne de confiance.

trusty *adj* fidèle, loyal; sûr.

truth *n* vérité *f*; **in ~** en vérité.

truthful *adj* véridique; qui dit la vérité.

truthfulness *n* véracité *f*.

try *vt* essayer, tâcher, chercher à; expérimenter; mettre à l'épreuve; tenter; juger; * *vi* essayer; **~ on** *vt* essayer; **~ out** *vt* essayer; * *n* tentative *f*; essai *m*.

trying *adj* pénible; fatigant.

tub *n* cuve *f*, bac *m*; baignoire *f*.

tuba *n* tuba *m*.

tube *n* tube *m*; métro *m*.

tuberculosis *n* tuberculose *f*.

tubing *n* tuyaux *mpl*.

tuck *n* pli *m*; * *vt* mettre.

tucker *vt* (US) fatiguer.

Tuesday *n* mardi *m*.

tuft *n* touffe *f*; houppe *f*.

tug *vt* remorquer; * *n* remorqueur *m*.

tuition *n* cours, enseignement *m*.

tulip *n* tulipe *f*.

tumble *vi* tomber, faire une chute; se jeter; * *vt* renverser; culbuter; * *n* chute *f*; culbute *f*.

tumbledown *adj* délabré.

tumbler *n* verre *m*.

tummy *n* ventre *m*.

tumour *n* tumeur *f*.

tumultuous *adj* tumultueux.

tuna *n* thon *m*.

tune *n* air *m*; accord *m*; harmonie *f*; * *vt* accorder; syntoniser.

tuneful *adj* mélodieux, harmonieux.

tuner *n* syntoniseur *m*.

tunic *n* tunique *f*.

tuning fork *n* (*mus*) diapason *m*.

tunnel *n* tunnel *m*; * *vt* creuser un tunnel dans.

turban *n* turban *m*.

turbine *n* turbine *f*.

turbulence *n* turbulence, agitation *f*.

turbulent *adj* turbulent, agité.

tureen *n* soupière *f*.

turf *n* gazon *m*; * *vt* gazonner.

turgid *adj* gonflé.

turkey *n* dinde *f*.

turmoil *n* agitation *f*; trouble *m*.

turn *vi* (se) tourner; devenir; changer; se retourner; se changer, se transformer; **~ around** se retourner; tourner; **~ back** revenir; **~ down** *vt* rejeter; rabattre; **~ in** aller se coucher; **~ off** *vi* tourner; *vt* éteindre; fermer; **~ on** *vt* allumer; ouvrir; **~ out** s'avérer; **~ over** *vi* se retourner; *vt* tourner; **~ up** *vi* arriver; se présenter; *vt* monter; * *n* tour *m*; tournure *f*; virage *m*; tendance *f*.

turncoat *n* renégat *m*.

turning *n* embranchement *m*.

turnip *n* navet *m*.

turn-off *n* sortie (d'autoroute) *f*; embranchement *m*.

turnout *n* production *f*.

turnover *n* chiffre d'affaires *m*.

turnpike *n* barrière *f* de péage.

turnstile *n* tourniquet *m*.

turntable *n* platine *f*.

turpentine *n* (essence de) térébenthine *f*.

turquoise *n* turquoise *f*.

turret *n* tourelle *f*.

turtle *n* tortue marine *f*.

turtledove *n* tourterelle *f*.

tusk *n* défense *f*.

tussle *n* lutte *f*.

tutor *n* professeur particulier *m*; directeur d'études *m*; * *vt* enseigner, donner des cours particuliers à.

tuxedo *n* smoking *m*.

twang *n* vibration *f*; ton nasillard *m*.

tweezers *npl* pince à épiler *f*.

twelfth *adj n* douzième *mf*.

twelve *adj n* douze *m*.

twentieth *adj n* vingtième *mf*.

twenty *adj n* vingt *m*.

twice *adv* deux fois.

twig *n* brindille *f*; * *vi* piger.

twilight *n* crépuscule *m*.

twin *n* jumeau *m* -elle *f*.

twine *vi* s'enrouler; serpenter; * *n* ficelle *f*.

twinge *vt* élancer; * *n* élancement *m*; remords *m*.

twinkle *vi* scintiller; clignoter.

twirl *vt* faire tournoyer; * *vi* tournoyer; * *n* tournoiement *m*.

twist *vt* tordre, tortiller; entortiller; * *vi* serpenter; * *n* torsion *f*; tournant *m*; rouleau *m*.

twit *n* (*sl*) crétin *m* -e *f*.

twitch *vi* avoir un mouvement nerveux; * *n* tic *m*.

twitter *vi* gazouiller; * *n* gazouillis *m*.

two *adj n* deux *m*.

two-door *adj* à deux portes.

two-faced *adj* hypocrite.

twofold *adj* double; * *adv* au double.

two-seater *n* voiture/avion à deux places *f/m*.

twosome *n* paire *f*; couple *m*.

tycoon *n* magnat *m*.

type *n* type *m*; caractère *m*; exemple *m*; * *vi* taper à la machine.

typecast *adj* enfermé dans un rôle.

typeface *n* police *f* de caractère.

typescript *n* texte dactylographié *m*.

typewriter *n* machine à écrire *f*.

typewritten *adj* dactylographié.

typical *adj* typique.

tyrannical *adj* tyrannique.

tyranny *n* tyrannie *f*.

tyrant *n* tyran *m*.

tyre *n* pneu *m*.

tyre pressure *n* pression *f* des pneus.

U

ubiquitous *adj* doué d'ubiquité.
udder *n* pis *m*.
ugh *excl* pouah!, berk!
ugliness *n* laideur *f*.
ugly *adj* laid; inquiétant.
ulcer *n* ulcère *m*.
ulterior *adj* ultérieur.
ultimate *adj* final; **~ly** *adv* finalement; à la fin.
ultimatum *n* ultimatum *m*.
ultramarine *n*, *adj* outremer *m*.
ultrasound *n* ultrason *m*.
umbilical cord *n* cordon ombilical *m*.
umbrella *n* parapluie *m*.
umpire *n* arbitre *m*.
umpteen *adj* un très grand nombre de, beaucoup de.
unable *adj* incapable.
unaccompanied *adj* non accompagné, seul.
unaccomplished *adj* inaccompli, inachevé.
unaccountable *adj* inexplicable.
unaccountably *adv* inexplicablement.
unaccustomed *adj* inaccoutumé, inhabituel.
unacknowledged *adj* non reconnu; (resté) sans réponse.
unacquainted *adj* qui ignore, qui n'a pas connaissance de.
unadorned *adj* sans ornement.
unadulterated *adj* pur; sans mélange.
unaffected *adj* sincère; non affecté.
unaided *adj* sans aide.
unaltered *adj* inchangé.
unambitious *adj* sans ambition.
unanimity *n* unanimité *f*.
unanimous *adj* **~ly** *adv* unanime(ment).
unanswerable *adj* incontestable.
unanswered *adj* sans réponse.
unapproachable *adj* inaccessible.
unarmed *adj* non armé, désarmé.
unassuming *adj* sans prétention, modeste.
unattached *adj* indépendant; libre.
unattainable *adj* inaccessible.
unattended *adj* sans surveillance.
unauthorised *adj* sans autorisation.
unavoidable *adj* inévitable.
unavoidably *adv* inévitablement.
unaware *adj* ignorant; inconscient.
unawares *adv* à l'improviste; par mégarde.

unbalanced *adj* déséquilibré; non soldé.
unbearable *adj* insupportable.
unbecoming *adj* malséant, déplacé, peu seyant.
unbelievable *adj* incroyable.
unbend *vi* se détendre; * *vt* redresser.
unbiased *adj* impartial.
unblemished *adj* sans tache, sans défaut.
unborn *adj* à naître, pas encore né.
unbreakable *adj* incassable.
unbroken *adj* non brisé; intact; ininterrompu; indompté.
unbutton *vt* déboutonner.
uncalled-for *adj* injustifié.
uncanny *adj* mystérieux.
unceasing *adj* incessant, continu.
unceremonious *adj* brusque.
uncertain *adj* incertain, douteux.
uncertainty *n* incertitude *f*.
unchangeable *adj* immuable.
unchanged *adj* inchangé.
unchanging *adj* invariable, immuable.
uncharitable *adj* peu charitable.
unchecked *adj* non maîtrisé.
unchristian *adj* peu chrétien.
uncivil *adj* impoli, grossier.
uncivilised *adj* barbare, non civilisé.
uncle *n* oncle *m*.
uncomfortable *adj* inconfortable; incommode; désagréable.
uncomfortably *adv* inconfortablement; mal; désagréablement.
uncommon *adj* rare, extraordinaire.
uncompromising *adj* intransigeant.
unconcerned *adj* indifférent.
unconditional *adj* inconditionnel, absolu.
unconfined *adj* illimité, sans bornes.
unconfirmed *adj* non confirmé.
unconnected *adj* sans rapport.
unconquerable *adj* invincible, insurmontable.
unconscious *adj* inconscient; **~ly** *adv* inconsciemment, sans s'en rendre compte.
unconstrained *adj* non contraint, libre.
uncontrollable *adj* irrésistible; qui ne peut être maîtrisé.
unconventional *adj* peu conventionnel.

unconvincing *adj* peu convaincant.
uncork *vt* déboucher.
uncorrected *adj* non corrigé.
uncouth *adj* grossier.
uncover *vt* découvrir.
uncultivated *adj* inculte.
uncut *adj* non taillé, intégral.
undamaged *adj* non endommagé, indemne.
undaunted *adj* intrépide.
undecided *adj* indécis.
undefiled *adj* pur, immaculé.
undeniable *adj* indéniable, incontestable; **~bly** *adv* incontestablement.
under *prep* sous; dessous; moins de; selon; * *adv* au-dessous, endessous.
under-age *adj* mineur.
undercharge *vt* ne pas faire payer assez.
underclothing *n* sous-vêtements *mpl*.
undercoat *n* première couche *f*.
undercover *adj* secret, clandestin.
undercurrent *n* courant sous-marin *m*.
undercut *vt* vendre moins cher que.
underdeveloped *adj* sous-développé, insuffisamment développé.
underdog *n* opprimé *m* -e *f*.
underdone *adj* pas assez cuit.
underestimate *vt* sous-estimer.
undergo *vt* subir; supporter.
undergraduate *n* étudiant(e) en licence *m(f)*.
underground *n* mouvement clandestin *m*.
undergrowth *n* broussailles *fpl*, sous-bois *m*.
underhand *adv* en cachette; * *adj* secret, clandestin.
underlie *vi* être à la base de.
underline *vt* souligner.
undermine *vt* saper.
underneath *adv* (en) dessous; * *prep* sous, au-dessous de.
underpaid *adj* sous-payé.
underprivileged *adj* défavorisé.
underrate *vt* sous-estimer.
undersecretary *n* sous-secrétaire *mf*.
undershirt *n* (US) maillot de corps *m*.
undershorts *npl* (US) caleçon *m*.

underside n dessous m.

understand vt comprendre.

understandable adj compréhensible.

understanding n compréhension f; intelligence f; entendement m; accord m; * adj compréhensif.

understatement n affirmation en dessous de la vérité f.

undertake vt entreprendre.

undertaking n entreprise f; engagement m.

undervalue vt sous-estimer.

underwater adj sous-marin; * adv sous l'eau.

underwear n sous-vêtements mpl, dessous mpl.

underworld n pègre f.

underwrite vt souscrire à; assurer contre.

underwriter n assureur m.

undeserved adj immérité; ~ly adv à tort, indûment.

undeserving adj peu méritant.

undesirable adj peu souhaitable.

undetermined adj indéterminé; indécis.

undigested adj non digéré.

undiminished adj non diminué.

undisciplined adj indiscipliné.

undisguised adj non déguisé.

undismayed adj non découragé.

undisputed adj incontesté.

undisturbed adj non dérangé, paisible.

undivided adj indivisé, entier.

undo vt défaire; détruire.

undoing n ruine f.

undoubted adj ~ly adv indubitable(ment).

undress vi se déshabiller.

undue adj excessif; injuste.

undulating adj ondulant.

unduly adv trop, excessivement.

undying adj éternel.

unearth vt déterrer.

unearthly adj surnaturel.

uneasy adj inquiet; troublé, gêné.

uneducated adj sans instruction.

unemployed adj au chômage.

unemployment n chômage m.

unending adj interminable.

unenlightened adj peu éclairé.

unenviable adj peu enviable.

unequal adj ~ly adv inégal(ement).

unequalled adj inégalé.

unerring adj ~ly adv infaillible(ment).

uneven adj inégal; impair; ~ly adv inégalement.

unexpected adj inattendu; inopiné; ~ly adv de manière inattendue; inopinément.

unexplored adj inexploré.

unfailing adj infaillible, certain.

unfair adj injuste; inéquitable; ~ly adv injustement.

unfaithful adj infidèle.

unfaithfulness n infidélité f.

unfaltering adj ferme, assuré.

unfamiliar adj peu familier, peu connu.

unfashionable adj démodé; ~bly adv sans se préoccuper de la mode.

unfasten vt détacher, défaire.

unfathomable adj insondable, impénétrable.

unfavourable adj défavorable.

unfeeling adj insensible, impitoyable.

unfinished adj inachevé, incomplet.

unfit adj inapte; impropre.

unfold vt déplier; révéler; * vi s'ouvrir.

unforeseen adj imprévu.

unforgettable adj inoubliable.

unforgivable adj impardonnable.

unforgiving adj implacable.

unfortunate adj malheureux, malchanceux; ~ly adv malheureusement, par malheur.

unfounded adj sans fondement.

unfriendly adj inamical.

unfruitful adj stérile; infructueux.

unfurnished adj non meublé.

ungainly adj gauche.

ungentlemanly adj peu galant.

ungovernable adj ingouvernable, indomptable.

ungrateful adj ingrat; peu reconnaissant; ~ly adv avec ingratitude.

ungrounded adj infondé.

unhappily adv malheureusemnt.

unhappiness n tristesse f.

unhappy adj malheureux.

unharmed adj indemne, sain et sauf.

unhealthy adj malsain; maladif.

unheard-of adj inédit, sans précédent.

unheeding adj insouciant; distrait.

unhook vt décrocher; dégrafer.

unhoped(-for) adj inespéré.

unhurt adj indemne.

unicorn n licorne f.

uniform adj uniforme; ~ly adv uniformément; * n uniforme m.

uniformity n uniformité f.

unify vt unifier.

unimaginable adj inimaginable.

unimpaired adj non diminué, intact.

unimportant adj sans importance.

uninformed adj mal informé.

uninhabitable adj inhabitable.

uninhabited adj inhabité, désert.

uninjured adj indemne, sain et sauf.

unintelligible adj inintelligible.

unintelligibly adv inintelligiblement.

unintentional adj involontaire.

uninterested adj indifférent.

uninteresting adj inintéressant.

uninterrupted adj ininterrompu, continu.

uninvited adj sans être invité.

union n union f; syndicat m.

unionist n syndicaliste mf.

unique adj unique, exceptionnel.

unison n unisson m.

unit n unité f.

unitarian n unitarien m -ne f.

unite vt unir; * vi s'unir.

unitedly adv conjointement, ensemble.

United States (of America) npl États-Unis mpl.

unity n unité, harmonie f, accord m.

universal adj ~ly adv universel(lement).

universe n univers m.

university n université f.

unjust adj ~ly adv injuste(ment).

unkempt adj négligé; débraillé.

unkind adj peu aimable; méchant.

unknowingly adv inconsciemment.

unknown adj inconnu.

unlawful adj illégal, illicite; ~ly adv illégalement.

unlawfulness n illégalité f.

unleash vt lâcher, déchaîner.

unless conj à moins que/de, sauf.

unlicensed adj illicite.

unlike adj différent, dissemblable.

unlikelihood n improbabilité f.

unlikely adj improbable; invraisemblable; adv improbablement.

unlimited adj illimité.

unlisted adj ne figurant pas sur une liste/sur l'annuaire.

unload vt décharger.

unlock vt ouvrir, déverrouiller.

unluckily adv malheureusement.

unlucky adj malchanceux.

unmanageable adj difficile, peu maniable, impossible.

unmannered adj mal élevé, impoli.

unmannerly adj rustre.

unmarried adj célibataire, qui n'est pas marié.

unmask vt démasquer.

unmentionable adj qu'il ne faut pas mentionner.

unmerited *adj* immérité.

unmindful *adj* oublieux, indifférent.

unmistakable *adj* indubitable; **~ly** *adv* sans aucun doute.

unmitigated *adj* absolu.

unmoved *adj* insensible, impassible.

unnatural *adj* non naturel; pervers; affecté.

unnecessary *adj* inutile, superflu.

unneighbourly *adj* peu aimable avec ses voisins, peu sociable.

unnoticed *adj* inaperçu.

unnumbered *adj* innombrable.

unobserved *adj* inaperçu.

unobtainable *adj* impossible à obtenir; introuvable.

unobtrusive *adj* discret.

unoccupied *adj* inoccupé.

unoffending *adj* inoffensif, innocent.

unofficial *adj* non officiel.

unorthodox *adj* hétérodoxe; peu orthodoxe.

unpack *vt* défaire; déballer.

unpaid *adj* non payé.

unpalatable *adj* désagréable au goût.

unparalleled *adj* incomparable; sans pareil.

unpleasant *adj* **~ly** *adv* désagréable(ment).

unpleasantness *n* caractère désagréable *m*.

unplug *vt* débrancher.

unpolished *adj* non ciré; fruste, rude.

unpopular *adj* impopulaire.

unpractised *adj* inexpérimenté, inexercé.

unprecedented *adj* sans précédent.

unpredictable *adj* imprévisible.

unprejudiced *adj* impartial.

unprepared *adj* qui n'est pas préparé.

unprofitable *adj* inutile; peu rentable.

unprotected *adj* sans protection; exposé.

unpublished *adj* inédit.

unpunished *adj* impuni.

unqualified *adj* non qualifié; inconditionnel.

unquestionable *adj* incontestable, indiscutable; **~ly** *adv* indiscutablement, sans conteste.

unquestioned *adj* incontesté, indiscuté.

unravel *vt* débrouiller.

unread *adj* qui n'a pas été lu; inculte.

unreal *adj* irréel.

unrealistic *adj* irréaliste.

unreasonable *adj* déraisonnable.

unreasonably *adv* déraisonnablement.

unregarded *adj* négligé; dont on fait peu de cas.

unrelated *adj* sans rapport; sans lien de parenté.

unrelenting *adj* implacable.

unreliable *adj* peu fiable.

unremitting *adj* inlassable, constant.

unrepentant *adj* impénitent.

unreserved *adj* sans réserve; franc; **~ly** *adv* sans réserve.

unrest *n* agitation *f*; troubles *mpl*.

unrestrained *adj* non contenu; non réprimé.

unripe *adj* vert, pas mûr.

unrivalled *adj* sans égal, sans pareil.

unroll *vt* dérouler.

unruliness *n* indiscipline *f*; turbulence *f*.

unruly *adj* indiscipliné.

unsafe *adj* dangereux, peu sûr.

unsatisfactory *adj* peu satisfaisant.

unsavoury *adj* désagréable, insipide.

unscathed *adj* indemne.

unscrew *vt* dévisser.

unscrupulous *adj* sans scrupules.

unseasonable *adj* hors de saison, inopportun.

unseemly *adj* inconvenant.

unseen *adj* invisible; inaperçu.

unselfish *adj* généreux.

unsettle *vt* perturber.

unsettled *adj* perturbé; instable; variable.

unshaken *adj* inébranlable, ferme.

unshaven *adj* non rasé.

unsightly *adj* disgracieux, laid.

unskilful *adj* maladroit, malhabile.

unskilled *adj* inexpérimenté.

unsociable *adj* insociable, sauvage.

unspeakable *adj* ineffable, indicible.

unstable *adj* instable.

unsteadily *adv* d'un pas chancelant; d'une manière mal assurée.

unsteady *adj* instable.

unstudied *adj* naturel; spontané.

unsuccessful *adj* infructueux, vain; **~ly** *adv* sans succès.

unsuitable *adj* peu approprié; inopportun.

unsure *adj* peu sûr.

unsympathetic *adj* peu compatissant.

untamed *adj* sauvage.

untapped *adj* non exploité.

untenable *adj* insoutenable.

unthinkable *adj* inconcevable.

unthinking *adj* irréfléchi, étourdi.

untidiness *n* désordre *m*.

untidy *adj* en désordre; peu soigné.

untie *vt* dénouer, défaire.

until *prep* jusqu'à; * *conj* jusqu'à ce que.

untimely *adj* intempestif.

untiring *adj* infatigable.

untold *adj* jamais révélé; indicible; incalculable.

untouched *adj* intact.

untoward *adj* fâcheux; inconvenant.

untried *adj* qui n'a pas été essayé *ou* mis à l'épreuve.

untroubled *adj* tranquille, paisible.

untrue *adj* faux.

untrustworthy *adj* indigne de confiance.

untruth *n* mensonge *m*, fausseté *f*.

unused *adj* neuf, inutilisé.

unusual *adj* inhabituel, exceptionnel; **~ly** *adv* exceptionnellement, rarement.

unveil *vt* dévoiler.

unwavering *adj* inébranlable.

unwelcome *adj* importun.

unwell *adj* indisposé, souffrant.

unwieldy *adj* peu maniable.

unwilling *adj* peu disposé; **~ly** *adv* de mauvaise grâce.

unwillingness *n* mauvaise grâce, mauvaise volonté *f*.

unwind *vt* dérouler; * *vi* se détendre.

unwise *adj* imprudent.

unwitting *adj* involontaire.

unworkable *adj* impraticable.

unworthy *adj* indigne.

unwrap *vt* défaire.

unwritten *adj* non écrit.

up *adv* en haut, en l'air; levé; * *prep* au haut de; plus loin.

upbringing *n* éducation *f*.

update *vt* mettre à jour.

upheaval *n* bouleversement *m*.

uphill *adj* difficile, pénible; * *adv* en montant.

uphold *vt* soutenir.

upholstery *n* tapisserie *f*.

upkeep *n* entretien *m*.

uplift *vt* élever.

upon *prep* sur.

upper *adj* supérieur; (plus) élevé.

upper-class *adj* aristocratique.

upper-hand *n* (*fig*) dessus *m*.

uppermost *adj* le plus haut, le plus élevé; **to be ~** prédominer.

upright *adj* droit, vertical; droit, honnête.

uprising *n* soulèvement *m*.

uproar *n* tumulte, vacarme *m*.

uproot *vt* déraciner.

upset *vt* renverser; déranger, bouleverser; * *n* désordre *m*; bouleversement *m*; * *adj* vexé; bouleversé.

upshot *n* résultat *m*; aboutissement *m*; conclusion *f*.

upside-down *adv* sens dessus dessous.

upstairs *adv* en haut (d'un escalier).

upstart *n* parvenu *m* -e *f*.

uptight *adj* très tendu.

up-to-date *adj* à jour.

upturn *n* amélioration *f*.

upward *adj* ascendant; **~s** *adv* vers le haut; en montant.

urban *adj* urbain.

urbane *adj* courtois.

urchin *n* gamin *m*; **sea ~** oursin *m*.

urge *vt* pousser; * *n* impulsion *f*; désir ardent *m*.

urgency *n* urgence *f*.

urgent *adj* urgent.

urinal *n* urinoir *m*.

urinate *vi* uriner.

urine *n* urine *f*.

urn *n* urne *f*.

us *pn* nous.

usage *n* utilisation *f*; usage *m*.

use *n* usage *m*; utilisation *f*, emploi *m*; * *vt* se servir de, utiliser.

used *adj* usagé.

useful *adj* **~ly** *adv* utile(ment).

usefulness *n* utilité *f*.

useless *adj* **~ly** *adv* inutile(ment).

uselessness *n* inutilité *f*.

user-friendly *adj* facile à utiliser.

usher *n* huissier *m*; placeur *m*.

usherette *n* ouvreuse *f*.

usual *adj* habituel, courant; **~ly** *adv* habituellement.

usurer *n* usurier *m* -ière *f*.

usurp *vt* usurper.

usury *n* usure *f*.

utensil *n* ustensile *m*.

uterus *n* utérus *m*.

utilise *vt* utiliser.

utility *n* utilité *f*.

utmost *adj* extrême, le plus grand; dernier.

utter *adj* complet; absolu; total; * *vt* prononcer; proférer; émettre.

utterance *n* expression *f*.

utterly *adv* complètement, tout à fait.

V

vacancy *n* chambre libre *f*.
vacant *adj* vacant; inoccupé; libre.
vacant lot *n* (US) terrain vague *m*.
vacate *vt* quitter; démissionner.
vacation *n* vacances *fpl*.
vacationer *n* vacancier *m* -ière *f*.
vaccinate *vt* vacciner.
vaccination *n* vaccination *f*.
vaccine *n* vaccin *f*.
vacuous *adj* vide.
vacuum *n* vide *m*.
vacuum bottle *n* thermos *m*.
vagina *n* vagin *m*.
vagrant *n* vagabond *m* -e *f*.
vague *adj* ~**ly** *adv* vague(ment).
vain *adj* vain, inutile; vaniteux.
valet *n* valet de chambre *m*.
valiant *adj* courageux, brave.
valid *adj* valide, valable.
valley *n* vallée *f*.
valour *n* courage *m*, bravoure *f*.
valuable *adj* précieux, de valeur; ~**s** *npl* objets de valeur *mpl*.
valuation *n* évaluation, estimation *f*.
value *n* valeur *f*; * *vt* évaluer; tenir à, apprécier.
valued *adj* précieux, estimé.
valve *n* soupape *f*.
vampire *n* vampire *m*.
van *n* camionnette *f*.
vandal *n* vandale *mf*.
vandalise *vt* saccager.
vandalism *n* vandalisme *m*.
vanguard *n* avant-garde *f*.
vanilla *n* vanille *f*.
vanish *vi* disparaître, se dissiper.
vanity *n* vanité *f*.
vanity case *n* vanity-case *m*.
vanquish *vt* vaincre.
vantage point *n* position avantageuse *f*.
vapour *n* vapeur *f*.
variable *adj* variable; changeant.
variance *n* désaccord, différend *m*.
variation *n* variation *f*.
varicose vein *n* varice *f*.
varied *adj* varié.
variety *n* variété *f*.
variety show *n* spectacle de variétés *m*.
various *adj* divers, différent.
varnish *n* vernis *m*; * *vt* vernir.
vary *vt* *vi* varier; *vi* changer.
vase *n* vase *m*.
vast *adj* vaste; immense.
vat *n* cuve *f*.

vault *n* voûte *f*; cave *f*, caveau *m*; saut *m*; * *vi* sauter.
veal *n* veau *m*.
veer *vi* (*mar*) virer.
vegetable *adj* végétal; * *n* végétal *m*; ~**s** *pl* légumes *mpl*.
vegetable garden *n* (jardin) potager *m*.
vegetarian *n* végétarien *m* -ne *f*.
vegetate *vi* végéter.
vegetation *n* végétation *f*.
vehemence *n* véhémence, fougue *f*.
vehement *adj* véhément, violent; ~**ly** *adv* avec véhémence.
vehicle *n* véhicule *m*.
veil *n* voile *m*; * *vt* voiler, dissimuler.
vein *n* veine *f*; nervure *f*; disposition *f*.
velocity *n* vitesse *f*.
velvet *n* velours *m*.
vending machine *n* distributeur automatique *m*.
vendor *n* vendeur *m*.
veneer *n* placage *m*; vernis *m*.
venerable *adj* vénérable.
venerate *vt* vénérer.
veneration *n* vénération *f*.
venereal *adj* vénérien.
vengeance *n* vengeance *f*.
venial *adj* véniel.
venison *n* venaison *f*.
venom *n* venin *m*.
venomous *adj* vénéneux; ~**ly** *adv* avec animosité.
vent *n* orifice *m*; conduit *m*; * *vt* (*fig*) décharger.
ventilate *vt* aérer.
ventilation *n* ventilation, aération *f*.
ventilator *n* ventilateur *m*.
ventriloquist *n* ventriloque *mf*.
venture *n* entreprise *f*; * *vi* s'aventurer; * *vt* risquer, hasarder.
venue *n* lieu *m* (de réunion).
veranda(h) *n* véranda *f*.
verb *n* (*gr*) verbe *m*.
verbal *adj* verbal, oral; ~**ly** *adv* verbalement.
verbatim *adv* textuellement, mot pour mot.
verbose *adj* verbeux.
verdant *adj* verdoyant.
verdict *n* (*law*) verdict *m*; jugement *m*.
verification *n* vérification *f*.

verify *vt* vérifier.
veritable *adj* véritable.
vermin *n* vermine *f*.
vermouth *n* vermout(h) *m*.
versatile *adj* doué de talents multiples; versatile.
verse *n* vers *m*; verset *m*.
versed *adj* versé.
version *n* version *f*.
versus *prep* contre.
vertebra *n* vertèbre *f*.
vertebral *adj* vertébral.
vertebrate *adj n* vertébré *m*.
vertex *n* sommet *m*.
vertical *adj* ~**ly** *adv* vertical-(ement).
vertigo *n* vertige *m*.
verve *n* verve *f*, brio *m*.
very *adj* vrai, véritable; exactement, même; * *adv* très, fort, bien.
vessel *n* récipient *m*; vase *m*; navire *m*.
vest *n* gilet *m*.
vestibule *n* vestibule *m*.
vestige *n* vestige *m*.
vestment *n* vêtement de cérémonie *m*; chasuble *f*.
vestry *n* sacristie *f*.
veteran *adj n* vétéran *m*.
veterinarian *n* vétérinaire *mf*.
veterinary *adj* vétérinaire.
veto *n* véto *m*; * *vt* opposer son véto à.
vex *vt* contrarier.
vexed *adj* contrarié.
via *prep* via, par.
viaduct *n* viaduc *m*.
vial *n* fiole, ampoule *f*.
vibrate *vi* vibrer.
vibration *n* vibration *f*.
vicarious *adj* par personne interposée.
vice *n* vice *m*; défaut *m*; étau *m*.
vice-chairman *n* vice-président *m*.
vice versa *adv* vice versa.
vicinity *n* voisinage *m*, proximité *f*.
vicious *adj* méchant; ~**ly** *adv* méchamment.
victim *n* victime *f*.
victimise *vt* prendre pour victime.
victor *n* vainqueur *m*.
victorious *adj* victorieux.
victory *n* victoire *f*.
video *n* vidéo *f*; vidéocassette *f*; magnétoscope *m*.
video tape *n* bande vidéo *f*.

viewer *n* téléspectateur *m* -trice *f*.
vie *vi* rivaliser.
view *n* vue *f*; perspective *f*; opinion *f*; panorama *m*; * *vt* voir; examiner.
viewfinder *n* viseur *m*.
viewpoint *n* point de vue *m*.
vigil *n* veille *f*; vigile *f*.
vigilance *n* vigilance *f*.
vigilant *adj* vigilant, attentif.
vigorous *adj* vigoureux; **~ly** *adv* vigoureusement.
vigour *n* vigueur *f*; énergie *f*.
vile *adj* vil, infâme; exécrable.
vilify *vt* diffamer.
villa *n* pavillon *m*; maison de campagne *f*.
village *n* village *m*.
villager *n* villageois *m* -e *f*.
villain *n* scélérat *m*.
vindicate *vt* venger, défendre.
vindication *n* défense *f*; justification *f*.
vindictive *adj* vindicatif.
vine *n* vigne *f*.
vinegar *n* vinaigre *m*.
vineyard *n* vignoble *m*.
vintage *n* millésime *m*; époque *f*.
vinyl *n* vinyle *m*.
viola *n* (*mus*) viole *f*.
violate *vt* violer.
violation *n* violation *f*.
violence *n* violence *f*.
violent *adj* violent; **~ly** *adv* violemment.
violet *n* (*bot*) violette *f*.
violin *n* (*mus*) violon *m*.
violinist *n* violiniste *mf*.
violoncello *n* (*mus*) violoncelle *m*.
viper *n* vipère *f*.
virgin *n, adj* vierge *f*.
virginity *n* virginité *f*.

Virgo *n* Vierge *f* (signe du zodiaque).
virile *adj* viril.
virility *n* virilité *f*.
virtual *adj* virtuel; quasiment; **~ly** *adv* de fait, pratiquement.
virtue *n* vertu *f*.
virtuous *adj* virtueux.
virulent *adj* virulent.
virus *n* virus *m*.
vis-à-vis *prep* vis-à-vis.
viscous *adj* visqueux, gluant.
visibility *n* visibilité *f*.
visible *adj* visible.
visibly *adv* visiblement.
vision *n* vision *f*; vue *f*.
visit *vt* visiter; * *n* visite *f*.
visitation *n* visite *f*.
visiting hours *npl* heures *fpl* de visite.
visitor *n* visiteur *m* -euse *f*; touriste *mf*.
visor *n* visière *f*.
vista *n* vue, perspective *f*.
visual *adj* visuel.
visual aid *n* support visuel *m*.
visualise *vt* s'imaginer.
vital *adj* vital; essentiel; indispensable; **~ly** *adv* vitalement; **~s** *npl* organes vitaux *mpl*.
vitality *n* vitalité *f*.
vital statistics *npl* statistiques démographiques *fpl*.
vitamin *n* vitamine *f*.
vitiate *vt* vicier.
vivacious *adj* vif.
vivid *adj* vif; vivant; frappant; **~ly** *adv* de façon éclatante; de façon frappante.
vivisection *n* vivisection *f*.
vocabulary *n* vocabulaire *m*.
vocal *adj* vocal.

vocation *n* vocation *f*; profession *f*, métier *m*; **~al** *adj* professionnel.
vocative *n* vocatif *m*.
vociferous *adj* bruyant.
vogue *n* vogue *f*; mode *f*.
voice *n* voix *f*; * *vt* exprimer.
void *adj* vide; * *n* vide *m*.
volatile *adj* volatile; versatile.
volcanic *adj* volcanique.
volcano *n* volcan *m*.
volition *n* volonté *f*.
volley *n* volée *f*; salve *f*; grêle *f*.
volleyball *n* volley-ball *m*.
voltage *n* voltage *m*.
voluble *adj* volubile, loquace.
volume *n* volume *m*.
voluntarily *adv* volontairement.
voluntary *adj* volontaire.
volunteer *n* volontaire *mf*; * *vi* se porter volontaire.
voluptuous *adj* voluptueux.
vomit *vt vi* vomir; * *n* vomissement *m*.
voracious *adj* **~ly** *adv* vorace(ment).
vortex *n* tourbillon *m*.
vote *n* vote, suffrage *m*; voix *f*; * *vt* voter.
voter *n* électeur *m* -trice *f*.
voting *n* vote *m*.
voucher *n* bon *m*.
vow *n* vœu *m*; * *vt* jurer.
vowel *n* voyelle *f*.
voyage *n* voyage par mer *m*; traversée *f*.
vulgar *adj* vulgaire; grossier.
vulgarity *n* grossièreté *f*; vulgarité *m*.
vulnerable *adj* vulnérable.
vulture *n* vautour *m*.

W

wad *n* tampon *m*; bouchon *m*, liasse *f*.

waddle *vi* se dandiner.

wade *vi* patauger.

wading pool *n* petit bassin (pour enfants) *m*.

wafer *n* gaufrette *f*; plaque *f*.

waffle *n* gaufre *f*.

waft *vt* porter, apporter; * *vi* flotter.

wag *vt vi* remuer.

wage *n* salaire *m*.

wage earner *n* salarié *m* -e *f*.

wager *n* pari *m*; * *vt* parier.

wages *npl* salaire *m*.

waggle *vt* remuer.

waggon *n* chariot *m*; (*rail*) wagon *m*.

wail *n* gémissement *m*, plainte *f*; * *vi* gémir.

waist *n* taille *f*.

waistline *n* taille *f*.

wait *vi* attendre; * *n* attente *f*; arrêt *m*.

waiter *n* serveur *m*.

waiting list *n* liste d'attente *f*.

waiting room *n* salle d'attente *f*.

waive *vt* renoncer à.

wake *vi* se réveiller; * *vt* réveiller; * *n* veillée *f*; (*mar*) sillage *m*.

waken *vt* réveiller; * *vi* se réveiller.

walk *vi* marcher, aller à pied; * *vt* parcourir; * *n* promenade *f*; marche *f*.

walker *n* marcheur *m* -euse *f*.

walkie-talkie *n* talkie-walkie *m*.

walking *n* marche à pied *f*.

walking stick *n* canne *f*.

walkout *n* grève *f* surprise.

walkover *n* (*sl*) victoire facile *f*, gâteau *m*.

walkway *n* passage pour piétons *m*.

wall *n* mur *m*; muraille *f*; paroi *f*.

walled *adj* muré.

wallet *n* portefeuille *m*.

wallflower *n* (*bot*) giroflée *f*.

wallow *vi* se vautrer.

wallpaper *n* papier peint *m*.

walnut *n* noix *f*; noyer *m*.

walrus *n* morse *m*.

waltz *n* valse *f*.

wan *adj* pâle.

wand *n* baguette (magique) *f*.

wander *vi* errer; aller sans but.

wane *vi* décroître.

want *vt* vouloir; demander; * *vi* manquer; * *n* besoin *m*; manque *m*.

wanting *adj* manquant, qui manque, qui fait défaut.

wanton *adj* lascif; capricieux.

war *n* guerre *f*.

ward *n* salle *f*; pupille *mf*.

wardrobe *n* garde-robe *f*, penderie *f*.

warehouse *n* entrepôt *m*.

warfare *n* guerre *f*.

warhead *n* ogive *f*.

warily *adv* avec circonspection.

wariness *n* circonspection, prudence *f*.

warm *adj* chaud; chaleureux; * *vt* réchauffer; ~ **up** *vi* se réchauffer; s'échauffer; s'animer; *vt* réchauffer.

warm-hearted *adj* affectueux.

warmly *adv* chaudement, chaleureusement.

warmth *n* chaleur *f*.

warn *vt* prévenir; avertir.

warning *n* avertissement *m*.

warning light *n* voyant lumineux *m*.

warp *vi* se voiler; * *vt* voiler; fausser.

warrant *n* garantie *f*; mandat *m*.

warranty *n* garantie *f*.

warren *n* terrier *m*.

warrior *n* guerrier *m* -ière *f*.

warship *n* navire de guerre *m*.

wart *n* verrue *f*.

wary *adj* prudent, circonspect.

wash *vt* laver; * *vi* se laver; * *n* lavage *m*; lessive *f*.

washable *adj* lavable.

washbowl *n* lavabo *m*.

washcloth *n* gant de toilette *m*.

washer *n* rondelle *f*.

washing *n* linge à laver *m*; lessive *f*.

washing machine *n* machine à laver *f*.

washing-up *n* vaisselle *f*.

wash-out *n* (*sl*) fiasco *m*.

washroom *n* toilettes *fpl*.

wasp *n* guêpe *f*.

wastage *n* gaspillage *m*; perte *f*.

waste *vt* gaspiller; dévaster, saccager; perdre; * *vi* se perdre; * *n* gaspillage *m*; détérioration *f*; terre inculte *f*; déchets *mpl*.

wasteful *adj* gaspilleur; prodigue; ~**ly** *adv* avec prodigalité.

waste paper *n* vieux papiers *mpl*.

waste pipe *n* tuyau d'échappement *m*.

watch *n* montre *f*; surveillance *f*; garde *f*; * *vt* regarder; observer; surveiller; faire attention à; * *vi* regarder; monter la garde.

watchdog *n* chien de garde *m*.

watchful *adj* vigilant; ~**ly** *adv* avec vigilance.

watchmaker *n* horloger *m*.

watchman *n* veilleur de nuit *m*; gardien *m*.

watchtower *n* tour de guet *f*.

watchword *n* mot de passe *m*; mot d'ordre *m*.

water *n* eau *f*; * *vt* arroser, mouiller; * *vi* pleurer, larmoyer.

water closet *n* W.C. *mpl*.

watercolour *n* aquarelle *f*.

waterfall *n* cascade *f*.

water heater *n* chauffe-eau *m invar*.

watering-can *n* arrosoir *m*.

water level *n* niveau de l'eau *m*.

waterlily *n* nénuphar *m*.

water line *n* ligne de flottaison *f*.

waterlogged *adj* imprégné d'eau.

water main *n* conduite principale d'eau *f*.

watermark *n* filigrane *m*.

watermelon *n* pastèque *f*.

watershed *n* (*fig*) moment *m* critique.

watertight *adj* étanche.

waterworks *npl* usine hydraulique *f*.

watery *adj* aqueux; détrempé; délavé.

wave *n* vague *f*; lame *f*; onde *f*; * *vi* faire signe de la main; onduler; * *vt* agiter.

wavelength *n* longueur d'ondes *f*.

waver *vi* vaciller, osciller.

wavering *adj* hésitant.

wavy *adj* ondulé.

wax *n* cire *f*; * *vt* cirer; * *vi* croître.

wax paper *n* papier paraffiné *m*.

waxworks *n* musée de cire *m*.

way *n* chemin *m*; voie *f*; route *f*; manière *f*; direction *f*; **to give ~** céder.

waylay *vt* attaquer, arrêter au passage.

wayward *adj* capricieux.

we *pn* nous.

weak *adj* ~**ly** *adv* faible(ment).

weaken *vt* affaiblir.

weakling *n* personne faible *f*.

weakness *n* faiblesse *f*; point faible *m*.

wealth *n* richesse *f*; abondance *f*.

wealthy *adj* riche.

wean *vt* sevrer.

weapon *n* arme *f*.

wear *vt* porter; user; * *vi* s'user; ~ **away** *vt* user; *vi* s'user; ~ **down** *vt* user; épuiser; ~ **off** *vi* s'effacer; ~ **out** *vi* s'user; s'épuiser; *vt* user; * *n* usage *m*; usure *f*.

weariness *n* lassitude *f*; fatigue *f*; ennui *m*.

wearisome *adj* fatigant.

weary *adj* las, fatigué; ennuyeux.

weasel *n* belette *f*.

weather *n* temps *m*; * *vt* surmonter.

weather-beaten *adj* ayant souffert des intempéries.

weathercock *n* girouette *f*.

weather forecast *n* prévisions météorologiques *fpl*.

weave *vt* tisser; entrelacer.

weaving *n* tissage *m*.

web *n* tissu *m*; toile *f* d'araignée; palmure *f*.

wed *vt* épouser; * *vi* se marier.

wedding *n* mariage *m*; noces *fpl*.

wedding day *n* jour du mariage *m*.

wedding dress *n* robe de mariée *f*.

wedding present *n* cadeau de mariage *m*.

wedding ring *n* alliance *f*.

wedge *n* cale *f*; * *vt* caler; enfoncer.

wedlock *n* mariage *m*.

Wednesday *n* mercredi *m*.

wee *adj* petit.

weed *n* mauvaise herbe *f*; * *vt* désherber.

weedkiller *n* désherbant *m*.

weedy *adj* envahi par les mauvaises herbes.

week *n* semaine *f*; **tomorrow** ~ demain en huit; **yesterday** ~ il y a eu une semaine hier.

weekday *n* jour de semaine, jour ouvrable *m*.

weekend *n* week-end *m*, fin de semaine *f*.

weekly *adj* de la semaine, hebdomadaire; * *adv* chaque semaine, par semaine.

weep *vt* *vi* pleurer.

weeping willow *n* saule pleureur *m*.

weigh *vt* *vi* peser.

weight *n* poids *m*.

weightily *adv* pesamment.

weightlifter *n* haltérophile *m*.

weighty *adj* lourd; important.

welcome *adj* opportun; ~! bienvenue !; * *n* accueil *m*; * *vt* accueillir.

weld *vt* souder; * *n* soudure *f*.

welfare *n* bien-être *m*; assistance sociale *f*.

welfare state *n* État-providence *m*.

well *n* source *f*; fontaine *f*; puits *m*; * *adj* bien, bon; * *adv* bien; **as ~ as** aussi bien que, en plus de, comme.

well-behaved *adj* bien élevé, sage.

well-being *n* bien-être *m*.

well-bred *adj* bien élevé.

well-built *adj* bien bâti, solide.

well-deserved *adj* bien mérité.

well-dressed *adj* bien habillé.

well-known *adj* connu, célèbre.

well-mannered *adj* poli, bien élevé.

well-meaning *adj* bien intentionné.

well-off *adj* aisé, dans l'aisance.

well-to-do *adj* aisé, riche.

well-wisher *n* admirateur *m* -trice *f*.

wench *n* jeune fille, jeune femme *f*.

west *n* ouest, Occident *m*; * *adj* ouest, de/à l'ouest; * *adv* vers/à l'ouest.

westerly, western *adj* (d')ouest.

westward *adv* vers l'ouest.

wet *adj* mouillé, humide; * *n* humidité *f*; * *vt* mouiller.

wetnurse *n* nourrice *f*.

wet suit *n* combinaison de plongée *f*.

whack *vt* donner un grand coup à; * *n* grand coup *m*.

whale *n* baleine *f*.

wharf *n* quai *m*.

what *pn* qu'est-ce qui,(qu'est-ce) que, quoi; que, qui; ce qui, ce que; quel(le), que; * *adj* quel(s), quelle(s); * *excl* quoi! comment!.

whatever *pn* quoi que; tout; n'importe quoi.

wheat *n* blé *m*.

wheedle *vt* cajoler, câliner.

wheel *n* roue *f*; volant *m*; gouvernail *m*; * *vt* tourner; pousser, rouler; * *vi* tourner en rond, tournoyer.

wheelbarrow *n* brouette *f*.

wheelchair *n* fauteuil roulant *m*.

wheelclamp *n* sabot *m*.

wheeze *vi* respirer bruyamment.

when *adv, conj* quand.

whenever *adv* quand; chaque fois que.

where *adv* où; * *conj* où; **any~** n'importe où; **every~** partout.

whereabout(s) *adv* où.

whereas *conj* tandis que; attendu que.

whereby *pn* par lequel (laquelle), au moyen duquel (de laquelle).

wherever *adv* où que.

whereupon *conj* sur quoi; après quoi.

wherewithal *npl* ressources *fpl*.

whet *vt* aiguiser.

whether *conj* si.

which *pn* lequel, laquelle; celui/celle(s)/ceux que, celui/celle(s)/ceux qui; ce qui, ce que; quoi, ce dont * *adj* quel(s), quelle(s).

whiff *n* bouffée, odeur *f*.

while *n* moment *m*; **a ~** quelque temps; * *conj* pendant que; alors que; quoique.

whim *n* caprice *m*.

whimper *vi* gémir, pleurnicher.

whimsical *adj* capricieux, fantasque.

whine *vi* gémir, se plaindre; * *n* gémissement *m*, plainte *f*.

whinny *vi* hennir.

whip *n* fouet *m*; cravache *f*; * *vt* fouetter; battre.

whipped cream *n* crème fouettée *f*.

whirl *vi* tourbillonner, tournoyer; aller à toute allure; * *vt* faire tourbillonner, faire tournoyer.

whirlpool *n* tourbillon *m*.

whirlwind *n* tornade *f*.

whisper *vi* chuchoter; murmurer.

whispering *n* chuchotement *m*; murmure *m*.

whistle *vi* siffler; * *n* sifflement *m*.

white *adj* blanc; pâle; * *n* blanc *m*; blanc d'œuf *m*.

white elephant *n* bibelot *m*.

white-hot *adj* chauffé à blanc.

white lie *n* petit mensonge, mensonge innocent *m*.

whiten *vt* *vi* blanchir.

whiteness *n* blancheur *f*; pâleur *f*.

whitewash *n* blanc de chaux *m*; * *vt* blanchir à la chaux; disculper.

whiting *n* merlan *m*.

whitish *adj* blanchâtre.

who *pn* qui.

whoever *pn* quiconque, qui que ce soit, quel(le) que soit.

whole *adj* tout, entier; intact, complet; sain; * *n* tout *m*; ensemble *m*.

wholehearted *adj* sincère.

wholemeal *adj* complet.

wholesale *n* vente en gros *f*.

wholesome *adj* sain, salubre.

wholewheat *adj* complet.

wholly *adv* complètement.

whom *pn* qui; que.

whooping cough *n* coqueluche *f*.

whore *n* putain *f*.

why *n* pourquoi *m*; * *conj* pourquoi; * *excl* eh bien!, tiens!

wick *n* mèche *f*.

wicked *adj* méchant, mauvais; **~ly** *adv* méchamment.

wickedness *n* méchanceté, perversité *f*.

wicker *n* osier *m*; * *adj* en osier.

wide *adj* large, ample; grand; **~ly** *adv* partout; **far and ~** de tous côtés.

wide-awake *adj* bien réveillé.

widen *vt* élargir, agrandir.

wide open *adj* grand ouvert.

widespread *adj* très répandu.

widow *n* veuve *f*.

widower *n* veuf *m*.

width *n* largeur *f*.

wield *vt* manier, brandir.

wife *n* femme *f*; épouse *f*.

wig *n* perruque *f*.

wiggle *vt* agiter; * *vi* s'agiter.

wild *adj* sauvage, féroce; désert; fou; furieux.

wilderness *n* étendue déserte *f*.

wild life *n* faune *f*.

wildly *adv* violemment; furieusement; follement.

wilful *adj* délibéré; entêté.

wilfulness *n* obstination *f*.

wiliness *n* ruse, astuce *f*.

will *n* volonté *f*; testament *m*; * *vt* vouloir.

willing *adj* prêt, disposé; **~ly** *adv* volontiers, de bon cœur.

willingness *n* bonne volonté *f*, empressement *m*.

willow *n* saule *m*.

willpower *n* volonté *f*.

wilt *vi* se fâner.

wily *adj* astucieux.

win *vt* gagner, conquérir; remporter.

wince *vi* tressaillir.

winch *n* treuil *m*.

wind *n* vent *m*; souffle *m*; gaz *mpl*.

wind *vt* enrouler; envelopper; donner un tour de; * *vi* serpenter.

windfall *n* fruit abattu par le vent *m*; (*fig*) aubaine *f*.

winding *adj* tortueux.

windmill *n* moulin à vent *m*.

window *n* fenêtre *f*.

window box *n* jardinière *f*.

window cleaner *n* laveur(-euse) *m(f)* de carreaux.

window ledge *n* appui *m* de fenêtre.

window pane *n* carreau *m*.

window sill *n* rebord *m* de fenêtre.

windpipe *n* trachée *f* artère.

windscreen *n* pare-brise *m invar*.

windscreen washer *n* lave-glace *m invar*.

windscreen wiper *n* essuie-glace *m invar*.

windy *adj* venteux.

wine *n* vin *m*.

wine cellar *n* cave (à vin) *f*.

wine glass *n* verre à vin *m*.

wine list *n* carte des vins *f*.

wine merchant *n* négociant en vins *m*.

wine tasting *n* dégustation de vins *f*.

wing *n* aile *f*.

winged *adj* ailé.

winger *n* ailier *m*.

wink *vi* faire un clin d'œil; * *n* clin d'œil *m*; clignement *m*.

winner *n* gagnant *m* -e *f*; vainqueur *m*.

winning post *n* poteau d'arrivée *m*.

winter *n* hiver *m*; * *vi* hiverner.

winter sports *npl* sports d'hiver *mpl*.

wintry *adj* d'hiver, hivernal.

wipe *vt* essuyer; effacer.

wire *n* fil *m*; télégramme *m*; * *vt* installer des fils électriques à; télégraphier.

wiring *n* installation électrique *f*.

wiry *adj* effilé et nerveux.

wisdom *n* sagesse, prudence *f*.

wisdom teeth *npl* dents de sagesse *fpl*.

wise *adj* sage, avisé, judicieux, prudent.

wisecrack *n* bon mot *m*, plaisanterie *f*.

wish *vt* souhaiter, désirer; * *n* souhait, désir *m*.

wishful *adj* désireux.

wisp *n* brin *m*; mince volute *f*.

wistful *adj* nostalgique, rêveur.

wit *n* esprit *m*, intelligence *f*.

witch *n* sorcière *f*.

witchcraft *n* sorcellerie *f*.

with *prep* avec; à; de; contre.

withdraw *vt* retirer; rappeler; annuler; * *vi* se retirer.

withdrawal *n* retrait *m*.

withdrawn *adj* réservé.

wither *vi* se flétrir, se faner.

withhold *vt* détenir, retenir, empêcher.

within *prep* à l'intérieur de; * *adv* dedans; à l'intérieur.

without *prep* sans.

withstand *vt* résister à.

witless *adj* sot, stupide.

witness *n* témoin *m*; témoignage *m*; * *vt* être témoin de; attester.

witness stand *n* barre des témoins *f*.

witticism *n* mot d'esprit *m*.

wittily *adv* spirituellement.

wittingly *adv* sciemment, à dessein.

witty *adj* spirituel, plein d'esprit.

wizard *n* sorcier, magicien *m*.

wobble *vi* trembler.

woe *n* malheur *m*; affliction *f*.

woeful *adj* triste, malheureux; **~ly** *adv* tristement.

wolf *n* loup *m*; **she ~** louve *f*.

woman *n* femme *f*.

womanish *adj* de femme.

womanly *adj* féminin, de femme.

womb *n* utérus *m*.

women's lib *n* mouvement de libération de la femme *m*.

wonder *n* merveille *f*; miracle *m*; émerveillement *m*; * *vi* s'émerveiller.

wonderful *adj* merveilleux; **~ly** *adv* merveilleusement.

wondrous *adj* merveilleux.

won't *abrev* de **will not**.

wont *n* coutume *f*.

woo *vt* faire la cour à.

wood *n* bois *m*.

wood alcohol *n* alcool méthylique *m*.

wood carving *n* sculpture sur bois *f*.

woodcut *n* gravure sur bois *f*.

woodcutter *n* bûcheron *m*.

wooded *adj* boisé.

wooden *adj* de bois, en bois.

woodland *n* région boisée *f*.

woodlouse *n* cloporte *m*.

woodman *n* forestier *m*; garde-forestier *m*.

woodpecker *n* pic *m*.

woodwind *n* (*mus*) bois *mpl*.

woodwork *n* menuiserie *f*.

woodworm *n* ver du bois *m*.

wool *n* laine *f*.

woollen *adj* de laine.

woollens *npl* lainages *mpl*.

woolly *adj* laineux, de laine.

word *n* mot *m*; parole *f*; * *vt* exprimer; rédiger.

wordiness *n* verbosité *f*.

wording *n* formulation *f*.

word processing *n* traitement *m* de texte.

word processor *n* machine *f* à traitement de texte.

wordy *adj* verbeux.

work *vi* travailler; opérer; fonctionner; fermenter; * *vt* (faire)

travailler, faire fonctionner; façonner; * ~ **out** *vi* marcher; * *vt*
résoudre; * *n* travail *m*; œuvre *f*;
ouvrage *m*; emploi *m*.
workable *adj* exploitable.
workaholic *n* drogué du travail
m.
worker *n* travailleur *m* -euse *f*;
ouvrier *m* -ère *f*.
workforce *n* main-d'œuvre *f*.
working-class *adj* ouvrier.
workman *n* ouvrier, artisan *m*.
workmanship *n* exécution *f*; qualité du travail *f*.
workmate *n* camarade de travail *mf*.
workshop *n* atelier *m*.
world *n* monde *m*; * *adj* du monde;
mondial.
worldliness *n* mondanité *f*; attachement aux choses matrielles
m.
worldly *adj* mondain; terrestre.
worldwide *adj* mondial.
worm *n* ver *m*.
worn-out *adj* épuisé; usé.
worried *adj* inquiet.
worry *vt* inquiéter; *n* souci *m*.
worrying *adj* inquiétant.
worse *adj adv* pire; * *n* le pire.
worship *n* culte *m*; adoration *f*; **your**

~ Monsieur le Maire, Monsieur le
Juge; * *vt* adorer, vénérer.
worst *adj* le pire; * *adv* le plus mal;
* *n* le pire *m*.
worth *n* valeur *f*, prix *m*; mérite *m*.
worthily *adv* dignement, à juste titre.
worthless *adj* sans valeur; inutile.
worthwhile *adj* qui vaut la peine;
louable.
worthy *adj* digne; louable.
would-be *adj* soi-disant.
wound *n* blessure *f*; * *vt* blesser.
wrangle *vi* se disputer; * *n* dispute
f.
wrap *vt* envelopper.
wrath *n* colère *f*.
wreath *n* couronne, guirlande *f*.
wreck *n* naufrage *m*; ruines *fpl*;
destruction *f*; épave *f*; * *vt* causer
le naufrage de; démolir.
wreckage *n* naufrage *m*; épave *f*,
débris *mpl*.
wren *n* roitelet *m*.
wrench *vt* tordre; forcer; tourner
violemment; * *n* clé *f*; torsion
violente *f*.
wrest *vt* arracher.
wrestle *vi* lutter.
wrestling *n* lutte *f*.

wretched *adj* malheureux, misérable.
wriggle *vi* remuer, se tortiller.
wring *vt* tordre; essorer; arracher.
wrinkle *n* ride *f*; * *vt* rider; * *vi* se
rider.
wrist *n* poignet *m*.
wristband *n* manchette de chemise *f*.
wristwatch *n* montre-bracelet *f*.
writ *n* écriture *f*; assignation *f*; acte
judiciaire *m*.
write *vt* écrire; composer; ~ **down**
consigner par écrit; ~ **off** annuler; réduire; ~ **up** rédiger.
write-off *n* perte *f*.
writer *n* écrivain *m*; auteur *m*.
writhe *vi* se tordre.
writing *n* écriture *f*; œuvres *fpl*;
écrit *m*.
writing desk *n* bureau *m*.
writing paper *n* papier à lettres *m*.
wrong *n* mal *m*; injustice *f*; tort *m*;
injure *f*; * *adj* mauvais, mal; injuste; inopportun; faux, erroné;
* *adv* mal, inexactement; * *vt* faire du tort à, léser.
wrongful *adj* injuste.
wrongly *adv* injustement.
wry *adj* ironique, narquois.

X, Y, Z

xenon *n* xénon *m.*
xenophobe *n* xénophobe *mf.*
xenophobia *n* xénophobie *f.*
xenophobic *adj* xénophobique.
Xmas *abbr* Noël *m.*
X-ray *n* rayon X *m.*
xylophone *n* xylophone *m.*
yacht *n* yacht *m.*
yachting *n* navigation de plaisance *f.*
Yankee *n* yankee *m.*
yard *n* yard (0.914 m) *m*; cour *f.*
yardstick *n* critère d'évaluation *m.*
yarn *n* longue histoire *f*; fil *m.*
yawn *vi* bâiller; * *n* bâillement *m.*
yawning *adj* béant.
yeah *adv* (*fam*) oui, ouais.
year *n* année *f.*
yearbook *n* annuaire *m.*
yearling *n* animal âgé d'un an *m.*
yearly *adj adv* annuel(lement).
yearn *vi* languir.
yearning *n* désir ardent *m.*
yeast *n* levure *f.*
yell *vi* hurler; * *n* hurlement *m.*
yellow *adj n* jaune *m.*
yellowish *adj* jaunâtre.

yelp *vi* japper, glapir; * *n* jappement *m.*
yes *adv, n* oui *m.*
yesterday *adv, n* hier (*m*).
yet *conj* pourtant; cependant; * *adv* encore.
yew *n* if *m.*
yield *vt* donner, produire; rapporter; * *vi* se rendre; céder; * *n* production *f*; récolte *f*; rendement *m.*
yoga *n* yoga *m.*
yog(h)urt *n* yaourt *m.*
yoke *n* joug *m.*
yolk *n* jaune d'œuf *m.*
yonder *adv* là-bas.
you *pn* vous; tu; te; toi.
young *adj* jeune; ~**er** *adj* plus jeune.
youngster *n* jeune *mf.*
your(s) *pn* ton, ta, tes; votre, vos; le tien, la tienne, les tiens, les tiennes; le/la vôtre, les vôtres; **sincerely ~s** je vous prie d'agréer, Monsieur/Madame, l'expression de mes sentiments les meilleurs.
yourself *pn* toi-même; vous-même(s).

youth *n* jeunesse, adolescence *f*; jeune homme *m.*
youthful *adj* jeune.
youthfulness *n* jeunesse *f.*
yuppie (*adj*) *n* (de) jeune cadre dynamique *m.*
zany *adj* farfelu.
zap *vt* flinguer.
zeal *n* zèle *m*; ardeur *f.*
zealous *adj* zélé.
zebra *n* zèbre *m.*
zenith *n* zénith *m.*
zero *n* zéro *m.*
zest *n* enthousiasme *m.*
zigzag *n* zigzag *m.*
zinc *n* zinc *m.*
zip, zipper *n* fermeture éclair *f.*
zip code *n* code postal *m.*
zodiac *n* zodiaque *m.*
zone *n* zone *f*; secteur *m.*
zoo *n* zoo *m.*
zoological *adj* zoologique.
zoologist *n* zoologiste *mf.*
zoology *n* zoologie *f.*
zoom *vi* vrombir.
zoom lens *n* zoom *m.*

French Vocabulary

The Body   Le corps

1

head	la tête
hair	les cheveux *m*
dark	brun
fair	blond
bald	chauve
brown (*hair*)	châtain
smooth	lisse
curly	frisé
grey hair	les cheveux *m* gris
scalp	le cuir chevelu

2

face	la figure
features	les traits *m*
forehead	le front
cheek	la joue
wrinkle	la ride
dimple	la fossette
chin	le menton
beautiful	belle
handsome	beau
pretty	joli

3

ugly	laid
ugliness	la laideur
beauty	la beauté
beauty spot	le grain de beauté
freckle	la tache de rousseur
ear	l'oreille *f*
hearing	l'ouïe *f*
to hear	entendre
to listen	écouter

4

listener	l'auditeur, l'auditrice
earlobe	le lobe de l'oreille
deaf	sourd
mute	muet
deaf-mute	sourd-muet
deafness	la surdité
to deafen	assourdir
deafening	assourdissant
eardrum	le tympan
sound	le son

5

noise	le bruit
eye	l'œil *m*
senses	les sens *m*
eyesight	la vue
tear	la larme
eyebrow	le sourcil
to frown	froncer les sourcils
eyelid	la paupière
eyelash	le cil
pupil	la pupille

6

retina	la rétine
iris	l'iris *m*
glance	le coup d'œil
to glance	jeter un coup d'oeil
to see	voir
to look	regarder
visible	visible
invisible	invisible
blind	aveugle
blindness	la cécité

7

to blind	aveugler
blind spot	le point aveugle
one-eyed	borgne
cross-eyed	qui louche
to observe	observer
to notice	remarquer
expression	l'expression *f*
to smile	sourire
smile	le sourire
to laugh	rire

8

laugh	le rire
laughing	riant
mouth	la bouche
tongue	la langue
lip	la lèvre
tooth	la dent
eyetooth	la canine supérieure
gum	la gencive
palate	le palais
to say	dire

9

saying	le proverbe
to speak	parler
to shout	crier
to be quiet	se taire
touch	le toucher
to touch	toucher
to feel	sentir
tactile	tactile
nose	le nez
nostril	la narine

10

bridge (nose)	l'arête *m* du nez
smell (sense)	l'odorat *m*
smell	l'odeur *f*
to smell (of)	sentir
to taste (of)	avoir le goût de
to taste	goûter
taste (sense)	le goût
taste bud	les papilles *f*
tasty	savoureux
tasting	la dégustation

11

moustache	la moustache
beard	la barbe
facial hair	les poils du visage
sideburns	les pattes
dandruff	les pellicules *f*
plait	la tresse
curl	la boucle
to shave	se raser
to grow a beard	se laisser pousser la barbe
bearded	barbu

12

clean-shaven	glabre
jaw	la mâchoire
throat	la gorge
neck	le cou
shoulder	l'épaule
back	le dos
chest	la poitrine
breast	le sein
to breathe	respirer
breath	le souffle

13

breathing	la respiration
lung	le poumon
windpipe	la trachée-artère
heart	le cœur
heartbeat	le battement de cœur
rib	la côte
side	le flanc
limb	le membre
leg	la jambe
lame	boiteux

14

to limp	boiter
thigh	la cuisse
calf	le mollet
tendon	le tendon
groin	l'aine *f*
muscle	le muscle
knee	le genou
kneecap	la rotule
to kneel	s'agenouiller
foot	le pied

15

heel	le talon
toe	l'orteil *m*
sole	la plante du pied
ankle	la cheville
instep	la cambrure du pied
arm	le bras
forearm	l'avant-bras *m*
right-handed	droitier
left-handed	gaucher
right	la droite

16

left	la gauche
hand	la main
to handle	manier
handshake	la poignée de main
handful	la poignée
finger	le doigt
index finger	l'index *m*
thumb	le pouce
palm	la paume
nail	l'ongle *m*

17

wrist	le poignet
elbow	le coude
fist	le poing
knuckle	l'articulation *f* du doigt
bone	l'os *m*
spine	la colonne vertébrale
skeleton	le squelette
skull	le crâne
blood	le sang
vein	la veine

18

artery	l'artère *f*
capillary	le vaisseau capillaire
liver	le foie
skin	la peau
pore	le pore
sweat	la sueur
to sweat	transpirer
scar	la cicatrice
wart	la verrue
complexion	le teint

19

brain	le cerveau
kidney	le rein
bladder	la vessie
spleen	la rate
gland	la glande
larynx	le larynx
ligament	le ligament
cartilage	le cartilage
womb	l'utérus *m*
ovary	l'ovaire *m*

20

height	la taille
big	grand
small	petit
tall	grand
short	petit
fat	gros
thin	mince
strong	fort
strength	la force
weak	faible

21

to be knock-kneed	avoir les genoux *m* cagneux
to be bow-legged	avoir les jambes *f* arquées
to stand	être debout
to stand up	se lever
to raise	lever
to lie down	s'allonger
to sleep	dormir
sleep	le sommeil
to be sleepy	avoir sommeil
to dream	rêver

22

to doze	somnoler
to fall asleep	s'endormir
asleep	endormi
to be awake	être éveillé
to wake up	se réveiller
drowsy	somnolent
dream	le rêve
nightmare	le cauchemar
conscious	conscient
unconscious	inconscient

Clothes   Les vêtements

23

jacket	la veste
trousers	le pantalon
jeans	le jean
dungarees	la salopette
overalls	la blouse
braces	les bretelles
sweater	le chandail
to darn	rapiécer
sock	la chaussette
raincoat	l'imperméable

24

overcoat	le manteau
to shelter	s'abriter
to protect	protéger
hat	le chapeau
brim	le bord
shadow	l'ombre *f*
cap	la casquette
glasses	les lunettes
earmuffs	le serre-tête
walking stick	la canne

25

umbrella	le parapluie
cloth	la toile
fine	fin
thick	épais
coarse	rude
shirt	la chemise
T-shirt	le T-shirt
tie	la cravate

handkerchief	le mouchoir
suit	le complet

26

waistcoat	le gilet
skirt	la jupe
miniskirt	la minijupe
blouse	le chemisier
stockings	les bas *m*
veil	le voile
beret	le béret
collar	le col
gloves	les gants
belt	la ceinture

27

scarf	l'écharpe *f*
button	le bouton
to button	boutonner
to unbutton	déboutonner
new	neuf, nouveau
second-hand	d'occasion
graceful	gracieux
narrow	étroit
broad	large

28

ready-made	de confection
to make	faire
to get made	faire faire
to wear	porter
to use	user
worn out	usé
useful	utile
useless	inutile
practical	pratique

29

housecoat	le peignoir
nightdress	la chemise de nuit
pyjamas	le pyjama
underpants	le slip
knickers	le slip
petticoat	le jupon
slip	la combinaison
bra	le soutien-gorge
leotard	le collant

30

coat hanger	le cintre
zip	la fermeture éclair
wristband	le poignet
sweatshirt	le sweatshirt
shorts	le short
tracksuit	le survêtement
dress	la robe
to dress	habiller
to dress oneself	s'habiller
to take off	ôter

31

to remove	enlever
to undress	se déshabiller
naked	nu
to put	mettre
to put on	mettre
sash	la ceinture à nœud
apron	le tablier
shawl	le châle
sleeve	la manche
to sew	coudre

32

seam	la couture
seamstress	la couturière
thread	le fil
needle	l'aiguille f
hole	le trou
scissors	les ciseaux m
ribbon	le ruban
linen	le lin
lace	la dentelle
velcro	le velcro

33

fur	la fourrure
furry	en peluche f
silk	la soie
silky	soyeux
velvet	le velours
cotton	le coton
nylon	le nylon
fan	l'éventail m
in fashion	à la mode
out of fashion	démodé

34

dressmaker	la couturière
pocket	la poche
bag	le sac
pin	l'épingle f
to tie	attacher, nouer
to untie	détacher, dénouer
to loosen	desserrer
sandal	la sandale
slipper	le chausson
pair	la paire

35

lace	le lacet
shoe	la chaussure
sole	la semelle
heel	le talon
to polish	cirer
shoe polish	le cirage
shoehorn	le chausse-pied
boot	la botte
leather	le cuir
rubber	le caoutchouc

36

suede	le daim
barefoot	nu-pieds
to put on one's shoes	se chausser
to take off one's shoes	se déchausser
footwear	les chaussures f
shoemaker	le chausseur
ring	l'anneau
diamond	le diamant
necklace	le collier
bracelet	le bracelet

Family and Relationships
La famille et les relations

37

father	le père
mother	la mère
parents	les parents m
son	le fils
daughter	la fille
children	les enfants m
brother	le frère
sister	la sœur
brotherhood	la fraternité
brotherly	fraternel

38

elder	aîné
younger	cadet
husband	le mari
wife	la femme
uncle	l'oncle m
aunt	la tante
nephew	le neveu
niece	la nièce
grandfather	le grand-père
grandmother	la grand-mère

39

grandparents	les grands-parents m
grandson	le petit-fils
granddaughter	la petite-fille
boy	le garçon
girl	la fille
cousin	le cousin, la cousine
twin	le jumeau, la jumelle
baby	le bébé
child	l'enfant m
to be born	naître

40

to grow up	grandir
name	le nom
surname	le nom de famille
birthday	l'anniversaire m
age	l'âge m
old	vieux

to get old	vieillir
old man	le vieil homme
old woman	la vieille dame
youth	le jeune

41

young	jeune
young man	le jeune homme
young woman	la jeune femme
father-in-law	le beau-père
mother-in-law	la belle-mère
son-in-law	le gendre
daughter-in-law	la bru
brother-in-law	le beau-frère
sister-in-law	la belle-sœur
orphan	l'orphelin, l'orpheline

42

stepfather	le beau-père
stepmother	la belle-mère
stepson	le beau-fils
stepdaughter	la belle-fille
stepbrother	le demi-frère
stepsister	la demi-sœur
bachelor	célibataire
spinster	célibataire
widower	le veuf
widow	la veuve

43

ancestors	les ancêtres
descendants	les descendants
boyfriend	le petit ami
girlfriend	la petite amie
couple	le couple
love	l'amour m
to fall in love	tomber amoureux, amoureuse
to marry	se marier
wedding	le mariage
honeymoon	la lune de miel

44

maternity	la maternité
paternity	la paternité
to be pregnant	être enceinte
to give birth	accoucher
childbirth	l'accouchement
nurse	la nourrice
child minder	la gardienne d'enfants
to baby-sit	garder les enfants
baby-sitter	le/la babysitter
godmother	la marraine

45

godfather	le parrain
baptism	le baptême
to baptise	baptiser
crèche	la crèche
to breastfeed	allaiter
infancy	la petite enfance

to spoil (child)	gâter
spoiled	gâté
divorce	le divorce
separation	la séparation

46

family planning	le planning familial
familiar	familier
contraception	la contraception
contraceptive	le contraceptif
contraceptive pill	la pilule anticoncep tionnelle
condom	le préservatif
abortion	l'avortement m
to have an abortion	se faire avorter
period	les règles f
to menstruate	avoir ses règles f
to conceive	concevoir

47

middle-aged	entre deux âges
menopause	la ménopause
to retire	prendre sa retraite
pensioner	le retraité, la retraitée
the aging process	le vieillissement
old age	le troisième âge
death	la mort, le décès
to die	mourir, décéder
dying	moribond
deathbed	le lit de mort

48

dead man	le mort
dead woman	la morte
death certificate	le certificat de décès
mourning	le deuil
burial	l'enterrement m
to bury	enterrer
grave	la tombe
cemetery	le cimetière
wake	la veillée funèbre
coffin	le cercueil

49

deceased	le défunt, la défunte
late	feu
to console	consoler
to weep	pleurer
to wear mourning	porter le deuil
to survive	survivre
crematorium	le crématorium
cremation	l'incinération f
to cremate	incinérer
ashes	les cendres f

Health   La santé

50

sickness	la maladie

nurse	l'infirmier, l'infirmière
infirmary	l'infirmerie f
sick	malade
hospital	l'hôpital m
patient	le patient, la patiente
cough	la toux
to cough	tousser
to injure	blesser
injury	la blessure

51

cramp	la crampe
to cut oneself	se couper
to dislocate	se démettre
to faint	s'évanouir
to be ill	être malade
to become ill	tomber malade
to look after	soigner
care	les soins m
careful	soigneux

52

carelessness	la négligence, l'imprudence
careless	négligent, imprudent
negligent	négligent
doctor	le médecin
medicine	le médicament
prescription	l'ordonnance f
pharmacist	le pharmacien, la pharma-cienne
pharmacy	la pharmacie
cure	le remède
curable	curable

53

incurable	incurable
to cure	guérir
to get well	se rétablir
healthy	sain
unhealthy	malsain
to recover	se remettre, se rétablir
pain	la douleur
painful	douloureux
to suffer	souffrir

54

diet	le régime
obesity	l'obésité f
obese	obèse
anorexic	anorexique
anorexia	l'anorexie f
obsession	l'obsession f
to get fat	grossir
headache	le mal de tête
toothache	la rage de dents
stomach ache	le mal de ventre

55

indigestion	l'indigestion f
aspirin	l'aspirine f
migraine	la migraine

food poisoning	l'intoxication f ali-mentaire
sore throat	le mal de gorge
hoarse	enroué
pale	pâle
to turn pale	pâlir
faintness	le malaise
cold (illness)	le rhume

56

to catch a cold	s'enrhumer
wound	la plaie
surgeon	le chirurgien
to heat	réchauffer
hot	chaud
temperature	la température
perspiration	la sueur
sweaty	en sueur
fever	la fièvre
germ	le germe

57

microbe	le microbe
contagious	contagieux
vaccine	le vaccin
to shiver	frissonner
madness	la folie
mad	fou
drug	la drogue
pill	le cachet
to scar	se cicatriser
stitches	les points m de suture

58

to relieve	soulager
swollen	enflé
boil	le furoncle
to bleed	saigner
blood	le sang
to clot	se coaguler
blood cell	la cellule sanguine
blood group	le groupe sanguin
blood pressure	la tension artérielle
blood test	l'analyse f de sang
check up	l'examen m médical

59

epidemic	l'épidémie f
plague	la peste
allergy	l'allergie f
allergic	allergique
angina	l'angine f
tonsillitis	l'amygdalite f
fracture	la fracture
cast	le plâtre
crutches	les béquilles f
wheelchair	le fauteuil roulant

60

haemophiliac	hémophile
haemophilia	l'hémophilie f

cholesterol	le cholestérol
vitamin	la vitamine
calorie	la calorie
handicapped persons	les handicapés
handicap	le désavantage
pneumonia	la pneumonie
heart attack	la crise cardiaque
bypass operation	le pontage

61

heart surgery	la chirurgie du cœur
microsurgery	la microchirurgie
pacemaker	le stimulateur cardiaque
heart transplant	la greffe du cœur
smallpox	la variole
stroke	l'apoplexie f
tumour	la tumeur
HIV positive	séropositif (au virus VIH)
AIDS	le sida
cancer	le cancer

62

breast cancer	le cancer du sein
chemotherapy	la chimiothérapie
screening	la visite de dépistage
diagnosis	le diagnostic
antibody	l'anticorps m
antibiotic	l'antibiotique m
depression	la dépression
depressed	déprimé
to depress	déprimer
to undergo an operation	subir une opération

63

painkiller	l'analgésique m
treatment	le traitement
anaesthetic	l'anesthésie f
anaesthetist	l'anesthésiste
donor	le donneur
genetic engineering	le génie génétique
test-tube baby	le bébé-éprouvette
surrogate mother	la mère-porteuse
infertile	stérile
hormone	l'hormone f

64

psychologist	le, la psychologue
psychology	la psychologie
psychoanalyst	le, la psychanalyste
psychoanalysis	la psychanalyse
psychosomatic	psychosomatique
hypochondriac	l'hypocondriaque
plastic surgery	la chirurgie esthétique
face-lift	le lissage
implant	l'implant m
self-esteem	l'amour-propre m

65

to smoke	fumer
passive smoking	le tabagisme passif
to inhale	avaler la fumée

withdrawal symptoms	l'état m de manque
alcohol	l'alcool m
hangover	la gueule de bois
alcoholic	l'alcoolique
drug addict	le toxicomane
drug addiction	la toxicomanie
drugs traffic	le trafic de drogue

66

heroin	l'héroïne f
cocaine	la cocaïne
drugs trafficker	le trafiquant de drogue
to launder money	blanchir de l'argent
syringe	la seringue
to inject	injecter
to take drugs	se droguer
clinic	la clinique
outpatient	le malade en consultation externe
therapy	la thérapie

Nature   La nature

67

world	le monde
natural	naturel
creation	la création
the Big Bang theory	la théorie du big-bang
supernatural	surnaturel
to create	créer
sky	le ciel
galaxy	la galaxie
the Milky Way	la voie lactée
the Plough	la Grande Ourse

68

astronomer	l'astronome
astronomy	l'astronomie
telescope	le téléscope
UFO	l'OVNI m (objet volant non identifié)
light year	l'année-lumière f
asteroid	l'astéroïde m
meteor	la météorite
comet	la comète
star	l'étoile f
starry	étoilé

69

to twinkle	scintiller
to shine	briller
planet	la planète
Earth	la Terre
Mercury	Mercure
Venus	Vénus
Mars	Mars
Jupiter	Jupiter
Saturn	Saturne
Uranus	Uranus

70

Neptune	Neptune
Pluto	Pluton
orbit	l'orbite f
to orbit	graviter autour de
gravity	la pesanteur
satellite	le satellite
moon	la lune
eclipse	l'éclipse f
sun	le soleil
sunspot	la tache solaire

71

ray	le rayon
radiate	irradier
radiant	radieux, rayonnant
midnight sun	le soleil de minuit
shining	brillant
brilliancy	l'éclat m
sunrise	le lever de soleil
to rise	se lever
sunset	le coucher de soleil
to set	se coucher

72

dawn	l'aube
to dawn	poindre
dusk	le crépuscule
nightfall	la tombée de la nuit
earthquake	le tremblement de terre
volcano	le volcan
eruption	l'éruption f
deserted	désert
desert	le désert
plain	la plaine

73

flat	plat
level	le niveau
valley	la vallée
hill	la colline
mountain	la montagne
mountainous	montagneux
peak	le pic
summit	le sommet
range of mountains	la chaîne de montagnes
crag	le rocher escarpé

74

rock	la roche
steep	abrupt
slope	la pente
coast	la côte
coastal	côtier
shore	le rivage
beach	la plage
cliff	la falaise
sea	la mer
tide	la marée

75

high tide	la marée haute
low tide	la marée basse
ebb tide	le reflux
flood tide	le flux
wave	la vague
foam	l'écume f
tempest	la tempête
hurricane	l'ouragan m
gulf	le golfe
bay	la baie

76

cape	le cap
straits	le détroit
island	l'île f
spring	la source
fountain	la fontaine
waterfall	la cascade
stream	le cours d'eau
river	la rivière
current	le courant
draught	le courant d'air

77

glacier	le glacier
iceberg	l'iceberg m
ice cap	la calotte glaciaire
icefloe	la banquise
to flood	inonder
border	le bord
lake	le lac
pond	l'étang m
marsh	le marais
marshy	marécageux

78

deep	profond
depth	la profondeur
weather	le temps
fine weather	le beau temps
climate	le climat
barometer	le baromètre
thermometer	le thermomètre
degree	le degré
air	l'air m
breeze	la brise

79

cool, fresh	frais
wind	le vent
windy	venteux
dampness	l'humidité f
damp	humide
to wet	mouiller
wet	mouillé
storm	la tempête, l'orage m
stormy	orageux
dry	sec

80

drought	la sécheresse
to dry	sécher
rainbow	l'arc-en-ciel *m*
rain	la pluie
rainy	pluvieux
to rain	pleuvoir
drop	la goutte
shower	l'ondée *f*
cloud	le nuage
cloudy	nuageux

81

to cloud over	se couvrir
to clear up	se dégager
lightning	la foudre
lightning conductor	le paratonnerre
flash of lightning	l'éclair *m*
sheet lightning	les éclairs *m* en nappe
fork lightning	les éclairs *m* en zigzag
harmful	nuisible
to harm	endommager
thunder	le tonnerre

82

to thunder	tonner
fog	le brouillard
mist	la brume
foggy	brumeux
misty	brumeux, embrumé
snow	la neige
snowstorm	la tempête de neige
snowfall	la chute de neige
hailstone	le grêlon

83

to hail	grêler
to freeze	geler
frozen	gelé
icicle	le glaçon
frost	la gelée blanche
to thaw	fondre
ice	la glace
thaw	le dégel
heatwave	la canicule
sultry	lourd

Minerals   Les minéraux

84

metal	le métal
mine	la mine
mineral	le minéral
forge	la forge
to forge	forger
steel	l'acier *m*
iron	le fer
iron *adj*	en fer

bronze	le bronze
brass	le laiton

85

copper	le cuivre
tin	l'étain *m*
lead	le plomb
zinc	le zinc
nickel	le nickel
aluminium	l'aluminium *m*
silver	l'argent *m*
gold	l'or *m*
platinum	le platine
mould	le moule

86

to extract	extraire
to exploit	exploiter
miner	le mineur
to melt, smelt	fondre
to mould	mouler
rust	la rouille
rusty	rouillé
to solder	souder
to alloy	allier
alloy	l'alliage *m*

87

stone	la pierre, le caillou
stony	caillouteux
quarry	la carrière
granite	le granit
to polish	polir
polished	poli
smooth	lisse
marble	le marbre
lime	la chaux
chalk	la craie

88

clay	l'argile *f*
sulphur	le soufre
jewel	le joyau
pearl	la perle
diamond	le diamant
ruby	le rubis
emerald	l'émeraude
mother-of-pearl	le nacre
enamel	l'émail *m*
sapphire	le saphir

89

agate	l'agate *f*
opal	l'opale *f*
lapis-lazuli	le lapis-lazuli
obsidian	l'obsidienne *f*
garnet	le grenat
alkali	l'alcali *m*
acid	l'acide *m*
acidity	l'acidité *f*

plutonium	le plutonium
radium	le radium

Animals   Les animaux

90

domestic	domestique
tame	apprivoisé
cat	le chat
kitten	le chaton
to mew	miauler
feline	le félin
claw	la griffe
dog	le chien
bitch	la chienne
puppy	le chiot

91

to bark	aboyer
canine	canin
watchful	vigilant
watchdog	le chien de garde
pet	l'animal *m* familier
breed	la race
greyhound	le lévrier
alsatian	le berger allemand
terrapin	la tortue d'eau douce
tropical fish	le poisson exotique

92

aquarium	l'aquarium *m*
aquatic	aquatique
horse	le cheval
to neigh	hennir
stallion	l'étalon *m*
mare	la jument
colt	le poulain
donkey	l'âne *m*
bray	braire
mule	le mulet

93

male	le mâle
female	la femelle
livestock	le bétail
horn	la corne
paw	la patte
hoof	le sabot
tail	la queue
flock	le troupeau
cow	la vache
ox	le bœuf

94

to low	mugir
bull	le taureau
calf	le veau
heifer	la génisse

lamb	l'agneau
sheep	le mouton
ram	le bélier
ewe	la brebis
goat	la chèvre
pig	le cochon

95

grunt	grogner
to fatten	engraisser
wild	sauvage
carnivorous	carnivore
herbivorous	herbivore
omnivorous	omnivore
quadruped	le quadrupède
biped	le bipède
mammal	le mammifère
warm-blooded	à sang chaud

96

predator	le prédateur
prey	la proie
lion	le lion
lioness	la lionne
cub	le lionceau
to roar	rugir
mane	la crinière
tiger	le tigre
tigress	la tigresse
cheetah	le guépard

97

leopard	le léopard
lynx	le lynx
mountain lion	le puma
hyena	la hyène
jackal	le chacal
to scavenge	dépecer une charogne
scavenger	le charognard
carrion	la charogne
jaguar	le jaguar
tapir	le tapir

98

buffalo	le buffle
mongoose	la mangouste
porcupine	le porc-épic
armadillo	le tatou
skunk	la mouffette
sloth	le paresseux
rhinoceros	le rhinocéros
hippopotamus	l'hippopotame *m*
wolf	le loup
pack	la meute

99

bear	l'ours *m*
to hibernate	hiberner
zebra	le zèbre
bison	le bison

Animals		Animals	
to graze	brouter	insect	l'insecte *m*
pasture	le pâturage	to hum	bourdonner
wild boar	le sanglier	humming	le bourdonnement
ferocious	féroce		
bristle (boar)	la soie	**105**	
elephant	l'éléphant *m*	antenna	l'antenne *f*
		worm	le ver
100		to worm	ramper
tusk	la défense	earthworm	le ver de terre
trunk	la trompe	tapeworm	le ver solitaire
camel	le chameau	parasite	le parasite
hump	la bosse	beetle	le scarabée
dromedary	le dromadaire	stag beetle	le lucane
llama	le lama	silkworm	le ver à soie
deer	le chevreuil	caterpillar	la chenille
doe	la biche		
stag	le cerf	**106**	
elk	l'élan *m*	chrysalis	la chrysalide
		metamorphosis	la métamorphose
101		to metamorphose	se métamorphoser
moose	l'orignal *m*	butterfly	le papillon
antlers	les bois *m*	moth	la mite
fox	le renard	fly	la mouche
cunning	rusé	bluebottle	la mouche bleue
craft, cunning	la ruse	spider	l'araignée *f*
hare	le lièvre	web	la toile d'araignée
badger	le blaireau	to spin	tisser sa toile
otter	la loutre		
dormouse	le loir	**107**	
shrew	la musaraigne	wasp	la guêpe
		hornet	le frelon
102		to sting	piquer
hedgehog	le hérisson	sting	la piqûre
weasel	la belette	bee	l'abeille *f*
mink	le vison	worker (bee, ant)	l'ouvrière *f*
beaver	le castor	bumblebee	le bourdon
dam	la digue	queen bee	la reine
mole	la taupe	beehive	la ruche
molehill	la taupinière	apiary	le rucher
mouse	la souris		
mousetrap	la souricière	**108**	
		apiarist	l'apiculteur *m*
103		drone	le faux-bourdon
rabbit	le lapin	honey	le miel
rat	le rat	honeycomb	le rayon de miel
bat	la chauve-souris	grasshopper	la sauterelle
nocturnal	nocturne	locust	la locuste
primates	les primates *m*	infest	infester
gorilla	le gorille	cricket	le grillon
monkey	le singe	glow-worm	le ver luisant
orang-utan	l'orang-outan *m*	ant	la fourmi
baboon	le babouin		
		109	
104		anthill	la fourmilière
gibbon	le gibbon	colony	la colonie
marsupial	le marsupial	to itch	démanger
kangaroo	le kangourou	itch	la démangeaison
koala	le koala	termite	la termite
giant panda	le panda géant	troublesome	gênant
invertebrate	invertébré	to molest	importuner
exoskeleton	l'exosquelette *m*	mosquito	le moustique

mosquito net	la moustiquaire
malaria	le paludisme

110

flea	la puce
earwig	le perce-oreille
praying mantis	la mante religieuse
scorpion	le scorpion
snail	l'escargot
slug	la limace
louse	le pou
lousy	pouilleux
centipede	le mille-pattes
millipede	le mille-pattes

111

reptile	le reptile
cold-blooded	à sang froid
tortoise	la tortue
turtle	la tortue marine
crocodile	le crocodile
alligator	l'alligator *m*
grass snake	la couleuvre
snake	le serpent
slowworm	l'orvet *m*
harmless	inoffensif

112

to crawl	ramper
viper	la vipère
fang	le crochet
python	le python
anaconda	l'anaconda *m*
rattlesnake	le serpent à sonnette
cobra	le cobra
poison	le venin
antidote	l'antidote *m*
poisonous	venimeux

113

bird	l'oiseau *m*
aviary	la volière
ostrich	l'autruche *f*
beak, bill	le bec
wing	l'aile *f*
to fly	voler
flight	le vol
flightless	coureur
to lay (eggs)	pondre (des œufs)
to nest	nicher

114

canary	le canari
robin redbreast	le rouge-gorge
chaffinch	le pinson
nightingale	le rossignol
sparrow	le moineau
swallow	l'hirondelle *f*
lark	l'alouette *f*
cuckoo	le coucou
magpie	la pie

115

blackbird	le merle
crow	le corbeau
to caw	croasser
seagull	la mouette
albatross	l'albatros *m*
cormorant	le cormoran
partridge	la perdrix
pheasant	le faisan
stork	la cigogne
owl	le hibou

116

rooster	le coq
cockcrow	au premier chant du coq
to crow	chanter
cock-a-doodle-doo	cocorico
hen	la poule
feather	la plume
to pluck	plumer
chicken	le poulet
to brood	couver
to breed (animals)	élever

117

pigeon	le pigeon
duck	le canard
goose	l'oie *f*
swan	le cygne
parrot	le perroquet
toucan	le toucan
turkey	la dinde
peacock	le paon
hummingbird	le colibri
bird of paradise	l'oiseau de paradis

118

rapacious	rapace
bird of prey	le rapace
eagle	l'aigle *m*
vulture	le vautour
peregrine	le faucon pèlerin
to swoop	s'abattre
falcon	le faucon
falconer	le fauconnier
falconry	la fauconnerie
condor	le condor

119

amphibious	amphibie
amphibian	l'amphibie *m*
frog	la grenouille
bullfrog	la grenouille d'Amérique
tadpole	le têtard
toad	le crapaud
salamander	la salamandre
crustacean	le crustacé
crab	le crabe
prawn	la langoustine

120

fish	le poisson
goldfish	le poisson rouge
piranha	le piranha
voracious	vorace
carp	la carpe
sturgeon	l'esturgeon *m*
caviar	le caviar
trout	la truite
hake	le merlu, le colin
herring	le hareng

121

sardine	la sardine
skate	la raie
cod	la morue
eel	l'anguille *f*
electric eel	l'anguille électrique *f*
elver	la civelle
salmon	le saumon
school (fish)	le banc
coral	le corail
coral reef	le récif de corail

122

flipper	la nageoire
fin	l'aileron *m*
gills	les ouïes *f*
shell	la coquille
scale	l'écaille *f*
squid	le calmar
octopus	la pieuvre
tentacle	le tentacule
cuttlefish	la seiche
crayfish	la langouste

123

lobster	le homard
sea urchin	l'oursin *m*
sea horse	l'hippocampe *m*
starfish	l'étoile de mer *f*
shellfish	les coquillages *m*
oyster	l'huître *f*
shark	le requin
whale	la baleine
killer whale	l'épaulard *m*
dolphin	le dauphin

124

seal	le phoque
sea lion	l'otarie *f*
walrus	le morse
natural selection	la sélection naturelle
survival of the fittest	la loi du plus fort
evolution	l'évolution *f*
to evolve	évoluer
zoology	la zoologie
zoologist	le zoologue
zoo	le zoo

125

habitat	l'habitat *m*
extinct	disparu
dinosaur	le dinosaure
mammoth	le mammouth
dodo	le dronte
yeti	le yéti
mythical	mythique
myth	le mythe
unicorn	la licorne
dragon	le dragon

Plants   Les plantes

126

to transplant	transplanter
to plant	planter
root	la racine
to root (pig, etc)	fouiller
to take root	prendre racine
to uproot	déraciner
radical	le radical
tendril	la vrille
stalk	la tige
sap	la sève

127

foliage	le feuillage
leaf	la feuille
leafy	feuillu
to shed leaves	perdre ses feuilles
deciduous	à feuilles caduques
evergreen	à feuilles persistantes
perennial	la plante vivace
thorn	l'épine
thorn tree	l'aubépine *f*
thorny	épineux

128

weed	la mauvaise herbe
to weed	désherber
to thin	éclaircir
thistle	le chardon
nettle	l'ortie *f*
briar	l'églantier *m*
hemlock	la ciguë
deadly nightshade	la belladone
Venus flytrap	la dionée
rush	le jonc

129

reed	le roseau
epiphyte	épiphyte
moss	la mousse
spider plant	le chlorophytum
bud	le bourgeon
to bud	bourgeonner
flower	la fleur
to flower	fleurir

blooming	en fleur
petal	le pétale

130

to wither	se flétrir, se faner
withered	flétri, fané
garland	la guirlande
scent	le parfum
garden	le jardin
gardener	le jardinier
landscape gardener	le paysagiste
to water	arroser
watering can	l'arrosoir *m*
irrigation	l'irrigation *f*

131

herb	l'aromate *m*
thyme	le thym
rosemary	le romarin
sage	la sauge
parsley	le persil
mint	la menthe
tarragon	l'estragon *m*
coriander	la coriandre
dill	le fenouil
watercress	le cresson

132

balsam	la balsamine
chicory	la chicorée
chives	la ciboulette
mustard	la moutarde
balm	la mélisse
clover	le trèfle
grass	l'herbe *f*
shrub	l'arbuste *m*
myrtle	le myrte
gorse	l'ajonc *m*

133

flowerbed	la plate-bande
pansy	la pensée
primrose	la primevère
daisy	la marguerite
anemone	l'anémone *f*
tulip	la tulipe
hyacinth	la jacinthe
lily	le lis
lily of the valley	le muguet
mignonette	le réséda

134

snowdrop	le perce-neige
crocus	le crocus
carnation	l'œillet *m*
bluebell	la campanule
poppy	le pavot
cornflower	le bleuet
buttercup	le bouton d'or
daffodil	la jonquille
forget-me-not	le myosotis

135

foxglove	la digitale
sunflower	le tournesol
dandelion	le pissenlit
snapdragon	la gueule-de-loup
marigold	le souci
orchid	l'orchidée *f*
bush	le buisson
magnolia	le magnolia
fuchsia	le fuchsia
rhododendron	le rhododendron

136

heather	la bruyère
undergrowth	le sous-bois
scrub	les broussailles *f*
broom	le genêt
mallow	la mauve
laurel	le laurier
privet	le troène
hedge	la haie
to enclose	clôturer

137

vegetables	les légumes *m*
kitchen garden	le jardin potager
mushroom	le champignon
fungus	le champignon
harmful	nocif
leek	le poireau
radish	le radis
lettuce	la laitue
celery	le céleri
rhubarb	la rhubarbe

138

chard	les bettes *f*
spinach	la blette, la bette
turnip	le navet
potato	la pomme de terre
to peel	éplucher
to scrape	gratter
green peas	les petits pois *m*
husk (peas)	la cosse
to husk	écosser
cabbage	le chou

139

fruit	le fruit
fruit tree	l'arbre *m* fruitier
to graft	greffer
graft	la greffe
to shake	secouer
to prune	tailler
pear tree	le poirier
pear	la poire
apple tree	le pommier
apple	la pomme
cherry tree	le cerisier

140

cherry	la cerise
plum	la prune
plum tree	le prunier
prune	le pruneau
stone	le noyau
to stone	dénoyauter
almond	l'amande f
almond tree	l'amandier m
peach	la pêche
peach tree	le pêcher

141

apricot	l'abricot m
apricot tree	l'abricotier m
walnut	la noix
walnut tree	le noyer
chestnut	la châtaigne
chestnut tree	le châtaignier
hazelnut	la noisette
hazelnut tree	le noisetier
lemon	le citron
lemon tree	le citronnier

142

orange tree	l'oranger m
orange	l'orange f
olive	l'olive f
olive tree	l'olivier m
date	la datte
palm tree	le palmier
pomegranate	la grenade
pomegranate tree	le grenadier
banana tree	le bananier
pineapple	l'ananas m

143

coconut	la noix de coco
coconut tree	le cocotier
sugar cane	la canne à sucre
yam	l'igname f
lychee	le litchi
kiwi fruit	le kiwi
ripe	mûr
to ripen	mûrir
juicy	juteux
strawberry	la fraise

144

strawberry plant	le fraisier
medlar	la nèfle
medlar tree	le néflier
raspberry	la framboise
raspberry bush	le framboisier
blackcurrant	le cassis
redcurrant	la groseille
gooseberry	la groseille à maquereau
grape	le raisin
raisins	les raisins secs m

145

vine	la vigne
vineyard	le vignoble
vintner	le vigneron
grape harvest	les vendanges f
to gather grapes	vendanger
press	le pressoir
to press	presser
forest trees	les arbres forestiers
wood	le bois
jungle	la jungle

146

woody	boisé
wild, uncultivated	inculte
ivy	le lierre
to climb	grimper
creeper	la plante grimpante
wisteria	la glycine
mistletoe	le gui
rosewood	le palissandre
juniper	le genièvre
fern	la fougère

147

tree	l'arbre m
bark	l'écorce f
branch	la branche
twig	la brindille
knot	le nœud
tree ring	l'anneau m
trunk	le tronc
oak	le chêne
acorn	le gland
holm oak	le chêne vert

148

beech	le hêtre
ash	le frêne
elm	l'orme m
poplar	le peuplier
aspen	le tremble
lime	le tilleul
birch	le bouleau
fir	le sapin
conifer	le conifère
coniferous	conifère

149

pine	le pin
cone	la pomme de pin
hop	le houblon
monkey puzzle	l'araucaria m
sycamore	le sycomore
maple	l'érable m
holly	le houx
alder	l'aulne m
bamboo	le bambou
eucalyptus	l'eucalyptus m

150		wildlife	la faune
acacia	l'acacia *m*	harmful	nuisible
rubber tree	l'hévéa *m*	atmosphere	l'atmosphère *f*
mahogany	l'acajou *m*	smog	le smog
ebony	l'ébène *m*	unleaded petrol	l'essence *f* sans plomb
cedar	le cèdre		
cactus	le cactus	**155**	
cacao tree	le cacaoyer	ecosystem	l'écosystème *m*
giant sequoia	le séquoia géant	ecology	l'écologie *f*
bonsai	le bonsaï	ecologist	l'écologiste
yew	l'if *m*	acid rain	les pluies *f* acides
		deforestation	le déboisement
151		to deforest	déboiser
weeping willow	le saule pleureur	rainforest	la forêt tropicale
azalea	l'azalée *f*	underdeveloped	sous-développé
catkin	le chaton	industrialised	industrialisé
spore	le spore	ozone layer	la couche d'ozone
pollination	la pollinisation		
to pollinate	polliniser	**156**	
pollen	le pollen	oil slick	la marée noire
to fertilise	féconder	greenhouse effect	l'effet *m* de serre
stock (species)	la giroflée	to recycle	recycler
hybrid	hybride	recycling	le recyclage
		renewable	renouvelable
		fossil fuels	les combustibles *m* fossiles

The Environment   L'environnement

		resource	la ressource
		landfill	la décharge
152			
environmental	de l'environnement	**157**	
environmentalist	l'écologiste	decibel	le décibel
environmentalism	la science de l'environne-ment	to soundproof	insonoriser
		radiation	la radiation
pollution	la pollution	radioactive	radioactif
to conserve	préserver	nuclear energy	l'énergie *f* nucléaire
conservation	la défense de l'environne-ment	fallout	les retombées *f* radio-actives
waste	les déchets *m*	reactor	le réacteur
to waste	gaspiller	fission	la fission
rubbish	les ordures *f*	fusion	la fusion
rubbish tip	la décharge	leak	la fuite

The Home   La maison

153		**158**	
sewage	les eaux usées *f*	house	la maison
oil spill	le déversement de pétrole	apartment block	l'immeuble *m*
poisonous	toxique	to let	louer
to poison	empoisonner	tenant	le, la locataire
industrial waste	les déchets *m* industriels	rent	le loyer
toxic	toxique	housing	le logement
pollutant	le polluant	to move house	déménager
to pollute	polluer	landlord, owner	le, la propriétaire
consumerism	le consumérisme	to own	être propriétaire de
consumerist	le consumériste	ownership	la propriété
154		**159**	
to consume	consommer		
solar panel	le panneau solaire	country house	la maison de campagne
windmill	le moulin à vent	farmhouse	la ferme
wind energy	l'énergie *f* éolienne		
wave energy	l'énergie *f* des vagues		

villa	la villa
cottage	le cottage
chalet	le chalet
terraced house	la rangée de maisons
semi-detached house	la maison jumelée
mansion	le manoir
palace	le palais

160

castle	le château
igloo	l'igloo *m*
teepee	le tipi
log cabin	la cabane en rondins
houseboat	la péniche aménagée
hut	la hutte, l'abri *m*
house trailer	la roulotte
penthouse	l'appartement-terrasse
lighthouse	le phare
shack	la cabane

161

building	le bâtiment *m*
to build	construire
building site	le chantier
building contractor	l'entrepreneur *m*
to repair	réparer
solid	solide
to destroy	détruire
to demolish	démolir
garage	le garage
shed	l'appentis *m*

162

door	la porte
doorknocker	le heurtoir
to knock at the door	frapper à la porte
doormat	le paillasson
doorbell	la sonnette
threshold	le seuil
bolt	le verrou
plan	le plan
foundations	les fondations *f*
to found	fonder

163

cement	le ciment
concrete	le béton
stone	la pierre
cornerstone	la pierre angulaire
antiquated	vétuste
modern	moderne
luxurious	luxueux
roomy	spacieux
whitewashed	blanchi à la chaux
neglected	mal tenu, à l'abandon

164

worm-eaten	vermoulu
moth-eaten	mité
shanty	la baraque
shantytown	le bidonville

brick	la brique
sand	le sable
slate	l'ardoise *f*
gutter	la gouttière
drainpipe	le tuyau d'écoulement
step	la marche

165

plaster	le plâtre
skirting	la plinthe
floor	le plancher
wall	le mur
partition	la cloison
wood	le bois
board	la planche
beam	la poutre
to sustain	soutenir
to contain, hold	contenir

166

facade	la façade
outside	l'extérieur *m*
inside	l'intérieur *m*
window	la fenêtre
windowsill	l'appui *m* de fenêtre
venetian blinds	les stores vénitiens *m*
shutters	les volets *m*
balcony	le balcon
windowpanes	la vitre
glass	le verre

167

porch	le porche
gate	la grille
hinge	le gond
front door	la porte d'entrée
doorkeeper	le, la concierge
to open	ouvrir
opening	l'ouverture *f*
entrance	l'entrée *f*
to enter	entrer
to go out	sortir

168

way out	la sortie
lock	la serrure
to shut, close	fermer
to lock up	fermer à clef
key	la clef
to lock	verrouiller
staircase	l'escalier *m*
upstairs	en haut
downstairs	en bas
landing	le palier

169

ladder	l'échelle *f*
bannisters	la rampe
lift	l'ascenseur *m*
to go up	monter
ascent	la montée

to go down	descendre
descent	la descente
low	bas
high	haut
storeys	les étages *m*

170
ground floor	le rez-de-chaussée
first floor	le premier étage
cellar	la cave
tile	la tuile
roof	le toit
ceiling	le plafond
floor	le plancher
to turn	tourner
to return	revenir
return	le retour

171
to give back	rendre
chimney	la cheminée
hearth	l'âtre *m*
fire	le feu
spark	l'étincelle *f*
to sparkle	étinceler
flame	la flamme
ashes	la cendre
stove	la cuisinière
smoke	la fumée

172
to smoke (fire)	fumer
to burn	brûler
to blaze	flamber
ardent	ardent
coal	le charbon
embers	les braises
to scorch	roussir
to glow	rougeoyer
firewood	le bois de chauffage

173
woodcutter	le bûcheron
shovel	la pelle
poker	le tisonnier
to poke	attiser
matches	les allumettes *f*
wax	la cire
to light	allumer
box	la boîte
drawer	le tiroir
chest of drawers	la commode

174
comfortable	confortable
uncomfortable	inconfortable
lighting	l'éclairage *m*
dazzle, splendour	la splendeur
to light up	allumer

to put out, extinguish	éteindre
light	la lumière
lamp	la lampe
lampshade	l'abat-jour *m*
wick	la mèche

175
candle	la bougie
candlestick	le chandelier
room	la pièce
to inhabit	habiter
inhabitant	l'habitant, l'habitante
to reside	demeurer
residence	la demeure
hall (large room)	le vestibule
furniture	le mobilier
a piece of furniture	le meuble

176
furnished	meublé
corridor	le couloir
hall, lobby	le hall, le vestibule
hall stand	le portemanteau
sitting room	le salon
lounge	le salon
to serve	servir
guest	l'invité, l'invitée
to invite	inviter
table	la table

177
seat	le siège
to sit down	s'asseoir
to be sitting	être assis
cushion	le coussin
stool	le tabouret
chair	la chaise
armchair	le fauteuil
rocking chair	la fauteuil à bascule
sofa	le sofa
couch	le canapé, le divan
bench	le banc

178
bookcase	la bibliothèque
bookshelf	le rayon
bookrest	le support à livres
library	la bibliothèque
office, study	le bureau
writing desk	le secrétaire
to write	écrire
handwriting	l'écriture
paper	le papier

179
record player	le tourne-disques
LP	le disque
hi-fi	la chaîne
television	la télévision
video recorder	le magnétoscope

radiator	le radiateur
radio	la radio
ornament	le bibelot
alarm clock	le réveil
grandfather clock	l'horloge f

180
tapestry	la tapisserie
a tapestry	une tapisserie
to hang	accrocher
to take down	décrocher
wallpaper	le papier peint
to wallpaper	tapisser
tile (decorative)	le carreau
floor tiles	les tommettes
tiling	le carrelage
picture	le tableau

181
frame	le cadre
portrait	le portrait
photograph	la photo
photograph album	l'album m de photos
dining room	la salle à manger
to eat	manger
meal	le repas
breakfast	le petit déjeuner
to breakfast	prendre le petit déjeuner
lunch	le déjeuner

182
dinner	le dîner
to lunch	déjeuner
to dine	dîner
supper	le souper
to have supper	souper
sideboard	le buffet
larder	le garde-manger
pantry	l'office f
shelf	l'étagère f
cup	la tasse
draining board	l'égouttoir m

183
sugarbowl	le sucrier
coffeepot	la cafetière
teapot	la théière
tray	le plateau
table service	le service de table
tablecloth	la nappe
napkin	la serviette
plate	l'assiette f
saucer	la soucoupe
serving dish	le plat

184
microwave	le micro-ondes
to microwave	faire cuire au micro-ondes
food mixer	le mixer
refrigerator	le frigidaire

grater	la râpe
flowerpot	le pot à fleurs
(drinking) glass	le verre
glassware	la verrerie
to cook	faire cuire
to boil	faire bouillir

185
gas cooker	la cuisinière à gaz
electric cooker	la cuisinière électrique
grill	le grill
barbecue grill	le grill au feu de bois
saucepan	la casserole
refuse, rubbish	les ordures f
washing machine	la machine à laver
sewing machine	la machine à coudre
washing powder	la lessive
vacuum cleaner	l'aspirateur

186
electricity	l'électricité f
fusebox	la boîte à fusibles
central heating	le chauffage central
light bulb	l'ampoule f
switch	l'interrupteur m
to switch on	allumer
to switch off	éteindre
plug	la prise (mâle)
socket	la prise (femelle), la douille
air conditioning	la climatisation

187
lid	le couvercle
to cover	couvrir
to uncover	découvrir
to uncork	déboucher
crockery	la vaisselle
discover	découvrir
spoon	la cuillère
teaspoon	la cuillère à café
spoonful	la cuillerée

188
fork	la fourchette
cutlery	les couverts m
knife	le couteau
to carve (meat)	découper
to cut	couper
sharp	coupant, affûté
bottle	la bouteille
cork	le bouchon
corkscrew	le tire-bouchon
bottle opener	l'ouvre-bouteille m

189
to pull out	enlever
to drink	boire
beverage	la boisson
to toast (health)	porter un toast

oven	le four
utensils	les ustensiles *m* de cuisine
pressure cooker	la cocotte minute
frying pan	la poêle à frire
cooking pot	la marmite
pitcher	la cruche

190

bucket	le seau
to pour out	verser
basket	le panier
to fill	remplir
full	plein
empty	vide
to empty	vider
broom	le balai
to sweep	balayer
to rub, scrub	frotter

191

to wash (dishes)	faire la vaisselle
bedroom	la chambre à coucher
to go to bed	se coucher
bed	le lit
bedspread	le couvre-lit
bunk beds	les lits superposés
cot	le lit d'enfant
mattress	le matelas
sheets	les draps *m*
electric blanket	la couverture chauffante

192

bolster	le traversin
pillow	l'oreiller *m*
carpet	le tapis
rug, mat	la carpette
to wake	réveiller
to awake	se réveiller
to get up early	se lever tôt
in the early hours	de bonne heure
curtain	les rideaux *m*
attic	le grenier

193

alarm clock	le réveil
hot-water bottle	la bouillotte
nightcap	le bonnet de nuit
to sleepwalk	être somnambule
sleepwalker	le, la somnambule
sleepwalking	le somnambulisme
wardrobe	la garde-robe
to keep	garder
dressing table	la coiffeuse
screen	le paravent

194

bathroom	la salle de bains
bath	le bain
bathtub	la baignoire
to bathe	prendre un bain
to wash	laver

to wash oneself	se laver
towel	la serviette
washbasin	le lavabo
shower	la douche
to take a shower	prendre une douche

195

tap	le robinet
to turn on (tap)	ouvrir
to turn off (tap)	fermer
sponge	l'éponge *f*
facecloth	le gant de toilette
toothbrush	la brosse à dents
toothpaste	le dentifrice
toothpick	le cure-dents
toilet paper	le papier hygiénique
toilet bowl	la cuvette des WC

196

soap	le savon
shampoo	le shampooing
makeup	le maquillage
face cream	la crème pour le visage
face pack	le masque de beauté
compact	le poudrier
lipstick	le rouge à lèvres
nail file	la lime à ongles
nail clippers	la pince à ongles
nail varnish	le vernis à ongles

197

hairpin	l'épingle *f* à cheveux
hairdryer	le séche-cheveux
hairspray	la laque
hairslide	la barrette
hairpiece	le postiche
hairnet	la résille
to wipe	essuyer
to clean	nettoyer
clean	propre
dirty	sale

198

mirror	le miroir
basin	la cuvette
jug	le broc
razor	le rasoir
smoke detector	le détecteur de fumée
razorblade	la lame de rasoir
electric razor	le rasoir électrique
shaving foam	la crème à raser
comb	le peigne
to comb oneself	se peigner

199

tools	les outils *m*
saw	la scie
to saw	scier
drill	la perceuse
drill bit	le foret, la mèche

sawdust	la sciure de bois
hammer	le marteau
nail	le clou
to nail	clouer
spade	la bêche
pickaxe	la pioche

200

screw	la vis
screwdriver	le tourne-vis
axe	la hache
paint	la peinture
paintbrush	le pinceau
to paint	peindre
glue	la colle
sander	la ponceuse
sandpaper	le papier de verre

Society

La société

201

street	la rue
walk, promenade	la promenade
to go for a walk	se promener
passer-by	le passant
avenue	l'avenue f
kiosk	le kiosque
native of	originaire de
compatriot	le, la compatriote
pavement	le trottoir
gutter	le caniveau

202

road	la route
high road	la grande route
street lamp	le lampadaire
traffic	la circulation
frequented	très fréquenté
to frequent	fréquenter
pedestrian	le piéton
pedestrian area	la zone piétonnière
square	la place
park	le parc

203

crossroads	le carrefour
corner	le coin
alley	la ruelle
quarter (of a town)	le quartier
slum	le taudis
outskirts	la banlieue
around	autour de
dormitory town	la ville-dortoir
premises	le local
warehouse	l'entrepôt m

204

cul-de-sac	le cul-de-sac
one-way	le sens unique

traffic jam	les embouteillages m
rush hour	les heures f de pointe
zebra crossing	le passage clouté
shop window	la vitrine
poster	l'affiche f
bus stop	l'arrêt m d'autobus
to queue	faire la queue
routine	la routine

205

shop	le magasin
shopkeeper	le commerçant, la commerçante
counter	le comptoir, le guichet
to show	montrer
inn	l'auberge f
innkeeper	l'aubergiste
to stay	séjourner
lodging house	la pension de famille
guest	le, la pensionnaire
board and lodgings	le gîte et le couvert

206

profession	la profession
trade	le métier
mechanic	le mécanicien
engineer	l'ingénieur m
electrician	l'électricien
workman	l'ouvrier
operative	l'opérateur, l'opératrice
apprentice	l'apprenti, l'apprentie
apprenticeship	l'apprentissage m
day labourer	le journalier

207

fireman	le sapeur-pompier
fire station	la caserne de pompiers
fire hydrant	la bouche d'incendie
shop assistant	la vendeuse, le vendeur
fishmonger	le poissonnier, la poissonnière
fishmonger's	la poissonnerie
street sweeper	le balayeur de rues
librarian	le, la bibliothécaire
notary	le notaire

208

policeman	l'agent m de police
police (force)	la police
police station	le commissariat de police
secretary	le, la secrétaire
plumber	le plombier
jeweller	le bijoutier
stonecutter	le tailleur de pierres précieuses
haberdasher	le mercier, la mercière
haberdashery	la mercerie

209

carpenter	le menuisier

ironmonger	le quincaillier	fertiliser	l'engrais *m*
miller	le meunier, la meunière	to fertilise (land)	amender
mill	le moulin	fertile	fertile
to grind	moudre	barren	stérile
baker	le boulanger, la boulangère	dry	aride
to knead	pétrir	to sow	semer
bakery	la boulangerie	seed	la semence
barber	le coiffeur	sowing	les semailles *f*
barbershop	la boutique de coiffeur		

210

215

tobacconist	le marchand de tabac	to scatter	semer à la volée
tobacconist's	le bureau de tabac	to germinate	germer
rag-and-bone-man	le chiffonnier	to mow	faucher
tailor	le tailleur	reaper	le moissonneur
butcher	le boucher	reaping machine	la moissonneuse
butcher's	la boucherie	combine harvester	la moissonneuse-bat-teuse
pork butcher's	la charcuterie		
milkman	le laitier	sickle	la faucille
dairy	la laiterie	scythe	la faux
glazier	le vitrier	to harvest	moissonner, récolter
		harvest	la moisson, la récolte

211

216

bricklayer	le maçon	rake	le râteau
stationer	le papetier	to rake	ratisser
stationery shop	la papèterie	spade	la bêche
upholsterer	le tapissier	to dig	bêcher
photographer	le photographe	hoe	la binette
blacksmith	le forgeron	meadow	le pré
horseshoe	le fer à cheval	silage	l'ensilage *m*
shepherd	le berger	wheat	le blé
cowboy	le vacher	oats	l'avoine *f*
		barley	l'orge *f*
		ear (of wheat)	l'épi *m*

212

217

farm	la ferme	maize	le maïs
to lease	louer à bail	rice	le riz
country estate	le domaine	alfalfa	la luzerne
courtyard	la cour	pile	le tas
well	le puits	to pile up	entasser
stable	l'étable *f*	tractor	le tracteur
hayfork	la fourche	harrow	la herse
straw	la paille	baler	la lieuse
hay	le foin	rotovator	le motoculteur
grain	les céréales *f*	milking machine	la trayeuse

213

218

agriculture	l'agriculture *f*	to milk	traire
agricultural	agricole	stockbreeder	l'éleveur, l'éleveuse
rustic	champêtre	stockbreeding	l'élevage *m*
countryside	la campagne	fodder, feed	le fourrage
peasant	le paysan, la paysanne	to irrigate	irriguer
farmer	le fermier, la fermière	greenhouse	la serre
to cultivate	cultiver	subsidy	la subvention
cultivation	la culture	grape harvest	les vendanges *f*
tillage	le labour	grape picker	le vendangeur
to plough	labourer		

214

219

plough	la charrue	commerce	le commerce
furrow	le sillon		

firm	l'entreprise *f*	unemployment	le chômage
branch	la succursale	unemployed	au chômage
export	l'exportation *f*	chief	le chef
import	l'importation *f*	typewriter	la machine à écrire
company	la société	typist	la dactylo
partner	l'associé, l'associée	typing	la dactylographie
to associate	s'associer	shorthand	la sténographie
businessman	l'homme d'affaires	shorthand typist	la sténo-dactylo
business	les affaires *f*	audiotypist	l'audiotypiste

220

subject	le sujet
to offer	offrir
offer	l'offre *f*
demand	la demande
account	le compte
current account	le compte courant
to settle	régler
order	la commande
to cancel	annuler
on credit	à crédit

225

chairman of the board	le président-directeur général , le P-D.G.
managing director	le directeur général
board of directors	le conseil d'admin-istration
shareholder	l'actionnaire
dividend	le dividende
takeover	le rachat
to list (shares)	coter
asset	l'actif *m*
liability	le passif
contract	le contrat

221

by instalments	à tempérament
for cash	comptant
market	le marché
deposit	le dépôt, les arrhes *f*
goods	les marchandises *f*
bargain	l'occasion *f*, l'affaire *f*
second-hand	d'occasion
cheap	bon marché
expensive	cher
to bargain, haggle	marchander

226

purchase	l'achat *m*
to buy	acheter
to sell	vendre
sale	la vente
buyer	l'acheteur *m*
seller	le vendeur
wholesale	en gros
retail	au détail
auction	la vente aux enchères
to bid	faire une offre

222

packaging	l'emballage *m*
to pack up	emballer
to unpack	déballer
to wrap	envelopper
to unwrap	défaire, ouvrir
transport	le transport
to transport	transporter
carriage	le port
portable	portatif
delivery	la livraison

227

to auction	vendre aux enchères
client	le client, la cliente
clientele	la clientèle
catalogue	le catalogue
price list	les tarifs *m*
quantity	la quantité
gross	brut
net	net
to cost	coûter
cost	le coût, le prix

223

to deliver	livrer
to dispatch	expédier
office	le bureau
manager	le directeur, le gérant
accountant	le comptable
clerk	l'employé, l'employée de bureau
to depend on	dépendre de, se fier à
to employ	employer
employee	l'employé, l'employée
employment	l'emploi *m*

228

free of charge	gratuit
to pay	payer
wages	le salaire
salary	le salaire
payment	le paiement
in advance	d'avance
invoice	la facture
checkout	la caisse
cashier	le caissier, la caissière
accounts	la comptabilité

224

employer	l'employeur *m*

229

balance sheet	le bilan
income	les revenus *m*
expenditure	les dépenses *f*
to spend	dépenser
to acknowledge receipt	accuser réception
to receive	recevoir
reception	la réception
profit	le bénéfice
loss	la perte
loan	le prêt, l'emprunt *m*

230

to borrow	emprunter
to lend	prêter
to prepare	préparer
to obtain	obtenir
creditor	le créancier
debt	la dette
debtor	le débiteur
to get into debt	s'endetter
to be in debt	être endetté
bankruptcy	la faillite

231

to go bankrupt	faire faillite
receiver	le syndic de faillite
banking	les opérations *f* de banque
bank	la banque
banknote	le billet de banque
banker	le banquier
bankcard	la carte de crédit
bank account	le compte en banque
savings bank	la caisse d'épargne *f*
savings book	le livret de caisse d'épargne

232

to save (money)	économiser
capital	le capital
interest	les intérêts *m*
income tax	l'impôt *m* sur le revenu
Stock Exchange	la Bourse
share	l'action *f*, le titre
bullish	haussier
bearish	baissier
exchange	le change
rate	le taux
to exchange	changer

233

to be worth	valoir
value	la valeur
to value	estimer
discount	la remise
to deduct	déduire
to cash a cheque	encaisser un chèque
payable on sight	payable à vue
signature	la signature
to sign	signer
draft	la traite

234

postal order	le mandat-poste
to fall due	venir à échéance
due	dû
date	la date
to date	dater
to inform	informer, aviser
warning	l'avertissement *m*
coin	la pièce
money	l'argent *m*
mint	la Monnaie

235

post office	le bureau de poste
mail	le courrier
by return of post	par retour du courrier
postcard	la carte postale
letter	la lettre
postman	le facteur
letterbox	la boîte aux lettres
collection	la levée
to collect	ramasser
registered	recommandé

236

to distribute	distribuer
envelope	l'enveloppe *f*
postage	l'affranchissement *m*
to frank	affranchir
to seal	cacheter
stamp	le timbre
postmark	le cachet de la poste
to stamp	timbrer
parcel	le colis
item	l'article *m*

237

to register	enregistrer
to forward	expédier
sender	l'expéditeur *m*
addressee	le destinataire
unknown	inconnu
to send	envoyer
sticker	la vignette
courier	le coursier
air mail	le courrier-avion
by airmail	par avion

238

pound sterling	la livre sterling
franc	le franc
mark	le mark
dollar	le dollar
cent	le centime
lira	la lire
ingot	le lingot
foreign currencies	les devises *f*
speculation	la spéculation
speculator	le spéculateur

239

wealthy	riche
wealth	la richesse
rich	riche
to get rich	s'enrichir
to acquire	acquérir
to possess	posséder, détenir
fortune	la fortune
fortunate	fortuné
poverty	la pauvreté
poor	pauvre
necessity	le besoin

240

to need	manquer de
misery	la misère
miserable	misérable
beggar	le mendiant
to beg	mendier
homeless	sans abri
squatter	le squatter
eviction	l'expulsion *f*
malnourished	sous-alimenté
disadvantaged	défavorisé

241

industry	l'industrie *f*
industrialist	l'industriel *m*
manufacture	la fabrication
to manufacture	fabriquer
factory	l'usine *f*
manufacturer	le fabricant
trademark	la marque
machine	la machine
machinery	les machines
to undertake	entreprendre

242

enterprise	l'entreprise *f*
expert	l'expert *m*
skill	la compétence, l'habileté *f*
skilful	habile
ability	l'aptitude *f*
clumsy	gauche
to keep busy	s'occuper
busy	occupé
lazy	paresseux
strike	la grève

243

striker	le, la gréviste
lock-out	la grève patronale
blackleg	le briseur de grève
picket	le piquet de grève
to go on strike	se mettre en grève
trade union	le syndicat
trade unionist	le, la syndicaliste
trade unionism	le syndicalisme
minimum wage	le salaire minimum
market economy	l'économie *f* de marché

244

government	le gouvernement
to govern	gouverner
politics	la politique
political	politique
politician	le politicien
socialist	socialiste
conservative	conservateur
social democrat	social-démocrate
fascist	fasciste
communist	communiste

245

monarchy	la monarchie
monarch	le monarque *m*
king	le roi
queen	la reine
viceroy	le vice-roi
to reign	régner
royal	royal
crown	la couronne
to crown	couronner
throne	le trône

246

court	la cour
courtier	le courtisan
chancellor	le chancelier
rank	le rang
prince	le prince
princess	la princesse
title	le titre
subject	le sujet
emperor	l'empereur *m*
empress	l'impératrice *f*

247

revolution	la révolution
guillotine	la guillotine
to guillotine	guillotiner
counterrevolution	la contre-révolution
aristocracy	l'aristocratie *f*
aristocrat	l'aristocrate
confiscate	confisquer
confiscation	la confiscation
secular	séculaire
secularisation	la sécularisation

248

republic	la république
republican	républicain
president	le président
embassy	l'ambassade *f*
ambassador	l'ambassadeur *m*
consul	le consul
consulate	le consulat
state	l'Etat *m*
city state	la ville-Etat
councillor	le conseiller

249

council	le conseil
to advise	conseiller
to administer	administrer
minister	le ministre
ministry	le ministère
cabinet	le conseil des ministres
deputy	le député
parliament	le parlement
senate	le sénat
senator	le sénateur

250

session	la séance
to deliberate	délibérer
dialogue	le dialogue
discuss	débattre de
adopt	adopter
decree	le décret
to decree	décréter
to proclaim	proclamer
election	l'élection f
referendum	le référendum

251

to elect	élire
to vote	voter
vote	le vote
town council	le conseil municipal
mayor	le maire
bailiff	l'huissier m
justice	la justice
just	juste, équitable
unjust	injuste
judge	le juge

252

to judge	juger
court	le tribunal
judgment	le jugement
injury	le préjudice
to protect	protéger
law	la loi
legal	légal
illegal	illégal
to bequeath	léguer
beneficiary	l'ayant droit, le légataire

253

to make a will	faire un testament
will	le testament
heir	l'héritier m
heiress	l'héritière f
to inherit	hériter
inheritance	l'héritage m
tribunal	le tribunal
to summons	assigner
summons	l'assignation f
appointment	le rendez-vous

254

trial	le procès
lawsuit	le procès
lawyer	l'avocat m
to advocate	préconiser
to swear	jurer
oath	le serment
witness	le témoin
to bear witness	attester
testimony	le témoignage
evidence	les preuves f

255

infringement	l'infraction f
indictment	l'acte m d'accusation
to plead	plaider
to accuse	accuser
accused	l'accusé, l'accusée
plaintiff	le demandeur
defendant	le défendeur
to sue	poursuivre en justice
fault	la faute
jury	le jury

256

crime	le crime
murderer	le meurtrier, l'assassin
to murder	assassiner
to kill	tuer
suicide	le suicide
to commit	commettre
offence	le délit
thief	le voleur
bandit	le bandit

257

theft	le vol
to steal	voler
traitor	le traître
treason	la trahison
fraud	l'escroquerie f
bigamy	la bigamie
bigamist	bigame
assault	coups m et blessures f
blackmail	le chantage
to blackmail	faire chanter

258

rape	le viol
rapist	le violeur
guilty	coupable
innocent	innocent
defence	la défense
to defend	défendre
to prohibit	interdire
acquittal	l'acquittement m
to acquit	acquitter

259

sentence	la sentence
to sentence	condamner

verdict	le verdict	guard, watch	la garde
fine	l'amende f	sentry	la sentinelle
conviction	la condamnation	garrison	la garnison
to condemn	condamner	barracks	la caserne
prison	la prison	regiment	le régiment
to imprison	emprisonner	detachment	le détachement
prisoner	le détenu, la détenue	reinforcement	les renforts m
to arrest	arrêter	battalion	le bataillon

260

		265	
capital punishment	la peine capitale	to equip	équiper
executioner	le bourreau	equipment	l'équipement
gallows	la potence	uniform	l'uniforme m
firing squad	le peloton d'exécution	flak jacket	le gilet pare-balles
electric chair	la chaise électrique	firearm	l'arme f à feu
pardon	l'amnistie f	to arm	armer
remission	la remise de peine	to disarm	désarmer
parole	la liberté surveillée	to load	charger
false imprisonment	la détention arbitraire	to unload	décharger
self-defence	la légitime défense	to shoot	tirer, faire feu

261

		266	
army	l'armée f	shot	le coup de feu
drill	les exercices m	bullet	la balle
military	militaire	bulletproof	anti-balles
soldier	le soldat	cartridge	la cartouche
conscription	la conscription	revolver	le révolver
conscript	le conscrit, l'appelé m	bayonet	la bayonette
conscientious objector	l'objecteur de conscience m	dagger	le poignard
recruit	la recrue	tank	le tank
flag	le drapeau	armoured car	le véhicule blindé
troops	la troupe	barded wire	le fil de fer barbelé

262

		267	
officer	l'officier m	Cold War	la Guerre froide
sergeant	le sergent	superpower	la superpuissance
corporal	le caporal	rocket	la roquette
rank	le grade	nuclear warhead	l'ogive f nucléaire
general	le général	blockade	le blocus
colonel	le colonel	holocaust	l'holocauste m
captain	le capitaine	friendly fire	le tir de son propre camp
lieutenant	le lieutenant	ceasefire	le cessez-le-feu
discipline	la discipline	disarmament	le désarmement
order	l'ordre m	pacifism	le pacifisme

263

		268	
disorder	le désordre	war	la guerre
infantry	l'infanterie f	warlike	guerrier, belliqueux
cavalry	la cavalerie	warrior	le guerrier
artillery	l'artillerie f	guerilla	le guérillero
cannon	le canon	guerilla warfare	la guérilla
grenade	la grenade	campaign	la campagne
to explode	exploser	siege	le siège
gunpowder	la poudre	to besiege	assiéger
ammunition	les munitions f	fort	le fort
bomb	la bombe	spy	l'espion, l'espionne

264

		269	
to shell	bombarder	attack	l'offensive f
bombardment	le bombardement	to attack	attaquer

assault	l'assaut *m*
ambush	l'embuscade *f*
to surrender	se rendre
surrender	la reddition
encounter	l'affrontement *m*
to meet	(se) rencontrer
fight	le combat
to fight	combattre

270

combatant	le combattant
exploit	le haut fait
battlefield	le champ de bataille
trench	la tranchée
to repel	repousser
retreat	la retraite
flight	la fuite
to flee	s'enfuir
defeat	la défaite
to defeat	vaincre

271

to pursue	poursuivre
pursuit	la poursuite
to conquer	conquérir
victor	le vainqueur
vanquished	le vaincu
armistice	l'armistice *m*
treaty	le traité
peace	la paix
captivity	la captivité
to escape	s'échapper

272

to encamp	camper
encampment	le campement
to manoeuvre	manœuvrer
wounded	le blessé
hero	le héros
heroine	l'héroïne *f*
medal	la médaille
pension	la pension
war memorial	le monument aux morts

273

navy	la marine
sailor	le matelot
admiral	l'amiral *m*
squadron	l'escadron *m*
fleet	la flotte
to float	flotter
to sail	naviguer
navigator	le navigateur
warship	le navire de guerre
battleship	le cuirassé

274

aircraft carrier	le porte-avions
fighter plane	l'avion de chasse
destroyer	le contre-torpilleur
minesweeper	le dragueur de mines

submarine	le sous-marin
aerodrome	l'aérodrome *m*
spotter plane	l'avion *m* de reconnaissance
air raid	le raid aérien
air-raid shelter	l'abri *m* antiaérien
parachute	le parachute

275

parachutist	le parachutiste
surface to air missile	le missile sol-air
helicopter	l'hélicoptère *m*
to bring down	abattre
anti-aircraft defence	la défense contre avions (DCA)
anti-aircraft gun	le canon de DCA
bomb disposal	la neutralisation des bombes
bomber (plane)	le bombardier
explosion	l'explosion *f*
shell	l'obus *m*

276

religion	la religion
religious	religieux, pieux
God	Dieu
goddess	la déesse
monk	le moine
nun	la religieuse
divine	divin
omnipotent	tout-puissant
saviour	le sauveur

277

safe	sauf
pagan	païen
Christianity	le christianisme
Christian	chrétien
Catholic	catholique
Catholicism	le catholicisme
Protestantism	le protestantisme
Protestant	protestant
Calvinism	le calvinisme
Calvinist	calviniste

278

Presbyterian	presbytérien
Mormonism	le mormonisme
Mormon	mormon
Bible	la Bible
Koran	le Coran
Islam	l'Islam *m*
Muslim	musulman
Hindu	hindou
Hinduism	l'hindouisme *m*
Buddhist	bouddhiste

279

Buddhism	le bouddhisme
Jewish	juif
Judaism	le judaïsme

Rastafarian	rastafari
Scientology	la scientologie
scientologist	scientologiste
to convert	convertir
sect	la secte
animism	l'animisme
voodoo	le vaudou

280

shaman	chaman
atheist	athée
atheism	l'athéisme *m*
agnostic	agnostique
agnosticism	l'agnosticisme *m*
heretic	hérétique
heresy	l'hérésie *f*
fundamentalist	intégriste
fundamentalism	l'intégrisme *m*
to believe	croire

281

believer	croyant
belief	la croyance
faith	la foi
church	l'église *f*
chapel	la chapelle
chalice	le calice
altar	l'autel *m*
mass	la messe
blessing	la bénédiction
to bless	bénir

282

to curse	maudire
clergy	le clergé
clergyman	l'écclésiastique *m*
to preach	prêcher
preacher	le prédicateur
sermon	le sermon
apostle	l'apôtre *m*
angel	l'ange *m*
holy	saint
saint	le saint, la sainte

283

blessed	béni
sacred	sacré
devil	le diable
devilish	diabolique
cult	le culte
solemn	solennel
prayer	la prière
to pray	prier
devout	dévot
fervent	fervent

284

sin	le péché
to sin	pécher
sinner	le pécheur, la pécheresse
repentant	pénitent

to repent	se repentir
pope	le pape
cardinal	le cardinal
bishop	l'évêque *m*
archbishop	l'archevêque *m*
priest	le prêtre, le curé

285

parish	la paroisse
abbot	l'abbé *m*
abbess	l'abbesse *f*
abbey	l'abbaye *f*
convent	le couvent
monastery	le monastère
minister	le pasteur
pilgrim	le pèlerin
pilgrimage	le pèlerinage
to celebrate	célébrer

The Intellect and Emotions
L'intelligence et les sentiments

286

mind	l'esprit *m*
thought	la pensée
to think of	penser à
to meditate	méditer
to remember	se souvenir
to agree with	être d'accord avec
agreement	l'accord *m*
soul	l'âme *f*
to come to mind	venir à l'esprit
recollection	le souvenir

287

renown	la renommée
to perceive	percevoir
to understand	comprendre
understanding	la compréhension
intelligence	l'intelligence *f*
intelligent	intelligent
clever	ingénieux
stupid	stupide, bête
stupidity	la stupidité, la bêtise
worthy	digne

288

unworthy	indigne
reason	la raison
reasonable	raisonnable
unreasonable	pas raisonnable
to reason	raisonner
to discuss	discuter
to convince	convaincre
opinion	l'opinion *f*
to affirm	affirmer
to deny	nier

289

certainty	la certitude
certain	certain
uncertain	incertain
sure	sûr
unsure	pas sûr
security	la sécurité
to risk	risquer
doubt	le doute
doubtful	douteux
mistake	l'erreur f

290

to make a mistake	se tromper
suspicion	le soupçon
to suspect	soupçonner
suspicious	suspect, soupçonneux
desire	le désir
to desire	désirer
to grant	accorder
will	la volonté
to decide	décider
undecided	indécis

291

hesitate	hésiter
capable	capable, apte
incapable	incapable, inapte
capability	la capacité, l'aptitude f
talent	le talent
disposition, temper	le tempérament
character	le caractère
to rejoice	se réjouir
cheerfulness	la gaieté
happiness	le bonheur

292

cheerful	gai, enjoué
sad	triste
sadness	la tristesse
to grieve	avoir du chagrin
enjoyment	la joie
happy	heureux
unhappy	malheureux
unfortunate	malheureux, malchanceux
contented	satisfait, content
discontented	mécontent

293

discontent	le mécontentement
displeased	contrarié
pleasure	le plaisir
to please	plaire
to displease	déplaire, mécontenter
pain	la douleur
painful	douloureux
sigh	le soupir
to sigh	soupirer
to complain	se plaindre

294

complaint	la plainte
to protest	protester
depressed	déprimé
to despair	se désespérer
despair	le désespoir
hope	l'espoir m
to hope	espérer
expectation	l'espérance f
consolation	la consolation
to comfort	réconforter

295

consoling	consolateur
calm	le calme, la tranquillité
calm	calme, tranquille
restless	agité
anxiety	l'inquiétude
fear	la crainte
to fear	craindre
to be afraid	avoir peur
to frighten	faire peur
to be frightened	avoir peur

296

terror	la terreur
to terrify	terrifier
frightful	épouvantable
to astonish	étonner, stupéfier
astonishment	l'étonnement, la stupéfaction
to encourage	encourager
to discourage	décourager
conscience	la conscience
scruple	le scrupule
remorse	le remords

297

repentance	le repentir
to regret	regretter
sentiment	le sentiment
consent	le consentement
to consent	consentir
mercy	la miséricorde
charitable	charitable
pity	la pitié
piety	la piété

298

impiety	l'impiété f
friendly	amical
unfriendly	hostile
favour	le service, la faveur
to favour	favoriser
favourable	favorable
unfavourable	défavorable
confidence	la confiance
trustful	confiant
mistrustful	méfiant

299

to trust	faire confiance à
friendship	l'amitié f
esteem	l'estime f
kind	aimable
friend	l'ami, l'amie
enemy	l'ennemi, l'ennemie
hatred	la haine
to hate	haïr, détester
hateful	odieux
contempt	le mépris

300

to despise	mépriser
to get angry	se mettre en colère f
quarrel	la querelle
to quarrel	se quereller
to reconcile	se réconcilier
quality	la qualité
virtue	la vertu
virtuous	vertueux
vice	le vice
vicious	méchant

301

addicted	adonné à
defect	le défaut
fault	la faute
to fail	échouer
custom	la coutume
to be necessary	être nécessaire
to become accustomed	s'accoutumer
habit	l'habitude f
to boast about	se vanter de
moderate	modéré

302

goodness	la bonté
kind	bon
affection	l'affection f
wickedness	la méchanceté
gratitude	la gratitude
ungrateful	ingrat
ingratitude	l'ingratitude f
grateful	reconnaissant
to thank	remercier
thank you	merci

303

honesty	la franchise, l'honnêteté f
honourable	honorable
to honour	honorer
to dishonour	déshonorer
honour	l'honneur m
dishonour	le déshonneur
honest	franc, honnête
dishonest	malhonnête

304

modesty	la pudeur

shame	la honte
shameful	honteux
to be ashamed	avoir honte
audacity	l'effronterie f
audacious	effronté
daring	hardi
boldness	l'intrépidité
fearless	sans peur
to dare	oser

305

reckless	téméraire
timid	timide
timidity	la timidité
rude	grossier
rudeness	la grossièreté
courtesy	la courtoisie
polite	poli
impolite	impoli
villain	le vaurien
envy	la jalousie

306

loyal	loyal, fidèle
disloyal	déloyal
generous	généreux
generosity	la générosité
selfishness	l'égoïsme m
selfish	égoïste
egoist	l'égoïste
greed	la cupidité
stingy	avare
miser	l'avare

307

truth	la vérité
true	vrai
to lie	mentir
liar	le menteur, la menteuse
lie	le mensonge
hypocritical	hypocrite
hypocrite	l'hypocrite
frank	franc
frankness	la franchise
accuracy	l'exactitude f

308

inaccuracy	l'inexactitude f
punctuality	la ponctualité
faithfulness	la fidélité
unfaithfulness	l'infidélité f
faithful	fidèle
unfaithful	infidèle
coward	lâche
cowardice	la lâcheté
anger	la colère
offence	l'offense f

309

to offend	offenser

to insult	insulter
excuse	l'excuse f
to excuse	excuser
humble	humble
humility	l'humilité f
pride	la fierté, l'orgueil m
proud	fier, orgueilleux
vain	vaniteux
to be obstinate	être têtu

310

obstinacy	l'entêtement m
whim	le caprice, la lubie
sober	sobre
sobriety	la sobriété
sensual	sensuel
sensuality	la sensualité
hedonistic	hédoniste
lust	la luxure
revenge	la vengeance
to revenge	venger

311

vindictive	vindicatif
jealous	jaloux
temperamental	fantasque
affectionate	affectueux
imaginative	imaginatif
extrovert	extraverti
introvert	introverti
demanding	exigeant
sincere	sincère
sincerity	la sincérité

312

optimistic	optimiste
optimist	l'optimiste
pessimistic	pessimiste
pessimist	le pessimiste
perceptive	perspicace
cautious	prudent
sensitive	sensible
sensitivity	la sensibilité
sensible	sensé, raisonnable
common sense	le bon sens

Education and Learning
L'enseignement et le savoir

313

to educate	éduquer, instruire
educational	éducatif
educationalist	le, la pédagogue
adult education	l'enseignement m pour adultes
mixed education	l'enseignement m mixte
primary school	l'école f primaire
to teach	enseigner

teacher (primary)	l'instituteur, l'institutrice
teacher (secondary)	le professeur
tutor	le précepteur
college	le lycée, le collège

314

university	l'université f
language laboratory	le laboratoire de langues
class	la classe
pupil	l'élève
boarder	l'interne
day pupil	l'externe
to study	étudier
student	l'étudiant, l'étudiante
grant	la bourse
scholarship holder	le boursier, la boursière
desk	le pupitre

315

blackboard	le tableau
chalk	la craie
pencil	le crayon
ink	l'encre f
pen	le stylo
ruler	la règle
line	la ligne
exercise book	le cahier
to bind (books)	relier
page	la page

316

to fold	plier
sheet of paper	le feuillet, la copie
cover (book)	la couverture
work	le travail
hard-working	travailleur
studious	studieux
lesson	la leçon
to learn	apprendre
to forget	oublier

317

forgetful	étourdi
forgetfulness	l'étourderie f
absentminded	distrait
course	le cours
attention	l'attention f
to be attentive	être attentif
inattention	l'inattention f
inattentive	inattentif
to explain	expliquer
explanation	l'explication f

318

task	la tâche
theme	le thème
thematic	thématique
exercise	l'exercice m
practice	la pratique
to practise	s'exercer
easy	facile

Education and Learning

easiness	la facilité
difficult	difficile

319

difficulty	la difficulté
progress	les progrès *m*
homework	les devoirs *m*
must	devoir
to owe	devoir
examination	l'examen *m*
to pass an examination	être reçu à un examen
to copy	copier
to swot	bûcher
to cram for an exam	bachoter
crammer	la boite à bachot

320

to examine	examiner
examiner	l'examinateur, l'examinatrice
proof	l'épreuve *f*
to try	essayer
to blame	blâmer
blame	le blâme
approve	approuver
disapprove	désapprouver
mark	la note
to note	noter

321

annotation	l'annotation *f*
to annotate	annoter
remarkable	remarquable
prize	le prix
to reward	récompenser
to praise	faire l'éloge de
praise	l'éloge *m*
holidays	les vacances *f*
conduct	la conduite
to behave	se conduire bien

322

to misbehave	se conduire mal
effort	l'effort *m*
to endeavour	s'efforcer de
obedience	l'obéissance *f*
obedient	obéissant
disobedience	la désobéissance
disobedient	désobéissant
to obey	obéir
to disobey	désobéir
laziness	la paresse

323

strict	sévère
severity	la sévérité
threat	la menace
to threaten	menacer
punishment	la punition
to punish	punir
to deserve	mériter
grammar	la grammaire

Education and Learning

to indicate	indiquer
indication	l'indication *f*

324

to point out	signaler
spelling	l'orthographe *f*
to spell	épeler
full stop	le point
colon	les deux points *m*
semicolon	le point-virgule
comma	la virgule
question mark	le point d'interrogation
exclamation mark	le point d'exclamation
to note down	noter, inscrire

325

to ask (question)	interroger
to ask for	demander
to answer	répondre
answer	la réponse
to admire	admirer
admiration	l'admiration *f*
to exclaim	s'exclamer
article	l'article *m*
noun	le nom, le substantif
to name	nommer

326

appointment	le rendez-vous
to call	appeler
to be called	s'appeler
reference	la référence
to relate to	se rapporter à
fixed	fixe
to fix	fixer
to join	relier, joindre
together	ensemble
join	la jonction, le raccord

327

to correspond	correspondre
correspondence	la correspondance
sentence	la phrase
language	la langue
idiomatic	idiomatique
idiom	la locution
speech	la parole
talkative	bavard
voice	la voix
word	le mot

328

to express	exprimer
expressive	expressif
vocabulary	le vocabulaire
dictionary	le dictionnaire
letter	la lettre
speech	le discours
lecture	la conférence
lecturer	le conférencier, la conférencière

orator	l'orateur *m*	to announce	annoncer
eloquence	l'éloquence *f*	advertisement (classified)	l'annonce *f*

329
eloquent	éloquent
elocution	la diction, l'élocution *f*
to converse	converser
conversation	la conversation
to understand	comprendre
to pronounce	prononcer
to correct	corriger
correction	la correction
example	l'exemple *m*
meaning	le sens

330
to mean	signifier
translation	la traduction
to translate	traduire
translator	le traducteur, la traductrice
interpreter	l'interprète
interpretative	interprétatif
interpretation	l'interprétation *f*
to imagine	imaginer
imagination	l'imagination *f*

331
idea	l'idée *f*
essay	l'essai *m*, la dissertation
essayist	l'essayiste
thesis	la thèse
thesis supervisor	le directeur de thèse
doctorate	le doctorat
to develop	développer
off the subject	hors sujet
object	l'objet *m*
subject	le sujet
to describe	décrire

332
description	la description
fable	la fable
drama	le théâtre
comedy	la comédie
comical	comique
chapter	le chapitre
to interest	intéresser
interesting	intéressant
attractive	attrayant
to attract	attirer

333
to publish	publier
to print	imprimer
printer	l'imprimeur *m*
printing	l'impression *f*
newspaper	le journal
journalist	le, la journaliste
magazine	la revue
news	les nouvelles *f*

334
history	l'histoire *f*
historian	l'historien, l'historienne
the Stone Age	l'âge *m* de la pierre
the Bronze Age	l'âge *m* du bronze
the Iron Age	l'âge *m* du fer
the Dark Ages	l'âge *m* des ténèbres
the Middle Ages	le moyen-âge
archaeology	l'archéologie *f*
archaeologist	l'archéologue
to excavate	faire des fouilles

335
carbon dating	la datation à l'aide du carbone 14
event	l'événement *m*
to happen	se produire
to civilise	civiliser
civilisation	la civilisation
knight	le chevalier
chivalry	la chevalerie
explorer	l'explorateur *m*
to explore	explorer
discovery	la découverte

336
to discover	découvrir
pirate	le pirate
piracy	la piraterie
treasure	le trésor
conquest	la conquête
conqueror	le conquérant
to conquer	conquérir
empire	l'empire *m*
imperial	impérial
slave	l'esclave

337
emancipation	l'émancipation *f*
to emancipate	émanciper
destiny	le destin
to destine	destiner
power	le pouvoir, la puissance
powerful	puissant
to be able, can	pouvoir
slavery	l'esclavage *m*
to free	libérer
reformation	la réforme

338
liberator	le libérateur
nationalism	le nationalisme
nationalist	nationaliste
alliance	l'alliance *f*
to ally	s'allier
ally	l'allié, l'alliée
to enlarge	agrandir

increase	la croissance
to increase	augmenter
to diminish	diminuer

339

decline	le déclin
to decay	décliner
renowned	célèbre
to disturb	déranger
to emigrate	émigrer
emigrant	l'émigrant, l'émigrante
rebel	le rebelle
rebellion	la révolte
rising	le soulèvement
independence	l'indépendance f

340

geography	la géographie
map	la carte
North Pole	le pôle nord
South Pole	le pôle sud
north	le nord
south	le sud
east	l'est m
west	l'ouest m
compass	la boussole
magnetic north	le nord magnétique

341

distant	lointain
distance	la distance
near	proche
to approach	approcher, s'approcher
neighbour	le voisin, la voisine
to determine	déterminer
limit	la limite
region	la région
country	le pays
compatriot	le, la compatriote

342

citizen	le citoyen, la citoyenne
city	la ville
population	la population
to people	peupler
populous	populeux
village	le village
people	les gens, le peuple
province	la province
provincial	provincial
place	le lieu

Places   Les lieux

343

Africa	l'Afrique f
African	africain
North America	l'Amérique f du Nord
North American	nord-américain

South America	l'Amérique f du Sud
South American	sud-américain
Central America	l'Amérique f Centrale
Central American	de l'Amérique f Centrale
Australia	l'Australie f
Australian	australien

344

Europe	l'Europe f
European	européen
Arctic	les régions f arctiques
Antarctica	l'Antarctique m
Oceania	l'Océanie f
Oceanian	océanien
Asia	l'Asie f
Asian	asiatique
New Zealand	la Nouvelle-Zélande
New Zealander	néo-zélandais

345

Spain	l'Espagne f
Spanish	espagnol
Germany	l'Allemagne f
German	allemand
Italy	l'Italie f
Italian	italien
Greece	la Grèce
Greek	grec
Russia	la Russie
Russian	russe

346

Switzerland	la Suisse
Swiss	suisse
Holland	la Hollande
Dutch	hollandais
Portugal	le Portugal
Portuguese	portugais
Belgium	la Belgique
Belgian	belge
Great Britain	la Grande-Bretagne
British Isles	les Iles Britanniques

347

United Kingdom	le Royaume-Uni
British	britannique
England	l'Angleterre f
English	anglais
Scotland	l'Ecosse f
Scottish	écossais
Wales	le Pays de Galles
Welsh	gallois
Northern Ireland	l'Irlande f du Nord
Northern Irish	de l'Irlande du Nord

348

Ireland	l'Irlande f
Irish	irlandais
France	la France
French	français
Austria	l'Autriche

Austrian	autrichien	Turin	Turin
Scandinavia	la Scandinavie	Cologne	Cologne
Scandinavian	scandinave		
Iceland	l'Islande *f*	**354**	
Icelandic	islandais	Hamburg	Hambourg
		Hanover	Hanovre
349		Basle	Bâle
Greenland	le Groenland	Vienna	Vienne
Greenlander	groenlandais	Viennese	viennois
Sweden	la Suède	Antwerp	Anvers
Swedish	suédois	Berlin	Berlin
Norway	la Norvège	Berlin *adj*	berlinois
Norwegian	norvégien	Geneva	Genève
Finland	la Finlande	Geneva *adj*	genévois
Finnish	finlandais, finnois		
Denmark	le Danemark	**355**	
Danish	danois	Athens	Athènes
		Brussels	Bruxelles
350		Strasbourg	Strasbourg
Bavaria	la Bavière	Bruges	Bruges
Bavarian	bavarois	Moscow	Moscou
Saxony	la Saxe	Muscovite	moscovite
Saxon	saxon	St Petersburg	Saint-Pétersbourg
Alsace	l'Alsace *f*	Warsaw	Varsovie
Alsatian	alsacien	Prague	Prague
Lorraine	la Lorraine	Budapest	Budapest
Dordogne	la Dordogne		
Auvergne	l'Auvergne *f*	**356**	
Provence	la Provence	Stockholm	Stockholm
		Oslo	Oslo
351		Copenhagen	Copenhague
London	Londres	New York	New York
London *adj*	londonien	New York *adj*	new-yorkais
Paris	Paris	Havana	La Havane
Parisian	parisien	Cairo	Le Caire
Madrid	Madrid	Cape Town	Le Cap
Madrid *adj*	madrilène	Beijing	Beijing
Edinburgh	Edimbourg	Mexico City	Mexico
The Hague	La Haye		
		357	
352		Poland	la Pologne
Toulouse	Toulouse	Polish	polonais
Milan	Milan	Czech Republic	la République Tchèque
Lisbon	Lisbonne	Czech	tchèque
Bordeaux	Bordeaux	Slovakia	la Slovaquie
Bordeaux *adj*	bordelais	Slovak	slovaque
Lyons	Lyon	Slovenia	la Slovénie
Lyons *adj*	lyonnais	Slovene	slovène
Marseilles	Marseille	Croatia	la Croatie
Marseilles *adj*	marseillais	Croatian	croate
353		**358**	
Rome	Rome	Hungary	la Hongrie
Roman	romain	Hungarian	hongrois
Venice	Venise	Bosnia	la Bosnie
Venetian	vénitien	Bosnian	bosniaque
Naples	Naples	Serbia	la Serbie
Neapolitan	napolitain	Serbian	serbe
Florence	Florence	Albania	l'Albanie *f*
Florentine	florentin	Albanian	albanais

Romania	la Roumanie	Palestine	la Palestine
Romanian	roumain	Palestinian	palestinien

359

Bulgaria	la Bulgarie
Bulgarian	bulgare
Macedonia	la Macédoine
Macedonian	macédonien
Moldova	la Moldavie
Moldovan	moldave
Belarus	la Biélorussie
Belorussian	biélorusse
Ukraine	l'Ukraine *f*
Ukrainian	ukrainien

360

Estonia	l'Estonie *f*
Estonian	estonien
Latvia	la Lettonie
Latvian	letton
Lithuania	la Lituanie
Lithuanian	lituanien
Armenia	l'Arménie *f*
Armenian	arménien
Azerbaijan	l'Azerbaïdjan *m*
Azerbaijani	Azerbaïdjanais

361

Georgia	la Géorgie
Georgian	géorgien
Siberia	la Sibérie
Siberian	sibérien
Turkey	la Turquie
Turkish	turc
Arabia	l'Arabie *f*
Arab	arabe
Morocco	le Maroc
Moroccan	marocain

362

Egypt	l'Egypte *f*
Egyptian	égyptien
China	la Chine
Chinese	chinois
India	l'Inde *f*
Indian	indien
Japan	le Japon
Japanese	japonais
Ghana	le Ghana
Ghanaian	ghanéen

363

Algeria	l'Algérie *f*
Algerian	algérien
Tunisia	la Tunisie
Tunisian	tunisien
South Africa	l'Afrique du Sud *f*
South African	sud-africain
Israel	Israël *m*
Israeli	israélien

364

Castile	la Castille
Castilian	castillan
Andalusia	l'Andalousie *f*
Andalusian	andalou
Catalonia	la Catalogne
Catalan	catalan
Galicia	la Galice
Galician	galicien
Basque Country	le Pays Basque
Basque	basque

365

United States	les Etats-Unis *m*
American	américain
Canada	le Canada
Canadian	canadien
Mexico	le Mexique
Mexican	mexicain
Colombia	la Colombie
Colombian	colombien
Peru	le Pérou
Peruvian	péruvien

366

Brazil	le Brésil
Brazilian	brésilien
Chile	le Chili
Chilean	chilien
Argentina	l'Argentine *f*
Argentinian	argentin
Uruguay	l'Uruguay *m*
Uruguayan	uruguayen
Bolivia	la Bolivie
Bolivian	bolivien

367

Pyrenees	les Pyrénées *f*
Alps	les Alpes *f*
Atlas Mountains	l'Atlas *m*
Dolomites	les Dolomites *f*
Carpathians	les Carpates *f*
Andes	les Andes *f*
Himalayas	l'Himalaya *m*
Mont Blanc	le Mont Blanc
Table Mountain	la Montagne de la Table
Everest	l'Everest *m*

368

Amazon	l'Amazone *f*
Nile	le Nil
Rhine	le Rhin
Rhône	le Rhône
Tagus	le Tage
Danube	le Danube
Thames	la Tamise
Seine	la Seine

Loire	la Loire
Volga	la Volga

369

Atlantic	l'Atlantique *m*
Pacific	le Pacifique
Arctic	l'océan glacial Arctique
Antarctic	l'océan glacial Antarctique
Mediterranean	la Méditerranée
North Sea	la mer du Nord
Black Sea	la mer Noire
Red Sea	la mer Rouge
Dead Sea	la mer Morte
Caribbean	la mer des Antilles

370

Baltic Sea	la mer Baltique
English Channel	la Manche
Bay of Biscay	le golfe de Gascogne
West Indies	les Antilles
Canaries	les îles Canaries
The Philippines	les Philippines
Sicily	la Sicile
Sardinia	la Sardaigne
Corsica	la Corse
Corsican	corse

371

Balearic Islands	les Baléares
Crete	la Crète
Cretan	crétois
Cyprus	Chypre *f*
Cypriot	cypriote
Dardanelles	les Dardanelles *f*
Bosphorus	le Bosphore
Channel Islands	les îles Anglo-Normandes
Falkland Islands	les Malouines

Science   La science

372

weights	les poids *m*
weight	le poids
to weigh	peser
heavy	lourd
light	léger
scales	la balance
to measure	mesurer
to compare	comparer
comparison	la comparaison

373

to contain	contenir
contents	le contenu
metric system	le système métrique
metre	le mètre
centimetre	le centimètre
millimetre	le millimètre
gram	le gramme

kilogram	le kilo
litre	le litre
hectare	l'hectare *m*

374

kilometre	le kilomètre
tonne	la tonne
inch	le pouce
foot	le pied
arithmetic	l'arithmétique *f*
mathematics	les mathématiques *f*
to calculate	calculer
to count	compter
number	le numéro, le nombre

375

figure	le chiffre
zero	zéro
addition	l'addition *f*
to add	additionner
subtraction	la soustraction
to subtract	soustraire
remainder	le reste
equal	égal
equality	l'égalité *f*
to multiply	multiplier
product	le produit

376

quotient	le quotient
divisor	le diviseur
to divide	diviser
part	la part
fraction	la fraction
half	la moitié
third	le tiers
quarter	le quart
dozen	la douzaine
double	double

377

triple	triple
geometry	la géométrie
algebra	l'algèbre *f*
space	l'espace *m*
spacious	spacieux
parallel	parallèle
perpendicular	perpendiculaire
horizontal	horizontal
horizon	l'horizon *m*
right angle	l'angle *m* droit

378

triangle	le triangle
square	le carré
curved	courbe
straight	droit
circumference	la circonférence
circle	le cercle
centre	le centre
diameter	le diamètre

problem	le problème
correct	exact

379

incorrect	inexact
wrong	faux
simple	simple
to complicate	compliquer
to demonstrate	démontrer
to solve	résoudre
result	le résultat
to result	résulter
physics	la physique
physical	physique

380

matter	la matière
pressure	la pression
phenomenon	le phénomène
strange	étrange
movement	le mouvement
to move	bouger
mobile	mobile
immobile	immobile
electric	électrique
electricity	l'électricité f

381

mechanics	la mécanique
invent	inventer
optics	l'optique f
optical	optique
microscope	le microscope
lens	la lentille
to reflect	réfléchir
reflection	la réflexion
chemistry	la chimie
chemical	chimique

382

biology	la biology
biological	biologique
biologist	le, la biologiste
to research	faire des recherches
researcher	le chercheur
element	l'élément m
oxygen	l'oxygène m
hydrogen	l'hydrogène m
atom	l'atome m
nucleus	le noyau, le nucléus

383

laboratory	le laboratoire
experiment	l'expérience f
mixture	le mélange
to decompose	décomposer
to compose	composer
compound	le composé
rare	rare
science	la science
scientific	scientifique

384

scientist	le scientifique
knowledge	la connaissance, le savoir
to know (something)	savoir
to know (somebody)	connaître
wisdom	la sagesse
wise	sage
sage	le sage
to be ignorant of	ignorer
experience	l'expérience f
inexperience	l'inexpérience f

Communications   Les communications

385

telegraph	le télégraphe
telegram	le télégramme
to telegraph	télégraphier
telex	le télex
telephone	le téléphone
to telephone	téléphoner
telephonist	le, la téléphoniste
call	l'appel m
receiver	le combiné
mouthpiece	le microphone

386

telephone booth	la cabine téléphonique
telephone exchange	le central téléphonique
telephone directory	l'annuaire m
telephone subscriber	l'abonné, l'abonnée
answerphone	le répondeur
to hang up	raccrocher
engaged	occupé
to dial	composer le numéro
radiotelephone	le radiotéléphone
videophone	le visiophone

387

fax	le fax, la télécopie
to fax	faxer
modem	le modem
electronic mail	le courrier électronique
information technology	l'informatique f
microelectronics	la microélectronique
screen	l'écran m
keyboard	le clavier
key	la touche
mouse	la souris

388

computer	l'ordinateur m
computer language	le langage de programmation
computer literate	initié à l'informatique
computer scientist	l'informaticien, l'informaticienne
computer game	le jeu électronique

computer animation	l'animation f sur ordina-teur
computer-aided design	la conception assistée par ordinateur
computerese	le jargon informatique
to computerise	informatiser
computerisation	l'informatisation f

389

to program	programmer
programmer	le programmeur, la pro-grammeuse
systems analyst	l'analyste fonctionnel
word processing	le traitement de texte
memory	la mémoire
disk drive	le lecteur de disques
software	le logiciel
hardware	le matériel
shareware	le share-ware
cursor	le curseur

390

menu	le menu
to store	mémoriser
file	le fichier
to file	classer
data	les données f
database	la base de données
desktop publishing	la publication assistée par ordinateur
to lay out	composer, mettre en page
silicon	le silicium
silicon chip	la puce électronique

391

user-friendly	convivial
laser printer	l'imprimante f à laser
ink-jet printer	l'imprimante f à jet d'encre
scanner	le scanner
circuit	le circuit
fibreoptics	la transmission par fibre optique
machine translation	la traduction automatique
to network	interconnecter
networking	l'interconnexion f
information superhighway	l'autoroute f de l'information

The Arts and Entertainment

Les arts et les spectacles

392

painting	la peinture
painter	le peintre
to paint	peindre
picturesque	pittoresque
artist	l'artiste
museum	le musée
engraving	la gravure

| print | l'estampe f |
| background | l'arrière-plan m |

393

foreground	l'avant-plan m
still life	la nature morte
drawing	le dessin
to draw	dessiner
draughtsman	le dessinateur
outline	l'esquisse f
to imitate	imiter
imitation	l'imitation f
abstract	abstrait
innovative	novateur

394

to innovate	innover
resemblance	la ressemblance
similar	similaire
forgery	le faux
forger	le faussaire
auction	la vente aux enchères
to bid	faire une offre
lot	le lot
reserve price	le prix minimum
exhibition	l'exposition f

395

antique	l'antiquité f
antique dealer	l'antiquaire
art dealer	le marchand de tableaux
palette	la palette
brush	le pinceau
easel	le chevalet
colour	la couleur
to colour	colorer
coloured	coloré, en couleur
dull	mat

396

multicoloured	multicolore
contrast	le contraste
to contrast	contraster
white	blanc
black	noir
light blue	bleu clair
dark green	vert foncé
yellow	jaune
brown	marron, brun
chestnut	marron

397

pink	rose
red	rouge
violet	violet
mauve	mauve
purple	violet, pourpre
gilt	doré
to gild	dorer

grey	gris	arch	l'arche *f*
patron	le mécène	column	la colonne
patronage	le mécénat	plinth	la plinthe

398

		403	
to patronise	patronner	nave	la nef
oils l'huile *f*		cathedral	la cathédrale
watercolour	l'aquarelle *f*	cathedral city	la ville épiscopale
fresco	la fresque	apse	l'abside *f*
triptych	le tryptique	stained glass	le vitrail
cartoon	la bande dessinée	transept	le transept
the Renaissance	la Renaissance	flying buttress	l'arc-boutant *m*
Renaissance Art	l'art *m* de la Renaissance	font	les fonts baptismaux *m*
crayon	le pastel	crypt	la crypte
canvas	la toile	basilica	la basilique

399

		404	
gallery	la galerie	Gothic	gothique
tone	le ton	Romanesque	roman
landscape	le paysage	Baroque	baroque
portrait	le portrait	mosque	la mosquée
portraitist	le portraitiste	minaret	le minaret
miniature	la miniature	synagogue	la synagogue
miniaturist	le, la miniaturiste	pagoda	la pagode
landscape painter	le, la paysagiste	mausoleum	le mausolée
impressionism	l'impressionisme *m*	pyramid	la pyramide
impressionist	impressioniste	Sphinx	le Sphinx

400

		405	
surrealism	le surréalisme	temple	le temple
surrealist	surréaliste	Corinthian	corinthien
cubism	le cubisme	Ionian	ionien
cubist	cubiste	Doric	dorique
symbol	le symbole	forum	le forum
to symbolise	symboliser	amphitheatre	l'amphithéâtre *m*
symbolic	symbolique	aqueduct	l'aqueduc *m*
sculpture	la sculpture	dolmen	le dolmen
sculptor	le sculpteur	menhir	le menhir
workshop	l'atelier *m*	cave painting	la peinture rupestre

401

		406	
to carve	tailler	illiterate	analphabète
model	le modèle	literate	qui sait lire et écrire
statue	la statue	oral history	la tradition orale
bust	le buste	ballad	la ballade
group	le groupe	saga	la saga
chisel	le ciseau	tradition	la tradition
cast	le moule	story	le conte
shape	la forme	storyteller	le raconteur
to shape	former	narrative	la narration
architecture	l'architecture *f*	to learn by heart	apprendre par cœur

402

		407	
architect	l'architecte	literature	la littérature
vault	la voûte	papyrus	le papyrus
dome	le dôme	parchment	le parchemin
pillar	le pilier	alphabet	l'alphabet *m*
arch	l'arc *m*	character	le signe, le personnage
tower	la tour	author	l'auteur *m*
scaffolding	l'échafaudage *m*	writer	l'écrivain *m*

editor	le rédacteur
edition	l'édition *f*
copyright	les droits *m* d'auteur, le copyright

408

style	le style
reader	le lecteur, la lectrice
biography	la biographie
biographer	le, la biographe
biographical	biographique
autobiography	l'autobiographie *f*
autobiographical	autobiographique
fiction	la fiction
fictional	fictif
science fiction	la science-fiction

409

novel	le roman
novelist	le romancier, la romancière
publisher	l'éditeur *m*
royalties	les droits *m* d'auteur
bookshop	la librairie
bookseller	le, la libraire
encyclopaedia	l'encyclopédie *f*
encyclopaedic	encyclopédique
paperback	le livre de poche
poetry	la poésie

410

poet	le poète, la poétesse
poetic	poétique
rhyme	la rime
to rhyme	rimer
metre	le mètre
stanza	la strophe
sonnet	le sonnet
assonance	l'assonance *f*
syllable	la syllabe
nursery rhyme	la comptine

411

fairy tale	le conte de fées
Cinderella	Cendrillon
Red Riding Hood	le Petit Chaperon Rouge
Snow White	Blanche-Neige
dwarf	le nain
goblin	le lutin
gnome	le gnome
elf	l'elfe *m*
Sleeping Beauty	la Belle au bois dormant
Snow Queen	la Reine des neiges

412

Puss in Boots	le Chat Botté
Bluebeard	Barbe-bleue
witch	la sorcière
wizard	le sorcier, l'enchanteur *m*
spell	le charme
to cast a spell	jeter un charme
magician	le magicien, la magicienne

magic	la magie
magical	magique
mermaid	la sirène

413

mythology	la mythologie
Homer	Homère
Homeric	homérique
Iliad	l'Iliade *f*
Odyssey	l'Odyssée *f*
Odysseus	Odusseus
Trojan	troyen
Trojan horse	le cheval de Troie
Achilles	Achille
Achilles' heel	le talon d'Achille

414

Cyclops	le cyclope
Atlantis	l'Atlantide *f*
Romulus	Romulus
Hercules	Hercule
Herculean	herculéen
The Arabian nights	les mille et une nuits
Armageddon	Armageddon *m*
Valhalla	Walhalla *m*
Thor	Tor *m*
rune	la rune

415

masterpiece	le chef d'œuvre
music	la musique
musician	le musicien, la musicienne
to play (an instrument)	jouer
composer	le compositeur
orchestra	l'orchestre *m*
symphony	la symphonie
aria	l'aria *m*
overture	l'ouverture *m*
march	la marche

416

soft	doux
stringed instrument	l'instrument *m* à cordes
wind instrument	l'instrument *m* à vent
brass instruments	les cuivres *m*
piano	le piano
pianist	le, la pianiste
organ	l'orgue *m*, les orgues *f*
organist	l'organiste
harmony	l'harmonie *f*
flute	la flûte

417

to blow	souffler
bagpipes	la cornemuse
cornet	le cornet
violin	le violon
auditorium	l'auditorium *m*
score	la partition
opera	l'opéra *m*

tenor	le ténor
soprano	le, la soprano
baritone	le bariton

418

bass	la contrebasse
conductor	le chef d'orchestre
instrumentalist	l'instrumentaliste
rehearsal	la répétition
viola	la viole d'amour
violinist	le, la violoniste
cello	le violoncelle
bow	l'archet *m*
guitar	la guitare

419

to strum	gratter
harp	la harpe
drum	le tambour
oboe	le hautbois
clarinet	la clarinette
bassoon	le basson
trumpet	la trompette
trombone	le trombone
French horn	le cor d'harmonie
tuba	le tuba

420

songbook	le recueil de chansons
singing	le chant
to sing	chanter
to enchant	enchanter
enchanting	charmant
spell, charm	le charme
singer	le chanteur
singer (woman)	la chanteuse, la cantatrice
choir	le chœur
to accompany	accompagner
accompaniment	l'accompagnement *m*

421

song	la chanson
refrain	le refrain
concert	le concert
to syncopate	syncoper
jazz	le jazz
beat	le rythme
saxophone	le saxophone
rock music	le rock
drums	la batterie

422

synthesiser	le synthétiseur
folk music	le folk
mandolin	la mandoline
banjo	le banjo
ocarina	l'ocarina *m*
accordion	l'accordéon *m*
xylophone	le xylophone
tambourine	le tambourin

zither	la cithare
concertina	le concertina

423

dance, dancing	la danse
to dance	danser
ball	le bal
dancer	le danseur, la danseuse
theatre	le théâtre
theatrical	théâtral
mask	le masque
box office	le guichet
seat, place	la place
stalls	l'orchestre *m*
box (theatre)	la loge

424

pit	l'orchestre
stage	la scène
scene	la scène
interval	l'entracte *m*
scenery	le décor
curtain	le rideau
play	la pièce
playwright	le dramaturge
character	le personnage

425

tragedy	la tragédie
comedy	la comédie
actor	l'acteur *m*
actress	l'actrice *f*
to play a role	jouer un rôle
to be word-perfect	maîtriser parfaitement son rôle
costume	le costume
lighting	l'éclairage *m*
denouement	le dénouement
to stage	mettre en scène

426

performance	la représentation
flop	le fiasco
to flop	faire un four
debut, first performance	le début
trapdoor	la trappe
to be a success	être un succès
audience	le public
spectator	le spectateur, la spectatrice
applause	les applaudissements *m*
whistling, hissing	les sifflets *m*

427

cinema	le cinéma
screen	l'écran *m*
to dub	doubler
to subtitle	sous-titrer
subtitles	les sous-titres *m*
sequel	la suite

director	le réalisateur
producer	le producteur
to censor	censurer
censorship	la censure

428

to whistle, hiss	siffler
amusements	les jeux
playground	la cour de récréation
to enjoy oneself	s'amuser
entertaining	divertissant
amusing	amusant
pastime	le passe-temps
rest	le repos
to rest	se reposer
weariness	la lassitude

429

to get tired	se fatiguer
tired	fatigué
to get bored	s'ennuyer
boring	ennuyeux
fair	la foire
festival	le festival
crowd	la foule
to assemble	se rassembler
circus	le cirque
trapeze	le trapèze

430

trapeze artist	le, la trapéziste
tightrope	la corde raide
tightrope walker	le, la funambule
acrobat	l'acrobate
acrobatic	acrobatique
acrobatics	les acrobaties f
clown	le clown
joke	la farce
lottery	la loterie
to be lucky	avoir de la chance

431

luck	la chance
swing	la balançoire
to swing (oneself)	se balancer
seesaw	la bascule
roundabout	le manège
game	le jeu
to play	jouer
player	le joueur, la joueuse
toy	le jouet
match	la partie, le match

432

to win	gagner
to lose	perdre
to draw	faire match nul
to cheat	tricher
deceit	la supercherie
deceitful	mensonger

meeting	la réunion
to meet	se réunir
to join	rejoindre
party	le groupe

433

to visit	visiter
visit	la visite
playing cards	les cartes f
to deal	distribuer les cartes
to shuffle	battre les cartes
suit	la couleur
billiards	le billard
cue	la queue de billard
cannon	le carambolage
spin	l'effet m

434

chess	les échecs m
piece	la pièce
pawn	le pion
rook	la tour
bishop	le fou
knight	le cavalier
chessboard	l'échiquier m
draughts	le jeu m de dames
dice	les dés m
jigsaw	le puzzle

Sport   Le sport

435

swimming	la natation
to swim	nager
swimmer	le nageur, la nageuse
breaststroke	la brasse
crawl	le crawl
backstroke	le dos m crawlé
butterfly stroke	la nage papillon
to dive	plonger

436

high diving	le plongeon de haut vol
to row	ramer
rower	le rameur
oar	l'aviron m
canoe	le canoë
canoeing	le canoë-kayak
canoeist	le, la canoéiste
paddle	la pagaie
skate	le patin
to skate	patiner

437

figure skating	le patinage artistique
rollerskates	les patins m à roulettes
skateboard	le skateboard
amateur	l'amateur m

fan le supporter	
bet	le pari
to bet	parier
odds	la cote
ball	la balle, le ballon
football (sport)	le football

438

football	le ballon de football
footballer	le footballeur
football pools	le jeu des pronostics
referee	l'arbitre *m*
penalty	le pénalty
corner	le corner
offside	hors-jeu
forward	l'avant *m*
defender	l'arrière *m*
midfielder	le demi

439

winger	l'ailier *m*
to score	marquer un but
to shoot	shooter
to dribble	dribbler
goal	(objectif) le but
goal (score)	le but
goalkeeper	le gardien de but
goalscorer	le buteur
goal kick	le dégagement
team	l'équipe *f*

440

league	la ligue
trophy	le trophée
knockout competition	la compétition à élimina-toires *f*
rugby	le rugby
to tackle	plaquer
scrum	la mêlée
scrum-half	le demi de mêlée
fly-half	le demi d'ouverture
prop	le pilier
fullback	l'arrière *m*

441

American football	le football américain
tennis	le tennis
lawn tennis	le tennis sur gazon
tennis player	le joueur, la joueuse de tennis
set	le set
volley	la volée
to serve	servir
table tennis	le ping-pong
boxing	la boxe

442

boxer	le boxeur
wrestling	la lutte
champion	le champion, la championne

fencing	l'escrime
fencer	l'escrimeur, l'escrimeuse
foil	le fleuret
gymnast	le, la gymnaste
gymnastics	la gymnastique
somersault	le saut périlleux
cycling	le cyclisme

443

cyclist	le cycliste
mountain bicycle	le vélo tout-terrain
time trial	la course contre la montre
stage	l'étape *f*
yellow jersey	le maillot jaune
horseriding	l'équitation *f*
showjumping	le concours hippique
dressage	le dressage
polo	le polo
horseman	la cavalier, la cavalière

444

grandstand	la tribune
racecourse	l'hippodrome *m*
race	la course
to run	courir
bullfight	la corrida
bullfighter	le toréador
motor racing	la course automobile
scrambling	le motocross
hockey	le hockey
bowls	le jeu de boules *f*

445

stadium	le stade
high jump	le saut en hauteur
long jump	le saut en longueur
triple jump	le triple saut
pole vault	le saut à la perche
long-distance runner	le coureur de fond
lap	le tour de piste
marathon	le marathon
training	l'entraînement *m*
athletics	l'athlétisme

446

athlete	l'athlète
sprinter	le sprinter, la sprinteuse
sprint	le sprint
to sprint	sprinter
starting blocks	le starting-block
hurdle	la haie
hurdler	le coureur de haies
javelin	le javelot
shotput	le poids
to put the shot	lancer le poids

447

discus	le disque
hammer	le marteau

relay race	la course de relais
baton	le témoin
Olympics	les Jeux Olympiques
triathlon	le triathlon
decathlon	le décathlon
decathlete	le décathlonien
pentathlon	le pentathlon
pentathlete	le pentathlonien

448

mountaineering	l'alpinisme *m*
mountaineer	l'alpiniste
rock climbing	l'escalade *f*
rock climber	le grimpeur
ice-axe	le piolet
skiing	le ski
to ski	skier
ski	le ski
cross-country skiing	le ski de randonnée *f*
winter sports	les sports *m* d'hiver

449

ski-lift	le télésiège
skier	le skieur, la skieuse
ski stick	le bâton de ski
ski-jump	le saut à skis
snowshoes	les raquettes *f*
ice hockey	le hockey sur glace
puck	le palet
toboggan	la luge
water-skiing	le ski nautique
outboard motor	le hors-bord

450

slalom	le slalom
to abseil	descendre en rappel
to fish	pêcher
angling	la pêche à la ligne
fishing rod	la canne à pêche
reel	le moulinet
bait	l'appât *m*
to bait	appâter
hook	le hameçon
fly fishing	la pêche à la mouche

Food and Drink

La nourriture et la boisson

451

food	la nourriture
provisions	les provisions *f*
to nourish	nourrir
appetite	l'appétit *m*
snack	le casse-croûte
to have a snack	casser la croûte
hunger	la faim
hungry	affamé
thirst	la soif
thirsty	assoiffé

452

to be hungry	avoir faim
to be thirsty	avoir soif
sweet	sucré
to have a sweet tooth	aimer les sucreries
sugar	le sucre
sugary	sucré
tasteless	insipide
bitter	amer
milk	le lait
to pasteurise	pasteuriser

453

skimmed milk	le lait écrémé
whole milk	le lait entier
cream	la crème
butter	le beurre
buttermilk	le babeurre
cheese	le fromage
egg	l'œuf *m*
yolk	le jaune d'œuf
egg white	le blanc d'œuf
shell	la coquille

454

soft-boiled egg	l'œuf *m* à la coque
scrambled eggs	les œufs *m* brouillés
omelette	l'omelette *f*
bread	le pain
brown bread	le pain bis
sliced bread	le pain en tranches
loaf	la miche
roll	le petit pain
crumb	la miette
crust	la croûte

455

health foods	les aliments naturels
organically grown	de culture biologique
vegetarian	végétarien
fibre	la fibre
wholemeal bread	le pain complet
rye bread	le pain de seigle
to slim	être au régime
lentils	les lentilles *f*
margarine	la margarine
polyunsaturated	polyinsaturé

456

fast food	le prêt-à-manger
hamburger	le hamburger
hot dog	le hot-dog
pizza	la pizza
fat	la matière grasse
fatty food	les aliments gras
frozen food	les surgelés *m*
french fries	les frites *f*
crisps	les chips *f*
confectionery	les pâtisseries *f*

457

vegetable	le légume
carrot	la carotte
broccoli	le brocoli
onion	l'oignon *m*
celery	le céleri
radish	le radis
spinach	les épinards *m*
asparagus	l'asperge *f*
cucumber	le concombre
gherkin	le cornichon

458

lettuce	la laitue
tomato	la tomate
peas	les petits pois *m*
chickpeas	les pois chiches *m*
bean	le haricot
french bean	le haricot vert
cauliflower	le chou-fleur
Brussels sprout	le chou de Bruxelles
aubergine	l'aubergine *f*

459

salad	la salade
mixed salad	la salade mélangée
corn	le maïs
beetroot	la betterave
green pepper	le poivron vert
mashed potato	la purée de pommes de terre
garlic	l'ail *m*
pumpkin	le potiron
courgette	la courgette
marrow	la courge

460

sweet potato	la patate douce
mushroom	le champignon
condiment	le condiment
spice	l'épice *f*
coriander	la coriandre
mustard	la moutarde
nutmeg	la noix de muscade
cinnamon	la cannelle
turmeric	le curcuma
saffron	le safran

461

soup	la soupe, le potage
soup tureen	la soupière
broth	le bouillon
beef	le bœuf
veal	le veau
steak	le steack
rare	bleu
well-done	à point
sauce	la sauce
gravy	le jus de viande

462

cutlet	la côtelette
ham	le jambon
bacon	le bacon
sausage	la saucisse
pepperoni	le saucisson épicé
blood sausage	le boudin
raw	cru
soft	tendre, mou
hard	dur
stew	le ragoût

463

tripe	les tripes *f*
cooking	la cuisson
cook	le cuisinier, la cuisinière
to cook	faire cuire
to roast	faire rôtir
roast	le rôti
to stew	dauber
to slice	couper en tranches
slice	la tranche
to fry	faire frire

464

fried	frit
chicken	le poulet
breast	le blanc
leg	la cuisse
ham	le jambon
to cure	saler
to smoke (food)	fumer
lamb	l'agneau *m*
pork	le porc
horse meat	le cheval
horse butcher	la boucherie chevaline

465

to grill	faire griller
to barbecue	faire griller au feu de bois
barbecue	le gril au feu de bois
to bake	faire cuire au four
breaded	pané
scampi	les scampi *m*
to stuff	farcir
spit	la broche
suckling pig	le cochon de lait
shank (lamb)	le jarret

466

fish	le poisson
haddock	l'églefin *m*
mussel	la moule
mullet	le rouget
mackerel	le maquereau
clam	la palourde
sole	la sole
tuna	le thon
salad	la salade
oil	l'huile *f*

467

vinegar	le vinaigre
sour	aigre
cruet stand	le flacon d'huile et de vinaigre
salt	le sel
saltcellar	la salière
pepper	le poivre
pepperpot	le poivrier
mustard	la moutarde
mayonnaise	la mayonnaise

468

jam	la confiture
marmalade	la marmelade
cake	le gâteau
pastry-cook	le pâtissier, la pâtissière
dough	la pâte
dessert	le dessert
pancake	la crêpe
rice pudding	le gâteau de riz
custard	la crème anglaise
roast apple	la pomme au four

469

caramel cream	la crème caramel
ice cream	la glace
chocolate	le chocolat
chocolate mousse	la mousse au chocolat
fritters	les beignets *m*
sponge cake	le gâteau de Savoie
fruit salad	la salade de fruits
whipped cream	la crème fouettée
cheesecake	le flan au fromage blanc
lemon meringue	la meringue au citron

470

pudding	le dessert
biscuit	le biscuit
baby food	les aliments pour bébés
flour	la farine
self-raising flour	la farine pour gâteaux
yeast	la levure
baking soda	le bicarbonate de soude
lard	le lard
peanut oil	l'huile *f* d'arachide
sunflower oil	l'huile *f* de tournesol

471

olive oil	l'huile *f* d'olive
rice	le riz
yoghurt	le yaourt
doughnut	le beignet
apple compote	la compote de pommes
sandwich	le sandwich
spaghetti	les spaghetti *m*
grated cheese	le fromage râpé
noodles	les nouilles *f*
frog legs	les cuisses *f* de grenouille

472

restaurant	le restaurant
menu	le menu
starter	le hors d'œuvre
main course	le plat de résistance
waiter	le serveur
waitress	la serveuse
drink	la boisson
to drink	boire
to sip	siroter
to gulp	engloutir

473

to empty	vider
empty	vide
nonalcoholic drink	la boisson non alcoolisée
wine	le vin
red wine	le vin rouge
rosé wine	le vin rosé
vintage	le millésime
beer	la bière
water	l'eau *f*
drinkable	potable

474

milkshake	le milk-shake
tonic	le Schweppes
juice	le jus
soft drink	la boisson non alcoolisée
sherry	le xérès, le sherry
dry	sec, dry
sherbet	le sorbet
orange squash	l'orangeade *f*
lemonade	la limonade
fizzy	gazeux
to uncork	déboucher

475

corkscrew	le tire-bouchon
liqueur	la liqueur
spirits	les spiritueux *m*
cognac	le cognac
tonic water	le Schweppes
lemon squash	la citronnade
mineral water	l'eau *f* minérale
cappuccino	le cappuccino
tea	le thé
camomile tea	la camomille

476

lemon tea	le thé citron
coffee	le café
coffee with milk	le café au lait
decaffeinated coffee	le café décaféiné
iced coffee	le café glacé
instant coffee	le café soluble
soda	le soda
whisky	le whisky
canned beer	la bière en boîte
bottled beer	la bière en bouteille

477

cider	le cidre
champagne	le champagne
vermouth	le vermouth
vodka	la vodka
rum	le rhum
Irish coffee	le café irlandais
anise	l'anis *m*
brandy	l'eau-de-vie *f*
cherry brandy	le kirsch
applejack	le calvados

Travel and Tourism

Les voyages et le tourisme

478

to travel	voyager
traveller	le voyageur, la voyageuse
travel agency	l'agence *f* de voyages
travel agent	l'agent de voyages
package holiday	les vacances *f* organisées
tourist	le, la touriste
tourist season	la saison touristique
hotel	l'hôtel *m*
hotelier	l'hôtelier, l'hôtelière
reception	la réception

479

information desk	le bureau de renseigements
lobby	le hall, le vestibule
service	le service
to book in advance	réserver d'avance
vacant	libre
bill	la note
tip	le pourboire
hostel	le foyer
youth hostel	l'auberge *f* de jeunesse
boarding house	la pension de famille

480

camping	le camping
campsite	l'emplacement *m*
to go camping	faire du camping
camp-chair	la chaise pliante
camping-van	le camping-car
air mattress	le matelas pneumatique
bottle-opener	l'ouvre-bouteilles *m*
camp bed	le lit de camp
tin-opener	l'ouvre-boîtes *m*

481

campfire	le feu de camp
flashlight	la lampe électrique
fly sheet	le double toit
ground	le sol
ground sheet	le tapis de sol
guy line	la corde
mallet	le maillet

shelter	l'abri *m*
to take shelter	s'abriter
to get wet	se mouiller

482

sleeping bag	le sac de couchage
to sleep out	dormir à la belle étoile
tent	la tente
tent peg	le piquet de tente
tent pole	le montant de tente
thermos flask	la bouteille thermos
caravan	la caravane
to go caravaning	faire du caravaning
to live rough	vivre à la dure
tramp	le vagabond

483

self-catering apartment	l'appartement *m* indépendant
day-tripper	l'excursionniste
trip	l'excursion *f*
railway	le chemin de fer
platform	le quai
to derail	dérailler
derailment	le déraillement
to collide	entrer en collision
collision	la collision
accident	l'accident *m*

484

timetable	les horaires
guidebook	le guide
train	le train
express train	le rapide
through train	le train direct
to arrive	arriver
arrival	l'arrivée *f*
to leave	partir
departure	le départ
departure board	le tableau des départs

485

underground railway	le métro
diesel	le gazole
steam	la vapeur
corridor	le corridor
to alight	descendre
halt	l'arrêt *m*
compartment	le compartiment
tunnel	le tunnel
viaduct	le viaduc
cutting	la tranchée

486

railway network	le réseau ferroviaire
railhead	la tête de ligne
railtrack	la voie ferrée
railworker	le cheminot
stationmaster	le chef de gare
waiting room	la salle d'attente
single ticket	l'aller simple *m*

return ticket	l'aller-retour *m*
to examine	contrôler
ticket inspector	le contrôleur

487

guard	le chef de train
engine driver	le mécanicien
signalman	l'aiguilleur *m*
locomotive	la locomotive
carriage	le wagon
dining car	le wagon-restaurant
sleeping car	le wagon-couchettes
luggage	les bagages *m*
to check in	enregistrer les bagages
left-luggage	la consigne

488

trunk	la malle
case	la valise
rucksack	le sac à dos
stop	l'arrêt *m*
to stop	s'arrêter
stay	le séjour
customs	la douane
customs officer	le douanier
examination	le contrôle, la visite
to examine	contrôler

489

duty	le droit de douane
tax	la taxe
to tax	taxer
to declare	déclarer
duty-free	hors taxe, duty-free
passport	le passeport
identity card	la carte d'identité
bus	l'autobus *m*
taxi	le taxi
taxi driver	le chauffeur de taxi

490

driving licence	le permis de conduire
to drive	conduire
motor car	la voiture
motoring	l'automobilisme *m*
motorist	l'automobiliste
to hire	louer
trailer	la remorque
to give someone a lift	déposer quelqu'un
hitchhiker	l'auto-stoppeur, l'auto-stoppeuse
to hitchhike	faire de l'auto-stop

491

hitchhiking	l'auto-stop *m*
sharp bend	le virage serré
to skid	déraper
door (vehicle)	la portière
window (vehicle)	la vitre
to park	se garer
to slow down	ralentir

to accelerate	accélérer
to start up	démarrer
to overtake	doubler, dépasser

492

aerial	l'antenne *f*
air filter	le filtre à air
alternator	l'alternateur *m*
antifreeze	l'antigel *m*
gearbox	la boîte de vitesses
axle	l'essieu *m*
battery	les accus *m*
flat	à plat
bonnet	le capot
boot	le coffre

493

brake fluid	le lockheed
bumper	le pare-chocs
carburettor	le carburateur
child seat	le siège pour enfants
choke	le starter
clutch	l'embrayage *m*
cylinder	le cylindre
horsepower	la puissance

494

disc brake	le frein à disques
distributor	le delco
dynamo	la dynamo
dynamic	dynamique
engine	le moteur
exhaust	le tuyau d'échappement
fan belt	la courroie de ventilateur
fuel gauge	la jauge d'essence
fuel pump	la pompe d'alimentation
fuse	le fusible

495

gear lever	le levier de vitesses
generator	la génératrice
to generate	générer
alternating current	le courant alternatif
hand brake	le frein à main
hazard lights	les feux *m* de détresse
horn	le klaxon
ignition	le contact
ignition key	la clef de contact
indicator	le clignotant

496

jack	le cric
silencer	le silencieux
number plate	la plaque minéralogique
oil filter	le filtre à huile
points	les vis platinées *f*
rear-view mirror	le rétroviseur
reflector	le cataphote
reverse light	les feux *m* de recul
roof-rack	la galerie
seat	le siège

497

seat belt	la ceinture de sécurité
shock absorbers	les amortisseurs *m*
socket wrench	la clef à pipe
spanner	la clef anglaise
spare part	la pièce détachée
spark plug	la bougie
speedometer	le compteur
starter motor	le démarreur
steering wheel	le volant
sunroof	le toit ouvrant

498

suspension	la suspension
towbar	la barre de remorquage
transmission	la transmission
tyre	le pneu
wheel	la roue
windscreen	le pare-brise
wipers	les essuie-glace *m*
wrench	la clef
air bag	l'air-bag *m*
four-wheel drive	le quatre-quatre

499

motorbike	la moto
helmet	le casque
bicycle	le vélo
racing cycle	le vélo de course
pedal	la pédale
to pedal	pédaler
tube	la chambre à air
puncture	la crevaison
chain	la chaîne
pannier bag	la sacoche

500

ship	le bateau, le navire
boat	le bateau
sail	la voile
to embark	embarquer
to disembark	débarquer
on board	à bord
disembarkment	le débarquement
to tow	remorquer
tug	le remorqueur
crossing	la traversée

501

to cross	traverser
passage	la traversée, le passage
passenger	le passager, la passagère
cabin	la cabine
deck	le pont
mast	le mât
pilot	le pilote
rudder	le gouvernail
crew	l'équipage *m*
anchor	l'ancre *f*

502

to cast anchor	jeter l'ancre *f*
anchorage	le mouillage
cargo	la cargaison
to sink	sombrer, couler
sinking	le naufrage
shipwreck	le naufrage, l'épave *f*
signal	le signal
to signal	transmettre un signal *m*
lighthouse	le phare
port	le port

503

quay	le quai
oil tanker	le pétrolier
to launch	lancer
salvage	le sauvetage
to salvage	sauver
free on board	franco à bord
waybill	la feuille de route
hovercraft	l'aéroglisseur *m*
hoverport	le hoverport

504

stern	la poupe
bows	l'avant *m*
prow	la proue
starboard	tribord
port	bâbord
keel	la quille
figurehead	la figure de proue
funnel	la cheminée
rigging	le gréement
sail	la voile

505

raft	le radeau
galley	la galère
clinker-built	à clins
galleon	la galion
clipper	le clipper
schooner	la goélette
whaler	le baleinier
trawler	le chalutier
to trawl	pêcher au chalut
factory ship	le navire-usine

506

hydrofoil	l'hydrofoil *m*
powerboat	le hors-bord
dinghy	le youyou
pontoon	le ponton
liferaft	le canot de sauvetage
aqualung	le scaphandre auto-nome
diver	le scaphandrier
navigation	la navigation
to navigate	naviguer
to weigh anchor	lever l'ancre *f*

507

balloon	le ballon
airship	le dirigeable
aviation	l'aviation *f*
airplane	l'avion *m*
flying boat	l'hydravion *m*
airport	l'aéroport *m*
air terminal	l'aérogare *f*
passenger	le passager, la passagère
business class	la classe affaires
tourist class	la classe touriste

508

farewell	les adieux *m*
air hostess	l'hôtesse de l'air *f*
to land	atterrir
forced landing	l'atterrissage *m* forcé
to take off	décoller
take-off	le décollage
seatbelt	la ceinture de sécurité
to fly	voler
propeller	l'hélice *f*
pilot	le pilote

509

autopilot	le pilotage automatique
black box	la boîte noire
runway	la piste
undercarriage	le train d'atterrissage
sound barrier	le mur du son
to crash	s'écraser
glider	le planeur
to glide	planer
hang-glider	le deltaplane
autogiro	l'autogire *m*

Days of the week Les jours de la semaine

Monday	lundi
Tuesday	mardi
Wednesday	mercredi
Thursday	jeudi
Friday	vendredi
Saturday	samedi
Sunday	dimanche

Months Les mois

January	janvier
February	février
March	mars
April	avril
May	mai
June	juin
July	juillet
August	août
September	septembre
October	octobre
November	novembre
December	décembre

Seasons Les saisons

spring	le printemps
summer	l'été *m*
autumn	l'automne *m*
winter	l'hiver *m*

Numbers les nombres

1	un, une
2	deux
3	trois
4	quatre
5	cinq
6	six
7	sept
8	huit
9	neuf
10	dix
11	onze
12	douze
13	treize
14	quatorze
15	quinze
16	seize
17	dix-sept
18	dix-huit
19	dix-neuf
20	vingt
21	vingt et un
22	vingt-deux
23	vingt-trois
24	vingt-quatre
25	vingt-cinq
26	vingt-six
27	vingt-sept
28	vingt-huit
29	vingt-neuf
30	trente
40	quarante
50	cinquante
60	soixante
70	soixante-dix
80	quatre-vingts
90	quatre-vingt-dix
100	cent
200	deux cents
300	trois cents
400	quatre cents
500	cinq cents
600	six cents
700	sept cents
800	huit cents
900	neuf cents
1000	mille

2000	deux mille
1000000	un million
1st	premier
2nd	deuxième, second
3rd	troisième
4th	quatrième
5th	cinquième
6th	sixième
7th	septième
8th	huitième
9th	neuvième
10th	dixième
11th	onzième
12th	douzième
13th	treizième
14th	quatorzième
15th	quinzième
16th	seizième
17th	dix-septième
18th	dix-huitième
19th	dix-neuvième
20th	vingtième
21st	vingt et unième
30th	trentième
31st	trente et unième
40th	quarantième
50th	cinquantième
60th	soixantième
70th	soixante-dixième
80th	quatre-vingtième
90th	quatre-vingt-dixième
100th	centième
200th	deux-centième
300th	trois-centième
400th	quatre-centième
500th	cinq-centièeme
600th	six-centième
700th	sept-centième
800th	huit-centième
900th	neuf-centième
1000th	millième
2000th	deux-millième
millionth	millionième
two millionth	deux-millionième

Proverbs and idioms

Proverbes et locutions

to be homesick	— avoir le mal du pays
to have pins and needles	— avoir des fourmis (dans)
don't mention it	— je vous en prie
it's none of your business	— ça ne vous regarde pas
it's all the same to me	— ça m'est égal
as deaf as a post	— sourd comme un pot
to sleep like a log	— dormir comme un loir

as drunk as a lord — saoûl comme un Polonais

at full speed — à toute vitesse

no sooner said than done — aussitôt dit, aussitôt fait l'auras

a chip off the old block — tel père, tel fils

out of sight, out of mind — loin des yeux, loin du cœur

at night all cats are grey — la nuit, tous les chats sont gris

practice makes perfect — c'est en forgeant qu'on devient forgeron

better late than never — mieux vaut tard que jamais

birds of a feather flock together — qui se ressemble s'assemble

to kill two birds with one stone — faire d'une pierre deux coups

every cloud has a silver lining — à quelque chose malheur est bon

he who laughs last laughs longest — rira bien qui rira le dernier

a bird in the hand is worth two in the bush — un tiens vaut mieux que deux tu l'auras

in the long run — à long terme

on the other hand — d'autre part

at first sight — à première vue

in the short term — à court terme

in my opinion — à mon avis

in fact — en réalité, en fait

in other words — en d'autres termes

First names   ### Prénoms

Alexander	Alexandre
Andrew	André
Anthony	Antoine
Bernard	Bernard
Charles	Charles
Christopher	Christophe
Edward	Edouard
Francis	Francis
George	Georges
Henry	Henri

James	Jacques
Joseph	Joseph
Lawrence	Laurent
Louis	Louis
Martin	Martin
Michael	Michel
Nicholas	Nicolas
Paul	Paul
Peter	Pierre
Philip	Philippe
Raymond	Raymond
Thomas	Thomas
Vincent	Vincent
Alice	Alice
Anne	Anne
Catherine	Catherine
Charlotte	Charlotte
Deborah	Deborah
Eleanor	Eléonore
Elizabeth	Elisabeth
Ellen	Hélène
Emily	Emilie
Esther	Esther
Josephine	Joséphine
Louise	Louise
Margaret	Marguerite
Mary	Marie
Matilda	Mathilde
Ophelia	Ophélie
Patricia	Patricia
Pauline	Pauline
Rachel	Rachel
Rose	Rose
Susan	Suzanne
Sylvia	Sylvie
Veronica	Véronique

Signs of the Zodiac

Les signes du zodiaque

Aquarius	Verseau
Pisces	Poissons
Aries	Mars
Taurus	Taureau
Gemini	Gémeaux
Cancer	Cancer
Leo	Lion
Virgo	Vierge
Libra	Balance
Scorpio	Scorpion
Sagittarius	Sagittaire
Capricorn	Capricorne

Prepositions, Adverbs and Conjunctions
Les prépositions, les adverbes
et les conjonctions

against	contre
at	à
between	entre
for	pour
from	de
in	dans, en
of	de
on	sur
to	à, dans, en
with	avec
without	sans
above	au-dessus de
down	en bas
under	sous
in front of	devant
opposite	en face de
forward	en avant
behind	derrière
backwards	en arrière
close to	près de
near	près de
far from	loin de
before	avant
after	après
here	ici
there	là
inside	dedans
within	à l'intérieur, dans
outside	dehors
where	où
during	pendant
except	sauf
towards	vers
until	jusqu'à
according to	selon, d'après
now	maintenant
often	souvent
then	alors
never	jamais
always	toujours
at once	tout de suite
soon	bientôt
still	encore
already	déjà
like	comme
how	comment
neither… nor	ni… ni
either… or	soit… soit
and	et
but	mais
why	pourquoi
because	parce que
if	si
yes	oui, si
no	non
well	bien
badly	mal

Prepositions, Adverbs and Conjunctions

quickly	vite	much	beaucoup
slowly	lentement	nothing	rien
enough	assez	nobody	personne
when	quand	perhaps	peut-être
too	aussi	once	une fois
more	plus	instead of	au lieu de
less	moins	at times	parfois

French Phrases

Key to Pronunciation

Guide to French pronunciation scheme

ah   as in bad, far, father
ai   as in met, excuse, well, mercy
ay   as in obey, day
aw   as in hot, blot, fought
ee   as in meal, feel, souvenir
er   as in the, tick, speaker
ew   as in beautiful*
oo   as in true, blue, glue
oh   as in note, boat

* There is no exact equivalent in English for the French 'closed' oo sound. Try with your lips to make the oo shape, while saying the ee sound through them.

The other area of French pronunciation without exact equivalents in English is the ng sounds, reduced here for simplicity to two:

an   as in French comprend (sounds like ong, as in song)

ern   as in French bien (sounds like ang, as in bang)

French consonants are pronounced much as in English.

Getting Started

Everyday words and phrases

Yes
Oui
wee

No
Non
non

Please
S'il vous plaît
seel voo play

Yes, please
Oui, s'il vous plaît
wee, seel voo play

No, thank you
Non, merci
non, mair-see

Thank you
Merci
mair-see

Good
Bien
byern

OK
Ça va
sah vah

Excuse me
Excusez-moi
aiks-kew-say-mwah

I am very sorry
Je suis désolé
jer swee day-soh-lay

Being understood

I do not understand
Je ne comprends pas
jer ner kohm-pran pah

I understand
Je comprends
jer kohm-pran

Do you understand?
Comprenez-vous?
kohm-prer-nay-voo?

I do not speak French
Je ne parle pas français
jer ner pahrl pah fran-say

Do you speak English?
Parlez-vous anglais?
par-lay-voo zan-glay

Can you help me, please?
Pouvez-vous m'aider, s'il vous plaît?
poo-vay-voo may-day, seel voo play

Could you repeat that?
Pourriez-vous répétez, s'il vous plaît?
poo-ryay-voo ray-pay-tay, seel voo play

Please repeat that slowly
Répétez lentement, s'il vous plaît
ray-pay-tay lan-ter-man, seel voo play

Please write it down
Notez-le, s'il vous plaît
noh-tay-ler, seel voo play

Can you translate this for me?
Pouvez-vous me traduire ceci?
poo-vay-voo me trah-dweer ser-see

Is there someone who speaks English?
Y a-t-il quelqu'un qui parle anglais?
ee-ah-teel kail-kern kee pahrl an-glay

Please point to the phrase in the book
Montrez-moi la phrase dans le livre, s'il vous plaît
mon-tray mwah la frahz dan ler leevr, seel voo play

It does not matter
Ce n'est rien
ser nai ryern

I do not mind
Ça ne me dérange pas
sa ner mer day-ranj pah

Greetings and exchanges

Hello
Bonjour
bon-joor

Hi
Salut
sah-lew

Good morning
Bonjour
bon-joor

Good evening
Bonsoir
bon-swahr

How are you?
Comment allez-vous?
koh-man tah-lay voo

I am very well, thank you
Très bien, merci
trai byern, mair-see

It is good to see you
Je suis heureux de vous voir
jer swee zer-rer der voo vwahr

It is nice to meet you
Heureux de faire votre connaissance
her-rer der fair vohtr koh-nay-sans

That is very kind of you
Vous êtes très aimable
voo zait trai zai-mahbl

You are very kind
Vous êtes bien aimable
voo zait byern ay-mahbl

You are very welcome
Je vous en prie
jer voo zan pree

Good night
Bonne nuit
bohner nwee

Goodbye
Au revoir
oh rer-vwahr

See you soon
A bientôt
ah byern-toh

My name is...
Je m'appelle...
jer mah-pail

What is your name?
Comment vous appelez-vous?
koh-man voo zah-play voo

Here is my son
Voici mon fils
vwah-see mon fees

This is	**— my daughter**
Voici	— ma fille
vwah-see	*— mah fee*

— my husband
— mon mari
— mon mah-ree

— my wife
— ma femme
— mah fahm

I am on holiday
Je suis en vacances
jer swee zan vah-kans

I am a student
Je suis étudiant
jer swee zay-tew-dyan

I live in London
J'habite à Londres
jah-beet ah londr

I am from — Britain
Je suis — Britannique
jer swee — bree-tah-neek

— England
— Anglais
— ang-lay

— Scotland
— Ecossais
— zay-koh-say

I am from — Wales
Je suis — Gallois
jer swee — gahl-wah

— Australia
— Australien
— *zoh-strah-lyern*

— Ireland
— Irlandais
— *zeer-lan-day*

— South Africa
— Sud-Africain
— *sewd-ahf-ree-kern*

— America
— Américain
— *zah-may-reek-ern*

— New Zealand
— Néo-Zélandais
— *nayoh-zay-lan-day*

Common questions

Where?
Où?
oo

How long will it take?
Il y en a pour combien de temps?
eel-yohn-ah poor kohm-byern der tan

Where is...?
Où se trouve...?
oo ser troov...

How much do I have to pay?
Combien dois-je payer?
kohm-byern dwah-jer pay-yay

Where are...?
Où se trouvent...?
oo ser troov...

What do you call this in French?
Comment appelez-vous ceci en français?
koh-man tah-play voo ser-see an fran-say

When?
Quand?
kan

What does this mean?
Que veut dire ceci?
ker ver deer ser-see

What?
Quoi/Comment?
kwah/koh-mon

What is the problem?
Quel est le problème?
kail ai ler proh-blaim

How?
Comment?
koh-man

What is this?
Qu'est-ce que c'est?
kais-ker say

How much?
Combien?
kohm-byern

What is wrong?
Qu'est-ce qui ne va pas?
kais-kee ner vah pah

Who?
Qui?
kee

What time do you close?
A quelle heure fermez-vous?
ah kail err fair-may voo

Why?
Pourquoi?
poor-kwah

Where can I change my clothes?
Où puis-je me changer?
oo pwee-jer mer shan-gay

Which?
Lequel?
ler-kail

Who did this?
Qui a fait cela?
kee ah fay ser-lah

Have you got any change?
Avez-vous de la monnaie?
ahvay voo der lah moh-nay

Who should I see about this?
A qui puis-je m'adresser?
ah kee pwee-jer mah-drai-say

Where can I buy a postcard?
Où puis-je acheter une carte postale?
oo pwee-jer ahsh-tay ewn kahrt pohs-tahl

How can I contact American Express/Diners Club?
Comment puis-je contacter American Express/
Diners Club?
koh-man pwee-jer kon-tahk-tay ah-may-ree-kan aik-sprais/dee-nairs kloob

Do you know a good restaurant?
Connaissez-vous un bon restaurant?
koh-nai-say voo zern bon rais-toh-ran

Do you mind if I...?
Est-ce que ça vous dérange si...?
ais-ker sah voo day-ranj see...

May I borrow your map?
Puis-je emprunter votre plan?
pwee-jer an-prern-tay vohtr plan

Asking the time

What time is it?
Quelle heure est-il?
kail err ay-teel

It is...
Il est...
eel ai

a quarter past ten
dix heures et quart
dee-zerr ay kahr

a quarter to eleven
onze heures moins le quart
on-zerr mwan ler kahr

after three o'clock
après trois heures
ah-prai trwah zerr

at about one o'clock
vers une heure
vair ewn err

at half past six
à six heures et demie
ah see-zerr ay der-mee

at night
la nuit
lah nwee

before midnight
avant minuit
ah-van mee-nwee

early
de bonne heure
der bohn err

eleven o'clock
onze heures
onz err

five past ten
dix heures cinq
deez err sank

five to eleven
onze heures moins cinq
onz err mwan sank

half past eight exactly
huit heures et demie pile
weet err zai der-mee peel

half past ten
dix heures et demie
deez err zai der-mee

in an hour's time
dans une heure
dan zewn err

in half an hour
dans une demi-heure
dan zewn der-mee err

late
tard
tahr

midnight
minuit
mee-nwee

nearly five o'clock
presque cinq heures
praisk sank err

soon
bientôt
byern-toh

ten o'clock
dix heures
dee zerr

ten past ten
dix heures dix
dee zerr dees

ten to eleven
onze heures moins dix
on zerr mwan dees

this afternoon
cet après-midi
sait ah-prai mee-dee

this evening
ce soir
ser swahr

this morning
ce matin
ser mahtern

tonight
cette nuit
sait nwee

twelve o'clock (midday)
midi
mee-dee

twenty-five past ten
dix heures vingt-cinq
dee zerr vern-sank

twenty to eleven
onze heures moins vingt
onz err mwan vern

two hours ago
il y a deux heures
eel ee ah derr zerr

Common problems

I have no currency
Je n'ai pas d'argent liquide
jer nay pah dahr-jan lee-keed

I have dropped a contact lens
J'ai laissé tomber une lentille
jay lay-say tohm-bay ewn lan-tee

I cannot find my driving licence
Je ne trouve pas mon permis de conduire
jer ner troov pah mon pair-mee der kon-dweer

I have lost my credit cards
J'ai perdu mes cartes de crédit
jay pair-dew may kahrt der kray-dee

I must see a lawyer
Je veux voir un avocat
jer ver vwahr ern ah-voh-kah

My car has been stolen
On m'a volé ma voiture
on mah voh-lay mah vwah-tewr

My handbag has been stolen
On m'a volé mon sac
on mah voh-lay mon sahk

My wallet has been stolen
On m'a volé mon portefeuille
on mah voh-lay mon pohrt-fery

At the Airport

The main airport in Paris is Charles de Gaulle, though some flights use the other airport at Orly. There are regular rail and coach services linking Paris to both airports. You can fly to Paris from various UK provincial airports, as well as from Heathrow and Gatwick. Other places you can fly to from the UK include Biarritz, Bordeaux, Clermont-Ferrand, Lyon, Marseille and Toulouse.

Buses connecting Charles de Gaulle Airport to the centre of Paris are regular and reasonably priced, although in heavy traffic the journey may take up to an hour (bear this in mind if you decide to take a taxi). Using the *RER* (suburban express train) is a quicker option and is also reasonably priced: departing from Roissy *TGV* station, or Gare du Nord and Châtelet where you can transfer to the Métro.

The airport at Orly also has a regular bus service to the centre and bus links to local train stations.

Arrival

Here is my passport
Voici mon passeport
vwah-see mon pahs-pohr

We have a joint passport
Nous avons un passeport conjoint
noo zah-von ern pahs-pohr kon-jwern

I am attending a convention
Je participe à une convention
jer pahr-tee-seep ah ewn con-van-syon

I am here on business
Je suis ici pour affaires
jer swee zee-see poor ahf-air

I will be staying here for eight weeks
Je reste huit semaines
jer raist wee ser-main

We are visiting friends
Nous sommes chez des amis
noo sohm shay day-zah-mee

I have nothing to declare
Je n'ai rien à déclarer
jer nay ryern ah day-klah-ray

I have the usual allowances
J'ai les quantités permises
jay lay kan-tee-tay pair-meez

This is for my own use
C'est pour mon usage personnel
sai poor mon ew-sahj pair-soh-nail

Common problems and requests

I have lost my ticket
J'ai perdu mon billet
jay pair-dew mon bee-yay

I have lost my traveller's cheques
J'ai perdu mes chèques de voyage
jay pair-dew may shaik der vohy-ahj

I have missed my connection
J'ai raté ma correspondance
jay rah-tay mah koh-rais-pon-dans

The people who were to meet me have not arrived
Les gens qui devaient venir me chercher ne sont pas arrivés
lay jan kee der-vay ver-neer mer shair-shay ner son pah zah-ree-vay

I am in a hurry
Je suis pressé
jer swee prai-say

I am late
Je suis en retard
jer swee zan rer-tahr

Where will I find the airline representative?
Où puis-je trouver l'agent de la compagnie aérienne?
oo pwee-jer troovai lah-jan der lah kon-pah-nee ai-ree-ain

I have lost my bag
J'ai perdu mon sac
jay pair-dew mon sahk

At the Airport

Where can I buy currency?
Où puis-je changer de l'argent?
oo pwee-jer shan-jay der lahr-jan

Where can I change traveller's cheques?
Où puis-je changer des chèques de voyage?
oo pwee-jer shan-jay day shaik der vohy-ahj

Where is	**— the bar?**
Où est	— le bar?
oo ai	*— ler bahr*

— the lounge?
— le salon d'attente?
— ler sah-lon dah-tant

— the transfer desk?
— le guichet de transit?
— ler gee-shay der tran-see

— the information desk?
— le bureau de renseignements?
— ler bew-roh der ran-sain-yer-man

	— the toilet?
Où sont	— les toilettes?
oo son	*— lay twah-lait*

Is there a bus into town?
Y a-t-il un autobus pour aller en ville?
ee-ah-teel ern oh-toh-bews poor ah-lay an veel

Can I upgrade to first class?
Puis-je prendre un billet de première classe?
pwee-jer prandr ern bee-yay der prer-mee-air klahs

Where do I get the connection flight to Nice?
Où dois-je prendre la correspondance pour Nice?
oo dwah-jer prandr lah koh-rais-pon-dans poor nees

Luggage

Where is the baggage from flight number...?
Où sont les bagages du vol numéro...?
oo son lay bah-gahj dew vohl new-may-roh...

My luggage has not arrived
Mes valises ne sont pas arrivées
may vah-leez ner son pah zah-ree-vay

Where is my bag?
Où est mon sac?
oo ai mon sahk

It is	— a large suitcase
C'est	— une grande valise
sai	*— tewn grand vah-leez*

— a rucksack
— un sac à dos
— tern sahk ah doh

— a small case
— une petite valise
— tewn per-teet vah-leez

These bags are not mine
Ces sacs ne sont pas à moi
say sahk ner son pah ah mwah

Where do I pick up my bags?
Où reprend-on ses bagages?
oo rer-pran-ton say bah-gahj

Are there any luggage trolleys?
Y a-t-il des chariots à bagages?
ee-ah-teel day shah-ryoh ah bah-gahj

Can I check in my bags?
Puis-je enregistrer mes bagages?
pwee-jan-ray-jees-tray may bah-gahj

Can I have help with my bag?
Y a-t-il un porteur?
ee-ah-teel ern pohr-terr

Careful, the handle is broken
Attention, la poignée est cassée
ah-tan-syon, lah pwah-nyay ai kah-say

This package is fragile
Ce paquet est fragile
ser pah-kay ai frah-jeel

I will carry that myself
Je porterai ceci moi-même
jer pohr-tai-ray ser-see mwah-maim

Is there a left-luggage office?
Y a-t-il une consigne?
ee-ah-teel ewn kon-seen

Is there any charge?
Faut-il payer?
foh-teel pay-yay

No, do not put that on top
Non, ne mettez pas ça en haut
non, ner mai-tay pah sah ohn-oh

Please take these bags to a taxi
Portez ces valises à un taxi, s'il vous plaît
pohr-tay say vah-leez ah ern tahk-see, seel voo play

At the Hotel

French hotels

In comparison with those in Britain, French hotels are good value – especially at the lower end of the market. But there are marked regional variations – the south coast is far more expensive than rural inland areas or other coasts of France.

The best-value hotels in France tend to be *auberges* or country inns. These are often delightful family-run establishments where they take pride in the quality of their food. In large towns and cities, the choice of hotels with character is not as good (Paris excepted) but you can nearly always find satisfactory chain hotels. At the luxury end of the market there are some splendid *châteaux*, beautifully converted mills, farms or priories – all elegantly furnished and often providing food of high quality.

Star ratings

Hotels in France are officially rated on a five-point scale, from simple one-star accommodation to four-star *de luxe*. (There are also basic unclassified hotels which are not categorised as *hôtels de tourisme*.) The French Tourist Office in London will provide you with a list of approved hotels. The star ratings are based on facilities (whether there's a lift, air conditioning, night porter, etc). They tell you roughly what prices to expect but give you no indication of what a place is really like.

Prices

Prices are controlled and should be displayed at reception and in every bedroom. Rates are quoted for the room, not per person, and are usually the same whether one or two people are using the room. Breakfast is rarely included in the price of the room.

Rates include service and tax, except in some deluxe hotels where the service is charged separately. It is quite normal in any hotel to ask to see a room before you agree to take it.

Most hotels offer rates for *pension complète* (all three meals) and *demi-pension* (breakfast and one meal). To qualify for *pension complète* you usually have to stay for a minimum of three days and the meals may be different from the other restaurant menus – with less choice.

Meals

The normal French breakfast consists of French bread or croissants and coffee – '*café complet*'. You can usually have it in your room, and occasionally you have no choice but to do so.

Although the hotel will expect you to take its breakfast, there is no legal obligation to do so and you will find that the coffee and croissants are a lot cheaper in the local café – and often better too. In the same way, many hotels will expect you to have an evening meal if you are staying the night, but under French law hoteliers are not allowed to insist that you do so. On the other hand, if it is a hotel that is renowned for its quality of cuisine you may not need to venture any farther.

Rooms and beds

In small hotels, double beds are the norm, though twins are becoming more common. In cheaper hotels, hard bolsters are used instead of pillows (but always check to see if there are pillows in the wardrobe) and there may be no soap provided.

A number of restaurants offer rooms that vary from basic to very luxurious. These restaurants-with-rooms are often very good value, but you cannot expect to stay in one unless you are planning to eat there.

Booking

Bookings for hotels need to be made well in advance during high season, particularly for Paris and other popular areas. In large towns, at stations and airports, there are offices known as *Accueil de France* which can book accommodation for you in their area or in main towns. Bookings can be made only up to a week ahead and for personal callers only.

Most hoteliers won't hold rooms after 6pm unless you've telephoned to say you will be late or have paid a deposit.

Bed and breakfast

With so many good-value hotels serving excellent food, it's not surprising that bed and breakfast has traditionally not been a prominent part of the French holiday scene. But that is changing, largely because the *Gîtes de France* organisation has set up a large-scale scheme to market bed and breakfast places. They're called *chambres d'hôtes*, and the roadside signs identifying them are now a common sight. The scheme promotes country homes offering bed and breakfast and 'a very warm family welcome' – ranging from cottages to small châteaux.

Another bed and breakfast organisation is *Café-Couette* (literally translated as Coffee-Duvet) offering over 1,000 homes to stay in. You are treated as one of the family and you can stay for as long as you like.

Guest membership of the organisation entitles you to the reservation service and the guide to all the bed and breakfasts available, in which they are graded from 2 to 5 'coffee pots'.

Reservations and enquiries

My name is…
Je m'appelle…
jer mah-pail

I have a reservation
J'ai réservé
jay ray-sair-vay

I am sorry I am late
Je suis en retard. Excusez-moi
jer swee zan rer-tahr. aiks-kew-say mwah

I was delayed at the airport
J'ai été retenu à l'aéroport
jay ay-tay rer-ter-new ah lahee-roh-pohr

My flight was late
Mon vol avait du retard
mon vohl ah-vay dew rer-tahr

I shall be staying until July 4th
Je reste jusqu'au quatre juillet
jer raist jews-koh kahtr joo-yay

I want to stay for 5 nights
Je veux rester cinq nuits
jer ver rais-tay sank nwee

There are five of us
Nous sommes cinq
noo sohm sank

Do you have — a single room?
Avez-vous — une chambre pour une personne?
ah-vay voo — zewn shanbr poor ewn pair-sohn

— a double room with a bath?
— une chambre pour deux person nes avec bain?
— zewn shanbr poor der pair-sohn ah-vaik bern

Do you have —	**a room with twin beds and a shower?**
Avez-vous —	une chambre avec lits jumeaux et douche?
ah-vay voo —	*zewn shanbr ah-vaik lee jew-moh ay doosh*
I need —	**a double room with a bed for a child**
Je veux—	une chambre pour deux personnes avec un lit d'enfant.
jer ver —	*ewn shanbr poor der pair-sohn ah-vaik ern lee dan-fan*
—	**a room with a double bed**
—	une chambre avec un grand lit.
—	*ewn shanbr ah-vaik ern gran lee*
—	**a room with twin beds and bath**
—	une chambre avec lits jumeaux et bain.
—	*ewn shanbr ah-vaik lee jew-moh aybern*
—	**a single room**
—	une chambre pour une personne
—	*ewn shanbr poor ewn pair-sohn*
—	**a single room with a shower or bath**
—	une chambre pour une personne avec douche ou bain.
—	*ewn shanbr poor ewn pair-sohn ah-vaik doosh oo bern*

Does the price include	**— room and breakfast?**
Est-ce que le tarif comprend	— la chambre et le petit déjeuner?
ais-ker ler tah-reef kohm-pran	— *lah shanbr ay ler per-tee day-jer-nay*
—	**room and all meals?**
—	la chambre et tous les repas?
—	*lah shanbr ay too lay rer-pah*
—	**room and dinner?**
—	la chambre et le dîner?
—	*la shanbr ay ler dee-nay*

How much is it for a child?
Cela coûte combien pour un enfant?
ser-lah koot kohm-byern poor ewn an-fan

How much is it	**— per night?**
Combien coûte	— par nuit?
kohm-byern koot	— *pahr nwee*
	— per person?
	— par personne?
	— *pahr pair-sohn*
	— full board?
	— la pension complète?
	— *lah pan-syon kohm-plait*
	— half-board?
	— la demi-pension?
	— *lah der-mee pan-syon*

Which floor is my room on?
A quel étage est ma chambre?
ah kail ay-tahj ai mah shanbr

Can we have breakfast in our room?
Pouvons-nous prendre le petit déjeuner dans la chambre?
poo-von noo prandr ler per-tee day-jer-nay dan la shanbr

Is this a safe area?
Est-ce que la région est sûre?
ais-ker lah ray-jeeon ai sewr

Can we have adjoining rooms?
Pouvons-nous avoir des chambres attenantes?
poo-von noo zah-vwahr day shanbr za-ter-nant

Are there other children staying at the hotel?
Y a-t-il d'autres enfants à l'hôtel?
ee-ah-teel dohtr zan-fan ah loh-tail

Are there supervised activities for the children?
Y a-t-il des activités surveillées pour les enfants?
ee-ah-teel day zahk-tee-vee-tay sewr-vay-yay poor lay zan-fan

Can my son sleep in our room?
Est-ce que mon fils peut dormir avec nous?
ais-ke mon fees per dohr-meer ah-vaik noo

Is the voltage 220 or 110?
Est-ce que le courant est à 220 ou 110 volts?
ais-ker ler koo-ran ai ah der san van oo san dee vohlt

Is there a trouser press I can use?
Puis-je faire repasser mon pantalon?
pwee-jer fair rer-pah-say mon pan-tah-lon

Is there	**— a television?**
Y a-t-il	— un poste de télévision?
ee-ah-teel	— *ern pohst der tay-lay-vee-syon*
	— a hairdryer?
	— un sèche-cheveux?
	—*ern saish-sher-ver*

Is there	— a minibar?
Y a-t-il	— un minibar?
ee-ah-teel	*— ern mee-nee-bahr*

— **a room service menu?**
— un menu servi dans les cham
bres?
— ern mer-new sair-vee dan lay shanbr

— **a telephone?**
— un téléphone?
— ern tay-lay-fohn

— **a casino?**
— un casino?
— ern kah-see-noh

— **a lift?**
— un ascenseur?
— ern ah-san-serr

— **a sauna?**
— un sauna?
— ern soh-nah

— **a swimming pool?**
— une piscine?
— ewn pee-seen

Do you have	— a cot for my baby?
Avez-vous	— un lit d'enfant pour mon bébé?
ah-vay voo	*— zan lee dan-fan poor mon bay-bay*

— **a laundry service?**
— un service de blanchisserie?
— zern sair-vees der blan-shee-ser-ree

— **a car park?**
— un parking?
— zern pahr-keeng

— **a safe for valuables?**
— un coffre pour les objets de
valeur?
*— ern kohfr poor lay-zohb-jay der vah-
lerr*

Is there	— a fax machine?
Y a-t-il	— un télécopieur?
ee-ah-teel	*— zern tay-lay-koh-pee-err*

— **a market in the town?**
— un marché en ville?
— ern mahr-shay an veel

— **a Chinese restaurant?**
— un restaurant chinois?
— ern rais-toh-ran sheen-wah

— **a Vietnamese restaurant?**
— un restaurant vietnamien?
— ern rais-toh-ran vyait-nah-myern

Do you have satellite TV?
Recevez-vous les programmes par satellite?
rer-ser-vay voo lay proh-grahm pahr sah-tay-leet

What time	— does the hotel close?
A quelle heure	— est-ce que l'hôtel ferme?
ah kail err	*— ais-ker loh-tail fairm*

— **does the restaurant close?**
— ferme le restaurant?
— fairm ler rais-toh-ran

— **is breakfast?**
— est le petit déjeuner?
— ai ler per-tee day-jer-nay

— **is lunch?**
— est le déjeuner?
— ai ler day-jer-nay

— **is dinner?**
— est le dîner?
— ai ler dee-nay

— **does the bar open?**
— ouvre le bar?
— oovr ler bahr

Service

Please fill the minibar
Remplissez le minibar, s'il vous plaît
ran-plee-say ler mee-nee-bahr, seel voo play

Please send this fax for me
Transmettez ce fax, s'il vous plaît
trans-mai-tay ser fahks, seel voo play

Please turn the heating off
Fermez le chauffage, s'il vous plaît
fair-may ler shoh-fahj, seel voo play

Please, wake me at 7 o'clock in the morning
Réveillez-moi à sept heures, s'il vous plaît
ray-vay-yay mwah ah sait err, seel voo play

Can I have	— an ashtray?
Je peux avoir	— un cendrier?
jer per ah-vwahr	*— ern san-dree-ay*

— **another blanket?**
— une autre couverture?
— ewn ohtr koo-vair-tewr

Can I have — another pillow?
Je peux avoir — un autre oreiller?
jer per ah-vwhar — ern ohtr oh-ray-yay

— my key, please?
— ma clef, s'il vous plaît?
— lah klay, seel voo play

— some coat hangers?
— des cintres?
— day serntr

— some note paper?
— du papier?
— dew pah-pyay

— a newspaper?
— un journal?
— an joor-nahl

Can I have my wallet from the safe?
Je peux avoir mon portefeuille du coffre?
jer per ah-vwahr mon pohrt-fery dew kohfr

Can I hire a portable telephone?
Puis-je louer un téléphone portatif?
pweej loo-ay ern tay-lay-fohn pohr-tah-teef

Can I make a telephone call from here?
Puis-je téléphoner d'ici?
pweej tay-lay-foh-nay dee-see

Can I send this by courier?
Puis-je envoyer ceci par coursier?
pweej an-vwah-yay ser-see pahr koor-syay

Can I use my credit card?
Puis-je utiliser ma carte de crédit?
pweej ew-tee-lee-say mah kahrt der kray-dee

Can you connect me with the international operator?
Pouvez vous me passer la standardiste internationale?
poo-vay voo mer pah-say lah stan-dahr-deest an-tair-nah-syo-nahl

Can I have an outside line, please?
Pouvez-vous me passer une ligne extérieure, s'il vous plaît?
poo-vay voo pah-say ewn leen aiks-tair-yerr, seel voo play

Can you recommend a good local restaurant?
Pouvez-vous me recommander un bon restaurant?
poo-vay voo mer rer-koh-man-day ern bon rais-toh-ran

Please charge this to my room
Mettez cela sur ma note, s'il vous plaît
mai-tay ser-lah sewr mah noht, seel voo play

Can I dial direct from my room?
Puis-je obtenir une ligne extérieure directement?
pweej ohb-ter-neer ewn leen aiks-tair-yerr dee-raik-ter-man

Can I use my personal computer here?
Puis-je utiliser mon PC ici?
pweej ew-tee-lee-say mon pay-say ee-see

I need an early morning call
Réveillez-moi de bonne heure
ray-vay-yay mwah der bohn err

I need — some soap
J'ai besoin — de savon
jay ber-zwern — der sah-von

— some towels
— de serviettes
— der sair-vyait

— a razor
– d'un rasoir
— dern rah-zwahr

I need some toilet paper
Il me faut du papier hygiénique
eel mer foh dew pah-pyay ee-jay-neek

I need to charge these batteries
Je veux recharger ces piles
jer ver rer-shahr-jay say peel

I want to press these clothes
Je veux faire repasser ces vêtements
jer ver fair rer-pah-say say vait-man

Has my colleague arrived yet?
Est-ce que mon collègue est arrivé?
ais-ker mon koh-laig ai tah-ree-vay

How do I use the telephone?
Comment fait-on pour téléphoner?
koh-man fai-ton poor tay-lay-foh-nay

I am expecting a fax
J'attends un fax
jah-tan ern fahks

Where can I send a fax?
Où peut-on envoyer un fax?
oo per-ton an-vwah-yay ern fahks

What is the charge?
Quel est le tarif?
kail ai ler tah-reef

Problems

Can I speak to the manager?
Puis-je parler au directeur?
pweej pahr-lay oh dee-raik-terr

Where is the manager?
Où est le directeur?
oo ai ler dee-raik-terr

I cannot close the window
La fenêtre ne ferme pas
lah fer-naitr ner fairm pah

I cannot open the window
La fenêtre ne s'ouvre pas
lah fer-naitr ner soovr pah

The air conditioning is not working
La climatisation ne marche pas
lah klee-mah-tee-zah-syon ner mahrsh pah

The bathroom is dirty
La salle de bains est sale
lah sahl der bern ai sahl

The heating is not working
Le chauffage ne marche pas
ler shoh-fahj ner mahrsh pah

The light is not working
La lumière ne marche pas
lah lew-myair ner mahrsh pah

The room is not serviced
On ne fait pas le ménage dans la chambre
on ner fai pah ler may-nahj dan lah shanbr

The room is too noisy
La chambre est trop bruyante
lah shanbr ai troh broo-yant

The room key does not work
La clef de la chambre ne marche pas
lah klay der lah shanbr ner mahrsh pah

There are no towels in the room
Il n'y a pas de serviettes dans la chambre
eel nyah pah der sair-vyait dan lah shanbr

There is no hot water
Il n'y a pas d'eau chaude
eel nyah pah doh shohd

There is no plug for the washbasin
Il n'y a pas de bonde dans le lavabo
eel nyah pah der bond dan ler lah-vah-boh

My daughter is ill
Ma fille est malade
mah fee ai mah-lahd

My son is lost
Mon fils s'est perdu
mon fees sai pair-dew

Checking out

Could you order me a taxi?
Appelez-moi un taxi, s'il vous plaît
ah-play mwah ern tahk-see, seel voo play

Please leave the bags in the lobby
Laissez les bagages dans le hall, s'il vous plaît
lay-say lay bah-gahj dan ler ahl, seel voo play

I want to stay an extra night
Je veux rester une nuit supplémentaire
jer ver rais-tay ewn nwee sew-play-man-tair

Do I have to change rooms?
Dois-je changer de chambre?
dwah jer shan-jay der shanbr

Can I have the bill please?
Puis-je avoir la note, s'il vous plaît?
pweej ah-vwahr lah noht, seel voo play

We will be leaving early tomorrow
Nous partons tôt demain matin
noo pahr-ton toh der-mern mah-tern

Thank you, we enjoyed our stay
Merci, nous avons fait un bon séjour
mair-see, noo zah-von fai tern bon say-joor

Other Accommodation

Self-catering

Self-catering holidays are very big business in France. There are simple rural cottages, stylish seaside villas, modern high-rise apartments, old farmhouses and barns – even apartments in grand *châteaux*.

Gîtes

Thousands of British families are now opting for holidays in *gîtes*. These are modestly priced simple country houses or apartments, offering a real taste of rural France. There are 30,000 altogether, many of them renovated farmhouses or country cottages. Some properties are quite remote, others in small villages, but there are very few which are not in rural locations and only a handful are near the sea. Properties are all inspected and graded by the *Gîtes de France* organisation but even the top-graded accommodation can't match the comforts of a 3-star hotel. What most *gîtes* can offer is rural charm and character. Each property is privately owned and sometimes the *gîte* may be a self-contained apartment in the owner's house.

Villas and apartments

The most popular area for villa and apartment holidays is the south of France. Here you find every type of holiday home, from studios and stylish villas to spanking new apartment blocks and Provençal-style cottages. In Languedoc-Roussillon the coast has been developed on a large scale with huge purpose-built complexes. Other popular coasts for self-catering are those of Brittany and the Atlantic.

Booking

If you want a *gîte* or any self-catering property in high season you must book well in advance. Seaside accommodation is usually snapped up by December or January, and even remote rural properties are booked up several months in advance. Lots of tour operators organise packages combining self-catering accommodation and car ferry, and there are also a number of air packages to the south of France.

Renting a house

We have rented this villa
Nous avons loué cette villa
noo zah-von loo-ee sait vee-lah

Here is our booking form
Voici notre bon de réservation
vwah-see nohtr bon der ray-sair-vah-syon

Can I contact you on this number?
Puis-je vous joindre à ce numéro?
pwee-jer voo jwandr ah ser new-may-roh

Can you send a repairman?
Pouvez-vous faire réparer?
poo-vay voo fair ray-pah-ray

How does this work?
Comment est-ce que ça marche?
koh-man ais-ker sah mahrsh

What is the voltage here?
Quelle est la tension, s'il vous plaît?
kail ai lah tan-syon, seel voo play

I cannot open the shutters
Les volets ne s'ouvrent pas
lay voh-lay ner soovr pah

Is the water heater working?
Est-ce que le chauffe-eau marche?
ais-ker ler shoh-foh mahrsh

Is the water safe to drink?
Est-ce que l'eau est potable?
ais-ker loh ai poh-tahbl

Is there any spare bedding?
Y a-t-il de la literie de rechange?
ee-ah-teel der lah lee-ter-ree der rer-shanj

The cooker does not work
La cuisinière ne marche pas
lah kwee-see-nyair ner mahrsh pah

The fridge does not work
Le frigo ne marche pas
ler free-goh ner mahrsh pah

The toilet is blocked
Les WC sont bouchés
lay doobl-vay-say son boo-shay

There is a leak
Il y a une fuite
eel-yah ewn fweet

We do not have any water
Nous n'avons pas d'eau
noo nah-von pah doh

We need two sets of keys
Il nous faut deux jeux de clefs
eel noo foh der jer der klay

When does the cleaner come?
La femme (**woman**)/l'agent (**man**) de ménage vient quand?
lah fahm/lah-jong der may-nahj vyern kan?

Where is Où est *oo ai*	**— the fuse box?** — la boîte à fusibles? *— lah bwaht ah few-zeebl*
	— the bathroom? — la salle de bains? *— lah sahl der bern*
	— the socket for my razor? — la prise pour le rasoir? *— lah preez poor ler rah-zwahr*
	— the key for this door? — la clef de cette porte? *— lah klay der sait pohrt*

Camping

Camping is extremely popular in France, and the main sites are very well organised. The weather, particularly in the south, is well suited to the outdoor life and the facilities available at some of the sites make camping as comfortable as staying in a simple *gîte*. Tents with double beds, fridges, electric lights, gas stoves and even indoor chemical toilets are available for rent through UK tour operators.

Family camping holidays are increasingly popular. The sites are good places for getting to know people, and some put on organised activities to keep children amused. Such sites will have a restaurant or take-away food service for families who don't want to have to cook every meal.

Camping packages

There are several tour operators who offer all-in camping packages, the price inclusive of Channel ferry tickets and camping accommodation in pre-erected tents. The sites are usually very well organised and equipped. There are special rates for children. The overall price for a family works out at roughly the same as that of a *gîte* holiday.

Site gradings

Camp sites are classified from one to four stars, depending on the amenities. All sites are required by law to display their star rating and prices at the entrance. The camping charges are worked out according to the star ratings. On 1- and 2-star sites there are normally separate charges per person, per car, per caravan and per pitch: on 3- or 4-star sites there are often fixed charges per pitch, regardless of how many of you there are and what equipment you have. Charges usually run from midday to midday, and if you stay on a site after noon you will normally be charged for an extra night.

On the simplest sites the only facilities you can expect are covered washing and toilet areas (often inadequate for the number of campers), while at the other end of the market the big 4-star sites might have a pool, tennis courts, shops, launderette, restaurant, bar, playground and more. In other words, you don't have to move far to enjoy yourself – but you may find you're paying hotel prices.

All graded sites have a minimum space allocated to each pitch, although the restrictions tend to be ignored in high season. It's therefore worth checking out the size of your plot before deciding to take it.

Where to go

The most popular areas for camping are Brittany, Normandy, the Atlantic coast, the Dordogne and the south coast. The south has over 300 officially recognised sites, most of them offering attractive locations and good facilities. The sites on the Mediterranean are notoriously crowded in July and August and it's important to reserve your pitch in advance; if you don't enjoy being cheek-by-jowl with your neighbours, the Mediterranean sites are best avoided at this time.

For those who want 'to get away from it all', France has ample inland camping sites, providing privacy and peace. There are sites in the grounds of *châteaux*, in the fields of farmhouses, beside rivers, lakes and streams. Some of the town camp sites are surprisingly cheap and attractively located, often beside a river. In popular tourist areas, farms offer *camping à la ferme*, which is likely to be on a simple, quiet and uncrowded site.

Off-site camping, or *le camping sauvage*, is prohibited in many areas and notably in the south. There are areas of inland France where you can set up a tent – but always ask permission first.

Choosing a site

The best source for finding a site is the Michelin guide *Camping Caravaning France*. It is written in French, but the facilities are given in symbols and there are English translations where necessary. It recommends a wide range of sites and gives all the facilities available. The national camping organisation, the *Fédération Française de Camping Caravaning*, publishes another useful guide to camp sites.

For upmarket camping it's worth considering the *Castels et Caravaning* group, which offers accommodation at 40 4-star sites, many set in the grounds of *châteaux* and historic houses.

If you are travelling independently and wish to make a reservation, you can write direct to the camp sites, enclosing an International Reply Coupon (available from post offices). But remember that some of the smaller sites don't take advance bookings.

Before going it's worth buying an International Camping Carnet which shows you have third party insurance cover. Some upmarket sites won't let you in without it. The carnet is available from motoring, camping and caravanning organisations.

Useful camping phrases

Can we camp in your field?
Pouvons-nous camper dans votre champ?
poo-von noo kan-pay dan vohtr shan

Can we camp near here?
Pouvons-nous camper près d'ici?
poo-von noo kan-pay prai dee-see

Can we park our caravan here?
Pouvons-nous garer notre caravane ici?
poo-von noo gah-ray nohtr kah-rah-vahn ee-see

Please can we pitch our tent here?
Pouvons-nous dresser notre tente ici?
poo-von noo drais-say nohtr tant ee-see

Where do I pay?
Où dois-je payer?
oo dwah jer pay-yay

Do I pay when I leave?
Dois-je payer au départ?
dwah-jer pay-yay oh day-pahr

Is there a more sheltered site?
Y a-t-il un emplacement plus abrité?
ee-ah-teel ern an-plahs-man plew zah-bree-tay

Is there a restaurant or a shop on the site?
Y a-t-il un restaurant ou un magasin sur place?
ee-ah-teel ern rais-toh-ran oo ern mah-gah-zan sewr plahs

Is there another campsite near here?
Y a-t-il un autre terrain de camping près d'ici?
ee-ah-teel ern ohtr tair-ran der kan-peeng prai dee-see

Is this the drinking water?
Est-ce bien l'eau potable?
ais byern loh poh-tahbl

The site is very wet and muddy
L'emplacement est très humide et boueux
lan-plahs-man ai trai zew-meed ay boo-er

Where are the toilets?
Où sont les toilettes?
oo son lay twah-lait

Where can I have a shower?
Où puis-je prendre une douche?
oo pweej prandr ewn doosh

Where can we wash our dishes?
Où pouvons-nous faire notre vaisselle?
oo poo-von noo fair nohtr vai-sail

Is there	— a paddling pool?
Y a-t-il	— une pataugeoire?
ee-ah-teel	— *ewn pah-toh-jwahr*

— a swing park?
— des balançoires?
— *day bah-lan-swahr*

— a swimming pool?
— une piscine?
— *ewn pee-seen*

Hostelling

Although often sited at the edge of town, or in difficult to reach rural areas, French youth hostels (*auberges de jeunesse*) provide good-value, basic accommodation for travellers on a budget, often in beautiful surroundings. As well as dormitory beds, rooms for couples are available in more modern hostels. To stay in a youth hostel you must be a member of the International Youth Hostel Federation (IYHF) or Hostelling International (HI). HI membership also covers two rival French youth hostel associations, the *Fédération Unie des Auberges de Jeunesse* and the *Ligue Française pour les Auberge de Jeunesse*.

Are you open during the day?
Etes-vous ouvert pendant la journée?
ait voo zoo-vair pan-dan lah joor-nay

What time do you close?
A quelle heure fermez-vous?
ah kail err fair-may voo

Can we stay five nights here?
Pouvons-nous rester ici cinq nuits?
poo-von noo rais-tay ee-see sank nwee

Can we stay until Sunday?
Pouvons-nous rester jusqu'à dimanche?
poo-von noo rais-tay jews-kah dee-mansh

Do you serve meals?
Servez-vous des repas?
sair-vay voo day rer-pah

Can I use the kitchen?
Puis-me me servir de la cuisine?
pweej mer sair-veer der lah kwee-zeen

Here is my membership card
Voici ma carte de membre
vwah-see mah kahrt der manbr

I do not have my card
Je n'ai pas ma carte sur moi
jer nay pah mah kahrt sewr mwah

Can I join here?
Puis-je m'inscrire ici?
pweej mern-skreer ee-see

Thank you, we enjoyed our stay
Merci, nous avons fait un bon séjour
mair-see, noo zah-von fai tern bon say-joor

Childcare

Can you warm this milk for me?
Pouvez-vous faire réchauffer ce lait, s'il vous plaît?
poo-vay voo fair ray-shoh-fay ser lai, seel voo play

Do you have a cot for my baby?
Avez-vous un lit d'enfant pour mon bébé?
ah-vay voo zan lee dan-fan poor mon bay-bay

Do you have a high chair?
Avez-vous une chaise haute?
ah-vay voo zewn shaiz oht

Is there a baby-sitter?
Y a-t-il une baby-sitter?
ee-ah-teel ewn bay-bay-see-tair?

My daughter is 7 years old
Ma fille a sept ans
mah fee ah sait an

My son is 10 years old
Mon fils a dix ans
mon fees ah dee zan

She goes to bed at nine o'clock
Elle se couche à neuf heures
ail ser koosh ah ner verr

We will be back in two hours
Nous serons de retour dans deux heures
noo ser-ron der rer-toor dan der zerr

Where can I buy some disposable nappies?
Où puis-je trouver des couches à jeter?
oo pweej troo-vay day koosh ah jer-tay

Where can I change the baby?
Où puis-je changer le bébé?
oo pweej shan-jay ler bay-bay

Where can I feed my baby?
Où puis-je nourrir mon bébé?
oo pweej noo-reer mon bay-bay

I am very sorry. That was very naughty of him
Je suis désolé : il a été très vilain
jer swee day-soh-lay : eel ah ay-tay trai vee-lern

It will not happen again
Cela ne se reproduira pas
ser-lah ner ser rer-proh-dwee-rah

Getting Around

Public Transport

France has a very comprehensive rail system covering the whole country. The SNCF (*Société Nationale de Chemins de Fer*), a nationally owned company, runs a fast, efficient, modern service. The TGV (*Train à Grande Vitesse*) is the fastest train in the world – from Paris to Lyon it takes just 2 hours, which means that from city centre to city centre it is faster than going by air. Bus services are mainly used to connect rural areas to the rail network. The inland air service is useful for very long journeys, particularly those not covered by high-speed trains. Public transport can be prone to disruption by strikes.

Getting around Paris

If you arrive by air at Charles de Gaulle airport, the easiest way to get to the centre of Paris is to take the airport coach to Porte Maillot, near the Place de l'Etoile. The cheaper alternative is to take the shuttle bus to Charles de Gaulle station, then a train to the Gare du Nord. If you arrive by train you can get straight on to the Métro system.

The Métro and the RER (*Réseau Express Régional*) suburban lines are quick, efficient and cheap. The system is quite simple as long as you remember that the lines are called by the names of the station at each end (there are two names for each line). When you want to change trains you follow signs saying *Correspondances*. Electronic maps will help you pinpoint the station you want and the fastest route to take. If you are making several journeys, a book of 10 tickets (called a *carnet*) works out cheaper than buying them individually. One ticket takes you as far as you want. There are also *Paris Visites* visitor's passes that allow unlimited travel for 2, 3 or 5 days around Paris and its suburbs. A *Carte Orange* (you'll need a passport photo) is valid from Monday to Sunday and allows unlimited travel within specific zones.

Buses are a less convenient form of transport than the Métro but may be preferable for the tourist because you get to see the layout of the city.

Asking for directions

Excuse me, please
Excusez-moi, s'il vous plaît
aik-skew-say mwah, seel voo play

Where is	**— the art gallery?**
Où est	— la galerie d'art?
oo ai	*— lah gah-lai-ree dahr*

— the police station?
— le commissariat de police?
— ler koh-mee-sah-ryah der poh-lees

— the post office?
— le bureau de poste?
— ler bew-roh der pohst

Can you tell me the way to the bus station?
Où est la gare routière?
oo ai lah gahr roo-tyair

Can you show me on the map?
Montrez-moi sur le plan, s'il vous plaît
mon-tray mwah sewr ler plan, seel voo play

I am looking for the Tourist Information Office
Je cherche l'Office de Tourisme
jer shairsh loh-fees der too-reesm

I am lost
Je suis perdu
jer swee pair-dew

I am lost. How do I get to the Hôtel de la Gare?
Je suis perdu. Où se trouve l'hôtel de la Gare?
jer swee pairdew. oo ser troov loh-tail der lah gahr

I am trying to get to the market
Je cherche le marché
jer shairsh ler mahr-shay

I want to go to the theatre
Je veux aller au théâtre
jer ver ah-lay oh tay-ahtr

Is this the right way to the supermarket?
C'est bien par ici, le supermarché?
sai byern pahr ee-see, ler sew-pair-mahr-shay

We are looking for a restaurant
Nous cherchons un restaurant
noo shair-shon zern rais-toh-ran

Where are the toilets?
Où sont les toilettes?
oo son lay twah-lait

Where do I get a bus for the city centre?
D'où part le bus pour le centre-ville?
doo pahr ler bews poor ler santr veel

How long does it take to get to the park?
Il y en a pour combien de temps pour aller au parc?
eel yan ah poor kohm-byern der tan poor ah-lay oh pahrk

Is it far?
Est-ce loin?
ais lwern

Can you walk there?
On peut y aller à pied?
on per tee ah-lay ah pyay?

By road

Where does this road go to?
Où mène cette route?
oo main sait root

Which road do I take to Bordeaux?
Quelle est la route de Bordeaux?
kail ai lah root der bohr-doh

How do I get onto the motorway (highway)?
Comment peut-on rejoindre l'autoroute (la grande route)?
koh-man per-ton rer-jwandr loh-toh-root (lah grand root)

How far is it to Nancy?
Il y a combien de kilomètres jusqu'à Nancy?
eel yah kohm-byern der kee-loh-maitr jewsk-ah nan-see

How long will it take to get there?
Dans combien de temps y serai-je?
dan kohm-byern der tan ee ser-raij

I am looking for the next exit
Je cherche la prochaine sortie
jer shairsh lah proh-shain sohr-tee

Is there a filling station near here?
Y a-t-il un poste d'essence près d'ici?
ee-ah-teel ern pohst dai-sans prai dee-see

Which is the best route to Lyon?
Quelle est la meilleure route pour aller à Lyon?
kail ai lah mai-yerr root poor ah-lay ah lee-on

Which is the fastest route?
Quelle est la route la plus rapide?
kail ai lah root lah plew rah-peed

Directions

Vous allez	**— à gauche**
voo zah-lay	*— ah gohsh*
You go	— left

	— à droite
	— ah drwaht
	— right

	— jusqu'à
	— jewsk-kah
	— as far as…

Vous allez	**— vers...**
voo zah-lay	*— vair...*
You go	— towards…

	— juste à côté
	— jewst ah koh-tay
	— around the corner

Continuez tout droit
kon-tee-nway too drwah
Keep going straight ahead

Suivez la direction	— de l'autoroute
swee-vay lah dee-raik-syon	*— der loh-toh-root*
Follow the signs for	— the motorway

	— du prochain carrefour
	— dew proh-shern kahr-foor
	— the next junction

Tournez à gauche
toor-nay ah gohsh
Turn left

Tournez à droite
toor-nay ah drwaht
Turn right

C'est	— au carrefour
sai	*— toh kahr-foor*
It is	— at the intersection

	— à côté du cinéma
	— ah koh-tay dew see-nay-mah
	— next to the cinema

	— à l'étage au-dessus/à l'étage au-dessous
	— ah lay-tahj oh der-sew/ ah lay-tahj oh der-soo
	— on the next floor (up)/on the next floor (down)

C'est	— en face de la gare
sai	*— an fahs der lah gahr*
It is	— opposite the railway station

	— là-bas
	— lah-bah
	— over there

Il faut régler le péage
eel foh ray-glay ler pay-ahj
You have to pay the toll

Prenez la première à droite
prer-nay lah prer-myair ah drwaht
Take the first road on the right

Prenez la route d'Albi
prer-nay lah root dahl-bee
Take the road for Albi

Prenez la deuxième à gauche
prer-nay lah der-zyaim ah gohsh
Take the second road on the left

Hiring a car

It is cheaper to organise the rental of a car before you leave home, but you can rent cars at airports and in most cities (there may be a surcharge included at the airport). Basic car insurance will be included in the rental fee, but beware of being sold unneccesary cover that may already be included in your travel insurance.

I want to hire a car
Je veux louer une voiture
jer ver loo-ay ewn vwah-tewr

Can I hire a car?
Puis-je louer une voiture?
pweej loo-ay ewn vwah-tewr

Can I hire a car with an automatic gearbox?
Puis-je louer une automatique?
pweej loo-ay ewn oh-toh-mah-teek

Can I pay for insurance?
Puis-je payer l'assurance?
pweej pay-yay lah-sew-rans

Do I have to pay a deposit?
Dois-je verser des arrhes?
dwah-jer vair-say day zahr

Do I pay in advance?
Dois-je payer d'avance?
dwah-jer pay-yay dah-vans

Is tax included?
Est-ce que la taxe est comprise?
ais-ker lah tahks ai kohm-preez

Is there a charge per kilometre?
Y a-t-il un tarif par kilomètre?
ee-ah-teel ern tah-reef pahr kee-loh-maitr

Do you have	— a large car?
Avez-vous	— une grosse voiture?
ah-vay voo	*— zewn grohs vwah-tewr*

	— a smaller car?
	— une voiture plus petite?
	— zewn vwah-tewr plew per-teet

	— an automatic?
	— une automatique?
	— zewn oh-toh-mah-teek

	— an estate car?
	— un break?
	— zan braik

I need it for 2 weeks
J'en ai besoin pour deux semaines
john ay ber-zwan poor der ser-main

We will both be driving
Nous conduirons tous les deux
noo kohn-dwe-ron too lay der

I need to complete this form
Je dois remplir ce formulaire
jer dwah ran-pleer ser fohr-mew-lair

I want to leave the car at the airport
Je veux laisser la voiture à l'aéroport
jer ver lai-say lah vwah-tewr ah lai-roh-pohr

I would like a spare set of keys
Je voudrais un jeu de clefs de rechange
jer voo-drai ern jer der klay der rer-shanj

Must I return the car here?
Faut-il ramener la voiture ici?
foh-teel rahm-nay lah vwah-tewr ee-see

Please explain the documents
Expliquez-moi ces documents, s'il vous plaît
aiks-plee-kay mwah say doh-kew-man, seel voo play

Please show me how to operate the lights
Montrez-moi comment fonctionnent les phares
mon-tray mwah koh-man fon-syonn lay fahr

Please show me how to operate the windscreen wipers
Montrez-moi comment fonctionnent les essuie-glace
mon-tray mwah koh-man fon-syonn lay zai-swee-glahs

Where is reverse gear?
Où est la marche arrière?
oo ai lah mahrsh ah-ryair

Where is the tool kit?
Où est la trousse à outils?
oo ai lah troos ah oo-tee?

How does the steering lock work?
Comment fonctionne l'antivol de direction?
koh-man fon-syohn lan-tee-vohl der dee-raik-syon

By taxi

As in this country, taxis can be picked up at a rank or will stop if you hail them. A tip of a few francs is expected.

Where can I get a taxi?
Où puis-je trouver un taxi?
oo pwee-jer troo-vay ern tahk-see?

Please show us around the town
Faites-nous faire un tour de la ville, je vous prie
fait noo fair ern toor der lah veel, jer voo pree

Please take me to this address
Conduisez-moi à cette adresse, s'il vous plaît
kon-dwee-zay mwah ah sait ah-drais, seel voo play

How much is it per kilometre?
C'est combien le kilomètre?
sai kohm-byern ler kee-loh-maitr?

Will you put the bags in the boot?
Mettez les valises dans le coffre, s'il vous plaît
mai-tay lay vah-leez dan ler kohfr, seel voo play

Please wait here for a few minutes
Attendez ici quelques minutes, s'il vous plaît
ah-tan-day ee-see kail-ker mee-newt, seel voo play

Please, stop at the corner
Arrêtez-vous au coin, s'il vous plaît
ah-rai-tay voo oh kwern, seel voo play

Please, wait here
Veuillez patienter un moment
ver-yay pah-syan-tay an moh-man

Take me to the airport, please
Conduisez-moi à l'aéroport, s'il vous plaît
kon-dwee-zay mwah ah lai-roh-pohr, seel voo play

The bus station, please
La gare routière, s'il vous plaît
lah gahr roo-tyair, seel voo play

I am in a hurry
Je suis pressé
jer swee prai-say

Please hurry, I am late
Depêchez-vous, je suis en retard
day-pai-shay voo, jer swee zan rer-tahr

Turn left, please
Tournez à gauche, s'il vous plaît
toor-nay ah gohsh, seel voo play

Turn right, please
Tournez à droite, s'il vous plaît
toor-nay ah drwaht, seel voo play

Wait for me please
Attendez-moi, s'il vous plaît
ah-tan-day mwah, seel voo play

Can you come back in one hour?
Pouvez-vous revenir dans une heure?
poo-vay voo rer-ver-neer dan zewn err

How much is that, please?
C'est combien, s'il vous plaît?
sai kohm-byern, seel voo play

Keep the change
Gardez la monnaie
gahr-day lah moh-nay

By bus

The most reliable bus services in France follow the SNCF network, and are useful for local journeys and connections to stations. In most cities they will operate a pay-as-you-enter system and accept travel cards. Privately run services to rural areas that are not reachable by a railway are sometimes infrequent and unreliable.

Does this bus go to the castle?
Est-ce que ce bus va au château?
ais-ker ser bews vah oh shah-toh

How frequent is the service?
Quelle est la fréquence du service?
kail ai lah fray-kans dew sair-vees

What is the fare to the city centre?
C'est combien pour le centre-ville?
sai kohm-byern poor ler santr veel

When is the last bus?
Quand part le dernier bus?
kan pahr ler dair-nyay bews

Where do I get the bus for the airport?
D'où part le bus pour l'aéroport?
doo pahr ler bews poor lai-roh-pohr

Which bus do I take for the football stadium?
Quel bus faut-il prendre pour aller au stade?
kail bews foh-teel prandr poor ah-lay oh stahd

Please tell me when to get off the bus
Dites-moi où je dois descendre, s'il vous plaît
deet mwah oo jer dwah day-sandr

By train

Travelling by Eurostar through the Channel Tunnel will take you directly from London Waterloo to Lille in about two hours, and to Paris Gard du Nord in about three hours.

The rail system in France is generally reliable and efficient. The TGV now extends over a wide network, including Lille, Rouen and Nice. The ride in the TGVs (and in the slower long-distance Corail trains) is smooth and comfortable. Prices are reasonable and trains normally arrive on time. Reservations can be made in Britain – check with your travel agent. In France they can be made at main railway stations or by telephone. Advance bookings for the TGV are compulsory but you can make these up to a few minutes before departure at special machines at the station.

All tickets bought in France must be validated at the orange machines at the entrance to the platform before you travel and again if you make a break in your journey of more than 24 hours.

For off-peak travel there are discounts. If you intend to make several train journeys, it's worth purchasing a *Euro Domino* ticket, giving unlimited travel on any 3, 5 or 10 days in a month and entitling you to a reduction on Eurostar. Rail cards that give a reduction can also be bought: for couples (*Carte Couple*, 25 per cent reduction), people over 60 (*Carte Vermeille*, 30 per cent reduction), people under 26 (*Carissimo*, 30 per cent reduction) and children under 16 (*Carte Kiwi*, 30 per cent reduction for ticket holder and up to four others of any age).

When is the next train to Calais?
Quand part le prochain train pour Calais?
kan pahr ler proh-shern trern poor kah-lay

Where can I buy a ticket?
Où puis-je acheter un billet?
oo pweej ash-tay ern bee-yay

Can I buy a return ticket?
Puis-je prendre un aller-retour?
pweej prandr ern ah-lay-rer-toor

A return (round-trip ticket) to Toulouse, please
Un aller-retour pour Toulouse, s'il vous plaît
ern ah-lay-rer-toor poor too-looz, seel voo play

A return to Paris, first class
Un aller-retour pour Paris, en première classe
ern ah-lay-rer-toor poor pah-ree, an prer-myair klahs

A single (one-way ticket) to Montpellier, please
Un aller simple pour Montpellier, s'il vous plaît
ern ah-lay-sernpl poor mon-per-lyay, seel voo play

A smoking compartment, first-class
Compartiment fumeurs, première classe
kohm-pahr-tee-man few-merr, prer-myair klahs

A non-smoking compartment, please
Compartiment non-fumeurs, s'il vous plaît
kohm-pahr-tee-man non-few-merr, seel voo play

Second class. A window seat, please
Deuxième classe. Côté fenêtre, s'il vous plaît
der-zyaim klahs. koh-tay fer-naitr, seel voo play

I have to leave tomorrow
Je dois partir demain
jer dwah pahr-teer der-man

I want to book a seat on the sleeper to Paris
Je veux réserver une couchette dans le train de
Paris
*jer ver ray-sair-vay ewn koo-shait dan ler trern der pah-
ree*

What are the times of the trains to Paris?
Quels sont les horaires des trains pour Paris?
kail son lay zoh-rair day trern poor pah-ree

Where is the departure board (listing)?
Où est le tableau des départs?
oo ai ler tah-bloh day day-pahr

Where should I change?
Où faut-il changer?
oo foh-teel shan-jay

Can I take my bicycle?
Puis-je emmener mon vélo?
pweej an-mer-nay mon vay-loh

Is there | **— a restaurant on the train?**
Y a-t-il | — un restaurant dans le train?
ee-ah-teel | — *ern rais-toh-ran dan ler trern*

— a buffet car (club car)?
— un buffet?
— *ern bew-fay*

— a dining car?
— un wagon-restaurant?
— *ern vah-gon rais-toh-ran*

Do I have time to go shopping?
Ai-je le temps de faire des courses?
ay-jer ler tan der fair day koors

Which platform do I go to?
C'est sur quel quai?
sai sewr kail kay

How long do I have before my next train leaves?
Il me reste combien de temps avant le prochain
train?
*eel mer raist kohm-byern der tan ah-van ler proh-shern
trern*

What time does the train leave?
A quelle heure part le train?
ah kail err pahr ler trern

What time is the last train?
A quelle heure part le dernier train?
ah kail err pahr ler dair-nyay trern

Where do I have to change?
Où faut-il changer?
oo foh-teel shan-jay

Is this the Marseilles train?
C'est bien le train de Marseille?
sai byern ler trern der mahr-say

Is this the platform for Grenoble?
C'est bien le quai pour le train de Grenoble?
sai byern ler kay poor ler trern der grer-nohbl

Is this a through train?
Est-ce un train direct?
ais ern trern dee-raikt

Are we at Orléans yet?
Sommes-nous arrivés à Orléans?
sohm noo zah-ree-vay ah ohr-lay-an

What time do we get to Nantes?
A quelle heure arrivons-nous à Nantes?
ah kail err ah-ree-von noo zah nant

Do we stop at Le Mans?
Est-ce que le train s'arrête au Mans?
ais-ker ler trern sah-rait oh man

Are we on time?
On est à l'heure?
on ais tah lerr

How long will the delay be?
Combien de temps faudra-t-il attendre?
kohm-byern der tan foh-drah-teel ah-tandr

How long will this take?
Il y en a pour combien de temps?
eel yan ah poor kohm-byern der tan

Can you help me with my bags?
Pouvez-vous m'aider avec mes bagages?
poo-vay voo may-day ah-vaik may bah-gahj

I want to leave these bags in the left-luggage
Je veux laisser ces bagages à la consigne
jer ver lai-say say bah-gahj ah lah kon-seen

I shall pick them up this evening
Je reviendrai les prendre ce soir
jer rer-vyern-drai lay prandr ser swahr

How much is it per bag/case?
C'est combien par sac/valise?
sai kohm-byern parh sahk/va-leez

May I open the window?
Puis-je ouvrir la fenêtre?
pweej oov-reer lah fer-naitr

Is this seat taken?
Est-ce que cette place est libre?
ais ker sait plahs ai leebr

My wife has my ticket
C'est ma femme qui a mon billet
sai mah fahm kee ah mon bee-yay

I have lost my ticket
J'ai perdu mon billet
jay pair-dew mon bee-yay

This is a non-smoking compartment
C'est un compartiment non-fumeurs
sai tern kohm-pahr-tee-man non-few-merr

This is my seat
C'est ma place
sai mah plahs

Where is the toilet?
Où sont les toilettes?
oo son lay twah-lait

Why have we stopped?
Pourquoi avons-nous stoppé?
poor-kwah ah-von noo stoh-pay

Driving

Driving in France is quite straightforward and can even be pleasurable. Most of the roads (even minor ones) are fast, straight and uncrowded – for most of the time, anyway – and traffic congestion is much less severe than in Britain. Getting used to driving on the right is not as big a problem as it may at first seem.

France has an impressively comprehensive network of motorways, though most have only two lanes per carriageway. Tolls are charged on almost all of them, and these can mount up to considerable sums. On high-summer weekends it's important to steer clear of the notorious traffic blackspots: the Paris ring-road and the motorway from Paris via Beaune and Lyon to the south.

The roads

There are two main types of ordinary road: a *route nationale* (national road), prefixed with an N, and a *route départementale* ('county' road), prefixed with a D. Many of the N roads have become D roads in the last few years, and although you'll find the new numbers indicated on up-to-date maps, a lot of the signposts haven't yet been changed and some maps are still out of date. The more important N roads – the country's major arteries before the motorways were built – are often straight and fast but can be very hazardous, particularly where they go through towns and villages.

Motorways paying tolls

Normally as you approach a motorway you'll be confronted by a number of gates: head for one with a green light, press a button and take the ticket that emerges. It records where you joined the motorway and determines how much you pay when you leave it. There are occasional toll barriers across the main motorways – usually as you approach a city – where there may be short stretches that are free or for which you pay a fixed charge. If you have the correct change you can opt to go through an automatic gate where you toss coins into a chute as you drive through. At manned booths you can pay by Eurocheque, and on some motorways Visa credit cards are accepted.

Service areas

Motorway service areas often have impressive catering facilities – a single service area may have everything from a snack-bar serving fresh-ground coffee and croissants to a waiter-service restaurant with four-course menus. The best-value meals are the *routier* ('truck-driver') menus. Holders of the current *Relais Routier Guide* can get a four-course meal with beer, mineral water or a quarter litre of wine for under ten pounds. Service areas are quite frequent, but in between you will often find an *aire de repos* – a rest area with parking, toilets (not always too salubrious) and probably a picnic area with a rustic bench or two.

Route-finding

French motorways are notorious for horrendous traffic jams at peak holiday times. But most holiday destinations can be reached using less crowded alternative routes, or *Itineraires Bis,* indicated by green arrows on white (north to south) and white on green (south to north). The alternative network is marketed under the name *Bison Futé* ('crafty bison'); there are free *Bison Futé* maps available at toll booths, information centres and some service areas. Watch for the *Bison Futé* signs – a Red Indian who is supposed to know when the palefaces (tourists) will be on the warpath. Watch out also for yellow arrows on blue, labelled *itineraires de délestage,* showing shorter alternative routes for avoiding traffic blackspots at peak periods.

Route-planning maps

The Michelin route-planning map, sheet 911, covers dozens of alternative routes through France using the extensive network of secondary roads (as well as motorways and major roads, of course). In addition there's information on distances and driving times between towns and the peak holiday times to avoid. Map 915, in booklet form, covers the major routes for the whole of France. An English version of the useful *Bison Futé* brochure is available from the French Tourist Office, ferry ports and the AA and RAC.

Touring maps

For use once you've arrived in a particular area, there are three good series of maps available. The yellow-covered Michelin maps, which have a scale of 2km to 1cm, have the advantage that they link with the Michelin Red Guide, identifying towns and villages that have an entry in the guide and so greatly simplifying the job of finding a good hotel or restaurant when you're on the road.

The two other series both have a scale of 2.5km to 1cm, covering a bit more ground in a given area of map. The excellent maps published in France by Recta Foldex are now widely available in Britain under the *Telegraph* name: they have an index of place-names printed on the back. The maps published by the *IGN* (the French equivalent of the Ordnance Survey) are also good but are sold here only in fairly specialist shops.

Town plans

Even if you don't plan to do much eating out, the *Michelin Red Guide* to hotels and restaurants is worth buying for its many invaluable town plans. The regional *Michelin Green Guides* (for sightseeing) also have some town plans. The plans in both types of guide are linked to the Michelin yellow-covered maps by a common system of numbering the main roads into each town.

The rules

The main rules

Driving on the right It's surprising how quickly you get used to the idea of hugging the right-hand kerb. The real danger comes when you stop, usually for petrol: if you drive out from the petrol station on to a deserted road, your instinct may be to begin driving on the left-hand side.

Priority to the right *Priorité à droite* (giving way to traffic on your right) is being phased out. Most main roads now have priority, indicated by a succession of yellow diamond signs with white borders; when you lose priority the yellow sign has a black bar across it.

Roundabouts

The *priorité* rule used to mean that cars approaching a roundabout had priority over those already on it. In 1984 the system was changed to give priority to cars already on the roundabout, with prominent signs on the approach roads saying *Vous n'avez pas la priorité* – 'you do not have priority'. Even so, you still have to watch out for tiny roundabouts – perhaps going round a village monument – where the old rules still apply.

Speed limits

Speed limits are slightly higher than in Britain except when it's wet. They are now quite strictly enforced. Exceeding the speed limit can result in an on-the-spot cash fine as large as 5000 francs. **Open roads** Unless road signs say otherwise, the following general limits apply: 90km/hr (56mph) on ordinary roads, 110km/hr (68mph) on dual carriageways and toll-free motorways and 130km/hr (80mph) on toll motorways. When it's wet, and for drivers with less than two years' experience, the limits are lowered to 110km/hr (68mph) on toll motorways and 80km/hr (50mph) on other roads. There is a minimum speed limit of 80km/hr (50mph) in the outside lane of motorways during daylight.

Towns The limit in built-up areas is 60km/hr (37mph); the place-name sign marks the beginning of a town for speed-limit purposes; the end is marked by the name crossed out with a red line.

Other rules

You have to be 18 to drive a car; and you can't drive on a British provisional licence.

Drinking and driving is vigorously policed. Random breath-testing is widespread, and fines can be high: pleading ignorance will get you nowhere. A conviction can affect your insurance rating in Britain and can result in a prison sentence in France. It's worth remembering that spirit measures in French cafés are twice as large as those in British pubs.

Safety belts are compulsory for the driver and front-seat passenger: if safety belts are fitted to the rear seats, passengers in those seats must use them; under-tens must not travel in the front seat of a car that has a back seat.

Overtaking on the brow of a hill is not permitted. After over-taking on a multi-lane road you must return to the inside lane.

Stopping on open roads is not allowed unless you can drive right off the road.

Fines There's a system of on-the-spot fines for many motoring offences. To be accurate, it's not a fine but a deposit system, and the police collect the money only from people who can't show that they are resident in France. You have to pay in cash and the amounts are steep. Theoretically, you can always attend the subsequent court hearing: if you're not found guilty your deposit will be returned.

Parking The rules are similar to those in Britain, except that instead of yellow lines on the road, you should look for yellow marks on the kerbs. In some town streets parking is allowed on one side early in the month and on the other late in the month.

An area controlled by parking meters or automatic ticket machines is called a *zone grise* ('grey zone'): you have to pay to park between 9.00am and 7.00pm. In most large towns you can park in a *zone bleue* ('blue zone') between 9.00am and 12.30pm, and 2.30pm and 7.00pm. You have to display a time disc, which allows up to an hour's parking. You can buy discs from police stations; some shops and tourist offices will give you one free.

On the road

Breakdowns Move the car to the verge and either switch on the hazard warning lights or put the red warning triangle about 30m behind the car (100m on a motorway). On a motorway, call the police from an emergency telephone – there's one every 2km. On other roads, it will normally be best to find the nearest garage, though you can ring the police if necessary (telephone number 17). The local *garagiste* is often a friendly and highly competent mechanic who will charge you very modest prices. Main dealers of major brands of car are listed for each town in the Michelin Red Guide. The AA publish a useful *Car Components Guide*, translating the names of nearly 500 car parts with illustrations.

Accidents Inform the police, particularly if someone is injured (telephone 17). Motorists involved in an accident must complete a *constat à l'amiable* (accident statement form). If one or other party refuses to sign, then the case is taken to a local *huissier* (bailiff) who prepares a written

report called a *constat d'huissier*. This may take several days and can be expensive.

Filling up If you ask for the tank to be filled, make sure you don't get charged for more than you've had. It's safer to specify how much you want, in francs if you prefer – e.g. *pour cinquante francs*. Self-service stations (which are not very common in France) are invariably cheaper than those with attendants, and petrol costs quite a lot more on motorways than on normal roads.

The most useful credit card is Visa (*Carte Bleue*), but acceptance is far from universal. Acceptance of Access cards is slowly improving.

Types of fuel *Pétrole* in French means crude oil or paraffin; *essence* graded *normale* or *super* is the stuff you put in the car – though the word *essence* alone will often be taken to mean *normale*. Octane ratings are not always shown on pumps: *normale* is 90 octane, a low 2-star; *super* is 98 octane, 4-star. Watch out for *super sans plomb*, unleaded petrol.

Road signs

Road sign symbols are more or less international these days, but there are a lot of written signs in France that you might not be familiar with. The main ones are given below. If you're going through a town and there are no signs pointing to the destination you want, follow signs saying *autres directions* (other directions) or *toutes directions* (all directions).

absence de marquage — no road markings
accotements non stabilisés/consolidés — soft verge
agglomération — built-up area
aire de service (de repos) — service (rest) area
autoroute à péage — toll motorway
attention aux travaux — danger – road works
autres directions — other directions
bifurcation — road fork
bouchon — bottleneck
boue — mud
cédez le passage — give way
centre-ville — town centre
chantier (travaux) — roadworks
chaussée déformée — poor road surface
chute de pierres — (possibility of) fallen stones
défense de stationner — no parking
déviation — diversion
éboulement — landslide
entrée interdite — no entry

essence — petrol
éteignez vos phares/feux — switch off lights
feux — traffic lights
fin de — end of
gravillons — loose chippings
interdit sauf aux livraisons (riverains) — no entry except for deliveries (residents)
itinéraire bis — alternative route
passage protégé — your right of way
péage — toll
poids lourds — heavy vehicles
priorité à droite — priority to the right
préparez votre monnaie — get your change ready
prochaine sortie — next exit
ralentir — slow down
route barrée — road closed
sens unique — one-way street
serrez à droite — keep to the right
sortie — exit
stationnement — parking
toutes directions — all directions
travaux — roadworks
un train peut en cacher un autre — (at level crossings) one train can hide another coming the other way
véhicules lents — slow vehicles
verglas — ice on road
virages — bends
voie sans issue — no through road

Traffic and weather conditions

Are there any hold-ups?
Y a-t-il des bouchons?
ee-ah-teel day boo-shon

Is the traffic one-way?
Est-ce une route à sens unique?
ais ewn root ah sans ew-neek

Is the pass open?
Est-ce que le col est ouvert?
ais ker ler kohl ai too-vair

Is the road to Annecy snowed up?
Est-ce que la route d'Annecy est enneigée?
ais ker lah root dahn-see ai tan-nai-jay

Is the traffic heavy?
Y a-t-il beaucoup de circulation?
ee-ah-teel boh-koo der seer-kew-lah-syon

Is there a different way to the stadium?
Y a-t-il une autre route pour aller au stade?
ee-ah-teel ewn ohtr root poor ah-lay oh stahd

Is there a toll on this motorway (highway)?
Est-ce que cette autoroute (route) est à péage?
ais ker sait oh-toh-root (root) ai tah pay-ahj

What is causing this traffic jam?
Pourquoi y a-t-il un embouteillage?
poor-kwah ee-ah-teel ern an-boo-tery-ahj

What is the speed limit?
Quelle est la limitation de vitesse?
kail ai lah lee-mee-tah-syon der vee-tais

When is the rush hour?
Quelles sont les heures de pointe?
kail son lay zerr der pwant

When will the road be clear?
Quand est-ce que la voie sera dégagée?
kan es ker lah vwah ser-ra day-gah-jay

Do I need snow chains?
Est-ce que j'ai besoin de chaînes?
ais ker jay ber-zwern der shain

Parking

Can I park here?
Puis-je me garer là?
pwee-jer mer gah-ray lah

Is it safe to park here?
Peut-on se garer ici sans risque?
per-ton ser gah-ray ee-see san reesk

Do I need a parking disc?
Ai-je besoin d'un disque de stationnement?
ai-jer ber-zwern dern deesk der stah-syonn-man

What time does the car park close?
A quelle heure ferme le parking?
ah kail err fairm ler pahr-keeng

Do I need coins for the meter?
Faut-il mettre des pièces dans le parcmètre?
foh-teel maitr day pyais dan ler pahrk-maitr

Where can I get a parking disc?
Où peut-on acheter un disque de stationnement?
oo per-ton ahsh-tay ern deesk der stah-syonn-man

Do I need parking lights?
Faut-il laisser les feux de position allumés?
foh-teel lai-say lay fer der poh-zee-syon ah-lew-may

Is there a car park?
Est-ce qu'il y a un parking?
ais keel-yah ern pahr-keeng

How long can I stay here?
Combien de temps puis-je stationner ici?
kohm-byern der tan pwee-jer stah-syonn-ay ee-see

At the service station

Fill the tank, please
Le plein, s'il vous plaît
ler plern, seel voo play

Check — **the oil, please**
Vérifiez — l'huile, s'il vous plaît
vay-ree-fyay — lweel, seel voo play

— 25 litres of 3 star
— 25 litres de super
— vernt-sank leetr der sew-pair

— the water, please
— l'eau, s'il vous plaît
— loh, seel voo play

— 25 litres of 4 star
— 25 litres de super-plus
— vernt-sank leetr der sew-pair-plews

— the tyre pressure, please
— les pneus, s'il vous plaît
— lay pner, seel voo play

— 25 litres of diesel
— 25 (vingt cinq) litres de gazole
— vernt-sank leetr der gah-zohl

The pressure should be 2.3 at the front and 2.5 at the rear
C'est 2,3 (deux virgule trois) à l'avant et 2,5 (deux virgule cinq) à l'arrière
sai der veer-gewl trwah ah lah-van ay der veer-gewl sank ah lah-ryair

— 25 litres of unleaded petrol
— 25 (vingt cinq) litres de sans plomb
— vernt-sank leetr der san plohm

Do you take credit cards?
Acceptez-vous les cartes de crédit?
ahk-saip-tay voo lay kahrt der kray-dee

Can you clean the windscreen?
Nettoyez le pare-brise, s'il vous plaît
nai-twah-yay ler pahr-breez, seel voo play

Breakdowns and repairs

Can you give me a can of petrol, please?
Avez-vous un bidon d'essence, s'il vous plaît?
ah-vay voo zern bee-don dai-sans, seel voo play

— a tow?
— me prendre en remorque?
— mer prandr an rer-mohrk

Can you give me — **a push?**
Pouvez-vous — me pousser?
poo-vay voo — mer poo-say

Can you send a recovery truck?
Pouvez-vous envoyer une dépanneuse?
poo-vay voo zan-vwah-yay ewn day-pah-nurz

Can you take me to the nearest garage?
Pouvez-vous me conduire au garage le plus proche?
poo-vay voo mer kohn-dweer oh gah-rahj ler plew prohsh

I have run out of petrol
Je suis en panne sèche
jer swee zan pahn saish

Is there a telephone nearby?
Y a-t-il un téléphone près d'ici?
ee-ah-teel ern tay-lay-fohn prai dee-see

Do you have an emergency fan belt?
Avez-vous une courroie de secours?
ah-vay voo zewn koo-rwah der ser-koor

Do you have jump leads?
Avez-vous un câble de démarrage?
ah-vay voo zan kahbl der day-mah-rahj

I have a flat tyre
J'ai un pneu crevé
jay ern pner krer-vay

I have blown a fuse
Un fusible a sauté
ern few-zeebl ah soh-tay

I have locked myself out of the car
Les clefs sont enfermées à l'intérieur
lay klay son tan-fair-may zah lan-tay-ryerr

I have locked the ignition key inside the car
La clef de contact est enfermée à l'intérieur
lah klay der kohn-tahkt ai tan-fair-may ah lan-tay-ryerr

I have lost my key
J'ai perdu ma clef
jay pair-dew mah klay

I need a new fan belt
Il me faut une courroie de ventilateur neuve
eel mer foh tewn koo-rwah der van-tee-lah-terr nerv

I think there is a bad connection
Je crois qu'il y a un mauvais contact
jer krwah keel yah ern moh-vai kohn-tahkt

Can you repair a flat tyre?
Pouvez-vous réparer un pneu crevé?
poo-vay voo ray-pah-ray ern pner krer-vay

My car   — has been towed away
Ma voiture   — a été emmenée à la fourrière
mah vwah-tewr — ah ay-tay an-mer-nay ah lah foo-ryair

              — has broken down
              — est en panne
              — ai tan pahn

My car   — will not start
Ma voiture   — ne démarre pas
mah vwah-tewr— ner day-mahr pah

My windscreen has cracked
Mon pare-brise est fêlé.
mon pahr-breez ai fai-lay

The air-conditioning does not work
La climatisation ne marche pas
lah klee-mah-tee-zah-syon ner mahrsh pah

The battery is flat
Les accus sont à plat
lay zah-kew son tah plah

The engine has broken down
Le moteur est en panne
ler moh-terr ai tan pahn

The engine is overheating
Le moteur chauffe
ler moh-terr shohf

The exhaust pipe has fallen off
J'ai perdu mon pot d'échappement
jay pair-dew mon poh day-shahp-man

There is a leak in the radiator
Il y a une fuite au radiateur
eel yah ewn fweet oh rah-dyah-terr

Can you replace the windscreen wiper blades?
Pouvez-vous changer les balais des essuie-glace?
poo-vay voo shan-jay lay bah-lay day zai-swee-glahs

There is something wrong
Il y a un problème
eel yah an proh-blaim

There is something wrong with the car
La voiture ne marche pas
lah vwah-tewr ner mahrsh pah

Is there a mechanic here?
Y a-t-il un mécanicien?
ee-ah-teel ern may-kah-nee-syern

Can you find out what the trouble is?
Savez-vous ce qui ne va pas?
sah-vay voo ser kee ner vah pah

Do you have the spare parts?
Avez-vous les pièces détachées?
ah-vay voo lay pyais day-tah-shay

Is it serious?
Est-ce grave?
ais grahv

Can you repair it for the time being?
Pouvez-vous faire une réparation temporaire?
poo-vay voo fair ewn ray-pah-rah-syon tan-poh-rair

Will it take long to repair it?
Combien de temps faudra-t-il pour les réparations?
kohm-byern der tan foh-drah-teel poor lay ray-pah-rah-syon

Accidents and the police

There has been an accident
Il y a eu un accident
eel ya ew ern ahk-see-dan

We must call an ambulance
Il faut appeler une ambulance
eel foh tah-play ewn an-bew-lans

We must call the police
Il faut appeler la police
eel foh tah-play lah poh-lees

What is your name and address?
Quel est votre nom et votre adresse?
kail ai vohtr nohm ay vohtr ah-drais

You must not move
Ne bougez pas
ner boo-jay pah

He did not stop
Il ne s'est pas arrêté
eel ner sai pah zah-rai-tay

He is a witness
Il est témoin
eel ai tay-mwan

He overtook on a bend
Il a doublé dans un virage
eel ah doo-blay dan zern vee-rahj

He ran into the back of my car
Il m'a embouti à l'arrière
eel mah an-boo-tee ah lah-ryair

He stopped suddenly
Il s'est arrêté brusquement
eel sai tah-rai-tay brewsk-man

He was moving too fast
Il roulait trop vite
eel roo-lay troh veet

Here are my insurance documents
Voici mes pièces d'assurance
vwah-see may pyais dah-sew-rans

Here is my driving licence
Voici mon permis de conduire
vwah-see mon pair-mee der kon-dweer

How much is the fine?
Quel est le montant de la contravention?
kail ai ler mon-tan der lah kon-trah-van-syon

I have not got enough money. Can I pay at the police station?
Je n'ai pas assez d'argent. Puis-je payer au commissariat de police?
jer nay pah ah-say dahr-jan. pweej pay-yay oh koh-mee-sah-ryah der poh-lees

I am very sorry. I am a visitor
Je suis désolé. Je suis de passage
jer swee day-soh-lay. jer swee der pah-sahj

I did not know about the speed limit
Je ne savais pas que la vitesse était limitée
jer ner sah-vay pah ker lah vee-tais ay-tay lee-mee-tay

I did not understand the sign
Je n'ai pas compris le panneau
jer nay pah kohm-pree ler pah-noh

I did not see the sign
Je n'ai pas vu le panneau
jer nay pah vew ler pah-noh

I did not see the bicycle
Je n'ai pas vu la bicyclette
jer nay pah vew lah bee-see-klait

I could not stop in time
Je n'ai pas pu m'arrêter à temps
jer nay pah pew mah-rai-tay ah tan

I have not had anything to drink
Je n'ai rien bu
jer nay ryern bew

I was only driving at 50 km/h
Je ne roulais qu'à 50 km/h (cinquante kilomètre à l'heure)
jer ner roo-lay kah san-kant kee-loh-maitr ah lerr

I was overtaking
J'étais en train de dépasser
jay-tay an trern der day-pah-say

I was parking
J'étais en train de me garer
jay-tay an trern der mer gah-ray

That car was too close
La voiture me suivait de trop près
lah vwah-tewr mer swee-vay der troh prai

The brakes failed
Les freins ont lâché
lay frern zon lah-shay

The car number (licence number) was...
Le numéro d'immatriculation était...
ler new-may-roh dee-mah-tree-kew-lah-syon ay-tay...

The car skidded
La voiture a dérapé
lah vwah-tewr ah day-rah-pay

The car swerved
La voiture a fait un écart
lah vwah-tewr ah fai tan ay-kahr

The car turned right without signalling
La voiture a tourné à droite sans prévenir
lah vwah-tewr ah toor-nay ah drwaht san pray-ver-neer

The road was icy
La route était verglacée
lah root ay-tay vair-glah-say

The tyre burst
Le pneu a éclaté
ler pner ah ay-klah-tay

Eating Out

Good value and good quality

Eating out is a national pastime for the French. Even small towns have at least one ambitious restaurant, and, by British standards, restaurant meals are excellent value. The emphasis is on fresh local produce and even the humblest, dowdiest-looking place may produce food of surprisingly good quality.

Meals and menus

Proper restaurants and hotel dining rooms (other than in the major cities) stick to pretty rigid hours, and meals are generally served earlier than in Britain. Lunch (*le déjeuner*) – traditionally a leisurely two-hour affair – is the main meal of the day. Popular restaurants start filling up soon after noon. Book ahead for Sunday lunch. Dinner (*le dîner*) is usually served from around 7pm or 7.30pm until 8.30pm or 9pm; in some areas it's difficult to get dinner after 8pm.

Cafés (and brasseries – larger and smarter) are usually open all day for snacks or more substantial meals, and are useful if you haven't time to linger over a three-course meal. Prices in fashionable places – particularly in Paris – are very high, though you can stay for as long as you like for the price of one drink.

The word 'menu' has a more precise meaning in France than in Britain: it means a meal consisting of several courses with a narrow choice of dishes, at a fixed all-in price. Most restaurants offer several such menus at a range of prices, and may or may not also offer a wider choice of individual dishes from *la carte*. Menus invariably offer better value. The English expression 'à la carte menu' is a contradiction in terms in France.

The French way

- meals are not meant to be rushed, so service may seem slow
- waiters aren't called *garçon* – use *monsieur, madame* or *mademoiselle*
- the French don't drink coffee or tea during meals
- a simple restaurant will expect you to use the same knife and fork throughout the meal
- you will automatically be given bread with your meal but not a side plate or butter
- vegetables are often served separately from the meat, salads invariably so
- meat is normally served very rare or *saignant*; if you want it practically raw, ask for it *bleu*; if you want it rare, ask for it *à point*, for medium *bien cuit*
- cheese comes before dessert

Food

Even if France had no other attractions for the visitor, the country would retain the loyalty of many British fans because of its food. The French attitude to food is quite different from that of the British – put simply, they care about it.

Serious students of French food identify different styles of cooking – in particular *haute cuisine*, the rich, expensive fare traditionally associated with top-notch restaurants, and *nouvelle cuisine*, the modern version, using much less cream and butter.

Styles of cooking and sauces

Alsacienne (à l') — usually with sauerkraut, ham and sausages

Armoricaine (à l') — with sauce of tomatoes, herbs, white wine, brandy

Anglaise (à l') — plain, boiled

ballotine — boned, stuffed and rolled into a bundle

Béarnaise — sauce flavoured with tarragon and vinegar

Bercy — sauce with wine, shallots and bone marrow

Berrichonne (à la) — with bacon, cabbage, onions and chestnuts

beurre blanc — butter sauce with shallots and dry wine or vinegar

beurre noir — browned butter with vinegar

bigarade — bitter orange sauce

bonne femme — poached in white wine with onions and mushrooms

Bordelaise — sauce of red wine and bone marrow

boulangère (à la) — braised or baked with onions and potatoes

bourgeoise (à la) — with carrots, onions and bacon

Bourguignonne (à la) — cooked with burgundy, onions and mushrooms

Bretonne (à la) — served with haricot beans, sometimes as a purée

cardinal — rich, red fish sauce with mushrooms, truffles (usually for lobster)

chasseur — with shallots, mushrooms, tomatoes

chemise(en) — wrapped, generally in pastry

confit(e) — preserved or candied

court-bouillon — aromatic poaching liquid

croûte (en) — pastry case (in a)

daube — meat slowly braised in wine and herbs

diable — highly seasoned sauce; also type of cooking pot

Dijonnaise (à la) — with mustard sauce

farci(e) — stuffed

fourré (au) — filled

galantine — cold pressed poultry, meat or fish in jelly

Hollandaise — sauce with butter, egg yolk and lemon juice

Lyonnaise (à la) — with onions

Normande (à la) — with cream and any or all of: calvados, cider, apples

Provençal (à la) — with tomatoes, oil and garlic

roulade (de) — roll (of)

rouille — strongly flavoured creamy sauce with fish soups

Cheese

Part of the fun of eating cheese in France is that there are always new varieties to discover and try out.'Try anything once' should be your motto. Be prepared for lots of pleasant surprises, a huge variety of flavours from all over the country and methods of cheesemaking that are quite diverse

are are often jealously guarded secrets. It is customary in France to eat the cheese course before the dessert. The cheeses will be served with bread but not butter. Wherever you are, be sure to sample the local produce.

Principal cheeses

You're likely to come across these major varieties of cheese anywhere in France.

Brie — Soft cheese always made in round discs, varying in size. A good one should be yellow, creamy but not runny. It is made by factories in Brie and other parts of France and often called by the name of the area where it is made, for example Brie de Meaux or Brie de Melun

bleu d'Auvergne — Blue mould cheese created by a 19th-century peasant

Camembert — Small circular soft cheese invented in about 1790 by a farmer's wife, Mme Harel, whose statue you can see in the village of Camembert, near Vimoutiers in Normandy

Livarot — Soft, strong cheese with orange rind, from a small market town in Normandy

Munster — Large, round, supple cheese with orange rind, matured for three to six weeks, with strong smell and spicy flavour. Made in Alsace

Pont-l'Evêque — Small, square, pungent cheese, made from whole or skimmed milk

Port-Salut — Creamy, yellow, whole-milk cheese, first made at the Trappist Monastery of Port du Salut in Brittany

Reblochon — Soft, smooth cows' milk cheese from Savoie, with mild, creamy flavour

Roquefort — The true Roquefort, made in the little town of the same name in the Massif Central, is manufactured exclusively from ewes' milk. The unique feature of this cheese is that the curds are mixed with a special type of breadcrumb, causing a green mould to develop. The cheeses are stored in damp, cool caves for 30 or 40 days. Experts say it should then be left to ripen for a year

Regional cheeses

bleu de Bresse — Factory-made blue cheese from the Lyonnais in the shape of a small cylinder; creamy and smooth

Brillat-Savarin — Mild, creamy cheese from Normandy, named after the gastronome

Cantal — Hard, strong, yellow cheese, with a nutty flavour, made in the Auvergne

Chabichou — Small, cone-shaped goats' milk cheese, with strong smell and flavour; from the Poitou area

Chaource — White, soft and creamy cheese from Burgundy, made in cylinders

Dauphin — Soft, herb-seasoned cheese from Champagne Ardennes area, said to be named after Louis XlV's son

Epoisses — Soft, whole-milk cheese with spicy smell and flavour made all over Burgundy and central France

Olivet bleu — Small, rich, fruity cheese with bluish skin, sometimes wrapped in plane tree leaves: it comes from the Loire

Rollot — Cheese in the form of a disc with yellow rind, spicy smell and flavour

Saint-Marcellin — Small, round, mild cheese made of cow's milk from Savoie

Tomme — Name for a large number of cheeses, mainly from the Alps. Usually mild

Ste-Mauré — Soft creamy goats' milk cheese from Touraine

St-Nectaire — Flat, round cheese with mild but aromatic flavour, made on the Dordogne

Reservations

Should we reserve a table?
Faut-il réserver une table?
foh-teel ray-sair-vay ewn tahbl

Can I book a table for four at 8 o'clock?
Je voudrais réserver une table pour quatre pour huit heures
jer voo-dray ray-sair-vay ewn tahbl poor kahtr poor weet err

Can we have a table for four?
Une table pour quatre, s'il vous plaît
ewn tahbl poor kahtr, seel voo play

We would like a table — **by the window**
Nous voudrions une table — près de la fenêtre
noo voo-dryon ewn tahbl — *prai der lah fer-naitr*

— **on the terrace**
— sur la terrasse
— *sewr lah tay-rahs*

I am a vegetarian
Je suis végétarien
jer swee vay-jay-tah-ryern

Useful questions

Do you have a local speciality?
Avez-vous une spécialité régionale?
ah-vay voo zewn spay-syah-lee-tay ray-jyon-ahl

Do you have a set menu?
Avez-vous un menu à prix fixe?
ah-vay voo ern mer-new ah pree feeks

What do you recommend?
Que recommandez-vous?
ker rer-koh-man-day voo

What is the dish of the day?
Quel est le plat du jour?
kail ai ler plah dew joor

What is the soup of the day?
Quelle est la soupe du jour?
kail ai lah soop dew joor

What is this called?
Comment s'appelle ce plat?
koh-man sah-pail ser plah

What is this dish like?
Ce plat, il est comment?
ser plah, eel ai koh mon

Is this good?
Est-ce que c'est bon?
ais ker sai bon

Which local wine do you recommend?
Quel vin de pays recommandez-vous?
kail vern der payy rer-koh-man-day voo

Are vegetables included?
Est-ce que les légumes sont inclus?
ais ker lay lay-gewm son tern-klew

Is the local wine good?
Est-ce que le vin de pays est bon?
ais ker ler vern der payy ai bon

Is this cheese very strong?
Ce fromage, est-il très fort?
ser froh-mahj ai-teel trai fohr

How much is this?
C'est combien?
sai kohm-byern

Do you have yoghurt?
Avez-vous du yaourt?
ah-vay voo dew yah-oor

How do I eat this?
Comment mange-t-on cela?
koh-man manj-ton ser-lah

Ordering your meal

The menu, please
Le menu, s'il vous plaît
ler mer-new, seel voo play

Can we start with soup?
De la soupe pour commencer, s'il vous plaît
der lah soop poor koh-man-say, seel voo play

That is for me
C'est pour moi
sai poor mwah

Can we have some bread?
Du pain, s'il vous plaît
dew pern, seel voo play

Could we have some butter?
Du beurre, s'il vous plaît
dew berr, seel voo play

I will have salad
Je prendrai de la salade
jer pran-drai der lah sah-lahd

I will take that
Je prendrai ceci
jer pran-drai ser-see

I will take the set menu
Je prendrai le menu à prix fixe
jer pran-drai ler mer-new ah pree feeks

I like my steak	**— rare**
J'aime mon steack	— saignant
jaim mon staik	*— sai-nyan*
	— medium rare
	— à point
	— ah pwan
	— very rare
	— bleu
	— bler
	— well done
	— bien cuit
	— byern kwee

Could we have some more bread please?
Encore du pain, s'il vous plaît
an-kohr dew pern, seel voo play

Can I see the menu again, please?
Repassez-moi le menu, s'il vous plaît
rer-pah-say mwah ler mer-new, seel voo play

Wine

Wine is an integral part of French life. The vineyards of France produce a significant proportion of the world's wine, and the people of France consume much of that volume themselves. The choice of wines is enormous: everything from *vin ordinaire* in plastic bottles, costing no more than mineral water, to the cream of the crop from Bordeaux and Burgundy – the best wines in the world.

Unless you are very familiar with French wines, choosing from the wine list (*la carte des vins*) can be an intimidating experience. Some restaurants produce off-putting lists with pages of wines and prices that are very high indeed.

But if the big-name Bordeaux and Burgundy wines are out of reach, there are nearly always plenty of much cheaper alternatives, even in the top restaurants; many wines from the Loire and Rhone valleys or from the south and south-west are now finding their way on to wine lists throughout the country.

The house wine – *vin réserve du patron* or *vin de la maison* –is almost always a good bet: if it carries the restaurant's own label, it will usually have been carefully selected.

Reading a label

The ways in which wines are described on labels vary widely from region to region. Running across all the variations is a national system of identification employing four classifications.

Appellation (d'Origine) Contrôlée (AC or AOC) — A guarantee of origin and authenticity, applied to all major wines. An *appellation* may apply to a whole region (for example Bourgogne), a part of a region (for example Côtes de Nuit), a specific village (e.g. Gevrey-Chambertin) or even a particular vineyard (e.g. Grand Cru Clos de Bèze). In general, within a given region, the larger the geographic area described on the label, the cheaper and lesser quality the wine.

Vin Délimité de Qualité Supérieure (VDQS) — The second rank of *appellations* for regions producing minor wines. Some are of very good quality, being denied an AC only because they employ non-traditional grapes. As these better wines gain AC status, the VDQS label is being phased out.

Vin de Pays — 'Country wine' from a specific area – which may be a village or a whole region. Standards vary enormously.

Vin de Table or Vin Ordinaire — Blended wine, usually sold under a brand name.

Wine vocabulary

Blanc de blancs — White wine made from white grapes

Cave — Cellar or any wine establishment

Cave coopérative — Wine growers' cooperative, often a very good place to taste and buy

Chai — Cellar at ground level, sometimes meaning a warehouse

Château — A wine-growing estate, with or without a grand house, particularly in the Bordeaux area

Clairet — Very light red wine

Claret — Traditional English term for red wine from Bordeaux

Clos — Prestigious vineyard, often walled, found particularly in Burgundy and Alsace

Côte(s)/côteaux — Hillsides, generally producing better wines than lower vineyards

Crémant — In Champagne, 'less sparkling'; elsewhere, high-quality sparkling wine made by the Champagne method

Cru (Growth) — A term used in classifying the wines of different vineyards. In Bordeaux there is an elaborate and confusing system of *crus*, rooted firmly in the 19th century and not an entirely useful guide to quality. In Burgundy and Champagne, *Grand Cru* indicates the most prestigious wines, *Premier Cru* the second rank

Cuve Close — Method of making sparkling wine, generally inferior to the Champagne method

Cuvée du patron — House wine

Domaine — A wine estate, particularly in Burgundy

Méthode champenoise — Sparkling wine made by the Champagne method

Mise (en bouteille) au château/à la propriété/au domaine —Bottled on the wine-maker 's premises; usually a good thing

Moelleux — Mellow, sweet

Mousseux — Sparkling

Négociant — Wine merchant

Perlant/perlé — Very slightly sparkling

Pétillant — Slightly sparkling

Primeur — Young wine

Propriétaire-Récoltant — Owner-manager

Récolte — Crop

Réserve de la maison/du patron— House wine in a restaurant

Vendange tardive — Late vintage, especially in Alsace – the grapes are picked only when they have reached a certain sweetness

Vignoble — Vineyard

Viticulteur — Vine-grower

Ordering drinks

The wine list, please
La carte des vins, s'il vous plaît
lah kahrt day vern, seel voo play

A bottle of house red wine, please
Une bouteille de la cuvée du patron, s'il vous plaît
ewn boo-tery der lah kew-vay dew pah-tron, seel voo play

A glass of dry white wine, please
Un verre de vin blanc, s'il vous plaît
ern vair der vern blan, seel voo play

Another bottle of red wine, please
Une autre bouteille de vin rouge, s'il vous plaît
ewn ohtr boo-tery der vern rooj, seel voo play

Another glass, please
Un autre verre, s'il vous plaît
ern ohtr vair, seel voo play

We will take the beaujolais
Nous prendrons le beaujolais
noo pran-dron ler boh-joh-lay

Two beers, please
Deux bières, s'il vous plaît
der byair, seel voo play

Some plain water, please
De l'eau du robinet, s'il vous plaît
der loh dew roh-bee-nay, seel voo play

Can we have some mineral water?
De l'eau minérale, s'il vous plaît
der loh mee-nay-rahl, seel voo play

Black coffee, please
Un café (noir), s'il vous plaît
ern kah-fay (nwahr), seel voo play

Coffee with milk, please
Un café-crème, s'il vous plaît
ern kah-fay kraim, seel voo play

Tea with milk, please
Un thé au lait, s'il vous plaît
ern tay oh lay, seel voo play

Paying the bill

What is the total?
Ça fait combien en tout?
sah fai kohm-byern an too

Do you accept traveller's cheques?
Acceptez-vous les chèques de voyage?
ahk-saip-tay voo lay shaik der vohy-ahj

I would like to pay with my credit card
Je voudrais payer avec ma carte de crédit
jer voo-dray pay-yay ah-vaik mah kahrt der kray-dee

Is there any extra charge?
Y a-t-il un supplément?
ee-ah-teel ern sew-play-man

Is service included?
Est-ce que le service est compris?
ais ker ler sair-vees ai kohm-pree

Can I have a receipt?
Puis-je avoir un reçu?
pwee-jer ah-vwahr ern rer-sew?

Can I have an itemised bill?
Puis-je avoir une note détaillée?
pwee-jer ah-vwahr ewn nawt day-tah-yay

You have given me the wrong change
Vous vous êtes trompé en me rendant monnaie
voo voo zait trohm-pay an mer ran-dan moh-nay

This is not correct
C'est inexact
sai tee-naig-sahkt

This is not my bill
C'est addition n'est pas à moi
sait ahdee-syan nay paz ah mwa

I do not have enough currency
Je n'ai pas assez de liquide
jer nay pah ah-say der lee-keed

I do not have enough money
Je n'ai pas assez d'argent
jer nay pah ah-say dahr-jan

Complaints and compliments

Waiter! We have been waiting for a long time
Monsiuer/Madame/Mademoiselle! Nous attendons depuis longtemps
mer-syer/ma-dam/mad-mwa-zel noo zah-tan-don der-pwee lon-tan

This is cold
C'est froid
sai frwah

This is not what I ordered
Ce n'est pas ce que j'ai commandé
ser nai pah ser ker jay koh-man-day

Can I have the recipe?
Puis-je avoir la recette?
pwee-jer ah-vwahr lah rer-sait

This is excellent
C'est délicieux
sai day-lee-syer

The meal was excellent
Le repas était délicieux
ler rer-pah ay-tai day-lee-syer

Menu reader

abricots
ahb-ree-koh
apricots

ail
ah-ee
garlic

ananas
ah-nah-nah
pineapple

artichaut
ahr-tee-shoh
artichoke

asperge
ahs-pairj
asparagus

aubergine
oh-bair-jeen
aubergine

aubergines farcies
oh-bair-jeen fahr-see
stuffed aubergines

avocat
ah-voh-kah
avocado

bananes
bah-nahn
bananas

basilic
bah-see-leek
basil

beignets
bay-nyay
doughnuts, fritters

betterave
bait-rahv
beetroot

beurre
berr
butter

bifteck
beef-taik
beefsteak

blanquette de veau
blan-kait der voh
veal in white sauce

boeuf bourguignon
berf boor-gee-nyon
beef stewed in red wine

boeuf braisé
berf bray-zay
braised beef

boeuf en daube
berf an dohb
beef stew

bouillabaisse
boo-yah-bais
spicy fish soup with garlic

bouillon de boeuf
boo-yon der berf
beef broth

bouillon de poulet
boo-yon der poo-lay
chicken broth

calmar
kahl-mahr
squid

canard
kah-nahr
duck

canard à l'orange
kah-nahr ah loh-ranj
duck with orange

carottes
kah-roht
carrots

cassis
kah-see
blackcurrants

céleri
say-lai-ree
celery

cerfeuil
sair-fery
chervil

cerises
ser-reez
cherries

champignons
shan-pee-nyon
mushrooms

champignons à l'ail
shan-peen-yon ah lah-ee
mushrooms with garlic

champignons en sauce
shan-peen-yon an sohs
mushrooms in sauce

chicorée
shee-koh-ray
chicory, endive

chou
shoo
cabbage

choucroute
shoo-kroot
sauerkraut

chou-fleur
shoo-fler
cauliflower

choux de Bruxelles
shoo der brew-sail
Brussels sprouts

ciboulette
see-boo-lait
chives

citron
see-tron
lemon

civet de lapin
see-vay der lah-pern
rabbit stew

compote de pommes
kohm-poht der pohm
apple compote

concombre
kon-kohmbr
cucumber

confiture
kon-fee-tewr
jam

coq au vin
kohk oh vern
coq au vin

cornichon
kohr-nee-shon
gherkin

côtelette d'agneau
koht-lait dahn-yoh
lamb cutlet

côtelette de porc
koht-lait der pohr
pork cutlet

côtelette de veau
koht-lait der voh
veal cutlet

côtelette grillée
koht-lait gree-yay
grilled cutlet

coulis de pommes
koo-lee der pohm
apple sauce

courge
koorj
squash

courgettes
koor-jait
courgettes

crème anglaise
kraim an-glayz
custard

crème caramel
kraim kah-rah-mail
caramel custard

cresson
krai-son
watercress

crêpes
kraip
thin pancakes

— à la confiture
— *ah lah kon-fee-tewr*
— with jam

— au chocolat
— *oh shoh-koh-lah*
— with chocolate

croque-monsieur
krohk-mer-syer
cheese and ham toasted sandwich

cuisses de grenouilles
kwees der grer-nooy
frogs' legs

dattes
daht
dates

dessert
day-sair
pudding

dinde
dernd
turkey

échalottes
ay-shah-loht
shallots

en sauce
an sohs
in sauce

épinards
ay-pee-nahr
spinach

estragon
ais-trah-gon
tarragon

faisan
fay-san
pheasant

feuille de laurier
fery der loh-ryay
bayleaf

fèves
faiv
broad beans

filet de boeuf
fee-lay der berf
steak fillet

filet de colin
fee-lay der koh-lern
hake fillet

flan au fromage blanc
flan oh froh-mahj blan
cheesecake

fondue savoyarde
fon-dew sah-voh-yahrd
cheese fondue

fraises
fraiz
strawberries

fraises à la crème fraîche
fraiz ah lah kraim fraish
strawberries with cream

framboises
fran-bwahz
raspberries

frites
freet
French fries/chips

fruits à la crème fouettée
frwee zah lah kraim fwai-tay
fruit with whipped cream

gâteau
gah-toh
cake

gâteau aux amandes
gah-toh oh zah-mand
almond cake

gâteau de riz
gah-toh der ree
rice pudding

gâteau de Savoie
gah-toh der sah-vwah
sponge cake

gigot d'agneau
jee-goh dahn-yoh
roast leg of lamb

glace
glahs
ice cream

grenades
grer-nahd
pomegranates

grillé/au feu de bois
gree-yay/oh fer der bwah
grilled/barbecued

hachis parmentier
ahshee pahr-man-tyay
shepherd's pie

haricots blancs
ah-ree-koh blan
haricot beans

haricots verts
ah-ree-koh vair
French beans

homard
oh-mahr
lobster

huile
weel
oil

huîtres
weetr
oysters

jambon fumé
jan-bon few-may
cured ham

jardinière de légumes
jahr-dee-nyair der lay-gewm
diced vegetables

jarret (d'agneau, etc)
jah-ray (dahn-yoh)
shank (of lamb etc)

laitue
lay-tew
lettuce

langouste
lan-goost
crayfish

langue
lang
tongue

lapin farci
lah-pern fahr-see
stuffed rabbit

légumes
lay-gewm
vegetables

maïs
mah-ees
sweet corn

maquereau
mahk-roh
mackerel

maquereau
mahk-roh
mackerel

melon
mer-lon
melon

menthe
mant
mint

meringue au citron
may-rerng oh see-tron
lemon meringue

moules
mool
mussels

mousse au chocolat
moos oh shoh-koh-lah
chocolate mousse

moules frites
mool freet
mussels and French fries

moules marinières
mool mah-ree-nyair
mussels in wine and garlic

navet
nah-vay
turnip

oeuf à la coque
erf ah lah kohk
soft boiled egg

oeufs au bacon
er zoh bah-kon
eggs with bacon

oeufs au jambon
er zoh jan-bon
eggs with ham

oeufs au plat
er zoh plah
fried eggs

oeufs brouillés
er brwee-yay
scrambled eggs

oie
wah
goose

oignons
wahn-yon
onions

olives
oh-leev
olives

oranges
oh-ranj
oranges

palourdes
pah-loord
clams

pamplemousse
panp-moos
grapefruit

panais
pah-nai
parsnip

pastèque
pahs-taik
watermelon

pâtes
paht
pasta

pâtes aux oeufs
paht oh zer
egg noodles

pêche
paish
peach

persil
pair-seel
parsley

petits pains
per-tee pern
bread rolls

petits pois
per-tee pwah
sweet, young peas

poire
pwahr
pear

poireaux
pwah-roh
leeks

poisson
pwah-son
fish

poisson mariné
pwah-son mah-ree-nay
marinated fish

poivron rouge
pwahv-ron rooj
red pepper

poivron vert
pwahv-ron vair
green pepper

pomme au four
pohm oh foor
roast apple

pommes
pohm
apples

pommes de terre dauphinoises
pohm der tair doh-fee-nwahz
sliced potatoes baked with cream and cheese

pommes rôties
pohm roh-tee
roast potatoes

potage aux champignons
poh-tahj oh shan-pee-nyon
cream of mushroom soup

potage aux haricots rouges
poh-tahj oh zah-ree-koh rooj
kidney-bean soup

potage aux poireaux
poh-tahj oh pwah-roh
leek soup

potage aux pois
poh-tahj oh pwah
pea soup

potage aux tomates
poh-tahj oh toh-maht
tomato soup

potage de légumes
poh-tahj der lay-gewm
cream of vegetable soup

potage de poulet
poh-tahj der poo-lay
chicken soup

poulet frit/pané
poo-lay freet/pah-nay
fried/breaded chicken

poulet rôti
poo-lay roh-tee
baked/roasted chicken

prunes
prewn
plums

purée de pommes de terre
pew-ray der pohm der tair
mashed potatoes

radis
rah-dee
radishes

ragoût de boeuf
rah-goo der berf
beef stew

ragoût de poulet
rah-goo der poo-lay
chicken stew

raisins
rai-zern
grapes

reines-claude
rain-klohd
greengages

rillettes
reel-ait
potted meat

rognons en sauce
roh-nyon an sohs
stewed kidney

romarin
roh-mah-rern
rosemary

rôti de porc
roh-tee der pohr
roast pork

rouget
roo-jay
mullet

salade
sah-lahd
salad

salade composée
sah-lahd kohm-poh-say
mixed salad

salade de concombre
sah-lahd der kon-kohmbr
cucumber salad

salade de fruits
sah-lahd der frwee
fruit salad

salade de maïs
sah-lahd der mah-ees
corn salad

salade de pommes de terre
sah-lahd der pohm der tair
potato salad

salade de tomates
sah-lahd der toh-maht
tomato salad

salade russe
sah-lahd rews
Russian salad

sandwich au jambon
san-weesh oh jan-bon
ham sandwich

sardines
sahr-deen
sardines

sauce à l'oignon
sohs ah loh-nyon
onion sauce

sauce au vin
sohs oh vern
wine sauce

sauce aux poivrons verts
sohs oh pwahv-ron vair
green pepper sauce

sauce tomate
sohs toh-maht
tomato sauce

saucisse
soh-sees
sausage

sauge
sohj
sage

scampi
skahm-pee
scampi

seiche
saish
cuttlefish

sole meunière
sohl mer-nyair
sole in butter with parsley

steack au poivre
staik oh pwahvr
pepper steak

steack frites
staik freet
steak and French fries

tarte
tahrt
pie

tarte aux pommes
tahrt oh pohm
apple tart

thon
ton
tuna

thym
tern
thyme

tomates
toh-maht
tomatoes

tripes
treep
tripe

truite
trweet
trout

truite au beurre
trweet oh berr
fried trout

truite grillée
trweet gree-yay
grilled trout

viande
vee-and
meat

viande grillée
vee-and gree-yay
grilled meat

vinaigre
vee-naigr
vinegar

wiener schnitzel (escalope de veau panée)
ais-kah-lohp der voh pah-nay
veal escalope

yaourt
yah-oor
yoghurt

Drinks

armagnac
ahr-mahn-yahk
armagnac

bière
byair
beer

bière brune
byair brewn
stout

bière en boîte
byair an bwaht
canned beer

bière en canette
byair an kah-nait
bottled beer

café
kah-fay
black coffee

café au lait
kah-fay oh lay
coffee with milk (breakfast)

café crème
kah-fay kraim
coffee with steamed milk

café glacé
kah-fay glah-say
iced coffee

café irlandais
kah-fay eer-lan-day
Irish coffee

café soluble
kah-fay soh-lewb
instant coffee

calvados
kahl-vah-dohs
apple brandy

camomille
kah-moh-meel
camomile tea

champagne
shan-pah-nyer
champagne

cidre
seedr
cider

coca-cola
koh-kah-koh-lah
coke

cognac
kohn-yahk
brandy

déca
day-kah
decaffeinated coffee

eau minérale
oh mee-nay-rahl
mineral water

express
aiks-prais
expresso coffee

jus d'orange
jew doh-ranj
orange juice

jus de pomme
jew der pohm
apple juice

jus de raisin
jew der rai-zern
grape juice

kir
keer
blackcurrant liqueur

kirsch
keersh
cherry brandy

limonade
lee-moh-nahd
lemonade

liqueur
lee-kerr
liqueur

nectar d'abricot
naik-tahr dah-bree-koh
apricot juice

nectar de pêche
naik-tahr der paish
peach juice

orangeade
oh-ran-jahd
orange drink

pastis
pahs-tee
aniseed spirit

rhum
ron
rum

sangria
sahn-gree-ah
sangria

Schweppes
shwaips
tonic water

soda
soh-dah
soda

thé au lait
tay oh lay
tea with milk

thé citron
tay see-tron
lemon tea

un cognac
an koh-nyahk
a brandy

un (verre de) vin blanc
ern vair der vern blan
a glass of white wine

un (verre de) vin rouge
ern vair der vern rooj
a glass of red wine

une bière
ewn byair
a large beer

vin rosé
vern roh-zay
rosé wine

whisky
wees-kee
whisky

Out and About

The weather

The climate of France is not generally the main reason why people visit the country – unless they have chosen a skiing holiday. The climate of northern France is not unlike our own and is prone to rain and unpredictable changes. The centre, east and south of France have warmer climates, while the west coast is cooled by its proximity to the Atlantic Ocean.

Isn't it a lovely day?
Belle journée, n'est-ce pas?
bail joor-nay, nais pah

Is it going to get any warmer?
Est-ce qu'il va faire plus chaud?
ais keel vah fair plew shoh

Is it going to stay like this?
Est-ce que ce temps va durer?
ais ker ser tan vah dew-ray

Is there going to be a thunderstorm?
Va-t-il y avoir un orage?
vah-teel ee ah-vwahr ern oh-rahj

It has stopped snowing
Il ne neige plus
eel ner naij plew

There is a cool breeze
Il y a un vent frais
eel yah ern van frai

What is the temperature?
Quelle est la température?
kail ai lah tan-pay-rah-tewr

Will the weather improve?
Est-ce que le temps va s'arranger?
ais ker ler tan vah sah-ran-jay

It is far too hot
Il fait beaucoup trop chaud
eel fai boh-koo troh shoh

It is foggy
Il y a du brouillard
eel yah dew brwee-yahr

It is going to be fine
Il va faire beau
eel vah fair boh

It is going to be windy
Il va faire du vent
eel vah fair dew van

It is going to rain
Il va pleuvoir
eel vah pler-vwahr

It is going to snow
Il va neiger
eel vah nai-jay

It is raining again
Il pleut de nouveau
eel pler der noo-voh

It is very cold
Il fait très froid
eel fai trai frwah

It is very windy
Il y a beaucoup de vent
eel yah boh-koo der van

Will the wind die down?
Est-ce que le vent va tomber?
ais-ker ler van vah tohm-bay

On the beach

Can you recommend a quiet beach?
Pouvez-vous nous recommander une plage tranquille?
poo-vay voo noo rer-koh-man-day ewn plahj tran-keel

Is it safe to swim here?
Peut-on se baigner ici sans danger?
per-ton ser bain-yay ee-see san dan-jay

Is the current strong?
Est-ce que le courant est fort?
ais ker ler koo-ran ai fohr

Is the sea calm?
Est-ce que la mer est calme?
ais ker lah mair ai kahlm

Is there a lifeguard here?
Y a-t-il un maître nageur?
ee-ah-teel an maitr nah-jerr

Is this beach private?
Est-ce que la plage est privée?
ais ker lah plahj ai pree-vay

When is	**— high tide?**
A quelle heure est	— la marée haute?
ah kail err ai	— *lah mah-ree oht*

	— low tide?
	— la marée basse?
	— *lah mah-ree bahs*

Can I rent	**— a sailing boat?**
Puis-je louer	— un voilier?
pweej loo-ay	— *ern vwah-lyay*

Can I rent	**— a rowing boat?**
Puis-je louer	— une barque?
pweej loo-ay	— *ewn bahrk*

Is it possible to go	**— sailing?**
Peut-on faire	— de la voile?
per-ton fair	— *der lah vwahl*

	— surfing?
	— du surf?
	— *dew sewrf*

	— water skiing?
	— du ski nautique?
	— *dew skee noh-teek*

	— wind surfing?
	— de la planche à voile?
	— *der lah plansh ah vwahl*

Sport and recreation

Can we play	**— tennis?**
Peut-on jouer	— au tennis?
per-ton joo-ay	— *oh tay-nees*

	— golf?
	— au golf?
	— *oh gohlf*

Can we play	**— volleyball?**
Peut-on jouer	— au volley-ball?
per-ton joo-ay	— *oh voh-lay-bohl*

Can I rent the equipment?
Puis-je louer le matériel?
pweej loo-ay ler mah-tay-ryail

Can we go riding?
Peut-on monter à cheval?
per-ton mon-tay ah sher-vahl

Where can we fish?
Où peut-on faire de la pêche?
oo per-ton fair der lah paish

Do I need a permit?
Ai-je besoin d'un permis?
ai-jer ber-zwern dern pair-mee

Is there a heated swimming pool?
Y a-t-il une piscine chauffée?
ee-ah-teel ewn pee-seen shoh-fay

Entertainment

Is there	**— a disco?**
Y a-t-il	— une disco(thèque)?
ee-ah-teel	— *ewn dees-koh(taik)*

	— a good nightclub?
	— une bonne boîte de nuit?
	— *ewn bohn bwaht der nwee*

	— a theatre?
	— un théâtre?
	— *ern tay-ahtr*

	— a casino?
	— un casino
	— *ern kah-see-noh*

Are there any films in English?
Y a-t-il des films en anglais?
ee-ah-teel day feelm zan an-glay

How much is it per person?
Ça coûte combien par personne?
Sah koot kohm-byern pahr pair-sohn

Two stall tickets, please
Deux orchestres, s'il vous plaît
der-zohr-kaistr, seel voo play

Two tickets, please
Deux billets, s'il vous plaît
der bee-yay, seel voo play

How much is it to get in?
C'est combien pour l'entrée?
sai kohm-byern poor lan-tray

Is there a reduction for children?
Y a-t-il une réduction pour les enfants?
ee-ah-teel ewn ray-dewk-syon poor lay zan-fan

Sightseeing

Are there any — boat trips on the river?
Y a-t-il — des promenades en bateau sur la
rivière?
*ee-ah-teel — day prohm-nahd an bah-toh sewr lah
reevyair*

— guided tours of the castle?
— des visites guidées du château?
— day vee-seet gee-day dew shah-toh

— guided tours?
— des visites guidées?
— day vee-seet gee-day

What is the admission charge?
Combien coûte le billet?
kohm-byern koot ler bee-yay

What is there to see here?
Qu'y a-t-il à voir par ici?
kyah-teel ah vwahr pahr ee-see

Can we go up to the top?
Peut-on aller jusqu'en haut?
per-ton ah-lay jewsk an oh

What time does the gallery open?
A quelle heure ouvre la galerie?
ah kail err oovr lah gah-lai-ree

Can I take photos?
Puis-je prendre des photos?
pweej prandr day foh-toh

Can I use flash?
Puis-je utiliser le flash?
pweej ew-tee-lee-zay ler flahsh

When is the bus tour?
A quelle heure est l'excursion en autocar?
ah kail err ai laiks-kewr-syon an oh-toh-kahr

How long does the tour take?
Combien de temps dure l'excursion?
kohm-byern der tan dewr laiks-kewr-syon

What is this building?
Cet édifice, qu'est-ce que c'est?
sait ay-dee-fees, kais ker sai

When was it built?
Quand a-t-il été construit?
kan tah-teel ay-tay kon-strwee

Is it open to the public?
Est-il ouvert au public?
ai-teel oo-vair oh pewb-leek

Can we go in?
Peut-on entrer?
per-ton an-tray

Do you have a guide book?
Avez-vous un guide?
ah-vay voo zern geed

Is there a tour of the cathedral?
Y a-t-il une visite de la cathédrale?
ee-ah-teel ewn vee-seet der lah kah-tay-drahl

Is there an English-speaking guide?
Y a-t-il un guide anglophone?
ee-ah-teel ern geed an-gloh-fohn

Is this the best view?
Est-ce le plus beau panorama?
ais ler plew boh pah-noh-rah-mah

Souvenirs

Where can I buy postcards?
Où puis-je acheter des cartes postales?
oo pweej ahsh-tay day kahrt pohs-tahl

Where can we buy souvenirs?
Où peut-on acheter des souvenirs?
oo per ton ahsh-tay day soo-ver-neer

Have you got an English guidebook?
Avez-vous un guide en anglais?
ah-vay voo zern geed an an-glay

Have you got any colour slides?
Avez-vous des diapos(itives) en couleur?
ah-vay voo day dyah-poh(see-teev) an koo-lerr

How much does that cost?
C'est combien, s'il vous plaît?
sai kohm-byern, seel voo play

Have you got anything cheaper?
Avez-vous quelque chose de moins cher?
ah-vay voo kail-ker shohz der mwan shair

Going to church

Where is — the Catholic church?
Où est — l'église catholique?
oo ai   — lay-gleez kah-toh-leek

— the Baptist church?
— l'église baptiste?
— lay-gleez bahp-teest

— the mosque?
— la mosquée?
— lah mohs-kay

— the Protestant church?
— le temple?
— ler tanpl

— the synagogue?
— la synagogue?
— lah seen-ah-gohg

What time is the service?
A quelle heure est la messe?
ah kail err ai lah mais

I would like to see   — a priest
Je voudrais voir   — un prêtre
jer voo-dray vwahr   — ern praitr

— a minister
— un pasteur
— ern pahs-terr

— a rabbi
— un rabbin
— ern rah-bern

Shopping

General information

Nowhere is the culture gap between Britain and France clearer than in the matter of shopping. Department stores and small supermarkets have little importance outside Paris and other very big city centres; instead, in every town and in most villages, there are small, specialised shops and boutiques, while on the outskirts of large towns can be found furniture and DIY warehouses and enormous hypermarkets.

It is the care and flair that the French put into the preparation of food that most visitors find remarkable. Stalls and counters provide a feast for the eyes and a delight to the nose. Every town and sizeable village has regular markets, from early morning to midday once or twice a week, which are the best source for fresh fruit and vegetables and often for cheese, meat and fish; prices are always lower than in the shops. The

hypermarkets, too, are cheap and offer a huge range of high-quality food plus all sorts of other goods. Among the best bargains are table wine, bottled beer, coffee beans, olive oil and cast-iron cookware.

Most shops open early in the morning and stay open well into the evening but have a long midday break; food shops – particularly bakers, cake shops and delicatessens – are often open on Sunday morning. Many shops close all day on Monday. Hypermarket opening hours are long – usually 8am or 10am to 10pm, including Mondays.

Les médicaments (medicines) are sold in *pharmacies*, cosmetics in *parfumeries*. You can get stamps (*des timbres*) from a general newsagent (*marchand de journaux*), a tobacconist (*bureau de tabac*) or a bookshop (*librairie*).

General phrases and requests

I would like that one
Je voudrais celui-là
jer voo-dray ser-lwee-lah

No, the other one
Non, l'autre
non, lohtr

I would like that one over there?
Je voudrais l'autre, là-bas
jer voo-dray lohtr, lah-bah

I would like the other one
Je voudrais l'autre
jer voo-dray lohtr

Can I have a carrier bag?
Avez-vous un sac?
ah-vay voo zern sahk

Can I pay for air insurance?
Puis-je payer l'assurance pour un colis avion?
pweej pay-yay lah-sew-rans poor ern koh-lee ah-vyon

Can I see that umbrella?
Puis-je regarder ce parapluie?
pweej rer-gahr-day ser pah-rah-plwee

Can I use traveller's cheques?
Puis-je utiliser des chèques de voyage?
pweej ew-tee-lee-zay day shaik der voh-yahj

Can you deliver it to my hotel?
Pouvez-vous le livrer à mon hôtel?
poo-vay voo ler leev-ray ah mon oh-tail

Have you got anything cheaper?
Avez-vous quelque chose de moins cher?
ah-vay voo kail-ker shohz der mwan shair

How much does that cost?
C'est combien, s'il vous plaît?
sai kohm-byern, seel voo play

How much is it per kilo?
C'est combien le kilo?
sai kohm-byern ler kee-loh

How much is it per metre?
C'est combien le mètre?
sai kohm-byern ler maitr

I am looking for a souvenir
Je cherche un souvenir
jer shairsh ern soov-neer

I do not like it
Cela ne me plaît pas
ser-lah ner mer plai pah

I like this one
Ceci me plaît
ser-see mer plai

I will take this one
Je vais prendre celui-ci
jer vai prandr ser-lwee-see

Is there a reduction for children?
Y a-t-il une réduction pour les enfants?
ee-ah-teel ewn ray-dewk-syon poor lay zan-fan

Please forward a receipt to this address
Envoyez un reçu à cette adresse, je vous prie
an-vwah-yay ern rer-sew ah sait ah-drais, jer voo pree

Please pack it for shipment
Emballez-le pour l'expédition, s'il vous plaît
an-bah-lay-ler poor laiks-pay-dee-syon, seel voo play

Please wrap it up for me
Emballez-le, je vous prie
an-bah-lay-ler, jer voo pree

There is no need to wrap it
Ce n'est pas la peine de l'emballer
ser nai pah lah pain der lan-bah-lay

We need to buy some food
Il faut acheter de la nourriture
eel foh ahsh-tay der lah noo-ree-tewr

Where can I buy cassette tapes and compact discs?
Où puis-je trouver des cassettes et des disques laser?
oo pwee-jer troo-vay day kah-sait ay day deesk lah-zair

Where can I buy some clothes?
Où puis-je acheter des vêtements?
oo pweej ahsh-tay day vait-man

Where can I buy tapes for my camcorder?
Où puis-je trouver des cassettes pour mon caméscope?
oo pweej troo-vay day kah-sait poor mon kah-may-skohp

Where can I get my camcorder repaired?
Où puis-je faire réparer mon caméscope?
oo pweej fair ray-pah-ray mon kah-may-skohp

Will you send it by air freight?
Pouvez-vous l'expédier par avion?
poo-vay voo laiks-pay-dyay pahr ah-vyon

Where is the children's department?
Où est le rayon enfants?
oo ai ler rah-yon an-fan

Where is the food department?
Où est le rayon alimentation?
oo ai ler rah-yon ah-lee-man-tah-syon

Specialist food shops

Boulangeries and pâtisseries
Bread and pastry shops Most French bread doesn't keep long, so it has to be very fresh. The traditional loaf is the long, thin, crusty white *baguette*, sold in various sizes; longer-lasting breads – wholemeal, rye and country loaves – are increasingly available. Breakfast treats include *croissants* and the sweet *brioche* and *pain au chocolat*, flaky pastry with chocolate filling.

Patisseries are for serious cakes, freshly made on the premises. Shops generally have a particular speciality – such as rich chocolate *gâteaux*, fruit tarts, fancy biscuits or hand-made chocolates.

Boucheries and charcuteries
Butchers' and delicatessens High quality and meticulous preparation are the trademarks of a French butcher so prices may seem high. The range of produce is usually much larger than at home – including a wider range of poultry, game, rabbits and hares – and cuts of meat may be different. Minced meat (*hâché*) can be prepared in several qualities, including the ultra-lean *tartare* for eating raw.

French delicatessens provide pâtés and terrines, quiches and pizzas, puddings and pies, hams and sausages, and ready-made *hors d'oeuvre* and sometimes main dishes such as beef cooked in wine.

Poissonneries

Fish shops There are far more fish stalls in France than proper fish shops. Even inland, there's a surprisingly good choice, ranging from the tiniest winkle to tunny fish of massive proportions, invariably very fresh. There are plenty of fish that you can take home and simply grill – sole, trout, prawns, fresh sardines, for example – and also many less familiar sights and some that are suitable only for soups and stews. Fishmongers will willingly clean and gut (*vider*) the fish for you.

Oysters are excellent value. By combining oysters with mussels, prawns, clams and other seafood you can make up your own *plateau de fruits de mer* – an expensive dish in any restaurant but one that you can put together fairly cheaply near the coast.

Crémeries, fromageries and épiceries

Dairy, cheese and grocers' shops In regions rich in dairy products, specialist *crémeries* (dairies) are common. Milk is commonly UHT – heat-treated and long-lasting, which bears no resemblance to real milk; non-UHT pasteurised milk is sometimes hard to find.

The widest variety of cheese comes from a *fromagerie*. Made from cows', goats' or ewes' milk, it ranges from mild to very strong and smelly; it's worth trying Brie or Camembert made from unpasteurised milk (*lait cru*), which is quite unlike the average supermarket product at home.

Grocers' shops (*épiceries*) are useful, particularly for high-quality tins or jars of vegetables or soups.

Buying groceries

I would like Je voudrais *jer voo-dray*	— **a kilo of potatoes** — un kilo de pommes de terre — *ern kee-loh der pohm der tair*	**Can I have** Je voudrais *jer voo-dray*	— **5 slices of ham, please?** — cinq tranches de jambon, s'il vous plaît — *sank transh der jan-bon, seel voo play*
	— **a bar of chocolate** — une tablette de chocolat — *ewn tah-blait der shoh-koh-lah*		— **100 g of ground coffee?** — cent grammes de café moulu, s'il vous plaît — *san grahm der kah-fay moo-lew, seel voo play*
	— **a litre of milk** — un litre de lait — *ern leetr der lay*		— **half a dozen eggs, please?** — six oeufs, s'il vous plaît — *see zer, seel voo play*
	— **two steaks** — deux biftecks — *der beef-taik*		— **half a kilo of butter, please?** — une livre de beurre, s'il vous plaît — *ewn leevr der berr, seel voo play*
Can I have Je voudrais *jer voo-dray*	— **some sugar, please?** — du sucre, s'il vous plaît — *dew sewkr, seel voo play*		
	— **a bottle of wine, please?** — une bouteille de vin, s'il vous plaît — *ewn boo-tery der vern, seel voo play*		

At the newsagent's

I would like Je voudrais *jer voo-dray*	— **some postage stamps** — des timbres — *day termbr*	**I need** Il me faut *eel mer foh*	— **some adhesive tape** — du scotch — *dew skohtsh*
	— **postcards** — des cartes postales — *day kahrt pohs-tahl*		— **a bottle of ink** — une bouteille d'encre — *zewn boo-tery dankr*

I need
Il me faut
eel me foh

— **a pen**
— un stylo
— *zern stee-loh*

— **a pencil**
— un crayon
— *zern kray-yon*

— **some envelopes**
— des enveloppes
— *day zan-vai-lohp*

— **some note paper**
— du papier à lettres
— *dew pah-pyay ah laitr*

Do you have
Avez-vous
ah-vay voo

— **English paperbacks?**
— des livres de poche anglais?
— *day leevr der pohsh an-glay*

— **a local map?**
— une carte de la région?
— *ewn kahrt der lah ray-jyon*

— **street maps?**
— des plans de ville?
— *day plan der veel*

Do you have
Avez-vous
ah-vay voo

— **a road map?**
— une carte routière?
— *zewn kahrt roo-tyair*

— **coloured pencils?**
— des crayons de couleur?
— *day kray-yon der koo-lerr*

— **felt pens?**
— des stylos-feutres?
— *day stee-loh fertr*

— **drawing paper?**
— du papier à dessin?
— *dew pah-pyay ah dai-sern*

— **English newspapers?**
— des journaux anglais?
— *day joor-noh zan-glay*

— **English books?**
— des livres anglais?
— *day leevr zan-glay*

At the tobacconist's

Do you have
Avez-vous
ah-vay voo

— **cigarette papers?**
— du papier à cigarettes?
— *dew pah-pyay ah see-gah-rait*

— **a box of matches?**
— une boîte d'allumettes?
— *ewn bwaht dah-lew-mait*

— **a cigar?**
— un cigare?
— *ern see-gahr*

— **a cigarette lighter?**
— un briquet?
— *ern bree-kay*

— **a pipe?**
— une pipe?
— *ewn peep*

— **a gas (butane) refill?**
— une cartouche de gaz?
— *ewn kahr-toosh der gahz*

— **a pouch of pipe tobacco?**
— un paquet de tabac à pipe?
— *ern pah-kay der tah-bahk ah peep*

Do you have
Avez-vous
ah-vay voo

— **some pipe cleaners?**
— des cure-pipes?
— *day kewr-peep*

A packet of...please
Un paquet de... s'il vous plaît
ern pah-kay der... seel voo play

A packet of...please, with filter tips
Un paquet de... s'il vous plaît, à bout filtre
ern pah-kay der... seel voo play, ah boo feeltr

A packet of...please, without filters
Un paquet de... s'il vous plaît, sans filtre
ern pah-kay der... seel voo play, san feeltr

Have you got any
Avez-vous
ah-vay voo

— **English brands?**
— des cigarettes anglaises?
— *day see-gah-rait an-glaiz*

— **American brands?**
— des cigarettes américaines?
— *day see-gah-rait ah-may-ree-kain*

— **rolling tobacco?**
— du tabac à cigarettes?
— *dew tah-bahk ah see-gaa-rait*

At the chemist's

I need some high-protection suntan cream
Je veux une crème solaire pour peau délicate
jer ver ewn kraim soh-lair poor poh day-lee-kaht

Do you sell sunglasses?
Vendez-vous des lunettes de soleil?
van-day voo day lew-nait der soh-lery

Can you give me something for— insect bites?
Avez-vous quelque chose contre— les piqûres
d'insectes?
*ah-vay voo kail-ker shohz kawntr   — lay pee-kewr
dern-saikt*

— an upset stomach?
— le mal à l'estomac?
— ler mahl ah lais-toh-mah

— a cold?
— un rhume?
— ern rewm

— a cough?
— une toux?
— ewn too

— a headache?
— les maux de tête?
— lay moh der tait

— a sore throat?
—un mal de gorge?
— ern mahl der gohrj

Can you give me something for — hay fever?
Avez-vous quelque-chose contre — le rhume des
foins?
*ah-vay voo kail-ker shohz kawntr   — ler rewm day
fwern*

— toothache?
— le mal aux dents?
— ler mahl oh dan

— sunburn?
— un coup de soleil?
— ern koo der soh-lery

Do I need a prescription?
Ai-je besoin d'une ordonnance?
ay-jer ber-zwern dewn ohr-doh-nans

How many do I take?
Combien de cachets dois-je prendre?
kohm-byern der kah-shay dwah-jer prandr

How often do I take them?
Je les prends tous les combien?
jer lay pran too lay kohm-byern

Are they safe for children to take?
Est-ce qu'ils conviennent aux enfants?
ais keel kon-vyain oh zan-fan

Shopping for clothes

I am just looking, thank you
Je ne fais que regarder, merci
jer ner fai ker rer-gahr-day, mair-see

I like that one there
J'aime bien celui-là
jaim byern ser-lwee-lah

I like the one in the window
J'aime bien celui qui est en vitrine
jaim byern ser-lwee kee ai an vee-treen

I like this one
J'aime bien celui-ci
jaim byern ser-lwee-see

I like it
Il me plaît
eel mer plai

I do not like it
Il ne me plaît pas
eel ner mer plai pah

I will take it
Je le prends
jer ler pran

Can I change it if it does not fit?
Puis-je le rapporter s'il ne me va pas?
pweej ler rah-pohr-tay seel ner mer vah pah

Can you please measure me?
Pouvez-vous prendre mes mesures, s'il vous plaît?
poo-vay voo prandr may mer-sewr, seel voo play

Have you got a larger size?
Avez-vous une taille plus grande?
ah-vay voo ewn tah-ee plew grand

Have you got this in other colours?
Avez-vous ceci dans une autre teinte?
ah-vay voo ser-see dan zewn ohtr ternt

I take a large shoe size
Je chausse grand
jer shohs gran

I take continental size ... 43
Je chausse du ... 43
jer shohs dew ... kah-rant trwah

I would like this suit
Je voudrais ce costume
jer voo-dray ser koh-stewm

I would like one with a zip
J'en voudrais un avec une fermeture éclair
jan voo-dray ern ah-vaik ewn fairm-tewr ay-klair

I would like this hat
Je voudrais ce chapeau
jer voo-dray ser shah-poh

I would like a smaller size
Je voudrais une taille plus petite
jer voo-dray ewn tah-ee plew per-teet

Where are the changing (dressing) rooms?
Où sont les cabines d'essayage?
oo son lay kah-been dai-say-yahj

Where can I try it on?
Où puis-je l'essayer?
oo pweej lai-say-yay

Is it too long?
Est-ce trop long?
ais troh lon

Is it too short?
Est-ce trop court?
ais troh koor

Is there a full-length mirror?
Y a-t-il un grand miroir?
ee-ah-teel ern gran meer-wahr

Is this all you have?
Est-ce tout ce que vous avez?
ais toos ker voo zah-vay

It does not fit
Ce n'est pas à ma taille
Ser nai pahz ah mah tahy

It does not suit me
Il ne me va pas
eel ner mer vah pah

May I see it in daylight?
Puis-je le regarder à la lumière du jour?
pwee-jer ler rer-gahr-day ah lah lew-myair dew joor

Is it drip-dry?
Faut-il le repasser?
foh-teel ler rer-pah-say

Is it dry-clean only?
Faut-il le nettoyer à sec seulement?
foh-teel ler nai-twah-yay ah saik serl-man

Is it machine washable?
Est-ce lavable à la machine?
ais lah-vahbl ah lah mah-sheen

What is it made of?
C'est en quel tissu?
sai tan kail tee-sew

Will it shrink?
Est-ce que ça rétrécit?
ais ker sah ray-tray-see

Photography

Can you develop this film, please?
Pouvez-vous développer cette pellicule, s'il vous plaît?
poo-vay voo dayv-loh-pay sait pay-lee-kewl, seel voo play

I would like this photo enlarged
Je voudrais un agrandissement de cette photo
jer voo-dray zern ah-gran-dees-man der sait foh-toh

I would like two prints of this one
Je voudrais deux copies de cette photo
jer voo-dray der koh-pee der sait foh-toh

When will the photos be ready?
Quand est-ce que les photos seront prêtes?
kan ais ker lay foh-toh ser-ron prait

I need a film for   **— this camera**
Je voudrais une pellicule pour — cet appareil
jer voo-dray zewn pay-lee-kewl poor — sait ah-pah-rery

         — this camcorder
         — ce caméscope
         — ser kah-may-skohp

I need a film for — this cine camera
Je voudrais une pellicule pour — cette caméra
er voo-dray zewn pay-lee-kewl poor— sait kah-may-rah

—this video camera
—cette caméra vidéo
—*sait kah-may-rah vee-dyoh*

I want a black and white film
Je veux une pellicule noir et blanc
jer ver ewn pay-lee-kewl nwahr ay blan

I want batteries for the flash
Je veux des piles pour le flash
jer ver day peel poor ler flahsh

I want a colour slide film
Je veux une pellicule couleur pour diapos(itives)
jer ver zewn pay-lee-kewl koo-lerr poor dyah-poh(-see-teev)

I want a colour print film
Je veux une pellicule couleur
jer ver zewn pay-lee-kewl koo-lerr

Camera repairs

I am having trouble with my camera
J'ai des problèmes avec mon appareil
jay day proh-blaim ah-vaik moh nah-pah-rery

There is something wrong with my camera
Mon appareil ne marche plus
moh nah-pah-rery ner mahrsh plew

This is broken
C'est cassé
sai kah-say

Where can I get my camera repaired?
Où puis-je faire réparer mon appareil?
oo pweej fair ray-pah-ray moh nah-pah-rery

Have you got a spare part for this?
Avez-vous une pièce de rechange pour ceci?
ah-vay voo zewn pyais der rer-shanj poor ser-see

The film is jammed
La pellicule est coincée
lah pay-lee-kewl ai kwern-say

Camera parts

accessory
accessoire
ahk-sai-swahr

blue filter
filtre bleu
feeltr bler

cassette
cassette
kah-sait

cartridge
cartouche
kahr-toosh

camcorder
caméscope
kah-may-skohp

cine camera
caméra
kah-may-rah

distance
distance
dees-tans

enlargement
agrandissement
ah-gran-dees-man

exposure
pose
pohz

exposure meter
posemètre
pohz-maitr

flash
flash
flahsh

flash bulb
ampoule de flash
an-pool der flahsh

flash cube
cube de flash
kewb der flahsh

focal distance
distance focale
dees-tans foh-kahl

focus
mise au point
meez oh pwan

in focus
net
nay

out of focus
flou
floo

image
image
ee-mahj

lens
objectif
ohb-jaik-teef

lens cover
bouchon d'objectif
boo-shon dohb-jaik-teef

over exposed
surexposé
sewr-aiks-poh-zay

picture
photo
foh-toh

projector
projecteur
proh-jaik-terr

print
épreuve
ay-prerv

negative
négatif
nay-gah-teef

red filter
filtre rouge
feeltr rooj

reel
bobine
boh-been

shade
nuance
new-ans

slide
diapositive
dyah-poh-zee-teef

shutter
obturateur
ohb-tew-rah-terr

shutter speed
vitesse d'obturateur
vee-tais dohb-tew-rah-terr

transparency
transparent
trans-pah-ran

tripod
tripode
tree-pohd

under exposed
sous-exposé
soo-zaiks-poh-zay

viewfinder
viseur
vee-zerr

wide-angle lens
objectif grand angle
ohb-jaik-teef gran tangl

At the hairdresser's

I would like to make an appointment
Je voudrais prendre rendez-vous
jer voo-dray prandr ran-day-voo

I want a haircut
Je veux me faire couper les cheveux
jer ver mer fair koo-pay lay sher-ver

Please cut my hair short
Coupez mes cheveux court, s'il vous plaît
koo-pay may sher-ver koor, seel voo play

Please cut my hair in a fringe
Coupez mes cheveux avec une frange
koo-pay may sher-ver ah-vaik ewn franjr

Take a little more off the back
Dégagez un peu plus à l'arrière
day-gah-jay ern per plews ah lah-ryair

I would like	**— a trim**
Je voudrais	— une coupe d'entretien
jer voo-dray	*— ewn koop dantr-tyern*
	— a conditioner
	— du baume démêlant
	— dew bohm day-mai-lan
	— a perm
	— une permanente
	— ewn pair-mah-nant

I would like	**— my hair streaked**
Je voudrais	— des mèches
jer voo-dray	*— day maish*

	— a blow-dry
	— un brushing
	— ern broo-sheeng

	— hair spray
	— de la laque
	— der lah lahk

	— my hair dyed
	— me les faire teindre
	— mer lay fair terndr

	— a shampoo and cut
	— un shampooing et une coupe
	— ern shahm-pweeng ay ewn koop

I would like	**— a shampoo and set**
Je voudrais	— un shampooing et une mise en plis
jer voo-dray	*— ern shahm pweeng ay ewn mee zan plee*

That is fine, thank you
C'est parfait, merci
sai pahr-fai, mair-see

Not too much off
Pas trop
pah troh

The dryer is too hot
Le séchoir est trop chaud
ler say-shwahr ai troh shoh

The water is too hot
L'eau est trop chaude
loh ai troh shohd

Laundry

Is there a launderette nearby?
Y a-t-il une laverie automatique près d'ici?
ee-ah-teel ewn lahv-ree oh-toh-mah-teek prai dee-see

Can you clean this skirt?
Pouvez-vous laver cette jupe?
poo-vay voo lah-vay sait jewp

Can you clean and press these shirts?
Pouvez-vous laver et repasser ces chemises?
poo-vay voo lah-vay ay rer-pah-say say sher-meez

Can you wash these clothes?
Pouvez-vous laver ces vêtements?
poo-vay voo lah-vay say vait-man

This stain is	**— oil**
Cette tache est	— de l'huile
sait tahsh ai	*— der lweel*

	— blood
	— du sang
	— dew san

	— coffee
	— du café
	— dew kah-fay

	— ink
	— de l'encre
	— der lankr

This fabric is	**— delicate**
Ce tissu est	— fin
ser tee-sew ai	*— fern*

This fabric is	**— damaged**
Ce tissu est	— endommagé
ser tee-sew ai	*— tan-doh-mah-jay*

	— torn
	— déchiré
	— day-shee-ray

Can you do it quickly?
Pouvez-vous le faire rapidement?
poo-vay voo ler fair rah-peed-man

When should I come back?
Quand dois-je revenir?
kan dwah-jer rerv-neer

When will my clothes be ready?
Quand puis-je passer prendre mes vêtements?
kan pwee-jer pah-say prandr may vait-man

How does the machine work?
Comment marche cette machine?
koh-man mahrsh sait mah-sheen

How long will it take?
Il y en a pour combien de temps?
eel yan ah poor kohm-byern der tan

I have lost my dry cleaning ticket
J'ai perdu mon coupon de nettoyage à sec
jay pair-dew mon koo-pon der nai-twah-yahj ah saik

General repairs

Can you repair it?
Pouvez-vous le réparer?
poo-vay voo ler ray-pah-ray

Can you repair them?
Pouvez-vous les réparer?
poo-vay voo lay ray-pah-ray

Would you have a look at this please?
Pourriez-vous y jeter un coup d'oeil, s'il vous plaît?
poo-ryay voo zee jer-tay an koo dery, seel voo play

Here is the guarantee
Voici la garantie
vwah-see lah gah-ran-tee

I need new heels on these shoes
Ces chaussures ont besoin de talons neufs
say shoh-sewr on ber-zwern der tah-lon nerf

I need them in a hurry
J'en ai besoin aussitôt que possible
john ay ber-zwern oh-see-toh ker poh-seebl

I will come back later
Je reviens plus tard
jer rer-vyern plew tahr

I will come back in an hour
Je reviens dans une heure
jer rer-vyern dan zewn err

Please send it to this address
Expédiez-le à cette adresse, s'il vous plaît
aiks-pay-dyay ler ah sait ah-drais, seel voo play

At the post office

Postage stamps are available at post offices (*bureaux de post* or *PTT* – pronounced *pay tay tay*) and from tobacconists (*tabacs*). Post boxes are painted yellow and are usually sited near *tabacs*.

Can I have a telegram form, please?
Donnez-moi un formulaire de télégramme, s'il vous plaît
doh-nay mwah ern fohr-mew-lair der tay-lay-grahm, seel voo play?

Can I have six stamps for postcards to Britain?
Donnez-moi six timbres pour cartes postales pour la Grande-Bretagne
doh-nay mwah see termbr poor kahrt pohs-tahl poor lah grand-brer-tahn

How much is a letter to	**— Britain?**
C'est combien pour une lettre pour	— la Grande-Bretagne?
say kohm-byern poor ewn laitr poor	— *la grand-brer-tahn*

     — **America?**
     — les États-Unis?
     — *lays-ayta-zewni*

12 stamps, please
Douze timbres, s'il vous plaît
dooz termbr, seel voo play

I need to send this by courier
Je voudrais envoyer ceci par coursier
jer voo-dray an-vwah-yay ser-see pahr koor-syay

I want to send a telegram
Je veux envoyer un télégramme
jer ver an-vwah-yay ern tay-lay-grahm

I want to send this by registered mail
Je veux envoyer ceci en recommandé
jer ver an-vwah-yay ser-see an rer-koh-man-day

I want to send this parcel
Je vex expédier ce colis
jer ver aiks-pay-dyay ser koh-lee

When will it arrive?
Quand arrivera-t-il à destination?
kan tah-reev-rah teel ah days-tee-nah-syon

Can I use my credit card?
Puis-je utiliser ma carte de crédit?
pweej ew-tee-lee-say mah kahrt der kray-dee

Using the telephone

When phoning from France to Britain you must dial 00, then 44, then the area code minus the initial 0, then the subscriber number. Coin boxes are being phased out so it is essential to buy a phone card (50- or 120-unit) although many call boxes also accept credit cards. Phone cards can be bought in *tabacs*, newsagents and post offices. If using a coin box, put the money in before dialling the number: they take 50-centimes, 1-franc, 5-franc or 10-franc pieces. For longer calls you may find it more convenient to phone from a major post office. You will be allocated a numbered kiosk with an ordinary phone and receive a bill at the end of the call. The drawback with this method is that you cannot keep track of what you are spending.

Can I use the telephone, please?
Puis-je me servir du téléphone, s'il vous plaît?
pweej mer sair-veer dew tay-lay-fohn, seel voo play

I must make a phone call to Britain
Il me faut téléphoner en Grande-Bretagne
eel mer foh tay-lay-foh-nay an grand-brer-tahn

I want to make a phone call
Je veux téléphoner
jer ver tay-lay-foh-nay

How much is it to phone to Paris?
C'est combien pour téléphoner à Paris?
sai kohm-byern poor tay-lay-foh-nay ah pah-ree

I would like to make a reversed charge (collect)
  call
Je voudrais téléphoner en PCV
jer voo-dray tay-lay-foh-nay an pay-say-vay

The number I need is…
Le numéro est le…
ler new-may-roh ai ler…

What is the code for   — Britain?
Quel est l'indicatif pour   — la Grande-Bretagne?
kail ai lern-dee-kah-teef poor   — lah grand-brer-tahn

           — America?
           — les États-Unis?
           — lays-ayta-zewni

Please, call me back
Rappelez-moi, s'il vous plaît
rah-play mwah, seel voo play

I am sorry. We were cut off
Je suis désolé. On nous a coupés
jer swee day-soh-lay. on noo zah koo-pay

What you may hear

J'essaie d'obtenir votre communication
jai-say dohb-ter-neer vohtr koh-mew-nee-kah-syon
I am trying to connect you

Je ne peux pas obtenir ce numéro
jer ner per pah zohb-ter-neer ser new-may-roh
I cannot get through to this number

Je vous passe Monsieur Brown
jer voo pahs mer-syer Broon
I am putting you through to Mr Brown

La ligne est occupée
lah leen ai toh-kew-pay
The line is engaged (busy)

Le numéro est en dérangement
ler new-may-roh ai an day-ranj-man
The number is out of order

Allez-y, vous êtes en ligne
ah-lay-zee, voo zait an leen
Please go ahead

Changing money

Can I change these traveller's cheques?
Puis-je changer ces chèques de voyage?
pweej shan-jay say shaik der voh-yahj

Can I change these notes (bills)?
Puis-je changer ces billets?
pweej shan-jay say bee-yay

Can I contact my bank to arrange for a transfer?
Puis-je contacter ma banque pour organiser un
  virement?
*pweej kon-tahk-tay mah bank poor ohr-gah-nee-zay ern
  veer-man*

Has my cash arrived?
Est-ce que mes fonds sont arrivés?
ais-ker may fon son tah-ree-vay?

Here is my passport
Voici mon passeport
vwah-see mon pahs-pohr

I would like to cash a cheque with my
  Eurocheque card
Je voudrais encaisser un chèque avec ma carte
  Eurochèque
*jer voo-dray an-kai-say ern shaik ah-vaik mah kahrt er-
  roh-shaik*

I would like to obtain a cash advance with my
  credit card
Je voudrais une avance en liquide sur ma carte de
  crédit
*jer voo-dray ewn ah-vans an lee-keed sewr mah kahrt der
  kray-dee*

This is the name and address of my bank
Voici le nom et l'adresse de ma banque
vwah-see ler nohm ay lah-drais der mah bank

What is the rate for sterling?
Quel est le taux de change pour la livre sterling?
kail ai ler toh der shanj poor lah leevr stair-leeng

What is the rate of exchange?
Quel est le taux de change?
kail ai ler toh der shanj

What is your commission?
Quelle est votre commission?
kail ai vohtr koh-mee-syon

Health

Health services

British travellers will need an E111 form, available in post offices, to be entitled to the same health services as French citizens. In France, every stage of treatment incurs a charge but employed French people are entitled to a refund of 70–75 per cent of medical and dental expenses. To qualify for this reimbursement of some of your expenses, find a doctor who is a *médecin conventionné* (the address of a doctor can be found at any *pharmacie*) whom you must ask for the relevant forms, but be prepared for a bit of paperwork when you return home. Prescriptions must be paid for at the *pharmacie*. All travellers, even those from the EU, would be wise to take out travel insurance and medical cover. The number to ring for a medical emergency is 15. The fire brigade are also able to deal with medical emergencies (telephone 18).

What's wrong?

Can I see a doctor?
Puis-je voir un médecin?
pwee-jer vwahr an mayd-sern

I need a doctor
Je veux voir un médecin
jer ver vwahr an mayd-sern

He has been badly injured
Il a été grièvement blessé
eel ah ay-tay gree-aiv-man blay-say

He has burnt himself
Il s'est brûlé
eel sai brew-lay

He has dislocated his shoulder
Il s'est démis l'épaule
eel sai day-mee lay-pohl

He is hurt
Il s'est fait mal
eel sai fai mahl

He is unconscious
Il a perdu connaissance
eel ah pair-dew koh-nai-sans

She has a temperature
Elle a de la fièvre
ail ah der lah fyaivr

She has been bitten
Elle a été mordue
ail ah ay-tay mohr-dew

She has sprained her ankle
Elle s'est tordu la cheville
ail sai tohr-dew lah sher-vee

My son has cut himself
Mon fils s'est coupé
mon fees sai koo-pay

My arm is broken
Mon bras est cassé
mon brah ai kah-say

I am badly sunburnt
J'ai attrapé un mauvais coup de soleil
jay ah-trah-pay ern moh-vai koo der soh-lery

I am ill
Je suis malade
jer swee mah-lahd

I am constipated
Je suis constipé
jer swee kon-stee-pay

I am a diabetic
Je suis diabétique
jer swee dyah-bay-teek

I am allergic to penicillin
Je suis allergique à la pénicilline
jer swee zah-lair-jeek ah lah pay-nee-see-leen

I have	— a headache
J'ai	— mal à la tete
jay	— *mahl ah lah tait*

I have
J'ai
jay

— **a pain here**
— mal là
— *mahl lah*

— **a rash here**
— une éruption là
— *ewn ay-rewp-syon lah*

— **sunstroke**
— une insolation
— *ewn ern-soh-lah-syon*

— **been stung**
— été piqué
— *ay-tay pee-kay*

— **a sore throat**
— mal à la gorge
— *mahl ah lah gohrj*

— **an earache**
— mal aux oreilles
— *oh zoh-rery*

— **cramp**
— une crampe
— *ewn krahmp*

— **diarrhoea**
— la diarrhée
— *lah dyah-ray*

— **been sick**
— J'ai vomi
— *jay voh-mee*

I have
Je me suis
jer mer swee

— **hurt my arm**
— fait mal au bras
— *fai mahl oh brah*

— **hurt my leg**
— fait mal à la jambe
— *fai mahl ah lah janb*

— **pulled a muscle**
— claqué un muscle
— *klah-kay ern mewskl*

— **cut myself**
— coupé
— *koo-pay*

It is
C'est
say

— **inflamed here**
— enflammé là
— *tan-flah-may lah*

— **painful to walk**
— douloureux de marcher
— *doo-loo-rer der mahr-shay*

It is
C'est
say

— **painful to breathe**
— douloureux de respirer
— *doo-loo-rer der rers-pee-ray*

— **painful to swallow**
— douloureux d'avaler
— *doo-loo-rers dah-vah-lay*

I feel dizzy
J'ai des étourdissements
jay day zay-toor-dees-man

I feel faint
Je me sens faible
jer mer san faibl

I feel nauseous
J'ai la nausée
jay lah noh-say

I fell
Je suis tombé
jer swee tohm-bay

I cannot sleep
Je n'arrive pas à dormir
jer nah-reev pah ah dohr-meer

I think I have food poisoning
Je crois que j'ai une intoxication alimentaire
jer krwah ker jay ewn ern-tohk-see-kah-syon ah-lee-man-tair

My stomach is upset
J'ai mal à l'estomac
jay mahl ah lais-toh-mah

My tongue is coated
J'ai la langue chargée
jay lah lan-g shahr-jay

There is a swelling here
C'est enflé là
sai tan-flay lah

I need some antibiotics
J'ai besoin d'antibiotiques
jay ber-zwan dan-tee-byoh-teek

I suffer from high blood pressure
Je fais de l'hypertension
jer fai der lee-pair-tan-syon

I am taking these drugs
Je prends ces médicaments
jer pran say may-dee-kah-man

Can you give me a prescription for them?
Pouvez-vous me donner une ordonnance pour ces médicaments?
poo-vay voo mer doh-nay ewn ohr-doh-nans poor say may-dee-kah-man?

I am on the pill
Je prends la pilule
jer pran lah pee-lewl

I am pregnant
Je suis enceinte
jer swee zan-cernt

My blood group is...
Mon groupe sanguin est...
mon groop san-gwern ai...

I do not know my blood group
Je ne sais pas quel est mon groupe sanguin
jer ner say pah kail ai mon groop san-gwern

At the hospital

Do I have to go into hospital?
Sera-t-il nécessaire de m'hospitaliser?
ser-ra-teel nay-say-sair der mohs-pee-tah-lee-zay

Do I need an operation?
Est-ce qu'il faudra m'opérer?
ais-keel foh-drah moh-pay-ray

Here is my E111 form
Voici mon formulaire E111
vwah-see mon fohr-mew-lair er san-tonz

How do I get reimbursed?
Comment serai-je remboursé?
koh-man ser-raij ran-boor-say

Must I stay in bed?
Dois-je garder le lit?
dwah-jer gahr-day ler lee

When will I be able to travel?
Quand serai-je en état de voyager?
kan ser-raij an ay-tah der voh-yah-jay

Will I be able to go out tomorrow?
Pourrai-je sortir demain?
poo-raij sohr-teer der-mern

At the dentist's

I have
J'ai
jay

— a toothache
— mal aux dents
— mahl oh dan

— broken a tooth
— une dent cassée
— ewn dan kah-say

I have to see the dentist
Il faut que je voie le dentiste
eel foh ker jer vwah ler dan-teest

My false teeth are broken
Mon dentier est cassé
mon dan-tyay ai kah-say

My gums are sore
J'ai mal aux gencives
jay mahl oh jan-seev

Can you find out what the trouble is?
Savez-vous ce qui ne va pas?
sah-vay voo ser kee ner vah pah

Please give me an injection
Donnez-moi une piqûre, s'il vous plaît
doh-nay- mwah ewn pee-kewr, seel voo play

That hurts
Ça fait mal
sah fai mahl

The filling has come out
Le plombage a sauté
ler pohm-bahj ah soh-tay

This one hurts
Celle-ci fait mal
sail-see fai mahl

Will you have to take it out?
Faudra-t-il l'arracher?
foh-drah-teel lah-rah-shay

Are you going to fill it?
Allez-vous la plomber?
ah-lay voo lah plohm-bay

For Your Information

Ordinals

1st	premier *prer-myay*	**4th**	quatrième *kaht-ryaim*
2nd	deuxième *der-zyaim*	**5th**	cinquième *sern-kyaim*
3rd	troisième *trwah-zyaim*	**n-th**	énième *ain-yaim*

Fractions and percentages

a half	un demi *an der-mee*	**two thirds**	deux tiers *der tyair*
a quarter	un quart *an kahr*	**10%**	dix pour cent *dee poor san*
a third	un tiers *an tyair*		

Dates

on Friday	vendredi *van-drer-dee*	**tomorrow**	demain *der-mern*
next Tuesday	mardi prochain *mahr-dee proh-shern*	**next week**	la semaine prochaine *lah ser-main proh-shain*
last Tuesday	mardi dernier *mahr-dee dair-nyay*	**in June**	en juin *an jwern*
yesterday	hier *ee-air*	**July 7th**	le sept juillet *ler sait jwee-yay*
today	aujourd'hui *oh-joor-dwee*	**last month**	le mois dernier *ler mwah dair-nyay*

Times of the year

in spring	au printemps *oh prern-tan*	**in autumn**	en automne *ohn oh-tohn*
in summer	en été *ohn ay-tay*	**in winter**	en hiver *ohn ee-vair*

Public holidays

New Year's Day, January 1
Le Jour de l'An
ler joor der lan

Easter Monday
Le lundi de Pâques
le lern-dee der pahk

Labour Day, May 1
La Fête du Travail
lah fait dew trah-vahee

Armistice Day 1945, May 8
Le 8 mai
le weet mai

Ascension Day (40 days after Easter)
La Fête de l'Ascension
lah fait der lah-san-syon

Whit Monday (7th Monday after Easter)
La Fête de la Pentecôte
lah fait der lah pant-koht

Bastille Day, July 14
Le 14 Juillet
ler kah-tohrz jwee-yay

Assumption Day, August 15
La Fête de l'Assomption
la fait der lah-sohmp-syon

All Saints Day, November 1
La Toussaint
lah too-san

Armistice Day 1918, November 11
Le 11 novembre
ler onz noh-vanbr

Christmas Day, December 25
Noël
noh-ail

Common adjectives

bad
mauvais
moh-vay

beautiful
beau/magnifique
boh/mah-nee-feek

big
grand
gran

cheap
bon marché
bon mahr-shay

cold
froid
frwah

expensive
cher
shair

difficult
difficile
dee-fee-seel

easy
facile
fah-seel

fast
rapide
rah-peed

good
bon/bien
bon/byern

high
haut
oh

hot
chaud
shoh

little
petit
per-tee

long
long
lon

new
nouveau/neuf
noo-voh/nerf

old
vieux
vee-er

short
court
koor

slow
lent
lan

small
petit
per-tee

ugly
laid
lay

Signs and notices

attention
ah-tan-syon
caution

ascenseur
ah-san-serr
lift/elevator

sortie
sohr-tee
exit

renseignements
ran-sain-man
information

soldes
sohld
sale

épuisé
ay-pwee-zay
sold out

occupé
oh-kew-pay
occupied

sonnez
soh-nay
please ring

poussez
poo-say
push

entrée
an-tray
entrance

entrez sans frapper
an-tray san frah-pay
enter without knocking

entrée gratuite
an-tray grah-tweet
no admission charge

téléphone
tay-lay-fohn
telephone

sapeurs-pompiers
sah-perr pohm-pyay
fire brigade

libre
leebr
vacant

Objets trouvés
ohb-jay troo-vay
Lost Property Office

entrée interdite
an-tray ern-tair-deet
No trespassing

danger
dan-jay
danger

fermé
fair-may
closed

poison
pwah-zon
poison

chaud
shoh
hot

froid
frwah
cold

caisse
kais
cashier

passage interdit
pah-sahj ern-tair-dee
no thoroughfare

entrée interdite
an-tray ern-tair-deet
no entry

hôpital
oh-pee-tahl
hospital

ambulance
an-bew-lans
ambulance

chemin privé
sher-mern pree-vay
private road

piste cyclable
peest seek-lahbl
cycle path

serrez à droite
sai-ray ah drwaht
keep to the right

381

souvenirs
soov-neer
souvenirs

agence de voyages
ahj-ans der voh-yahj
travel agency

offre spéciale
ohfr spay-syahl
special offer

eau potable
oh poh-tahbl
drinking water

déviation
day-vyah-syon
diversion

tirez
tee-ray
pull

à vendre
ah vandr
for sale

à louer
ah loo-ay
to let/for hire

tarifs
tah-reef
price list

bienvenue
byern-ver-new
welcome

réservé aux...
ray-sair-vay oh...
allowed only for...

chien méchant
beware of the dog
shee-ern may-shan

police
poh-lees
police

risque d'incendie
reesk dern-san-dee
danger of fire

départs
day-pahr
departures

détritus
day-tree-tews
litter

ouvert
oo-vair
open

sonnez
soh-nay
ring

arrivées
ah-ree-vay
arrivals

école
ay-kohl
school

entrée
an-tray
entrance

horaires
oh-rair
timetable

messieurs
may-syer
gentlemen

dames
dahm
ladies

douane
doo-ahn·
customs

bagages
bah-gahj
baggage

banque
bank
bank

police
poh-lees
police

urgence
oor-jans
emergency

réservé
ray-sair-vay
reserved

danger de mort
dan-jay der mohr
danger of death

espace fumeurs
ais-pahs few-merr
smoking area

interdiction de marcher sur le gazon
ern-tair-deek-syon der mahr-shay sewr ler gah-zon
keep off the grass

pour usage externe seulement
poor ew-zahj aiks-tairn serl-man
for external use only

ne pas parler au conducteur en cours de route
ner pah pahr-lay oh kon-dewk-terr an koor der root
It is forbidden to speak to the driver while the bus is moving

ne pas toucher
ner pah too-shay
do not touch

avertisseur d'incendie
ah-vair-tee-serr dern-san-dee
fire alarm

sortie de secours
sohr-tee der ser-koor
emergency exit

sonnette d'alarme
soh-nait dah-lahrm
communication cord (rail)

interdiction de photographier
ern-tair-deek-syon der foh-toh-grah-fyay
no picture taking

réservé au personnel
ray-sair-vay oh pair-soh-nail
employees only

parking réservé aux résidents
pahr-keeng ray-sair-vay oh ray-zee-dan
parking for residents only

compartiment fumeurs
kohm-pahr-tee-man few-merr
smoking compartment

liquidation des stocks
lee-kee-dah-syon day stohk
closing-down sale

fermé l'après-midi
fair-may lah-prai-mee-dee
closed in the afternoon

ne pas se pencher au dehors
ner pah ser pan-shay oh der-ohr
do not lean out

interdiction de fumer
ern-tair-deek-syon der few-may
no smoking

In an Emergency

Fire brigade Pompiers *pohm-pyay*:   telephone 18

Ambulance Ambulance *an-bew-lans*: telephone 15

Police Police *poh-lees:*   telephone 17

Call	–	**an ambulance**
Appelez	–	une ambulance
ah-play	–	*ewn an-bew-lans*
	–	**the fire brigade**
	–	les pompiers
	–	*lay pohm-pyay*
	–	**the police**
	–	la police
	–	*lah poh-lees*

There is a fire
Il y a un incendie
eel-yah ern ern-san-dee

Get a doctor
Appelez un médecin
ah-play ern mayd-sern

My son is lost
Mon fils s'est perdu
mon fees sai pair-dew

My daughter is ill
Ma fille est malade
mah fee ai mah-lahd

Who speaks English?
Qui parle anglais?
kee pahrl an-glay

Where is the British consulate?
Où se trouve le consulat de Grande-Bretagne?
oo ser troov ler kon-sew-lah der grand-brer-tahn

French Verbs

Verb Forms

Auxiliary

Auxiliary verbs are used to form compound tenses of verbs, eg *have* in *I have seen*. The auxiliary verbs in French are *avoir* and *être*.

Compound

Compound tenses are verb tenses consisting of more than one element. In French, compound tenses are formed by the *auxiliary* verb and the *past participle*, eg *il a écrit – he has written*.

Conditional

The conditional is introduced in English by the auxiliary *would*, eg *I would come if I had the time*. In French, this is rendered by a single verb form, eg *je viendrais*.

Imperative

The imperative is used for giving orders, eg *sois sage – be good*, or making suggestions, eg *allons – let's go*.

Imperfect indicative

In French, this tense describes past habitual or continuous action, eg *elle chantait – she was singing*.

Indicative

The normal form of a verb, as in *j'aime – I like, il est venu – he has come, j'essaie – I am trying*.

Past historic

This tense, specific to French, is only used in narration in the formal written language.

Past participle

This is the form used after the auxiliary *have* in English, eg *eaten – mangé* in *j'ai mangé – I have eaten*.

Perfect indicative

This is the standard past tense of conversation, comprising the *auxiliary* (*avoir* or *être*), and the *past participle*, eg *j'ai vu – I have seen, nous sommes descendus – we have descended*.

Pluperfect indicative

In French and English, this tense expresses an action which happened in the past before another past action. In French, this comprises the *imperfect indicative* of *avoir* or *être* and the *past participle*, eg *il avait vu – he had seen, vous étiez arrivés – you had arrived*.

Present participle

This is the form which ends in *-ing* in English, eg *allant – going*.

Subjunctive

This is rarely used in English. It survives in expressions such as *if I were you*, and *God save the Queen*. In French, the subjunctive generally follows the conjunction *que* after expressions of doubt, fear, emotion, etc.

absoudre
to absolve

Present participle
absolvant

Past participle
absous (-te)

Present indicative
j'absous
tu absous
il absout
nous absolvons
vous absolvez
ils absolvent

Imperfect indicative
j'absolvais
tu absolvais
il absolvait
nous absolvions
vous absolviez
ils absolvaient

Past historic
–
–
–
–
–
–

Future
j'absoudrai
tu absoudras
il absoudra
nous absoudrons
vous absoudrez
ils absoudront

Perfect indicative
j'ai absous
tu as absous
il a absous
nous avons absous
vous avez absous
ils ont absous

Pluperfect indicative
j'avais absous
tu avais absous
il avait absous
nous avions absous
vous aviez absous
ils avaient absous

Present subjunctive
que j'absolve
que tu absolves
qu'il absolve
que nous absolvions
que vous absolviez
qu'ils absolvent

Conditional
j'absoudrais
tu absoudrais
il absoudrait
nous absoudrions
vous absoudriez
ils absoudraient

Imperative
absous
absolvons
absolvez

accueillir
to greet, welcome

Present participle
accueillant

Past participle
accueilli

Present indicative
j'accueille
tu accueilles
il accueille
nous accueillons
vous accueillez
ils accueillent

Imperfect indicative
j'accueillais
tu accueillais
il accueillait
nous accueillions
vous accueilliez
ils accueillaient

Past historic
j'accueillis
tu accueillis
il accueillit
nous accueillîmes
vous accueillîtes
ils accueillirent

Future
j'accueillerai

tu accueilleras
il accueillera
nous accueillerons
vous accueillerez
ils accueilleront

Perfect indicative
j'ai accueilli
tu as accueilli
il a accueilli
nous avons accueilli
vous avez accueilli
ils ont accueilli

Pluperfect indicative
j'avais accueilli
tu avais accueilli
il avait accueilli
nous avions accueilli
vous aviez accueilli
ils avaient accueilli

Present subjunctive
que j'accueille
que tu accueilles
qu'il accueille
que nous accueillions
que vous accueilliez
qu'ils accueillent

Conditional
j'accueillerais
tu accueillerais
il accueillerait
nous accueillerions
vous accueilleriez
ils accueilleraient

Imperative
accueille
accueillons
accueillez

acheter
to buy

Present participle
achetant

Past participle
acheté

Present indicative
j'achète
tu achètes
il achète

nous achetons
vous achetez
ils achètent

Imperfect indicative
j'achetais
tu achetais
il achetait
nous achetions
vous achetiez
ils achetaient

Past historic
je achetai
tu achetas
il acheta
nous achetâmes
vous achetâtes
ils achetèrent

Future
j'achèterai
tu achèteras
il achètera
nous achèterons
vous achèterez
ils achèteront

Perfect indicative
j'ai acheté
tu as acheté
il a acheté
nous avons acheté
vous avez acheté
ils ont acheté

Pluperfect indicative
j'avais acheté
tu avais acheté
il avait acheté
nous avions acheté
vous aviez acheté
ils avaient acheté

Present subjunctive
que j'achète
que tu achètes
qu'il achète
que nous achetions
que vous achetiez
qu'ils achètent

Conditional
je achèterais
tu achèterais
il achèterait

nous achèterions
vous achèteriez
ils achèteraient

Imperative
achète
achetons
achetez

acquérir
to acquire

Present participle
acquérant

Past participle
acquis

Present indicative
j'acquiers
tu acquiers
il acquiert
nous acquérons
vous acquérez
ils acquièrent

Imperfect indicative
j'acquérais
tu acquérais
il acquérait
nous acquérions
vous acquériez
ils acquéraient

Past historic
j'acquis
tu acquis
il acquit
nous acquîmes
vous acquîtes
ils acquirent

Future
je acquerrai
tu acquerras
il acquerra
nous acquerrons
vous acquerrez
ils acquerront

Perfect indicative
j'ai acquis
tu as acquis
il a acquis

nous avons acquis
vous avez acquis
ils ont acquis

Pluperfect indicative
j'avais acquis
tu avais acquis
il avait acquis
nous avions acquis
vous aviez acquis
ils avaient acquis

Present subjunctive
que j'acquière
que tu acquières
qu'il acquière
que nous acquérions
que vous acquériez
qu'ils acquièrent

Conditional
j'acquerrais
tu acquerrais
il acquerrait
nous acquerrions
vous acquerriez
ils acquerraient

Imperative
acquiers
acquérons
acquérez

admettre
to admit, acknowledge

Present participle
admettant

Past participle
admis

Present indicative
j'admets
tu admets
il admet
nous admettons
vous admettez
ils admettent

Imperfect indicative
j'admettais
tu admettais
il admettait

nous admettions
vous admettiez
ils admettaient

Past historic
j'admis
tu admis
il admit
nous admîmes
vous admîtes
ils admirent

Future
j'admettrai
tu admettras
il admettra
nous admettrons
vous admettrez
ils admettront

Perfect indicative
j'ai admis
tu as admis
il a admis
nous avons admis
vous avez admis
ils ont admis

Pluperfect indicative
j'avais admis
tu avais admis
il avait admis
nous avions admis
vous aviez admis
ils avaient admis

Present subjunctive
que j'admette
que tu admettes
qu'il admette
que nous admettions
que vous admettiez
qu'ils admettent

Conditional
j'admettrais
tu admettrais
il admettrait
nous admettrions
vous admettriez
ils admettraient

Imperative
admets
admettons
admettez

aider
to help, assist

Present participle
aidant

Past participle
aidé

Present indicative
j'aide
tu aides
il aide
nous aidons
vous aidez
ils aident

Imperfect indicative
j'aidais
tu aidais
il aidait
nous aidions
vous aidiez
ils aidaient

Past historic
j'aidai
tu aidas
il aida
nous aidâmes
vous aidâtes
ils aidèrent

Future
j'aiderai
tu aideras
il aidera
nous aiderons
vous aiderez
ils aideront

Perfect indicative
j'ai aidé
tu as aidé
il a aidé
nous avons aidé
vous avez aidé
ils ont aidé

Pluperfect indicative
j'avais aidé
tu avais aidé
il avait aidé
nous avions aidé
vous aviez aidé
ils avaient aidé

Present subjunctive
que j'aide
que tu aides
qu'il aide
que nous aidions
que vous aidiez
qu'ils aident

Conditional
j'aiderais
tu aiderais
il aiderait
nous aiderions
vous aideriez
ils aideraient

Imperative
aide
aidons
aidez

aimer
to love, like

Present participle
aimant

Past participle
aimé

Present indicative
j'aime
tu aimes
il aime
nous aimons
vous aimez
ils aiment

Imperfect indicative
j'aimais
tu aimais
il aimait
nous aimions
vous aimiez
ils aimaient

Past historic
j'aimai
tu aimas
il aima
nous aimâmes
vous aimâtes
ils aimèrent

Future
j'aimerai

tu aimeras
il aimera
nous aimerons
vous aimerez
ils aimeront

Perfect indicative
j'ai aimé
tu as aimé
il a aimé
nous avons aimé
vous avez aimé
ils ont aimé

Pluperfect indicative
j'avais aimé
tu avais aimé
il avait aimé
nous avions aimé
vous aviez aimé
ils avaient aimé

Present subjunctive
que j'aime
que tu aimes
qu'il aime
que nous aimions
que vous aimiez
qu'ils aiment

Conditional
j'aimerais
tu aimerais
il aimerait
nous aimerions
vous aimeriez
ils aimeraient

Imperative
aime
aimons
aimez

aller
to go

Present participle
allant

Past participle
allé

Present indicative
je vais
tu vas
il va

nous allons
vous allez
ils vont

Imperfect indicative
j'allais
tu allais
il allait
nous allions
vous alliez
ils allaient

Past historic
j'allai
tu allas
il alla
nous allâmes
vous allâtes
ils allèrent

Future
j'irai
tu iras
il ira
nous irons
vous irez
ils iront

Perfect indicative
je suis allé
tu es allé
il est allé
nous sommes allés
vous êtes allés
ils sont allés

Pluperfect indicative
j'étais allé
tu étais allé
il était allé
nous étions allés
vous étiez allés
ils étaient allés

Present subjunctive
que j'aille
que tu ailles
qu'il aille
que nous allions
que vous alliez
qu'ils aillent

Conditional
j'irais
tu irais
il irait
nous irions
vous iriez
ils iraient

Imperative
va
allons
allez

apercevoir
to see, notice

Present participle
apercevant

Past participle
aperçu

Present indicative
j'aperçois
tu aperçois
il aperçoit
nous apercevons
vous apercevez
ils aperçoivent

Imperfect indicative
j'apercevais
tu apercevais
il apercevait
nous apercevions
vous aperceviez
ils apercevaient

Past historic
j'aperçus
tu aperçus
il aperçut
nous aperçûmes
vous aperçûtes
ils aperçurent

Future
j'apercevrai
tu apercevras
il apercevra
nous apercevrons
vous apercevrez
ils apercevront

Perfect indicative
j'ai aperçu
tu as aperçu
il a aperçu
nous avons aperçu
vous avez aperçu
ils ont aperçu

Pluperfect indicative
j'avais aperçu

tu avais aperçu
il avait aperçu
nous avions aperçu
vous aviez aperçu
ils avaient aperçu

Present subjunctive

que j'aperçoive
que tu aperçoives
qu'il aperçoive
que nous apercevions
que vous aperceviez
qu'ils aperçoivent

Conditional

j'apercevrais
tu apercevrais
il apercevrait
nous apercevrions
vous apercevriez
ils apercevraient

Imperative

aperçois
apercevons
apercevez

apparaître
to appear

Present participle

apparaissant

Past participle

apparu

Present indicative

j'apparais
tu apparais
il apparaît
nous apparaissons
vous apparaissez
ils apparaissent

Imperfect indicative

j'apparaissais
tu apparaissais
il apparaissait
nous apparaissions
vous apparaissiez
ils apparaissaient

Past historic

j'apparus
tu apparus
il apparut

nous apparûmes
vous apparûtes
ils apparurent

Future

j'apparaîtrai
tu apparaîtras
il apparaîtra
nous apparaîtrons
vous apparaîtrez
ils apparaîtront

Perfect indicative

j'ai apparu
tu as apparu
il a apparu
nous avons apparu
vous avez apparu
ils ont apparu

Pluperfect indicative

j'avais apparu
tu avais apparu
il avait apparu
nous avions apparu
vous aviez apparu
ils avaient apparu

Present subjunctive

que j'apparaisse
que tu apparaisses
qu'il apparaisse
que nous apparaissions
que vous apparaissiez
qu'ils apparaissent

Conditional

j'apparaîtrais
tu apparaîtrais
il apparaîtrait
nous apparaîtrions
vous apparaîtriez
ils apparaîtraient

Imperative

apparais
apparaissons
apparaissez

appartenir
to belong

Present participle

appartenant

Past participle

appartenu

Present indicative

j'appartiens
tu appartiens
il appartient
nous appartenons
vous appartenez
ils appartiennent

Imperfect indicative

j'appartenais
tu appartenais
il appartenait
nous appartenions
vous apparteniez
ils appartenaient

Past historic

j'appartins
tu appartins
il appartint
nous appartînmes
vous appartîntes
ils appartinrent

Future

j'appartiendrai
tu appartiendras
il appartiendra
nous appartiendrons
vous appartiendrez
ils appartiendront

Perfect indicative

j'ai appartenu
tu as appartenu
il a appartenu
nous avons appartenu
vous avez appartenu
ils ont appartenu

Pluperfect indicative

j'avais appartenu
tu avais appartenu
il avait appartenu
nous avions appartenu
vous aviez appartenu
ils avaient appartenu

Present subjunctive

que j'appartienne
que tu appartiennes
qu'il appartienne
que nous appartenions
que vous apparteniez
qu'ils appartiennent

Conditional

j'appartiendrais

tu appartiendrais
il appartiendrait
nous appartiendrions
vous appartiendriez
ils appartiendraient

Imperative

appartiens
appartenons
appartenez

appeler
to call

Present participle

appelant

Past participle

appelé

Present indicative

j'appelle
tu appelles
il appelle
nous appelons
vous appelez
ils appellent

Imperfect indicative

j'appelais
tu appelais
il appelait
nous appelions
vous appeliez
ils appelaient

Past historic

j'appelai
tu appelas
il appela
nous appelâmes
vous appelâtes
ils appelèrent

Future

j'appellerai
tu appelleras
il appellera
nous appellerons
vous appellerez
ils appelleront

Perfect indicative

j'ai appelé
tu as appelé
il a appelé

nous avons appelé
vous avez appelé
ils ont appelé

Pluperfect indicative

j'avais appelé
tu avais appelé
il avait appelé
nous avions appelé
vous aviez appelé
ils avaient appelé

Present subjunctive

que j'appelle
que tu appelles
qu'il appelle
que nous appelions
que vous appeliez
qu'ils appellent

Conditional

j'appellerais
tu appellerais
il appellerait
nous appellerions
vous appelleriez
ils appelleraient

Imperative

appelle
appelons
appelez

apporter
to bring

Present participle

apportant

Past participle

apporté

Present indicative

j'apporte
tu apportes
il apporte
nous apportons
vous apportez
ils apportent

Imperfect indicative

j'apportais
tu apportais
il apportait

nous apportions
vous apportiez
ils apportaient

Past historic

j'apportai
tu apportas
il apporta
nous apportâmes
vous apportâtes
ils apportèrent

Future

j'apporterai
tu apporteras
il apportera
nous apporterons
vous apporterez
ils apporteront

Perfect indicative

j'ai apporté
tu as apporté
il a apporté
nous avons apporté
vous avez apporté
ils ont apporté

Pluperfect indicative

j'avais apporté
tu avais apporté
il avait apporté
nous avions apporté
vous aviez apporté
ils avaient apporté

Present subjunctive

que j'apporte
que tu apportes
qu'il apporte
que nous apportions
que vous apportiez
qu'ils apportent

Conditional

j'apporterais
tu apporterais
il apporterait
nous apporterions
vous apporteriez
ils apporteraient

Imperative

apporte
apportons
apportez

apprécier
to appreciate

Present participle
appréciant

Past participle
apprécié

Present indicative
j'apprécie
tu apprécies
il apprécie
nous apprécions
vous appréciez
ils apprécient

Imperfect indicative
j'appréciais
tu appréciais
il appréciait
nous appréciions
vous appréciiez
ils appréciaient

Past historic
j'appréciai
tu apprécias
il apprécia
nous appréciâmes
vous appréciâtes
ils apprécièrent

Future
j'apprécierai
tu apprécieras
il appréciera
nous apprécierons
vous apprécierez
ils apprécieront

Perfect indicative
j'ai apprécié
tu as apprécié
il a apprécié
nous avons apprécié
vous avez apprécié
ils ont apprécié

Pluperfect indicative
j'avais apprécié
tu avais apprécié
il avait apprécié
nous avions apprécié
vous aviez apprécié
ils avaient apprécié

Present subjunctive
que j'apprécie
que tu apprécies
qu'il apprécie
que nous appréciions
que vous appréciiez
qu'ils apprécient

Conditional
je apprécierais
tu apprécierais
il apprécierait
nous apprécierions
vous apprécieriez
ils apprécieraient

Imperative
apprécie
apprécions
appréciez

apprendre
to learn

Present participle
apprenant

Past participle
appris

Present indicative
j'apprends
tu apprends
il apprend
nous apprenons
vous apprenez
ils apprennent

Imperfect indicative
j'apprenais
tu apprenais
il apprenait
nous apprenions
vous appreniez
ils apprenaient

Past historic
j'appris
tu appris
il apprit
nous apprîmes
vous apprîtes
ils apprirent

Future
j'apprendrai
tu apprendras
il apprendra
nous apprendrons
vous apprendrez
ils apprendront

Perfect indicative
j'ai appris
tu as appris
il a appris
nous avons appris
vous avez appris
ils ont appris

Pluperfect indicative
j'avais appris
tu avais appris
il avait appris
nous avions appris
vous aviez appris
ils avaient appris

Present subjunctive
que j'apprenne
que tu apprennes
qu'il apprenne
que nous apprenions
que vous appreniez
qu'ils apprennent

Conditional
j'apprendrais
tu apprendrais
il apprendrait
nous apprendrions
vous apprendriez
ils apprendraient

Imperative
apprends
apprenons
apprenez

arriver
to arrive

Present participle
arrivant

past participle
arrivé

Present indicative
j'arrive
tu arrives
il arrive

nous arrivons
vous arrivez
ils arrivent

Imperfect indicative

j'arrivais
tu arrivais
il arrivait
nous arrivions
vous arriviez
ils arrivaient

Past historic

j'arrivai
tu arrivas
il arriva
nous arrivâmes
vous arrivâtes
ils arrivèrent

Future

j'arriverai
tu arriveras
il arrivera
nous arriverons
vous arriverez
ils arriveront

Perfect indicative

je suis arrivé
tu es arrivé
il est arrivé
nous sommes arrivés
vous êtes arrivés
ils sont arrivés

Pluperfect indicative

j'étais arrivé
tu étais arrivé
il était arrivé
nous étions arrivés
vous étiez arrivés
ils étaient arrivés

Present subjunctive

que j'arrive
que tu arrives
qu'il arrive
que nous arrivions
que vous arriviez
qu'ils arrivent

Conditional

j'arriverais
tu arriverais
il arriverait

nous arriverions
vous arriveriez
ils arriveraient

Imperative

arrive
arrivons
arrivez

s'asseoir
to sit down

Present participle

s'asseyant

Past participle

assis

Present indicative

je m'assieds
tu t'assieds
il s'assied
nous nous asseyons
vous vous asseyez
ils s'asseyent

Imperfect indicative

je m'asseyais
tu t'asseyais
il s'asseyait
nous nous asseyions
vous vous asseyiez
ils s'asseyaient

Past historic

je m'assis
tu t'assis
il s'assit
nous nous assîmes
vous vous assîtes
ils s'assirent

Future

je m'assiérai
tu t'assiéras
il s'assiéra
nous nous assiérons
vous vous assiérez
ils s'assiéront

Perfect indicative

je me suis assis
tu t'es assis
il s'est assis

nous nous sommes assis
vous vous êtes assis
ils se sont assis

Pluperfect indicative

je m'étais assis
tu t'étais assis
il s'était assis
nous nous étions assis
vous vous étiez assis
ils s'étaient assis

Present subjunctive

que je m'asseye
que tu t'asseyes
qu'il s'asseye
que nous nous asseyions
que vous vous asseyiez
qu'ils s'asseyent

Conditional

je m'assiérais
tu t'assiérais
il s'assiérait
nous nous assiérions
vous vous assiériez
ils s'assiéraient

Imperative

assieds-toi
asseyons-nous
asseyez-vous

atteindre
to reach

Present participle

atteignant

Past participle

atteint

Present indicative

j'atteins
tu atteins
il atteint
nous atteignons
vous atteignez
ils atteignent

Imperfect indicative

j'atteignais
tu atteignais
il atteignait

nous atteignions
vous atteigniez
ils atteignaient

Past historic

j'atteignis
tu atteignis
il atteignit
nous atteignîmes
vous atteignîtes
ils atteignirent

Future

j'atteindrai
tu atteindras
il atteindra
nous atteindrons
vous atteindrez
ils atteindront

Perfect indicative

j'ai atteint
tu as atteint
il a atteint
nous avons atteint
vous avez atteint
ils ont atteint

Pluperfect indicative

j'avais atteint
tu avais atteint
il avait atteint
nous avions atteint
vous aviez atteint
ils avaient atteint

Present subjunctive

que j'atteigne
que tu atteignes
qu'il atteigne
que nous atteignions
que vous atteigniez
qu'ils atteignent

Conditional

j'atteindrais
tu atteindrais
il atteindrait
nous atteindrions
vous atteindriez
ils atteindraient

Imperative

atteins
atteignons
atteignez

attendre
to wait

Present participle

attendant

Past participle

attendu

Present indicative

j'attends
tu attends
il attend
nous attendons
vous attendez
ils attendent

Imperfect indicative

j'attendais
tu attendais
il attendait
nous attendions
vous attendiez
ils attendaient

Past historic

j'attendis
tu attendis
il attendit
nous attendîmes
vous attendîtes
ils attendirent

Future

j'attendrai
tu attendras
il attendra
nous attendrons
vous attendrez
ils attendront

Perfect indicative

j'ai attendu
tu as attendu
il a attendu
nous avons attendu
vous avez attendu
ils ont attendu

Pluperfect indicative

j'avais attendu
tu avais attendu
il avait attendu
nous avions attendu
vous aviez attendu
ils avaient attendu

Present subjunctive

que j'attende
que tu attendes
qu'il attende
que nous attendions
que vous attendiez
qu'ils attendent

Conditional

j'attendrais
tu attendrais
il attendrait
nous attendrions
vous attendriez
ils attendraient

Imperative

attends
attendons
attendez

avoir
to have

Present participle

ayant

Past participle

eu

Present indicative

j'ai
tu as
il a
nous avons
vous avez
ils ont

Imperfect indicative

j'avais
tu avais
il avait
nous avions
vous aviez
ils avaient

Past historic

j'eus
tu eus
il eut
nous eûmes
vous eûtes
ils eurent

Future

j'aurai

tu auras
il aura
nous aurons
vous aurez
ils auront

Perfect indicative
j'ai eu
tu as eu
il a eu
nous avons eu
vous avez eu
ils ont eu

Pluperfect indicative
j'avais eu
tu avais eu
il avait eu
nous avions eu
vous aviez eu
ils avaient eu

Present subjunctive
que j'aie
que tu aies
qu'il ait
que nous ayons
que vous ayez
qu'ils aient

Conditional
j'aurais
tu aurais
il aurait
nous aurions
vous auriez
ils auraient

Imperative
aie
ayons
ayez

battre
to beat

Present participle
battant

Past participle
battu

Present indicative
je bats
tu bats
il bat

nous battons
vous battez
ils battent

Imperfect indicative
je battais
tu battais
il battait
nous battions
vous battiez
ils battaient

Past historic
je battis
tu battis
il battit
nous battîmes
vous battîtes
ils battirent

Future
je battrai
tu battras
il battra
nous battrons
vous battrez
ils battront

Perfect indicative
j'ai battu
tu as battu
il a battu
nous avons battu
vous avez battu
ils ont battu

Pluperfect indicative
j'avais battu
tu avais battu
il avait battu
nous avions battu
vous aviez battu
ils avaient battu

Present subjunctive
que je batte
que tu battes
qu'il batte
que nous battions
que vous battiez
qu'ils battent

Conditional
je battrais
tu battrais
il battrait

nous battrions
vous battriez
ils battraient

Imperative
bats
battons
battez

boire
to drink

Present participle
buvant

Past participle
bu

Present indicative
je bois
tu bois
il boit
nous buvons
vous buvez
ils boivent

Imperfect indicative
je buvais
tu buvais
il buvait
nous buvions
vous buviez
ils buvaient

Past historic
je bus
tu bus
il but
nous bûmes
vous bûtes
ils burent

Future
je boirai
tu boiras
il boira
nous boirons
vous boirez
ils boiront

Perfect indicative
j'ai bu
tu as bu
il a bu
nous avons bu
vous avez bu
ils ont bu

Pluperfect indicative

j'avais bu
tu avais bu
il avait bu
nous avions bu
vous aviez bu
ils avaient bu

Present subjunctive

que je boive
que tu boives
qu'il boive
que nous buvions
que vous buviez
qu'ils boivent

Conditional

je boirais
tu boirais
il boirait
nous boirions
vous boiriez
ils boiraient

Imperative

bois
buvons
buvez

céder
to yield

Present participle
cédant

Past participle
cédé

Present indicative
je cède
tu cèdes
il cède
nous cédons
vous cédez
ils cèdent

Imperfect indicative
je cédais
tu cédais
il cédait
nous cédions
vous cédiez
ils cédaient

Past historic
je cédai

tu cédas
il céda
nous cédâmes
vous cédâtes
ils cédèrent

Future
je céderai
tu céderas
il cédera
nous céderons
vous céderez
ils céderont

Perfect indicative
j'ai cédé
tu as cédé
il a cédé
nous avons cédé
vous avez cédé
ils ont cédé

Pluperfect indicative
j'avais cédé
tu avais cédé
il avait cédé
nous avions cédé
vous aviez cédé
ils avaient cédé

Present subjunctive
que je cède
que tu cèdes
qu'il cède
que nous cédions
que vous cédiez
qu'ils cèdent

Conditional
je céderais
tu céderais
il céderait
nous céderions
vous céderiez
ils céderaient

Imperative
cède
cédons
cédez

choisir
to choose

Present participle
choisissant

Past participle
choisi

Present indicative
je choisis
tu choisis
il choisit
nous choisissons
vous choisissez
ils choisissent

Imperfect indicative
je choisissais
tu choisissais
il choisissait
nous choisissions
vous choisissiez
ils choisissaient

Past historic
je choisis
tu choisis
il choisit
nous choisîmes
vous choisîtes
ils choisirent

Future
je choisirai
tu choisiras
il choisira
nous choisirons
vous choisirez
ils choisiront

Perfect indicative
j'ai choisi
tu as choisi
il a choisi
nous avons choisi
vous avez choisi
ils ont choisi

Pluperfect indicative
j'avais choisi
tu avais choisi
il avait choisi
nous avions choisi
vous aviez choisi
ils avaient choisi

Present subjunctive
que je choisisse
que tu choisisses
qu'il choisisse
que nous choisissions
que vous choisissiez
qu'ils choisissent

Conditional

je choisirais
tu choisirais
il choisirait
nous choisirions
vous choisiriez
ils choisiraient

Imperative

choisis
choisissons
choisissez

combattre
to fight

Present participle

combattant

Past participle

combattu

Present indicative

je combats
tu combats
il combat
nous combattons
vous combattez
ils combattent

Imperfect indicative

je combattais
tu combattais
il combattait
nous combattions
vous combattiez
ils combattaient

Past historic

je combattis
tu combattis
il combattit
nous combattîmes
vous combattîtes
ils combattirent

Future

je combattrai
tu combattras
il combattra
nous combattrons
vous combattrez
ils combattront

Perfect indicative

j'ai combattu

tu as combattu
il a combattu
nous avons combattu
vous avez combattu
ils ont combattu

Pluperfect indicative

j'avais combattu
tu avais combattu
il avait combattu
nous avions combattu
vous aviez combattu
ils avaient combattu

Present subjunctive

que je combatte
que tu combattes
qu'il combatte
que nous combattions
que vous combattiez
qu'ils combattent

Conditional

je combattrais
tu combattrais
il combattrait
nous combattrions
vous combattriez
ils combattraient

Imperative

combats
combattons
combattez

commencer
to begin

Present participle

commençant

Past participle

commencé

Present indicative

je commence
tu commences
il commence
nous commençons
vous commencez
ils commencent

Imperfect indicative

je commençais
tu commençais
il commençait

nous commencions
vous commenciez
ils commençaient

Past historic

je commençai
tu commenças
il commença
nous commençâmes
vous commençâtes
ils commencèrent

Future

je commencerai
tu commenceras
il commencera
nous commencerons
vous commencerez
ils commenceront

Perfect indicative

j'ai commencé
tu as commencé
il a commencé
nous avons commencé
vous avez commencé
ils ont commencé

Pluperfect indicative

j'avais commencé
tu avais commencé
il avait commencé
nous avions commencé
vous aviez commencé
ils avaient commencé

Present subjunctive

que je commence
que tu commences
qu'il commence
que nous commencions
que vous commenciez
qu'ils commencent

Conditional

je commencerais
tu commencerais
il commencerait
nous commencerions
vous commenceriez
ils commenceraient

Imperative

commence
commençons
commencez

comprendre
to understand, include

Present participle
comprenant

Past participle
compris

Present indicative
je comprends
tu comprends
il comprend
nous comprenons
vous comprenez
ils comprennent

Imperfect indicative
je comprenais
tu comprenais
il comprenait
nous comprenions
vous compreniez
ils comprenaient

Past historic
je compris
tu compris
il comprit
nous comprîmes
vous comprîtes
ils comprirent

Future
je comprendrai
tu comprendras
il comprendra
nous comprendrons
vous comprendrez
ils comprendront

Perfect indicative
j'ai compris
tu as compris
il a compris
nous avons compris
vous avez compris
ils ont compris

Pluperfect indicative
j'avais compris
tu avais compris
il avait compris
nous avions compris
vous aviez compris
ils avaient compris

Present subjunctive
que je comprenne
que tu comprennes
qu'il comprenne
que nous comprenions
que vous compreniez
qu'ils comprennent

Conditional
je comprendrais
tu comprendrais
il comprendrait
nous comprendrions
vous comprendriez
ils comprendraient

Imperative
comprends
comprenons
comprenez

conclure
to conclude

Present participle
concluant

Past participle
conclu

Present indicative
je conclus
tu conclus
il conclut
nous concluons
vous concluez
ils concluent

Imperfect indicative
je concluais
tu concluais
il concluait
nous concluions
vous concluiez
ils concluaient

Past historic
je conclus
tu conclus
il conclut
nous conclûmes
vous conclûtes
ils conclurent

Future
je conclurai

tu concluras
il conclura
nous conclurons
vous conclurez
ils concluront

Perfect indicative
j'ai conclu
tu as conclu
il a conclu
nous avons conclu
vous avez conclu
ils ont conclu

Pluperfect indicative
j'avais conclu
tu avais conclu
il avait conclu
nous avions conclu
vous aviez conclu
ils avaient conclu

Present subjunctive
que je conclue
que tu conclues
qu'il conclue
que nous concluions
que vous concluiez
qu'ils concluent

Conditional
je conclurais
tu conclurais
il conclurait
nous conclurions
vous concluriez
ils concluraient

Imperative
conclus
concluons
concluez

conduire
to drive, lead

Present participle
conduisant

Past participle
conduit

Present indicative
je conduis
tu conduis
il conduit

nous conduisons
vous conduisez
ils conduisent

Imperfect indicative
je conduisais
tu conduisais
il conduisait
nous conduisions
vous conduisiez
ils conduisaient

Past historic
je conduisis
tu conduisis
il conduisit
nous conduisîmes
vous conduisîtes
ils conduisirent

Future
je conduirai
tu conduiras
il conduira
nous conduirons
vous conduirez
ils conduiront

Perfect indicative
j'ai conduit
tu as conduit
il a conduit
nous avons conduit
vous avez conduit
ils ont conduit

Pluperfect indicative
j'avais conduit
tu avais conduit
il avait conduit
nous avions conduit
vous aviez conduit
ils avaient conduit

Present subjunctive
que je conduise
que tu conduises
qu'il conduise
que nous conduisions
que vous conduisiez
qu'ils conduisent

Conditional
je conduirais
tu conduirais
il conduirait
nous conduirions
vous conduiriez
ils conduiraient

Imperative
conduis
conduisons
conduisez

connaître
to know

Present participle
connaissant

Past participle
connu

Present indicative
je connais
tu connais
il connaît
nous connaissons
vous connaissez
ils connaissent

Imperfect indicative
je connaissais
tu connaissais
il connaissait
nous connaissions
vous connaissiez
ils connaissaient

Past historic
je connus
tu connus
il connut
nous connûmes
vous connûtes
ils connurent

Future
je connaîtrai
tu connaîtras
il connaîtra
nous connaîtrons
vous connaîtrez
ils connaîtront

Perfect indicative
j'ai connu
tu as connu
il a connu
nous avons connu
vous avez connu
ils ont connu

Pluperfect indicative
j'avais connu

tu avais connu
il avait connu
nous avions connu
vous aviez connu
ils avaient connu

Present subjunctive
que je connaisse
que tu connaisses
qu'il connaisse
que nous connaissions
que vous connaissiez
qu'ils connaissent

Conditional
je connaîtrais
tu connaîtrais
il connaîtrait
nous connaîtrions
vous connaîtriez
ils connaîtraient

Imperative
connais
connaissons
connaissez

conquérir
to conquer

Present participle
conquérant

Past participle
conquis

Present indicative
je conquiers
tu conquiers
il conquiert
nous conquérons
vous conquérez
ils conquièrent

Imperfect indicative
je conquérais
tu conquérais
il conquérait
nous conquérions
vous conquériez
ils conquéraient

Past historic
je conquis
tu conquis
il conquit

nous conquîmes
vous conquîtes
ils conquirent

Future
je conquerrai
tu conquerras
il conquerra
nous conquerrons
vous conquerrez
ils conquerront

Perfect indicative
j'ai conquis
tu as conquis
il a conquis
nous avons conquis
vous avez conquis
ils ont conquis

Pluperfect indicative
j'avais conquis
tu avais conquis
il avait conquis
nous avions conquis
vous aviez conquis
ils avaient conquis

Present subjunctive
que j'conquière
que tu conquières
qu'il conquière
que nous conquérions
que vous conquériez
qu'ils conquièrent

Conditional
je conquerrais
tu conquerrais
il conquerrait
nous conquerrions
vous conquerriez
ils conquerraient

Imperative
conquiers
conquérons
conquérez

consentir
to consent, agree

Present participle
consentant

Past participle
consenti

Present indicative
je consens
tu consens
il consent
nous consentons
vous consentez
ils consentent

Imperfect indicative
je consentais
tu consentais
il consentait
nous consentions
vous consentiez
ils consentaient

Past historic
je consentis
tu consentis
il consentit
nous consentîmes
vous consentîtes
ils consentirent

Future
je consentirai
tu consentiras
il consentira
nous consentirons
vous consentirez
ils consentiront

Perfect indicative
j'ai consenti
tu as consenti
il a consenti
nous avons consenti
vous avez consenti
ils ont consenti

Pluperfect indicative
j'avais consenti
tu avais consenti
il avait consenti
nous avions consenti
vous aviez consenti
ils avaient consenti

Present subjunctive
que je consente
que tu consentes
qu'il consente
que nous consentions
que vous consentiez
qu'ils consentent

Conditional
je consentirais

tu consentirais
il consentirait
nous consentirions
vous consentiriez
ils consentiraient

Imperative
consens
consentons
consentez

construire
to build

Present participle
construisant

Past participle
construit

Present indicative
je construis
tu construis
il construit
nous construisons
vous construisez
ils construisent

Imperfect indicative
je construisais
tu construisais
il construisait
nous construisions
vous construisiez
ils construisaient

Past historic
je construisis
tu construisis
il construisit
nous construisîmes
vous construisîtes
ils construisirent

Future
je construirai
tu construiras
il construira
nous construirons
vous construirez
ils construiront

Perfect indicative
j'ai construit
tu as construit
il a construit

nous avons construit
vous avez construit
ils ont construit

Pluperfect indicative
j'avais construit
tu avais construit
il avait construit
nous avions construit
vous aviez construit
ils avaient construit

Present subjunctive
que je construise
que tu construises
qu'il construise
que nous construisions
que vous construisiez
qu'ils construisent

Conditional
je construirais
tu construirais
il construirait
nous construirions
vous construiriez
ils construiraient

Imperative
construis
construisons
construisez

contenir
to contain

Present participle
contenant

Past participle
contenu

Present indicative
je contiens
tu contiens
il contient
nous contenons
vous contenez
ils contiennent

Imperfect indicative
je contenais
tu contenais
il contenait

nous contenions
vous conteniez
ils contenaient

Past historic
je contins
tu contins
il contint
nous contînmes
vous contîntes
ils continrent

Future
je contiendrai
tu contiendras
il contiendra
nous contiendrons
vous contiendrez
ils contiendront

Perfect indicative
j'ai contenu
tu as contenu
il a contenu
nous avons contenu
vous avez contenu
ils ont contenu

Pluperfect indicative
j'avais contenu
tu avais contenu
il avait contenu
nous avions contenu
vous aviez contenu
ils avaient contenu

Present subjunctive
que je contienne
que tu contiennes
qu'il contienne
que nous contenions
que vous conteniez
qu'ils contiennent

Conditional
je contiendrais
tu contiendrais
il contiendrait
nous contiendrions
vous contiendriez
ils contiendraient

Imperative
contiens
contenons
contenez

contredire
to contradict

Present participle
contredisant

Past participle
contredit

Present indicative
je contredis
tu contredis
il contredit
nous contredisons
vous contredisez
ils contredisent

Imperfect indicative
je contredisais
tu contredisais
il contredisait
nous contredisions
vous contredisiez
ils contredisaient

Past historic
je contredis
tu contredis
il contredit
nous contredîmes
vous contredîtes
ils contredirent

Future
je contredirai
tu contrediras
il contredira
nous contredirons
vous contredirez
ils contrediront

Perfect indicative
j'ai contredit
tu as contredit
il a contredit
nous avons contredit
vous avez contredit
ils ont contredit

Pluperfect indicative
j'avais contredit
tu avais contredit
il avait contredit
nous avions contredit
vous aviez contredit
ils avaient contredit

Present subjunctive

que je contredise
que tu contredises
qu'il contredise
que nous contredisions
que vous contredisiez
qu'ils contredisent

Conditional

je contredirais
tu contredirais
il contredirait
nous contredirions
vous contrediriez
ils contrediraient

Imperative

contredis
contredisons
contredisez

convaincre
to convince

Present participle

convainquant

Past participle

convaincu

Present indicative

je convaincs
tu convaincs
il convainc
nous convainquons
vous convainquez
ils convainquent

Imperfect indicative

je convainquais
tu convainquais
il convainquait
nous convainquions
vous convainquiez
ils convainquaient

Past historic

je convainquis
tu convainquis
il convainquit
nous convainquîmes
vous convainquîtes
ils convainquirent

Future

je convaincrai

tu convaincras
il convaincra
nous convaincrons
vous convaincrez
ils convaincront

Perfect indicative

j'ai convaincu
tu as convaincu
il a convaincu
nous avons convaincu
vous avez convaincu
ils ont convaincu

Pluperfect indicative

j'avais convaincu
tu avais convaincu
il avait convaincu
nous avions convaincu
vous aviez convaincu
ils avaient convaincu

Present subjunctive

que je convainque
que tu convainques
qu'il convainque
que nous convainquions
que vous convainquiez
qu'ils convainquent

Conditional

je convaincrais
tu convaincrais
il convaincrait
nous convaincrions
vous convaincriez
ils convaincraient

Imperative

convaincs
convainquons
convainquez

coudre
to sew

Present participle

cousant

Past participle

cousu

Present indicative

je couds
tu couds
il coud

nous cousons
vous cousez
ils cousent

Imperfect indicative

je cousais
tu cousais
il cousait
nous cousions
vous cousiez
ils cousaient

Past historic

je cousis
tu cousis
il cousit
nous cousîmes
vous cousîtes
ils cousirent

Future

je coudrai
tu coudras
il coudra
nous coudrons
vous coudrez
ils coudront

Perfect indicative

j'ai cousu
tu as cousu
il a cousu
nous avons cousu
vous avez cousu
ils ont cousu

Pluperfect indicative

j'avais cousu
tu avais cousu
il avait cousu
nous avions cousu
vous aviez cousu
ils avaient cousu

Present subjunctive

que je couse
que tu couses
qu'il couse
que nous cousions
que vous cousiez
qu'ils cousent

Conditional

je coudrais
tu coudrais
il coudrait

nous coudrions
vous coudriez
ils coudraient

Imperative
 couds
cousons
cousez

courir
to run

Present participle
courant

Past participle
couru

Present indicative
je cours
tu cours
il court
nous courons
vous courez
ils courent

Imperfect indicative
je courais
tu courais
il courait
nous courions
vous couriez
ils couraient

Past historic
je courus
tu courus
il courut
nous courûmes
vous courûtes
ils coururent

Future
je courrai
tu courras
il courra
nous courrons
vous courrez
ils courront

Perfect indicative
j'ai couru
tu as couru
il a couru
nous avons couru
vous avez couru
ils ont couru

Pluperfect indicative
j'avais couru
tu avais couru
il avait couru
nous avions couru
vous aviez couru
ils avaient couru

Present subjunctive
que je coure
que tu coures
qu'il coure
que nous courions
que vous couriez
qu'ils courent

Conditional
je courrais
tu courrais
il courrait
nous courrions
vous courriez
ils courraient

Imperative
cours
courons
courez

couvrir
to cover

Present participle
couvrant

Past participle
couvert

Present indicative
je couvre
tu couvres
il couvre
nous couvrons
vous couvrez
ils couvrent

Imperfect indicative
je couvrais
tu couvrais
il couvrait
nous couvrions
vous couvriez
ils couvraient

Past historic
je couvris
tu couvris
il couvrit

nous couvrîmes
vous couvrîtes
ils couvrirent

Future
je couvrirai
tu couvriras
il couvrira
nous couvrirons
vous couvrirez
ils couvriront

Perfect indicative
je suis couvert
tu es couvert
il est couvert
nous sommes couverts
vous êtes couverts
ils sont couverts

Pluperfect indicative
j'étais couvert
tu étais couvert
il était couvert
nous étions couverts
vous étiez couverts
ils étaient couverts

Present subjunctive
que je couvre
que tu couvres
qu'il couvre
que nous couvrions
que vous couvriez
qu'ils couvrent

Conditional
je couvrirais
tu couvrirais
il couvrirait
nous couvririons
vous couvririez
ils couvriraient

Imperative
couvre
couvrons
couvrez

craindre
to fear

Present participle
craignant

Past participle
craint

Present indicative
je crains
tu crains
il craint
nous craignons
vous craignez
ils craignent

Imperfect indicative
je craignais
tu craignais
il craignait
nous craignions
vous craigniez
ils craignaient

Past historic
je craignis
tu craignis
il craignit
nous craignîmes
vous craignîtes
ils craignirent

Future
je craindrai
tu craindras
il craindra
nous craindrons
vous craindrez
ils craindront

Perfect indicative
j'ai craint
tu as craint
il a craint
nous avons craint
vous avez craint
ils ont craint

Pluperfect indicative
j'avais craint
tu avais craint
il avait craint
nous avions craint
vous aviez craint
ils avaient craint

Present subjunctive
que je craigne
que tu craignes
qu'il craigne
que nous craignions
que vous craigniez
qu'ils craignent

Conditional
je craindrais

tu craindrais
il craindrait
nous craindrions
vous craindriez
ils craindraient

Imperative
crains
craignons
craignez

créer
to create

Present participle
créant

Past participle
créé

Present indicative
je crée
tu crées
il crée
nous créons
vous créez
ils créent

Imperfect indicative
je créais
tu créais
il créait
nous créions
vous créiez
ils créaient

Past historic
je créai
tu créas
il créa
nous créâmes
vous créâtes
ils créèrent

Future
je créerai
tu créeras
il créera
nous créerons
vous créerez
ils créeront

Perfect indicative
j'ai créé
tu as créé
il a créé

nous avons créé
vous avez créé
ils ont créé

Pluperfect indicative
j'avais créé
tu avais créé
il avait créé
nous avions créé
vous aviez créé
ils avaient créé

Present subjunctive
que je crée
que tu crées
qu'il crée
que nous créions
que vous créiez
qu'ils créent

Conditional
je créerais
tu créerais
il créerait
nous créerions
vous créeriez
ils créeraient

Imperative
crée
créons
créez

croire
to believe, think

Present participle
croyant

Past participle
cru

Present indicative
je crois
tu crois
il croit
nous croyons
vous croyez
ils croient

Imperfect indicative
je croyais
tu croyais
il croyait
nous croyions
vous croyiez
ils croyaient

Past historic
je crus
tu crus
il crut
nous crûmes
vous crûtes
ils crurent

Future
je croirai
tu croiras
il croira
nous croirons
vous croirez
ils croiront

Perfect indicative
j'ai cru
tu as cru
il a cru
nous avons cru
vous avez cru
ils ont cru

Pluperfect indicative
j'avais cru
tu avais cru
il avait cru
nous avions cru
vous aviez cru
ils avaient cru

Present subjunctive
que je croie
que tu croies
qu'il croie
que nous croyions
que vous croyiez
qu'ils croient

Conditional
je croirais
tu croirais
il croirait
nous croirions
vous croiriez
ils croiraient

Imperative
crois
croyons
croyez

croître
to grow, increase

Present participle
croissant

Past participle
crû

Present indicative
je croîs
tu croîs
il croît
nous croissons
vous croissez
ils croissent

Imperfect indicative
je croissais
tu croissais
il croissait
nous croissions
vous croissiez
ils croissaient

Past historic
je crûs
tu crûs
il crût
nous crûmes
vous crûtes
ils crûrent

Future
je croîtrai
tu croîtras
il croîtra
nous croîtrons
vous croîtrez
ils croîtront

Perfect indicative
j'ai crû
tu as crû
il a crû
nous avons crû
vous avez crû
ils ont crû

Pluperfect indicative
j'avais crû
tu avais crû
il avait crû
nous avions crû
vous aviez crû
ils avaient crû

Present subjunctive
que je croisse
que tu croisses
qu'il croisse
que nous croissions
que vous croissiez
qu'ils croissent

Conditional
je croîtrais
tu croîtrais
il croîtrait
nous croîtrions
vous croîtriez
ils croîtraient

Imperative
croîs
croissons
croissez

cueillir
to pick

Present participle
cueillant

Past participle
cueilli

Present indicative
je cueille
tu cueilles
il cueille
nous cueillons
vous cueillez
ils cueillent

Imperfect indicative
je cueillais
tu cueillais
il cueillait
nous cueillions
vous cueilliez
ils cueillaient

Past historic
je cueillis
tu cueillis
il cueillit
nous cueillîmes
vous cueillîtes
ils cueillirent

Future
je cueillerai
tu cueilleras
il cueillera
nous cueillerons
vous cueillerez
ils cueilleront

Perfect indicative
j'ai cueilli
tu as cueilli
il a cueilli

nous avons cueilli
vous avez cueilli
ils ont cueilli

Pluperfect indicative

j'avais cueilli
tu avais cueilli
il avait cueilli
nous avions cueilli
vous aviez cueilli
ils avaient cueilli

Present subjunctive

que je cueille
que tu cueilles
qu'il cueille
que nous cueillions
que vous cueilliez
qu'ils cueillent

Conditional

je cueillerais
tu cueillerais
il cueillerait
nous cueillerions
vous cueilleriez
ils cueilleraient

Imperative

cueille
cueillons
cueillez

cuire
to cook

Present participle

cuisant

Past participle

cuit

Present indicative

je cuis
tu cuis
il cuit
nous cuisons
vous cuisez
ils cuisent

Imperfect indicative

je cuisais
tu cuisais
il cuisait
nous cuisions
vous cuisiez
ils cuisaient

Past historic

je cuisis
tu cuisis
il cuisit
nous cuisîmes
vous cuisîtes
ils cuisirent

Future

je cuirai
tu cuiras
il cuira
nous cuirons
vous cuirez
ils cuiront

Perfect indicative

j'ai cuit
tu as cuit
il a cuit
nous avons cuit
vous avez cuit
ils ont cuit

Pluperfect indicative

j'avais cuit
tu avais cuit
il avait cuit
nous avions cuit
vous aviez cuit
ils avaient cuit

Present subjunctive

que je cuise
que tu cuises
qu'il cuise
que nous cuisions
que vous cuisiez
qu'ils cuisent

Conditional

je cuirais
tu cuirais
il cuirait
nous cuirions
vous cuiriez
ils cuiraient

Imperative

cuis
cuisons
cuisez

débattre
to discuss, debate

Present participle

débattant

Past participle

débattu

Present indicative

je débats
tu débats
il débat
nous débattons
vous débattez
ils débattent

Imperfect indicative

je débattais
tu débattais
il débattait
nous débattions
vous débattiez
ils débattaient

Past historic

je débattis
tu débattis
il débattit
nous débattîmes
vous débattîtes
ils débattirent

Future

je débattrai
tu débattras
il débattra
nous débattrons
vous débattrez
ils débattront

Perfect indicative

j'ai débattu
tu as débattu
il a débattu
nous avons débattu
vous avez débattu
ils ont débattu

Pluperfect indicative

j'avais débattu
tu avais débattu
il avait débattu
nous avions débattu
vous aviez débattu
ils avaient débattu

Present subjunctive

que je débatte
que tu débattes
qu'il débatte
que nous débattions
que vous débattiez
qu'ils débattent

Conditional
je débattrais
tu débattrais
il débattrait
nous débattrions
vous débattriez
ils débattraient

Imperative
débats
débattons
débattez

décevoir
to disappoint

Present participle
décevant

Past participle
déçu

Present indicative
je déçois
tu déçois
il déçoit
nous décevons
vous décevez
ils déçoivent

Imperfect indicative
je décevais
tu décevais
il décevait
nous décevions
vous déceviez
ils décevaient

Past historic
je déçus
tu déçus
il déçut
nous déçûmes
vous déçûtes
ils déçurent

Future
je décevrai
tu décevras
il décevra
nous décevrons
vous décevrez
ils décevront

Perfect indicative
j'ai déçu

tu as déçu
il a déçu
nous avons déçu
vous avez déçu
ils ont déçu

Pluperfect indicative
j'avais déçu
tu avais déçu
il avait déçu
nous avions déçu
vous aviez déçu
ils avaient déçu

Present subjunctive
que je déçoive
que tu déçoives
qu'il déçoive
que nous décevions
que vous déceviez
qu'ils déçoivent

Conditional
je décevrais
tu décevrais
il décevrait
nous décevrions
vous décevriez
ils décevraient

Imperative
déçois
décevons
décevez

décrire
to describe

Present participle
décrivant

Past participle
décrit

Present indicative
je décris
tu décris
il décrit
nous décrivons
vous décrivez
ils décrivent

Imperfect indicative
je décrivais
tu décrivais
il décrivait

nous décrivions
vous décriviez
ils décrivaient

Past historic
je décrivis
tu décrivis
il décrivit
nous décrivîmes
vous décrivîtes
ils décrivirent

Future
je décrirai
tu décriras
il décrira
nous décrirons
vous décrirez
ils décriront

Perfect indicative
j'ai décrit
tu as décrit
il a décrit
nous avons décrit
vous avez décrit
ils ont décrit

Pluperfect indicative
j'avais décrit
tu avais décrit
il avait décrit
nous avions décrit
vous aviez décrit
ils avaient décrit

Present subjunctive
que je décrive
que tu décrives
qu'il décrive
que nous décrivions
que vous décriviez
qu'ils décrivent

Conditional
je décrirais
tu décrirais
il décrirait
nous décririons
vous décririez
ils décriraient

Imperative
décris
décrivons
décrivez

décroître
to decrease

Present participle
décroissant

Past participle
décrû

Present indicative
je décroîs
tu décroîs
il décroît
nous décroissons
vous décroissez
ils décroissent

Imperfect indicative
je décroissais
tu décroissais
il décroissait
nous décroissions
vous décroissiez
ils décroissaient

Past historic
je décrûs
tu décrûs
il décrût
nous décrûmes
vous décrûtes
ils décrûrent

Future
je décroîtrai
tu décroîtras
il décroîtra
nous décroîtrons
vous décroîtrez
ils décroîtront

Perfect indicative
j'ai décrû
tu as décrû
il a décrû
nous avons décrû
vous avez décrû
ils ont décrû

Pluperfect indicative
j'avais décrû
tu avais décrû
il avait décrû
nous avions décrû
vous aviez décrû
ils avaient décrû

Present subjunctive
que je décroisse
que tu décroisses
qu'il décroisse
que nous décroissions
que vous décroissiez
qu'ils décroissent

Conditional
je décroîtrais
tu décroîtrais
il décroîtrait
nous décroîtrions
vous décroîtriez
ils décroîtraient

Imperative
décroîs
décroissons
décroissez

déduire
to deduce, infer

Present participle
déduisant

Past participle
déduit

Present indicative
je déduis
tu déduis
il déduit
nous déduisons
vous déduisez
ils déduisent

Imperfect indicative
je déduisais
tu déduisais
il déduisait
nous déduisions
vous déduisiez
ils déduisaient

Past historic
je déduisis
tu déduisis
il déduisit
nous déduisîmes
vous déduisîtes
ils déduisirent

Future
je déduirai
tu déduiras
il déduira
nous déduirons
vous déduirez
ils déduiront

Perfect indicative
j'ai déduit
tu as déduit
il a déduit
nous avons déduit
vous avez déduit
ils ont déduit

Pluperfect indicative
j'avais déduit
tu avais déduit
il avait déduit
nous avions déduit
vous aviez déduit
ils avaient déduit

Present subjunctive
que je déduise
que tu déduises
qu'il déduise
que nous déduisions
que vous déduisiez
qu'ils déduisent

Conditional
je déduirais
tu déduirais
il déduirait
nous déduirions
vous déduiriez
ils déduiraient

Imperative
déduis
déduisons
déduisez

défaire
to undo

Present participle
défaisant

Past participle
défait

Present indicative
je défais
tu défais
il défait

nous défaisons
vous défaites
ils défont

Imperfect indicative
je défaisais
tu défaisais
il défaisait
nous défaisions
vous défaisiez
ils défaisaient

Past historic
je défis
tu défis
il défit
nous défîmes
vous défîtes
ils défirent

Future
je déferai
tu déferas
il défera
nous déferons
vous déferez
ils déferont

Perfect indicative
j'ai défait
tu as défait
il a défait
nous avons défait
vous avez défait
ils ont défait

Pluperfect indicative
j'avais défait
tu avais défait
il avait défait
nous avions défait
vous aviez défait
ils avaient défait

Present subjunctive
que je défasse
que tu défasses
qu'il défasse
que nous défassions
que vous défassiez
qu'ils défassent

Conditional
je déferais
tu déferais
il déferait

nous déferions
vous déferiez
ils déferaient

Imperative
défais
défaisons
défaites

démentir
to deny

Present participle
démentant

Past participle
démenti

Present indicative
je démens
tu démens
il dément
nous démentons
vous démentez
ils démentent

Imperfect indicative
je démentais
tu démentais
il démentait
nous démentions
vous démentiez
ils démentaient

Past historic
je démentis
tu démentis
il démentit
nous démentîmes
vous démentîtes
ils démentirent

Future
je démentirai
tu démentiras
il démentira
nous démentirons
vous démentirez
ils démentiront

Perfect indicative
j'ai démenti
tu as démenti
il a démenti
nous avons démenti
vous avez démenti
ils ont démenti

Pluperfect indicative
j'avais démenti
tu avais démenti
il avait démenti
nous avions démenti
vous aviez démenti
ils avaient démenti

Present subjunctive
que je démente
que tu démentes
qu'il démente
que nous démentions
que vous démentiez
qu'ils démentent

Conditional
je démentirais
tu démentirais
il démentirait
nous démentirions
vous démentiriez
ils démentiraient

Imperative
démens
démentons
démentez

dépenser
to spend

Present participle
dépensant

Past participle
dépensé

Present indicative
je dépense
tu dépenses
il dépense
nous dépensons
vous dépensez
ils dépensent

Imperfect indicative
je dépensais
tu dépensais
il dépensait
nous dépensions
vous dépensiez
ils dépensaient

Past historic
je dépensai

tu dépensas
il dépensa
nous dépensâmes
vous dépensâtes
ils dépensèrent

Future

je dépenserai
tu dépenseras
il dépensera
nous dépenserons
vous dépenserez
ils dépenseront

Perfect indicative

j'ai dépensé
tu as dépensé
il a dépensé
nous avons dépensé
vous avez dépensé
ils ont dépensé

Pluperfect indicative

j'avais dépensé
tu avais dépensé
il avait dépensé
nous avions dépensé
vous aviez dépensé
ils avaient dépensé

Present subjunctive

que je dépense
que tu dépenses
qu'il dépense
que nous dépensions
que vous dépensiez
qu'ils dépensent

Conditional

je dépenserais
tu dépenserais
il dépenserait
nous dépenserions
vous dépenseriez
ils dépenseraient

Imperative

dépense
dépensons
dépensez

descendre
to go down, descend

Present participle

descendant

Past participle

descendu

Present indicative

je descends
tu descends
il descend
nous descendons
vous descendez
ils descendent

Imperfect indicative

je descendais
tu descendais
il descendait
nous descendions
vous descendiez
ils descendaient

Past historic

je descendis
tu descendis
il descendit
nous descendîmes
vous descendîtes
ils descendirent

Future

je descendrai
tu descendras
il descendra
nous descendrons
vous descendrez
ils descendront

Perfect indicative

je suis descendu
tu es descendu
il est descendu
nous sommes descendus
vous êtes descendus
ils sont descendus

Pluperfect indicative

j'étais descendu
tu étais descendu
il était descendu
nous étions descendus
vous étiez descendus
ils étaient descendus

Present subjunctive

que je descende
que tu descendes
qu'il descende
que nous descendions
que vous descendiez
qu'ils descendent

Conditional

je descendrais
tu descendrais
il descendrait
nous descendrions
vous descendriez
ils descendraient

Imperative

descends
descendons
descendez

détenir
to hold, detain

Present participle

détenant

Past participle

détenu

Present indicative

je détiens
tu détiens
il détient
nous détenons
vous détenez
ils détiennent

Imperfect indicative

je détenais
tu détenais
il détenait
nous détenions
vous déteniez
ils détenaient

Past historic

je détins
tu détins
il détint
nous détînmes
vous détîntes
ils détinrent

Future

je détiendrai
tu détiendras
il détiendra
nous détiendrons
vous détiendrez
ils détiendront

Perfect indicative

j'ai détenu

détruire

tu as détenu
il a détenu
nous avons détenu
vous avez détenu
ils ont détenu

Pluperfect indicative

j'avais détenu
tu avais détenu
il avait détenu
nous avions détenu
vous aviez détenu
ils avaient détenu

Present subjunctive

que je détienne
que tu détiennes
qu'il détienne
que nous détenions
que vous déteniez
qu'ils détiennent

Conditional

je détiendrais
tu détiendrais
il détiendrait
nous détiendrions
vous détiendriez
ils détiendraient

Imperative

détiens
détenons
détenez

détruire
to destruct

Present participle

détruisant

Past participle

détruit

Present indicative

je détruis
tu détruis
il détruit
nous détruisons
vous détruisez
ils détruisent

Imperfect indicative

je détruisais
tu détruisais
il détruisait

nous détruisions
vous détruisiez
ils détruisaient

Past historic

je détruisis
tu détruisis
il détruisit
nous détruisîmes
vous détruisîtes
ils détruisirent

Future

je détruirai
tu détruiras
il détruira
nous détruirons
vous détruirez
ils détruiront

Perfect indicative

j'ai détruit
tu as détruit
il a détruit
nous avons détruit
vous avez détruit
ils ont détruit

Pluperfect indicative

j'avais détruit
tu avais détruit
il avait détruit
nous avions détruit
vous aviez détruit
ils avaient détruit

Present subjunctive

que je détruise
que tu détruises
qu'il détruise
que nous détruisions
que vous détruisiez
qu'ils détruisent

Conditional

je détruirais
tu détruirais
il détruirait
nous détruirions
vous détruiriez
ils détruiraient

Imperative

détruis
détruisons
détruisez

devenir
to become

Present participle

devenant

Past participle

devenu

Present indicative

je deviens
tu deviens
il devient
nous devenons
vous devenez
ils deviennent

Imperfect indicative

je devenais
tu devenais
il devenait
nous devenions
vous deveniez
ils devenaient

Past historic

je devins
tu devins
il devint
nous devînmes
vous devîntes
ils devinrent

Future

je deviendrai
tu deviendras
il deviendra
nous deviendrons
vous deviendrez
ils deviendront

Perfect indicative

je suis devenu
tu es devenu
il est devenu
nous sommes devenus
vous êtes devenus
ils sont devenus

Pluperfect indicative

j'étais devenu
tu étais devenu
il était devenu
nous étions devenus
vous étiez devenus
ils étaient devenus

Present subjunctive
que je devienne
que tu deviennes
qu'il devienne
que nous devenions
que vous deveniez
qu'ils deviennent

Conditional
je deviendrais
tu deviendrais
il deviendrait
nous deviendrions
vous deviendriez
ils deviendraient

Imperative
deviens
devenons
devenez

devoir
must, to owe

Present participle
devant

Past participle
dû

Present indicative
je dois
tu dois
il doit
nous devons
vous devez
ils doivent

Imperfect indicative
je devais
tu devais
il devait
nous devions
vous deviez
ils devaient

Past historic
je dus
tu dus
il dut
nous dûmes
vous dûtes
ils durent

Future
je devrai

tu devras
il devra
nous devrons
vous devrez
ils devront

Perfect indicative
j'ai dû
tu as dû
il a dû
nous avons dû
vous avez dû
ils ont dû

Pluperfect indicative
j'avais dû
tu avais dû
il avait dû
nous avions dû
vous aviez dû
ils avaient dû

Present subjunctive
que je doive
que tu doives
qu'il doive
que nous devions
que vous deviez
qu'ils doivent

Conditional
je devrais
tu devrais
il devrait
nous devrions
vous devriez
ils devraient

Imperative
dois
devons
devez

dire
to say, tell

Present participle
disant

Past participle
dit

Present indicative
je dis
tu dis
il dit

nous disons
vous dites
ils disent

Imperfect indicative
je disais
tu disais
il disait
nous disions
vous disiez
ils disaient

Past historic
je dis
tu dis
il dit
nous dîmes
vous dîtes
ils dirent

Future
je dirai
tu diras
il dira
nous dirons
vous direz
ils diront

Perfect indicative
j'ai dit
tu as dit
il a dit
nous avons dit
vous avez dit
ils ont dit

Pluperfect indicative
j'avais dit
tu avais dit
il avait dit
nous avions dit
vous aviez dit
ils avaient dit

Present subjunctive
que je dise
que tu dises
qu'il dise
que nous disions
que vous disiez
qu'ils disent

Conditional
je dirais
tu dirais
il dirait

nous dirions
vous diriez
ils diraient

Imperative
dis
disons
dites

disjoindre
to take apart, disconnect

Present participle
disjoignant

Past participle
disjoint

Present indicative
je disjoins
tu disjoins
il disjoint
nous disjoignons
vous disjoignez
ils disjoignent

Imperfect indicative
je disjoignais
tu disjoignais
il disjoignait
nous disjoignions
vous disjoigniez
ils disjoignaient

Past historic
je disjoignis
tu disjoignis
il disjoignit
nous disjoignîmes
vous disjoignîtes
ils disjoignirent

Future
je disjoindrai
tu disjoindras
il disjoindra
nous disjoindrons
vous disjoindrez
ils disjoindront

Perfect indicative
j'ai disjoint
tu as disjoint
il a disjoint
nous avons disjoint
vous avez disjoint
ils ont disjoint

Pluperfect indicative
j'avais disjoint
tu avais disjoint
il avait disjoint
nous avions disjoint
vous aviez disjoint
ils avaient disjoint

Present subjunctive
que je disjoigne
que tu disjoignes
qu'il disjoigne
que nous disjoignions
que vous disjoigniez
qu'ils disjoignent

Conditional
je disjoindrais
tu disjoindrais
il disjoindrait
nous disjoindrions
vous disjoindriez
ils disjoindraient

Imperative
disjoins
disjoignons
disjoignez

disparaître
to disappear

Present participle
disparaissant

Past participle
disparu

Present indicative
je disparais
tu disparais
il disparaît
nous disparaissons
vous disparaissez
ils disparaissent

Imperfect indicative
je disparaissais
tu disparaissais
il disparaissait
nous disparaissions
vous disparaissiez
ils disparaissaient

Past historic
je disparus

tu disparus
il disparut
nous disparûmes
vous disparûtes
ils disparurent

Future
je disparaîtrai
tu disparaîtras
il disparaîtra
nous disparaîtrons
vous disparaîtrez
ils disparaîtront

Perfect indicative
j'ai disparu
tu as disparu
il a disparu
nous avons disparu
vous avez disparu
ils ont disparu

Pluperfect indicative
j'avais disparu
tu avais disparu
il avait disparu
nous avions disparu
vous aviez disparu
ils avaient disparu

Present subjunctive
que je disparaisse
que tu disparaisses
qu'il disparaisse
que nous disparaissions
que vous disparaissiez
qu'ils disparaissent

Conditional
je disparaîtrais
tu disparaîtrais
il disparaîtrait
nous disparaîtrions
vous disparaîtriez
ils disparaîtraient

Imperative
disparais
disparaissons
disparaissez

dissoudre
to dissolve

Present participle
dissolvant

Past participle
dissous (-te)

Present indicative
je dissous
tu dissous
il dissout
nous dissolvons
vous dissolvez
ils dissolvent

Imperfect indicative
je dissolvais
tu dissolvais
il dissolvait
nous dissolvions
vous dissolviez
ils dissolvaient

Past historic
–
–
–
–
–
–

Future
je dissoudrai
tu dissoudras
il dissoudra
nous dissoudrons
vous dissoudrez
ils dissoudront

Perfect indicative
j'ai dissous
tu as dissous
il a dissous
nous avons dissous
vous avez dissous
ils ont dissous

Pluperfect indicative
j'avais dissous
tu avais dissous
il avait dissous
nous avions dissous
vous aviez dissous
ils avaient dissous

Present subjunctive
que je dissolve
que tu dissolves
qu'il dissolve
que nous dissolvions
que vous dissolviez
qu'ils dissolvent

Conditional
je dissoudrais
tu dissoudrais
il dissoudrait
nous dissoudrions
vous dissoudriez
ils dissoudraient

Imperative
dissous
dissolvons
dissolvez

distraire
to distract, entertain

Present participle
distrayant

Past participle
distrait

Present indicative
je distrais
tu distrais
il distrait
nous distrayons
vous distrayez
ils distraient

Imperfect indicative
je distrayais
tu distrayais
il distrayait
nous distrayions
vous distrayiez
ils distrayaient

Past historic
–
–
–
–
–
–

Future
je distrairai
tu distrairas
il distraira
nous distrairons
vous distrairez
ils distrairont

Perfect indicative
j'ai distrait

tu as distrait
il a distrait
nous avons distrait
vous avez distrait
ils ont distrait

Pluperfect indicative
j'avais distrait
tu avais distrait
il avait distrait
nous avions distrait
vous aviez distrait
ils avaient distrait

Present subjunctive
que je distraie
que tu distraies
qu'il distraie
que nous distrayions
que vous distrayiez
qu'ils distraient

Conditional
je distrairais
tu distrairais
il distrairait
nous distrairions
vous distrairiez
ils distrairaient

Imperative
distrais
distrayons
distrayez

donner
to give

Present participle
donnant

Past participle
donné

Present indicative
je donne
tu donnes
il donne
nous donnons
vous donnez
ils donnent

Imperfect indicative
je donnais
tu donnais
il donnait

nous donnions
vous donniez
ils donnaient

Past historic

je donnai
tu donnas
il donna
nous donnâmes
vous donnâtes
ils donnèrent

Future

je donnerai
tu donneras
il donnera
nous donnerons
vous donnerez
ils donneront

Perfect indicative

j'ai donné
tu as donné
il a donné
nous avons donné
vous avez donné
ils ont donné

Pluperfect indicative

j'avais donné
tu avais donné
il avait donné
nous avions donné
vous aviez donné
ils avaient donné

Present subjunctive

que je donne
que tu donnes
qu'il donne
que nous donnions
que vous donniez
qu'ils donnent

Conditional

je donnerais
tu donnerais
il donnerait
nous donnerions
vous donneriez
ils donneraient

Imperative

donne
donnons
donnez

dormir
to sleep

Present participle

dormant

Past participle

dormi

Present indicative

je dors
tu dors
il dort
nous dormons
vous dormez
ils dorment

Imperfect indicative

je dormais
tu dormais
il dormait
nous dormions
vous dormiez
ils dormaient

Past historic

je dormis
tu dormis
il dormit
nous dormîmes
vous dormîtes
ils dormirent

Future

je dormirai
tu dormiras
il dormira
nous dormirons
vous dormirez
ils dormiront

Perfect indicative

j'ai dormi
tu as dormi
il a dormi
nous avons dormi
vous avez dormi
ils ont dormi

Pluperfect indicative

j'avais dormi
tu avais dormi
il avait dormi
nous avions dormi
vous aviez dormi
ils avaient dormi

Present subjunctive

que je dorme
que tu dormes
qu'il dorme
que nous dormions
que vous dormiez
qu'ils dorment

Conditional

je dormirais
tu dormirais
il dormirait
nous dormirions
vous dormiriez
ils dormiraient

Imperative

dors
dormons
dormez

écrire
to write

Present participle

écrivant

Past participle

écrit

Present indicative

j'écris
tu écris
il écrit
nous écrivons
vous écrivez
ils écrivent

Imperfect indicative

j'écrivais
tu écrivais
il écrivait
nous écrivions
vous écriviez
ils écrivaient

Past historic

j'écrivis
tu écrivis
il écrivit
nous écrivîmes
vous écrivîtes
ils écrivirent

Future

j'écrirai

tu écriras
il écrira
nous écrirons
vous écrirez
ils écriront

Perfect indicative

j'ai écrit
tu as écrit
il a écrit
nous avons écrit
vous avez écrit
ils ont écrit

Pluperfect indicative

j'avais écrit
tu avais écrit
il avait écrit
nous avions écrit
vous aviez écrit
ils avaient écrit

Present subjunctive

que j'écrive
que tu écrives
qu'il écrive
que nous écrivions
que vous écriviez
qu'ils écrivent

Conditional

j'écrirais
tu écrirais
il écrirait
nous écririons
vous écririez
ils écriraient

Imperative

écris
écrivons
écrivez

élire
to elect

Present participle

élisant

Past participle

élu

Present indicative

j'élis
tu élis
il élit

nous élisons
vous élisez
ils élisent

Imperfect indicative

j'élisais
tu élisais
il élisait
nous élisions
vous élisiez
ils élisaient

Past historic

j'élus
tu élus
il élut
nous élûmes
vous élûtes
ils élurent

Future

j'élirai
tu éliras
il élira
nous élirons
vous élirez
ils éliront

Perfect indicative

j'ai élu
tu as élu
il a élu
nous avons élu
vous avez élu
ils ont élu

Pluperfect indicative

j'avais élu
tu avais élu
il avait élu
nous avions élu
vous aviez élu
ils avaient élu

Present subjunctive

que j'élise
que tu élises
qu'il élise
que nous élisions
que vous élisiez
qu'ils élisent

Conditional

j'élirais
tu élirais
il élirait
nous élirions
vous éliriez
ils éliraient

Imperative

élis
élisons
élisez

emporter
to take, carry away

Present participle

emportant

Past participle

emporté

Present indicative

j'emporte
tu emportes
il emporte
nous emportons
vous emportez
ils emportent

Imperfect indicative

j'emportais
tu emportais
il emportait
nous emportions
vous emportiez
ils emportaient

Past historic

j'emportai
tu emportas
il emporta
nous emportâmes
vous emportâtes
ils emportèrent

Future

j'emporterai
tu emporteras
il emportera
nous emporterons
vous emporterez
ils emporteront

Perfect indicative

j'ai emporté
tu as emporté
il a emporté
nous avons emporté
vous avez emporté
ils ont emporté

Pluperfect indicative

j'avais emporté

tu avais emporté
il avait emporté
nous avions emporté
vous aviez emporté
ils avaient emporté

Present subjunctive
que j'emporte
que tu emportes
qu'il emporte
que nous emportions
que vous emportiez
qu'ils emportent

Conditional
j'emporterais
tu emporterais
il emporterait
nous emporterions
vous emporteriez
ils emporteraient

Imperative
emporte
emportons
emportez

entendre
to hear

Present participle
entendant

Past participle
entendu

Present indicative
j'entends
tu entends
il entend
nous entendons
vous entendez
ils entendent

Imperfect indicative
j'entendais
tu entendais
il entendait
nous entendions
vous entendiez
ils entendaient

Past historic
j'entendis
tu entendis
il entendit

nous entendîmes
vous entendîtes
ils entendirent

Future
j'entendrai
tu entendras
il entendra
nous entendrons
vous entendrez
ils entendront

Perfect indicative
j'ai entendu
tu as entendu
il a entendu
nous avons entendu
vous avez entendu
ils ont entendu

Pluperfect indicative
j'avais entendu
tu avais entendu
il avait entendu
nous avions entendu
vous aviez entendu
ils avaient entendu

Present subjunctive
que j'entende
que tu entendes
qu'il entende
que nous entendions
que vous entendiez
qu'ils entendent

Conditional
j'entendrais
tu entendrais
il entendrait
nous entendrions
vous entendriez
ils entendraient

Imperative
entends
entendons
entendez

entreprendre
to undertake

Present participle
entreprenant

Past participle
entrepris

Present indicative
j'entreprends
tu entreprends
il entreprend
nous entreprenons
vous entreprenez
ils entreprennent

Imperfect indicative
j'entreprenais
tu entreprenais
il entreprenait
nous entreprenions
vous entrepreniez
ils entreprenaient

Past historic
j'entrepris
tu entrepris
il entreprit
nous entreprîmes
vous entreprîtes
ils entreprirent

Future
j'entreprendrai
tu entreprendras
il entreprendra
nous entreprendrons
vous entreprendrez
ils entreprendront

Perfect indicative
j'ai entrepris
tu as entrepris
il a entrepris
nous avons entrepris
vous avez entrepris
ils ont entrepris

Pluperfect indicative
j'avais entrepris
tu avais entrepris
il avait entrepris
nous avions entrepris
vous aviez entrepris
ils avaient entrepris

Present subjunctive
que j'entreprenne
que tu entreprennes
qu'il entreprenne
que nous entreprenions
que vous entrepreniez
qu'ils entreprennent

Conditional

j'entreprendrais
tu entreprendrais
il entreprendrait
nous entreprendrions
vous entreprendriez
ils entreprendraient

Imperative

entreprends
entreprenons
entreprenez

entrer
to go, come in

Present participle

entrant

Past participle

entré

Present indicative

j'entre
tu entres
il entre
nous entrons
vous entrez
ils entrent

Imperfect indicative

j'entrais
tu entrais
il entrait
nous entrions
vous entriez
ils entraient

Past historic

j'entrai
tu entras
il entra
nous entrâmes
vous entrâtes
ils entrèrent

Future

j'entrerai
tu entreras
il entrera
nous entrerons
vous entrerez
ils entreront

Perfect indicative

je suis entré
tu es entré
il est entré
nous sommes entrés
vous êtes entrés
ils sont entrés

Pluperfect indicative

j'étais entré
tu étais entré
il était entré
nous étions entrés
vous étiez entrés
ils étaient entrés

Present subjunctive

que j'entre
que tu entres
qu'il entre
que nous entrions
que vous entriez
qu'ils entrent

Conditional

j'entrerais
tu entrerais
il entrerait
nous entrerions
vous entreriez
ils entreraient

Imperative

entre
entrons
entrez

envoyer
to send

Present participle

envoyant

Past participle

envoyé

Present indicative

j'envoie
tu envoies
il envoie
nous envoyons
vous envoyez
ils envoient

Imperfect indicative

j'envoyais

tu envoyais
il envoyait
nous envoyions
vous envoyiez
ils envoyaient

Past historic

j'envoyai
tu envoyas
il envoya
nous envoyâmes
vous envoyâtes
ils envoyèrent

Future

j'enverrai
tu enverras
il enverra
nous enverrons
vous enverrez
ils enverront

Perfect indicative

j'ai envoyé
tu as envoyé
il a envoyé
nous avons envoyé
vous avez envoyé
ils ont envoyé

Pluperfect indicative

j'avais envoyé
tu avais envoyé
il avait envoyé
nous avions envoyé
vous aviez envoyé
ils avaient envoyé

Present subjunctive

que j'envoie
que tu envoies
qu'il envoie
que nous envoyions
que vous envoyiez
qu'ils envoient

Conditional

je enverrais
tu enverrais
il enverrait
nous enverrions
vous enverriez
ils enverraient

Imperative

envoie
envoyons
envoyez

essuyer
to wipe

Present participle
essuyant

Past participle
essuyé

Present indicative
j'essuie
tu essuies
il essuie
nous essuyons
vous essuyez
ils essuient

Imperfect indicative
j'essuyais
tu essuyais
il essuyait
nous essuyions
vous essuyiez
ils essuyaient

Past historic
j'essuyai
tu essuyas
il essuya
nous essuyâmes
vous essuyâtes
ils essuyèrent

Future
j'essuierai
tu essuieras
il essuiera
nous essuierons
vous essuierez
ils essuieront

Perfect indicative
j'ai essuyé
tu as essuyé
il a essuyé
nous avons essuyé
vous avez essuyé
ils ont essuyé

Pluperfect indicative
j'avais essuyé
tu avais essuyé
il avait essuyé
nous avions essuyé
vous aviez essuyé
ils avaient essuyé

Present subjunctive
que j'essuie
que tu essuies
qu'il essuie
que nous essuyions
que vous essuyiez
qu'ils essuient

Conditional
j'essuierais
tu essuierais
il essuierait
nous essuierions
vous essuieriez
ils essuieraient

Imperative
essuie
essuyons
essuyez

éteindre
to put out, switch off

Present participle
éteignant

Past participle
éteint

Present indicative
j'éteins
tu éteins
il éteint
nous éteignons
vous éteignez
ils éteignent

Imperfect indicative
j'éteignais
tu éteignais
il éteignait
nous éteignions
vous éteigniez
ils éteignaient

Past historic
j'éteignis
tu éteignis
il éteignit
nous éteignîmes
vous éteignîtes
ils éteignirent

Future
j'éteindrai

tu éteindras
il éteindra
nous éteindrons
vous éteindrez
ils éteindront

Perfect indicative
j'ai éteint
tu as éteint
il a éteint
nous avons éteint
vous avez éteint
ils ont éteint

Pluperfect indicative
j'avais éteint
tu avais éteint
il avait éteint
nous avions éteint
vous aviez éteint
ils avaient éteint

Present subjunctive
que j'éteigne
que tu éteignes
qu'il éteigne
que nous éteignions
que vous éteigniez
qu'ils éteignent

Conditional
j'éteindrais
tu éteindrais
il éteindrait
nous éteindrions
vous éteindriez
ils éteindraient

Imperative
éteins
éteignons
éteignez

être
to be

Present participle
étant

Past participle
été

Present indicative
je suis
tu es
il est

nous sommes
vous êtes
ils sont

Imperfect indicative
j'étais
tu étais
il était
nous étions
vous étiez
ils étaient

Past historic
je fus
tu fus
il fut
nous fûmes
vous fûtes
ils furent

Future
je serai
tu seras
il sera
nous serons
vous serez
ils seront

Perfect indicative
j'ai été
tu as été
il a été
nous avons été
vous avez été
ils ont été

Pluperfect indicative
j'avais été
tu avais été
il avait été
nous avions été
vous aviez été
ils avaient été

Present subjunctive
que je sois
que tu sois
qu'il soit
que nous soyons
que vous soyez
qu'ils soient

Conditional
je serais
tu serais
il serait
nous serions
vous seriez
ils seraient

Imperative
sois
soyons
soyez

exclure
to exclude

Present participle
excluant

Past participle
exclu

Present indicative
j'exclus
tu exclus
il exclut
nous excluons
vous excluez
ils excluent

Imperfect indicative
j'excluais
tu excluais
il excluait
nous excluions
vous excluiez
ils excluaient

Past historic
j'exclus
tu exclus
il exclut
nous exclûmes
vous exclûtes
ils exclurent

Future
j'exclurai
tu excluras
il exclura
nous exclurons
vous exclurez
ils excluront

Perfect indicative
j'ai exclu
tu as exclu
il a exclu
nous avons exclu
vous avez exclu
ils ont exclu

Pluperfect indicative
j'avais exclu

tu avais exclu
il avait exclu
nous avions exclu
vous aviez exclu
ils avaient exclu

Present subjunctive
que j'exclue
que tu exclues
qu'il exclue
que nous excluions
que vous excluiez
qu'ils excluent

Conditional
j'exclurais
tu exclurais
il exclurait
nous exclurions
vous excluriez
ils excluraient

Imperative
exclus
excluons
excluez

expliquer
to explain

Present participle
expliquant

Past participle
expliqué

Present indicative
j'explique
tu expliques
il explique
nous expliquons
vous expliquez
ils expliquent

Imperfect indicative
j'expliquais
tu expliquais
il expliquait
nous expliquions
vous expliquiez
ils expliquaient

Past historic
j'expliquai
tu expliquas
il expliqua

nous expliquâmes
vous expliquâtes
ils expliquèrent

Future
j'expliquerai
tu expliqueras
il expliquera
nous expliquerons
vous expliquerez
ils expliqueront

Perfect indicative
j'ai expliqué
tu as expliqué
il a expliqué
nous avons expliqué
vous avez expliqué
ils ont expliqué

Pluperfect indicative
j'avais expliqué
tu avais expliqué
il avait expliqué
nous avions expliqué
vous aviez expliqué
ils avaient expliqué

Present subjunctive
que j'explique
que tu expliques
qu'il explique
que nous expliquions
que vous expliquiez
qu'ils expliquent

Conditional
j'expliquerais
tu expliquerais
il expliquerait
nous expliquerions
vous expliqueriez
ils expliqueraient

Imperative
explique
expliquons
expliquez

extraire
to extract, pull out

Present participle
extrayant

Past participle
extrait

Present indicative
j'extrais
tu extrais
il extrait
nous extrayons
vous extrayez
ils extraient

Imperfect indicative
j'extrayais
tu extrayais
il extrayait
nous extrayions
vous extrayiez
ils extrayaient

Past historic
–
–
–
–
–
–

Future
j'extrairai
tu extrairas
il extraira
nous extrairons
vous extrairez
ils extrairont

Perfect indicative
j'ai extrait
tu as extrait
il a extrait
nous avons extrait
vous avez extrait
ils ont extrait

Pluperfect indicative
j'avais extrait
tu avais extrait
il avait extrait
nous avions extrait
vous aviez extrait
ils avaient extrait

Present subjunctive
que j'extraie
que tu extraies
qu'il extraie
que nous extrayions
que vous extrayiez
qu'ils extraient

Conditional
j'extrairais

tu extrairais
il extrairait
nous extrairions
vous extrairiez
ils extrairaient

Imperative
extrais
extrayons
extrayez

faire
to do, make

Present participle
faisant

Past participle
fait

Present indicative
je fais
tu fais
il fait
nous faisons
vous faites
ils font

Imperfect indicative
je faisais
tu faisais
il faisait
nous faisions
vous faisiez
ils faisaient

Past historic
je fis
tu fis
il fit
nous fîmes
vous fîtes
ils firent

Future
je ferai
tu feras
il fera
nous ferons
vous ferez
ils feront

Perfect indicative
j'ai fait
tu as fait
il a fait

nous avons fait
vous avez fait
ils ont fait

Pluperfect indicative

j'avais fait
tu avais fait
il avait fait
nous avions fait
vous aviez fait
ils avaient fait

Present subjunctive

que je fasse
que tu fasses
qu'il fasse
que nous fassions
que vous fassiez
qu'ils fassent

Conditional

je ferais
tu ferais
il ferait
nous ferions
vous feriez
ils feraient

Imperative

fais
faisons
faites

finir
to finish, end

Present participle

finissant

Past participle

fini

Present indicative

je finis
tu finis
il finit
nous finissons
vous finissez
ils finissent

Imperfect indicative

je finissais
tu finissais
il finissait
nous finissions
vous finissiez
ils finissaient

Past historic

je finis
tu finis
il finit
nous finîmes
vous finîtes
ils finirent

Future

je finirai
tu finiras
il finira
nous finirons
vous finirez
ils finiront

Perfect indicative

j'ai fini
tu as fini
il a fini
nous avons fini
vous avez fini
ils ont fini

Pluperfect indicative

j'avais fini
tu avais fini
il avait fini
nous avions fini
vous aviez fini
ils avaient fini

Present subjunctive

que je finisse
que tu finisses
qu'il finisse
que nous finissions
que vous finissiez
qu'ils finissent

Conditional

je finirais
tu finirais
il finirait
nous finirions
vous finiriez
ils finiraient

Imperative

finis
finissons
finissez

fournir
to supply, provide

Present participle

fournissant

Past participle

fourni

Present indicative

je fournis
tu fournis
il fournit
nous fournissons
vous fournissez
ils fournissent

Imperfect indicative

je fournissais
tu fournissais
il fournissait
nous fournissions
vous fournissiez
ils fournissaient

Past historic

je fournis
tu fournis
il fournit
nous fournîmes
vous fournîtes
ils fournirent

Future

je fournirai
tu fourniras
il fournira
nous fournirons
vous fournirez
ils fourniront

Perfect indicative

j'ai fourni
tu as fourni
il a fourni
nous avons fourni
vous avez fourni
ils ont fourni

Pluperfect indicative

j'avais fourni
tu avais fourni
il avait fourni
nous avions fourni
vous aviez fourni
ils avaient fourni

Present subjunctive

que je fournisse
que tu fournisses
qu'il fournisse
que nous fournissions
que vous fournissiez
qu'ils fournissent

Conditional

je fournirais
tu fournirais
il fournirait
nous fournirions
vous fourniriez
ils fourniraient

Imperative

fournis
fournissons
fournissez

garder
to keep

Present participle

gardant

Past participle

gardé

Present indicative

je garde
tu gardes
il garde
nous gardons
vous gardez
ils gardent

Imperfect indicative

je gardais
tu gardais
il gardait
nous gardions
vous gardiez
ils gardaient

Past historic

je gardai
tu gardas
il garda
nous gardâmes
vous gardâtes
ils gardèrent

Future

je garderai
tu garderas
il gardera
nous garderons
vous garderez
ils garderont

Perfect indicative

j'ai gardé

tu as gardé
il a gardé
nous avons gardé
vous avez gardé
ils ont gardé

Pluperfect indicative

j'avais gardé
tu avais gardé
il avait gardé
nous avions gardé
vous aviez gardé
ils avaient gardé

Present subjunctive

que je garde
que tu gardes
qu'il garde
que nous gardions
que vous gardiez
qu'ils gardent

Conditional

je garderais
tu garderais
il garderait
nous garderions
vous garderiez
ils garderaient

Imperative

garde
gardons
gardez

haïr
to hate

Present participle

haïssant

Past participle

haï

Present indicative

je hais
tu hais
il hait
nous haïssons
vous haïssez
ils haïssent

Imperfect indicative

je haïssais
tu haïssais
il haïssait

nous haïssions
vous haïssiez
ils haïssaient

Past historic

je haïs
tu haïs
il haït
nous haïmes
vous haïtes
ils haïrent

Future

je haïrai
tu haïras
il haïra
nous haïrons
vous haïrez
ils haïront

Perfect indicative

j'ai haï
tu as haï
il a haï
nous avons haï
vous avez haï
ils ont haï

Pluperfect indicative

j'avais haï
tu avais haï
il avait haï
nous avions haï
vous aviez haï
ils avaient haï

Present subjunctive

que je haïsse
que tu haïsses
qu'il haïsse
que nous haïssions
que vous haïssiez
qu'ils haïssent

Conditional

je haïrais
tu haïrais
il haïrait
nous haïrions
vous haïriez
ils haïraient

Imperative

hais
haïssons
haïssez

inclure
to include

Present participle
incluant

Past participle
inclu

Present indicative
j'inclus
tu inclus
il inclut
nous incluons
vous incluez
ils incluent

Imperfect indicative
j'incluais
tu incluais
il incluait
nous incluions
vous incluiez
ils incluaient

Past historic
j'inclus
tu inclus
il inclut
nous inclûmes
vous inclûtes
ils inclurent

Future
j'inclurai
tu incluras
il inclura
nous inclurons
vous inclurez
ils incluront

Perfect indicative
j'ai inclu
tu as inclu
il a inclu
nous avons inclu
vous avez inclu
ils ont inclu

Pluperfect indicative
j'avais inclu
tu avais inclu
il avait inclu
nous avions inclu
vous aviez inclu
ils avaient inclu

Present subjunctive
que j'inclue
que tu inclues
qu'il inclue
que nous incluions
que vous incluiez
qu'ils incluent

Conditional
j'inclurais
tu inclurais
il inclurait
nous inclurions
vous incluriez
ils incluraient

Imperative
inclus
incluons
incluez

inscrire
to write down, register

Present participle
inscrivant

Past participle
inscrit

Present indicative
j'inscris
tu inscris
il inscrit
nous inscrivons
vous inscrivez
ils inscrivent

Imperfect indicative
j'inscrivais
tu inscrivais
il inscrivait
nous inscrivions
vous inscriviez
ils inscrivaient

Past historic
j'inscrivis
tu inscrivis
il inscrivit
nous inscrivîmes
vous inscrivîtes
ils inscrivirent

Future
j'inscrirai
tu inscriras
il inscrira
nous inscrirons
vous inscrirez
ils inscriront

Perfect indicative
j'ai inscrit
tu as inscrit
il a inscrit
nous avons inscrit
vous avez inscrit
ils ont inscrit

Pluperfect indicative
j'avais inscrit
tu avais inscrit
il avait inscrit
nous avions inscrit
vous aviez inscrit
ils avaient inscrit

Present subjunctive
que j'inscrive
que tu inscrives
qu'il inscrive
que nous inscrivions
que vous inscriviez
qu'ils inscrivent

Conditional
j'inscrirais
tu inscrirais
il inscrirait
nous inscririons
vous inscririez
ils inscriraient

Imperative
inscris
inscrivons
inscrivez

instruire
to educate, instruct

Present participle
instruisant

Past participle
instruit

Present indicative
j'instruis
tu instruis
il instruit

nous instruisons
vous instruisez
ils instruisent

Imperfect indicative
j'instruisais
tu instruisais
il instruisait
nous instruisions
vous instruisiez
ils instruisaient

Past historic
j'instruisis
tu instruisis
il instruisit
nous instruisîmes
vous instruisîtes
ils instruisirent

Future
j'instruirai
tu instruiras
il instruira
nous instruirons
vous instruirez
ils instruiront

Perfect indicative
j'ai instruit
tu as instruit
il a instruit
nous avons instruit
vous avez instruit
ils ont instruit

Pluperfect indicative
j'avais instruit
tu avais instruit
il avait instruit
nous avions instruit
vous aviez instruit
ils avaient instruit

Present subjunctive
que j'instruise
que tu instruises
qu'il instruise
que nous instruisions
que vous instruisiez
qu'ils instruisent

Conditional
j'instruirais
tu instruirais
il instruirait
nous instruirions
vous instruiriez
ils instruiraient

Imperative
instruis
instruisons
instruisez

interdire
to forbid

Present participle
interdisant

Past participle
interdit

Present indicative
j'interdis
tu interdis
il interdit
nous interdisons
vous interdisez
ils interdisent

Imperfect indicative
j'interdisais
tu interdisais
il interdisait
nous interdisions
vous interdisiez
ils interdisaient

Past historic
j'interdis
tu interdis
il interdit
nous interdîmes
vous interdîtes
ils interdirent

Future
j'interdirai
tu interdiras
il interdira
nous interdirons
vous interdirez
ils interdiront

Perfect indicative
j'ai interdit
tu as interdit
il a interdit
nous avons interdit
vous avez interdit
ils ont interdit

Pluperfect indicative
j'avais interdit

tu avais interdit
il avait interdit
nous avions interdit
vous aviez interdit
ils avaient interdit

Present subjunctive
que j'interdise
que tu interdises
qu'il interdise
que nous interdisions
que vous interdisiez
qu'ils interdisent

Conditional
j'interdirais
tu interdirais
il interdirait
nous interdirions
vous interdiriez
ils interdiraient

Imperative
interdis
interdisons
interdisez

intervenir
to intervene

Present participle
intervenant

Past participle
intervenu

Present indicative
j'interviens
tu interviens
il intervient
nous intervenons
vous intervenez
ils interviennent

Imperfect indicative
j'intervenais
tu intervenais
il intervenait
nous intervenions
vous interveniez
ils intervenaient

Past historic
j'intervins
tu intervins
il intervint

nous intervînmes
vous intervîntes
ils intervinrent

Future

j'interviendrai
tu interviendras
il interviendra
nous interviendrons
vous interviendrez
ils interviendront

Perfect indicative

je suis intervenu
tu es intervenu
il est intervenu
nous sommes intervenus
vous êtes intervenus
ils sont intervenus

Pluperfect indicative

j'étais intervenu
tu étais intervenu
il était intervenu
nous étions intervenus
vous étiez intervenus
ils étaient intervenus

Present subjunctive

que j'intervienne
que tu interviennes
qu'il intervienne
que nous intervenions
que vous interveniez
qu'ils interviennent

Conditional

j'interviendrais
tu interviendrais
il interviendrait
nous interviendrions
vous interviendriez
ils interviendraient

Imperative

interviens
intervenons
intervenez

introduire
to introduce

Present participle

introduisant

Past participle

introduit

Present indicative

j'introduis
tu introduis
il introduit
nous introduisons
vous introduisez
ils introduisent

Imperfect indicative

j'introduisais
tu introduisais
il introduisait
nous introduisions
vous introduisiez
ils introduisaient

Past historic

j'introduisis
tu introduisis
il introduisit
nous introduisîmes
vous introduisîtes
ils introduisirent

Future

j'introduirai
tu introduiras
il introduira
nous introduirons
vous introduirez
ils introduiront

Perfect indicative

j'ai introduit
tu as introduit
il a introduit
nous avons introduit
vous avez introduit
ils ont introduit

Pluperfect indicative

j'avais introduit
tu avais introduit
il avait introduit
nous avions introduit
vous aviez introduit
ils avaient introduit

Present subjunctive

que j'introduise
que tu introduises
qu'il introduise
que nous introduisions
que vous introduisiez
qu'ils introduisent

Conditional

j'introduirais

tu introduirais
il introduirait
nous introduirions
vous introduiriez
ils introduiraient

Imperative

introduis
introduisons
introduisez

jeter
to throw

Present participle

jetant

Past participle

jeté

Present indicative

je jette
tu jettes
il jette
nous jetons
vous jetez
ils jettent

Imperfect indicative

je jetais
tu jetais
il jetait
nous jetions
vous jetiez
ils jetaient

Past historic

je jetai
tu jetas
il jeta
nous jetâmes
vous jetâtes
ils jetèrent

Future

je jetterai
tu jetteras
il jettera
nous jetterons
vous jetterez
ils jetteront

Perfect indicative

j'ai jeté
tu as jeté
il a jeté

nous avons jeté
vous avez jeté
ils ont jeté

Pluperfect indicative

j'avais jeté
tu avais jeté
il avait jeté
nous avions jeté
vous aviez jeté
ils avaient jeté

Present subjunctive

que je jette
que tu jettes
qu'il jette
que nous jetions
que vous jetiez
qu'ils jettent

Conditional

je jetterais
tu jetterais
il jetterait
nous jetterions
vous jetteriez
ils jetteraient

Imperative

jette
jetons
jetez

joindre
to join, attach

Present participle
joignant

Past participle
joint

Present indicative

je joins
tu joins
il joint
nous joignons
vous joignez
ils joignent

Imperfect indicative

je joignais
tu joignais
il joignait
nous joignions
vous joigniez
ils joignaient

Past historic

je joignis
tu joignis
il joignit
nous joignîmes
vous joignîtes
ils joignirent

Future

je joindrai
tu joindras
il joindra
nous joindrons
vous joindrez
ils joindront

Perfect indicative

j'ai joint
tu as joint
il a joint
nous avons joint
vous avez joint
ils ont joint

Pluperfect indicative

j'avais joint
tu avais joint
il avait joint
nous avions joint
vous aviez joint
ils avaient joint

Present subjunctive

que je joigne
que tu joignes
qu'il joigne
que nous joignions
que vous joigniez
qu'ils joignent

Conditional

je joindrais
tu joindrais
il joindrait
nous joindrions
vous joindriez
ils joindraient

Imperative

joins
joignons
joignez

jouer
to play

Present participle
jouant

Past participle
joué

Present indicative

je joue
tu joues
il joue
nous jouons
vous jouez
ils jouent

Imperfect indicative

je jouais
tu jouais
il jouait
nous jouions
vous jouiez
ils jouaient

Past historic

je jouai
tu jouas
il joua
nous jouâmes
vous jouâtes
ils jouèrent

Future

je jouerai
tu joueras
il jouera
nous jouerons
vous jouerez
ils joueront

Perfect indicative

j'ai joué
tu as joué
il a joué
nous avons joué
vous avez joué
ils ont joué

Pluperfect indicative

j'avais joué
tu avais joué
il avait joué
nous avions joué
vous aviez joué
ils avaient joué

Present subjunctive

que je joue
que tu joues
qu'il joue
que nous jouions
que vous jouiez
qu'ils jouent

Conditional
je jouerais
tu jouerais
il jouerait
nous jouerions
vous joueriez
ils joueraient

Imperative
joue
jouons
jouez

laver
to wash

Present participle
lavant

Past participle
lavé

Present indicative
je lave
tu laves
il lave
nous lavons
vous lavez
ils lavent

Imperfect indicative
je lavais
tu lavais
il lavait
nous lavions
vous laviez
ils lavaient

Past historic
je lavai
tu lavas
il lava
nous lavâmes
vous lavâtes
ils lavèrent

Future
je laverai
tu laveras
il lavera
nous laverons
vous laverez
ils laveront

Perfect indicative
j'ai lavé

tu as lavé
il a lavé
nous avons lavé
vous avez lavé
ils ont lavé

Pluperfect indicative
j'avais lavé
tu avais lavé
il avait lavé
nous avions lavé
vous aviez lavé
ils avaient lavé

Present subjunctive
que je lave
que tu laves
qu'il lave
que nous lavions
que vous laviez
qu'ils lavent

Conditional
je laverais
tu laverais
il laverait
nous laverions
vous laveriez
ils laveraient

Imperative
lave
lavons
lavez

lever
to lift, raise

Present participle
levant

Past participle
levé

Present indicative
je lève
tu lèves
il lève
nous levons
vous levez
ils lèvent

Imperfect indicative
je levais
tu levais
il levait

nous levions
vous leviez
ils levaient

Past historic
je levai
tu levas
il leva
nous levâmes
vous levâtes
ils levèrent

Future
je lèverai
tu lèveras
il lèvera
nous lèverons
vous lèverez
ils lèveront

Perfect indicative
j'ai levé
tu as levé
il a levé
nous avons levé
vous avez levé
ils ont levé

Pluperfect indicative
j'avais levé
tu avais levé
il avait levé
nous avions levé
vous aviez levé
ils avaient levé

Present subjunctive
que je lève
que tu lèves
qu'il lève
que nous levions
que vous leviez
qu'ils lèvent

Conditional
je lèverais
tu lèverais
il lèverait
nous lèverions
vous lèveriez
ils lèveraient

Imperative
lève
levons
levez

se lever
to get up, stand up

Present participle
se levant

Past participle
levé

Present indicative
je me lève
tu te lèves
il se lève
nous nous levons
vous vous levez
ils se lèvent

Imperfect indicative
je me levais
tu te levais
il se levait
nous nous levions
vous vous leviez
ils se levaient

Past historic
je me levai
tu te levas
il se leva
nous nous levâmes
vous vous levâtes
ils se levèrent

Future
je me lèverai
tu te lèveras
il se lèvera
nous nous lèverons
vous vous lèverez
ils se lèveront

Perfect indicative
je me suis levé
tu t'es levé
il s'est levé
nous nous sommes levés
vous vous êtes levés
ils se sont levés

Pluperfect indicative
je m'étais levé
tu t'étais levé
il s'était levé
nous nous étions levés
vous vous étiez levés
ils s'étaient levés

Present subjunctive
que je me lève
que tu te lèves
qu'il se lève
que nous nous levions
que vous vous leviez
qu'ils se lèvent

Conditional
je me lèverais
tu te lèverais
il se lèverait
nous nous lèverions
vous vous lèveriez
ils se lèveraient

Imperative
lève-toi
levons-nous
levez-vous

lire
to read

Present participle
lisant

Past participle
lu

Present indicative
je lis
tu lis
il lit
nous lisons
vous lisez
ils lisent

Imperfect indicative
je lisais
tu lisais
il lisait
nous lisions
vous lisiez
ils lisaient

Past historic
je lus
tu lus
il lut
nous lûmes
vous lûtes
ils lurent

Future
je lirai

tu liras
il lira
nous lirons
vous lirez
ils liront

Perfect indicative
j'ai lu
tu as lu
il a lu
nous avons lu
vous avez lu
ils ont lu

Pluperfect indicative
j'avais lu
tu avais lu
il avait lu
nous avions lu
vous aviez lu
ils avaient lu

Present subjunctive
que je lise
que tu lises
qu'il lise
que nous lisions
que vous lisiez
qu'ils lisent

Conditional
je lirais
tu lirais
il lirait
nous lirions
vous liriez
ils liraient

Imperative
lis
lisons
lisez

manger
to eat

Present participle
mangeant

Past participle
mangé

Present indicative
je mange
tu manges
il mange

nous mangeons
vous mangez
ils mangent

Imperfect indicative
je mangeais
tu mangeais
il mangeait
nous mangions
vous mangiez
ils mangeaient

Past historic
je mangeai
tu mangeas
il mangea
nous mangeâmes
vous mangeâtes
ils mangèrent

Future
je mangerai
tu mangeras
il mangera
nous mangerons
vous mangerez
ils mangeront

Perfect indicative
j'ai mangé
tu as mangé
il a mangé
nous avons mangé
vous avez mangé
ils ont mangé

Pluperfect indicative
j'avais mangé
tu avais mangé
il avait mangé
nous avions mangé
vous aviez mangé
ils avaient mangé

Present subjunctive
que je mange
que tu manges
qu'il mange
que nous mangions
que vous mangiez
qu'ils mangent

Conditional
je mangerais
tu mangerais
il mangerait
nous mangerions
vous mangeriez
ils mangeraient

Imperative
mange
mangeons
mangez

marcher
to walk

Present participle
marchant

Past participle
marché

Present indicative
je marche
tu marches
il marche
nous marchons
vous marchez
ils marchent

Imperfect indicative
je marchais
tu marchais
il marchait
nous marchions
vous marchiez
ils marchaient

Past historic
je marchai
tu marchas
il marcha
nous marchâmes
vous marchâtes
ils marchèrent

Future
je marcherai
tu marcheras
il marchera
nous marcherons
vous marcherez
ils marcheront

Perfect indicative
j'ai marché
tu as marché
il a marché
nous avons marché
vous avez marché
ils ont marché

Pluperfect indicative
j'avais marché

tu avais marché
il avait marché
nous avions marché
vous aviez marché
ils avaient marché

Present subjunctive
que je marche
que tu marches
qu'il marche
que nous marchions
que vous marchiez
qu'ils marchent

Conditional
je marcherais
tu marcherais
il marcherait
nous marcherions
vous marcheriez
ils marcheraient

Imperative
marche
marchons
marchez

maudire
to curse

Present participle
maudissant

Past participle
maudit

Present indicative
je maudis
tu maudis
il maudit
nous maudissons
vous maudissez
ils maudissent

Imperfect indicative
je maudissais
tu maudissais
il maudissait
nous maudissions
vous maudissiez
ils maudissaient

Past historic
je maudis
tu maudis
il maudit

nous maudîmes
vous maudîtes
ils maudirent

Future

je maudirai
tu maudiras
il maudira
nous maudirons
vous maudirez
ils maudiront

Perfect indicative

j'ai maudit
tu as maudit
il a maudit
nous avons maudit
vous avez maudit
ils ont maudit

Pluperfect indicative

j'avais maudit
tu avais maudit
il avait maudit
nous avions maudit
vous aviez maudit
ils avaient maudit

Present subjunctive

que je maudisse
que tu maudisses
qu'il maudisse
que nous maudissions
que vous maudissiez
qu'ils maudissent

Conditional

je maudirais
tu maudirais
il maudirait
nous maudirions
vous maudiriez
ils maudiraient

Imperative

maudis
maudissons
maudissez

mentir
to (tell a) lie

Present participle

mentant

Past participle

menti

Present indicative

je mens
tu mens
il ment
nous mentons
vous mentez
ils mentent

Imperfect indicative

je mentais
tu mentais
il mentait
nous mentions
vous mentiez
ils mentaient

Past historic

je mentis
tu mentis
il mentit
nous mentîmes
vous mentîtes
ils mentirent

Future

je mentirai
tu mentiras
il mentira
nous mentirons
vous mentirez
ils mentiront

Perfect indicative

j'ai menti
tu as menti
il a menti
nous avons menti
vous avez menti
ils ont menti

Pluperfect indicative

j'avais menti
tu avais menti
il avait menti
nous avions menti
vous aviez menti
ils avaient menti

Present subjunctive

que je mente
que tu mentes
qu'il mente
que nous mentions
que vous mentiez
qu'ils mentent

Conditional

je mentirais

tu mentirais
il mentirait
nous mentirions
vous mentiriez
ils mentiraient

Imperative

mens
mentons
mentez

mettre
to put

Present participle

mettant

Past participle

mis

Present indicative

je mets
tu mets
il met
nous mettons
vous mettez
ils mettent

Imperfect indicative

je mettais
tu mettais
il mettait
nous mettions
vous mettiez
ils mettaient

Past historic

je mis
tu mis
il mit
nous mîmes
vous mîtes
ils mirent

Future

je mettrai
tu mettras
il mettra
nous mettrons
vous mettrez
ils mettront

Perfect indicative

j'ai mis
tu as mis
il a mis

nous avons mis
vous avez mis
ils ont mis

Pluperfect indicative

j'avais mis
tu avais mis
il avait mis
nous avions mis
vous aviez mis
ils avaient mis

Present subjunctive

que je mette
que tu mettes
qu'il mette
que nous mettions
que vous mettiez
qu'ils mettent

Conditional

je mettrais
tu mettrais
il mettrait
nous mettrions
vous mettriez
ils mettraient

Imperative

mets
mettons
mettez

mordre
to bite

Present participle

mordant

Past participle

mordu

Present indicative

je mords
tu mords
il mord
nous mordons
vous mordez
ils mordent

Imperfect indicative

je mordais
tu mordais
il mordait
nous mordions
vous mordiez
ils mordaient

Past historic

je mordis
tu mordis
il mordit
nous mordîmes
vous mordîtes
ils mordirent

Future

je mordrai
tu mordras
il mordra
nous mordrons
vous mordrez
ils mordront

Perfect indicative

j'ai mordu
tu as mordu
il a mordu
nous avons mordu
vous avez mordu
ils ont mordu

Pluperfect indicative

j'avais mordu
tu avais mordu
il avait mordu
nous avions mordu
vous aviez mordu
ils avaient mordu

Present subjunctive

que je morde
que tu mordes
qu'il morde
que nous mordions
que vous mordiez
qu'ils mordent

Conditional

je mordrais
tu mordrais
il mordrait
nous mordrions
vous mordriez
ils mordraient

Imperative

mords
mordons
mordez

moudre
to grind

Present participle

moulant

Past participle

moulu

Present indicative

je mouds
tu mouds
il moud
nous moulons
vous moulez
ils moulent

Imperfect indicative

je moulais
tu moulais
il moulait
nous moulions
vous mouliez
ils moulaient

Past historic

je moulus
tu moulus
il moulut
nous moulûmes
vous moulûtes
ils moulurent

Future

je moudrai
tu moudras
il moudra
nous moudrons
vous moudrez
ils moudront

Perfect indicative

j'ai moulu
tu as moulu
il a moulu
nous avons moulu
vous avez moulu
ils ont moulu

Pluperfect indicative

j'avais moulu
tu avais moulu
il avait moulu
nous avions moulu
vous aviez moulu
ils avaient moulu

Present subjunctive

que je moule
que tu moules
qu'il moule
que nous moulions
que vous mouliez
qu'ils moulent

mourir

to die

Conditional

je moudrais
tu moudrais
il moudrait
nous moudrions
vous moudriez
ils moudraient

Imperative

mouds
moulons
moulez

mourir

to die

Present participle

mourant

Past participle

mort

Present indicative

je meurs
tu meurs
il meurt
nous mourons
vous mourez
ils meurent

Imperfect indicative

je mourais
tu mourais
il mourait
nous mourions
vous mouriez
ils mouraient

Past historic

je mourus
tu mourus
il mourut
nous mourûmes
vous mourûtes
ils moururent

Future

je mourrai
tu mourras
il mourra
nous mourrons
vous mourrez
ils mourront

Perfect indicative

je suis mort

tu es mort
il est mort
nous sommes morts
vous êtes morts
ils sont morts

Pluperfect indicative

j'étais mort
tu étais mort
il était mort
nous étions morts
vous étiez morts
ils étaient morts

Present subjunctive

que je meure
que tu meures
qu'il meure
que nous mourions
que vous mouriez
qu'ils meurent

Conditional

je mourrais
tu mourrais
il mourrait
nous mourrions
vous mourriez
ils mourraient

Imperative

meurs
mourons
mourez

naître

to be born

Present participle

naissant

Past participle

né

Present indicative

je nais
tu nais
il naît
nous naissons
vous naissez
ils naissent

Imperfect indicative

je naissais
tu naissais
il naissait

nous naissions
vous naissiez
ils naissaient

Past historic

je naquis
tu naquis
il naquit
nous naquîmes
vous naquîtes
ils naquirent

Future

je naîtrai
tu naîtras
il naîtra
nous naîtrons
vous naîtrez
ils naîtront

Perfect indicative

je suis né
tu es né
il est né
nous sommes nés
vous êtes nés
ils sont nés

Pluperfect indicative

j'étais né
tu étais né
il était né
nous étions nés
vous étiez nés
ils étaient nés

Present subjunctive

que je naisse
que tu naisses
qu'il naisse
que nous naissions
que vous naissiez
qu'ils naissent

Conditional

je naîtrais
tu naîtrais
il naîtrait
nous naîtrions
vous naîtriez
ils naîtraient

Imperative

nais
naissons
naissez

nuire
to harm, damage

Present participle
nuisant

Past participle
nui

Present indicative
je nuis
tu nuis
il nuit
nous nuisons
vous nuisez
ils nuisent

Imperfect indicative
je nuisais
tu nuisais
il nuisait
nous nuisions
vous nuisiez
ils nuisaient

Past historic
je nuisis
tu nuisis
il nuisit
nous nuîsimes
vous nuîsites
ils nuisirent

Future
je nuirai
tu nuiras
il nuira
nous nuirons
vous nuirez
ils nuiront

Perfect indicative
j'ai nui
tu as nui
il a nui
nous avons nui
vous avez nui
ils ont nui

Pluperfect indicative
j'avais nui
tu avais nui
il avait nui
nous avions nui
vous aviez nui
ils avaient nui

Present subjunctive
que je nuise
que tu nuises
qu'il nuise
que nous nuisions
que vous nuisiez
qu'ils nuisent

Conditional
je nuirais
tu nuirais
il nuirait
nous nuirions
vous nuiriez
ils nuiraient

Imperative
nuis
nuisons
nuisez

offrir
to offer

Present participle
offrant

Past participle
offert

Present indicative
j'offre
tu offres
il offre
nous offrons
vous offrez
ils offrent

Imperfect indicative
j'offrais
tu offrais
il offrait
nous offrions
vous offriez
ils offraient

Past historic
j'offris
tu offris
il offrit
nous offrîmes
vous offrîtes
ils offrirent

Future
j'offrirai

tu offriras
il offrira
nous offrirons
vous offrirez
ils offriront

Perfect indicative
j'ai offert
tu as offert
il a offert
nous avons offert
vous avez offert
ils ont offert

Pluperfect indicative
j'avais offert
tu avais offert
il avait offert
nous avions offert
vous aviez offert
ils avaient offert

Present subjunctive
que j'offre
que tu offres
qu'il offre
que nous offrions
que vous offriez
qu'ils offrent

Conditional
j'offrirais
tu offrirais
il offrirait
nous offririons
vous offririez
ils offriraient

Imperative
offre
offrons
offrez

ouvrir
to open

Present participle
ouvrant

Past participle
ouvert

Present indicative
j'ouvre
tu ouvres
il ouvre

nous ouvrons
vous ouvrez
ils ouvrent

Imperfect indicative
j'ouvrais
tu ouvrais
il ouvrait
nous ouvrions
vous ouvriez
ils ouvraient

Past historic
j'ouvris
tu ouvris
il ouvrit
nous ouvrîmes
vous ouvrîtes
ils ouvrirent

Future
j'ouvrirai
tu ouvriras
il ouvrira
nous ouvrirons
vous ouvrirez
ils ouvriront

Perfect indicative
j'ai ouvert
tu as ouvert
il a ouvert
nous avons ouvert
vous avez ouvert
ils ont ouvert

Pluperfect indicative
j'avais ouvert
tu avais ouvert
il avait ouvert
nous avions ouvert
vous aviez ouvert
ils avaient ouvert

Present subjunctive
que j'ouvre
que tu ouvres
qu'il ouvre
que nous ouvrions
que vous ouvriez
qu'ils ouvrent

Conditional
j'ouvrirais
tu ouvrirais
il ouvrirait
nous ouvririons
vous ouvririez
ils ouvriraient

Imperative
ouvre
ouvrons
ouvrez

paraître
to seem, appear

Present participle
paraissant

Past participle
paru

Present indicative
je parais
tu parais
il paraît
nous paraissons
vous paraissez
ils paraissent

Imperfect indicative
je paraissais
tu paraissais
il paraissait
nous paraissions
vous paraissiez
ils paraissaient

Past historic
je parus
tu parus
il parut
nous parûmes
vous parûtes
ils parurent

Future
je paraîtrai
tu paraîtras
il paraîtra
nous paraîtrons
vous paraîtrez
ils paraîtront

Perfect indicative
j'ai paru
tu as paru
il a paru
nous avons paru
vous avez paru
ils ont paru

Pluperfect indicative
j'avais paru

tu avais paru
il avait paru
nous avions paru
vous aviez paru
ils avaient paru

Present subjunctive
que je paraisse
que tu paraisses
qu'il paraisse
que nous paraissions
que vous paraissiez
qu'ils paraissent

Conditional
je paraîtrais
tu paraîtrais
il paraîtrait
nous paraîtrions
vous paraîtriez
ils paraîtraient

Imperative
parais
paraissons
paraissez

parler
to speak, talk

Present participle
parlant

Past participle
parlé

Present indicative
je parle
tu parles
il parle
nous parlons
vous parlez
ils parlent

Imperfect indicative
je parlais
tu parlais
il parlait
nous parlions
vous parliez
ils parlaient

Past historic
je parlai
tu parlas
il parla

nous parlâmes
vous parlâtes
ils parlèrent

Future
je parlerai
tu parleras
il parlera
nous parlerons
vous parlerez
ils parleront

Perfect indicative
j'ai parlé
tu as parlé
il a parlé
nous avons parlé
vous avez parlé
ils ont parlé

Pluperfect indicative
j'avais parlé
tu avais parlé
il avait parlé
nous avions parlé
vous aviez parlé
ils avaient parlé

Present subjunctive
que je parle
que tu parles
qu'il parle
que nous parlions
que vous parliez
qu'ils parlent

Conditional
je parlerais
tu parlerais
il parlerait
nous parlerions
vous parleriez
ils parleraient

Imperative
parle
parlons
parlez

partir
to leave

Present participle
partant

Past participle
parti

Present indicative
je pars
tu pars
il part
nous partons
vous partez
ils partent

Imperfect indicative
je partais
tu partais
il partait
nous partions
vous partiez
ils partaient

Past historic
je partis
tu partis
il partit
nous partîmes
vous partîtes
ils partirent

Future
je partirai
tu partiras
il partira
nous partirons
vous partirez
ils partiront

Perfect indicative
je suis parti
tu es parti
il est parti
nous sommes partis
vous êtes partis
ils sont partis

Pluperfect indicative
j'étais parti
tu étais parti
il était parti
nous étions partis
vous étiez partis
ils étaient partis

Present subjunctive
que je parte
que tu partes
qu'il parte
que nous partions
que vous partiez
qu'ils partent

Conditional
je partirais

tu partirais
il partirait
nous partirions
vous partiriez
ils partiraient

Imperative
pars
partons
partez

payer
to pay

Present participle
payant

Past participle
payé

Present indicative
je paie
tu paies
il paie
nous payons
vous payez
ils paient

Imperfect indicative
je payais
tu payais
il payait
nous payions
vous payiez
ils payaient

Past historic
je payai
tu payas
il paya
nous payâmes
vous payâtes
ils payèrent

Future
je paierai
tu paieras
il paiera
nous paierons
vous paierez
ils paieront

Perfect indicative
j'ai payé
tu as payé
il a payé

nous avons payé
vous avez payé
ils ont payé

Pluperfect indicative
j'avais payé
tu avais payé
il avait payé
nous avions payé
vous aviez payé
ils avaient payé

Present subjunctive
que je paie
que tu paies
qu'il paie
que nous payions
que vous payiez
qu'ils paient

Conditional
je paierais
tu paierais
il paierait
nous paierions
vous paieriez
ils paieraient

Imperative
paie
payons
payez

peindre
to paint

Present participle
peignant

Past participle
peint

Present indicative
je peins
tu peins
il peint
nous peignons
vous peignez
ils peignent

Imperfect indicative
je peignais
tu peignais
il peignait
nous peignions
vous peigniez
ils peignaient

Past historic
je peignis
tu peignis
il peignit
nous peignîmes
vous peignîtes
ils peignirent

Future
je peindrai
tu peindras
il peindra
nous peindrons
vous peindrez
ils peindront

Perfect indicative
j'ai peint
tu as peint
il a peint
nous avons peint
vous avez peint
ils ont peint

Pluperfect indicative
j'avais peint
tu avais peint
il avait peint
nous avions peint
vous aviez peint
ils avaient peint

Present subjunctive
que je peigne
que tu peignes
qu'il peigne
que nous peignions
que vous peigniez
qu'ils peignent

Conditional
je peindrais
tu peindrais
il peindrait
nous peindrions
vous peindriez
ils peindraient

Imperative
peins
peignons
peignez

penser
to think

Present participle
pensant

Past participle
pensé

Present indicative
je pense
tu penses
il pense
nous pensons
vous pensez
ils pensent

Imperfect indicative
je pensais
tu pensais
il pensait
nous pensions
vous pensiez
ils pensaient

Past historic
je pensai
tu pensas
il pensa
nous pensâmes
vous pensâtes
ils pensèrent

Future
je penserai
tu penseras
il pensera
nous penserons
vous penserez
ils penseront

Perfect indicative
j'ai pensé
tu as pensé
il a pensé
nous avons pensé
vous avez pensé
ils ont pensé

Pluperfect indicative
j'avais pensé
tu avais pensé
il avait pensé
nous avions pensé
vous aviez pensé
ils avaient pensé

Present subjunctive
que je pense
que tu penses
qu'il pense
que nous pensions
que vous pensiez
qu'ils pensent

Conditional

je penserais
tu penserais
il penserait
nous penserions
vous penseriez
ils penseraient

Imperative

pense
pensons
pensez

perdre
to lose

Present participle

perdant

Past participle

perdu

Present indicative

je perds
tu perds
il perd
nous perdons
vous perdez
ils perdent

Imperfect indicative

je perdais
tu perdais
il perdait
nous perdions
vous perdiez
ils perdaient

Past historic

je perdis
tu perdis
il perdit
nous perdîmes
vous perdîtes
ils perdirent

Future

je perdrai
tu perdras
il perdra
nous perdrons
vous perdrez
ils perdront

Perfect indicative

j'ai perdu

tu as perdu
il a perdu
nous avons perdu
vous avez perdu
ils ont perdu

Pluperfect indicative

j'avais perdu
tu avais perdu
il avait perdu
nous avions perdu
vous aviez perdu
ils avaient perdu

Present subjunctive

que je perde
que tu perdes
qu'il perde
que nous perdions
que vous perdiez
qu'ils perdent

Conditional

je perdrais
tu perdrais
il perdrait
nous perdrions
vous perdriez
ils perdraient

Imperative

perds
perdons
perdez

permettre
to allow, enable

Present participle

permettant

Past participle

permis

Present indicative

je permets
tu permets
il permet
nous permettons
vous permettez
ils permettent

Imperfect indicative

je permettais
tu permettais
il permettait

nous permettions
vous permettiez
ils permettaient

Past historic

je permis
tu permis
il permit
nous permîmes
vous permîtes
ils permirent

Future

je permettrai
tu permettras
il permettra
nous permettrons
vous permettrez
ils permettront

Perfect indicative

j'ai permis
tu as permis
il a permis
nous avons permis
vous avez permis
ils ont permis

Pluperfect indicative

j'avais permis
tu avais permis
il avait permis
nous avions permis
vous aviez permis
ils avaient permis

Present subjunctive

que je permette
que tu permettes
qu'il permette
que nous permettions
que vous permettiez
qu'ils permettent

Conditional

je permettrais
tu permettrais
il permettrait
nous permettrions
vous permettriez
ils permettraient

Imperative

permets
permettons
permettez

plaindre
to pity

Present participle
plaignant

Past participle
plaint

Present indicative
je plains
tu plains
il plaint
nous plaignons
vous plaignez
ils plaignent

Imperfect indicative
je plaignais
tu plaignais
il plaignait
nous plaignions
vous plaigniez
ils plaignaient

Past historic
je plaignis
tu plaignis
il plaignit
nous plaignîmes
vous plaignîtes
ils plaignirent

Future
je plaindrai
tu plaindras
il plaindra
nous plaindrons
vous plaindrez
ils plaindront

Perfect indicative
j'ai plaint
tu as plaint
il a plaint
nous avons plaint
vous avez plaint
ils ont plaint

Pluperfect indicative
j'avais plaint
tu avais plaint
il avait plaint
nous avions plaint
vous aviez plaint
ils avaient plaint

Present subjunctive
que je plaigne
que tu plaignes
qu'il plaigne
que nous plaignions
que vous plaigniez
qu'ils plaignent

Conditional
je plaindrais
tu plaindrais
il plaindrait
nous plaindrions
vous plaindriez
ils plaindraient

Imperative
plains
plaignons
plaignez

plaire
to please

Present participle
plaisant

Past participle
plu

Present indicative
je plais
tu plais
il plaît
nous plaisons
vous plaisez
ils plaisent

Imperfect indicative
je plaisais
tu plaisais
il plaisait
nous plaisions
vous plaisiez
ils plaisaient

Past historic
je plus
tu plus
il plut
nous plûmes
vous plûtes
ils plurent

Future
je plairai

tu plairas
il plaira
nous plairons
vous plairez
ils plairont

Perfect indicative
j'ai plu
tu as plu
il a plu
nous avons plu
vous avez plu
ils ont plu

Pluperfect indicative
j'avais plu
tu avais plu
il avait plu
nous avions plu
vous aviez plu
ils avaient plu

Present subjunctive
que je plaise
que tu plaises
qu'il plaise
que nous plaisions
que vous plaisiez
qu'ils plaisent

Conditional
je plairais
tu plairais
il plairait
nous plairions
vous plairiez
ils plairaient

Imperative
plais
plaisons
plaisez

porter
to carry

Present participle
portant

Past participle
porté

Present indicative
je porte
tu portes
il porte

nous portons
vous portez
ils portent

Imperfect indicative

je portais
tu portais
il portait
nous portions
vous portiez
ils portaient

Past historic

je portai
tu portas
il porta
nous portâmes
vous portâtes
ils portèrent

Future

je porterai
tu porteras
il portera
nous porterons
vous porterez
ils porteront

Perfect indicative

j'ai porté
tu as porté
il a porté
nous avons porté
vous avez porté
ils ont porté

Pluperfect indicative

j'avais porté
tu avais porté
il avait porté
nous avions porté
vous aviez porté
ils avaient porté

Present subjunctive

que je porte
que tu portes
qu'il porte
que nous portions
que vous portiez
qu'ils portent

Conditional

je porterais
tu porterais
il porterait

nous porterions
vous porteriez
ils porteraient

Imperative

porte
portons
portez

poursuivre
to continue, pursue

Present participle

poursuivant

Past participle

poursuivi

Present indicative

je poursuis
tu poursuis
il poursuit
nous poursuivons
vous poursuivez
ils poursuivent

Imperfect indicative

je poursuivais
tu poursuivais
il poursuivait
nous poursuivions
vous poursuiviez
ils poursuivaient

Past historic

je poursuivis
tu poursuivis
il poursuivit
nous poursuivîmes
vous poursuivîtes
ils poursuivirent

Future

je poursuivrai
tu poursuivras
il poursuivra
nous poursuivrons
vous poursuivrez
ils poursuivront

Perfect indicative

j'ai poursuivi
tu as poursuivi
il a poursuivi
nous avons poursuivi
vous avez poursuivi
ils ont poursuivi

Pluperfect indicative

j'avais poursuivi
tu avais poursuivi
il avait poursuivi
nous avions poursuivi
vous aviez poursuivi
ils avaient poursuivi

Present subjunctive

que je poursuive
que tu poursuives
qu'il poursuive
que nous poursuivions
que vous poursuiviez
qu'ils poursuivent

Conditional

je poursuivrais
tu poursuivrais
il poursuivrait
nous poursuivrions
vous poursuivriez
ils poursuivraient

Imperative

poursuis
poursuivons
poursuivez

pousser
to push

Present participle

poussant

Past participle

poussé

Present indicative

je pousse
tu pousses
il pousse
nous poussons
vous poussez
ils poussent

Imperfect indicative

je poussais
tu poussais
il poussait
nous poussions
vous poussiez
ils poussaient

Past historic

je poussai

tu poussas
il poussa
nous poussâmes
vous poussâtes
ils poussèrent

Future

je pousserai
tu pousseras
il poussera
nous pousserons
vous pousserez
ils pousseront

Perfect indicative

j'ai poussé
tu as poussé
il a poussé
nous avons poussé
vous avez poussé
ils ont poussé

Pluperfect indicative

j'avais poussé
tu avais poussé
il avait poussé
nous avions poussé
vous aviez poussé
ils avaient poussé

Present subjunctive

que je pousse
que tu pousses
qu'il pousse
que nous poussions
que vous poussiez
qu'ils poussent

Conditional

je pousserais
tu pousserais
il pousserait
nous pousserions
vous pousseriez
ils pousseraient

Imperative

pousse
poussons
poussez

pouvoir
can, to be able to

Present participle

pouvant

Past participle

pu

Present indicative

je peux
tu peux
il peut
nous pouvons
vous pouvez
ils peuvent

Imperfect indicative

je pouvais
tu pouvais
il pouvait
nous pouvions
vous pouviez
ils pouvaient

Past historic

je pus
tu pus
il put
nous pûmes
vous pûtes
ils purent

Future

je pourrai
tu pourras
il pourra
nous pourrons
vous pourrez
ils pourront

Perfect indicative

j'ai pu
tu as pu
il a pu
nous avons pu
vous avez pu
ils ont pu

Pluperfect indicative

j'avais pu
tu avais pu
il avait pu
nous avions pu
vous aviez pu
ils avaient pu

Present subjunctive

que je puisse
que tu puisses
qu'il puisse
que nous puissions
que vous puissiez
qu'ils puissent

Conditional

je pourrais
tu pourrais
il pourrait
nous pourrions
vous pourriez
ils pourraient

Imperative

—

prédire
to predict

Present participle

prédisant

Past participle

prédit

Present indicative

je prédis
tu prédis
il prédit
nous prédisons
vous prédisez
ils prédisent

Imperfect indicative

je prédisais
tu prédisais
il prédisait
nous prédisions
vous prédisiez
ils prédisaient

Past historic

je prédis
tu prédis
il prédit
nous prédîmes
vous prédîtes
ils prédirent

Future

je prédirai
tu prédiras
il prédira
nous prédirons
vous prédirez
ils prédiront

Perfect indicative

j'ai prédit
tu as prédit
il a prédit

nous avons prédit
vous avez prédit
ils ont prédit

Pluperfect indicative

j'avais prédit
tu avais prédit
il avait prédit
nous avions prédit
vous aviez prédit
ils avaient prédit

Present subjunctive

que je prédise
que tu prédises
qu'il prédise
que nous prédisions
que vous prédisiez
qu'ils prédisent

Conditional

je prédirais
tu prédirais
il prédirait
nous prédirions
vous prédiriez
ils prédiraient

Imperative

prédis
prédisons
prédisez

prendre
to take

Present participle

prenant

Past participle

pris

Present indicative

je prends
tu prends
il prend
nous prenons
vous prenez
ils prennent

Imperfect indicative

je prenais
tu prenais
il prenait
nous prenions
vous preniez
ils prenaient

Past historic

je pris
tu pris
il prit
nous prîmes
vous prîtes
ils prirent

Future

je prendrai
tu prendras
il prendra
nous prendrons
vous prendrez
ils prendront

Perfect indicative

j'ai pris
tu as pris
il a pris
nous avons pris
vous avez pris
ils ont pris

Pluperfect indicative

j'avais pris
tu avais pris
il avait pris
nous avions pris
vous aviez pris
ils avaient pris

Present subjunctive

que je prenne
que tu prennes
qu'il prenne
que nous prenions
que vous preniez
qu'ils prennent

Conditional

je prendrais
tu prendrais
il prendrait
nous prendrions
vous prendriez
ils prendraient

Imperative

prends
prenons
prenez

prescrire
to prescribe

Present participle

prescrivant

Past participle

prescrit

Present indicative

je prescris
tu prescris
il prescrit
nous prescrivons
vous prescrivez
ils prescrivent

Imperfect indicative

je prescrivais
tu prescrivais
il prescrivait
nous prescrivions
vous prescriviez
ils prescrivaient

Past historic

je prescrivis
tu prescrivis
il prescrivit
nous prescrivîmes
vous prescrivîtes
ils prescrivirent

Future

je prescrirai
tu prescriras
il prescrira
nous prescrirons
vous prescrirez
ils prescriront

Perfect indicative

j'ai prescrit
tu as prescrit
il a prescrit
nous avons prescrit
vous avez prescrit
ils ont prescrit

Pluperfect indicative

j'avais prescrit
tu avais prescrit
il avait prescrit
nous avions prescrit
vous aviez prescrit
ils avaient prescrit

Present subjunctive

que je prescrive
que tu prescrives
qu'il prescrive
que nous prescrivions
que vous prescriviez
qu'ils prescrivent

Conditional

je prescrirais
tu prescrirais
il prescrirait
nous prescririons
vous prescririez
ils prescriraient

Imperative

prescris
prescrivons
prescrivez

présenter
to present, introduce

Present participle

présentant

Past participle

présenté

Present indicative

je présente
tu présentes
il présente
nous présentons
vous présentez
ils présentent

Imperfect indicative

je présentais
tu présentais
il présentait
nous présentions
vous présentiez
ils présentaient

Past historic

je présentai
tu présentas
il présenta
nous présentâmes
vous présentâtes
ils présentèrent

Future

je présenterai
tu présenteras
il présentera
nous présenterons
vous présenterez
ils présenteront

Perfect indicative

j'ai présenté

tu as présenté
il a présenté
nous avons présenté
vous avez présenté
ils ont présenté

Pluperfect indicative

j'avais présenté
tu avais présenté
il avait présenté
nous avions présenté
vous aviez présenté
ils avaient présenté

Present subjunctive

que je présente
que tu présentes
qu'il présente
que nous présentions
que vous présentiez
qu'ils présentent

Conditional

je présenterais
tu présenterais
il présenterait
nous présenterions
vous présenteriez
ils présenteraient

Imperative

présente
présentons
présentez

prévenir
to warn, prevent

Present participle

prévenant

Past participle

prévenu

Present indicative

je préviens
tu préviens
il prévient
nous prévenons
vous prévenez
ils préviennent

Imperfect indicative

je prévenais
tu prévenais
il prévenait

nous prévenions
vous préveniez
ils prévenaient

Past historic

je prévins
tu prévins
il prévint
nous prévînmes
vous prévîntes
ils prévinrent

Future

je préviendrai
tu préviendras
il préviendra
nous préviendrons
vous préviendrez
ils préviendront

Perfect indicative

je suis prévenu
tu es prévenu
il est prévenu
nous sommes prévenus
vous êtes prévenus
ils sont prévenus

Pluperfect indicative

j'étais prévenu
tu étais prévenu
il était prévenu
nous étions prévenus
vous étiez prévenus
ils étaient prévenus

Present subjunctive

que je prévienne
que tu préviennes
qu'il prévienne
que nous prévenions
que vous préveniez
qu'ils préviennent

Conditional

je préviendrais
tu préviendrais
il préviendrait
nous préviendrions
vous préviendriez
ils préviendraient

Imperative

préviens
prévenons
prévenez

prévoir
to foresee, anticipate

Present participle
prévoyant

Past participle
prévu

Present indicative
je prévois
tu prévois
il prévoit
nous prévoyons
vous prévoyez
ils prévoient

Imperfect indicative
je prévoyais
tu prévoyais
il prévoyait
nous prévoyions
vous prévoyiez
ils prévoyaient

Past historic
je prévis
tu prévis
il prévit
nous prévîmes
vous prévîtes
ils prévirent

Future
je prévoirai
tu prévoiras
il prévoira
nous prévoirons
vous prévoirez
ils prévoiront

Perfect indicative
j'ai prévu
tu as prévu
il a prévu
nous avons prévu
vous avez prévu
ils ont prévu

Pluperfect indicative
j'avais prévu
tu avais prévu
il avait prévu
nous avions prévu
vous aviez prévu
ils avaient prévu

Present subjunctive
que je prévoie
que tu prévoies
qu'il prévoie
que nous prévoyions
que vous prévoyiez
qu'ils prévoient

Conditional
je prévoirais
tu prévoirais
il prévoirait
nous prévoirions
vous prévoiriez
ils prévoiraient

Imperative
prévois
prévoyons
prévoyez

produire
to produce

Present participle
produisant

Past participle
produit

Present indicative
je produis
tu produis
il produit
nous produisons
vous produisez
ils produisent

Imperfect indicative
je produisais
tu produisais
il produisait
nous produisions
vous produisiez
ils produisaient

Past historic
je produisis
tu produisis
il produisit
nous produisîmes
vous produisîtes
ils produisirent

Future
je produirai
tu produiras
il produira
nous produirons
vous produirez
ils produiront

Perfect indicative
j'ai produit
tu as produit
il a produit
nous avons produit
vous avez produit
ils ont produit

Pluperfect indicative
j'avais produit
tu avais produit
il avait produit
nous avions produit
vous aviez produit
ils avaient produit

Present subjunctive
que je produise
que tu produises
qu'il produise
que nous produisions
que vous produisiez
qu'ils produisent

Conditional
je produirais
tu produirais
il produirait
nous produirions
vous produiriez
ils produiraient

Imperative
produis
produisons
produisez

promettre
to promise

Present participle
promettant

Past participle
promis

Present indicative
je promets
tu promets
il promet

nous promettons
vous promettez
ils promettent

Imperfect indicative
je promettais
tu promettais
il promettait
nous promettions
vous promettiez
ils promettaient

Past historic
je promis
tu promis
il promit
nous promîmes
vous promîtes
ils promirent

Future
je promettrai
tu promettras
il promettra
nous promettrons
vous promettrez
ils promettront

Perfect indicative
j'ai promis
tu as promis
il a promis
nous avons promis
vous avez promis
ils ont promis

Pluperfect indicative
j'avais promis
tu avais promis
il avait promis
nous avions promis
vous aviez promis
ils avaient promis

Present subjunctive
que je promette
que tu promettes
qu'il promette
que nous promettions
que vous promettiez
qu'ils promettent

Conditional
je promettrais
tu promettrais
il promettrait
nous promettrions
vous promettriez
ils promettraient

Imperative
promets
promettons
promettez

proscrire
to proscribe, prohibit

Present participle
proscrivant

Past participle
proscrit

Present indicative
je proscris
tu proscris
il proscrit
nous proscrivons
vous proscrivez
ils proscrivent

Imperfect indicative
je proscrivais
tu proscrivais
il proscrivait
nous proscrivions
vous proscriviez
ils proscrivaient

Past historic
je proscrivis
tu proscrivis
il proscrivit
nous proscrivîmes
vous proscrivîtes
ils proscrivirent

Future
je proscrirai
tu proscriras
il proscrira
nous proscrirons
vous proscrirez
ils proscriront

Perfect indicative
j'ai proscrit
tu as proscrit
il a proscrit
nous avons proscrit
vous avez proscrit
ils ont proscrit

Pluperfect indicative
j'avais proscrit

tu avais proscrit
il avait proscrit
nous avions proscrit
vous aviez proscrit
ils avaient proscrit

Present subjunctive
que je proscrive
que tu proscrives
qu'il proscrive
que nous proscrivions
que vous proscriviez
qu'ils proscrivent

Conditional
je proscrirais
tu proscrirais
il proscrirait
nous proscririons
vous proscririez
ils proscriraient

Imperative
proscris
proscrivons
proscrivez

recevoir
to receive, entertain

Present participle
recevant

Past participle
reçu

Present indicative
je reçois
tu reçois
il reçoit
nous recevons
vous recevez
ils reçoivent

Imperfect indicative
je recevais
tu recevais
il recevait
nous recevions
vous receviez
ils recevaient

Past historic
je reçus
tu reçus
il reçut

nous reçûmes
vous reçûtes
ils reçurent

Future

je recevrai
tu recevras
il recevra
nous recevrons
vous recevrez
ils recevront

Perfect indicative

j'ai reçu
tu as reçu
il a reçu
nous avons reçu
vous avez reçu
ils ont reçu ˙

Pluperfect indicative

j'avais reçu
tu avais reçu
il avait reçu
nous avions reçu
vous aviez reçu
ils avaient reçu

Present subjunctive

que je reçoive
que tu reçoives
qu'il reçoive
que nous recevions
que vous receviez
qu'ils reçoivent

Conditional

je recevrais
tu recevrais
il recevrait
nous recevrions
vous receviez
ils recevraient

Imperative

reçois
recevons
recevez

reconduire
to renew, drive home

Present participle

reconduisant

Past participle

reconduit

Present indicative

je reconduis
tu reconduis
il reconduit
nous reconduisons
vous reconduisez
ils reconduisent

Imperfect indicative

je reconduisais
tu reconduisais
il reconduisait
nous reconduisions
vous reconduisiez
ils reconduisaient

Past historic

je reconduisis
tu reconduisis
il reconduisit
nous reconduisîmes
vous reconduisîtes
ils reconduisirent

Future

je reconduirai
tu reconduiras
il reconduira
nous reconduirons
vous reconduirez
ils reconduiront

Perfect indicative

j'ai reconduit
tu as reconduit
il a reconduit
nous avons reconduit
vous avez reconduit
ils ont reconduit

Pluperfect indicative

j'avais reconduit
tu avais reconduit
il avait reconduit
nous avions reconduit
vous aviez reconduit
ils avaient reconduit

Present subjunctive

que je reconduise
que tu reconduises
qu'il reconduise
que nous reconduisions
que vous reconduisiez
qu'ils reconduisent

Conditional

je reconduirais

tu reconduirais
il reconduirait
nous reconduirions
vous reconduiriez
ils reconduiraient

Imperative

reconduis
reconduisons
reconduisez

reconnaître
to recognise, acknowledge

Present participle

reconnaissant

Past participle

reconnu

Present indicative

je reconnais
tu reconnais
il reconnaît
nous reconnaissons
vous reconnaissez
ils reconnaissent

Imperfect indicative

je reconnaissais
tu reconnaissais
il reconnaissait
nous reconnaissions
vous reconnaissiez
ils reconnaissaient

Past historic

je reconnus
tu reconnus
il reconnut
nous reconnûmes
vous reconnûtes
ils reconnurent

Future

je reconnaîtrai
tu reconnaîtras
il reconnaîtra
nous reconnaîtrons
vous reconnaîtrez
ils reconnaîtront

Perfect indicative

j'ai reconnu
tu as reconnu
il a reconnu

nous avons reconnu
vous avez reconnu
ils ont reconnu

Pluperfect indicative

j'avais reconnu
tu avais reconnu
il avait reconnu
nous avions reconnu
vous aviez reconnu
ils avaient reconnu

Present subjunctive

que je reconnaisse
que tu reconnaisses
qu'il reconnaisse
que nous reconnaissions
que vous reconnaissiez
qu'ils reconnaissent

Conditional

je reconnaîtrais
tu reconnaîtrais
il reconnaîtrait
nous reconnaîtrions
vous reconnaîtriez
ils reconnaîtraient

Imperative

reconnais
reconnaissons
reconnaissez

réduire
to reduce

Present participle

réduisant

Past participle

réduit

Present indicative

je réduis
tu réduis
il réduit
nous réduisons
vous réduisez
ils réduisent

Imperfect indicative

je réduisais
tu réduisais
il réduisait
nous réduisions
vous réduisiez
ils réduisaient

Past historic

je réduisis
tu réduisis
il réduisit
nous réduisîmes
vous réduisîtes
ils réduisirent

Future

je réduirai
tu réduiras
il réduira
nous réduirons
vous réduirez
ils réduiront

Perfect indicative

j'ai réduit
tu as réduit
il a réduit
nous avons réduit
vous avez réduit
ils ont réduit

Pluperfect indicative

j'avais réduit
tu avais réduit
il avait réduit
nous avions réduit
vous aviez réduit
ils avaient réduit

Present subjunctive

que je réduise
que tu réduises
qu'il réduise
que nous réduisions
que vous réduisiez
qu'ils réduisent

Conditional

je réduirais
tu réduirais
il réduirait
nous réduirions
vous réduiriez
ils réduiraient

Imperative

réduis
réduisons
réduisez

refaire
to redo, renovate

Present participle

refaisant

Past participle

refait

Present indicative

je refais
tu refais
il refait
nous refaisons
vous refaites
ils refont

Imperfect indicative

je refaisais
tu refaisais
il refaisait
nous refaisions
vous refaisiez
ils refaisaient

Past historic

je refis
tu refis
il refit
nous refîmes
vous refîtes
ils refirent

Future

je referai
tu referas
il refera
nous referons
vous referez
ils referont

Perfect indicative

j'ai refait
tu as refait
il a refait
nous avons refait
vous avez refait
ils ont refait

Pluperfect indicative

j'avais refait
tu avais refait
il avait refait
nous avions refait
vous aviez refait
ils avaient refait

Present subjunctive

que je refasse
que tu refasses
qu'il refasse
que nous refassions
que vous refassiez
qu'ils refassent

Conditional
je referais
tu referais
il referait
nous referions
vous referiez
ils referaient

Imperative
refais
refaisons
refaites

rejoindre
to get back to, meet up with

Present participle
rejoignant

Past participle
rejoint

Present indicative
je rejoins
tu rejoins
il rejoint
nous rejoignons
vous rejoignez
ils rejoignent

Imperfect indicative
je rejoignais
tu rejoignais
il rejoignait
nous rejoignions
vous rejoigniez
ils rejoignaient

Past historic
je rejoignis
tu rejoignis
il rejoignit
nous rejoignîmes
vous rejoignîtes
ils rejoignirent

Future
je rejoindrai
tu rejoindras
il rejoindra
nous rejoindrons
vous rejoindrez
ils rejoindront

Perfect indicative
j'ai rejoint

tu as rejoint
il a rejoint
nous avons rejoint
vous avez rejoint
ils ont rejoint

Pluperfect indicative
j'avais rejoint
tu avais rejoint
il avait rejoint
nous avions rejoint
vous aviez rejoint
ils avaient rejoint

Present subjunctive
que je rejoigne
que tu rejoignes
qu'il rejoigne
que nous rejoignions
que vous rejoigniez
qu'ils rejoignent

Conditional
je rejoindrais
tu rejoindrais
il rejoindrait
nous rejoindrions
vous rejoindriez
ils rejoindraient

Imperative
rejoins
rejoignons
rejoignez

relire
to read again, over

Present participle
relisant

Past participle
relu

Present indicative
je relis
tu relis
il relit
nous relisons
vous relisez
ils relisent

Imperfect indicative
je relisais
tu relisais
il relisait

nous relisions
vous relisiez
ils relisaient

Past historic
je relus
tu relus
il relut
nous relûmes
vous relûtes
ils relurent

Future
je relirai
tu reliras
il relira
nous relirons
vous relirez
ils reliront

Perfect indicative
j'ai relu
tu as relu
il a relu
nous avons relu
vous avez relu
ils ont relu

Pluperfect indicative
j'avais relu
tu avais relu
il avait relu
nous avions relu
vous aviez relu
ils avaient relu

Present subjunctive
que je relise
que tu relises
qu'il relise
que nous relisions
que vous relisiez
qu'ils relisent

Conditional
je relirais
tu relirais
il relirait
nous relirions
vous reliriez
ils reliraient

Imperative
relis
relisons
relisez

reluire
to shine, gleam

Present participle
reluisant

Past participle
relui

Present indicative
je reluis
tu reluis
il reluit
nous reluisons
vous reluisez
ils reluisent

Imperfect indicative
je reluisais
tu reluisais
il reluisait
nous reluisions
vous reluisiez
ils reluisaient

Past historic
je reluis
tu reluis
il reluit
nous reluîmes
vous reluîtes
ils reluirent

Future
je reluirai
tu reluiras
il reluira
nous reluirons
vous reluirez
ils reluiront

Perfect indicative
j'ai relui
tu as relui
il a relui
nous avons relui
vous avez relui
ils ont relui

Pluperfect indicative
j'avais relui
tu avais relui
il avait relui
nous avions relui
vous aviez relui
ils avaient relui

Present subjunctive
que je reluise
que tu reluises
qu'il reluise
que nous reluisions
que vous reluisiez
qu'ils reluisent

Conditional
je reluirais
tu reluirais
il reluirait
nous reluirions
vous reluiriez
ils reluiraient

Imperative
reluis
reluisons
reluisez

rendre
to give back

Present participle
rendant

Past participle
rendu

Present indicative
je rends
tu rends
il rend
nous rendons
vous rendez
ils rendent

Imperfect indicative
je rendais
tu rendais
il rendait
nous rendions
vous rendiez
ils rendaient

Past historic
je rendis
tu rendis
il rendit
nous rendîmes
vous rendîtes
ils rendirent

Future
je rendrai
tu rendras
il rendra
nous rendrons
vous rendrez
ils rendront

Perfect indicative
j'ai rendu
tu as rendu
il a rendu
nous avons rendu
vous avez rendu
ils ont rendu

Pluperfect indicative
j'avais rendu
tu avais rendu
il avait rendu
nous avions rendu
vous aviez rendu
ils avaient rendu

Present subjunctive
que je rende
que tu rendes
qu'il rende
que nous rendions
que vous rendiez
qu'ils rendent

Conditional
je rendrais
tu rendrais
il rendrait
nous rendrions
vous rendriez
ils rendraient

Imperative
rends
rendons
rendez

rentrer
to return

Present participle
rentrant

Past participle
rentré

Present indicative
je rentre
tu rentres
il rentre

nous rentrons
vous rentrez
ils rentrent

Imperfect indicative
je rentrais
tu rentrais
il rentrait
nous rentrions
vous rentriez
ils rentraient

Past historic
je rentrai
tu rentras
il rentra
nous rentrâmes
vous rentrâtes
ils rentrèrent

Future
je rentrerai
tu rentreras
il rentrera
nous rentrerons
vous rentrerez
ils rentreront

Perfect indicative
je suis rentré
tu es rentré
il est rentré
nous sommes rentrés
vous êtes rentrés
ils sont rentrés

Pluperfect indicative
j'étais rentré
tu étais rentré
il était rentré
nous étions rentrés
vous étiez rentrés
ils étaient rentrés

Present subjunctive
que je rentre
que tu rentres
qu'il rentre
que nous rentrions
que vous rentriez
qu'ils rentrent

Conditional
je rentrerais
tu rentrerais
il rentrerait
nous rentrerions
vous rentreriez
ils rentreraient

Imperative
rentre
rentrons
rentrez

répondre
to answer, reply

Present participle
répondant

Past participle
répondu

Present indicative
je réponds
tu réponds
il répond
nous répondons
vous répondez
ils répondent

Imperfect indicative
je répondais
tu répondais
il répondait
nous répondions
vous répondiez
ils répondaient

Past historic
je répondis
tu répondis
il répondit
nous répondîmes
vous répondîtes
ils répondirent

Future
je répondrai
tu répondras
il répondra
nous répondrons
vous répondrez
ils répondront

Perfect indicative
j'ai répondu
tu as répondu
il a répondu
nous avons répondu
vous avez répondu
ils ont répondu

Pluperfect indicative
j'avais répondu

tu avais répondu
il avait répondu
nous avions répondu
vous aviez répondu
ils avaient répondu

Present subjunctive
que je réponde
que tu répondes
qu'il réponde
que nous répondions
que vous répondiez
qu'ils répondent

Conditional
je répondrais
tu répondrais
il répondrait
nous répondrions
vous répondriez
ils répondraient

Imperative
réponds
répondons
répondez

reprendre
to take back, resume

Present participle
reprenant

Past participle
repris

Present indicative
je reprends
tu reprends
il reprend
nous reprenons
vous reprenez
ils reprennent

Imperfect indicative
je reprenais
tu reprenais
il reprenait
nous reprenions
vous repreniez
ils reprenaient

Past historic
je repris
tu repris
il reprit

nous reprîmes
vous reprîtes
ils reprirent

Future
je reprendrai
tu reprendras
il reprendra
nous reprendrons
vous reprendrez
ils reprendront

Perfect indicative
j'ai repris
tu as repris
il a repris
nous avons repris
vous avez repris
ils ont repris

Pluperfect indicative
j'avais repris
tu avais repris
il avait repris
nous avions repris
vous aviez repris
ils avaient repris

Present subjunctive
que je reprenne
que tu reprennes
qu'il reprenne
que nous reprenions
que vous repreniez
qu'ils reprennent

Conditional
je reprendrais
tu reprendrais
il reprendrait
nous reprendrions
vous reprendriez
ils reprendraient

Imperative
reprends
reprenons
reprenez

reproduire
to reproduce

Present participle
reproduisant

Past participle
reproduit

Present indicative
je reproduis
tu reproduis
il reproduit
nous reproduisons
vous reproduisez
ils reproduisent

Imperfect indicative
je reproduisais
tu reproduisais
il reproduisait
nous reproduisions
vous reproduisiez
ils reproduisaient

Past historic
je reproduisis
tu reproduisis
il reproduisit
nous reproduisîmes
vous reproduisîtes
ils reproduisirent

Future
je reproduirai
tu reproduiras
il reproduira
nous reproduirons
vous reproduirez
ils reproduiront

Perfect indicative
j'ai reproduit
tu as reproduit
il a reproduit
nous avons reproduit
vous avez reproduit
ils ont reproduit

Pluperfect indicative
j'avais reproduit
tu avais reproduit
il avait reproduit
nous avions reproduit
vous aviez reproduit
ils avaient reproduit

Present subjunctive
que je reproduise
que tu reproduises
qu'il reproduise
que nous reproduisions
que vous reproduisiez
qu'ils reproduisent

Conditional
je reproduirais

tu reproduirais
il reproduirait
nous reproduirions
vous reproduiriez
ils reproduiraient

Imperative
reproduis
reproduisons
reproduisez

résoudre
to solve, resolve

Present participle
résolvant

Past participle
résolu

Present indicative
je résous
tu résous
il résout
nous résolvons
vous résolvez
ils résolvent

Imperfect indicative
je résolvais
tu résolvais
il résolvait
nous résolvions
vous résolviez
ils résolvaient

Past historic
je résolus
tu résolus
il résolut
nous résolûmes
vous résolûtes
ils résolurent

Future
je résoudrai
tu résoudras
il résoudra
nous résoudrons
vous résoudrez
ils résoudront

Perfect indicative
j'ai résolu
tu as résolu
il a résolu

nous avons résolu
vous avez résolu
ils ont résolu

Pluperfect indicative

j'avais résolu
tu avais résolu
il avait résolu
nous avions résolu
vous aviez résolu
ils avaient résolu

Present subjunctive

que je résolve
que tu résolves
qu'il résolve
que nous résolvions
que vous résolviez
qu'ils résolvent

Conditional

je résoudrais
tu résoudrais
il résoudrait
nous résoudrions
vous résoudriez
ils résoudraient

Imperative

résous
résolvons
résolvez

ressentir
to feel, experience

Present participle

ressentant

Past participle

ressenti

Present indicative

je ressens
tu ressens
il ressent
nous ressentons
vous ressentez
ils ressentent

Imperfect indicative

je ressentais
tu ressentais
il ressentait

nous ressentions
vous ressentiez
ils ressentaient

Past historic

je ressentis
tu ressentis
il ressentit
nous ressentîmes
vous ressentîtes
ils ressentirent

Future

je ressentirai
tu ressentiras
il ressentira
nous ressentirons
vous ressentirez
ils ressentiront

Perfect indicative

j'ai ressenti
tu as ressenti
il a ressenti
nous avons ressenti
vous avez ressenti
ils ont ressenti

Pluperfect indicative

j'avais ressenti
tu avais ressenti
il avait ressenti
nous avions ressenti
vous aviez ressenti
ils avaient ressenti

Present subjunctive

que je ressente
que tu ressentes
qu'il ressente
que nous ressentions
que vous ressentiez
qu'ils ressentent

Conditional

je ressentirais
tu ressentirais
il ressentirait
nous ressentirions
vous ressentiriez
ils ressentiraient

Imperative

ressens
ressentons
ressentez

restreindre
to restrict

Present participle

restreignant

Past participle

restreint

Present indicative

je restreins
tu restreins
il restreint
nous restreignons
vous restreignez
ils restreignent

Imperfect indicative

je restreignais
tu restreignais
il restreignait
nous restreignions
vous restreigniez
ils restreignaient

Past historic

je restreignis
tu restreignis
il restreignit
nous restreignîmes
vous restreignîtes
ils restreignirent

Future

je restreindrai
tu restreindras
il restreindra
nous restreindrons
vous restreindrez
ils restreindront

Perfect indicative

j'ai restreint
tu as restreint
il a restreint
nous avons restreint
vous avez restreint
ils ont restreint

Pluperfect indicative

j'avais restreint
tu avais restreint
il avait restreint
nous avions restreint
vous aviez restreint
ils avaient restreint

Present subjunctive

que je restreigne
que tu restreignes
qu'il restreigne
que nous restreignions
que vous restreigniez
qu'ils restreignent

Conditional

je restreindrais
tu restreindrais
il restreindrait
nous restreindrions
vous restreindriez
ils restreindraient

Imperative

restreins
restreignons
restreignez

revenir
to come back

Present participle

revenant

Past participle

revenu

Present indicative

je reviens
tu reviens
il revient
nous revenons
vous revenez
ils reviennent

Imperfect indicative

je revenais
tu revenais
il revenait
nous revenions
vous reveniez
ils revenaient

Past historic

je revins
tu revins
il revint
nous revînmes
vous revîntes
ils revinrent

Future

je reviendrai

tu reviendras
il reviendra
nous reviendrons
vous reviendrez
ils reviendront

Perfect indicative

je suis revenu
tu es revenu
il est revenu
nous sommes revenus
vous êtes revenus
ils sont revenus

Pluperfect indicative

j'étais revenu
tu étais revenu
il était revenu
nous étions revenus
vous étiez revenus
ils étaient revenus

Present subjunctive

que je revienne
que tu reviennes
qu'il revienne
que nous revenions
que vous reveniez
qu'ils reviennent

Conditional

je reviendrais
tu reviendrais
il reviendrait
nous reviendrions
vous reviendriez
ils reviendraient

Imperative

reviens
revenons
revenez

revivre
to live again, to be revived

Present participle

revivant

Past participle

revécu

Present indicative

je revis
tu revis
il revit

nous revivons
vous revivez
ils revivent

Imperfect indicative

je revivais
tu revivais
il revivait
nous revivions
vous reviviez
ils revivaient

Past historic

je revécus
tu revécus
il revécut
nous revécûmes
vous revécûtes
ils revécurent

Future

je revivrai
tu revivras
il revivra
nous revivrons
vous revivrez
ils revivront

Perfect indicative

j'ai revécu
tu as revécu
il a revécu
nous avons revécu
vous avez revécu
ils ont revécu

Pluperfect indicative

j'avais revécu
tu avais revécu
il avait revécu
nous avions revécu
vous aviez revécu
ils avaient revécu

Present subjunctive

que je revive
que tu revives
qu'il revive
que nous revivions
que vous reviviez
qu'ils revivent

Conditional

je revivrais
tu revivrais
il revivrait
nous revivrions
vous revivriez
ils revivraient

Imperative
revis
revivons
revivez

rire
to laugh

Present participle
riant

Past participle
ri

Present indicative
je ris
tu ris
il rit
nous rions
vous riez
ils rient

Imperfect indicative
je riais
tu riais
il riait
nous riions
vous riiez
ils riaient

Past historic
je ris
tu ris
il rit
nous rîmes
vous rîtes
ils rirent

Future
je rirai
tu riras
il rira
nous rirons
vous rirez
ils riront

Perfect indicative
j'ai ri
tu as ri
il a ri
nous avons ri
vous avez ri
ils ont ri

Pluperfect indicative
j'avais ri

tu avais ri
il avait ri
nous avions ri
vous aviez ri
ils avaient ri

Present subjunctive
que je rie
que tu ries
qu'il rie
que nous riions
que vous riiez
qu'ils rient

Conditional
je rirais
tu rirais
il rirait
nous ririons
vous ririez
ils riraient

Imperative
ris
rions
riez

rompre
to break (off)

Present participle
rompant

Past participle
rompu

Present indicative
je romps
tu romps
il rompt
nous rompons
vous rompez
ils rompent

Imperfect indicative
je rompais
tu rompais
il rompait
nous rompions
vous rompiez
ils rompaient

Past historic
je rompis
tu rompis
il rompit

nous rompîmes
vous rompîtes
ils rompirent

Future
je romprai
tu rompras
il rompra
nous romprons
vous romprez
ils rompront

Perfect indicative
j'ai rompu
tu as rompu
il a rompu
nous avons rompu
vous avez rompu
ils ont rompu

Pluperfect indicative
j'avais rompu
tu avais rompu
il avait rompu
nous avions rompu
vous aviez rompu
ils avaient rompu

Present subjunctive
que je rompe
que tu rompes
qu'il rompe
que nous rompions
que vous rompiez
qu'ils rompent

Conditional
je romprais
tu romprais
il romprait
nous romprions
vous rompriez
ils rompraient

Imperative
romps
rompons
rompez

savoir
to know

Present participle
sachant

Past participle
su

savoir

Present indicative

je sais
tu sais
il sait
nous savons
vous savez
ils savent

Imperfect indicative

je savais
tu savais
il savait
nous savions
vous saviez
ils savaient

Past historic

je sus
tu sus
il sut
nous sûmes
vous sûtes
ils surent

Future

je saurai
tu sauras
il saura
nous saurons
vous saurez
ils sauront

Perfect indicative

j'ai su
tu as su
il a su
nous avons su
vous avez su
ils ont su

Pluperfect indicative

j'avais su
tu avais su
il avait su
nous avions su
vous aviez su
ils avaient su

Present subjunctive

que je sache
que tu saches
qu'il sache
que nous sachions
que vous sachiez
qu'ils sachent

Conditional

je saurais

tu saurais
il saurait
nous saurions
vous sauriez
ils sauraient

Imperative

sache
sachons
sachez

séduire
to seduce, charm

Present participle

séduisant

Past participle

séduit

Present indicative

je séduis
tu séduis
il séduit
nous séduisons
vous séduisez
ils séduisent

Imperfect indicative

je séduisais
tu séduisais
il séduisait
nous séduisions
vous séduisiez
ils séduisaient

Past historic

je séduisis
tu séduisis
il séduisit
nous séduisîmes
vous séduisîtes
ils séduisirent

Future

je séduirai
tu séduiras
il séduira
nous séduirons
vous séduirez
ils séduiront

Perfect indicative

j'ai séduit
tu as séduit
il a séduit

nous avons séduit
vous avez séduit
ils ont séduit

Pluperfect indicative

j'avais séduit
tu avais séduit
il avait séduit
nous avions séduit
vous aviez séduit
ils avaient séduit

Present subjunctive

que je séduise
que tu séduises
qu'il séduise
que nous séduisions
que vous séduisiez
qu'ils séduisent

Conditional

je séduirais
tu séduirais
il séduirait
nous séduirions
vous séduiriez
ils séduiraient

Imperative

séduis
séduisons
séduisez

sentir
to smell, feel

Present participle

sentant

Past participle

senti

Present indicative

je sens
tu sens
il sent
nous sentons
vous sentez
ils sentent

Imperfect indicative

je sentais
tu sentais
il sentait
nous sentions
vous sentiez
ils sentaient

Past historic
je sentis
tu sentis
il sentit
nous sentîmes
vous sentîtes
ils sentirent

Future
je sentirai
tu sentiras
il sentira
nous sentirons
vous sentirez
ils sentiront

Perfect indicative
j'ai senti
tu as senti
il a senti
nous avons senti
vous avez senti
ils ont senti

Pluperfect indicative
j'avais senti
tu avais senti
il avait senti
nous avions senti
vous aviez senti
ils avaient senti

Present subjunctive
que je sente
que tu sentes
qu'il sente
que nous sentions
que vous sentiez
qu'ils sentent

Conditional
je sentirais
tu sentirais
il sentirait
nous sentirions
vous sentiriez
ils sentiraient

Imperative
sens
sentons
sentez

servir
to serve

Present participle
servant

Past participle
servi

Present indicative
je sers
tu sers
il sert
nous servons
vous servez
ils servent

Imperfect indicative
je servais
tu servais
il servait
nous servions
vous serviez
ils servaient

Past historic
je servis
tu servis
il servit
nous servîmes
vous servîtes
ils servirent

Future
je servirai
tu serviras
il servira
nous servirons
vous servirez
ils serviront

Perfect indicative
j'ai servi
tu as servi
il a servi
nous avons servi
vous avez servi
ils ont servi

Pluperfect indicative
j'avais servi
tu avais servi
il avait servi
nous avions servi
vous aviez servi
ils avaient servi

Present subjunctive
que je serve
que tu serves
qu'il serve
que nous servions
que vous serviez
qu'ils servent

Conditional
je servirais
tu servirais
il servirait
nous servirions
vous serviriez
ils serviraient

Imperative
sers
servons
servez

sortir
to go out, leave

Present participle
sortant

Past participle
sorti

Present indicative
je sors
tu sors
il sort
nous sortons
vous sortez
ils sortent

Imperfect indicative
je sortais
tu sortais
il sortait
nous sortions
vous sortiez
ils sortaient

Past historic
je sortis
tu sortis
il sortit
nous sortîmes
vous sortîtes
ils sortirent

Future
je sortirai
tu sortiras
il sortira
nous sortirons
vous sortirez
ils sortiront

Perfect indicative
je suis sorti

tu es sorti
il est sorti
nous sommes sortis
vous êtes sortis
ils sont sortis

Pluperfect indicative

j'étais sorti
tu étais sorti
il était sorti
nous étions sortis
vous étiez sortis
ils étaient sortis

Present subjunctive

que je sorte
que tu sortes
qu'il sorte
que nous sortions
que vous sortiez
qu'ils sortent

Conditional

je sortirais
tu sortirais
il sortirait
nous sortirions
vous sortiriez
ils sortiraient

Imperative

sors
sortons
sortez

souffrir
to suffer

Present participle

souffrant

Past participle

souffert

Present indicative

je souffre
tu souffres
il souffre
nous souffrons
vous souffrez
ils souffrent

Imperfect indicative

je souffrais
tu souffrais
il souffrait

nous souffrions
vous souffriez
ils souffraient

Past historic

je souffris
tu souffris
il souffrit
nous souffrîmes
vous souffrîtes
ils souffrirent

Future

je souffrirai
tu souffriras
il souffrira
nous souffrirons
vous souffrirez
ils souffriront

Perfect indicative

j'ai souffert
tu as souffert
il a souffert
nous avons souffert
vous avez souffert
ils ont souffert

Pluperfect indicative

j'avais souffert
tu avais souffert
il avait souffert
nous avions souffert
vous aviez souffert
ils avaient souffert

Present subjunctive

que je souffre
que tu souffres
qu'il souffre
que nous souffrions
que vous souffriez
qu'ils souffrent

Conditional

je souffrirais
tu souffrirais
il souffrirait
nous souffririons
vous souffririez
ils souffriraient

Imperative

souffre
souffrons
souffrez

sourire
to smile

Present participle

souriant

Past participle

souri

Present indicative

je souris
tu souris
il sourit
nous sourions
vous souriez
ils sourient

Imperfect indicative

je souriais
tu souriais
il souriait
nous souriions
vous souriiez
ils souriaient

Past historic

je souris
tu souris
il sourit
nous sourîmes
vous sourîtes
ils sourirent

Future

je sourirai
tu souriras
il sourira
nous sourirons
vous sourirez
ils souriront

Perfect indicative

j'ai souri
tu as souri
il a souri
nous avons souri
vous avez souri
ils ont souri

Pluperfect indicative

j'avais souri
tu avais souri
il avait souri
nous avions souri
vous aviez souri
ils avaient souri

Present subjunctive
que je sourie
que tu souries
qu'il sourie
que nous souriions
que vous souriiez
qu'ils sourient

Conditional
je sourirais
tu sourirais
il sourirait
nous souririons
vous souririez
ils souriraient

Imperative
souris
sourions
souriez

souscrire
to subscribe

Present participle
souscrivant

Past participle
souscrit

Present indicative
je souscris
tu souscris
il souscrit
nous souscrivons
vous souscrivez
ils souscrivent

Imperfect indicative
je souscrivais
tu souscrivais
il souscrivait
nous souscrivions
vous souscriviez
ils souscrivaient

Past historic
je souscrivis
tu souscrivis
il souscrivit
nous souscrivîmes
vous souscrivîtes
ils souscrivirent

Future
je souscrirai

tu souscriras
il souscrira
nous souscrirons
vous souscrirez
ils souscriront

Perfect indicative
j'ai souscrit
tu as souscrit
il a souscrit
nous avons souscrit
vous avez souscrit
ils ont souscrit

Pluperfect indicative
j'avais souscrit
tu avais souscrit
il avait souscrit
nous avions souscrit
vous aviez souscrit
ils avaient souscrit

Present subjunctive
que je souscrive
que tu souscrives
qu'il souscrive
que nous souscrivions
que vous souscriviez
qu'ils souscrivent

Conditional
je souscrirais
tu souscrirais
il souscrirait
nous souscririons
vous souscririez
ils souscriraient

Imperative
souscris
souscrivons
souscrivez

soustraire
to subtract

Present participle
soustrayant

Past participle
soustrait

Present indicative
je soustrais
tu soustrais
il soustrait

nous soustrayons
vous soustrayez
ils soustraient

Imperfect indicative
je soustrayais
tu soustrayais
il soustrayait
nous soustrayions
vous soustrayiez
ils soustrayaient

Past historic
–
–
–
–
–

Future
je soustrairai
tu soustrairas
il soustraira
nous soustrairons
vous soustrairez
ils soustrairont

Perfect indicative
j'ai soustrait
tu as soustrait
il a soustrait
nous avons soustrait
vous avez soustrait
ils ont soustrait

Pluperfect indicative
j'avais soustrait
tu avais soustrait
il avait soustrait
nous avions soustrait
vous aviez soustrait
ils avaient soustrait

Present subjunctive
que je soustraie
que tu soustraies
qu'il soustraie
que nous soustrayions
que vous soustrayiez
qu'ils soustraient

Conditional
je soustrairais
tu soustrairais
il soustrairait
nous soustrairions
vous soustrairiez
ils soustrairaient

Imperative
soustrais
soustrayons
soustrayez

soutenir
to support

Present participle
soutenant

Past participle
soutenu

Present indicative
je soutiens
tu soutiens
il soutient
nous soutenons
vous soutenez
ils soutiennent

Imperfect indicative
je soutenais
tu soutenais
il soutenait
nous soutenions
vous souteniez
ils soutenaient

Past historic
je soutins
tu soutins
il soutint
nous soutînmes
vous soutîntes
ils soutinrent

Future
je soutiendrai
tu soutiendras
il soutiendra
nous soutiendrons
vous soutiendrez
ils soutiendront

Perfect indicative
j'ai soutenu
tu as soutenu
il a soutenu
nous avons soutenu
vous avez soutenu
ils ont soutenu

Pluperfect indicative
j'avais soutenu

tu avais soutenu
il avait soutenu
nous avions soutenu
vous aviez soutenu
ils avaient soutenu

Present subjunctive
que je soutienne
que tu soutiennes
qu'il soutienne
que nous soutenions
que vous souteniez
qu'ils soutiennent

Conditional
je soutiendrais
tu soutiendrais
il soutiendrait
nous soutiendrions
vous soutiendriez
ils soutiendraient

Imperative
soutiens
soutenons
soutenez

se souvenir
to remember

Present participle
se souvenant

Past participle
souvenu

Present indicative
je me souviens
tu te souviens
il se souvient
nous nous souvenons
vous vous souvenez
ils se souviennent

Imperfect indicative
je me souvenais
tu te souvenais
il se souvenait
nous nous souvenions
vous vous souveniez
ils se souvenaient

Past historic
je me souvins
tu te souvins
il se souvint

nous nous souvînmes
vous vous souvîntes
ils se souvinrent

Future
je me souviendrai
tu te souviendras
il se souviendra
nous nous souviendrons
vous vous souviendrez
ils se souviendront

Perfect indicative
je me suis souvenu
tu t'es souvenu
il s'est souvenu
nous nous sommes souvenus
vous vous êtes souvenus
ils se sont souvenus

Pluperfect indicative
je m'étais souvenu
tu t'étais souvenu
il s'était souvenu
nous nous étions souvenus
vous vous étiez souvenus
ils s'étaient souvenus

Present subjunctive
que je me souvienne
que tu te souviennes
qu'il se souvienne
que nous nous souvenions
que vous vous souveniez
qu'ils se souviennent

Conditional
je me souviendrais
tu te souviendrais
il se souviendrait
nous nous souviendrions
vous vous souviendriez
ils se souviendraient

Imperative
souviens-toi
souvenons-nous
souvenez-vous

suffire
to be sufficient

Present participle
suffisant

Past participle
suffi

Present indicative

je suffis
tu suffis
il suffit
nous suffisons
vous suffisez
ils suffisent

Imperfect indicative

je suffisais
tu suffisais
il suffisait
nous suffisions
vous suffisiez
ils suffisaient

Past historic

je suffis
tu suffis
il suffit
nous suffîmes
vous suffîtes
ils suffirent

Future

je suffirai
tu suffiras
il suffira
nous suffirons
vous suffirez
ils suffiront

Perfect indicative

j'ai suffi
tu as suffi
il a suffi
nous avons suffi
vous avez suffi
ils ont suffi

Pluperfect indicative

j'avais suffi
tu avais suffi
il avait suffi
nous avions suffi
vous aviez suffi
ils avaient suffi

Present subjunctive

que je suffise
que tu suffises
qu'il suffise
que nous suffisions
que vous suffisiez
qu'ils suffisent

Conditional

je suffirais

tu suffirais
il suffirait
nous suffirions
vous suffiriez
ils suffiraient

Imperative

suffis
suffisons
suffisez

suivre
to follow

Present participle

suivant

Past participle

suivi

Present indicative

je suis
tu suis
il suit
nous suivons
vous suivez
ils suivent

Imperfect indicative

je suivais
tu suivais
il suivait
nous suivions
vous suiviez
ils suivaient

Past historic

je suivis
tu suivis
il suivit
nous suivîmes
vous suivîtes
ils suivirent

Future

je suivrai
tu suivras
il suivra
nous suivrons
vous suivrez
ils suivront

Perfect indicative

j'ai suivi
tu as suivi
il a suivi

nous avons suivi
vous avez suivi
ils ont suivi

Pluperfect indicative

j'avais suivi
tu avais suivi
il avait suivi
nous avions suivi
vous aviez suivi
ils avaient suivi

Present subjunctive

que je suive
que tu suives
qu'il suive
que nous suivions
que vous suiviez
qu'ils suivent

Conditional

je suivrais
tu suivrais
il suivrait
nous suivrions
vous suivriez
ils suivraient

Imperative

suis
suivons
suivez

surprendre
to surprise

Present participle

surprenant

Past participle

surpris

Present indicative

je surprends
tu surprends
il surprend
nous surprenons
vous surprenez
ils surprennent

Imperfect indicative

je surprenais
tu surprenais
il surprenait
nous surprenions
vous surpreniez
ils surprenaient

Past historic
je surpris
tu surpris
il surprit
nous surprîmes
vous surprîtes
ils surprirent

Future
je surprendrai
tu surprendras
il surprendra
nous surprendrons
vous surprendrez
ils surprendront

Perfect indicative
j'ai surpris
tu as surpris
il a surpris
nous avons surpris
vous avez surpris
ils ont surpris

Pluperfect indicative
j'avais surpris
tu avais surpris
il avait surpris
nous avions surpris
vous aviez surpris
ils avaient surpris

Present subjunctive
que je surprenne
que tu surprennes
qu'il surprenne
que nous surprenions
que vous surpreniez
qu'ils surprennent

Conditional
je surprendrais
tu surprendrais
il surprendrait
nous surprendrions
vous surprendriez
ils surprendraient

Imperative
surprends
surprenons
surprenez

survivre
to survive

Present participle
survivant

Past participle
survécu

Present indicative
je survis
tu survis
il survit
nous survivons
vous survivez
ils survivent

Imperfect indicative
je survivais
tu survivais
il survivait
nous survivions
vous surviviez
ils survivaient

Past historic
je survécus
tu survécus
il survécut
nous survécûmes
vous survécûtes
ils survécurent

Future
je survivrai
tu survivras
il survivra
nous survivrons
vous survivrez
ils survivront

Perfect indicative
j'ai survécu
tu as survécu
il a survécu
nous avons survécu
vous avez survécu
ils ont survécu

Pluperfect indicative
j'avais survécu
tu avais survécu
il avait survécu
nous avions survécu
vous aviez survécu
ils avaient survécu

Present subjunctive
que je survive
que tu survives
qu'il survive
que nous survivions
que vous surviviez
qu'ils survivent

Conditional
je survivrais
tu survivrais
il survivrait
nous survivrions
vous survivriez
ils survivraient

Imperative
survis
survivons
survivez

suspendre
to suspend, hang

Present participle
suspendant

Past participle
suspendu

Present indicative
je suspends
tu suspends
il suspend
nous suspendons
vous suspendez
ils suspendent

Imperfect indicative
je suspendais
tu suspendais
il suspendait
nous suspendions
vous suspendiez
ils suspendaient

Past historic
je suspendis
tu suspendis
il suspendit
nous suspendîmes
vous suspendîtes
ils suspendirent

Future
je suspendrai
tu suspendras
il suspendra
nous suspendrons
vous suspendrez
ils suspendront

Perfect indicative
j'ai suspendu

tu as suspendu
il a suspendu
nous avons suspendu
vous avez suspendu
ils ont suspendu

Pluperfect indicative
j'avais suspendu
tu avais suspendu
il avait suspendu
nous avions suspendu
vous aviez suspendu
ils avaient suspendu

Present subjunctive
que je suspende
que tu suspendes
qu'il suspende
que nous suspendions
que vous suspendiez
qu'ils suspendent

Conditional
je suspendrais
tu suspendrais
il suspendrait
nous suspendrions
vous suspendriez
ils suspendraient

Imperative
suspends
suspendons
suspendez

se taire
to be quiet, silent

Present participle
se taisant

Past participle
tu

Present indicative
je me tais
tu te tais
il se tait
nous nous taisons
vous vous taisez
ils se taisent

Imperfect indicative
je me taisais
tu te taisais
il se taisait

nous nous taisions
vous vous taisiez
ils se taisaient

Past historic
je me tus
tu te tus
il se tut
nous nous tûmes
vous vous tûtes
ils se turent

Future
je me tairai
tu te tairas
il se taira
nous nous tairons
vous vous tairez
ils se tairont

Perfect indicative
je me suis tu
tu t'es tu
il s'est tu
nous nous sommes tus
vous vous êtes tus
ils se sont tus

Pluperfect indicative
je m'étais tu
tu t'étais tu
il s'était tu
nous nous étions tus
vous vous étiez tus
ils s'étaient tus

Present subjunctive
que je me taise
que tu te taises
qu'il se taise
que nous nous taisions
que vous vous taisiez
qu'ils se taisent

Conditional
je me tairais
tu te tairais
il se tairait
nous nous tairions
vous vous tairiez
ils se tairaient

Imperative
tais-toi
taisons-nous
taisez-vous

tendre
to tighten

Present participle
tendant

Past participle
tendu

Present indicative
je tends
tu tends
il tend
nous tendons
vous tendez
ils tendent

Imperfect indicative
je tendais
tu tendais
il tendait
nous tendions
vous tendiez
ils tendaient

Past historic
je tendis
tu tendis
il tendit
nous tendîmes
vous tendîtes
ils tendirent

Future
je tendrai
tu tendras
il tendra
nous tendrons
vous tendrez
ils tendront

Perfect indicative
j'ai tendu
tu as tendu
il a tendu
nous avons tendu
vous avez tendu
ils ont tendu

Pluperfect indicative
j'avais tendu
tu avais tendu
il avait tendu
nous avions tendu
vous aviez tendu
ils avaient tendu

Present subjunctive

que je tende
que tu tendes
qu'il tende
que nous tendions
que vous tendiez
qu'ils tendent

Conditional

je tendrais
tu tendrais
il tendrait
nous tendrions
vous tendriez
ils tendraient

Imperative

tends
tendons
tendez

tenir
to hold

Present participle

tenant

Past participle

tenu

Present indicative

je tiens
tu tiens
il tient
nous tenons
vous tenez
ils tiennent

Imperfect indicative

je tenais
tu tenais
il tenait
nous tenions
vous teniez
ils tenaient

Past historic

je tins
tu tins
il tint
nous tînmes
vous tîntes
ils tinrent

Future

je tiendrai

tu tiendras
il tiendra
nous tiendrons
vous tiendrez
ils tiendront

Perfect indicative

j'ai tenu
tu as tenu
il a tenu
nous avons tenu
vous avez tenu
ils ont tenu

Pluperfect indicative

j'avais tenu
tu avais tenu
il avait tenu
nous avions tenu
vous aviez tenu
ils avaient tenu

Present subjunctive

que je tienne
que tu tiennes
qu'il tienne
que nous tenions
que vous teniez
qu'ils tiennent

Conditional

je tiendrais
tu tiendrais
il tiendrait
nous tiendrions
vous tiendriez
ils tiendraient

Imperative

tiens
tenons
tenez

tirer
to pull

Present participle

tirant

Past participle

tiré

Present indicative

je tire
tu tires
il tire

nous tirons
vous tirez
ils tirent

Imperfect indicative

je tirais
tu tirais
il tirait
nous tirions
vous tiriez
ils tiraient

Past historic

je tirai
tu tiras
il tira
nous tirâmes
vous tirâtes
ils tirèrent

Future

je tirerai
tu tireras
il tirera
nous tirerons
vous tirerez
ils tireront

Perfect indicative

j'ai tiré
tu as tiré
il a tiré
nous avons tiré
vous avez tiré
ils ont tiré

Pluperfect indicative

j'avais tiré
tu avais tiré
il avait tiré
nous avions tiré
vous aviez tiré
ils avaient tiré

Present subjunctive

que je tire
que tu tires
qu'il tire
que nous tirions
que vous tiriez
qu'ils tirent

Conditional

je tirerais
tu tirerais
il tirerait
nous tirerions
vous tireriez
ils tireraient

Imperative
tire
tirons
tirez

traduire
to translate

Present participle
traduisant

Past participle
traduit

Present indicative
je traduis
tu traduis
il traduit
nous traduisons
vous traduisez
ils traduisent

Imperfect indicative
je traduisais
tu traduisais
il traduisait
nous traduisions
vous traduisiez
ils traduisaient

Past historic
je traduisis
tu traduisis
il traduisit
nous traduisîmes
vous traduisîtes
ils traduisirent

Future
je traduirai
tu traduiras
il traduira
nous traduirons
vous traduirez
ils traduiront

Perfect indicative
j'ai traduit
tu as traduit
il a traduit
nous avons traduit
vous avez traduit
ils ont traduit

Pluperfect indicative
j'avais traduit

tu avais traduit
il avait traduit
nous avions traduit
vous aviez traduit
ils avaient traduit

Present subjunctive
que je traduise
que tu traduises
qu'il traduise
que nous traduisions
que vous traduisiez
qu'ils traduisent

Conditional
je traduirais
tu traduirais
il traduirait
nous traduirions
vous traduiriez
ils traduiraient

Imperative
traduis
traduisons
traduisez

transcrire
to transcribe

Present participle
transcrivant

Past participle
transcrit

Present indicative
je transcris
tu transcris
il transcrit
nous transcrivons
vous transcrivez
ils transcrivent

Imperfect indicative
je transcrivais
tu transcrivais
il transcrivait
nous transcrivions
vous transcriviez
ils transcrivaient

Past historic
je transcrivis
tu transcrivis
il transcrivit

nous transcrivîmes
vous transcrivîtes
ils transcrivirent

Future
je transcrirai
tu transcriras
il transcrira
nous transcrirons
vous transcrirez
ils transcriront

Perfect indicative
j'ai transcrit
tu as transcrit
il a transcrit
nous avons transcrit
vous avez transcrit
ils ont transcrit

Pluperfect indicative
j'avais transcrit
tu avais transcrit
il avait transcrit
nous avions transcrit
vous aviez transcrit
ils avaient transcrit

Present subjunctive
que je transcrive
que tu transcrives
qu'il transcrive
que nous transcrivions
que vous transcriviez
qu'ils transcrivent

Conditional
je transcrirais
tu transcrirais
il transcrirait
nous transcririons
vous transcririez
ils transcriraient

Imperative
transcris
transcrivons
transcrivez

vaincre
to vanquish

Present participle
vainquant

Past participle
vaincu

vaincre

Present indicative
je vaincs
tu vaincs
il vainc
nous vainquons
vous vainquez
ils vainquent

Imperfect indicative
je vainquais
tu vainquais
il vainquait
nous vainquions
vous vainquiez
ils vainquaient

Past historic
je vainquis
tu vainquis
il vainquit
nous vainquîmes
vous vainquîtes
ils vainquirent

Future
je vaincrai
tu vaincras
il vaincra
nous vaincrons
vous vaincrez
ils vaincront

Perfect indicative
j'ai vaincu
tu as vaincu
il a vaincu
nous avons vaincu
vous avez vaincu
ils ont vaincu

Pluperfect indicative
j'avais vaincu
tu avais vaincu
il avait vaincu
nous avions vaincu
vous aviez vaincu
ils avaient vaincu

Present subjunctive
que je vainque
que tu vainques
qu'il vainque
que nous vainquions
que vous vainquiez
qu'ils vainquent

Conditional
je vaincrais

tu vaincrais
il vaincrait
nous vaincrions
vous vaincriez
ils vaincraient

Imperative
vaincs
vainquons
vainquez

valoir
to be worth

Present participle
valant

Past participle
valu

Present indicative
je vaux
tu vaux
il vaut
nous valons
vous valez
ils valent

Imperfect indicative
je valais
tu valais
il valait
nous valions
vous valiez
ils valaient

Past historic
je valus
tu valus
il valut
nous valûmes
vous valûtes
ils valurent

Future
je vaudrai
tu vaudras
il vaudra
nous vaudrons
vous vaudrez
ils vaudront

Perfect indicative
j'ai valu
tu as valu
il a valu

nous avons valu
vous avez valu
ils ont valu

Pluperfect indicative
j'avais valu
tu avais valu
il avait valu
nous avions valu
vous aviez valu
ils avaient valu

Present subjunctive
que je vaille
que tu vailles
qu'il vaille
que nous valions
que vous valiez
qu'ils vaillent

Conditional
je vaudrais
tu vaudrais
il vaudrait
nous vaudrions
vous vaudriez
ils vaudraient

Imperative
vaux
valons
valez

vendre
to sell

Present participle
vendant

Past participle
vendu

Present indicative
je vends
tu vends
il vend
nous vendons
vous vendez
ils vendent

Imperfect indicative
je vendais
tu vendais
il vendait
nous vendions
vous vendiez
ils vendaient

venir
to come

Past historic
je vendis
tu vendis
il vendit
nous vendîmes
vous vendîtes
ils vendirent

Future
je vendrai
tu vendras
il vendra
nous vendrons
vous vendrez
ils vendront

Perfect indicative
j'ai vendu
tu as vendu
il a vendu
nous avons vendu
vous avez vendu
ils ont vendu

Pluperfect indicative
j'avais vendu
tu avais vendu
il avait vendu
nous avions vendu
vous aviez vendu
ils avaient vendu

Present subjunctive
que je vende
que tu vendes
qu'il vende
que nous vendions
que vous vendiez
qu'ils vendent

Conditional
je vendrais
tu vendrais
il vendrait
nous vendrions
vous vendriez
ils vendraient

Imperative
vends
vendons
vendez

venir
to come

Present participle
venant

Past participle
venu

Present indicative
je viens
tu viens
il vient
nous venons
vous venez
ils viennent

Imperfect indicative
je venais
tu venais
il venait
nous venions
vous veniez
ils venaient

Past historic
je vins
tu vins
il vint
nous vînmes
vous vîntes
ils vinrent

Future
je viendrai
tu viendras
il viendra
nous viendrons
vous viendrez
ils viendront

Perfect indicative
je suis venu
tu es venu
il est venu
nous sommes venus
vous êtes venus
ils sont venus

Pluperfect indicative
j'étais venu
tu étais venu
il était venu
nous étions venus
vous étiez venus
ils étaient venus

Present subjunctive
que je vienne
que tu viennes
qu'il vienne
que nous venions
que vous veniez
qu'ils viennent

Conditional
je viendrais
tu viendrais
il viendrait
nous viendrions
vous viendriez
ils viendraient

Imperative
viens
venons
venez

vivre
to live

Present participle
vivant

Past participle
vécu

Present indicative
je vis
tu vis
il vit
nous vivons
vous vivez
ils vivent

Imperfect indicative
je vivais
tu vivais
il vivait
nous vivions
vous viviez
ils vivaient

Past historic
je vécus
tu vécus
il vécut
nous vécûmes
vous vécûtes
ils vécurent

Future
je vivrai
tu vivras
il vivra
nous vivrons
vous vivrez
ils vivront

Perfect indicative
j'ai vécu

tu as vécu
il a vécu
nous avons vécu
vous avez vécu
ils ont vécu

Pluperfect indicative

j'avais vécu
tu avais vécu
il avait vécu
nous avions vécu
vous aviez vécu
ils avaient vécu

Present subjunctive

que je vive
que tu vives
qu'il vive
que nous vivions
que vous viviez
qu'ils vivent

Conditional

je vivrais
tu vivrais
il vivrait
nous vivrions
vous vivriez
ils vivraient

Imperative

vis
vivons
vivez

voir
to see

Present participle

voyant

Past participle

vu

Present indicative

je vois
tu vois
il voit
nous voyons
vous voyez
ils voient

Imperfect indicative

je voyais
tu voyais
il voyait

nous voyions
vous voyiez
ils voyaient

Past historic

je vis
tu vis
il vit
nous vîmes
vous vîtes
ils virent

Future

je verrai
tu verras
il verra
nous verrons
vous verrez
ils verront

Perfect indicative

j'ai vu
tu as vu
il a vu
nous avons vu
vous avez vu
ils ont vu

Pluperfect indicative

j'avais vu
tu avais vu
il avait vu
nous avions vu
vous aviez vu
ils avaient vu

Present subjunctive

que je voie
que tu voies
qu'il voie
que nous voyions
que vous voyiez
qu'ils voient

Conditional

je verrais
tu verrais
il verrait
nous verrions
vous verriez
ils verraient

Imperative

vois
voyons
voye

vouloir
to want

Present participle

voulant

Past participle

voulu

Present indicative

je veux
tu veux
il veut
nous voulons
vous voulez
ils veulent

Imperfect indicative

je voulais
tu voulais
il voulait
nous voulions
vous vouliez
ils voulaient

Past historic

je voulus
tu voulus
il voulut
nous voulûmes
vous voulûtes
ils voulurent

Future

je voudrai
tu voudras
il voudra
nous voudrons
vous voudrez
ils voudront

Perfect indicative

j'ai voulu
tu as voulu
il a voulu
nous avons voulu
vous avez voulu
ils ont voulu

Pluperfect indicative

j'avais voulu
tu avais voulu
il avait voulu
nous avions voulu
vous aviez voulu
ils avaient voulu

Present subjunctive	*Conditional*	*Imperative*
que je veuille	je voudrais	veuille
que tu veuilles	tu voudrais	voulons
qu'il veuille	il voudrait	voulez/veuillez
que nous voulions	nous voudrions	
que vous vouliez	vous voudriez	
qu'ils veuillent	ils voudraient	

Irregular English Verbs

Present tense	Past tense	Past participle
arise	arose	arisen
awake	awoke	awaked, awoke
be [I am, you/we/they are, he/she/it is, *gérondif* being]	was, were	been
bear	bore	borne
beat	beat	beaten
become	became	become
begin	began	begun
behold	beheld	beheld
bend	bent	bent
beseech	besought, beseeched	besought, beseeched
beset	beset	beset
bet	bet, betted	bet, betted
bid	bade, bid	bid, bidden
bite	bit	bitten
bleed	bled	bled
bless	blessed, blest	blessed, blest
blow	blew	blown
break	broke	broken
breed	bred	bred
bring	brought	brought
build	built	built
burn	burnt, burned	burnt, burned
burst	burst	burst
buy	bought	bought
can	could	(been able)
cast	cast	cast
catch	caught	caught
choose	chose	chosen
cling	clung	clung
come	came	come
cost	cost	cost
creep	crept	crept
cut	cut	cut
deal	dealt	dealt
dig	dug	dug
do [he/she/it does]	did	done
draw	drew	drawn
dream	dreamed, dreamt	dreamed, dreamt
drink	drank	drunk
drive	drove	driven
dwell	dwelt, dwelled	dwelt, dwelled
eat	ate	eaten
fall	fell	fallen
feed	fed	fed
feel	felt	felt
fight	fought	fought
find	found	found
flee	fled	fled
fling	flung	flung
fly [he/she/it flies]	flew	flown
forbid	forbade	forbidden
forecast	forecast	forecast
forget	forgot	forgotten
forgive	forgave	forgiven
forsake	forsook	forsaken
forsee	foresaw	foreseen

Present tense	Past tense	Past participle
freeze	froze	frozen
get	got	got, (US) gotten
give	gave	given
go [he/she/it goes]	went	gone
grind	ground	ground
grow	grew	grown
hang	hung, hanged	hung, hanged
have [I/you/we/they have, he/she/it has, *gérondif* having]	had	had
hear	heard	heard
hide	hid	hidden
hit	hit	hit
hold	held	held
hurt	hurt	hurt
keep	kept	kept
kneel	knelt	knelt
know	knew	known
lay	laid	laid
lead	led	led
lean	leant, leaned	leant, leaned
leap	leapt, leaped	leapt, leaped
learn	learnt, learned	learnt, learned
leave	left	left
lend	lent	lent
let	let	let
lie [*gérondif* lying]	lay	lain
light	lighted, lit	lighted, lit
lose	lost	lost
make	made	made
may	might	-
mean	meant	meant
meet	met	met
mistake	mistook	mistaken
mow	mowed	mowed, mown
must	(had to)	(had to)
overcome	overcame	overcome
pay	paid	paid
put	put	put
quit	quit, quitted	quit, quitted
read	read	read
rid	rid	rid
ride	rode	ridden
ring	rang	rung
rise	rose	risen
run	ran	run
saw	sawed	sawn, sawed
say	said	said
see	saw	seen
seek	sought	sought
sell	sold	sold
send	sent	sent
set	set	set
sew	sewed	sewn, sewed
shake	shook	shaken
shall	should	

Present tense	Past tense	Past participle
shear	sheared	sheared, shorn
shed	shed	shed
shine	shone	shone
shoot	shot	shot
show	showed	shown, showed
shrink	shrank	shrunk
shut	shut	shut
sing	sang	sung
sink	sank	sunk
sit	sat	sat
slay	slew	slain
sleep	slept	slept
slide	slid	slid
sling	slung	slung
smell	smelt, smelled	smelt, smelled
sow	sowed	sown, sowed
speak	spoke	spoken
speed	sped, speeded	sped, speeded
spell	spelt, spelled	spelt, spelled
spend	spent	spent
spill	spilt, spilled	spilt, spilled
spin	spun	spun
spit	spat	spat
split	split	split
spoil	spoilt	spoilt
spread	spread	spread
spring	sprang	sprung
stand	stood	stood
steal	stole	stolen
stick	stuck	stuck
sting	stung	stung
stink	stank	stunk
stride	strode	stridden
strike	struck	struck
strive	strove	striven
swear	swore	sworn
sweep	swept	swept
swell	swelled	swelled, swollen
swim	swam	swum
swing	swung	swung
take	took	taken
teach	taught	taught
tear	tore	torn
tell	told	told
think	thought	thought
throw	threw	thrown
thrust	thrust	thrust
tread	trod	trodden, trod
understand	understood	understood
upset	upset	upset
wake	woke	woken
wear	wore	worn
weave	wove,	wove, woven
wed	wedded	wed, wedded

Present tense	Past tense	Past participle
weep	wept	wept
win	won	won
wind	wound	wound
withdraw	withdrew	withdrawn
withhold	withheld	withheld
withstand	withstood	withstood
wring	wrung	wrung
write	wrote	written